MW00978742

COLLECTOR'S
INFORMATION
CLEARINGHOUSE

ANTIQUES &
COLLECTIBLES
RESOURCE
DIRECTORY

COLLECTOR'S
INFORMATION
CLEARINGHOUSE

ANTIQUES & COLLECTIBLES RESOURCE DIRECTORY

DAVID J. MALONEY, Jr.

WALLACE-HOMESTEAD BOOK COMPANY
Radnor, Pennsylvania

To my patient, supportive and understanding wife, Barbara

Designed by Adrianne Onderdonk Dudden
Manufactured in the United States of America

Library of Congress Cataloging in Publication Data
Maloney, David J.
    Collector's information clearinghous antiques & collectibles
resource directory / David J. Maloney.
        p.   cm.
    Includes index.
    ISBN 0-87069-611-4 (hc)—ISBN 0-87069-610-6 (pb)
        1. Antiques—Information services—United States—Directories.
    I. Title.   II. Title: Collector's information clearinghouse antiques
and collectibles resource directory.
NK1127.M34   1991
745.1′025′73—dc20   91-26412
                                                          CIP

1 2 3 4 5 6 7 8 9 0   0 9 8 7 6 5 4 3 2

CONTENTS

FOREWORD

The key to the 1990s is information. Nowhere in this more evident than in the antiques and collectibles field. In the past two decades, the growth in the number of collecting categories, collectors, and dealers has increased significantly. No individual can track the entire field. The age of the antiques and collectibles generalist is past.

Specialization is the key to survival in today's market. Entire collecting communities, e.g., baseball cards, dolls, firearms, and toys, have fragmented from the main body. Even within these groups, sub-specialization occurs. If items were encountered in select groups, this would not present a problem. Alas, this is usually not the case.

When an appraiser, auctioneer, or dealer enters a house filled with a wide range of items, determining a value for each and every one is overwhelming.

When an individual wants to have an object restored, how to find a competent appraiser?

When someone breaks a piece of china in the family service, how does he obtain a replacement piece?

When a bank, acting as estate executor, needs an appraisal of a specialized collection, to whom does it turn?

All need answers—ideally from *one* source. Prior to publication of the *Collector's Information Clearinghouse Antiques & Collectibles Resource Directory*, some information was scattered among a wide variety of sources and locations. Within the field there were a few books listing collectors and dealers who buy in specialized categories and a book on restoration sources. A trip to the library to consult general reference books on clubs and organizations might result in identifying a collector's club. Assembled listings for manufacturers of reproductions and copycats, operating supplies, and research sources simply did not exist.

As the owner of Rinker Enterprises, Inc., the largest privately held resource and research center in the antiques and collectibles field, I am in a better position than anyone else to appreciate the enormity of the task that David J. Maloney undertook. The logistics of assembling and checking the information stagger the imagination. When David first approached me about the project, I had no trouble recognizing the need for and potential of such a directory, but felt David a bit mad for even contemplating such a project.

As one of the nation's leading appraisers, David had already begun to assemble vast quantities of information for his own business use, storing it and updating it in a database. A review of the printouts indicated that all that was needed for general use was to refine the data. David's willingness to respond to suggestions from a variety of sources greatly strengthen this book.

Collector's Information Clearinghouse Antiques & Collectibles Resource Directory is a tool. Once its applicability has been discovered, it will be a difficult tool to put down. Hopefully, it will become an extension of its user.

This resource directory will sit on my desk next to the general price guides that I consult almost daily. It will be used heavily. How do I know?

In the early 1980s, just as I assumed the position of editor of *Warman's Antiques and their Prices*, Ralph and Terry Kovel published a resource directory. Imagine my delight when I discovered that one of my principal rivals willingly provided me with access to all their research sources for less than fifteen dollars. I wore out three copies in the first year.

If you have followed my work in the antiques and collectibles field during the past decade, you know what I was able to do with the information that the Kovels so graciously provided. May you enjoy the same success with the information in this book.

Harry L. Rinker
Zionsville, Pennsylvania
October, 1991

PREFACE

The *Collector's Information Clearinghouse Antiques & Collectibles Resource Directory* is a monumental undertaking designed to provide users with a comprehensive, all-in-one, up-to-date compendium of resource information to aid in the location, study and authentication, replacement, repair, valuation, and buying and selling of over 2000 categories of art, antiques, collectibles and other types of personal property.

The recent past has witnessed an unprecedented explosion in the values of—and interest in—antiques and collectibles. From lunch boxes and toy banks to whiskey flasks and art glass, our collecting habits and our fascination with yesteryear's throwaways, furnishings, decorations, and cultural artifacts has resulted in a highly fragmented and specialized assortment of collector interest groups. Consequently, the collectibility of such diverse items as decoys, limited edition plates, and Civil War artifacts has spawned or supported a plethora of specialized services, talents and products now available to both the collecting and non-collecting public.

Specialized resources include buyers, collectors, dealers, experts, appraisers, periodicals, conservation suppliers, repair and refinishing suppliers, reproduction sources, manufacturers, distributors, and producers, clubs, societies and associations, museums and libraries, centers for specialized research, mail-bid and gallery auctions.

Having been a full-time appraiser and claims representative for the past ten years, I am very familiar with the need for a readily available, comprehensive, and current reference source. Each year I am required to locate specific information about thousands of different pieces of personal property such as antiques, collectibles, limited editions, household contents, automobiles or business property. In the course of my work—as well as during speaking engagements—the public poses a constant stream of questions: "I collect automobile license plates. Is there a club I can join or a newsletter that focuses on my interest?"; "Where can I go to get my old toys repaired?"; "Is there an auction service that conducts specialized sales of art glass?"; "What is the value of my old Coca-Cola machine?"; "Is there a dealer or collector who would like to buy my old B&O Railroad china?"; and, most frequently, "How and where can I sell my antiques and collectibles for the most money?"

CIC's Antiques & Collectibles Resource Directory is a compilation of over 7000 entries covering over 700 primary classifications (further divided into over 2000 subclassifications) of antiques and collectibles. The compilation was made over the course of a two-year period with a verification mailing being sent to all potential entries just prior to publication to ensure accuracy and completeness. An asterisk adjacent to an entry denotes listings for which verification returns were not received prior to the April 1, 1991, deadline but for which we are confident of the accuracy nonetheless. No charge was made for inclusion within this directory. A listing should not be considered an endorsement, and no guarantee is made as to satisfaction of service received. Comments regarding service will be weighed, however, in considering those to be included in future editions.

CIC's Antiques & Collectibles Resource Directory is designed to be of help to a myriad of individuals and professional groups. My experience demonstrates quite dramatically that most of the non-collecting public is unaware of the collectibility and value of many of their own possessions. Even if they are aware that their collectible items are of interest to others, they are often at a loss as how best to go about setting a price and finding a buyer should they choose to sell, or in locating sources of information should they desire to learn more about their collectible. The *Antiques & Collectibles Resource Directory* is an ideal source of information for locating potential buyers. Individual buyers are listed, as are clubs and periodicals which are themselves excellent sources for information about potential buyers. In addition, the listed auction services (often specializing in a narrow area) provide alternatives to selling to an individual. Specialty museum and library collections, as well as hundreds of collector clubs, periodicals and book sources that cater to a wide range of collector interests, are also listed should one develop an interest in collecting or a desire to learn more about a specific subject.

For professionals, such as appraisers, dealers, estate liquidators, repairers, attorneys, and claims adjusters, *CIC's Antiques & Collectibles Resource Directory* provides an unrivaled source of information to aid in the successful authentication and valuation of antiques and collectibles or to help with the successful resolution of a claim. Experts found among dealers, collectors, collector clubs and specialized periodicals offer an unparalleled source of expertise to help in confirming bona fide claims or in disproving fraudulent ones.

The goal of this book is to place as much information as possible at the user's fingertips to allow him to make decisions based on knowledge and fact. For sellers, I strongly recommend Dr. H. A. Hyman's book, *I'll Buy That* (Treasure Hunt Publications, 1991, $23.95 ppd.; Box 699, Claremont, CA 91711) and Ralph & Terry Kovel's *Kovel's Guide to Selling Your Antiques and Collectibles* (Crown Publishing, 1990, $9.95) for inside tips on selling your antiques. Following their guidelines will make selling enjoyable as well as profitable. For additional buyers you may also wish to obtain *Who's Who in Collecting and Antiques* (Collectors Connection and Registry [CCR], 1991, $7.95; P.O. Box 54, South San Francisco, CA 94083-0054 [800-777-1078]). CCR also offers a worldwide computer database for real-time matching of buyers and sellers.

Veteran dealers and collectors are well aware that knowledge and information are the keys to success in the world of antiques and collectibles. Unfortunately, such informational sources are widely scattered and often short-lived or frequently changing. Heretofore there was no organized method to capture, preserve, collate, and distribute collector resource information in such a way as to efficiently keep the public accurately informed on a continuing basis. The *Collector's Information Clearinghouse Antiques and Collectibles Resource Directory* is designed to overcome this shortfall through daily updating and regular publication.

We are continuing to research and implement enhancements, and your feedback is important to us. We are always interested in correcting, updating and adding sources of information, and in improving category nomenclature and structure, so please write to us or give us a call (phone 301-695-8544 or fax 301-695-6491) with your suggestions for changes. At the end of the *Directory* you will find a Listing Application Form. Submit the latter at any time to either change your existing listing or to add a new one.

A special thanks to all those listed and to our users for their feedback, suggestions, survey responses and overwhelming positive encouragement. We continue to strive for excellence in providing a thorough, accurate and all-encompassing resource directory. I encourage and welcome your comments and suggestions.

David J. Maloney, ISA
Editor
Collector's Information Clearinghouse
P.O. Box 2049
Frederick, MD 21702-1049

USER'S GUIDE TO THE DIRECTORY

DESCRIPTION OF THE GENERAL LISTINGS

The main section of this directory contains specific information about each entry listed within the appropriate category. There are over 2000 categories, listed alphabetically by primary classification (or collecting category) in capital letters. Subclassifications appear where there are recognized subcategories.

ADVERTISING COLLECTIBLES

(see also BUTTONS, Pinback; GLASSES; LABELS; MAGAZINES, Covers & Tear Sheets; PAPER COLLECTIBLES; POCKET MIRRORS; TIN COLLECTIBLES; WATCH FOBS)
Figurals
Firearms-Related
Signs

AGRICULTURE RELATED ITEMS

AIRLINE MEMORABILIA

Pilots Wings

ART, African & Tribal

Of particular importance is the extensive and comprehensive cross-referencing system: it directs the user to related subject matter and is unique to this publication.

Each entry in the General Listings has as much information as is applicable, and includes the following in a typical entry:

PRIMARY CLASSIFICATION

Sub-Classification

Entry Type (i.e., Dealer, Collector, Club)
Contact name
Business, Organization, Club, Museum, name
Periodical type and name
Address
Phone and fax numbers
Descriptive comment

Classification

Of critical importance to this directory was the establishment of a classification system which employs a well-defined system that is also sensitive to nomenclature currently in vogue within the collecting community. A bilevel system of nomenclature which includes primary classifications and, where necessary, subclassifications, was adopted. Additional flexibility is afforded within either level by employing terms inside parentheses such as *CERAMICS (AMERICAN)*, *Stoneware,* or *GLASS, Carnival (Post-1960).*

Some entries may be found under their unique classification, as well as within one or more specialty areas:

■ Auction houses are listed under the classification *AUCTION SERVICES* and also within the specialty classifications which apply (if any), e.g., *DOLLS, TOYS,* etc.

■ New-book sellers are listed under *BOOKS, Collector,* as well as under any specialty classification which applies.

■ Repair, restoration and conservation services (no distinction is made among the three) will be found under *REPAIRS & RESTORATIONS* or within their specialy classification, e.g., *TRAINS, Toy.*

■ Objects made of fired clay (pottery, earthenware, stoneware and porcelain) will be found under the primary classification *CERAMICS,* which is further subdivided by place of origin and type, e.g., *CERAMICS (AMERICAN ART POTTERY), Roseville Pottery Co..* By cross-reference, users are directed to related areas such as *COOKIE JARS, FAIRINGS* and *DINNERWARE* (a generic classification which contains most "china" matching services). The *Resource Directory* accommodates the misnomer "china" as it refers to porcelain and other types of tableware by including a *CHINA* classification which merely directs the user to appropriate categories such as *CERAMICS* and *DINNERWARE.* In deference to the current vogue, however, the term "china" as it refers to dishes is retained in the classifications *RAILROAD COLLECTIBLES, China* and *WHITE HOUSE COLLECTIBLES, China.*

■ Matching services locate replacement pieces for dinnerware, glassware and flatware services. *TABLEWARE* will direct the reader to the classifications in which matching services can be found (*DINNERWARE; FLATWARE; GLASS, Elegant*).

■ Sports-related collectibles are listed alphabetically by sport (Baseball, Auto Racing) under the primary classification of *SPORTS COLLECTIBLES.*

■ Contemporary collectibles, including limited editions, can be found under *COLLECTIBLES (MODERN).*

■ Supplies for dealers and collectors can be found under *ANTIQUES DEALERS & COLLECTORS, Supplies for.*

■ *COMPUTER PROGRAMS, Collectors'* lists software programs for maintaining collections.

■ *APPRAISAL ASSOCIATIONS* lists societies to contact, such as the International Society of Appraisers, Ltd., to locate a qualified personal property apppraiser.

■ *MOVING & STORAGE ASSOCIATIONS* lists associations involved with the moving and storage industry. The Claims Prevention and Procedure Council, Inc., for instance, is an ideal source for locating quality repair and restoration services in your area.

■ *REPRODUCTION SOURCES* (sometimes catering only to the wholesale trade) lists businesses offering copies of antiques and collectibles, from R.S. Prussia porcelain and oak furniture to Diamond Dye lithographed tins and jukeboxes.

Entry Type

The entry type identifies the listing as an auction service, bookseller, collector's club, periodical, collector, dealer, expert, matching service, manufacturer/distributor/producer, miscellaneous service of special interest, museum or library, repair/

restoration/conservation service, reproduction source, supplier or vendor. Entries are *alphabetical by type*, then in *ZIP code order* for ease in locating services or other collectors in your area.

If, for instance, you see six dealers (or nine repair services) listed in the category of interest, then search for the ZIP code closest to your own to find the nearest dealer (or repair service).

ZIP Code Ranges	ZIP Abbre-viations	State	ZIP Code Ranges	ZIP Abbre-viations	State	ZIP Code Ranges	ZIP Abbre-viations	State
010-027	☐ MA	Massachusetts	320-349	☐ FL	Florida	680-693	☐ NE	Nebraska
028-029	☐ RI	Rhode Island	350-369	☐ AL	Alabama	700-714	☐ LA	Louisiana
030-038	☐ NH	New Hampshire	370-385	☐ TN	Tennessee	716-729	☐ AR	Arkansas
039-049	☐ ME	Maine	386-397	☐ MS	Mississippi	730-749	☐ OK	Oklahoma
050-059	☐ VT	Vermont	400-427	☐ KY	Kentucky	750-799	☐ TX	Texas
060-069	☐ CT	Connecticut	430-458	☐ OH	Ohio	800-816	☐ CO	Colorado
070-089	☐ NJ	New Jersey	460-479	☐ IN	Indiana	820-831	☐ WY	Wyoming
100-149	☐ NY	New York	480-499	☐ MI	Michigan	833-838	☐ ID	Idaho
150-196	☐ PA	Pennsylvania	500-528	☐ IA	Iowa	840-847	☐ UT	Utah
197-199	☐ DE	Delaware	530-549	☐ WI	Wisconsin	850-865	☐ AZ	Arizona
200-205	☐ DC	District of Col.	550-567	☐ MN	Minnesota	870-884	☐ NM	New Mexico
206-219	☐ MD	Maryland	570-577	☐ SD	South Dakota	890-898	☐ NV	Nevada
220-246	☐ VA	Virginia	580-588	☐ ND	North Dakota	900-961	☐ CA	California
247-268	☐ WV	West Virginia	590-599	☐ MT	Montana	967-968	☐ HI	Hawaii
270-289	☐ NC	North Carolina	600-629	☐ IL	Illinois	970-979	☐ OR	Oregon
290-299	☐ SC	South Carolina	630-658	☐ MO	Missouri	980-994	☐ WA	Washington
300-319	☐ GA	Georgia	660-679	☐ KS	Kansas	995-999	☐ AK	Alaska

"Suppliers" are sources of replacement parts or supplies for the classification within which they are located. Included in this category and vendors who cater to the needs of collectors, dealers, repairers and restorers, conservators, etc.

"Experts" have a high degree of knowledge or skill in a particular subject area. Although normally listed only once, "experts" are usually "collectors" and often-times "dealers" as well, i.e., they buy, sell and collect.

Similarly, "dealers" are often "collectors" and will buy as well as sell.

Always check the comment section of each entry to locate collectors or experts who might also supply parts, do repairs or provide other services relevant to the classification.

"Man./Dist./Prod." are businesses which either manufacture, distribute or produce items such as modern collectibles, e.g., *COLLECTIBLES (MODERN)*.

As a general rule, only "periodicals" (newsletters, magazines, newspapers, journals) issued more than once a year are included in this directory. Price guides and books are not listed. Such reference sources are available through your local library or from the booksellers listed in the directory. "Periodicals" appear under that heading *unless* issued by a club or society, in which case they are listed under the club. Many fine club periodicals are available to members only, so you may wish to join in order to receive them.

Names, Addresses and Phone Numbers

Some listings name a contact, some do not, while some wish to be listed only as an anonymous "collector" or "dealer." The individual's name is followed by the business and periodical name, address, phone and fax numbers, and comment line.

Comments

Most entries include a comment line to amplify information and users will find them to be extremely valuable. Comment space was limited, so at times editorial license was taken to shorten or otherwise modify comments submitted by the applicants.

THE APPENDIXES

Several often-consulted categories of services are grouped in the appendixes, as well as listed under specialty categories. This provides the user with a second convenient way to quickly look up the following:

Appendix A: Auction Services
Appendix B: Matching Services
Appendix C: Repair & Restoration Services
Appendix D: Suppliers

THE INDEXES

The directory offers two indexes for locating specific subject areas. The first index lists subjects alphabetically, as do The General Listings: PRIMARY, Secondary. A second index is done alphabetically by secondary or subclassification, so that the reader may find a special subject, such as Baseball (listed under SPORTS) or Faberge (listed under RUSSIAN ITEMS).

USEFUL SUGGESTIONS

When requesting a reply, always send a long self-addressed and stamped envelope (LSASE) to ensure and expedite a reply. Most collector's clubs operate on a shoestring budget and require an LSASE when information is requested; others will appreciate your courtesy. If you are requesting information about a particular item, include a description (material, dimensions, drawings and color of maker's mark, etc.), and a photo, sketch or photocopy of the item in question.

Due to frequent fluctuations in membership dues, costs of brochures, samples of periodicals, etc., such information was purposely excluded from this publication. Remember, always ask if charges apply to your request. Also, if contacting a party by phone, *do not call collect* unless specifically instructed to do so. There may also be charges for catalogs, lists, samples or brochures.

If no expert is listed for your particular area of interest, try contacting a collector's club or periodical. Often the club's contact or the periodical's editor or publisher are experts and excellent sources of information.

If you wish to be listed in future editions of the *Resource Directory*, complete the form on the last page of this book.

GENERAL LISTINGS

A & P ITEMS

Collector

C.T. Peters, Inc.
C.T. Peters
P.O. Box 2120
Red Bank, NJ 07701
Wants give-aways, brochures, trading cards, publications, etc. from The Great Atlantic & Pacific Tea Company (A&P); pre-1964. *

ABRAHAM LINCOLN ITEMS

(see also PERSONALITIES (HISTORICAL), Abraham Lincoln)

ADDING MACHINES

(see also CALCULATORS; TYPEWRITERS)

Club/Association

Early Typewriter Collectors Association
Magazine: ETCetera
Darryl Rehr, Ed.
11433 Rochester Ave. #303
Los Angeles, CA 90025
Phone: 213-477-5229
An internt'l. club for collectors of old office equipment; provides contact with worldwide network of over 500 members; free ads.

Collector

Peter Frei
P.O. Box 500
Brimfield, MA 01010
Phone: 800-942-8968
Wants old typewriters, adding machines, sewing machines, and old vacuum cleaners, etc.

Collector

Edward Stuart
3025 Ontario Road NW #203
Washington, DC 20009
Phone: 202-332-6511
Wants old adding machines, key driven non-listing models only such as Comptometer or Burroughs Arithometer.

Collector

Arthur Cheslock
514 Paul St.
Baltimore, MD 21202
Phone: 301-962-8580
Wants pre-1945 machines. *

Collector

Darryl Rehr
11433 Rochester Ave. #303
Los Angeles, CA 90025
Phone: 213-447-5229
Wants adding machines (machines that only add) of unusual and early designs; send SASE for free information packet.

ADS

Magazine

(see also ADVERTISING COLLECTIBLES; MAGAZINES, Covers & Tear Sheets)

ADVERTISING COLLECTIBLES

(see also BUTTONS, Pinback; GLASSES; LABELS; MAGAZINES, Covers & Tear Sheets; PAPER COLLECTIBLES; POCKET MIRRORS; TIN COLLECTIBLES; WATCH FOBS)

Auction Service

James D. Julia, Inc.
P.O. Box 830
Fairfield, ME 04937
Phone: 207-453-7904   FAX: 207-453-2502
Specialized auctions of advertising and country stone items, dolls, toys.

Auction Service

Dave Beck
P.O. Box 435
Mediappolis, IA 52637
Phone: 319-394-3943
Conducts mail auctions of advertising watch fobs, mirrors, pinback buttons, etc.; send stamp for illustrated auction catalog.

Club/Association

Ephemera Society of America Inc., The
Newsletter: Ephemera News
P.O. Box 37
Schoharie, NY 12157
Phone: 518-295-7978
Focuses on the preservation and study of ephemera (short-lived printed matter); also publishes "The Ephemera Journal" annually.

Club/Association

National Association of Paper & Advertising Collectors
Newsletter: NAPAC Newsletter
P.O. Box 500
Mount Joy, PA 17552
Phone: 717-653-9797

Club/Association

Antique Advertising Association
Newsletter: AAA Newsletter
P.O. Box 1121
Morton Grove, IL 60053
Phone: 708-446-0904
Dedicated to collecting ALL forms of quality advertising: tobacco, whiskey, beer, candy, gum, clocks, country store, cabinets, etc.

Club/Association

Tin Container Collectors Association
Newsletter: Tin Type
P.O. Box 44010
Aurora, CO 80044

Collector

House of Stewart
Box 387
Huntington, NY 11743 *

Collector

Barry
2300 Meadowlane Dr.
Easton, PA 18042
Beer, soda, whiskey, other advertising lithos: calendars, signs, trays, match holders.

Collector

Dolly Yanolko
2333 S. Third St.
Allentown, PA 18103 *

Collector

Jerry A. Phelps
6013 Innes Trace Rd.
Louisville, KY 40222
Phone: 502-425-4765
Wants pre-1900 country store and advertising items: signs, broadsides, clocks, tins, bins, display cases, etc.

Collector

Mike & Shirley Sembric
3743 Willow Run
Westlake, OH 44155
Phone: 216-734-2827
Specializes in country store advertising items.

Collector

Steve Ketcham
Box 24114
Edina, MN 55424
Phone: 612-920-4205
Seeking pre-1940 advertising signs, trays, mirrors, posters, etc. for all types of products.

Collector

Roger V. Baker
P.O. Box 620417
Woodside, CA 94062
Phone: 415-851-7188
Wants signs, calendars, trays, etc. from firearms and ammunition, beer, whiskey, tobacco, and general store companies.

Dealer

Alice's Advertising Antiques
Alice Kasten
131 Allenwood Road
Great Neck, NY 11023
Phone: 516-466-8954
Offers computerized search for advertising items such as cigarette silks, almanacs, advertising mirrors, trays, etc.; also buys.

Dealer

C.C. Cowboys
Marion Lathan
Rt. 1, Box 430
Chester, SC 29706
Phone: 803-377-8225 or 803-581-3000
Wants advertising signs, machines, clocks, displays, etc.; also soft drink, gum, ice cream, auto-related, etc. advertising items.

Dealer

Robert M. Levine
14342 S. Outer 40 Drive
Chesterfield, MO 63017
Phone: 314-469-6322   FAX: 314-469-6383
Buys, sells, trades and collects advertising items with company logo; must be at least 25 years old.

Expert

Dennis & George Collectibles
Dennis O'Brien
3407 Lake Montebello Dr.
Baltimore, MD 21218
Phone: 301-889-3964
With George Goehring runs collectibles mail order firm; collectors and dealers of upright pocket tobacco tins, advertising, etc.

Expert

Hoosier Peddler, The
Dave Harris
5400 S. Webster St.
Kokomo, IN 46902
Phone: 317-453-6172
*Specializing in rare comic toys & tin wind-ups, antique advertising & Disneyana. ***

Museum/Library

Warsaw Collection of Business Americana
Smithsonian Institution
Washington, DC 20560

Museum/Library

American Advertising Museum
9 NW Second Ave.
Portland, OR 97209
Phone: 503-226-0000   FAX: 503-226-2635
The AAM exhibits and preserves the history of the advertising industry; its history, different media, and most memorable campaigns.

Periodical

Newsletter: Tole House Newsletter, The
P.O. Box 8091
Erie, PA 16505
Phone: 814-838-9180
*A Newsletter for serious collectors of commercial collectibles. ***

Alka Seltzer

Collector

Darlene Shidler
58999 Lower Dr.
Goshen, IN 46526
Phone: 219-533-6102

Wants Alka Seltzer and Miles Laboratories, Inc. (Elkhart, IN) items: bottles, boxes, toys, "Speedy" figures, advertising, etc.

Beer & Soda

Museum/Library

Museum of Beverage Containers &
Advertising, The
1055 Ridgecrest Drive
Goodlettsville, TN 37072
Phone: 615-859-5236   FAX: 615-859-5238
The largest collection of soda and beer cans in the world; buy, sell, trade beer & soda advertising items.

Creamers

Periodical

Newsletter: Creamers
Lloyd B. Bindscheattle
P.O. Box 11
Lake Villa, IL 60046
A quarterly, 20 page newsletter dealing with glass, advertising, individual, dairy and coffee creamers; free ads; $4/yr.

Eating Utensils

Collector

Larry August
P.O. Box 1202
Marshalls Creek, PA 18335
Phone: 771-722-0242
Wants to buy spoons, forks, knives etc. with imprints from stores, firms, railroads, airlines, etc.; all conditions.

Figurals

Collector

Neil Berliner, M.D.
18-05 215 St.
Bayside, NY 11360
Phone: 718-279-2318
Wants rare 3-D advertising figurals: RCA Radiotron, Hotpoint Man, Squirt Boy, nodders, s/p, and store displays; trades welcome.

Firearms Related

Collector

Bill Bramlett
Box 1105
Florence, SC 29503
Phone: 803-393-7390
*Advertising items such as calendars, trade signs, posters from Remington, Marlin, Peters, U.M.C., Winchester, etc.; pre-1935. ***

Movie Related

Periodical

Magazine: Movie Advertising Collector
George Reed
P.O. Box 28587
Philadelphia, PA 19149

M.A.C. provides information concerning movie advertising; a non-profit organization for collector and non-collector alike.

Piano Related

Collector

Philip Jamison
17 Sharon Alley
West Chester, PA 19382
Phone: 215-696-8449
*Wants piano advertising; also wants old pianos. ***

Collector

Richard Howe
73 Saddlebrook Lane
Houston, TX 77024
*Wants piano/organ catalogs, trade cards, post cards, advertising items, roll catalogs, etc. ***

Posters

Dealer

Poster America
Jack Banning
138 West 18th St.
New York, NY 10011
Phone: 212-206-0499
*Specializing in vintage advertising posters from 1890 to 1950. ***

Expert

Miscellaneous Man
George Theofiles
Box 1776
New Freedom, PA 17349
Phone: 717-235-4766   FAX: 717-235-2853
Since 1970 offering catalogs of rare posters and early advertising and ephemera on hundreds of subjects. Descriptive flyer available.

Signs

Collector

Alex Caiola
84 Seneca
Emerson, NJ 07630
Phone: 201-262-7030
Wants bottling company soda or beer signs marked Seilheimer, Satteley, Taylor or Carldsadt.

Collector

Terry Allen
1705 2nd Ave.
Manchester, TN 37355
*Wants signs made of wood, tin, glass and paper. ***

Collector

Michael Bruner
8482 Huron River Drive
Union Lake, MI 48386
Phone: 313-674-0433 or 313-661-2359
Wants pre-1950 American or Canadian porcelain signs with good colors or graphics.

Collector
Richard Trautwein
437 Dawson St.
Sault Ste. Marie, MI 49783
Phone: 906-635-0356
Especially interested in porcelain advertising signs, neon clocks, and Coca Cola items.

Dealer
Darrow's Fun Antiques
Gary Darrow
309 E. 61st St.
New York, NY 10021
Phone: 212-838-0730
Buys & sells antique toys, ad signs, animated art, jukeboxes, slot machines, comic watches, bicycles & memorabilia of all types.

Museum/Library
Museum of Transportation
15 Newton Street
Brookline, MA 02146
Phone: 617-522-6140

Repro. Source
Attic Antiques, The
2301 Peach Orchard Rd.
Augusta, GA 30906
Sells reproduction paper and cardboard advertising signs.

Repro. Source
New Century Galleries, Inc.
10613 Lorain Ave.
Cleveland, OH 44111
Sells reproduction paper and cardboard advertising signs.

Repro. Source
Desperate Enterprises
Box 312
Wadsworth, OH 44281
Phone: 216-334-1897   FAX: 216-334-0153
Reproduces over 122 different nostalgia advertising signs on tin and over 725 nostalgia sepia toned 11"x14" photos.

Repro. Source
AAA Sign Co.
354 S. State Line Rd.
Lowellville, OH 44436
Phone: 216-536-8834 or 412-964-8394
Manufacturers and carries over 300 different reproduction embossed tin sign designs; full color catalog $2.

Tin Vienna Art Plates
Expert
Howard & Jean Hazelcorn
P.O. Box 1066
Teaneck, NJ 07666
Phone: 201-836-6293
Authors of "Hazelcorn's Price Guide to Tin Vienna Art Plates"; tin advertising plates made from the 1890's to the 1950's.

Trade Cards
Auction Service
Murray Cards (International) Ltd.
51 Watford Way
Hendon Central
London NW4 3JH England
Stocks and auctions trade cards; also publishes "Cigarette Card Values" - a catalog of cigarette and other trade cards.

Collector
Guy C. Weaver
302 South Newton St.
Pooler, GA 31322
Phone: 912-748-6002
Wants old trade cards, especially for bottled products.

Expert
Kit Barry
143 Main St.
Brattleboro, VT 05301
Phone: 802-254-2195

Periodical
Journal: Trade Card Journal, The
Kit Barry
143 Main St.
Brattleboro, VT 05301
Phone: 802-254-2195
A quarterly publication providing a centralized source of information about advertising trade card history and collecting.

Trade Cards (Tobacco)
Auction Service
Murray Cards (International) Ltd.
Newsletter: Cigarette Cards
51 Watford Way
Hendon Central
London NW4 3JH England
Stocks in excess of 20M cigarette & trade cards; monthly specialist auctions; publisher of card values & books on card collecting.

Collector
Paul Davis
306 Landsende Rd.
Devon, PA 19333
Phone: 215-644-1216
Wants insert and trade cards of tobacco companies; also wants Liebig and Au Bon Marche trade cards.

Periodical
Magazine: Cigarette Card Monthly
15 Debdale Lane
Keyworth
Nottingham NG12 5HT England *

Typewriter Related
Collector
Darryl Rehr
11433 Rochester Ave. #303
Los Angeles, CA 90025
Phone: 213-447-5229
Wants pre-1920 ads for typewriters and office equipment; also trade catalogs and business magazines, e.g. "Business Man's Monthly."

AGRICULTURE RELATED ITEMS
(see also FARM COLLECTIBLES; FARM MACHINERY; TOYS, Farm; TRACTORS)

AIR LABELS
(see also AIRLINE MEMORABILIA)

AIRLINE MEMORABILIA
(see also AIRPLANES; AVIATION; AVIATION MEMORABILIA; STAMP COLLECTING, Air Mail Related; TOYS, Airplane Related; TRANSPORTATION COLLECTIBLES)

Club/Association
World Airline Historical Society
Magazine: Captain's Log
Paul F. Collins, Pres.
3381 Apple Tree Lane
Erlanger, KY 41018
Phone: 606-342-9039
Members are interested in the collecting of airline memorabilia and in the study of airlines and airliners.

Club/Association
Aeronautica & Air Label Collectors Club
c/o Aerophilatelic Federation
P.O. Box 1239
Elgin, IL 60121
Phone: 708-888-1907
AALCC specializes in air labels, aviation postcards, timetables (schedules) and other airline memorabilia; issues air label catalogs.

Collector
Len Yafonsky
71-50 Parsons
Flushing, NY 11365
*Wants airline swizzle sticks, kiddie wings, cigarette lighters. *

Collector
Bob Shives
P.O. Box 976
Chambersburg, PA 17201-0976
Phone: 717-263-9316
Buying "Aero-Mini" metal airliner models; also buying most items from National, Eastern and Piedmont airlines.

Collector

Randy Ridgely
447 Oglethorpe Ave.
Athens, GA 30606
Wants railroad, steamship and airline items.

Collector

Bill Rosenbloom
1893 Worcester
St. Paul, MN 55116
Phone: 612-699-2784
Wants all older logoed airline items: playing cards, schedules, posters, kiddie wings, and all other logo-marked items.

Collector

Dick Wallin
P.O. Box 1784
Springfield, IL 62705
Phone: 217-498-9297
Wants airline dishes, glassware, silver serving pieces, playing cards, wings, badges, travel agent plane models, etc.

Dealer

JB Airline Collectibles
P.O. Box 1489
Lanesborough, MA 01237

Expert

John R. Joiner
245 Ashland Trail
Tyrone, GA 30290
Phone: 404-487-3732
Wants wings, hat badges, display models, postcards, timetables, pins, playing cards; anything old.

Expert

Stan Baumwald
2430 NE 35th St.
Lighthouse Point, FL 33064
Phone: 305-946-1315
Collector of airline memorabilia, especially wings, kiddie wings, playing cards, postcards; author of "Junior Crew Member Wings."

Baggage I.D. Labels

Collector

H. Van Dyk
7 Birchwood Ave.
Peabody, MA 01960
Wants airline baggage I.D. labels (for travelers' name/address); 1st Class, cabin baggage, crew, fragile, etc.; no destination labels.

Expert

H. Van Dyk
7 Birchwood Ave.
Peabody, MA 01960
Author of "Catalog of Baggage I.D. Labels, Vol. 1, U.S.A. & Canada" and "Catalog of Baggage I.D. Labels, Vol. 2, Europe & Middle East."

Junior Crew Member Wings

Collector

Todd Kelton
P.O. Box 28158
Sacramento, CA 95828
Phone: 916-383-4643
Wants "airline freebie" type; metal and plastic. *

Models (Desk)

(see also TOYS, Airplane)

Collector

Larry McLaughlin
17 Seventh Ave.
Smithtown, NY 11787
Phone: 516-265-9224
Wants to buy airplane, rocket, missle desk models: manufacturers' display models, travel agency models, commercial or military, etc.

Collector

David Ostrowski
5411 Masser Lane
Fairfax, VA 22032

Man./Prod./Dist.

Daron Worldwide Trading, Inc.
P.O. Box 1375
Roslyn Heights, NY 11577
Phone: 516-742-2323   FAX: 516-742-2353
Sells Wooster collectors' scale model aircraft; same models as produced for the airlines; most popular commercial aircraft.

Pan-American Airways

Club/Association

Pan American Airmail Collectors Club
c/o Aerophilatelic Federation
P.O. Box 1239
Elgin, IL 60121-1239
Phone: 708-888-1907
Members interested in Pan American Airways including covers, cachets, labels, charts, posters, timetables, china dinner service, etc.

Pilots Wings

Collector

Lee
Box 587
Hope Mills, NC 28348
Wings: military and civilian, airline model planes; also law enforcement badges. *

Expert

Col. L.G. Frazier, Ret.
Route 2, Box 401D
Dale, TX 78616
Expert on pilot qualification badges. *

Playing Cards

Expert

Top Flite information
Fred Chan
P.O. Box 473
Burtonsville, MD 20866
Phone: 301-381-4626
Author of "Airline Playing Cards" with supplements; buys and sells airline playing cards (decks and singles).

AIRPLANES

(see also AIRLINE MEMORABILIA;
AVIATION; AVIATION MEMORABILIA)

Club/Association

Antique Airplane Association, Inc.
Magazine: Antique Airplane News & Digest
Robert Taylor, Pres.
Rt. 2, Box 172
Ottumwa, IA 52501
Phone: 515-938-2773

Collector

Bruce Pike
RD #1, Box 291
Aliquippa, PA 15001
Phone: 412-378-0449
Wants old ignition model airplane engines, parts and related items. *

Museum/Library

Reynolds Aviation Museum
Byron E. Reynolds
4110 - 57 Street
Wetaskiwin
Alberta T9A 2B6 Canada

Museum/Library

New England Air Museum of the
Connecticut Aeronautical Historical
Bradley International Airport
Windsor Locks, CT 06096
Phone: 203-623-3305

Museum/Library

National Air & Space Museum
6th St. & Independence Ave. SW
Washington, DC 20560
Phone: 202-357-2700

Museum/Library

Experimental Aircraft Association
Aviation Foundation, Inc.
Whittman Air Field
Oshkosh, WI 54093
Phone: 414-426-4800

Museum/Library

Museum of Science & Industry
Keith R. Gill
57th St. & Lake Shore Drive
Chicago, IL 60637
Phone: 312-684-1414   FAX: 312-684-5580

Periodical

Sky Books International Inc.
Magazine: FlyPast
48 East 50th St.
New York, NY 10022
England's top selling aviation monthly.

Periodical

World War I Aeroplanes, Inc.
Journal: WWI Aero
15 Crescent Road
Poughkeepsie, NY 12601
Phone: 914-473-3679
A bi-monthly magazine for collectors, restorers, replica builders, historians, and modelers focusing on 1900-1919 aircraft.

Periodical

World War I Aeroplanes, Inc.
Journal: Skyways
15 Crescent Road
Poughkeepsie, NY 12601
Phone: 914-473-3679
A bi-monthly magazine for collectors, restorers, replica builders, historians, and modelers focusing on 1920-1940 aircraft.

Periodical

Magazine: Air Wars
8931 Kittyhawk Ave.
Los Angeles, CA 90045
Focuses on the restoration of classic (1919-1939) fighter planes; how-to articles and photos, museum articles, plans for models, etc.

Ford Tri-Motors

Collector

Tim O'Callaghan
46878 Bettyhill
Plymouth, MI 48170
Phone: 313-459-4636
Buys any item related to the Tri-motor airplanes built be Ford Motor Co. from 1926-1932.

Military

Periodical

Business Press Inter., Ltd.
Magazine: Aeroplane Monthly
205 East 42nd St.
New York, NY 10017
Articles on the veterans of WWI, the Spitfires, Hurricanes, Heinkels and Messerschmitts of WWII; preservation, competition, photos, etc.

Periodical

Magazine: Windsock
4314 West 238th St.
Torrance, CA 90505
The journal for WWI aeroplane enthusiasts and modelers.

Model

(see also MODELS; MODEL KITS)

Club/Association

Society of Antique Modelers
Newsletter: Sam Speaks
2538 N. Spurgeon St.
Santa Anna, CA 92706
Phone: 714-542-8294
Focuses on the collecting, restoring and operating of antique model airplanes.

Periodical

Magazine: Model Aviation
1810 Samuel Morse Dr.
Reston, VA 22090
Magazine written for all four categories of scale model aircraft: radio control, r/c giant, control line, and free flight.

Model (Remote Control)

Periodical

Magazine: R/C Modeler Magazine
P.O. Box 487
Sierra Madre, CA 91024
Complete R/C publication for the remote control enthusiast; construction, how-to's; equipment, contests, etc.

Periodical

Magazine: Model Builder
898 W. 16th St.
Newport Beach, CA 92663
Up to the minute articles about the hobby, plans, construction, contests, etc.

Sailplanes

Club/Association

Vintage Sailplane Association
Magazine: Bungee Cord
Rt. 1 Box 239
Lovettesville, VA 22080
Phone: 703-822-5504
Soaring enthusiasts who are keeping our gliding history and heritage alive by building, restoring, flying gliders from the past.

Collector

J. Scott
Scott Airpark
Rt. 1 Box 239
Lovettesville, VA 22080
Phone: 703-822-5504
Private collector of rare and restorable gliders.

Waco

Club/Association

International Waco Association, The
Magazine: IWA Magazine
Alan & Drina Abel
806 Lockport Rd.
P.O. Box 2065
Terre Haute, IN 47802
Phone: 812-232-1042

Maintains large file of air airplane history and photos; contributions of related material welcomed.

AIRSHIPS

Balloons

(see also STAMP COLLECTING, Covers (Balloon Related))

Club/Association

Lighter-Than-Air Society
1800 Triplett Blvd.
Akron, OH 44206 *

Collector

John Dillon
850 Meadow Lane
Camp Hill, PA 17011
Phone: 717-761-6895
*Wants ballooning related items: plates, posters, etc. **

Dirigibles & Zeppelins

Club/Association

Zeppelin Collectors Club
Newsletter: Zeppelin Collector
c/o Aerophilatelic Federation
P.O. Box 1239
Elgin, IL 60121-1239
Phone: 708-888-1907
Members collect anniversary covers of the Zepplin flights; also related memorabilia: china, cards, photos, labels, tickets, etc.

Collector

Hank Loescher
52 Melrose Ave.
Bridgeport, CT 06605-3056
Phone: 203-368-4983
Wants zeppelin or dirigible related items: books, charts, photos, relics, souvenirs, fabric, personal items, info., etc.

Dealer

Dealer
6001 Riverdale Ave.
Bronx, NY 10471 *

Expert

Art Bink
Zepplin
P.O. Box 2502
Cinnaminson, NJ 08077
Phone: 609-829-3959
Historian not dealer wants airship items: zeppelin, blimp, dirigible memorabilia; pieces, toys, photos, books, medals, china, etc.

Museum/Library
Navy Lakehurst Historical Society
Art Bink
Zepplin
P.O. Box 2502
Cinnaminson, NJ 08077
Phone: 609-829-3959

ALARM BOXES

Collector
Tom Mills
Bellevue Rd.
Berlin, MA 01503
*Wants fire alarm and police boxes, cast iron signs and U.S.P.O. pickup boxes; also wants porcelain license plates and signs. ***

ALASKA COLLECTIBLES

Expert
Alaskan Heritage Bookshop
174 S. Franklin
P.O. Box 22165
Juneau, AK 99802
Phone: 907-586-6748 or 907-789-8450
Buys/sells books, maps, stereo views, prints, photos, souvenirs, Klondike, letters, ephemera, etc.; anything Alaska/Yukon/Klondike.

ALCOHOLICS ANONYMOUS ITEMS

Collector
Clark Phelps
390 "K" Street
Salt Lake City, UT 84103
Phone: 801-355-1394
Historian wants AA books, pamphlets, etc. before 1974.

Expert
Bishop of Books, The
Charles Bishop, Jr.
46 Eureka Ave.
Wheeling, WV 26003
Phone: 304-242-2937
Buy, sell, appraise books, magazines, posters, postcards, etc. relating to alcoholism or Alcoholics Anonymous.

ALMANACS

(see also BOOKS)

ALUMINUM

Hammered

Club/Association
Aluminum Collectors
Newsletter: Aluminist, The
Dannie Woodard
P.O. Box 1347
Weatherford, TX 76086
Phone: 817-594-4680

Newsletter provides updated information on prices, patterns, ads and companies; group organized in 1990; 200 members.

Expert
Dannie Woodard
P.O. Box 1347
Weatherford, TX 76086
Phone: 817-594-4680
Co-author with Billie Wood of "Hammered Aluminum - Hand Wrought Collectibles."

AMISH ITEMS

Collector
Linda Grunewald
P.O. Box 311
Utica, MI 48087
Phone: 313-739-4053
*Wants anything Amish pre-1930's: quilts, rag dolls, etc. ***

AMUSEMENT PARK ITEMS

(see also CAROUSELS & CAROUSEL FIGURES; COIN-OPERATED MACHINES, Arcade Games; ROLLER COASTERS; TARGETS, Shooting Gallery)

Auction Service
Norton Auctioneers of Michigan, Inc.
David A. Norton
Pearl at Monroe
Coldwater, MI 49036
Phone: 517-279-9063   FAX: 517-279-9191
Specializing in the auctioning of amusement rides, carousels, amusement parks, arcades, museums, etc.

Club/Association
International Association of Amusement
Parks & Attractions
1448 Duke St.
Alexandria, VA 22314
Phone: 703-836-4800   FAX: 703-836-4801

Club/Association
Historic Amusement Foundation
Newsletter: HAF Times
4410 North Keystone Ave.
Indianapolis, IN 46205
Phone: 317-841-7677

Club/Association
National Amusement Park Historical
Association
Newsletter: National Amusement Park
   Historical News
P.O. Box 83
Mount Prospect, IL 60056 *

Collector
Tom Keefe
P.O. Box 464
Tinley Park, IL 60477

*Wants signs, tickets, carousel horses, tokens, photos, movies, letterheads, ride manufacturer's catalogs, posters, advertising items. ***

Expert
Prize Publishers
Thomas G. Morris
P.O. Box 8307
Medford, OR 97504
Phone: 503-779-3164
Specializing in chalkware figures, knock-down figures, shooting gallery targets, etc.

ANGELS

Club/Association
Angels Collectors Club of America
Newsletter: Halo Everybody!
Mary Winemniller
2706 Green Acre Dr.
Sebring, FL 33870

ANIMAL COLLECTIBLES

(see also CAT COLLECTIBLES; DOG COLLECTIBLES; ELEPHANT COLLECTIBLES; FROGS COLLECTIBLES; HORSE COLLECTIBLES; INSECTS; VETERINARY MEDICINE ITEMS)

Dealer
Just Animals
Barbara Framke
15525 Fitzgerald
Livonia, MI 48154
Phone: 313-464-8493
Buys and sells animal collectibles, especially figurines; features and special orders "Stone Critters."

Plastic Models

Collector
Chelle Fulk
3007 Darden Rd.
Greensboro, NC 27407-6801
Phone: 919-299-7261
Wants plastic horses, dogs, cattle, wildlife, etc.; especially Breyer; any size, condition or color.

ANIMAL TROPHIES

(see also SKELETONS; SPORTING COLLECTIBLES)

Collector
Gene Harris
7123 S.W. 117 Ave.
Miami, FL 33183
Phone: 305-274-4044
Wants ivory, antlers, skulls, horns, animal mounts, pelts, skins, fossils, feathers, or art made form the above.

Dealer

Randall Thompson
654 Lela Pl.
Grand Junction, CO 81504
African trophies, European type skull mounts on plaques, warthog, reedbuck, warthog teeth, American antlers, small horns and antlers.

ANIMATION FILM ART

(see also CARTOON ART)

Club/Association

Greater Washington Animation Collectors Club
Nancy S. McClellan, Pres
12423 Hedges Run Dr. #184
Lake Ridge, VA 22192

Dealer

Animation Gallery, Ltd.
Don Bell
1977 Queen St. East, 2nd Floor
Toronto
Ontario M4L 1J1 Canada *

Dealer

Gifted Images Gallery
68 Seaman Ave.
Rockville Ctr., NY 11570
Phone: 516-536-6886 or 800-726-6708
FAX: 516-763-5213
Buys and sells original animation art from the Walt Disney Studios.

Dealer

Cartoon Carnival Gallery, The
Stu & Miriam Reisbord
2 Rabbit Run
Wallingford, PA 19086
Phone: 215-566-4343 or 215-566-1292
FAX: 215-566-2727
Specializing in Disney vintage drawings, cels and backgrounds for over 20 years; also original pen & ink classic syndicated art.

Dealer

Seaside Gallery
Melanie Oehrli
P.O. Box 1
Nags Head, NC 27959
Phone: 919-441-5418 or 800-828-2444
FAX: 919-441-8563
Wants original oils, graphics, sculpture, and animation film art; also buys and sells old and new animation art.

Dealer

One-of-a-Kind Cartoon Art
Elvena Greet
775 Livingstone Place
Decatur, GA 30030
Phone: 404-377-3333 *

Dealer

Art To Cel
6161 28th St. SE
Grand Rapids, MI 49546
Phone: 616-940-3665 or 616-940-1832
Original cels and drawings; also limited editions.
*

Expert

Thomas R. Horvitz
Suite 601
255 N. El Cielo
Palm Springs, CA 92262
Phone: 619-320-9599 *

Museum/Library

Museum of Modern Art, The
11 W. 53rd. Street
New York, NY 10019
Phone: 212-708-9889

Museum/Library

Museum of Cartoon Art
Comly Ave.
Rye Brook, NY 10573
Phone: 914-939-0234
Acknowledged by most as the premier repository of animation art and history in the U.S.

Museum/Library

Baltimore Museum of Art, The
Art Museum Drive
Baltimore, MD 21218
Phone: 301-396-7101

Museum/Library

Walt Disney Archives
500 South Buena Vista St.
Burbank, CA 91521

Periodical

Magazine: American Cartoon Art
P.O. Box 425
Lodi, NJ 07644
Phone: 201-925-2458
Focuses on all types of comic art. *

ANTIQUES

(see also COLLECTIBLES)

Club/Association

Antique Collectors' Club, Ltd.
Magazine: Antique Collecting
Jean Johnson, Mgr.
5 Church Street
Woodbridge
Suffolk IP12 1DS England
A sophisticated magazine of the Antique Collectors' Club, the parent organization for dozens of regional antiques clubs within the U.K.

Club/Association

Questers, The
Magazine: Quester Quarterly
210 S. Quince St.
Philadelphia, PA 19107
Phone: 215-923-5183
Promotes the study and appreciation of antiques and objects of art and of their historical background; regional chapters. *

Club/Association

American Antique Arts Association,
Alexandria Chapter
Newsletter: A.A.A.A. journal
P.O. Box 426
Temple Hills, MD 20748-2413
Phone: 301-449-5372
The AAAA is devoted to the appreciation, study and preservation of American antiques, architecture, art, crafts and local history.

Club/Association

Victorian Homeowner's Association
Newsletter: Victorian Homeowner's
Association Newsletter
P.O. Box 846
Sutter Creek, CA 95685
Phone: 209-267-0774
For owners of Victorian homes; home renovation, antiques and collecting info.

Expert

George E. Michael
P.O. Box 2087
Merrimack, NH 03054-2087
Phone: 603-424-7400
Specialist in fine arts and antiques: expert witness, auctioneer, writer, editor, consultant, lecturer and instructor.

Misc. Service

Artfact, Inc.
Stephen J. Abt, III
Suite E104
1130 Ten Rod Rd.
North Kingstown, RI 02852
Phone: 401-295-2658
A computerized library recording auction sales of art and antiques; complete descriptions, prices realized, on-screen images.

Misc. Service

Antique Researchers
P.O. Box 79
Waban, MA 02168
Phone: 617-969-6238
Research detectives specializing in all types of questions, problems, or issues relating to art and antiques; do not buy or sell.

Misc. Service

Amherst Management Associates
Irene M. Spaulding
P.O. Box 38
Amherst, NH 03031
Phone: 603-472-2371
A lecture bureau representing some of the finest guest speakers in the antiques and collectibles field.

Misc. Service

Edward J. Pfeiffer
361 Lovely St.
Avon, CT 06001
Phone: 203-673-6678   FAX: 203-676-9481
Writing & public relations services for auctions, shows, dealers, museums; publicity, event promotion, speeches, scripts, presentations.

Misc. Service

Centrox World Auction Monitor
Pierre Sernet
17 E. 767th St.
New York, NY 10021
Phone: 212-772-9173
Subscription service notifying subscribers of articles of interest appearing in upcoming auctions; covers over 175 auction houses

Misc. Service

Period Antiques Delivery Service, Inc.
Donald L. Raleigh
397 Cypress St.
P.O. Box L
Millington, MD 21651
Phone: 301-778-4357 or 800-962-1424
Specializes in the professional transportation of antiques and works of art.

Misc. Service

Timeless Treasures Publishing
Catalog: For Collectors Only
Robert Dabbs
P.O. Box 341
Lexington, MO 64067
Phone: 816-584-7411
A one-stop ordering service for SAMPLES of hundreds of antiques & collectibles related catalogs and periodicals.

Misc. Service

Hansen's Academy
Elizabeth Hansen
P.O. Box 1330
Freedom, CA 95019
A non-profit academy for learning about antiques and collectibles, and about being an antiques dealer.

Museum/Library

Shelburne Museum, Inc.
U.S. Route 7
Shelburne, VT 05482
Phone: 802-985-3346

37 historic structures; diverse collection of American folk, fine, decorative and utilitarian art.

Museum/Library

Henry Francis DuPont Winterthur Museum
P.O. Box 90
Winterthur, DE 19735-0001
Phone: 800-448-3883 or 302-888-4741

Museum/Library

Henry Ford Museum & Greenfield Village
P.O. Box 1970
Dearborn, MI 48121
Phone: 313-271-1620

Periodical

Quartet Publications
Magazine: Antique & Collectors Fayre
149 North Street
Romford
Essex RM1 1ED England
*An English monthly magazine for the antiques and collectibles trade. **

Periodical

Newspaper: Collectors Gazette
17 Adbolton Lodge
Carlton
Nottingham, England **

Periodical

Quadrant Subscription Services, Ltd.
Directory: Antique Dealer & Collectors Guide, The
35 Perrymount Rd.
Haywards Heath
RH16 3DH England
Glossy international monthly magazine for dealers and collectors: articles, ads, auction reports, etc.

Periodical

Amis-Gibbs Publications, Ltd.
Magazine: Antique Showcase
Barbara Sutton-Smith, Ed
P.O. Box 260
Bala
Ontario POC 1AO Canada
Phone: 205-762-5631
National monthly magazine with diverse articles, show and auction reports, museum exhibits, book reviews, upcoming trends, etc.

Periodical

Newspaper: Antiques Trade Gazette
17 Whitcomb Street
London WC2H 7PL England
A substantial weekly newspaper with articles, calendar of shows and sales, ads, etc. focusing on the English market.

Periodical

Kollectrama Publications
Magazine: Collectors Mart
Old Railway Station
Horringford, Arreton
Isle Of Wight P030 3AP England
A colorful magazine with collectibles articles on breweriana, advertising, bottles, coronation wares, whisky pitchers, signs, etc.

Periodical

Newspaper: Insight On Collectibles
R.R. 1, P.O. Box 130
Durham
Ontario N0G 10R Canada **

Periodical

Magazine: World of Antiques & Fine Arts
234 King's Road
London SW3 5UA England **

Periodical

Newspaper: New England Antiques Journal
Jody Young, GM
P.O. Box 120
Ware, MA 01082
Phone: 413-967-3505   FAX: 413-967-6009

Periodical

Victorian Homes
Magazine: Victorian Homes
P.O. Box 61
Millers Falls, MA 01349
Phone: 413-659-3785   FAX: 413-659-3113
Glossy magazine with information sources for locating special items for restoring and decorating Victorian homes.

Periodical

Newspaper: MassBay Antiques
Shannon Aaron, Ed.
9 Page St.
P.O. Box 293
Danvers, MA 01923
Phone: 508-777-7070   FAX: 508-774-6365
Circulation of 20,000 plus 5000 more during big show months; shows, auctions, people, research articles, extensive calendar section.

Periodical

Newspaper: Cape Cod Antiques & Arts
P.O. Box 400
Yarmouth Port, MA 02675
A monthly supplement to The Register concentrating on art & antiques in the Cape Cod area.

Periodical

Magazine: New England Antiques & Art Magazine
100 Commercial St. #106
Portland, ME 04101

Periodical
Maine Antique Digest, Inc.
Newspaper: Maine Antique Digest
Sam & Salley Pennington
P.O. Box 645
Waldoboro, ME 04572
Phone: 207-832-7534
The major monthly newspaper on antiques, art and antiques.

Periodical
Newton Bee Publishing Co.
Newspaper: Antiques & the Arts Weekly (The Newtown Bee)
5 Church Hill Rd.
Newtown, CT 06470-9987
Phone: 203-426-3141

Periodical
Sotheby's Subscriptions
Magazine: Preview
P.O. Box 5111
Norwalk, CT 06856-9851
Phone: 203-447-6843
A magazine exploring the history, forms, styles, techniques, etc. of the world of art; meet the collectors, experts & specialists.

Periodical
Newsletter: Auction Forum U.S.A.
341 West 12th Street
New York, NY 10014
Phone: 212-627-1372 or 800-388-3878
The monthly buyer's guide to regional auctions and antiques sources in America; includes auction previews, results and calendar.

Periodical
GCR Publishing
Magazine: Country Accents
Marilyn Hansen, Ed.
1700 Broadway
New York, NY 10019
Phone: 212-541-7100 or 212-245-1242
A monthly magazine that focuses on decorating, crafts, collectibles, and antiques.

Periodical
Magazine: Country Living
224 W. 57th Street
New York, NY 10019
A monthly magazine that focuses on decorating, crafts, collectibles, and antiques.

Periodical
Magazine: Colonial Homes
1790 Broadway
New York, NY 10019 *

Periodical
Brant Publications, Inc.
Magazine: Magazine Antiques, The
980 Madison Ave.
New York, NY 10021
Phone: 800-247-2160

Periodical
Newspaper: Treasure Chest
253 W. 72 St. #211A
New York, NY 10023
Phone: 212-496-2234
The information source & marketplace for collectors & dealers of antiques and collectibles.

Periodical
Magazine: Antiques & Collectibles Magazine
P.O. Box 268
Greenvale, NY 11548 *

Periodical
Newspaper: New York Antique Almanac
P.O. Box 335
Lawrence, NY 11559
Phone: 716-924-4040
Antiques newspaper with ads, articles, auction and show reports; concentrating in the Northeast.

Periodical
Newspaper: Mountain Heritage & Antiques
Bridge Street
Hunter, NY 12442 *

Periodical
Antique Collectors' Club, Ltd.
Magazine: Antique Collecting
Market Street Industrial Park
Wappingers' Falls, NY 12590
Phone: 914-297-0003 or 800-252-5231
    FAX: 914-297-0068
Sophisticated magazine of ACC; the parent organization for dozens of regional U.K. antiques clubs.

Periodical
Newspaper: Collectors World
35 Fort Hill Avenue
Canandriqua, NY 14424 *

Periodical
Wolfe Publications
Newspaper: New York-Pennsylvania Collector, The
Andrew D. Wolfe, Pub.
Drawer C
Fishers, NY 14453
Phone: 716-924-4040   FAX: 716-924-7734
Informative articles on art, antiques & Americana; show and auction reviews; annual subject index in Jan.; calendar of events.

Periodical
Historical Times, Inc.
Magazine: Early American Life
P.O. Box 8200
Harrisburg, PA 17105-8200
Phone: 717-657-9555
Magazine devoted to arts, crafts, collecting, travel and furnishings.

Periodical
Joel Sater Publications
Newspaper: Antiques & Auction News
Doris Ann Johnson, Editor
P.O. Box 500, Route 230 West
Mount Joy, PA 17552
Phone: 717-653-9797 or 800-428-4211
    FAX: 717-653-5606
A weekly newspaper featuring antiques, collectibles, auctions, sales, shows and exhibits.

Periodical
Newspaper: Antique Catalog
207 N. Bowman Ave.
Merion Station, PA 19066 *

Periodical
Newspaper: Renninger's Antique Guide
P.O. Box 495
Lafayette Hill, PA 19444
Phone: 215-828-4614 or 215-825-6392
Newspaper covering antique shows, shops, flee markets and auctions catering primarily to the mid-Atlantic region.

Periodical
Smithsonian Institution
Magazine: Smithsonian Magazine
900 Jefferson Drive NW
Washington, DC 20560
Phone: 202-357-1300

Periodical
Newspaper: Antique Market Tabloid
10822 Child's Court
Silver Spring, MD 20901 *

Periodical
Collectors' Information Clearinghouse (CIC)
Directory: CIC's Antiques & Collectibles Resource Directory
David J. Maloney, ISA
P.O. Box 2049
Frederick, MD 21702-1049
Phone: 301-695-8544 or 301-663-0818
    FAX: 301-695-6491
Publishes major information source for collectors, sellers, claims adjusters, etc.: Experts, Buyers, Collector Clubs, Periodicals,

Periodical
Oxford University Press, Inc.
Journal: Journal of the History of Collections
c/o Journals Marketing Dept.
2001 Evans Road
Cary, NC 27513
An English journal dedicated to the study of collections from palaces and household accumulations to systematic museum collections.

Periodical
Newspaper: MidAtlantic Antiques Magazine
Lydia A. Tucker, Ed.
P.O. Box 908
Henderson, NC 27536
Phone: 916-492-4001   FAX: 919-430-0125
A monthly newspaper for collectibles and the antiques trade; listing upcoming shows & auctions; display ads for shops and mail order

Periodical
Newspaper: Carolina Antique News
P.O. Box 241114
Charlotte, NC 28224 *

Periodical
Newspaper: Southern Antiques
P.O. Drawer 1107
Decatur, GA 30031-1107
Phone: 404-289-0054
The South's leading monthly antiques and collectibles newspaper.

Periodical
Newspaper: Antiques & Crafts Gazette, The
Bob & Betty Morck
P.O. Box 181
Cumming, GA 30130
Phone: 404-887-3563
*"The Gazette" is a quarterly newspaper serving the Southern U.S. *

Periodical
Newsmagazine: Antique Monthly
2100 Powers Ferry Road
Atlanta, GA 30339
Phone: 404-955-5656   FAX: 404-952-0669
Monthly newsmagazine covering the fine antiques market; color photos, ads, auction results, show calendar, etc.

Periodical
Newspaper: Antique Shoppe
P.O. Box 2335
Inverness, FL 32651-2335 *

Periodical
Newspaper: Antiquarian, The
223 SE 37th Ave.
Ocala, FL 32671-3045

Periodical
Newspaper: Antique Press, The
12403 N. Florida Ave.
Tampa, FL 33612
Phone: 813-935-7577
*Florida's newspaper of antiques and collectibles. Published 18 times per year. *

Periodical
Newspaper: Antiques & Collectibles Buyer
P.O. Box 320014
Tampa, FL 33679 *

Periodical
Turner Publishing Co.
Newspaper: Antique Gazette
Suite 106
6949 Charlotte Pike
Nashville, TN 37209-4208
Phone: 615-352-0941   FAX: 615-352-0941
Complete antiques guide; shop/mall locator, show calendar, classifieds, articles; nationwide distribution.

Periodical
Schroeder's Publishing Co., Inc.
Newsletter: Schroeder's Insider & Price Update
P.O. Box 3009
Paducah, KY 42001
*A monthly newsletter published for the antique and collectible marketplace. *

Periodical
Newspaper: Buckeye Marketeer, The
P.O. Box 954
Westerville, OH 43081
Phone: 614-895-1663
A monthly newspaper focusing on antiques and collectibles shows, flea markets, auctions and festivals.

Periodical
Newspaper: Antique Review
P.O. Box 538
Worthington, OH 43085
Phone: 800-992-9757

Periodical
Americana Magazine Inc.
Magazine: Americana
205 West Center St.
Marion, OH 43302

Periodical
Magazine: Western Reserve Magazine
2101 Superior Ave.
Cleveland, OH 44114
Phone: 216-241-7639
*Magazine featuring antiques, local history and historic preservation. *

Periodical
Kovels on Antiques and Collectibles
Newsletter: Kovels On Antiques & Collectibles
Ralph & Terry Kovel
P.O. Box 22200
Beachwood, OH 44122
                         FAX: 216-742-3115
Focuses on antiques, decorative arts and collectibles; identification and buying tips, prices, reproduction alerts, etc.

Periodical
Farm & Dairy Publishers
Newspaper: Antique Collector & Auction Guide, The
P.O. Box 38
Salem, OH 44460
Phone: 216-337-3419 or 216-337-3164
                         FAX: 216-337-9550
A weekly insert to "Farm and Dairy" newspaper; serving the antiques and collectibles trade; ads, auctions, articles, etc.

Periodical
Mayhill Publications, Inc.
Newspaper: AntiqueWeek
Tom Hoepf, Mng. Ed.
P.O. Box 90
Knightstown, IN 46148
Phone: 317-345-5133 or 800-876-5133
                         FAX: 800-876-5133
A leading antiques, auctions and collectors' newspaper published weekly every Monday in two regional editions: Eastern and Central.

Periodical
Antique & Collectible News Service
Newsletter: Inside Antiques
Robert Reed, Ed.
P.O. Box 204
Knightstown, IN 46148
Phone: 317-345-7479
Monthly newsletter focusing on antiques and collectibles; feature articles, lists of new books, information of interest to collectors.

Periodical
Newspaper: Collectors Guide
21101 East 11 Mile Road
St. Clair Shores, MI 48081 *

Periodical
Newspaper: Auction & Antique News
Tony Baird, Ed.
909 Buckingham Ave.
Flint, MI 48507
Phone: 313-743-1571   FAX: 313-744-3290
A bi-monthly 12-pg. newspaper with articles, shows, events, auction reports, contemporary collectibles, ads, etc.

Periodical
Magazine: Country Home Magazine
1716 Locust Avenue
Des Moines, IA 50336 *

Periodical
Magazine: Art & Antiques
P.O. Box 11697
Des Moines, IA 50340
Phone: 800-274-7594
Glossy magazine focusing on the fine and decorative arts and in antiques: colorful ads, articles, auction reports, etc.

Periodical

Yankee, Inc.
Magazine: Yankee Magazine
P.O. Box 10531
Des Moines, IA 50347-0531

Periodical

Newspaper: Collectors News
Cherie Henn, Pub.
P.O. Box 156
Grundy Center, IA 50638
Phone: 319-824-6981   FAX: 319-824-3414
The monthly publication for antiquers & collectors nationwide; complete show & sale calendar, articles, expert advice, values, etc.

Periodical

Newsletter: Antiquing U.S.A.
Route 2, Box 11
Fontanelle, IA 50846-9702 *

Periodical

Newspaper: Antique Trader Weekly, The
P.O. Box 1050
Dubuque, IA 52001
Phone: 319-588-2073   FAX: 319-588-0888
A weekly newspaper (about 100 pgs.) with ads, articles and news on the antiques and collectibles hobby.

Periodical

Price Guide: Antique Trader Price Guide To Antiques, The
P.O. Box 1050
Dubuque, IA 52001
Phone: 319-588-2073
*A monthly newsmagazine-format price guide for the antiques and collectibles trade. **

Periodical

Newspaper: Antiques Journal
P.O. Box 1046
Dubuque, IA 52001 *

Periodical

CarPac Publishing Co.
Newspaper: Collectors Journal
Keith Knaack
1800 W. D St.
P.O. Box 601
Vinton, IA 52349-0601
Phone: 319-472-4763 or 319-472-4764
              FAX: 319-472-3117
Weekly auction paper for collectors and antique lovers; weekly auction and flea market calendar, auction results, and articles.

Periodical

Antique American, Inc. Mall
Newsletter: Antique America News
Cheryle Frye
702 W. 76th St.
Davenport, IA 52806
Phone: 319-386-3430 or 800-747-0474

A monthly newsletter put out by the mall; ads, articles about antiques and collectibles, reproduction alerts.

Periodical

Magazine: Nostalgia Magazine
9401 West Beloit Road, # 311
Milwaukee, WI 53227 *

Periodical

Newspaper: Antiques Dealer Digest
P.O. Box 109
Madison, WI 53701 *

Periodical

Newspaper: Northern Collector
Box 189
Govnick, MN 56644 *

Periodical

Magazine: Antiques Advertiser U.S.A.
37419 Hwy. 45
Lake Villa, IL 60046
Phone: 312-356-1035   FAX: 312-356-8961
*Monthly paper with classifieds & articles about the antiques and collectibles trade. **

Periodical

Newspaper: Keystone Country Peddler
P.O. Box 467
Richmond, IL 60071 *

Periodical

Lightner Publishing Corp.
Magazine: Antiques & Collecting Hobbies
Dale K. Graham, Pub.
1006 S. Michigan Ave.
Chicago, IL 60605
Phone: 312-939-4767   FAX: 312-939-0053
Informative articles on antiques & collectors items; up-to-the-minute news in the field, auction results, ads, book reviews.

Periodical

Magazine: Victorian Accents
P.O. Box 508
Mt. Morris, IL 61054-7995
*A monthly magazine that focuses on decorating, crafts, collectibles, and antiques. **

Periodical

Journal: American Collectors Journal, The
204 W. 4th St.
P.O. Box 407
Kewanee, IL 61443
Phone: 309-852-2602
A bi-monthly publication focusing on antiques, nostalgia, collectibles and hobbies.

Periodical

Newspaper: Collector, The
105 S. Buchanan
Box 158
Heyworth, IL 61745
Phone: 309-473-2466 or 309-473-2414

Monthly newspaper for those interested in antiques and collectibles; flea markets, shows, articles, event reviews, etc.

Periodical

WEB Communications, Inc.
Magazine: Antique Market Report
Debra Roark
P.O. Box 12830
Wichita, KS 67270
Phone: 316-946-0600   FAX: 331-694-0675
Bi-monthly magazine focusing on prices being realized in the antiques industry and particularly on the results of auction house

Periodical

Newspaper: Old News is Good News Antiques Gazette, The
Bill Alexander, Ed.
P.O. Box 65292
Baton Rouge, LA 70896
Phone: 504-923-0575   FAX: 504-923-0576
A monthly newspaper focusing on the heritage, antiques, collectibles and attractions of the South.

Periodical

Newspaper: Antiques & Collectible News
P.O. Box 171713
Arlington, TX 76003 *

Periodical

Newspaper: Southwest Antiques News
P.O. Box 66402
Houston, TX 77006 *

Periodical

Newspaper: Antique & Collectors Guide
8510 Frazier Drive
Beaumont, TX 77707
*Antiques guide to the Gulf states. **

Periodical

Newspaper: Mountain States Collector
Box 2525
Evergreen, CO 80439 *

Periodical

Arizona Antique News
Newspaper: Arizona Antique News & Southwest Antiques Journal
Ron Smisek, Ed.
P.O. Box 26536
Phoenix, AZ 85068
Phone: 602-943-9137
A monthly publication designed for collectors and dealers; syndicated writers offer regional perspectives of the antiques hobby.

Periodical

Newspaper: West Coast Peddler
P.O. Box 5134
Whittier, CA 90607
Phone: 213-698-1718
Oldest monthly newspaper about antiques, the arts, and collectibles serving the Pacific States.

Periodical

Newspaper: <u>Antique & Collectibles</u>
Sandy Pasqua, Ed.
P.O. Drawer 1565
El Cajon, CA 92022
Phone: 619-593-2925 or 619-593-2916
                          FAX: 619-442-4043
13th year of publishing; concentrating on antiques and collectibles of southern CA: auctions, shows, articles, ads, etc.

Periodical

Magazine: <u>Antique Collector, The</u>
Jim Lance
Box 271369
Escondido, CA 92027
Phone: 619-747-8327   FAX: 619-432-6560
Beautifully illustrated British magazine with authoritative articles over the whole range of fine and decorative arts.

Periodical

Collectors Connection & Registry
Directory: <u>Who's Who In Collecting & Antiques</u>
P.O. Box 54
South San Francisco, CA 94083-0054
Phone: 800-777-1078
Offers a network for collectors to buy and sell by means of a worldwide directory and referral service.

Periodical

Newspaper: <u>Antiques West</u>
3315 Sacramento St. #618
San Francisco, CA 94118
Phone: 415-221-4645
A monthly source of information about the antiques and art markets in the Western United States.

Periodical

Magazine: <u>Antiques & Fine Art</u>
Suite 120
255 North Market Street
San Jose, CA 95110
*A monthly magazine serving the antiques and art communities. ***

Periodical

Kruse Publishing
Newspaper: <u>Antiques Today</u>
Elaine Kruse, Pub.
16430 Creekside Dr.
Sonora, CA 95370-9117
Phone: 209-532-8870   FAX: 209-532-8870
Monthly newspaper covering mainly Northern California and Nevada with articles, news, features, calendar, classifieds, show info.

Periodical

Newspaper: <u>Old Stuff</u>
Donna L. Miller
P.O. Box 1084
McMinnville, OR 97128
Phone: 503-434-5386 or 503-472-2139
                          FAX: 503-472-2601
Published 5 times/year; a newspaper about the history, nostalgia, antiques, and collectibles of the Northwest U.S.

Repro. Source

Renovator's Supply
Millers Falls, MA 01349
Phone: 413-659-2241   FAX: 413-659-3796
Offers catalog of Victorian reproduction accessories, lighting, hardware, bath fixtures, and door, window and cabinet hardware.

British

Periodical

The British Connection
Magazine: <u>Realm</u>
P.O. Box 215
Landisburg, PA 17040-9989
A glossy magazine featuring articles about the land, history, peoples, and arts and sciences of England.

French

Dealer

Ambiance Galleries, Inc.
Ellen Coopersmith
7818 Old Georgetown Rd.
Bethesda, MD 20814
Phone: 301-656-1512
Wants fine, ornate 18th to early 20th century French and Continental antiques.

Mexican

Dealer

Shop, The
Ed Barry
208 W. San Francisco
Santa Fe, NM 87501
Phone: 505-983-4823 or 800-525-5764
Along with Rick Griego, specializes in primitives and unusual small pieces of antique furniture from Mexico and New Mexico.

ANTIQUES DEALERS & COLLECTORS

Supplies For

(see also AUCTION CATALOGS; REPAIRS & RESTORATIONS; REPRODUCTION SOURCES)

Man./Prod./Dist.

Display Products, Inc.
Suite 300
10632 Little Patuxent Pkwy.
Columbia, MD 21044
Phone: 301-964-8022 or 800-628-2352
Distributes Allstate aluminum showcases.

Man./Prod./Dist.

Vector, Inc.
P.O. Box 857
Sturgis, MI 49091
Phone: 616-651-9941
Manufactures multi-drawer collectibles display cabinets from oak or walnut.

Supplier

Ship's Treasurers
P.O. Box 590
Milton, MA 02186
Phone: 617-964-8010
Carries baseball card polypropylene sleeves.

Supplier

Russell Norton
P.O. Box 1070
New Haven, CT 06504-1070
Phone: 203-562-7800
Carries clear 2.5 mil polypropylene archival sleeves.

Supplier

Flip Cards & Supplies
181 Route 46 West
Lodi, NJ 07644
Phone: 201-472-8077   FAX: 201-472-6559
Carries supplies for the sports card and memorabilia collector: snap-tight card holders, top load and screw down card holders, etc.

Supplier

Antique Dealers Supply
Warren Abrams
P.O. Box 717
Matawan, NJ 07747
Phone: 908-583-3345   FAX: 908-290-9345
Carries table covers, aluminum show cases, canopies, lights, alarms, etc.

Supplier

Mylan Enterprises
P.O. Box 194
Morris Plains, NJ 07950
Phone: 201-538-6186
Carries a wide assortment of wrapping pads, and bubble pacs and bags.

Supplier

Source, The
P.O. Box 350349
Brooklyn, NY 11235

Supplier

Intense Tents
Box 538
Round Lake, NY 12151
Phone: 518-899-6190
Supplier of canopy tent units.

Supplier

Seidman Supply Co.
3366 Kensington Ave.
Philadelphia, PA 19134
Phone: 215-423-8896   FAX: 215-423-9242
Carries supplies for the sports card and memorabilia collector: ball cubes and holders; sorting trays, shoeboxes, acrylic card holders.

Supplier

John P. Scott Woodworking
1300 Evergreen Ave.
Richmond, VA 23224
Phone: 804-231-1942
Manufacturers lighted bases to display paperweights, glass and crystal.

Supplier

Corbox Co.
6701 Hubbard Avenue
Cleveland, OH 44127
Phone: 800-321-7286
*Supplier of Corbox carry-all boxes with attached covers. **

Supplier

Roberts Colonial House, Inc.
Paul B. Roberts
570 W. 167th Street
South Holland, IL 60473
Phone: 312-331-6233   FAX: 708-331-0538
Sells plate hangers, plate stands, plexiglass display cubes, quilted vinyl china cases, and over 1600 other items; send for catalog.

Supplier

J-Mounts/Militaria Promotions
Suite 160
6427 W. Irving Park Rd.
Chicago, IL 60634
Phone: 312-777-0499
Sell J-mount display boxes; glass-top display boxes for small collectibles: jewelry, watches, buttons, badges, etc.; all sizes.

Supplier

Garrett's
Rt. 1, Box 97
Eudora, KS 66025
Phone: 913-542-2339 or 800-447-7508
Sells black collector frames and aluminum or cherry sales/display/show cases.

Supplier

Collectors Supply Company
8415 "G" Street
Omaha, NE 68127
Phone: 401-592-1786   FAX: 402-592-9015

Album pages, plastic bags, displays, etc.

Supplier

Charlie's
4908 E. 15th St.
Tulsa, OK 74112
Phone: 918-749-1010 or 800-433-7083
Sells hand-crafted aluminum display cases.

Supplier

Jones West Packaging Co.
Dept. DL-1
P.O. Box 1084
Rohnert Park, CA 94927
Phone: 707-795-8552
Supplier of all sizes of ZIP CLOSE plastic bags in small or large quantities; since 1981; credit cards accepted.

ANTIQUES SHOP DIRECTORIES

Periodical

Antique Press, The
Guide: Sloan's Green Guide to Antiquing in New England
Susan P. Sloan
9 Brimmer St.
Boston, MA 02108
Phone: 617-723-3001 or 800-552-5632
                    FAX: 617-248-0185
2500 listings of antiques dealers, auction houses, antiquarian booksellers, shops, flea markets, tours, collections in New England.

Periodical

Antiques & Art Around, Inc.
Guide: Antiques & Art Around Florida
Joan Bryant, Ed.
P.O. Box 2481
Fort Lauderdale, FL 33303-2481
Phone: 305-768-9430 or 800-248-9430
Full color guide to Florida's antique shops; maps, shows, museums, flea markets; feature articles on antiques and FL heritage.

Periodical

Guide: AntiqueWeek Antique Shop Directory
Connie Swaim, Ed.
P.O. Box 90
Knightstown, IN 46148
Phone: 317-345-5133 or 800-876-5133
                    FAX: 800-876-5133
AntiqueWeek Shop Guide is an annual directory that lists antique shops and malls; two editions are published: Eastern and Central.

Periodical

Guide: Stewarts Guide to Antiques Shops
Steve Stewart
P.O. Box 166
Huntington Beach, CA 92648
Phone: 714-536-2223
Lists antique antiques and collectibles shops in Southern California.

ANTIQUITIES

(see also ARCHAEOLOGICAL ARTIFACTS; COINS & CURRENCY, Coins (Ancient))

Auction Service

Hesperia Arts
Jonathan Rosen
29 West 57th Street
New York, NY 10019
Specializing in the sale of antiquities.

Dealer

Hurst Gallery
Norman Hurst
53 Mount Auburn St.
Cambridge, MA 02138
Phone: 617-491-6888
*Antiquities and ethnographic art. **

Dealer

Classica Antiquities
Frank J. Wagner
P.O. Box 509
Syracuse, NY 13201
Phone: 315-687-0036 or 315-457-7249
For over 25 years buying/selling ancient Greek, Roman, Egyptian, Near Eastern coins and antiquities.

Museum/Library

Abbe Museum
Box 286
Bar Harbor, ME 04609
Phone: 207-288-3519

Periodical

Magazine: Minerva
7 Davies St.
London W1Y ILL England
A bi-monthly illustrated magazine focusing on ancient art, antiquities, archaeology and numismatic discoveries worldwide.

Periodical

Classical Association of the United States
Newsletter: Classical World
Department Of Classics
Duquesne University
Pittsburgh, PA 15282
Phone: 412-434-6452 *

Periodical

Magazine: Celator, The
P.O. Box 123
Lodi, WI 53555
Phone: 608-592-4684   FAX: 608-592-4682
A monthly magazine focusing on antiquities and ancient coins; ads, articles, auction reports, etc.

Greek & Roman

Expert
Nancy Terrizini
977 Clark Ave. #C
Mountain View, CA 94040

APOLLO XI MEMORABILIA

(see also SPACE EXPLORATION)

Collector
Ronald Ulrich
114 East Benton
Mt. Olive, IL 62069
Wants Apollo XI (first moon landing) items; plates, cups, dishes, coins, books, glasses, etc.

Collector
Bernard Passion
3517 1/2 Kinney St.
Los Angeles, CA 90065
Phone: 213-386-3300
Wants Apollo XI (first moon landing) items.

APPLE PEELERS

(see also KITCHEN COLLECTIBLES)

Collector
Johnny Appleseed
8060 Sierra St.
Fair Oaks, CA 95628
Apple peelers wanted; give patent dates, model and description.

APPRAISAL ASSOCIATIONS

Misc. Service
Canadian Association of Personal
Property Appraisers
2 Briar Place
Halifax
Nova Scotia B3M 2X2 Canada

Misc. Service
New England Appraisers Association
104 Charles Street
Boston, MA 02114
Phone: 617-523-6272

Misc. Service
Art Dealers Association of America
575 Madison Avenue
New York, NY 10022
Phone: 212-940-8590
The Art Dealers Association is helpful in locating an expert to authenticate a valuable work of art.

Misc. Service
Appraisers Association of America
60 East 42nd St.
New York, NY 10165
Phone: 212-867-9775

Misc. Service
American Society of Appraisers
P.O. Box 17265
Washington, DC 20041
Phone: 703-478-2228

Misc. Service
International Society of Appraisers
Newsletter: Appraisers Information Exchange
P.O. Box 726
Hoffman Estates, IL 60195
Phone: 708-882-0706
Largest association of professional personal property appraisers.

Misc. Service
International Society of Fine Arts
Appraisers, Ltd.
Newsletter: Evaluator, The
Elizabeth Carr
P.O. Box 280
River Forest, IL 60305
Phone: 708-848-3340
An interntaional society for professional appraisers; quarterly newsletter free to members.

Misc. Service
National Association of Jewelry
Appraisers, The
Newsletter: Jewelry Appraiser, The
4210 North Brown Ave.
Scottsdale, AZ 85251
Phone: 602-941-8088
Members perform gem and jewelry valuations exclusively.

Misc. Service
Antique Appraisers Association of America
11361 Garden Grove Blvd.
Garden Grove, CA 92643
Phone: 714-530-7090

AQUARIUMS

Victorian & Art Deco
Collector
Myron Palay
4242 Lorain Ave.
Cleveland, OH 44113-3771
Phone: 216-961-7903
Wants aquariums and things aquatic including books and catalogs; aquariums of any size, need not hold water.

ARCHAEOLOGICAL ARTIFACTS

(see also ANTIQUITIES; ARROWHEADS & POINTS; NATURAL HISTORY; FOSSILS; MINERALS; PREHISTORIC ARTIFACTS; TREASURE HUNTING)

Museum/Library
Kelsey Museum of Ancient & Mediaeval
Archaeology
434 S. State St.
Ann Arbor, MI 48109
Phone: 313-764-9304

Museum/Library
Kampsville Archaeological Museum
P.O. Box 366
Kampsville, IL 62053
Phone: 618-653-4316

Museum/Library
Bade Institute of Biblical Archaeology
1798 Scenic Ave.
Berkeley, CA 94709
Phone: 415-848-0529

Periodical
Magazine: Archaeology Magazine
P.O. Box 58556
Boulder, CO 80321-8556
A bi-monthly magazine focusing on archaeological history, digs, sites and artifacts.

ARCHITECTURAL ELEMENTS

(see also STAINED GLASS)

Dealer
Architectural Antiques
H. Weber Wilson
24 Franklin St.
Newport, RI 02840
Phone: 401-846-7010
Sells architectural antiques; also repairs leaded stained glass.

Dealer
United House Wrecking
535 Hope Street
Stamford, CT 06906
Sells architectural elements; stained and beveled glass, brass & copper, plumbing & lighting fixtures, Victorian gingerbread, etc.

Periodical
Old-House Journal Corp., The
Magazine: Old-House Journal, The
P.O. Box 58017
Boulder, CO 80322-8017
Phone: 800-234-3797
Monthly magazine focusing on the repair of old houses; publishes "The Old-Journal Catalog"- hundreds of sources for products &

Plumbing
Dealer
Roy Electric Co., Inc.
1054 Coney Island Ave.
Brooklyn, NY 11230
Phone: 718-434-7002 or 800-366-3347
Sells vintage plumbing hardware. •

ARCTIC EXPLORERS

Museum/Library

Bowdoin College, Perry-MacMillan Arctic
Museum
Hubbard Hall
Brunswick, ME 04011
Phone: 207-725-3416

ARMS & ARMOR

(see also FIREARMS; KNIVES; MILITARIA;
POWDER HORNS; SWORDS)

Auction Service

Wallis & Wallis
West Street Auction Galleries
Lewes
East Sussex BN7 2NJ England
*Britain's specialist auctioneers of arms, armour,
militaria and military orders.*

Museum/Library

Higgins Armory Museum
100 Barber Avenue
Worcester, MA 01606
Phone: 617-853-6015

Periodical

Magazine: Man at Arms
Andrew Mowbray, Pub.
1525 Old Louisquisset Pike
P.O. Box 460
Lincoln, RI 02865
Phone: 401-726-8011
*"Man at Arms" is the official arms collecting
periodical of the NRA. A non-shooting magazine
focusing on collectible arms and armor.*

Repro. Source

Museum Replicas Limited
P.O. Box 840
Conyers, GA 30207
*Sells authentic replica edged weapons, battle
gear, period clothing; swords, daggers, axes,
shields, helmets, tunics, etc.*

Japanese

Book Seller

Alan D. Meaux
P.O. Box 1271
Oak Harbor, WA 98277-1271
Phone: 206-675-8429
*Specializes in rare and hard to find books dealing
with Japanese arms and armor and related sub-
jects.*

Collector

Raymond Macy
P.O. Box 11
W. Alex, OH 45381
Phone: 513-839-5721
*Wants Japanese swords, daggers, sword parts,
matchlock guns, anything samurai.*

Collector

Don Beck
Box 15305
Ft. Wayne, IN 46885
Phone: 219-486-3010
*Wants Japanese swords and sword items, guns,
medals, daggers, head gear, from any war 1860 to
1945.*

Collector

Alan D. Meaux
P.O. Box 1271
Oak Harbor, WA 98277-1271
Phone: 206-675-8429
*Wants items related to the Japanese samurai such
as swords, armor, clothing, woodblock prints as
well as unusual items.*

Expert

Alan D. Meaux
P.O. Box 1271
Oak Harbor, WA 98277-1271
Phone: 206-675-8429
*Specializes in and appraises Japanese arms and
armor.*

Japanese (Swords)

Club/Association

Token Kenkyu Kai
5519 Farquhar Ln.
Dallas, TX 75209
Phone: 214-352-4674
Focuses on Japanese swords. •

Club/Association

Japanese Sword Society of the United
States, Inc.
Newsletter: Japanese Sword Society of U. S.
Newsletter
Dr. T.C. Ford, Ed.
P.O. Box 712
Breckenridge, TX 76024
*Focuses on the study and preservation of Japanese
swords.*

Club/Association

North West Token Kai
Newsletter: North West Token Kai Newsletter
Alan D. Meaux
P.O. Box 1271
Oak Harbor, WA 98277-1271
Phone: 206-675-8429
*The N.W.T.K. is an organization formed to pro-
mote the preservation of the Japanese sword and
related samurai artifacts.*

Collector

R. Lighter
P.O. Box 320042
Cocoa Beach, FL 32932-0042
Phone: 407-783-0314
*Japanese swords and sword items; also guns, me-
dals, daggers, head gear; member NBTHK, To-
kyo.* •

Collector

K. Wiley
719 Baldwin SE
Grand Rapids, MI 49503
Phone: 616-451-8410
*Wants Japanese swords, daggers, sword parts.
Also German 3rd Reich daggers, swords, bayo-
nets. References available.*

Repro. Source

Frank
P.O. Box 50026
New Orleans, LA 70150
*Japanese samurai swords handmade by T.
Ogawa, famous master sword maker from Japan.*

Miniature

Club/Association

Miniature Arms Collectors/Makers
Society
Newsletter: MAC/MS Newsletter
104 White Sand Ln.
Racine, WI 53402 •

ARROWHEADS & POINTS

(see also INDIAN ITEMS)

Expert

Rich Relics
Richard B. Troyanowski
P.O. Box 432
Sandia Park, NM 87047
Phone: 505-281-2611 or 505-281-2329
*Specializes in prehistoric lithics (stone items, e.g.
arrowheads, points, clubs, bowls, etc.)*

ART

(see also BRONZES; CARTOON ART;
FOLK ART; ILLUSTRATORS; MEDALLIC
SCULPTURES; ORIENTALIA; PRINTS;
REPAIRS & RESTORATIONS; WESTERN
ART & CRAFTS)

Auction Service

James R. Bakker
370 Broadway Street
Cambridge, MA 02139
Phone: 617-864-7067 •

Auction Service

Philip C. Shute Gallery
Philip Shute
50 Turnpike Street
West Bridgewater, MA 02379
Phone: 508-588-0022 or 508-588-7833
*Antique and custom furniture, art, silver, glass
and china, collectibles, etc.*

Auction Service

Young Fine Art Gallery, Inc.
P.O. Box 313
North Berwick, ME 03906 •

Auction Service

Mystic Fine Arts
47 Holmes Street
Mystic, CT 06255
Phone: 203-572-8873

Auction Service

Swann Galleries, Inc.
104 E. 25th St.
New York, NY 10010
Phone: 212-254-4710   FAX: 212-979-1017
Oldest/largest U.S. auctioneer specializing in rare books, autographs & manuscripts, Judaica, photographs, and works of art on paper.

Auction Service

Christie's East
219 E. 67th St.
New York, NY 10021
Phone: 212-606-0400

Auction Service

Sotheby's
1334 York Ave. at 72nd Street
New York, NY 10021
Phone: 212-606-7000

Auction Service

Christie's
502 Park Ave.
New York, NY 10022
Phone: 212-546-1000

Auction Service

William Doyle Galleries
175 E. 87th St.
New York, NY 10128
Phone: 212-427-2730

Auction Service

Weschler's
William P. Weschler, Jr.
909 E Street NW
Washington, DC 20004
Phone: 202-628-1281 or 800-331-1430
               FAX: 202-628-2366
Conducts specialized auction sales of art, paintings, prints and graphics.

Auction Service

Frank Boos Gallery, Inc.
420 Enterprise Court
Bloomfield Hills, MI 48013
Phone: 313-332-1500

Auction Service

Chicago Art Gallery, Inc.
Richard Friedman
6039 Oakton Street
Skokie, IL 60077
Phone: 708-677-6080 or 708-677-6081

Auction Service

Selkirk Galleries
4166 Olive Street
St. Louis, MO 63108
Phone: 314-533-1700

Auction Service

Western Heritage Sale
1416 Avenue K
Plano, TX 75074
Phone: 214-423-1500

Auction Service

Texas Art Gallery
1400 Main Street
Dallas, TX 75202
Phone: 214-747-8158

Book Seller

Sound View Press
Pete Falk
170 Boston Post Rd., Box 150
Madison, CT 06443
Phone: 203-245-2246
Researches and writes about artists listed in "Who's Who in American Art"; also publishes art reference dictionaries.

Book Seller

Dealer's Choice Books
P.O. Box 710
Land O' Lakes, FL 34639
Phone: 813-996-6599 or 800-238-8288
               FAX: 813-996-5226
Sells collector and art reference books: "Art Sales Index", "Who Was Who in American Art", "Signatures of American Artists", etc.

Dealer

Vose Galleries of Boston, Inc.
238 Newbury Street
Boston, MA 02116
Phone: 617-536-6176
Specializes in 18th, 19th, and 20th century art. *

Dealer

Henry B. Holt
21 Village Drive
P.O. Box 442
Montville, NJ 07045
Phone: 201-316-8883 or 201-316-8929
               FAX: 201-402-9735
Buys and sells American art, oils or watercolors; conservation and framing available; wants marines, still life, Hudson River, etc.

Dealer

Kennedy Galleries
40 West 57th Street, 5th Floor
New York, NY 10019
Phone: 212-541-9600
Specializes in 18th, 19th, and 20th century art. *

Dealer

Graham Gallery
1014 Madison Avenue
New York, NY 10021
Phone: 212-535-5767
Specializes in 18th, 19th, and 20th century art.

Dealer

Alexander Gallery
996 Madison Avenue
New York, NY 10021
Phone: 212-472-1636
Specializes in 18th, 19th, and 20th century art. Wants to buy paintings and prints.

Dealer

Coe Kerr Gallery
49 East 82nd Street
New York, NY 10028
Phone: 212-628-1340
Specializes in 18th, 19th, and 20th century art. *

Dealer

Antique Art Galleries, Inc.
David Harrison
17214 Birdsong Lane
Gaithersburg, MD 20878
Phone: 301-258-9317 or 301-946-2152
               FAX: 301-963-1272
Buys, sells, trades, restores, accepts consignments of 19th century European and American oil paintings.

Dealer

Aunti-Q
A. Thomas Fleming
2200 Columbia Pike, Apt. #105
Arlington, VA 22204-4422
Phone: 703-920-9093

Dealer

Gallery Mayo, Inc.
Robert B. Mayo
5705 Grove Ave.
Richmond, VA 23336
Phone: 804-288-2109
Buys and sells late 19th through early 20th century American art, with a specialty in Southern and sporting art.

Dealer

Keny & Johnson Gallery
300 East Beck Street
Columbus, OH 43206
Phone: 614-464-1228
Specializes in 18th, 19th, and 20th century art. *

Dealer

R.H. Love Gallery
100-108 East Ohio Street
Chicago, IL 60611
Phone: 312-664-9620
Specializes in 18th, 19th, and 20th century art. *

Dealer

Goldfield Galleries
8400 Melrose Avenue
Los Angeles, CA 90069
Phone: 213-651-1122
*Specializes in 18th, 19th, and 20th century art. ***

Dealer

De Ville Galleries
8751 Melrose Avenue
Los Angeles, CA 90069
Phone: 213-652-0525
*Specializes in 18th, 19th, and 20th century art. ***

Dealer

Petersen Galleries
332 N. Rodeo Dr.
Beverly Hills, CA 90210
Phone: 213-274-6705
*Specializes in 18th, 19th, and 20th century art. ***

Expert

Van Cline & Davenport, Ltd.
Stephen Van Cline
792 Franklin Ave.
Franklin Lakes, NJ 07417
Phone: 201-891-4588   FAX: 201-891-2824
Specializes in paintings, watercolors, drawings, bronze & marble sculpture; appraisals, authentication, lectures, expert testimony.

Expert

Fer-Duc Inc.
Joseph Ferrara
Box 1303
Newburgh, NY 12550
Phone: 914-565-5990

Expert

McKittrick Fine Arts
Price Guide: Mckittrick's Art Price Guide
Michael & Rose Mckittrick
P.O. Box 461
Sewickley, PA 15143
Phone: 412-741-0743
Publishes an annual comprehensive listing of art auction sales results including over 28,000 works of art.

Expert

National Gallery of Art
Wilford Scott
6th & Constitution Ave. NW
Washington, DC 20565
Phone: 202-842-6246
*Expert on 19th century American landscape painters. ***

Expert

Geolat & Associates
C. Van Northrup
14110 Dallas Pkwy., #200
Dallas, TX 75240
Phone: 214-239-9314   FAX: 214-404-1359

American, European & Mexican fine art; modern paintings, drawings, watercolors; old & modern prints; modern sculpture.

Expert

Tucker Appraisal Associates
Sally Tucker
P.O. Box 13605
Houston, TX 77219
Phone: 713-529-8878
Specializes in fine art, sculpture, paintings, watercolors, and drawings.

Misc. Service

Art Sales Index, Ltd.
Database: Artquest Computer Service
1 Thames Street
Weybridge
Surrey KT13 8JG England
ARTQUEST on-line computer art sales database; also the Annual Art Sales Index, and Auction Prices of American Artists.

Misc. Service

Telepraisal
M. Barden Prisant
P.O. Box 20686
New York, NY 10009
Phone: 212-614-9090 or 800-645-6002
Computerized works of art data base search for art auctions and prices realized.

Misc. Service

International Foundation for Art
Research (IFAR)
Magazine: IFAR Reports
46 East 70th St.
New York, NY 10021
Phone: 212-879-1780 or 212-879-1781
                        FAX: 212-734-4174
Clearinghouse for information on art theft, fraud, forgery; promotes recovery of stolen art & prevention of circulation of forged works.

Misc. Service

National Museum & Gallery Registration
Association
Suite 320
655 15th St. NW
Washington, DC 20005
Phone: 202-639-4311
*Records ownerships; also current retail value of works of fine art; maintaining biographical archive covering member artists. ***

Misc. Service

American Institute for Conservation of
Historic & Artistic Works
Directory: AIC Directory
Suite #340
1400 16th St. NW
Washington, DC 20036
Phone: 202-232-6636
Purpose is to advance the knowledge and practice of the conservation of cultural property.

Misc. Service

Art Data Bank
200 N. Andrews Ave.
Ft. Lauderdale, FL 33301
Phone: 800-327-9630
Offers a buyer-seller matching service for fine art in the price range of $5000 and up; paintings, prints, sculptures, drawings, etc.

Misc. Service

National Gallery of Art
Dept. of Education Resources
6th & Constitution Ave. NW
Washington, DC 20565
Phone: 202-842-6273
FREE loan program of VHS, 16mm film, and slide/tape programs covering many facets of art and antiques. Send for free catalog.

Museum/Library

Frick Collection, The
1 East 70th Street
New York, NY 10021
Phone: 212-288-8700
Contains a wealth of art resources.

Museum/Library

Pennsylvania Academy of Fine Arts
1301 Cherry St.
Philadelphia, PA 19102
Phone: 215-972-7600

Museum/Library

National Museum of American Art
Catalog: Smithsonian Art Index
8th & G Sts. NW
Washington, DC 20560
Phone: 202-357-2504
Identifies drawings, prints, paintings and sculpture in Smithsonian divisions but not part of the museum collection.

Museum/Library

National Portrait Gallery
Catalog: Catalog of American Portraits
8th & F Streets NW
Washington, DC 20560
Phone: 202-357-1407

Museum/Library

National Museum of American Art
Catalog: Peter A. Juley & Son Collection
8th & G Sts. NW
Washington, DC 20560
Phone: 202-357-2504
Over 127,000 photographic negatives of art now lost, destroyed or altered.

Museum/Library

National Museum of American Art
Catalog: Slide & Photograph Archives
8th & G Sts. NW
Washington, DC 20560
Phone: 202-357-2504

Over 60,000 35mm color slides and over 200,000 photographs and negatives for visual documentation of American art.

Museum/Library
National Museum of American Art
Catalog: Pre-1877 Art Exhibition Catalogue Index
8th & G Sts. NW
Washington, DC 20560
Phone: 202-357-2504
A computerized index from over 700 rare catalogs of exhibitions held between 1790 and 1876; art unions, fairs, museums, etc.

Museum/Library
National Museum of American Art
Catalog: Permanent Collection Data Base
8th & G Sts. NW
Washington, DC 20560
Phone: 202-357-2504
A computerized listing providing information on the over 300,000 objects in the museum's permanent collection.

Museum/Library
National Portrait Gallery, Archives of American Art Headquarters
Journal: Archives of American Art Journal
8th & F Streets NW
Washington, DC 20560
Phone: 202-357-1407
Important source of biographical material on American artists. Regional offices in Boston, Detroit, Houston, NY City, San Francisco.

Museum/Library
Chrysler Museum, Art Reference Library, The
Olney Rd. & Mowbray Arch
Norfolk, VA 23510
Phone: 804-622-1211

Periodical
Auction Index, Inc.
Price Guide: Leonard's Annual Price Index of Art Auctions
30 Valentine Park
Newton, MA 02165
Phone: 617-964-2876
*Annual directory covering over 38,000 sales representing over 16,000 artists. ***

Periodical
Review Magazine, Inc., The
Magazine: Review Magazine, The
60 Ben. Franklin Way - Unit C
Barnstable, MA 02601
Phone: 508-775-7001   FAX: 508-775-7001
A magazine specializing in the art and antiques of the Cape Cod region.

Periodical
Newsletter: Art/Antiques Investment Report, The
99 Wall Street
New York, NY 10005 *

Periodical
Art & Auction Magazine
Directory: International Directory for Collectors, The
250 West 57th St., Room 215
New York, NY 10019
*A comprehensive list of reputable art dealers in the U.S. and abroad. ***

Periodical
Magazine: Art in America
980 Madison Avenue
New York, NY 10021
Phone: 800-247-2160
A colorful magazine focusing primarily on contemporary art.

Periodical
Newsletter: ARTnews
P.O. Box 969
Farmingdale, NY 11737 *

Periodical
Magazine: American Artist
1 Color Court
Marion, OH 43302 *

Periodical
Gale Research, Inc.
Directory: International Directory of Arts
835 Penobscot Bldg.
Detroit, MI 48226
Phone: 313-961-2242 or 800-877-4253
FAX: 313-961-6082
Art reference almanac: lists art museums, book publishers, artists, universities, schools, art and antique organ., restorers, etc.

Periodical
Magazine: Art & Auction
P.O. Box 11344
Des Moines, IA 50340
Phone: 800-777-8718
A monthly magazine of the international art markets.

Periodical
Magazine: Connoisseur, The
P.O. Box 10107
Des Moines, IA 50350 *

Periodical
WEB Publications, Inc.
Magazine: Art Today
Debra Roark
P.O. Box 12830
Wichita, KS 67277
Phone: 316-946-0600   FAX: 316-946-0675

The magazine of new art forms and design in pottery, wood, fiber, paper, furniture, glass, ceramics, rugs, jewelry, and metal.

Periodical
Magazine: Latin American Art
P.O. Box 9888
Scottsdale, AZ 85252-3888
*Art from or artists who painted in Latin America, e.g. Frederick Church. ***

Periodical
Magazine: Antiques & Fine Art
Suite 120
255 North Market Street
San Jose, CA 95110
*A monthly magazine serving the antiques and art communities. ***

African & Tribal
Collector
Richard McCoy
1119 Michigan Ave.
St. Joseph, MI 49085
Wants African and South American artifacts: spears, masks, shields, arrows, weapons, skins, mounts, ivory, art, tools, body adornments.

Dealer
Antiques by Susan Akins
Susan Akins
3740 Howard Ave.
Kensington, MD 20895
Phone: 301-946-4609
All Oriental items including Indonesia, Southeast Asia and India; also African items.

Museum/Library
African Art Museum of the S.M.A. Fathers
23 Bliss Ave.
Tenafly, NJ 07670
Phone: 201-567-0450

Museum/Library
Museum of Classical Antiques & Primitive Arts
Joe Liberkowski
P.O. Box 2161
Medford Lakes, NJ 08055
Wants African and American Indian items; also pre-1940 Mexican and South American Santos, Retablos, Ex Votos, crucifixes, religious.

Museum/Library
National Museum of African Art
Smithsonian Institution
950 Independence Ave.
Washington, DC 20560
Phone: 202-357-4600

Periodical

African Studies Center
Magazine: African Art
University Of California
Los Angeles, CA 90024-1310
Phone: 213-825-1218 *

Repro. Source

Artifactory
641 Indiana Ave. NW
Washington, DC 20004
Phone: 202-393-2727
Sells new African and other foreign souvenir, arts and craft items including carvings and textiles.

Asian

(see also ART, Oriental)

Collector

John Rudak
P.O. Box 832
Norwich, CT 06360
Phone: 203-442-2147
Wants Buddhist and Hindu art of Southeast Asia; all representations desired.

British

Museum/Library

Yale Center for British Art
Duncan Robinson, Pres.
Box 2120 Yale Station
New Haven, CT 06520
Phone: 203-432-2800 or 203-432-2850
                        FAX: 203-432-9695
Largest museum and research center for British paintings, sculpture, prints, drawings, and rare books outside England; no decorative arts.

Periodical

Magazine: Bvrlington, The
Jim Lance
c/o Publishers Mini Systems
P.O. Box 301369
Escondido, CA 92030-9957
Phone: 619-747-8327   FAX: 619-432-6560
The best English art journal printed for the collector or individual interested in art or art history.

Byzantine

Museum/Library

Dumbarton Oaks Research Library & Collection
1703 32nd St. NW
Washington, DC 20007
Phone: 202-342-3200

Contemporary

Dealer

Fischbach Gallery
24 West 57th Street
New York, NY 10019
Phone: 212-759-2345 *

Dealer

Allan Frumkin Gallery
50 West 57th Street
New York, NY 10019
Phone: 212-757-6655 *

Dealer

Marlborough Gallery
40 West 57th Street
New York, NY 10019
Phone: 212-541-4900 *

Dealer

Knoedler & Company
19 East 70th Street
New York, NY 10021
Phone: 212-794-0050   FAX: 212-772-6932

Dealer

Pace Gallery, The
32 East 57th Street
New York, NY 10022
Phone: 212-421-3292 *

Dealer

Andre Emmerich Gallery
41 East 57th Street
New York, NY 10022
Phone: 212-752-0124

Expert

Holtzman & Gould
Karen Holtzman
4201 Cathedral Ave. NW #707E
Washington, DC 20016
Phone: 202-966-5877
Art consultant.

Misc. Service

Art Information Center
Suite 412
280 Broadway
New York, NY 10007
Phone: 212-227-0282
*A free clearinghouse of information on contemporary artists. Maintains files on 65,000 living artists and their gallery affiliations. ***

Museum/Library

Museum of Modern Art, The
11 W. 53rd. Street
New York, NY 10019
Phone: 212-708-9889

Periodical

New Art Association
Magazine: New Art Examiner
20 W. hubbard St. 2W
Chicago, IL 60610
Phone: 312-836-0330   FAX: 312-836-0222
Magazine reporting on contemporary visual arts.

Periodical

Newspaper: West Art
P.O. Box 6868
Auburn, CA 95604
Phone: 916-885-0969
West Coast bi-weekly art publication; information and photographs of current West Coast fine art and craft exhibitions.

German

Museum/Library

Busch-Reisinger Museum
32 Quincy Street
Cambridge, MA 02138
Phone: 617-495-2317

Jewish

(see also JUDAICA)

Museum/Library

Center for Jewish Art, The
Journal: Jewish Art
P.O. Box 4262
Jerusalem 91042, Israel

Oriental

(see also BRONZES, Oriental; CERAMICS (ORIENTAL); ORIENTALIA; PRINTS, Woodblock (Japanese))

Auction Service

Weschler's
William P. Weschler, Jr.
909 E Street NW
Washington, DC 20004
Phone: 202-628-1281 or 800-331-1430
                        FAX: 202-628-2366
Conducts specialized auction sales of antique Oriental Art.

Expert

Rosenzweig & Assoc.
Dr. Daphne L. Rosenzweig
P.O. Box 16187
Temple Terrace, FL 33617-6187
Phone: 813-988-0880
Consultant dealing with Oriental Art, gems and minerals; author of "Selected Works from the Fine Arts Group of Later Chinese Painting."

Museum/Library

Freer Gallery of Art
Smithsonian Institution
12th & Jefferson Dr. SW
Washington, DC 20560
Phone: 202-357-2104

Museum/Library

Arthur M. Sackler Gallery
Smithsonian Institution
1050 Independance Ave.
Washington, DC 20560
Phone: 202-357-4880

Periodical

Magazine: Arts of Asia
1309 Kowloon Centre
29-39 Ashley Road
Kowloon, Hong Kong
A fully illustrated, scholarly magazine about the Oriental arts.

Periodical

Newsletter: Newsletter, East Asian Art & Archaeology
Tappan Hall, Rm. 50
University of Michigan
Ann Arbor, MI 48109-1357
Phone: 313-764-5555 or 313-936-2539
Published several times annually, NEAAA focuses on current exhibitions, symposia, newly published books, scholarly news, etc.

Periodical

Magazine: Orientations
Jim Lance
c/o Publishers Mini Systems
P.O. Box 301369
Escondido, CA 92030-9957
Phone: 619-747-8327   FAX: 619-432-6560
A monthly full color perfect bound art journal for collectors of fine and rare Oriental art; published in Hong Kong.

Repair Service

Dobson Studios
Janice & Dennis Dobson
810 N. Daniel St.
Arlington, VA 22201
Phone: 703-243-7363
Conservator of Oriental screens, scrolls and wood block prints; repairs and restoration to other paper items as well.

Paintings

Dealer

Hirschl & Adler Galleries, Inc.
21 East 70th St.
New York, NY 10021
Phone: 212-535-8810   FAX: 212-772-7237

Dealer

Vixseboxse Art Galleries
12413 Cedar Rd.
Cleveland, OH 44106
Phone: 216-791-2727 *

Dealer

Don Treadway
2128 Madison Rd.
Cincinnati, OH 45208
Phone: 513-321-6742   FAX: 513-871-7722

Misc. Service

Massachusetts Materials Research, Inc.
P.O. Box 326
West Boylston, MA 01583
Phone: 617-835-6262

This firm will analyze paint on antique furniture and paintings to determine age and composition.
*

Museum/Library

National Museum of American Art
Catalog: Inventory of Amer. Paintings
  Executed Before 1914
8th & G Sts. NW
Washington, DC 20560
Phone: 202-357-2504
A computerized index of over 230,000 records of pre-1914 paintings in public and private collections; artist, location, subject, photo.

Repro. Source

Bianco Collection
Suite 604-256
4279 Roswell Rd.
Atlanta, GA 30342
Phone: 404-436-5832
Offers framed oil paintings on canvas in the exact style of John Singer Sargent. *

Paintings (Marine)

Dealer

Karl Gabosh
125 Calamint Hill Rd, North
Princeton, MA 01541
Phone: 508-464-2093
Specializes in American marine paintings. *

Dealer

Oliphant & Company
360 E. 55th St.
New York, NY 10022
Phone: 212-935-6324

Paintings (Primitive)

Dealer

Barbara N. Cohen Galleries
Leonard & Barb Cohen
115 E. Main St.
Waterloo, NY 13165-1432
Phone: 315-539-3032 or 315-539-3372
Wants 1820-1840 primitive paintings of children alone or with other children, people, cats, toys, etc.; oil, watercolor, pastels.

Peale Papers

Museum/Library

National Portrait Gallery
Catalog: Charles Wilson Peale Papers
8th & F Streets NW
Washington, DC 20560
Phone: 202-357-1407
Specializing in documenting and cataloging all Peale family paintings and manuscripts.

Portraits (Miniature)

Dealer

Remembrance of Things Past
Dorothy Blitzer
269 Bloomfield Ave.
Windsor, CT 06095
Buys, sells and collects portrait miniatures, especially those on ivory.

Expert

Galerie Nouvelle
Lester E. Sender
3482 Lee Road
Shaker Heights, OH 44120
Phone: 216-752-2435   FAX: 216-991-7461
Buys and sells portrait miniatures on paper, ivory, canvas, porcelain or metal from the 17th century thru 1930, American and Continental.

Pre-Columbian

Museum/Library

Dumbarton Oaks Research Library & Collection
1703 32nd St. NW
Washington, DC 20007
Phone: 202-342-3200

R. Atkinson Fox

Club/Association

Fox Club, The
Barb Kratz
2208 Ground Blvd.
Cedar Falls, IA 50613
R. Atkinson Fox (1860-1927) was a Canadian artist. *

Club/Association

R. Atkinson Fox Society
Newsletter: Fox Hunt Newsletter
Sherri Fountain
1511 W. 4th Ave.
Hutchinson, KS 67501
Phone: 316-663-4293

Expert

Rita Mortenson
727 North Spring
Independence, MO 64050
R. Atkinson Fox (1860-1927) was a Canadian artist. Rita Mortenson is author of "R. Atkinson Fox: His Life and Work."

Remington

Dealer

Museum Collections By Schulenburg, Inc.
Fred Schulenburg
P.O. Box 2369
Shelton, CT 06484
Phone: 508-349-9169 or 800-243-6229
Specializes in Remington bronzes and collector plates.

Museum/Library

Frederic Remington Art Museum
303 Washington Street
Ogdensburg, NY 13669
Phone: 315-393-2425

Rodin

Museum/Library

Rodin Museum
c/o Philadelphia Museum Of Art
P.O. Box 7646
Philadelphia, PA 19101
Phone: 215-763-8100

Spanish

Museum/Library

Hispanic Society of America, The
Broadway & 155th Street
New York, NY 10033
Phone: 212-926-2234

Sporting

(see also SPORTING COLLECTIBLES)

Collector

Gallery Mayo, Inc.
Robert B. Mayo
5705 Grove Ave.
Richmond, VA 23336
Phone: 804-288-2109
Wants American sporting art thru the mid-20th century; author of "America, The Sporting View."

Dealer

Ravenwood Gallery
38745 Butternut Ridge Rd.
Elyria, OH 44035
Phone: 216-458-4929
Wants wildlife, hunting, fishing paintings, prints and books.

Sports

(see also SPORTS COLLECTIBLES)

Museum/Library

University of New Haven National Art Museum of Sport, Inc.
Newsletter: Museum of Sport Newsletter
300 Orange St.
West Haven, CT 06516
Phone: 203-932-7197
Promotes sports art, e.g. paintings, sculptures, prints depicting fishing, track, boxing, racquet games, auto racing, baseball, etc.

Tattoo

Museum/Library

Tattoo Art Museum, The
Magazine: Tattoo Historian
Lyle Tuttle
837 Columbus Ave.
San Francisco, CA 94133
Phone: 415-775-4991 or 415-775-1262

Largest collection of tattoo art and related antiques & collectibles; buys/sells machines, designs, artifacts, photos, paintings, etc.

Western

(see also WESTERN AMERICANA; WESTERN ART & CRAFTS)

Museum/Library

National Cowboy Hall of Fame
Magazine: Persimon Hill
M.J. VanDeventer
1700 N.E. 63rd St.
Oklahoma City, OK 73111
Phone: 405-478-2250 or 405-478-4714
NCHA represents 17 western states; preserves the rich heritage of the Old West and the memory of those who contributed to it.

Museum/Library

Amon Carter Museum of Western Art
P.O. Box 2365
Fort Worth, TX 76113
Phone: 817-738-1933
Has large and distinguished collection of paintings and sculpture by Frederic Remington and Charles M. Russell.

Periodical

Duerr & Tierney, inc.
Magazine: Art of the West
Suite 235
15612 Hwy. 7
Minnetonka, MN 55345
Phone: 612-935-5850   FAX: 612-935-6546
Magazine featuring art of the West: cowboys, American landscapes, western wildlife, etc.

Wildlife

Periodical

Magazine: Wildlife Art News
Suite 2
1245 Carlson Lake Lane
Eagan, MN 55123

ART DECO

(see also CERAMICS; FURNITURE; GEMS & JEWELRY; GLASS)

Auction Service

Gallery 68 Auctions
3 Southvale Drive
Toronto
Ontario M46 1G1 Canada *

Auction Service

Christie's East
219 E. 67th St.
New York, NY 10021
Phone: 212-606-0400
Christie's East is well known in the collecting field for its Art Deco auctions.

Auction Service

Phillips Fine Art & Auctioneers
406 East 79th St.
New York, NY 10022
Phone: 212-570-4830   FAX: 212-570-2207
Specializes in the sale of jewelry, paintings, prints, silver, coins, stamps, toys (especially lead soldiers), and movie memorabilia.

Auction Service

William Doyle Galleries
175 E. 87th St.
New York, NY 10128
Phone: 212-427-2730
Conducts four annual "Belle Epoque" auctions featuring Art Deco.

Auction Service

Saugerties Auction Service
16 Livingston Street
Saugerties, NY 12477
Phone: 914-246-9928
*Conducts specialized Art Deco auctions twice a year. *

Auction Service

Savoia & Fromm Auction Services
Route 23
South Cairo, NY 12482
Phone: 518-622-8000   FAX: 518-622-9453

Auction Service

Art Deco Auctions, Ltd.
19528 Ventura Blvd. #153
Tarzana, CA 91356
Phone: 818-996-3509
*Specializes in Art Deco posters, lithographs, etchings, and original paintings including artists Icart and Erte. *

Club/Association

Art Deco Trust
Robert McGregor, Pres.
P.O. Box 248
Napier, New Zealand

Club/Association

Art Deco Society of New South Wales
Mary Nilsson, Pres.
P.O. Box 753
Willoughby
New South Wales 1068, AUS.

Club/Association

Art Deco Society of Western Australia
Vyonne Geneve, Pres.
182 Broome Street
Cottesloe 6011
Western Australia

Club/Association
Canadian Art Deco Society
Don Luxton
P.O. Box 183
Station E, Victoria
Brit. Col. V8W 2M6 Canada

Club/Association
Thirties Society, The
Alan Powers
58 Crescent Lane
London SWA England

Club/Association
Art Deco Society of Boston
Newsletter: Motif
Tony Fusco, Pres.
One Murdock Terrace
Brighton, MA 02135
Phone: 617-787-2637 FAX: 617-782-4430
Purpose is to educate, and to preserve items and architecture relating to the Art Deco period.

Club/Association
Art Deco Society of New York
David Gibson, Pres.
c/o Ryan Gibson Bauer
90 West Street, 14th Floor
New York, NY 10036
Phone: 212-395-2744

Club/Association
Art Deco Society of Washington
Newsletter: Trans Lux
Richard Striner, Pres.
P.O. Box 11090
Washington, DC 20008
Phone: 202-231-3793

Club/Association
Baltimore Deco Society
Sherry Cucchiella, Pr.
7123 Pheasant Cross Rd.
Baltimore, MD 21209

Club/Association
Art Deco Society of the Palm Beaches
Sharon Koskoff, Pres.
820 Lavers Circle #G203
Del Ray Beach, FL 23444
Phone: 407-276-9925

Club/Association
Chicago Art Deco Association
Lynn Abbie, Pres.
823 Lake St.
Oak Park, IL 60301
Phone: 312-848-2237

Club/Association
Art Deco Society of Los Angeles
James Zink
P.O. Box 972
Hollywood, CA 90078
Phone: 213-659-DECO

Club/Association
Art Deco Society of San Diego
Helen Hobbs-Halmay
P.O. Box 33762
San Diego, CA 92103
Phone: 619-296-3322

Club/Association
Art Deco Society of California
Newsletter: Sophisticate, The
Jeffery Tucker, Pres.
100 Bush St., #511
San Francisco, CA 94104
Phone: 415-982-DECO
Dedicated to the preservation of California's Art Deco (1920's-1940's) artistic expression heritage.

Dealer
Full Swing
Michelle Mancini
474 Thames
Newport, RI 02840
Phone: 401-849-9494
*Specializing in 1920-1950's furnishings and accessories: Art Deco living rooms, dining rooms, bedrooms, wicker, kitchenware, etc. ***

Dealer
Detour
Irena Urdang De Tour
92 Main Street
Deep River, CT 06417
Phone: 203-526-9797
*Specializing in vintage clothing, accessories, and vintage luggage by Vuitton and Oshkosh. ***

Dealer
Friedman Gallery
Mike Friedman
135 Post Road East
Westport, CT 06880
Phone: 203-226-5533
*Specializing in chrome, clocks, jewelry, glass and other objects. ***

Dealer
Historical Design Collection
Dennis Gallion
305 East 61st Street #209
New York, NY 10021
Phone: 212-593-4528
Interested in periods impacted by Japanese design: Arts & Crafts, Art Nouveau, Symbolism, Vienna Secession, Cubism, Art Deco, Bauhaus, etc.

Dealer
Deco Deluxe
Sandi Berman
125 East 57th Street
New York, NY 10022
Phone: 212-688-2677 *

Dealer
Times & Moments Antiques & Collectibles
Ron Savino
349 Atlantic Ave.
Brooklyn, NY 11217
Phone: 718-625-3145 or 718-497-4529
Specializes in Art Deco furniture, 1920's-30's gas stoves, enamel-top kitchen tables, waterfall furniture, Bakelite & Catalin radios, etc.

Dealer
Warehouse, The
Paul Fuhrman
120 Gordon Street
Allentown, PA 18102
Phone: 215-770-0702
Specializes in Art Deco upholstered furniture especially American furnishings from 1930-1940's.
*

Dealer
Ken Forster & Inglett-Watson
Ken Forster
884 Park Avenue
Baltimore, MD 21201
Phone: 301-244-8064
*Specializing in American machine age furnishings, Georg Jensen silver, Viennese Secession, Wiener Werkstatte, etc. ***

Dealer
First 1/2
Jacques Caussin
12150 E. Outer Dr.
Detroit, MI 48224
Phone: 313-886-3443
Specializing in 1930's Industrial Design: American chrome and metal furnishings from Bel Geddes, Schoen, and others.

Expert
Fusco & Four, Associates
Tony Fusco
One Murdock Terrace
Brighton, MA 02135
Phone: 617-787-2637 FAX: 617-782-4430
Author of "The Official Identification and Price Guide to Art Deco"; offers curatorial services for 1909-1939 Art Deco collectors.

Expert
Mary Gaston
Box 342
Bryan, TX 77806
*Author of "Collector's Guide to Art Deco." ***

Museum/Library
Victoria & Albert Museum
Cromwell Road
London SW7 England

Museum/Library
Musee Des Arts Decoratifs
Palais du Louvre
107 Rue de Rivoli
75001 Paris, France

Museum/Library
Walter Gropius House
141 Cambridge St.
Boston, MA 02114
Phone: 617-227-3956
Mailing address is as above, but located at 68 Baker Bridge Rd., Lincoln, MA.

Museum/Library
Isabella Stewart Gardner Museum
2 Palace Road
Boston, MA 02115
Phone: 617-566-1401

Museum/Library
Newark Museum, The
P.O. Box 540
Newark, NJ 07101
Phone: 201-596-6550

Museum/Library
Cooper-Hewitt Museum, The Smithsonian Institution's Nat. Museum of Design
2 East 91st St.
New York, NY 10128
Phone: 212-860-6868

Museum/Library
Virginia Museum of Fine Arts
Frederick R. Brandt
2800 Grove Ave.
Richmond, VA 23221-2466
Phone: 804-367-0888   FAX: 804-367-9393
Fine arts museum covering the entire range of history of art.

Museum/Library
Detroit Institute of Art, The
5200 Woodward Avenue
Detroit, MI 48202
Phone: 313-833-7900

Repro. Source
Sun Foundry
Kenneth F. Kalbleish, Sr.
299 S. Lake St.
Burbank, CA 91502
Phone: 818-841-7979 or 800-367-3479
Manufactures bronze statues and ceramic plates; send for catalog of reproduction Art Deco items.

Repro. Source
Art Deco Decor
17303 Santa Lucia Street
Fountain Valley, CA 92708-3117
Phone: 714-842-6457
Send for catalog of Art Deco reproduction items. Large collection of Tiffany style and Art Nouveau bronze and cut lead glass lamps.

Chase Co. Brass & Copper

Expert
Richard Kilbride
81 Willard Terrace
Stamford, CT 06903
Phone: 203-322-0568
*Specializes in Art Deco chrome. ***

ART NOUVEAU

(see also CERAMICS; FURNITURE; GEMS & JEWELRY; GLASS)

Collector
Bird-in-the-Cage
201 King St.
Alexandria, VA 22314
*Wants paper items, vintage clothing, glass, etc. from the 1880's to 1915 Art Nouveau period. ***

Dealer
Antiques & Art Galleries
Steve Whysel
101 N. Main
Bentonville, AR 72712
Phone: 501-273-7701 or 501-444-9911
Wants Art Nouveau pottery, art glass, lamps, furniture, paintings, etchings, jewelry, bronze statues, marble figures, vases, bowls, etc.

Museum/Library
Virginia Museum of Fine Arts
Frederick R. Brandt
2800 Grove Ave.
Richmond, VA 23221-2466
Phone: 804-367-0888   FAX: 804-367-9393
Fine arts museum covering the entire range of history of art.

ART POTTERY

(see also CERAMICS (AMERICAN ART POTTERY); CERAMICS (ENGLISH), Art Pottery)

ART TEFT & FRAUD

Misc. Service
International Foundation for Art Research (IFAR)
Magazine: IFAR Reports
46 East 70th St.
    New York, NY 10021
Phone: 212-879-1780 or 212-879-1781
                 FAX: 212-734-4174
Clearinghouse for information on art theft, fraud, forgery; promotes recovery of stolen art & prevention of circulation of forged works.

Misc. Service
Federal Trade Commission
Public Reference
Washington, DC 20580
*Free fact sheet about scam artists. ***

ARTS & CRAFTS

(see also FRANK LLOYD WRIGHT; FURNITURE, Stickley; COPPER ITEMS, Stickley)

Auction Service
David Rago's American Arts & Crafts Auction
Station E
P.O. Box 3592
Trenton, NJ 08629
Phone: 609-585-2546
Specializing in the sale of American art pottery and Arts and Crafts items.

Auction Service
Don Treadway Auctions
Don Treadway
2128 Madison Rd.
Cincinnati, OH 45208
Phone: 513-321-6742   FAX: 513-871-7722
Specializes in the sale of Arts and Crafts pottery.

Club/Association
Roycrofters-At-Large Association/Elbert Hubbard Foundation
Newsletter: Newsletter To Members
31 S. Grove St.
East Aurora, NY 14052
Phone: 716-652-3333 *

Dealer
ARK Antiques
Rosalie & Aram Berberian
Box 3133
New Haven, CT 06515
Phone: 203-387-3754
Wants American craftsman silver, jewelry and metal of the first half of the 20th century.

Dealer
David Rago Arts & Crafts
David Rago
Station E
P.O. Box 3592
Trenton, NJ 08629
Phone: 609-585-2546
Wants American art pottery, and Arts and Crafts items such as furniture and metal items by Stickley, Rohlfs, Wright, Roycroft, etc.

Dealer
Harvey Kaplan
40 First St.
Troy, NY 12180
Phone: 518-272-3456
*Wants Limbert, Roycroft; also Stickley furniture, clocks, lighting and architects' drawings. ***

Dealer
Bob Berman
441 S. Jackson St.
Media, PA 19063
Phone: 215-843-1516

Wants mission oak and Arts & Crafts furniture by Craftsman, Gustav Stickley, Roycroft, Limbert; also pottery by Dedham, Teco, etc.

Dealer
Don Treadway
2128 Madison Rd.
Cincinnati, OH 45208
Phone: 513-321-6742   FAX: 513-871-7722

Dealer
John Toomey
818 North Blvd.
Oak Park, IL 60302
Phone: 708-383-5234
Conducts Arts and Crafts auctions in association with Don Treadway.

Dealer
Dealer
1706 North Bissell St.
Chicago, IL 60614
Phone: 312-915-0277
*Furniture, lamps, accessories 1900-1920: Rohlf, Roycroft, Stickley, Wright, Van Erp lamps, Teco and George Ohr pottery, Jarvie candlesticks. **

Expert
ARK Antiques
Rosalie Berberian
Box 3133
New Haven, CT 06515
Phone: 203-387-3754
Specializing in American Arts & Crafts Movement silver, jewelry and metal items.

Expert
Bruce Johnson
P.O. Box 6660
Durham, NC 27708
Phone: 919-286-9522
Writes furniture repair/refinishing column. Wrote price guide to arts and crafts movement items.

Periodical
Newsletter: Arts & Crafts Quarterly
David Rago
Station E
P.O. Box 3592
Trenton, NJ 08629
Phone: 609-585-2546

Roycroft
(see also BOOKS, Roycroft)

Museum/Library
Elbert Hubbard Library-Museum
Village Hall
571 Main St.
East Aurora, NY 14052
Phone: 716-652-6000

Van Erp-Style Lamps
Repro. Source
Mission Oak Shop, The
Jerry Cohen
123 Main St.
Putnam, CT 06260
Phone: 203-928-6662   FAX: 203-928-1039
Makes hammered copper and mica light fixtures in the Arts & Crafts style of Dick Van Erp and Gustav Stickley.

ASH TRAYS
Tire Shaped
Collector
Jeff McVey
P.O. Box 201
Mofett Field, CA 94035
*Wants rubber tire ash trays. **

ASTRONOMICAL ITEMS
(see also BOOKS, Collector (Natural History); INSTRUMENTS & DEVICES, Scientific)

Collector
Crossley
556 Allenview Dr.
Mechanicsburg, PA 17055
Phone: 717-697-1714
*Wants astronomical antiques: telescopes, books, globes, paper ephemera, postcards, stereo views showing observatories, etc. **

ATLANTIC CITY COLLECTIBLES
Collector
Mitchell Cohen
P.O. Box 629
Huntingdon Valley, PA 19006
Wants antiques and memorabilia: Hotel, Pier, Fralinger Piggy Bank, Heinz Pickle Pins, anything Atlantic City.

ATLASES
(see also MAPS)

Collector
Mayer
Box 11302
Pittsburgh, PA 15238
U.S. atlases before 1875, state and county atlases before 1900, pocket maps, globes, etc.; anything relating to Pittsburgh, PA.

Collector
J. Hanna
4016 Woodland Rd.
Annandale, VA 22003
Phone: 703-941-8256
*Wants atlases, books or ephemera with maps, U.S. documents with maps and large single maps; pre-1900. **

AUCTION CATALOGS
Book Seller
Catalog Kid
Debbie Schwartz
555 Old Long Ridge Rd.
Stamford, CT 06903
Phone: 203-322-7854
Distributes post sale auction catalogs.

Book Seller
Auction Catalog, Co., The
Burton Hem
634 5th Ave.
San Rafael, CA 94901
Phone: 415-457-0428 or 800-487-0428
            FAX: 415-457-4489
Sells most definitive, up-to-date reference in art, antiques & collectible market: Sotheby, Christie, Skinner post auction catalogs.

AUCTION SERVICES
(see also ART; BOOKS; BOTTLES; COINS & CURRENCY; COLLECTIBLES; DECOYS; DOLLS; GAMES; GLASS; MILITARIA; POSTCARDS; STEINS; TOYS; etc.)

Auction Service
Christie's South Kensington, Ltd.
85 Old Brompton Road
London SW7 3LD England
Regular sales of furniture, paintings, silver, jewelry, ceramics, textiles, books and collectibles; free verbal valuations weekdays.

Auction Service
Phillips Auction Gallery
101 New Bond Street
London W1Y 0AS England

Auction Service
Pioneer Auction of Amherst
Jct. Rt. 111 & 63
N. Amherst, MA 01059
Phone: 413-253-9914 *

Auction Service
Caropreso Gallery
136 High Street
Lee, MA 01238
Phone: 413-243-3424 *

Auction Service
Douglas Auctioneers
Douglas B. Bilodeau
Route 5
South Deerfield, MA 01373
Phone: 413-665-3530   FAX: 413-665-2877
Auction sales year-round, specializing in antiques, fine art, estates, and appraising; also conducts Auctioneering School.

Auction Service

Skinner, Inc.
357 Main Street
Bolton, MA 01740
Phone: 508-779-6241 or 617-236-1700
                    FAX: 508-779-5144
Established in 1962, Skinner Inc. is the fifth largest auction house in the US.

Auction Service

Willis Henry Auctions
22 Main St.
Marshfield, MA 02059
Phone: 617-834-7774
Specializes in American antiques, esp. Shaker, early American, and American Indian.

Auction Service

F.B. Hubley & Co., Inc.
364 Broadway
Cambridge, MA 02139
Phone: 617-876-2030 *

Auction Service

Marc J. Matz Gallery
366-B Broadway
Cambridge, MA 02139
Phone: 617-661-6200 *

Auction Service

Robert C. Eldred & Co.
P.O. Box 796
East Dennis, MA 02641
Phone: 508-385-3116

Auction Service

Richard A. Bourne Auction Co., Inc.
P.O. Box 141
Hyannis Port, MA 02647
Phone: 508-775-0797

Auction Service

Arman Absentee Auctions
P.O. Box 3239
Newport, RI 02840
Phone: 401-683-3100   FAX: 401-683-4044
Specialize in mail-bid auctions for historical staffordshire, quimper, American glass, paperweights, bottles, etc.

Auction Service

Gustave White Auctioneers
P.O. Box 59
Newport, RI 02840
Phone: 401-847-4250 *

Auction Service

Richard W. Withington, Inc.
R.D. 2, Box 440
Hillsboro, NH 03244
Phone: 603-464-3232

Auction Service

Northeast Auctions
Ronald Bourgeault
694 Lafayette Road
Hampton, NH 03842
Phone: 603-926-9800   FAX: 603-926-3545 *

Auction Service

Paul McInnis
356 Exeter Road
Hampton Falls, NH 03844
Phone: 603-778-8989 *

Auction Service

Sanders & Mock Associates, Inc.
Mark Hanson
P.O. Box 37
Tamworth, NH 03886
Phone: 603-323-8749 or 603-323-8784

Auction Service

Richard W. Oliver Auctions
Route One, Plaza One
Kennebunk, ME 04043
Phone: 207-985-3600   FAX: 207-985-7734

Auction Service

F.O. Bailey Auction Gallery
Joy Piscopo
141 Middle Street
Portland, ME 04101
Phone: 207-744-1479   FAX: 207-774-7914 *

Auction Service

James D. Julia, Inc.
P.O. Box 830
Fairfield, ME 04937
Phone: 207-453-7904   FAX: 207-453-2502

Auction Service

Duane Merrill
32 Beacon Street
S. Burlington, VT 05403
Phone: 802-878-2625 *

Auction Service

Winter Associates, Inc.
Regina Madigan
P.O. Box 823
Plainville, CT 06062
Phone: 203-793-0288 or 800-962-2530
Conducts estate liquidations of antiques, fine furniture, paintings, jewelry, porcelain, glass, etc.

Auction Service

Litchfield Auction Gallery
Clarence W. Pico
425 Bantam Rd.
P.O. Box 1337
Litchfield, CT 06759
Phone: 203-567-3126   FAX: 203-567-3266
Auction announcements and catalogs available upon request (no subscription).

Auction Service

Berman's Auction Gallery
33 West Blackwell Street
Dover, NJ 07081
Phone: 201-361-3110

Auction Service

Bob Koty Professional Auctioneers
Bob & Clara Koty
P.O. Box 625
Freehold, NJ 07728
Phone: 908-780-1265
Specializes in the auction sale of antiques, collectibles, household contents, estates, etc.

Auction Service

Castner Auction & Appraisal Service
Leon Castner, Pres.
6 Wantage Ave.
Branchville, NJ 07826
Phone: 201-948-3868
Specializing in the sale of local estate contents including antiques and residential contents.

Auction Service

Swann Galleries, Inc.
104 E. 25th St.
New York, NY 10010
Phone: 212-254-4710   FAX: 212-979-1017
Oldest/largest U.S. auctioneer specializing in rare books, autographs & manuscripts, Judaica, photographs, and works of art on paper.

Auction Service

Lubin Galleries, Inc.
Irwin Lubin
30 West 26th Street
New York, NY 10010
Phone: 212-924-3777   FAX: 212-366-9190
Sells furniture, antiques, silver, bronzes, porcelains, oriental rugs, ethnographic art, jewelry, etc.

Auction Service

Christie's East
219 E. 67th St.
New York, NY 10021
Phone: 212-606-0400

Auction Service

Sotheby's
1334 York Ave. at 72nd Street
New York, NY 10021
Phone: 212-606-7000

Auction Service

Guernsey's Auction
108 1/2 East 73rd St.
New York, NY 10021
Phone: 212-794-2280   FAX: 212-744-3638
Auctions unique commodities and collections, e.g. vintage automobiles, marine art, animation cels, Soviet art, posters, etc.

Auction Service
Sotheby's Arcade Auction
1334 York Ave. at 72nd Street
New York, NY 10021
Phone: 212-606-7409
Focuses on the sale of collectibles: toys, dolls, games, banks, etc.

Auction Service
Christie's
502 Park Ave.
New York, NY 10022
Phone: 212-546-1000

Auction Service
Phillips Fine Art & Auctioneers
406 East 79th St.
New York, NY 10022
Phone: 212-570-4830   FAX: 212-570-2207
Specializes in the sale of jewelry, paintings, prints, silver, coins, stamps, toys (especially lead soldiers), and movie memorabilia.

Auction Service
Harmer Rooke Galleries
3 East 57th Street
New York, NY 10022
Phone: 212-751-1900   FAX: 212-758-1713

Auction Service
William Doyle Galleries
175 E. 87th St.
New York, NY 10128
Phone: 212-427-2730

Auction Service
South Bay Auctions, Inc.
485 Montauk Highway
East Moriches, NY 11940
Phone: 516-878-2909 or 516-878-2933
     FAX: 516-878-1863

Auction Service
Marvin Cohen Auctions
Box 425, Routes 20 & 22
New Lebanon, NY 12125
Phone: 518-794-7477

Auction Service
Savoia & Fromm Auction Services
Route 23
South Cairo, NY 12482
Phone: 518-622-8000   FAX: 518-622-9453

Auction Service
Mid-Hudson Auction Galleries
1 Idlewild Ave.
Cornwall-On-Hudson, NY 12520
Phone: 914-534-7828 *

Auction Service
Doyle Auctioneers
R.D. 3 Box 137
Fishkill, NY 12524
Phone: 914-896-9492

Auction Service
Iroquois Auction Gallery
Box 66
Port Henry, NY 12974
Phone: 518-546-7003 *

Auction Service
Mapes Auctioneers & Appraisers
David W. Mapes
1600 Vestal Parkway West
Vestal, NY 13850
Phone: 607-754-9193   FAX: 607-786-3549

Auction Service
Collectors Auction Services
P.O. Box 13732
Seneca, PA 16346
Phone: 814-677-6070   FAX: 814-677-6070
An absentee mail bid auction handling quality antiques and collectibles.

Auction Service
Roan Bros. Auction Gallery
R.D. 3 Box 118
Cogan Station, PA 17728
Phone: 717-494-0170

Auction Service
Freeman/Fine Arts of Phila.
Leslie Lynch Lynch, ASA
1808-10 Chestnut St.
Philadelphia, PA 19103
Phone: 215-563-9275 or 215-563-9453
     FAX: 215-563-8236
A full-service auction tradition since 1805 with new ideas to serve both buyer and seller with auction and appraisal services.

Auction Service
Alderfer Auction Company
501 Fairground Road
Hatfield, PA 19440
Phone: 215-368-5477   FAX: 215-368-9055

Auction Service
Pennypacker Auction Center
1540 New Holland Rd.
Reading, PA 19607 *

Auction Service
Weschler's
William P. Weschler, Jr.
909 E Street NW
Washington, DC 20004
Phone: 202-628-1281 or 800-331-1430
     FAX: 202-628-2366
A full service auction service for art, antiques, decorative accessories, household furnishings, and commercial liquidations.

Auction Service
Sloan's
Ben Hastings
4920 Wyaconda Rd.
Rockville, MD 20852
Phone: 301-468-4911

Auction Service
Richard Opfer Auctioneering, Inc.
1919 Greenspring Dr.
Timonium, MD 21093
Phone: 301-252-5035   FAX: 301-252-5863

Auction Service
Harris Auction Galleries
8783-875 N. Howard St.
Baltimore, MD 21201
Phone: 301-728-7040 *

Auction Service
Fredericktowne Auction Gallery
Thom Pattie
5305 Jefferson Pike
Frederick, MD 21701
Phone: 301-473-5566 or 800-962-1305

Auction Service
Jim Depew Galleries
1860 Piedmont Road, NE
Atlanta, GA 30324
Phone: 404-874-2286 *

Auction Service
Garth's Auction, Inc.
P.O. Box 369
Delaware, OH 43015
Phone: 614-362-4771

Auction Service
Wolf's Auctioneers
1239 West 6th St.
Cleveland, OH 44113
Phone: 216-575-9653 or 800-526-1991
     FAX: 216-621-8011

Auction Service
Dumouchelle Art Galleries
Lawrence Dumouchelle
409 East Jefferson Ave.
Detroit, MI 48226
Phone: 313-963-6255 or 313-963-0248
     FAX: 313-963-8199
A fine arts auction house; rugs, paintings, jewelry, porcelain, silver, art glass, toys, dolls, furniture, books, sculpture, etc.

Auction Service
Dunning's Auction Service, Inc.
755 Church Rd.
Elgin, IL 60123
Phone: 312-741-3483   FAX: 708-741-3589
Premier mid-American auction firm selling antiques, fine art, jewelry, American Indian art, and real estate.

Auction Service

Hanzel Galleries, Inc.
1120 South Michigan Avenue
Chicago, IL 60605
Phone: 312-922-6234

Auction Service

Chase Gilmore Art Galleries
724 West Washington
Chicago, IL 60606
Phone: 312-648-1690 *

Auction Service

Leslie Hindman Auctions
215 West Ohio St.
Chicago, IL 60610
Phone: 312-670-0010   FAX: 312-670-4248

Auction Service

Manion's Auction House
P.O. Box 12214
Kansas City, KS 66112
Phone: 913-299-6692   FAX: 913-299-6792
A mail-bid auction company specializing in militaria, baseball cards, toys, glass, railroad items, and other collectibles.

Auction Service

Woody Auction Company
P.O. Box 618
Douglass, KS 67039
Phone: 316-746-2694

Auction Service

Morton M. Goldberg Auction Galleries, Inc.
547 Baronne St.
New Orleans, LA 70113
Phone: 504-592-2300   FAX: 504-592-2311 *

Auction Service

Pettigrew Auction Company
1645 South Tejon Street
Colorado Springs, CO 80906
Phone: 719-633-7963

Auction Service

Butterfield & Butterfield
7601 Sunset Blvd.
Los Angeles, CA 90046
Phone: 213-850-7500

Auction Service

Butterfield & Butterfield
220 San Bruno Ave.
San Francisco, CA 94103
Phone: 415-861-7500
Specialties: posters, toys decorative arts, furniture, photography. Largest full-service auction in the West.

Periodical

Magazine: Auction World
417 W. Stanton
P.O. Box 745
Fergus Falls, MN 56537
Phone: 218-739-4408   FAX: 218-736-7474
The monthly newsmagazine for professional auctioneers featuring news, feature stories and columns on auctions all over the U.S.

AUTO RACING MEMORABILIA

(see also SPORTS MEMORABILIA, Auto Racing)

AUTOGRAPHS

(see also HISTORICAL AMERICANA; MANUSCRIPTS; PAPER COLLECTIBLES; PLAYBOY ITEMS; SPORTS COLLECTIBLES)

Auction Service

T. Vennett-Smith Chartered Auctioneer
Richard Davie
11 Nottingham Road, Gotham
Nottingham NG11 OHE England
Great Britain's leading professional autograph auction house, specializing in bi-monthly auctions of fine and varied autographs.

Auction Service

Swann Galleries, Inc.
104 E. 25th St.
New York, NY 10010
Phone: 212-254-4710   FAX: 212-979-1017
Oldest/largest U.S. auctioneer specializing in rare books, autographs & manuscripts, Judaica, photographs, and works of art on paper.

Club/Association

Autographics International
Box 543
Tilsonburg
Ontario N5G 4J1 Canada *

Club/Association

Universal Autograph Collectors Club
Newsletter: Pen & Quill, The
P.O. Box 6181
Washington, DC 20044-6181
The UACC has over 2000 members; offers a bi-monthly newsletter with reports on facsimiles, forgeries, authentication, auctions, etc.

Club/Association

Manuscript Society, The
Magazine: Manuscripts
350 N. Niagara St.
Burbank, CA 91505
An organization of collectors, dealers, librarians, archivists, scholars and others interested in autographs and manuscripts.

Collector

Stan Block
128 Cynthia Rd.
Newton, MA 02159
Wants autographs, banners, leathers, political pins, baseball cards, silks, sports memorabilia.

Collector

Edward Bomsey
7317 Farr St.
Annandale, VA 22003
Wants letters, photographs, signatures of personalities in politics, military, science, entertainment, music, arts, etc.

Collector

Will Paulsen
969 Rock Creek Rd.
Charlottesville, VA 22903
Phone: 804-971-6864
Wants autographs in the Civil War, Early American Patriots, and American Presidents categories.
*

Collector

Joseph Maddalena
Suite 704
9440 Santa Monica Blvd.
Beverly Hills, CA 90210
Phone: 800-942-8856
Wants original letters, manuscripts, rare books of famous people. Cash paid. Serious inquiries only.

Collector

Michael Reese II
P.O. Box 5704
South San Francisco, CA 94083
Phone: 415-541-5920
Wants autographs: early aviation (1910-1939), letters, Presidents letters, any Civil War (Union or Confederate).

Dealer

Kenneth W. Rendell, Inc.
Kenneth Rendell
125 East 57th St.
New York, NY 10022
Phone: 800-447-1007 or 617-431-1776
                          FAX: 617-237-1492
Wants letters, documents of authors, presidents, statesmen, etc.; "Guide to Values of Autographs" available upon request.

Dealer

Paul Longo Americana
Paul Longo
P.O. Box 490
South Orleans, MA 02662
Phone: 508-255-5482
Wants autographs of Presidents, famous athletes, world famous inventors, statesmen, actors and actresses, etc.

Dealer

Mark Vardakis
Box 1430
Coventry, RI 02816
Phone: 401-823-8440 or 800-342-0301
FAX: 401-823-8861
Buying and selling presidents, authors, musicians, celebrities, scientists, etc.; also conducts autograph auctions.

Dealer

La Barre Galleries
George H. La Barre
P.O. Box 746
Hollis, NH 03049
Phone: 603-882-2411
Major dealer and expert in autographs, and stocks and bonds.

Dealer

Jerry Granat Manuscripts
Jerry & Ellen Granat
P.O. Box 92
Woodmere, MY 11598
Phone: 516-374-7809
Buys and sells letters and autographs from famous people; issues autograph catalogs.

Dealer

Pages of History
Jerry Docteur
P.O. Box 2840
Binghamton, NY 13902
Phone: 607-724-4983
Wants presidential and other historical autographs and material.

Dealer

Robert Batchelder
1 West Butler Avenue
Ambler, PA 19002
Phone: 215-643-1430
Wants autograph letters, manuscripts & documents (American & European in all fields): Presidents, historical, literary, musical, etc.

Dealer

Catherine Barnes
2031 Walnut St., 3rd Floor
P.O. Box 30117
Philadelphia, PA 19103
Phone: 215-854-0175
Wants autographs, letters, documents, etc. signed by historic individuals, e.g. Presidents, government, science, law, etc.

Dealer

Rare Books & Manuscripts
Carmen D. Valentino
2965 Richmond St.
Philadelphia, PA 19134
Phone: 215-739-6056
Antiquarian bookseller specializing in rare books, manuscripts, documents, early newspapers, ephemera, broadsides; pre-WWI.

Dealer

Autos & Autos
B.C. West, Jr.
P.O. Box 280
Elizabeth City, NC 27909
Phone: 919-335-1117
Wants autographs of famous aviators, scientists, doctors, Presidents, etc.; author of "The Autograph Collector Checklist."

Dealer

Autographs Incorporated
Ed London
9408 NW 70 Street
Tamarac, FL 33321
Phone: 305-726-4107 or 305-724-4294
Buys and sells autographs; free giant super sale autograph catalog available upon request.

Dealer

Linda Payne Autographs
Linda Payne
3619 Standish Ln.
Racine, WI 53405-4377
Phone: 414-554-1229   FAX: 414-554-6781
Wants all items signed by famous people; from 1 item to entire collections, especially good vintage items; catalog available.

Dealer

Robert A. LeGresley
P.O. Box 1199
Lawrence, KS 66044
Phone: 913-749-5458 or 913-843-3644
FAX: 913-841-1777
Buys and sells autographs, specializing in historical, scientific, literary, musicians, composers, aviation, Civil War, entertainers.

Dealer

Lone Star Autographs
P.O. Drawer 500
Kaufman, TX 75142
*Buy, sell, trade; wants autographed letters, documents, signed photographs; free catalog available. Member of Manuscript Society. ***

Dealer

Autographs of America
Tim Anderson
P.O. Box 461
Provo, UT 84603
Phone: 801-226-1787
Buy, sell, trade autographs: historical, Mormons, sports figures, etc.; specializing in movie stars of the 1930's, '40's and '50's.

Dealer

Celebrity Access
Thomas Burford
20 Sunnyside Ave. Ste. #A241
Mill Valley, CA 94941
Phone: 415-389-8133

Publishes annual directory of celebrity addresses; buys/sells/trades autographs; publishes catalog of autographs for sale.

Dealer

Linda's Autographs
Linda Murphy-Anthony
P.O. Box 1
Umpqua, OR 97486
Phone: 503-459-4730 or 503-673-8379
FAX: 503-459-4730
Autographs of famous people bought and sold.

Expert

Brian Kathenes
P.O. Box 77296
West Trenton, NJ 08628
Phone: 609-530-1350   FAX: 609-530-0660
Full service autograph business; buying, selling & appraising autographs, rare books & historically significant collectibles.

Expert

Charles Hamilton
c/o Harper & Row Publishers
10 E. 53rd St.
New York, NY 10022 *

Misc. Service

Jim Weaver
405 Dunbar
Pittsburgh, PA 15235
FREE AUTOGRAPHS! Almost 1000 personal addresses of celebrities who will usually send FREE, autographed photo. $12 for list.

Museum/Library

Pierpoint Morgan Library, The
29 E. 36th St.
New York, NY 10016
Phone: 212-685-0008

Museum/Library

New York Public Library, The
5th Ave. & 42nd Street
New York, NY 10018
Phone: 212-930-0800

Periodical

Walter R. Benjamin Autographs, Inc.
Magazine: Collector
P.O. Box 255
Hunter, NY 12442

Periodical

Newsletter: Autograph Review, The
Jeffrey Morey
305 Carlton Road
Syracuse, NY 13207
Phone: 315-474-3516
A bi-monthly publication for the serious collector; collector growth oriented: sports, military, actors addresses.

Periodical

Magazine: Autograph Collector's Magazine, The

Joe Kraus
P.O. Box 55328
Stockton, CA 95205
Phone: 209-473-0570 or 209-942-2131
FAX: 209-368-1549
Covers autograph/historical document collecting in all fields: entertainment, sports, historical, etc.; for all ages; lots of ads.

Periodical

Magazine: Autograph Quarterly & Buyers Guide

Joe Kraus
P.O. Box 55328
Stockton, CA 95205
Phone: 209-473-0570 or 209-942-2131
FAX: 209-368-1549
Features advertising & catalog offerings of dealers worldwide plus articles by experts about what's happening in the autograph market.

Periodical

Price Guide: Autograph Dealers Price Guide
Suite 269
1224 NE Walnut
Roseburg, OR 97470
A monthly publication; current market value for thousands of famous names; Rev. War, politicians, military, artists, business, etc.

Sports Related

Dealer

Bud Glick
2846 Lexington Lane
Highland Park, IL 60035
Phone: 708-576-3521 or 708-433-7484
Buys and sells sports autographs as well as autographs from famous people in all fields.

AUTOMOBILES

(see also AUTOMOBILIA; BUSES; MODELS; SPORTS COLLECTIBLES, Auto Racing; TAXI RELATED COLLECTIBLES; TRACTORS & RELATED ITEMS; TRUCKS)

Appraisals

Auto Appraisal Group
Larry Batton
Suite 240
2 Boar's Head Place
Charlottesville, VA 22901
Phone: 804-295-1722   FAX: 804-295-7918

Appraisals

Auto Evaluators
R.W. "Bob" Ryan
Suite 225
5078 S. 108th St.
Omaha, NE 68137
Phone: 402-895-2881 or 402-681-2968

Appraisals

Fast Appraisal Service Team, Inc.
Les Ferris
Suite 11A
574 Boston Rd.
Billerica, MA 01821
Phone: 508-670-2446 or 508-667-8002
FAX: 508-670-5220

Appraisals

Bob Lichty
1851 Spring Rd.
Carlisle, PA 17013
Phone: 717-249-0455 or 717-249-7347

Appraisals

New England Appraisal Service
Arthur B. Shorts
P.O. Box 187
Manchester, CT 06040
Phone: 203-647-0409

Appraisals

Quentin Craft
P.O. Drawer 1139
Indiana, PA 15701
Phone: 412-463-1530

Appraisals

M & M Automobile Appraisers, Inc.
Mike & Mary Grippo
RR1, Box 220
Beecher, IL 60401-9757
Phone: 708-258-6662   FAX: 708-258-9675
Special interest, collectible and antique cars; member International Society of Appraisers.

Appraisals

Marion Associates
4400 Washington St. W.
Charleston, WV 25313
Phone: 304-744-1211

Appraisals

Appraisal Network, The
Suite 1139
13700 Alton Pkwy.
Irvine, CA 92718
Phone: 714-586-1992

Appraisals

Automotive Legal Service
P.O. Box 626
Dresher, PA 19025
Phone: 800-487-4947

Appraisals

Kruse International
Dean Kruse
P.O. Box 190
Auburn, IN 46706
Phone: 800-328-0771   FAX: 219-925-5467

Auction Service

ACS International Collector Vehicle Auctions
227 West Highway 36
St. Paul, MN 55113
Phone: 612-633-9655   FAX: 612-633-3212
Conducts consignment auctions, appraisals, private sales, liquidations.

Auction Service

International Classic Auctions
9 North Roosevelt
Chandler, AZ 85226
Phone: 602-899-2222   FAX: 602-961-1540
Conducts auctions of special interest automobiles and related memorabilia.

Auction Service

Specialty Sales
4321 First St.
Pleasanton, CA 94566
Phone: 415-484-2262   FAX: 415-426-8535
Auctions antiques, classics, exotics; indoor showrooms.

Auction Service

Kruse International
P.O. Box 190
Auburn, IN 46706
Phone: 219-925-5600 or 800-328-0771
FAX: 219-925-5467
Specializes in auctioning antique, classic and other special interest automobiles, planes, motorcycles, trucks, etc.

Club/Association

Antique Automobile Club of America
Magazine: Antique Automobile
P.O. Box 417
Hershey, PA 17033-0417
Phone: 717-534-1910
*Focusing on "antique" cars; usually 1900-1925 (or by state registration a vehicle at least 30 years old.) ***

Club/Association

Mid-American Old Time Automobile Association
Magazine: Antique Car Times
P.O. Box 2995
Jackson, TN 38302
Phone: 901-424-2809
M.O.T.A.A. represents approximately 32 affiliated antique car clubs; "Antique Car Times" filled with articles featuring antique cars.

Club/Association

Veteran Motor Car Club of America
Magazine: Bulb Horn
William E. Donze, ExSec
P.O. Box 360788
Strongsville, OH 44136
Phone: 216-238-2771

A hobby club organized in 1938 to serve the needs of those interested in the preservation of collector vehicles and related memorabilia.

Club/Association

Milestone Car Society
Magazine: Mile Post
P.O. Box 24612
Indianapolis, IN 46224
Focuses on "milestone" cars; certain club-approved 1946-1970 cars which are gaining popularity with the passage of time.

Club/Association

Society of Automotive Historians
Journal: Society of Automotive Historians Journal
5201 Woodward Ave.
Detroit, MI 48202 *

Club/Association

Horseless Carriage Club of America
Magazine: Horseless Carriage Gazette
7210 Jordan Ave.
Canoga Park, VA 91303
Phone: 818-704-4253 *

Dealer

Duffy's Collectible Cars
250 Classic Car Court S.W.
Cedar Rapids, IA 52404
Phone: 319-364-7000   FAX: 319-364-4036

Museum/Library

Sturbridge Auto Museum
P.O. Box 486
Sturbridge, MA 01566
Phone: 617-867-2217

Museum/Library

Heritage Plantation Auto Museum
P.O. Box 566
Sandwich, MA 02563
Phone: 617-888-3300

Museum/Library

Volvo Antique Auto Museum & Village
27640 W. Hwy. 120
Volvo, IL 60073
Phone: 815-385-3644

Museum/Library

Museum of Science & Industry
Keith R. Gill
57th St. & Lake Shore Drive
Chicago, IL 60637
Phone: 312-684-1414   FAX: 312-684-5580

Museum/Library

Antiques, Inc. Car Museum
P.O. Box 1887
Muskogee, OK 74402
Phone: 918-687-4447

Museum/Library

National Automobile Museum
10 Lake St. South
Reno, NV 89501
Phone: 702-333-9300   FAX: 702-333-9309
A complete museum depicting the history of automobiles.

Periodical

Hemmings Motor News
Magazine: Special Interest Autos
Box 196
Bennington, VT 05201-9940
Phone: 802-442-3101
A bi-monthly magazine focusing on special interest vehicles.

Periodical

Hemmings Motor News
Magazine: Hemmings Motor News
P.O. Box 100
Bennington, VT 05201-9980
Phone: 802-442-3101
Newsmagazine for antique and special interest auto enthusiasts; auctions, ads, services, insurance, restorations, etc.

Periodical

Newsletter: Car Collecting & Investing
Bill Gillette, Ed.
Suite 300
2315 Broadway
New York, NY 10024
Phone: 212-873-5900 or 800-537-1158
                    FAX: 212-799-1728
Only bi-weekly newsletter for news, forecasts, auction results, and developments in collector car field; $37.50/yr. (50% CIC discount).

Periodical

Automobile Quarterly, Inc
Magazine: Automobile Quarterly's Quatrefoil
Rt. 222 & Sharadin Rd.
P.O. Box 348
Kutztown, PA 19530
Phone: 215-683-3169 or 800-523-0236
                    FAX: 215-683-3287
Glossy magazine featuring articles about classic foreign and domestic cars; also carries a large assortment of classic car posters.

Periodical

National Automobile Dealers Association
Price Guide: N.A.D.A. Official Used Car Guide
8400 Westpark Drive
McLean, VA 22102
Phone: 800-544-6232
A series of value guides for domestic and foreign cars, trucks, vans, RV's, mobile homes, motorcycles, snowmobiles, and boats.

Periodical

Magazine: Car Collector & Car Classics
Suite 144
8601 Dunwoody Place
Atlanta, GA 30350 *

Periodical

Magazine: DuPont Registry
2502 N. Rocky Point Dr., #1095
Tampa, FL 33607
Phone: 800-262-2886 or 800-233-1731
A monthly report of Kruse Auction Co. car sales results.

Periodical

Magazine: Auto Trader Old Car Book
14549 62nd St. North
Clearwater, FL 34620
Phone: 800-422-1160 or 800-331-0190
A comprehensive monthly listing with photo ads of cars for sale nationwide; also classified and display ads for the car enthusiast.

Periodical

Amos Press, Inc.
Magazine: Cars & Parts
P.O. Box 452
Sidney, OH 45365
Phone: 513-498-0803
For the collector of special interest & muscle cars; restoration, automotive history, how-to articles, show & auction coverage, etc.

Periodical

Krause Publications, Inc.
Newspaper: Old Cars Weekly
Brad Bowling, Ed.
700 East State St.
Iola, WI 54990
Phone: 800-258-0929 or 715-445-2214
                    FAX: 715-445-4087
Concerning antique automobiles of all ages; auction reports, hobby events, car shows, swap meets, ads, club activities, etc.

Periodical

Krause Publications, Inc.
Newspaper: Old Cars News & Marketplace
700 E. State St.
Iola, WI 54990
Phone: 800-258-0929 or 715-445-2214
                    FAX: 715-445-4087
Only weekly periodical serving collectors of antique and collectible cars of the past 100 years; restorations, auction results, ads, etc.

Periodical

Krause Publications, Inc.
Magazine: Old Cars Price Guide
Kenneth Buttolph, Ed.
700 E. State St.
Iola, WI 54990
Phone: 800-258-0929 or 715-445-2214
                    FAX: 715-445-4087

Lists current values in five grading categories for all American cars made from 1901-1979.

Periodical

Krause Publications, Inc.
Magazine: Car Corral
700 E. State St.
Iola, WI 54990
Phone: 800-258-0929 or 715-445-2214
FAX: 715-445-4087
Monthly marketplace for buyers/sellers of late model and collector cars; listing arranged for easy location; ads, restorers, parts, etc.

Periodical

Magazine: Deals on Wheels
P.O. Box 205
Sioux Falls, SD 57101
Phone: 605-338-7666 or 800-334-1886
A comprehensive monthly listing with photo ads of cars for sale nationwide; also classified and display ads for the car enthusiast.

Periodical

Magazine: Collectible Automobile
7373 North Cicero
Lincolnwood, IL 60646 *

Periodical

Magazine: Skinned Knuckles
175 May Avenue
Monrovia, CA 91016
*Monthly magazine for car restorers. **

Periodical

Newspaper: Coast Car Collector
5800 Shellmound St.
Emeryville, CA 94608
*Monthly color newspaper focusing on the West Coast car market. **

Repair Service

Classic Coach Works
Bob Burroughs
4937-C Green Valley Rd.
Monrovia, MD 21770
Phone: 301-831-6666
Restores classic automobiles.

Repair Service

Realistic Auto Restorations, Inc.
2519 6th Ave. S.
St. Petersburg, FL 33712
Phone: 813-327-5162
Offers restoration services for antiques, classics, street rods, Corvettes and all sports cars.

Repair Service

Classic Car Co., The
442 Distribution Parkway
Collierville, TN 38017
Phone: 901-854-6501
Offers complete classic and antique car sales and restoration.

Repair Service

Beckley Auto Restoration
David Ten Brink
4405 S.W. Capital
Battle Creek, MI 49017
Phone: 616-979-3013
Offers complete classic and antique car restoration.

Amphibious

Club/Association

Amphibious Auto Club of America
Newsletter: AACA Newsletter
3281 Elk Ct.
Yorktown Heights, NY 10598
Phone: 914-245-7541 *

British Cabs

Club/Association

American British Cab Society
4470 Cerritos Ave.
Long Beach, CA 90807
Phone: 213-424-4302 *

Chryslers

Club/Association

Chrysler 300 Club, Inc.
Magazine: Brute Force
9238 Mayfair Lane
Orland Park, IL 60462
Of particular interest to owners of Chrysler 300 series automobiles.

Contemporary Historical

Club/Association

Contemporary Historical Vehicle Association
Newsletter: Action Era Vehicle
16944 Dearborn St.
Sepulveda, CA 91343
Phone: 912-477-4410
*Interested in preservation, collection, and acclamation of road vehicles at least 25 years old. **

Corvettes

Club/Association

National Corvette Owners Association
Newsletter: NCOA Newsletter
900 S. Washington St.
Falls Church, VA 22046
Over 15,000 members strong.

Customized Show Cars

Club/Association

International Show Car Association
Magazine: Show Stopper
Hayne Dominick
32385 Mally Dr.
Madison Heights, MI 48071
Phone: 313-588-5568   FAX: 313-588-6007

Sanctioning body for 125 annual MAGNA Auto Shows involving over 27,000 privately owned custom vehicles; judging, competition services.

Fords (Model A)

Club/Association

Model "A" Restorers Club
Magazine: Model "A" News, The
24822 Michigan Ave.
Dearborn, MI 48124
Phone: 313-278-1455
To encourage members to acquire, preserve, restore, exhibit and make use of Model A Fords (1928-1931).

Muscle Cars

Periodical

Amos Press, Inc.
Magazine: Muscle Cars of the 60's/70's
P.O. Box 4251
Sidney, OH 45365
Phone: 513-498-0803
A bi-monthly magazine for collectors, restorers & admirers of super cars of yesteryear; articles, maintenance, restoring details, etc.

Mustang

Club/Association

Mustang Club of America, Inc.
Magazine: Mustang Times
P.O. Box 447
Lithonia, GA 30058-0447
Phone: 404-482-4822
An association for the Ford Mustang and Shelby collector, restorer and enthusiast.

Periodical

Magazine: Mustang
P.O. Box 3286
Los Angeles, CA 90078 *

Professional

Club/Association

Professional Car Society
Magazine: Professional Car
P.O. Box 09636
Columbus, OH 43209
Phone: 614-221-6831
*Interested in vintage funeral, rescue, livery, and related professional vehicles. **

Sports Cars

Club/Association

Vintage Sports Car Club of America
Magazine: Vintage Sports Car
170 Wetherill Rd.
Garden City, NY 11530 *

Steam

Club/Association

Steam Automobile Club of America
Newsletter: Steam Automobile
P.O. Box 285
Niles, MI 49120 *

Street Rods

Club/Association

National Street Rod Association
Magazine: Streetscene Magazine
4030 Park Ave.
Memphis, TN 38111
Phone: 901-452-4030 *

Periodical

Magazine: American Rodder
P.O. Box 551
Mt. Morris, IL 61054
Focuses on latest trends and techniques in the field
of street rodding.

AUTOMOBILIA

(see also FORD MOTOR COMPANY
ITEMS; MODELS)

Collector

Donald Fehr
Box 872
Northfield, NJ 08225
Phone: 609-641-5910
Wants automobilia on specific cars, e.g. sales,
owners, accessories, hood ornaments, shop man-
uals, jewelry, etc.

Collector

Greg Wolfe
Box 333
Conyngham, PA 18219
Phone: 717-788-2007
Wants automotive/aviation books, magazines &
sales literature 1930-1965; also wants auto and
aviation toys and unbuilt kits, etc. *

Collector

Arnold Levin
P.O. Box 223
Northbrook, IL 60062
Phone: 708-564-2893
Wants classic car accessories such as carbide and
brass lights, hood ornaments, etc. *

Dealer

Ron & Deb Ladley
1850 Valley Forge Road
Lansdale, PA 19446
Phone: 215-584-1665
Wants auto, truck and motorcycle literature, ephemera, catalogs, brochures, manuals, signs,
dealership items, etc.; any age.

Dealer

Aquarius Antiques
Jim & Nancy Schaut
P.O. Box 10781
Glendale, AZ 85318
Phone: 602-878-4293
Publishes a quarterly catalog of one-of-a-kind
transportation toys and memorabilia; toys, board
games, trains; buy and sell.

Museum/Library

Museum of Transportation
15 Newton St.
Brookline, MA 02146
Phone: 617-522-6140

Museum/Library

Swigart Museum
Rte. 22 E
Huntingdon, PA 16652
Phone: 814-643-3000

Buick Related Items

Collector

Alvin Heckard
R.D. 1, Box 88
Lewistown, PA 17044
Phone: 717-248-7071 or 717-248-2816
Wants Buick promotional items, paperweights,
desk sets, ash trays, key chains, promotional
models, matchbooks, awards, literature, etc.

Hood Ornaments

Collector

Craig Emmerson
Suite 1200
10505 N. 69th St.
Scottsdale, AZ 85253
Phone: 602-998-2213 or 602-991-9638
FAX: 602-998-8968
Wants "car mascots", pre-war; premium paid for
humorous or signed hood ornaments.

Collector

Dan Smith
438 Camino Del Rio So. #213
San Diego, CA 92108
Phone: 619-291-6624 or 619-442-4314
Wants hood ornaments/mascots from 1910
through 1930's; also wants related literature, ads,
signs, etc.

Hubcaps

Club/Association

Hubcap Collectors Club
Newsletter: Hubcapper
Dennis Kuhn
P.O. Box 54
Buckley, MI 49620
Phone: 616-269-3555
Focus on the older threaded hubcaps.

Dealer

Ken Byrd's Hub Cap Center
Ken Byrd
703 Frederick St.
Hagerstown, MD 21740
Phone: 301-797-1367
Carries over 25,000 wheel covers; also rebuilds
wire wheels.

Ignition Parts

Collector

Myron Palay
4242 Lorain Ave.
Cleveland, OH 44113-3771
Phone: 216-961-7903
Wants early brass-era vibrator coils, coil boxes and
switches from pre-1913 automobiles.

Instruments

Repair Service

John Wolf & Co.
4550 Wood St.
Willoughby, OH 44094

Literature

Collector

Bob Johnson
21 Blandin Ave.
Framingham, MA 01701
Phone: 508-872-9173 or 800-229-2886
Automobile literature wanted: brochures, man-
uals; sales, service & parts books; dealer items, etc.

Collector

Walter Miller
6710 Brooklawn Pkwy.
Syracuse, NY 13211
Phone: 315-432-8282   FAX: 315-422-2554
Buys 1900-1975 automobile sales brochures, repair manuals, parts catalogs, showroom items or
any other related literature.

Collector

Glen Pancoma
1205-B Melroseway
Vista, CA 92083
Wants original automobile literature 1904-1988:
sales brochures, ads, shop and owners' manuals,
misc. *

Collector

Penning
Box 16171
Fresno, CA 93755
Automobile, truck dealers showroom brochures
wanted 1900 - 1970; also factory service, owner's
manuals.

Model A Advertising

Dealer

Jim Thomas
8165 Glenmill Ct.
Cincinnati, OH 45249
Phone: 513-489-7430
Wants 1928-1931 Ford Model "A" car and truck advertising, sales literature, posters, dealer items, memorabilia; buy/sell/trade.

Objects D'art

Club/Association

Automobile Objects D'Art Club
David K. Bausch
252 N. 7th St.
Allentown, PA 18102
Phone: 215-820-3001 or 215-432-3355
A club for collectors interested in early automobile history as shown through art and objects of art.

Signs

Dealer

Automotive Memorabilia Gallery
Bob & Judy
P.O. Box 776
Middleboro, MA 02346
Phone: 508-947-7287
*Wants automotive signs for automobiles, trucks, motorcycles, buses, gasoline, motor oil, Klaxon horns, tire companies, etc. ***

Spark Plugs

Club/Association

Spark Plug Collectors of America
Magazine: Ignitor, The
Steve McPherson
8241 NE 110th Place
Kirkland, WA 98034
Dedicated to the promotion of spark plug collecting and research, and the preservation of spark plug history.

AVIATION

(see also AIRSHIPS; PERSONALITIES (FAMOUS), Charles A. Lindbergh; STAMP COLLECTING, Air Mail Related)

Book Seller

Aviation Heritage Books
Alan & Drina Abel
806 Lockport Rd.
P.O. Box 2065
Terre Haute, IN 47802
Phone: 812-232-1042
Publishes and distributes books about aviation.

Book Seller

Historic Aviation
1401 Kings Wood Rd.
Eagan, MN 55122
Phone: 800-225-5575

Expert

Don Thomas
1801 Oak Creek Dr.
Dunedin, FL 34698
Phone: 813-784-3029
Author of "Nostalgia Panamerica", "Poster Art of the Airlines", "Lindbergh and Commercial Aviation, "Nostalgia North Americana."

Museum/Library

Aviation Heritage Research Center
Newsletter: Drina's Hanger Flyer
Alan & Drina Abel
806 Lockport Rd.
P.O. Box 2065
Terre Haute, IN 47802
Phone: 812-232-1042
Maintains large file of air airplane history and photos as well as a small museum; contributions of related material welcome.

Museum/Library

Stephan Remington
2555 Robert Fowler Way, #A
San Jose, CA 95148
Associated with aviation for over 40 years; has his own art gallery and museum of aircraft recognition items.

Periodical

Magazine: In Flight Aviation News
Nick Veronico
P.O. Box 620447
Woodside, CA 94062
Phone: 415-364-8110   FAX: 415-364-1359
A 120 page newspaper devoted to aviation & aviation history; editors will answer questions about memorabilia and refer sellers to buyers.

Art

Dealer

Aviation Arts
533 South Coast Hwy.
Laguna Beach, CA 92651
Offers new aviation related art of interest to collectors.

Military

Museum/Library

U.S. Army Aviation Museum
P.O. Box 610
Fort Rucker, AL 36362
Phone: 205-255-4507

Museum/Library

U.S. Air Force Museum
Richard L. Uppstrom, Dir.
Wright-Patterson A.F.B, OH 45433-6518
Phone: 513-255-3286   FAX: 513-255-3910
World's largest aviation museum with 10 1/2 acres of aircraft and other exhibits under roof.

Museum/Library

Confederate Air Force
Box CAF
Harlingen, TX 78551
Phone: 512-425-1057

Museum/Library

American Fighter Aces Museum Foundation
Newsletter: American Fighter Aces Bulletin
4636 Fighter Aces Dr.
Mesa, AZ 85205
Phone: 602-830-4540

AVIATION MEMORABILIA

(see also AIRLINE MEMORABILIA; AIRPLANES; AVIATION; MINIATURES, Airplanes; STAMP COLLECTING, Air Mail Related; TOYS, Airplane Related)

Auction Service

Dale C. Anderson Co.
Dale C. Anderson
4 W. Confederate Ave.
Gettysburg, PA 17325
Conducts mail bid auctions of military and civilian aviation memorabilia.

Club/Association

American Aviation Historical Society
Journal: AAHS Journal
2333 Otis St.
Santa Ana, CA 92704
Phone: 714-549-4818
*For the aviation buff; personalities, unit histories, equipment, etc. ***

Collector

Greg Wolfe
Box 333
Conyngham, PA 18219
Phone: 717-788-2007
*Wants automotive/aviation books, magazines & sales literature 1930-1965; also wants auto and aviation toys and unbuilt kits, etc. ***

Collector

Mike Kirkpatrick
17501 NE 33rd Pl.
Redmond, WA 98052
Phone: 206-881-5739 or 206-949-5019
Buys and sells military and commercial pilots and aviation clocks, watches, chronographs, and pilots wings; also submarine badges.

Museum/Library

Southern Museum of Flight
4343 N. 73rd St.
Birmingham, AL 35026
Phone: 205-833-8226

Museum/Library

Pima Museum
6400 S. Wilmot Rd.
Tucson, AZ 85706
Phone: 602-574-0462

Military

Club/Association
F-4 Phantom II Society
Newsletter: Smoke Trails
P.O. Box 261043
Pland, TX 75026
Phone: 214-867-4335
Focuses on the F-4 Phantom II.

Collector
Charles Donald
P.O. Box 822
Union City, NJ 07087-0822
Phone: 201-330-9619
Wants WWI squadron memorial volumes and squadron histories 1914 to 1918; also wants aviation-related photos from 1920's to 1940's.

Military (Pilots Wings)

Collector
Robert Missero
4 Kakiat Lane
Spring Valley, NY 10977-2009
Phone: 914-425-0013
Wants all types of WWII sterling silver U.S. Army Air Force wings; 1", 2", 3"; also wing bracelets.

AVON COLLECTIBLES

(see also BOTTLES; CALIFORNIA PERFUME COMPANY)

Club/Association
National Association of Avon Collectors, Inc.
Newsletter: Avon Times
Bill Armstrong, Pres.
P.O. Box 68
West Newton, IN 46183

Club/Association
Bud Hastin's National Avon Collectors Club
Newsletter: Avon Times
P.O. Box 9868
Kansas City, MO 64134

Club/Association
World Wide Avon Collectors Club
Newspaper: World Wide Avon News
44021 Seventh Street East
Lancaster, CA 93534
Phone: 805-948-8849
The newspaper contains ads for the buying and selling of Avon related items. *

Club/Association
Western World Avon Collectors Club
Newsletter: Western World Avon Collectors Newsletter
P.O. Box 23785
Pleasant Hills, CA 94523
Phone: 415-825-1042

Collector
Linda Weeks
P.O. Box 123
Centre Harbor, NH 03226
Phone: 603-253-7509
Wants Avon tall ships, cars, and steins. *

Museum/Library
Nicholas Avon Museum
MTD Rt. Box 71
Clifton, VA 24422

BABY CARRIAGES

(see also PERAMBULATORS)

BADGES

(see also FRATERNAL ORGANIZATION ITEMS; MEDALS, ORDERS & DECORATIONS; MILITARIA; POLICE & SHERIFF MEMORABILIA; PATCHES; VETERANS, Civil War)

Chauffeurs

Collector
Dr. Edward H. Miles
888 Eighth Ave.
New York, NY 10019
Phone: 212-765-2660

Collector
Trent Culp
P.O. Box 550
Misenheimer, NC 28109
Phone: 704-279-6242
Collects chauffeurs' badges from all states and all years, especially badges from the Southern states.

BANANA COLLECTIBLES

Club/Association
International Banana Club
Newsletter: Woddis Newsletter
L. Ken Bannister, T.B.
2524 N. El Molino Ave.
Altadena, CA 91001
Phone: 818-798-2272
A "fun" humorous club founded in 1972; purpose is to keep people smiling and excercising their sense of humor each day.

BANK CHECKS

(see also COINS & CURRENCY; STAMP COLLECTING, Revenue & Tax Stamps)

Club/Association
American Society of Check Collectors
Magazine: Check Collector
Charles Kemp, Sec.
P.O. Box 71892
Madison Heights, MI 48091
Founded in 1969, ASCC is open to collectors of all types of fiscal paper: engravings, revenue stamps on checks; over 400 members.

Club/Association
Check Collectors Round Table
Newsletter: Check List, The
2075 Nicholas Ct.
Warren, MI 48092
Phone: 313-573-0796
Interested in old and new banking paper such as checks, drafts, certificates of deposit, gold dust receipts, stocks and bonds. *

Collector
Bob Pyne
P.O. Box 149064
Orlando, FL 32814
Wants older bank checks; also Confederate money, stocks and bonds.

Periodical
Krause Publications, Inc.
Newspaper: Bank Note Reporter
Dave Harper, Ed.
700 East State St.
Iola, WI 54990
Phone: 800-258-0929 or 715-445-2214
FAX: 715-445-4087
Monthly news source and marketplace for collectors of U.S. and world paper money, notes, checks and related fiscal paper.

BANKS

Collector
Bob Brady
1375 Harrisburg Pike
Lancaster, PA 17601
Phone: 717-569-7408
Wants to buy mechanical and still banks.

Collector
Jim Rocheleau
1137 Cadieux
Grosse Point, MI 48230
Phone: 313-885-7805
Wants mechanical and still banks.

Collector
Mike Henry
P.O. Box 435
Chicago Heights, IL 60411
Mechanical and still banks wanted.

Collector
Don Eigenberg
1595 Beverly
Gering, NE 69341
Wants cast iron, tin, glass, and wood banks. *

Expert
Richard Friz
RFD 2, Box 155
Peterborough, NH 03458
Phone: 603-563-8155 *

Expert
Sy Schreckinger
P.O. Box 104
East Rockaway, NY 11518
Buy/sell mechanical and still banks: cast iron, tin, wood or lead; also wooden bank shipping boxes, bank trade cards, catalogs, etc.

Expert
Reynolds Toys
Charles Reynolds
2836 Monroe St.
Falls Church, VA 22042
Phone: 703-533-1322
Specializes in mechanical and still banks.

Expert
Bill Norman
2601 Empire Ave.
Burbank, CA 91504 *

Expert
Long's Americana
Earnest & Ida Long
P.O. Box 90
Mokelumne Hill, CA 95245
Phone: 209-286-1348
Specializes in toys, banks, games and other children's items; publishes "Dictionary of Toys, Vol I & II" and "Penny Lane."

Repair Service
Sy Schreckinger
P.O. Box 104
East Rockaway, NY 11518
Offers professional, museum quality repair, restoration and cleaning of iron and tin mechanical and still banks.

Book-Shaped
Collector
Kraker
9800 McMillan Ave.
Silver Spring, MD 20910
*Pencil sharpeners, figural, hand-held; also unusual book banks. *

Glass
Collector
Bonnie Hare
311 Fairview St.
Carlisle, PA 17013
Phone: 717-243-5378 *

Mechanical
Club/Association
Mechanical Bank Collectors of America
Newsletter: Mechanical Banker
Rick Muhlhiem, Sec.
P.O. Box 128
Allegan, MI 49010
Phone: 616-673-4509

Collector
Jeff Bradfield
745 Hillview Dr.
Dayton, VA 22821
Phone: 703-879-9961
Wants original banks in good condition with original paint.

Dealer
Bill Bertoia
1217 Glenwood Drive
Vineland, NJ 08630
Phone: 609-692-4092 *

Dealer
Kittelberger Galleries
Bryan Kittelberger
82 1/2 E. Main St.
Webster, NY 14580
Phone: 716-265-1230

Expert
Mark Suozzi
P.O. Box 102
Ashfield, MA 01330
Phone: 413-628-3241
Antique penny banks, 1 cent arcade machines, advertising signs, mechanical folk art, and wind up American clockwork toys.

Expert
James Maxwell
P.O. Box 367
Lampeter, PA 17537
Phone: 717-464-5573 *

Expert
Dr. Greg Zeminick
Suite 160
1350 Kirts
Troy, MI 48084
Phone: 313-642-8129   FAX: 313-244-9495
Wants mechanical banks, any condition or completeness; wooden or cardboard packing boxes; trade cards, catalogs; also bell toys.

Repro. Source
Reynolds Toys
Charles Reynolds
2836 Monroe St.
Falls Church, VA 22042
Phone: 703-533-1322
Offers limited editions of new original penny bank reproductions of sand-cast aluminum; over 100 editions produced from 1970-1990.

Oil-Can (Miniature)
Collector
Peter Capell
1838 West Grace St.
Chicago, IL 60613-2724
Phone: 312-871-8735   FAX: 312-871-8735
Wants tin or tin with paper label miniature oil-can banks produced as promotional giveaways for gasoline and motor oil dealers.

Registering
Expert
Robert L. McCumber
201 Carriage Dr.
Glastonbury, CT 06033
Author of "Registering Banks"; registering banks (e.g. pocket tube banks) show amount as coins are deposit.

Still
Club/Association
Still Bank Collectors Club
Magazine: Penny Bank Post
153 Scott Ave.
Bloomsburg, PA 17815
Phone: 717-784-3946
The magazine is published three times per year.

BARBED WIRE
(see also FENCE COLLECTIBLES)

Club/Association
American Barbed Wire Collectors Society
1023 Baldwin Rd.
Bakersfield, CA 93304
The only national association for collectors of barbed wire and associated fencing tools.

Club/Association
New Mexico Barbed Wire Collectors
Association
Newsletter: Wire Barb & Nail
Box 102
Stanley, NM 87056 *

Expert
Schoolmaster Auctions
Ken Norris
P.O. Box 476
Grandfalls, TX 79742
Phone: 915-547-2421 *

Museum/Library
Barbed Wire Museum
P.O. Box 716
La Crosse, KS 67548
Phone: 913-222-3116

Museum/Library
Historical Museum of Barbed Wire &
Related Fencing Tools
Delbert Trew, Dir.
P.O. Box 290
McLean, TX 79057
The museum is the newest and largest wire and fence museum in the world.

Museum/Library
National Cowboy Hall of Fame & Western
Heritage Center
Magazine: Persimon Hill
1700 N.E. 63rd St.
Oklahoma City, OK 73111
Phone: 405-478-2250   FAX: 405-478-4714

NCHA represents 17 western states; preserves the rich heritage of the Old West and the memory of those who contributed to it.

BARBER SHOP COLLECTIBLES

(see also BOTTLES, Barber; SHAVING COLLECTIBLES)

Auction Service

Nard Auctions
Tony Nard
U.S. Route 220
Milan, PA 18831
Phone: 717-888-9404   FAX: 717-888-7723
Conducts specialized auctions of occupational shaving mugs, barber bottles, razors, country store and advertising items.

Collector

Burto Handelsman
18 Hotel Dr.
White Plains, NY 10605
Phone: 914-428-4480   FAX: 914-428-2145
Wants to buy shaving mugs, personalized barber bottles decorated with glass labels, barber shop photos and related catalogs.

Collector

Bill Campesi
Box 140
Merrick, NY 11566
Phone: 516-546-9630
Collector of straight razors, especially fancy handles; also wants related trade catalogs, advertising, show cases, postcards, etc.

Collector

Ken Mead
P.O. Box 229
Moline, MI 49335
Phone: 616-877-4285
Wants any barber shop related item. *

Expert

Robert Doyle
R.D. 3 Box 137
Fishkill, NY 12524
Phone: 914-896-9492 *

Barber Poles

Supplier

William Marvy Company
Robert Marvy
1540 St. Clair Ave.
St. Paul, MN 55105
Phone: 612-698-0726   FAX: 612-698-4048
Manufacturers barber poles and replacement parts: domes, motors, glass and paper cylinders, etc.

Shaving Mugs

Club/Association

National Shaving Mug Collectors Association
Newsletter: Barber Shop Collectibles Newsletter
E. Maxine Cook
818 S. Knight Ave.
Park Ridge, IL 60068
Phone: 708-823-3490

Club/Association

National Shaving Mug Collectors Society
Newsletter: Barber Shop Collectibles Newsletter
Edward D. Moore, Sec.
420 South Plum St.
Troy, OH 45373
Phone: 513-335-8879

Collector

Ralph Nix
Box 655
Red Bay, AL 35582
Phone: 205-356-2997
Wants old, personalized shaving mugs.

Collector

Mike Griffin
11 Walton Ave.
White Plains, NY 10606
Buys early shaving mugs; editor of the "National Shaving Mug Collectors Association Newsletter."

Expert

Edward Leach
381 Trenton Ave.
Paterson, NJ 07503
Phone: 201-684-5398 *

Expert

Burto Handelsman
18 Hotel Dr.
White Plains, NY 10605
Phone: 914-428-4480   FAX: 914-428-2145
Author of the "Shaving Mugs" section in the Time-Life "Encyclopedia of Collectibles" series.

Museum/Library

Atwater Kent Museum - the History Museum of Philadelphia
15 S. 7th St.
Philadelphia, PA 19143
Phone: 215-922-3031

Museum/Library

Lightner Museum
P.O. Box 334
St. Augustine, FL 32085
Phone: 904-824-2874

Periodical

Newsletter: Barber Shop Collectibles Newsletter
R.D. 6, Box 176
Bedford, PA 15522 *

Shaving Mugs (Occupational)

Dealer

Burto Handelsman
18 Hotel Dr.
White Plains, NY 10605
Phone: 914-428-4480   FAX: 914-428-2145
Buys and sells occupational shaving mugs; also personalized barber bottles.

BAROMETERS

(see also INSTRUMENTS & DEVICES, Scientific)

Expert

Charles Edwin Antiques
Chuck Probst
P.O. Box 1340
Louisa, VA 23093
Phone: 703-967-0416
Buys, sells, repairs.

Repair Service

Den of Antiquity
138 Charles Street
Boston, MA 02114
Phone: 617-367-6190
Repairs and restores antique mercury barometers.
*

Repair Service

Henry Witzenberger
15 Po Lane
Hicksville, NY 11801
Phone: 516-935-7432
Repairs and restores antique mercury and aneroid barometers; also repairs clocks. *

Repair Service

Charles Edwin Antiques
Chuck Probst
P.O. Box 1340
Louisa, VA 23093
Phone: 703-967-0416
Buys, sells, repairs.

BASEBALL CAPS

(see CAPS)

BASKETS

(see also KITCHEN COLLECTIBLES)

Museum/Library

Old Salem, Inc.
Drawer F
Salem Station
Winston-Salem, NC 27108
Phone: 919-723-3688

Museum/Library
Heard Museum, The
22 E. Monte Vista Rd.
Phoenix, AZ 85004
Phone: 602-252-8845

Supplier
Connecticut Cane & Reed Co.
134 Pine St.
P.O. Box 762
Manchester, CT 06040
Phone: 203-646-6586   FAX: 203-649-2221
Largest selection of materials and books; source for cane, wicker and basket supplies; all types of materials to reseat a chair.

BATHING BEAUTIES

Nudies & Naughties
(see also FIGURINES, Lady)

Collector
S. Weintraub
2924 Helena
Houston, TX 77006
Phone: 713-520-1262
Wants pre-1930 bisque or china bathing beauties, nudes & naughties; high quality (no Japanese); also old catalogs & advertising for same.

BATTERSEA ENAMEL BOXES

Expert
Melvin & Barb Alpern
14 Carter Rd.
West Orange, NJ 07052
Phone: 201-731-9427 *

Repro. Source
Halcyon Days, London Ltd.
14 Brook St.
London W1Y 1AA England
Handpainted enamel boxes, paperweights, eggs, sculpture, candlesticks and special editions. *

BEADS

(see also GEMS & JEWELRY)

Club/Association
Center for Bead Research
Newsletter: Margaretologist
Peter Francis, Jr
4 Essex Street
Lake Placid, NY 12946
Phone: 518-523-1794

Club/Association
Chicago Midwest Bead Society
Newsletter: Chicago Midwest Bead Society
Naomi Rubin
1020 Davis
Evanston, IL 60201
Phone: 708-329-4040
Focuses on native American and foreign beads and beadwork.

Club/Association
Bead Society, The
Newsletter: Bead News
P.O. Box 2513
Culver City, CA 90231 *

Club/Association
Center for the Study of Beadwork
P.O. Box 13716
Portland, OR 97213

Dealer
Lauren Enterprises, Ltd.
Mary Roody
12 North Third St.
St. Charles, IL 60174
Phone: 708-513-7306 or 708-584-3899
An international bead bazaar; specializing in rare beads, pendants, textiles and Oriental antiques.

Dealer
Ari Imports
Suite 2008
8 South Michigan Ave.
Chicago, IL 60603
Phone: 312-332-1988
Bead importer and distributor.

Museum/Library
Museum of the American Indian, Heye Foundation
Broadway & 155th Street
New York, NY 10032
Phone: 212-283-2420

Museum/Library
Corning Museum of Glass, The
One Museum Way
Corning, NY 14830-2253
Phone: 607-937-5371   FAX: 607-937-3352
Over 24,000 glass objects, innovative exhibits, videos, models; glass history, archaeology, and early manufacturing.

Museum/Library
Bead Museum, The
140 South Montezuma
Prescott, AZ 86301
Phone: 602-445-2431

Supplier
Gampel Supply Corp.
39 West 37th St.
New York, NY 10018 *

Supplier
Har Man Importing Company
48 West 37th St.
New York, NY 10018 *

Supplier
Berger Specialty Company
413 East 8th St.
Los Angeles, CA 90010 *

Supplier
Bead Store, The
417 Castro St.
San Francisco, CA 94114 *

Supplier
Venerable Bead, The
2990 Adeline
Berkeley, CA 94703 *

Trade

Collector
Wade
3632 55th St.
Lubbock, TX 79413
Trade beads wanted that are more than 200 years old. *

Expert
Gary L. Fogelman
RD 1, Box 240
Turbotville, PA 17772
Phone: 717-437-3698
Author of "Glass Trade Beads in the Northeas and Including Aboriginal Bead Industries."

BEAM BOTTLES

(see also BOTTLES, Special Ed. (Beam))

BEARS

(see also SMOKEY THE BEAR ITEMS; TEDDY BEARS)

Grizzly

Dealer
Bear Den
P.O. Box 238
Shrewsbury, MA 01545
Phone: 508-795-1321
Wants grizzly bear art work: sculptures, prints, etc. *

BEER CANS

(see also BREWERIANA)

Club/Association
Beer Can Collectors of America
Newsletter: Beer Can Collectors News
Don Hicks, Pres.
747 Merus Court
Fenton, MO 63026
Phone: 314-343-6486   FAX: 314-343-6486

Collector
John Conrad
3245N-650 East
Churubusco, IN 46723
Phone: 219-693-3507
Old beer cans & advertisements; also 1 qt. old metal oil cans.

Dealer

AAACRC
P.O. Box 8061
Saddle Brook, NJ 07662
Buys, trades and sells beer cans, complete sets; bottom opened; will sell or trade for silver coins. 12 oz size only, US.

Expert

Owen's Collectibles
Lowell Owens
12 Bonnie Ave.
New Hartford, NY 13413
Wants items advertising beer brands or breweries.
*

Museum/Library

Museum of Beverage Containers &
Advertising, The
1055 Ridgecrest Drive
Goodlettsville, TN 37072
Phone: 615-859-5236   FAX: 615-585-5238
The largest collection of soda and beer cans in the world; also cleans and removes rust from old beer cans.

Periodical

Newsletter: Beer Can Advertiser & News
   Report, The
P.O. Box 373
Independence, MO 64051 *

Supplier

Soda Mart - Can World
1055 Ridgecrest Dr.
Goodlettsville, TN 37072
Phone: 615-859-5236   FAX: 615-859-5238
Sells breweriana books; also cleans and de-rusts on cans, and sells supplies for the beer can collector.

BEER RELATED COLLECTIBLES

(see also BEER CANS; BREWERIANA)

BELLS

Club/Association

American Bell Association
Newsletter: Bell Tower, The
Charles Blake
P.O. Box 172
Shoreham, VT 05770

Collector

George Coupe
1243 1st St. S.E.
Washington, DC 20003
Phone: 202-554-1000 or 800-368-5466
                          FAX: 202-863-0775
Wants unusual bells, tap bells, figural, but no bells with handles.

Dealer

Bob Brosamer
195 S. Main St.
Brooklyn, MI 49230
Phone: 517-467-2793
Buys and sells bronze church bells & bells of all kinds; early dates and foundries. *

Expert

World of Bells
Dorothy Malone Anthony
802 S. Eddy
Ft. Scott, KS 66701
Phone: 316-223-3404
Over 200 bells in color in each of the seven books published to date in the "World of Bells" book series; flyer on request.

BELT BUCKLES

Club/Association

Buckle Buddies International
Bob Bracken
501 Dauphin St.
Riverside, NJ 08075
Phone: 609-461-6421

Collector

D. Foust
639 County Road 139
Van Buren, OH 45889 *

Expert

Bob Bracken
501 Dauphin St.
Riverside, NJ 08075
Phone: 609-461-6421
President of Buckle Buddies Int.; appraises, buys, sells, reproduces belt buckles; former staff writer for Buckle Buddies Magazine.

Periodical

Newsletter: Buckle Exchange
Box 121
Collins, IA 50055 *

Periodical

Toy Farmer Ltd.
Magazine: Buckle Buddies
Claire D. Scheibe
HC 2 Box 5
LaMoure, ND 58458
Phone: 701-883-5206 or 701-883-5207
                          FAX: 701-883-5208
Only publication in the world that publishes information on belt buckles.

John Deere

Club/Association

International Association of John Deere
Buckle Collectors
John Cooklin
2120 22 1/2 Ave.
Rock Island, IL 61201
Phone: 309-786-9747

BERMUDA COLLECTIBLES

Collector

Ernest E. Roberts
5 Corsa St.
Dix Hills, NY 11746
Wants pre-1950 postcards, covers, hotel stationary, maps, prints, old books, photographs, and other paper ephemera relating to Bermuda.

BIBLES

(see also BOOKS)

Museum/Library

American Bible Society
1865 Broadway
New York, NY 10023
Phone: 212-408-1204 or 212-408-1512
Collection of nearly 40,000 bibles, testaments, and scripture portions in approximately 1,900 languages, dating from the 15th cent.

Periodical

Magazine: Bible Collectors World
Box 311
Oak Creek, WI 53154 *

BICYCLE MEMORABILIA

Collector

Beth Dituillo
216 Cedar Ave.
Horsham, PA 19044
Phone: 215-672-6416
Wants pre-1920 bicycle memorabilia; clubs, medals, cups, mugs, photos, prints, paintings, accessories. *

License Plates

Collector

Roy Klotz
3251 Lenape Dr.
Dresher, PA 19025
Phone: 215-884-0808
Wants bicycle license plates; any town, any year.

BICYCLES

(see also TOYS, Pedal Vehicles;
TRICYCLES; WAGONS)

Auction Service

Bill's Classic Cyclery
Bill Feasel
712 Morrison St.
Fremont, OH 43420
Phone: 419-334-7844   FAX: 419-334-2845
Conducts auctions specializing in the sale of classic bicycles, tricycles, wagons and toy pedal vehicles.

Club/Association
International Veteran Cycle Association
Robert B. Balcomb
248 Highland Dr.
Findlay, OH 45840-1207
Phone: 419-423-2760
Umbrella organization for international clubs of bicycle collectors, historians, enthusiasts; promotes the heritage of the bicycle.

Club/Association
Wheelmen, The
Magazine: Wheelmen Magazine, The
George Garrettson
216 E Sedgewick
Philadelphia, PA 19117
Phone: 215-247-1075
A club with about 800 members dedicated to the enjoyment and preservation of our bicycle heritage.

Club/Association
Classic Bicycle & Whizzer Club of America
35769 Simon
Fraser, MI 48026
Phone: 313-791-5594
This organization is dedicated to the preservation, restoration and enjoyment of special-interest bicycles and the Whizzer

Club/Association
National Pedal Vehicle Association
Bruce Beimers
1720 Rupert, N.E.
Grand Rapids, MI 49505
Phone: 616-361-9887
Focuses on bicycles and pedal cars.

Club/Association
Cascade Classic Cycle Club
John McDonald, Sec.
7935 SE Market Street
Portland, OR 97215-3655
Phone: 503-775-2688
A club devoted to riding and restoring classic bicycles; offers members seminars, technical trips and tours.

Collector
Richard Roy
P.O. Box 280
Branchville, NJ 07826
Wants old pre-1900 bicycles, tricycles and related items.

Collector
J. Carpenter
RD 5 Box 275
Montague, NJ 07827
Phone: 201-293-7297
Wants old bicycles and related memorabilia. *

Collector
John Lannis
P.O. Box 5600
Pittsburgh, PA 15207
Phone: 412-461-5099
Wants bicycles or related literature 1860-1880.

Collector
Art Bransky
R.D. 2, Box 558
Breinigsville, PA 18031
Phone: 215-285-6180
Wants 1930-1960 Deluxe balloon tire bicycles; also any delivery bicycle or tricycle or bicycle sidecars.

Collector
Robert Olds
364 Vinewood
Tallmadge, OH 44278
Phone: 216-633-5938 *

Dealer
Bill's Classic Cyclery
Bill Feasel
712 Morrison St.
Fremont, OH 43420
Phone: 419-334-7844   FAX: 419-334-2845
Buys/sells antique and classic bicycles, pedal cars, motorbikes and motorcycles; mail order catalog of parts, decals, etc.

Expert
Leon Dixon
P.O. Box 765
Huntington Beach, CA 92648
Phone: 714-997-7744
Wants old deluxe, streamlined (1920-1965) bicycles, bicycle literature, memorabilia, catalogs, parts, etc.

Periodical
Magazine: National Antique & Classis Bicycle
John Lannis
P.O. Box 5600
Pittsburgh, PA 15207
Phone: 412-461-5099
A monthly publication for buying and selling antique and classic bicycles.

Periodical
Magazine: Antique/Classic Bicycle News
P.O. Box 1049
Ann Arbor, MI 48106
Phone: 312-404-8443   FAX: 312-404-8443
The "Voice for the Hobby" bimonthly; information on companies, reprints from catalogs, ads, and event notices.

Periodical
Newsletter: Classic Bicycle & Whizzer News
Leon Dixon
P.O. Box 765
Huntington Beach, CA 92648
Phone: 714-997-7744

CBWN published since 1977; started and defined the hobby of collecting "Classic Bicycles"; authentic details, photos.

Repro. Source
Art Bransky
R.D. 2, Box 558
Breinigsville, PA 18031
Phone: 215-285-6180
Makes repro. parts for Schwinn, Roadmaster & Ross cycle trucks: baskets, brackets, store name plates, kickstands, fender clips.

BILLIARD RELATED ITEMS
Collector
Carl Ames
539 Lyme Rock Rd.
Bridgewater, NJ 08807
Wants billiard-related photos, advertisements, catalogs, books, two-piece pool cues, etc. *

Collector
Classic Billiards
Ken Hash
4302 Chapel Rd.
Perry Hall, MD 21128
Phone: 301-256-0765
Wants antique pool tables or related items.

Dealer
Ed Lanza Billiard Co.
209 W. Evesham Ave.
Magnolia, NJ 08049
Antique billiard and pool table accessories. *

Dealer
Tony Giammatteo
509 Woodlawn Ave.
Newark, DE 19711
Phone: 302-453-8788 or 713-251-5993
Dealer in antique pool and billiard tables, pool room accessories: cues, chairs, lights, memorabilia; brochures available.

Periodical
Magazine: Pool & Billiard Magazine
Suite 207
109 Fairfield Way
Bloomingdale, IL 60108

BINOCULARS
(see also OPTICAL ITEMS)

Collector
Edward Stuart
3025 Ontario Road NW #203
Washington, DC 20009
Phone: 202-332-6511
Wants old binoculars, American or European, prism type only.

BIRD HOUSES

Dealer

Birdnest of Ridgefield
Susie Fisk Stern
2 Big Shop Lane
Ridgefield, CT 06877
Phone: 203-431-9889
Wants antique bird houses. *

BIRTH RELATED ITEMS

Collector

Fran Barnes
25 Fifth Ave. 9B
New York, NY 10003
Phone: 212-505-2720
Wants books, art, advertising, etc. (no large toys or furniture), both medical and consumer, related to pregnancy, birth, newborn.

BLACKLIGHTS

Man./Prod./Dist.

UVP Inc.
P.O. Box 1501
San Gabriel, CA 91778
Phone: 818-285-3123
Suppliers of all styles of high quality blacklights.

Misc. Service

Kit: Collectors Blacklight Guide, The
Karl Gabosh
125 Calamint, Hill Rd., North
Princeton, MA 01541
A guide to explain the peculiar things seen under a blacklight; complete with text and samples. *

BLACK MEMORABILIA

(see also DOLLS, Black; SLAVERY ITEMS)

Club/Association

Black Memorabilia Collectors
Association
Edward McIntosh
822 4th St. NE, Apt.2
Washington, DC 20002
Phone: 202-543-3794
An organization which supports the preservation of African-American artifacts and which represents black memorabilia collectors.

Collector

Jan Thalberg
23 Mountain View Dr.
Weston, CT 06883
Phone: 203-227-8175

Collector

Dr. E Maynard
R.D. 7, Box 370
Monroe, NY 10950
Phone: 914-783-1552
Wants black American books and memorabilia: history, biography, fiction, non-fiction.

Collector

Margaret Betts
P.O. Box 21790
Detroit, MI 48221

Collector

Judy Posner
R.D. 1 Box 273
Effort, PA 18330
Phone: 717-629-6583   FAX: 717-629-0521
Wants black Mammy and Chef cookie jars, salt & pepper shakers and kitchen items.

Collector

Collector
P.O. Box 8853
Elkins Park, PA 19117
Wants black items; especially insulting items: toys, figurines, prints, grocery items, signs, etc. *

Collector

William Perkins
4937 Catherinc St.
Philadelphia, PA 19143 *

Collector

Pete Levine
1916 Piedmont Circle
Atlanta, GA 30324
Phone: 404-233-5028 *

Collector

Mike Kranz
659 O'Neill Rd.
Hudson, WI 54016
Phone: 715-386-7333
Wants cookie jars, string holders, toys, salt & peppers, linens, advertising, etc.

Collector

Tim Schnitzer
P.O. Box 5512
Yuma, AZ 85364
Phone: 602-783-4816
Wants nearly all Black items. *

Dealer

Basia Kirschner
P.O. Box 371
Newton, NJ 07860
Specializing in black memorabilia. *

Dealer

UNICA Shows Unlimited
Malinda Saunders
5406 9th St. NW
Washington, DC 20011
Specializing in black memorabilia and in the promotion of black memorabilia shows.

Expert

Kit Barry
143 Main St.
Brattleboro, VT 05301

Expert

Lewis & Blalock Collection of Black
Memorabilia
Steven D. Lewis
Box 28561
Washington, DC 20005
Phone: 202-332-3082
Exhibitions and lectures relating to black memorabilia; also wants to buy black memorabilia.

Expert

Canadian Antiques
Gloria & Joe Canada
10812 Southall Drive
Largo, MD 20772
Phone: 301-350-0982
Collector seeking advanced items of Black Americana: porcelains, dolls, bisque, advertising, art, etc.

Expert

Black Doll Networks
Patikii Gibbs
Box 158472
Nashville, TN 37215
Author of "Black Collectibles."

Expert

Black Relics, Inc.
Darrell A. Smith
P.O. Box 24954
Tempe, AZ 85282
Phone: 602-921-2129
Author of "Black Americana." *

Misc. Service

Lewis & Blalock Collection of Black
Memorabilia
Steven D. Lewis
Box 28561
Washington, DC 20005
Phone: 202-332-3082
The Lewis & Blalock Collection was established in 1981 and is housed in Wash., DC; call for further information on lectures and exhibits.

Misc. Service

Ethnic Treasures Corp.
Jeannette Carson
1401 Asbury Court
Hyattsville, MD 20782
Phone: 301-559-6363
Sponsors a series of Ethnic Treasures Shows which specialize in black collectibles.

Museum/Library

Museum of African American History
301 Frederick Douglass St.
Detroit, MI 48202
Phone: 313-833-9800

Periodical

Magazine: Black Ethnic Collectibles
Jeannette Carson
1401 Asbury Court
Hyattsville, MD 20782
Phone: 301-559-6363

BLACKSMITHING ITEMS

(see also TOOLS)

Collector

Richard L. Weiss
R.D. #2, Box 641
Breinigsville, PA 18031
Phone: 215-285-4122
Wants rare and unusual blacksmithing tools, literature, advertising signs and related items.

BLIMPS

(see also AIRSHIPS)

BOATS

(see also OUTBOARD MOTORS; TOYS, Boats & Outboards)

Club/Association

Antique Boat Society
Learning Place
Manset, ME 04656
Phone: 207-244-5015 *

Club/Association

Antique & Classic Boat Society
Newsletter: Rusty Rudder
P.O. Box 831
Lake George, NY 12845 *

Club/Association

Chris Craft Antique Boat Club, Inc.
Newsletter: Brass Bell
Wilson W. Wright
217 South Adams Street
Tallahassee, FL 32301
Phone: 904-224-5169 or 904-224-1033
Focuses on collecting, restoring and maintaining antique boats; quarterly magazine has lots of ads for antique boats for sale.

Dealer

Classic Boat Connection, The
Mitch LaPointe
1733 Gull Ln.
Mound, MN 55364
Phone: 612-472-6122
Free publication lists boats for sale and offers restoration tips.

Expert

Wilson W. Wright
217 South Adams Street
Tallahassee, FL 32301
Phone: 904-224-5169 or 904-224-1033
Specializes in antique boats.

Museum/Library

Maine Maritime Museum
963 Washington Street
Bath, ME 04530
Phone: 207-443-1316

Periodical

Magazine: Messing About In Boats
Bob Hicks
29 Burley St.
Wenham, MA 01984
Phone: 508-774-0906
Great bi-weekly magazine about interesting boats & people who design, build, restore and/or use them - sail, oar, antique, steam, etc.

Periodical

Magazine: Classic Boat
Jim Lance
c/o Publishers Mini Systems
P.O. Box 301369
Escondido, CA 92030-9957
Phone: 619-747-8327   FAX: 619-432-6560
British magazine about restoration & preservation of classic boats: technical pages, history, affordable boats, books, sources.

Periodical

Magazine: Antique & Classic Boat
P.O. Box 1634
Colton, CA 92324-0881
A bi-monthly magazine mostly about mahogany runabouts.

Canoes

Club/Association

Wooden Canoe Heritage Association
Magazine: Wooden Canoe
P. Christopher Merigold, Pres.
Box 226
Blue Mountain Lake, NY 12812
Phone: 414-294-3725 or 803-648-7655
Non-profit association dedicated to preserving, studying, building, restoring and using wooden and birch bark canoes.

Steam

Club/Association

International Steamboat Society
Journal: Steamboating
Rt. 1, Box 262
Middlebourne, WV 26149-9748
Phone: 304-386-4434   FAX: 304-386-4868

Yachts

Club/Association

Classic Yacht Association
Newsletter: Classic Boating Newsletter
P.O. Box 372
Napa, CA 94558
Phone: 707-255-0349
*Interested in the preservation and maintenance of pre-1942 power driven pleasure boats. **

BOB'S BIG BOY ITEMS

Collector

Connie Wolf
P.O. Box 1111
Norwalk, CA 90650
Wants Big Boy items: menus, ashtrays, matches, nodders, lamps, anything unusual.

Collector

Steve Soelberg
29126 Laro Dr.
Agoura Hills, CA 91301
Phone: 818-889-9909
Wants Bob's Big Boy lamps, lunch boxes, cookie jars, counter displays, buttons, nodders, menus, ash trays, salt/peppers, etc.

BOOK ARTS

(see also BOOKS, Repair Service; PRINTING EQUIPMENT)

Museum/Library

University of California, Special
Collections Department
P.O. Box 5900
Riverside, CA 92517
Phone: 714-787-3233 or 714-784-7324
                          FAX: 714-787-3285
Collection on the Book Arts, especially book binding, papermaking, fine presses, forgeries, etc.

BOOKMARKS

Collector

Joan Huegel
1002 West 25th St.
Erie, PA 16502 *

Periodical

Newsletter: Bookmark Collector
Joan L. Huegel
1002 West 25th St.
Erie, PA 16502

BOOKPLATES

Club/Association

American Society of Bookplate
Collectors & Designers
Newsletter: Bookplates in the News
Audrey Spencer Arellanes, Ed.
605 N. Stoneman Ave., No. F
Alhambra, CA 91801
Phone: 213-283-1936
Quarterly newsletter features articles on contemporary bookplate artists & collectors, news of exhibitions, competitions, literature.

BOOKS

(see also ALMANACS; AUCTION CATALOGS; BIBLES; BOOK ARTS; COMIC BOOKS; COOKBOOKS; GULLIVER'S TRAVELS; ILLUSTRATORS)

Auction Service

New Hampshire Book Auctions
Richard & Mary Sykes
92 Woodbury Rd.
P.O. Box 86
Weare, NH 03281
Phone: 603-529-1700 or 603-529-7432
Specializes in the auction of books, maps, prints and ephmera.

Auction Service

Swann Galleries, Inc.
104 E. 25th St.
New York, NY 10010
Phone: 212-254-4710   FAX: 212-979-1017
Oldest/largest U.S. auctioneer specializing in rare books, autographs & manuscripts, Judaica, photographs, and works of art on paper.

Auction Service

Waverly Auctions
Dale Sorenson
4931 Cordell Ave.
Bethesda, MD 20814
Phone: 301-951-8883   FAX: 301-718-8375
Specializes in the auction of graphic art, books, paper, atlases, prints, postcards and other paper ephemera.

Auction Service

Baltimore Book Co., Inc.
Chris Bready
2112 N. Charles St.
Baltimore, MD 21218
Phone: 301-659-0550
Buys and auctions books, prints, paintings, autographs, photographs, and ephemera.

Auction Service

Samuel Yudkin & Associates
2109 Popkins Lane
Alexandria, VA 22307
Phone: 703-768-1858
Booksellers who conduct book and print auctions.
*

Auction Service

California Book Auction Galleries, Inc.
5225 Wilshire Blvd. #324
Los Angeles, CA 90036
Phone: 213-939-6202

Auction Service

California Book Auction Galleries, Inc.
Suite 730
965 Mission St.
San Francisco, CA 94103
Phone: 415-243-0650   FAX: 415-243-0789
Specialty auction house dealing in fine and rare books, manuscripts and maps.

Club/Association

National Book Collectors Society
Magazine: National Book Collector, The
Daniel M. McAdam
Suite 349
65 High Ridge Road
Stamford, CT 06905
Phone: 203-325-1872
Dedicated to disseminating information on and fostering interest in book collecting.

Club/Association

Antiquarian Booksellers Association of America
50 Rockefeller Plaza
New York, NY 10020
Phone: 212-757-9395   FAX: 212-459-0307
Offers an illustrated list of commonly faked newspapers, broadsides, and letters; also publishes a membership directory.

Collector

Joseph W. Toti, Esg.
4719 Easthill Dr., SW
Roanoke, VA 24018
Collects primarily signed first edition books; however, also a collector of all genre of books.

Collector

D. Edmond Miller
P.O. Box 4516
Durham, NC 27706-4516
Books and autograph material by Truman Capote, F. Scott Fitzgerald, Reynolds Price and William Styron.

Dealer

Imperial Fine Books, Inc.
Bibi Mohamed
790 Madison Ave. Suite 200
New York, NY 10021
Phone: 212-861-6620
Fine books bought and sold; sets, fine and decorative bindings, first editions, fore-edge paintings, childrens & illustrated books, etc.

Dealer

Rare Books & Manuscripts
Carmen D. Valentino
2965 Richmond St.
Philadelphia, PA 19134
Phone: 215-739-6056
Antiquarian bookseller specializing in rare books, manuscripts, documents, early newspapers, ephemera, broadsides; pre-WWI.

Dealer

Monocacy Books
John & Anne Olson
P.O. Box 647
Mt. Airy, MD 21771
Phone: 301-831-6052
Wants Civil-War books, new and out of print, documents and paper items.

Dealer

Judge of Mysteries (J.O.M.) Books
P.O. Box 803
Roanoke, VA 24004
Buys and sells all sorts of books; offers periodic catalog listing items for sale.

Dealer

Peddler's Wagon
Bob & Beverlee Reimers
P.O. Box 109
Lamar, MO 64759-0109
Phone: 417-682-3734
Buys and sells books on quilting, needlework, children's illustrated books, Little Golden books, and Frank Lloyd Wright.

Expert

Quill & Brush
Pat & Allen Ahearn
P.O. Box 5365
Rockville, MD 20853
Phone: 301-460-3700   FAX: 301-871-5425
Author of "Book Collecting, A Comprehensive Guide" and "Collecting Books, The Guide to Values."

Expert

Chapel Hill Rare Books
Douglas O'Dell
Suite 310
143 W. Franklin Street
Chapel Hill, NC 27516
Phone: 919-929-8351
Fine rare books in all fields, first editions in literature and Americana; inscribe copies, bindings, travels, etc.; author on books.

Expert

Kubik Antiquarian Books
Owen Kubik
3474 Clar-Von Dr.
Dayton, OH 45430
*Writes column for Antique week. Personal replies seldom possible. ***

Misc. Service

BookQuest/SerialsQuest
Magazine: Matchmaker, The
Edward Johnson
135 Village Queen Dr.
Owings Mills, MD 21117
Phone: 800-627-2216
The Online Book Network database links buyers and sellers of out-of-print, used and rare books; also a directory of book dealers.

Museum/Library

Library of Congress
10 First St. SE
Washington, DC 20540
Phone: 202-287-5000

Periodical

Magazine: A.B. Bookman's Weekly
P.O. Box AB
Clifton, NJ 07015
Phone: 201-772-0020
A weekly magazine for libraries and the trade; includes news about auctions, books wanted, books for sale, and more. *

Periodical

Magazine: American Book Collector
P.O. Box 867
Ossining, NY 10562 *

Periodical

Magazine: Book Source Monthly
John C. Huckans, Ed.
P.O. Box 567
Cazenovia, NY 13035
Phone: 315-655-8499 or 315-655-9654
            FAX: 315-655-4249
Book Source Monthly serves both members of the antiquarian book trade and private collectors; nationwide BOOKQUEST database exposure.

Periodical

Price Guide: Collectors Price Index
Box 2515
Chattanooga, TN 37409 *

Periodical

Newspaper: Book Shopper Monthly
P.O. Box 309
Fraser, MI 48026 *

Repair Service

Book Doctor, The
P.O. Box 68
Harrisburg, OH 43126
Phone: 800-848-7918
Does handcrafted bookbinding, family bible restorations, book restoration, leather binding, etc. *

Repair Service

Harden Ballantine Bookcrafts
202 North Walnut St.
Yellow Springs, OH 45387
Phone: 513-767-7417
Bookbinder. Disbound books repaired. *

Repair Service

Don E. Sanders Bookbiner
Don E. Sanders
1116 Pinion Dr.
Austin, TX 78748
Phone: 512-282-4774
20 years experience; custom binding & cases, restoration and repair.

Repair Service

Adolphus Bindery
P.O. Box 2085
Austin, TX 78768
Phone: 512-444-6616
Bookbinder specializing in restoration. *

Antiques

Book Seller

John Ives Antiquarian Books
5 Normanhurst Dr.
Twickenham
Middlesex TW1 1NA England
Supplies specialist reference books on antiques and collecting to customers all over the world; send for free catalog.

Collector

Frderick Appraisal Services
David Maloney
1612 Shookstown Rd.
Frederick, MD 21702
Phone: 301-695-8544 or 301-663-0818
            FAX: 301-695-6491
Wants used reference books about antiques & collectibles; prefers less than 15 years old; specific subjects (no encyclopedias).

Baseball

Collector

R. Plapinger
P.O. Box 1062
Ashland, OR 97520
Phone: 503-488-1220
Wants any book about baseball: non-fiction, fiction, adult, juvenile, especially turn-of-the-century; send SASE for list of most

Big Little

Club/Association

Big Little Book Collectors Club of America
Newsletter: Big Little Times
Larry Lowery
P.O. Box 1242
Danville, CA 94526
Phone: 415-837-2086
Club provides a conduit among collectors and dealers; publishes research and other information pertaining to Big Little Books.

Expert

Saturday Matinee
Ron Donnelly
P.O. Box 7047
Panama City, FL 32413 *

Expert

Larry Lowery
P.O. Box 1242
Danville, CA 94526
Phone: 415-837-2086
Author of "The Collector's Guide to Big Little and Similar Books."

Boys'

Collector

Ruttar
3116 Teesdale
Philadelphia, PA 19152

Wants boys books: Andy Blake, Trigger Berg, Poppy Ott, Jerry Todd, Hal Keen, Racer Boys, Sam Steele series. *

Children's

Collector

Margery Wilder
Box 175
Nordland, WA 98358
Wants Tasha, Tudor, Beatrix Potter and various other charming illustrated books including Sambo's.

Dealer

Deer Park Books
Barbara & Dick DePalma
27 Deer Park Rd.
Danbury, CT 06811
Phone: 203-743-2246
Buys and sells illustrated children's books; catalogs and lists sent upon requests.

Dealer

Marvelous Books
Helmar/ Dorothy Kern
P.O. Box 1510
Ballwin, MO 63022
Phone: 314-458-3301
Buy/sell quality children's books; search service available; 4 catalogs for $5; want list available; friendly service for 15 years.

Dealer

Ruppert Books
5909 Darnell
Houston, TX 77074
Phone: 713-774-2202 or 713-666-1344
Wants books: Nancy Drew, Hardy Boys, Little Black Sambo, Raggedy Ann, Dick and Jane Readers, OZ, early illustrated children's books.

Expert

Margaret Tyrell
117 North 40th St.
Allentown, PA 18104
Phone: 215-395-9364 *

Expert

E. Lee Baumgarten
943 Bonifant St., No. 3
Silver Spring, MD 20910
Phone: 301-588-5571
Specializes, collects, buys and sells children's books; author of "Price Guide for Children's & Illustrated Books (1880-1940)."

Museum/Library

American Antiquarian Society
185 Salisbury Street
Worcester, MA 01609
Phone: 508-755-5221

Museum/Library
Free Library of Philadelphia
Logan Square
Philadelphia, PA 19103
Phone: 215-686-5322

Periodical
Newsletter: Martha's KidLit Newsletter
P.O. Box 1488
Ames, IA 50010 *

Collector (Antiques)

Book Seller
Bill Sacks
5435 Rosedale Avenue
Montreal
Quebec H4V 2H7 Canada *

Book Seller
Joslin Hall Rare Books
P.O. Box 516
Concord, MA 01742
Phone: 508-371-3101
Specialists in rare books on the decorative arts and American fine art.

Book Seller
Bethlehem Book Company
249 East St.
Bethlehem, CT 06751 *

Book Seller
Books About Antiques
Greg Johnson
139 Main Street North
Woodbury, CT 06798
Phone: 203-263-0241

Book Seller
Jo-D Books
81 Willard Terrace
Stamford, CT 06903
Phone: 203-322-0568
Books on antiques, collectibles and memorabilia.

Book Seller
Sotheby's Publications
c/o Rizzoli Inter. Pub.
300 Park Ave. South
New York, NY 10010
Phone: 212-982-2300 or 800-433-1238
Source for antiques related books and price guides published by Sotheby's.

Book Seller
C. Richard Becker, Bookseller
C. Richard Becker
London Terrace Station
P.O. Box 20261
New York, NY 10011
Phone: 212-243-3789
Specialist in books on the decorative and applied arts; standard reference works on antiques, original art work and collecting.

Book Seller
House of Collectibles
201 East 50th St.
New York, NY 10022
Phone: 800-638-6460

Book Seller
Christie's Publications
21-44 44th Ave.
Long Island City, NY 11101
Phone: 718-784-1480

Book Seller
Art Books Services, Inc.
P.O. Box 360
Hughsonville, NY 12537
Phone: 914-297-1312   FAX: 914-297-0068
Carries the best books on the fine and decorative arts; also on architecture and garden design.

Book Seller
Antique Collectors' Club, Ltd.
Market Street Industrial Park
Wappingers' Falls, NY 12590
Phone: 914-297-0003 or 800-252-5231
                         FAX: 914-297-0068
Offers only the highest quality standard reference works on antiques, art, gardening and architecture.

Book Seller
ArtBooks
Doris Motta
P.O. Box 665
Cooperstown, NY 13326
Phone: 607-547-9748
Books and catalogs on fine and decorative arts.

Book Seller
Hotchkiss House
P.O. Box 239
Fairport, NY 14450

Book Seller
Collectors Shelf of Books
P.O. Box 6
Westfield, NY 14787
Phone: 716-326-3676

Book Seller
Reference Rack, The
Box 445
Orefield, PA 18069
Phone: 800-722-7279
Books on antiques, art and collectibles; issues two catalogs per year.

Book Seller
Wallace-Homestead Book Co.
Jeanine LaBorne
201 King of Prussia Rd.
Radnor, PA 19089
Phone: 215-964-4710 or 800-345-1214
                         FAX: 215-964-4100

Publisher of a line of collectibles and antiques books including the well-known "Warman's Price Guides."

Book Seller
Museum Books & Prints
P.O. Box 7832
Reading, PA 19603
Phone: 215-372-0642
*Sells books on antiques, decorative and fine arts; free search service available. ***

Book Seller
Henry Francis DuPont Winterthur Museum
P.O. Box 90
Winterthur, DE 19735-0001
Phone: 800-448-3883 or 302-888-4741

Book Seller
Homebiz News & More
B.J. Hicks
2919 Mistwood Forest Dr.
Chester, VA 23831-7043
Offers antique and collectible reference books; send $1 for catalog on discount collector books.

Book Seller
Collector Books
P.O. Box 3009
Paducah, KY 42002-3009
Phone: 800-626-5420   FAX: 502-898-8890
Offers large selection of collector books and books on antiques.

Book Seller
Kovels on Antiques and Collectibles
Ralph & Terry Kovel
P.O. Box 22200
Beachwood, OH 44122
                         FAX: 216-742-3115
Focuses on antiques, decorative arts and collectibles; identification and buying tips, prices, reproduction alerts, etc.

Book Seller
Green Gate Books
P.O. Box 934
Lima, OH 45802
Phone: 419-225-3816 or 800-228-3816
Collector books wholesale only.

Book Seller
L-W Book Sales
P.O. Box 69
Gas City, IN 46933
Phone: 800-777-6450

Book Seller
Library, The
Nancy Johnson
P.O. Box 37
Des Moines, IA 50301
Phone: 515-262-6714   FAX: 515-263-8116

Reference books on antiques, collectibles and the decorative arts; foreign and private presses; over 3500 titles in stock.

Collector (Art)

Book Seller

New England Gallery
R.F.D. 2
Wolfeboro, NH 03894
Phone: 603-569-3501 *

Book Seller

Museum Gallery Book Shop
360 Mine Hill Road
fairfield, CT 06530
Phone: 203-259-7114
Sells and art reference books; publishes catalog of current offerings.

Book Seller

Hacker Art Books
54 West 57th Street
New York, NY 10019
*Sells and art reference books; publishes catalog of current offerings. *

Book Seller

Olana Gallery
Drawer 9
Brewster, NY 10509
Phone: 914-279-8077
*Offers books and catalogs exclusively on American art and artists; new, out-of-print, reprints, rare; Want lists invited. *

Book Seller

Art World International
69 N. Federal Highway
Dania, FL 33004
Phone: 305-923-3001
*Offers books and catalogs on American art and artists; contact for current catalog of offerings. *

Book Seller

Dealer's Choice Books
P.O. Box 710
Land O' Lakes, FL 34639
Phone: 813-996-6599 or 800-238-8288
FAX: 813-996-5226
Sells collector and art reference books: "Art Sales Index", "Who Was Who in American Art", "Signatures of American Artists", etc.

Collector (Art, Asian)

Book Seller

Paragon Book Gallery
237 West 72nd St.
New York, NY 10023
Phone: 212-496-2378   FAX: 212-496-2379
Carries a large selection of books and catalogs on Asian art.

Book Seller

Rare Oriental Book Co.
Jerrald Stanoff
P.O. Box 1599
Aptos, CA 95001-1599
Carries a large selection of books on Japanese prints and other Asian Art.

Collector (Autographs)

Book Seller

Autograph Collector's Magazine, The
Joe Kraus
P.O. Box 55328
Stockton, CA 95205
Phone: 209-473-0570 or 209-942-2131
FAX: 209-368-1549

Collector (Barbed Wire)

Book Seller

Schoolmaster Auctions
Ken Norris
P.O. Box 476
Grandfalls, TX 79742
Phone: 915-547-2421
*Wants books, periodicals, and articles about barbed wire. *

Collector (Breweriana)

Book Seller

Soda Mart - Can World
1055 Ridgecrest Dr.
Goodlettsville, TN 37072
Phone: 615-859-5236   FAX: 615-859-5238
Sells breweriana books; also cleans and de-rusts on cans, and sells supplies for the beer can collector.

Collector (Cameras)

Book Seller

Centennial Photo
Rt. 3, Box 1125
Grantsburg, WI 54840 *

Book Seller

Kaleido-Cam
William P. Carroll
8500 La Entrada
Whittier, CA 90605
Phone: 213-693-8421   FAX: 213-947-8499
Antique and classic cameras for sale; also repairs; offers new and used books on kaleidoscopes, cameras and the history of

Collector (Cars)

Book Seller

Classic Motorbooks
P.O. Box 1
Osceola, WI 54020
Phone: 800-826-6600   FAX: 715-294-4448
The best selections of books about special interest cars, tractors, trucks, motorcycles, etc.

Collector (Ceramics)

Book Seller

Hayden & Fandetta
John-Peter J. Hayden
Radio City Station
P.O. Box 1200
New York, NY 10101-1200
Phone: 212-581-8520
Foremost source on rare, out-of-print, and new books on pottery and porcelain.

Book Seller

Antique Publications
David Richardson
P.O. Box 553
Marletta, OH 45750-0553
Phone: 614-373-9959 or 800-533-3433
FAX: 614-373-5530
Offers a wide selection of books about pottery and glass.

Collector (Clocks)

Book Seller

Adams Brown Company
P.O. Box 357
Cranbury, NJ 08512
Phone: 800-257-5278
*Issues catalog of horological books and literature; also books on furniture, silver and the decorative arts. *

Book Seller

S. LaRose, Inc.
234 Commerce Place
Greensboro, NC 27420
Phone: 919-275-0462
*Issues catalog of horological books and literature.
*

Book Seller

Heart of America Press
P.O. Box 9808
Kansas City, MO 64134
Phone: 816-761-0080
*Issues catalog of horological books and literature.
*

Collector (Clothing)

Book Seller

Wooden Porch Books
Rt. 1, Box 262
Middlebourne, WV 26149-9748
Phone: 304-386-4434   FAX: 304-386-4868
6 catalogs per year listing approximately 2400 out-of-print books and magazines on the fiber arts and kindred subjects.

Book Seller

R.L. Shep Books
Box 668
Mendocino, CA 95460
Phone: 717-937-1436

Reprints of Victorian and Edwardian costume books stressing patterns, instructions, embroidery, etc.; women and men; practical manuals.

Collector (Coin-Operated)

Book Seller

TAJ Distributing
621 Miller St.
Luzerne, PA 18709
Carries a large supply of books and literature related to coin-operated machines. ★

Book Seller

Mr. Russell
2404 West 111th St.
Chicago, IL 60655
Carries a large supply of books related to coin-operated machines. ★

Book Seller

Coin Slot, The
P.O. Box 612
Wheatridge, CO 80033
Books, old catalog reprints, posters, service manuals, etc. on antique coin-operated machines. ★

Book Seller

Hoflin Publishing Ltd.
4401 Zephyr St.
Wheat Ridge, CO 80033-3299
Phone: 303-420-2222 or 800-352-5678
Books, old catalog reprints, posters, service manuals, etc. on antique coin-operated machines.

Collector (Collectibles)

Book Seller

Blystone Books
William Blystone
Dept. CIC
2132 Delaware Ave.
Pittsburgh, PA 15218
Phone: 412-371-3511
Sells in print & out of print collectibles books by mail; specialty areas are dolls, toys and train books; looking for new book sources.

Collector (Dolls)

Book Seller

Hobby House Press, Inc.
Paul Ruddell
900 Frederick St.
Cumberland, MD 21502-9985
Phone: 301-759-3770   FAX: 301-759-4940
Specializes on books dealing with Dolls, Teddy Bears, Paper Dolls, Vintage Clothing.

Collector (Firearms)

Book Seller

INFO-ARM
Newsletter: INFO-ARM Newsletter
P.O. Box 1262
Champlain, NY 12919

Specializing in books on handguns, rifles, shotguns, ammunition, edged weapons, etc.

Book Seller

Ray Riling Arms Books Co.
P.O. Box 18925
Philadelphia, PA 19119
Carries every gun book in print.

Collector (Fishing Items)

Book Seller

Highwood Bookshop
Lewis & Wilma Razek
P.O. Box 1246
Traverse City, MI 49684
Phone: 616-271-3898
Offers books about fish decoy collecting, fishing tackle collecting, and decoy and related carving.

Collector (Gems/Jewelry)

Book Seller

Gemstone Press
Monica Wilson
P.O. box 237
Woodstock, VT 05091
Phone: 802-457-4000 or 800-962-4544
                        FAX: 802-457-4504
Internt'l. source for books and other items designed to help people in the gem trade and consumers learn more about gems & jewelry.

Book Seller

Jewelers' Circular-Keystone Book Club
Newsletter: Jewelers' Book Club News
One Chilton Way
Radnor, PA 19089-0140
Phone: 215-964-4480
Offers books about gems and jewelry.

Book Seller

Gemological Institute of America
Bookstore
1660 Stewart St.
Santa Monica, CA 90404
Phone: 800-421-7250

Book Seller

Gems, Etc.
P.O. Box 6237
Whittier, CA 90609
Phone: 213-943-0090 or 800-443-4182
Sells books about gems and jewelry.

Collector (Glass)

Book Seller

Antique Publications
David Richardson
P.O. Box 553
Marietta, OH 45750-0553
Phone: 614-373-9959 or 800-533-3433
                        FAX: 614-373-5530
Offers a wide selection of books about pottery and glass.

Collector (Indian Items)

Book Seller

Hothem House
Lar Hothem
P.O. Box 458
Lancaster, OH 43130
Phone: 614-653-9030
Buys and sells Indian related books covering archaeology, artifacts, earthworks, U.S. prehistory.

Collector (Japanese Prints)

Book Seller

Ukiyo-E Books
Chris Uhlenbeck
Langebrug 34
Leiden 2311 TM Holland

Collector (Jukeboxes)

Book Seller

Newspaper: Always Jukin'
Michael F. Baute
221 Yesler Way
Seattle, WA 98104
Phone: 206-233-9460   FAX: 206-233-9871
Sells books about jukeboxes, jukebox service manuals and records.

Collector (Knives)

Book Seller

Knife World Books
P.O. Box 3395
Knoxville, TN 37927
Phone: 615-523-3339   FAX: 615-637-7123
Specializes in books about knives.

Book Seller

Weyer International - Book Division
Louise Weyer
333 14th St.
Toledo, OH 43624
Phone: 419-241-5454 or 800-448-8424
                        FAX: 419-241-2637
Specializes in books about knives.

Collector (Militaria)

Book Seller

Portrayal Press
P.O. Box 1913-24
Bloomfield, NJ 07003
Phone: 201-743-1851
Carries a wide selection of books on every aspect of military history and military science. ★

Book Seller

Military Bookman, The
29 East 93rd Street
New York, NY 10128
Phone: 212-348-1280
Deals exclusively in military, naval and aviation history o/p books, with related pictorial items; by mail or on site; catalogs available.

Book Seller

Antheil Booksellers
2177 Isabelle Court
North Bellmore, NY 11710
Phone: 516-826-2094
*Offers over 1500 mostly out-of-print military,
maritime and aviation books; catalog subscription
$5 for 4 issues.*

Book Seller

Phoenix Militaria, Inc. Military
Bookstore
Rt. 1, Box 287
Mertztown, PA 19539
Phone: 215-682-1010 or 800-446-0909
               FAX: 215-682-1066
*Sells a wide variety of military-related books and
publications.*

Book Seller

Nautical & Aviation Publishing Co.
Suite 314
101 West Read Street
Baltimore, MD 21201
Phone: 301-659-0220   FAX: 301-539-8832
*Carries naval, aviation and Civil War military
books; many titles are primary sources, i.e. mem-
oirs, biographies, etc.*

Book Seller

Military Book Club, The
P.O. Box 6355
Indianapolis, IN 46209-9478
*Focuses on books about wars, strategies, battles
and weapons.*

Book Seller

Zenith Books
P.O. Box One
Osceola, WI 54020
Phone: 800-826-6600   FAX: 715-294-4448
*World's best selection of aviation, modeling, radio
control model aircraft, and military books and
videos.*

Collector (Nautical)

Book Seller

Columbia Trading Company
Bob Glick
504 Main St.
West Barnstable, MA 02668
Phone: 508-362-8966
*Issues 6 catalogs a year each offering 500 nautical,
boating, and naval books, magazines and eph-
emera for sale.*

Collector (Postcards)

Book Seller

Deltiologists of America
Magazine: Postcard Classics
Dr. James Lewis Lowe, Dir.
P.O. Box 8
Norwood, PA 19074
Phone: 215-485-8572

*International postcard society for collectors,
dealers, librarians, and archivist; offers several
postcard related books for sale.*

Collector (Radios)

Book Seller

Vintage Radio
Morgan McMahon
P.O. Box 2045
Palos Verdes, CA 90274
Sells books about old radios. *

Collector (Records)

Book Seller

Jellyroll Publications
P.O. Box 255
Port Townsend, WA 98363
Phone: 206-385-3029
*Offers an assortment of publications for the record
collector.* *

Collector (Silver)

Book Seller

Silver Magazine
Diane Cramer
P.O. Box 1243
Whittier, CA 90609
Phone: 213-696-6738
*New and out of print books and catalogs relating
to silver and silverplate; the source for books by
Tardy and Rainwater.*

Collector (Teddy Bears)

Book Seller

Hobby House Press, Inc.
Paul Ruddell
900 Frederick St.
Cumberland, MD 21502-9985
Phone: 301-759-3770   FAX: 301-759-4940
*Specializes on books dealing with Dolls, Teddy
Bears, Paper Dolls, Vintage Clothing.*

Collector (Tools)

Book Seller

Tool Merchant
John Walter
P.O. Box 6471
Akron, OH 44312
Phone: 800-542-1993
Sells about old tools. *

Collector (Vintage Clothing)

Book Seller

Hobby House Press, Inc.
Paul Ruddell
900 Frederick St.
Cumberland, MD 21502-9985
Phone: 301-759-3770   FAX: 301-759-4940
*Specializes on books dealing with Dolls, Teddy
Bears, Paper Dolls, Vintage Clothing.*

Collector (Watches)

Book Seller

Heart of America Press
P.O. Box 9808
Kansas City, MO 64134
Phone: 816-761-0080
Issues catalog of horological books and literature.
*

Coloring

Expert

Norm & Cathy Vigue
62 Bailey St.
Stoughton, MA 02072
Phone: 617-344-5441

Fashion

Collector

Beatrix Brockerman
730 W. Gaines St.
Tallahassee, FL 32324
*Wants pre-1950's pattern books by Vogue, Sim-
plicity, etc.* *

First Editions

Dealer

Family Album, The
Ron Lieberman
R.D. 1, Box 42
Glen Rock, PA 17327
Phone: 717-235-2134   FAX: 717-235-8042
*Buys and sells fine books in all fields, specializing
in American first editions.*

Dealer

Quill & Brush
Pat & Allen Ahearn
P.O. Box 5365
Rockville, MD 20853
Phone: 301-460-3700   FAX: 301-871-5425
*Book dealer specializing in 19th & 20th century
first editions.*

German

Collector

R.L. Rice
612 E. Front St.
Bloomington, IL 61701
*Wants illustrated German language books in-
cluding Bibles, children's and travel books; also
art books 1830's -1920's.*

Heraldry

Dealer

Antiques & Art Galleries
Steve Whysel
101 N. Main
Bentonville, AR 72712
Phone: 501-273-7701 or 501-444-9911
*Wants coat of arms (family crests) on fabric,
wood, cups, plates, tile, paper, etc.; also wants
books on heraldry.*

Horatio Alger, Jr.

(see also PERSONALITIES (LITERARY),
Horatio Alger, Jr.)

Collector

Newsletter: Newsboy
George Owens
HCR 72, Box 166A
Glenwood, AR 71943
Wants Horatio Alger, Jr. books; state title, publisher, condition and price.

Ian Fleming

Collector

Albert Mendez
142-35 38th Ave.
Flushing, NY 11354
Phone: 718-961-2866
Wants any books by author Ian Fleming including "James Bond" novels, books and magazines.

Illustrated

(see also ILLUSTRATORS)

Dealer

Mashburn Books & Cards
P.O. Box 609
Enka, NC 28728
Phone: 704-667-1427
Wants books with illustrations by Harrison Fisher, Coles Phillips, Clarence Underwood, Henry Hutt, Howard C. Christy, Charles Gibson. *

Juvenile Series

Club/Association

Series Book Collectors Society
Newsletter: SBCS Newsletter
60 Turner Ave.
Riverside, RI 02915
Phone: 313-694-2196
Interested in series books such as Hardy Boys, Nancy Drew, Tom Swift, etc. *

Club/Association

Society of Phantom Friends
Newsletter: Whispered Watchword
519 S. 7th St.
Moorhead, MI 56560
For collectors of girls' series books. *

Periodical

Yellowback Press
Magazine: Yellowback Library
Gil O'Gara
P.O. Box 36172
Des Moines, IA 50315
Phone: 515-287-0404
Focuses on juvenile series books and dime novels; largest circulation in the hobby.

Periodical

Magazine: Mystery & Adventure Series
  Review
Fred Woodworth, Ed.
P.O. Box 3488
Tucson, AZ 85722
Quarterly magazine devoted to collecting and preserving c.1925-1965 series-books, e.g. Hardy Boys, Ken Holt & Rick Brant.

Law

Misc. Service

E. (Ned) DeRussy
7612 Club Rd.
Ruxton, MD 21201
Phone: 301-825-1306
Appraiser of Maryland law books.

Little Golden

Club/Association

Little Golden Book Collectors Club
P.O. Box 5672
Baltimore, MD 21210 21210
Phone: 301-243-3747 *

Collector

Laura Fadem
6116 S. Gary Ave.
Tulsa, OK 74136 *

Collector

Gloria Flager
5966 Barcelona Dr. S.E.
Salem, OR 97301
Wants certain Little Golden Books to complete collection; write for want list; also has duplicates for sale.

Expert

Kathie Diehl
P.O. Box 5672
Baltimore, MD 21210 21210
Phone: 301-243-3747 *

Expert

Steve Santi
19626 Ricardo Ave.
Hayward, CA 94541
Phone: 415-481-2586
Buys and sells Little Golden Books by Books Americana; author of "Collecting Little Golden Books."

Medical & Dental

(see also MEDICAL, DENTAL &
PHARMACEUTICAL)

Dealer

M.B. Raskin & Co.
11 Edgemere Dr.
Albertson, NY 11507
Wants pre-1940 medical and dental books. *

Military History

(see also MILITARY HISTORY)

Dealer

Book Castle, Inc.
Paul Hunt
P.O. Box 10907
Burbank, CA 91510
Phone: 818-845-1563 or 818-842-6816
                        FAX: 818-845-0460
Buys and sells books, specialty: movie & TV memorabilia, and military and history.

Miniature

Expert

Family Album, The
Ron Lieberman
R.D. 1, Box 42
Glen Rock, PA 17327
Phone: 717-235-2134   FAX: 717-235-8042

Movie & TV Related

Dealer

Book Castle, Inc.
Paul Hunt
P.O. Box 10907
Burbank, CA 91510
Phone: 818-845-1563 or 818-842-6816
                        FAX: 818-845-0460
Buys and sells books, specialty: movie & TV memorabilia, and military and history.

Paperback

Expert

Hancer's Bookstore
Kevin Hancer
5813 York Ave.
Edina, MN 55410
Phone: 612-922-9144 *

Periodical

Journal: Dime Novel Round-Up
Edward T. LeBlanc
87 School St.
Fall River, MA 02720
Phone: 508-672-2082
A magazine devoted to the collecting, preservation and literature of the old-time dime and nickel novels and popular story papers.

Periodical

Magazine: Golden Perils
Howard Hopkins, Ed.
5 Milliken Mills Road
Scarboro, ME 04074
A tri-annual magazine focusing on serials and pulp magazines.

Periodical

Gryphon Publications
Magazine: <u>Paperback Parade</u>
Gary Lavisi
P.O. Box 209
Brooklyn, NY 11228
Phone: 718-646-6126
A magazine for Pb readers and collectors; news, articles, lists, interviews; a hobby publication full of news and info about the Pb's.

Periodical

Magazine: <u>Books Are Everything!</u>
302 Martin Drive
Richmond, KY 40475 *

Periodical

Magazine: <u>Echoes</u>
504 E. Morris Street
Seymour, TX 76380
Focuses on dime novels and pulp magazines. *

Pop-Ups

Collector

James P. Harold
2122 Mass. Ave. NW #522
Washington, DC 20008-2833
Phone: 202-296-6527
Wants "toy" and "moveable" books (pop-ups).

Collector

Margery Wilder
Box 175
Nordland, WA 98358
Collecting pop-up, mechanical, fold-out, unusual children's books.

Roycroft

Dealer

Antiquarian Archive, The
David B. Ogle
160 S. Murphy Ave.
Sunnyvale, CA 94086
Phone: 408-739-5633
Specialist in Western Americana, railroadiana, nautical & maritime, military history & memoirs, books of the Roycroft printing shop.

Sports

Collector

John Buonaguidi
2830 Rockridge Dr.
Pleasant Hill, CA 94523
Wants 19th century non-fiction books about baseball, football, or boxing. *

BOTTLE CAPS

Milk

(see also BOTTLES, Milk; DAIRY COLLECTIBLES)

Collector

Jerry Jerard
402 Western Avenur
Brattleboro, VT 05301

Collector

Dennis Osborn
P.O. Box 1335
Ashtabula, OH 44004
Wants to buy milk caps; send photo copies.

BOTTLE OPENERS

Figural

(see also CORKSCREWS)

Club/Association

Figural Bottle Opener Collectors Club
Newsletter: <u>Opener, The</u>
Donna Kitzmiller
117 Basin Hill Road
Duncannon, PA 17020
Formed to promote interest in and knowledge about figural bottle openers.

Club/Association

Just for Openers
Newsletter: <u>Just for Openers Newsletter</u>
John Stanley
605 Windsong Lane
Durham, NC 27713
Phone: 919-493-9802 or 919-966-5794
Just for Openers is a club for bottle and corkscrew collectors; the quarterly newsletter covers all types of both.

Collector

Phyllis Eisenach
13018 Clarion Rd.
Fort Washington, MD 20744
Phone: 301-292-2328

Collector

John Stanley
605 Windsong Lane
Durham, NC 27713
Phone: 919-493-9802 or 919-966-5794
Wants any bottle opener or corkscrew from the Southeast U.S.

Expert

Barbara Rosen
6 Shoshone Trail
Wayne, NJ 07470 *

Expert

Reynolds Toys
Charles Reynolds
2836 Monroe St.
Falls Church, VA 22042
Phone: 703-533-1322
An advanced collector paying top dollar for openers, e.g. wall mount boy winking, Amish Man, Skull, Coyote, Standing College Figures, etc.

Expert

Cracker Barrel Antiques
Rita & John Ebner
4540 Helen Rd.
Columbus, OH 43232
Wants cast iron figural bottle openers. *

Repro. Source

Charles Reynolds
2836 Monroe St.
Falls Church, VA 22042
Phone: 703-533-1322
Offers limited editions of new original figural bottle opener reproductions of sand-cast aluminum; flyer on request.

BOTTLES

(see also INFANT FEEDERS; INKWELLS & INKSTANDS; SODA FOUNTAIN COLLECTIBLES; SOFT DRINK COLLECTIBLES)

Auction Service

B.B.R. Auctions
2 Strafford Ave., Elsescar
Barnsley
S. Yorkshire S74 8AA England
England's leading specialists and auction house for antique bottles, pot lids and related advertising material.

Auction Service

Norman C. Heckler & Company
79 Bradford Corner Road
Woodstock Valley, CT 06282
Phone: 203-974-0682 or 203-974-1634
Specializes in the sale of early glass and bottles; Heckler & Co. sold a single bottle for $40,700 at auction in 1990.

Auction Service

Glass Works Auctions
James Hagenbuch
P.O. Box 187
East Greenville, PA 18041
Phone: 215-679-5849
Specializes in the auction of bottles, flasks, barber bottles, jars, bitters bottles, scent bottles, shaving mugs, and related go-withs.

Club/Association

New Jersey Antique Bottle Collectors Association
Joe Maggi
117 Lincoln Pl.
Waldwick, NJ 07463

Club/Association

Baltimore Antique Bottle Club
Newsletter: <u>Baltimore Bottle Digger</u>
P.O. Box 36061
Townson, MD 21286-6061
Monthly meetings include displays, selling/trading and speaker programs about bottles & related items: jugs, fruit jars, etc.

Club/Association

My Bottle Club
Charles O. Benton
1200 Jacobs Rd.
DeLand, FL 32724
Phone: 904-734-3651

Club/Association

Midwest Antique Fruit Jar & Bottle Club
Newsletter: Glass Chatter
P.O. Box 38
Flat Rock, IN 47234
*Sponsors two fruit and bottle shows each year in
Indianapolis.*

Club/Association

Federation of Historical Bottle Clubs
Newsletter: Federation Glass Works, The
Barbara A. Harms
14521 Atlantic
Riverdale, IL 60627
Phone: 312-841-4068
*Provides news of the National Bottle Museum,
bottles, jars, flasks, glass, and other related items.*

Collector

Douglas Anderson
112 South Commerce St.
Centerville, MD 21617
Phone: 301-758-3278 *

Collector

Steve Ketcham
Box 24114
Edina, MN 55424
Phone: 612-920-4205
*Buying pre-1900 American bottles with embossed
or paper labels: especially flasks, bitters, cures,
figurals, barber bottles, etc.*

Collector

Jim Hall
549 Williamsburg Ct.
Wheeling, IL 60090
Phone: 312-541-5788
*Wants historical flasks, bitters, inks, etc. *

Collector

Krol's Rock City and Mobile Park
Ed Krol
Star Rt. 2, Box 15A
Derning, NM 88030
Phone: 505-546-4368
*Hutchinson sodas, embossed & painted milks,
inks, Coca Colas, cures, hairs, seltzer, beers, baby
bottles, whiskeys, druggist, etc.*

Dealer

Antique Bottles & Stoneware Shop
Don Dzuro
3566 Copley Rd.
Akron, OH 44321
Phone: 216-666-8170
*Buys, sells and trades bottles, jars and pottery;
author of "Ohio Bottles."*

Museum/Library

National Bottle Museum
Alan Blakeman
Eslecar Workshops, Elsecar
Barnsley
S. Yorkshire S74 8AA England
*Specialist museum covering all areas of bottles:
wines, medicines, inks, brewery, etc.*

Museum/Library

National Bottle Museum
P.O. Box 621
Ballston Spa, NY 12020
Phone: 518-885-7589

Museum/Library

Toledo Museum of Art, The
P.O. Box 1013
Toledo, OH 43620
Phone: 419-255-8000

Museum/Library

Hawaii Bottle Museum
Newsletter: Hawaii Bottle Museum News
P.O. Box 25152
Honolulu, HI 96825
Phone: 808-395-4671

Periodical

B.B.R. Publishing
Magazine: British Bottle Review
A.R. Blakeman
2 Strafford Ave., Elsescar
Barnsley
S. Yorkshire S74 8AA England
*The world's longest continuous running publica-
tion covering the multitudinous areas of antique
bottles; including world news.*

Periodical

Magazine: Antique Bottle & Glass Collector
James Hagenbuch
P.O. Box 187
East Greenville, PA 18041
Phone: 215-679-5849   FAX: 215-679-3068
*A monthly magazine for the glass and bottle
collector.*

Periodical

Magazine: Pictorial Bottle Review
P.O. Box 2161
Palos Verdes Peninsula, CA 90274
*For collectors of modern bottles. *

Periodical

Bottles & Extras Magazine
Magazine: Bottles & Extras
Scott Grandstaff
P.O. Box 154
Happy Camp, CA 96039
Phone: 916-493-2032
*A monthly mag. for collectors of old bottles and
related antiques; articles on private collections,
digging news, auctions, etc.*

Periodical

Magazine: Old Bottle Magazine
P.O. Box 243
Bend, OR 97701 *

Barber

(see also BARBER SHOP COLLECTIBLES)

Collector

George Coupe
1243 1st St. S.E.
Washington, DC 20003
Phone: 202-554-1000 or 800-368-5466
                    FAX: 202-863-0775
Wants barber bottles; must be in good condition.

Bitters

Expert

Carlyn Ring
203 Kensington Rd.
Hampton Falls, NH 03844-2213
*Author of "For Bitters Only Up-Date and Price
Guide."*

Expert

Robert Daly
10341 Jewell Lake Ct.
Fenton, MO 48430 *

Ginger Beer

Expert

Sven Stau
P.O. Box 1135
Buffalo, NY 14211
*Author of "The Illustrated Stone Ginger Beer." *

Historical Flasks

Expert

Mark Vuono
306 Mill Road
Stamford, CT 06903
Phone: 203-329-8744
*Specializes in historical flasks, blown-3-mold,
and blown American glass. *

Expert

John Crary
P.O. Box 417
Canton, NY 13617
*Author of "Guide to the Value of Historical
Flasks."*

Expert

Robert Daly
10341 Jewell Lake Ct.
Fenton, MO 48430 *

Japanese

Collector

Al Sparacino
743 La Huerta Way
San Diego, CA 92154
Phone: 619-690-3632

Wants Japanese figural sake, wine, liquor bottles: House of Koshu, Kikukawa, Kamotsuru, Kikkoman, Sasaiti Shuzo, Okura Shuzu, etc.

Japanese/German Give-Away

Collector

Paul Stookey
3015 W. St. Rt. 571
Troy, OH 45373
Phone: 513-698-3392
Wants Japanese and German give-a-way bottles.

Milk

(see also BOTTLE CAPS, Milk; DAIRY COLLECTIBLES)

Club/Association

National Association of Milk Bottle Collectors, Inc.
Newsletter: Milk Route, The
Thomas Gallagher
4 Ox Bow Rd.
Westport, CT 06880-2602
Phone: 203-277-5244
Focuses on the milk and dairy history and related memorabilia; membership includes the newsletter and history of fluid milk industry.

Collector

Alex Caiola
84 Seneca
Emerson, NJ 07630
Phone: 201-262-7030
Wants New Jersey tin-top and pre-1915 milk bottles from Englewood, Hackensack, Ridgewood, Hohokus, Harington Park, Teaneck.

Collector

Dick Chenoweth
2917 Putty Hill Ave.
Baltimore, MD 21234
Phone: 301-668-3426 *

Expert

Thomas Gallagher
4 Ox Bow Rd.
Westport, CT 06880-2602
Phone: 203-277-5244

Expert

Tony Knipp
P.O. Box 105
Blooming Grove, NY 10914
Phone: 914-496-6841

Expert

Ralph Riovo
686 Franklin Street
Alburtis, PA 18011-9578
Phone: 215-966-2536
Buying and selling milk and dairy items for 16 years; wants milk bottles with Hopalong Cassidy, Annie Oakley, Disney characters, etc.

Expert

John Tutton
Rt. 4, Box 929
Front Royal, VA 22630
Phone: 703-635-7058
Involved in milk bottles for 23 years; covering collecting, buying and selling; lecturer and author of three books on milk bottles.

Miniature

Collector

Tony Natelli
151-20 88th St.
Howard Beach, NY 11414
Phone: 718-738-3344
Advanced collector wants to buy and trade with collectors from Spain, Italy, Holland, France, Australia, New Zealand and South America.

Collector

Lee Weiss
5626 Corning Ave.
Los Angeles, CA 90056
Wants miniature bottles such as whiskey, beer, liquor and pop containers.

Dealer

Flask, The
12194 Ventura Blvd.
Studio City, CA 91604
Phone: 818-761-5373
Carries large selection of minis.

Periodical

Newsletter: Miniature Bottle Mart
24 Gertrude Lane
West Haven, CT 06516
For collectors of old or new miniature bottles. *

Periodical

Briscoe Publications
Newsletter: Miniature Bottle Collector, The
P.O. Box 2161
Palos Verdes Peninsula, CA 90274
For collectors of modern or old miniature bottles.

Miniature Beer & Soda

Collector

John Carver
4668 Evelyn St.
Milton, FL 32570
Phone: 904-994-9419
Wants miniature beer and soda bottles 1900-1963. *

Miniature Liquor

Auction Service

Frank Callan
P.O. Box 777
Brewster, MA 02631
Phone: 508-896-6491
Specializes in mini liquor bottles & figurals from all over the world; quarterly catalog.

Club/Association

Miniature Cognac Club
Newsletter: Cognac Newsletter
P.O. Box 32145
Oklahoma City, OK 73123 *

Club/Association

Lilliputian Bottle Club, The
Newsletter: Gulliver's Gazette
Thomas F. Nagelin, MemCh.
13271 Clinton St.
Garden Grove, CA 92643
Phone: 714-638-3041 or 714-554-8000
FAX: 714-554-1798
215 member club is 20 years old and very active; meets monthly, sponsors a mini-bottle show and sale each October.

Collector

Paul Stookey
3015 W. St. Rt. 571
Troy, OH 45373
Phone: 513-698-3392
Wants miniature whiskey jugs and older miniature whiskey bottles.

Collector

Roscoes Restaurant
Bill Costas
22746 Roscoe Blvd.
West Hills, CA 91304
Phone: 818-883-5597
1000's of mini's on display.

Collector

Thomas F. Nagelin, Sr.
13271 Clinton St.
Garden Grove, CA 92643
Phone: 714-638-3041 or 714-554-8000
FAX: 714-554-1798
Wants miniature liquor bottles; 1930's and 1940's; has collection of over 11,000 minis.

Collector

John Goetz
P.O. Box 1570
Cedar Ridge, CA 95924
Phone: 916-272-4644
Buy/sell ceramic & glass figural mini bottles: dancers, pigs, drunks, Santas, octopus and other whimsical figures; sorry, no Beam types.

Perfume & Scent

Club/Association

Perfume & Scent Bottle Collectors
Newsletter: Perfume & Scent Bottle Collectors Newsletter
Jeane Parris
2022 E. Charleston Blvd.
Las Vegas, NV 89104
Phone: 702-385-6059

Dealer

Cocktails & Laughter Antiques
Randall Monsen
P.O. Box 1503
Arlington, VA 22210
Phone: 703-938-2129
*Wants all kinds, especially with original labels: by Guerlain, Coty, Nina Ricci, Dior, Corday, Lalique, etc. *

Expert

Madeleine France Antiques
Newsletter: Newsletter On Rene Lalique Perfume Bottles
Madeleine France
P.O. Box 15555
Plantation, FL 33318
Phone: 305-584-0009   FAX: 305-584-0014
Wants perfume bottles and boudoir items: Lalique, Baccarat, Viard, St. Louis, Moser, Sterling Scents, Steuben, Victorian laydowns, etc.

Expert

Emily Hart Killian
Suite 131
1211 E. Front St.
Traverse City, MI 49684-2997
Author of "Perfume Bottles Remembered."

Expert

Glass House, The
Jean L. Sloan
Box 5342
Madison, WI 53705
Phone: 608-233-9493 *

Supplier

Paradise & Co.
2902 Neal Road
Paradise, CA 95969
Phone: 916-872-5020   FAX: 916-872-5020
Repairs; also replacement hardware and atomizer bulbs and tassels for perfume bottles.

Poison

Expert

Mr. Poison
Noel Cook
6601 Woodbine Rd.
Woodbine, MD 21797
Phone: 301-781-7013
Buys trades, and sells embossed poison bottles from anywhere in the world; willing to help any new poison bottle collector.

Saratoga-Type

Club/Association

Saratoga-Type Bottle Collectors Society
Newsletter: Spouter
Star Route 1, Box 3A
Sparrow Bush, NY 12780

Soda

Periodical

Newsletter: Nagy's International Hutchinson Newsletter
3540 Northwest 23rd St.
Oklahoma City, OK 73107 *

Special Ed.

Dealer

Heartland of Kentucky Specialties
P.O. Box 428
Lebanon Jct., KY 40105
Phone: 502-833-2827
Hundreds of whiskey decanters by Jim Beam, Wild turkey, Ski Country, McCormick and others; also beer steins, neon lights, mirrors, clocks.

Special Ed. (Beam)

Club/Association

Cape Codders Jim Beam Bottle & Specialty Club
Angelo J. Triantafellow
80 Lincoln Road
Rockland, MA 02370

Club/Association

Space Coast Jim Beam Bottle & Specialties Club
Fred H. Horn, Pres.
2280 Cox Road
Cocoa, FL 32926

Club/Association

Music City Beam Bottle Club
George Gebhardt
2008 June Drive
Nashville, TN 37214
*A district chapter of the International Association Of Jim Beam Bottle & Specialties Club. *

Club/Association

International Association of Jim Beam Bottle & Specialties Club
Newsletter: Beam Around the World
Shirley Sumbles, Sec.
5013 Chase Ave.
Downers Grove, IL 60515
Phone: 708-963-8980

Special Ed. (Ezra Brooks)

Club/Association

National Ezra Brooks Bottle & Specialties Club
Newsletter: NEBBSC Newsletter
420 West 1st Street
Kewanee, IL 61443 *

Special Ed. (Hoffman)

Club/Association

Hoffman National Collectors Club
P.O. Box 37341
Cincinnati, OH 45222 *

Special Ed. (Michter)

Club/Association

Michter's International Collectors Society
Newsletter: Michter's Collector, The
P.O. Box 481
Schaefferstown, PA 17088
*A company-produced newsletter of interest to collectors of Michter bottles. *

Special Ed. (Mt. Hope)

Club/Association

Mount Hope Collectors Society
P.O. Box 8
Cornwall, PA 17016 *

Special Ed. (Ski Country)

Club/Association

National Ski Country Bottle Club
Newsletter: Ski Country Collector, The
1224 Washington Ave.
Golden, CO 80401
Phone: 303-279-3373 or 800-792-6452
Designed as a source of information on collectors decanters, old and new; newsletter features articles about a broad range of decanters.

BOXES

(see also BATTERSEA ENAMEL BOXES; CHEESE BOXES; CIGAR BANDS, BOXES & LABELS; ORIENTALIA; RUSSIAN ITEMS; STAMP BOXES)

Collector

Betty Bird
107 Ida St.
Mount Shasta, CA 96067
Phone: 916-926-4331
Wants any type of figural or unusual boxes and containers: enamels, glass, porcelain, metal; also small scent containers.

Plastic

Collector

A. Behrendt
10100 Cambridge
Westchester, IL 60154
Phone: 708-345-8593
Collects decorative celluloid glove, collar, trinket, dresser set boxes and celluloid autograph albums; must be in mint condition.

Seed

Collector

Lynn Anderson
15500 S.E. Royer Rd.
Clackmas, OR 97015
Wants seed boxes; must have colorful paper labels on the inside.

Trinket

Expert
Melvin & Barb Alpern
14 Carter Rd.
West Orange, NJ 07052
Phone: 201-731-9427 *

BOY SCOUT MEMORABILIA

(see also GIRL SCOUT MEMORABILIA)

Club/Association
International Badgers Club
Magazine: Badgers Club Magazine
Robert Hass
7760 NW 50th St.
Lauder Hill, FL 33351
Phone: 305-741-5835
Members interested in collecting Scout and Guide badges of the entire world.

Club/Association
National Scouting Collectors Society
Newsletter: Scouting Collectors Quarterly
806 E. Scott St.
Tuscola, IL 61953 *

Club/Association
Southern California Association of
Traders
Jean S. Amster
5521 Saloma Avenue
Van Nuys, CA 91411 *

Club/Association
American Scouting Traders Association,
Inc.
Newsletter: American STAR, The
Dave Minnihan, Pres.
P.O. Box 92
Kentfield, CA 94914-0092
Phone: 415-665-2871
ASTA members share an interest in the collecting and trading of Scouting memorabilia; for Scouts and Scouters only.

Collector
Bruce White
3 Woodfern Ave.
Trenton, NJ 08628
Phone: 609-882-5584
Wants Boy Scouts of America patches, pins, literature, WWW items, jamboree, etc.

Collector
Fran & Carl Holden
257 Church St.
Doylestown, OH 44230
Phone: 216-658-2793
Wants old or unusual pins, badges, medals, O/A, Jamboree, Senior Scouts; also uniforms, games, official literature, postcards, etc.

Collector
John Blair
3215 Moyer Dr.
Franklin, OH 45005
Phone: 513-746-1963
Wants Boy Scout memorabilia.

Collector
Larry Ruehlen
22005 Raymond
Saint Clair Shores, MI 48082
Phone: 313-296-6447
Wants Boy Scout merit badges, patches, all square scout badges, uniforms, sashes, medals, ranks, books, Air Scout, etc.

Collector
Doug Bearce
Box 4742
Salem, OR 97302
Phone: 503-399-9872
Wants Boy Scout items: books, uniforms, patches, pins, OA items, Jamboree, etc.

Dealer
Scout Collectors Shop
James W. Clough
7763 Elmwood Drive
South Glen Falls, NY 12801
Phone: 518-793-4029
Wants Boy Scout items.

Expert
Jim & Bea Stevenson
316 Sage Lane
Euless, TX 76039
Phone: 817-354-8903
Wants Boy Scout handbooks, paper items, Jamboree items, uniforms, insignia, Sea Scouts, Skippers, Order of the Arrow, etc.

Museum/Library
Lawrence L. Lee Scout Museum & Max
Silber Scouting Library
Magazine: Scout Memorabilia
Dr. Edward Rowan, Ed.
P.O. Box 1121
Manchester, NH 03105
Phone: 603-627-1492 or 603-669-8919
FAX: 603-625-2467
Home to one of the finest collections of Boy Scout memorabilia; "Scout Memorabilia" has insert listing sales, auctions, ads, etc.

Museum/Library
Murray State University National Museum
of the Boy Scouts of America
Murray, KY 42071
Phone: 502-762-3383

Museum/Library
Zitelman Scout Museum
Mrs. Ralph Zitelman
708 Seminary St.
Rockford, IL 61104
Phone: 815-962-3999
Worldwide Scouting: patches, books, uniforms & equipment including Boy and Girl Scouts, Brownies, Explorers, Scoutmasters, etc.

Periodical
Magazine: Scout Collectors' Quarterly
806 E. Scott
Tuscola, IL 61953

Periodical
Magazine: Fleur-de-Lis
Ken Wiltz
126 Seagull Row
Novato, CA 94945-4515
An international scouting memorabilia magazine.

BRASS ITEMS

(see also BELLS; CANDLEHOLDERS;
GARDEN HOSE NOZZLES;
INSTRUMENTS & DEVICES; LAMPS &
LIGHTING; MEDICAL, DENTAL &
PHARMACEUTICAL)

Expert
Mary Gaston
Box 342
Bryan, TX 77806 *

Repair Service
Brass & Copper Polishing Shop
Don Reedy
13 South Carroll St.
Frederick, MD 21701
Phone: 301-663-4240 or 301-662-5503
Repairs and polishes brass and copper items.

Repro. Source
Virginia Metalcrafters
1010 East Main St.
Waynesboro, VA 22980
Makes and sells andirons, fireplace tools and fenders, fire marks, chandeliers, candlesticks, sconces, etc.

BREWERIANA

(see also ADVERTISING COLLECTIBLES;
BEER CANS; BOTTLES; PROHIBITION
ITEMS; SALOON COLLECTIBLES;
STEINS)

Auction Service
Lynn Geyer Auctions
Lynn Geyer
329 West Butler Dr.
Phoenix, AZ 85021
Phone: 602-943-2283

Conducts annual specialized auction on all aspects of breweriana and soda-pop; also contemporary steins, mugs & drinking glasses.

Club/Association

East Coast Breweriana Association
Newsletter: <u>ECBA Newsletter</u>
Gene Fink
2010 N. Broad St.
Lansdale, PA 19446

Club/Association

American Breweriana Association, Inc.
Journal: <u>American Breweriana Journal</u>
Christine Galloway, ExDir
P.O. Box 11157
Pueblo, CO 81001
Phone: 719-544-9267
For ordinary people with an extraordinary love for beer, brewing, brewing history and breweriana; exchange services, library, etc.

Collector

Ron Leese
R.D. 7 Box 393
Hanover, PA 17331
Phone: 717-637-1983 *

Collector

Bill Weaver
P.O. Box 1061
Grand Rapids, MI 49501
Phone: 616-454-6037
*Drewrys beer glasses, pitchers, signs and any memorabilia. **

Collector

Steve Ketcham
Box 24114
Edina, MN 55424
Phone: 612-920-4205
Wants pre-prohibition brewery memorabilia: calendar, publications, brewery signs, trays, glasses, posters, pocket mirrors, steins, etc.

Dealer

Bob Miller
386 Pennsylvania Ave.
Mineola, NY 11501
Phone: 516-741-5679
Wants old beer advertising items such as match safes, corkscrews, unusual bottle openers, paperweights, signs, etched glassware, etc.

Dealer

Binau's Breweriana & Collectibles
Alvin Binau
121 Gaywood Dr.
Hagerstown, MD 21740
Phone: 301-733-2010
Wants cans, glasses, mugs, lights, signs; old and new.

Advertising

Club/Association

National Association of Breweriana
Advertising
Newsletter: <u>Breweriana Collector</u>
Roger E. Jaeger
2343 Mat-Tu-Wee Lane
Wauwatosa, WI 53226
Phone: 414-257-0158
Focuses on anything with the word "Beer" or "Brewery" on it.

Collector

Roger E. Jaeger
2343 Mat-Tu-Wee Lane
Wauwatosa, WI 53226
Phone: 414-257-0158
Wants any advertising item with the word "Beer" or "Brewery" on it.

Dealer

David Donovan
2900 Cedarcrest Ave.
Baltimore, MD 21219
Phone: 301-388-1228
*Wants all types of brewery advertising items. **

Expert

Owen's Collectibles
Lowell Owens
12 Bonnie Ave.
New Hartford, NY 13413
*Wants items advertising beer brands or breweries. **

Dixie Beer Items

Collector

Jim Haag
3449 Tisdale Ct.
Lexington, KY 40503
Phone: 606-223-5288
*Wants Dixie Beer items from Lexington. **

Hamm's Beer

Collector

Pete Nowicki
1531 39th Ave.
San Francisco, CA 94122
Phone: 415-566-7506
Collector desires to obtain older Hamm's Beer advertising: glasses, signs, neons, etc.; the older the better.

Historian

Expert

Tycho's Nose Antiques
James D. Robertson
57 Heights Terrace
Fair Haven, NJ 07704
Phone: 908-741-7770 or 908-747-3251
Wine and beer historian and collector interested in breweriana.

BRICKS

Club/Association

International Brick Collectors
Association
Journal: <u>International Brick Collectors
Association Journal</u>
8357 Somerset Dr.
Prairie Village, KS 66207
Phone: 913-341-8842

Museum/Library

Museum of Ancient Brick, The
General Shale Corp.
3211 North Roan Street
Johnson City, TN 37601
Phone: 615-282-4661

BRIDAL COLLECTIBLES

Periodical

Newsletter: <u>Bridal Collector's Roster</u>
Ann C. Bergin
P.O. Box 105
Amherst, NH 03031
Phone: 603-673-1885
Wants wedding and bride related pictorial books, dolls, music boxes, etc.; also first communions, Christenings, "rites" of passage.

BROMO-SELTZER ITEMS

Collector

Ludwig
606 Worcester Rd.
Towson, MD 21204
Phone: 301-821-1281
*Emerson Drug Co., Baltimore. MD items - Bromo, Ginger-Mint Julep/Gum, Aperio Laxative, etc. **

BRONZES

(see also ART; ORIENTALIA)

Dealer

Steve Newman Fine Arts
201 Summer St.
Stamford, CT 06905
Phone: 203-323-7799
*Wants American, Deco, Nouveau, Animalier, Impressionistic. **

Expert

Van Cline & Davenport, Ltd.
Stephen Van Cline, CAPP
792 Franklin Ave.
Franklin Lakes, NJ 07417
Phone: 201-891-4588   FAX: 201-891-2824
Specializes in paintings, watercolors, drawings, bronze & marble sculpture; appraisals, authentication, lectures, expert testimony.

Repro. Source

Juratone London, Inc.
High Gorses, Henley Down
Battle
East Sussex TN33 9BP England
Makers of reproduction Art Deco bronzes and scrimshaw "ivory" (whales' teeth, elephant tusks, tortoise shells, etc.) *

Repro. Source

Jim Solk Co., Inc.
3770 Selby Ave.
P.O. Box 34092
Los Angeles, CA 90034
Phone: 213-559-1800 or 800-835-3600
                FAX: 213-559-1856
Extensive selection of reproduction bronzes after famous artists.

Repro. Source

EMI, Inc.
Dru McBride
401 E. Cypress
Visalia, CA 93277
Phone: 209-732-8126   FAX: 209-732-5961
Buy foundry direct bronze sculptures by Remington, Russell, Mene, Bonhuer; over 200 pieces; color catalog available for $10.

Oriental

Repro. Source

Eisler Porcelain
Luanne R. Eisler
RD #3, Box 200R
Slippery Rock, PA 16057
Phone: 412-794-5004
Importer/wholesaler of reproduction Oriental bronzes, cast by the lost wax method; originals date from Ming Dynasty.

Remington

Repro. Source

Ben Shaool Wholesale
Ben Shaool
28 S. Potomac St.
Hagerstown, MD 21740
Phone: 301-797-5800
Importer of Oriental ivory, porcelain, reverse paintings, rugs; also Remington recast bronzes, clocks, lacquered furniture.

Repro. Source

Manny's Oriental Rugs
Manny Shaool
72 W. Washington St.
Hagerstown, MD 21740
Phone: 301-797-7434
Importer of Oriental ivory, porcelain, reverse paintings, rugs; also Remington recast bronzes, clocks, lacquered furniture.

Repro. Source

Henry Bonnard Bronze Co. & Associates
4305 S. Highway 17-92
Casselberry, FL 32707
Phone: 407-339-9103 or 800-521-3179
Offers large selection of Frederic Remington bronzes; call or write for color catalog.

Repro. Source

Plaza Art & Bronze Gallery
658 Central Ave.
St. Petersburg, FL 33701
Phone: 813-898-1965
Sells recast Remington bronzes; $599 while they last. *

BROWNIES BY PALMER COX

Collector

Norm & Judy Sherbert
3805 S. Valley Dr.
Evergreen, CO 80439 *

Expert

Faye Pisello
577 Lake St.
Wilson, NY 14172 *

BUBBLE GUM & CANDY WRAPPERS

(see also CANDY BARS; TRADING CARDS, Non-Sport)

Club/Association

Bubble Gum & Candy Wrapper Collectors
Newsletter: Wrapper, The
P.O. Box 573
St. Charles, IL 60174
Phone: 708-377-7921
Focuses on non-sports cards, wrappers and related items.

BUBBLE GUM CARDS

(see also TRADING CARDS, Non-Sport)

Collector

Mark Angert
Suite 206
2121 E. Commercial Blvd.
Ft. Lauderdale, FL 33308
Phone: 305-920-5102
Wants gum, candy, tobacco, trade & premium cards: baseball, war, Superman, comic character, Indian, airplane, Lone Ranger, space, etc.

Garbage Pail Kids

Collector

Doug Bramlett
213 Belvin St.
Darlington, SC 29532-2105
Phone: 803-393-7390
Wants Garbage Pail Kids gum cards; especially interested in cards from the first and second series.
*

BUCKLES

(see also BELT BUCKLES)

BUMPER STICKERS

Radio Station

Collector

Doreen Lynn Olson
28 Drewberry Lane
Duluth, MN 55810-1913
Phone: 218-628-3462
Collector/trader of bumper stickers from AM/FM radio stations in the USA, Canada and Mexico; will trade other promo items for stickers.

BURGER-SHAPED COLLECTIBLES

Collector

Harry Speir
1360 N. Nova Rd.
Daytona Beach, FL 32117
Phone: 904-254-8753   FAX: 904-255-2460
Wants burgers and burger-related items: candles, banks, toys, anything!

BURMA SHAVE COLLECTIBLES

Collector

Steve Soelberg
29126 Laro Dr.
Agoura Hills, CA 91301
Phone: 818-889-9909

BUS LINE COLLECTIBLES

(see also TRANSPORTATION COLLECTIBLES)

BUSES

Club/Association

Bus History Association
Magazine: Bus Industry Magazine
Bernard Drovillard
965 McEwan
Windsor
Ontario N9B 2G1 Canada
Phone: 519-977-0664
Founded to preserve and record data, information and other materials related to the bus industry in North America and worldwide.

Club/Association

International Bus Collectors Club
Newsletter: IBCC Newsletter
Robert B. Redden, Sr.
1518 "C" Trailee Drive
Charleston, SC 29407
Phone: 803-571-2489
The definitive bus club in the U.S.; work as consultants to the movie industry and media; produces the only American line of bus models.

BUSINESS CARDS

Club/Association

Business Card Collectors International
Newsletter: My Card
P.O. Box 466
Hollywood, FL 33022
Phone: 305-920-8256 *

Club/Association

American Business Card Club
Newsletter: Card Talk
Avery N. Pitzak
P.O. Box 460297
Aurora, CO 80046-0297
Phone: 303-690-6496
The American Business Card Club is a unique resource for business people and collectors alike.

Expert

Avery N. Pitzak
P.O. Box 460297
Aurora, CO 80046-0297
Phone: 303-690-6496
Author of "The Definitive Book on Business Cards."

Famous Personalities

Club/Association

Famous Personalities' Business Card
Collectors of America
Newsletter: FPBCCA Newsletter
P.O. Box 8028
Ann Arbor, MI 48107 *

BUTTER MOLDS

(see also KITCHEN COLLECTIBLES, Molds
(Butter))

BUTTONHOOKS

Club/Association

Buttonhook Society, The
Newsletter: Boutonneur, The
2 Romney Place
Maidstone
Kent ME15 6LE England
To promote interest and research in the history, origins, uses and the collecting of buttonhooks; newsletters, exhibitions.

Collector

Paul Moorehead
2 Romney Place
Maidstone
Kent ME15 6LE England
Seeks unusual buttonhooks singles or in sets.

Collector

Richard Mathes
P.O. Box 1408
Springfield, OH 45501
Wants all types of buttonhooks to add to substantial collection; boot/shoe hooks, glove hooks, loop buttoners, or collar buttoners.

BUTTONS

Club/Association

National Button Society
Newsletter: National Button Bulletin
Lois Pool, Sec.
2733 Juno Place
Akron, OH 44333-4137
Phone: 216-864-3296
A non-profit organization devoted to the hobby of button collecting; newsletter printed five times a year.

Collector

A. Barth
1120 Laurelwood Dr.
McLean, VA 22102
Phone: 703-734-0306
Wants fine quality 19th century buttons of all materials and sizes. *

Dealer

Newsletter: Olympic Collectors Newsletter,
The
Bill Nelson
P.O. Box 41630
Tucson, AZ 85717-1630
Phone: 602-629-0860 or 602-629-0387
Monthly newsletter with news, tips, and sources; for collectors of Olympic, Sports, Disney, Coca Cola pins; large selection in stock.

Dealer

Foxes' Den Antiques
Georgia Fox
P.O. Box 846
Sutter Creek, CA 95685
Phone: 209-267-0774
Wants antique clothing buttons: porcelain, metal, gilt and Satsuma buttons with pictures, fables, buildings, and heads of famous people.

Expert

Lois Pool
2733 Juno Place
Akron, OH 44313
Phone: 216-535-9186 *

Museum/Library

Waterbury Company Button Museum
32 Mattatuck Heights
Waterbury, CN 06705
Phone: 203-597-1812

Museum/Library

Judith Basin Museum
P.O. Box 299
Stanford, MT 59479
Phone: 406-566-2572
50,000 item button collection.

Museum/Library

Gay Nineties Button & Doll Museum
Rte. 4, Box 420
Eureka Springs, AR 72632
Phone: 501-253-9321

Periodical

Newsletter: Creative Button Bulletin
26 Meadowbrook Lane
Chalfont, PA 18914
For collectors of modern or old buttons. *

Military

Collector

Daniel J. Binder
927 20th St.
Rockford, IL 61104-3508
Phone: 815-226-9056 or 815-877-3041
Wants 1812-1865 U.S. military buttons, especially Confederate States, Southern State seals, and Southern military school buttons.

Pinback

(see also PINS; POLITICAL
COLLECTIBLES)

Collector

Bob Cereghino
Suite 170A-319
6400 Baltimore National Pike
Baltimore, MD 21228
Phone: 301-766-7593
Wants advertising, entertainment and political pinback buttons.

Pinback (Advertising)

Dealer

Dave Beck
P.O. Box 435
Mediappolis, IA 52637
Phone: 319-394-3943
Buys and sells advertising watch fobs, mirrors and pinbacks; send stamp for illustrated mail auction catalog.

Railroad/Transit Uniform

Expert

Donald P. Van Court
41 Hillcrest Road
Madison, NJ 07940-2559
Phone: 201-377-2676
Author of "Transportation Uniform Buttons"; the monograms, sets of initials, and "trademarks" that appear on railroad uniform buttons.

CABINET CARDS

(see also PHOTOGRAPHS)

CALCULATORS

(see also ADDING MACHINES;
TYPEWRITERS)

Expert

Darryl Rehr
11433 Rochester Ave. #303
Los Angeles, CA 90025
Phone: 213-447-5229

Wants early calculators (they subtract, multiply, divide and add) such as the "Comptometer", "Curta", and "Milionaire."

CALENDAR PLATES

Collector
Jane M. Cummings
37943 Wright St.
Willoughby, OH 44094
Phone: 216-949-2174
Wants any '20's, '30's & '40's or earlier calendar plates, especially the unusual or pre-1906.

CALENDARS
(see also PAPER COLLECTIBLES)

Periodical
Magazine: Paper Collectors' Marketplace
Doug Watson
P.O. Box 12899
Scandinavia, WI 54977
Phone: 715-467-2379
Monthly magazine for collectors of autographs, paperbacks, postcards, advertising, photographica, magazines; all types of paper

CALIFORNIA PERFUME COMPANY
(see also AVON COLLECTIBLES)

Collector
Patrick Brady
210 Fulton St.
Elmira, NY 14904
Phone: 607-732-2894
Wants CPC paper, tins, bottles, anything.

Expert
Dick Pardini
3107 N. El Dorado St.
Stockton, CA 95204
Phone: 209-466-5550
Wants certain CPC items (1886 to 1929); no AVON; will help with CPC prices and identification; enclose LSASE for information.

CALLIGRAPHY

Club/Association
Society for Calligraphy
Newsletter: Bulletin
P.O. Box 64174
Los Angeles, CA 90064
Phone: 213-380-6975
Interested in the collecting and studying of penmanship samples; also in calligraphy. *

CALLING CARDS
(see also BUSINESS CARDS)

CAMERAS & CAMERA EQUIPMENT
(see also 3-D PHOTOGRAPHICA; PHOTOGRAPHS; PHOTOGRAPHY; STEREO VIEWERS & STEREOGRAPHS)

Auction Service
Christie's South Kensington, Ltd.
Michael Pritchard
85 Old Brompton Road
London SW7 3LD England
An international auction house specializing in the sale of rare and collectible cameras, photographic equipment and optical toys.

Club/Association
Photographic Collectors Club of Great Britain
Magazine: Photographica World
Michael Pritchard, Ed.
5 Station Industrial Estate
Prudhoe
Northumberland NE42 6NP Eng.
Club aims to promote the study and collection of photographic equipment and images by publications, meetings, auctions and shows.

Club/Association
American Society of Camera Collectors
4918 Alcove Ave.
North Hollywood, CA 91607
Phone: 818-769-6160
An educational society dedicated to the restoration and preservation of all types of photographica.

Collector
Pearl Dearkin
P.O. Box 2405
Morristown, NJ 07960
Wants old, odd, very large or very small cameras; or with three of more lenses; no Kodaks or Polaroids; also camera books and catalogs. *

Collector
Levin
7440 East Prairie Rd.
Skokie, IL 60076
Phone: 312-675-7440
Wants modern and antique cameras, lenses, accessories, stereo cameras and viewers. *

Dealer
John S. Craig
P.O. Box 1637
Torrington, CT 06790
Phone: 203-496-9791
Buys and sells antique and collectible photographica: cameras, daguerrotypes, stereos, literature.

Dealer
Kaleido-Cam
William P. Carroll
8500 La Entrada
Whittier, CA 90605
Phone: 213-693-8421   FAX: 213-947-8499

Antique and classic cameras for sale; also repairs; offers new and used books on kaleidoscopes, cameras and the history of

Periodical
Camerashopper
Magazine: Camera Shopper Magazine
1 Magnolia Hill
West Hartford, CT 06117-2022
Phone: 203-233-9922   FAX: 203-233-5122
Buy, sell, trade magazine for used, classic and antique photographica including vintage photographs.

Periodical
Magazine: Shutterbug
Box F
Titusville, FL 32781
Phone: 407-268-5010   FAX: 407-267-7216
Geared to the advanced to professional photographer; articles about new/old equip. & access., collectibles and new products; many ads.

Repair Service
Cameratek
Cliff Ratcliff
1780 N. Market St.
Frederick, MD 21701
Phone: 301-695-9733
Professional repair service; also buy, sell, trade, used cameras.

Kodak

Club/Association
International Kodak Historical Society
P.O. Box 21
Flourtown, PA 19301 *

Leica

Club/Association
Leica Historical Society of America
2314 W. 53rd St.
Minneapolis, MN 55410 *

Nikon

Club/Association
Nikon Historical Society
Magazine: Nikon Journal, The
Robert J. Rotoloni
P.O. Box 3213
Munster, IN 46321
Phone: 708-895-5319   FAX: 708-868-2352
Focuses on the history of Nikon cameras; magazine contains articles and ads for the Nikon collector.

Expert
Robert J. Rotoloni
P.O. Box 3213
Munster, IN 46321
Phone: 708-895-5319   FAX: 708-868-2352
Author of "The Nikon..An Illustrated History of the Nikon Camera", founder of the Nikon Historical Society.

Subminiature

Collector
Bob Johnson
P.O. Box 71687
Marietta, GA 30007-1687
Serious collector of very small (subminiature) cameras including those built into binoculars, lighters, radios, rings, pencils, etc.

Zeiss

Club/Association
Zeiss Historical Society
P.O. Box 631
Clifton, NJ 07012
Dedicated to the study & exchange of information on the history of Carl Zeiss Optical Co., its people and products from 1846 to present.

CAMPBELL SOUP COLLECTIBLES

Collector
Dorothy Ference
124 College Hwy.
Southwick, MA 01077
Phone: 413-569-3215
Buys, sells, trades Campbell soup premiums, games, playing cards, etc.; anything related to Campbell soup.

Collector
Newsletter: Kids Illustrated Drayton
   Supplement (K.I.D.S.)
G.L. Wine
649 Bayview Drive
Akron, OH 44319-1502
Newsletter for collectors of Campbell Kid Dolls and related items; also memorabilia about the Kids' creator, Grace G. Drayton & her art.

Museum/Library
Campbell Museum
Campbell Place
Camden, NJ 08101
Phone: 609-342-6440
Large collection of soup tureens, ladles, spoons and soup dishes made of porcelain, china, earthenware, silver, and pewter.

CAN OPENERS

Collector
Richard M. Bueschel
414 N. Prospect Manore Ave.
Mt. Prospect, IL 60056
Phone: 708-253-0791
Wants cast iron can openers that cut metal, c. 1850-1930; any size, shape or form; also images, photos, advertising of openers in use.

Collector
John Young
Box 587
Elgin, IL 60121
Phone: 312-695-8635
*Interested in tin can openers. **

CANAL COLLECTIBLES

Club/Association
American Canal Society, Inc.
Newsletter: American Canals
Charles W. Derr, Sec.
117 Main St.
Freemansburg, PA 18017
Focuses on the preservation, restoration, interpretation and use of the historic navigational canals of the Americas.

Club/Association
Pennsylvania Canal Society Canal Museum
Newsletter: Canal Currents
P.O. Box 877
Easton, PA 18042 *

CUB/Association
Canal Society of Ohio
Newsletter: Towpaths
550 Copley Road
Akron, OH 44320
*Focuses on the Miami and Erie and the Ohio and Erie canals. **

Collector
Harry L. Rinker
P.O. Box 248
Zionsville, PA 18092
Phone: 215-965-1122 or 215-966-5544
                FAX: 215-965-1124
Seeks artifacts, books, paper ephemera and commemorative objects associated with America's mule-drawn canal era.

Museum/Library
Erie Canal Museum
318 Erie Blvd.
Syracuse, NY 13202
Phone: 315-471-0593

Museum/Library
Canal Society of New York State, Inc.
311 Montgomery St.
Syracuse, NY 13202
Phone: 315-428-1862

Museum/Library
Canal Museum & Hugh Moore Park
P.O. Box 877
Easton, PA 18044-0877
Phone: 215-250-6700

Museum/Library
Illinois & Michigan Canal Museum
803 S. State St.
Lockport, IL 60441
Phone: 815-838-5080

CANCELLATIONS

Postal
(see also STAMP COLLECTING, Postmarks)

CANDLEHOLDERS

Dealer
Phyllis Van Aufeen
10425 Fawcett St.
Kensington, MD 20895
Phone: 301-933-3772
Specializes in antique brass candleholders; English, American, Continental.

Museum/Library
Frick Art Museum, The
P.O. Box 86190
Pittsburgh, PA 15221
Phone: 412-371-0600

CANDY BARS
(see also BUBBLE GUM & CANDY WRAPPERS)

Club/Association
Great American Candy Bar Club
Newsletter: Candy Bar Gazebo
Six Edge Street
Ipswich, MA 01938 *

CANDY CONTAINERS
(see also PEZ CONTAINERS)

Club/Association
Candy Container Collectors of America
Newsletter: Candy Gram, The
Douglas Dezso
864 Paterson Ave.
Maywood, NJ 07607
Phone: 201-845-7707

Collector
Sacks Appeal
Ross Hartsough
98 Bryn Mar Rd.
Winnipeg
Manitoba R3T 3P5 Canada
Phone: 204-269-1022
Wants glass and plastic figural candy containers, especially PEZ containers.

Collector
Douglas Dezco
864 Paterson Ave.
Maywood, NJ 07607
Phone: 201-845-7707 *

Collector
Jeff Bradfield
745 Hillview Dr.
Dayton, VA 22821
Phone: 703-879-9961
Wants rare or unusual candy containers especially with good paint.

Dealer

Childhood Memories, Inc.
Vincent G. Krug
P.O. Box 96
Ashford, CT 06278
Phone: 203-429-8876
Wants uncommon glass, tin, and papier-mache candy containers.

Museum/Library

Cambridge Glass Museum, The
812 Jefferson Ave.
Cambridge, OH 43725
Phone: 614-432-3045
Over 5000 pieces of Cambridge glass on display; also 100 pieces of Cambridge Art Pottery; private museum.

CANES & WALKING STICKS

(see also UMBRELLAS)

Club/Association

Placibo Press
Newsletter: Walking Stick News
Suite 231
4051 East Olive Rd.
Pensacola, FL 32514
Phone: 904-477-3995
Focuses on walking sticks and related items for stick makers, dealers, users, collectors and rhabdophiles.

Collector

Frances Monek
950 E. Westminster
Lake Forest, IL 60045 *

Collector

Larry Love
4125 Sperry
Dallas, TX 75214
Phone: 214-821-1688
*Wants items advertising barb wire, gates and other fence related items: e.g. walking canes, salesman samples, patent models, etc. *

Collector

Scher
1637 Market St.
San Francisco, CA 94103-1217
Phone: 415-863-4344
Wants dual purpose, container, weapon, gadget, fancy carved ivory, gold or silver canes.

Expert

Whitehall Shop
David P. Lindquist
1215 E. Franklin Street
Chapel Hill, NC 27514
Phone: 919-942-3179

Expert

Catherine Dike
4121 Forest Park
St. Louis, MO 63108

Museum/Library

Essex Institute
132 Essex St.
Salem, MA 01970
Phone: 617-744-3390

Museum/Library

Remington Gun Museum
P.O. Box 179
Ilion, NY 13357
Phone: 315-894-9961
Affiliated with the Remington Arms Company, Inc.

Museum/Library

Valley Forge Historical Society, The
P.O. Box 122
Valley Forge, PA 19481
Phone: 215-783-0535

Repair Service

Uncle Sam Umbrella Shop
161 West 57th St.
New York, NT 10019
Phone: 212-582-1977
Repairs canes and umbrellas.

CANNING JARS

(see also BOTTLES; FRUIT JARS; JELLY CONTAINERS)

CANNONS

(see also MILITARIA)

Club/Association

Cannon Hunters Association of Seattle
Newsletter: CHAOS
13547 Linden Ave. N.
Seattle, WA 98133
Phone: 206-362-2425 *

Collector

Chuck Kratz
17821 Golfview
Homewood, IL 60430
Phone: 708-799-8478
Wants old muzzle loading cannons in any condition; also wooden artillery carriages and ammunition chests.

CANS

(see also BEER CANS; BREWERIANA; OYSTER RELATED COLLECTIBLES; SOFT-DRINK COLLECTIBLES, Soft Drink Cans)

CANTON

(see also CERAMICS (ORIENTAL), Chinese Export Porcelain)

CAP GUNS

(see also TOYS, Cap Pistols)

CAPS

Club/Association

National Cap & Patch Association
Newsletter: NCPA Newsletter
Rt. 1 P.O. Box 164
Deer Park, WI 54007
Phone: 715-269-5411 *

CARDS

(see also SPORTS COLLECTIBLES; TRADING CARDS, Non-Sport)

CARNEGIE HALL ITEMS

Collector

Carnegie Hall Corporation
Gino Francesconi
881 Seventh Ave.
New York, NY 10019
Phone: 212-903-9629
Wants house programs, stagebills, photographs of building, posters of events, other early memorabilia.

CAROUSELS & CAROUSEL FIGURES

(see also FOLK ART)

Auction Service

Guernsey's Auction
108 1/2 East 73rd St.
New York, NY 10021
Phone: 212-794-2280   FAX: 212-744-3638
Specializes in the sale of carousel figures.

Auction Service

Auction Under the Big Top
Tommy Sciortino
3723 N. Nebraska Aave.
Tampa, FL 33603
Phone: 818-248-5387 or 813-932-1782
                    FAX: 813-248-5387
Specializes in the sale of circus equipment and memorabilia, carousels, amusement devices, coin-ops, toys, etc.

Club/Association

American Carousel Society
Newsletter: American Carousel Society Newsletter
Robin Frielich
60 East 8th St. #12K
New York, NY 10003
The goal of the ACS is to preserve the carousel art, both the individual figures or the complete carousel.

Club/Association

National Carousel Association
Newsletter: Merry-Go-Roundup
J. Blake, ExSec.
P.O. Box 4333
Evansville, IN 47724-0333
Primary goal is to protect existing operating carousels.

Collector
Dave Boyle
36 Andrews Trace
New Castle, PA 16102
Phone: 412-656-8181 *

Dealer
Rader's Horse House
Phil & Molly Rader
2277 Ogden Rd.
Wilmington, OH 45177
Phone: 513-382-3266 or 513-865-4498
Buys, sells and trades carousel horses; also creates original carousel and equestrian paintings, prints and T-shirt apparel.

Dealer
Class Menagerie
55 Windsor Terrace
Yonkers, NY 10703
Phone: 914-423-8477 *

Dealer
Musical Mounts & Arts, Inc.
Box 83
Phillipsburg, OH 45354
Phone: 513-884-7051 *

Dealer
Merry-Go-Art
Don Snider
2606 Jefferson
Joplin, MO 64804
Phone: 417-624-7281
Buys and sells carousel figures.

Dealer
Pegi O. Sanders
5802 E. Shea Blvd.
Scottsdale, AZ 85254
Phone: 602-948-3268 *

Dealer
Wooden Horse, The
920 West Mescalero Road
Roswell, NM 88201
Phone: 505-622-7397 *

Dealer
Daniel's Den
720 Mission St.
South Pasadena, CA 91030
Phone: 213-682-3557 *

Dealer
Flying Tails
John & June Reely
1209 Indiana Ave.
South Pasadena, CA 91030
Phone: 213-256-8657
Send SASE for supply catalog: hair tails and stands, etc.

Expert
William Manns
P.O. Box 47
Millwood, NY 10546
Phone: 914-245-2926   FAX: 914-962-1945
Author of "Painted Ponies, American Carousel Art." Send photo and request for information about your carving and its authenticity.

Expert
Carousel Corner
Jon & Barbara Abbott
Box 420
Clarkston, MI 48016
Phone: 313-625-1233
Collector, dealer, appraiser of carousel horses for many years. *

Museum/Library
Heritage Plantation of Sandwich
P.O. Box 566
Sandwich, MA 02563
Phone: 617-888-3300

Museum/Library
New England Carousel Museum, Inc.
Arthur Caffee
95 Riverside Ave.
Bristol, CT 06010
Phone: 203-585-5411

Museum/Library
Herschell Carrousel Factory Museum
180 Thompson St.
P.O. Box 672
North Tonawanda, NY 14120-0672
Phone: 716-693-1885
Allen Herschell carousel, c. 1916, and original Allan Herschell factory site; exhibits, gift shop, carving demonstrations.

Museum/Library
Merry-Go-Round Museum
Howard E. Guenther, Dir.
P.O. Box 718
Sandusky, OH 44870
Phone: 419-626-6111 or 419-627-5412
Restoration services for carousel animals & band organs; no charge for restoration to pieces loaned to museum for 3 years.

Museum/Library
Indianapolis Childrens Museum
3010 North Meridian
Indianapolis, IN 46208

Museum/Library
Circus World Museum Library & Research Center
Robert L. Parkinson, Lib.
426 Water St.
Baraboo, WI 53913
Phone: 608-356-8341   FAX: 608-356-1800
Working carousel, Herschell portable, c. 1929.

Museum/Library
Dickinson County Historical Society
P.O. Box 506
Abilene, KS 67410
Phone: 913-263-2681
Has a working carousel - Parker track machine c. 1895.

Museum/Library
Carousel Museum of America
665 Beach Street
San Francisco, CA 94109

Museum/Library
International Museum of Carousel Art
Carol Perron
P.O. Box 14942
Portland, OR 97214
Phone: 503-241-2252
Historical museum dedicated to preserving the carousel.

Periodical
Zon International Publishing
Directory: Carousel Shopper
William Manns
P.O. Box 47
Millwood, NY 10546
Phone: 914-245-2926   FAX: 914-962-1945
A carousel resource directory: suppliers, museums, carousel events, shows, restorers, auctions, reproductions, cards, posters, etc.

Periodical
Magazine: Carousel News & Trader, The
Walter & Nancy Loucks
Suite 206
87 Park Avenue West
Mansfield, OH 44902
Phone: 419-529-4999   FAX: 419-529-2321
Monthly magazine serving the carousel enthusiast since 1985; color photos, ads, stories, auctions, restoring, events, etc.

Periodical
Magazine: Carousel Art Magazine
P.O. Box 992
Garden Grove, CA 92642
For those interested in carousels and related memorabilia; focuses on the restoring, collecting, and displaying of carousel carvings.

Repair Service
R & F Designs, Inc.
William R. Finkenstein
95 Riverside Ave.
Bristol, CT 06010
Phone: 203-585-5411
Considered the best carousel restoration firm, examples: New Orleans, City Park, Derby Ride, Playland, Rye, NY.

Repair Service
Bill Hamlet
614 Polk Street
Raleigh, NC 27604
Restores old carousel figures and carves new figures. *

Repair Service
Rosa P. Ragan
905 W. Johnson
Raleigh, NC 27605 *

Repair Service
Gray Sales, Inc.
P.O. Box 14732
Surfside Beach, SC 29587
Phone: 803-238-0251
Does carousel figure restorations and appraisals. *

Repair Service
Joe Leonard Custom Woodworking
P.O. Box 510
Burton, OH 44021
Restores old carousel figures and carves new figures. *

Repair Service
Floyd Girtz
1500 N. Pecan Avenue
Roswell, NM 88201
Restores old carousel figures and carves new figures. *

Repair Service
Carol Perron
P.O. Box 14942
Portland, OR 97214
Phone: 503-235-2252

Repro. Source
Carvers Inc.
William R. Finkenstein
95 Riverside Ave.
Bristol, CT 06010
Phone: 203-585-5411
Specializing in carving carousel figures in an existing or new design.

Supplier
Sally Craig
336 W. High Street
Elizabeth, PA 17022
Carries hair tails and stirrups. *

Supplier
Brass Ring, The
5746 La Cumbre Road
Somis, CA 93066
Carries custom stands. *

Organs
Club/Association
American Band Organ Association
Fred Dahlinger
1030 Chestnut Blvd.
Chesterton, IN 46304

CARRIAGES
(see also HORSE-DRAWN VEHICLES, Carriages)

CARS
(see also AUTOMOBILES; MODELS, Cars; SPORTS COLLECTIBLES, Auto Racing)

CARTES-DE-VISITES
(see also PHOTOGRAPHS)

CARTOON ART
(see also ANIMATION FILM ART; COMIC BOOKS; COMIC STRIPS, Sunday Newspaper)

Auction Service
Russ Cochran
P.O. Box 469
West Plains, MO 65775
Phone: 417-256-2224
Conducts phone bid auctions of original comic art and illustrations.

Dealer
Cartoon Museum
Jim Ivey
4300 S. Semoran Blvd. #109
Orlando, FL 32822
Phone: 407-273-0141
Buys and sells original cartoon art of all types; also "spin offs": books, collectibles, comic books, magazines, etc.

Dealer
Robert A. LeGresley
P.O. Box 1199
Lawrence, KS 66044
Phone: 913-749-5458 or 913-843-3644
FAX: 913-841-1777
Buys and sells original comic art.

Dealer
Comics Paradise Gallery
P.O. Box 1540
Studio City, CA 91604 *

Dealer
Comic Gallery
4224 Balboa Ave.
San Diego, CA 92117 *

Dealer
Comic Castle
107 W. Amerige
Fullerton, CA 92632 *

Misc. Service
King Features Syndicate
235 E. 45th Street
New York, NY 10017
A major comic strip syndicator. *

Misc. Service
Newspaper Enterprise Association
200 Park Avenue
New York, NY 10166
A major comic strip syndicator. *

Misc. Service
United Feature Syndicate
200 Park Avenue
New York, NY 10166
A major comic strip syndicator. *

Misc. Service
Washington Post Writers Group
1150 15th Street NW
Washington, DC 20071
A major comic strip syndicator. *

Misc. Service
Tribune Media Services
64 E. Concord Street
Orlando, FL 32801
A major comic strip syndicator. *

Misc. Service
Universal Press Syndicate
4900 Main Street, 9th Floor
Kansas City, MO 64112
A major comic strip syndicator. *

Misc. Service
News America Syndicate
1703 Kaiser Avenue
Irvine, CA 92714
A major comic strip syndicator. *

Museum/Library
Museum of Cartoon Art
Comly Ave.
Rye Brook, NY 10573
Phone: 914-939-0234
Acknowledged by most as the premier repository of animation art and history in the U.S.

Walt Kelly
Club/Association
Steve Thompson
6908 Wentworth Ave. South
Richfield, MN 55423
Phone: 612-869-6320
Internationally-known bibliographer and biographer of Walt Kelly and "Pogo"; active collector of unusual and esoteric Kellyana.

CASH REGISTERS

Collector
Gill
Box 3811
Clifton Park, NY 12065
Phone: 518-871-6035
Brass or wood in any condition; also literature, ads, sales brochures.

Collector
Hayne Dominick
2996 Shannon Drive
Oakland, MI 48363
Phone: 313-693-3358
Buying early and unusual cash registers; specializing in National Cash Register, related memorabilia & advertising; sales & repairs.

Expert
John Apple Antiques
John Apple
1720 College Ave.
Racine, WI 53043
Phone: 414-633-3086
*Specializes in brass cash registers and parts. ***

Expert
Play It Again Sam's, Inc.
Sam Robins
5310 W. Devon
Chicago, IL 60646
Phone: 312-763-1771
Buys, sells, trades machines; has extensive register parts inventory; also offers a full restoration service for cash registers.

Expert
Antique Registers
Henry Bartsch
P.O. Box 444
Rockaway Beach, OR 97136
Phone: 503-355-2932
Author of "Antique Cash Registers 1880-1920"; offers antique cash register sales and service.

CASINO COLLECTIBLES
(see also GAMBLING COLLECTIBLES)

CAST IRON ITEMS
(see also BANKS; FIREBACKS; GARDEN FURNITURE; KITCHEN COLLECTIBLES; STOVES; TARGETS; TOYS; WATER SPRINKLERS; WINDMILL COLLECTIBLES, Weights)

Collector
J.M. Ellwood
8220 E. San Miguel
Scottsdale, AZ 85250
Phone: 602-947-6220
Wants trivets, match holders, irons, banks, children's stoves and irons, advertising items, cigar cutters, corkscrews, cap exploders.

Expert
Craig Dinner
P.O. Box 455
Valley Stream, NY 11582
Phone: 516-825-0145
*Wants cast iron doorstops, figural bottle openers, tie backs, figural miniatures, doorknockers, paperweights, etc. ***

Periodical
Newsletter: Cast Iron Cookware News
Steve Stephens
28 Angela Ave.
San Anselmo, CA 94960
Phone: 415-453-7790
A bi-weekly, 6-page illustrated newsletter packed with information focusing on cast iron kitchen cookware (incl. Griswold).

Griswold

Expert
PRS Harned
Denise & Bill Harned
P.O. Box 10373
Elmwood, CT 06110
Authors of "Griswold Cast Collectibles" a history and value guide.

CASTOR SETS

Collector
Bird of Paradise
Juanita Wilkins
430 S. Cole St.
Lima, OH 45805-3367
Wants art glass or colored pattern-glass shakers, cruets, syrup pitchers, and castor sets.

CATALOGS

Mail Order

Dealer
Hesson Country Crafts & Collectables
Judy Hesson
1261 S. Lloyd
Lombard, IL 60148
Phone: 708-627-3298
Buys & sells mail order catalogs: Sears, Montgomery Ward, Penny, Aldens, Spiegel: 1935-1990; also other catalogs; list costs $2.

Medical

Museum/Library
Armed Forces Medical Museum
Michael Rhode
Bldg. 54
Walter Read Medical Center
Washington, DC 20306
Phone: 202-576-2438 or 202-576-0401
FAX: 202-576-2164
Federal government museum archives that collects catalog material related to the history of medicine, especially military medicine.

Trade
(see also ADVERTISING COLLECTIBLES; MACHINERY & EQUIPMENT, Catalogs; MAGAZINES)

Collector
Richard M. Bueschel
414 N. Prospect Manor Ave.
Mt. Prospect, IL 60056
Phone: 708-253-0791
Wants 1850-1950 trade catalogs of amusement rides, coin machines & other products for use in saloons, diners, restaurants, hotels.

Dealer
Steve Finer
P.O. Box 758
Greenfield, MA 01302
Phone: 413-773-5811

Dealer
David Belcher
231 S. Main St.
Orange, MA 01364 *

Dealer
High Ridge Books
P.O. Box 286
Rye, NY 10580 *

Dealer
Riverow Bookshop
John D. Spencer
204 Front St.
Owego, NY 13827 *

Dealer
George Fink
P.O. Box 241
Camden, DE 19934 *

Dealer
Kenneth Schneringer
271 Sabrina Ct.
Woodstock, GA 30188 *

Dealer
Hillcrest
Dick Hyatt
P.O. Box 1143
Wharton, TX 77488 *

Repro. Source
Harold Barker
3108 Klingler Rd.
Ada, OH 45810
Phone: 419-634-7328
Specializes in the sale of high quality photocopies of old catalogs and manuals, especially in the field of woodworking.

Trade (Silver)

Repro. Source

Diane Cramer
P.O. Box 1243
Whittier, CA 90609
Phone: 213-696-6738
Reproductions of 19th cent. American silver, silverplate & jeweler's catalogs, e.g. "1869 Simpson, Hall, Miller", 144 pgs., 11"x17".

CAT COLLECTIBLES

(see also ANIMAL COLLECTIBLES)

Club/Association

Cat Collectors
Newsletter: Cat Talk
Marilyn Dipboye
31311 Blair Drive
Warren, MI 48092
Phone: 313-264-0285
Focuses on all types of cat collectibles; offers catalog of extensive line of new cat collectibles for sale.

Collector

Jackie Durham
P.O. Box 2426
Rockville, MD 20852
Wants Chessie and other cat related items; also wants Lou Wain cat illustrations.

Dealer

Barbara N. Cohen Galleries
Leonard & Barb Cohen
115 E. Main St.
Waterloo, NY 13165-1432
Phone: 315-539-3032 or 315-539-3372
Wants unusual antique cat figurines and figures of all materials; also cat or cat grouping paintings in oil or watercolor.

Expert

Marilyn Dipboye
31311 Blair Drive
Warren, MI 48092
Phone: 313-264-0285
Wants figurines by Royal Doulton or Rosenthal; also Currier & Ives, playing cards, cat sheet music, etc.

Museum/Library

Historic James Russell Webster Mansion Inn
Leonard & Barb Cohen
115 E. Main St.
Waterloo, NY 13165-1432
Phone: 315-539-3032 or 315-539-3372
The only Cat Figurine Museum in the U.S.: over 500 figurines and paintings fro the 18th cent.; tours done on advance notice for $10.

Periodical

Newsletter: Cats Newsletter
Zoe Marchand
1443 Overing St.
Bronx, NY 10461
A small quarterly newsletter for cat lovers: poetry, short-stories, b&w photos.

Goebel Figurines

Collector

Linda Nothnagel
Rt. 3
Shelbina, MO 63468
Phone: 314-588-4958
Wants out-of-production Goebel cat figurines.

CELLULOID ITEMS

(see also BOXES, Plastic; CHARMS, Plastic; PLASTIC COLLECTIBLES)

CELS

(see also ANIMATION FILM ART)

CERAMICS

(see also CALENDAR PLATES; DINNERWARE; FAIRINGS; FIGURINES; POT LIDS; REPAIRS & RESTORATIONS; RAILROAD COLLECTIBLES, China; STEINS)

Club/Association

American Ceramic Circle
Journal: American Ceramic Circle Journal & Newsletter
Grand Central Station
P.O. Box 1495
New York, NY 10163 *

Dealer

Heritage Antiques
Marilyn Stellberg
Box 844
Bellville, TX 77418
Wants pre-1880 English or American porcelain, pottery of stoneware, etc. of any type; also offers antiques research by mail.

Expert

Tova's Treasurers
Martin Spickler, PhD
909 W. Nolcrest Dr.
Silver Spring, MD 20903
Phone: 301-593-6492
Specializes in glass, ceramics and Oriental antiques.

Expert

Country Peasants, The
Susan & Al Bagdade
3136 Elder Ct.
Northbrook, IL 60062
Phone: 708-498-1468 *

Misc. Service

Frandon Enterprises, Inc.
Donald Wallace
P.O. Box 300321
Seattle, WA 98103
Sells a kit, similar to that used by FDA inspectors, to check the lead content of ceramic dinnerware; $29.95 plus $3.50 S&H.

Museum/Library

Jones Museum of Glass & Ceramics, The
Douglas Hill, ME 04024
Phone: 207-787-3370
Unique museum, over 7000 examples of glass & ceramics ranging from antiquity to present; covers all types from all periods.

Museum/Library

National Museum of American History
14th & Constitution Ave. NW
Washington, DC 20560
Phone: 202-357-2700

Museum/Library

National Museum of Ceramic Art
250 W. Pratt St.
Baltimore, MD 21201
Phone: 301-837-2529

Periodical

Newsletter: Dishpatch
P.O. Box 106
Buttzville, NJ 07829
Phone: 210-453-3491
*Focuses on 20th century dishes. *

Repro. Source

Design-Technics Ceramics, Inc.
150 East 58th St.
New York, NY 10155
Phone: 212-355-3183
*Museum reproductions of ceramic products. *

Repro. Source

Foreign Advisory
P.O. Box 86
Princess Anne, MD 21853
*Produces reproductions of blue and white, polychrome "Old Delft", Royal Holland Pewter and classical creamware. *

Belleek

Club/Association

Belleek Collectors Society, The
Newsletter: Belleek Collector, The
Martina Kerr-Bromley
c/o Reed & Barton Co.
144 West Britannia St.
Taunton, MA 02780
Phone: 508-824-6611   FAX: 508-822-7269
Carries Irish Belleek.

Dealer

Richard Lewis
23 Bank Street
Medford, NJ 08055
Buys and sells American Belleek. *

Expert

Mary Beth Appert
525 W. Broad St.
Quakertown, PA 18951
Phone: 215-538-0976 or 215-538-9638
Collector of black mark and green mark Irish Belleek; also all makes of American Belleek.

Expert

Mary Gaston
Box 342
Bryan, TX 77806
Specializes in American Belleek. *

Museum/Library

Museum of Ceramics at East Liverpool
Donna Juszczak
400 E. 5th Street
East Liverpool, OH 43920
Phone: 216-386-6001
Detailed exhibit of the local ceramic industry; "The City of Hills & Kilns" by Wm. Gates, Jr. can be obtained by contacting the museum.

Blue & White Pottery

Club/Association

Blue & White Pottery Club
Newsletter: Blue & White Pottery Club
    Newsletter
224 12th St. NW
Cedar Rapids, IA 52405
Phone: 319-362-8116

Expert

Kathryn McNearny
502 Kettering Way
Orange Park, FL 32073 *

Expert

Upper Loft Antiques
Gregg Ellington
47 Columbus St.
Wilmington, OH 45177
Phone: 513-382-4311
Buys, sells, trades and collects graniteware and American ceramics including mochaware, yellowware, spongeware, etc.

Blue Willow Pattern

Club/Association

Toronto Willow Society
359 Danenport Rd.
Toronto
Ontario M5R 1K5 Canada *

Expert

Joshua D. Young
P.O. Box 188
Reeds Spring, MO 65737
Phone: 417-272-3507
Author of "The Blue Willowware Book and Appraisal Guide."

Copper Lustre

Expert

Richard G. Marden
Box 524
Wolfeboro, NH 03894
Phone: 603-569-3209 *

Corn Shaped

Collector

Mike Thomas
623 Burnside Dr.
Miamisburg, OH 45342
Buying corn pottery - Shawnee Corn King, Terrace ceramics, Stanford Corn. *

Flow Blue

Club/Association

Flow Blue International Collectors Club
Newsletter: Blueberry Notes
Don & Larie Hensley
28 Irene St.
Brooksville, FL 34601
Phone: 904-796-8244

Collector

Barbara Amster
15 Bellevue Ave.
Bass River, MA 02664
Wants all pre-1910 pieces as well as damaged pieces from 1840-1880. *

Collector

Collector
P.O. Box 274
El Dorado Springs, MO 64744 *

Dealer

Louise M. Loehr
163 W. Main St.
P.O. Box 208
Kutztown, PA 19530
Phone: 215-683-8370
Co-author of "Willow Pattern China." Specializing in willow, flow blue, and early children's china. Wants one piece or collections.

Dealer

Antique Place, The
1524 S. Glenstone
Springfield, MO 65804
Phone: 417-887-3800 *

Matching Service

Country Oaks Antiques
7116 Shadow Oaks
Memphis, TN 38125
Buys and sells flow blue on national market; provides locator service; send $2 and LSASE for inventory list.

Gaudy Dutch

Expert

John Querry
R.D. 2 Box 137B
Martinsburg, PA 16662
Phone: 814-793-3185 *

Expert

Bea Cohen
Box 825
Easton, PA 18044-0825
Phone: 215-252-1098 *

Ironstone

Expert

Hospice House Antiques
William Durham
9633 Beaver Valley Rd.
Belvidere, IL 61008
Phone: 815-547-5128

Ironstone (Mulberry)

Collector

Barbara Amster
15 Bellevue Ave.
Bass River, MA 02664 *

Expert

Mary Gaston
Box 342
Bryan, TX 77806 *

Ironstone (Tea Leaf)

Club/Association

Tea Leaf Club International
Newsletter: Tea Leaf Readings
P.O. Box 2204
Columbus, IN 47202-2204
Phone: 812-379-4518   FAX: 614-592-4650
Purpose is to inform membership about Tea Leaf Ironstone and its copper lustre variants.

Collector

Julie Rich
9720 Whiskey Run
Laurel, MD 20707
Wants to buy tea leaf ironstone; editor of the Tea Leaf Club International's newsletter, "Tea Leaf Readings".

Expert

Julie Rich
9720 Whiskey Run
Laurel, MD 20723
Phone: 301-490-7604

Editor of "Tea Leaf Readings", the official publication of the Tea Leaf Club International.

Expert

LeRoy Bruggink
313 Ramaker Ave.
Cedar Grove, WI 53013 *

Expert

Hospice House Antiques
William Durham
9633 Beaver Valley Rd.
Belvidere, IL 61008
Phone: 815-547-5128

Lustre Ware (Pink)

Collector

James P. Harold
2122 Mass. Ave. NW #522
Washington, DC 20008-2833
Phone: 202-296-6527

Majolica

Auction Service

Michael G. Strawser
P.O. Box 332
Wolcottville, IN 46795
Phone: 219-854-2895 or 219-854-3979
Specializing in Majolica auctions in the U.S.

Club/Association

Majolica International Society
Newsletter: Majolica International Society
  Newsletter
Michael G. Strawser, Pres.
Suite 103
1275 First Ave.
New York, NY 10021
Phone: 219-854-2895 or 219-854-3979
Conventions held in April/May each year with speakers and show/sale.

Club/Association

Majolica Collectors Association
P.O. Box 332
Wolcottville, IN 46795 *

Dealer

Majolica Wares
Marlene Humberd
2314 Guthrie Ave., N.W.
Cleveland, TN 37311
Phone: 615-339-3975 or 615-479-6364
Collects originals in order to make reproductions; buys and sells antique Victorian majolica upon availability and request.

Expert

Hardy Hudson
108 Green Leaf Lane
Altamonte Springs, FL 32714 *

Expert

Linda & Kenneth Ketterling Antiques
Linda & Ken Ketterling
3202 E. Lincolnshire Blvd.
Toledo, OH 43606
Phone: 419-536-5531
Buys and sells English and American majolica, good condition; unusual pieces particularly desired.

Repro. Source

Majolica Wares
Marlene Humberd
2314 Guthrie Ave., N.W.
Cleveland, TN 37311
Phone: 615-339-3975 or 615-479-6364
Produces high-quality American-made majolica reproductions.

Military Related

Collector

Rex Stark
49 Wethersfield Rd.
Bellingham, MA 02019
Phone: 508-966-0994
Wants to buy china with American political and military portraits or scenes; Liverpool, lustreware, parian ware, Staffordshire, etc.

Mochaware

Expert

Bea Cohen
Box 825
Easton, PA 18044-0825
Phone: 215-252-1098 *

Expert

Upper Loft Antiques
Gregg Ellington
47 Columbus St.
Wilmington, OH 45177
Phone: 513-382-4311
Buys, sells, trades and collects graniteware and American ceramics including mochaware, yellowware, spongeware, etc.

Painted

Club/Association

World Organization of China Painters,
The
Magazine: China Painter, The
Pamela Garrity
2641 N.W. 10th St.
Oklahoma City, OK 73107
Phone: 405-521-1234
Organization with 7000 members, 10,000 sq. ft. museum dedicated to hand-painted porcelain china; seminars, courses, library.

Museum/Library

World Organization of China Painters,
The
Magazine: China Painter, The
Pamela Garrity
2641 N.W. 10th St.
Oklahoma City, OK 73107
Phone: 405-521-1234
10,000 sq. ft. museum houses examples of hand-painted porcelain china from all over the U.S. and from several foreign countries.

Picasso Editions

Collector

Albert Merola
211 Bradford St.
Provincetown, MA 02657
Phone: 508-487-2546 *

Collector

James Balla
211 Bradford St.
Provincetown, MA 02657
Phone: 508-487-2546
*Wants Picasso ceramic editions made at Madoura. *

Political Related

Collector

Rex Stark
49 Wethersfield Rd.
Bellingham, MA 02019
Phone: 508-966-0994
Wants to buy china with American political and military portraits or scenes; Liverpool, lustreware, parian ware, Staffordshire, etc.

Redware

Expert

Barbara Rosen
6 Shoshone Trail
Wayne, NJ 07470 *

Souvenir & Commemorative

(see also SOUVENIR & COMMEMORATIVE ITEMS)

Periodical

Newsletter: Antique Souvenir Collectors News
Box 562
Great Barrington, MA 01230
Phone: 413-528-5490
The nationwide marketplace for antique souvenirs of all kinds: souvenir china, spoons, photos, glass, postcards - anything souvenir.

Periodical

Newspaper: Travel Collector
P.O. Box 40
Manawa, WI 54949-0040
Phone: 414-596-1944

Monthly newspaper that focuses on souvenir and commemorative glass and ceramic items in addition to other souvenir collectibles.

Spatterware
Expert
Bea Cohen
Box 825
Easton, PA 18044-0825
Phone: 215-252-1098 *

Spongeware
Expert
Bea Cohen
Box 825
Easton, PA 18044-0825
Phone: 215-252-1098 *

Expert
Upper Loft Antiques
Grcgg Ellington
47 Columbus St.
Wilmington, OH 45177
Phone: 513-382-4311
Buys, sells, trades and collects graniteware and American ceramics including mochaware, yellowware, spongeware, etc.

Willow Pattern
Club/Association
Willow Society
Newsletter: Willow Transfer Quarterly
39 Medhurst Rd.
Toronto
Ontario M4B 1B2 Canada
Phone: 416-757-0634 *

Club/Association
International Willow Collectors
Harry J. Hall, Pres.
145 Maple Drive
Springboro, OH 45066
Phone: 513-748-0446 or 513-435-2134
Members interested in collecting and studying of ceramics and other materials decorated with the willow pattern.

Dealer
Louise M. Loehr
163 W. Main St.
P.O. Box 208
Kutztown, PA 19530
Phone: 215-683-8370
Co-author of "Willow Pattern China." Specializing in willow, flow blue, and early children's china. Wants one piece or collections.

Expert
Connie Rogers
1733 Chase St.
Cincinnati, OH 45223
Phone: 513-541-2013
Editor of "American Willow Report" 7/87 thru 5/90.

Expert
Lois Misiewicz
2062 Trevino
Oceanside, CA 92056
Phone: 619-757-2062 *

Periodical
Newsletter: Willow Word, The
Mary Linda Berndt, Ed.
P.O. Box 13382
Arlington, TX 76094
A newsletter having full-color photographs of willowware.

Yellowware
Expert
Upper Loft Antiques
Gregg Ellington
47 Columbus St.
Wilmington, OH 45177
Phone: 513-382-4311
Buys, sells, trades and collects graniteware and American ceramics including mochaware, yellowware, spongeware, etc.

CERAMICS (AMERICAN)
Club/Association
American Ceramic Arts Society
71 W. 23rd St.
New York, NY 10010
Phone: 212-727-1760

Collector
Harvey Duke
115 Montague St.
Brooklyn, NY 11201
Wants to buy Brayton figurines, Fraunfelter, Porcelier, and American china & pottery dealer signs and related material.

Dealer
Naomi's
1817 Polk Street
San Francisco, CA 94109
Phone: 415-775-1207
Buys/sells American dinnerware: Hall, Bauer, Tepco, Wallace, Coors, Autumn Leaf, Russel Wright, American Modern, Iroquois, etc.

Expert
Buttzville Center
Harvey Duke
Box 106
Butzville, NJ 07829
Author of "Price Guide to Pottery and Porcelain"; 60 collectible American potteries; be an expert; $12.95 + $1.50 P&H.

Expert
Pat Thomas Antiques
Pat Thomas
501 E. North Street
Chapel Hill, NC 27514
Phone: 919-942-6720 *

Expert
Lorrie Kitchen
3905 Torrance Dr.
Toledo, OH 43612
Phone: 419-478-3815
Specializing in American dinnerware such as Hall China, Fiesta, Blue Ridge and Shawnee.

Expert
Dan Tucker
3905 Torrance Dr.
Toledo, OH 43612
Phone: 419-478-3815
Specializing in Hall china, Fiesta, Blue Ridge, Shawnee.

Expert
Woody Griffith
4107 White Ash Rd.
Crystal Lake, IL 60014
Phone: 815-459-7808
Specializes in Jewel Tea, Noritake, Hall China. *

Expert
Briggerman Antiques
Lawrence Briggerman
1309 E. St.
Charleston, IL 61920
Phone: 217-345-2543
Specializing in Fiesta, Jewel Tea, Heisey, Cambridge Pottery, etc. *

Museum/Library
Everson Museum of Art of Syracuse & Onondaga County
401 Harrison Street
Syracuse, NY 13202
Phone: 315-474-6064

Museum/Library
Museum of Ceramics at East Liverpool
Donna Juszczak
400 E. 5th Street
East Liverpool, OH 43920
Phone: 216-386-6001
Detailed exhibit of the local ceramic industry; "The City of Hills & Kilns" by Wm. Gates, Jr. can be obtained by contacting the museum.

Museum/Library
Scio Pottery Museum
38250 Crimm Rd.
Scio, OH 43988
Phone: 614-945-3111

Periodical
Newsletter: Studio Potter
Box 70
Goffstown, NH 03045 *

Periodical
Magazine: American Ceramics
15 West 44th Street
New York, NY 10036
Phone: 212-944-2180

A magazine about ceramic art. *

Periodical

Magazine: Glaze, The
P.O. Box 4782
Birmingham, AL 35206
Phone: 205-833-9853
A bi-monthly magazine devoted to American dinnerware, china and pottery.

Periodical

Depression Glass Daze, Inc.
Newspaper: Daze, The
Teri Steele, Ed.
275 State Rd.
Box 57
Otisville, MI 48463-0057
Phone: 313-631-4593
A monthly newspaper catering to the dealers and collectors of glass, china and pottery from the 1920's and 1930's.

Periodical

Magazine: American Clay Exchange
800 Murray Dr.
El Cajon, CA 92020 *

Art Deco

Museum/Library

Cowan Pottery Museum at the Rocky River
Public Library
1600 Hampton Road
Rocky River, OH 44116-2699
Phone: 216-333-7610

Museum/Library

Cranbrook Academy of Art Museum
P.O. Box 801
Bloomfield Hills, MI 48013
Phone: 313-645-3323

Bennington

(see also CERAMICS (AMERICAN), Stoneware)

Expert

Upper Loft Antiques
Gregg Ellington
47 Columbus St.
Wilmington, OH 45177
Phone: 513-382-4311
Buys, sells, trades and collects graniteware and American ceramics including mochaware, yellowware, spongeware, etc.

Museum/Library

Bennington Museum, The
W. Main St.
Bennington, VT 05201
Phone: 802-447-1571

Black Cats

Expert

Pamela Ford
1609 Lynkirk La.
Kirkwood, MO 63122
Phone: 314-984-0525 or 314-531-4321
Interested in Shafford-style black cats especially on teapots, mugs, egg cups, spice racks, unusual pieces.

Illinois

Club/Association

Foundation for Historical Research of
Illinois Potteries
Eva Mounce
704 E. Twelfth St.
Streator, IL 61364
Phone: 815-672-2827
Purpose of the Foundation is to research and document the history of the Illinois pottery industry, c. 1830-1930.

Club/Association

Collectors of Illinois Pottery &
Stoneware
Newsletter: Collectors of Ill. Pottery &
Stoneware Newsletter
David A. McGuire
1527 East Converse St.
Springfield, IL 62702
Phone: 217-544-9048
An organization for persons interested in collecting Illinois pottery; quarterly newsletter features photos and information.

Collector

David A. McGuire
1527 East Converse St.
Springfield, IL 62702
Phone: 217-544-9048
Paying top dollar for early salt glaze or unusual Illinois pottery.

Ott & Brewer

Expert

Mary Gaston
Box 342
Bryan, TX 77806 *

Pennsylania German

Museum/Library

Hershey Museum
James McMahon
170 W. Hersheypark Dr.
Hershey, PA 17033
Phone: 717-534-3439
Focused collection of objects detailing the town of Hershey history, regional PA German heritage, native American material culture.

Russel Wright Designs

(see also RUSSEL WRIGHT)

Expert

Ann M. Kerr
P.O. Box 437
Sidney, OH 45365
Phone: 513-492-6369
Wants Russel Wright dinnerware, stainless, chrome; Bauer art ware, etc.; Author of "Collector's Encyclopedia of Russell Wright

Shawnee Pottery Co.

Periodical

Newsletter: Shawnee Pottery Newsletter
Pam Curran
P.O. Box 713
New Smyrna Beach, FL 32170-0713
Send LSASE for information.

Southern Folk Pottery

Club/Association

Southern Folk Pottery Collectors
Society
Newsletter: SFPCS Newsletter
Roy Thompson
1224 Main Street
Glastonbury, CT 06033
Phone: 203-633-3121 or 203-659-3695
Quarterly newsletter provides articles and latest auction results; periodic offerings of special limited editions by famous potters.

Expert

Roy Thompson
1224 Main Street
Glastonbury, CT 06033
Phone: 203-633-3121 or 203-659-3695
Author of "Face Jugs, Chickens and Other Whimseys."

Stoneware

Auction Service

Marlin G. Denlinger Auctions
R.R. 3, Box 3775
Morrisville, VT 05661
Phone: 802-888-2774
Conducts specialized auctions of decorated stoneware. *

Auction Service

Arthur Auctioneering
Wayne Arthur
R.D. 2 Box 155
Hughesville, PA 17737
Phone: 717-584-3697
Conducts specialized sales of decorated stoneware.

Collector

Steve Ketcham
Box 24114
Edina, MN 55424
Phone: 612-920-4205

Primarily interested in crocks, jugs, etc. which carry name of product or advertising such as liquor dealers, medicines, etc.

Collector

Peter M. Naysmith
Mounted Rt., Box 444
Two Harbors, MN 55616
Phone: 218-834-4770
Will pay up to $50 for stoneware (jugs preferred) with advertising on the side and the name of the pottery company maker on the bottom.

Dealer

3 Behrs
RD #8 Horsepound Road
Carmel, NY 10512
*Stoneware specialists; also publishes periodic mail-order catalog of decorated stoneware. ***

Dealer

Troy & Black, Inc.
Carl McCann
P.O. Box 228
Red Creek, NY 13143
Phone: 315-754-8115
Buys and sells high quality American stoneware, coverlets and figured maple furniture.

Dealer

Antiques & Americana
Vicki & Bruce Waasdorp
10931 Main Street
Clarence, NY 14031
Phone: 716-759-2361 *

Dealer

Tinder Box Antiques
Ivy & Geoff Bean
8200 Mountain Laurel Ln.
Gaithersburg, MD 20879
Phone: 301-963-7469
Wants blue decorated American stoneware: crocks, jugs, jars, etc.

Man./Prod./Dist.

Rowe Pottery Works
404 England St.
Cambridge, WI 53523
Phone: 608-764-5435   FAX: 608-423-4273
Produces authentic reproductions of 19th century salt-glaze stoneware plates, figurines, miniatures and steins.

Museum/Library

Bennington Museum, The
W. Main St.
Bennington, VT 05201
Phone: 802-447-1571

Museum/Library

Museum of Ceramics at East Liverpool
Donna Juszczak
400 E. 5th Street
East Liverpool, OH 43920
Phone: 216-386-6001
Detailed exhibit of the local ceramic industry; "The City of Hills & Kilns" by Wm. Gates, Jr. can be obtained by contacting the museum.

Stoneware (New Jersey)

Collector

Alex Caiola
84 Seneca
Emerson, NJ 07630
Phone: 201-262-7030
Wants marked stoneware from New Jersey towns Hackensack & Englewood; also quart-size stenciled stoneware jugs from anywhere in U.S.

Willets

Expert

Mary Gaston
Box 342
Bryan, TX 77806 *

CERAMICS (AMERICAN ART POTTERY)

Club/Association

Pottery Lovers Reunion
Newsletter: Pottery Lovers Newsletter
Pat Sallaz
4969 Hudson Drive
Stow, OH 44224
Publishes a quarterly newsletter describing activities and plans for the upcoming Pottery Lovers Reunion and show.

Club/Association

American Art Pottery Association
Magazine: Journal of the AAPA
Jean Oberkirsch
125 E. Rose Ave.
St. Louis, MO 63119
Phone: 413-968-0708

Collector

Collector
Box 126
Flourtown, PA 19031
Phone: 215-247-7317
*Wants Roseville middle period, Rookwood, Van Briggle, Hampshire, etc.; also unmarked pottery if "right look." ***

Collector

Bill Holland
107 S. 18th St.
Philadelphia, PA 19103
Phone: 215-647-7099 *

Dealer

Edward E. Stump
6 High Street
Mullica Hill, NJ 08062
Phone: 609-478-4488 or 609-467-1265
Wants Roseville and Weller art pottery.

Dealer

David Rago Arts & Crafts
David Rago
Station E
P.O. Box 3592
Trenton, NJ 08629
Phone: 609-585-2546
Wants American art pottery; also Arts & Crafts items such as furniture and metal items by Stickley, Rohlfs, Wright, Roycroft, etc.

Dealer

Caren Fine
11603 Gowrie Ct.
Potomac, MD 20854
Phone: 310-299-2116
Wants Clarice Cliff English art pottery from the 1920's and 1930's; also Rookwood, Newcomb, Van Briggle, Grubey, Teco, Roseville, etc.

Dealer

Dorothy Daniel
4020 N. 25th St.
Arlington, VA 22207
Phone: 703-243-0322 *

Dealer

McCormack & Company
Tony McCormak
P.O. Box 13645
Atlanta, GA 30324
Phone: 404-266-8411
Always buying Rookwood, Grueby, Newcomb College, Teco, Marblehead, Overbeck; dated Van Briggle, George Ohr, Weller & Roseville pottery.

Dealer

Ray Thomas
5155 Manchester Dr.
Zanesville, OH 43701
*Buys and sells American art pottery. ***

Dealer

Cincinnati Art Galleries
635 Main St.
Cincinnati, OH 45202
Phone: 513-381-2128
Rookwood is their specialty; also want Van Briggle, Newcomb, Grueby, etc.

Dealer

Don Treadway
2128 Madison Rd.
Cincinnati, OH 45208
Phone: 513-321-6742   FAX: 513-871-7722

Expert

Fer-Duc Inc.
Joseph Ferrara
Box 1303
Newburgh, NY 12550
Phone: 914-896-9492
Specializing in American art pottery: Ohr, Rookwood, Zanesville, etc.

Expert

Marnette Antiques
Marvin Stofft
45 12th St.
Tell City, IN 47586
Phone: 812-547-5707
Wants to buy Ohio-made American art pottery.

Expert

Norman Haas
264 Clizbe Rd.
Quincy, MI 49082
Phone: 517-639-8537 *

Expert

Nichols Art Pottery
Harold Nichols
632 Agg Ave.
Ames, IA 50010
Phone: 515-292-9167
*Specializes in American art pottery: Roseville, Weller, McCoy etc. *

Expert

Steve Schoneck
P.O. Box 56
Newport, MN 55055
Phone: 612-459-2980
*Specializes in Handicraft Guild of Minneapolis, American art pottery, and Arts & Crafts. *

Expert

Mary Weldi-Skinner
1656 W. Farragut Ave.
Chicago, IL 60640-2010
Phone: 312-271-0236
*Specializing in American and European Art Pottery. *

Expert

Wes-Jan Antiques
Wesley Garton
P.O. Box 780985
Wichita, KS 67278
Phone: 316-778-1948 *

Expert

California Spectrum
Jack Chipman
P.O. Box 1429
Redondo Beach, CA 90278
Phone: 213-376-2964 or 213-831-6775
Specializes in 20th century American ceramics.

Expert

Robert Bettinger
N.P.S. Box 8611
Monterey, CA 93943
Phone: 408-443-5554 *

Museum/Library

Everson Museum of Art of Syracuse & Onondaga County
401 Harrison Street
Syracuse, NY 13202
Phone: 315-474-6064

Museum/Library

Zanesville Art Center
620 Military Road
Zanesville, OH 43701
Phone: 614-452-0741

Museum/Library

Cincinnati Art Museum
Eden Park
Cincinnati, OH 45202
Phone: 513-721-5204

Museum/Library

Newcomb College Art Gallery
1229 Broadway
New Orleans, LA 70118
Phone: 504-865-5327

American Art Clay Co.

Expert

Virginia Heiss
7777 N. Alton Ave.
Indianapolis, IN 46268
Phone: 317-875-6797
Specializes in pottery made by the American Art Clay Co., Indianapolis, IN.

Cowan Pottery Co.

Collector

Ann M. Kerr
P.O. Box 437
Sidney, OH 45365
Phone: 513-492-6369
Wants Cowan figural items done by Guy Cowan, Gregory, Schrekengast, Winter, etc.

Museum/Library

Cowan Pottery Museum at the Rocky River Public Library
1600 Hampton Road
Rocky River, OH 44116-2699
Phone: 216-333-7610
Features a collection of over 8000 pieces by the artists of the Cowan Pottery Studio of Lakewood and Rocky River, Ohio, 1912-1932.

Dedham Pottery Co.

Expert

Robert W. Skinner, Inc.
Marilee Meyer
Route 117
Bolton, MA 01740
Phone: 508-779-6241 *

Expert

Bea Cohen
Box 825
Easton, PA 18044-0825
Phone: 215-252-1098 *

Repro. Source

Potting Shed Inc., The
P.O. Box 1287
Concord, MA 10742
Phone: 508-369-1382 or 800-722-4287
                    FAX: 508-369-1416
Hand made Dedham reproduction pottery; each piece signed by the artist.

Fulper Pottery Co.

Collector

Terry Seger
5778 Breezewood Dr.
Cincinnati, OH 45248
Phone: 513-451-3784
*Wants large examples of Fulper pottery. *

Expert

Classic Interiors & Antiques
Douglas White
2144 Edgewater Dr.
Orlando, FL 32804
Phone: 407-841-6681 *

Houghton/Dalton

Club/Association

Houghton-Dalton Collectors Society
Newsletter: Houghton-Dalton Collectors
    Newsletter
Jim & Mira Houdeshell
1801 N. Main St.
Findlay, OH 45840
Phone: 419-423-2895 or 419-424-4551

Expert

JMJ Antiques
Jim & Mira Houdeshell
1801 N. Main St.
Findlay, OH 45840
Phone: 419-423-2895 or 419-424-4551
Author of "Houghton and Dalton Pottery."

Newcomb College

Dealer

David Rago Arts & Crafts
David Rago
Station E
P.O. Box 3592
Trenton, NJ 08629
Phone: 609-585-2546
Wants American art pottery, and Arts and Crafts items such as furniture and metal items by Stickley, Rohlfs, Wright, Roycroft, etc.

Dealer

David Chase Gallery
Cliff Catania
P.O. Box 330
Ephrata, PA 17522
Phone: 717-733-4243   FAX: 717-733-4243
Buy and sell Newcomb pottery; special interest in early, high-glaze pieces.

North Dakota School Of Mines

Expert

Antique Gallery
Robert Barr
300 West Main
Mandan, ND 58554 *

Owens Pottery Co.

Expert

Marnette Antiques
Marvin Stofft
45 12th St.
Tell City, IN 47586
Phone: 812-547-5707

Rookwood Pottery Co.

Collector

Margaret Peck
4550 N. Flowing Wells Rd., #174
Tucson, AZ 85705
Phone: 602-887-9734
Author of "Second Book of Rookwood Pottery."

Man./Prod./Dist.

Rookwood Pottery
4515 Page Ave.
Michigan Center, MI 49254
*Company makes new pottery. *

Roseville Pottery Co.

Collector

Barbara Rendina
27171 Lake Shore
Euclid, OH 44132 *

Dealer

Fenner's Antiques
Osna & Jim Fenner
2611 Ave. S
Brooklyn, NY 11229 *

Dealer

Ruman
292 Pershing Ave.
Leechburg, PA 15656
Phone: 412-845-7275

Expert

Marnette Antiques
Marvin Stofft
45 12th St.
Tell City, IN 47586
Phone: 812-547-5707

Expert

Sharon & Bob Huxford
1202 7th St.
Covington, IN 47932 *

Expert

Gordon Hoppe
10120 32nd Ave. N.
Plymouth, MN 55441
Phone: 612-546-7461 *

Van Briggle Pottery Co.

Man./Prod./Dist.

Van Briggle Pottery Co.
P.O. Box 96
Colorado Springs, CO 80901
Phone: 303-633-7729
Beautiful figurines and pottery made as copies of original Van Briggle pieces from the early 1900's.

Weller Pottery Co.

Expert

Dr. Ann G. McDonald
Box 7321
Arlington, VA 22207
Author of "All About Weller."

Expert

Marnette Antiques
Marvin Stofft
45 12th St.
Tell City, IN 47586
Phone: 812-547-5707

Expert

Sharon & Bob Huxford
1202 7th St.
Covington, IN 47932 *

CERAMICS (AMERICAN DINNERWARE)

Buffalo Pottery Co.

Expert

Seymour&Violet Altman
8970 Main St.
Clarence, NY 14031
Phone: 716-634-4488 *

Expert

Ruth & Dale Van Kuren Antiques
Ruth & Dale Van Kuren
5990 Goodrich Rd.
Clarence Center, NY 14032
Phone: 716-741-2606 *

Man./Prod./Dist.

Buffalo China, Inc.
658 Bailey Ave.
Buffalo, NY 14206
Phone: 716-824-8515 or 800-828-7033

Coors Porcelain Co.

Collector

Ed Bour
11496 W. Florida Place
Denver, CO 80232
Phone: 303-989-4540
Wants Coors Pottery items: vases, Rosebud, Rockmount, Thermoporcelain, etc.

Expert

Newsletter: Coors Pottery Newsletter
Robert Schneider
3808 Carr Pl. N.
Seattle, WA 98103-8126
Author of "Coors Rosebud Pottery."

Gladding-McBean/Franciscan

Expert

Terry Telford
192 Sixth Ave.
New York, NY 10013
*Specializing in Franciscan (trade name used by Gladding McBean and Co.) dinnerware. *

Matching Service

Deleen Enge
912 N. Signal
Ojai, CA 93203
Phone: 805-646-2549
Specializing in mail order sales of Franciscan (trade name used by Gladding McBean and Co.) dinnerware; author of "Franciscan Ware."

Gorham

Man./Prod./Dist.

Gorham, Inc.
P.O. Box 906
Mount Kisco, NY 10549
Phone: 914-242-9300 or 800-225-1460
FAX: 914-242-9379

Hall China Co./Autumn Leaf

Club/Association

National Autumn Leaf Collectors Club
Beverly Robbins, Sec.
7346 Shamrock Dr.
Indianapolis, IN 46217
Phone: 317-881-8932

Specializes in Hall China Company's Autumn Leaf pattern that was designed for the Jewel Tea Company; also Jewel Tea Co. items.

Expert

ELO Books
Harvey Duke
Box 627 - M
Brooklyn, NY 11202
Author of "Superior Quality Hall China" & "Hall 2", the authoritative books on the Hall China Company; $14.95 + $1.50 P&H each.

Expert

Margaret & Kenn Whitmyer
Box 30806
Gahanna, OH 43230
Author of "The Collector's Guide to Hall China." *

Expert

Elizabeth Boyce
38 Carlotia Dr.
Jeffersonville, IN 47130
Phone: 812-282-8697
Hall china columnist for the "Glaze."

Expert

Ben Moulton
RR 21, Box 103
Terra Haute, IN 47802
Phone: 812-234-3870
Specializes in Hall China: refrigeratorware, kitchenware, dinnerware, novelties, tea pots, etc.

Expert

Jo Cunningham
535 E. Normal
Springfield, MO 65807
Phone: 417-831-1320
Author of "The Autumn Leaf Story."

Man./Prod./Dist.

Hall China Company, The
P.O. Box 989
East Liverpool, OH 43920
Maker of Hall China since 1903.

Homer Laughlin China Co.

Collector

Robert Green
P.O. Box 222
San Anselmo, CA 94960 *

Dealer

Edward E. Stump
6 High Street
Mullica Hill, NJ 08062
Phone: 609-478-4488 or 609-467-1265
Specializes in Homer Laughlin China Company's Fiesta, Harlequin and Riviera patterns; buying and selling.

Man./Prod./Dist.

Homer Laughlin Co., The
Newell, WV 26050
Phone: 304-387-1300

Homer Laughlin/Fiesta

Dealer

Gus Gustafson
P.O. Box 106
Butzville, NJ 07829
Specializes in Homer Laughlin China Company's Fiesta pattern. *

Expert

Fiesta Monitor
P.O. Box 846
Edensburg, PA 15931
Has done extensive research not found in books on Fiesta; will answer questions for SASE plus $1; full refund if question not answered.

Expert

Sharon & Bob Huxford
1202 7th St.
Covington, IN 47932 *

Homer Laughlin/Harlequin

Expert

Sharon & Bob Huxford
1202 7th St.
Covington, IN 47932 *

Lenox

Man./Prod./Dist.

Lenox China Shop
53 Commerce Dr.
Cranberry, NJ 08512
Phone: 609-395-8054 or 800-367-7467
Retail showroom selling open stock on current stemware, dinnerware, and giftware patterns.

Man./Prod./Dist.

Lenox China & Crystal Consumer Service
100 Lenox Dr.
Lawrenceville, NJ 08648
Phone: 609-896-2800 or 800-635-3669
Offers Matching Services List of dealers who offer replacements for current of discontinued Lenox items; also gives insurance estimates.

Lenox/Ceramic Art Co.

Expert

Mary Gaston
Box 342
Bryan, TX 77806
Specializes in the Ceramic Art Co., Trenton, NJ, established in 1899 by J. Coxon and W. Lenox; early maker of American belleek. *

Lewistown Pottery Co.

Collector

Scott Armstrong
R.D.4, Box 115
Lewistown, PA 17044
Phone: 717-248-5285
Wants pieces marked Lewistown Pottery.

Metlox Potteries

Dealer

Karen Silversmintz
1908 Antwerp Ave.
Plano, TX 75025 *

Man./Prod./Dist.

Metlox Potteries
P.O. Box 8
Manhattan Beach, CA 90266
Phone: 213-545-4516

Pennsbury Pottery Co.

Collector

David Angelocci
47 Maddock Ave.
Trenton, NJ 08610
Phone: 609-888-3243
Wants Pennsbury Pottery: dinnerware, lamps, tiles, plaques, cruets, canister & spice sets, pie plates, birds, unusual items, etc. *

Collector

Mark Supnick
8524 NW 2nd St.
Coral Springs, FL 33071
Phone: 305-755-3448
Author of "Shawnee Pottery", and "Collecting Hull's Little Red Riding Hood."

Expert

B.A. Wellman
#9 Corsage St.
Southboro, MA 01772 *

Pfaltzgraff Pottery Co.

Expert

Pfaltzgraff Co., The
Dave Walsh
140 East Market
York, PA 17401 *

Pickard China Co.

Expert

Lois & Milt Steinfeld
Box 457
Westfield, NJ 07091 *

Man./Prod./Dist.

Pickard China Co.
782 Corona Ave.
Antioch, IL 60002-1574
Phone: 708-395-3800   FAX: 708-395-3827 *

Purinton Pottery Co.

Dealer

Bob Hoover
RD 4, Box 94
Blairsville, PA 15717 *

Expert

Pat Dole
P.O. Box 4782
Birmingham, AL 35206
Phone: 205-833-9853
Author of "Purinton Pottery Book II."

Red Wing Pottery Co.

Club/Association

Red Wing Collectors Society, Inc.
Newsletter: Red Wing Collectors Newsletter
David Newkirk
Rte. 3, Box 146
Monticello, MN 55362

Expert

David Newkirk
Rt. 3, Box 146
Monticello, MN 55362

Reed & Barton

Man./Prod./Dist.

Reed & Barton
144 W. Britannia Street
Taunton, MA 02780
Phone: 508-824-6611   FAX: 508-822-7269
Produces china, crystal, silver, silverplate, and stainless flatware, collectible plates, bells, dolls, ornaments and accessories.

Southern Potteries/Blue Ridge

Collector

Norma Lilly
144 Highland Dr.
Blountville, TN 37617
Phone: 615-323-5247
Wants Blue Ridge china made by Southern Potteries, Inc.; any unusual form or pattern.

Expert

Susan Moore
3046 H Clairmont Rd. NE
Atlanta, GA 30329 *

Expert

Betty Newbound
4567 Chadsworth
Union Lake, MI 48085
Specializes in Blue Ridge dinnerware (made by Southern Potteries) and other collectible china and glass. *

Periodical

Newsletter: National Blue Ridge Newsletter
Norma Lilly
144 Highland Dr.
Blountville, TN 37617
Phone: 615-323-5247
10 pre-punched pages; Q&A up-date, articles, new patterns, readers comment section.

Stangl Pottery Co.

Dealer

Edward E. Stump
6 High Street
Mullica Hill, NJ 08062
Phone: 609-478-4488 or 609-467-1265
Wants Stangl dinnerware and Stangl birds.

Expert

Popkorn Antiques
Robert & Nancy Perzel
4 Mine St.
P.O. Box 1057
Flemington, NJ 08822
Phone: 908-782-9631
Offers a Stangl Pottery dinner matching service; also Stangl birds and Artware.

Taylor, Smith & Taylor/Lu-Ray

Dealer

Edward E. Stump
6 High Street
Mullica Hill, NJ 08062
Phone: 609-478-4488 or 609-467-1265
Specializes in Taylor, Smith and Taylor Company's Lu-Ray Pastels line.

Dealer

Popkorn Antiques
Robert & Nancy Perzel
4 Mine St.
P.O. Box 1057
Flemington, NJ 08822
Phone: 908-782-9631

Expert

Ed Nenstiel
4905 Bristow Dr.
Annandale, VA 22003
Specializes in Taylor, Smith and Taylor Company's Lu-Ray Pastels line. *

Expert

Shirley Suber-Moore
2161 S. Owasso Place
Tulsa, OK 74114
Phone: 918-747-4164
Specializes in Taylor, Smith and Taylor Company's Lu-Ray Pastels line. *

Vernon Kilns Co.

Expert

Maxine Nelson
873 Marigold Ct.
Carlsbad, CA 92009
Author of "Versatile Vernon Kilns, Book II."

Periodical

Newsletter: Vernon Views
P.O. Box 945
Scottsdale, AZ 85252
The newsletter for collectors of Vernon Kilns pottery; recent finds, free ads, interesting articles.

Warwick China Co.

Club/Association

Warwick China Collectors Club
1291 N. Elmwood Dr.
Aurora, IL 60506
Phone: 312-859-3435 *

Expert

Pat & Don Hoffman
1291 N. Elmwood Dr.
Aurora, IL 60506
Phone: 312-859-3435 *

Matching Service

Ackerman Antiques
Box 2310
Athens, OH 45701

Watt Pottery Co.

Collector

David Hagen
Star Rt., Box 116
Sarona, WI 54870
Phone: 715-469-3306
Wants plates, cups and saucers, canister sets, glasses, etc. *

Expert

Glenn Seabolt
130 Collingwood Dr.
Bristol, TN 37620 *

CERAMICS (AMERICAN FIGURES)

Ceramic Art Studio

Expert

B.A. Wellman
#9 Corsage St.
Southboro, MA 01772
Specializes in pieces made by the Ceramic Art Studio of Madison, WI (1941-1957). *

Expert

Gunther Schmidt
1440 Boston Post Rd.
Larchmont, NY 10538 *

Expert
Daniel Fortney
Suite 173 Chalet at The River
823 N. 2nd St.
Milwaukee, WI 53203 *

Florence

Expert
Jeanne Fredericks
12364 Downey Ave.
Downey, CA 90242 *

Kay Finch

Expert
Al Alberts
2645 California St. #101
Mountain View, CA 94040 *

CERAMICS (AMERICAN PRODUCTION ARTWARE)

Abingdon

Club/Association
Abingdon Pottery Club
Newsletter: Abingdon Pottery Collectors
   Newsletter
Penny Vaughan, Pres.
212 South Fourth
Monmouth, IL 61462
Phone: 309-734-2337

Collector
Mary Weldi-Skinner
1656 W. Farragut Ave.
Chicago, IL 60640-2010
Phone: 312-271-0236 *

Expert
Robert Rush
210 N. Main St.
Abingdon, IL 61410 *

Expert
Elaine Westover
Rt. 1
Abingdon, IL 61410 *

California Potteries

Expert
California Spectrum
Jack Chipman
P.O. Box 1429
Redondo Beach, CA 90278
Phone: 213-376-2964 or 213-831-6775
Specializes in 20th century American ceramics.

Camark Pottery Co.

Expert
B & B Antiques
Doris & Burdell Hall
P.O. Box 1501
Fairfield Bay, AR 72088
Phone: 501-884-6571 or 309-263-2988
Specializing in Camark pottery and American dinnerware.

Cliftwood

Expert
B & B Antiques
Doris & Burdell Hall
P.O. Box 1501
Fairfield Bay, AR 72088
Phone: 501-884-6571 or 309-263-2988
Specializing in Morton pottery and American dinnerware.

Frankoma Pottery Co.

Expert
Tom & Phyllis Bess
14535 East 13th St.
Tulsa, OK 74108
Phone: 918-437-7776
Authors of "Frankoma Treasurers" with price guide; $22 postpaid.

Man./Prod./Dist.
Frankoma Pottery, Inc.
P.O. Box 789
Sapulpa, OK 74067
Phone: 918-224-5511

Haeger/Royal Haeger

Expert
Lee Garmon
1529 Whittier St.
Springfield, IL 62704
Phone: 217-789-9574
Specializes in Royal Haeger and Royal Hickman American ceramics. *

Hull Pottery/Red Riding Hood

Dealer
Lee Feenstra
Box 419
Hull, IA 51239 *

Expert
Mark Supnick
8524 NW 2nd St.
Coral Springs, FL 33071
Phone: 305-755-3449
Author of "Shawnee Pottery", and "Collecting Hull's Little Red Riding Hood."

Expert
Antiquity Collectibles
Mike Zimpfer
3714 Lexington Rd.
Michigan City, IN 46360
Phone: 219-879-0409   FAX: 219-874-7296
Buying Hull pottery especially Bowknot, Red Riding Hood, all baskets and large vases, advertising materials; also Fiesta Ware.

Expert
Joan Gray Hull
1376 Nevada S.W.
Huron, SD 57350
Phone: 605-352-1685
Author of "Hull—The Heavenly Pottery."

Expert
Brenda Roberts
R.R. 2 Hwy 65 South
Marshall, MO 65340
Phone: 816-886-8888
Author of "The Collector's Encyclopedia of Hull Pottery."

McCoy Pottery Co.

Collector
Kathy Lynch
12704 Lockleven Lane
Woodbridge, VA 22192
Phone: 703-590-0274
Wants all McCoy Pottery items especially cookie jars.

Expert
Judy Posner
R.D. 1 Box 273
Effort, PA 18330
Phone: 717-629-6583   FAX: 717-629-0521

Expert
Sharon & Bob Huxford
1202 7th St.
Covington, IN 47932 *

Periodical
Newsletter: Our McCoy Matters
Kathy Lynch
12704 Lockleven Lane
Woodbridge, VA 22192
Phone: 703-590-0274
A bimonthly newsletter for McCoy collectors: classifieds, current market trends, articles, etc.

Periodical
Newsletter: McCoy Reunion News
Kathy Lynch
12704 Lockleven Lane
Woodbridge, VA 22192
Phone: 703-590-0274
A quarterly newsletter for McCoy collectors focusing on the planning, execution & follow-up to the annual McCoy Lovers Reunion, Zanesville.

Morton Potteries

Expert

B & B Antiques
Doris & Burdell Hall
P.O. Box 1501
Fairfield Bay, AR 72088
Phone: 501-884-6571 or 309-263-2988
Specializing in Morton pottery and American dinnerware; author of "Morton's Potteries: 99 Years."

Muncie Pottery Co.

Expert

Virginia Heiss
7777 N. Alton Ave.
Indianapolis, IN 46268
Phone: 317-875-6797

Shawnee Pottery Co.

Expert

Mark Supnick
8524 NW 2nd St.
Coral Springs, FL 33071
Phone: 305-755-3448
Author of "Shawnee Pottery", and "Collecting Hull's Little Red Riding Hood."

Uhl Pottery Co.

Club/Association

Uhl Collectors Society
Newsletter: Uhl Family Happenings
Roger Shelton
607 Willow Drive
Shelbyville, IN 46176 *

CERAMICS (CONTINENTAL)

Expert

William Brinkley
401 S. Washington Ave.
McLeansboro, IL 62859
Phone: 618-643-3427
*Specializes in Meissen, Dresden, and other European porcelains; also Cybis porcelains. **

Museum/Library

Wadsworth Atheneum
600 Main Street
Hartford, CT 06103
Phone: 203-278-2670

Dutch

Periodical

Newsletter: Dutch Potter, The
Gail Comer
47 London Terrace
New Rochelle, NY 10804
Phone: 914-636-6416   FAX: 212-491-8905
Articles on Dutch Art Nouveau & Art Deco pottery, 1880-1940 Royal Delft, Gouda, Rozenburg, Purmerend, etc.; shows, ads, photos, Q&A.

Haviland

(see also CERAMICS (EUROPEAN), Limoges)

Club/Association

Haviland Collectors Internationale
Shirley Powers, Sec.
Box 728
Ogden, IA 50212
Phone: 515-432-2600
An organization dedicated to the study and promotion of porcelain and pottery made by the Haviland companies of France and America.

Expert

Harrison's Antiques
Peg Harrison
2417 Edgewater Dr.
Orlando, FL 32804
Phone: 305-425-6481

Expert

Dee's China Shop
Dee & Maurice Hooks
P.O. Box 142
Lawrenceville, IL 62439
Phone: 618-943-2741

Expert

Mary Gaston
Box 342
Bryan, TX 77806 *

Man./Prod./Dist.

Haviland & Co.
21 Spielman Rd.
Fairfield, NJ 07006
Phone: 201-227-4511   FAX: 201-882-1094

Matching Service

Harrison's Antiques
Peg Harrison
2417 Edgewater Dr.
Orlando, FL 32804
Phone: 305-425-6481
*Matching service for Haviland, china, sterling and antique decorative accessories. **

Matching Service

Walker's Matching Service
Box 357
Athens, OH 45701
Phone: 614-593-5631
Buys and sells French or American patterns of Haviland.

Matching Service

E.C. Sales
Ed Cunningham
47 Coventry
Anderson, IN 46012
Phone: 317-643-4127
*If possible, please send Schleiger number with your request. **

Matching Service

Seekers, The
9014 Roos Road
Houston, TX 77036
Phone: 713-777-4430
*Send for list of all Haviland China matching services. **

Matching Service

Auld Lang Syne
7600 Highway 120
Jamestown, CA 94237
Phone: 209-984-DISH
Pattern locators.

Herend

Man./Prod./Dist.

Martin's Herend Imports, Inc.
1524 Spring Hill Rd.
McLean, VA 22102
Phone: 703-821-8515   FAX: 703-790-5531

Hutschenreuther

Expert

Gray's Gallery
Jack Gunsaulus
583 W. Ann Arbor Trail
Plymouth, MI 48170
Phone: 313-455-2373

Limoges

Expert

Mary Gaston
Box 342
Bryan, TX 77806 *

Meissen/Dresden

Dealer

Meissen Shop, The
329 Worth Ave.
Palm Beach, FL 33480
Phone: 407-832-2504
Devoted exclusively to antique Meissen porcelain.

Expert

Henry Pachter
267 East Township Line Rd.
Upper Darby, PA 19082
Phone: 215-789-0999
*Specializes in European porcelains particularly Meissen. **

Expert

Crossed Swords Exchange
Charles Bernstein
3301 Pierson St.
Oakland, CA 94619
Phone: 415-261-2425 *

Mottahedeh

Man./Prod./Dist.

Mottahedeh & Co.
225 Fifth Ave.
New York, NY 10010
Phone: 215-685-3050   FAX: 212-889-9483

Old Ivory

Periodical

Newsletter: Old Ivory Newsletter
Pat Fitzwater
P.O. Box 1004
Wilsonville, OR 97070
Focuses on the Old Ivory patterns of porcelain
dinnerware produced in Germany during the late
1800's; send a SASE for a sample copy.

Quimper

Dealer

Shop On Main, The
Betty & John Lucas
15 W. Friend St.
Columbiana, OH 44408
Phone: 216-482-0111

Expert

Sandra Bondhus
Box 100
Unionville, CT 06085
Phone: 203-678-1808
Author of "Quimper Pottery"; specializes in 19th
& 20th century Quimper of fine artistic merit;
always buying and selling Quimper.

Expert

Merry Walk Antiques
Joan Datesman
Box 746
Newtown, PA 18940
Phone: 215-968-1762   FAX: 215-579-2748
Author of "Collecting Quimper; Quimper Collec-
tions"; trips to France maintains large 1860-1930
inventory; rustic to elaborate designs.

Expert

Country Peasants, The
Susan & Al Bagdade
3136 Elder Ct.
Northbrook, IL 60062
Phone: 708-498-1468
Buys and sells Quimper pottery, especially un-
usual pieces: figures and early decorative exam-
ples; authors, lecturers, staff writers.

Man./Prod./Dist.

Quimper Faience
141 Water St.
Stonington, CT 06378
Phone: 203-535-1515
The American branch of the French Quimper
factory. *

R.S. Prussia

Club/Association

International Association of R. S.
Prussia Collectors Inc.
Newsletter: IARSPC Newsletter
c/o Martin Auction Co.
109 W. 5th St.
Durant, IA 52747

Collector

Collector
P.O. Box 274
El Dorado Springs, MO 64744
Wants R.S. Prussia: portraits, animals, birds or
unusual floral patterns. *

Expert

Bird of Paradise
Juanita Wilkins
430 S. Cole St.
Lima, OH 45805-3367

Expert

Marnette Antiques
Marvin Stofft
45 12th St.
Tell City, IN 47586
Phone: 812-547-5707

Expert

Dee's China Shop
Dee & Maurice Hooks
P.O. Box 142
Lawrenceville, IL 62439
Phone: 618-943-2741
Has been buying and selling R.S. Prussia for 20
years.

Rosenthal

Man./Prod./Dist.

Rosenthal USA Limited
66-26 Metropolitan Ave.
Middle Village, NY 11379
Phone: 718-417-3400   FAX: 718-417-3407

Royal Bayreuth

Collector

Eric Sidman
P.O. Box 634
Medway, MA 02053
Phone: 617-884-7520 or 401-333-3008
Wants Royal Bayreuth: Tapestry, Sunbonnets,
figurals; unusual or rare items; will pay for photos;
prompt reply.

Collector

Bird of Paradise
Juanita Wilkins
430 S. Cole St.
Lima, OH 45805-3367

Expert

L. Brenner Antiques
Larry Brenner
1005 Chestnut St.
Manchester, NH 03104
Phone: 603-625-8203 *

Expert

Dee's China Shop
Dee & Maurice Hooks
P.O. Box 142
Lawrenceville, IL 62439
Phone: 618-943-2741

Royal Copenhagen

Man./Prod./Dist.

Royal Copenhagen/Bing & Grondahl Co.
27 Holland Ave.
White Plains, NY 10603
Phone: 914-428-8222 or 800-431-1992
                    FAX: 914-428-8251
Manufactures dinnerware, cobalt blue underglaze collector plates, figurines, bells, dolls,
ornaments and gift accessories.

Scandinavian

Dealer

Gallerie Ani'tiques
Anita L. Grashof
Stage House Village
Park & Front Streets
Scotch Plains, NJ 07076
Phone: 908-322-7085 or 201-377-3032
Wants Swedish art pottery such as Argenta by
Kage, Gustavsberg.

Dealer

Phil Anderson
2147 W. Farwell
Chicago, IL 60645
Phone: 312-338-1758
Buys and sells porcelain figurines and vases from
the Scandinavian countries, especially from Copenhagen, Denmark.

Schlegelmilch

(see also CERAMICS (EUROPEAN), R.S.
Prussia)

Expert

Mary Gaston
Box 342
Bryan, TX 77806
Includes pieces marked "R.S. Germany", "R.S.
Poland", "R.S. Russia", "R.S. Suhl", and "R.S.
Tillowitz." *

Teplitz-Turn

Expert
Gray's Gallery
Jack Gunsaulus
583 W. Ann Arbor Trail
Plymouth, MI 48170
Phone: 313-455-2373
Buys and sells Teplitz-Turn art pottery, e.g. items made by the Amphora Porcelain Works and Alexandra Works.

Villory & Boch

Man./Prod./Dist.
Villory & Boch Co.
8000 Harwin Dr. #150
Houston, TX 77036
Phone: 713-785-0761   FAX: 212-481-0283

Zsolnay

Collector
Drawing Room, The
221 Spring St.
Newport, RI 02840
Phone: 401-841-5060
Wants Hungarian Zsolnay pottery; send photos and price; can buy from photo.

Expert
Laszlo Gyugyi
P.O. Box 17329
Pittsburgh, PA 15235 •

CERAMICS (ENGLISH)

Club/Association
Wedgwood International Seminar
Newsletter: WIS Newsletter
Delores M. Martin, Pres.
12526 Martindale Rd.
Houston, TX 77048
Phone: 713-991-2608
An educational association sharing the latest information in the field of English ceramics; also publishes the "Annual Proceedings."

Dealer
Wynn A. Sayman
Old Fields
Richmond, MA 01254
Phone: 413-698-2272
Specializes in early English pottery & porcelains.

Dealer
Sly Fox
Paul Fox
P.O. Box 371
Suitland, MD 20746
Specializes in early English transfer underglaze pottery and porcelain. •

Expert
Terence A. Lockett
6 Tideswell Road
Hazel Grove
Stockport SK7 6JG England
Author of "Davenport."

Art Pottery

Expert
Mary Weldi-Skinner
1656 W. Farragut Ave.
Chicago, IL 60640-2010
Phone: 312-271-0236
Specializing in American and European Art Pottery. •

Clarice Cliff

Club/Association
Clarice Cliff Collectors Club
Leonard Griffin
Fantasque House
Tennis Drive, The Park
Nottingham NG7 1AE England •

Collector
Darryl Rehr
11433 Rochester Ave. #303
Los Angeles, CA 90025
Phone: 213-477-5229
Wants hand-painted "Bizarre-Ware" only; many patterns including "Fantasque", "Cruise Ware" and others; please send photos.

Dealer
Halifax Antique Center
Muir Hewitt
Queens Road/Gibbet Street
Queens Road Mills
Halifax HX1 4LR Canada •

Dealer
Caren Fine
11603 Gowrie Ct.
Potomac, MD 20854
Phone: 310-299-2116
Wants Clarice Cliff English art pottery from the 1920's and 1930's; also Rookwood, Newcomb, Van Briggle, Grubey, Teco, Roseville, etc.

Expert
Meisel Primavera Gallery
Louis & Susan Meisel
133 Prince St.
New York, NY 10012 •

Doulton & Royal Doulton
(see also FIGURINES, Royal Doulton; COLLECTIBLES (MODERN), Royal Doulton)

Club/Association
Mid-America Doulton Collectors
Newsletter: MADCAP
Betty J. Weir, Pres.
P.O. Box 2434
Joliet, IL 60434
Phone: 815-725-7348
The bi-monthly MADCAP newsletter is devoted to serious Doulton collectors, with an active buy, sell and trade section.

Dealer
Mainly Doulton
Rita Leiter
40 Chestnut Hill
North Hills, NY 11576
Phone: 516-365-1836
Buys and sells discontinued jugs, whiskey pieces, series ware, etc.

Dealer
Yesterdays South, Inc.
P.O. Box 161083
Miami, FL 33116
Phone: 800-368-5866 or 305-251-1988
                    FAX: 305-254-5977
Send SASE for list of almost 1000 Doultons for sale.

Expert
Gourmet Antiques Inc.
Nicki Budin
703 S. Main St.
Mansfield, OH 44907
Phone: 800-331-8543 •

Periodical
B.B.R. Publishing
Magazine: Collecting Doulton
A.R. Blakeman
2 Strafford Avenue, Elsecar
Barnsley
S. Yorkshire S74 8AA England
Leading magazine for the coverage of all aspects of Royal Doulton pottery: character jugs, figurines, advertising items, etc.

Goss Pottery Co./Crested Ware

Club/Association
Goss Collectors Club
Magazine: Goss Hawks, The
Brenda Robertson
4 Khasiaberry
Walnut Tree
Milton Keynes MK7 7DP England
Worldwide membership with regional meetings held in England.

Club/Association
Crested Circle
26 Urswick Road
Dagenhem
Essex RM9 6EA England •

Liverpool

Expert

Richard G. Marden
Box 524
Wolfeboro, NH 03894
Phone: 603-569-3209 *

Moorcroft

Collector

Poole
P.O. Box 692
Mill City, OR 97360 *

Royal Doulton

(see also CERAMICS (ENGLISH), Doulton
& Royal Doulton; FIGURINES, Royal
Doulton)

Man./Prod./Dist.

Royal Doulton USA Inc.
700 Cottontail Lane
Somerset, NJ 08873
Phone: 908-356-7929 or 800-582-2102
FAX: 908-356-9567

Shelley Potteries

Club/Association

Shelley Group
Newsletter: Shelley Group Newsletter
228 Croyland Road
Lower Edmonton
London N9 7BG England

Expert

Lustre Pitcher Antiques
Fern Kao
Box 312
Bowling Green, OH 43402
Phone: 419-352-5928 *

Staffordshire

Expert

Van Cline & Davenport, Ltd.
Stephen Van Cline, CAPP
792 Franklin Ave.
Franklin Lakes, NJ 07417
Phone: 201-891-4588   FAX: 201-891-2824
*Specializes in English Staffordshire & Wedgwood
ceramics; appraisals, authentication, lectures, expert testimony.*

Museum/Library

Hershey Museum of American Life
170 West Hershey Park Drive
Hershey, PA 17033
Phone: 717-534-3439
Large collection of 19th century English Staffordshire tableware made for export to the U.S.

Staffordshire (Historical)

Dealer

William/Teresa Kurau
P.O. Box 457
Lampeter, PA 17537
Phone: 717-464-0731
*Wants dark blue and lighter colors; Arms of the
States by Mayer; Erie Canal and Liverpool
pitchers; list of items for sale available.*

Expert

Richard G. Marden
Box 524
Wolfeboro, NH 03894
Phone: 603-569-3209 *

Expert

David & Linda Arman
R.D. #1, Box 353A
Woodstock, CT 06281
Phone: 203-928-5838
Wants Historical Staffordshire. *

Susie Cooper China Ltd.

Collector

Darryl Rehr
11433 Rochester Ave. #303
Los Angeles, CA 90025
Phone: 213-477-5229
*Wants Art Deco style patterns and shapes; please
send photo and SASE for guaranteed reply.*

Torquay Terra-Cotta Co.

Club/Association

North American Torquay Society
Magazine: Torquay Collector, The
Joseph D. Brewer
P.O. Box 397
Dalton, GA 30722
Phone: 404-226-3691
*For the enhancement of knowledge and enjoyment
of Torquay pottery; magazine offers articles, ads,
convention news.*

Club/Association

Torquay Pottery Collectors Society
Newsletter: Torquay Pottery Collectors Society
Newsletter
Beth Pulsipher
Box 373
Schoolcraft, MI 49087
Phone: 616-679-4195

Collector

Barbara Treat
479 Burley Road
Collierville, TN 38017
*U.S. and Canada coordinator for the Torquay
Pottery Collectors' Society.* *

Wade

Expert

Ian Warner
P.O. Box 55
Brampton
Ontario L6V 2K7 Canada
Specializing in Wade porcelain and swankyswigs.
*

Wedgwood

Club/Association

Wedgwood Society
The Roman Villa
Rockbourne, Fordingbridge
Hents SP6 3PG England *

Club/Association

Wedgwood Collectors Society
Newsletter: Wedgwood Collectors Society
Newsletter
P.O. Box 14013
Newark, NJ 07198

Dealer

Lydia's Antiques
P.O. Box 462
Newbury Park, CA 91319
Phone: 805-496-7805
*Specializes in antique and collectors' Jasper,
Fairyland, Creamware, Basalts, Dry Bodies,
Majolica; all shapes.*

Dealer

Carol's Antique Gallery
Carol Payne
14455 Big Basin Way
Saratoga, CA 95070
Phone: 408-867-7055
*Wants Wedgwood Jasperware & fancy wares both
modern & antique, especially black jasper, basalt,
& multi-colors.*

Expert

Van Cline & Davenport, Ltd.
Stephen Van Cline, CAPP
792 Franklin Ave.
Franklin Lakes, NJ 07417
Phone: 201-891-4588   FAX: 201-891-2824
*Specializes in English Staffordshire & Wedgwood
ceramics; appraisals, authentication, lectures, expert testimony.*

Man./Prod./Dist.

Waterford Wedgwood USA Inc.
P.O. Box 1454
Wall, NJ 07719
Phone: 201-938-5800   FAX: 201-938-6915

Museum/Library

Buten Museum
246 N. Bowman Ave.
Merion, PA 19066
Phone: 215-664-6601

Museum/Library
Birmingham Museum of Art
2000 8th Ave. N.
Birmingham, AL 35203
Phone: 205-254-2565

Whisky Pitchers
Collector
Alan Blakeman
Eslecar Workshops, Elsecar
Barnsley
S. Yorkshire S74 8AA England
*Wants pottery whisky pitchers, especially with
coloured tops or coloured transfer decorations; will
trade.*

CERAMICS (ORIENTAL)

Chinese Export Porcelain
Dealer
Mellin's Antiques
P.O. Box 134
Redding, CT 06875
Specializes in Canton porcelain. *

Dealer
James Gallery
112 Centennial Ave.
Rahns, PA 19426
Phone: 215-489-2828

Expert
Hobart Van Deusen
28 The Green
Watertown, CT 06795
Phone: 203-945-3456
Specializes in Canton porcelain.

Expert
Bea Cohen
Box 825
Easton, PA 18044-0825
Phone: 215-252-1098
Specializes in Canton porcelain. *

Expert
Mark Saville
26 Brookmawr Rd.
Newton Square, PA 19073-2001
Phone: 215-353-5506
Specializes in Canton porcelain. *

Expert
Elinor Gordon
P.O. Box 211
Villanova, PA 19085
Phone: 215-525-0981

Expert
Hobart D. Van Deusen
28 The Green
Watertown, CT 06795
Phone: 203-945-3456

*Wants to buy rare & unusual forms of blue &
white Canton; willing to assist others in identifying and pricing their pieces.*

Museum/Library
Peabody Museum of Salem
East India Square
Salem, MA 01970
Phone: 617-745-1876

Museum/Library
Captain Robert Bennet Forbes House
Dr. Dana D. Ricciardi
215 Adams St.
Milton, MA 02186
Phone: 617-696-1815
*A Boston China trade merchant's country man-
sion; 19th century artifacts: Chinese export porce-
lain, prints, paintings, furniture, etc.*

Museum/Library
Western Reserve Historical Society
10825 East Blvd.
Cleveland, OH 44106
Phone: 216-721-5722

Geisha Girl Pattern
Expert
E. Litts
P.O. Box 394
Morris Plains, NJ 07950
*Author of "The Collector's Encyclopedia of Geisha
Girl Porcelain."*

Mikasa
Man./Prod./Dist.
Mikasa
1 Gilbert Dr.
Secaucus, NJ 07094
Phone: 201-867-9210

Nippon
Club/Association
Canadian Nippon Collectors Association
Box 759
Allison
Ontario LOM TAOO Canada *

Club/Association
New England Nippon Collectors Club
Stephen Costa
145 Londonderry Rd.
Windham, NH 03087

Club/Association
International Nippon Collectors Club
Newsletter: INCC Newsletter
Nat Goldstein, Sec.
46-45 188th St.
New York, NY 11358
Phone: 718-961-5674

Club/Association
Long Island Nippon Collectors Club
Rhonda Perroncino
3372 Hewlett Ave.
Merrick, NY 11566

Club/Association
Great Lakes Nippon Collectors Club
Kathy Wojciechowski
P.O. Box 230
Peotone, IL 60468
Phone: 708-258-6105

Collector
Stephen Costa
145 Londonderry Rd.
Windham, NH 03087

Dealer
Mark Griffin
1768 Maple Ave.
Ft. Myers, FL 33901
Phone: 813-334-0083
*Buys quality Nippon: chocolate & tea sets,
molded, portraits, wall plaques, coralene, urns,
jugs, moriage, figural, Deco Noritake.*

Expert
c/o Infinity
Wilf Pegg
744 Dundas Street East
Toronto
Ontario M5A 2C3 Canada
*Advanced collector specializing in early "blown-
out" or relief-molded Nippon (1891-1921); features animals, birds and humans in relief.*

Expert
Joan Van Patten
Box 102
Rexford, NY 12148 *

Expert
Quality Nippon
Kathy Wojciechowski
P.O. Box 230
Peotone, IL 60468
Phone: 708-258-6105
*Pays top dollar for high quality undamaged Nip-
pon: large vases, urns, portraits, moriage,
coralene, tapestry, dresser sets, dolls, etc.*

Noritake
Dealer
Allenwood Americana Antiques
Ken & Gloria Kipp
Box 116
Allenwood, PA 17810
Phone: 717-538-1440
*Wants the Azalea pattern & scenic Noritake
china; established dealer with over 20 years experi-
ence; always buying & selling.*

Dealer

Rocking Chair Treasures
Vance Etzler
111 South Carroll St.
Frederick, MD 21701
Phone: 301-695-9304

Expert

Joan Van Patten
Box 102
Rexford, NY 12148 *

Matching Service

Noritake Co., Inc.
75 Seaview Drive
Secaucus, NJ 07094
Phone: 201-319-0600   FAX: 201-319-1962 *

Periodical

Newsletter: Noritake News
David H. Spain
1237 Federal Avenue East
Seattle, WA 98102
Phone: 206-323-8102
Color-filled quarterly newsletter for all Noritake dealers and collectors; emphasis on Art Deco.

Phoenix Bird Pattern

Club/Association

Phoenix Bird Collectors of America
Newsletter: Phoenix Bird Discoveries
Joan Oates
5912 Kingsfield Dr.
West Bloomfield, MI 48322
Phone: 313-661-2335
Members interested in ceramics decorated in the blue-and-white Phoenix Bird pattern and variants.

Expert

Joan Van Patten
Box 102
Rexford, NY 12148 *

Expert

Joan Oates
5912 Kingsfield Dr.
West Bloomfield, MI 48322
Phone: 313-661-2335
Author of "Phoenix Bird Chinaware" Books I, II, III and IV; available for $15 each plus postage ($1.25 for one/two; $1.50 for three/four.)

CEREAL BOX PREMIUMS

Collector

David Welch
RR 2, Box 233
Murphysboro, IL 62966
Phone: 618-687-2282
Wants all give-away or send-away items offered through cereal boxes and relating to TV, sports, comic, cartoon or movie characters.

Expert

Tomart Publications
Tom Tumbusch
P.O. Box 292102
Dayton, OH 45429
Phone: 513-294-2250
Buys radio, cereal, comic book, etc. premiums, i.e. rings, badges, etc.; author of "Illustrated Radio Premium Catalog & Price Guide."

CEREAL BOX PRIZES

Collector

Lee Woolf
321 Meeting House Lane
Narberth, PA 19072
Phone: 215-667-9378
*Wants cereal box toy cars made by F.F. Tool, Ohio; other cars by Kelloggs, Post, 1900's, 1950's, & 1960's. *

Collector

Graham Trievel
P.O. Box 4811, Rt. 113
Lionville, PA 19353
*Wants cereal box prizes from 1960's and 1970's. *

CEREAL BOXES

Auction Service

Memory Tree
1546-10 Simpson St.
Madison, WI 53713
Phone: 608-222-2418   FAX: 608-222-6935
Conducts specialty mail auctions of cereal boxes and backs, character items, premiums, rings and classes.

Collector

Scott Bruce
P.O. Box 87
Somerville, MA 02143
*Wants cereal boxes, store displays, and cereal box premiums. *

Collector

David Welch
RR 2, Box 233
Murphysboro, IL 62966
Phone: 618-687-2282
Wants any pre-1975 food boxes showing TV, movie, cartoon, sports, or comic characters or premium offers.

Collector

Don Marris
P.O. Box 111266
Arlington, TX 76007
Phone: 817-261-8745
Wants nice condition cereal boxes; should have front, back and sides.

Dealer

Toy Scouts, Inc.
Bill & Joanne Bruegman
330 Merriman Rd.
Akron, OH 44303-1552
Phone: 216-836-0668 or 216-864-6751
Want boxes that feature the Lone Ranger, cartoon characters, sports, movie stars, and radio show premiums.

Periodical

Newsletter: Flake
P.O. Box 481
Cambridge, MA 02140
Focuses on cereal boxes, store displays, and cereal box premiums; Jay Ward, Disney, cowboy, Hanna-Barbera boxes; articles, profiles, etc.

Periodical

Newsletter: Free Inside
Michael Vollmer
P.O. Box 178844
San Diego, CA 92117
Phone: 619-276-6977
Focuses on cereal boxes, store displays, and cereal box premiums; features articles and commentary on hobby of old & new cereal boxes.

CHALKWARE

(see also AMUSEMENT PARK ITEMS; FOLK ART)

Expert

Prize Publishers
Thomas G. Morris
P.O. Box 8307
Medford, OR 97504
Phone: 503-779-3164
Author of "The Carnival Chalk Prize."

CHARACTER COLLECTIBLES

(see also COMIC BOOKS; COMIC STRIPS; DISNEY COLLECTIBLES; MOVIE MEMORABILIA; RADIO SHOW PREMIUMS; TELEVISION SHOWS & MEMORABILIA; TOYS, Character)

Auction Service

Memory Tree
1546-10 Simpson St.
Madison, WI 53713
Phone: 608-222-2418   FAX: 608-222-6935
Conducts specialty mail auctions of cereal boxes and backs, character items, premiums, rings and classes.

Dealer

Joe & Juanita Reese
511 Dair Ave.
Harrison, OH 45030
*Wants character collectibles and Madame Alexander dolls; also western collectibles and pocket knives. *

Alice In Wonderland

Club/Association

Alice in Wonderland Collectors Network
Newsletter: Alice in Wonderland Collectors
    Network Newsletter
Bill Birenbaum
2486 Brunswick Circle A1
Woodridge, IL 60517
Phone: 708-968-0664
An organization of collectors, buyers and sellers of Alice & Lewis Carroll items.

Beanie & Cecil

Club/Association

Beanie & Cecil Collectors Fan Club
Newsletter: Beanie & Cecil Collectors Fan
    Club Newsletter
20159 Cohasset Street, #5
Canoga Park, CA 91306

Betty Boop

Collector

M. Zingre
Rt. 4 Box 229
Hendersonville, NC 28739
Wants any Betty Boop item. *

Cartoon & Comic

Auction Service

Comic Strip & Character Memorabilia
P.O.Box 385H
La Mirada, CA 90637
Phone: 213-943-9380
Conducts mail-bid auctions of cartoon and comic character memorabilia. *

Collector

Character Toys
Elmer & Viola Reynolds
P.O. Box 2183
Clarksville, IN 47131
Wants Kewpies, all comic character toys, banks, tin wind-ups, bisques, and Disneyana. *

Dealer

Cartoon Museum
Jim Ivey
4300 S. Semoran Blvd. #109
Orlando, FL 32822
Phone: 407-273-0141
Buys and sells original cartoon art of all types; also "spin offs": books, collectibles, comic books, magazines, etc.

Expert

Norm & Cathy Vigue
62 Bailey St.
Stoughton, MA 02072
Phone: 617-344-5441
Wants Popeye, Dick Tracy, Flintstones, Jetsons, Roy Rogers, Howdy Doody, Buck Rogers, Flash Gordon, Tarzan, Superman, Hoppy, etc.

Repro. Source

Warner Bros. Collections
4000 Warner Blvd.
Burbank, CA 91522
Send for catalog of Looney Tunes memorabilia.

Dick Tracy

Collector

Chester Gould
P.O. Box 183
Erwin, NC 28339
Dick Tracy comics wanted. *

Collector

Nay Russo
One South Main St.
Chagrin Falls, OH 44022
Phone: 216-247-7035
Wants all Dick Tracy related items: toys, premiums, books, carmel cards, games, puzzles, etc.

Expert

Larry Doucet
2351 Sultana Dr.
Yorktown Heights, NY 10598
A leading collector of all types of Dick Tracy collectibles; co-author of "The Authorized Guide to Dick Tracy Collectibles."

Howdy Doody

Dealer

Terry & Jeannie Quadnau
23 Hereford St.
Cincinnati, OH 45216-1107
Wants Howdy Doody, Hopalong Cassidy, character paper dolls and coloring books, board games and character items.

James Bond 007

Club/Association

James Bond Fan Club
Magazine: Bondage Quarterly
P.O. Box 414
Bronxville, NY 10708
Interested in the collection of memorabilia relating to James Bond, Secret Agent 007, his movies, and the actors who played him. *

Orphan Annie

Collector

Donna Walker
1560 N. Sandburg Terrace
Chicago, IL 60610
Wants Orphan Annie collectibles exclusively. *

Peanuts Characters

Club/Association

Peanuts Collector Club
Newsletter: Peanuts Collector Club Newsletter
Andrea C. Podley
P.O. Box 94
North Hollywood, CA 91603

Dedicated to the art & memorabilia associated with Charles M. Schulz, creator of "Peanuts"; also related characters in the strip.

Expert

Freddi Margolin
P.O. Box 5124
Bay Shore, NY 11706
Wants Peanuts related items: music boxes, pianos, Pop-Up books by Hallmark, Cartoon Maker and Talking Story Book by Mattel, etc. *

Expert

Andrea C. Podley
P.O. Box 94
North Hollywood, CA 91603
Author of "The Official Price Guide to Peanuts Collectibles."

Pogo

Club/Association

Pogo Fan Club
Magazine: Fort Mudge Most, The
Steve Thompson
6908 Wentworth Ave. South
Richfield, MN 55423
Phone: 612-869-6320
Inter. club explores all aspects of Walt Kelly's career; magazine reprints scarce and unpublished Kellyana, ads, letters, strip.

Popeye

Club/Association

Popeye Fan Club
Newsletter: PFC Newsletter
Suite 151
5995 Stage Road
Bartlett, TN 38134

Rocky & Bullwinkle

Collector

Bob Janci
10 Oak Crest Lane
Coplay, PA 18037
Wants Rocky, Bullwinkle, Boris, Natasha collectibles: photos, records, pins, etc. *

Sherlock Holmes

Club/Association

Confederation of Wisteria Lodge, The
13 Lindsey Terrace NW
Rome, GA 30161 *

Collector

Robert C. Hess
Robert Hess
559 Potter Blvd.
Brightwaters, NY 11718
Phone: 516-665-8365
Wants Sherlock Holmes/Sir Arthur Conan Doyle items: figurines, sculpture, statuary, dolls, original artwork, illustrations, etc.

Smurf

Club/Association

Smurf Collectors Club International
Newsletter: Smurf Collectors Newsletter
24 Cabot Road West
Massapequa, NY 11758
Phone: 516-799-3221
Focuses on Smurf memorabilia from 56 countries.

Collector

S. Lund
24CH Cabot Road W.
Massapequa, NY 11758
Phone: 516-799-3221
Wants European items only; post cards, metal
cars, books, figurines; must have "Peyo" (creator's
name) license mark.

Tarzan

Club/Association

Jungle Club
5813 York Ave.
Edina, MN 55410
Phone: 612-922-9144 *

Expert

Hancer's Bookstore
Kevin Hancer
5813 York Ave.
Edina, MN 55410
Phone: 612-922-9144 *

Museum/Library

University of Louisville, Belknap
Campus Library
c/o Ekstrom Library
Rare Book Room
Louisville, KY 40292
Phone: 502-588-5555

Three Stooges

Club/Association

Northern Ohio Three Stooges Fan
Association
586 Wilkes Lane
Richmond Heights, OH 44143
Phone: 216-481-9446

Collector

Gary Lassin
P.O. Box 747
Gwynedo Valley, PA 19437
Wants 3 Stooges memorabilia; toys, games, posters, stills, anything.

Collector

Harry S. Ross
586 Wilkes Ln.
Richmond Hts., OH 44143
Phone: 216-481-9446
Serious Three Stooges collector seeks rare, unusual
memorabilia: toys, games, paper, advertising,
personal items, animation cels, etc.

Collector

Peter Moment
537 Bright St.
San Francisco, CA 94132
Wants Three Stooges items: books, lobby cards,
autographs, letters, canceled checks, films, hand
puppets, gum cards, scripts, etc. *

Man./Prod./Dist.

Soitenly Stooges
Harry S. Ross
586 Wilkes Ln.
Richmond Hts., OH 44143
Phone: 216-481-9446
Catalog of new Three Stooges gifts - dolls, books,
videos, posters, T-shirts, buttons, jewelry, magnets, magnets, photos, clocks, etc.

Yellow Kid

Club/Association

Yellow Kid Society
Newsletter: Yellow Kid Notes
Richard Olson
103 Doubloon Drive
Slidell, LA 70461
Phone: 504-641-5173

Collector

Richard Olson
103 Doubloon Drive
Slidell, LA 70461
Phone: 504-641-5173
Wants all Yellow Kid items including pinbacks,
gum cards, toys, ads, magazines, comic supplements, etc.

CHARMS

Plastic

(see also PLASTIC COLLECTIBLES)

Collector

D. Brandt
2425 Sandpiper Way
Cameron Park, CA 95682
Phone: 916-677-4376
Wants celluloid (plastic) charms from the 1930's-
40's: Disney, Popeye, Betty Boop, Kewpie, Mobil,
Schmoo, Pop-Eyed, etc.

Collector

Poole
P.O. Box 692
Mill City, OR 97360
Wants older plastic charms. *

CHECKS

(see also BANK CHECKS; COINS &
CURRENCY)

CHEESE BOXES

Collector

Mitch Kaidy
921 Crittenden Rd.
Rochester, NY 14623
Phone: 716-424-4746
Wants cheese boxes, cheese kegs, Phoenix, Old
English, Breakstone, Kraft. *

CHESS SETS

(see also GAMES)

Club/Association

Chess Collectors International
Newsletter: Chess Collector, The
Dr. George Dean, Pres.
P.O. Box 166
Commack, NY 11725
Phone: 516-543-1330   FAX: 516-543-7901
International membership interested in collecting
chess sets, chess stamps, chess books, chess art, and
other chess related items.

Club/Association

Chess Collectors Association
Newsletter: Checkmate
P.O. Box 99444
Louisville, KY 40299
Phone: 502-267-5357 *

Collector

Jeffrey Litwin
141 Stine Dr.
Collegeville, PA 19426
Phone: 215-489-9322
Wants antique or unusual chess sets; please send
description and photo.

Expert

Floyd Sarisohn
P.O. Box 166
Commack, NY 11725
Phone: 516-543-1330   FAX: 516-543-7901

Museum/Library

Long Island Chess Museum
Bernice & Floyd Sarisohn
P.O. Box 166
Commack, NY 11725
Phone: 516-543-1330   FAX: 516-543-7901
Private museum of over 300 chess sets; viewing by
appointment only.

CHILDREN'S THINGS

(see also BOOKS; DR. SEUSS ITEMS;
PERAMBULATORS; MINIATURES)

Club/Association

Children's Things Collectors Society
Newsletter: CTCS Newsletter
Linda Martin
P.O. Box 983
Durant, IA 52747

Expert
Rosella Tinsley
105 15 St.
Osawatomie, KS 66064
Specializing in dishes, tea sets, and furniture. *

Alphabet Plates
Collector
Walter Lozoski
910 4th Ave. N. #102
Seattle, WA 98109
Phone: 206-285-4986
Wants children's alphabet (A.B.C.) plates.

Dishes
Collector
D.M. Diabo
19953 Great Oaks Circle S.
Mt. Clemens, MI 48043 *

Dealer
Louise M. Loehr
163 W. Main St.
P.O. Box 208
Kutztown, PA 19530
Phone: 215-683-8370
Co-author of "Willow Pattern China." Specializing in willow, flow blue, and early children's china. Wants one piece or collections.

Expert
Margaret & Kenn Whitmyer
Box 30806
Gahanna, OH 43230 *

Expert
Lorraine Punchard
P.O. Box 20543
Bloomington, MN 55420
Phone: 612-888-1079   FAX: 612-888-8527
Author of "Child's Play."

CHINA
(see also CERAMICS; DINNERWARE)

CHINESE ITEMS
(see also ORIENTALIA)

CHOCOLATE MOLDS
(see also KITCHEN COLLECTIBLES, Molds)

Collector
Shirley Baumann
21090 Floyd Ave.
Iowa Falls, IA 50126
Wants any two-piece mold.

CHRISTMAS COLLECTIBLES
(see also HOLIDAY COLLECTIBLES;
COLLECTIBLES (MODERN), Ornaments)

Auction Service
Robert J. Connelly, ASA
666 Chenango St.
Binghamton, NY 13901
Phone: 607-722-9593   FAX: 607-722-1266
Conducts specialty Christmas sales.

Auction Service
Bruce & Shari Knight
2475 Signal Hill Road
Springfield, OH 45504
Conducts specialty Christmas sales. *

Club/Association
Golden Glow of Christmas Past
Newsletter: Golden Glow of Christmas Past
P.O. Box 14808
Chicago, IL 60614
Network of Christmas antique collectors focusing on 1870-1950; annual convention.

Collector
Bob Merck
44 Newtown Turnpike
Weston, CT 06883
Wants pre-1940 figural glass or paper ornaments; Santa Claus figures, Santa blocks & games, figural glass light bulbs (need not work.)

Collector
Holiday Auction, The
Cindy Chipps
4027 Brooks Hill Rd.
Brooks, KY 40109
Phone: 502-955-9238
Wants figural light bulbs, Matchless Wonder Stars; also other Christmas items, electrical or mechanical.

Collector
J. W. & Treva Courter
R.R. #1
Simpson, IL 62985
Phone: 618-949-3884
Wants German Christmas glass figural ornaments, old Father Christmas and Wonder Stars.

Collector
John & Jenny Tarrant
10221 Squire Meadows
St. Louis, MO 63123
Wants feather trees, unusual ornaments, cotton ornaments, Santas, paper or cardboard ornaments, and candy containers.

Dealer
Bettie Petzoldt
RR #1 Box 249
New Park, PA 17352
Phone: 717-382-1416
Collect/buy/sell early Christmas ornaments: glass, diecut, Dresden, cotton, lights, Santas; monthly illustrated sales list available.

Dealer
Charles & Grace Gottschall
5761 Route 202
Lahaska, PA 18931 *

Expert
Holiday Antiques
Lissa & Dick Smith
Box 208 R.D. 1
Danville, PA 17821
Phone: 717-275-7796 *

Expert
Margaret & Kenn Whitmyer
Box 30806
Gahanna, OH 43230
Author of "Christmas Collectibles." *

Periodical
Magazine: Deck the Halls
P.O. Box 476879
Chicago, IL 60647 *

Repro. Source
Kurt S. Adler, Inc.
1107 Broadway
New York, NY 10010
Carries assorted ornaments. *

Mail Order Catalogs
Dealer
Hesson Country Crafts & Collectables
Judy Hesson
1261 S. Lloyd
Lombard, IL 60148
Phone: 708-627-3298
Buys & sells Christmas mail order catalogs: Sears, Montgomery Ward, Penny, Aldens, Spiegel: 1935-1990; also other catalogs; list $2.

CIGAR BANDS

BOXES & LABELS
(see also LABELS)

Club/Association
International Seal, Label & Cigar Band Society
Newsletter: Inter. Seal, Label & Cigar Band Soc. Bulletin
8915 E. Bellevue St.
Tucson, AZ 85715
Phone: 602-296-1048
Interested in hotel, cigar box, beer, fruit crate, etc. labels; also matchcovers, charity stamps, Christmas seals, sugar packets, etc.

Collector
Cerebro
David & Barbara Freiberg
P.O. Box 1221
Lancaster, PA 17603
Phone: 717-656-7875 or 800-69L-ABEL

Wants cigar box, cigar bands, old adver. labels: fire cracker labels, baggage labels, US cigarette cards, advertising poster stamps.

Collector
Joseph Hruby
1511 Lyndhurst Road
Lyndhurst, OH 44124
Wants old cigar band collections in good condition.

Collector
Shapiro
3201 So. Monroe
Denver, CO 80210
Wants old cigar band collections, cigar box labels, baseball cards. *

Expert
Steve C. Jones
Box 6093
Syracuse, NY 13217
Phone: 607-753-8822
Buys and sells old unused cigar box labels, lithographer's cigar box sample labels, sample books, proof labels; any amount; catalog.

Expert
Aaron Industries
Joe Davidson
5185 Windfall Rd.
Medina, OH 44256
Phone: 216-723-7172
Author and expert specializing in stone lithography especially cigar box labels.

Expert
Dr. Tony Hyman
Box 699
Claremont, CA 91711
Phone: 714-621-5952 FAX: 714-621-7525
Collector, dealer, expert, author; wants pre-1020 cigar box labels, cans & all else related to cigar making, selling or smoking.

Museum/Library
Metropolitan Museum of Art, The
Jefferson Burdich Collection
5th Avenue & 82nd Street
New York, NY 10028
Phone: 212-879-5500

Periodical
Arnot Art Museum
Magazine: C.I.G.A.R. Quarterly
235 Lake St.
Elmira, NY 14901
A quarterly journal devoted to histories of the cigar, box and printing industries. *

CIGAR STORE COLLECTIBLES

(see also CIGAR BANDS, BOXES & LABELS; SMOKING COLLECTIBLES)

Collector
Dr. Greg Zeminick
Suite 160
1350 Kirts
Troy, MI 48084
Phone: 313-642-8129 FAX: 313-244-9495
Wants cigar store items: Indians, figures, cigar cutters, lighters, photos, blinking eye clocks, cast iron items: anything cigar store.

Museum/Library
New York Public Library, Arnet Collections, The
5th Ave. & 42nd Street
New York, NY 10018
Phone: 212-930-0800

Museum/Library
National Tobacco-Textile Museum
P.O. Box 541
Danville, VA 24543
Phone: 804-797-9437

CIGARETTE COLLECTIBLES

(see also LIGHTERS; SMOKING COLLECTIBLES)

Collector
John Hale
293 Varick St.
Jersey City, NJ 07302
Phone: 201-435-8298
Wants cigarette lighters, boxes, packs, fluid cans, the unusual and bizarre. *

Cards

Collector
Robert Hess
559 Potter Blvd.
Brightwaters, NY 11718
Wants pre-WWII cigarette cards with any theme or art; also English and German cigarette cards. *

Cigarette Boxes

Dealer
Lenore Monleon
33 Fifth Ave.
New York, NY 10003
Phone: 212-475-7871 or 212-838-1004
Wants enamel and sterling match safes and cigarette boxes.

Match Safes

Collector
Betty Bird
107 Ida St.
Mount Shasta, CA 96067
Phone: 916-926-4331

Dealer
Lenore Monleon
33 Fifth Ave.
New York, NY 10003
Phone: 212-475-7871 or 212-838-1004
Wants enamel and sterling match safes and cigarette boxes.

Packs

Club/Association
Cigarette Pack Collectors' Association
Newsletter: Brandstand
61 Searle St.
Georgetown, MA 01833
Phone: 508-352-7377
For those interested in cigarette packs, tins, boxes and related advertising items; especially obsolete U.S. brands.

Stands

Collector
Lawrence Hartnell
Box 352
Collingwood
Ontario L9Y 3Z7 Canada
Wants footed cigarette holders (stands) (1920-1935) shaped like wine glasses; some have the foot rolled up to serve as an ashtray.

CIRCUS COLLECTIBLES

(see also CLOWN COLLECTIBLES)

Auction Service
Auction Under the Big Top
Tommy Sciortino
3723 N. Nebraska Aave.
Tampa, FL 33603
Phone: 818-248-5387 or 813-932-1782
FAX: 813-248-5387
Specializes in the sale of circus equipment and memorabilia, carousels, amusement devices, coin-ops, toys, etc.

Club/Association
Circus Fans of America
Magazine: White Tops
4 Center Drive
Camp Hill, PA 17011 *

Collector
Ross Wandrey
1603 Morse
Houston, TX 77019
Wants posters, programs, lithographs, window cards, photographs, negatives, route cards, books, toys, etc.

Museum/Library
P.T. Barnum Museum
820 Main St.
Bridgeport, CT 06604
Phone: 203-576-7320

Museum/Library

John & Mable Ringling Museum of Art
5401 Bayshore Rd.
Sarasota, FL 34243
Phone: 813-355-5101

Museum/Library

Circus City Festival Museum
154 North Broadway
Peru, IN 46970
Phone: 317-472-3918

Museum/Library

Circus World Museum Library & Research
Center
Robert L. Parkinson, Lib.
426 Water St.
Baraboo, WI 53913
Phone: 608-356-8341   FAX: 608-356-1800
*Large collection of circus lithographs, route books,
circus programs, circus photos and b/w negatives,
circus trade journals, etc.*

Museum/Library

Emmett Kelly Historical Museum
202 E. Main
Sedan, KS 67361
Phone: 316-725-3470

Periodical

Newsletter: Circus Report
Don Marcks
525 Oak Street
El Cerrito, CA 94530-3699
Phone: 415-525-3332
A weekly newsletter devoted to the circus.

Ricketts Circus

Dealer

Bill Ricketts
P.O. Box 9605-B
Ashville, NC 28805
Phone: 704-669-2205 or 704-669-8881
*Wants to buy any posters, newspaper ads, etc.
which advertise the Ricketts Circus (first circus in
the US - Phila., PA).*

CIRCUS EQUIPMENT

Miniature Models Of

Club/Association

Circus Model Builders International
Newsletter: Little Circus Wagon
Sally Conover Weitlauf
347 Lonsdale Ave.
Dayton, OH 45419-3249
Phone: 513-299-0515
*For builders and collectors of miniature models of
circus equipment.*

CIVIL WAR

Club/Association

Civil War Society, The
Magazine: Civil War Magazine
P.O. Box 798
Berryville, VA 22611
Phone: 800-247-6253
*An international organization of Civil War en-
thusiasts; publishes full-color "Civil War Maga-
zine" bi-monthly.*

Club/Association

Civil War Round Table, The
Newsletter: Civil War Roundtable Newsletter
357 W. Chicago Ave.
Chicago, IL 60610
Phone: 312-944-3085
*The nation's leading organization dedicated to
the study of Civil War history.*

Club/Association

Heritagepac
Jerry L. Russell
P.O. Box 7388
Little Rock, AR 72217
Phone: 501-225-3996   FAX: 501-225-5167
*A national political action committee dedicated to
the preservation of Civil War battlefields.*

Club/Association

Civil War Round Table Associates
Jerry L. Russell, NatCh.
P.O. Box 7388
Little Rock, AR 72217
Phone: 501-225-3996   FAX: 501-225-5167
*The nation's leading battlefield preservation orga-
nization.*

Club/Association

Confederate Historical Institute, The
Newsletter: CHI Dispatch
Jerry L. Russell
P.O. Box 7388
Little Rock, AR 72217
Phone: 501-225-3996   FAX: 501-225-5167
*The only organization devoted to the study of the
history of The Confederate States of America.*

Club/Association

Society of Civil War Historians, The
Jerry L. Russell, ExSec.
P.O. Box 7388
Little Rock, AR 72217
Phone: 501-225-3996   FAX: 501-225-5167
*The only organization for the teachers of Civil War
history.*

Misc. Service

National Archives & Records
Administration
7th & Pennsylvania Ave. NW
Washington, DC 20408
*For locating military records of Civil War veter-
ans.*

Misc. Service

Veterans Administration, Director of
National Cemetery System
818 Vermont Ave. NW
Washington, DC 20420
*Contact to find out where a Civil War ancestor
was buried during or after the Civil War.*

Misc. Service

Marie Varrelman Melchiori, CGRS
121 Tapawingo Rd. SW
Vienna, VA 22180
Phone: 703-938-7279
*Certified genealogical record searcher, specializes
in Civil War research.*

Periodical

Newspaper: Civil War News, The
P.O. Box C
Arlington, MA 02174
Phone: 617-646-2010   FAX: 617-643-1864
*A newspaper published nine times per year for
people with an active interest in Civil War history.*

Periodical

Distant Frontier Press
Newsletter: Mail Call
P.O. Box 5031
South Hackensack, NJ 07606
*Published bi-monthly, each issue is filled with
letters, stories and poems written to, by or about
Civil War soldiers.*

Periodical

Magazine: Courier, The
P.O. Box 1863
Williamsville, NY 14231-1863
Phone: 716-634-8324
*A bi-monthly magazine containing classified ads,
articles, events, calendar, book reviews, and
goods/services for Civil War buffs.*

Periodical

Magazine: North South Trader's Civil War
   Magazine
Stephen W. Sylvia, Pub.
P.O. Drawer 631
Orange, VA 22960
Phone: 703-67C-IVIL
*The bimonthly magazine for Civil War relic hun-
ters, collectors, reenactors and historians.*

Periodical

Newsletter: Grave Matters
Steve Davis
1163 Warrenhall Lane
Atlanta, GA 30319
*A newsletter for Civil War buffs who carry their
hobby to the ultimate dead end!*

Periodical

Magazine: Blue & Gray Magazine
P.O. Box 28685
Columbus, OH 43228
Phone: 800-541-0956

A bi-monthly full-color magazine focusing on the Civil War.

Periodical

Magazine: Civil War Times Illustrated
P.O. Box 1863
Mt. Morris, IL 61054-9947
Phone: 815-734-6309 or 800-435-9610
A bi-monthly magazine focusing on the historical aspects of the great conflict.

Periodical

Magazine: Confederate Veteran
8506 Braesdale
Houston, TX 77701
Includes scholarly articles about the battles, leaders and soldiers of the War Between the States; images, Southern heritage, etc.

Artillery

Periodical

Magazine: Artilleryman, The
4 Water Street
P.O. Box C
Arlington, MA 02174
Published quarterly, the only magazine exclusively for the artillery enthusiast: artillery history, unit profiles, shell

Cavalry

Museum/Library

U.S. Horse Cavalry Association & Museum
P.O. Box 2325
Fort Riley, KS 66442-0325
Phone: 913-784-5759   FAX: 913-784-5797
Collects, preserves and displays the uniforms, weapons and equipment used by cavalry soldiers from the Revolutionary War through WWII.

Periodical

Journal: Civil War Cavalry Review
P.O. Box 63
Mt. Sidney, VA 24467
A quarterly journal devoted exclusively to the indepth and accurate portrayal of the Civil War horse soldier.

Reenactors

Club/Association

North-South Skirmish Association
1238 Ronald Street
Vandalia, OH 45377
Phone: 513-890-0910
For those interested in Civil War reenacting.

Periodical

Newspaper: Union Times, The
7214 Laurel Hill Road
Orlando, FL 32818
Phone: 407-295-7510
Carries the latest information on all Southeastern events: shows, reenactments, book fairs; for historians, reenactors, buffs in S.E.

Periodical

Newspaper: Camp Chase Gazette
P.O. Box 707
Marietta, OH 45750
Phone: 614-373-1865
For 17 years the voice of the Civil War reenactor: recruiting, events, equipment, etc.

Periodical

Magazine: Reenactor's Journal
P.O. Box 1864
Varna, IL 61375
A concise, to-the-point magazine for reenactors of the War Between the States; for military or civilian reenactor.

Periodical

Newspaper: Yesteryears Chronicle
P.O. Box 132
Sullivan, IL 61951
Phone: 217-728-7128
The leading interpretive historical publication for period fashion and living: reciepts, fashion, poems, needlework, activities, etc.

CIVIL WAR ARTIFACTS

(see also EXONUMIA; MEDICAL, DENTAL & PHARMACEUTICAL, Civil War)

Club/Association

Company H 119th NY Volunteers
Historical Association
Newsletter: Hempstead Volunteer, The
Glenn F. Sitterly, Pres.
2306 Rockwood Ave.
Baldwin, NY 11510
Phone: 516-868-4521
Focuses on photos, letters, possessions, records of the original 119th N.Y. Civil War soldiers, 11th and later 20th Corps.

Collector

Gil Barrett
8322 Sperry Court
Laurel, MD 20723
Phone: 301-498-1412
Wants Civil War photos and memorabilia particularly Maryland Union, 6th and 8th Mass. Infantry, and Boston Light Artillery.

Collector

Barry Smith
1707 Brookcliff Dr.
Greensboro, NC 27408
Phone: 919-288-4375
Wants Union or Confederate Civil War memorabilia: letters, documents, autographs, photos, etc.

Collector

David Taylor
P.O. Box 87
Sylvania, OH 43560
Phone: 419-882-5547 *

Collector

James Mejdrich
128 N. Knollwood Dr.
Wheaton, IL 60187
Wants Civil War photos, letters, diaries, and personal items.

Dealer

Gunsight Antiques & Americana
P.O. Box 1056
Westbrook, ME 04092
Phone: 207-839-3825
Buys and sells weapons, uniforms, headgear, accouterments, personal presentation & identified items, etc.; specializes in Civil War.

Dealer

Bob & Pat Bartosz
Box 226
Wenonah, NJ 08090
Phone: 609-468-0866
*Any old 1800's paper items, Civil War letters, bank checks, slave documents, fire department items, early baseball. **

Dealer

Blue & Gray Relic Shop
Mike & Rose Klinepeter
Route 1, Box 26
Big Cove Tannery, PA 17212
Phone: 717-294-3326 *

Dealer

Will Gorges Civil War Items
Will Gorges
308 Simmons St.
New Bern, NC 28560
Phone: 919-638-4913 or 919-636-3039
Full time dealer in Civil War artifacts; firearms, accouterments, edged weapons, dug items, coins, etc.; catalog available.

Dealer

Antique Scientifica
Alex Peck
P.O. Box 710
Charleston, IL 61920
Phone: 217-348-1009
Wants surgical and bloodletting instruments, any Civil War (and pre-1890) medical gear, USA Hosp. Dept., etc.; anything Civil War.

Expert

Antiques Americana
K.C. Owings
Box 19
N. Abington, MA 02351
Phone: 617-857-1655
Wants Civil War, Colonial American documents, books, autographs and related collectibles; send $1 for three catalog issues.

Expert

Courtney Wilson
8398 Court Ave.
Ellicott City, MD 21043
Phone: 301-465-6827
Military antiques 1700-1900: appraiser, consultant, broker, dealer; arms, uniforms, equipment, memorabilia - especially Civil War.

Museum/Library

Grand Army of the Republic Memorial
Museum & Library
4278 Griscom St.
Philadelphia, PA 19124-3954
Phone: 215-673-1688 or 215-289-6484
Civil War Museum & Library; artifacts, personal memorabilia, paintings, G.A.R. & S.U.V.C.W. records; open first Sunday or by appt.

Museum/Library

Museum of the Confederacy, The
1201 East Clay St.
Richmond, VA 23219
Phone: 804-649-1861

Museum/Library

New Bern Civil War Museum
Will Gorges
301 Metcalf St.
New Bern, NC 28560
Phone: 919-633-2818 or 919-636-3039
Houses one of the finest in-depth private collections of Civil War memorabilia and weapons in the U.S. and open to the public.

Museum/Library

Confederate Research Center
Dr. B.D. Patterson
P.O. Box 619
Hillsboro, TX 76645
Phone: 817-582-2555
Large collection of Civil War artifacts; museum provides information about Confederate soldiers & capsule histories of Confed. regiments.

Periodical

Directory: Militaria Directory
David C. Williams
2237 Brookhollow Dr.
Abilene, TX 79605
Publishes a directory of military dealers, collectors, genealogical research, artifact restoration, etc. for Rev. War through Civil War.

Repro. Source

Regimental Quartermaster, The
Box 553
Hatboro, PA 19040
Civil War reproduction muskets, uniforms, equipment, accouterments, shooting supplies, leather goods, etc.; send $2 for list.

Repro. Source

Staley's Sundries
710 Caroline Street
Fredericksburg, VA 22401
Phone: 703-373-8349
*Carries American Revolution and Civil War era gifts, flags, music, costumes, accessories, costume patterns, accouterments, etc. ***

Confederate

Dealer

Brian Michael Green
Brian & Maria Green
P.O. Box 1816
Kernersville, NC 27285-1816
Phone: 919-993-5100
Buy & sell Confederate States autographs and documents, especially military related; also photos, CDV's and other memorabilia.

Confederate Bonds

Collector

Jule Dews
7703 Baltimore National Pike
Frederick, MD 21702
Phone: 301-473-8287
Wants Confederate bonds. Custom framing available for same. Author of book about Confederate Bonds.

Confederate Money

Collector

Bob Pyne
P.O. Box 149064
Orlando, FL 32814
Wants older bank checks; also Confederate money, stocks and bonds.

Confederate Swords

Collector

Steve Hess
P.O. Box 3476
De Land, FL 32720-3476
Phone: 904-736-1067

Currency

Dealer

S C Coin & Stamp Co. Inc.
Cy Phillips, Jr.
P.O. Drawer 3069
Arcadia, CA 91006
Phone: 818-445-8277 or 800-367-0779
Wants Confederate stamps, Civil War tokens, medals, currency, encased postage, etc.

Paper Items

Collector

Wayne Styles
P.O. Box 8019
Atlantic City, NJ 08404
Phone: 609-927-7050 *

Collector

Jack Dohahue
P.O. Box 123
Bayside, NY 11361
Phone: 718-225-4067
*Wants Civil War autographs, letters, diaries, arms; North and South. ***

Dealer

Bob & Pat Bartosz
Box 226
Wenonah, NJ 08090
Phone: 609-468-0866
Wants Civil War paper items, e.g. letters, diaries, slave papers. Author of "The Civil War Letter of Geo. R. White 19th Mass. Vol."

Photographs

Collector

Pete Falk
170 Boston Post Rd., Box 150
Madison, CT 06443
Phone: 203-245-2246
Wants important vintage Civil War photographs, especially of notable figures such as Abraham Lincoln, Grant, Lee, etc.

Misc. Service

Department of the Army
Michael Whitney, Cur.
U.S. Army Military Institution
Carlisle Barracks, PA 17013-5009
*Wants to make copies of photos of Civil War veterans. Loan your photo and get 8x10 copy made for free. Write them first for info. ***

Tokens

Club/Association

Civil War Token Society
Journal: Civil War Token Journal
Cindy Grellman
P.O. Box 951988
Lake Mary, FL 32795-1988
Phone: 407-321-8747
Purpose is to promote the study of Civil War tokens along educational, historic and scientific lines.

Veterans

(see also VETERANS, Civil War)

CIVILIAN CONSERVATION CORPS ITEMS

Club/Association

Association of Civilian Conservation
Corps Alumni
P.O. Box 16429
St. Louis, MO 63125
A group of over 10,000 members founded in 1977.

Collector
Jake Eckenrode
R.D. 3 Box 421
Bellefonte, PA 16823
Phone: 814-355-8769
Wants CCC items from the 1930's.

Collector
Larry Jarvinen
313 Condon Rd.
Manistee, MI 49660
Phone: 616-723-5063

Collector
Thomas W. Pooler
22152 McCourtney Rd.
Grass Valley, CA 95949-7661
Phone: 916-268-9545
Wants all CCC material: medals, flags, rings, tokens, insignia (especially numbered company patches.) Send description AND price.

Dealer
Allenwood Americana Antiques
Ken & Gloria Kipp
Box 116
Allenwood, PA 17810
Phone: 717-538-1440
Established dealer with over 20 years experience; always buying and selling.

CLOCKS

(see also INSTRUMENTS & DEVICES, Scientific; WATCHES)

Club/Association
Antiquarian Horological Society
Magazine: Antiquarian Horology
New Houses, High Street
Ticehurst, Wadhurst
Sussex TN5 7AL England *

Club/Association
National Association of Watch & Clock
Collectors, Inc.
Magazine: Bulletin of the NAWCC
Thomas J. Bartels, ExDir
514 Poplar St.
Columbia, PA 17512-2130
Phone: 717-684-8261   FAX: 717-684-0878
The NAWCC is a non-profit and scientific association founded in 1943 and now serving the horological interests of 35,000 hobbyists.

Collector
Jerry Boxenhorn
2045 Legion St.
South Bellmore, NY 11710
Phone: 516-221-2723
*Wants one clock or a collection; also movements, parts; all clock related items. *

Collector
Myron Palay
4242 Lorain Ave.
Cleveland, OH 44113-3771
Phone: 216-961-7903
Wants contents of watch and clock repair shops, 1 item or entire shop; also wants pre-1700 watches and clocks in any condition.

Collector
Larry Spilkin
P.O. Box 5039
Southfield, MI 48086-5039
Phone: 313-642-3722
Wants Lawson, Herman-Miller, Howard-Miller clocks.

Collector
Dennis Kickhofel
20863 Lancaster Rd.
Harper Woods, MI 48225
*Wants various types of Regulator schoolhouse clocks *

Collector
Jim Rocheleau
1137 Cadieux
Grosse Point, MI 48230
Phone: 313-885-7805
Wants cast iron blinking eye clocks, plus all others.

Dealer
Meurs Renehan
101 East Main St.
Clinton, CT 06413
Phone: 203-669-7055

Dealer
Barbara N. Cohen Galleries
Leonard & Barb Cohen
115 E. Main St.
Waterloo, NY 13165-1432
Phone: 315-539-3032 or 315-539-3372
Wants 16th-early 19th century European clocks: lantern, bracket, grandfather, automation, chinoiserie, fusee chain, inlaid, ormolu.

Dealer
Timesavers
P.O. Box 171
Wheeling, IL 60090
Phone: 312-394-4818
*A dealer who offers new clocks but specializes in the reproduction of American antique clocks. *

Expert
Robert O. Stuart
Box 104, Jo Joy Road
Limington, ME 04049
Phone: 207-793-4522 *

Expert
Eric Chandlee Wilson
16 Bondsville Road
Thorndale, PA 19372
Phone: 215-383-5597
Tallcase clock dealer specializing in Chester County, PA clocks and an expert on clocks by the Chandlee's.

Expert
Harvey Flemister
512 Highgate Terrace
Silver Spring, MD 20904
Phone: 301-622-3686

Expert
Olde Time Antiques
Joe & Wilma Clark
2088 Creekview Ct.
Reynoldsburg, OH 43068
Phone: 614-863-2637 *

Expert
Martha Tipps
7012 Blackwood Dr.
Dallas, TX 75231
Phone: 214-348-0075

Museum/Library
Willard House & Clock Museum, Inc.
P.O. Box 156
Grafton, MA 01519
Phone: 617-839-3500

Museum/Library
American Clock & Watch Museum
Journal: Timepiece Journal
100 Maple St.
Bristol, CT 06010-5092
Phone: 203-583-6070
Preserves the history of American horology, especially Connecticut and Bristol's role; large displays of clocks & watches.

Museum/Library
National Association of Watch & Clock
Collectors Museum, Inc., The
Patricia Tomes
514 Poplar St.
Columbia, PA 17512-2130
Phone: 717-684-8261   FAX: 717-684-0878
The NAWCC museum strives to illustrate the history of timekeeping with a collection of more than 8000 horological items.

Museum/Library
National Museum of American History
14th & Constitution Ave. NW
Washington, DC 20560
Phone: 202-357-2700

Museum/Library
Greensboro Clock Museum
300 Bellemeade St.
Greensboro, NC 27401
Phone: 919-275-0462

Museum/Library
Bily Clock Exhibit
Spillville, IA 52168
Phone: 319-562-3569

Museum/Library
Time Museum, The
Dorothy Mastricola
7801 E. State St.
P.O. Box 5285
Rockford, IL 61125
Phone: 815-398-6000
Has an extensive collection of time-measuring devices from all parts of the world dating from ancient instruments to the atomic clock.

Museum/Library
Old Clock Museum
929 E. Preston St.
Pharr, TX 78577
Phone: 512-787-1923

Periodical
Magazine: Antique Clocks
Wolsey House, Wolsey Road
Hemel Hempstead HP24SS England *

Periodical
Magazine: Clocks
Wolsey House, Wolsey Rd.
Hemel Hempstead
Herts, England
The British monthly magazine for clock enthusiasts; feature articles on clock history and restoration.

Periodical
Magazine: Horological Times
P.O. Box 11011
Cincinnati, OH 45211 *

Periodical
Magazine: Watch & Clock Review
2403 Champa St.
Denver, CO 80205
Phone: 303-296-1600   FAX: 303-295-2159
Monthly magazine primarily for new and vintage watch and clock retailers; features articles on watches, clocks and shops.

Repair Service
Burt Dial Company
P.O. Box 774
Raymond, NH 03077
Phone: 603-895-2879
Specializes in reverse painting on glass for clock tablets and doors, and in the restoring of clock dials.

Repair Service
Charles Miller
1721 Stanton St.
York, PA 17404
Phone: 843-0363
Member NAWCC, AWI. *

Repair Service
Antique Clock Repair
Joel Vernick
10807 Kenilworth Ave.
P.O. Box 81
Garrett Park, MD 20896
Phone: 301-933-0654 or 301-933-4689
Over 30 years experience in clock repair.

Repair Service
Harvey Flemister
512 Highgate Terrace
Silver Spring, MD 20904
Phone: 301-622-3686
Many years experience in the repair and restoration of antique clocks and watches.

Repair Service
Dorothy Briggs
410 Ethan Allen Ave.
Takoma Park, MD 20912
Phone: 301-270-4166
Specializes in the restoration of painted clock dials as well as reverse painting on glass. *

Repair Service
Old Clockworks, The
Lee M. Flemister
10201 Kings Arms Tavern Court
Ellicott City, MD 21043
Phone: 301-854-5514

Repair Service
Dial House, The
Martha & Dick Smallwood
2287 Buchanan Highway
Dallas, GA 30132
Phone: 404-445-2877
Antique clock dials only; preserved, restored or replaced; call or write before shipping.

Repro. Source
Foster Campos
213 Schoosett St., Route 139
Pembroke, MA 02359
Phone: 617-826-8577
A dealer who offers new clocks but specializes in the reproduction of American antique clocks. *

Repro. Source
S. LaRose, Inc.
234 Commerce Place
Greensboro, NC 27420
Phone: 919-275-0462
A dealer who offers new clocks but specializes in the reproduction of American antique clocks. *

Repro. Source
Tec Specialties
P.O. Box 909
Smyrna, GA 30081
Phone: 404-952-4842
Makes replacement clock dials, decals, backboard labels and calendar strips for antique clocks; also carries supplies for the hobbyist.

Repro. Source
Ken Kyckelhahn
252 California Ave.
Oakdale, CA 95361
Phone: 209-847-1337
A dealer who offers new clocks but specializes in the reproduction of American antique clocks. *

Repro. Source
Aubrey A. Aramaki
331 N.W. Gilman Blvd.
Issaquah, WA 98027
Phone: 206-392-5200
A dealer who offers new clocks but specializes in the reproduction of American antique clocks. *

Supplier
Mason & Sullivan Co. Classics in the Making
586 Higgins Crowell Road
West Yarmouth, Cape Cod, MA 02673
Phone: 800-227-7418
Mail order source for quality kits; boats, guitars, steam engines, kaleidoscopes, instruments, etc.; also supplies.

Supplier
Dome Wood Company
1705 Rimpau Ave. #101
Corona, CA 91719
Phone: 800-292-5522 or 714-540-3662
                         FAX: 714-540-3512
Carries a large line of watch stands and glass domes; will custom make domes to your specifications.

Supplier
Modern Technical Tools & Supply Company
211 Nevada Street
Hicksville, NY 11801
Phone: 516-931-7875
Carries clock movements and related tools and materials for the clockmaker, hobbyist or technician. *

Supplier
S. LaRose, Inc.
234 Commerce Place
Greensboro, NC 27420
Phone: 919-275-0462
Carries a complete line of clock parts. *

Supplier

M. Beresh, Inc.
Suite 353
21770 Greenfield
Oak Park, MI 48237
Phone: 313-968-2930
Carries complete line of clock parts. *

Supplier

KLOCKIT
P.O. Box 636
Lake Geneva, WI 53147
Phone: 800-556-2548
Mail order source for clock movements, hands, faces, hardware, music boxes, barometers, parts, tools, etc.

Supplier

American Clockmaker, The
P.O. Box 326
Clintonville, WI 54929
Phone: 715-823-5101
Mail order source for clock movements, kits, parts and supplies; including shelf, grandfather and German cuckoo clocks.

Supplier

Turncraft Clock Imports Co.
P.O. Box 27288
Golden Valley, MN 55427-0288
Phone: 800-544-1711
Mail order source of fine clock movements, kits, parts and supplies.

Supplier

Bernard Edwards Dial Co.
1331 Southwind Drive
Northbrook, IL 60062
Phone: 708-272-2563
Specializing in clock dials only. *

Supplier

Timesavers
P.O. Box 171
Wheeling, IL 60090
Phone: 312-394-4818
Carries a complete line of clock parts. *

Supplier

Aguilar Jewelers' Supply
520 "E" Street, Room 408
San Diego, CA 92101
Phone: 714-232-2993
Carries complete line of clock parts. *

Supplier

Otto Frei - Jules Borel
Box 796
Oakland, CA 94604
Phone: 415-832-0355
Carries complete line of clock parts.

Character/Comic

Collector

David Welch
RR 2, Box 233
Murphysboro, IL 62966
Phone: 618-687-2282
Wants watches/clocks relating to sports, TV, cartoon, comic, movie characters with original boxes ONLY; also wants empty boxes.

Expert

Howard S. Brenner
106 Woodgate Terrace
Rochester, NY 14625
Phone: 716-482-3641
Specializes in mint/boxed examples of comic watches; author of "Collecting Comic Character Clock & Watches."

Cuckoo

Repro. Source

Cuckoo Clock Center
Heerstrasse 131
5401 St. Goar
Rhein, Germany *

Electric

Club/Association

Electrical Horology Society
Journal: Electric Horology Society Journal
1910 Coney Island Ave.
Brooklyn, NY 11203
Phone: 718-375-2700
Purpose is to inform members of the various types of electrical clocks. *

European

Expert

Brielle Galleries
Frank Vitale
707 Union Ave.
Brielle, NJ 08730
Phone: 908-528-9300
Foremost collector and dealer of 17th, 18th, and 19th century European clocks.

Kitchen Plate Wall Clocks

Collector

C. Marron
61 Creek Rd.
Christiana, PA 17509
Phone: 215-593-6102
Wants German or American clocks: ceramic of enameled tin face. *

Novelty Animated

Collector

Kaifer
Box 232
Bethania, NC 27010
Wants clocks by Lux, Keebler, Westclox. *

Collector

Ben Yellin
24 Quarterdeck St.
Marina Del Rey, CA 90292
Phone: 213-873-1016
Animated alarm clocks. *

Self Winding

Club/Association

Self Winding Clock Association
Newsletter: Catalyst
P.O. Box 7704
Long Beach, CA 90807
Phone: 213-427-8001
Interested in historical horological information, particularly about the Self Winding Clock Company, NY, which operated 1886-1971. *

CLOISONNE

(see also ORIENTALIA)

Club/Association

Cloisonne Collectors Club
Newsletter: Cloison, The
1631 Minnulus Way
La Jolla, CA 92037
Phone: 619-454-0595 *

Museum/Library

George Walter Vincent Smith Art Museum
222 State Street
Springfield, MA 01103
Phone: 413-733-4214

Ceramic Body

Collector

Sousa
5904 Wellesley Ave.
Pittsburgh, PA 15206 *

CLOTHING & ACCESSORIES

(see also BUTTONS; BUTTON HOOKS; COMBS & HAIR ACCESSORIES; HATPINS & HATPIN HOLDERS; LUGGAGE; SEWING ITEMS & GO-WITHS; TEXTILES)

Expert

Irene Spaulding
P.O. Box 38
Amherst, NH 03031
Specialist in antique purses and vintage clothing.

Neckties

Expert

Dr. Ron Spark
Box 43414
Tucson, AZ 85733
Author of "Fit-To-Be-Tied" (Abbeville, 1988) specializes in 1940's neckties.

Vintage

Club/Association

Costume Society, The
63 Salisbury Rd.
Liverpool L19 0PH England

Club/Association

Vintage Fashion/Costume Jewelry Club
Newsletter: VFCJ Newsletter
David Baron
P.O. Box 265
Glen Oaks, NY 11004
For those interested in vintage jewelry and clothing; newsletter carries dealer listings, buy & sell ads, classifieds, etc.

Club/Association

Costume Society of America, The
Newsletter: Costume Society of America
  Newsletter
55 Edgewater Dr.
P.O. Box 73
Earleville, MD 21919
Phone: 301-275-2329   FAX: 301-275-8936
Dedicated to creating understanding of the field of costume and to the study and preservation of historic dress.

Club/Association

Textile & Costume Guild
Newsletter: Textures
c/o Fullerton Museum Center
301 North Pomona Ave.
Fullerton, CA 92632
Phone: 714-738-6545
Guild meets 2nd Sat. of the month Sept.-June; extensive costume collection; womens and mens from 1820's to the present.

Collector

Lynda Long
8517 Crestview Dr.
Fairfax, VA 22031
*Wants dresses, suits and accessories from the 1940's. ***

Collector

Linda Hood
5828 Brentwood Trace
Brentwood, TN 37027
*Wants women and children clothing 1850-1950: crinolines, bustles, hobble skirts, flapper dresses, Gibson-girl and WWII styles. ***

Collector

Terry McCormick
P.O. Box 1422
Corvallis, OR 97339

Dealer

Vintage, Etc.
1796 Massachusetts Ave.
Cambridge, MA 02140
Phone: 617-497-1516

*Carries men's and women's clothing from the late 1920's to the 1950's; specializes in formal wear and outerwear. ***

Dealer

Yesterday's Threads
564 Main Street
Branford, CT 06405
Phone: 203-481-6452
*Specializes in women's clothing and accessories from early 1800's to the 1940's; also some men's and children's. ***

Dealer

Pahaka
Pahaka September
19 Fox Hill
Upper Saddle River, NJ 07458
Phone: 201-327-1464
Buys and sells women's, men's and children's clothing 1880-1950's; also jewelry, hats, shoes, and patterns.

Dealer

Dressing Screen, The
2 Manning Avenue
Troy, NY 12180
Phone: 518-274-2885
*Carries men's and women's clothing and accessories from 1860's through 1940's. ***

Dealer

Carol Canty
7 North Court St.
Frederick, MD 21701
Phone: 301-694-0513
Wants vintage clothing, accessories, and jewelry.

Dealer

Fashions of Yesteryear
1780 Newmans-Cardington Rd. E.
Waldo, OH 43356
Phone: 614-726-2425
*Civil War & Victorian to 1940 clothing, hats, jewelry, shoes, parasols, laces, purses, fans. ***

Dealer

Modern Times
5363 N. College Ave.
Indianapolis, IN 46220
Phone: 317-253-8108
*Women's and men's vintage clothing from the late 1940's to the early 1960's. ***

Dealer

Carrie's Vintage Clothing
204 E. Neil
Champagne, IL 61820
*A complete range of 20th century stock through the 1950's. ***

Dealer

Diane McGee Estate Clothing Company
Diane McGee
5225 Jackson
Omaha, NE 68106
Phone: 402-551-0727
Mail order only; complete line from 1850's to 1960's.

Dealer

Somewhere in Time
Sarah Fox
103 Newcastle Dr.
Lafayette, LA 70503
Phone: 318-235-1081 or 318-984-9863
Wants buttons, belt buckles, ornamental sew-on or clamp-on handbag frames, Art Nouveau or Art Deco jewelry; offers clothes 1850-1960.

Dealer

Puttin' On the Ritz
313 Knox
Dallas, TX 75205
Phone: 212-522-8030
*Carries men's and women's clothing and accessories from 1860's through 1960's. ***

Dealer

Honey Buns
5801 N. 7th Street
Phoenix, AZ 85014
Phone: 602-266-4353
*Specializes in 1920's to 1950's women's (some men's) clothing. ***

Dealer

Lacis
2982 Adeline Street
Berkeley, CA 94703
Phone: 415-843-7178
*Specializes in women's clothing and accessories from Victorian through the 1930's. ***

Expert

Elizabeth S. Brown
45 Whippoorwill Way
R.D. 2, Box 238
Belle Mead, NJ 08502
Phone: 908-359-3395 or 908-874-7590
Lecturer, appraiser & costume consultant on various aspects of clothing collecting & conservation; uses own collection for lectures.

Expert

Creative Clothes
Kathi Reynolds
330 N. Church St.
Thurmont, MD 21788-1640
Phone: 301-695-5340
Specializes in the dating and identification of period/vintage clothing.

Expert

Ruth Osborne
Box 85
Higginsport, OH 45131
Phone: 513-375-6605 *

Expert

Diane McGee
5225 Jackson
Omaha, NE 68106
Phone: 402-551-0727
Author of "A Passion for Fashion: Antique, Collectible, & Retro Clothes 1850-1950"; 200 pgs., over 190 photos; send $24.95 + $2 UPS.

Expert

Maryanne Dolan
138 Belle Avenue
Pleasant Hill, CA 94523
Phone: 415-935-2366
Author of "Vintage Clothing 1880-1960", a fully illustrated identification and value guide.

Museum/Library

Boston Museum of Fine Arts, The
465 Huntington Avenue
Boston, MA 02115
Phone: 617-267-9300

Museum/Library

Museum of Costume
Keeper of Costume
4 Circus, Bath
Avon BA1 2EW England
The museum's collection includes all aspects of fashion from the 16th century to the present—handmade, ready-to-wear and designer.

Museum/Library

Museum of Art, Rhode Island School of Design
224 Benefit St.
Providence, RI 02903
Phone: 401-331-3511

Museum/Library

Wadsworth Atheneum
600 Main Street
Hartford, CT 06103
Phone: 203-278-2670

Museum/Library

Fashion Institute of Technology, Edward C. Blum Design Laboratory
227 West 27th Street
New York, NY 10001
Phone: 212-760-7970

Museum/Library

Metropolitan Museum of Art, The Costume Institute
5th Avenue & 82nd Street
New York, NY 10028
Phone: 212-879-5500

Museum/Library

Museums at Stony Brook, The
Newsletter: Dialogue
1208 Rte. 25A
Stony Brook, NY 11790
Phone: 516-751-0066   FAX: 516-751-0353
Large collection of American Art, decoys, horse-drawn vehicles, costumes, and miniature period rooms; museum shop.

Museum/Library

Philadelphia College of Textiles & Science, The Goldey Paley Design Center
4200 Henry Avenue
Philadelphia, PA 19144

Museum/Library

National Museum of American History
14th & Constitution Ave. NW
Washington, DC 20560
Phone: 202-357-2700

Museum/Library

Valentine Museum
1015 East Clay
Richmond, VA 23219
Phone: 804-649-0711

Museum/Library

Western Reserve Historical Society
10825 East Blvd.
Cleveland, OH 44106
Phone: 216-721-5722

Museum/Library

Indianapolis Museum of Art, Indiana Fashion Design Collection
1200 W. 38th Street
Indianapolis, IN 46208
Phone: 317-923-1331

Museum/Library

Detroit Historical Museum
5401 Woodward Ave.
Detroit, MI 48202
Phone: 313-833-1805

Museum/Library

Chicago Historical Society
Clark Street at North Avenue
Chicago, IL 60614
Phone: 312-642-4600

Museum/Library

Missouri Historical Society
Jefferson Memorial Bldg.
Forest Park
St. Louis, MO 63112
Phone: 314-361-1424

Museum/Library

Phoenix Art Museum, The Arizona Costume Institute
1625 North Central Ave.
Phoenix, AZ 85004
Phone: 602-257-1880

Museum/Library

Museum of Vintage Fashion
1712 Chapparal Lane
Lafayette, CA 94549
Phone: 415-945-1896

Periodical

Hobby House Press, Inc.
Magazine: Vintage Fashions
Rene M. Trezise
900 Frederick St.
Cumberland, MD 21502-9985
Phone: 301-759-3770   FAX: 301-759-4940
A colorful bi-monthly magazine with original research articles focusing on pre-Victorian-1960 clothing, jewelry, accessories.

Periodical

Newsletter: Biasline
Bobbi Ann Loper
115 South Manhattan
Tampa, FL 33609
*Costume Tech puts out this newsletter for theatrical costumers, amateur and professional. *

Periodical

Newsletter: Glass Slipper, The
653 S. Orange Ave.
Sarasota, FL 34236-7503

Periodical

Booklet: Vintage Lill's Newsletter
Jacqueline Horning
7501 School Road, - 26
Cincinnati, OH 45249

Periodical

Newsletter: Vintage Clothing Newsletter
Terry McCormick
P.O. Box 1422
Corvallis, OR 97339
Phone: 503-752-7456
First national publication on vintage clothing; published since 1984; ads, information, personality profiles, tips, etc.

Repro. Source

Creative Clothes
Kathi Reynolds
330 N. Church St.
Thurmont, MD 21788-1640
Phone: 301-695-5340
Makes all styles of period costume for men, women, and children.

Repro. Source

Past Patterns
Dept. CIC
P.O. Box 7587
Grand Rapids, MI 49510
Phone: 616-245-9456
Sells clothing patterns from the years 1830-1949 in woman's sizes 8-20; also men's and children's patterns available; free information.

Repro. Source

Dazians
2014 Commerce Street
Dallas, TX 75201
Phone: 214-748-3450
*Supplier to theatrical costumers, carries variety of unusual fabrics and findings, including hat forms, trims, and fabrics. ***

Repro. Source

Heidi's Pages & Petticoats
Heidi Marsh
810 El Caminito
Livermore, CA 94550
Men's, women's, and children's patterns from the Civil War era; many taken from Godey's Lady Book diagrams and patterns.

Supplier

Mini-Magic
3675 Reed Road
Columbus, OH 43220
*Focus on fabrics and supplies for doll people but also sells acid-free tissue and other conservation supplies. ***

Vintage Corsets

Collector

VVC
Suite 192
8351 Roswell Rd.
Atlanta, GA 30350
Phone: 404-939-7291
*Wants corsets; Victorian to 1960's; any number; also related advertising, etc. ***

Vintage Hats

Collector

Linda Hood
5828 Brentwood Trace
Brentwood, TN 37027
*Wants "millinery madness" woman's and children's hats - the crazier the better. ***

Museum/Library

Colonial Williamsburg Millinery Shop
P.O. Box C
Williamsburg, VA 23185
Phone: 804-229-1000

CLOWN COLLECTIBLES

(see also CIRCUS COLLECTIBLES; COLLECTIBLES (MODERN), Figurines (Emmett Kelly, Jr.))

Periodical

Newsletter: Hendersons Clown Collectors
  Newsletter
Box 5125
Garden Grove, CA 92645 *

Emmett Kelly

Museum/Library

Emmett Kelly Historical Museum
202 E. Main
Sedan, KS 67361
Phone: 316-725-3470

Emmett Kelly, Jr.

Collector

N. Neill
P.O. Box 9352
Greensboro, NC 27429
Wants anything related to Emmett Kelly, Jr.: advertising, postcards. etc.

COAL CARVINGS

Collector

Robert Gormley
334 Brownsburg Rd.
Newtown, PA 18940
*Wants anthracite coal carvings and jewelry; old only. ***

Collector

Linda Franklin
2716 Northfield
Charlottesville, VA 22901

COAT OF ARMS

(see also BOOKS, Heraldry)

Dealer

Antiques & Art Galleries
Steve Whysel
101 N. Main
Bentonville, AR 72712
Phone: 501-273-7701 or 501-444-9911
Wants coat of arms (family crests) on fabric, wood, cups, plates, tile, paper, etc.; also wants books on heraldry.

COCA-COLA COLLECTIBLES

(see also SOFT DRINK COLLECTIBLES, Coca-Cola)

COCKTAIL SHAKERS

(see also SALOON COLLECTIBLES)

Expert

Stephen Visakay Cocktail Shakers
Steve Visakay
P.O. Box 1517
W. Caldwell, NJ 07007
Free appraisals, identification and history of the maker of your cocktail shaker; SASE for reply.

COFFINS

Collector

David Adams
203 Meng Rd.
Schwenksville, PA 19473
*Antique coffins wanted circa 1700-1870; knowledgeable in prices and originality. ***

COIN-OPERATED MACHINES

Auction Service

Home Amusement Co., Inc.
11910 Parklawn Drive
Rockville, MD 20852
Phone: 301-468-0070
Specialized auctions of carousel horses, slot machines, juke boxes, arcade games, collectibles, country store, trade stimulators, etc.

Auction Service

Auction Under the Big Top
Tommy Sciortino
3723 N. Nebraska Aave.
Tampa, FL 33603
Phone: 818-248-5387 or 813-932-1782
                    FAX: 813-248-5387
Specializes in the sale of circus equipment and memorabilia, carousels, amusement devices, coin-ops, toys, etc.

Club/Association

Pinball Owners Association
POA 465 Cranbrook Road
Ilford
Essex 192 6EW England
For those interested in pinball machines, jukeboxes and slot machines.

Club/Association

Society for the Preservation of
Historical Coin Operated Machines
100 North Central Ave.
Hartsdale, NY 10630
Phone: 914-428-2600 *

Collector

Richard O. Gates
P.O. Box 187
Chesterfield, VA 23832
Phone: 804-748-0382 or 804-794-5146
Wants coin-operated machines including jukeboxes, pinballs, Coca Cola machines & signs or literature related to any of the above.

Collector

Mike Gorski
1770 Dover Rd.
Westlake, OH 44145
Phone: 216-871-6071
Slot machines, old penny arcade machines; Wurlitzer 78 RPM jukeboxes, odd vending machines;Regina musical boxes, old coin-operated

Collector

Richard McCoy
1119 Michigan Ave.
St. Joseph, MI 49085
Wants slot machines, trade stimulators, gumball machines, pinball machines, pop machines, arcade games, etc.

Collector

Arnold Levin
P.O. Box 223
Northbrook, IL 60062
Phone: 708-564-2893 *

Collector

John Anderson
15500 S.E. Royer Rd.
Clackamas, Oregon 97015
Phone: 503-658-3607
Wants slot machines or other coin-operated machines.

Dealer

Darrow's Fun Antiques
Gary Darrow
309 E. 61st St.
New York, NY 10021
Phone: 212-838-0730
Buys & sells antique toys, ad signs, animated art, jukeboxes, slot machines, comic watches, bicycles & memorabilia of all types.

Dealer

Ken Durham
909 26th St. NW
Washington, DC 20037
Phone: 202-338-1342   FAX: 202-338-1342
Buy/sell/trade countertop coin-operated machines: trade stimulators, vending machines, arcade machines, punchboards, books on same.

Dealer

Michael Plitt
591 Hillcrest Dr.
Frederick, MD 21702
Phone: 301-694-8648

Dealer

David Evans
7999 Keller Rd.
Cincinnati, OH 45243 *

Dealer

Quicksilver Oddities Antique Coin-Ops & Collectibles
Harold Daniel
2322 Rollins
Grand Blanc, MI 48439
Wants slot machines 25 yrs. old or older; also antique coin-operated gaming devices, trade stimulators, vending machines, arcade games.

Dealer

Coin Machine Trader
Ted & Betty Salveson
569 Kansas SE
P.O. Box 602
Huron, SD 57350
Phone: 605-352-3870
Buys, sells and repairs various types of coin-operated machines: slots, pinball, jukeboxes, gumballs, arcade games, etc.

Dealer

MANtiques
Harold Adler
14572 Deervale
Sherman Oaks, CA 91403
Phone: 818-990-2461
Buys & sells pre-1950 coin-operated vending machines: games of skill, chance, 3 reel, dice, etc., counter models.

Expert

Joseph S. Jancuska
619 Miller St.
Luzerne, PA 18709
Phone: 717-287-3478
Buys, sells, repairs and appraises slot machines, trade stimulators, gum & nut machines & other coin-operated machines.

Expert

Bill Enes
8520 Lewis Dr.
Lenexa, KS 66227
Phone: 913-441-1492 or 913-441-1502
                    FAX: 913-441-1502
Author of "Silent Salesmen - an Encyclopedia of Collectible Gum, Candy & Nut Machines."

Periodical

Magazine: Coin Slot International
P.O. Box 57, Daltry Street
Oldham
Manchester OL1 4BB England
The U.K.'s premier weekly magazine for the coin-op industry.

Periodical

Newsletter: Coin-Op Newsletter
Ken Durham
909 26th St. NW
Washington, DC 20037
Phone: 202-338-1342   FAX: 202-338-1342

Focuses on countertop arcade machines, trade stimulators, vending machines, jukeboxes, and slot machines; send SASE for info.

Periodical

Magazine: Gameroom Magazine
1014 Mount Tabor Road
New Albany, IN 47150
Phone: 800-462-4263   FAX: 812-945-6966
A great source of information for the collector and dealer of jukeboxes, pinballs, coke machines and other gameroom collectibles.

Periodical

Coin Machine Trader
Newsletter: Coin Machine Trader
Ted & Betty Salveson
569 Kansas SE
P.O. Box 602
Huron, SD 57350
Phone: 605-352-3870
A monthly newsletter featuring articles on various types of coin-op. machines: slots, pinball, jukeboxes, gumballs, arcade games, etc.

Periodical

Hoflin Publishing Ltd.
Magazine: Coin Slot, The
4401 Zephyr St.
Wheat Ridge, CO 80033-3299
Phone: 303-420-2222 or 800-352-5678
Focuses on antique vending machines, slot machines, pinball machines, arcade games, coin-operated musical instruments, etc.

Periodical

Magazine: Loose Change
1515 South Commerce St.
Las Vegas, NV 89102-2703
Phone: 702-387-8750 or 702-387-8752
A monthly magazine with articles on coin-operated music machines, jukeboxes, trade stimulators, gaming machines, etc.

Repair Service

Joseph S. Jancuska
619 Miller St.
Luzerne, PA 18709
Phone: 717-287-3478
Buys, sells, repairs and appraises slot machines, trade stimulators, gum & nut machines & other coin-operated machines.

Supplier

Evans & Frink
Rick Frink
2977 Eager
Howell, MI 48843
Supplies reelstrips, pay cards, decals, instruction sheets, and mint wrappers for slot machines and trade stimulators.

Advertising

Expert

Richard M. Bueschel
414 N. Prospect Manor Ave.
Mt. Prospect, IL 60056
Phone: 708-253-0791
Wants photos of coin machines (vending, scales, jukeboxes, arcade, slot machines), advertising, literature, catalogs, etc.; author.

Gumball Machines

Collector

Don L. Reedy
251 East Patrick St.
Frederick, MD 21701
Phone: 301-663-4240 or 301-662-5503
Buy, sell, trade gumball and peanut machines; also Coca-Cola advertising items and novelty radios.

Jukeboxes

Club/Association

Amusement & Music Operators Association
Suite 600
111 E. Wacker Dr.
Chicago, IL 60601 *

Collector

Joe Weber
604 Centre St.
Ashland, PA 17921
Phone: 717-875-4787 or 717-875-4401
Wants early Capehart & Wurlitzer jukeboxes which play 78 rpm records; will arrange pickup; all letters answered; will offer advise.

Collector

Frank Sansome
P.O. Box 94
Brick, NJ 08723
Phone: 201-840-1094
*Wants any jukeboxes, 40's, 50's, 60's; also slot machines and arcade games. **

Collector

Keith Andree
47 Louisa Ct.
Northport, NY 11768
Phone: 516-757-2615 *

Collector

John Chamblin
2233 Kingsridge Dr.
Wilmington, DE 19810
Phone: 302-475-8462
*Wurlitzers, jukeboxes or parts wanted; also old slot machines. **

Collector

Mike Gorski
1770 Dover Rd.
Westlake, OH 44145
Phone: 216-871-6071

Slot machines, old penny arcade machines; Wurlitzer 78 RPM jukeboxes, odd vending machines;Regina musical boxes, old coin-operated

Collector

Arnold Levin
P.O. Box 223
Northbrook, IL 60062
Phone: 708-564-2893 *

Dealer

Johnston's Jukebox Classics & Vintage
Slot Machines, Inc.
John & Wendy Johnston
6742 Fifth Ave.
Brooklyn, NY 11220
Phone: 718-833-8455
*Has over 2000 cookie jars. She and her husband are also jukebox and vintage slot machine dealers. **

Dealer

Lloyd's Jukeboxes
Lloyd Thoburn
22900 Shaw Rd. #106
Sterling, VA 22170
Phone: 703-834-6699 or 703-834-9080
Buys jukeboxes in any condition; free phone appraisal of wholesale values; has over 300 jukeboxes in stock.

Dealer

Zygmut & Associates (Jukeboxes)
Illinois Antique Slot Machine Co.
Frank Zygmut
P.O. Box 542
Westmont, IL 60559
Phone: 708-985-2742 or 708-971-1015
 FAX: 708-985-5151
Buys and sells slot machines and jukeboxes; 150-200 slot machines & Wurlitzer jukeboxes in stock; Wurlitzer One More Time distributor.

Expert

Rick Botts
2545 SE 60th Ct.
Des Moines, IA 50317-5099
Phone: 515-265-8324 FAX: 515-265-1980

Expert

A.M.R. Publishing Co.
Frank Adams
P.O. Box 3007
Arlington, WA 98223
Phone: 206-659-6434 FAX: 206-659-5994
Publishes jukebox books and service manuals; also buys and sells; author of "Jukeboxes, 1900-1990 The Other American Manufacturers."

Periodical

Newspaper: Slot Machine & Jukebox Gazette
Ken Durham
909 26th St. NW
Washington, DC 20037
Phone: 202-338-1342 FAX: 202-338-1342

Semi-annual newspaper focusing on slot machines and jukeboxes; lots of ads, articles, shows, auctions; send SASE for info.

Periodical

Newspaper: Jukebox Trader
P.O. Box 1081
Des Moines, IA 50311 *

Periodical

Magazine: Jukebox Collector
Rick Botts
2545 SE 60th Ct.
Des Moines, IA 50317-5099
Phone: 515-265-8324 FAX: 515-265-1980
A monthly magazine with large classified ad department, reprinted articles, repair information, shows, auctions, etc.

Periodical

Newspaper: Always Jukin'
Michael F. Baute
221 Yesler Way
Seattle, WA 98104
Phone: 206-233-9460 FAX: 206-233-9871
Largest circulation monthly jukebox publication; photos, show reports, ads, new products, restoring guides, etc.

Repro. Source

Nostalgic Music Company
Edward Cadmus
58 Union Ave.
New Providence, NJ 07974
Phone: 908-464-5538
Sells the Antique Apparatus line of reproduction jukeboxes and speakers; specializing in 45 and CD jukeboxes.

Supplier

Jukebox Junction
P.O. Box 1081
Des Moines, IA 50311
*Publishes a catalog of reproduction jukebox parts and literature. **

Jukeboxes (Film)

Expert

Fred Bingaman
810 Courtland Drive
Manchester, MO 63021
Phone: 314-391-6651
Wants audio visual (film) jukeboxes (scopitones), and related advertising items, films, spare parts, etc.

Periodical

Newsletter: Scopitone Newsletter, The
Fred Bingaman
810 Courtland Drive
Manchester, MO 63021
Phone: 314-391-6651

Pinball Machines

Expert

Gordon A. Hasse, Jr.
140 East 95th St., 6-D
New York, NY 10128
Phone: 212-996-3825
Expert & collector of pinball machines with access to most of the country's collectors; fair value for machines of interested.

Expert

John Fetterman
Box 625, R.D. #1
Elysburg, PA 17824
Phone: 717-672-3176 *

Expert

Coin Machine Trader
Ted Salveson
569 Kansas SE
P.O. Box 602
Huron, SD 57350
Phone: 605-352-3870
Specializes in all types of pinball machines from Bingo type to Flipper, electrical mechanical and solid state; 50 years experience.

Expert

Richard M. Bueschel
414 N. Prospect Manor Ave.
Mt. Prospect, IL 60056
Phone: 708-253-0791
Wants pinball related photos showing games in use, photo post cards, sales literature, advertising, manuals, operator reminiscences,

Periodical

Newsletter: Pinball Trader
Jack Simonton
P.O. Box 1795
Campbell, CA 95009-1795
Phone: 408-554-8737
A monthly newsletter dedicated to informing pinball collectors of games for sale and trade; also hints for maintenance and renovations.

Prophylactic Machines

Collector

Mr. Condom
11417 27th Ave.
Trevor, WI 53179
Phone: 414-862-6797
Buys/sells collectible prophylactic and feminine hygiene vending equipment and related items; catalog $2.

Slot Machines

Collector

Grand Illusions
Martin Roenigk
26 Barton Hill
East Hampton, CT 06424
Phone: 203-267-8682

Slot machines and other coin-operated machines; also Wurlitzer 78 rpm jukeboxes.

Collector

Mike Gorski
1770 Dover Rd.
Westlake, OH 44145
Phone: 216-871-6071
Slot machines, old penny arcade machines; Wurlitzer 78 RPM jukeboxes, odd vending machines;Regina musical boxes, old coin-operated

Collector

Ryan
7217 N. Jersey
Portland, OR 97203
Phone: 503-286-3597
*Wants slot machines and related literature and advertisements. *

Dealer

Johnston's Jukebox Classics & Vintage
Slot Machines, Inc.
John & Wendy Johnston
6742 Fifth Ave.
Brooklyn, NY 11220
Phone: 718-833-8455
Has over 2000 cookie jars. She and her husband are also jukebox and vintage slot machine dealers.
*

Dealer

Zygmut & Associates (Jukeboxes)
Illinois Antique Slot Machine Co.
Frank Zygmut
P.O. Box 542
Westmont, IL 60559
Phone: 708-985-2742 or 708-971-1015
　　　　　　　　　　FAX: 708-985-5151
Buys and sells slot machines and jukeboxes; 150-200 slot machines & Wurlitzer jukeboxes in stock; Wurlitzer One More Time distributor.

Dealer

St. Louis Slot Machine Company
Tom Kolbrener
2111 S. Brentwood
St. Louis, MO 63144
Phone: 314-961-4612
$3 for 32 page color catalog of fully-restored antique slot machines for sale.

Expert

Newsletter: Slot Machine Newsletter
Richard Reddock
P.O. Box 524
North Bellmore, NY 11710
*Author of "Price Guide to Antique Slot Machines." *

Expert

Richard M. Bueschel
414 N. Prospect Manor Ave.
Mt. Prospect, IL 60056
Phone: 708-253-0791

Wants slot machine photos showing games in use, photo post cards, sales literature, advertising, manuals, operator reminiscences, etc.

Expert

Liberty Belle Saloon Saloon &
Restaurant
Marshall Frey
4250 South Virginia Street
Reno, NV 89502
Phone: 702-825-1776
Collector of antique slot machines for 32 years; author of "Slot Machine - A Pictorial History of the First 100 Years."

Museum/Library

Liberty Belle Saloon & Slot Machine
Collection
Marshall Frey
4250 South Virginia Street
Reno, NV 89502
Phone: 702-825-1776
Nations largest display of antique slot machines; also other antiques; free admission.

Periodical

Newspaper: Slot Machine & Jukebox Gazette
Ken Durham
909 26th St. NW
Washington, DC 20037
Phone: 202-338-1342　　　FAX: 202-338-1342
Semi-annual newspaper focusing on slot machines and jukeboxes; lots of ads, articles, shows, auctions; send SASE for info.

Supplier

Antique Slot Machine Part Co.
Tom Krahl
140 N. Western Ave.
Carpentersville, IL 60110
Phone: 708-428-8476
Publishes a catalog of reproduction slot machine parts; also repairs.

Vending Machines

Collector

Brian L. Carter
29750 N. Hilltop
Orange Village, OH 44022
Phone: 216-831-4684
Wants gumball, peanut & slot machines; also penny arcade games and other old coin operated vending machines; also wants parts.

Collector

Mike Gorski
1770 Dover Rd.
Westlake, OH 44145
Phone: 216-871-6071
Slot machines, old penny arcade machines; Wurlitzer 78 RPM jukeboxes, odd vending machines;Regina musical boxes, coin-operated

Expert

Bill Enes
8520 Lewis Dr.
Lenexa, KS 66227
Phone: 913-441-1492 or 913-441-1502
FAX: 913-441-1502
Author of "Silent Salesmen - Encyclopedia of Collectible Gum, Candy, and Nut Machines"; buys and sells.

COINS & CURRENCY

(see also BANK CHECKS; CIVIL WAR; CREDIT CARDS & CHARGE COINS; ELONGATED COINS; EXONUMIA; MACERATED CURRENCY; STOCKS & BONDS; TOKENS; WOODEN MONEY)

Auction Service

Spink & Son, Ltd.
King Street
St. James's
london SW1Y 6QS England
Auctioneers and dealers of coins (ancient to present), medals, orders, tokens, decorations and other numismatic items.

Auction Service

Kurt R. Krueger Auctions
Kurt R. Krueger
160 N. Washington St.
Iola, WI 54945
Phone: 715-445-3845   FAX: 715-445-4100
Specializing in the mail-bid auction of tokens, advertising, brewery items, Western Americana, autographs, sports, coins & currency, etc.

Auction Service

Bowers & Merena, Inc.
Box 1224
Wolfeboro, NH 03894
Phone: 603-569-5095 or 800-458-4646
FAX: 603-569-5319
Specializes in coin auctions.

Auction Service

Stack's Coin Galleries
123 West 57th St.
New York, NY 10019
Phone: 212-582-5955   FAX: 212-245-5018
Specializes in coin auctions.

Auction Service

Superior Galleries
9478 West Olympic Blvd.
Beverly Hills, CA 90212-4299
Phone: 800-421-0754   FAX: 213-203-0496
Specialists in the auctioning of coins. Offers grading services. *

Club/Association

American Numismatic Society, The
Newsletter: American Numismatic Society Newsletter, The
Broadway & 155th St.
New York, NY 10032
Phone: 212-234-3130
Focuses on American coins. *

Club/Association

John Reich Collectors Society
Journal: John Reich Journal
David J. Davis
P.O. Box 205
Ypsilanti, MI 48197
Phone: 313-845-3866
The purpose of the JRCS is to encourage the study of numismatics, particularly US gold and silver coins minted before 1838.

Club/Association

Chinese Banknote Collectors Society
Box 350
Kenilworth, IL 60043 *

Club/Association

Fremont Coin Club, Inc.
1722 E. 19th St.
Fremont, NE 68025

Club/Association

Jefferson County Coin Club
Newsletter: JCCC Newsletter
George Van Trump, Jr.
P.O. Box 260170
Lakewood, CO 80226
Phone: 303-985-3508

Club/Association

American Numismatic Association
Magazine: Numismatist, The
Robert J. Leuver, ExDir
818 N. Cascade Ave.
Colorado Springs, CO 80903-3279
Phone: 719-632-2646 or 800-367-9723
FAX: 719-632-2646
Worldwide assoc. of collectors of coins, paper money, medals and tokens; over 33,000 members; offers collector services and benefits.

Club/Association

American British Numismatic Society
Box 652
Saugus, CA 91350 *

Collector

Wilson's Syngraplics
John & Nancy Wilson
P.O. Box 27185
Milwaukee, WI 53227
Phone: 414-545-8636
Wants any pre-1934 paper money issued in the U.S.; also wants any postcards depicting banks.

Collector

Bob Cochran
P.O. Box 1085
Florissant, MO 63031
Collector of U.S. paper money; also banking history.

Dealer

Littleton Coin Company
253 Union St.
Littleton, NH 03561
Wants estates, accumulations; especially American coins, gold and silver. *

Dealer

Peak A/C
Steven Peak
Box 173
East Meadow, NY 11554
Phone: 516-271-5847
Buy, sell, trade all coins, tokens, medals and currency; wants better numismatic items for inclusion in brochure.

Dealer

Tangible Investments of America, Inc.
Mark E. Mitchell
3002 Winter Pine Ct.
Fairfax, VA 22031
Phone: 703-591-3150   FAX: 703-395-3152
Interested in investment grade coins.

Dealer

San Juan Precious Metals Corp.
Ron Gordon
4818 San Juan Ave.
Jacksonville, FL 32210-3232
Phone: 904-387-3486

Dealer

Florida Currency & Coins
Ed Kuszmar
19 East Palmetto Park Road
Boca Raton, FL 33432
Phone: 800-447-4590 or 407-368-7422
Interested in coins, currency, paper Americana ephemera, and 1893 Columbia Exposition items *

Dealer

Numismatic Assets Co., Inc.
P.O. Box 27004
Indianapolis, IN 46227
Phone: 317-786-7150 *

Dealer

MCS
Box 18061
West St. Paul, MN 55118
Phone: 612-641-9909
Stamps and coins bought. *

Dealer

Maple City Coin
Dr. R.A. Heitt
Drawer 80
Monmouth, IL 61462
Phone: 309-734-3212   FAX: 309-734-8083
Buys and sells all coins and numismatic items; also knives, Indian artifacts, fishing lures, old pens.

Dealer

S C Coin & Stamp Co. Inc.
Cy Phillips, Jr.
P.O. Drawer 3069
Arcadia, CA 91006
Phone: 818-445-8277 or 800-367-0779
Tokens, medals, coins, currency, badges, expo. and fair items, scrap gold and silver.

Expert

Milton Mitchell
3401 Hallaton Ct.
Silver Spring, MD 20906
Phone: 301-598-7959

Expert

Coin Investment Councilors
Guy Whidden
7504 Rockwood Rd.
Frederick, MD 21701
Phone: 301-473-8375
Specializes in coin identification and values; many years of experience.

Man./Prod./Dist.

Kennedy Mint, Inc., The
12102 Pearl Road
Strongsville, OH 44136
Phone: 800-442-6468
Sells individual and proof sets of early and new commemorative U.S. coins.

Misc. Service

Numismatic Guaranty Corporation of America
P.O. Box 1776
Parsippany, NJ 07054
Phone: 201-984-6222
*Professional coin graders. ***

Misc. Service

International Numismatic Society
Newsletter: Numorum
Charles R. Hoskins
1707 L St., NW Suite 250
P.O. Box 66555
Washington, DC 20035
Phone: 202-223-4496 or 215-492-1981
                      FAX: 202-429-5275
The INS offers authentication and grading of rare coins and paper money to the public for a nominal fee.

Misc. Service

NumisNet(sm)
L.D. Mitchell, Pres.
Laurel Centre Station
P.O. Box 5100
Laurel, MD 20726
Phone: 301-498-8542
24-hr. computer bulletin board service on 301-498-8205 for numismatic collectors; electronic messaging/programs for 2 dozen

Misc. Service

Professional Coin Grading Service
P.O. Box 9458
Newport Beach, CA 92658
*Offers authentication service for coins from all countries. ***

Museum/Library

American Numismatic Society, The
Newsletter: American Numismatic Society Newsletter, The
Broadway & 155th St.
New York, NY 10032
Phone: 212-234-3130

Museum/Library

National Museum of American History
14th & Constitution Ave. NW
Washington, DC 20560
Phone: 202-357-2700

Museum/Library

Museum of the American Numismatic Association
Magazine: Numismatist, The
Robert W. Hoge, Cur.
818 N. Cascade Ave.
Colorado Springs, CO 80903
Phone: 719-632-2646   FAX: 719-634-4085
A museum collection including 400,000 items; largest numismatic circulating library with books and A/V material free to members.

Museum/Library

Old Mint Museum
Olga K. Widnes
5th & Mission Sts.
San Francisco, CA 94103
Phone: 415-744-6830   FAX: 415-744-9355
The Old Mint Museum is a National Historic Landmark; open free M-F 10-5, closed holidays.

Periodical

Newsletter: Restrike, The
RFD 1, Box 530
Winthrop, ME 04364

Periodical

Newsletter: Coin Previewer
Bob Leuchten
P.O. Box 8655
Coral Springs, FL 33075
Phone: 305-755-3012

Numismatic investment newsletter; recommendations for the prudent collector or investor, sound advise, ads, monthly specials, events.

Periodical

Newspaper: Coin World
P.O. Box 150
Sydney, OH 45367 *

Periodical

Krause Publications, Inc.
Magazine: Coin Prices
Bob Wilhite, Ed.
700 East State St.
Iola, WI 54990
Phone: 800-258-0929 or 715-445-2214
                      FAX: 715-445-4087
Provides complete current market prices for U.S. coins; values listed for up to 12 grades of preservation; frequently updated pricings.

Periodical

Krause Publications, Inc.
Magazine: Coins
Arlyn G. Sieber
700 East State St.
Iola, WI 54990
Phone: 800-258-0929 or 715-445-2214
                      FAX: 715-445-4087
Leading monthly newsstand magazine provides in-depth features on U.S. coins with color photos; collector columns, articles, values, ads.

Periodical

Krause Publications, Inc.
Newspaper: Numismatic News
Bob Whilhite, Ed.
700 E. State St.
Iola, WI 54990
Phone: 800-258-0929 or 715-445-2214
                      FAX: 715-445-4087
A weekly guide to the coin collecting hobby serving active collectors of U.S. coins with timely news; values, ads, calendar.

Periodical

Krause Publications, Inc.
Magazine: World Coin News
Dave Harper, Ed.
700 E. State St.
Iola, WI 54990
Phone: 800-258-0929 or 715-445-2214
                      FAX: 715-445-4087
The only bi-weekly guide serving world coin collectors; news, historical features, huge ad section, coin values, show calendar.

Periodical

Newsletter: Coin Value Research Guide
David Lisot, Ed.
P.O. Box 3040
Santa Monica, CA 90408
A quarterly newsletter containing pricing for most gold and silver proof and uncirculated modern coins.

Periodical

Newsletter: Certified Coin Dealer Newsletter
(The "Bluesheet")
P.O. Box 11099
Torrance, CA 90510
A weekly report on the certified coin market; unbiased wholesale information on rare coins for the coin hobby and business.

Periodical

Newsletter: Coin Dealer Newsletter, The (The "Greysheet")
P.O. Box 11099
Torrance, CA 90510
A weekly report on the certified coin market; unbiased wholesale information on rare coins for the coin hobby and business.

Periodical

Newsletter: Currency Dealer Newsletter, The
(The "Greensheet")
P.O. Box 11099
Torrance, CA 90510
A monthly newsletter reporting on the currency market.

Periodical

Magazine: Coinage
2660 E. Main St.
Ventura, CA 93003

Cents

Club/Association

Society of Lincoln Cent Collectors
Dr. Sol Taylor, Pres.
P.O. Box 5465
North Hollywood, CA 91616
Phone: 818-789-7805
Collectors of U.S. small cents.

Coin Errors

Club/Association

Combined Organization of Numismatic
Error Collectors of America
Newsletter: Errorscope
Box 932
Savannah, GA 31402
Phone: 912-232-8655
Interested in mint errors and varieties on U.S. and foreign coins. *

Periodical

Magazine: Error Trends Coin Magazine
Arnold Margolis
P.O. Box 158
Oceanside, NY 11572
Phone: 516-764-8063
A monthly magazine focusing on coin errors.

Coins (Ancient)

Auction Service

Classic Numismatic Group, Inc.
Box 245
Quarryville, PA 17566-0245
Phone: 717-786-4013
Specializes in the auction sale of classical coins: Greek, Roman, Byzantine, Medieval, British, foreign, etc.

Dealer

Classica Antiquities
Frank J. Wagner, MngDir
P.O. Box 509
Syracuse, NY 13201
Phone: 315-687-0036
For over 25 years buying/selling ancient Greek, Roman, Egyptian, Near Eastern coins and antiquities.

Periodical

Magazine: Celator, The
P.O. Box 123
Lodi, WI 53555
Phone: 608-592-4684   FAX: 608-592-4682
A monthly magazine focusing on antiquities and ancient coins; ads, articles, auction reports, etc.

Coins (Copper)

Club/Association

Early American Coppers
Newsletter: Penny-Wise
P.O. Box 15782
Cincinnati, OH 45215
Phone: 513-771-0696
Interested in early American copper coinage. *

Coins (Liberty Seated)

Club/Association

Liberty Seated Collectors Club
Journal: Gobrecht Journal
5718 King Arthur Dr.
Kettering, OH 45429 *

Coins (World Proof)

Club/Association

World Proof Numismatic Association
Newsletter: Proof Collectors Corner
Gail P. Gray, Pres.
P.O. Box 4094
Pittsburgh, PA 15201
Phone: 412-782-4477   FAX: 412-782-4477
WPNA is dedicated to the collector of proof coinage; purpose is to bring forth the latest news on new coin issues, medals, etc.

Croatian

Club/Association

Croatian Numismatic Society
254 Crestwood Dr.
Hobart, IN 46342

Focuses on the numismatic history of Croatia, Serbia, Slovenia and Yugoslavia.

Latin American

Club/Association

Latin American Paper Money Society
Newsletter: LANSA
Arthur C. Matz
3304 Milford Mill Rd.
Baltimore, MD 21207
Phone: 301-655-3109
A booklet issued three times a year for those interested in Latin American and Iberia paper money.

Paper Money

Club/Association

International Bank Note Society
Journal: International Bank Note Society
Journal
Milan Alusic, GenSec
P.O. Box 1642
Racine, WI 53401
Phone: 414-554-6255
Members interested in worldwide bank notes and paper currencies; journal published quarterly with articles, ads, etc.

Club/Association

Society of Paper Money Collectors
Magazine: Paper Money
Bob Cochran, Sec.
P.O. Box 1085
Florissant, MO 63031
Interested in all aspects of collecting paper currency; welcomes opportunity to help non-collectors, but PLEASE send SASE for reply.

Dealer

William Barrett
Box 9
Victoria Station
Montreal H3Z 2V4 Canada
Specialist in British, French, Portuguese, Spanish and Danish colonies; Chinese foreign banks, all proof and specimen notes.

Dealer

Tom Knebl, Inc.
P.O. Box 3689
Carson City, NV 89702-3689
Wants all world bank notes; also U.S. large size notes and military currency; U.S. fractional currency; Colonial currency, etc.

Expert

Lance K. Campbell
P.O. Box 204
Mary Esther, FL 32569
Editor of "Inside IBNS", the monthly newsletter of the International Bank Note Society.

Periodical

Token Publishing, Ltd.
Magazine: Bond & Banknote News
84 High Street
Honiton
Devon EX14 8JW England
An English publication focusing on paper money.

Periodical

Krause Publications, Inc.
Newspaper: Bank Note Reporter
Dave Harper, Ed.
700 East State St.
Iola, WI 54990
Phone: 800-258-0929 or 715-445-2214
        FAX: 715-445-4087
Monthly news source and marketplace for collectors of U.S. and world paper money, notes, checks and related fiscal paper.

Paper Money (World)

Expert

Neil Shafer
P.O. Box 17138
Milwaukee, WI 53217
Phone: 414-352-5962
Editor of "Standard Catalog of World Paper Money."

Primitive

Club/Association

International Primitive Money Society
Journal: International Primitive Money Society Journal
P.O. Box 1510
Redlands, CA 92373
Interested in primitive monies such as trading stones, metal rings, animal pelts, shells, and other primitive objects. *

Souvenir Cards

Club/Association

Souvenir Card Collectors Society
Journal: Souvenir Card Journal
P.O. Box 4155
Tulsa, OK 74159
Phone: 918-747-6724
Souvenir cards are 8 1/2" ;ts 11" cards with engraved reproductions of philatelic or numismatic designs from original plates.

Topical

Club/Association

Topical Numismatics Society
Dennis G. Rainey
3708 Nipomo Ave.
Long Beach, CA 90808
Phone: 213-429-4153
Focuses on coins and bank notes that are based on themes or topics such as transportation, birds, plants, sports events, etc.

Travelers Checks

Collector

Gary Snover
P.O. Box 3034
San Bernardino, CA 92413
Phone: 714-883-5849
Wants world wide travelers checks for collection; specimens, proofs or canceled issues.

COLLECTIBLES

(see also CHARACTER COLLECTIBLES;
COWBOY HEROES; POLITICAL
COLLECTIBLES; RADIO SHOW
PREMIUMS; SUPER HEROES;
TELEVISION SHOWS & MEMORABILIA;
etc.)

Auction Service

Nostalgia Publications, Inc.
Allan Petretti
21 South Lake Dr.
Hackensack, NJ 07601
Phone: 201-488-4536
Conducts mail-bid auctions of Coca-Cola and other advertising memorabilia and collectibles. *

Auction Service

Historicana
Robert Coup
P.O. Box 348
Leola, PA 17540-0348
Phone: 717-656-7780
Mail-bid auctions of Disneyana, historical & political Americana, toys, premiums, character collectibles; sample catalogs $2.

Auction Service

Doyle Auctioneers
R.D. 3 Box 137
Fishkill, NY 12524
Phone: 914-896-9492

Auction Service

Hake's Americana & Collectibles Auction
Ted Hake
P.O. Box 1444
York, PA 17405
Phone: 717-848-1333   FAX: 717-848-4977
Specializing in mail-bid auctions of Disneyana, historical Americana, toys, premiums, political items, character and other collectibles.

Auction Service

Kurt R. Krueger Auctions
Kurt R. Krueger
160 N. Washington St.
Iola, WI 54945
Phone: 715-445-3845   FAX: 715-445-4100
Specializing in the mail-bid auction of tokens, advertising, brewery items, Western Americana, autographs, sports, etc.

Auction Service

Mail Bid Auction
G.E. Moore
P.O. Box 414
Yucca Valley, CA 92286
        FAX: 619-365-9668
Conducts mail-bid auctions of collectibles: books, coins, medals, Disney, theater, valentines, art, railroad, medical/dental, etc.

Club/Association

Trivial Group, The
Newsletter: Unique & Unusual Collection, The
603 E. 105th St.
Kansas City, MO 64131
Interested in a wide range of collectible categories: hornets' nests, cat cards, almanacs, etc. *

Expert

Rinker Enterprises, Inc.
Harry L. Rinker
P.O. Box 248
Zionsville, PA 18092
Phone: 215-965-1122   FAX: 215-965-1124
Maintains research files, library (books, periodicals, etc.), photos and slides covering over 1200 antiques & collectibles categories.

Misc. Service

Timeless Treasures Publishing
Directory: Collection Connections
Robert Dabbs
P.O. Box 341
Lexington, MO 64067
Phone: 816-584-7411
WANTED classifieds; serious buyers for dozens of categories of collectibles.

Misc. Service

Rinker Enterprises, Inc.
Harry L. Rinker
P.O. Box 248
Zionsville, PA 18092
Phone: 215-965-1122   FAX: 215-965-1124
Antiques & collectibles resource center devoted to research & education; offers publications, teaching, consultations, etc.

Misc. Service

Advision, Inc.
David Lisot
3100 Arrowwood Lane
Boulder, CO 80303
Phone: 303-444-2320
Advision specializes in producing and distributing videotapes about coins and collectibles; currently over 100 video titles

Museum/Library

Wicomico Country Free Library
Arthur H. Goetz, Dir.
P.O. Box 4148
Salisbury, MD 21803
Phone: 301-749-3612   FAX: 301-548-2968

Offers a wide variety of antique and collecting books and information including identification and values, contacts, etc.

Periodical
Newsletter: Hobbyist Bulletin Board
K.J. Smith
140 Waite Road
Boxborough, MA 01719
A monthly publication with classifieds advertising crafts, collectibles, books, etc. *

Periodical
Newsletter: Collecting Newsletter
Robert F. Masterson
P.O. Box 859
Everett, MA 02149-3425
Phone: 617-387-7882
A quarterly with a circulation of 500; for the hobbyist and serious collector of all types of collectibles.

Periodical
Newsletter: Northeast Hobbies
Robert F. Masterson
P.O. Box 859
Everett, MA 02149-3425
Phone: 617-387-7882
A quarterly with a circulation of 500; for the hobbyist and serious collector of all types of collectibles.

Periodical
Newsletter: Collectors' Classified
William Margolin
P.O. Box 347
Holbrook, MA 02343-0347
Phone: 617-961-1463
All collectibles, especially cards, coins, stamps, books, memorabilia; published since 1975; 4 issues $1; free subscriber ads.

Periodical
Crafts & Collections
Newsletter: All Hobbies Ad Sheet
P.O. Box 291
Portland, CT 06480
Phone: 203-342-1969
Classified advertisements.

Periodical
Newspaper: Collectors Marketplace, The
Dorothy J. Graf, Ed.
P.O. Box 25
Stewartsville, NJ 08886
Phone: 908-479-4614
A bi-monthly publication for collectors and dealers; classifieds and display ads for buying and selling all collectibles.

Periodical
Magazine: Inside Collector, The
657 Meacham Ave.
Elmont, NY 11003
Phone: 516-326-9393 or 800-828-1429

Glossy, color magazine on today's most popular antiques and collectibles; collector profiles, shows, auctions, trends, ads, etc.

Periodical
J.L.C. Publications
Newsletter: Hobby News
Box 258
Ozone Park, NY 11416
A bi-monthly crafts newsletter. *

Periodical
Rinker Enterprises, Inc.
Newsletter: Rinker's Antiques & Collectibles Market Report
Harry L. Rinker
P.O. Box 248
Zionsville, PA 18092
Phone: 215-965-1122   FAX: 215-965-1124
A monthly antiques & collectible newsletter offering market analyses, collecting tips, reproduction information & editorial comment.

Periodical
Collectors' Information Clearinghouse (CIC)
Directory: CIC's Antiques & Collectibles Resource Directory
David J. Maloney, ISA
P.O. Box 2049
Frederick, MD 21702-1049
Phone: 301-695-8544 or 301-663-0818
FAX: 301-695-6491
Publishes major information source for collectors, sellers, claims adjusters, etc.: Experts, Buyers, Collector Clubs, Periodicals,

Periodical
Journal: Hobby Journal
Barry Younce
P.O. Box 176
Patterson, NC 28661
A publication for hobbyists. *

Periodical
Cumberland Communications
Magazine: Collections
Shane Rhyne
P.O. Box 333
Tazewell, TN 37879
Phone: 615-626-8250   FAX: 615-626-8253
A quarterly magazines focusing on collectibles.

Periodical
Newsletter: Hobby News & Homemakers Magazine
Marjorie Scott
Rt. 2, Box 42
McCall Creek, MS 39647
A bi-monthly publications for collectors, craft persons, pen-pals, etc. *

Periodical
Newspaper: National Hobby News, The
Col. "Woody" Russell
125 3 St. NW
P.O. Box 612
New Philadelphia, OH 44663-0612
Phone: 216-339-6338
A quarterly publication; lots and lots of get-rich-quick and mail order ads; a few short articles of interest to the collector.

Periodical
Newspaper: Flea Marketeer
P.O. Box 686
Southfield, MI 48037
Phone: 313-351-9910   FAX: 313-351-9037
A bi-monthly newsletter with articles about collectibles and hobbies; also tips on buying, selling, and trading.

Periodical
Newspaper: Travel Collector
P.O. Box 40
Manawa, WI 54949-0040
Phone: 414-596-1944
Monthly newspaper that focuses on souvenir and commemorative glass and ceramic items in addition to other souvenir collectibles.

Periodical
Newspaper: Yesteryear
P.O. Box 2
Princeton, WI 54968
Phone: 414-787-4808
A monthly newspaper featuring articles and ads about antiques & collectibles; shops, shows, flea markets, etc.

Periodical
Newsletter: Classified Ads Newsletter
W. Bartlett
P.O. Box 644
Park Forest, IL 60466
A newsletter of collectibles classifieds from around the country. *

Periodical
Newsletter: Collectors Exchange
P.O. Box 193
Berwick, LA 70342
Monthly paper for collectors; buy-sell-trade ads for antiques and collectibles. *

Periodical
Magazine: Collectors' Showcase
James R. Brackin, Pub.
Suite 210
7130 S. Lewis Ave.
Tulsa, OK 74136
Phone: 928-496-7406 or 800-341-1522
FAX: 918-496-7485
America's premier collectors' magazine; published monthly; featuring articles about toys, dolls and collectibles.

Periodical
Magazine: American Flea Market Journal
M.H. Sparks
1911 Ave. D
Brownwood, TX 76801
Phone: 915-643-6418
Need flea market roducts? AFMJ is full of wholesale merchandise sources, ideas and inside information; $3 for sample copy.

COLLECTIBLES (INTERNATIONAL)

Periodical
Newsletter: Amazing News
Biem, 103-3 Dosu-Dong
Uisong, Kyungbuk
Seoul 769-800, Korea
*An international hobby magazine with ads, collectors, articles, etc. ***

Periodical
Newsletter: JH All Hobbies
Jacques Herrijgers
1 Nachtegaallaan, B-1701
Itterbeek, Belgium
A quarterly international publications for hobbyists, collectors and pen-pal seekers; a bilingual publication (English and French.)

Periodical
Magazine: Traders Classified
Box 5215
Windsor
Ontario N9J 2L3 Canada
Monthly newsprint ad magazine from Canada covering a wide variety of mail order collectibles; coins, WWII, railroad, stamps,

COLLECTIBLES (MODERN)

(see also DOLLS; FIGURINES; STEIFF)

Dealer
Maurice Nasser Co.
New London Shopping Center
New London, CT 06320
Phone: 203-443-6523 or 800-243-0895

Dealer
Pandoras Box
200 Hamilton Ave.
White Plains, NY 10601
Phone: 914-949-2467 *

Dealer
Gift Gallery, The
Sy Schreck
1546 Northern Blvd.
Manhasset, NY 11030
Phone: 516-627-6500 or 800-443-8322
Deals in collectibles: Precious Moments, Dept. 56 cottages, Hummels, plates, Boehm, Swarovski, Krystonia, David Winter, Anri, etc.

Dealer
Limited Edition, The
2170 Sunrise Highway
Merrick, NY 11566
Phone: 516-623-4400 or 800-645-2864
Specializes in suspended and retired Precious Moments figurines.

Dealer
Elwell Exchange
295 Italy Turnpike
Naples, NY 14512
Phone: 716-374-6452 *

Dealer
Magdalena Interiors
3235 Chestnut St. NW
Washington, DC 20015
Phone: 202-966-8755

Dealer
Tiara Gifts
Wheaton Plaza
Wheaton, MD 20902
Phone: 301-949-0210

Dealer
Biggs Collectibles
Donny Biggs
6223 Lakeside Ave.
Richmond, VA 23228
Phone: 804-266-7744 or 800-637-0704
                              FAX: 804-266-7775
Carries lots of limited edition dolls (Ashton Drake dealer of the year); also Chilmark, Hummel, David Winter, etc.

Dealer
Dealer
Box 486
Greenville, OH 45331
Phone: 513-548-4006
*Wants Precious Moments and Hummels; any size collection; buys dealers overstocks. ***

Dealer
Collectibles etc., Inc.
Sandy Forgach
8362 N. 49th St.
Brown Deer, WI 53223
Phone: 414-355-4545 or 800-558-5594
Specializes in old and new Precious Moments figurines, old and new collector plates, Ashton Drake and Perillo dolls, accessories.

Dealer
Gifts 'n Things, Inc.
St. Charles, MO 63301
Phone: 314-946-6896 or 341-532-9532
Buy, sell, trade retired figurines & cottages: Precious Moments, Jan Hagara, Tom Clark, D. Winter and Lilliput Cottages, Dept. 56, etc.

Dealer
Eloise's Gifts & Antiques
722 South Goliad
Rockwall, TX 75087
Phone: 214-771-6371
Carries Cairn, All Gods, Armani, L. Davis, Dept. 56, Duncan Royale, Frumps, EKJ, Hummel, M. Humphrey, Hagara, Sarahs, D. Winter, etc.

Dealer
Opa's Haus, Inc.
Newsletter: OHI Exchange
1600 River Road
New Braunfels, TX 78132
Phone: 512-629-1191 or 800-627-1600
                              FAX: 512-629-0153
Collector's source for buying/selling major retired collectibles: Dept. 56, David Winter, Lowell Davis, Hummel, Duncan Royale, etc.

Dealer
Collections Unlimited
Ms. Mickey Kaz
4867 1/2 Topanga Canyon Blvd.
Woodland Hills, CA 91364
Phone: 818-713-9390 or 800-366-1819
                              FAX: 818-713-9390

Man./Prod./Dist.
Georgetown Collection
P.O. Box 9730
Portland, ME 04104
Phone: 207-775-4800   FAX: 207-775-6457
A direct mail marketer of heirloom quality collectibles, including porcelain dolls and figurines.

Man./Prod./Dist.
ArtAffects
P.O. Box 98
Staten Island, NY 10307
Phone: 718-948-6767   FAX: 718-967-4521
ArtAffects produces fine collectibles and graphics including plates, bells, dolls, ornaments, figurines and steins.

Man./Prod./Dist.
Anna-Perenna, Inc.
71-73 Weyman Ave.
New Rochelle, NY 10805
Phone: 914-633-3777 or 800-627-2550
Manufacturers and publishes limited edition prints, figurines and plates by artists such as P. Buckley Moss.

Man./Prod./Dist.
Reco
138-150 Haven Ave.
Port Washington, NY 11050
Phone: 516-767-2400   FAX: 516-767-2409
Producer of prints, plates, figurines, bells, dolls, ornaments, music boxes, fans and accessories.

Man./Prod./Dist.

United States Historical Society
First & Main Streets
Richmond, VA 23219
Phone: 804-648-4736   FAX: 804-648-0002
Direct mail marketer of collectibles in stained glass, pewter, porcelain and other materials.

Man./Prod./Dist.

Flambro Imports, Inc.
Aded Zyssman
1260 Collier Road, NW
Atlanta, GA 30318
Phone: 404-352-1381   FAX: 404-352-2150
Importer of collectible clowns (Emmett Kelly, Jr.) and circus-related items, plates, ornaments, figurines and miniatures.

Man./Prod./Dist.

Hamilton Collection, The
P.O. Box 2567
Jacksonville, FL 32232
Phone: 904-723-6000   FAX: 904-725-8997
Formerly The Hamilton Mint, produces collectible plates, figurines and dolls.

Man./Prod./Dist.

Viking Import House, Inc.
690 NE 13th Street
Fort Lauderdale, FL 33304
Phone: 305-763-3388 or 800-327-2297
                    FAX: 305-462-2317
Distributes prints, plates, figurines, bells, dolls, ornaments, etc. for most manufacturers of limited edition collectibles.

Man./Prod./Dist.

Munro Collectibles
5242 Angola Rd.
Toledo, OH 43615
Phone: 419-536-5792   FAX: 419-536-6623
Produces and distributes fantasy and wildlife figurines and miniatures.

Man./Prod./Dist.

Midwest Importers of Cannon Falls, Inc.
P.O. Box 20
Cannon Falls, MN 55009-0020
Phone: 507-263-4261
Imports and wholesales unique gifts from around the world - bells, paperweights, dolls, ornaments, figurines, German nutcrackers, etc.

Man./Prod./Dist.

ENESCO Corp.
Eugene Freedman, Pres.
One Enesco Plaza
Elk Grove Village, IL 60007
Phone: 708-640-5200 or 800-323-0636
                    FAX: 708-640-6151
Giftware company produces/designs fine gifts & collectibles: figurines, musicals, waterballs, etc. by Precious Moments and others.

Man./Prod./Dist.

American Artists
Suite 7
42 Sherwood Terrace
Lake Bluff, IL 60044
Phone: 312-295-5355   FAX: 312-295-5491
Manufacturers and distributes limited edition plates, figurines and prints by artists such as Fred Stone, Donald Zolan and Susan Leigh.

Man./Prod./Dist.

Band Creations
Suite F
28427 Ballard Dr.
Lake Forest, IL 60045
Phone: 708-816-0900   FAX: 708-816-3695
Produces figurines and dolls by artists including Lori Davis, Karen Moore and Sue Shanahan.

Man./Prod./Dist.

Bello Creations
7503 W. Diversey Ave.
Elmwood Park, IL 60137
Phone: 708-456-6669   FAX: 708-456-6687
Produces/distributes original porcelain dolls, art works and glass designed by Yolando Bello, Kathy Hippensteel and Khaim Pinkhasik.

Man./Prod./Dist.

Roman, Inc.
555 Lawrence Ave.
Rosell, IL 60172-1599
Phone: 708-529-3000   FAX: 708-529-1121
Produces figurines, plates, lithographs, bells, dolls, music boxes, etc. Exclusive importer of Fontanini nativity sets and plates.

Man./Prod./Dist.

Hollywood Limited Editions, Inc.
6990 Central Park Ave.
Lincolnwood, IL 60645
Phone: 708-673-3250 or 800-323-1413
                    FAX: 708-673-4037
Distributes an extensive line of collector plates, figurines, bells, ornaments and accessories.

Man./Prod./Dist.

Dave Grossman Creations
1608 N. Warson Rd.
St. Louis, MO 63132
Phone: 314-423-5600   FAX: 314-423-7620
Producer of collectible plates, ornaments and figurines including Rockwell, Gone With the Wind, Wizard of Oz, and Emmett Kelly, Sr.

Man./Prod./Dist.

John Hine Studios, Inc.
P.O. Box 801207
Houston, TX 77280-7030
Phone: 713-690-4477   FAX: 713-462-7030
Distributor of David Winter Cottages, Malcolm Cooper Pubs, Maurice Wideman's American collection, and Christopher Lawrence's Mushrooms.

Man./Prod./Dist.

CREART U.S.
4517 Manzanillo Drive
Austin, TX 78749
Phone: 512-280-3143   FAX: 512-280-0695
Produces limited edition wildlife and animal figurine figurines from bonded marble.

Man./Prod./Dist.

American West Galleries
1302 N. Cleveland Ave.
Loveland, CO 80537
Phone: 303-667-4800
Manufacturers and distributes limited edition plates, bells, dolls, original art, figurines and prints by various artists.

Man./Prod./Dist.

Hamilton Gifts Limited
Kathy Harty
800 W. Walnut
Compton, CA 90224-4369
Phone: 800-626-1850
Produces/designs fine gifts & collectibles: figurines, mugs, dolls, plates, ornaments, TV show memorabilia: Simpsons, Maud Humphrey, etc.

Man./Prod./Dist.

Incolay Studios, Inc.
S.G. Bright
445 North Fox Street
San Fernando, CA 91340
Phone: 818-365-2521   FAX: 818-365-9599
Manufacturer of handcrafted reproductions of antiques, music boxes and accessories in variegated stone cameo relief (Wedgwood-style.)

Man./Prod./Dist.

Porter & Price, Inc.
148 South Vinewood St.
Escondido, CA 92029-1921
Phone: 619-741-8700   FAX: 619-745-6070
Produces prints, plates, figurines, steins and plaques by artists such as Susie Morton, Alan Murray, and Darrell Burchfield.

Man./Prod./Dist.

Finelt Hooper Asociates
Suite 536
20503 Yorba Linda Blvd.
Yorba Linda, CA 92686
Phone: 714-693-0132
Manufactures precious and non-precious medallions, jewelry, coins, figurines and miniatures for the Walt Disney Co., the U.N.,

Man./Prod./Dist.

Rarities Mint, Inc.
3873 Eagle Dr.
Anaheim, CA 92807
Phone: 800-USA-MINT   FAX: 714-630-9337
Manufactures limited editions bronze medallions under license to Disney, Warner Bros., Paramount Pictures, MCA, and Universal Studios.

Periodical

Magazine: Collector Editions
Joan M. Pursley, Ed.
170 Fifth Ave. - 12 Floor
New York, NY 10010
Phone: 212-989-8700 or 800-347-6969
FAX: 212-645-8976
A bi-weekly consumer magazine covering contemporary collector plates, figurines, prints and glass objects; companies, artists, etc.

Periodical

Newsletter: Classifieds for Collectors
P.O. Box 1864
Waukesha, WI 53187
*A publication offering the collector an opportunity to buy, sell and exchange collectibles. ***

Periodical

Rosie Wells Enterprises, Inc.
Magazine: Collectors' Bulletin
Rosie Wells
R.R. 1
Canton, IL 61520
Phone: 309-668-2565   FAX: 309-668-2795
Articles about today's collectibles: Lowell Davis, Anri, Dept. 56, Precious Moments, Jan Hagara, Maud Humphrey, David Winter, etc.

Periodical

WEB Publications, Inc.
Magazine: Collector's Mart Magazine
Bette Peters
P.O. Box 12830
Wichita, KS 67277
Phone: 316-946-0600   FAX: 316-946-0675
Quarterly magazine for limited-edition art and collectibles: classifieds, articles, dealers ads, club notices, etc.

Bessie Pease Gutmann

Club/Association

Gutmann Collectors Club
P.O. Box 4743
Lancaster, PA 17604-4743
Phone: 717-293-2779   FAX: 717-293-2781
Focuses on the works of Bessie Pease Gutmann. Sponsored by The Balliol Corp.

Bing & Grondahl

Man./Prod./Dist.

Royal Copenhagen/Bing & Grondahl Co.
27 Holland Ave.
White Plains, NY 10603
Phone: 914-428-8222 or 800-431-1992
FAX: 914-428-8251
Manufactures dinnerware, cobalt blue underglaze collector plates, figurines, bells, dolls, ornaments and gift accessories.

Bob Olszewski

Club/Association

Club Olszewski, Inc.
Newsletter: Small Talk
Jacci & Wallie Bednar
P.O. Box 29067
Parma, OH 44129-0067
FAX: 216-433-7071
A fan club for Robert Olszewski with the primary purpose of sharing personal information on this talented artist & his miniatures.

Clarissa Johnson

Man./Prod./Dist.

Clarissa's Creations
Clarissa Johnson
18111 Meyers
Detroit, MI 48235
Phone: 313-341-7762
Produces original Afro American artwork: prints, collector plates, and note and greeting cards designed by Clarissa Johnson.

Collector Plates

Club/Association

International Plate Collectors Guild
Newsletter: Platter Platter
Marjorie M. Rosenberg, Pr.
P.O. Box 487
Artesia, CA 90702-0487
Phone: 213-924-6335
A monthly newsletter for plate collectors.

Man./Prod./Dist.

Christian Fantasy Collectibles
Robert Dailey
125 Woodland Ave.
Rutherford, NJ 07070
Phone: 201-933-4836
Producer of the "Realms of Wonder" series of fantasy collectible plates designed by Tim and Rita Hildebrandt.

Man./Prod./Dist.

Cambridge Collection
P.O. Box 21416
Pikesville, MD 21208
Phone: 301-358-7951
Produces and distributes collector plates by artists Steve Leonardi and Debra Colburn.

Man./Prod./Dist.

Bradford Exchange, The
9301 N. Milwaukee Ave.
Niles, IL 60648
Phone: 312-966-2770
Pioneered in direct mail marketing of collector plates and created an organized secondary market trading exchange for collector plates.

Museum/Library

Bradford Museum of Collector's Plates, The
9333 N. Milwaukee Ave.
Niles, IL 60648
Phone: 708-966-2770

Periodical

Plate Collector's Stock Exchange
Newsletter: Plate-O-Holic
478 Ward Street Extension
Wallingford, CT 06492
Phone: 203-265-1722
*A newsletter for dealers with articles focusing on the forecasting of collector plate values. ***

Periodical

Magazine: Plate World
Brian J. Taylor, Pub.
9200 North Maryland Ave.
Niles, IL 60648
Phone: 312-763-7773   FAX: 708-966-9463
The largest publication in its field and the only magazine with editorial content dealing primarily with limited edition plates.

Collector Plates (Bareuther)

Man./Prod./Dist.

WARA Intercontinental Co.
20101 West 8 Mile Road
Detroit, MI 48219
Phone: 313-535-9110
Sole importer and distributor of Bareuther cobalt blue collector plates and bells.

Cottages

Man./Prod./Dist.

Department 56
P.O. Box 5562
Hopkins, MN 55343
Phone: 800-548-8696   FAX: 612-944-8313
Produces "Snow Village", "Dickens' Village" and other lighted houses and accessories.

Cottages (David Winter)

Club/Association

David Winter Cottages Collectors Guild
Magazine: Cottage Country
P.O. Box 800667
Houston, TX 77280-0667
Phone: 713-690-4477   FAX: 713-462-7030
Focuses on the English collectible miniature cottages by David Winter. Sponsored by John Hine Studios, Inc., the U.S. distributor.

Cottages (Windy Meadows)

Club/Association

Windy Meadows Pottery Collector Club
Jan Richardson
c/o Windy Meadows Pottery
1036 Valley Road
Knoxville, MD 21758
Phone: 301-834-8857 or 800-527-6274
FAX: 301-663-0612
Specializes in the hand-built stoneware Windy Meadows candlehouses & cottages designed by Jan Richardson. A company-sponsored club.

Crystal

Club/Association

Crystal World Collectors Society, The
c/o Happy World Products
3 Cesar Place
Moonachie, NJ 07074
Phone: 201-896-0336   FAX: 201-896-0795
Focuses on Austrian crystal figurines, paperweights, bells & prisms. Sponsored by Happy World Products/The Crystal World Co.

Man./Prod./Dist.

Iris Arc Crystal
114 East Haley St.
Santa Barbara, CA 93101
Phone: 805-963-3661 or 800-392-7546
FAX: 805-965-2458
Designs and manufactures full lead crystal collectibles including paperweights, cottages, ornaments, figurines, miniatures, etc.

Man./Prod./Dist.

Crystallite
625 DuBois St.
San Rafael, CA 94901
Phone: 800-999-9856   FAX: 415-459-5141
Distributes Austrian crystal figurines by Charles Castelli and cold-cast porcelain fantasy figurines by Mark Newman and Randy Bowen.

Crystal (Swarovski)

Club/Association

Swarovski Collectors Society
c/o Swarovski America, Ltd.
2 Slater Road
Cranston, RI 02920
Phone: 800-556-6478 or 800-426-3088
FAX: 401-463-8459
Focuses on Austrian Swarovski crystal figurines and giftware. Sponsored by Swarovski America, Ltd.

Danbury Mint

Man./Prod./Dist.

Danbury Mint, The
47 Richards Ave.
Norwalk, CT 06856
Phone: 203-853-2000 or 800-243-4664

A direct mail marketer of collector plates. Also produces miniatures, dolls, figurines and other collectibles.

Decoupage Giftware

Man./Prod./Dist.

Tomorrow Today Corporation
Milton Reach, III
Box 612
Westfield, MA 01086
Phone: 413-562-2465 or 800-253-3456
FAX: 413-562-6778
Designs and manufactures fine decoupage giftware such as ornaments and musicals; also stationary and potpourri.

Decoys

Man./Prod./Dist.

Beaver Dam Decoys
1662 Beaver Dam Road
Point Pleasant, NJ 08742
Phone: 201-892-2542
Manufacturers wooden decoys, birds and fish.

Dept. 56

Collector

Sue Coffee
10 Saunders Hollow
Old Lyme, CT 06371
Phone: 203-434-5641
Wants new Dept. 56 items especially waterglobes and nite-lites.

Dolls

(see also DOLLS)

Man./Prod./Dist.

C.V. Gambina, Inc.
2005 Gentilly Blvd.
New Orleans, LA 70119
Phone: 504-947-0626   FAX: 504-947-7542
Manufactures porcelain, rag and vinyl dolls designed by C.V. Gambina and Joel Eguigure.

Periodical

Newsletter: Doll Collectors' Market Report
P.O. Box 128
Headland, AL 36345-0128
A bi-monthly market analysis report of surveyed prices for collectible & vinyl modern dolls.

Dolls (Ashton-Drake)

Man./Prod./Dist.

Ashton-Drake Galleries, The
212 West Superior Street
Chicago, IL 60610-9948
Phone: 708-966-2770   FAX: 708-966-3121
Direct mail marketer of dolls by various designers such as Yolando Bello, Dianna Effner, Cindy M. McClure, and Kathy Hippensteel.

Dolls (Bradley)

Club/Association

Bradley Doll Club, The
Newsletter: Bradley Doll Club Newsletter
Joanna Harstein
1424 North Spring St.
Los Angeles, CA 90014
Phone: 213-221-4162   FAX: 213-221-4162
Focuses on the collectible dolls issued by Bradley Collectibles. A manufacturer-sponsored club.

Dolls (Dynasty)

Man./Prod./Dist.

Cardinal, Inc./Dynasty Doll Collection
Stanley & Irene Wahlberg
P.O. Box 99
Port Reading, NJ 07064
Phone: 908-636-6160   FAX: 908-636-0017
Imports the Dynasty Doll collection and Concord miniatures.

Dolls (Franklin Mint)

Club/Association

Franklin Mint Doll Collector Club
c/o The Franklin Mint
U.S. Route 1
Franklin Center, PA 19091
Phone: 800-523-7622
Focuses on the dolls issued by Franklin Mint. Sponsored by The Franklin Mint.

Dolls (Good-Kruger)

Man./Prod./Dist.

Good-Kruger Dolls
1320 Village Road
Strasburg, PA 17579
Phone: 717-687-7208   FAX: 717-687-6195
Manufactures dolls designed by Julie Good-Kruger.

Dolls (Gorham)

Man./Prod./Dist.

Gorham, Inc.
P.O. Box 906
Mount Kisco, NY 10549
Phone: 914-242-9300 or 800-225-1460
FAX: 914-242-9379

Dolls (Jan Goodyear)

Man./Prod./Dist.

Doll Workshop, The
3560 Aurora Road
Melbourne, FL 32934
Phone: 407-242-2678
Manufactures limited edition dolls by Jan Goodyear.

Dolls (Jerri)

Club/Association

Jerri Collectors Club
c/o Dolls By Jerri
P.O. Box 561748
Charlotte, NC 28256
Phone: 704-333-3211
Collectors are interested in dolls by Jerri. Sponsored by Dolls by Jerri.

Dolls (Lee Middleton)

Man./Prod./Dist.

Middleton Doll Company
1301 Washington Blvd.
Belpre, OH 45714
Phone: 614-423-1717   FAX: 614-423-5983
The sole manufacturer and producer of original porcelain and vinyl dolls designed by artist and sculptor, Lee Middleton.

Dolls (Madame Alexander)

Club/Association

Madame Alexander Fan Club
Newsletter: Madame Alexander Fan Club
    Newsletter
Earl Meisinger
11 South 767 Book Rd.
Naperville, IL 60564
Members receive the "Madame Alexander Shopper" which is devoted to buying and selling Madame Alexander dolls and accessories.

Collector

Elaine DeVylder
2 Weed Circle
Stamford, CT 06902
Wants cloth or vinyl "Robin Woods" dolls; also Madame Alexander dolls.

Dealer

Joe & Juanita Reese
511 Dair Ave.
Harrison, OH 45030
Wants character collectibles and Madame Alexander dolls; also western collectibles and pocket knives. *

Dolls (Phyllis Parkins)

Club/Association

Phyllis' Collectors Club
Newsletter: PCC Newsletter
Phyllis Parkins
c/o The Collectables, Inc.
Rt. 4, Box 503
Rolla, MO 65401
Phone: 314-364-7849   FAX: 314-364-2448
Focuses on the Phyllis Parkins' collectible dolls. Sponsored by The Collectables, Inc.

Dolls (Robin Holland)

Man./Prod./Dist.

Starshine Dolls
1724 Hull Street
Ft. Collins, CO 80526
Phone: 303-225-1654
Manufactures limited edition Native American dolls in vinyl and porcelain designed by artist Robin Holland.

Dolls (Robin Woods)

Club/Association

Robin Woods Doll Club
c/o Robin Woods, Inc.
6592 Hamilton Ave.
Pittsburgh, PA 15206
Phone: 412-361-3655   FAX: 412-361-3806
Focuses on the rotationally molded vinyl dolls designed by Robin Woods. sponsored by Robin Woods, Inc.

Collector

Elaine DeVylder
2 Weed Circle
Stamford, CT 06902
Wants cloth or vinyl "Robin Woods" dolls; also Madame Alexander dolls.

Dolls (Rotraud Schrott)

Club/Association

Rotraud Schrott Fan Club
c/o Great American Doll Co.
1620 South Sinclair St.
Anaheim, CA 92806
Phone: 800-669-3655   FAX: 714-978-7315
Focuses on collectible dolls designed by Rotraud Schrott. Sponsored by the Great American Doll Company.

Dolls (Susan Wakeen)

Man./Prod./Dist.

Susan Wakeen Doll Company, Inc.
532 Hopemeadow St.
Simsbury, CT 06070
Phone: 203-658-5859
Manufactures collectible vinyl and porcelain dolls designed by Susan Wakeen.

Donald Zolan

Club/Association

Donald Zolan Collectors Society
133 E. Carrillo St.
Santa Barbara, CA 93101
Phone: 805-963-1371   FAX: 805-962-0605
Focuses on the collectible plates, lithographs, etc. designed by artist Donald Zolan. Sponsored by Pemberton & Oakes Gallery.

Duncan Royale

Club/Association

Duncan Royale Collectors Club
Newsletter: Royale Courier
c/o Duncan Royale Co.
1141 South Acacia Ave.
Fulerton, CA 92631
Phone: 714-879-1360   FAX: 714-879-4611
Focuses on the collectible figurines, graphics and plates issued by Duncan Royale. Sponsored by Duncan Royale Co.

Edna Hibel

(see also PERSONALITIES (ARTISTS), Edna Hibel)

Man./Prod./Dist.

Edna Hibel Studio
P.O. Box 9967
Riveria Beach, FL 33419
Phone: 407-848-9633   FAX: 407-848-9640
Publishes and distributes fine arts, collectibles, reproductions, gift items, and fashion and accessories designed Edna Hibel.

Eggshell Porcelain

Man./Prod./Dist.

Eisler Porcelain
Luanne R. Eisler
RD #3, Box 200R
Slippery Rock, PA 16057
Phone: 412-794-5004
Importer/wholesaler of bowls, cups & vases of handpainted "eggshell" porcelain; must be .5mm thin or less; first made in Ming Dynasty.

Figurines

Club/Association

Silvertip Collectors Society
c/o Silvertip Studios, Inc.
Route 1, 2763 East, 3400 North
Twin Falls, ID 83301
Phone: 208-734-3440
Focuses on the bronze and pewter sculptures by Danny D. Edwards. Sponsored by Silvertip Studios, Inc.

Dealer

Colonial House Antiques
Stan Worrey
182 Front St.
Berea, OH 44017
Phone: 216-826-4169 or 800-344-9299
                        FAX: 216-826-0839
Specializes in old Royal Doultons, Hummels, David Winter & Lilliput Lane Cottages; mails catalogs three times a year.

Man./Prod./Dist.

United Design Corp.
P.O. Box 1200
Nobel, OK 73068
Phone: 405-872-3468   FAX: 405-360-4442

A producer of figurines by sculptors Donna Kennicutt, Suzan Bradford, Larry Miller, Ken Memoli and Penni Jo Jonas.

Figurines (Adorables)

Club/Association

Adorables Collectors Society
P.O. Box 1846
New Rockelle, NY 10801
Focuses on Adorables figurines. Sponsored by Anna-Perenna, Inc.

Figurines (Animal)

Man./Prod./Dist.

Sandicast, Inc.
8480 Miralani Drive
San Diego, CA 92126
Phone: 619-695-9611   FAX: 619-695-0615
Manufacturer of animal figurines noted for their lifelike appearance and designed by artist Sandra A. Brue.

Figurines (Anri)

Club/Association

Club ANRI
Newsletter: Club ANRI Newsletter
c/o Schmid, Inc.
55 Pacella Park Drive
Randolph, MA 02368
Phone: 617-961-3000   FAX: 617-986-8168
Focuses on Anri maple-carved wooden figurines. Sponsored by SCHMID, Inc.

Figurines (Armani)

Club/Association

G. Armani Society
Magazine: G. Armani Review
Connie Ribaudo, ExDir
300 Mac Lane
Keasbey, NJ 08832 .
Phone: 908-417-0330 or 800-327-6264
                        FAX: 908-417-0031
For fans and collectors of the works (sculptures) of master sculptor Giuseppe Armani.

Figurines (Artina)

Man./Prod./Dist.

Artina Collectibles
1112 NW 19th Ave.
Portland, OR 97209
Phone: 503-274-1055 or 800-222-4966
Manufactures original characters from Rien Poortvliet's books "Gnomes" and "The Book of the Sandman."

Figurines (Cairn)

Club/Association

Cairn Collector Society, The
c/o Cairn Studio, Ltd.
P.O. Box 400
Davidson, NC 28036
Phone: 704-892-5859

Focuses on collectible figurines such as Tom Clark's Gnomes issued by Cairn Studio Ltd. Sponsored by Cairn Studio, Ltd.

Club/Association

Cairn Studio Ltd.
P.O. Box 400
Davidson, NC 28036
Phone: 704-892-5859
Manufacturers gnomes and other character figurines by artists such as Tom Clark.

Figurines (Carousels)

Man./Prod./Dist.

WACO Products Corp.
One North Corporate Dr.
Riverdale, NJ 07457-0160
Phone: 201-616-1660   FAX: 201-616-1621
Manufactures moving hand-painted porcelain carousels as part of their "Melody in Motion" series.

Man./Prod./Dist.

Willits Designs
P.O. Box 750009
Petaluma, CA 94975
Phone: 707-778-7211
Produces The American Carousel limited edition collections by Tobin Fraley; also other collectibles including plates, figurines, etc.

Figurines (Chilmark)

Club/Association

Chilmark Registry
Newsletter: Chilmark Report
Cyndi Gavin McNally
c/o Lance Corp.
321 Central Street
Hudson, MA 01749
Phone: 508-568-1401   FAX: 508-568-8741
Focuses on Chilmark pewter sculptures. Sponsored by the Lance Corp. The "Chilmark Report" reports on after-market values.

Figurines (Constance Guerra)

Man./Prod./Dist.

Constance Collection
Rt. 1, Box 538
P.O. Box 250
Midland, VA 22728
Phone: 703-788-4500 or 800-722-3511
Produces figurines, ornaments and miniatures from crushed pecan wood resin designed by Constance Angela Guerra.

Figurines (Don Polland)

Club/Association

Polland Collectors Society
c/o Polland Studios
P.O. Box 2468
Prescott, AZ 86302
Phone: 602-778-1900   FAX: 602-778-4034

Focuses on Don Polland's pewter sculpture collectible figurines. Sponsored by Polland Studios (Gerard Corp.).

Figurines (Elfin Glen)

Club/Association

Elfin Glen Collectors Guild
c/o Elfin Glen Studio, Inc.
4401 South Pinemont, Suite 220
Houston, TX 77041
Phone: 713-462-4116
Focuses on the Elfin Glen figurine series entitled "The Citizens of Elfin Glen" designed by D.A. Snuffer. A manufacturer-sponsored club.

Figurines (Emmett Kelly, Jr.)

(see also CLOWN COLLECTIBLES)

Club/Association

EKJ Collectors Society
Journal: EK Journal
Dorietta Oaklief
P.O. Box 93507
Atlanta, GA 30377-0507
Phone: 404-352-1381
Focuses on the Emmett Kelly, Jr. clown figurines. Sponsored by Flambro Imports, Inc.; journal, binder, pin, "members only" plaque.

Club/Association

Emmett's Friends
c/o Frankenmuth Gallery
568 South Main Street
Frankenmuth, MI 48734
Focuses on the clown figurines issued by Flambro Imports, Inc.

Periodical

Cumberland Communications
Magazine: Collections
Shane Rhyne
P.O. Box 333
Tazewell, TN 37879
Phone: 615-626-8250   FAX: 615-626-8253
A quarterly collectibles magazine containing the "Emmett Kelly, Jr. Collectors Edition" supplement/value guide.

Figurines (Goebel)

Man./Prod./Dist.

Goebel Inc.
P.O. Box 10
Pennington, NJ 08534
Phone: 609-737-8777 or 800-366-4632
                        FAX: 609-737-8685
Distributors of Goebel and other figurines.

Figurines (Goebel-Friar Tuck)

Club/Association

Friars Club
102 Ketewamoke Ave.
Babylon, NY 11702
Phone: 516-661-8363

For collectors interested in the Goebel Friar Tuck figurines.

Figurines (Goebel-Miniatures)

Dealer

Country Cousin, Inc.
Newsletter: Magnifier, The
Betty & Ray Olszewski
12532 Dillingham Square
Lake Ridge, VA 22192
Phone: 703-590-5400 or 703-791-5538
Provides collectors with information about the artist, the product, and availability of product through mail order sales.

Man./Prod./Dist.

Goebel Miniatures
4820 Adohr Lane
Camarillo, CA 93012
Phone: 805-484-4351 FAX: 805-482-2143
Produces fine hand-painted limited edition Goebel miniature figurines.

Figurines (Krystonia)

Club/Association

Krystonia Collectors Club
c/o Precious Art/Panton, Inc.
110 E. Ellsworth Rd.
Ann Arbor, MI 48108
Phone: 313-677-3510 or 313-677-3412
FAX: 313-677-3411
Focuses on the Krystonia dragon, gnome & elf collectibles. Sponsored by Precious Art/Panton, Inc.; "members' only" pieces available.

Figurines (Lilliput Lane)

Club/Association

Land of Legend Collectors Fellowship, The
Claire Golata
c/o Gift Link/Lilliput
9052 Old Annapolis Rd.
Columbia, MD 21045
Phone: 301-964-2202 FAX: 301-964-5673
Focuses on the Britain's Lilliput Lane fantasy figurines. Sponsored by Gift Link, Inc./Lilliput Lane, Ltd.

Figurines (Maud Humphrey)

Man./Prod./Dist.

Hamilton Gifts Limited Maud Humphrey Collectors' Club
Donna Carucci
P.O. Box 4009
Compton, CA 90224-4009
Phone: 800-626-1850
Members receive membership figurine, information on the Maud Humphrey Collection, and newsletter; can acquire "Members Only" figurines.

Figurines (Memories Of Yesdy')

Club/Association

Enesco Memories of Yesterday Collectors' Society
Newsletter: Sharing Memories...
Diana C. Derbas
One Enesco Plaze
P.O. Box 245
Elk Grove Village, IL 60009-0245
Phone: 708-640-5200 or 800-323-0636
FAX: 708-640-6151
Society members receive symbol of membership figurine, newsletter, opportunity to acquire "Members Only" figurine.

Figurines (Michael Garman)

Man./Prod./Dist.

Michael Garman Productions, Inc.
2418 West Colorado Ave.
Colorado Springs, CO 80904
Phone: 800-874-7144
Manufactures three-dimensional sculptures of people who have shaped America: cowboys, aviators, soldiers, policemen, wino, heroes, etc.

Figurines (Sebastian)

Club/Association

Sebastian Miniatures Collectors Society
Newsletter: Sebastian Miniatures Collectors Society News
Cyndi Gavin McNally
c/o The Lance Corp.
321 Central St.
Hudson, MA 01749
Phone: 508-568-1401 FAX: 508-568-8741
Focuses on the Sebastian collectible figurines. Sponsored by the Lance Corp.; members receive free miniature, annual value guide.

Dealer

Blossom Shop
Jim Waite
112 No. Main
Farmer City, IL 61842
Phone: 309-928-3222 or 800-842-2593
Buys and sells old and new Sebastian miniatures by P.W. Baston, private issues, commercial & Marblehead, MA.; sponsor Sebastian fair.

Periodical

Price Guide: Sebastian Exchange
Paul J. Sebastian
2072 Pine Drive
Lancaster, PA 17601
Phone: 717-394-3874
Issue three newsletters each year covering the secondary market; also publishes annual Sebastian "Value Register Handbook."

Figurines (Wee Forest Folk)

Club/Association

Wee Forest Folk Collector's Club
Newsletter: Folktales
Betty Jo Royster, Pres.
511 Clayton Rd.
Durham, NC 27703
Phone: 919-596-6456
Club provides information about Wee Forest Folk figurines, past and present; helps locate figurines from 1978 to present.

Folk Art

Man./Prod./Dist.

Vaillancourt Folk Art
P.O. Box 582
Millbury, MA 01527
Phone: 508-865-9183
Creates limited edition chalkware replicas cast from antique chocolate molds and ice cream forms.

Franklin Mint

Club/Association

Franklin Mint Collectors Society
Newsletter: Franklin Mint Almanac, The
c/o The Franklin Mint
U.S. Route 1
Franklin Center, PA 19091
Phone: 800-523-7622
Focuses on the quality jewelry, crystal, collectibles, and sculpture issued by The Franklin Mint which sponsors the Society.

Dealer

AAACRC
P.O. Box 8061
Saddle Brook, NJ 07662
Wants silver coins, complete sets or single piece from Franklin Mint or any other mint.

Man./Prod./Dist.

Franklin Mint Customer Service Department
U.S. Route 1
Franklin Center, PA 19091
Phone: 215-459-6000 or 800-523-7622
FAX: 215-459-7002
Designs, manufactures and markets collectibles including jewelry, sculpture, dolls, figurines, bells, ornaments, arms replicas, etc.

Museum/Library

Franklin Mint Museum, The
U.S. Route 1
Franklin Center, PA 19091
Phone: 800-523-7622

Glassware

Man./Prod./Dist.

Via Vermont
Ben Ptashnik, Pres
P.O. Box 670
Norwich, VT 05055
Phone: 802-649-1008 or 800-642-1008
Designs and produces fine art glass giftware such as music boxes, jewelry boxes, display cases, kaleidoscopes and sun catchers.

Gregory Perillo

Club/Association

Perillo Collectors Club
c/o ArtAffects, Inc.
P.O. Box 98
Staten Island, NY 10307
Phone: 718-948-6767   FAX: 718-967-4521
Focuses on the collectibles designed by Gregory Perillo. Sponsored by ArtAffects, Inc.

Jan Hagara

Club/Association

Jan Hagara Collectors Club
c/o Royal Orleans
40114 Industrial Park
Georgetown, TX 78626
Phone: 512-863-8318   FAX: 512-863-0833
For collectors of Hagara prints, figurines, porcelain dolls, miniatures. Sponsored by Royal Orleans, Inc.

Man./Prod./Dist.

B & J Company, The
P.O. Box 67
Georgetown, TX 78627
Phone: 512-863-8318 or 800-722-3996
                    FAX: 512-863-0833
Produces and distributes prints, porcelain dolls, cards and collector plates by Jan Hagara.

Legends

Club/Association

Legends Collectors Society
c/o Legends, Inc.
1602 North Indiana
Los Angeles, CA 90063
Phone: 213-266-2941   FAX: 213-266-2582
Interested in the bronze, pewter and 24 karat gold vermeil sculptures made by Legends. Sponsored by Legends, Inc.

Lenox

Man./Prod./Dist.

Lenox Collections
P.O. Box 519
Langhorne, PA 19047-0519
Phone: 215-750-6900 or 800-225-1779
                    FAX: 215-750-7362
Direct-mail marketing division of Lenox Corp. selling doll, ornament, figurines and giftware collectibles issued by Lenox.

Lithophanes

Man./Prod./Dist.

Schmidt-Failing, Ltd.
David N. Failing
10579 Miller Rd.
Utica, NY 13502
Phone: 315-724-1139 or 800-448-5366
David Failing is the only American artist skilled in the creation of original porcelain lithophanes; all are signed, numbered & limited.

Lowell Davis

Club/Association

Lowell Davis Farm Club
Newsletter: Lowell Davis Farm Club Gazette
c/o Schmid, Inc.
55 Pacella Park Drive
Randolph, MA 02368
Phone: 617-961-3000   FAX: 617-986-8168
Focuses on the collectible plates and figurines designed by artist Lowell Davis. Sponsored by Schmid Co.

Marine Corps

Man./Prod./Dist.

Annelin, Ltd.
309 Christopher Court
Lansdale, PA 19446
Phone: 215-362-8397
Produces porcelain figurines of Marine corps figurines designed by Col. Charles Waterhours, USMCR, tracing the Corp's history.

Maruri

Man./Prod./Dist.

Maruri USA
7541 Woodman Place
Van Nuys, CA 91405
Phone: 818-780-0704
Producer and distributor of high quality porcelain plates and figurines.

Music Boxes

Man./Prod./Dist.

Splendid Music Box Co.
225 Fifth Ave.
New York, NY 10010
Phone: 212-532-9304   FAX: 212-532-9334
Imports over 1000 types of music boxes from all over the world.

Norman Rockwell

(see also ILLUSTRATORS, Norman Rockwell)

Periodical

Norman Rockwell Memorial Society
Newsletter: Norman Rockwell Memorial Society Newsletter
P.O. Box 270328
Tampa, FL 33688
Phone: 813-961-8834

*Members list new Rockwell items for sale. ***

Ornaments

Club/Association

Del-Mar-Pa Ornament Kollector's Klub
Newsletter: DOKK Newsletter
Bob Glover, Pres.
131 South Tartan Drive
Elkton, MD 21921
Phone: 302-366-5145 or 301-398-1674
                    FAX: 302-366-5236
For those interested in collecting Hallmark, Enesco, Precious Moments, and other ornaments.

Club/Association

Hand & Hammer Collectors Club
c/o Hand & Hammer
2610 Morse Lane
Woodbridge, VA 22192
Phone: 703-491-4866
Focuses on the sterling silver collectibles designed by Chip deMatteo. Sponsored by Hand & Hammer, Co.

Club/Association

Hallmarkers Holiday Happening
S.K. Holland
6151 Main Street
Springfield, OR 97478
Phone: 503-726-0740
Monthly meetings; members discuss new Hallmark and Enesco ornaments; members want to buy; send list of items for sale.

Man./Prod./Dist.

Ostrom Company
P.O. Box 4279
Portland, OR 97208-4729
Phone: 503-281-6460 or 800-688-8148
                    FAX: 503-281-6469
Specializes in art works in photo-engraved metal and glass. Produces the Abigail Lefferts Lloyd ornament series.

Periodical

Rosie Wells Enterprises, Inc.
Magazine: Ornament Collector, The
Rosie Wells
R.R. 1
Canton, IL 61520
Phone: 309-668-2565   FAX: 309-668-2795
The magazine specializing in Ornament Collector news, especially in Hallmark, Enesco, Carlton ornaments; ads, articles, photos, etc.

Ornaments (Hallmark)

Club/Association

Hallmark Collectors Club Connection
P.O. Box 110
Fenton, MI 48430

Club/Association
Central Wisconsin Ornament Collectors
Club
Nancy M. Soddy
401 Novak St.
Mosinee, WI 54455
Phone: 715-693-4135
*Members interested primarily in collecting Hall-
mark Christmas ornaments; some members have
other areas of interest as well.*

Club/Association
St. Louis Hallmarketeers
Carole Kleitz
673 Huntley Heights Dt.
Manchester, MO 63021
Phone: 314-227-1394

Club/Association
Hallmark Keepsake Ornament Collectors
Club
P.O. Box 412734
Kansas City, MO 64141-2734
*Focuses on Hallmark Ornaments. A manufac-
turer-sponsored club.*

Dealer
Christmas Shop
P.O. Box 5221
Cary, NC 27511
*Buys and sells Hallmark Christmas Ornaments;
1975-1988 ***

Dealer
Hallmark Collector
307 East Main
Fowler, IN 47944
*Buy and sell Ornaments, Merry Miniatures, etc.
(1973-1988). ***

Expert
Baggage Car
Hals & Meredith DeGood
513 Elm St.
West Des Moines, IA 50265
Phone: 515-225-3070 *

Expert
Rosie Wells
R.R. 1
Canton, IL 61520
Phone: 309-668-2565   FAX: 309-668-2795
*Author of "Secondary Market Price Guide for
Hallmark Ornaments and Merry Miniatures."*

Expert
David & Pennie Scheirer
Suite 299
700-U E. Redlands Blvd.
Redlands, CA 92373
Phone: 714-794-9233
*Authors of the "Green Guide", a definitive secon-
dary market price guide to Hallmark ornaments
and Merry Miniatures.*

Matching Service
David & Pennie Scheirer
Suite 299
700-U E. Redlands Blvd.
Redlands, CA 92373
Phone: 714-794-9233
*Will find lowest priced dealers for any particular
Hallmark ornament or Merry Miniature; avoid
the middleman markups; send SASE for info.*

Museum/Library
Hallmark Visitors Center
P.O. Box 580
Kansas City, MO 64141
Phone: 816-274-5672

Periodical
Carousel Collectibles
Newsletter: Twelve Months of Christmas
Joan Ketterer
P.O. Box 97172
Pittsburgh, PA 15229
Phone: 412-367-2352
*A bi-weekly newsletter for new and long-time
Hallmark collectors.*

Periodical
Baggage Car
Newsletter: Hallmark Newsletter
Hals & Meredith DeGood
513 Elm St.
West Des Moines, IA 50265
Phone: 515-225-3070 *

Periodical
Magazine: Ornament Trader Magazine
Alan Forbush, Pub.
P.O. Box 879
Placentia, CA 92670
*A bi-monthly magazine bringing Hallmark orna-
ment collectors together: current secondary orna-
ment prices, ads, articles, etc.*

Ornaments (Silver)

Collector
Overtons
200 Ave. Santa Margarita
San Clemente, CA 92672
Phone: 714-498-5330
*Wants sterling and silverplated Christmas orna-
ments which have been made by many silver
companies since 1970.*

Expert
Perry & Arthur Hart
P.O. Box 1804
Springfield, VA 22151
*Co-authors with Don and Lea Galyean of "All
That Glitters", an illustrated book about sterling
silver ornaments.*

P. Buckley Moss

Club/Association
P. Buckley Moss Society
P.O. Box 486
Wayne, MI 48184
Phone: 313-721-9198
*Focuses on the collectible figurines, plates and
graphics designed by P. Buckley Moss. Sponsored
by The Moss Portfolio.*

Man./Prod./Dist.
Moss Portfolio, The
1055 Thomas Jefferson St., NW
Washington, DC 20007
Phone: 202-338-5598
*Publisher and distributor of watercolors, original
prints, offset lithographs, plates, dolls, and figu-
rines by P. Buckley Moss.*

Pickard China Co.

Man./Prod./Dist.
Pickard China Co.
782 Corona Ave.
Antioch, IL 60002-1574
Phone: 708-395-3800   FAX: 708-395-3827
*In addition to dinnerware, manufactures collect-
ible plates, bells, ornaments, steins and bowls.*

PJ's

Club/Association
PJ's Carousel Collectors Club
Jim Hennon
c/o PJ's, Inc.
P.O. Box 532
Newbern, VA 24126
Phone: 703-674-4300   FAX: 703-674-2356
*Focuses on the miniature replica carousel animals
from the turn of the century. Sponsored by PJ's,
Inc.*

Precious Moments

Club/Association
Precious Moments Collectors' Club, The
Newsletter: Goodnewsletter
Shonnie Bilin, VP
P.O. Box 1466
Elk Grove, IL 60007
Phone: 708-640-5200 or 800-323-0636
                    FAX: 708-640-6151
*Focuses on Precious Moments collectible figu-
rines; members can buy "Members' Only" figu-
rines. An ENESCO manufacturer-sponsored*

Club/Association
Precious Moments Collectors
Magazine: Precious Collectibles
Rosie Wells
R.R. 1
Canton, IL 61520
Phone: 309-668-2565   FAX: 309-668-2795
*A glossy magazine with ads, articles, collector
interviews, etc.; published exclusively for Precious
Moments collectors.*

Misc. Service

Collectibles etc., Inc. Match Service
Sandy Forgach
8362 N. 49th St.
Brown Deer, WI 53223
Phone: 414-355-4545 or 800-558-5594
A specialized service matching buyers and sellers of older Precious Moments.

Misc. Service

Rosie Wells Enterprises, Inc.
R.R. 1
Canton, IL 61520
Phone: 900-535-7700
Rosie's Instant Hot Top Line has news flashes & hot tips for Precious Moments collectors; message changes Thursdays at noon; $2/min.

Prints

(see also PRINTS)

Club/Association

Pelican Art Club
Tom & Rosemarie Prendergast
c/o Pelican Art Prints
One Nasturtium Ave.
Glenwood, NJ 07418
Phone: 201-764-7149 or 914-986-8113
Focuses on the collectible conservation prints, Duck Prints and time-limited prints. Sponsored by Pelican Art Prints.

Club/Association

Original Print Collectors Group, Ltd.
19 East 70th Street
New York, NY 10021

Prints (Fred Stone)

Club/Association

Fred Stone Collectors Club
c/o American Artists
42 Sherwood Terrace, Suite 7
Lake Bluff, IL 60044
Phone: 312-295-5355   FAX: 312-295-5491
Focuses on the collectible prints by Fred Stone. Sponsored by American Artists.

Prints (Irene Spencer)

Man./Prod./Dist.

Irene Spencer, Inc.
Irene Spencer
1202 Star View Drive
Vista, CA 92084
Phone: 619-727-0847 or 617-727-0092
Produces and publishes the lithographs and plates of artist Irene Spencer.

Reed & Barton

Man./Prod./Dist.

Reed & Barton
144 W. Britannia Street
Taunton, MA 02780
Phone: 508-824-6611   FAX: 508-822-7269

Produces china, crystal, silver, silverplate, and stainless flatware, collectible plates, bells, dolls, ornaments and accessories.

Remington

Man./Prod./Dist.

Museum Collections By Schulenberg, Inc.
P.O. Box 2369
Shelton, CT 06484
Phone: 203-736-2639 or 800-243-6229
Manufactures plates and bronzes. Official reproducer of Frederic Remington design bronze sculptures.

Robert Bourgeault

Man./Prod./Dist.

Art World of Bourgeault
Robert A. Bourgeault
20538 Theresa Dr.
Mt. Clemens, MI 48083
Phone: 313-791-8569
Artist Robert Bourgeault designs and produces an intern. line of limited edition prints, plates and giftware for dealers & collectors.

Royal Copenhagen

Man./Prod./Dist.

Royal Copenhagen/Bing & Grondahl Co.
27 Holland Ave.
White Plains, NY 10603
Phone: 914-428-8222 or 800-431-1992
                    FAX: 914-428-8251
Manufactures dinnerware, cobalt blue underglaze collector plates, figurines, bells, dolls, ornaments and gift accessories.

Royal Doulton

Club/Association

Royal Doulton International Collectors Club
Magazine: Royal Doulton Inter. Collectors
    Club Newsletter
Mrs. Patricia O'Brien
850 Progress Ave.
Scarborough
Ontario M1H 3C4 Canada
Phone: 416-431-4202   FAX: 416-431-0089
Focuses on the Royal Doulton collectibles; a manufacturer-sponsored club; members entitled to purchase "member only" figurines.

Club/Association

Royal Doulton International Collectors
Club
Newsletter: Royal Doulton Inter. Collectors
    Club Newsletter
c/o Royal Doulton, Inc.
P.O. Box 1815
Somerset, NJ 08873
Phone: 908-356-7929 or 800-582-2102
                    FAX: 908-256-9467
Focuses on Royal Doulton plates, bells, paperweights, figurines, character and Toby jugs, etc. Sponsored by Royal Doulton, Inc.

Sculptures

Man./Prod./Dist.

Imhoff's Fine Art
RD 2 Box 194A
Spartansburg, PA 16434
Phone: 814-827-6052
Designs, sculpts and reproduces limited edition bronze and cold-cast terra-cotta series.

Skippy

Club/Association

Skippy Collectors Club
Newsletter: Skippy Newsletter
c/o Skippy, Inc.
74 Willow Grove Rd.
Brunswick, ME 04011
Phone: 207-721-0936
Focuses on the Skippy print and doll collectibles. Sponsored by Skippy, Inc.

Spangler's Realm

Man./Prod./Dist.

Spangler's Realm Collectors Club
c/o Realms, Inc.
11733 Lackland Rd.
Maryland Heights, MO 63146
Phone: 314-991-0793   FAX: 314-991-0958
Focuses on the Spangler's Realm line of figurines, bells, ornaments and prints. Sponsored by Realms, Inc.

Sports Related

Club/Association

Sports Impressions Collectors Club
c/o Collectible Resource Group
3911 SW 47th Ave., #914
Fort Lauderdale, FL 33314
Phone: 305-791-1264   FAX: 305-791-1269
Focuses on the Sports Impressions line of sports figurines and plates collectibles. Sponsored by Collectible Resource Group.

Club/Association

Collectors League
c/o Gartlan USA
15502 Graham Street
Huntington Beach, CA 92649
Phone: 714-897-0090   FAX: 714-892-1034
Focuses on the Gartlan sports collectibles. Sponsored by Gartlan USA.

Man./Prod./Dist.

Sports Impressions
82 Bridge Road
Central Islip, NY 11722
Phone: 516-234-9124   FAX: 516-234-9182
Produces figurines and plates in fine china and porcelain featuring baseball, football and basketball stars.

Man./Prod./Dist.

Collectible Resource Group, Inc.
Newsletter: CRGram
3911 SW 47th Ave., #914
Ft. Lauderdale, FL 33314
Phone: 305-791-1264   FAX: 305-791-1269
*Distributor of porcelain baseball collectibles including prints, plates, figurines, miniatures, steins, and ceramic baseball cards. ***

Steins

Man./Prod./Dist.

Caroline Connection, The
1502 North 23rd St.
Wilmington, ND 28405
Phone: 919-251-1110 or 800-457-9700
                    FAX: 919-343-0449
Manufacturers collectible steins of high quality.

Man./Prod./Dist.

Opa's Haus, Inc.
1600 River Road
New Braunfels, TX 78132
Phone: 512-629-1191 or 800-627-1600
                    FAX: 512-629-0153
OHI offers exclusive limited edition steins and mugs for the discerning collector.

Ted DeGrazia

Man./Prod./Dist.

Artists of the World
2915 N. 67th Place
Scottsdale, AZ 85251
Phone: 602-946-6361   FAX: 602-941-8918
Produces collector plates, figurines, ornaments and miniatures based on the work of Ted De-Grazia.

COLLEGE COLLECTIBLES

Expert

Kevin McCandless
1776 Valley Rd.
Champaign, IL 61820
Phone: 217-356-6266 *

Humor Magazines

Collector

Michael Gessel
P.O. Box 748
Arlington, VA 22216
Phone: 703-532-4261
Wants magazines (bound or individual copies); also posters and anthologies.

COLORADO COLLECTIBLES

Dealer

Powder Cache Antiques
Leo Stambaugh
612 6th St. - Unit C
P.O. Box 984 - A
Georgetown, CO 80444
Phone: 303-569-2848 or 303-569-2109

Buy, sell, trade Colorado historical photos, paper, medals, bottles, tokens, mining artifacts, paper and lamps, etc.

COMBS & HAIR ACCESSORIES

(see also HATPINS & HATPIN HOLDERS)

Club/Association

Antique Comb Collectors Club
Newsletter: Antique Comb Collector
Belva Green, Ed.
3748 Sunray Dr.
Holiday, FL 34691
Phone: 813-942-7354
Organization dedicated to sharing research and information about antique and ornamental accessories for the hair from any culture.

Expert

Belva Green
3748 Sunray Dr.
Holiday, FL 34691
Phone: 813-942-7354
Historian, researcher, lecturer on combs, jewelry and accessories for the hair.

Expert

Evelyn Haertig
P.O. Box 5457
Carmel-By-The-Sea, CA 93921 *

Museum/Library

Leominister Historical Society, Field
School Museum
Paul J. Benoit
17 School Street
Leominster, MA 01453
Phone: 508-534-5375
One of the best comb collections in the U.S.

Museum/Library

Miller's Museum of Antique Combs
Box 316
Homer, AK 99603
Phone: 907-235-8819
The entire museum is dedicated to combs and headdress.

COMIC ART

(see also CARTOON ART)

COMIC BOOKS

(see also SCIENCE FICTION
COLLECTIBLES; SUPER HEROES)

Collector

Stephen Fisher
7920 19th Ave.
Brooklyn, NY 11214
Phone: 718-837-2538 *

Collector

S.A. Geppi
1718-M Belmont Ave.
Baltimore, MD 21207
Phone: 301-298-2981
Golden Age, DC's, Timelys, Marvels, all 10 cent and 12 cent comics pre-1968; also baseball cards or related items.

Dealer

Richard Semowich
R.D. #8, Box 94
Binghamton, NY 13901
Phone: 607-648-4025
Wants old comic books from 1933 to 1970; buying any size collection; contact for the best price.

Dealer

Geppi's Comic World, Inc.
Robert Cook
7019 Security Blvd.
Baltimore, MD 21207
Phone: 301-298-1759 or 301-298-1758

Dealer

American Collectibles Exchange
Jon Warren
P.O. Box 2512
Chattanooga, TN 37409
Phone: 615-821-8121
Wants comics, also wants cartoon art, Disney, Big Little Books, Pulp Magazines, Baseball and Non-Sport Cards.

Dealer

Comics Unlimited
Box 1414
Oklahoma City, OK 73101
Phone: 405-236-5303
Wants pre-1965 comic books.

Expert

Overstreet Publications Inc.
Robert Overstreet
780 Hunt Cliff Dr. NW
Cleveland, TN 37311
Phone: 615-472-4135 *

Periodical

Newsletter: Marvel Comics
387 Park Ave. S.
New York, NY 10016
Phone: 212-696-0808 *

Periodical

Magazine: Comicist
P.O. Box 233
Loveland, OH 45140 *

Periodical

Krause Publications, Inc.
Newspaper: Comics Buyer's Guide
Don & Maggie Thompson, Ed.
700 E. State St.
Iola, WI 54990
Phone: 715-445-2214 or 800-258-0929
FAX: 715-445-4087
Only weekly newspaper serving comics fans, collectors, and the entire comics industry: articles about artists, buy/sell ads, calendar,

Periodical

Krause Publications, Inc.
Price Guide: Comics Buyer's Guide Price
   Guide
700 E. State St.
Iola, WI 54990
Phone: 715-445-2214 or 800-258-0929
FAX: 715-445-4087
A quarterly price guide with all the latest market information; more than 25,000 comic values, color-grading guide, articles, ads, etc.

Periodical

Newspaper: Buyer's Guide for Comic
   Fandom, The
15800 Route 84 North
East Moline, IL 61244
Phone: 309-496-2353
A weekly newspaper. *

Super Heroes

(see also SUPER HEROES)

Dealer

Adventure Ink
Tom Burkert
97 Woodmere Rd.
Stamford, CT 06905
Phone: 914-741-2510
Interested in super hero comic books.

COMIC STRIPS

Sunday Newspaper

Expert

David Begin
138 Lansberry Ct.
Los Gatos, CA 95032
Buys and sells Sunday newspaper comics from 1890-1980's.

COMPACTS

Club/Association

Compact Collectors Club
Newsletter: Powder Puff
Roselyn Gerson
P.O. Box Letter S
Lynbrook, NY 11563
Phone: 516-887-9349 or 516-593-8746
FAX: 516-593-0611

An international club whose members collect compacts, vanities, necessaires, etc.; newsletter contains articles, buy/sell ads, etc.

Collector

Bruce Axler
Ansonia Station
P.O. Box 1288
New York, NY 10023
Wants ladies' compacts with mult-functions, i.e. compacts combined with other items such as cigarette lighters, flashlights, etc.

Expert

Roselyn Gerson
P.O. Box 100
Malverne, NY 11565
Phone: 516-593-8749
Wants unusual gadget compacts: cane/compact, hatpin/compact, gun/compact; also compact advertising; author of book on subject.

COMPUTER PROGRAM

Collectors'

Man./Prod./Dist.

BDL Homeware
Bette Laswell
2509 N. Campbell #328N
Tucson, AZ 85719
Phone: 602-577-1435 or 800-BDL-4BDL
Sells software for collectors and dealers; no computer skills required; inventories collections for insurance, etc.; free catalog.

Man./Prod./Dist.

ByteSize Software
D.A. Heitzman
P.O. Box 4515
West Hills, CA 91308-4515
Phone: 818-340-5125
Sells sophisticated, user-friendly program to monitor your collectibles; many features; well organized; IBM and compatibles.

Man./Prod./Dist.

Third Rail
3377 Cimarron Drive
Santa Ynez, CA 93460
Phone: 805-688-7370
Sells computer inventory program for collectors; organize your collectibles; up to 225,000 items; for IBM PC/PCjr/XT/AT.

COMPUTERS

Museum/Library

Computer Museum
300 Congress St.
Boston, MA 02210
Phone: 617-426-2800

CONESTOGA WAGONS

(see also HORSE-DRAWN VEHICLES)

CONSERVATORS

(see also REPAIRS & RESTORATIONS)

CONSTRUCTION EQUIPMENT

(see also INDUSTRY RELATED ITEMS;
MACHINERY & EQUIPMENT)

Club/Association

Historical Construction Equipment
   Association
Newsletter: Equipment Echoes
P.O. Box 328
Grand rapids, OH 43522
Phone: 419-832-0808
Dedicated to preserving the history of construction, surface mining and dredging equipment and related memorabilia, trade

COOKBOOKS

(see also BOOKS; COOKIES & COOKIE
SHAPING; MENUS)

Club/Association

Cook Book Collectors Club of America, Inc.
Newsletter: Cook Book Gossip
Bob & Jo Ellen Allen
231 E. James Blvd.
P.O. Box 85
St. James, MO 65559
Phone: 314-265-8296
Focuses on cookbooks & advertising cook books and recipe publications by many companies such as Jell-O, Pillsbury, Betty Crocker, etc.

Collector

Bernice Stafford
332 Vinyard Rd.
Warwick, RI 02889
Wants cookbooks by famous chefs (first editions only). *

Collector

Sue Erwin
P.O. Box 32369
San Jose, CA 95152-2369
Phone: 408-259-8657

Dealer

Deer Park Books
Barbara & Dick DePalma
27 Deer Park Rd.
Danbury, CT 06811
Phone: 203-743-2246
Buys and sells pre-1950 cook books; catalogs and lists sent upon request.

Expert

Bob & Jo Ellen Allen
231 E. James Blvd.
P.O. Box 85
St. James, MO 65559
Phone: 314-265-8296

Wants cookbooks & advertising cook books and recipe publications by many companies such as Jell-O, Pillsbury, Betty Crocker, etc.

Expert
Loraine Perier
P.O. Box 1
Vancouver, WA 98666

Periodical
Heritage Publications
Directory: Just Cookbooks!
Mary Barile
P.O. Box 642
Arkville, NY 12406
Phone: 914-586-3810   FAX: 914-586-2797
Offers "Just Cookbooks!", a directory to the world of American cookbooks; for collectors, dealers, sellers, etc.

Periodical
Newspaper: Cookbook Collectors' Exchange
Sue Erwin
P.O. Box 32369
San Jose, CA 95152-2369
Phone: 408-259-8657
Lists cookbooks for sale or trade; voluntarily assist in locating items; non-commercial ads are free to collectors; articles, etc.

COOKIE JARS
Collector
Darryl Rehr
11433 Rochester Ave. #303
Los Angeles, CA 90025
Phone: 213-447-5229
Buys interesting pre-1960 figural cookie jars: Pearl China Chef, Abington Witch and many, many others.

Collector
Carl & Gari McCallum
918 Rosewood
Wasco, CA 93280
Phone: 805-758-5630
Buy, sell, trade cookie jars; collects all types but prefers figural and advertising jars.

Dealer
Judy Posner
R.D. 1 Box 273
Effort, PA 18330
Phone: 717-629-6583   FAX: 717-629-0521
Wants FIGURAL cookie jars: comic characters, Disney, Black Mammys, Chefs, Butlers, etc.; send for illustrated want list.

Expert
Wendy Johnston
6742 Fifth Ave.
Brooklyn, NY 11220
Phone: 718-833-8455
Has over 2000 cookie jars. She and her husband are also jukebox and vintage slot machine dealers.
*

Expert
Nichols Art Pottery
Harold Nichols
632 Agg Ave.
Ames, IA 50010
Phone: 515-292-9167
Specializes in American art pottery: Roseville, Weller, McCoy etc. *

Expert
Ermagene Westfall
R.R. #1 Box 222
Richmond, MO 64085
Author of "An Illustrated Value Guide to Cookie Jars." *

Museum/Library
Cookie Jar Museum, The
Lucille Bromberek
111 Stephen St.
Lemont, IL 60439
Phone: 708-257-5012
Only Cookie Jar Museum in the world; over 2000 jars from U.S. and all over the world; also buys and sells.

Periodical
Newsletter: Crazed Over Cookie Jars
Maureen Saxby
P.O. Box 130
German Valley, IL 61039
Phone: 815-362-2941
A monthly publication about cookie jars and full of facats, fun, wants and buys.

COOKIES & COOKIE SHAPING
(see also KITCHEN COLLECTIBLES)

Club/Association
Cookie Cutter Collectors Club
Newsletter: Cookie Crumbs
Ruth Capper
1167 Teal Road S.W.
Dellroy, OH 44620
Phone: 216-735-2839 or 202-966-0869
Focusing on cookie cutters, boards and rollers.

Expert
Phyllis S. Wetherill
5426 27th Street NW
Washington, DC 20015
Phone: 202-966-0869
Buys/collects cookie shaping items and anything related to cookies: cutters, molds, presses, irons, photographs, postcards, ads, etc.

Expert
Mark Winchester
8408 Kay Ct.
Annandale, VA 22003
Phone: 703-280-1049
Specializes in cookie cutters in large human and animal figure shapes. *

Periodical
Newsletter: Cookies
Phyllis S. Wetherill
5426 27th Street NW
Washington, DC 20015
Phone: 202-966-0869
In its 19th year, "Cookies" contains historical information about the shaping of cookies: new and old cutters, molds, irons, presses, etc.

Periodical
Newsletter: Around Ohio Newsletter
Milli Simerli
P.O. Box 14
Bloomingburg, OH 43106
Phone: 614-437-7400
Newsletter contains new cutter sources, old cutter research, area and national events, Q & A column.

COPPER ITEMS
(see also ARTS & CRAFTS, Roycroft)

Expert
Mary Gaston
Box 342
Bryan, TX 77806 *

Stickley
Collector
Terry Seger
5778 Breezewood Dr.
Cincinnati, OH 45248
Phone: 513-451-3784 *

CORKPULLERS
(see also CORKSCREWS)

CORKSCREWS
(see also BOTTLE OPENERS, Figural)

Club/Association
Canadian Corkscrew Collectors Club
Joseph C. Paradi
670 Meadow Wood Rd.
Mississauga
Ontario L5J 2S6 Canada
Phone: 416-823-3754 or 416-978-6934
                    FAX: 416-823-3775
Worldwide membership, mostly from the U.S.; write for application form.

Club/Association
International Correspondence of Corkscrew Addicts
Donald A. Bull
20 Fairway Dr.
Stamford, CT 06903
Phone: 203-968-1925
Membership limited to 50; members interested in corkscrews as well as wine paraphernalia such as decanters, wine strainers, funels, etc.

Collector

Paul P. Luchsinger
104 Deer Run
Williamsville, NY 14211
Phone: 716-689-6580
Wants old and unusual corkscrews as well as other wine related items.

Collector

John Young
Box 587
Elgin, IL 60121
Phone: 312-695-8635 *

Collector

Lynette McCormack
15500 S.E. Royer Rd.
Clackamas, OR 97015 *

Expert

Joseph C. Paradi
670 Meadow Wood Rd.
Mississauga
Ontario L5J 2S6 Canada
Phone: 416-823-3754 or 416-978-6934
                          FAX: 416-823-3775
Buys/sells; wants European and American corkscrews and corkpullers; especially mechanical pieces with makers' marks; send photocopy.

Expert

Donald A. Bull
20 Fairway Dr.
Stamford, CT 06903
Phone: 203-968-1925
Buys corkscrews or anything picturing corkscrews; author of "A Price Guide to Beer Advertising Openers and Corkscrews."

Expert

Baker's Lady Luck Emporium
Roger V. Baker
P.O. Box 620417
Woodside, CA 94062
Phone: 415-851-7188
Specializing in saloon collectibles: gambling, bar bottles, shaving mugs, razors, Bowie knives, daggers, barber items, match safes.

Advertising

Collector

Joseph C. Paradi
670 Meadow Wood Rd.
Mississauga
Ontario L5J 2S6 Canada
Phone: 416-823-3754 or 416-978-6934
                          FAX: 416-823-3775
Wants any corkscrew or corkpuller with beer or other advertising on it; buys single items or entire collections; send photocopy of item.

CORN COLLECTIBLES

Club/Association

Corn Items Collectors Association Inc.
Newsletter: Bang Board, The
E. Eloise Alton, Ed.
613 N. Long St.
Shelbyville, IL 62565
Phone: 217-774-5002
Association collecting and studying anything having to do with corn, i.e. inventions, corn collectibles, etc.

Corn Shellers

Collector

Robert Rauhauser
Box 766
Thomasville, PA 17364-9622
Wants corn shellers: handheld, table mounted, box mounted; any unusual corn shellers; also popcorn shellers.

Collector

Don Monnier
P.O. Box 772
Sidney, OH 45365
Phone: 513-492-1420
Wants corn shellers; also hand crank rope makers.
*

CORONATION MEMORABILIA

(see also ROYALTY COLLECTIBLES, British)

COSTUME JEWELRY

(see also GEMS & JEWELRY, Costume)

COUNTERFEIT DETECTING ITEMS

Collector

Donald Gorlick
P.O. Box 24541
Seattle, WA 98124
Wants counterfeit currency detectors, scales, scanners, grids, books, reporters, recorders, magnifiers, Detectographs, etc.

COUNTRY STORE COLLECTIBLES

(see also ADVERTISING COLLECTIBLES; BOTTLES; CIGAR BANDS, BOXES & LABELS; LABELS; STRING HOLDERS; TIN CONTAINERS)

COVERED BRIDGES

Club/Association

Newsletter: Portals
Russell J. Holmes
Box 95
Seven Valleys, PA 17360
Society is committed to saving and preserving covered bridges; monthly meeting held for collectors of bridge related material.

Collector

Marie Ward
365 Neiffer Rd.
Schwenksville, PA 19473
Phone: 215-287-9495
Wants items relating to covered bridges.

COVERLETS

(see also FOLK ART; LOOMS; REPAIRS & RESTORATIONS, Textiles; TEXTILES)

Club/Association

Colonial Coverlet Guild of America
Barbara Frisbee
5617 Blackstone
La Grange, IL 60525
Phone: 708-352-3812
Members are interested in coverlets or antique textiles, their preservation and in the present revival of weaving.

Dealer

Troy & Black, Inc.
Carl McCann
P.O. Box 228
Red Creek, NY 13143
Phone: 315-754-8115
Buys and sells high quality American stoneware, coverlets and figured maple furniture.

Expert

Looms, The
Newsletter: Looms, The
Ken Colwell
154 High St.
Mineral Point, WI 53565
Phone: 608-987-2277 or 608-348-2766
Offers workshops, books and tours related to weaving; also sells antique looms and equipment.

Museum/Library

Museum of American Textile History
800 Massachusetts Ave.
North Andover, MA 01845
Phone: 617-686-0191

Repro. Source

Family Heir-Loom Weavers
David C. Kline
R.D. #3, Box 59E
Red Lion, PA 17356
Phone: 717-246-2431 or 717-244-5921
Makers of fancy jacquard coverlets, ingrain carpets & other historic textiles; send $2.50 for brochure.

Miniature

Man./Prod./Dist.

Rev./Mrs. John Grim
Willow Spring Farms
Brownsville, MD 21715
Makes handwoven miniature coverlets. *

COWBOY COLLECTIBLES

(see also WESTERN AMERICANA)

COWBOY HEROES

(see also CHARACTER COLLECTIBLES;
COLLECTIBLES; MOVIE MEMORABILIA;
RADIO SHOW PREMIUMS; TELEVISION
SHOWS & MEMORABILIA; WESTERN
AMERICANA)

Collector

Harry L. Rinker
P.O. Box 248
Zionsville, PA 18092
Phone: 215-965-1122 or 215-966-5544
FAX: 215-965-1124
*Collects all forms of TV cowboy memorabilia
spanning the period from 1948 to 1975 with
special emphasis on Hopalong Cassidy.*

Collector

Phil Ellis
P.O. Box 11042
Santa Rosa, CA 95406
Phone: 707-544-6050
*Wants Hopalong Cassidy, Roy Rogers, Gene
Autry; comic toys, Disneyana, radio premiums,
TV Westerns, etc.*

Expert

Saturday Matinee
Ron Donnelly
Box 7047
Panama City, FL 32413 *

Periodical

Westerns & Serials Fan Club
Magazine: Favorite Westerns & Serial World
Norman Kietzer
Route One, Box 103
Vernon Center, MN 56090
Phone: 507-549-3677
*A club for collectors as well as non-collectors
interested in westerns and serials, and in related
memorabilia.*

Annie Oakley

Collector

Gordon Becker
1210 N. Jefferson
Dixon, IL 61021
Phone: 815-288-1629
*Wants Buffalo Bill and Annie Oakley items, pre-
1920; also other Old West lawmen, outlaw, gun-
fighter items. *

Buffalo Bill

Club/Association

Buffalo Bill Memorial Association
Newsletter: BBMA Newsletter
P.O. Box 1000
Cody, WY 82414
Phone: 307-587-4771 *

Collector

Melvin Schulte
211 Fourth Ave. SW
Pocahantas, IA 50574
*Wants Buffalo Bill memorabilia: programs, pho-
tos, business paper, advertising, pre-1918 clippings, miscellaneous of all kinds. *

Collector

Gordon Becker
1210 N. Jefferson
Dixon, IL 61021
Phone: 815-288-1629
*Wants Buffalo Bill and Annie Oakley items, pre-
1920; also other Old West lawmen, outlaw, gun-
fighter items. *

Museum/Library

Buffalo Bill Museum of LeClaire, Iowa,
Inc.
P.O. Box 284
LeClaire, IA 52753
Phone: 319-289-5580

Museum/Library

Buffalo Bill Memorial Museum
987 1/2 Lookout Mtn. Road
Golden, CO 80401
Phone: 303-526-0747 or 303-526-0744
*Dedicated to the history of William F. Cody; large
collection of personal belongings, photos and documents.*

Gene Autry

Museum/Library

Gene Autry Museum
Bobby Newton
c/o Chamber of Commerce
P.O. Box 158
Gene Autry, OK 73436
Phone: 405-389-5350
*Museum of Gene Autry memorabilia including
photos, posters, etc.; also local memorabilia.*

Museum/Library

Gene Autry Western Heritage Museum
Newsletter: Spur
4700 Western Heritage Way
Los Angeles, CA 90027-1462
Phone: 213-677-2000   FAX: 213-660-5721
*Collects items relating to the American West,
including Western film memorabilia.*

Periodical

Gene Autry Development Association
Newspaper: Gene Autry Star Telegram
Bobby Newton
c/o Chamber of Commerce
P.O. Box 158
Gene Autry, OK 73436
Phone: 405-389-5350
*An annual tabloid to promote the community &
the man; very big with collectors world over; in-
cludes phots and stories relating to both.*

Hopalong Cassidy

Club/Association

Friends of Hoppy Club
Newsletter: Hoppy Talk
Laura Bates
6310 Friendship Drive
New Concord, OH 43762-9708
Phone: 614-826-4850
*Club organized to establish a museum in Cam-
bridge, OH (boyhood home of Wm. Boyd); news-
letter contains, articles, buy/sell ads, etc.*

Club/Association

Hopalong Cassidy Fan Club
Newsletter: Hopalong Cassidy Newsletter
P.O. Box 1361
Boyes Hot Springs, CA 95416

Collector

Rick Fields
225 Windsor Dr.
Mt. Sterling, KY 40353 *

Dealer

Terry & Jeannie Quadnau
23 Hereford St.
Cincinnati, OH 45216-1107
*Wants Howdy Doody, Hopalong Cassidy,
character paper dolls and coloring books, board
games and character items.*

Lone Ranger

Collector

Karl L. Rommel
737 Cloverleaf Rd.
Lansing, MI 48906
Phone: 517-484-7865
Wants all "Lone Ranger" memorabilia.

Expert

Dave Holland
17142 Index St.
Granada Hills, CA 91344 *

Periodical

Newsletter: Silver Bullet
Jerry & Kay Klepey
P.O. Box 553
Forks, WA 98331
Phone: 206-327-3726
*Not a club. Run free "buy/sell ads" for subscribers;
also mail orders Lone ranger related memorabilia;
always buying Lone ranger items.*

Red Ryder

Collector

Gabby Talkington
4703 Upland Dr.
Richmond, CA 94803
Phone: 415-223-1142 or 415-273-3268
*Wants Red Ryder games, books, guns, puzzles,
etc. for private collection.*

Roy Rogers & Dale Evans

Club/Association

Roy Rogers - Dale Evans Collectors
Association
Newsletter: RRDECA Newsletter
Nancy Horsley, ExSec
P.O. Box 1166
Portsmouth, OH 45662
Phone: 614-353-2146 or 614-353-0900

MUSEUM/Library

Roy Rogers Hometwn Exhibit
c/o Chamber of Commerce
P.O. Box 509
Portsmouth, OH 45662
Phone: 614-353-1116

Museum/Library

Roy Rogers & Dale Evans Museum
15650 Seneca Rd.
Victorville, CA 92392
Phone: 619-243-4547

Tom Mix

Museum/Library

Tom Mix Museum
721 North Delaware
Dewey, OK 74029
Phone: 918-534-1555

COW COLLECTIBLES

Periodical

Cowtree Collector
Newsletter: Moosletter
Carol J. Peiffer, Pub.
240 Wahl Ave.
Evans City, PA 16033
*Quarterly newsletter with cow talk, cartoons, mail
order sources for whatever has been produced using
the cow theme.*

Creamers

Collector

LuAnn Riggs
3302 Colonel Court Dr.
Richmond, TX 77469-6864
*Wants 18th and 19th century ceramic creamers
made in Holland, Germany, France, Japan, Occupied Japan, Staffordshire England, etc.*

CRACKER JACK TOYS

Collector

Wes Johnson
P.O. Box 169001
Louisville, KY 40216-9001
*Advanced collector wants tin, cast metal, plastic
toy prizes, old paper items; also ANGELUS
Marshmallows, CHECKERS Confection items.*

Collector

Harriet Joyce
16144 Woodhaven Ct.
Granger, IN 46530
*Wants pre-1948 Cracker Jack prizes; especially
1920's through 1930's vintage.* *

CREDIT CARDS & CHARGE COINS

Collector

Gary Olsen
505 S. Royal Ave.
Front Royal, VA 22630
Phone: 703-635-7157 or 703-635-7158
                                   FAX: 703-635-1818
*Collecting since 1960's; will pay $1 each plus
postage for any age, quantity or condition of expired credit cards; plastic, paper, metal.*

Collector

Gerri Lonchar
6330 Pineshade
Houston, TX 77008
Wants charge coins. *

Collector

"The Credit Card Collector"
T.L. Helgeson
1645 W. Valencia Rd. Box 432
Tucson, AZ 85746
Phone: 602-294-6865   FAX: 602-573-1509
*Wants all credit cards, paper or plastic; also other
credit/charge related items such as charge coins,
plates or tokens.*

Expert

Edward L. Dence
8627 Crispin Dr.
Philadelphia, PA 19136-2013
Author of "Store Charge Coins." *

Expert

Greg Tunks
150 Hohldale
Houston, TX 77022
Phone: 713-691-1387
*Wants pre-1970 plastic or paper credit cards; au-
thor of "Credit Card Collecting Bonanza."*

Periodical

Newsletter: Credit Card Collector
Greg Tunks
150 Hohldale
Houston, TX 77022
Phone: 713-691-1387
*A monthly newsletter dedicated to credit card and
charge coin collectibles.*

CRESTED WARE

(see also CERAMICS (ENGLISH), Goss
Pottery Co./Crested Ware)

CROCHET HOOKS

Collector

Hicker' Nut Hill Antiques
Genie Prather
Rt. 2, Box 532
Tyler, TX 75704
*Want older, elegant and unusual hooks made of
ivory or are handmade.* *

CRUETS

(see also GLASS, Pattern; GLASS, Art)

Expert

Cruets, Cruets, Cruets
Elaine Ezell
P.O. Box 342
Annapolis Junction, MD 20701
Phone: 301-255-6777 or 301-420-6859
*Advanced collector and co-author with George
Newhouse of "Cruets, Cruets, Cruets"; buys/sells
art glass and colored Victorian cruets.*

CRYSTAL

(see also GLASS, Crystal)

CUBAN COLLECTIBLES

Collector

Gustavo Tapanes
2011 8th St.
North Bergen, NJ 07047
*Wants Cuban postcards: also books, photos from
Cuba and Spanish American War on.* *

Collector

Manuel Bustillo
27 E. 94th St.
New York, NY 10128
*Wants old Cuban postcards and books: except on
Spanish American War.* *

Expert

Albert Mendez
142-35 38th Ave.
Flushing, NY 11354
Phone: 718-961-2866
*Specializes in and collects pre-1959 Cuban mili-
tary and police badges; also medals, swords, paper
goods, photos, books, etc.*

CUP PLATES

Club/Association

Pairpoint Cup Plate Collectors of America
Newsletter: Mini Thistle
Box 52
East Weymouth, MA 02189
*An organization for collectors of cup plates; pub-
lishes "Thistle" semi-annually and "Mini-This-
tle" bi-monthly;*

Expert
John E. Bilane
109 Normandy Village
Union, NJ 07083
Phone: 908-686-3060
Buys and sells antique glass cup plates.

Contemporary

Expert
Laurie Verge
11801 Crestwood Ave.
Brandywine, MD 20613
Phone: 301-372-8240 *

CZECHOSLOVAKIAN COLLECTIBLES

Collector
Delores Saar
45 5th Ave. NW
Hutchinson, MN 55350
*Wants items marked "Made in Czechoslovakia": glass, pottery and porcelain, etc. ***

Expert
Ruth Forsythe
Box 327
Galena, OH 43201 *

DAIRY COLLECTIBLES

(see also BOTTLE CAPS, Milk; BOTTLES, Milk; COW CREAMERS; ELSIE THE BORDON COW ITEMS; FARM COLLECTIBLES)

Club/Association
National Association of Milk Bottle Collectors, Inc.
Newsletter: Milk Route, The
Thomas Gallagher
4 Ox Bow Rd.
Westport, CT 06880-2602
Phone: 203-277-5244
Focuses on the milk and dairy history and related memorabilia; membership includes the newsletter and history of fluid milk industry.

Dealer
Ralph Riovo
686 Franklin Street
Alburtis, PA 18011-9578
Phone: 215-966-2536
Adlactilist and dealer in milk and dairy memorabilia; wants milk bottles, dairy advertising and related memorabilia.

Expert
Thomas Gallagher
4 Ox Bow Rd.
Westport, CT 06880-2602
Phone: 203-277-5244

Expert
Tony Knipp
P.O. Box 105
Blooming Grove, NY 10914
Phone: 914-496-6841

Expert
Time Travelers
Leigh Giarde
P.O. Box 366
Bryn Mawr, CA 92318
Phone: 714-792-8681
Mail order sales and purchases of milk bottles and go-withs; author of "Glass Milk Bottles: Their Makers and Marks."

Museum/Library
New York State Historical Association and The Farmers' Museum, Inc., The
P.O. Box 800
Cooperstown, NY 13326
Phone: 607-547-2593 or 607-547-2533

Periodical
Lenga Dairy Collectibles
Newsletter: Udder Collectibles, The
HC 73 Box 1
Smithville Flats, NY 13841-9502
Focuses on dairy collectibles such as milk bottles, cow facts and more.

Cream Separators

Club/Association
Cream Separator Association
Newsletter: Cream Separator News
Dr. Paul Dettloff, Sec.
Rt. 3 Box 189
Arcadia, WI 54612
Phone: 608-323-7470
For those interested in cream separators and other dairy items; newsletter contains articles, free ads for subscribers, photos, etc.

Dairy Case Tags

Collector
Betty R. Foley
227 Union Ave.
Pittsburgh, PA 15202
Phone: 412-761-0685
Wants porcelain dairy tags; these were attached to old wooden milk crates to advertise the names of the dairies; usually 1 1/2" x 5".

DANCE MEMORABILIA

(see also THEATRICAL MEMORABILIA)

DATE NAILS

Club/Association
Texas Date Nail Collectors Association
Newsletter: Nailer News
501 W. Horton
Brenham, TX 77833
Phone: 409-830-1495

Date nails are about 2" long; dime-size heads are marked with a date number; driven into railroad ties, telephone poles, etc.

DAUGERREOTYPES

(see also PHOTOGRAPHS)

DECANTERS

Special Edition Whiskey

(see also BOTTLES, Special Ed.)

DECORATED OBJECTS

(see also FOLK ART; FURNITURE, Painted)

Club/Association
Historical Society of Early American Decoration
Journal: Decorator
19 Dove St.
Albany, NY 12210
Phone: 518-462-1676
*Interested in early American decorated items such as tinware, furniture, stenciling; country painting, metal leaf, pontypool, etc. ***

DECORATIVE ARTS

(see also ANTIQUES, General)

Museum/Library
Daughters of the American Revolution Museum
1776 D Street NW
Washington, DC 20006
Phone: 202-879-3254

Museum/Library
National Museum of American History
Branch Library
Smithsonian Institution
Washington, DC 20560
Phone: 202-357-2414
Books/journals/trade catalogs on material culture, decorative arts, domestic & community life, applied science, engineering, technology.

Museum/Library
Museum of Early Southern Decorative Arts
Journal: Journal of Early Southern Decorative Arts
P.O. Box 10310
Winston-Salem, NC 27108
Phone: 919-722-7360
Focuses on Southern decorative arts; has Research Center, Catalog of Early Southern Decorative Arts, and Index of Southern Artists.

Periodical

Decorative Arts Trust
Newsletter: Decorative Arts Trust Newsletter
106 Bainbridge St.
Philadelphia, PA 19147
Phone: 215-627-2859
Study and preservation of American decorative arts; features private collections, museums, restorations, and preservation.

Periodical

Museum of Early Southern Decorative
Arts
Journal: Journal of Early Southern Decorative
Arts
P.O. Box 10310
Winston-Salem, NC 27108
Phone: 919-722-7360
Focuses on Southern decorative arts; has Research Center, Catalog of Early Southern Decorative Arts, and Index of Southern Artists.

DECOYS

(see also FOLK ART; SPORTING COLLECTIBLES)

Misc. Service

Dick's Duck Den
Richard C. Motzer
2878 Saddleback
Cincinnati, OH 45244-3915
Phone: 513-231-5953
Sells contemporary decoy carvings; also gives carving instructions.

Bird

Auction Service

Richard W. Oliver Auctions
Route One, Plaza One
Kennebunk, ME 04043
Phone: 207-985-3600   FAX: 207-985-7734

Auction Service

James D. Julia, Inc.
Frank M. Schmidt
P.O. Box 830
Fairfield, ME 04937
Phone: 207-453-7904   FAX: 207-453-2502 *

Club/Association

Midwest Decoy Collectors Association
1100 Bayview Dr.
Fox River Grove, IL 60021
Phone: 312-639-9392 *

Dealer

RJG Antiques
Russ & Karen Goldberger
P.O. Box 2033
Hampton, NH 03842
Phone: 603-926-1770
Specializes in quality working decoys, folk art and original American paintings.

Dealer

Peace Antiques
John Cook
HC 3 Box 13A
Remer, MN 56672
Has specialized in buying and selling fish and duck decoys for 20 years.

Expert

Jackson Parker
76 Berkshire Rd.
Newtonville, MA 02160 *

Museum/Library

Museums at Stony Brook, The
Newsletter: Dialogue
1208 Rte. 25A
Stony Brook, NY 11790
Phone: 516-751-0066   FAX: 516-751-0353
Large collection of American Art, decoys, horse-drawn vehicles, costumes, and miniature period rooms; museum shop.

Museum/Library

Salisbury State College, North American Wildfowl Art Museum of the Ward Found.
655 South Salisbury Blvd.
Salisbury, MD 21801
Phone: 301-742-4988

Museum/Library

Cleveland Museum of Natural History
Wade Oval, University Circle
Cleveland, OH 44106
Phone: 216-231-4600

Periodical

Decoy Magazine
Magazine: Decoy Magazine
Joe Engers
P.O. Box 277
Burtonsville, MD 20866
Phone: 301-890-0262
Only bi-monthly magazine serving the decoy collecting market; classifieds, calendar, auction news, carver profiles, full color.

Periodical

Magazine: Decoy World
R.F.D. 1, Box 5
Trappe, MD 21673
Phone: 301-476-3092

Periodical

Ward Foundation
Journal: Wild Fowl Art Journal
655 South Salisbury Blvd.
Salisbury, MD 21801 *

Periodical

Magazine: Decoy Hunter, The
901 North 9th
Clinton, IN 47842
Phone: 317-832-2525

Repro. Source

Will Kirkpatrick Shorebird Decoys, Inc.
124 Forest Ave.
Hudson, MA 01749
Phone: 508-562-7871
*Authentic reproductions of antique decoys. *

Repro. Source

J.J. Decoy Co.
P.O. Box 60
Fairfield, ME 04937
Phone: 207-453-9460
*Sells carved and painted decoys, shore birds, and animals: wood fish, cows, roosters, geese, swans, black ducks, etc. *

Repro. Source

Duane Sylor
49 Horner Rd.
Angelica, NY 14709
Phone: 716-466-7700
Sells handcarved carved and painted duck and shorebird decoys; copies of original working decoys.

Fish

(see also FISHING COLLECTIBLES)

Club/Association

Great Lakes Fish Decoy Collectors & Carvers Association
Frank R. Baron, Sec.
35824 West Chicago
Livonia, MI 48150
Phone: 313-427-7768
Regular meetings and newsletter; long range goal is to establish a permanent display of spearfishing artifacts.

Club/Association

American Fish Decoy Association
Newsletter: American Fish Decoy Forum, The
John E. Shoffner
624 Merritt St.
Fife Lake, MI 49633
Phone: 616-879-3912
9 month old association is the largest fish decoy collectors association with approx. 160 members; newsletter has color photos.

Dealer

Great Lakes Ice Decoys
Frank R. Baron
35824 West Chicago
Livonia, MI 48150
Phone: 313-427-7768
Buys, sells, trades fish decoys; quarterly list of decoys for sale; author of "Bud Stewart, Michigan's Legendary Lure Maker."

Dealer

Nick's Wood Shop
Dominic Torella
134 Michigan Ave.
Au Gres, MI 48703
Phone: 517-876-7075 *

Dealer
Nick's Wood Shop
John E. Shoffner
624 Merritt St.
Fife Lake, MI 49633
Phone: 616-879-3912
*Issues 6 lists a year with approx. 600 fish decoys
and antique fishing tackle items for sale.*

Dealer
Ronald J. Fritz
P.O. Box 70
Williamsburg, MI 49690
Phone: 616-267-5752
*Buying and selling old working fish decoys by
carvers from Michigan, New York as well as from
other areas.*

Dealer
Mikko's Bait Shop
Mikko Cowdrey
P.O. Box 100
Osakis, MN 56360
Phone: 612-859-3536
Buys/sells authentic fish decoys.

Dealer
Peace Antiques
John Cook
HC 3 box 13A
Remer, MN 56672
*Has specialized in buying and selling fish and
duck decoys for 20 years.*

Expert
Ronald J. Fritz
P.O. Box 70
Williamsburg, MI 49690
Phone: 616-267-5752
*Specialist in the fish decoy carvings of Michigan
carvers Peterson, Nelson, Ramey, Hulbert &
Bruning; author of book on subject.*

DIMESTORE SOLDIERS
(see also SOLDIERS, Toy)

DINNERWARE
(see also CERAMICS; FLATWARE; GLASS,
Elegant; GLASS, Crystal; REPAIRS &
RESTORATIONS; TABLEWARE)

Matching Service
William Ashley Ltd.
Suite 209
50 Bloor St.
West Toronto M4W 3L8 Canada
Phone: 416-964-2500   FAX: 416-964-2500
Discontinued pattern service.

Matching Service
Old China Patterns Ltd.
1560 Brimley Rd.
Scarborough
Ontario M1P 3G6 Canada
Phone: 416-299-8880   FAX: 416-299-4721
*International matching service for dinnerware by
major English and American manufacturers.*

Matching Service
Ross Simmons
136 Route 5
Warwick, RI 02886
Phone: 401-463-3100 or 800-556-7376
                         FAX: 401-463-8599
*Sells new, active patterns of Royal Doulton,
Minton, Wedgwood, Noritake, Villeroy & Boch,
Royal Worcester, Lenox, etc.*

Matching Service
Thurber's
2158 Plainfield Pike, Unit 1
Cranston, RI 02921
Phone: 401-942-0488 or 800-848-7237
                         FAX: 401-942-5601

Matching Service
China By Pattern
P.O. Box 129
Farmington, CT 06034
Phone: 203-678-7079
*Locating china, crystal & glassware: Lenox,
Spode, Doulton, Syracuse, Wedgwood,
Haviland, Noritake, Johnson Bros., etc.*

Matching Service
Lanac Sales
73 Canal St.
New York, NY 10002
Phone: 212-925-6422 *

Matching Service
Past & Presents
65-07 Fitchess St.
Rego Park, NY 11374
Phone: 718-896-5146
*Matching and locating service for Coalport,
Derby, Franciscan, Gorham, Lenox, Metlox,
Mikasa, Minton, Noritake, and others.*

Matching Service
Pattern Finders
P.O. Box 206
Port Jefferson Station, NY 11776
Phone: 516-928-5158
*All major brands of dinnerware and crystal
stocked in huge inventory; locating service for hard
to find patterns; Rosenthal specialists.*

Matching Service
Old China Patterns Ltd.
Dept. CIC
P.O. Box 290
Fineview, NY 13640
Phone: 315-482-3829 or 800-525-7390
                         FAX: 315-482-5827
*Buys and sells internationally; since 1966; spe-
cializing in English & American china; charter
member Inter. Assoc. of Dinnerware Matchers.*

Matching Service
China Match
Freda Bell
9 Elmford Rd.
Rochester, NY 14606
Phone: 716-426-2783 or 716-338-3781
*Replacements of discontinued china, stoneware,
glass and crystal stemware.*

Matching Service
Replacements Ltd.
Lea Ann Mills
P.O. Box 26029
Greensboro, NC 27420
Phone: 919-697-3000   FAX: 919-697-3100
*China, crystal and flatware (obsolete, active and
inactive).*

Matching Service
China Cabinet
P.O. Box 266
Clearwater, SC 29822
Phone: 803-593-9655
*Features a number of Metlox Potteries patterns. **

Matching Service
China Chasers
2380 Peachtree Corners Circle
Norcross, GA 30092
Phone: 404-441-9146
*China and crystal replacements. **

Matching Service
Johnson Brothers Replacements
3576 Clairmont Rd.
Atlanta, GA 30319
Phone: 404-634-1194 *

Matching Service
Joyful Ventures
P.O. Box 4995
Ocala, FL 32678 *

Matching Service
Abrahante's Tableware Matching Service
Suite 209
7175 SW 47th St.
Miami, FL 33155
Phone: 305-661-1456
*American, English and Japanese manufacturers
of discontinued patterns of china, crystal and
flatware.*

Matching Service
Jewel Box
P.O. Box 145
Albertville, AL 35950
Phone: 205-878-3301 *

Matching Service
China Mater
99 West Carlos Rd.
Memphis, TN 38117
Phone: 901-685-6983 *

Matching Service
Barron's
P.O. Box 994
Novi, MI 48376
Phone: 800-538-6340

Matching Service
Jacquelynn's China Matching Service
Jacquelynn Ives
219 N. Milwaukee St.
Milwaukee, WI 53202
Phone: 414-272-8880
Discontinued Coalport, Franciscan, Lenox, Minton, Spode, Royal Doulton, Wedgwood, Pickard, and other china patterns bought & sold.

Matching Service
China & Crystal Replacements
P.O. Box 187
Excelsior, MN 55331
Phone: 612-474-6418
Discontinued and active china, dinnerware and crystal bought and sold.

Matching Service
Patterns of the Past
513 S. Main St.
Princeton, IL 61356
Phone: 805-875-1944 *

Matching Service
Dining Elegance, Ltd.
Dept. CIC
P.O. Box 4203
St. Louis, MO 63163
Phone: 314-865-1408
Listing of patterns in stock sent upon request; $1.

Matching Service
International Dinnerware Matchers
Association
E. Wallace
P.O. Box 4203
St. Louis, MO 63163
*An association of dinnerware matchers. **

Matching Service
Locators, Inc.
908 Rock St.
Little Rock, AR 72202
Phone: 501-371-0858 or 800-367-9690

Carries out-of-production (discontinued) china and crystal, and discontinued as well as active sterling flatware patterns.

Matching Service
Seekers, The
9014 Roos Road
Houston, TX 77036
Phone: 713-523-9710 *

Matching Service
Ettelman's Discontinued China & Crystal
Mrs. David Solka, Pres.
P.O. Box 6491
Corpus Christi, TX 78466
Phone: 512-888-8391
Buy/sell inactive patterns of china by Caselton, Flintridge, Franciscan, Haviland, Lenox, Oxford and Syracuse.

Matching Service
International Association of Dinnerware
Matchers
P.O. Box 50125
Austin, TX 78763-0125
Phone: 512-472-1548
IADM is a group of independent dinnerware matchers in the US & Canada organized to promote honesty and integrity within the profession.

Matching Service
A&A Dinnerware Locators
Larry & Anne McDonald
P.O. Box 50222
Austin, TX 78763-0222
Phone: 512-472-1548 or 512-264-1054
Locate/match discontinued china, earthenware, etc.; all major manufacturers: American, European, Japanese; primarily mail order.

Matching Service
Jo Hancock
2318 61st
Lubbock, TX 79412
Phone: 806-792-2557 *

Matching Service
Walter Drake Silver & China Exchange
94 Drake Building
Colorado Springs, CO 80940
Phone: 719-596-3140 or 800-525-9291
FAX: 719-593-5321
Active and inactive silver and china tableware replacements. For their Insurance Replacement Department call 800-525-2274.

Matching Service
Wood Jewelers
848 East Main St.
Santa Paula, CA 93060
Phone: 805-525-5547 *

Matching Service
China Traders
Suite 220
690 Los Angeles Ave.
Simi Valley, CA 93065
Phone: 805-527-5440
A discontinued china replacement service; buys and sells most discontinued china patterns.

Matching Service
Silver Lane Antiques
P.O. Box 322
San Leandro, CA 94577
Phone: 415-483-0632
Buys and sells discontinued patterns by major American and English china companies; also American sterling flatware.

Matching Service
Table Treasures
P.O. Box 4265
Stockton, CA 95204
Phone: 209-463-3607
Buy, sell and locate discontinued patterns in china, earthenware and crystal. American, English and Japanese manufacturers.

Matching Service
Patterns Unlimited International
Warren & Betty Roundhill
Dept. CIC
P.O. Box 15238
Seattle, WA 98115
Phone: 206-523-9710
Buy, sell and appraise discontinued tableware patterns of china, silver and glass.

DIRIGIBLES

(see also AIRSHIPS)

DIRILYTE FLATWARE

(see also FLATWARE)

DISCONTINUED TABLEWARE PATTERNS

(see also FLATWARE; DINNERWARE; GLASS, Elegant; GLASS, Crystal)

DISNEY COLLECTIBLES

(see also CHARACTER COLLECTIBLES)

Club/Association
Mouse Club East
Newsletter: Mouse Club East Newsletter
474 Main Street
Willmington, MA 01887
Phone: 508-657-6576

Club/Association

National Fantasy Fan Club for Disneyana
Collectors & Enthusiasts
Journal: Fantasyline
P.O. Box 19212
Irvine, CA 92713
Phone: 818-509-1687
To preserve the legacy of Walt Disney through collecting and preserving of Disney memorabilia, research and sharing of information.

Club/Association

Mouse Club
Newsletter: Mouse Club, The
Kim & Julie McEuen
2056 Cirone Way
San Jose, CA 95124
Phone: 408-377-2590
A bi-monthly newsletter devoted to articles about Disneyana collecting; sponsors semi-annual show and sale of strickly Disneyana.

Collector

Bob Havey
P.O. Box 183
W. Sullivan, ME 04689
Phone: 207-442-3083
Disney collector buys all nice 1930's/40's items; excellent prices paid.

Collector

Ferdinand Dolfi
247 1/2 Porter St.
Waynesburg, PA 15370
Phone: 412-852-2830 *

Collector

Character Toys
Elmer & Viola Reynolds
P.O. Box 2183
Clarksville, IN 47131
Wants Kewpies, all comic character toys, banks, tin wind-ups, bisques, and Disneyana. *

Collector

David Welch
RR 2, Box 233
Murphysboro, IL 62966
Phone: 618-687-2282
Wants milk bottles ONLY if showing Disney characters, (no Hilo Dairy, please); also Disney silverware if with original box, toy or stand.

Collector

Sandy & Don Madden
1315 Shanessey Rd.
El Cajon, CA 92019
Phone: 619-444-8531
Wants Disneyana; battery and wind-ups. *

Dealer

Mouse Man Ink, The
P.O. Box 3195
Wakefield, MA 01880
Phone: 617-246-3876

Buys and sells, specializing in pre-1941 Disney; large catalog available for $1.

Dealer

Toy Scouts, Inc.
Bill & Joanne Bruegman
330 Merriman Rd.
Akron, OH 44303-1552
Phone: 216-836-0668 or 216-864-6751
Wants all 1930's Disney items featuring Mickey Mouse and friends: figurines, dolls, toys, paper, radios, lamp, advertising, etc.

Expert

Mel Morrison
P.O. Box 1177
No. Windham, ME 04062
Co-author of "Price Guide to Walt Disney Collectables." *

Expert

Hake's Americana & Collectibles Auction
Ted Hake
P.O. Box 1444
York, PA 17405
Phone: 717-848-1333   FAX: 717-848-4977
Specializing in mail-bid auctions of Disneyana, historical Americana, toys, premiums, political items, character and other collectibles.

Expert

Tomart Publications
Tom Tumbusch
P.O. Box 292102
Dayton, OH 45429
Phone: 513-294-2250
Buys Disneyana items; author of "Tomart's Illustrated Disneyana Catalog and Price Guide" series depicting 20,000 items in color.

Expert

Hoosier Peddler, The
Dave Harris
5400 S. Webster St.
Kokomo, IN 46902
Phone: 317-453-6172
Specializing in rare comic toys & tin wind-ups, antique advertising & Disneyana. *

Museum/Library

Walt Disney Archives
500 South Buena Vista St.
Burbank, CA 91521

Periodical

Magazine: Storyboard Magazine
2512 Artesia Blvd.
Redondo Beach, CA 90278-9984
A bi-monthly full-color magazine for Disneyana collectors. *

Ceramics

Dealer

Judy Posner
R.D. 1 Box 273
Effort, PA 18330
Phone: 717-629-6583   FAX: 717-629-0521
Wants Disney bisque figures, Disney dinnerware, character cookie jars & shakers; send $1 for catalog; send for wants list.

DIVING EQUIPMENT

(see also NAUTICAL COLLECTIBLES)

Helmets

Collector

Larry Pitman
5424 Bryan Station Rd.
Paris, KY 40361
Phone: 606-299-5022
Wants diving helmets. *

DOG COLLECTIBLES

(see also ANIMAL COLLECTIBLES)

Collector

Mary Devlin
9726 Philadelphia Rd.
Baltimore, MD 21237-
Phone: 301-686-9212
Wants dog-related items on any breed. *

Dealer

Denise Hamilton
2835 Carson Dr.
Elmira, NY 14903
Phone: 607-562-8564
Buys/sells Russian Wolfhound or Greyhound items: all breed Erphila, Morten studio figurines: doggy jewelry, buttons, statues, etc.

Expert

Joselyn Butterer
137 South Main St.
Quakerstown, PA 18951
Phone: 215-536-9211 *

Museum/Library

American Kennel Club, Inc. Library
Roberta Vesley, Lib.
51 Madison Ave.
New York, NY 10010
Phone: 212-696-8245   FAX: 216-696-8299
Research library open to the public; 17,000 volumes on dogs and related areas.

Museum/Library

Dog Museum, The
1721 S. Mason Rd.
St. Louis, MO 63131
Phone: 314-821-3647

Periodical

Magazine: Canine Collectors Companion
P.O. Box 2948
Portland, OR 97208-2948 *

Figurines (Mortens Studios)

Collector

Collector
2330 Linden Ave.
South Plainfield, NJ 07080
Wants Mortens Studio dog figurines. *

German Shepherds

Collector

Edythe Shephard
1334 E. Suncrest Dr.
Tucson, AZ 85706 *

Plastic Models

Collector

Collector
3007 Darden Rd.
Greensboro, NC 27407
Phone: 919-299-7261
Wants plastic horses, dogs, etc.: Breyer, Hartland, others; any size, condition, color. *

Scotties

Club/Association

Wee Scots, Inc.
Newsletter: Scottie Sampler
Dept. 91-8
P.O. Box 1512
Columbus, IN 47202-1512
A quarterly newsletter with historical data, current market prices, photos, ads, etc. for Scottie collectors and dealers.

Collector

Wee Scots, Inc.
Donna & Jim Newton
Dept. 91-8
P.O. Box 1512
Columbus, IN 47202-1512
Wants items with Scottie designs: glassware, old greeting cards, post cards, playing cards, books, hooked rugs, advertising, etc.

Dealer

Van M. Jones
2847 Madison Rd.
Cincinnati, OH 45209
Phone: 513-531-0244
Interested in all kinds of Scotty memorabilia, especially bronzes, porcelains, etchings & fine art, playing cards with Scotty motif.

Dealer

L & W Antiques
5760 West Irving Park Rd.
Chicago, IL 60634
Phone: 312-545-6338 *

DOLL HOUSES & FURNISHINGS

(see also MINIATURES)

Collector

Sharon Wilkins
1105 Burnham St.
Cocoa, FL 32922 *

Expert

Barbara Rosen
6 Shoshone Trail
Wayne, NJ 07470 *

Man./Prod./Dist.

Open House
Noel & Pat Thomas
Box 213
Seaview, WA 98644
Makes unique, authentic and very detailed doll houses. *

Museum/Library

Strong Museum, The
1 Manhattan Square
Rochester, NY 14607
Phone: 716-263-2700

Museum/Library

Washington Dolls' House & Toy Museum
5236 44th Street NW
Washington, DC 20015
Phone: 202-244-0024

Periodical

Magazine: International Dolls' House News
June Stowe, Ed.
P.O. Box 79
Southampton S09 7EZ England
In publication for over 24 years; specialist magazine devoted to doll houses and miniatures both old and new.

Periodical

Magazine: Doll Castle News
P.O. Box 247
Washington, NJ 07882
Phone: 201-689-6513 or 201-689-7042
A magazine focusing on dolls, miniatures, doll houses and related items; ads, paper doll section, needlework, patterns, etc.

DOLLS

(see also BROWNIES BY PALMER COX; COLLECTIBLES (MODERN), Dolls; DOLL HOUSES & FURNISHINGS; GOLLIWOGGS & DUTCH DOLLS; TEDDY BEARS; TOYS; TROLLS)

Auction Service

Sotheby's
34-35 New Bond Street
London W1A 2AA England

Conducts specialty auctions of tinplate toys, diecasts, trains, antique dolls, teddy bears, automata.

Auction Service

Richard W. Withington, Inc.
R.D. 2, Box 440
Hillsboro, NH 03244
Phone: 603-464-3232

Auction Service

Theriault's Auction
P.O. Box 151
Annapolis, MD 21404
Phone: 301-224-3655   FAX: 301-224-2515

Auction Service

Cobb's Doll Auction
David M. Cobb
803 Franklin Ave.
Columbus, OH 43205
Phone: 614-252-8844
Conducts quarterly antique doll auctions; send $22 for catalog; send address for advance notice flyer.

Auction Service

McMasters' Auction
James E. McMasters
P.O. Box 1755
Cambridge, OH 43725
Phone: 800-842-3526 or 614-432-4320
                              FAX: 614-432-3191
Specializes in autions of antique and collectible dolls.

Auction Service

International Doll Exhibitions & Auctions, Ltd.
P.O. Box 54
Morton Grove, IL 60053 *

Auction Service

Frasher's
Rt. 1, Box 142
Oak Grove, MO 64075
Phone: 816-625-3786 *

Auction Service

J & J Galleries
Paul Johnson
P.O. Box 20764
Kansas City, MO 64195-0764
Phone: 816-386-2972 or 312-878-0928
Specializing in antique dolls and related items. *

Club/Association

Doll Collectors of America
Newsletter: Bulletin
14 Chestnut Rd.
Westford, MA 01886
Phone: 617-692-8392 *

Club/Association

Doll Artisan Guild
Magazine: Doll Artisan, The
35 Main Street
Oneonta, NY 13820
Phone: 607-432-4977
Focusing on new dolls and the art of doll making; patterns, tips, new products, auction news, museums, dollmaking seminars, etc.

Club/Association

Ginny Doll Club
Newsletter: Ginny Doll Club News
Jeanne Niswonger
305 West Beacon Rd.
Lakeland, FL 33803
Phone: 813-687-8015
Focuses on Ginny dolls and club news.

Club/Association

Modern Doll Club
Journal: Modern Doll Club journal
Jeanne Niswonger
305 West Beacon Road
Lakeland, FL 33803
A corresponding club for doll collectors.

Club/Association

National Organization of Miniaturists & Dollers
Newsletter: NOMAD Dolletter
Sara Patterson
1300 Schroder
Normal, IL 61761
Stories, articles, illustrations, patterns, and how-to information.

Club/Association

United Federation of Doll Clubs
Newsletter: Doll News
P.O. Box 14146
Parkville, MO 64152
Write for a list of the standardized terms used by doll collectors. *

Dealer

Aladdin Antiques
Liz Olimpio
Governor's Rd.
Sanbornville, NH 03872
Phone: 603-522-8503   FAX: 603-522-8933
Buy, sells, repairs antique dolls.

Dealer

Judie's Dolls
Judie Littlefield
6908 Colonial Drive
Thurmont, MD 21788
Phone: 301-898-7084
Buys and sells old collectible dolls, new porcelain reproduction and collectible dolls, doll clothes, shoes and wigs.

Dealer

Melton's Antiques
Julia Melton
4201 Indian River Rd.
Chesapeake, VA 23325
Phone: 800-736-6251 or 800-736-6310 *

Dealer

Clark's Antiques
Betty Clark
Rt. 2, Box 106
Houston, MS 38851
Wants any doll: jointed bisque dolls, celluloid dolls, Indian dolls, or rag dolls. *

Dealer

Enchanted World Doll Museum
Cynthia R. Decker
615 North Main
Mitchell, SD 57301
Phone: 605-996-9896   FAX: 605-996-0210
Buys and sells antique and collectible dolls and accessory items; specializes in 1800 to early 1900's bisque and china dolls.

Dealer

Donna Purkey
2430 W. Random Dr.
Anaheim, CA 92804
Phone: 714-828-5909
Wants older collectible dolls: Barbies, Shirley Temple, Kewpie, Ginny, Storybook, GI Joes, Toni, Terri Lee, etc.; also accessories.

Expert

My Dear Dolly
Patricia Snyder
P.O. Box 303
Sparta, NJ 07871
Phone: 201-729-8087
Updated & accurately described listings for antique and collectible dolls and toys mailed quarterly to collectors; wants character dolls.

Expert

House of Collectibles
Julie Collier
201 East 50th Street
New York, NY 10022
Phone: 212-872-8120

Expert

Flanigan's Antiques
Vicki Flanigan
P.O. Box 1662
Winchester, VA 22601 *

Expert

Mary Jo Walczak
5312 Brophy Dr.
Toledo, OH 43611 *

Expert

Gems of the Doll World
Mary Gorham
9399 Shelly Lane
Montgomery, OH 45243
Writes "Gems of the Doll World" column about dolls. Send SASE along with drawing of mold marks and photographs for identification.

Misc. Service

Doll Detective, The
Linda Holderbaum
107 North 32nd
Battle Creek, MI 49015
Phone: 616-963-6291
Lectures, appraise, organizes exhibitions; restoration and conservation work formerly a museum curator.

Museum/Library

Bethnel Green Museum of Childhood
Cambridge Heath Road
London E2 9PA England

Museum/Library

Victoria & Albert Museum
Cromwell Road
London SW7 England

Museum/Library

Wenhem Historical Association & Museum, Inc.
132 Main Street
Wenhem, MA 01984
Phone: 508-468-2377

Museum/Library

Yesteryears Museum
Newsletter: Yesteryears Museum News
P.O. Box 609
Sandwich, MA 02563
Phone: 617-888-1711

Museum/Library

Doll Museum, The
520 Thames St.
Newport, RI 02840
Phone: 401-849-0405
Featuring a fine collection of antique and modern dolls; museum toy shop carries antiques, collectibles, etc.; offers repairs.

Museum/Library

Fairfield Historical Society
636 Old Post Road
Fairfield, CT 06430
Phone: 203-259-1598

Museum/Library

Doll Castle Doll Museum
P.O. Box 247
Washington, NJ 07882
Phone: 201-689-6513 or 201-689-7042
Houses hundreds of dolls and related items collected by the staff of "Doll Castle News."

Museum/Library
Museum of the City of New York
5th Avenue at 103rd St.
New York, NY 10029
Phone: 212-534-1672

Museum/Library
Aunt Len's Doll House, Inc.
6 Hamilton Terrace
New York, NY 10031
Phone: 212-926-4172

Museum/Library
Town of Yorktown Museum
1974 Commerce Street
Yorktown Heights, NY 10598
Phone: 914-962-2811

Museum/Library
Victorian Doll Museum & Chili Doll
Hospital
Linda Greenfield
4332 Buffalo Road
North Chili, NY 14514
Phone: 716-247-1030
*A wonderland exhibiting over 2000 identified
dolls from mid-1800's to present; puppet show, toy
circus, doll houses, paper dolls, etc.*

Museum/Library
Strong Museum, The
1 Manhattan Square
Rochester, NY 14607
Phone: 716-263-2700

Museum/Library
Mary Merritt Doll Museum, The
Marjorie Darrah
Route 422
Douglassville, PA 19518
Phone: 215-385-3809

Museum/Library
Washington Dolls' House & Toy Museum
5236 44th Street NW
Washington, DC 20015
Phone: 202-244-0224

Museum/Library
National Museum of American History
14th & Constitution Ave. NW
Washington, DC 20560
Phone: 202-357-2700

Museum/Library
Milan Historical Museum, Inc.
P.O. Box 308
Milan, OH 44846
Phone: 419-499-2968

Museum/Library
Enchanted World Doll Museum
Eunice T. Reese
615 North Main
Mitchell, SD 57301
Phone: 605-996-9896   FAX: 605-996-0210
*4000 antique and collectible dolls in display; gift
shop has Madame Alexander, and Bradley dolls;
also Dept. 56 Dickens Village houses.*

Museum/Library
House of a Thousand Dolls
P.O. Box 136
Loma, MT 59460
Phone: 406-739-4338

Museum/Library
Eugene Field House & Toy Museum
634 Broadway St.
St. Louis, MO 63102
Phone: 314-421-4689

Museum/Library
Toy & Miniature Museum of Kansas City
Sandi Russell
5235 Oak St.
Kansas City, MO 64112
Phone: 816-333-2055
*Museum housed in an elegant mansion features
collections of miniatures, antique dolls' houses
and antique toys.*

Museum/Library
Prairie Museum of Art & History
P.O. Box 465
Colby, KS 67701
Phone: 913-462-6972

Museum/Library
Gay Nineties Button & Doll Museum
Rte. 4, Box 420
Eureka Springs, AR 72632
Phone: 501-253-9321

Museum/Library
Geuther Doll Museum
188 N. Main St.
Eureka Springs, AR 72632
Phone: 501-253-8501

Museum/Library
Eliza Cruce Hall Doll Museum
Grand at E. Northwest
Ardmore, OK 73401
Phone: 405-223-8290

Museum/Library
Franks Antique Doll Museum
Francis & Clara Franks
410 N. Grove St.
Marshall, TX 75670
Phone: 903-935-3065 or 903-935-3070

Museum/Library
McCurdy's Historical Doll Museum
246 North 100th Street East
Provo, UT 84601

Museum/Library
Hobby City Doll & Toy Museum
1238 South Beach Blvd.
Anaheim, CA 92804
Phone: 714-527-2323

Museum/Library
Museum of Modern Mythology
Suite 900
693 Mission Street
San Francisco, CA 94105
Phone: 415-546-0202

Periodical
Newsletter: Doll Investment Newsletter
P.O. Box 1982
Centerville, MA 02632
*Reports on recent doll sales and auctions, repairs,
fakes, and other issues of interest to the doll
investor.* •

Periodical
Directory: Doll Castle News Doll Directory,
The
P.O. Box 247
Washington, NJ 07882
Phone: 201-689-6513 or 201-689-7042
*Lists classified ads for hundreds of sources of
interest to the doll collector.*

Periodical
Magazine: Doll Castle News
P.O. Box 247
Washington, NJ 07882
Phone: 201-689-6513 or 201-689-7042
*A magazine focusing on dolls, miniatures, doll
houses and related items; ads, paper doll section,
needlework, patterns, etc.*

Periodical
Magazine: Dolls - The Collectors Magazine
Joan M. Pursley, Ed.
170 Fifth Ave. - 12th Floor
New York, NY 10010
Phone: 212-989-8700 or 800-347-6969
                      FAX: 212-645-8976
*Covers antique and contemporary collector dolls
and the artists that designed them; auction re-
ports, current prices, museum collections.*

Periodical
Magazine: Dollmaking
170 Fifth Ave. - 12th Floor
New York, NY 10010
Phone: 212-989-8700 or 800-347-6969
                      FAX: 212-645-8976
*A quarterly magazine of dollmaking projects and
plans; beautifully and lavishly illustrated.*

Periodical

Magazine: Costume Quarterly
118-01 Sutter Ave.
Jamaica, NY 11420-2407
For doll collectors.

Periodical

Newsletter: Dollmasters, The
Florence Theriault
P.O. Box 151
Annapolis, MD 21404
Phone: 301-224-3655   FAX: 301-224-2515
"The Dollmasters" is published quarterly and contains articles about doll market news as well as recent auction reports.

Periodical

Hobby House Press, Inc.
Magazine: Doll Reader
Rene M. Trezise
900 Frederick St.
Cumberland, MD 21502-9985
Phone: 301-759-3770   FAX: 301-759-4940
Focusing on new and old dolls; latest research on old dolls and current prices; also projects, costume patterns, shows, sales, etc.

Periodical

Hobby House Press, Inc.
Magazine: Doll Artistry
Rene M. Trezise
900 Frederick St.
Cumberland, MD 21502-9985
Phone: 301-759-3770   FAX: 301-759-4940

Periodical

Newspaper: Collectors United
P.O. Box 1160
Chatsworth, GA 30705 *

Periodical

Magazine: Dolls of Sunybrook, The
576 Greenlawn Ave.
Columbus, OH 43223
*A bimonthly magazine about dolls and paper dolls with buy/sell ads, articles, and show and auction announcements. **

Periodical

Newsletter: Doll Shop Talk
Rt. 1, Box 100
Evanston, IN 47531
Phone: 812-529-8561 *

Periodical

House of White Birches
Magazine: Women's Circle Doll Designs
Rebekah Montgomery, Ed.
P.O. Box 11302
Des Moines, IA 50340-1302
Phone: 800-888-6833
Focuses on dollcrafting; instructions for creating dolls in every medium; patterns for doll costumes and how-to's for repair/restoring.

Periodical

House of White Birches
Magazine: International Doll World
Rebekah Montgomery, Ed.
P.O. Box 11302
Des Moines, IA 50340-1302
Phone: 800-888-6833
Covers many aspects of dolls and doll collecting: articles on doll history, interviews with doll artists, how-to articles, doll ID, etc.

Periodical

House of White Birches
Magazine: Doll Collector's Price Guide
Rebekah Montgomery, Ed.
P.O. Box 11302
Des Moines, IA 50340-1302
Phone: 800-888-6833
Focuses on antique and collectible dolls, identification, fakes, auction results, ads, investing, teddy bears, etc.

Periodical

Directory: National Catalogue of Doll Shows, The
8488 Dam Road
Minocqua, WI 54548
Phone: 714-356-6149
*An annual listing by states and dates of doll, toy and miniature shows and sales. **

Periodical

Magazine: Bambini
P.O. Box 33
Highland, IL 62249
Phone: 618-675-3497 *

Periodical

Newsletter: Costume Quarterly for Doll Collectors
May Wenzel
38 Middlesex Dr.
Brentwood, MO 63144
*Contains patterns for doll dresses. **

Periodical

Newspaper: Doll Times, The
218 W. Woodbin
Dallas, TX 75224
*A monthly newspaper with ads and articles about dolls, auctions, and shows. **

Periodical

Newspaper: National Doll & Teddy Bear Collector
Harmony Coburn, Pub.
215 Greenbridge Drive, #117
Lake Oswego, OR 97035
Phone: 503-636-5960
A monthly newspaper with a West Coast perspective; for doll and teddy bear collectors, dealers and artists.

Periodical

Newspaper: Western Doll Collector
P.O. Box 2061
Portland, OR 97208 *

Repair Service

Victorian Doll Museum & Chili Doll Hospital
Linda Greenfield
4332 Buffalo Road
North Chili, NY 14514
Phone: 716-247-1030
Recognized expert in doll restoration; repairs all types of dolls; restringing, leather body repair, replacement of cloth bodies.

Repair Service

Doll Heaven
502 Broadway
New Haven, IN 46774
Phone: 219-493-6428
Doll restoration & repair; specializing in broken bisque and composition dolls; modern, antique, collector dolls; all materials.

Repair Service

International Doll Restoration Artists Association
Magazine: IDRAA Workshop
Route 2, Box 7
Worthington, MN 56187 *

Supplier

Dollspart Supply Co.
46-50 54th Ave.
Maspeth, NY 11378
Phone: 718-361-1833 or 800-336-3655
                         FAX: 718-361-5833
Sells full range of doll books and parts: eyes, wigs, bodies, clothing, tools, etc.

Supplier

Joyce's Doll House Parts
20188 Williamson
Mt. Clemens, MI 48043-7498
Phone: 313-791-0469   FAX: 313-791-6193
Replacement limbs for the collector; nearly 300 styles in porcelain, bisque or china, wigs, eyes, sewing needs, etc.; catalog.

Advertising

Expert

Quilted Keepsakes & Unique Dolls Exhibit
Mary Jane Lamphier
577 Main St.
Arlington, IA 50606
Phone: 319-633-5885
Buys, sells and trades advertising dolls and characters such as Jolly Green Giant, the Ronald McDonald collection, Campbell Soup Kids, etc.

Expert

Joleen A. Robinson
502 Lindley Dr.
Lawrence, KS 66049
Wants advertising dolls (trademark or promotional dolls): Dough Boy, Green Giant, Aunt Jemima, etc.

Museum/Library

Quilted Keepsakes & Unique Dolls Exhibit
Mary Jane Lamphier
577 Main St.
Arlington, IA 50606
Phone: 319-633-5885
Has museum of advertising dolls (trademark or promotional dolls): Pillsbury Dough Boy, M & M dolls, Green Giant, Aunt Jemima, etc.

Annalee

Club/Association

Annalee Doll Society
Magazine: Collector, The
June Rogier
P.O. Box 1137
Meredith, NH 03253-1137
Phone: 800-433-6557
A collectors club sponsored by the Annalee Doll Co.; conducts annual Annalee doll auction; sells Annalees dolls on consignment.

Collector

Bobbi Stavros
730 Boston Rd.
Billerica, MA 01866
Phone: 617-677-1187
Wants Annalee dolls and doll catalogs.

Collector

Sue Coffee
10 Saunders Hollow
Old Lyme, CT 06371
Phone: 203-434-5641
Wants Annalee dolls, catalogs, advertising material; the older the better; send photo or description.

Collector

Margie Motzer
2878 Saddleback
Cincinnati, OH 45244-3915
Phone: 513-231-5953
Buys, sells, trades Annalee Dolls and or catalogs; whole collections or individual pieces; send SASE for special price list.

Dealer

Annalee Antique & Collectible Doll Shoppe
P.O. Box 1137
Meredith, NH 03253
Phone: 800-433-6557
A company-sponsored shop.

Man./Prod./Dist.

Annalee Mobilitee Dolls, Inc.
P.O. Box 708
Meredith, NH 03253
Phone: 607-279-3333   FAX: 603-279-6659
Creates, produces and distributes posable felt dolls of distinction which contain wire armatures for flexibility and repositioning.

Museum/Library

Annalee Doll Museum
Reservoir Road, Box 1137
Meredith, NH 03253
Phone: 603-279-4144

Periodical

Newsletter: Chatter Box News
100 Middleton Rd. #48
Bohemia, NY 11716
Phone: 516-563-4957 or 516-225-2591
A newsletter that specializes in Annalee Dolls: secondary market ads and retail prices; swap, trade, and buy ads; articles, raffles, etc.

Automatons

Collector

Cindy Oakes
34025 W. 6 Mile
Livonia, MI 48152
Phone: 313-591-3252
Wants bisque automatons or bisque dolls on music boxes; any condition; 1890-1900's.

Barbie

Auction Service

Remember When Auctions
Irene Davis
SR Box 11
Oak Hall, VA 23416
Phone: 804-824-5524
Conducts annual auctions of Barbie and related items.

Collector

Irene Davis
SR Box 11
Oak Hall, VA 23416
Phone: 804-824-5524
Wants dolls from 1959 to 1965; also clothes, cars and other Barbie related items.

Collector

Lois Burger
2323 Lincoln
Beatrice, NE 68310
Phone: 402-228-2797
Wants pre-1966 Barbie clothes, accessories, Ken, Midge, Skipper & their clothes; also anything Barbie related such as comics, cars.

Collector

Marcie Melillo
10089 West Fremont Ave.
Littleton, CO 80127

Barbie and family dolls, clothes, etc.

Dealer

Marl & Barbie
Marl Davidson
5707 39th St., Circle East
Bradenton, FL 34203
Phone: 813-751-6275
Specializing in hard to find Barbie dolls, accessories, fashions; complete line of Barbie & family items; catalog $1.50 + LSASE.

Dealer

Gretchen & Wildrose Playdolls
5816 Steeplewood Dr.
North Richland Hills, TX 76180
Phone: 817-485-7189 *

Dealer

Anne Henderson
13629 Victory
Van Nuys, CA 91401
Phone: 818-785-1177
Barbie and family dolls, clothes, etc.

Periodical

Newsletter: Barbie Talks Some More!
Jacqueline Horning
7501 School Road, - 26
Cincinnati, OH 45249

Periodical

Barbie Bazaar, Inc.
Magazine: Barbie Bazaar
5617 6th Ave.
Kenosha, WI 53140-5101

Betsy McCall

Collector

David & Marci Van Ausdall
666-840 Spring Creek Dr.
Westwood, CA 96137
Phone: 916-256-3041
Wants to buy 8" Betsy McCall dolls, clothing and accessories.

Black

(see also BLACK MEMORABILIA)

Dealer

Afro-American Doll Gallery
Erlene Reed
1794 Verbena St., NW
Washington, DC 20012
Phone: 202-829-7170
Wants Black-related dolls, plates, banks, door stops, folk art, etc.

Expert

Black Doll Networks
Patikii Gibbs
Box 158472
Nashville, TN 37215
Author of "Black Dolls."

Bobbin' Head

Expert

Minnie Memories
Patrick Flynn
122 Shadywood Ave.
Mankato, MN 56001
Author of "Bobbin Head Dolls/Hartland Statues."

Buddy Lee

Collector

Marion Lathan
Rt. 1, Box 430
Chester, SC 29706
Phone: 803-377-8225 or 803-581-3000
Wants "Buddy Lee" dolls, with or without uniforms; also wants all advertising dolls.

Cabbage Patch

Club/Association

Cabbage Patch Kids Collectors Club
P.O. Box 714
Cleveland, GA 30528
Phone: 404-865-2171   FAX: 404-865-5862
Focuses on the Cabbage Patch dolls by Xavier Roberts. Sponsored by Original Appalachian Artworks.

Chatty Cathy

Club/Association

Chatty Cathy Collectors Club
Newsletter: CCCC Newsletter
Lisa Eisenstein
2610 Dover St.
Piscataway, NJ 08854-4437

Collector

Lisa
2610 Dover St.
Piscataway, NJ 08854-4437
Phone: 201-463-9085
Wants Chatty Cathy items: clothes, case, accessories; books and all other related items. *

Cloth

Periodical

Magazine: Cloth Doll Magazine, The
Leta Bergman
P.O. Box 1089
Mt. Shasta, CA 96067
Phone: 916-926-5009 or 916-926-4621
A quarterly magazine on cloth/fabric dolls: articles, collector information, sources of supplies, book reviews, patterns, etc.

Periodical

Magazine: Designer's Notebook
Leta Bergman
P.O. Box 1089
Mt. Shasta, CA 96067
Phone: 916-926-5009 or 916-926-4621

A new newsletter about the cloth/fabric doll industry and business.

Dawn

Collector

Joedi Johnson
2901 E. Nutwood Ave. C-13
Fullerton, CA 92631
Phone: 714-996-0943
Wants to buy all "Dawn" doll related items: dolls, accessories, outfits, etc.

Eloise Wilkin

(see also ILLUSTRATORS, Eloise Wilkin)

GI Joe

Club/Association

GI Joe Collectors Club
Newsletter: GI Joe Collectors Club Newsletter
James DeSimone, Pres.
150 S. Glenoaks Blvd.
Burbank, CA 91510
Phone: 818-953-4239
100's of members worldwide; the source for GI Joe information and service.

Collector

Joseph Nardozza
690 Edel Ave.
Maywood, NJ 07607
Wants one doll or entire collections. *

Expert

GI Joe Nostalgia Co.
Joe Bodnarchuk
62 McKinley Ave.
Kenmore, NY 14217
Phone: 716-873-0264 or 800-5GI-JOES
                              FAX: 716-873-0264
GI Joe enthusiast and collector since 1964; pays big $$$$ for mint collections of any size; quality a must.

Half

Collector

Sharon Wilkins
1105 Burnham St.
Cocoa, FL 32922
Wants half dolls: porcelain half dolls decorated a lady's dresser in the 20's and 30's. *

Kewpie

(see also ROSE O'NEILL COLLECTIBLES)

Collector

Character Toys
Elmer & Viola Reynolds
P.O. Box 2183
Clarksville, IN 47131
Wants Kewpies, all comic character toys, banks, tin wind-ups, bisques, and Disneyana. *

Nesting

Expert

Michele Lyons Lefkovitz
c/o Books Americana
Florence, AL 35630
"Matreshka" are the wooden nesting dolls made in the Soviet Union. *

Paper

Club/Association

Original Paper Doll Artists Guild, The
Magazine: OPDAG News
Judy M. Johnson
P.O. Box 176
Skandia, MI 49885
Phone: 906-942-7865
An organization of paper doll enthusiasts to promote the PD hobby; magazine has PD news, how-tos, paper dolls, artist features, etc.

Collector

Loretta Willis
808 Lee Ave.
Tifton, GA 31794
Deals with many paper doll and doll collectors who collect PD's as a hobby; wants PD movie stars, nostalgia, new & old for collection.

Collector

R.H. Stevens
17838 South East Hwy. 452
Umatilla, FL 32784
Paper dolls wanted: cut or uncut.

Collector

Fran VanVynckt
433 Split Rail-H
Valparaiso, IN 46383
Paper dolls wanted: cut or uncut; pre-1950. *

Collector

Sharon Rogers
1813 Junius
Fort Worth, TX 76103
Wants pre-1970 paper dolls, cut or uncut, sorted or unsorted; celebrities, antique, advertising, etc.; please describe & price.

Collector

Shirley Harwood
P.O. Box 33454
Granada Hills, CA 91344
Wants uncut 1950-1970 celebrity and non-celebrity paper dolls. *

Dealer

Gepetto's Doll House
U.S. Hwy. 441
P.O. Box 524
Cherokee, NC 28719

Dealer
Johana's Dolls, Etc.
Johana Gast Anderton
828 Geneva Drive
P.O. Box 786
Oviedo, FL 32765
Phone: 407-365-4178
Specializes in original & antique paper dolls, antique dolls and teddy bears, original doll clothes; a one-time $2 for all catalogs.

Dealer
Judy M. Johnson
P.O. Box 176
Skandia, MI 49885
Phone: 906-942-7865
Buys, sells, collects and designs paper dolls and PD books; wants paper dolls, especially original art and unique or comic paper dolls.

Dealer
Journal: Celebrity Doll Journal
Loraine Burdick
5 Court Place
Puyallup, WA 98372
Celebrity Doll Journal features research on collectibles and creators; also offers sales list of paper dolls.

Expert
Mary Young
1040 Greenbridge Dr.
Kettering, OH 45429 *

Expert
Denis C. Jackson
P.O. Box 1958
Sequim, WA 98382
Phone: 206-683-2559
Author of "The Price & ID Guide to Old Magazine Paperdolls"; with a strong focus on the golden age of paper, 'teens through the 1920's.

Man./Prod./Dist.
Brain Maps
Charlotte Whatley
224 Fishback Ave.
Fort Collins, CO 80521
Phone: 303-493-4485
Designs and markets contemporary line of paper dolls.

Periodical
Newsletter: Loretta's Place Paper Doll Newsletter
Loretta Willis
808 Lee Ave.
Tifton, GA 31794
A PD collector's newsletter with lots of paper dolls, PD artwork, artists featured, doll info, articles, buy/sell/trade ads, etc.

Periodical
Newsletter: Paper Doll Gazette
Route #2, Box 52
Princeton, IN 47670
Phone: 812-385-4080
*A quarterly newsletter with drawings and articles about paper dolls. ***

Periodical
Newsletter: Midwest Paper Dolls & Toys Quarterly
Janie Varsolona
P.O. Box 131
Galesburg, KS 66740
Phone: 316-763-2247 or 316-763-2561
A quarterly newsletter filled with interest to collectors of paper dolls; also buys, sells, collects and conducts specialty PD auctions.

Periodical
Newsletter: Paper Doll News
Ema Terry
P.O. Box 807
Vivian, LA 71082
A bi-monthly newsletter sharing news of the paper doll world.

Periodical
Magazine: Paper Doll & Paper Toy Quarterly Bulletin
3135 Oakcrest Drive
Hollywood, CA 90068
Phone: 213-851-2772
*A quarterly magazine for paper doll collectors. ***

Repro. Source
Creative Clothes
Kathi Reynolds
330 N. Church St.
Thurmont, MD 21788-1640
Phone: 301-695-5340
Creates authentically 1660-1760 period costumed paper dolls.

Parts
Collector
Dorothy Grinewitlki
3428 Napier Rd.
Benton Harbor, MI 49022
*Wants bisque dolls, heads or parts; also complete dolls. ***

Pincushion
Expert
Susan Endo
P.O. Box 4051
Covina, CA 91723
Author of "2nd Price Guide to Pincushion Dolls."

Raggedy Ann & Andy
Dealer
Gwen Daniel
18 Belleau Lake Ct.
O'Fallon, MO 63366
Phone: 314-281-3190
Wants Raggedy Ann & Andy's, books and related items; also teddy bears, Lulu & Tubby, Nancy & Sluggo, Howdy Doody and Barbie.

Periodical
Newsletter: Rags
Barbara Barth
P.O. Box 823
Atlanta, GA 30301
A quarterly newsletter devoted to the creations of Johnny Gruelle; ads, articles, photos, etc. for Raggedy Ann and other cloth dolls.

Storyteller
Expert
Jamie Saloff
3440 State Route 6N
Edinboro, PA 16412
Daughter of the creator of Storyteller Dolls, Iaulanda Turner Downey; high quality, handcrafted felt dolls made in the 1960's;en'70's.

Strawberry Shortcake
Club/Association
Strawberry Shortcake Collectors' Club
Newsletter: Berry-Bits
Peggy Jimenez
1409 72nd St.
North Bergen, NJ 07047

DOOR KNOCKERS
Expert
Cracker Barrel Antiques
Rita & John Ebner
4540 Helen Rd.
Columbus, OH 43232 *

DOOR PUSH PLATES
Collector
Edward Foley
227 Union Ave.
Pittsburgh, PA 15202
Phone: 412-761-0685
Wants porcelain door push (or pull) plates with advertising; attached to old wooden porch doors; Red Rose Tea, Chesterfields, etc.

DOORKNOBS
Club/Association
Antique Doorknob Collectors of America
Newsletter: Doorknob Collector, The
P.O. Box 126
Eola, IL 60519-0126
Phone: 312-357-2381

Collector

Richard C. Hubbard
162 Poplar Ave.
Hackensack, NJ 07601
Phone: 201-342-1274
Wants to buy old doorknobs; historical, figural or emblematic knobs; please describe and price.

Collector

Charles W. Wardell
P.O. Box 195
Trinity, NC 27370
Phone: 919-434-1145
Wants ornate doorknobs, escutcheon plates, store door handles, push plates, door knockers, doorbells, mail slots, etc.; 1870-1920.

Collector

Collector
3434 No. 47th Way
Phoenix, AZ 85018
*Wants porcelains, faces, animals, birds, lodges, cut glass, colored glass, gutta-percha, etc. doorknobs. ***

DOORSTOPS

Dealer

Nancy Smith
22021 Peach Tree Rd.
Boyds, MD 20841
Phone: 301-972-6250

Expert

Cracker Barrel Antiques
Rita & John Ebner
4540 Helen Rd.
Columbus, OH 43232 *

Repro. Source

Yield House
Dept. 1000
North Conway, NH 03860

DR. SEUSS COLLECTIBLES

Collector

Michael Gessel
P.O. Box 748
Arlington, VA 22216
Phone: 703-532-4261
Wants Dr. Seuss books, pamphlets, posters, advertising, ephemera, original illustrations, anything related to Dr. Seuss.

DRACULA

(see also MOVIE MEMORABILIA, Horror Films)

Club/Association

Count Dracula Fan Club
Journal: Dracula News
Dr. M. Jeanne Youngson
29 Washington Square West
New York, NY 10011
Phone: 212-982-6754
Vampires are us. Keeps members of the CDFC up on everything happening in the world of the undead; also publishes other newsletters.

DREDGING EQUIPMENT

Club/Association

Historical Construction Equipment Association
Newsletter: Equipment Echoes
P.O. Box 328
Grand rapids, OH 43522
Phone: 419-832-0808
Dedicated to preserving the history of construction, surface mining and dredging equipment and related memorabilia, trade

DUCK DECOYS

(see also DECOYS, Bird)

EAGLES

(see also FOLK ART)

Dealer

Eagles Eye
Suite 110
1200 E. Alosta Ave.
Glendora, CA 91740
Phone: 818-914-2584
*Wants fine gifts and artwork featuring the American Bald Eagle: bronze, crystal, porcelain, brass, wood, prints, plates, etc. ***

Museum/Library

Mariners' Museum, The
100 Museum Drive
Newport News, VA 23606
Phone: 804-595-0368

EASTER COLLECTIBLES

(see also HOLIDAY COLLECTIBLES; RUSSIAN ITEMS, Faberge)

EDGED WEAPONS

(see also ARMS & ARMOR; SWORDS; KNIVES; MILITARIA)

Expert

Thomas T. Wittmann
1253 N. Church St.
Morrestown, NJ 08057
Phone: 609-235-0622 or 609-866-8733
Buys and sells edged weapons: daggers, swords and certain bayonets; specializing in German 3rd Reich or Imperial period weapons.

EGG BEATERS

Collector

Darryl Rehr
11433 Rochester Ave. #303
Los Angeles, CA 90025
Phone: 213-447-5229
Wants old mechanical egg beaters (manual); please send photo or drawing; include SASE for reply.

EGGCUPS

Periodical

Pastimes
Newsletter: Eggcup Collectors' Corner
Dr. Joan M. George
67 Stevens Ave.
Old Bridge, NJ 08857
A quarterly newsletter for eggcup collectors.

ELECTRICAL APPLIANCES

(see also FANS, Mechanical; TOASTERS, Electric; VACUUM CLEANERS; WASHING MACHINES)

Club/Association

Electric Breakfast Club, The
P.O. Box 306
White Mills, PA 18473-0306
*Devoted to the collecting of vintage electric appliances used at the breakfast table: toasters, waffle irons, percolators, etc. ***

Expert

Mitchell, Inc.
K. M. Scotty Mitchell
2112 Lipscomb
Ft. Worth, TX 76110
Phone: 817-923-3275
Collector of small electrical kitchen appliances (1893-1940): toaster, waffle irons, coffee makers and specialty items, etc.

Expert

Mitchell, Inc.
Gary L. Miller
2112 Lipscomb
Ft. Worth, TX 76110-2047
Phone: 817-923-3275
Collector of small electrical kitchen appliances (1893-1940): toaster, waffle irons, coffee makers and specialty items, etc.

ELECTRICAL COLLECTIBLES

Museum/Library

Edison National Historic Site
Main St. at Lakeside Ave.
West Orange, NJ 07052
Phone: 201-736-5050
A museum with exhibits in all fields of Edison's contributions.

Museum/Library

National Museum of American History
14th & Constitution Ave. NW
Washington, DC 20560
Phone: 202-357-2700
The most extensive research facility in the U.S. for electric relics; trade catalogs, electric razors, refrigerators, TV's, radios, etc.

Museum/Library

Edison Winter Home & Museum
2350 McGregor Blvd.
Fort Myers, FL 33901
Phone: 813-334-3614
Contains Edison-related displays: appliances, early bulbs, and scientific equipment.

Museum/Library

Thomas Edison Birthplace Museum
P.O. Box 451
Milan, OH 44846
Phone: 419-499-2135
An Edison exhibit featuring phones, lamps, fans, photos, and other items related to Thomas Edison.

Museum/Library

Dayton Power & Light Company Museum
P.O. Box 1247-Courthouse Sq.
Dayton, OH 45401
Phone: 513-224-6428
Over 1000 electrical and non-electrical appliances and historical artifacts pertaining to the gas & electric utility industry.

Museum/Library

Baaken, The
3537 Zenith Avenue South
Minneapolis, MN 55416
Phone: 612-927-6508

Museum/Library

Masden Electric Museum
3251 E. Washington Blvd.
Los Angeles, CA 90023

ELECTRICITY RELATED ITEMS

(see also INSULATORS)

Club/Association

Telsa Coil Builders' Association
Newsletter: TCBA News
Harry Goldman
3 Amy Lane
Queensbury, NY 12804
Phone: 518-792-1003
TCBA is a clearinghouse on the history of electricity, wireless, etc.; acts as consultants for high voltage historical equipment.

Collector

Collector
RD3 Box 181
Glens Falls, NY 12801
*Wants books, magazines on electricity, induction coils, wireless telegraphy, electrotherapy, etc. ***

Museum/Library

Rocky Beach Dam, Gallery of Electricity
P.O. Box 1231
Wenatchee, WA 98801
Phone: 509-663-8121
The museum features communications and power relics.

ELEPHANT COLLECTIBLES

Club/Association

National Elephant Collectors Society, The
Newsletter: Jumbo Jargon
Richard W. Massiglia
380 Medford St.
Somerville, MA 02145-3810
Phone: 617-625-4067

Expert

Richard W. Massiglia
380 Medford St.
Somerville, MA 02145-3810
Phone: 617-625-4067

ELONGATED COINS

Club/Association

Elongated Collectors, The
Newsletter: TEC News
Raymond Dillard, Pres.
P.O. Box 161
Fenton, MI 48430
Focuses on coins of all dominations plus tokens & foreign coins that were run under pressure onto a die to strech into elongated shape.

ELSIE THE BORDON COW ITEMS

(see also DAIRY COLLECTIBLES)

Collector

Ron Selcke
P.O. Box 237
Bloomington, IL 60108
Phone: 708-543-4848
Wants Elsie toys, neons, Christmas cards, signs, calendars, bottles, etc.; send price and describe.

Collector

Marci Van Ausdall
666-840 Spring Creek Dr.
Westwood, CA 96137
Phone: 916-256-3041
Wants Bordon and Elsie Cow items: bottles, trade cards, related items.

EMBROIDERY

(see also TEXTILES)

ENGINES

(see also FARM MACHINERY; STEAM-OPERATED, Models & Equipment)

Gasoline

Periodical

Stemgas Publishing Co.
Magazine: Gas Engine Magazine
P.O. Box 328
Lancaster, PA 17603
Phone: 717-392-0733   FAX: 717-392-1341
G.E.M. is the leading magazine for antique tractor and gas engine collectors; articles, ads, restoration tips, histories, etc.

Supplier

Starbolt Engine Supplies
Bill Starky
3403 Buckeystown Pike
Adamstown, MD 21710
Phone: 301-874-2821
Sells parts for old gas engines. Mail order only.

Steam & Gasoline

Expert

Owls Head Transportation Museum
Charles Chiarchiaro
Rt. 73, Box 277
Owls Head, ME 04854
Phone: 207-594-4418
Mr. Chiarchiaro is an expert in pre-1910 internal combustion and steam engines.

Museum/Library

Antique Gas & Steam Engine Museum, Inc.
2040 Santa Fe Ave.
Vista, CA 92083
Phone: 619-941-1791 *

EQUIPMENT

(see also MACHINERY & EQUIPMENT)

ESTATE JEWELRY

(see also GEMS & JEWELRY)

EXIT GLOBES

Collector

Michael Bruner
8482 Huron River Drive
Union Lake, MI 48386
Phone: 313-674-0433 or 313-661-2359
Wants exit globes in all style, shapes and colors.

EXONUMIA

(see also TOKENS)

Auction Service

C & D Gale
2404 Berwyn Rd.
Wilmington, DE 19810
Phone: 302-478-0872
Conducts mail bid auctions of medals, tokens, religious items, trade checks, miscellaneous items, Civil War tokens and other exonumia.

FAIRINGS

Expert

Melvin & Barb Alpern
14 Carter Rd.
West Orange, NJ 07052
Phone: 201-731-9427 *

Expert

Daniel M. Sourbeer Antiques
Daniel Sourbeer
Box 10614
St. Petersburg, FL 33733
Phone: 813-866-3873 *

FAIRY LAMPS

(see also LAMPS & LIGHTING, Miniature;
NIGHT LIGHTS)

FANS

(see also ELECTRICAL APPLIANCES)

Hand

Club/Association

Fan Circle International
Magazine: Fans
79A Falcondale Rd.
Westbury-on-Trym
Bristol BS9 3JW England
A worldwide society to promote the interest and knowledge in all aspects of fan collecting.

Club/Association

East Bay Fan Guild
Newsletter: East Bay Fan Guild Newsletter
P.O. Box 1054
El Cerrito, CA 94530
Focuses on the collecting of women's and men's hand fans. *

Club/Association

Fan Association of North America
Newsletter: FANA Quarterly
Grace R. Grayson
2133 Pine Knoll Dr. #16
Walnut Creek, CA 94595
Phone: 415-256-0949
Non-profit educational organization; promotes fans as art objects and historical artifacts; holds annual conferences.

Collector

Gretchen Walberg
P.O. Box 130
Sunbury, PA 17801
Phone: 717-286-1617   FAX: 717-286-9686
Collects antique hand fans of fine quality; decorative, historical, or unusual.

Expert

Skinner, Inc.
Ellen Dennis
357 Main Street
Bolton, MA 01740
Phone: 508-779-6241 or 617-236-1700
FAX: 508-779-5144

Expert

Flanigan's Antiques
Vicki Flanigan
P.O. Box 1662
Winchester, VA 22601 *

Expert

Grace R. Grayson
2133 Pine Knoll Dr.
Walnut Creek, CA 94595
Phone: 415-256-0949
A FAN-atic! Collects antique and contemporary fans; European, Oriental, ethnic, etc.; also fan related advertising and literature.

Man./Prod./Dist.

Flamenco Importers, Inc.
P.O. Box 387
Willoughby, OH 44094
Phone: 216-946-4099
Imports hand painted Spanish fans for collectors.

Museum/Library

Colonial Williamsburg
P.O. Box C
Williamsburg, VA 23185
Phone: 804-229-1000
Specializes in early American furniture and the decorative arts.

Mechanical

Club/Association

American Fan Collectors Association
Newsletter: Fan Collector Newsletter, The
Michael Breedlove
P.O. Box 804
South Bend, IN 46624
Phone: 219-272-1231
Interested in water powered, steam, electric, and other types of mechanical fans; the AFCA sponsors an annual convention.

Collector

Kevin Shail
30 Old Middle Road
Brookfield, CT 06804
Interested in old mechanical fans, hot-air (kerosene) powered fans. *

Collector

Michael Breedlove
15633 Cold Spring Ct.
Granger, IN 46530
Phone: 219-272-1231
Collector seeks old antique or unusual electrical and mechanical fans; also seeking fan advertising items and photos; please call!

Expert

Fan Man, The
Kurt House
4614 Travis
Dallas, TX 75205
Phone: 214-559-4440
Author of "Ant. Mechanical Fans." Repairs, sells, buys, antique mechanical fans of all types including electrical, fuel-driven, etc.

Repair Service

Light Ideas
1037 Taft Street
Rockville, MD 20850
Phone: 301-424-5483   FAX: 301-424-5791
Repairs early electric fans; also carries parts.

FARM COLLECTIBLES

(see also CORN COLLECTIBLES; FARM
MACHINERY; WATCH FOBS, Farm
Related; WEANERS, Calf & Cow)

Museum/Library

Billings Farm & Museum
Esther Munroe Smith, Lib.
P.O. Box 489
Woodstock, VT 05091
Phone: 802-457-2355
Museum of farm life & technology of the late 19th century; darying, haying, general store, ice cutting, apple orchard, etc.

Museum/Library

New York State Historical Association
and The Farmers' Museum, Inc., The
P.O. Box 800
Cooperstown, NY 13326
Phone: 607-547-2593 or 607-547-2533

Museum/Library

Landis Valley Farm Museum
2451 Kissel Hill Rd.
Lancaster, PA 17601
Phone: 717-569-0401

Museum/Library

Carroll County Farm Museum
500 S. Center St.
Westminster, MD 21157
Phone: 301-848-7775
Focuses on Victoriana in rural America.

Museum/Library

National Agricultural Center & Hall of
Fame
W. Vernon, Dir.
630 Hall of Fame Dr.
Bonner Springs, KS 66012
Phone: 913-721-1075 or 913-721-3355
FAX: 913-721-1075
Collection of a wide range of farming and farm family related items: plows, tools, implements, art, dishes, schoolhouse items, etc.

Periodical

Newspaper: <u>Country Wagon Journal, The</u>
600 Otterhold Rd.
P.O. Box 331
West Milford, NJ 07480
Produced by folks who enjoy country values and like to work the soil; enjoyable articles and earthy tips.

Periodical

Magazine: <u>Farm Antiques News</u>
Gary Van Hoozer, Ed.
414 Main St.
P.O. Box 96
Tarkio, MO 64491-0096
Phone: 816-736-5668 or 816-736-4528
　　　　　　　　　　FAX: 816-736-5700
For collectors, restorers, traders of all types/sizes of old (pre-1950) farm items: tractors, horse & other machinery, toys, etc.

Cast Iron Seats

Club/Association

Cast Iron Seat Collectors Association
Newsletter: <u>CISCA Newsletter</u>
RFD #2, Box 40
Le Center, MN 56057
Phone: 612-357-6142 *

Expert

John Friedly, Jr.
Box 14
Ionia, MO 65335
Phone: 816-285-3451
*Interested in cast iron seats, box lids, tool boxes, corn planters, etc.; author of "Cast Iron Implement Seats." **

FARM MACHINERY

(see also ENGINES; HORSE-DRAWN VEHICLES; STEAM-OPERATED, Models & Equipment; TRACTORS & RELATED ITEMS)

Auction Service

Blaine Renzel
P.O. Box 222
Emigsville, PA 17318
Phone: 717-764-6412
Specializes in the sale of old and new farm machinery and equipment.

Auction Service

Waverly Sale Co.
Bill Dean
Box 355
Waverly, IA 50677
Phone: 319-352-3177
Specializes in the sale of old and new farm machinery and equipment.

Club/Association

Antique Engine, Tractor & Toy Club
Newsletter: <u>AETTC Newsletter</u>
David Semmel
Box 385, RT. #1 Pine Street
Slatington, PA 18080
Phone: 215-767-4768
Organized in 1986 with over 425 members; dedicated to preservation and enjoyment of old time farm engines, tractors and related toys.

Club/Association

Midwest Old Settlers & Threshers
Association
Newsletter: <u>Threshers Chaff</u>
Rt. 1 Threshers Rd.
Mt. Pleasant, IA 52641
Phone: 319-385-8937
*Interested in old steam equipment, threshers, gas engines, farm tractors, and other artifacts of early agriculture and pioneer days. **

Misc. Service

Austin's
Route 4, Box 241
Butler, MO 64730
Phone: 816-679-4080
Send $10 for a directory listing names, addresses, phone numbers of 600 used agri-parts yards; for new used and antique farm equipment.

Museum/Library

Mercer Museum of the Bucks County
Historical Society
Pine & Ashland Streets
Doylestown, PA 18901
Phone: 215-345-0210

Museum/Library

Makoti Threshers Museum
P.O. Box 94
Makoti, ND 58756
Phone: 701-726-5693

Periodical

Kelsey Publishing Ltd.
Magazine: <u>Stationary Engine</u>
Kelsey House, 77 High St.
Beckenham
Kent BR3 1AN England
A 28-page illustrated monthly magazine dealing with all types of gas engines, history, information, news and views, etc.

Periodical

Magazine: <u>Vintage Tractor Magazine</u>
Merrivale, Main Street
Carlton
Nuneaton CV13 OBZ England *

Periodical

Stemgas Publishing Co.
Magazine: <u>Iron Man Album</u>
P.O. Box 328
Lancaster, PA 17603
Phone: 717-392-0733　　　FAX: 717-392-1341
Carries articles, ads, auctions for steam traction machinery: tractors, threashers, trucks & automobiles, steam engines, etc.

Periodical

Stemgas Publishing Co.
Directory: <u>Steam & Gas Engine Show</u>
　　　<u>Directory</u>
P.O. Box 328
Lancaster, PA 17603
Phone: 717-392-0733　　　FAX: 717-392-1341
The annual show directory guides old-time farming enthusiasts to over 500 shows in the U.S. and Canada.

Periodical

Magazine: <u>Belt Pulley, The</u>
P.O. Box 83E
Nokomis, IL 62075
Features farm machinery, all makes and models, 1900;en1950; antique tractors, farm machinery and equipment.

Periodical

Magazine: <u>Magazine for Vintage Trucks &</u>
<u>Tractors</u>
P.O. Box 537
Severn, MD 21144 *

Periodical

Magazine: <u>Engineers & Engines</u>
1118 N. Raynor Ave.
Joliet, IL 60435 *

Periodical

Magazine: <u>Rusty Iron Monthly</u>
Shawn Rogers
P.O. Box 342
Sandwich, IL 60548
Focuses on the old iron marketplace: early gas and steam engines, tractors and related equipment.

Periodical

Magazine: <u>Strictly, I.C.</u>
25204 45th Ave. South
Kent, WA 98032 *

International Harvester

Club/Association

International Harvester Collectors
RR 2 Box 286
Winamac, IN 46996
An association of IH enthusiasts.

Salesman Samples

Collector

Allan Hoover
2133 14th St.
Peru, IL 61354
Wants samples of walking plows, hay mowers, hay rakes, bailors, cultivators, binders, reapers, windmills, silos, pitch forks, etc. *

Steam-Operated

Club/Association

Rough & Tumble Engineers' Historical
Association
Newsletter: Whistle
Box 9
Kinzers, PA 17535
Phone: 717-442-4249
Interested in gas and steam-operated engines and farm machinery. *

FAST FOODS COLLECTIBLES

(see also BURGER-SHAPED
COLLECTIBLES)

Expert

David Stone
P.O. Box 162281
Sacramento, CA 95816
Phone: 916-451-0243 *

Periodical

Newsletter: For Here Or To Go
David Stone
P.O. Box 162281
Sacramento, CA 95816
Phone: 916-451-0243

McDonald's

Club/Association

McDonald's Collectors Club
Jim Wolfe, Sec.
2315 Ross Dr.
Stow, OH 44224
Phone: 216-688-9343
Members focus on the collecting of all kinds of memorabilia, advertising and give-aways relating to McDonald's; Newsletter.

Collector

Meredith Williams
Box 633
Joplin, MO 64802
Phone: 417-624-2518 or 417-781-3855
Wants to buy McDonald's items: buttons, postcards, displays, old uniforms, kids clothes, Happy Meal boxes, toys, annual reports, etc.

Museum/Library

McDonald's Museum, The
400 Lee Street
Des Plaines, IL 60016

The first McDonald's; limited openings; across the street is an active McDonald's restaurant with lots of memorabilia.

Museum/Library

McDonald's World Corporate
Headquarters, The Ray Crock Museum
McDonald's Plaza
Oak Brook, IL 60521

Periodical

Newsletter: Collecting Tips Newsletter
Meredith Williams
Box 633
Joplin, MO 64802
Phone: 417-624-2518 or 417-781-3855
A monthly newsleter filled with up-to-date information about old and new McDonald's restaurant collectibles; also buy, sell and trade

FENCE COLLECTIBLES

(see also BARBED WIRE)

Collector

Larry Love
4125 Sperry
Dallas, TX 75214
Phone: 214-821-1688
Wants items advertising barb wire, gates and other fence related items: e.g. walking canes, salesman samples, patent models, etc. *

Museum/Library

Post Rock Museum, The
P.O. Box 473
La Crosse, KS 67548
Phone: 913-222-2719
Displays a variety of posts used to support barbed-wire fences.

FIGURINES

(see also ANIMAL COLLECTIBLES;
CERAMICS; COLLECTIBLES (MODERN);
REPAIRS & RESTORATIONS)

Dealer

Richard Hebel
Box 1116
Carmel, IN 46032
Phone: 317-848-2977
Wants limited edition collectibles. Wants old cameras, Spike Jones, '33 World's Fair Memorabilia. *

Boehm

Club/Association

Boehm Porcelain Society, The
P.O. Box 5051
Trenton, NJ 08638
Phone: 609-392-2207 or 800-257-9410
FAX: 609-392-1437
A Boehm manufacturer-sponsored club.

Club/Association

Boehm Guild Advisory
Magazine: Boehm Guild Advisory, The
P.O. Box 5051
Trenton, NJ 08638
Phone: 609-392-2207 or 800-257-9410
FAX: 609-392-1437

Dealer

Re Vann Galleries
Gwendolyn R. Van Zile
1501 Boardwalk at NY Ave.
Atlantic City, NJ 08401
Phone: 609-345-7474   FAX: 609-345-4398
Largest Boehm dealer in the U.S. Specializes in the Boehm secondary market.

Man./Prod./Dist.

Boehm Porcelain, Inc.
25 Fairfax St.
Trenton, NJ 08638
Phone: 609-392-2207 or 800-257-9410
FAX: 609-392-1437

Bossons

Club/Association

International Bossons Collectors
Society, Inc.
Newsletter: Bossons Briefs
Dr. Robert E. Davis, ExDir
21 John Maddox Drive
Rome, GA 30161
Phone: 404-232-1266
Bossons character heads or figurines.

Collector

Andy Jackson
823 Carlson Ave.
West Chester, PA 19382
Phone: 215-692-0269 or 215-272-7900
Wants all Bossons artware: face masks, dogs, animals and plaques; will buy, sell or trade.

Expert

Dr. Robert E. Davis
21 John Maddox Drive
Rome, GA 30161
Phone: 404-232-1266
Author of "The Imagical World of Bossons."

Cybis

Expert

Brinkley Interiors & Galleries
William Brinkley
401 S. Washington Ave.
McLeansboro, IL 62859
Specializes in Cybis porcelains; also Meissen, Dresden, and other European porcelains. *

Man./Prod./Dist.

Cybis Porcelains
65 Norman Ave.
Trenton, NJ 08618
Phone: 609-392-6074

Creates fine porcelain sculptures. Contact for purchasing or appraising limited or open edition figurines.

Hartland

Expert

Minnie Memories
Patrick Flynn
122 Shadywood Ave.
Mankato, MN 56001
Author of "Bobbin Head Dolls/Hartland Statues."

Hummel

(see also COLLECTIBLES (MODERN), Figurines (Goebel))

Club/Association

M.I. Hummel Club of Canada
100 Carnforth Road
Toronto
Ontario M4A2K7 Canada
Sales promotion and marketing arm of Goebel Canada; special Hummel editions available only through membership in M.I. Hummel Club.

Club/Association

M.I. Hummel Club
Newsletter: Insights
Goebel Plaze, Rte. 31
Pennington, NJ 08534-0011
Phone: 609-737-8777 or 800-666-2582
Oldest collectors club of its kind; members receive information on Hummel figurines, plates & bells history & artistry.

Club/Association

"Hummel" Collector's Club, Inc.
Newsletter: "Hummel" Collector's Club
  Quarterly
Dorothy Dous, Pres.
1261 University Dr.
Yardley, PA 19067-2857
Phone: 215-493-6204 or 215-493-6705
                    FAX: 215-321-7367
Specializing in M.I. Hummel figurines, plates and bells; fact filled newsletter includes new releases, discontinued and older figurines.

Collector

Audrey Domenick
7735 E. Jefferson Place
Denver, CO 80237
Phone: 303-779-5221 *

Dealer

Figurine Finders
Newsletter: Hummel Insider
Joe Idoni
20405 Cabana Dr.
Germantown, MD 20876
Phone: 301-972-3501 or 301-972-4985
                    FAX: 301-972-3275

Buying and selling 1 to 1000 pieces; largest dealer/collector; fair prices; many one of a kind; rare to current figurines.

Dealer

Cindy Oakes
34025 W. 6 Mile
Livonia, MI 48152
Phone: 313-591-3252
Wants complete set of Hummel plates; also Hummel figurines from crown mark to present.

Expert

Carl Luckey
R.R. 4, Box 301
Killen, AL 35645

Expert

Miller's Gift Gallery
Dean Genth
1322 N. Barron St.
Eaton, OH 45320
Phone: 513-456-4151   FAX: 513-456-3426
Offers replacements and loss claim analysis; author of the "Price Guide to M.I. Hummel"

Man./Prod./Dist.

Schmid, Inc.
55 Pacella Park Drive
Randolph, MA 02368
Phone: 617-961-3000   FAX: 617-986-8168
Distributor of collectibles including Hummel and Lowell Davis figurines, woodcarvings by Anri, Walt Disney, Beatrix Potter, etc.

Kaiser

Man./Prod./Dist.

Kaiser Porcelain (US) Inc.
2045 Niagara Falls Blvd.
Units 11 & 12
Niagara Falls, NY 14304
Phone: 716-297-2331   FAX: 716-297-2749

Lady

(see also BATHING BEAUTIES, Nudies & Naughties)

Collector

Ann M. Kerr
P.O. Box 437
Sidney, OH 45365
Phone: 513-492-6369
Always looking for fine quality lady figurines; must be signed and in perfect condition.

Lladro

Club/Association

Lladro Collectors Society
Magazine: Expressions
Hugh Robinson, Dir.
c/o Lladro Co.
43 West 57th Street
New York, NY 10019
Phone: 212-755-2377 or 800-345-5433
                    FAX: 212-758-1928
Focuses on the collectible Lladro figurines. Sponsored by Lladro Co.

Expert

Austin-Brown Gallery
Ted Brown
2410 East Airport Freeway
Irving, TX 75062

Man./Prod./Dist.

Lladro Co.
43 West 57th Street
New York, NY 10019
Phone: 212-755-2377 or 800-345-5433
                    FAX: 212-758-1928
Manufactures and distributes quality handcrafted porcelains from Valencia, Spain.

Museum/Library

Lladro Museum & Galleries
43 West 57th Street
New York, NY 10019
Phone: 212-755-2377 or 800-345-5433

Periodical

International Art Associates, Inc.
Newsletter: Work of Art
Joan Lewis
7-11 Legion Dr.
Valhalla, NY 10595
Phone: 914-948-4655   FAX: 914-948-4367
Focuses on secondary market Lladro prices; also auction prices and articles about the care, display and history of Lladro figurines.

Monks

Collector

Joseph
P.O. Box 32145
Oklahoma City, OK 73123
Wants monk-shaped character figurines.

Royal Doulton

Dealer

Colonial House Antiques
Stan Worrey
182 Front St.
Berea, OH 44017
Phone: 216-826-4169 or 800-344-9299
                    FAX: 216-826-0839
Specializes in old and new Royal Doulton figurines and character jugs.

FIREARMS

(see also ARMS & ARMOR; CIVIL WAR
ARTIFACTS; MILITARIA; POWDER
HORNS; TARGET SHOOTING
MEMORABILIA)

Auction Service

J.C. Devine, Inc. Auctioneers
Savage Road
P.O. Box 413
Milford, NH 03055
Phone: 603-673-4967   FAX: 603-672-0328
*Specializes in the sale of antique firearms and
edged weapons.* *

Collector

Bill Bramlett
Box 1105
Florence, SC 29503
Phone: 803-393-7390
Remington, Marlin, Peters, U.M.C., Winchester, pre-1935. *

Dealer

Ordnance Chest, The
P.O. Box 905
Madison, CT 06443
*Offers sales catalog of antique firearms, edged
weapons, accouterments, books, firearms parts,
images, posters, etc.*

Dealer

Ace Sporting Goods Inc.
88 S. Main St.
Washington, PA 15301
Buy, sell, trade antique and modern fire arms. *

Dealer

Donn's Gun Room
Route 309
Montgomeryville, PA 18936
Phone: 215-362-1257
*Wants rifles, pistols, swords, daggers, military
items, ammunition, binoculars, etc.* *

Dealer

Morton Swimmer
44 E. Randall St.
Baltimore, MD 21230
Phone: 301-727-2277
Wants antique guns; singles or collections. *

Dealer

Gun Center, The
William A. Kelley, Jr.
5831 Buckeystown Pike
Frederick, MD 21701
Phone: 301-694-6887
*A full service gun store offering special order services, gunsmithing, and firearms appraisals; buy,
sell, trade, consignment.*

Dealer

David Condon, Inc.
Dave Condon
Box 7
Middleburg, VA 22117
Phone: 703-687-5642 or 703-689-1363
Antique firearms bought and sold.

Dealer

Pete Montgomery
P.O. Box 194
Osteen, FL 32764
Phone: 305-321-3083
Wants antique guns; singles or collections. *

Dealer

Antique American Firearms
Douglas R. Carlson
P.O. Box 71035
Des Moines, IA 50325
Phone: 515-224-6552
*Offers antique firearms catalogs every 12 weeks;
hundreds of items per issue.*

Dealer

Seven Acres Antique Village & Museum
Randy Donley
8512 S. Union Rd.
Union, IL 60180
Phone: 815-923-2214
*Buys, sells and collects antique firearms of all
sorts.*

Dealer

Collectors Gun Shop
587 E. Main St.
Galesburg, IL 61401
Phone: 309-342-5800
*Wants antique firearms, Civil War carbines and
muskets, Colts, European muskets, Derringers,
Winchester, etc.*

Expert

Norm Flayderman
P.O. Box 2446
Ft. Lauderdale, FL 33303
Phone: 305-761-8855
Offers annual catalog of antique arms for sale.

Museum/Library

Springfield Armory National Historic
Site
1 Armory Square
Springfield, MA 01105
Phone: 413-734-6477

Museum/Library

National Firearms Museum
1600 Rhode Island Ave.
Washington, DC 20036
Phone: 202-828-6194

Museum/Library

Seven Acres Antique Village & Museum
Randy Donley
8512 S. Union Rd.
Union, IL 60180
Phone: 815-923-2214

Museum/Library

Herman's House of Guns
P.O. Box 191
Dorris, CA 96023
Phone: 916-397-2611

Periodical

Magazine: Gun Week
P.O. Box 488
Buffalo, NY 14209
*Covers all aspects of the shooting sport: new products, hunting regulations, gun legislation, shows
and collecting.*

Periodical

National Rifle Association
Magazine: American Rifleman
1600 Rhode Island Ave. NW
Washington, DC 20036
Phone: 202-828-6000 *

Periodical

Krause Publications, Inc.
Newspaper: Gun List
Bob Lemke, Pub.
700 East State St.
Iola, WI 54990
Phone: 800-258-0929 or 715-445-2214
                    FAX: 715-445-4087
*Huge marketplace for buying/selling collectible
firearms; over 50,000 guns in each issue.*

Periodical

Krause Publications, Inc.
Magazine: Gun Show Calendar
Bob Lemke, Pub.
700 East State St.
Iola, WI 54990
Phone: 800-258-0929 or 715-445-2214
                    FAX: 715-445-4087
*Largest listing of gun shows available; lists shows
throughout the U.S. and Canada; listings updated quarterly.*

Periodical

World-Wide Gun Report, Inc.
Magazine: Gun Report, The
P.O. Box 38
Aledo, IL 61231-0038
Phone: 309-582-5311
*The monthly magazine serving the antique and
semi-modern gun collector and dealer for over 35
years.*

Periodical

Snell Publishing Co., Inc.
Newspaper: Shotgun News
P.O. Box 669
Hastings, NE 68902
Phone: 800-345-6923
*The trading post for guns, bows (anything that shoots) and accessories. ***

Periodical

Magazine: Machine Gun News
201-C Franklin
P.O. Box 761
Hot Springs, AR 71913
Phone: 501-623-9832 or 501-623-4951
A monthly magazine providing a centralized source of information about automatic weapons for the shooting and collecting public.

Periodical

Magazine: Arms Gazette
13063 Ventura Blvd.
Studio City, CA 91604
*A magazine about guns. ***

Periodical

Magazine: Sporting Gun
Jim Lance
c/o Publishers Mini Systems
P.O. Box 301369
Escondido, CA 92030-9957
Phone: 619-747-8327   FAX: 619-432-6560
British magazine covers technical questions on clay & field shooting, competition coverage, and reviews of guns, cartridges & equipment.

Supplier

Knife & Gun Finishing Supplies
P.O. Box 13522
Arlington, TX 76013
Carries equipment and supplies for buffing, polishing, and making guns.

Colt

Collector

Coltania
7831 Peachtree Ave.
Panorama City, CA 91402
Wants Colt factory items: original catalogs, pamphlets, advertising & promotional, books, posters: anything Colt, his factory or guns.

Gunsmithing

Repair Service

Gun Center, The
William A. Kelley, Jr.
5831 Buckeystown Pike
Frederick, MD 21701
Phone: 301-694-6887
Offers a full line of gunsmithing services: repair, hot blueing, custom metal and stock work, etc.

Repair Service

Dilliott Gunsmithing, Inc.
Route 3, Box 3430
Dandridge, TN 37725
Phone: 615-397-9204
Repair and restoration of antique firearms; make obsolete parts; bluing and parkerizing.

Repair Service

Scott's Creek Armory, Inc.
Richard Binger
Rt. 1, Box 70
Morgantown, IN 46160
Phone: 317-878-5489
Buys and sells flintlocks and cartridge rifles and muskets; specializing in gunsmithing and restoration.

Japanese Matchlock

Collector

Mark Fletcher
P.O. Box 1526
Hampton, VA 23661
Phone: 804-244-1442
Collects Japanese matchlock and Japanese percussion firearms; also antique guns with Japanese markings.

Collector

Raymond Macy
P.O. Box 11
W. Alex, OH 45381
Phone: 513-839-5721
Wants Japanese swords, daggers, sword parts, matchlock guns, anything samurai.

Machine Guns

Dealer

J. Curtis Earl
5512 North Sixth Street
Phoenix, AZ 85102
Phone: 802-264-3166
A knowledgeable dealer of machine guns. Issues catalogs that are of interest to the beginning collector and to the advanced collector.

Pistols

Club/Association

National Automatic Pistol Collectors
Association
Newsletter: Auto Mag
P.O. Box 15738
St. Louis, MO 63163
Phone: 314-771-1160
For the automatic hand gun enthusiast.

Remington

Museum/Library

Remington Gun Museum
P.O. Box 179
Ilion, NY 13357
Phone: 315-895-9961

Affiliated with the Remington Arms Company, Inc.

Rifles

Expert

Scott's Creek Armory, Inc.
Richard Binger
Rt. 1, Box 70
Morgantown, IN 46160
Phone: 317-878-5489
Member NRA, life member American Single Shot Rifle Assn., National Muzzle Loading Rifle Assn., Ohio Gun Collectors Assn.

Winchester

Club/Association

Winchester Arms Collectors Association,
Inc.
Journal: Winchester, The
Robert A. Berg
P.O. Box 6754
Great Falls, MT 59406
Phone: 406-452-5315 or 406-771-8948
For collectors of Winchester firearms, ammunitions, and accessories.

Dealer

LeRoy Merz
Rt. 1, Nirschi Addition #3
Fergus Falls, MN 56537
Phone: 218-739-3255
Wants to buy fine antique Winchesters.

Museum/Library

Winchester Mystery House, Historic
Firearms Museum
525 South Winchester Blvd.
San Jose, CA 95128
Phone: 408-247-2000

FIREBACKS

Repro. Source

New England Firebacks
P.O. Box 162
Woodbury, CT 06798
Phone: 203-263-4328
Makes and sells reproduction solid cast iron firebacks.

FIRECRACKERS

(see also FIREWORKS MEMORABILIA)

FIRE FIGHTING MEMORABILIA

Auction Service

Maritime Auctions
Chuck Deluca
P.O. Box 322
York, ME 03909
Phone: 207-363-4247
Author of "Firehouse Memorabilia - A Collector's Reference."

Club/Association
Fire Bell Club of New York
Newsletter: Bell Club News Notes
150 E. 23rd St.
New York, NY 10010
Phone: 212-505-2681 *

Club/Association
Fire Collectors Club
Newsletter: FCC Newsletter
David Cerull
P.O. Box 992
Milwaukee, WI 53201
Collectors of Fire Service memorabilia: patches,
badges, medals, helmets, stamps, etc.

Club/Association
National Historical Fire Foundation
6101 E. Van Buren
Phoenix, AZ 85008
Phone: 602-275-3473 *

Collector
M. Gimley
P.O. Box 244
Oakland, NJ 07436
Wants items from the 1800's to 1920's: gold &
silver badges, buckets, engine lights, helmets,
lanterns, tintypes, statues of firemen, etc.

Collector
Jonathan Thomas
1208 Main St.
Southbury, CT 06488-2159
Wants to buy and trade firemen's hats, trumpets,
photos, scale model fire equipment, signs and
posters.

Collector
Joe Fox
39 Willowlawn
Cheektowaga, NY 14206
Phone: 716-824-5327
Wants fireman's lanterns, helmets, badges, trum-
pets, etc. *

Collector
David Cerull
P.O. Box 992
Milwaukee, WI 53201
Wants Fire Service medals from any country; send
detailed description, rubbing or photocopy along
with price.

Dealer
Cary Station Antiques
Robert H. Harper
22 Spring St.
Cary, IL 60013
Phone: 708-639-7434
Wants helmets, trumpets, presentation badges,
painted leather buckets, lamps, parade hats,
alarm equipment, etc.

Expert
Little Century
H. Thomas & Pat Laun
215 Paul Ave.
Syracuse, NY 13206
Phone: 315-437-4156 or 315-654-3244
Buys and sells fire related antiques and collect-
ibles, any number; supplies and manufactures
parts for firematic items; also

Museum/Library
New England Fire & History Museum
1439 Main St.
Brewster, MA 02631
Phone: 617-896-5711

Museum/Library
New York City Fire Museum, The
Newsletter: Housewatch, The
278 Spring St.
New York, NY 10013
Phone: 212-691-1303

Museum/Library
American Museum of Fire Fighting
Box 413
Corton Falls, NY 10519
Phone: 518-828-7695
The mailing address is as noted above, but located
on Harry Howard Ave., Hudson, NY.

Museum/Library
Hershey Museum
James McMahon
170 W. Hersheypark Dr.
Hershey, PA 17033
Phone: 717-534-3439
Focused collection of objects detailing the town of
Hershey history, regional PA German heritage,
native American material culture.

Museum/Library
Fire Museum of Maryland
1301 York Rd.
Lutherville, MD 21093
Phone: 301-321-7500

Museum/Library
Oklahoma Firefighters Museum
P.O. Box 11507
Oklahoma City, OK 73136
Phone: 405-424-3440

Museum/Library
Hall of Flame
3634 Civic Center Plaza
Scottsdale, AZ 85251
Phone: 602-275-3473
Mailing address is as noted above, but located at
6101 E. Van Buren, Phoenix, AZ.

Museum/Library
San Francisco Fire Deptartment Memorial
Museum
260 Golden Gate Ave.
San Francisco, CA 94102
Phone: 415-861-8000

Repair Service
Little Century
H. Thomas & Pat Laun
215 Paul Ave.
Syracuse, NY 13206
Phone: 315-437-4156 or 315-654-3244
Repairs fire fighting antiques and collectibles;
wood and metal parts fabricated.

Apparatus
Club/Association
Society for the Preservation of Antique
Motor Fire Apparatus in America
Newsletter: Engine! Engine!
P.O. Box 2005
Syracuse, NY 13220
Phone: 914-343-4219 *

Collector
Bob Ward
365 Neiffer Rd.
Schwenksville, PA 19473
Phone: 215-287-9495

FIRE INSURANCE RELATED
COLLECTIBLES
(see also FIRE MARKS)

Collector
Third Alarm
Box 805
Orleans, MA 02653
Wants fire insurance memorabilia: old signs, fire
marks, pre-1900 policies, blotters, paper weights,
etc. *

FIRE MARKS
Club/Association
Fire Mark Circle of the Americas, The
Newsletter: Fire Mark Circle of the Americas
    Newsletter, The
Glenn Hartley
2859 Marlin Dr.
Chamblee, GA 30341-5119
Phone: 404-451-2651
Contains club news, auction prices, and articles
about fire marks.

Collector
Third Alarm
Box 805
Orleans, MA 02653
Wants fire insurance memorabilia: old signs, fire
marks, pre-1900 policies, blotters, paper weights,
etc. *

FIREWORKS MEMORABILIA

Collector

Collectors Exchange, Inc.
Barry Zecker
P.O. Box 1022
Mountainside, NJ 07092
Phone: 908-232-6100
Wants old firecracker packs, labels, catalogs, salesmen's display boards and samples, sparkler and cap boxes; any related artifacts.

Collector

Stuart Schneider
P.O. Box 64
Teaneck, NJ 07666
Phone: 201-261-1983
Wants old firecracker pack labels.

Collector

R. Scheurer
1 Milburn Rd. R.D. #3
Goshen, NY 10924
*Wants firecrackers, packs, labels, catalogs; also Fourth of July memorabilia; prior to 1967. ***

Collector

Ricks
740 Southampton
Auburn Hills, MI 48057
*Wants old fireworks packs, labels, catalogs, etc. ***

Collector

William Scales
130 Fordham Circle
Pueblo, CO 81005
Phone: 719-561-0603
Especially wants old firecracker packs, labels, catalogs, etc.

Collector

Dennis
Box 2010
Saratoga, CA 95070
Phone: 408-996-1963
*Wants fireworks catalogs, firecracker packs, salute boxes, 4th of July toys, cannons, cap pistols (cast iron), posters; collections. ***

Expert

Karen Lea Rose
4420 Wisconsin Ave.
Tampa, FL 33616-1031
Phone: 813-839-6245
Wants old packs of fireworks or old firecracker catalogs.

FISHING COLLECTIBLES

(see also DECOYS, Fish; SPORTING
COLLECTIBLES)

Auction Service

Richard A. Bourne Auction Co., Inc.
P.O. Box 141
Hyannis Port, MA 02647
Phone: 508-775-0797

Auction Service

Richard W. Withington, Inc.
R.D. 2, Box 440
Hillsboro, NH 03244
Phone: 603-464-3232

Club/Association

National Fishing Lure Collectors Club
Newsletter: NFLCC Gazette
Rich Treml, Sec.
P.O. Box 1791
Dearborn, MI 48121
Phone: 313-842-2589
3000 members; fosters awareness of lure collecting as a hobby; assists members in identification, location and valuing lures, etc.

Collector

Collector
P.O. Box 784
Blairstown, NJ 07825
Phone: 201-362-9168 *

Collector

Collector
6 Carol Ave.
Fredonia, NY 14063
*Wants fishing tackle, old lures, fish decoys, reels, catalogs, advertising pieces, etc. ***

Collector

Mike Royster
418 Beechtree Rd.
Columbus, OH 43213
Phone: 614-239-8079
*Old fishing items, lures, reels, pre-1950. ***

Collector

James Anderson
P.O. Box 12704
New Brighton, MN 55112
Phone: 612-484-3198
Wants old fishing related items: lures, reels, posters, calendars, pins, envelopes, bobbers, etc.

Collector

Randy Deerdoff
10222 Lafferty Oaks
Houston, TX 77013
*Wants lures, fly rods, reels, tackle boxes, fish hooks, bobbers, etc. ***

Dealer

Bob & Shirley's Antiques
Bob Greenbaum
6151 Beverly Hills Rd.
Coopersburg, PA 18036
Phone: 215-282-4881
Wants all items related to the sport of fishing.

Dealer

Nick's Wood Shop
John E. Shoffner
624 Merritt St.
Fife Lake, MI 49633
Phone: 616-879-3912
Issues 6 lists a year with approx. 600 fish decoys and antique fishing tackle items for sale.

Expert

Al Munger
2235 Ritter St.
Philadelphia, PA 19125 *

Expert

David A. Gladwell
P.O. Box 238
Bedford, VA 24523
Phone: 703-586-1488 or 703-586-9575
Wants old fishing tackle, especially lures or plugs.

Expert

Fishing Co., The
J.L. Smith
P.O. Box 142
Westerville, OH 43081

Expert

Aardvark Publications
Jim Art
P.O. Box 252
Boulder Junction, WI 54512 *

Expert

Bean Town Antiques
Randy Hilst
1221 Florence #4
Pekin, IL 61554
Phone: 309-346-2710
*Wants lures, rods, reels; also old wooden duck calls. ***

Expert

Gabby Talkington
4703 Upland Dr.
Richmond, CA 94803
Phone: 415-223-1142 or 415-273-3268
Longtime buyer/seller of vintage fishing tackle: wood fishing lures, reels, rods, advertising and catalogs; sale list available.

Museum/Library

American Museum of Fly Fishing
Magazine: American Fly Fisher, The
P.O. Box 42
Manchester, VT 05254
Phone: 802-362-3300
Non-profit educational institution dedicated to preserving the rich history of fly fishing and American angling.

Museum/Library

National Fresh Water Fishing Hall of
Fame
Newsletter: Splash, The
One Fame Drive
P.O. Box 33
Hayward, WI 54843
Phone: 716-634-4440
*Custodian of historical sport fishing artifacts;
world record qualifier; clearinghouse for contemporary & historical fishing facts.*

Periodical

Newsletter: Antique Angler
P.O. Box K
Stockton, NJ 08559-0350 *

Periodical

Newsletter: Sporting Classics
P.O. Box 1017
Camden, SC 29020 *

Reels

Collector

Royal E. Fox
64 Colifield
Staten Island, NY 10302
*Wants spinning reels; working or not; parts,
boxes, literature, brochures, manuals.*

FLAGS & RELATED COLLECTIBLES

Club/Association

Flag Research Center
Newsletter: Flag Bulletin
P.O. Box 580
Winchester, MA 01890
Phone: 617-729-9410
*A research center specializing in information
about national and international flags. **

Club/Association

North American Vexillological
Association
3 Edgehill Road
Winchester, MA 01890 *

Collector

Tom Rentschler
1030 New London Rd.
Hamilton, OH 45013
Phone: 513-863-8633
*Wants U.S. flags; also Army Navy "E" flags
(WWII flag given industry for efficient production.) **

Collector

Mark Sutton
2035 St. Andrews Circle
Carmel, IN 46032
Phone: 317-844-5648
*Buys/trades old cloth American flags with 47 or
less than 45 stars; wants original flags from 6" to
HUGE; also unusual star patterns.*

Expert

Dan Grégor
P.O. Box 398
Gettysburg, PA 17325 *

Expert

Stars & Stripes
Robert Banks
18901 Gold Mine Court
Brookeville, MD 20833
Phone: 301-774-7850
*Seeking antique American flags with 37 stars or
less; also wants unique of uncommon examples of
any period.*

Expert

Dick Bitterman
1701 West Chase Ave.
Chicago, IL 60626
Phone: 312-743-3330 *

Museum/Library

Tumbling Waters Museum of Flags, Inc.
P.O. Drawer O
Prattville, AL 36067
Phone: 205-365-7392

FLASHLIGHTS

Collector

Kent Myers
Box 4074
Cave Creek, AZ 85331
Phone: 602-488-1616
*Flashlight collector wants to buy pre-1920
flashlights, related literature, etc.; please send
photo and price.*

Collector

Bill Utley
7616 Brookmill Rd.
Downey, CA 90241
*Wants flashlights or catalogs from flashlight companies. **

FLATWARE

(see also SILVER; SILVERPLATE;
TABLEWARE)

Dirilyte

Matching Service

Mrs. Kay's Sterling, Stainless &
Silverplate
Dept. JA1-92
P.O. Box 74184
Los Angeles, CA 90004-0184
Phone: 213-661-6279
*Matching service for DISCONTINUED
FLATWARE only; takes trade-in's; does insurance appraisals; nation-wide network of pickers,
suppliers.*

Silverplate

Matching Service

Barron's
P.O. Box 994
Novi, MI 48376
Phone: 800-538-6340

Matching Service

Walter Drake Silver & China Exchange
94 Drake Building
Colorado Springs, CO 80940
Phone: 719-596-3140 or 800-525-9291
　　　　　　　　　　　FAX: 719-593-5321
*Active and inactive silver and china tableware
replacements. For their Insurance Replacement
Department call 800-525-2274.*

Matching Service

Mrs. Kay's Sterling, Stainless &
Silverplate
Dept. JA1-92
P.O. Box 74184
Los Angeles, CA 90004-0184
Phone: 213-661-6279
*Matching service for DISCONTINUED
FLATWARE only; takes trade-in's; does insurance appraisals; nation-wide network of pickers,
suppliers.*

Matching Service

Abbey's Perfect Match
Attn: Coleen
P.O. Box 75603
Los Angeles, CA 90075
Phone: 213-913-3472
*Purchases store closeouts of discontinued flatware;
also offers great discounts on current patterns.*

Stainless Steel

Matching Service

Barron's
P.O. Box 994
Novi, MI 48376
Phone: 800-538-6340

Matching Service

Mrs. Kay's Sterling, Stainless &
Silverplate
Dept. JA1-92
P.O. Box 74184
Los Angeles, CA 90004-0184
Phone: 213-661-6279
*Matching service for DISCONTINUED
FLATWARE only; takes trade-in's; does insurance appraisals; nation-wide network of pickers,
suppliers.*

Matching Service

Abbey's Perfect Match
Attn: Coleen
P.O. Box 75603
Los Angeles, CA 90075
Phone: 213-913-3472

Purchases store closeouts of discontinued flatware; also offers great discounts on current patterns.

Sterling Silver

Expert

Maryanne Dolan
138 Belle Avenue
Pleasant Hill, CA 94523
Phone: 415-935-2366
Author of "American Sterling Silver Flatware."

Matching Service

Ross Simmons
136 Route 5
Warwick, RI 02886
Phone: 401-463-3100 or 800-556-7376
                FAX: 401-463-8599
Sells new, active patterns for Gorham, Reed & Barton, Wallace, Towle, Lunt, Kirk-Stieff, International.

Matching Service

R.S. Goldberg
67 Beverly Rd.
Hawthorne, NJ 07506
Phone: 800-252-6655
Hundreds of patterns in stock; always buying and selling.

Matching Service

Thurber's
2158 Plainfield Pike, Unit 1
Cranston, RI 02921
Phone: 401-942-0488 or 800-848-7237
                FAX: 401-942-5601

Matching Service

Lanac Sales
73 Canal St.
New York, NY 10002
Phone: 212-925-6422 *

Matching Service

Past & Presents
65-07 Fitchess St.
Rego Park, NY 11374
Phone: 718-896-5146
Matching and locating service for Coalport, Derby, Franciscan, Gorham, Lenox, Metlox, Mikasa, Minton, Noritake, and others.

Matching Service

Edward G. Wilson Inc.
Edward Wilson
1802 Chestnut St.
Philadelphia, PA 19103
Phone: 215-563-7369
Replaces active, inactive, and obsolete sterling and coin silver.

Matching Service

Kent Lambert
113 N. Charles St.
Baltimore, MD 21202
Phone: 301-355-3390 *

Matching Service

Replacements Ltd.
Lea Ann Mills
P.O. Box 26029
Greensboro, NC 27420
Phone: 919-697-3000   FAX: 919-697-3100
China, crystal and flatware (obsolete, active and inactive).

Matching Service

Beverly Bremer Silver Shop
3164 Peachtree Road NE
Atlanta, GA 30305
Phone: 404-261-4009
Appraises, buys, sells and matches sterling silver flatware; also buys and sells new and antique sterling silver holloware & giftware.

Matching Service

Abrahante's Tableware Matching Service
Suite 209
7175 SW 47th St.
Miami, FL 33155
Phone: 305-661-1456
American, English and Japanese manufacturers of discontinued patterns of china, crystal and flatware.

Matching Service

Barron's
P.O. Box 994
Novi, MI 48376
Phone: 800-538-6340

Matching Service

Jane Rosenow
Rt. #1, Box 177
Galva, IL 61434
Phone: 309-932-3953
*100's of patterns. *

Matching Service

Locators, Inc.
908 Rock St.
Little Rock, AR 72202
Phone: 501-371-0858 or 800-367-9690
Carries out-of-production (discontinued) china and crystal, and discontinued as well as active sterling flatware patterns.

Matching Service

Walter Drake Silver & China Exchange
94 Drake Building
Colorado Springs, CO 80940
Phone: 719-596-3140 or 800-525-9291
                FAX: 719-593-5321
Active and inactive silver and china tableware replacements. For their Insurance Replacement Department call 800-525-2274.

Matching Service

Mrs. Kay's Sterling, Stainless & Silverplate
Dept. JA1-92
P.O. Box 74184
Los Angeles, CA 90004-0184
Phone: 213-661-6279
Matching service for DISCONTINUED FLATWARE only; takes trade-in's; does insurance appraisals; nation-wide network of pickers, suppliers.

Matching Service

Silver Lane Antiques
P.O. Box 322
San Leandro, CA 94577
Phone: 415-483-0632
Buys and sells discontinued patterns by major American and English china companies; also American sterling flatware.

Matching Service

Sterling Shop, The
P.O. Box 595
Silverton, OR 97381
Phone: 503-873-6315
Sterling and silverplate flatware matching service.

Matching Service

Patterns Unlimited International
Warren & Betty Roundhill
Dept. CIC
P.O. Box 15238
Seattle, WA 98115
Phone: 206-523-9710
Buy, sell and appraise discontinued tableware patterns of china, silver and glass.

FLOORCLOTHS

Repro. Source

Olde Virginia Floorcloth & Trading Co.
Sharon & Roger Mason
6605 Richmond Rd.
P.O. Box 438
Williamsburg, VA 23185
Phone: 804-564-0600 or 804-488-7299
Painted canvas floorcloths created in 18th cent. style; 100% cotton canvas heavily primed, decorated with oils, varnished; supplies.

Repro. Source

Home Place Collections'
Rt. 3, Box 697
Thomasville, NC 27360
*Offers hand-painted canvas floorcloths. *

FLORIDA COLLECTIBLES

Collector

Dan McKenna
Box 2357
De Land, FL 32721
*Wants anything related to Florida: pre-1925 photos, stereoviews, paintings, prints, souvenirs, promotional material, etc. *

FLOWER "FROGS"

Collector

Dr. William G. Sommer, MD
9 W. 10th St.
New York, NY 10011
Phone: 212-260-0999
Wants ceramic figural flower "frogs": dancing ladies or nudes American (Cowan, Fulper, Rookwood) or European (Germany, England).

FOLK ART

(see also CAROUSELS; COVERLETS; DECOYS; EAGLES; FIRE MARKS; FRAKTURS; QUILTS; RUGS, Hooked; SAMPLERS; SCRIMSHAW; SILHOUETTES; TRAMP ART)

Club/Association

Folk Art Society of America
Newsletter: Folk Art Messenger
P.O. Box 17041
Richmond, VA 23226
Non-profit organization formed to discover, study, promote, preserve, exhibit, and document folk art, folk artists, and their environment.

Dealer

Steven Score Antiques
Steven Score
159 Main St.
Essex, MA 01929

Dealer

RJG Antiques
Russ & Karen Goldberger
P.O. Box 2033
Hampton, NH 03842
Phone: 603-926-1770
Specializes in quality working decoys, folk art and original American paintings.

Dealer

Kenneth & Ida Manko
P.O. Box 20
Moody, ME 04054 *

Dealer

Gary Guyette
Box 522
W. Farmington, ME 04992
Phone: 207-778-6256

Dealer

Marguerite Riordan Antiques
Marguerite Riordan
8 Pearl Street
Stonington, CT 06378
Phone: 203-535-2511 or 203-535-3431
                          FAX: 203-535-3431
Specializes in Folk Art, American furniture, paintings and decorative accessories; by appointment.

Dealer

Peter H. Tillou Fine Arts
Prospect Street
Litchfield, CT 06759
Phone: 203-567-5706

Dealer

American Hurrah Antiques
766 Madison Avenue
New York, NY 10021
Phone: 212-535-1930

Dealer

America's Folk Heritage Gallery
Jay Johnson
1044 Madison Avenue
New York, NY 10021
Phone: 212-628-7280

Dealer

Muleskinner Antiques
10626 Main Street
Clarence, NY 14031
Buys and sells redware, antique lighting, fold art, game boards, primitives, weathervanes, early glass, decoys, trade signs, etc.

Dealer

Fae B. Haight Antiques
P.O. Box 294
Lahaska, PA 18931 *

Dealer

Old Hope Antiques, Inc.
Edwin Hild
Box 209, Route 202
New Hope, PA 18938
Phone: 215-862-5055

Dealer

M. Finkel & Daughter
936 Pine Street
Philadelphia, PA 19107
Phone: 215-627-7797   FAX: 215-627-8199

Dealer

John C. Newcomer & Assoc.
John C. Newcomer
P.O. Box 130
Funkstown, MD 21734
Phone: 301-790-1327

Dealer

Main Street Antiques and Art
Louis Picek
110 West Main
Box 340
West Branch, IA 52358
Phone: 319-643-2065
Buys and sells folk art; offers a monthly list of items for sale.

Dealer

Frank & Barbara Pollack
1214 Green Bay Road
Highland Park, IL 60035
Phone: 312-433-2213
Buys and sells American primitives: paintings, furniture, toleware, folk art, textiles, etc.

Expert

Fendelman & Schwartz
Helaine Fendelman
1248 Post Rd.
Scarsdale, NY 10583
Phone: 914-725-0292
Appraises and liquidates estates; author of the "Official Identification and Price Guide to American Folk Art."

Museum/Library

Fruitlands Museums, Inc.
Robert D. Farwell, Dir.
102 Prospect Hill Rd.
Harvard, MA 01451
Phone: 508-456-3924
A 19th century American art and history museum complex.

Museum/Library

Boston Museum of Fine Arts, The
465 Huntington Avenue
Boston, MA 02115
Phone: 617-267-9300

Museum/Library

Yale University Art Gallery, Garvan Collection
Box 2006 Yale Station
New Haven, CT 06520
Phone: 203-432-0600

Museum/Library

Museum of American Folk Art
61 W. 62nd St.
New York, NY 10023
Phone: 212-977-7170

Museum/Library

New York Historical Society, The
170 Central Part West
New York, NY 10024
Phone: 212-873-3400   FAX: 212-874-8706
An unparalleled resource for the study and appreciation of American art, history, and culture.

Museum/Library

Albany Institute of History & Art
125 Washington Avenue
Albany, NY 12210
Phone: 518-463-4478

Museum/Library
New York State Historical Association
and The Farmers' Museum, Inc., The
P.O. Box 800
Cooperstown, NY 13326
Phone: 607-547-2533 or 607-547-2533

Museum/Library
Landis Valley Farm Museum
2451 Kissel Hill Rd.
Lancaster, PA 17601
Phone: 717-569-0401

Museum/Library
Mercer Museum of the Bucks County
Historical Society
Pine & Ashland Streets
Doylestown, PA 18901
Phone: 215-345-0210

Museum/Library
Pennsylvania Academy of Fine Arts
1301 Cherry St.
Philadelphia, PA 19102
Phone: 215-972-7600

Museum/Library
Historical Society of Pennsylvania
1300 Locust Street
Philadelphia, PA 19107
Phone: 215-732-6200

Museum/Library
Daughters of the American Revolution
Museum
1776 D Street NW
Washington, DC 20006
Phone: 202-879-3254

Museum/Library
National Museum of American History
14th & Constitution Ave. NW
Washington, DC 20560
Phone: 202-357-2700

Museum/Library
Abby Aldrich Rockefeller Folk Art
Center
P.O. Box C
Williamsburg, VA 23187
Phone: 804-220-7670

Museum/Library
Museum of Early Southern Decorative
Arts
Journal: Journal of Early Southern Decorative
Arts
P.O. Box 10310
Winston-Salem, NC 27108
Phone: 919-722-6148
*Focuses on Southern decorative arts; has Research
Center, Catalog of Early Southern Decorative
Arts, and Index of Southern Artists.*

Museum/Library
Bayou Bend Collection, The
P.O. Box 130157
Houston, TX 77219
Phone: 713-529-8773

Museum/Library
Museum of International Folk Art
P.O. Box 2087
Santa Fe, NM 87504
Phone: 505-827-8350

Periodical
Museum of American Folk Art
Magazine: Clarion, The
61 W. 62nd St.
New York, NY 10023
Phone: 212-977-7170

Contemporary

Museum/Library
Craft & Folk Art Museum
Joan M. Bendetti, Lib.
6067 Wilshire Blvd.
Los Angeles, CA 90036
Phone: 213-937-5544 or 213-934-7239
　　　　　　　　　　FAX: 213-937-5576
*Specializing in contemporary craft, design, folk
art: clay, fiber, wood, glass, paper, costume, dolls,
masks, etc.; artist's registry.*

Periodical
Gallery Press
Newsletter: Folk Art Finder
117 N. Main St.
Essex, CT 06426
Phone: 203-767-0313
*FAF is devoted to news and information on con-
temporary folk art; calendar, feature stories,
readers exchange, new artists, ads, etc.*

Southern

Dealer
Adams Et Al, Inc.
Joe Adams
P.O. Box 3075
Hilton Head, SC 29928
Phone: 803-785-7100　　FAX: 803-671-9107
*Wants Southern Folk Art (paintings, carvings,
etc.), crafts by Southern artisans (contemporary
and antique), slave quilts.*

Tinware

Museum/Library
Cooper-Hewitt Museum, The Smithsonian
Institution's Nat. Museum of Design
2 East 91st St.
New York, NY 10128
Phone: 212-860-6868

Weathervanes

Museum/Library
Heritage Plantation of Sandwich
P.O. Box 566
Sandwich, MA 02563
Phone: 617-888-3300

Repro. Source
Copper House, The
R.R. 1, Box 4
Epsom, NH 03234
Phone: 603-736-9798
*Handmade copper reproduction lighting fixtures
and weathervanes. No imports. Catalog $3 de-
ducted from purchase.*

Repro. Source
Ivan Barnett Collection
RD #1
Stevens, PA 17578
Phone: 717-738-1590
Handmade weathervanes of metal and wood. *

FOOD COLLECTIBLES

Museum/Library
World Food Museum, The
Journal: World Food
Meredith & Tom Hughes
P.O. Box 791
Great Falls, VA 22066
Phone: 703-759-6714
*Forming a network with other food museums and
collections; seek all collectibles, ephemera and
crafts relating to food.*

Chili

Misc. Service
National Chili Museum
Chuck Thompson
P.O. Box 11652
Houston, TX 77293
Phone: 713-442-7200
*Displays chili related memorabilia; old and un-
usual labels, photos, advertisements, chili parlor
menus, books, and other ephemera.*

Chuck Wagon Related

Misc. Service
Food Celebrity Service
Newsletter: Packaged Chili & Jerky Report
Chuck Thompson
P.O. Box 11652
Houston, TX 77293
Phone: 713-442-7200
*Cowboy Chuck Wagon food researcher, historian,
storyteller; wants postcards of old chuck wagons;
columnist and lecturer.*

Fake Food

Man./Prod./Dist.

Fake Food
Box 184
Telford, PA 18969
The first food-art product line of this kind in the country; pies, miniature fake food products, etc.

FORD MOTOR COMPANY ITEMS

Collector

Tim O'Callaghan
46878 Bettyhill
Plymouth, MI 48170
Phone: 313-459-4636
Buys, sells, trades all Ford Motor Company memorabilia: postcards, books, pins, badges, etc.

FOSSILS

(see also ARCHAEOLOGICAL ARTIFACTS; MINERALS; NATURAL HISTORY; PREHISTORIC ARTIFACTS)

Dealer

Langs' Fossils & Meteorites
326 Manor Ave.
Cranford, NJ 07016
Phone: 201-276-2155 *

Dealer

American Fossil Company
121-12 Dupont Street
Plainview, NY 11803 *

Dealer

J.F. Ray
P.O. Box 1364
Ocala, FL 32678
Catalog sales of fossils; supplies museums, shops, schools; since 1962.

Dealer

Rich Relics
Richard B. Troyanowski
P.O. Box 432
Sandia Park, NM 87047
Phone: 505-281-2611 or 505-281-2329
Buys/sells prehistoric/historic Indian artifacts, cowboy, militaria, old world antiquities & coins, fossils & ethnographic collectibles.

Museum/Library

Fick Fossil & History Museum
700 W. 3rd St.
Oakley, KS 67748
Phone: 913-672-4839

Museum/Library

John Day Fossil Beds National Monument
420 W. Main St.
John Day, OR 97845
Phone: 503-575-0721

FOURTH OF JULY ITEMS

(see also FIREWORKS MEMORABILIA; HOLIDAY COLLECTIBLES)

FRAKTURS

(see also FOLK ART)

Expert

Family Album, The
Ron Lieberman
R.D. 1, Box 42
Glen Rock, PA 17327
Phone: 717-235-2134   FAX: 717-235-8042
Buys, sells and appraises German Americana: fraktur, books, manuscripts, artwork, etc.

Expert

Pstr. Frederick Weiser
55 Kohler School Rd.
New Oxford, PA 17350-9415
Phone: 717-624-4106

Museum/Library

Free Library of Philadelphia
Logan Square
Philadelphia, PA 19103
Phone: 215-686-5322
The Henry S. Borneman collection of Pennsylvania German Fraktur.

FRAMES

(see also REPAIRS & RESTORATIONS, Gilding)

Dealer

Eli Wilner & Co.
Eli Wilner
1525 York Ave.
New York, NY 10028
Phone: 212-744-6521
Sells, buys and restores old picture frames.

Repair Service

Restoration of Antique Frames
R. Wayne Reynolds
P.O. Box 28
Stevenson, MD 21153
Phone: 301-484-1028
Conserves and restores gessoed and gold-leafed items such as frames, plaster items, moldings, etc.
*

FRANKART

Expert

Geode, Ltd.
Walter Glenn
3393 Peachtree Rd.
Atlanta, GA 30326
Phone: 404-261-9346
Buys and sells Frankart items; also advisor to collectors, dealers, auction houses, etc.

FRANK LLOYD WRIGHT

(see also ARTS & CRAFTS)

Dealer

Struve Gallery
Michael Fitzsimmons
309 West Superior Street
Chicago, IL 60610
Phone: 312-787-0563
*Specializing in 20th century architecture and decorative arts especially Frank Lloyd Wright and the Prairie School of design. *

Museum/Library

National Center for the Study of Frank Lloyd Wright
P.O. Box 444
Ann Arbor, MI 48106
Phone: 313-995-4504

Periodical

Newsletter: Wright Flyer
Jerry A. McCoy
1960 Biltmore St. NW #5
Washington, DC 20009-1538
Phone: 202-462-4790
"Wright Flyer" is a bi-monthly newsletter for admirers of Frank Lloyd Wright; send SASE for subscription info.; also buys Wright ephemera.

Periodical

Newsletter: Frank Lloyd Wright Newsletter
P.O. Box 2100
Oak Park, IL 60303
Phone: 312-328-6552 *

FRATERNAL ORGANIZATION ITEMS

Knights Of Columbus

Museum/Library

Knights of Columbus Headquarters Museum
One Columbus Plaza
New Haven, CT 06507
Phone: 203-772-2130

Masonic

Collector

Dave
P.O. Box 522
Manhattan, KS 66502
Phone: 913-776-1433
Wants Masonic/Shriners jewelry, coins, tokens, books, paper items, memorabilia, anything Masonic needed for collection.

Expert

George B. Spielman
1604 Rohrersville Rd.
Knoxville, MD 21758
Author of "Masonic Collectables."

Museum/Library

Museum of Our National Heritage
Clement M. Silvestro, Dir.
33 Marrett Rd.
P.O. Box 519
Lexington, MA 02173
Phone: 617-861-6559
Research library specializing in the history of Freemasonry and related fraternal organizations in the U.S.

Museum/Library

Iowa Masonic Library & Museum
P.O. Box 279
Cedar Rapids, IA 52406
Phone: 319-365-1438

Museum/Library

Masonic Grand Lodge Library & Museum of Texas
P.O. Box 446
Waco, TX 76703
Phone: 817-753-7395

Odd Fellows

Museum/Library

Odd Fellows Historical Society
2055 Center Ave.
Payepte, ID 83661
Phone: 208-459-2091
Mailing address is as noted above. Museum is located in Caldwell, ID.

FRETWORK

Collector

Rick Ralston
99-969 Iwaena St.
Aiea, HI 96701
Phone: 800-367-7044   FAX: 808-486-1276
Wants to buy fretwork models; trains, buses, boats, etc.

FRISBEES

Club/Association

Flying Disc Collectors Association
Newsletter: Flying Disc Collectors Assoc. Newsletter
Donn Blake
225 Circle Dr.
Las Vegas, NV 89101
Phone: 702-384-1769 *

FROG COLLECTIBLES

Club/Association

Frog Pond, The
Newsletter: Ribbit Ribbit
Ms. Merelaine Haskett, Ed.
P.O. Box 193
Beech Grove, IN 46107
Newsletter has articles and buy/sell/trade ads; open to all who are interested in collecting frog related items.

Club/Association

Chicago Herpetological Society
2001 North Clark St.
Chicago, IL 60614
Affiliated with the Chicago Academy of Sciences; focuses on the study of reptiles and amphibians; offers books about frogs and reptiles.

Dealer

Frog Fantasies Museum & Gift Shop
Louise Mesa
151 Spring St.
Eureka Springs, AR 72632
Phone: 501-253-7227

Museum/Library

Frog Fantasies Museum
Louise Mesa
151 Spring St.
Eureka Springs, AR 72632
Phone: 501-253-7227

FRUIT JARS

(see also BOTTLES; JELLY CONTAINERS)

Club/Association

Midwest Antique Fruit Jar & Bottle Club
Newsletter: Glass Chatter
P.O. Box 38
Flat Rock, IN 47234
Sponsors two fruit and bottle shows each year in Indianapolis.

Club/Association

Ball Collectors Club
Newsletter: Ball Collectors Club Newsletter
Mason Bright
22203 Doncaster
Riverview, MI 48192
Phone: 313-283-5965 or 313-479-1040
Focuses on collecting Ball fruit jars and GO-WITHS; newsletter includes information on Ball jars; lists jars for sale by members.

Collector

Art Snyder
110 White Oak Drive
Butler, PA 16001-3446
Phone: 412-287-0278
Buys/sells/trades all types of fruit jars especially Ball jars, odd closures, pint sizes, midgets and highly whittled quart size samples.

Collector

Collector
Box 71
Wallburg, NC 27373
Wants old fruit jars. One or a collection.

Collector

Harry Fisher
Rt. 1, Box 197
Owensville, MO 65066

*Wants Globe, Lightning, Masons amber, Millville Atmospherics and Improveds, Princess, Perfections, The Darling, Royal Amber, etc. ***

Expert

Jerry McCann
5003 West Berwin
Chicago, IL 60630
Phone: 312-777-0443
Wants to buy unusual fruit jars.

Expert

Hathaway's Antiques
John Hathaway
R-2 Box 220
Bryant Pond, ME 04219
Phone: 207-665-2124
Buys and sells fruit jars; hundreds of rare jars to inexpensive jars in all categories.

Expert

Dick Roller
364 Gregory Avenue
West Orange, NJ 07052-3743
Author of "Standard Fruit Jar Reference."

Expert

Jacqueline C. Linscott
3557 Nicklaus Dr.
Titusville, FL 32780
Phone: 407-267-9170
Specializes in Ball canning jars and other Ball items; must be embossed "Ball."

Expert

Mason Bright
22203 Doncaster
Riverview, MI 48192
Phone: 313-283-5965 or 313-479-1040
Specialist and collector of BALL fruit jars; wants jars, letterheads, advertising items, GO-WITHS; has largest collection in the U.S.

Expert

Alice Creswick
0-8525 Kenowa SW
Grand Rapids, MI 49504
Phone: 616-453-9565
Author of "Red Book No. 6: The Collector's Guide to Old Fruit Jars"; also sells books about old canning jars.

Expert

Bob & Jo Ellen Allen
231 E. James Blvd.
P.O. Box 85
St. James, MO 65559
Phone: 314-265-8296
Author of "Ball Blue Books & Ball Advertising 1914-1989" and "Kerr home Canning Books & Kerr Advertising 1903-1990."

Periodical

Newsletter: Fruit Jar Newsletter
Dick Roller
364 Gregory Avenue
West Orange, NJ 07052-3743
Covers new finds, glass factory histories, jar news in general plus want ads, for-sale page and show dates.

Periodical

Bottles & Extras Magazine
Magazine: Bottles & Extras
Scott Grandstaff
P.O. Box 154
Happy Camp, CA 96039
Phone: 916-493-2032
A monthly mag. for collectors of old bottles and related antiques; articles on private collections, digging news, auctions, etc.

FURNITURE (ANTIQUE)

(see also ARTS & CRAFTS; ART DECO; ART NOUVEAU; GARDEN FURNITURE; ORIENTALIA; REPAIRS & RESTORATIONS; SHAKER ITEMS; WICKER)

Dealer

Steven Score Antiques
Steven Score
159 Main St.
Essex, MA 01929

Dealer

Robert O. Stuart
P.O. Box 104
Limington, ME 04049
Phone: 207-793-4522

Dealer

Fae B. Haight Antiques
P.O. Box 294
Lahaska, PA 18931
Phone: 215-794-5890 or 215-766-2334

Dealer

Philip H. Bradley Co.
Philip Bradley
Route 30
Downingtown, PA 19335
Phone: 215-269-0427

Dealer

Peter Eaton 18 Century Furniture
39 State St.
P.O. Box 632
Newburyport, MA 01950
Phone: 508-465-2754

Dealer

James B. Grievo Fine American Antiques
RR 5, Box 52
Califon, NJ 07830
Phone: 908-439-2147

Dealer

Campbell House Antiques
Judy & Bill Campbell
160 E. Dow Run Rd.
Kennet Square, PA 19348
Phone: 215-347-6756

Dealer

Nathan Liverant & Son
168 South Main St.
P.O. Box 103
Colchester, CT 06415
Phone: 203-537-2409 or 203-537-2060

Dealer

John Keith Russell Antiques, Inc.
Spring St.
South Salem, NY 10590
Phone: 914-763-8144 or 203-537-2060
FAX: 914-763-3553

Dealer

R. Jorgensen Antiques
R.R. 1, Box 1125 Rte. 1
Wells, ME 04090
Phone: 207-646-9444

Dealer

Martin J. Conlon American Antiques
P.O. Box 3070
Providence, RI 02906
Phone: 401-831-1810

Dealer

Chalfant & Chalfant
1352 Paoli Pike
West Chester, PA 19380
Phone: 215-696-1862

Dealer

Boyertown Antiques
Richard & Lois Maimberg
1283 Weisstown Road
Boyertown, PA 19512
Phone: 215-367-2452

Dealer

John C. Newcomer & Assoc.
John C. Newcomer
P.O. Box 130
Funkstown, MD 21734
Phone: 301-790-1327

Expert

Heritage Antiques, Inc.
Suzy McLennan Anderson
65 East Main St.
Holmdel, NJ 07733
Phone: 908-946-8801
Authentication service offered for pre-1840 American furniture; also buys and sells.

Expert

J. Robert Boykin, III
Box 7440
Wilson, NC 27895
Phone: 919-237-1700
Specializing in Southern, Centennial and period antique furniture.

Expert

Van Cline & Davenport, Ltd.
Stephen Van Cline, CAPP
792 Franklin Ave.
Franklin Lake, NJ 07417
Phone: 201-891-4588   FAX: 201-891-2824
Specializes in 18th & early 19th cent. furniture & accessories; appraisals, authentication, lectures, expert testimony.

Misc. Service

Massachusetts Materials Research, Inc.
P.O. Box 326
West Boylston, MA 01583
Phone: 617-835-6262
This firm will analyze paint on antique furniture and paintings to determine age and composition.
*

Museum/Library

Society for the Preservation of New England Antiquities, The
141 Cambridge St.
Boston, MA 02114
Phone: 617-227-3956
Specializes in New England furniture and the decorative arts.

Museum/Library

Colonial Williamsburg
P.O. Box C
Williamsburg, VA 23187
Phone: 804-229-1000
Specializes in early American furniture and the decorative arts.

Periodical

Newsletter: EAGLES
Bill & Karen Goggin
P.O. Box 277
New Market, MD 21774
A monthly newsletter market guide devoted exclusively to pre-1840 Americana and accessories.

Repro. Source

Mack S. Headley & Sons
Rt. 1 Box 1245 Senseny Rd.
Berryville, VA 22611
Phone: 703-955-2022
Fine, handcrafted reproduction furniture; also antique restorations.

Adirondack

Expert

Joseph R. Dillon
P.O. Box 1642
Martinsville, IN 46151
Phone: 317-342-3795

Museum/Library

Adirondack Museum, The
Route 30
Blue Mountain Lake, NY 12812
Phone: 518-352-7311

American

Expert

James Wilhoit
29 Maryland Ave.
Annapolis, MD 21401
Phone: 301-268-1268 *

Arts & Crafts

Expert

Bruce Johnson
P.O. Box 6660
Durham, NC 27708
Phone: 919-286-9522
Writes furniture repair/refinishing column. Wrote price guide to arts and crafts movement items.

Beds

Dealer

Mendes Antiques
Rte. 44
52 Blanding Rd.
Rehoboth, MA 02769
Phone: 508-336-7381
Specializing in antique four-poster beds, all sizes.

Beds (Brass)

Repair Service

Bedpost, The
32 S. High St.
East Bajor, PA 18013
Phone: 215-588-4667
Manufactures brass and iron beds; also repairs antique brass beds and provides parts.

Belter

Dealer

Richard & Eileen Dubrow Antiques
Richard &Eileen Dubrow
P.O. Box 128
Bayside, NY 11361
Phone: 718-767-9758
Specializing in 19th century American cabinet maker furniture and decorative arts; will identify pieces as to maker by photo.

English

Expert

Whitehall Shop
David P. Lindquist
1215 E. Franklin Street
Chapel Hill, NC 27514
Phone: 919-942-3179

Figured Maple

Dealer

Troy & Black, Inc.
Carl McCann
P.O. Box 228
Red Creek, NY 13143
Phone: 315-754-8115
Buys and sells high quality American stoneware, coverlets and figured maple furniture.

French

Dealer

Orion Antique Importers, Inc.
Shelley & David Stevens
1435 Slocum Street
Dallas, TX 75207
Phone: 214-748-1177   FAX: 214-748-1491
Offers fine quality French furniture, chandeliers, mirrors, paintings, and architecturals; also in-house restoration

Haywood-Wakefield

Dealer

South Beach Furniture Company
Leonard Riforgiator
125 Fifth Street
Miami, FL 33139
Specializes in researching buying, selling and refinishing Haywood-Wakefield birch furniture from the 1930's.

Kitchen Cabinets

Expert

Hoosier Emporium, The
Rick Zirpoli
Route 529, Box 264
Milanville, PA 18443
Phone: 717-729-7080
Buys/sells kitchen cabinets; the most extensive line of parts & supplies; authority on Hoosier and Hoosier-type kitchen cabinets.

Oak

Museum/Library

Grand Rapids Public Museum
54 Jefferson SE
Grand Rapids, MI 49503
Phone: 616-456-3977

Repro. Source

Royola Pacific Corp.
Richard Liu
965 Jefferson Ave.
Union, NJ 07083
Phone: 201-686-8440 or 201-686-8465
                    FAX: 201-686-8712
Offers oak chairs, tables and desks to the trade only.

Patented

Expert

Glenn McAndrews
402 E. Warren St.
Lebanon, OH 45036
Phone: 513-932-5448

Sofas

Club/Association

National Antique Sofa Association
P.O. Box 110099
Aurora, CO 80011 *

Stickley

Repro. Source

L. & J.G. Stickley, Inc.
P.O. Box 480
Manlius, NY 13104-0480 *

Victorian

Museum/Library

Newark Museum, Ballantine House
P.O. Box 540
Newark, NJ 07101
Phone: 201-596-6550

Museum/Library

Lyndhurst
635 S. Broadway
Tarrytown, NY 10591
Phone: 914-631-0046

Wallace Nutting

Museum/Library

Wadsworth Atheneum
600 Main Street
Hartford, CT 06103
Phone: 203-278-2670

Windsors

Repro. Source

Olde Virginia Floorcloth & Trading Co.
Sharon & Roger Mason
6605 Richmond Rd.
P.O. Box 438
Williamsburg, VA 23185
Phone: 804-564-0600 or 804-465-1515
Makes a line of handcrafted reproduction 18th century style windsor chairs and settees.

Wooton Desks

Club/Association

Wooton Desk Owners Society, Inc.
Newsletter: <u>Wooton Desk Owners Society
Newsletter, The</u>
Richard &Eileen Dubrow
P.O. Box 128
Bayside, NY 11361
Phone: 718-767-9758
Archival records, authentication, and sales of Wooton desks.

FURS

Dealer

Barbara N. Cohen Galleries
Leonard & Barb Cohen
115 E. Main St.
Waterloo, NY 13165-1432
Phone: 315-539-3032 or 315-539-3372
Wants fox coats, silver and red, as well as lynx and other long-haired furs.

Misc. Service

Fur Appraisers & Consultants, Inc.
Richard A. Newman
350 Seventh Ave.
New York, NY 10001
Phone: 212-564-4733   FAX: 212-564-4735
Fur appraiser.

Museum/Library

Museum of the Fur Trade
Magazine: <u>MFT Quarterly</u>
HC 74, Box 18
Chadron, NE 69337
Phone: 308-432-3843
Dedicated to the study of the American fur trade from colonial times to the present; not involved with present day trapping.

G-MAN

Collector

Harry Whitworth
3608 Locust Circle West
Prospect, KY 40059
*Wants Melvin Purvis knife or pen/pencil; also anything G-man. ***

G.A.R. MEMORABILIA

(see also VETERANS, Civil War)

GAMBLING COLLECTIBLES

(see also COIN-OPERATED MACHINES, Slot Machines; PLAYING CARDS)

Auction Service

Full House
Gene Hochman
P.O. Box 4057
Boynton Beach, FL 33424-4057
*Conducts mail auctions specializing in playing cards and other gambling memorabilia. ***

Collector

Robert Eisenstadt
P.O. Box 020767
Brooklyn, NY 11202
Phone: 718-625-3553 or 718-522-1087
Wants gambling supply catalogs, old gambling related books and postcards, unique and antique chip holders, old gambling equipment.

Collector

John A. Greget
1124 Cymry Dr.
Berwyn, PA 19312
Phone: 215-296-2664
Buys and appraises gambling books or equipment.

Collector

R.E. White
7501 Grandview Ave.
Arvada, CO 80002
*Wants early, unusual items relating to gambling and gambling halls: playing card trimmers, dice-making tools, trade stimulators, etc. ***

Expert

Robert Doyle
R.D. 3 Box 137
Fishkill, NY 12524
Phone: 914-896-9492 *

Poker Chips

Collector

Robert Eisenstadt
P.O. Box 020767
Brooklyn, NY 11202
Phone: 718-625-3553 or 718-522-1087
Buys, sells, trades, and collects ivory and clay-composition poker chips; inlaid, engraved, embossed and catalin (bakelite) chips.

Expert

Dale Seymour
11170 Mora Dr.
Los Altos, CA 94024
Phone: 415-948-0948   FAX: 415-941-3695
Wants old poker chips; ivory, clay, or casino; also tokens; no paper, plain or plastic chips wanted. Author of book on same.

Periodical

Newsletter: <u>Poker Chip Newsletter</u>
P.O. Box 3491
Westlake Village, CA 91362 *

GAMES

(see also BILLIARD RELATED ITEMS; CHESS SETS; FRISBEES; GAMBLING COLLECTIBLES; MARBLES; PLAYING CARDS; PUZZLES; TOYS)

Auction Service

Richard W. Withington, Inc.
R.D. 2, Box 440
Hillsboro, NH 03244
Phone: 603-464-3232

Club/Association

Antique Toy Collectors of America, Inc., The
Newsletter: <u>Toy Chest</u>
Robert R. Grew
c/o Carter, Ledyard & Milburn
Two Wall St. - 13th Floor
New York, NY 10005
Phone: 212-238-8803   FAX: 212-732-3232
An organization focusing on antique toys and games.

Club/Association

American Game Collectors Association
Newsletter: <u>Game Times</u>
Joe Angiolillo, Pr.
4628 Barlow Dr.
Bartlesville, OK 74006
Focuses on board games as well as puzzles, playing cards, tops, toys, dolls, yo-yos, and outdoor and tabletop action games.

Collector

Joseph Angiolillo
21 Kenwood Dr.
Manchester, CT 06040 *

Expert

Richard Friz
RFD 2, Box 155
Peterborough, NH 03458
Phone: 603-563-8155 *

Expert

Lee Dennis
Spring Road
Peterborough, NH 04458
Phone: 603-924-6710 *

Expert

Bob Cereghino
Suite 170A-319
6400 Baltimore National Pike
Baltimore, MD 21228
Phone: 301-766-7593

Expert

Long's Americana
Earnest & Ida Long
P.O. Box 90
Mokelumne Hill, CA 95245
Phone: 209-286-1348
Specializes in toys, banks, games and other children's items; publishes "Dictionary of Toys, Vol I & II" and "Penny Lane."

Museum/Library

University of Waterloo Museum & Archive
of Games
Waterloo
Ontario N2L 3G1 Canada

Museum/Library

Washington Dolls' House & Toy Museum
5236 44th Street NW
Washington, DC 20015
Phone: 202-244-0024

Board

Club/Association

American Game Collectors Association
Newsletter: Game Times
Joe Angiolillo, Pr.
4628 Barlow Dr.
Bartlesville, OK 74006
Focuses on board games as well as puzzles, playing cards, tops, toys, dolls, yo-yos, and outdoor and tabletop action games.

Collector

Bill Smith
56 Locust Street
Douglas, MA 01516
Phone: 508-476-2015
Wants all board games; any age or theme.

Collector

Tom Allman
6 Towbridge St.
Newton, MA 02159
Phone: 617-965-0977
*Wants Sergeant Preston, Park and Shop, Nancy Drew, and other board games. ***

Collector

Michael
1729 35th St. #23
Washington, DC 20007
Phone: 202-333-1495
*Wants 1930's Monopoly, other Parker Bros. games; Hot Wheels and Matchbox cars. ***

Dealer

Debra Krim
16 Herbert Ave.
West Peabody, MA 01960
Phone: 508-535-3140   FAX: 508-535-7522
Wants boxed & board games from 1843 to 1970: McLoughlin, Ives, Bliss and other companies; baseball and TV games; cartoon strip games.

Expert

Lee Dennis
Spring Road
Peterborough, NH 04458
Phone: 603-924-6710
*Former curator-owner of the country's largest collections of board games; also baseball board games. ***

Expert

Big Game Hunter, The
Bruce Whitehill
299 Woosamonsa Rd.
Pennington, NJ 08534
Phone: 609-737-0795
One of the world's foremost authorities on American games; has large collection of antique American games and advertisements.

Museum/Library

Game Preserve, The
110 Spring Road
Peterborough, NH 03458
Phone: 603-924-6710

Board (TV Show Related)

Expert

Norm & Cathy Vigue
62 Bailey St.
Stoughton, MA 02072
Phone: 617-344-5441
Author of "Name of the Game." Buys & sells board games from TV cartoons, comedies, westerns, adventure, comic strip, detective, etc.

Croquet

Dealer

Allen Scheuch
356 W. 20th St.
New York, NY 10011
Phone: 212-929-2299 or 718-486-8136
Wants croquet photographs, booklets, unusual mallets & wickets, postcards; anything related to the game of croquet.

Punchboards

Expert

Amusement Sales
Clark Phelps
127 North Main
Midvale, UT 84047
Phone: 801-255-4731

Tiddledywinks

Collector

Larry Gage
3100 Loughboro Road, NW
Washington, DC 20016 *

GANGSTER RELATED COLLECTIBLES

(see also PERSONALITIES (CRIMINAL);
PROHIBITION ITEMS)

GARDEN FURNITURE

Furniture & Ornaments

Dealer

New England Garden Ornaments
38 East Brookfield Rd.
North Brookfield, MA 01535
Phone: 508-867-4474

Carries old and new garden architecture and ornamentation: sundials, statuary, planters, urns, wrought iron, pedestals, birdbaths, etc.

Dealer

Barbara N. Cohen Galleries
Leonard & Barb Cohen
115 E. Main St.
Waterloo, NY 13165-1432
Phone: 315-539-3032 or 315-539-3372
Wants antique or other quality statues, furniture, urns, fountains, etc.

Expert

Garden Accents
Elizabeth Schumacher
947 Longview Rd.
Gulph Mills, PA 19406
Phone: 215-525-3287 or 215-825-5525
                    FAX: 215-825-1958
Buys and sells best assortment of antique garden accessories: urns, planters, statuary, benches, fountains; bronze, iron, lead, etc.

Repro. Source

Robinson Iron
John C. Allen, Jr.
P.O. Box 1119
Alexander City, AL 35010
Phone: 205-329-8486
Makes reproduction furniture and fountains; catalog $5.

GARDEN HOSE NOZZLES

(see also WATER SPRINKLERS)

Collector

Dale Schmidt
610 Howell Prairie Rd. SE
Salem, OR 97301
Phone: 503-364-0499
Wants brass and copper garden hose nozzles.

GAS STATION COLLECTIBLES

(see also TOYS, Gas Station Related)

Club/Association

International Petroliana Collectors
Association
Magazine: Check the Oil!
P.O. Box 1000-F
Westerville, OH 43081-7000
Pumps, oil cans, signs, oil bottles, pens, pump globes; anything to do with the petroleum industry of days gone by.

Club/Association

American Petroleum Collectors/Iowa Gas
Magazine: Gas Line
John Logsdon
6555 Colby Ave.
Des Moines, IA 50311
Phone: 515-255-5265 or 515-276-2099

Sponsors annual convention, swap meet and auction for collectors of petroleum and automobile advertising items: signs, globes, cans, etc.

Club/Association
Oil Products & Ephemera Collectors
Box 25763
Colorado Springs, CO 80936 *

Collector
Peter Capell
1838 West Grace St.
Chicago, IL 60613-2724
Phone: 312-871-8735 or 312-871-8735
Collects gasoline company/service station items: pump globes, give-aways such as banks, thermometers, salt & pepper gas pump sets.

Expert
Scott Anderson
c/o Chilton Book Company
1 Chilton Way
Radnor, PA 19089 *

Repro. Source
Weber's Nostalgia Supermarket
1121 S. Main St.
Fort Worth, TX 76104
Phone: 817-335-3833
Sells gas pump items; globes for old gas pumps, brass nozzles, white cloth hoses; also enamel-on-steel advertising signs. *

Gulf Oil
Collector
Charles Whitworth
2522 Utica Sellersburg Rd.
Jeffersonville, IN 47130
Wants Gulf items: toys, doll dressed as service attendant; also cans; anything Gulf Oil. *

Pumps & Globes
Collector
Gary Hildman
3240 Sevier Rd.
Marcellus, NY 13108
Phone: 315-673-2535
Wants gasoline pump globes and related items: inserts, glass and metal bodies; also wants porcelain, tin, and neon signs.

Collector
Bob Fousek
Rt. 2 Box 73
Grantsville, MD 21536
Phone: 301-245-4277
Wants complete globes or parts; also gas advertising, tins, etc.

Collector
Kent Blaine
P.O. Box 596
Winona, MS 38967
Phone: 601-283-3510 or 601-283-3524

Wants gas station items thru 1950's; especially flat ad glass from 1930's-'50's gas pumps; 11"x4" with company logos, e.g. Texaco.

Collector
Scott Benjamin
7250 Franklin Ave. #216
Los Angeles, CA 90046
Phone: 213-876-2056
Wants gasoline globes, inserts, etched globes, aviation, marine and others. *

Repro. Source
Steve Staub
22 N. 2nd St.
Tripp City, OH 45371
Phone: 513-667-5975
Handmade antique-style gas pumps, trimmed in brass, wide selection of colors, 35 oil company globes to chose from.

Repro. Source
Doug Pray Enterprises
P.O. Box 1715
Broken Arrow, OK 74013
Phone: 918-251-3316
Handmade antique-style gas pumps, trimmed in brass, wide selection of colors, 35 oil company globes to chose from. *

GEMS & JEWELRY
(see also BEADS; LAPIDARY; MINERALS)

Club/Association
Accredited Gemologists Assoc.
1615 South Foothill Drive
Salt Lake City, UT 84108
Phone: 801-581-9900 *

Club/Association
American Gem Society
5901 W. 3rd.
Los Angeles, CA 90036

Club/Association
Gemological Institute of America
1660 Stewart St.
Santa Monica, CA 90404
Phone: 800-421-7250

Dealer
Kurt E. Knab, G.G.
P.O. Box 31
Camp Hill, PA 17011
Phone: 717-766-9302
Buys/sells modern, antique and estate jewelry; especially wants antique jewelry, diamonds, colored stones, Russian objects.

Dealer
Victorian Manor
Carol & Eugene Rooney, GG
33 Main St.
New Market, MD 21774
Phone: 301-865-3083

Buys and sells antique and estate jewelry; repairs, restores, re-enameling, remounting, restring, and custom design jewelry.

Dealer
Memory Lane Antiques
Betty Bird
107 Ida St.
Mount Shasta, CA 96067
Phone: 916-926-4331
Buys antique and collectible jewelry; prefers Victorian through 1950 especially signed pieces.

Expert
Timeless, Inc.
Gail B. Levine, GG
P.O. Box 7683
Rego Park, NY 11374-5020
Phone: 718-897-7305   FAX: 718-997-9057
Graduate Gemologist, appraiser, lecturer, assoc. editor of "JPR", a quarterly jewelry price, condition, quality report.

Expert
Metro Gem Consultants
Thomas J. Terpilak, G.G.
c/o Rings 'N' Things
4550 Montgomery Ave.
Bethesda, MD 20814
Phone: 301-654-0838 or 301-654-8678
Gemological consultant and professional appraiser.

Expert
Heller Antiques, Ltd.
Israel Heller
5454 Wisconsin Ave.
Chevy Chase, MD 20815
Phone: 301-654-0218
Specializes in jewelry, silver and Judaica.

Expert
Arthur Guy Kaplan
P.O. Box 1942
Baltimore, MD 21203
Phone: 301-752-2090 or 301-664-8350
                              FAX: 301-783-2723
Author of "The Official Price Guide to Antique Jewelry."

Expert
Nina Woolford, GG
P.O. Box 35
Rockville, VA 23146-0035
Phone: 804-749-4367   FAX: 718-997-9057
Graduate Gemologist, appraiser, lecturer, instructor; publisher of "JPR", a quarterly jewelry price, condition, quality report.

Expert
Athena Antiques
Elaine Luartes, GG
100 Beta Dr.
Franklin, TN 37064
Phone: 615-377-3442

Specializes in antique and estate jewelry; teaches ISA antique jewelry course; wants jewelry emphasizing craftsmanship and design.

Expert

Estate Jewelry
Gary Durow
1259 W. Grand River
Okemos, MI 48864
Phone: 517-349-1515
Specializes in antique and estate jewelry. *

Expert

Geolat & Associates
Patti J. Geolat, FGA, GG
14110 Dallas Pkwy., #200
Dallas, TX 75240
Phone: 214-239-9314   FAX: 214-404-1359
Specializes in gemology and gemstones; jewelry (antique and modern), diamonds.

Expert

Hoefers' Gemological Services
William D. Hoefer, FGA, GG
#G-176
1101 S. Winchester Blvd.
San Jose, CA 95128
Phone: 408-241-7688 or 408-241-7687
Specializes in the appraisal of gemstones, diamonds, and contemporary jewelry; also offers expert testimony for attorneys, court, etc.

Periodical

Jewelers' Circular-Keystone
Magazine: Heritage
Charles Bond, Pub.
One Chilton Way
Radnor, PA 19089
Phone: 215-964-4474 or 215-964-4489
                    FAX: 215-964-4273
A distinctive quarterly supplement on antique and period jewelry and watches; for the buyer, seller, collector and appraiser.

Periodical

Jewelers' Circular-Keystone
Magazine: Jewelers' Circular-Keystone
    Magazine
P.O. Box 2085
Radnor, PA 19089-9906
A monthly magazine focusing on new and antique gems, jewelry, and watches.

Periodical

Magazine: Collectors Clocks & Jewelry
Box E
Exton, PA 19341-9990
A bi-monthly magazine dedicated to clocks and jewelry. *

Periodical

C.M. Woolford Co.
Magazine: JPR
Nina Woolford, Pub.
P.O. Box 35
Rockville, VA 23146-0035
Phone: 804-749-4367   FAX: 718-997-9057
A timely jewelry price report on auction sales of antique and period jewelry.

Periodical

Jewelry & Personal Adornment
Magazine: Ornament
P.O. Box 35029
Los Angeles, CA 90035-0029
Phone: 213-652-9914 *

Repair Service

Thompsons Studio, Inc.
Back Meadow Road
Damariscotta, ME 04543
Phone: 207-563-5280
Repairs jewelry of any period. *

Supplier

Kassoy
32 W. 47th Street
New York, NY 10036
Phone: 800-452-7769
Mail order source for tools, supplies and instruments for the jewelry trade.

Supplier

Nasco
901 Janesville Ave.
Fort Atkinson, WI 53538
Phone: 414-563-2446 or 800-558-9595
Carries supplies for jewelry arts and crafts: wire, chains, tools, findings, beads, etc. *

Supplier

American Gem & Mineral Suppliers
Association
1299 Armando St.
Upland, CA 91789
Phone: 714-981-8588
Members are retailers, manufacturers, wholesalers, importers, distributors, or publishers in the gem, mineral, lapidary fields.

Art Deco

Repro. Source

Herzog & Adams
37 West 47th St.
New York, NY 10036 *

Costume

Club/Association

Vintage Fashion/Costume Jewelry Club
Newsletter: VFCJ Newsletter
David Baron
P.O. Box 265
Glen Oaks, NY 11004

Focuses on vintage costume jewelry; articles, book reviews, repair tips, special events, dealer listings, seekers, sellers and swappers.

Expert

Maryanne Dolan
138 Belle Avenue
Pleasant Hill, CA 94523
Phone: 415-935-2366
Author of "Collecting Rhinestone Jewelry."

GENEALOGY

Misc. Service

Genealogical Society of Utah, Family
History Library, State College, PA
P.O. Box 224
State College, PA 16801
Phone: 814-238-4560 *

Misc. Service

Genealogical Society of Utah, Family
History Library, Newark, DE Branch
22 Minquuil Dr.
Newark, DE 19713 *

Misc. Service

Genealogical Society of Utah, Family
History Library, Kensington,MD Branch
100000 Stoneybrook Dr.
Kensington, MD 20895
Phone: 301-587-0042 *

Misc. Service

Marie Varrelman Melchiori, CGRS
121 Tapawingo Rd. SW
Vienna, VA 22180
Phone: 703-938-7279
Certified genealogical record searcher, specializes in Civil War research.

Misc. Service

Rea Clodfelter Whicker
P.O. Box 93
Kaysville, UT 84037
Phone: 801-544-9447
Genealogical research in world's largest resource library; 26 years experience; references furnished upon request.

Misc. Service

Genealogical Society of Utah, Family
History Library
50 East North Temple St.
Salt Lake City, UT 84150
Check your local library for a copy of "News of the Family History Library" to learn about the LDS Library holdings.

GIRL SCOUT MEMORABILIA

(see also BOY SCOUT MEMORABILIA)

Collector

D. Nordlinger Stern
1336 54th Ave., N.E.
St. Petersburg, FL 33703
Phone: 813-527-1212   FAX: 813-525-4090
*Wants girl scout memorabilia; please send list of
items and prices.*

Collector

Fran & Carl Holden
257 Church St.
Doylestown, OH 44230
Phone: 216-658-2793
*Wants old or unusual pins, badges, medals,
Brownies, Senior Scouts, Roundups, Adult offi-
cials, Councils, literature, etc.*

Expert

Girl Scouts of the U.S.A.
Mary Degenhar
c/o National Equipment Service
830 Third Ave.
New York, NY 10022
Phone: 212-940-7500
Authority on Girl Scout items.

Expert

Girl Scouts of the U.S.A.
Judy Kirsch
c/o National Equipment Service
830 Third Ave.
New York, NY 10022
Phone: 212-940-7500
Authority on Girl Scout items.

Museum/Library

Zitelman Scout Museum
Mrs. Ralph Zitelman
708 Seminary St.
Rockford, IL 61104
Phone: 815-962-3999
*Worldwide Scouting: patches, books, uniforms &
equipment including Boy and Girl Scouts,
Brownies, Explorers, Scoutmasters, etc.*

GLASS

(see also CUP PLATES; GLASS KNIVES;
GLASSES; POWDER JARS; REPAIRS &
RESTORATIONS; REPAIRS &
RESTORATIONS, Glass; TABLEWARE)

Auction Service

Skinner, Inc.
357 Main St.
Bolton, MA 01740
Phone: 508-779-6241 or 617-236-1700
                         FAX: 508-779-5144
*Established in 1962, Skinner Inc. is the fifth
largest auction house in the US.*

Auction Service

Richard A. Bourne Auction Co., Inc.
P.O. Box 141
Hyannis Port, MA 02647
Phone: 508-775-0797

Auction Service

Arman Absentee Auctions
P.O. Box 3239
Newport, RI 02840
Phone: 401-683-3100   FAX: 401-683-4044
*Specializing in mail-bid auctions of early Ameri-
can glass, historical Staffordshire, paperweights.*

Auction Service

Glass Works Auctions
James Hagenbuch
P.O. Box 187
East Greenville, PA 18041
Phone: 215-679-5849
*Specializes in the auction of bottles, flasks, barber
bottles, jars, bitters bottles, scent bottles, shaving
mugs, and related go-withs.*

Club/Association

Glass Research Society of New Jersey
Wheaton Village
Glasstown Rd.
Millville, NJ 08332
Phone: 609-327-6800

Club/Association

National Early American Glass Club, The
Journal: Glass Club Bulletin, The
Francis Allen
7417 Allison St.
Hyattsville, MD 20784
*The Bulletin is published three times per year;
subscribed to by 50 major museums in the U.S.*

Club/Association

Glass Collectors Club of Toledo
c/o 2727 Middlesex Dr.
Toledo, OH 43606

Club/Association

Antique & Historical Glass Foundation
P.O. Box 7413
Toledo, OH 43615 *

Expert

Orva Walker
6213 Joyce Drive
Camp Springs, MD 20748-2413
Phone: 301-449-5372
*Lectures about glass at seminars, conventions,
universities, etc.; also conducts "I.D." clinics.*

Expert

Pleasant Valley Antiques
Barbara M. Lessig
21000 Georgia Ave.
Brookeville, MD 20833
Phone: 301-924-2293
*Specialist in appraising and selling all types of
glass ware.*

Expert

Susan Marth
13509 Glen Mill Rd.
Rockville, MD 20850
Phone: 301-294-9536

Man./Prod./Dist.

House of Glass, Inc., The
Joe Rice
R.R. 3, Box 153
Elwood, IN 46036
Phone: 317-552-6841
*Makes paperweights all signed by owner, Joe Rice;
also makes all sorts of other solid glass: ashtrays,
pears, ringholders, etc.*

Museum/Library

Jones Museum of Glass & Ceramics, The
Douglas Hill, ME 04024
Phone: 207-787-3370
*Unique museum, over 7000 examples of glass &
ceramics ranging from antiquity to present; covers
all types from all periods.*

Museum/Library

Bennington Museum, The
W. Main St.
Bennington, VT 05201
Phone: 802-447-1571

Museum/Library

Wheaton Historical Village Association
Museum of Glass
Glasstown Rd.
Millville, NJ 08332
Phone: 609-327-6800

Museum/Library

Corning Museum of Glass, The
Journal: Jounal of Glass Studies
One Museum Way
Corning, NY 14830-2253
Phone: 607-937-5371   FAX: 607-937-3352
*Over 24,000 glass objects, innovative exhibits,
videos, models; glass history, archaeology, and
early manufacturing.*

Museum/Library

Chrysler Museum, The
Olney Rd. & Mowbray Arch
Norfolk, VA 23510
Phone: 804-622-1211
*Fine collection of early to 20th century glass; also
ancient to modern artifacts from all over the
world.*

Museum/Library

Toledo Museum of Art, The
P.O. Box 1013
Toledo, OH 43697
Phone: 419-255-8000

Museum/Library

Glass Museum, The
309 S. Franklin
Dunkirk, IN 47336
Phone: 317-768-6809

Museum/Library

Bergstrom-Mahler Museum
Alex Vance, ExDir
165 N. Park Ave.
Neenah, WI 54956
Phone: 414-751-4658 or 414-751-4672
Extensive collection of glass paperweights, Bohemia, art glass, and Tiffany glass.

Museum/Library

Historical Glass Museum
1157 N. Orange
Redlands, CA 92373
Phone: 714-797-1528
A breathtaking display of American glassware.

Periodical

New York Experimental Glass Workshop, Inc.
Magazine: Glass Magazine
Suzanne Ramljak, Ed.
142 Mulberry St.
New York, NY 10013

Periodical

Magazine: Antique Bottle & Glass Collector
James Hagenbuch
P.O. Box 187
East Greenville, PA 18041
Phone: 215-679-5849   FAX: 215-679-3068
A monthly magazine for the glass and bottle collector.

Periodical

National Early American Glass Club, The
Newsletter: Glass Shards
P.O. Box 8489
Silver Spring, MD 20907
The semi-annual newsletter of the NEAGC; covers glass exhibits, chapter activities, etc.

Periodical

Antique Publications
Magazine: Glass Collector's Digest
David Richardson
P.O. Box 553
Marietta, OH 45750-0553
Phone: 614-373-9959 or 800-533-3433
                    FAX: 614-373-5530
A bi-monthly magazine focusing on the glass collecting specialties.

Periodical

Depression Glass Daze, Inc.
Newspaper: Daze, The
Teri Steele, Ed.
275 State Rd.
Box 57
Otisville, MI 48463-0057
Phone: 313-631-4593
A monthly newspaper catering to the dealers and collectors of glass, china and pottery from the 1920's and 1930's.

Periodical

Rudi Publishing
Magazine: Antique Glass Quarterly
Ruth Grizel, Ed.
P.O. Box 1364
Iowa City, IA 52244
A magazine for collectors; AQI covers a broad spectrum of American glass: pressed, art carnival through glass of the depression era.

Repro. Source

Wholesale Glass Dealers
Phil & Helen Rosso
1815 Trimble Ave.
Port Vue, PA 15133
Phone: 412-678-7352
*Sells reproduction pattern glass, Westmoreland glass, milk glass, reamers, measuring cups, candlesticks, carnival glass, etc. ***

Repro. Source

Treasure House
P.O. Box 774
Claremore, OK 74017
Phone: 918-342-2555
*Sells reproduction pattern glass, toothpick holders, salts, etc. ***

Akro Agate/Westite

Club/Association

Akro Agate Art Association
Newsletter: Akro Agate Gem, The
Joseph Bourque
P.O. Box 758
Salem, NH 03079

Collector

Albert Morin
668 Robbins Ave. #23
Dracut, MA 01826
Phone: 508-454-7907
Wants either Akro Agate or Westite items.

Animals

Expert

Lee Garmon
1529 Whittier St.
Springfield, IL 62704
Phone: 217-789-9574
*Specializes in Royal Haeger and Royal Hickman American ceramics. ***

Art

Auction Service

Early Auction Co.
123 Main St.
Milford, OH 45150
Phone: 513-831-4833

Collector

Carol Haley
760 Madison Ave.
New York, NY 10021
Phone: 212-988-5181
*Wants Galle, Daum, Tiffany, etc. ***

Dealer

Lenore Monleon
33 Fifth Ave.
New York, NY 10003
Phone: 212-475-7871 or 212-838-1004
Wants Galle, Lalique, silver overlay, Art Deco, Art Nouveau.

Dealer

Caren Fine
11603 Gowrie Ct.
Potomac, MD 20854
Phone: 310-299-2116
Wants glass and lamps by Renee Lalique, Tiffany, Galle, Handel, Quezal, Venni, Steuben.

Expert

Burmese Cruet
Clarence/Betty Maier
P.O. Box 432
Montgomeryville, PA 18936
Phone: 215-855-5388
*Wants art glass, e.g. Crown Milano, Royal Flemish, Burmese, Coralene, Peach Blow, pomona, Wave Crest, Mt. Washington, etc. ***

Expert

St. John Antiques
Virgil & Betty St. John
Box 400
Le Grand, IA 50142
Phone: 515-479-2952
*Specializes in carnival glass, Victorian colored glass, toys, and Maxwell Parrish prints. ***

Expert

Look Nook Antiques
Marge Musgrave
R.R. 3, Box 352
Mountain Home, AR 72653
Phone: 501-499-5283 ***

Museum/Library

Currier Gallery of Art, The
192 Orange St.
Manchester, NH 03104
Phone: 603-669-6144

Museum/Library

Wadsworth Atheneum
600 Main Street
Hartford, CT 06103
Phone: 203-278-2670

Art (1950's)

Collector

Dennis Boyd
211 S. Mulberry St.
Richmond, VA 23220
Wants 1950's art glass by Venini, Sarpaneva, Tapio Wirkkala, Kosta, Orrefors, Kaj Franck, Nutajari-Notsjo, Flysfors, Leerdam, Toso, etc. *

Baccarat

(see also PAPERWEIGHTS)

Man./Prod./Dist.

Baccarat Inc.
625 Madison Ave.
New York, NY 10022
Phone: 212-826-4100
Only Baccarat store in the U.S.; Baccarat also sold through Bailey, Banks & Biddle stores.

Black

Expert

Marlena Toohey
c/o Antiques Publications
P.O. Box 533
Marietta, OH 45750-0553
Phone: 614-373-9959 or 800-533-3433
FAX: 614-373-5530
Author of "A Collector's Guide to Black Glass."

Blenko

Museum/Library

Blenko Glass Visitor Center Museum and Wholesale Outlet
P.O. Box 67
Milton, WV 25541
Phone: 304-743-9081   FAX: 304-743-0547
Museum and outlet for nationally known blown glassware.

Cambridge

Club/Association

National Cambridge Collectors, Inc.
Newsletter: Cambridge Crystal Ball
J.D. Hanes, Sec.
P.O. Box 416
Cambridge, OH 43725-0416
Phone: 614-432-4245 or 614-432-6794
Preserves and studies the products of the Cambridge Glass Co., Cambridge, OH.

Museum/Library

Cambridge Glass Museum, The
812 Jefferson Ave.
Cambridge, OH 43725
Phone: 614-432-3045

Over 5000 pieces of Cambridge glass on display; also 100 pieces of Cambridge Art Pottery; private museum.

Museum/Library

Museum of the National Cambridge Collectors, Inc.
P.O. Box 416
Cambridge, OH 43725-0416
Phone: 614-432-4245 or 614-432-6794
Preserves and studies the products of the Cambridge Glass Co., Cambridge, OH.

Cameo

Collector

A.A. Merber
901 E. Camino Real
Boca Raton, FL 33432
Phone: 407-368-5690
Wants cameo glass by Galle, Daum-Nancy, etc., also English cameo glass. *

Candlewick

Club/Association

National Candlewick Collector's Club, The
Newsletter: Candlewick Collector Newsletter, The
Virginia R. Scott
275 Milledge Terrace
Athens, GA 30606
Phone: 404-548-5966
The newsletter is devoted to the Candlewick pattern, collectors, finds, prices, questions answered, look-alikes and repros. discussed.

Club/Association

Michiana Association of Candlewick Collectors
Newsletter: Spyglass
Lucille R. Geisler, Sec.
17370 Battles Rd.
South Bend, IN 46614
Phone: 219-291-9245

Club/Association

California Candlewick Collectors
Laura Murphy
1360 Lomay Place
Pasadena, CA 91103
An association for the purpose of sharing information and learning about Imperial Candlewick glass.

Collector

Laura Murphy
1360 Lomay Place
Pasadena, CA 91103
Advanced collector wants the more rare and difficult to find pieces of Imperial Candlewick pattern glass, especially colored pieces.

Dealer

Kathy Burch
221 N. Maple
Ithaca, MI 48847
Phone: 517-875-3138
Buys and sells unusual pieces of Candlewick glass including colored pieces; send SASE for sale list featuring Candlewick, Cape Cod, etc.

Expert

Virginia R. Scott
275 Milledge Terrace
Athens, GA 30606
Phone: 404-548-5966
Author of "The Collector's Guide to Imperial Candlewick."

Expert

Mary Wetzel
c/o Lucille Geisler
17370 Battles Rd.
South Bend, IN 46614
Author of "Candlewick - The Jewel of Imperial."

Matching Service

Ackerman Antiques
Box 2310
Athens, OH 45701

Carnival

Auction Service

Woody Auction Company
P.O. Box 618
Douglass, KS 67039
Phone: 316-746-2694

Club/Association

New England Carnival Glass Club
Eva Backer
12 Sherwood Rd.
West Hartford, CT 06117 *

Club/Association

American Carnival Glass Association
Newsletter: American Carnival Glass News
Dennis Runk, Sec.
P.O. Box 235
Littlestown, PA 17340
Phone: 717-359-7205
Learn about highly collectible carnival glass; news, conventions; send SASE for full color brochure.

Club/Association

International Carnival Glass Association
Newsletter: Town Pump, The
R.R. #1 Box 14
Mentone, IN 46539
Phone: 219-353-7678
Promotes interest in collecting old Carnival Glass; holds annual convention featuring displays, seminars and banquet.

Club/Association

Heart of America Carnival Glass
Association
Newsletter: HOACGA Bulletin
C. Lucille Britt
3048 Tamarak Dr.
Manhattan, KS 66502

Collector

W. Warren
38 Mosher Dr.
Tonawanda, NY 14150
Phone: 716-692-2886
Wants all colors of carnival glass; one piece or a collection.

Collector

Betsy Booth
4579 Clover Hill Circle
Walnutport, PA 18088
Phone: 215-767-9182 *

Dealer

Antique Place, The
1524 S. Glenstone
Springfield, MO 65804
Phone: 417-887-3800 *

Expert

Bill Edwards
423 N. Main
Rushville, IL 46173 *

Museum/Library

Fenton Art Glass Company, The
700 Elizabeth St.
Williamstown, WV 26187
Phone: 304-375-6122   FAX: 304-375-6459
Large attractive display of early Fenton and Upper Ohio Valley glass.

Periodical

Newsletter: Encore
P.O. Box 11734
Kansas City, MO 64138 *

Carnival (Post-1960)

Club/Association

Collectible Carnival Glass Association
Wilma Thurston
2360 N. Old S.R. 9
Columbus, IN 47203
Phone: 812-546-5724
Club formed for collectors of the newer carnival glass made after 1960; quarterly newsletter, annual convention with sale and seminars.

Commemorative Historical

Collector

Forrest Gesswein
9514 Powderhorn Lane
Baltimore, MD 21234
Phone: 301-668-7890

Collects American glass that commemorates people, places and events in our Nations history.

Crystal

Matching Service

Thurber's
2158 Plainfield Pike, Unit 1
Cranston, RI 02921
Phone: 401-942-0488 or 800-848-7237
FAX: 401-942-5601

Matching Service

Past & Presents
65-07 Fitchess St.
Rego Park, NY 11374
Phone: 718-896-5146
Matching and locating service for Coalport, Derby, Franciscan, Gorham, Lenox, Metlox, Mikasa, Minton, Noritake, and others.

Matching Service

Pattern Finders
P.O. Box 206
Port Jefferson Station, NY 11776
Phone: 516-928-5158
All major brands of dinnerware and crystal stocked in huge inventory; locating service for hard to find patterns; Rosenthal specialists.

Matching Service

China Match
Freda Bell
9 Elmford Rd.
Rochester, NY 14606
Phone: 716-338-3781
Replacements of discontinued china, stoneware, glass and crystal stemware.

Matching Service

Replacements Ltd.
Lea Ann Mills
P.O. Box 26029
Greensboro, NC 27420
Phone: 919-697-3000   FAX: 919-697-3100
China, crystal and flatware (obsolete, active and inactive).

Matching Service

China Chasers
2380 Peachtree Corners Circle
Norcross, GA 30092
Phone: 404-441-9146
China and crystal replacements. *

Matching Service

Abrahante's Tableware Matching Service
Suite 209
7175 SW 47th St.
Miami, FL 33155
Phone: 305-661-1456
American, English and Japanese manufacturers of discontinued patterns of china, crystal and flatware.

Matching Service

Barron's
P.O. Box 994
Novi, MI 48376
Phone: 800-538-6340

Matching Service

China & Crystal Replacements
P.O. Box 187
Excelsior, MN 55331
Phone: 612-474-6418
Discontinued and active china, dinnerware and crystal bought and sold.

Matching Service

Dining Elegance, Ltd.
Dept. CIC
P.O. Box 4203
St. Louis, MO 63163
Phone: 314-865-1408
List of patterns in stock available upon request; $1.

Matching Service

Locators, Inc.
908 Rock St.
Little Rock, AR 72202
Phone: 501-371-0858 or 800-367-9690
Carries out-of-production (discontinued) china and crystal, and discontinued as well as active sterling flatware patterns.

Matching Service

A&A Dinnerware Locators
Larry & Anne McDonald
P.O. Box 50222
Austin, TX 78763-0222
Phone: 512-472-1548 or 512-264-1054
Locate/match discontinued crystal patterns; all major manufacturers: American, European, Japanese; primarily mail order.

Matching Service

Table Treasures
P.O. Box 4265
Stockton, CA 95204
Phone: 209-463-3607
Buy, sell and locate discontinued patterns in china, earthenware and crystal. American, English and Japanese manufacturers.

Matching Service

Patterns Unlimited International
Warren & Betty Roundhill
Dept. CIC
P.O. Box 15238
Seattle, WA 98115
Phone: 206-523-9710
Buy, sell and appraise discontinued tableware patterns of china, silver and glass.

Curved

Supplier

B & L Antiqurie, Inc.
P.O. Box 453-6217
Lexington, MI 48450-0453
Phone: 800-523-6523   FAX: 313-359-7498
Curved glass for china cabinets & convex picture frame glass; special bends and cuts such as serpentine and J bends quoted on request.

Supplier

M.D. King
403 E. Montgomery
Knoxville, IA 50138
Phone: 515-842-6394
Curved glass for china cabinets; all sizes; will ship.

Supplier

Hoffer Glass
George J. Hoffer
613 W. College Ave.
Appleton, WI 54911
Phone: 414-731-8101
Curved glass for china cabinets; send width, length and a radius template; will quote picked up or shipped UPS.

Supplier

Universal Glass Co.
P.O. Box 2097
Alma, AR 72921
Phone: 800-446-5504
Curved glass for china cabinets; call for quote or brochure.

Custard

Collector

Delores Saar
45 5th Ave. NW
Hutchinson, MN 55350 *

Cut

Club/Association

American Cut Glass Association
Newsletter: Hobstar, The
Sam Story, Pres.
3228 South Blvd. Suite 271
P.O. Box 1775
Edmond, OK 73083-1775
Phone: 405-340-2110
Focuses on the Brilliant Period (1880-1915) of American glass.

Collector

John Cocco
62 First St.
Dupont, PA 18641
Phone: 717-655-1027
Wants single piece or entire estate. *

Collector

Charles Blanton
118 Magothy Bridge Rd.
Severna Park, MD 21146
Phone: 301-647-2841
Advanced collector wants one piece or entire collection.

Expert

Arthur Wilk
7261 Clinton Street
Elma, NY 14059
Appraises Brilliant Period American cut glass. *

Expert

Chet Cassel
910 Pheasant Run
Newark, DE 19711
Phone: 302-737-3819
Buys, sells (retail;shwholesale) and collects examples of fine cut glass.

Expert

From the Cutter's Wheel Antiques
Joan & Dick Randles
P.O. Box 285
Webster, NY 14580-0285
Phone: 716-671-3760
Specializes, buys and sells American Brilliant period cut glass and engraved glass; members ACGA; eves and weekends best time to call.

Museum/Library

High Museum of Art, The
1280 Peachtree St.
Atlanta, GA 30309
Phone: 404-892-3600   FAX: 404-898-8578

Museum/Library

Lightner Museum
P.O. Box 334
St. Augustine, FL 32085
Phone: 904-824-2874

Cut (American)

Expert

Marnette Antiques
Marvin Stofft
45 12th St.
Tell City, IN 47586
Phone: 812-547-5707

Czechoslavokian

Periodical

Arita
Magazine: Glass Review
Zdenka Kalabisova
Ve Smeckach 30,111 27
Prague 1., Czechoslovakia
Brief, well illustrated articles in English covering all aspects of Czechoslovakian glass; production glass, art glass, plus artists.

Daum (Nancy)

Man./Prod./Dist.

Daum Inc.
41 Madison Ave.
9th Floor
New York, NY 10010
Phone: 212-481-0288 *

Degenhart

Club/Association

Friends of Degenhart
Newsletter: Heartbeat
65323 Highland Hills Rd.
P.O. Box 186
Cambridge, OH 43725
Phone: 614-432-2626
Open to all Dagenhart collectors and supporters; free museum admission, 5% discount on most purchases, newsletter, annual "Gathering."

Museum/Library

Degenhart Paperweight & Glass Museum, Inc.
65323 Highland Hills Rd.
P.O. Box 186
Cambridge, OH 43725
Phone: 614-432-2626
History of glass in the Ohio valley; video, exhibits, research library, gift shop.

Depression

Club/Association

National Depression Glass Association, The
Newsletter: News & Views
Anita Wood
P.O. Box 69843
Odessa, TX 79769
Phone: 915-337-1297
A central organization for depression glass collectors; sponsors an annual show and sale in July.

Dealer

Popkorn Antiques
Robert & Nancy Perzel
4 Mine St.
P.O. Box 1057
Flemington, NJ 08822
Phone: 908-782-9631

Dealer

Fenner's Antiques
Osna & Jim Fenner
2611 Ave. S
Brooklyn, NY 11229 *

Dealer

Monkey House of Trash & Treasure
Juanita McGuire
31887 O'neil Dr.
Springfield, LA 70462
Phone: 504-294-3950

Expert

Gene Florence
Box 22186
Lexington, KY 40522 *

Expert

Margaret & Kenn Whitmyer
Box 30806
Gahanna, OH 43230
*Specializing in Depression era bedroom and bath-room glassware. Author of "Bedroom & Bathroom Glassware of the Depression Years." *

Expert

John & Judy Bine
32 San Carlos
St. Charles, MO 63303
Phone: 314-724-1568 *

Periodical

Depression Glass Daze, Inc.
Newspaper: Daze, The
Teri Steele, Ed.
275 State Rd.
Box 57
Otisville, MI 48463-0057
Phone: 313-631-4593
A monthly newspaper catering to the dealers and collectors of glass, china and pottery from the 1920's and 1930's.

Drinking

Dealer

Clint's Collectibles
Box 2082
Statesboro, GA 30458-2082
Phone: 912-681-1086
Buys/sells cartoon and advertising glasses; all sorts of contemporary collectibles: Tasmaninan Devils, Jungle Book, Super Heroes, etc.

Duncan & Miller

Club/Association

National Duncan Glass Society
Journal: National Duncan Glass Journal
P.O. Box 965
Washington, PA 15301
Phone: 412-222-6376
Focuses on the glassware produced by the Duncan & Miller Glass Co.

Early American

Auction Service

Norman C. Heckler & Company
79 Bradford Corner Road
Woodstock Valley, CT 06282
Phone: 203-974-0682 or 203-974-1634
Specializes in the sale of early glass and bottles; Heckler & Co. sold a single bottle for $40,700 at auction in 1990.

Expert

Mark Vuono
306 Mill Road
Stamford, CT 06903
Phone: 203-329-8744
*Specializes in historical flasks, blown-3-mold, and blown American glass. *

Expert

Wes-Jan Antiques
Wesley Garton
P.O. Box 780985
Wichita, KS 67278
Phone: 316-778-1948 *

Museum/Library

Sandwich Glass Museum
Newsletter: Cullet, The
129 Main St.
P.O. Box 103
Sandwich, MA 02563
Phone: 508-888-0251
The museum preserves and displays the glass man-ufactured in Sandwich 1825-1907.

Elegant

Matching Service

Red Horse Inn Antiques
420 1st Ave. N.W.
Plainview, MN 55964
Phone: 507-534-3511
Specializes in matching glass by Cambridge, Fostoria, Morgantown, Heisey, Tiffin, Duncan and Fry; no European glass companies in stock.

Matching Service

China By Pattern
P.O. Box 129
Farmington, CT 06034
Phone: 203-678-7079
Locating crystal & glassware: Fostoria, Cam-bridge, etc.

Matching Service

Milbra's Crystal Matching
P.O. Box 363
Rio Vista, TX 76093
Phone: 817-645-6066 or 817-373-2468
Crystal matching: Fostoria, Tiffin, Lenox & others; buy and sell.

Matching Service

Ettelman's Discontinued China & Crystal
P.O. Box 6491
Corpus Christi, TX 78466
Phone: 512-888-8391
Buys/sells inactive patterns of elegant glassware by Cambridge, Duncan, Fostoria, Heisey, Lenox and Tiffin.

European

Dealer

F.T.S. Inc.
Ron Fox
416 Throop St.
N. Babylon, NY 11704
Phone: 516-669-7232   FAX: 516-669-7232
Wants old European glass: transparent or opaque enamel, wheel cut, engraved, overlay, iridescent, etc.

Fenton

Club/Association

Fenton Art Glass Collectors of America, Inc.
Newsletter: Butterfly Net, The
P.O. Box 384
Williamstown, WV 26187
Phone: 304-375-6196
FAGCA is a non-profit educational corporation dedicated to learning about Fenton art glass.

Club/Association

National Fenton Glass Society
Newsletter: Fenton Flyer, The
P.O. Box 4008
Marietta, OH 45750

Expert

Ferill Rice
302 Pheasant Run
Kaukauna, WI 54130
Phone: 414-766-9176 *

Expert

Dick & Waunita Bosworth
7303 N.W. 75th St.
Kansas City, MO 64152 *

Man./Prod./Dist.

Fenton Art Glass Company, The
700 Elizabeth St.
Williamstown, WV 26187
Phone: 304-375-6122   FAX: 304-375-6459
Currently manufactures plates, figurines, bells, ornaments and a "Connoisseur Collection."

Findlay

Club/Association

Collectors of Findlay Glass
P.O. Box 256
Findlay, OH 45839-0256
Club for members to share information about Findlay Glass and the current activity in the marketplace.

Flowers

Museum/Library

Botanical Museum of Harvard University, The Blaschka Collection
24 Oxford Street
Cambridge, MA 02138
Phone: 617-495-2326

Life-like handcrafted glass replicas of plants and flowers.

Fostoria

Club/Association
Fostoria Glass Society, The
Newsletter: Facets of Fostoria
Clifford Bucy
P.O. Box 826
Moundsville, WV 26041
Phone: 304-845-2788

Club/Association
Fostoria Glass Society of Southern
California
Melanie Hildreth
3547 Toyon St.
West Covina, CA 91792
Phone: 818-912-1112
The FGSSC is a study group and a Chapter of the Fostoria Glass Society of America; monthly meetings; visitors welcome.

Dealer
Judy Giangiuli
RD 6, Box 292
New Castle, PA 16101
Phone: 412-652-5806
Wants Fostoria stemware. *

Expert
Michael Baker
P.O. Box 826
Moundsville, WV 26041 *

Museum/Library
Fostoria Glass Museum
Clifford Bucy
P.O. Box 826
Moundsville, WV 26041
Phone: 304-845-2788

Fry

Club/Association
H.C. Fry Glass Society
P.O. Box 41
Beaver, PA 15009 *

Gorham

Man./Prod./Dist.
Gorham, Inc.
P.O. Box 906
Mount Kisco, NY 10549
Phone: 914-242-9300 or 800-225-1460
FAX: 914-242-9379

Greentown

Club/Association
National Greentown Glass Association
Newsletter: National Greentown Glass
Association Newsletter
LeAnne Miliser
19596 Glendale Ave.
South Bend, IN 46637

Expert
JMJ Antiques
Jim & Mira Houdeshell
1801 N. Main St.
Findlay, OH 45840
Phone: 419-423-2895 or 419-424-4551

Museum/Library
Greentown Glass Museum
112 N. Meridian
P.O. Box 161
Greentown, IN 46936
Phone: 317-628-7818
An exhibit from the old Indiana Tumbler & Goblet Co. (1894-1903).

Museum/Library
Grand Rapids Public Museum
54 Jefferson SE
Grand Rapids, MI 49503
Phone: 616-456-3977

Hawkes

Expert
Marnette Antiques
Marvin Stofft
45 12th St.
Tell City, IN 47586
Phone: 812-547-5707

Heisey

Club/Association
Heisey Collectors of America
Newsletter: Heisey News, The
169 W. Church St.
Newark, OH 43055
Phone: 614-345-2932

Museum/Library
National Heisey Glass Museum, The
P.O. Box 27
Newark, OH 43055
Phone: 614-345-2932
Owned and operated by Heisey Collectors of America; hundreds of patterns of glass made by A.H. Heisey & Co. 1895-1957 on display.

Periodical
Heisey Publications
Newsletter: Newscaster, The
Ralph & Sandra McKelvey
P.O. Box 102
Plymouth, OH 44865
Phone: 419-935-0338

A quarterly newsletter on identification and research.

Imperial

Club/Association
National Imperial Glass Collectors
Society
Newsletter: Glasszette
P.O. Box 534
Bellaire, OH 43906
Members interested in glassware produced by the Imperial Glass Corp.; conducts an annual convention offering "members only" auction.

Jenkins

Expert
Joyce Ann Hicks
P.O. Box 2501
Kokomo, IN 46904
Author of "Jenkins Glass Price Guide."

Kosta Boda

Man./Prod./Dist.
Kosta Boda USA Ltd. (Div. of Orrefors)
233 West Parkway
Pompton Plains, NJ 07444
Phone: 201-831-1166

Lalique

Club/Association
Lalique Society of America
c/o Jacques Jugeat Co.
11 East 26th Street
New York, NY 10010
Phone: 212-684-6760 or 800-CRI-STAL
Focuses on the collectibles issued by Lalique. A Jacques Jugeat Co. marketer-sponsored club.

Collector
C.T. Peters, Inc.
C.T. Peters
P.O. Box 2120
Red Bank, NJ 07701 *

Collector
Jeff Myers
P.O. Box 26151
Charlotte, NC 28221
Phone: 800-327-9654
Wants to buy R. Lalique glass; also wants Galle, Daum and Tiffany glass.

Expert
Cocktails & Laughter Antiques
Randall Monsen
P.O. Box 1503
Arlington, VA 22210
Phone: 703-938-2129
Wants vases and perfumes by Lalique; prefers pre-1940 pieces by Rene Lalique but will consider earlier pieces. *

Expert
John Danis
11028 Raleigh Ct.
Rockford, IL 61111
Phone: 815-877-6098 *

Man./Prod./Dist.
Jacques Jugeat Co.
11 East 26th Street
New York, NY 10010
Phone: 212-684-6760
Distributor of Lalique in U.S.; patterns are never discontinued. Lalique also sold through Bailey, Banks & Biddle stores.

Matching Service
Tops & Bottoms Club
Madeleine France
P.O. Box 15555
Plantation, FL 33318
Phone: 305-584-0009   FAX: 305-584-0014
Matches Lalique perfume bottle tops and bottoms.

Museum/Library
Musee Des Arts Decoratifs
Palais du Louvre
107 Rue de Rivoli
75001 Paris, France

Lenox

Man./Prod./Dist.
Lenox China & Crystal Consumer Service
100 Lenox Dr.
Lawrenceville, NJ 08648
Phone: 609-896-2800 or 800-635-3669
Offers Matching Services List of dealers who offer replacements for current of discontinued Lenox items; also gives insurance estimates.

Man./Prod./Dist.
Lenox Shop
Rt. 3 East
Mt. Pleasant, PA 15666
Phone: 800-842-3681
Factory where crystal is made. Call to place custom orders for inactive pattern replacements.

Libbey

Man./Prod./Dist.
Libbey Glass
One Sea Gate
Toledo, OH 43666
Phone: 419-247-5000 *

Mercury

Expert
Dorothy Daniel
4020 N. 25th St.
Arlington, VA 22207
Phone: 703-243-0322 *

Milk

Club/Association
National Milk Glass Collectors Society
Newsletter: Opaque News
1113 Birchwood Dr.
Garland, TX 75043
Dedicated to the study, collection and preservation of milk glass items.

Expert
Barbara Joyce Kaye
158 Maple Ave.
Metuchen, NJ 08840
*Author of "White Gold: A Primer for Previously Unlisted Milk Glass, Book 1." **

Museum/Library
Houston Antique Museum, The
201 High St.
Chattanooga, TN 37403
Phone: 615-267-7176

Monart & Vasart

Club/Association
Monart & Vasart Collectors Club
Newsletter: Ysartnews
Peter Pfersick
869 Cleveland Street
Oakland, CA 94606 *

Moser

Expert
A Touch of Glass
Gary Baldwin
P.O. Box 213
Simpsonville, MD 21150
Phone: 301-788-21150
Buys, sells and collects European enameled glass; co-author with Lee Carno of "Moser - Artistry in Glass."

Mount Washington

Museum/Library
New Bedford Glass Museum
P.O. Box F-655
New Bedford, MA 02740
Phone: 617-994-0115

Mugs

Collector
Brent Godlewski
4551 NW 70th St,
Four Lauderdale, FL 33319-4043
Wants hand-blown, pressed with applied handles, purple slag, carnival, historical, nursery rhymes, geometrics, advertising, etc. mugs.

New Bedford

Museum/Library
New Bedford Glass Museum
P.O. Box F-655
New Bedford, MA 02740
Phone: 617-994-0115

Old Morgantown

Club/Association
Old Morgantown Glass Collectors' Guild
Newsletter: Old Morgantown Topics
Jerry Gallagher,Pres.
420 1st Ave. N.W.
Plainview, MN 55964
Phone: 507-534-3511
Guild goals are to research and preserve the history of the Morgantown, WV Glass Works.

Orrefors

Man./Prod./Dist.
Orrefors, Inc.
140 Bradford Dr.
Berlin, NJ 08009
Phone: 609-768-5400   FAX: 609-768-9726

Paden City

Expert
Michael Krumme
P.O. Box 5542
Santa Monica, CA 90409-5542
Send $1 & large SASE for Paden City Fact Sheet which answers commonly asked questions about Paden City Glass (but not Paden City Pottery.)

Pairpoint

Man./Prod./Dist.
Pairpoint Glass Works
851 Sandwich Rd.
Sagamore, MA 02561
Phone: 617-888-2344
Blowing room open to visitors; catalog $2 (refundable).

Pattern

Expert
Dendara's Antiques
Darryl Reilly
P.O. Box 1203
Pepperel, MA 01463
Phone: 617-433-8718 *

Expert
John & Alice Ahlfeld
2634 Royal Rd.
Lancaster, PA 17603
Phone: 717-397-7313 *

Expert
Golden Webb Antiques, Inc.
William Jenks
P.O. Box 1274
Wilkes-Barre, PA 18703
Phone: 717-288-3039 *

Expert
Jerry Baker
P.O. Box 13081
St. Petersburg, FL 33733
Phone: 813-323-5524 *

Expert
Mike Anderton
6619 52nd St. NE
Marysville, WA 98270
Phone: 206-334-1902 *

Matching Service
Kieningers
5159 Ridge Rd. East, R.D. 3
Williamson, NY 14589
Has thousands of pieces in stock; hundreds of patterns; will try to match. *

Pattern (Opalescent)

Expert
Jim Broom
Box 65
Effingham, IL 62401 *

Phoenix

Expert
Kelly Collection
Kathy Kelly
1621 Princess Ave.
Pittsburgh, PA 15216 *

Pressed

Museum/Library
Schminck Memorial Museum
128 South E St.
Lakeview, OR 97630
Phone: 503-947-3134
Large collection of American pressed glass, 1830-1920.

Reed & Barton

Man./Prod./Dist.
Reed & Barton
144 W. Britannia Street
Taunton, MA 02780
Phone: 508-824-6611   FAX: 508-822-7269
Produces china, crystal, silver, silverplate, and stainless flatware, collectible plates, bells, dolls, ornaments and accessories.

Sandwich

Expert
Richard G. Marden
Box 524
Wolfeboro, NH 03894
Phone: 603-569-3209 *

Museum/Library
Sandwich Glass Museum
Journal: Acorn, The
129 Main St.
P.O. Box 103
Sandwich, MA 02563
Phone: 508-888-0251
The museum contains and studies glass associated with the Sandwich Factory era.

Scandinavian Art

Dealer
Gallerie Ani'tiques
Anita L. Grashof
Stage House Village
Park & Front Streets
Scotch Plains, NJ 07076
Phone: 908-322-7085 or 201-377-3032
Wants Swedish (Orrefors, Kosta, glass by Gate, Thald, Lindstand) and Finish (Karhula, Iitala, glass by Wirkkala, Sarpaneva) art glass.

Sinclaire

Expert
Marnette Antiques
Marvin Stofft
45 12th St.
Tell City, IN 47586
Phone: 812-547-5707

Slag (Marble)

Expert
Dorothy Daniel
4020 N. 25th St.
Arlington, VA 22207
Phone: 703-243-0322 *

Souvenir & Commemorative

(see also SOUVENIR & COMMEMORATIVE ITEMS)

Periodical
Newspaper: Travel Collector
P.O. Box 40
Manawa, WI 54949-0040
Phone: 414-596-1944
Monthly newspaper that focuses on souvenir and commemorative glass and ceramic items in addition to other souvenir collectibles.

Steuben

Man./Prod./Dist.
Steuben Glass
5th Ave. at 56th Street
New York, NY 10022
Phone: 212-752-1441 *

Museum/Library
Rockwell Museum, The
Cedar St. at Denison Pkwy.
Corning, NY 14830
Phone: 607-937-5386
Large collection of glass made by Frederic Carder while he was with Steuben Glass Works; also large collection of western Americana.

St. Louis

(see also PAPERWEIGHTS)

Stretch

Club/Association
Stretch Glass Society
Newsletter: SGS Newsletter
Joanne Rodgers
P.O. Box 770643
Lakewood, OH 44107
For collectors of stretch glass; annual convention 1st week in May; newsletter contains articles submitted by membership.

Studio

Periodical
Verlsganstaly Handwerk GmbH
Magazine: Nues Glaz/New Glass
Gunter Nicola
Auf'm Tetelberg 7
Postfach 8120, 4000
Dusseldorf 1, Germany
Many well illustrated bilingual articles on European as well as U.S. studio glass.

Studio (Contemporary)

Dealer
Glass Gallery
Sarah Hansen
4720 Hampden
Bethesda, MD 20814
Phone: 301-657-3478
Retails one-of-a-kind contemporary glass pieces of art.

Sulphides-Cameos In Glass

Museum/Library
Bergstrom-Mahler Museum
Alex Vance, ExDir
165 N. Park Ave.
Neenah, WI 54956
Phone: 414-751-4658 or 414-751-4672

Tiffin

Club/Association

Tiffin Glass Collectors' Club
Newsletter: Tiffin Glassmasters
P.O. Box 554
Tiffin, OH 44883
Phone: 419-447-4452

Expert

Distel's Antiques
Ginny Distel
4041 S.C.R. 22
Tiffin, OH 44883
Phone: 419-447-5832 *

Val St. Lambert

Matching Service

Establishment Dubois
Avenue Brugman 219, 1180
Brussels, Belgium
Val St. Lambert also sold in the US through Bailey, Banks & Biddle stores. *

Viking

Man./Prod./Dist.

Viking Glass
P.O. Box 29
New Martinsville, WV 26155
Phone: 304-455-2900 *

Waterford

Man./Prod./Dist.

Waterford Wedgwood USA Inc.
P.O. Box 1454
Wall, NJ 07719
Phone: 201-938-5800   FAX: 201-938-6915

Wave Crest

Collector

Betty Bird
107 Ida St.
Mount Shasta, CA 96067
Phone: 916-926-4331

Westmoreland

Club/Association

National Westmoreland Glass Collectors Club
Newsletter: Towne Crier, The
P.O. Box 372
Export, PA 15632

Club/Association

Westmoreland Glass Collectors Club
Newsletter: Westmoreland Glass Collectors Newsletter
P.O. Box 143
North Liberty, IA 52317
Sponsors annual Westmoreland Glass convention, auction and souvenir limited edition items.

Museum/Library

Westmoreland Glass Museum
Phillip Rosso
1815 Trimble Ave.
Port Vue, PA 15133
Phone: 412-678-7352
Over 4,000 pieces on display; original photos, tools, molds, etc.; also wholesales glass.

Whimsies

Club/Association

Whimsey Club, The
Newsletter: Whimsical Notions
Chris Davis
522 Woodhill
Newark, NY 14513
Phone: 315-331-4078 or 716-652-7752
Interested in hand blown glass whimsies such as smoke bells, flip flops, witch balls, canes, rolling pins, etc.

Collectors

Jeff & Mary Waterhouse
22 Meadowbrook Rd.
Williamsville, NY 14221
Phone: 716-626-5703
Interested in hand blown glass whimsies such as smoke bells, flip flops, witch balls, canes, rolling pins, etc.

Witches Balls

Collector

J. Gurfein
2111 Jeff Davis Highway
Arlington, VA 22202
Wants witches balls and solid glass newel posts. *

GLASS (MODERN)

Club/Association

Glass Art Society
Journal: Glass Art Society Journal
Alice Rooney
P.O. Box 1364
Corning, NY 14830
Phone: 607-936-0530   FAX: 607-936-0530
An international organization to encourage excellence and to advance the appreciation, understanding and development of the glass arts.

GLASS EYES

Collector

Donald Gorlick
P.O. Box 24541
Seattle, WA 98124
Wants human glass eyes, either left or right, colors and size unimportant, just human eyes.

GLASS KNIVES

Club/Association

Glass Knife Collectors Club
Newsletter: Cutting Edge, The
Adrienne S. Escoe
P.O. Box 342
Los Alamitos, CA 90720
Phone: 213-430-6479
Focuses on the history of glass knives, identification of patterns, current pricing, articles about members, and buy/sell ads.

Collector

Macomber
RD 3, Box 201
Delta, PA 17314
Wants glass knives, please price and describe.

Collector

Gary Crabtree
3165 McKinley
San Bernardino, CA 92404
Wants glass knives, especially those with colored and ribbed handles.

GLASSES

Drinking

(see also STEINS (MODERN); SWANKYSWIGS)

Auction Service

Glasses, Mugs & Steins Auction
Pete Kroll
P.O. Box 207
Sun Prairie, WI 53590
Phone: 608-837-4818
A semi-annual mail auction featuring collectible advertising glasses, mugs, & steins: beer, soda, cartoon, Disney, rootbeer, sports, etc.

Collector

Tom Hoder
444 S. Cherry
Itasca, IL 60143
Phone: 708-773-2635
Specializing in cartoon and character decorated drinking glasses.

Collector

Carol Markowski
3141 W. Platte Ave.
Colorado Springs, CO 80904
Phone: 719-633-7399
Wants to buy drinking glasses with cartoon figures on them: Pepsi, Coke, fast food logos, early Disney, sports, etc.

Expert

Michael J. Kelly
408 Franklin St.
Slippery Rock, PA 16057
Phone: 412-794-6420

Buys and sells cartoon, sports, and fast-food drinking glasses: Disney, super heroes from 30's to present; author of books on same.

Expert
Mark E. Chase
RD #3 Box 360
New Wilmington, PA 16142
Phone: 412-946-8126
Buying cartoon, sports and fast-food drinking glasses from the 30's to the present.

Expert
John Hervey
P.O. Box 1373
Frisco, TX 75034
*Interested in Pepsi, Disney, Star Trek, etc. promotional glasses; also co-author of "Collector's Guide to Glass Collecting." ***

Periodical
Newsletter: Collector Glass News
Michael J. Kelly
P.O. Box 308
Slippery Rock, PA 16057
Phone: 412-946-8126 or 412-794-6420
Devoted exclusively to contemporary fast-food restaurant glassware, promotional glassware and food product tumblers.

Spirit (Advertising)
Expert
Barbara Edmonson
701 E. Lassen Ave. #308
Chico, CA 95926
Phone: 916-343-8460
*Author of "Old Advertising Spirits Glasses." ***

GLIDERS
(see also AIRPLANES, Sailplanes)

GLOBES
Dealer
Richard Arkway, Inc.
538 Madison Ave.
New York, NY 10022
Phone: 800-453-0045
*Wants pre-1900 globes; pre-1880 atlases; pre-1860 maps. ***

GOLD RUSH MEMORABILIA
Dealer
S C Coin & Stamp Co. Inc.
Cy Phillips, Jr.
P.O. Drawer 3069
Arcadia, CA 91006
Phone: 818-445-8277 or 800-367-0779
Wants gold rush items; also historical trail items; old west town tokens.

Museum/Library
Klondike Gold Rush National Historical Park
117 S. Main
Seattle, WA 98104
Phone: 206-442-7220

GOLLIWOGGS & DUTCH DOLLS
Expert
Sigourney's Antiques
Henry & Doris Sigourney
P.O. Box 447
Cavendish, VT 05142
Phone: 802-226-7713
*Golliwoggs are black characters originally adopted as an advertising character by an English manufacturer of jams and jellies. ***

GRANITEWARE
(see also KITCHEN COLLECTIBLES)

Club/Association
National Graniteware Society
Newsletter: National Graniteware News
P.O. Box 10013
Cedar Rapids, IA 52410-0013
For collectors to share information about graniteware.

Collector
Patricia Peltz
10091 Stilbite
Fountain Valley, CA 92708
*Wants blue graniteware. ***

Expert
Helen's Antiques
Helen Greguire
103 Trimmer Rd.
Hilton, NY 14468
Phone: 716-392-2704
*Author of "The Collector's Encyclopedia of Granite Ware." ***

Expert
Upper Loft Antiques
Gregg Ellington
47 Columbus St.
Wilmington, OH 45177
Phone: 513-382-4311
Buys, sells, trades and collects graniteware and American ceramics including mochaware, yellowware, spongeware, etc.

Expert
Blue Boar Antiques
Pamela & Allan Luttig
P.O. Box 423
Grand Ledge, MI 48837

GRAVESTONES
Club/Association
Association for Gravestone Studies
Newsletter: AGS Newsletter
Miranda Levin, ExDir
30 Elm Street
Worcester, MA 01609
Phone: 508-831-7753
The AGS offers information and restoration referrals for gravestones; NOTE: Respect gravestones; they are sacred and not collectible!

GREETING CARDS
(see also HOLIDAY COLLECTIBLES; POST CARDS; VALENTINES)

GULLIVER'S TRAVELS
Collector
Meredith & Tom Hughes
P.O. Box 791
Great Falls, VA 22066
Phone: 703-759-6714
Wants anything related to "Gulliver's Travels": games, toys, books and especially pop-up books.

GUNS
(see also ADVERTISING, Firearms Related; ARMS & ARMOR; CIVIL WAR ARTIFACTS; FIREARMS; MILITARIA; TOYS, BB Guns; TOYS, Cap Pistols)

HALLOWEEN COLLECTIBLES
(see also HOLIDAY COLLECTIBLES)

Collector
C.J. Russell
P.O. Box 499
Winchester, NH 03470 *

Collector
David Welch
RR 2, Box 233
Murphysboro, IL 62966
Phone: 618-687-2282
Wants rubber monster masks (sold through famous monster magazines only); also '50's-'60's monster, TV, movie, comic, cartoon costumes.

Collector
John & Jenny Tarrant
10221 Squire Meadows
St. Louis, MO 63123
Wants Halloween items, especially those made in Germany.

HANDBAGS
(see also PURSES)

HANDS

Wooden

Collector

Donald Gorlick
P.O. Box 24541
Seattle, WA 98124
Wants wooden hands with articulated fingers; may be a glove stretcher mold for sizing gloves; wooden with fingers and thumb that move.

HATPINS & HATPIN HOLDERS

Club/Association

International Club for Collectors of
Hatpins & Hatpin Holders
Newsletter: Points
Lillian Baker
15237 Chanera Ave.
Gardena, CA 90249
Phone: 213-329-2619

Collector

Gold Hatpin, The
Diane Richardson
P.O. Box 993
Oak Park, IL 60303-0993
Phone: 708-848-3247
Wants all types hatpins & holders: Satsuma, vanity, enameled, figural, fancy & the unusual; no repros.

Collector

Collector
P.O. Box 93
Canoga Park, CA 91305
Wants very ornate, standing or wall-type holders; also hatpins.

Dealer

Bits & Pieces of Yesterday & Today
Sharon Hood
46060 Warren
Canton, MI 48187
Phone: 313-453-5071
Wants hatpins and hatpin holders.

Dealer

L & W Antiques
5760 West Irving Park Rd.
Chicago, IL 60634
Phone: 312-545-6338
*Wants hatpins and hatpin holders. *

Expert

Robert Larsen
3214 19th St.
Columbus, NE 68601 *

Expert

Lillian Baker
15237 Chanera Ave.
Gardena, CA 90249
Phone: 213-329-2619

Specializes in high fashion costume jewelry, hatpins and hatpin holders, and miniatures; author of book on hatpins and holders.

Repro. Source

P.O. Box 24606
Philadelphia, PA 19111
Phone: 215-372-3887
Sells reproduction hat pins.

HAWAIIAN COLLECTIBLES

Collector

Gene Snyder
991 McLean St.
Dunedin, FL 34699-8
Wants Hawaiian memorabilia: postcards, 1950's shirts, anything.

Collector

Collector
75-5744 Alii Dr.
Kailua-Kona, HI 96740
*Wants Hawaiian vintage jewelry, menus, chalk and ceramic hula dancers, palm tree items, etched glass, TV lamps, shirts, etc. *

Collector

Cedric Felix
46 Market St.
Wailuku, HI 96793
*Wants Hawaiian artifacts, wooden carvings, dolls, drums, whaling items, documents, photo albums, hula items, maps, etc. *

Dealer

Wholesale Rug
2448 Lincoln Hwy.
East Lancaster, PA 17602
Phone: 717-295-9078
*Wants cultural art and artifacts from all the Polynesian islands; war clubs, items of personal adornment; also pre-1925 Hawaiian items. *

HEALTH & BEAUTY DEVICES

Devices To Restore

Collector

O. Lindan
1404 Dorsh Rd.
Cleveland, OH 44121
Phone: 216-382-7113
Wants old electrotherapeutic and controversial healing devices and related literature; also wants medical, scientific instruments.

HEBRAICA

(see also JUDAICA)

HI FI

Components

Collector

S. McDaniel
1 Edgewood Place
North Brunswick, NJ 08902
Phone: 201-249-3738
*Wants old audio equipment or speakers. *

Collector

J. McCarter
125 Harmony
West Grove, PA 19390
Phone: 215-869-2042
*Wants HI FI stereo components: nice 50's, 60's toners, amps, speakers, McIntosh, Marantz, Audio Research, Electro Voice, etc. *

HIGHWAY COLLECTIBLES

Club/Association

Society for Commercial Archeology,
National Museum of American History
14th & Constitution Ave., NW
Room 5010
Washington, DC 20560
Phone: 202-357-2700 *

Club/Association

2-Lane America
Newsletter: 2-Lane America Newsletter
Dr. Thomas J. Snyder
P.O. Drawer 5323
Oxnard, CA 93030
Phone: 805-485-9923
Organization focusing on protecting and promoting Rt. 66 (The Mother Road) and other U.S. roads; also collecting items relating thereto.

Route 66 Items

Club/Association

Route 66 Association of Illinois
Laura & Jeff Meyer
P.O. Box 8262
Rolling Meadows, IL 60008
Phone: 708-392-0860
Organization focusing on protecting and promoting Rt. 66 (The Mother Road) and collecting items relating thereto.

Signs & Traffic Devices

Periodical

Newsletter: Signpost
Jeff Francis
P.O. Box 41381
St. Petersburg, FL 33743
Phone: 813-345-4431 or 813-343-8977
An association focusing on the research and preservation of traffic devices.

HISTORICAL AMERICANA

(see also AUTOGRAPHS; GLASS,
Commemorative; MANUSCRIPTS; PAPER
COLLECTIBLES; POLITICAL
COLLECTIBLES)

Auction Service

Ben Corning
10 Lilian Road Ext.
Framingham, MA 01701
Phone: 617-872-2229
*Specializes in mail-bid auctions of political items
and historical Americana. ***

Auction Service

Rex Stark Auctions
49 Wethersfield Road
Bellingham, MA 02019
Phone: 508-966-0994
*Conducts mail auctions of quality historical
Americana: political, early military, advertising,
sports, etc.*

Auction Service

Rita-Mobley Auctions Inc.
P.O. Box 53
South Glastonbury, CT 06073
Phone: 203-633-3076
Specializing in historical items, ephemera, autographs, photographs, etc.

Auction Service

William A. Fox Auctions, Inc.
676 Morris Avenue
Springfield, NJ 07081
Phone: 201-467-2366
*Specializes in the sale of Americana, ephemera,
and U.S. and foreign stamps and covers.*

Auction Service

David Frent
P.O. Box 455
Oakhurst, NJ 07755
Phone: 201-922-0768
*Specializes in mail-bid auctions of political items
and historical Americana. ***

Auction Service

Swann Galleries, Inc.
104 E. 25th St.
New York, NY 10010
Phone: 212-254-4710   FAX: 212-979-1017
*Oldest/largest U.S. auctioneer specializing in rare
books, autographs & manuscripts, Judaica, photographs, and works of art on paper.*

Auction Service

Historicana
Robert Coup
P.O. Box 348
Leola, PA 17540-0348
Phone: 717-656-7780
*Specializes in mail-bid auctions of character
collectibles, Disneyana, political items & historical Americana; sample catalog $2.*

Auction Service

Ohio Boys Video Auction - the Dixeys
626 Arlington Avenue
Mansfield, OH 44903
*Specializes in mail-bid auctions of political items
and historical Americana. ***

Auction Service

Anderson Auction
Al Anderson
P.O. Box 644
Troy, OH 45373
Phone: 513-339-0850
*Specializes in mail-bid auctions of political items
and historical Americana.*

Auction Service

Political Gallery, The
Tom Slater
1325 W. 86th St.
Indianapolis, IN 46260
Phone: 317-257-0863
*Specializing in mail-bid auctions of Disneyana,
historical Americana, toys, political items, and
other collectibles.*

Auction Service

U.I. "Chick" Harris
Box 20614
St. Louis, MO 63139
Phone: 314-352-8623
Collector/specialist in all types of political Americana; conducts specialized mail-auctions of political and historical Americana.

Dealer

Rex Stark
49 Wethersfield Road
Bellingham, MA 02019
Phone: 508-966-0994
*Buys & sells historical Americana; wants 1770-
1870 Amer. historical pottery; offers catalog of
historical/political Americana for*

Dealer

Remember When Antiquities
P.O. Box 629
Acton, ME 04001
Phone: 207-477-8111
*Wants autographs, books, historical ephemera,
sports memorabilia. ***

Dealer

Peter Hlinka Historical Americana
Peter Hlinka
P.O. Box 310
New York, NY 10028-0003
Phone: 212-409-6407
*Publishes a large catalog of militaria, insignia,
war relics and other political and historical Americana; also foreign.*

Dealer

Macdonald's Historical Collections
J.F. Macdonald
1316 NE 113th
P.O. Box 56371
Portland, OR 97220
Phone: 503-255-7256
Buys/sells items on aviation, Am. History, medical, sports, wildlife, western, space, music, holidays, Civil War, black history, etc.

Expert

Hake's Americana & Collectibles Auction
Ted Hake
P.O. Box 1444
York, PA 17405
Phone: 717-848-1333   FAX: 717-848-4977
*Specializing in mail-bid auctions of Disneyana,
historical Americana, toys, premiums, political
items, character and other collectibles.*

HOBO COLLECTIBLES

(see also TRAMP ART)

Club/Association

National Hobo Association
Newsletter: Hobo Times
World Way Center
Box 90430
Los Angeles, CA 90009
Phone: 213-645-1500 *

HOLIDAY COLLECTIBLES

(see also CHRISTMAS COLLECTIBLES;
COLLECTIBLES (MODERN), Ornaments;
VALENTINES)

Auction Service

Holiday Auction, The
Cindy Chipps
4027 Brooks Hill Rd.
Brooks, KY 40109
Phone: 502-955-9238
*Holds monthly mail auction of a wide variety of
holiday items from the common to the very rare;
send #10 SASE for free catalog.*

Dealer

Bettie Petzoldt
RR #1 Box 249
New Park, PA 17352
Phone: 717-382-1416
*Wants pre-1940 Christmas items: unusual,
collectible (figural) Christmas ornaments, lights,
Santas; other holiday items too.*

Dealer

Holly-Daze
Jenny Tarrant
10221 Squire Meadows
St. Louis, MO 63123
*Wants papier-mache Halloween candy containers
& lanterns; also Santas, cotton people, bubble
lights; send LSASE for want list.*

Expert

Jackie Chamberlain
1520 Foothill Blvd.
La Canada, CA 91011
Phone: 818-790-5416 *

HOLLOWARE

(see also SILVER; SILVERPLATE)

HOLOGRAPHY

Museum/Library

Museum of Holography
11 Mercer Street
New York, NY 10013
Phone: 212-925-0581

HORNS & WHISTLES

(see also STEAM-OPERATED, Models &
Equipment)

Club/Association

Air Horn & Steam Whistle Enthusiasts
Magazine: Horn & Whistle
Richard J. Weisenberger
2655 North Friendship, Lot 18
Paducah, KY 42001
Phone: 502-554-1328
*Dedicated to the history of horns and whistles
presently used in marine, industry, railroad ser-
vice, general signaling and warnings.*

Collector

Lin Chapman
58 Blakeslee Rd.
Wallingford, CT 06492

HORSE COLLECTIBLES

(see also ANIMAL COLLECTIBLES;
SADDLES; WESTERN AMERICANA)

Club/Association

U. S. Horse Cavalry Association
Newsletter: Crossed Sabers
P.O. Box 6253
Fort Bliss, TX 79906
Phone: 915-565-3378
*Focuses on the history of cavalry units and equip-
ment and on the activities of the U.S. Cavalry
Museum. ***

Dealer

Just Animals
Barbara Framke
15525 Fitzgerald
Livonia, MI 48154
Phone: 313-464-8493
*Buys porcelain and ceramic horse figurines, espe-
cially by Hagen-Renaker, Beswick and Goebel;
also wants horse related books.*

Expert

Aquarius Antiques
Jim & Nancy Schaut
P.O. Box 10781
Glendale, AZ 85318
Phone: 602-878-4293
*Author of "Horsin' Around" (LW Books, 1990), a
price guide to equine collectibles (including toys).*

Museum/Library

American Saddle Horse Museum
Association
Keith D. Bartz, Dir.
4093 Iron Works Pike
Lexington, KY 40511
Phone: 606-259-2746
*To learn about the American saddlebred horse,
and to preserve and maintain artifacts pertinent
to the history of the breed.*

Museum/Library

International Museum of the Horse
4089 Iron Works Pike
Lexington, KY 40511
Phone: 606-233-4304

Museum/Library

Stradling Museum of the Horse, Inc.
P.O. Box 413
Patagonia, AZ 85624
Phone: 602-394-2264

Art

Dealer

Bear Den
P.O. Box 238
Shrewsbury, MA 01545
Phone: 508-795-1321
*Wants Quarter, Morgan, Thoroughbred, etc.
sculptures, prints, etc.; all art. ***

Models

Collector

Jessica Prior
2972 Russell Dr.
Howell, MI 48843
Phone: 517-546-4033
*Wants Breyer and Hartland plastic model horses,
rider and animal models; will buy collections.*

Dealer

Bentley Sales Company
642 Sandy Lane
Des Plaines, IL 60016
Phone: 708-439-2049
*Carries entire Bryer Model Horse line plus limited
editions, discontinued and special run models.*

Dealer

Edythe Shepherd
1334 E. Suncrest Dr.
Tucson, AZ 85706
*Wants Breyer plastic horses. ***

Periodical

Magazine: Just About Horses
Peter Stone, Pub.
34 Owens Dr.
Wayne, NJ 07470
Phone: 201-956-9555   FAX: 201-956-0077
*Offers information on model horse collecting and
hobbying including customization, vintage
models & horse model showing; no paid ads.*

HORSE-DRAWN VEHICLES

(see also CONESTOGA WAGONS; FARM
MACHINERY)

Auction Service

Carrollton Sleigh & Wagon Auction
P.O. Box 323
Carrollton, OH 44615
Phone: 800-452-8452
*Conducts auctions of horse-drawn carriages, bug-
gies, hitch wagons, tack and other horse-related
items.*

Auction Service

Shipshewana Annual Mid-West Carriage
Auction
P.O. Box 185
Shipshewana, IN 46565
*Conducts an annual (May/June) auction of
horse-drawn vehicles and related items.*

Auction Service

Sweeney's Horse & Carriage Sale
P.O. Box 67
Waukon, IA 52172

Auction Service

Martin Auctioneers Inc.
Larry L. Martin
P.O. Box 477
Intercourse, PA 17534
Phone: 717-768-8108   FAX: 717-768-7714
*Specializes in the sale of horse drawn carriages,
buggies, hitch wagons, tack and other horse-re-
lated items.*

Collector

Jack Day
2139 Corbett
Monkton, MD 21111
Phone: 301-472-9041
*Wants unusual horse drawn vehicles, coach
lamps, harnesses, literature, accessories. ***

Dealer

Dealer
P.O. Box 1392
Santa Rosa, CA 95402-1392
*Wants horse-drawn wagons, fifth-wheel farm
wagons, light delivery wagons, stagecoaches, etc.*

Periodical

Magazine: Draft Horse Journal
P.O. Box 670
Waverly, IA 50677

Periodical

Magazine: Driving Digest Magazine
P.O. 467
Brooklyn, CT 06234
A magazine for horsemen interested in competitive driving of a single horse, pairs and four-in-hands.

Carriages

Auction Service

Martin Auctioneers, Inc.
P.O. Box 71
Blue Ball, PA 17506
Phone: 717-768-8108
Specializes in the sale of carriages, sleds and other horse-drawn vehicles.

Club/Association

Carriage Association of America
Journal: Carriage Journal, The
R.D. 1 Box 115
Salem, NJ 08079
Phone: 609-935-1616
To foster knowledge, collecting, restoring, driving and research of horse-drawn vehicles.

Club/Association

American Driving Society
Magazine: Whip, The
P.O. Box 160
Metamora, MI 48455
Phone: 800-233-9806
Promotes the sport of carriage driving and horse training for sport and pleasure; articles, ads, competitions, carriage maintenance.

Club/Association

British Driving Society, The
Newsletter: British Driving Society Newsletter
Mrs. Jenny Dillon, Sec.
27 Dugard Place
Barford
Warwick CV35 8DX England
Focuses on carriage driving and horse training.

Museum/Library

Museums at Stony Brook, The
Newsletter: Dialogue
1208 Rte. 25A
Stony Brook, NY 11790
Phone: 516-751-0066   FAX: 516-751-0353
Large collection of American Art, decoys, horse-drawn vehicles, costumes, and miniature period rooms; museum shop.

Periodical

Magazine: Driving West
P.O. Box 2675
China, CA 91708
A monthly publication serving all driving enthusiasts; send for one free sample.

Repair Service

Chimney Farm Carriages
Charles C. Bent
R.F.D. 2
North Canaan, NH 03741
Phone: 603-523-4259
Restores horse-drawn vehicles. *

Repair Service

Woodlyn Coach Co.
Ivan Burkholder
4410 TR 628
Millersburg, OH 44654
Phone: 216-674-9124
Specializes in the repair and complete restoration of horse drawn carriages, buggies and wagons; also builds new hitch wagons.

Repair Service

A & D Buggy Shop
Alvin Raber
4682 RT. 5 TR 628
Millersburg, OH 44654
Phone: 614-599-6131
Specializes in the repair and restoration of horse drawn carriages and buggies.

Supplier

Plank & Sons
RR 2, Box C-23AA
Arthur, IL 61911
Phone: 217-543-3307
Carries buggy restoration and supply parts.

Supplier

Woodlyn Coach Co.
Ivan Burkholder
4410 TR 628
Millersburg, OH 44654
Phone: 216-674-9124
Carries buggy restoration and supply parts; send for catalog.

HOTEL COLLECTIBLES

Collector

Steve Rushmore
372 Willis Ave.
Mineola, NY 11501
Phone: 516-248-8828 or 800-366-7487
Wants hotel key tags; also hotel memorabilia; old or new; must show name of hotel.

HUMMELS

(see also FIGURINES, Hummel)

HUNGARIAN COLLECTIBLES

Collector

Dale Zelina
1527 West Clifton Blvd.
Lakewood, OH 44107
Anything from Hungary: Herend, Fischer, Zsolnay porcelains; pre-1940 marked Hungarian items; census lists, Hungarian settlements in PA.

HUNTING

(see also SPORTING COLLECTIBLES)

HYMNS

(see also BOOKS; SHEET MUSIC)

Club/Association

Hymn Society of America
Texas Christian University
Ft. Worth, TX 76129

ICE CREAM MEMORABILIA

(see also SODA FOUNTAIN COLLECTIBLES)

ICE SKATING COLLECTIBLES

Collector

Keith Pendell
1230 N. Cypress
La Habra, CA 90631
Phone: 213-619-8055
Wants antique ice skates: swan's head, big turn up, brass blades; also china with skating motif, skater's lanterns, books, etc.

ICONS

(see also RUSSIAN ITEMS)

Expert

The Icons Restoration Company
Tadas & Helen Sviderskis
730 Fifth Ave., 9th Floor
New York, NY 10019
Phone: 212-333-8638   FAX: 212-333-8720
Specializing in Byzantine, Greek & Russian icon paintings; subject search, consultation, iconography, attribution, appraisal, etc.

Repair Service

The Icons Restoration Company
Tadas & Helen Sviderskis
730 Fifth Ave., 9th Floor
New York, NY 10019
Phone: 212-333-8638   FAX: 212-333-8720
Professional museum experience in Byzantine, Greek & Russian icon conservation and restoration using ancient method of icon painting.

ILLUSTRATORS

(see also ART; BOOKS, Illusrated; MAGAZINES; PAPER COLLECTIBLES, Illustrated; PIN-UP ART; PRINTS)

Dealer

Judy Goffman Fine Art
18 East 77th Street
New York, NY 10021
Phone: 212-744-5190
Specializes in works by American illustrators.

Museum/Library
Society of Illustrators Museum of
American Illustration
128 E. 63rd. St.
New York, NY 10021
Phone: 212-838-2560

Alphonse Mucha

Collector
Don Kurtz
8471 Buffalo Dr.
Union Lake, MI 48387
Phone: 313-363-3039
Buys, sells Art Nouveau magazine covers, menus, etc. especially with covers by Alphonse Mucha; also Mucha illustrated books.

Coles Phillips

Expert
Denis C. Jackson
P.O. Box 1958
Sequim, WA 98382
Phone: 206-683-2559
Author of "The Price & ID Guide to Coles Phillips."

Eloise Wilkin

Club/Association
Eloise Wilkin Collectors Club
Newsletter: EWCC Newsletter
Joanne Arnold
1040 S. Kenilworth
Oak Park, IL 60304
Eloise Wilkin (1904-1987) was a doll designer, and an illustrator of children's books, advertisements, posters, and postcards.

Collector
Joanne Arnold
1040 S. Kenilworth
Oak Park, IL 60304
Wants items illustrated by Eloise Wilkin: pre-1960 children's books posters, paper dolls, puzzles, advertisements, etc.

Fern Bisel Peat

Expert
David W. Peat
1225 Carroll White
Indianapolis, IN 46219
Phone: 317-357-6895 or 317-351-4606
Wants books, tin toys, other metal or paper childrens' items from 1927-1947 illustrated by my aunt, Fern Bisel Peat.

J.C. & F.X. Leyendecker

Expert
Denis C. Jackson
P.O. Box 1958
Sequim, WA 98382
Phone: 206-683-2559

Author of "The Price Guide to JC & FX Leyendecker."

Joan Walsh Anglund

Periodical
Newsletter: Joan Walsh Anglund Collectors News
Ann C. Bergin
P.O. Box 105
Amherst, NH 03031
Phone: 603-673-1885
An annual newsletter containing information on children's book illustrator Joan Walsh Anglund; free buy, sell ad for subscribers.

Maxfield Parrish

Collector
Ed Meschi
Box 550
Monroeville, NJ 08343
Phone: 609-358-7293
Wants Maxfield Parrish prints.

Collector
John Crawford
3442 Manor Hill
Cincinnati, OH 45220
Phone: 513-221-6050

Dealer
Ruman
292 Pershing Ave.
Leechburg, PA 15656
Phone: 412-845-7275

Dealer
Parrish House, The
John Goodspeed Stuart
1740 Marion St.
Denver, CO 80218
Phone: 303-831-0055
Wants anything Maxfield Parrish.

Expert
Dick & Jaunita Bosworth
7303 N.W. 75th St.
Kansas City, MO 64152 *

Expert
Denis C. Jackson
P.O. Box 1958
Sequim, WA 98382
Phone: 206-683-2559
Author of "The Price and Identification Guide to Maxfield Parrish."

Norman Rockwell

(see also COLLECTIBLES (MODERN), Norman Rockwell)

Club/Association
Rockwell Society of America
Newsletter: Rockwell Society News
597 Saw Mill River Road
Ardsley, NY 10502
Focuses on Norman Rockwell and his art. *

Expert
Denis C. Jackson
P.O. Box 1958
Sequim, WA 98382
Phone: 206-683-2559
Author of "The Price Guide to Norman Rockwell."

Museum/Library
Norman Rockwell Museum at Stockbridge, The
P.O. Box 308
Stockbridge, MA 01262
Phone: 413-298-3944

Museum/Library
Norman Rockwell Museum
601 Walnut St.
Philadelphia, PA 19106
Phone: 215-922-4345

Museum/Library
Museum of Norman Rockwell Art
Joyce Devore
227 S. Park
Reedsburg, WI 53959
Phone: 608-524-2123

Sam Snelling

Collector
Collector
907 Prentiss Rd.
Waldorf, MD 20602
Wants Sam Snelling illustrations. *

William Pogany

Collector
Collector
907 Prentiss Rd.
Waldorf, MD 20602
Wants William Pogany illustrations. *

IMPLEMENT SEATS

(see also FARM COLLECTIBLES, Cast Iron Seats)

INDIAN ITEMS

(see also BEADS, Trade; INDIAN WARS; PREHISTORIC ARTIFACTS; WESTERN AMERICANA)

Auction Service
Robert W. Skinner, Inc.
357 Main St.
Bolton, MA 01740
Phone: 508-779-6241 *

Auction Service

Jack Sellner
P.O. Box 308
Fremont, CA 94537-0308
Conducts annual Indian auctions.

Club/Association

Indian Arts & Crafts Association
Newsletter: IACA Newsletter
Helen Skredergard
Suite B
122 Laveta NE
Albuquerque, NM 87108
Phone: 505-265-9149 or 505-255-6032
To collect, promote, preserve, protect and enhance the understanding of authentic American Indian crafts and arts.

Collector

T.L. Schafer
Rt. #2 Box 270
Marietta, OH 45750
Phone: 614-374-2807
Wants old Indian items: baskets, blankets, beadwork, pottery and relics.

Collector

Indian Rock Arts
John W. Barry
P.O. Box 583
Davis, CA 95616
Phone: 916-758-2561
Wants Indian baskets, pottery, beadwork, carvings, bows, arrows, masks, Kachinas, Navajo rugs, etc. NOTE: Respect sacred items.

Dealer

Indian Shop, The
Newsletter: Dig: The Archaeological
   Newsletter
Van Hilliard
P.O. Box 246
Independence, KY 41051
Phone: 606-428-2485
Publishes at least 4 large catalogs (50-80 pgs.) per year.

Dealer

D.S. Ellis
R.R. #3
Dundas
Ontario L9H 5E3 Canada
Phone: 519-756-9515
Wants to buy old Indian items: beadwork, pipes, wood or stone clubs, Eskimo artifacts, wooden masks, blankets, ivory, quillwork, etc.

Dealer

Cincinnati Art Galleries
635 Main St.
Cincinnati, OH 45202
Phone: 513-381-2128

Dealer

White Deed Indian Traders
Conrad "Duke" Glodowski
1834 Red Pine Lane
Stevens Point, WI 54481
Phone: 715-344-9217
Buys and sells Native American Indian arts and crafts; offers a search service for artifacts and contemporary North American crafts.

Dealer

World City, Inc.
6935 James Ave. South
Minneapolis, MN 55423
Wants beaded items, pottery, rugs; both pre-historic and historic.

Dealer

Naranjo's World of American Indian Art
Suite 150
4617 Montrose
Houston, TX 77006
Phone: 713-660-9690   FAX: 713-660-9690
Specializes in ancient and contemporary Indian arts and crafts; also appraises, restores and custom designs gold & silver jewelry.

Dealer

Two Stars Collection
Jan Duggan
P.O. Box 90075-243
Houston, TX 77290
Phone: 713-440-9120   FAX: 713-893-7907
Buys, sells and collects classic old American Indian baskets, beadwork and Navajo textiles.

Dealer

Arnold & Irving
Chuck Arnold
P.O. Box 18725
Denver, CO 80218
Phone: 800-369-3415
Buys and sells old Navajo, Pueblo & Hispanic textiles, Southwestern pottery, baskets, beadwork, etc.

Dealer

Primitive Arts
Michael Higgins
3026 E. Broadway
Tucson, AZ 85716
Phone: 602-326-4852 *

Dealer

Rich Relics
Richard B. Troyanowski
P.O. Box 432
Sandia Park, NM 87047
Phone: 505-281-2611 or 505-281-2329
Buys/sells prehistoric/historic Indian artifacts, cowboy, militaria, old world antiquities & coins, fossils & ethnographic collectibles.

Dealer

Adobe Gallery
Alexander Anthony, Jr.
413 Romero NW
Albuquerque, NM 87104
*Specializing in art of the Southwest Indian. *

Dealer

Broken Arrow Indian Arts & Crafts
222 North Plaza
Taos, NM 87571 *

Expert

Dawn Reno
R.R. 1, Box 500
Montgomery Center, VT 05471
Phone: 802-326-4707 *

Expert

Gary L. Fogelman
RD 1, Box 240
Turbotville, PA 17772
Phone: 717-437-3698
Specializes in and buys Indian artifacts: single pieces or entire collections.

Expert

Mary Elizabeth McDonald
620 Sierra Dr. SE
Albuquerque, NM 87108
Phone: 505-265-2842

Misc. Service

Indian Arts & Crafts Board
U.S. Dept. Of The Interior
Room 4004
Washington, DC 20240-0001
Phone: 202-208-3773
Write for a free "Source Directory" book which lists legitimate Indian-owned arts & crafts marketing firms throughout the country.

Museum/Library

Museum of Our National Heritage
Clement M. Silvestro, Dir.
33 Marrett Rd.
P.O. Box 519
Lexington, MA 02173
Phone: 617-861-6559
Innovative exhibits on American history and culture.

Museum/Library

Museum of the American Indian, Heye Foundation
Broadway & 155th Street
New York, NY 10032
Phone: 212-283-2420

Museum/Library

Hershey Museum
James McMahon
170 W. Hersheypark Dr.
Hershey, PA 17033
Phone: 717-534-3439

Focused collection of objects detailing the town of Hershey history, regional PA German heritage, native American material culture.

Museum/Library
The U.S. Department of the Interior Museum
18th & C Streets
Washington, DC 20240
Phone: 202-343-3477

Museum/Library
Indian Museum, The
650 Seneca
Wichita, KS 67203
Phone: 316-262-5221

Museum/Library
Colorado River Indian Tribes Museum
Route 1, Box 23-B
Parker, AZ 85344
Phone: 602-669-9211

Museum/Library
Amerind Foundation, Inc., The
P.O. Box 248
Dragoon, AZ 85609
Phone: 602-586-3003

Museum/Library
Wheelwright Museum of the American Indian, The
Newsletter: Messenger, The
Jonathan Batkin
P.O. Box 5153
Santa Fe, NM 87502
Phone: 505-982-4636

Periodical
Magazine: Indian-Artifact Magazine
RD 1, Box 240
Turbotville, PA 17772-9599
Phone: 717-437-3698
An easy reading quarterly focusing on American Indian prehistory: artifacts, tools, lifestyles, customs, archaeology, book reviews.

Periodical
American Indian Art, Inc.
Magazine: American Indian Art Magazine
7314 E. Osborn Dr.
Scottsdale, AZ 85251
Phone: 602-994-5445
Quarterly art journal devoted to native American art from prehistoric to modern.

Periodical
Newspaper: Indian Trader, The
Martin Link, Pub.
P.O. Box 1421
Gallup, NM 87305
Phone: 505-722-6694 or 800-748-1624
Focuses on old and new Indian art and artifacts.

Periodical
Magazine: American Indian Basketry Magazine
John M. Gogol
P.O. Box 66124
Portland, OR 97266
Phone: 503-233-8131
A magazine dedicated to American Indian basketry and other native arts. *

Repair Service
White Deed Indian Traders
Conrad "Duke" Glodowski
1834 Red Pine Lane
Stevens Point, WI 54481
Phone: 715-344-9217
Specializes in the repair and conservation of American Indian artifacts.

Repair Service
Salvatore Macri
5518 East Pinchot Ave.
Phoenix, AZ 85018
Phone: 602-959-1933
Restores fine porcelain and prehistoric and historic Indian artifacts. *

Artifacts & Arrowheads

Museum/Library
Favell Museum of Western Art & Indian Artifacts
P.O. Box 165
Klamath Falls, OR 97601
Phone: 503-882-9996

Museum/Library
National Museum of Natural History
10th St. & Constitution Ave.
Washington, DC 20560
Phone: 202-357-1300

Museum/Library
Field Museum of Natural History
Roosevelt Rd. at Lake Shore Dr
Chicago, IL 60605
Phone: 312-642-4600

Eskimo & Northwest Coast

Dealer
Alaska Shop
31 E. 74th St.
New York, NY 10021
Phone: 212-879-1782
Wants 1940's-1960's soapstone carvings; pre-1920 Eskimo masks, ivories, and amulets; pre-1920 NWC rattles, bowls, masks, etc. *

Dealer
Jeffrey R. Myers, Primitive Arts
Jeffrey R. Myers
16 East 82nd St.
New York, NY 10028
Phone: 212-472-0115   FAX: 212-288-1103

Wants pre-1915 NW masks, rattles, frontlets, bowls, textiles, boxes; pre-1915 Eskimo masks, carved boxes, bow drills, figural pieces, etc.

Expert
Mary Malloy
P.O. Box 491
Sharon, MA 02067
Phone: 617-784-3280
Author "Souvenirs of the Fur Trade 1799-1832."

Museum/Library
Samuel K. Fox Museum
P.O. Box 10021
Dillingham, AK 99576
Phone: 907-842-5601

Museum/Library
Sheldon Jackson Museum
P.O. Box 479
Sitka, AK 99835
Phone: 907-747-5228

Museum/Library
Totem Heritage Center
629 Dock St.
Ketchikan, AK 99901
Phone: 907-225-5900

Navajo

Collector
Ronald Wiener
Packard Bldg. - 12th Floor
111 S. 15th St.
Philadelphia, PA 19102
Phone: 215-977-2266   FAX: 215-977-2346
Wants rugs, blankets, baskets, pottery, etc.

Collector
Andrew Nagen
P.O. Box 1306
Corrales, NM 87408
Phone: 505-898-5058
Wants Navajo rugs and blankets; also Rio Grande, Pueblo, and Mexican textiles.

Museum/Library
Navajo National Monument
8C63 Box 3
Tonalea, AZ 86004
Phone: 602-672-2366

Pottery

Expert
Indian Rock Arts
John Barry
P.O. Box 583
Davis, CA 95616
Phone: 916-758-2561
Specializes in Pueblo Indian pottery; author of "American Indian Pottery."

Museum/Library
Cherokee National Museum
P.O. Box 515
Tahlequah, OK 74465
Phone: 918-456-6007

Museum/Library
Heard Museum, The
22 E. Monte Vista Rd.
Phoenix, AZ 85004
Phone: 602-252-8845

Museum/Library
Institute of American Indian Arts
Museum
P.O. Box 20007
Santa Fe, NM 87504
Phone: 509-988-6281

Pueblo
Collector
Indian Rock Arts
John W. Barry
P.O. Box 583
Davis, CA 95616
Phone: 916-758-2561
Wants traditional Pueblo paintings, prints, photos; books on Pueblos and exploration of Southwest; surveys of the SW; Yellowstone

Souvenirs
Expert
D. Irons Antiques
Abby Irons
223 Covered Bridge Rd.
Northampton, PA 18067
Phone: 215-262-9335

Souvenirs (Beadwork)
Expert
D. Irons Antiques
Marty & Mike Irons
223 Covered Bridge Rd.
Northampton, PA 18067
Phone: 215-262-9335

Weavings
Dealer
Campbell-Belikove Gallery
7045 Third Ave.
Scottsdale, AZ 85251
Phone: 602-994-0405 or 505-983-9707
                    FAX: 602-423-9595
Buys and sells antique Navajo, Pueblo and Hispanic weavings.

INDIAN WARS ITEMS
(see also INDIAN ITEMS; MILITARIA; MILITARY HISTORY)

Club/Association
Order of the Indian Wars, The
Jerry L. Russell, NatCh.
P.O. Box 7388
Little Rock, AR 72217
Phone: 501-225-3996   FAX: 501-225-5167
The only national organization devoted to the study & preservation of Indian Wars history.

INDUSTRY RELATED ITEMS
(see also CONSTRUCTION EQUIPMENT; FARM MACHINERY; LOGGING; MACHINERY & EQUIPMENT; MILLING; MINING; SCRIP; TOOLS; WHISKEY INDUSTRY ITEMS)

Club/Association
Early American Industries Association, The
Newsletter: Shavings, The
John S. Watson, Treas.
Empire State Plaza Station
P.O. Box 2128
Albany, NY 12220-0128
Phone: 518-439-2215
Interested in old tools, implements, utensils, vehicles, "Whatsits"; and to discover, identify and preserve same.

Museum/Library
Museum of Science & Industry
Keith R. Gill
57th St. & Lake Shore Drive
Chicago, IL 60637
Phone: 312-684-1414   FAX: 312-684-5580
Archives contains documents & photos of the 1893 Columbian Exposition.

INDY 500
(see also SPORTS COLLECTIBLES, Auto Racing (Indy 500))

INFANT FEEDERS
(see also BOTTLES)

Club/Association
American Collectors of Infant Feeders
Newsletter: Keeping Abreast
Jo Ann Todd
5161 West 59th Street
Indianapolis, IN 46254
Phone: 317-291-5850
Founded in 1973 for those interested in feeding infants and the devices used therefore: nursers, baby bottles, infant/invalid feeders.

Collector
Jo Ann Todd
5161 West 59th Street
Indianapolis, IN 46254
Phone: 317-291-5850

Wants infant/invalid feeders; nursers, baby bottles, etc.; made of horn, wood, pewter, silver, glass, plastic or pottery.

Collector
Pat Van Gaabeek
631 Randolph
Topeka, KS 66606
Wants ceramic or silver pap boats (invalid or infant feeders). *

Man./Prod./Dist.
Playtex Family Products, Inc.
215 College Rd.
Paramus, NJ 07652
Provides order forms for collectible baby bottles.

INKWELLS & INKSTANDS
(see also BOTTLES)

Club/Association
Society of Inkwell Collectors, The
Newsletter: Stained Finger, The
Vince McGraw
5136 Thomas Ave. So.
Minneapolis, MN 55410
Phone: 612-922-2792
Features articles about inkwells, pens and writing accessories; has catalog offering repro. inkwells, rocker blotters, pens, etc.

Collector
Schonstedt Instrument Co.
Erick Schonstedt
1775 Wiehle Ave.
Reston, VA 22090
Phone: 703-471-1050 *

Expert
Ted Rivera
Box 163
Torrington, CT 06790
Phone: 203-489-4325 *

Expert
Karen Bauman
P.O. Box 415
Hammond, IN 46325
Phone: 219-836-1957 *

Museum/Library
Bennington Museum, The
W. Main St.
Bennington, VT 05201
Phone: 802-447-1571

INSECTS
Museum/Library
University of California, Berkeley,
Essig Museum of Entomology
311 Wellman Hall
Berkeley, CA 94720
Phone: 415-642-4779

Butterflies

Museum/Library

Treasure of El Camino Real
P.O. Box 1047
Atascadero, CA 93423
Phone: 805-466-0142
The Victor Clemence butterfly collection.

INSTRUMENTS & DEVICES

Scientific

(see also ASTRONOMICAL ITEMS;
BAROMETERS; MEDICAL, DENTAL &
PHARACEUTICAL; MICROSCOPES;
SCALES; SLIDE RULES; SURVEYING
INSTRUMENTS)

Club/Association

Zeiss Historical Society
P.O. Box 631
Clifton, NJ 07012
Dedicated to the study & exchange of information on the history of Carl Zeiss Optical Co., its people and products from 1846 to present.

Club/Association

Maryland Microscopical Society
Dr. Sam Koslov
8621 Polk St.
McLean, VA 22102
Phone: 301-953-5591
Focuses on instruments and devices: medical, surveying, photographic, microscopical, navigational, horological, astronomical, etc.

Collector

Paul Ferraglio
3332 W. Lake Rd.
Canandaigua, NY 14424
Phone: 716-394-7663
Buys old scientific instruments: microscopes, surveying instruments, mineralogical & other optical instruments; also books & catalogs.

Collector

Dr. Allan Wissner
P.O. Box 102
Ardsley, NY 10502
Phone: 914-693-4628
Wants microscopes, medical, scientific instruments: Zentmayer, Grunow, Bullock, McAllister, Gundlack, McIntosh, Tolles, Queen,

Dealer

Tesseract
Box 151
Hastings-Hudson, NY 10706
Phone: 914-478-2594
Issues a series of well illustrated catalogs of early scientific instruments: calculation, computation, adding, navigation, etc.

Dealer

Hardings
Lynn Harding
103 West Aliso St.
Ojai, CA 93023
Phone: 805-646-0204
Specializes in buying and selling mechanical, industrial and scientific artifacts; also sells finely engineered replicas.

Dealer

History Associates
1115 NE 4th Ave.
Fort Lauderdale, FL 33304
Phone: 305-763-3843
Wants old scientific instruments related to land surveying and engineering, i.e. transits, chains, compasses, or old text books. *

Dealer

Scientific Americana
Jonathan Thomas
1208 Main St.
Southbury, CT 06488-2159
Buys/sells surveying compasses, mini. & table top globes, calculators & mechanical math devices, telescopes, drawing devices, etc.

Expert

Tools of Distinction
Jim Calison
60 Reservoir Rd.
Wallkill, NY 12589
Phone: 914-895-8035 *

Expert

James Kennedy Antiques, Ltd.
James Kennedy
Brightleaf Square
Durham, NC 27701
Phone: 919-682-1040 *

Museum/Library

National Museum of American History
Branch Library
Smithsonian Institution
Washington, DC 20560
Phone: 202-357-2414
Books/journals/trade catalogs on material culture, decorative arts, domestic & community life, applied science, engineering, technology.

Periodical

Greybird Publishing
Newsletter: Scientific, Medican & Mechanical Antiques
11824 Taneytown Pike
Taneytown, MD 21787
Phone: 301-447-2680
A quarterly newsletter for those interested in scientific, medical and mechanical devices; ads, auction reports, articles.

INSULATORS

Club/Association

National Insulator Association
Newsletter: Drip Point
John DeSousa
5 Brownstone Rd.
East Granby, CT 06026
An organization for those interested in collecting electrical insulators and other artifacts connected with related industries.

Club/Association

Yankee Polecat Insulator Club, The
Newsletter: YPIC Newslsetter
Doug MacGillvary
79 New Boltom Rd.
Manchester, CT 06040
Phone: 203-649-0477
Oldest continuing insulator club in the country; members throughout New England and surrounding areas; annual show, swap meets.

Club/Association

Capital District Insulator Club
Newsletter: Pilgrim Hat, The
Kevin Lawless, Sec.
41 Crestwood Dr.
Schenectady, NY 12306
Phone: 518-355-5688 or 518-356-0300
FAX: 518-356-1947
Club for collectors of antique electrical insulators; membership based in Northeast U.S.; annual show; regular club swaps and meetings.

Club/Association

Chesapeake Bay Insulator Club
Ken Wehr
10 Ridge Road
Catonsville, MD 21228
Members are collectors of glass and ceramic electrical insulators.

Club/Association

Lone Star Insulator Club
Newsletter: Lone Star Lines
Elton Gish
P.O. Box 1317
Buna, TX 77612
Phone: 409-994-5662 or 409-989-7161
FAX: 409-989-7774
Meets monthly on the 3rd Friday in Houston, TX; educational programs offered at each meeting.

Dealer

Doug MacGillvary
79 New Boltom Rd.
Manchester, CT 06040
Phone: 203-649-0477
Glass & porcelain insulators, collections or singles bought/sold/traded; a reputation built on twenty years of honest dealing.

Expert

Kevin Lawless
41 Crestwood Dr.
Schenectady, NY 12306
Phone: 518-355-5688 or 518-356-0300
FAX: 518-356-1947
Buys and sells all types of antique insulators; glass, porcelain, threadless, foreign, colored, rare, common, singles or collections.

Expert

Len. L. Linscott
3557 Nicklaus Dr.
Titusville, FL 32780
Phone: 407-267-9170
Wants "eared" glass electrical insulators; especially CD#250-CD#270; also those with rare colors of embossing errors.

Expert

Michael Bruner
8482 Huron River Drive
Union Lake, MI 48386
Phone: 313-674-0433 or 313-661-2359
Wants rare or unusual style insulators; single or entire collections; also wants related telephone/ telegraph items such as signs,

Expert

John & Carol McDougald
Box 1003
St. Charles, IL 60174-1003
Phone: 708-513-1544
Buys, sells, trades insulators and telephone related items and lightning rod balls and weathervanes.

Expert

Marilyn Albors
14715 Oak Bend Drive
Houston, TX 77079
Phone: 713-497-4146
Co-author of "Glass Insulators From Outside North America", "Worldwide Porcelain Insulators"; specialist in foreign insulators.

Expert

Elton Gish
P.O. Box 1317
Buna, TX 77612
Phone: 409-994-5662 or 409-989-7161
FAX: 409-989-7774
Wants 1890-1930 uni- or multipart porcelain insulators; author of "Multipart Porcelain Insulators"; specialist in porcelain insulators.

Periodical

Magazine: Crown Jewels of the Wire
John & Carol McDougald
Box 1003
St. Charles, IL 60174-1003
Phone: 708-513-1544
60-page monthly magazine of insulator and telephone history; glass, porcelain; foreign columns; classified ads, show dates, etc.

INSURANCE MEMORABILIA

Collector

Byron Gregerson
P.O. Box 951
Modesto, CA 95353
Phone: 209-523-3300 or 209-522-3963
FAX: 209-523-3399
Collector wants insurance memorabilia especially advertising signs: reverse-painting-on-glass, tin & lithography; mostly pre-1920.

INVALID FEEDERS

(see also BOTTLES; INFANT FEEDERS)

Collector

Ken Odiorne
Rt. 2, Box 22
Bertram, TX 78605
Phone: 512-355-2542
Wants invalid feeders: "cup", "boat" or "Aladdin's" lamp shapes; no plain white in "cup" or "boat" shapes unless unusual shape or mark.

IRONS

Pressing

(see also KITCHEN COLLECTIBLES)

Club/Association

Midwest Sad Iron Collectors Club
Newsletter: Midwest Sad Iron Collectors Club Newsletter
Paul W. Conrad, Pres.
11940 Lavida Ave.
St. Louis, MO 63138
Phone: 314-741-4171 *

Club/Association

Club of the Friends of Ancient Smoothing Irons
P.O. Box 215
Carlsbad, CA 92018
Phone: 619-729-1740

Expert

D. Irons Antiques
David & Sue Irons
223 Covered Bridge Rd.
Northampton, PA 18067
Phone: 215-262-9335
Buys and sells; issues semi-annual catalog of irons for sale.

Expert

Rosella Tinsley
105 15 St.
Osawatomie, KS 66064 *

Expert

Iron Lady, The
Carol & Jimmy Walker
501 N. 5th St.
Waelder, TX 78959
Phone: 512-665-7166

Buy and sell antique pressing irons; sale lists available upon request.

IVORY

(see also NEUTSKE; ORIENTALIA; SCRIMSHAW)

Dealer

Ed Tripp
Rt. 2 Box 78
Blue Ridge, TX 75004
*Importer of ivory, hardstone carvings, diamond jewelry. *

Periodical

Newsletter: Netsuke & Ivory Carving Newsletter-Video
Joan L. Cervi
3203 Adams Way
Ambler, PA 19002
Phone: 215-628-2026
A wholesaler who offers VHS videos and a monthly newsletter about imported netsuke, ivory carvings and other Orientalia.

Repro. Source

Juratone London, Inc.
High Gorses, Henley Down
Battle
East Sussex TN33 9BP England
*Makers of reproduction Art Deco bronzes and scrimshaw "ivory" (whales' teeth, elephant tusks, tortoise shells, etc.) *

Repro. Source

Artek, Inc.
Elm Avenue
Antrim, NH 03440
Phone: 603-588-6825
*Sells reproduction sperm whale teeth; also sells scrimshaw kits and supplies. *

JADE

(see also ORIENTALIA)

Periodical

Newsletter: Jade Collector, The
33112 Lake Road
Avon Lake, OH 44012
Phone: 216-933-6553 *

JAPANESE ITEMS

(see also ART, Oriental; ARMS & ARMOR, Japanese; FIREARMS, Japanese Matchlock; OCCUPIED JAPAN; ORIENTALIA; PRINTS, Woodblock (Japanese))

JARS

(see also FRUIT JARS)

JELL-O MEMORABILIA

Expert
Bob Allen
231 E. James Blvd.
P.O. Box 85
St. James, MO 65559
Phone: 314-265-8296

JELLY CONTAINERS

(see also FRUIT JARS)

Club/Association
Jelly Jammers
Journal: Jelly Jammers' Journal
Art Snyder
110 White Oak Drive
Butler, PA 16001-3446
Phone: 412-287-0278
Jelly Jammers focuses on collecting jelly jars, glasses, molds, cups, mugs and samples or miniatures, and on the education of its members.

Collector
Art Snyder
110 White Oak Drive
Butler, PA 16001-3446
Phone: 412-287-0278
Buys/sells/trades all types of jelly glasses, jars, molds and cups, especially patented examples; also wants all related material.

JEWELRY

(see also GEMS & JEWELRY)

JUDAICA

(see also ART, Jewish; TEXTILES,
Needlework (Judaic))

Auction Service
Swann Galleries, Inc.
104 E. 25th St.
New York, NY 10010
Phone: 212-254-4710   FAX: 212-979-1017
Oldest/largest U.S. auctioneer specializing in rare books, autographs & manuscripts, Judaica, photographs, and works of art on paper.

Collector
Mark Tanenbaum
824 Poplar St.
Erie, PA 16502
Phone: 814-452-2567 *

Collector
M. Margvlies
Box 7376
Washington, DC 20044 *

Dealer
Gary Niederkorn Silver
Newspaper: Silver Edition
Gary Niederkorn
2005 Locust St.
Philadelphia, PA 19103
Phone: 215-567-2606
Specializes in 19th and 20th cent. silver novelties, jewelry napkin rings, Judaica, picture frames, etc.; also Tiffany, Jensen, Mexican.

Dealer
Holy Land Treasures
Suite D
1200 Edgehill Drive
Burlingame, CA 94010
Phone: 415-343-9578
Wants to buy Jewish rare books, manuscripts, documents, antique ritual silver, Hanukah lamps, candlesticks, art, paintings, etc.

Expert
Heller Antiques, Ltd.
Israel Heller
5454 Wisconsin Ave.
Chevy Chase, MD 20815
Phone: 301-654-0218
Specializes in jewelry, silver and Judaica.

Expert
Arthur Feldman
1815 St. Johns Ave.
Highland Park, IL 60035
Phone: 312-432-2075 *

Museum/Library
Yeshiva University Museum
2520 Amsterdam Ave.
New York, NY 10033
Phone: 212-960-5390

Museum/Library
Jewish Museum, The
1109 5th Ave.
New York, NY 10128
Phone: 212-860-1888

Museum/Library
National Museum of American Jewish
History
55 N. 5th St.
Philadelphia, PA 19106
Phone: 215-923-3811

Museum/Library
B'nai B'rith Klutznick Museum
1640 Rhode Island Ave. NW
Washington, DC 20036
Phone: 202-857-6583

Museum/Library
Judaic Museum
6125 Montrose Rd.
Rockville, MD 20852
Phone: 301-881-0100

Museum/Library
Spertus Museum of Judaica
618 S. Michigan Ave.
Chicago, IL 60605
Phone: 312-922-9012

Museum/Library
Morton B. Weiss Museum of Judaica
1100 Hyde Park Blve.
Chicago, IL 60615
Phone: 312-924-1234

Museum/Library
Plotkin Judaica Museum of Greater
Phoenix
3310 No. 10th Ave.
Phoenix, AZ 85013
Phone: 602-264-4428

Museum/Library
Juddah L. Magnes Memorial Museum
2911 Russell St.
Berkeley, CA 94705
Phone: 415-849-2710

KALEIDOSCOPES

(see also OPTICAL TOYS)

Club/Association
Brewster Society
Suite 605
100 Severn Ave.
Annapolis, MD 21403

Collector
Grand Illusions
Martin Roenigk
26 Barton Hill
East Hampton, CT 06424
Phone: 203-267-8682
Buys and repairs high quality kaleidoscopes from the 1800's made of wood, leather, brass by Bush, Brewster, Bate, Carpenter, etc.

Dealer
Kaleido-Cam
William P. Carroll
8500 La Entrada
Whittier, CA 90605
Phone: 213-693-8421   FAX: 213-947-8499
Buys, sells and collects modern, top quality kaleidoscopes and, at times, antique kaleidoscopes.

Expert
Cozy Baker
Suite 605
100 Severn Ave.
Annapolis, MD 21403

KANSAS COLLECTIBLES

Dealer

Dearing Country Antiques
Billy & Jeane Jones
P.O. Box 82
Dearing, KS 67340
Phone: 316-948-6389
Want ceramic or glass souvenirs, plates, advertising items, calendars, vases, view cards - anything related to Kansas.

KEY CHAINS

Club/Association

License Plate Key Chain & Mini License
Plate Collectors
Newsletter: Key Chain News
Dr. Edward H. Miles
888 Eighth Ave.
New York, NY 10019
Phone: 212-765-2660
Focuses on miniature key chains, chauffeurs' badges, gum cards featuring license plates, windshield stickers, mini license plates.

KEY FOBS

Expert

Toy Farmer Ltd.
Claire D. Scheibe
HC 2 Box 5
LaMoure, ND 58458
Phone: 701-883-5206 or 701-883-5207
                    FAX: 701-883-5208

KEYS

(see also LOCKS)

Club/Association

Key Collectors International
Journal: Key Collector Journal
Don Stewart
P.O. Box 9397
Phoenix, AZ 85068
Phone: 602-942-0043
Focuses on locks, keys, handcuffs, and other restraints; also publishes "Padlock Quarterly" (mag.) and "Chain Gang" (newsletter).

Collector

Jimmy L. Smith
2405 S. Fourth
Effingham, IL 62401
Collects keys and some restraining devices.

Expert

Don Stewart
P.O. Box 9397
Phoenix, AZ 85068
Phone: 602-942-0043
Author of "Standard Guide to Key Collecting."

KITCHEN COLLECTIBLES

(see also CAST IRON ITEMS; CASTOR SETS; CHOCOLATE MOLDS; COOKIES & COOKIE SHAPING; COOKIE JARS; EGG BEATERS; GRANITEWARE; IRONS; PIE BIRDS)

Collector

Monitor Top
Murray Hill Station
Box 911
Malaga, NJ 08328
Phone: 609-697-9142
Wants kitchen collectibles, gadgets and appliances of the 1920-1930 era. *

Dealer

Popkorn Antiques
Robert & Nancy Perzel
4 Mine St.
P.O. Box 1057
Flemington, NJ 08822
Phone: 908-782-9631

Expert

Rosella Tinsley
105 15 St.
Osawatomie, KS 66064 *

Museum/Library

Kern County Museum
3801 Chester Ave.
Bakersfield, CA 93301
Phone: 805-861-2132

Coffee Mills

Collector

Dennis Kickhofel
20863 Lancaster Rd.
Harper Woods, MI 48225
Wants various types of Regulator schoolhouse clocks *

Expert

Terry Friend
R.R. 4, Box 152-D
Galax, VA 24333
Phone: 703-236-9027 *

Egg Beaters

Expert

Don Thornton
1345 Poplar Ave.
Sunnyvale, CA 94087 *

Molds

Expert

Ruth & Dale Van Kuren Antiques
Ruth & Dale Van Kuren
5990 Goodrich Rd.
Clarence Center, NY 14032
Phone: 716-741-2606

Specializing in chocolate, hard candy, maple sugar, ice cream, and other molds of all materials.
*

Molds (Butter)

Collector

Mrs. Wilson Taylor
154 Files Creek Rd.
Beverly, WV 26253 *

Expert

Rosella Tinsley
105 15 St.
Osawatomie, KS 66064 *

Repro. Source

M & M Enterprises
P.O. Box 185
Atkins, VA 24311
Sells 1/2 lb. round reproduction wooden butter molds with either a starburst or a cow design.

Molds (Candy)

Museum/Library

Wilbur's Americana Candy Museum
64 N. Broad Street
Litiz, PA 17543
Phone: 717-626-1131

Reamers

Club/Association

Mid-American Reamer Collectors
Newsletter: Juicy Journal
Winnie Cerbin, Sec.
2262 Clay St.
Austinburg, OH 44010
Phone: 216-275-1115
Club is an affiliate of the National Reamers Collectors Association; membership in the NRCA is a prerequisite to joining the MARC.

Club/Association

National Reamer Collectors Association (NRCA)
Newsletter: NRCA Quarterly Review
Rt. 3 Box 67
Frederic, WI 54837
Phone: 715-327-4365
A non-profit organization devoted to promoting citrus and juice reamer collecting and sharing information about reamers.

Club/Association

West-Coast Branch, Reamer Collectors Association
10837 Chiminess
Northbridge, CA 91326 *

Collector

Betty Franks
1831 Penthley Ave.
Akron, OH 44312
Phone: 216-784-2869

Wants old and unusual glass, china or pottery reamers; domestic or foreign, especially figurals.

Collector
Terry McDuffee
1478 West Cyprus Ave.
Redlands, CA 92373
Phone: 714-793-9534
Buys and sells reamers, juicers and kitchen glassware; rare and unusual items wanted; please price and describe.

Expert
Dee Long
112 S. Center
Lacon, IL 61540 *

Sausage Stuffers
Collector
Dale Schmidt
610 Howell Prairie Rd. SE
Salem, OR 97301
Phone: 503-364-0499
Wants all types; complete or parts.

Wire Ware
Expert
Rosella Tinsley
105 15 St.
Osawatomie, KS 66064 *

Repro. Source
Mathews Wire
654 West Morrison
Frankfort, IN 46041
Phone: 800-826-9650   FAX: 317-659-1059
Wholesale supplier of wire reproductions; egg baskets, display racks, etc.

KITS
(see also MODEL KITS)

KNIVES
(see also ARMS & ARMOR)

Club/Association
Fight'n Rooster Cutlery Club
Newsletter: FRCC Newsletter
Box 936
Lebanon, TN 37087
Phone: 615-444-8070
There are many more local and regional knife collectors clubs throughout the U.S.

Club/Association
Dare Blade Collectors' Society
Jim Goes
3938 Pineway Dr.
Kitty Hawk, NC 27949
Phone: 919-261-1149
Interested in all knives, from ancient native American stone artifacts to historic military blades & modern custom made knives.

Club/Association
National Knife Collectors Association
Magazine: National Knife Magazine
P.O. Box 21070
Chattanooga, TN 37421
Phone: 800-548-1442 or 800-548-3907
Focuses mainly on new knives but also carries some articles about old knives.

Club/Association
American Blade Collectors Association
P.O. Box 22007
Chattanooga, TN 37422
Phone: 615-894-0339   FAX: 615-892-7254
Membership includes annual club knife offer, annual commemorative Blade Show and Cutlery fair knife.

Club/Association
American Edge Collectors Association
Newsletter: AECA Newsletter
P.O. Box 2565
Country Club Hills, IL 60478

Collector
Bill Campesi
Box 140
Merrick, NY 11566
Phone: 516-546-9630
Buy, sell, trade all cutlery and related advertising: catalogs, postcards, cutlery display items; pocket, sheath, Bowie knives.

Collector
John
7808 Kiwanis Rd.
Harrisburg, PA 17112
Phone: 717-540-5522
*Wants knife collections, cased knife displays, knife ad and showcase items. ***

Collector
Gerald A. Shaw
1928 Causton Bluff Rd.
Savannah, GA 31404
Phone: 912-232-0771
Wants knives by Remington, Boker, Winchester, CASE, Russell, Western, Ka-Bar, etc.; also wants razors, books, daggers, hunting knives, etc.

Dealer
Blue Ridge Knives
Phil Martin
Rt. 6 Box 185
Marion, VA 24354
Phone: 703-783-6143   FAX: 703-783-9298
Will buy single knives or entire collection; also wholesales contemporary knives.

Dealer
Tony Foster
5926 Willard Drive
Honahan, SC 29406 *

Dealer
M.C. Matthews Cutlery
P.O. Box 33095
Decatur, GA 30033 *

Dealer
Atlanta Cutlery Corporation
Box 839
Conyers, GA 30207 *

Dealer
Charlie Mattox
P.O. Box 1565
Gallatin, TN 37066 *

Dealer
Paul Davis
P.O. Box 9354
Chattanooga, TN 37412 *

Dealer
Heritage Antique Knives
P.O. Box 22171
Chattanooga, TN 37422
Editor *

Dealer
Smoky Mountain Knife Works
204 Parkway
Sevierville, TN 37862 *

Dealer
Star Sales
1803 N. Central St.
Knoxville, TN 37901
*Offers mail order knife sales. ***

Dealer
W.E. Shockley
P.O. Box 99151
Jeffersontown, KY 40229 *

Expert
Jim Weyer
333 14th St.
Toledo, OH 43624
Phone: 419-241-5454 or 800-448-8424
                    FAX: 419-241-2637
Author of the "Knives: Points of Interest" book series which focuses on custom made knives.

Expert
Charles D. Stapp
7037 Haynes Rd.
Georgetown, IN 47122
Phone: 812-923-3483
Advisor to "Schroeder's Antique Price Guide."

Expert
A.G. Russell
1705 Highway 71 North
Springdale, AR 72764
Phone: 501-751-7341 *

Expert
Charles Clements
1741 Dallas St.
Aurora, CO 80010
Phone: 303-363-0403 *

Expert
Bernard Levine
P.O. Box 2404
Eugene, OR 97402
Phone: 503-484-0294
Identification and appraisal, museum consultation, expert witness, research, writing.

Museum/Library
National Knife Collectors Museum
P.O. Box 21070
Chattanooga, TN 37421
Phone: 800-548-1442 or 800-548-3907

Periodical
Magazine: Blade, The
P.O. Box 22007
Chattanooga, TN 37422
Phone: 615-894-0339   FAX: 615-892-7254
A bi-monthly magazine focusing on all aspects of knives, razors, pocket knives, knife-making, care, sharpening, etc.

Periodical
Newsletter: Blue Mill Blade, The
203 East Mineral Street
Newport, TN 37821 *

Periodical
Newspaper: Knife World
P.O. Box 3395
Knoxville, TN 37927
Phone: 615-523-3339   FAX: 615-637-7123
Ads, shows, knife makers, articles of interest to collectors and knife historians; has knife identification and value columns.

Periodical
Magazine: Knives Illustrated
2145 W. LaPalma Ave.
Anaheim, CA 92801
Phone: 714-635-9040 *

Repair Service
Garry L. Wackerhagen
2910 McNutt Ave.
Maryville, TN 37801
Phone: 615-977-WACK
Knife repair and restorations; reasonable rates.

Repair Service
Wendell Carson
Rt. 4, Box 314
New Albany, MS 38652 *

Repair Service
Charles Jones
P.O. Box 282
Belton, TX 76513

*Specializes in the repair of Case knives. ***

Repair Service
Skip Bryan
1852 Albany
Loveland, CO 80537
*Specializes in the repair of old knives. ***

Supplier
Masecraft Supply
902 Colony Road
Meriden, CT 06450
*Carries equipment and supplies for buffing, polishing, and making knives. ***

Supplier
Anderson Cutlery & Supply Co.
Box 383
Newton, CT 06470
*Carries equipment and supplies for buffing, polishing, and making knives. ***

Supplier
Sheffield Knifemakers Supplies
P.O. Box 141
De Land, FL 32720
*Carries equipment and supplies for buffing, polishing, and making knives. ***

Supplier
Knife & Gun Finishing Supplies
P.O. Box 13522
Arlington, TX 76013
Carries equipment and supplies for buffing, polishing, and making knives.

Case
Club/Association
Case Collectors Club
Newsletter: CCC Newsletter
Owens Way
Bradford, PA 16701 *

Colonel Coon
Club/Association
Colonel Coon Collectors Club
P.O. Box 1676
Dyersburg, TN 38025
Phone: 901-627-9659 *

Ka-Bar
Club/Association
Ka-Bar Knife Collectors Club
Newsletter: Bulletin
P.O. Box 406
Olean, NY 14760
Phone: 716-372-5611 or 800-321-9334
Purpose is to contribute to and promote the hobby of knife collecting.

Pocket
Club/Association
Canadian Knife Collectors Club
3141 Jessuca Court
Mississauga
Ontario L5C1X7 Canada *

Collector
Steve Deer
P.O. Box 477
Greencastle, IN 46135
Phone: 317-653-9437
Wants tricky openers; also picture handled carnival or punchboard knives.

Dealer
Joe & Juanita Reese
511 Dair Ave.
Harrison, OH 45030
*Wants character collectibles and Madame Alexander dolls; also western collectibles and pocket knives. ***

Dealer
Harrell Braddock
1412 Los Colinos
Graham, TX 76046
Buys and sells all pocket knives, any condition, any number; send SASE for list of knives for sale.

Expert
Charles D. Stapp
7037 Haynes Rd.
Georgetown, IN 47122
Phone: 812-923-3483
Advisor to "Schroeder's Antique Price Guide."

Periodical
Magazine: Edges
P.O. Box 22007
Chattanooga, TN 37422
Phone: 615-894-0339   FAX: 615-892-7254
The bi-monthly journal of American knife collecting: antique & contemporary pocket knives & folders, collector profiles, club info.

Repair Service
Ken Lukes
405 E. Wake Ham Ave.
Santa Ana, CA 92701
Phone: 714-542-8553

KU KLUX KLAN COLLECTIBLES
Collector
Roger Henry
RR #1, Box 192
Smithshire, IL 61478
Wants KKK books and other KKK items.

Dealer
Historical Collections
P.O. Box 42
Waynesboro, PA 17268
Phone: 717-762-3068

Wants KKK material and items.

LABELS

(see also ADVERTISING COLLECTIBLES; AVIATION MEMORABILIA; CIGAR BANDS, BOXES & LABELS; MATCHBOXES & LABELS)

Club/Association

American Antique Graphics Society
Joe Davidson
5185 Windfall Rd.
Medina, OH 44256
Phone: 216-723-7172
Members interested in graphic arts prints: from medieval, natural history to cigar labels.

Club/Association

International Seal, Label & Cigar Band Society
Newsletter: Inter. Seal, Label & Cigar Band
  Soc. Bulletin
8915 E. Bellevue St.
Tucson, AZ 85715
Phone: 602-296-1048
Interested in hotel, cigar box, beer, fruit crate, etc. labels; also matchcovers, charity stamps, Christmas seals, sugar packets, etc. *

Dealer

Cerebro
David & Barbara Freiberg
P.O. Box 1221
Lancaster, PA 17603
Phone: 717-656-7875 or 800-69L-ABEL
Wants cigar labels, pictorial cigar bands, fruit crate labels, firecracker labels, can labels, and other graphically pleasing labels.

Expert

Archives of Louisiana Trade Labels, Inc.
Sharon Dinkins
2317 Highway 190 West
Slidell, LA 70460
Phone: 504-649-6153   FAX: 504-649-6153
Specializes in colorful advertising food labels from the Walle Co. 1886-1950's.

Periodical

Newsletter: Southern Label Collectors
  Newsletter
P.O. Box 24811
Tampa, FL 33623

Repro. Source

Archives of Louisiana Trade Labels, Inc.
Sharon Dinkins
2317 Highway 190 West
Slidell, LA 70460
Phone: 504-649-6153   FAX: 504-649-6153
Produces authentic reproductions of early food label; accurately replicating the colors and details of early stone lithography.

Bread End

Collector

Don Shelley
P.O. Box 11
Fitchville, CT 06334
Phone: 203-887-6163
Bread labels and albums - Howdy Doody, spaceman, movie stars, Hoppy, Autry, Cisco Kid, Rough Rider, Lone Ranger, sports, Disney, etc.

Canned Salmon

Collector

Karen Hofstad
Box 203
Petersburg, AK 99833
Phone: 907-772-4770
Wants canned salmon labels; will accept collect calls; call evenings.

Fruit Crate (Citrus)

Club/Association

Citrus Label Society, The
Newsletter: Citrus Peal
Noel Gilbert, Sec.
131 Miramonte Dr.
Fulerton, CA 92365
Phone: 714-871-2864
Members concentrate on the collection of citrus fruit crate labels and on the history of the citrus fruit industry.

LAMPS & LIGHTING

(see also LIGHT BULBS; MINING RELATED ITEMS, Lamps; RAILROAD COLLECTIBLES, Lanterns; REPAIRS & RESTORATIONS, Lamps & Lighting)

Auction Service

Richard A. Bourne Auction Co., Inc.
P.O. Box 141
Hyannis Port, MA 02647
Phone: 508-775-0797

Auction Service

James D. Julia, Inc.
P.O. Box 830
Fairfield, ME 04937
Phone: 207-453-7904   FAX: 207-453-2502

Club/Association

Historical Lighting Society of Canada
Magazine: Illuminator
P.O. Box 561
Postal Station R, Toronto
Ontario M4G 4E1 Canada *

Club/Association

Rushlight Club Inc., The
Newsletter: Rushlight, The
Suite 196
1657 The Fairway
Jenkintown, PA 19046

One of the oldest organizations focusing on early lighting including lighting devices and fuels.

Club/Association

Incadescent Lamp Collectors
Association, The
Hugh F. Hicks, Cur.
c/o Museum of Lighting
717 Washington Place
Baltimore, MD 21201
Phone: 301-752-8586 or 301-837-1705

Collector

Anthony Glab
4154 Falls Road
Baltimore, MD 21211
Phone: 301-235-1777
Wants carbide or oilwick lamps: miners, railroad, general purpose lanterns or household lamps. *

Dealer

Pine Bough
Joanne Furst
Main Street
Northeast Harbor, ME 04662
Phone: 207-276-5079 or 207-244-7060
Specialists in early lighting devices.

Dealer

Chester Antique Center
Trudy Chatlos
32 Grove Street
P.O. Box 253
Chester, NJ 07930
Phone: 908-879-4331   FAX: 908-766-0386
Carries large selection of quality period lighting, hanging fixtures, table and floor lamps; wants to buy unrestored period fixtures.

Dealer

A-Bit-of-Antiquity
Richard Dudley
1412 Forest Lane
Woodbridge, VA 22191
Phone: 703-491-2878
Huge inventory of table, piano, student, hanging, bracket and banquet lights; many new and old parts for oil lamps; buys and sells.

Dealer

Historic Lighting Restoration Service & Sales
10341 Jewell Lake Ct.
Fenton, MI 48430
Phone: 313-629-4934
Wants old lighting fixtures and catalogs; also repairs. *

Dealer

Betty Lamp, The
Betty Schoon
Box 1038
Georgetown, CO 80444
Wants all kinds of primitive, pre-kerosene (1850) lighting devices used. *

Dealer

Greg's Antique Lighting
12005 Wilshire Blvd.
Los Angeles, CA 90025
Carries an outstanding selection of original Victorian chandeliers, wall sconces and other lighting devices.

Expert

Pat Thomas Antiques
Pat Thomas
501 E. North Street
Chapel Hill, NC 27514
Phone: 919-942-6720 *

Expert

Ruth Osborne
Box 85
Higginsport, OH 45131
Phone: 513-375-6605 *

Periodical

Newsletter: Light Revival
35 West Elm Ave.
Quincy, MA 02170
The newsletter for collectors and dealers of medium-priced lamps with a focus on late 19th and early 20th century lighting. *

Repro. Source

Copper House, The
R.R. 1, Box 4
Epsom, NH 03234
Phone: 603-736-9798
Handmade copper reproduction lighting fixtures and weathervanes. No imports. Catalog $3 deducted from purchase.

Repro. Source

Authentic Designs
36 The Mill Road
West Rupert, VT 05776
Phone: 802-394-7713
Makers of Colonial and Early American lighting fixtures. *

Repro. Source

American Period Lighting
Jack Cunningham
3004 Columbia Ave.
Lancaster, PA 17603
Phone: 717-392-5649
Sells complete line of reproduction period style lighting fixtures; also offers restoration of antiques lamps and lighting fixtures.

Aladdin

Club/Association

Aladdin Knights of the Mystic Light
Newsletter: Mystic Light, The
J. W. Courter
R.D. #1
Simpson, IL 62985
Phone: 618-949-3884

Purpose is to preserve Aladdin kerosene and electric lamps and Aladdin advertising history and memorabilia.

Expert

J. W. Courter
R.R. #1
Simpson, IL 62985
Phone: 618-949-3884
Wants Aladdin and Angle lamps.

Repair Service

A-Bit-of-Antiquity
Richard Dudley
1412 Forest Lane
Woodbridge, VA 22191
Phone: 703-491-2878
Expert restoration, repair, deplating & polishing of gas and electric lamps; specializing in oil lighting; carries old parts & shades.

Supplier

Phillips
172 Main St.
Toronto
Ontario M4E 2W1 England
Phone: 416-691-7372
Parts & expert repairs for Aladdin lamps; wickes, chimneys, mantles, holders, decorated glass shades, electric adaptors; catalog $5.

Carriage

Collector

Larry Sluiter
4186 East Lamm Rd.
Freeport, IL 61032
Phone: 815-235-1249
Wants carriage lamps in pairs; and horse-drawn carriages.

Chandeliers

Supplier

Lighting Designs
1500 Rockville Pike
Rockville, MD 20852
Phone: 301-468-7300
Carries large selection of crystal chandeliers and parts for same.

Cobalt Blue

Collector

John Moore
P.O. Box 23012
Alexandria, VA 22304
Wants cobalt blue oil lamps of any size. *

Kerosene

Expert

LeRoy Bruggink
313 Ramaker Ave.
Cedar Grove, WI 53013 *

Museum/Library

Kerosene Lamp Museum
100 Old Waterbury Turnpike
Winchester Center, CT 06094
Phone: 203-379-2612

Periodical

Newsletter: Font & Flue
P.O. Box 68
Pattonsburg, MO 64670
Phone: 816-367-2215 or 816-367-2201
A bi-monthly about kerosene lamps. *

Miniature

Club/Association

Night Light
Newsletter: Night Light Newsletter
Bob Culver
38619 Wakefield Ct.
Northville, MI 48167
Phone: 313-473-8575 or 313-594-7878
The goal of Night Light is to further the hobby of collecting miniature oil lamps.

Collector

Dr. Ann G. McDonald
Box 7321
Arlington, VA 22207
Wants miniature oil lamps; old colored glass night lamps with burners, chimneys, wicks to burn kerosene, matching shades.

Neon

Museum/Library

Neon Museum of Philadelphia
Len Davidson
860 N. 26th St.
Philadelphia, PA 19130
Phone: 215-232-0478
Museum restores & displays antique neon signs.

Museum/Library

Museum of Neon Art
704 Traction Ave.
Los Angeles, CA 90013
Phone: 213-617-1580

Revolving

Collector

Amy Kanis
5000 W. 96th St.
Indianapolis, IN 46268
Phone: 317-873-2727
Wants 1930's-60's revolving lamps, i.e. plastic or glass w/light bulb-heat propelled inner cylinder; all applications desired.

Tiffany/Handel/Pairpoint

Collector

Harvey Weinstein
22 Halifax Dr.
Morganville, NJ 07751
Phone: 201-536-4467 or 800-321-0204

Wants lamps and glass by Tiffany, Galle, Daum Nancy, Handel, Loetz, Pairpoint, Lalique, etc.

Collector
Mark
P.O. Box 2260
New York, NY 10008
Phone: 800-626-1752
Wants Pairpoint puffies, painted scenes; also Handel painted lamps and accessories.

Collector
Alan Grodsky
642 Franklin Ave.
Garden City, NY 11530
Phone: 516-413-8255 or 800-835-0008
Wants Pairpoint Puffies and painted scenic lamps; also Handel painted lamps; and accessories.

Collector
Dr. Neil Superfon
2121 W. Indian School Rd.
Phoenix, AZ 85015
Phone: 602-277-1449
*Wants Handel, Galle, Pairpoint, Tiffany lamps and glass. ***

Dealer
H & D Press, Inc.
Carole Hibel
P.O. Box 1284
Staten Isl., NY 10314
Phone: 800-HAN-DLES
Wants Handel, Tiffany, Pairpoint lamps and accessories.

Dealer
Robert Ogorek
5534 Richfield Rd.
Flint, MI 48506
Phone: 313-743-5258
*Also wants any signed lamp base; also Tiffany or cameo art glass. ***

Expert
Daniel Batchelor
R.D. #3, Box 10
Oswego, NY 13126
Phone: 315-342-1511
Buys and sells Pairpoint, Handel, and Bradley & Hubbard lamps.

Expert
Carl Heck Antiques
Carl Heck
Box 8416
Aspen, CO 81612
Phone: 303-925-8011
*Specializes in antique stained and beveled glass and Tiffany windows; also leaded and reverse-painted lamps. ***

Museum/Library
Pairpoint Lamp Museum
Edward Malakoff
276 Princeton Dr.
River Edge, NJ 07661
Phone: 201-487-1989

Repair Service
Joan Meyer
104 Colwyn Lane
Bala Cynwyd, PA 19004
Phone: 215-664-3174
*Expert craftsmanship, only Tiffany glass used, all work guaranteed; also wants Tiffany glass, sheets, scraps. ***

LANTERNS
(see also LAMPS & LIGHTING; MINING RELATED ITEMS, Lamps; RAILROAD COLLECTIBLES, Lanterns)

LAPIDARY
(see also GEMS & JEWELRY; MINERALS)

Club/Association
Rollin' Rock Club
Magazine: <u>Rollin' Rock Club Newsletter</u>
15 Kennington Dr.
Warrington, FL 32507-1099
Phone: 904-455-6424
*Interest is in lapidary: cutting, shaping and polishing of stones. ***

Museum/Library
Lizzadro Museum of Lapidary Art
220 Cottage Hill Ave.
Elmhurst, IL 60126
Phone: 312-833-1616

Repair Service
Hegeman & Co.
Richard P. Hegeman
Suite 307
334 Westminster St.
Providence, RI 02903
Phone: 401-831-6812
Cutters of all precious/semi-precious stones; specializing in the repair & restoration of all types of jewelry & gemstone replacements.

LAW ENFORCEMENT MEMORABILIA
(see also POLICE & SHERIFF MEMORABILIA)

LEAD SOLDIERS
(see also SOLDIER, Toy)

LETTER OPENERS
Expert
Diane Levine
P.O. Box 11708
Chicago, IL 60611

FAX: 312-943-0025
Buys and sells old letter openers.

LICENSE PLATE ATTACHMENTS
Automobile
Collector
Edward Foley
227 Union Ave.
Pittsburgh, PA 15202
Phone: 412-761-0685
Wants cast or steel license plate attachments (bolts to top of a plate): cities, beaches, tourist meccas, oil company, porcelain, etc.

LICENSE PLATES
Collector
Trent Culp
P.O. Box 550
Misenheimer, NC 28109
Phone: 704-279-6242
Collects license plates from all states: porcelain, early tin, motorcycle, Presidential Inauguration, early Alaskan & Hawaiian, etc.

Automobile
Club/Association
Automobile License Plate Collectors Association, Inc.
Newsletter: <u>ALPCA Newsletter</u>
Gary Brent Kincade
P.O. Box 712
Weston, WV 26452
Phone: 304-842-3773
A non-profit organization to promote interest in the collecting of motor vehicle license plates and to share information among members.

Collector
Dave Lincoln
Box 331
Yorklyn, DE 19736
Phone: 215-444-4144
Active hobbyist interested in expired plates from anywhere; any type, any number, any vintage; 30 years collecting; sells or swaps extras.

Dealer
Conrad Hughson
P.O. Box 399
Brattleboro, VT 05302
Phone: 802-387-4498
Collector of U.S. and Canadian license plates since 1952; will buy entire collections of early plates; many duplicates.

Repro. Source

Personalized AutoArt Products, Inc.
Suite D
2046 Park Place
Stone Mountain, GA 30087
Phone: 800-237-8510
*Makers of replicas and authentic-looking personalized license plates. ***

Automobile (Delaware)

Collector

Dave Lincoln
Box 331
Yorklyn, DE 19736
Phone: 215-444-4144
Collector seeks Delaware plates of all types, variety, and vintage for comprehensive display and forthcoming book.

Automobile (Porcelain)

Collector

Tom Mills
Bellevue Rd.
Berlin, MA 01503
*Wants fire alarm and police boxes, cast iron signs and U.S.P.O. pickup boxes; also wants porcelain license plates and signs. ***

Collector

Stephen S. Uss
60 Homecrest Ave.
Yonkers, NY 10703
Phone: 914-423-0442
Wants early porcelain, leather and tin auto or motorcycle license plates; also chauffeurs badges and dashboard registration discs.

Collector

Carl Malsahn
1610 Van Buren
Saginaw, MI 48602
Phone: 517-793-6961
Porcelain license plates any state, Michigan plates before 1945.

Bicycle

Collector

James C. Case
RR 1 box 68
Lindley, NY 14858
Phone: 607-524-6606
Wants pre-1940 sidepath tags (early bike licenses) from all states but especially New York.

Government

Collector

Jake Eckenrode
R.D. 3 Box 421
Bellefonte, PA 16823
Phone: 814-355-8769
Wants old U.S. Government license plates from any agency including old Civilian Conservation Corps (CCC) signs.

Miniature

Club/Association

License Plate Key Chain & Mini License
Plate Collectors
Newsletter: Key Chain News
Dr. Edward H. Miles
888 Eighth Ave.
New York, NY 10019
Phone: 212-765-2660
Focuses on miniature key chains, chauffeurs' badges, gum cards featuring license plates, windshield stickers, mini license plates.

Collector

Donald Fehr
P.O. Box 872
Northfield, NJ 08225
Phone: 609-641-5910
Wants DAV or BF Goodrich miniature license plates.

Collector

Edward Foley
227 Union Ave.
Pittsburgh, PA 15202
Phone: 412-761-0685
Wants B.F. Goodrich keychain license plates from all states, 1939 - 1942; many painted brass with B.F. Goodrich on back; 1 3/4" x 3/4".

LICENSES

(see also LICENSE PLATES)

Animal

Club/Association

International Society of Animal License
Collectors
Newsletter: Paw Prints
Trudy K. Doll, Pres.
278 Amal Dr.
York, PA 17403
Phone: 717-741-3049
Animal license (primarily dog) collectors united for the exchange of hobby material; annual convention in various areas of the U.S.

Collector

Trudy & Marty Doll
278 Amal Dr.
York, PA 17403
Phone: 717-741-3049
Wants any and all kinds of animal licenses, primarily dog.

Expert

Karen Lea Rose
4420 Wisconsin Ave.
Tampa, FL 33616-1031
Phone: 813-839-6245
Collects paper or metal animal licenses; tags or certificates.

Dog

Collector

James C. Case
RR 1 Box 68
Lindley, NY 14858
Phone: 607-524-6606
Wants log licenses and dog tags dated before 1920; especially interested in pre-1917 tags from New York state.

Hunting & Fishing

Collector

James C. Case
RR 1 Box 68
Lindley, NY 14858
Phone: 607-524-6606
Wants hunting, fishing, trapping licenses and license buttons as well as guide badges from all states (mainly pre-1945.)

Collector

Ron Brownawell
Box 337
Shermans Dale, PA 17090
Phone: 775-822-088
Wants hunting and fishing licenses: especially PA related; also pinback type licenses from all states and Canada.

Dealer

Frank's Antiques
P.O. Box 516
Hilliard, FL 32046
Phone: 904-845-2870
Wants hunting, fishing, trapping license buttons, any state; also Ducks Unl. buttons; gun co. of fishing tackle co. buttons, posters.

PA Licensed Operator

Collector

Edward Foley
227 Union Ave.
Pittsburgh, PA 15202
Phone: 412-761-0685
Wants PA Licensed Operator badges 1910-1929. The 1910 is keystone shape, 1911-1928 oval, 1929 is round; also special Licensed Driver.

LIDS

(see also POT LIDS)

Supplier

Abercombie & Co.
9159A Brookeville Rd.
Silver Spring, MD 20910
Phone: 301-585-2385
Carries replacement metal tops for bottles and shakers.

Supplier

Lid Lady, The
Virginia Bodiker
7790 East Ross Road
New Carlisle, OH 45344
Carries replacement lids for ceramic, glass, metal, and plastic vessels and containers.

LIGHT BULBS

(see also LAMPS & LIGHTING)

Collector

Little
670 Rose Dr.
Paramus, NJ 07652
Wants pointed tips, any lighting/electrical commemoratives, meters, sockets, primitives, Edison/ Westinghouse, etc. *

Collector

Joseph Kimbell
29-A Rivoli St.
San Francisco, CA 94117
Wants unusual light bulbs or old bulbs with evacuation teat; also figural and bubble Christmas bulbs, and special neon bulbs. *

Museum/Library

Mt. Vernon Museum of Incadescent
Lighting
Hugh F. Hicks, Cur.
717 Washington Place
Baltimore, MD 21201
Phone: 301-752-8586 or 301-837-1705
Museum with display of electric light bulbs depicting the entire industry which spans 110 years.

Repro. Source

Kyp-Go, Inc.
P.O. Box 247
St. Charles, IL 60174
Phone: 312-548-8181
Reproduction replicas of the old fashioned carbon filament light bulbs with evacuation teat. *

Repro. Source

P.A. Stammer Co.
824 L St.
Arcata, CA 95521
Phone: 707-822-5424   FAX: 707-882-0935
Makes reproductions of the 1930's light bulbs with decorative filaments inside such as flowers, hearts, religious styles, etc.

Glow Lights

Expert

Cindy Chipps
4027 Brooks Hill Rd.
Brooks, KY 40109
Phone: 502-955-9238
Buys/sells Glow Lights; made by Aerolux, Birdseye, Luxram and others; also wants advertising for same; author of book on Glow

Repro. Source

Loyal-T-Lites
Cindy Chipps
4027 Brooks Hill Rd.
Brooks, KY 40109
Phone: 502-955-9238
Sells reproductions of the 1930's Glow Lights; light bulbs with decorative filaments inside such as flowers and hearts.

LIGHTERS

(see also CIGARETTE COLLECTIBLES; SMOKING COLLECTIBLES)

Club/Association

Lighter Club of Great Britain, The
Newsletter: Blaze, The
Richard Ball
30 Heathfield Rd.
Croydon
Surrey CR0 1EU England

Club/Association

Pocket Lighter Preservation Guild &
Historical Society, Inc.
Newsletter: Flint & Flame
L.D. Marshall
36 Four Seasons
Chesterfield, MO 63017
Phone: 314-878-8708
With R.F. Eyerkuss publishes the bi-monthly "Flint & Flame", the most comprehensive lighter collector publication in the world.

Club/Association

On The Lighter Side, International
Lighter Collectors
Newsletter: On The Lighter Side
Judith Sanders, Sec.
Route 3, 136 Circle Drive
Quitman, TX 75783
Phone: 903-763-2795
Members collect cigar & cigarette lighters & research lighter history; bi-monthly newsletter; send SASE for information.

Collector

Ira Pilossof
7002 Ridge Blvd.
Brooklyn, NY 11209
Phone: 718-921-2516
Avid collector of cigarette lighters wants to buy any unusual lighter from the 1880's-1940's, especially Dunhill lighters.

Collector

Jim Lohr
140 14th Ave. No.
Wisconsin Rapids, WI 54494
Wants cigarette lighters, war era, novelty, watch, cigar, cord, bullet, car, gun, cannon lighters, etc. *

Dealer

Jack Seiderman
1050 N.E. 120 St.
Miami, FL 33161
Phone: 305-893-1047   FAX: 305-893-1047
Buys, sells, & collects collectible lighters, accessories, advertising, catalogs, books, brochures, instruction sheets, etc.

Expert

Jack Seiderman
1050 N.E. 120 St.
Miami, FL 33161
Phone: 305-893-1047   FAX: 305-893-1047
Author of "Lighter Encyclopedia."

Zippo

Club/Association

Zippy Collectors Club, Inc.
118 West 6th Ave.
York, PA 17404 *

LIGHTNING BALLS & RODS

(see also LIGHTNING PROTECTION COLLECTIBLES)

LIGHTNING PROTECTION COLLECTIBLES

Collector

John Gephart
1 Firestone Ct.
Fairfield, OH 45014
Lightning rods, balls, arrows, vanes, all related catalogs, paper and advertising.

Collector

Antiques By Daly
10341 Jewell Lake Ct.
Fenton, MO 48430
Wants old lightning fixtures, catalogs and books. *

Collector

Larry Bergman
Rt. 2
Whitehall, WI 54773
Phone: 715-985-3310
Wants lightning rod arrows with glass tails: by Black Swan Co., Shinn, D&S, Barnett. *

Expert

Michael Bruner
8482 Huron River Drive
Union Lake, MI 48386
Phone: 313-674-0433 or 313-661-2359
Wants lightning rod balls, catalogs, installation tags, rods, braces, etc.; co-author of "The Complete Book of Lightning Rod Balls."

Expert

Rod Krupka
2615 Echo Lane
Ortonville, MI 48462
Phone: 313-627-6351
Buys, sells lightning rod balls, weathervanes, related catalogs and ads; co-author of "The Complete Book of Lightning Rod Balls."

Periodical

Newsletter: Crown Point, The
Rod Krupka
2615 Echo Lane
Ortonville, MI 48462
Phone: 313-627-6351
Devoted to the history of lightning protection and the collecting of related items.

LIMITED EDITIONS

(see also COLLECTIBLES (MODERN))

LIPTON TEA COLLECTIBLES

Collector

Masten
149 Hillside Ave.
Cresskill, NJ 07626
*Wants Lipton Tea unusual memorabilia, signs, posters; also Lipton Soup, Knox Gelatin, Good Humor items. ***

LITHOPHANES

(see also COLLECTIBLES (MODERN), Lithophanes)

Club/Association

Lithophane Collectors Club - Blair
Museum of Lithophanes & Carved Waxes
Newsletter: Lithophane Collectors Bulletin
Laurel Blair, Curator
2030 Robinwood Ave.
P.O. Box 4557
Toledo, OH 43620
Phone: 419-243-4115

Collector

Blair Museum of Lithophanes & Carved
Waxes
Laurel Blair, Curator
2030 Robinwood Ave.
P.O. Box 4557
Toledo, OH 43620
Phone: 419-243-4115
Wants plaques, lamp shades, fairy lights, single cast shades.

Collector

Donald Gorlick
P.O. Box 24541
Seattle, WA 98124
Wants "Berlin transparencies": looks like bisque but when turned to light it has a picture in it; in tea sets, lamp shades, beer steins.

Museum/Library

Blair Museum of Lithophanes & Carved
Waxes
Laurel Blair, Curator
2030 Robinwood Ave.
P.O. Box 4557
Toledo, OH 43620
Phone: 419-243-4115

LOCKS

(see also KEYS; RESTRAINT DEVICES; SAFES)

Club/Association

American Lock Collectors Association
Newsletter: American Lock Collectors
  Association Newsletter
Charles Chandler
36076 Grennada
Livonia, MI 48154
Phone: 313-522-0920
Club newsletter reports on coming lock shows, also articles on locks, keys, handcuffs; prices, unusual items, historical info.

Club/Association

West Coast Lock Collectors
Newsletter: West Coast Lock Collectors
  Newsletter
Bob Heilemann
1427 Lincoln Blvd.
Santa Monica, CA 90401
Phone: 213-454-7295

Collector

Richard C. Hubbard
162 Poplar Ave.
Hackensack, NJ 07601
Phone: 201-342-1274
Interested in old US key or combination padlocks, embossed RR locks, figural shapes and unusual mechanisms or early patent dates.

Collector

Tim Bolender
123 W. Vorhees
Reading, OH 45215
Buys, sells, trades locks and keys.

Dealer

Wheeler-Tanner ESCAPES
Joseph & Pamela Tanner
P.O. Box 349
Great Falls, MT 59403
Phone: 406-453-4961
Wants padlocks of all sizes and shapes; figural, combination, round pancake types, railroad, Winchester, Wells Fargo, Express Co's., etc.

Expert

Bob Heilemann
1427 Lincoln Blvd.
Santa Monica, CA 90401
Phone: 213-454-7295
Collector and historian of antique padlocks.

Expert

Collector, The
Franklin Arnall
P.O. Box 253
Claremont, CA 91711
Phone: 714-621-2461
Wants to buy antique padlocks: brass railroad and express, odd miniatures, any unusual cast iron of brass; any quantity.

Museum/Library

Lock Museum of America, Inc.
Newsletter: Lock Museum of America
  Newsletter
130 Main St.
Terryville, CT 06786
Phone: 203-589-6359

Periodical

Newsletter: Padlock Quarterly
Don Stewart
P.O. Box 9397
Phoenix, AZ 85068
Phone: 602-942-0043

Repro. Source

Colonial Lock Co.
172 Main St.
Terryville, CT 06786
Phone: 203-584-0311
Makes old style wood-covered locks.

LOGGING RELATED ITEMS

(see also SCRIP)

Museum/Library

Ashland Logging Museum, Inc.
Box 348
Ashland, ME 04732
Phone: 207-435-3281

Museum/Library

Hoo-Hoo International Forestry Museum
P.O. Box 118
Gurdon, AR 71743
Phone: 501-353-4554

LOOMS

(see also COVERLETS)

Expert

Looms, The
Newsletter: Looms, The
Ken Colwell
154 High St.
Mineral Point, WI 53565
Phone: 608-987-2277 or 608-348-2766
Offers workshops, books and tours related to weaving; also sells books plus antique looms and other related weaving equipment.

LOTTERY TICKETS

Instant (Used)

Club/Association

Lottery Collectors Society
Newsletter: Lottery Collectors Newsletter
Bill Pasquino
1824 Lyndon Ave.
Lancaster, PA 17602
Phone: 717-393-0843
Unites lottery collectors and provides services such as newsletters, ticket catalog, and trading roster.

Collector

Bill Pasquino
1824 Lyndon Ave.
Lancaster, PA 17602
Phone: 717-393-0843
Wants losing instant lottery tickets; instant rub off lottery tickets from the 1970's and early 1980's.

Collector

Karen Lea Rose
4420 Wisconsin Ave.
Tampa, FL 33616-1031
Phone: 813-839-6245

LUGGAGE

(see also CLOTHING & ACCESSORIES)

Periodical

Newsletter: On the Move
The Manor House, Westhay
Glastonbury
Somerset, England
Focuses on luggage, picnic items, sporting and campaign items. *

Louis Vuitton

Dealer

Les Meilleurs
6461 SE Thorburn
Portland, OR 97215
Phone: 503-238-6888
Wants pre-1950 Louis Vuitton trunks and luggage.

LUNCH BOXES

Collector

Peter Reginato
60 Green St.
New York, NY 10012
Phone: 212-925-9787
Wants lunch boxes from 1950's through 1970's.

Collector

Box-A-Rama
Bill Henry
104 Davidson Lane
Oak Ridge, TN 37830
Phone: 615-483-0769

Wants to buy lunch boxes; also sponsors an annual show and auction, Box-A-Rama, specializing in lunch boxes.

Collector

David Reed
841 West Main St.
Madison, OH 44052
Phone: 216-428-6666
Wants Jetsons, Lost in Space, Westerns, TV Shows, Space: metal and vinyl.

Expert

Scott Bruce
P.O. Box 87
Somerville, MA 02143
Wants older lunch boxes.

Expert

Bob Cereghino
Suite 170A-319
6400 Baltimore National Pike
Baltimore, MD 21228
Phone: 301-766-7593

Expert

Allan Smith
1806 Shields Dr.
Sherman, TX 75090
Phone: 214-893-3626 *

Periodical

Newsletter: Hot Boxing
Scott Bruce
P.O. Box 87
Somerville, MA 02143

LURES

(see also FISHING COLLECTIBLES)

MACERATED CURRENCY ITEMS

Collector

Great American Co.
Bertram M. Cohen
169 Marlborough St.
Boston, MA 02116-1830
Phone: 617-247-4754
Wants items made from macerated U.S. money 1880-1940.

Collector

Donald Gorlick
P.O. Box 24541
Seattle, WA 98124
Wants macerated currency - items made up of ground-up money pulp; usually souvenir items, statues, plates, animals; often with a tag.

MACHINERY & EQUIPMENT

(see also CONSTRUCTION EQUIPMENT; FARM MACHINERY; INDUSTRY RELATED ITEMS; LOOMS; TOOLS; WASHING MACHINES)

Museum/Library

American Precision Museum Association, Inc.
P.O. Box 679
Windsor, VT 05089
Phone: 802-674-5781

Catalogs

(see also CATALOGS, Trade)

Collector

Marvin McKinley
1652 Rt. 9
Ashland, OH 44805
Wants old sales catalogs and manuals for machinery, steam engines, gas engines, windmills, farm machinery, buggies, sleighs, etc.

Collector

Clarence Goodburn
R 2 A-3
Madelia, MN 56062
Phone: 507-642-3281
Wants old sales catalogs, brochures, memorabilia, signs, magazines, for farm tractors, heavy construction equipment, cranes, shovels. *

Dealer

Broken Kettle Book Service
702 East Madison St.
Fairfield, IA 52556
Wants old sales catalogs and manuals for machinery, steam engines, gas engines, windmills, farm machinery, buggies, sleighs, etc.

Construction

Auction Service

Vilsmeier Auction Company, Inc.
Walter Vilsmeier
Rt. 309
Montgomeryville, PA 18936
Phone: 215-699-5833
Specializes in the sale of used machinery and equipment; tractor crawlers, loader backhoes, air compressors, graders, etc.

Auction Service

Forke Brothers
830 NBC Center
Lincoln, NE 68508
Phone: 402-475-3631
Specializes in the sale of used machinery and equipment; tractor crawlers, loader backhoes, air compressors, graders, etc. *

Auction Service

Miller & Miller
2525 Ridgmar Blvd.
Fort Worth, TX 76116
Phone: 817-732-4888
Specializes in the sale of used machinery and equipment; tractor crawlers, loader backhoes, air compressors, graders, etc. *

Auction Service

Ritchie Bros.
821 Weld County Rd. 27
Brighton, CO 80601
Phone: 800-547-3555
*Specializes in the sale of used machinery and equipment; tractor crawlers, loader backhoes, air compressors, graders, etc. ***

Club/Association

Historical Construction Equipment
Association
Newsletter: Equipment Echoes
P.O. Box 328
Grand Rapids, OH 43522
Phone: 419-832-0808
Dedicated to preserving the history of construction, surface mining and dredging equipment and related memorabilia, trade

Periodical

Dataquest
Magazine: Green Guide Auction Reports
1290 Ridder Dr.
San Jose, CA 95131-2398
Phone: 408-971-9000   FAX: 408-971-9003
A bi-monthly comprehensive review of construction equipment auction results.

Woodworking

Club/Association

Antique Woodworking Power Tool
Association
Journal: Journal of the AWPTA
Walt Vinoski
22900 Circle J Ranck Rd. #56
Santa Clarita, CA 91350
Phone: 805-254-3547 or 805-254-8970
Provides membership with advice on research, acquisition, restoration, and operation of old woodworking equipment.

Expert

Mr. Dana Martin Batory
402 E. Bucyrus St.
Crestline, OH 44827
Wants catalogs, photographs, advertising, manuals, reminiscences, etc. pertaining to woodworking machinery manufacturers.

MAGAZINES

(see also COLLEGE COLLECTIBLES,
Humor Magazines)

Collector

Bob Havey
P.O. Box 183
W. Sullivan, ME 04689
Phone: 207-442-3083
Wants many magazines from the 1800's to 1950: Movie Magazine, Vogue, Pictorial Review, Esquire, Good Housekeeping, McCall's, etc.

Collector

Gary Olsen
505 S. Royal Ave.
Front Royal, VA 22630
Phone: 703-635-7157 or 703-635-7158
　　　　　　　　　　FAX: 703-635-1818
Wants pre-1970 Life, Look, Colliers, Post, etc. especially with WWI and/or WWII stories and articles.

Collector

Pauline Harry
11493 Spring Hill Dr.
Spring Hill, FL 34609
Phone: 904-686-9418 *

Dealer

Magazine Man, The
Charles Zayic
P.O. Box 57
Ellsworth, ME 04605
Phone: 207-677-7342
Wants old magazines from 1900 thru 1950.

Dealer

Bits & Pieces of Yesterday & Today
Sharon Hood
46060 Warren
Canton, MI 48187
Phone: 313-453-5071
Wants magazines from the 1800's to 1930: Saturday Evening Post, Life, Look, Silver Screen, Harper's Bazaar, The Flapper, etc.

Expert

Denis C. Jackson
P.O. Box 1958
Sequim, WA 98382
Phone: 206-683-2559
Author of "The Masters Price & Identification Guide to Old Magazines."

Periodical

Newspaper: Vintage Collectibles
P.O. Box 5072
Chattanooga, TN 37406 *

Black Mask

Collector

Frank Vogel
60 Cindy Cove
Gulfport, MS 39503
Wants Black Mask magazines 1933 to 1940; describe and price.

Covers & Tear Sheets

Expert

Past & Present
Susan Nicholson
P.O. Box 595
Lisle, IL 60532
Phone: 708-964-5240

Buys and sells rare and unusual postcards, Victorian valentines, periodicals, advertising trade cards, etc.

Periodical

Magazine: Paper Collectors' Marketplace
Doug Watson
P.O. Box 12899
Scandinavia, WI 54977
Phone: 715-467-2379
Monthly magazine for collectors of autographs, paperbacks, postcards, advertising, photographica, magazines; all types of paper

Life

Collector

Roy Silva
318 S. Detroit St. #403
Los Angeles, CA 90036
*Wants Life magazines from 1883-1930. ***

MAD

Dealer

Toy Scouts, Inc.
Bill & Joanne Bruegman
330 Merriman Rd.
Akron, OH 44303-1552
Phone: 216-836-0668 or 216-864-6751

Men's (Girlie)

Expert

Denis C. Jackson
P.O. Box 1958
Sequim, WA 98382
Phone: 206-683-2559
Author of "The Price Guide & Identification Guide to Men's (Girlie) Magazines"; also issues 6 sale catalogs/year of magazines for sale.

Monster

Collector

Steve Dolnick
P.O. Box 69
East Meadow, NY 11554
Phone: 516-486-5085
Buys, sells and trades monster magazines; wants Monster Parade, World Famous Creatures, Thriller, Famous Monsters, and others.

Movie

(see also MOVIE MEMORABILIA)

Collector

Glen Arvin
Box 107
Celestine, IN 47521
Wants 30's-70's magazines with movie stars on cover: TV Guides, Personal Romances, etc.; Marilyn Monroe, Jayne Mansfield, etc.

National Geographic

Dealer

Don Smith's National Geographic
Magazines
Don Smith
3930 Rankin St.
Louisville, KY 40214-1748
Phone: 502-366-7504
Wants magazines from 1888. Buying and selling. Author of "Natl. Geo. Magazines (1888-1988) For Collectors" price guide booklet.

Periodical

Baxbaum Geographics
P.O. Box 465
Wilmington, DE 19899
Phone: 302-994-2663
Deals with the hobby of collecting National Geographic magazines.

Office Related

Collector

Darryl Rehr
11433 Rochester Ave. #303
Los Angeles, CA 90025
Phone: 213-447-5229
Wants pre-1920 magazines & articles relating to old office equipment: "System", "Business Man's Monthly", "Phonographic World", etc.

Outdoor

Collector

Martin Korsak
RD 2 Box 77 Mason Rd.
Vestal, NY 13850
Phone: 607-748-1651
*Pre-1940 outdoor magazines; Big Game Hunting Books; Gun Co. ads; WWI posters; Trench Art; Pocketknives; occupational shaving mugs. *

Dealer

Highwood Bookshop
Lewis & Wilma Razek
P.O. Box 1246
Traverse City, MI 49684
Phone: 616-271-3898
Buys and sells back issues of sporting magazines: hunting, fishing, archery, hunting dog, gun relates; late 1800's to present.

Playboy

Dealer

Centerfold Shop, The
Douglas L. Tracy
Suite 2-C
1220 23rd St.
San Diego, CA 92102-1960
Since 1968 specializing in Playboy magazines from the 1950's; mail order only; send $5 for catalog; want issues Vol. 1 No. 1 thru 1957.

Pulp

Collector

Jack Deveny
6805 Cheyenne Trail
Edina, MN 55439-1158
Phone: 612-941-2457
Wants Spider, Shadow, Doc Savage, Spicy, Detective, Mystery, Horror, Terror, etc.

Expert

Hancer's Bookstore
Kevin Hancer
5813 York Ave.
Edina, MN 55410
Phone: 612-922-9144 *

Periodical

Magazine: Pulp Collector
8417 Carrolton Pkwy.
New Carrolton, MD 20784 *

Periodical

Newsletter: Pulp & Paperback Market
Kevin Hancer
5813 York Ave.
Edina, MN 55410
Phone: 612-922-9144 *

Radio & Wireless

(see also TELEGRAPH ITEMS)

Collector

Paul Thompson
315 Larkspur Dr.
Santa Maria, CA 93455
Phone: 805-934-2778
Wants radio and wireless magazines before 1940.

Scandal/Cult/R 'n' R

Expert

Shake Books
Alan Betrock
449 12 St.
Brooklyn, NY 11215
Phone: 718-499-6941
Author of "Unseen America-The Greatest Cult Exploitation Magazines 1950-1966."

Trade

Collector

Richard M. Bueschel
414 N. Prospect Manore Ave.
Mt. Prospect, IL 60056
Phone: 708-253-0791
Wants trade magazines, e.g. saloons (Bar & Buffet, 1899-1910), drug stores (American Druggist) and coin machines (Coin Magazine

MAGIC LANTERNS & SLIDES

Club/Association

Magic Lantern Society of the U. S. &
Canada
Newsletter: Magic Lantern Bulletin
897 Belmont St.
Watertown, MA 02172
Phone: 617-489-5123 *

Collector

Elizabeth Gerber
21 Royal Dominion Ct.
Bethesda, MD 20817
Phone: 301-469-5016
*Wants magic lanterns and slides. *

Collector

Sherry L. Werdon
400 N. Washington
Lowell, MI 49331
Phone: 616-897-9580
Wants unusual magic lanterns or color magic lantern slides; also round extra large slides and wooden viewers, pantoscope, etc.

MAGICIANS PARAPHERNALIA

Club/Association

New England Magic Collectors
Association
Edward Hill
P.O. Box 30
Harmony, RI 02829
Phone: 401-231-1215
Association of serious collectors of magic who reside in the New England area; three meetings/ year; all collectors welcome as guests.

Club/Association

Magic Collectors Association
Newsletter: Magicol
19 Logan St.
New Britain, CT 06051
Phone: 203-224-1583 *

Collector

Frank Herman
710 Anchor Way
Carlsbad, CA 92008
Wants posters, programs, Mysto Magic sets, toys; also mentalists, escape artists, ventriloquists, fire eaters, spiritualists.

Collector

Ron Kohl
2316 W Sacramento Ave.
Chico, CA 95926
*Wants books, posters, magazines, equipment, etc.; singles or collection. *

Expert

John A. Greget
1124 Cymry Dr.
Berwyn, PA 19312
Phone: 215-296-2664

*Buys and appraises magic books, posters, maga-
zines, ephemera, equipment, etc.; singles or collection.*

Museum/Library

Houdini Magical Hall of Fame
Niagara Falls
Ontario L2E 6V6 Canada

Museum/Library

American Museum of Magic
Robert Lund
107 E. Michigan
P.O. Box 5
Marshall, MI 49068
Phone: 616-781-7666 or 616-781-7674
*Museum with holdings of approx. 250,000 items,
all on magic; interested in acquiring any material
on magicians.*

Houdini

Collector

Kevin Connolly
7 Warwick Court
River Edge, NJ 07661
Phone: 201-489-2838
*Wants anything Houdini or about magic: books,
posters, autographs, tricks, tokens, sets, apparatus, etc.*

Dealer

International Handcuff Exchange
Michael Griffin
356 W. Powell Rd.
Powell, OH 43065
Phone: 614-846-0585
*Buys/sells Houdini memorabilia and old collect-
ible magic; also handcuffs, leg irons, etc.; list of
items for sale available.*

Dealer

Wheeler-Tanner ESCAPES
Joseph & Pamela Tanner
P.O. Box 349
Great Falls, MT 59403
Phone: 406-453-4961
*Wants Houdini & other escape artist items: autog-
raphs, posters, letters, postcards, books, photos,
playbills, equipment, etc.*

MAGNETS

Refrigerator Door

Collector

Karen Lea Rose
4420 Wisconsin Ave.
Tampa, FL 33616-1031
Phone: 813-839-6245
*Collector wants to trade for refrigerator door-type
magnets that ADVERTISE a company, business
or product.*

MAILBOXES

Collector

Charles W. Wardell
P.O. Box 195
Trinity, NC 27370
Phone: 919-434-1145
*Wants 1870-1940 cast iron mailboxes; these boxes
were fancy in design and served on homes and
shops; usually with many coats of paint.*

MANNEQUINS

Collector

Gwen Daniel
18 Belleau Lake Ct.
O'Fallon, MO 63366
Phone: 314-281-3190
*Wants Victorian thru 1950's mannequins;, heads
only or full mannequins; send photos first if possible.*

Museum/Library

Mannequin Museum, The
Marsha Bentley Hale
P.O. Box 2555
Malibu, CA 90265

MANUSCRIPTS

(see also AUTOGRAPHS; BOOKS;
HISTORICAL AMERICANA; PAPER
COLLECTIBLES)

Club/Association

Manuscript Society, The
Journal: Manuscripts
350 N. Niagara St.
Burbank, CA 91505
*An organization of collectors, dealers, librarians,
archivists, scholars and others interested in autographs and manuscripts.*

Dealer

Rare Books & Manuscripts
Carmen D. Valentino
2965 Richmond St.
Philadelphia, PA 19134
Phone: 215-739-6058
*Antiquarian bookseller specializing in rare books,
manuscripts, documents, early newspapers, eph-
emera, broadsides; pre-WWI.*

Pennsylvania

Expert

Family Album, The
Ron Lieberman
R.D. 1, Box 42
Glen Rock, PA 17327
Phone: 717-235-2134   FAX: 717-235-8042
*Buys, sells, appraises all Pennsylvania related
books, manuscripts, artwork, etc.*

MAPS

(see also ATLASES; PAPER
COLLECTIBLES; GLOBES; STAMP
COLLECTING, Topical (Map Related))

Club/Association

International Map Collectors Society
Journal: International Map Collectors Society
Journal
Catherine Batchelor
Pikes, The Ridgeway
Oxshott, Leatherhead
Surrey KT22 0LG, England *

Club/Association

Association of Map Memorabilia
Collectors
Newsletter: Cartomania
Siegfried Feller
8 Amherst Rd.
Pelham, MA 01002
Phone: 413-253-3115
*For collectors & lovers of maps: on postcards,
stamps/envelopes, postmarks/cancels, labels, fab-
rics, trays/plates, etc.*

Club/Association

Chicago Map Society, The
Newsletter: Mapline
60 W. Walton St.
Chicago, IL 60610
Phone: 312-943-9090
Oldest map society in North America.

Collector

J. Hanna
4016 Woodland Rd.
Annandale, VA 22003
Phone: 703-941-8256
*Wants atlases, books or ephemera with maps,
U.S. documents with maps and large single maps;
pre-1900. *

Dealer

Cartomania Plus
Siegfried Feller
8 Amherst Rd.
Pelham, MA 01002
Phone: 413-253-3115
*Buys and sells maps and map related
memorabilia.*

Dealer

Thomas Baxter
P.O. Box 677
Wheatley Heights, NY 11798
Phone: 516-293-2576
*Wants old maps and atlases. *

Dealer

Old Print Gallery, The
James & Judith Blakely
1220 31st St. NW
Washington, DC 20007
Phone: 202-965-1818   FAX: 202-965-1869

Wants antique maps: American or foreign, 16th to 19th centuries.

Dealer

Antiquarian Books & Maps
Murray Hudson
109 S. Church St.
P.O. Box 163
Halls, TN 38040
Phone: 901-836-9057 or 800-748-9946
Buys and sells maps, especially wall, pocket, U.S. Civil War, R.R.; also books with maps: pre-1900 atlases, travel guides, etc.

Expert

David C. Jolly, Publishers
David C. Jolly
P.O. Box 931
Brookline, MA 02146
Phone: 617-232-6272
Author of "Antique Maps, Sea Charts, City Views, Celestial Charts & Battle Plans Price Record & Handbook."

Museum/Library

Hermon Dunlap Smith Center for the History of Cartography
Newberry Library
Chicago, IL 60610

Periodical

Newberry Library, Hermon D. Smith Center for the History of Cartography
Newsletter: Mapline
60 West Walton Street
Chicago, IL 60610
Phone: 312-943-9090 *

MARBLES

Auction Service

Block's Box
Robert S. Block
P.O. Box 51
Trumbull, CT 06611
Phone: 203-261-3223 or 203-783-1690
Conducts mail-bid auctions of marbles received from collectors, dealers, estates, museums and others.

Auction Service

Dan & Gretchen Turner
P.O. Box 210992
Nashville, TN 37221
Phone: 615-952-3699
Conducts marble mail auctions using VHS video tape/catalog.

Club/Association

Marble Collectors Unlimited
Newsletter: Marble Mart/Newsletter
P.O. Box 206
Northboro, MA 01532
Phone: 508-393-2923

The newsletter is published for and by members of MCU; contains items of interest such as meets, auctions, member buy/sell/trade ads, etc.

Club/Association

Marble Collectors Society of America
Newsletter: Marble Mania
Stanley Block
P.O. Box 222
Trumbull, CT 06611
Phone: 203-261-3223
Established to gather and disseminate information and to perform services to further the hobby of marbles and marble collecting.

Club/Association

National Marble Club of America
Newsletter: National Marble Club of America Newsletter
Jim Ridpath
440 Eaton Rd.
Drexel Hill, PA 19026
Phone: 215-622-4444
To keep marble collectors informed, to encourage children to once again play the game, and to advise members on all aspects of marbles.

Club/Association

Buckeye Marble Collectors Club
Newsletter: BMC Newsletter
437 Meadowbrook Dr.
Newark, OH 43055
Phone: 614-366-7002
Active club sponsoring annual convention in Columbus, OH; newsletter contains articles, buy/sell ads, calendar of events, etc.

Club/Association

Southern California Marble Collectors Society
Newsletter: SCMCS Bulletin
P.O. Box 84179
Los Angeles, CA 90073 *

Club/Association

Southern California Marble Club
18361-1 Strathern St.
Reseda, CA 91335

Collector

Beverly Brule
P.O. Box 206
Northboro, MA 01532
Phone: 508-393-2923
Buy/sell/trade marbles and marble related items.

Collector

Great American Co.
Bertram M. Cohen
169 Marlborough St.
Boston, MA 02116-1830
Phone: 617-247-4754
Marbles bought and sold; also wants postcards showing children playing with marbles.

Collector

Jack Whistance
288 Route 28
Kingston, NY 12401
Phone: 914-338-4397
Wants all old and pre-1930 machine made marbles for collection: swirls, onionskins, Lutz, slags, opaques, micas, sulphides, etc.

Collector

Sousa
5904 Wellesley Ave.
Pittsburgh, PA 15206
*Wants glass swirl marbles; also trophies and awards from marble tournaments, pre-1942; also glass marbles in original boxes. **

Collector

Mark Howard
6756 Perry Penny Dr.
Annandale, VA 22003
Phone: 703-642-5334 *

Collector

Gary & Sally Dolly
Box 2044
New Smyrna Beach, FL 32070 *

Collector

Frank Gardenhire
3608 Koons Rd.
Chattanooga, TN 37412
Phone: 615-867-5440 *

Collector

Edwin Snyder
P.O. Box 156
Lancaster, KY 40444
Phone: 606-792-4816
Akro agate and other old marbles in original boxes/packages; also mach. made: Oxbloods, Bricks, Lemonades, Cork Screws, Guineas, Large

Collector

Harold Hogue
5570 Hoffman Rd.
Milford, OH 45150 *

Collector

Collector
1021 East Wylie St.
Bloomington, IN 47401
Old sulphide or swirl marbles.

Collector

Lynn Christian
1114 Wilson Ave.
Ames, IA 50010
Phone: 515-232-2222
Wants old figurals, sulfides, swirls, etc.; also prizes from marble tournaments and contests.

Collector

Bob Hanson
Rt. 1, Box 222
Wapato, WA 98951
Phone: 509-848-2345 *

Dealer

Bill Sweet
14 Diaua Drive
P.O. Box 4736
Rumford, RI 02916
Phone: 401-434-4548

Dealer

Thomas Baxter
P.O. Box 677
Wheatley Heights, NY 11798
Phone: 516-293-2576
Wants handmade marbles from 1870-1920. *

Dealer

Wayne Sanders
2202 Livingston St.
Jefferson City, MO 65101
Phone: 314-636-7515 *

Expert

Block's Box
Stanley & Bob Block
P.O. Box 51
Trumbull, CT 06611
Phone: 203-261-3223 or 203-783-1690
Buys and sells; offers twelve page list of marbles currently available; send LSASE with 52 cents postage.

Expert

Everett Grist
734 12th St.
Charleston, IL 61920 *

Expert

Castle's Fair
Larry Castle
885 Taylor Ave.
Ogden, UT 84404
Phone: 801-393-8131
Advanced collector and nationally recognized expert with over 10 years experience with marbles; buys, appraises and repairs marbles.

Museum/Library

Children's Museum
67 East Kirby
Detroit, MI 48202
Phone: 313-494-1210

Repair Service

Jack Leslie
Rt. 4, Box 60
Liberty, MO 64068
Phone: 816-455-2110
Restores and regrinds glass marbles. *

Repair Service

Castle's Fair
Larry Castle
885 Taylor Ave.
Ogden, UT 84404
Phone: 801-393-8131
Restores and regrinds glass marbles; over ten years experience and more that 6000 marbles restored.

Sulphides

Collector

Lothar Ruepp
P.O. Box 349
Lake Hiawatha, NJ 07034
Wants colored sulphide marbles in good condition. *

MARDI GRAS ITEMS

New Orleans

Collector

Arthur Hardy
P.O. Box 8058
New Orleans, LA 70182
Wants ball invitations, post cards, carnival bulletins (parade papers), photos, illustrated feature articles, brochures, etc. *

Museum/Library

Mardi Gras World
P.O. Box 6307
New Orleans, LA 70174
Phone: 504-362-8211

MARINE CORPS ITEMS

Collector

J.K. Williams
6025 Makely Dr.
Fairfax Station, VA 22039
Phone: 703-250-8421
Wants U.S. Marine Corps WWII-era recruiting posters, including bus/trolley cards, tin signs, brochures, advertisements, etc.

MARITIME ANTIQUES

(see also NAUTICAL COLLECTIBLES)

MATCHBOXES & LABELS

Periodical

Newsletter: Vesta
18 Bain Ave.
Camberley GU15 2RR England
A monthly about matchbox labels. *

MATCHCOVERS

Club/Association

Trans Canada Matchcover Club
George Gyokery, Sec.
Box 219
Caledonia
Ontario NOA 1AO Canada
Phone: 416-765-4696

Club/Association

Liberty Bell Matchcover Club
Newsletter: Liberty Bell Crier
Marie E. Harbison, Trea.
6048 N. Water St.
Philadelphia, PA 19120
Phone: 215-424-5218
Members are interested in the collecting of matchcovers & matchboxes; hosts annual national convention; holds all-day shows, auctions.

Club/Association

American Matchcover Association
Newsletter: Front Striker Bulletin, The
Bill Retskin
3417 Clayborne Ave.
Alexandria, VA 22306-1410
Phone: 703-768-1051   FAX: 703-768-4719
Covers history and current status of the matchbook industry as well as the matchcover collecting hobby.

Club/Association

Rathkamp Matchbook Society
Newsletter: Rathkamp Matchbook Society Bulletin
John C. Williams
Dept. CH
1359 Surrey Road
Vandalia, OH 45377-1646
Phone: 513-890-8684
Devoted to collecting matchcovers and, to a limited extent, match boxes. Free information packet available.

Expert

Wray Martin
221 Upper Paradise
Hamilton
Ontario L9C 5C1 Canada
Phone: 416-383-0454

Expert

Bill Retskin
3417 Clayborne Ave.
Alexandria, VA 22306-1410
Phone: 703-768-1051   FAX: 703-768-4719
Author of "The Matchcover Resource Book and Price Guide."

Periodical

Newsletter: Match Hunter, The
Michael Zaun
740 Poplar
Boulder, CO 80304
Phone: 303-449-8547

20-page quarterly newsletter; letters, ads, articles about matchcovers and collections, games, etc.

MEDALLIC SCULPTURES

(see also MEDALS, ORDERS & DEORATIONS)

Club/Association

Society of Medalists
Old Ridgebury Rd.
Danbury, CT 00813
Interested in high relief medallic sculptures. *

Club/Association

American Medallic Sculpture Association
Newsletter: Members Exchange
George Cuhaj, Treas.
P.O. Box 6021
Astoria, NY 11106
A group of sculptors, collectors, suppliers, producers and scholars interested in high relief medallic sculptures.

MEDALS, ORDERS & DECORATIONS

(see also HISTORICAL AMERICANA; VETERANS, Civil War; MILITARIA; TOKENS)

Auction Service

Wallis & Wallis
West Street Auction Galleries
Lewes
East Sussex BN7 2NJ England
Britain's specialist auctioneers of arms, armour, militaria and military orders.

Auction Service

Spink & Son, Ltd.
King Street
St. James's
london SW1Y 6QS England
Auctioneers and dealers of coins (ancient to present), medals, orders, tokens, decorations and other numismatic items.

Club/Association

Token & Medal Society
Journal: Token & Medal Society Journal
Cindy Grellman
P.O. Box 951988
Lake Mary, FL 32795
Phone: 407-321-8747
Promote and stimulates "exonumia", the study of non-government issue tokens and medals.

Club/Association

American Numismatic Association
Magazine: Numismatist, The
Robert J. Leuver, ExDir
818 N. Cascade Ave.
Colorado Springs, CO 80903-3279
Phone: 719-632-2646 or 800-367-9723
FAX: 719-632-2646

Worldwide assoc. of collectors of coins, paper money, medals and tokens; over 33,000 members; offers collector services and benefits.

Collector

Stanley Steinberg
P.O. Box 512
Malden, MA 02148
Wants tokens and all engraved awards and medals: military, political, merchant advertising, associations, expositions, life-saving awards. *

Collector

Jerome Schaeper
705 Philadelphia St.
Covington, KY 41011
Phone: 606-581-3729
Tokens, medals, badges, pocket mirrors.

Dealer

Peter Hlinka Historical Americana
Peter Hlinka
P.O. Box 310
New York, NY 10028-0003
Phone: 212-409-6407
Publishes a large catalog of militaria, medals, insignia, war relics and other political and historical Americana; also foreign.

Dealer

Jeffrey B. Floyd
P.O. Box 9791
Alexandria, VA 22304
Phone: 703-461-9582
Buy, sell, trade all military medals & decorations; specializing in Imperial German, British and American awards; all periods.

Dealer

S C Coin & Stamp Co. Inc.
Cy Phillips, Jr.
P.O. Drawer 3069
Arcadia, CA 91006
Phone: 818-445-8277 or 800-367-0779
Tokens, medals, coins, currency, badges, expo. and fair items, scrap gold and silver.

Dealer

Ackley Unlimited
P.O. Box 82144
Portland, OR 97282-0144
Phone: 503-659-4681
Buys, sells, trades orders, decorations and medals.

Expert

Steve Johnson Militaria
Steve Johnson
P.O. Box 34682
Chicago, IL 60634
Wants military medals and decorations from all periods, any country.

Museum/Library

American Numismatic Society, The
Newsletter: American Numismatic Society Newsletter, The
Broadway & 155th St.
New York, NY 10032
Phone: 212-234-3130

Museum/Library

Museum of the American Numismatic Association
Magazine: Numismatist, The
Robert W. Hoge, Cur.
818 N. Cascade Ave.
Colorado Springs, CO 80903-3279
Phone: 719-632-2646   FAX: 719-634-4085
A museum collection including 400,000 items; collection includes medals, orders and decorations from all countries and time periods.

Museum/Library

Military Medal Museum & Research Center
448 N. San Pedro St.
San Jose, CA 95110
Phone: 408-298-1100

MEDICAL, DENTAL & PHARMACEUTICAL

(see also BOOKS, Medical & Dental; VETERINARY MEDICINE ITEMS)

Club/Association

Scientific Instrument Society
Magazine: Bulletin of the Scientific Instrument Society
P.O. Box 15
Worcestershire WR102TD England *

Club/Association

Medical Collectors Association
Newsletter: Medical Collectors Association Newsletter
Dr. M. Donald Blaufox, MD
1300 Morris Park Ave.
Bronx, NY 10461
The association meets once a year and issues its newsletter semi-annually.

Club/Association

Maryland Microscopical Society
Dr. Sam Koslov
8621 Polk St.
McLean, VA 22102
Phone: 301-953-5591
Focuses on instruments and devices; medical, surveying, photographic, microscopical, navigational, horological, astronomical, etc.

Collector

Norman B. Meadow
225 E. 64th St.
New York, NY 10021
Phone: 212-628-0032
Wants pre-1900 medical and surgical instruments or medical books.

Collector

Dr. Allan Wissner
P.O. Box 102
Ardsley, NY 10502
Phone: 914-693-4628
Wants microscopes, medical, scientific instruments: Zentmayer, Grunow, Bullock, Mc-Allister, Gundlack, McIntosh, Tolles, Queen, Pike.

Collector

Jerry A. Phelps
6013 Innes Trace Rd.
Louisville, KY 40222
Phone: 502-425-4765
Wants medical and apothecary antiques; also pre-1900 country store items and advertising items.

Collector

Greybird Publishing
Richard Van Vleck
11824 Taneytown Pike
Taneytown, MD 21787
Phone: 301-447-2680
Wants medical and scientific antiques of all sorts; especially microscopes, eye-related instruments, laboratory and demo devices.

Collector

Dr. Gimesh
Box 53788
Fayetteville, NC 28305
Wants medical, dental, apothecary items, spectacles, books, etc. *

Collector

Jerry A. Phelps
6013 Innes Trace Rd.
Louisville, KY 40222
Wants medical and apothecary antiques; also pre-1900 country store items.

Collector

Dale Beeks
Box 2515H
Coeur D'Arlene, ID 83814
Phone: 208-667-0830
Wants transits, compasses, link-chains; also fine microscopes, pre-1900 typewriters, calculating devices, medical items & quackery. *

Collector

Doug Johnston
529 W. Encanto
Phoenix, AZ 85003
Wants medical and pharmaceutical advertising (pre-1900), trade cards, calendars, journals, photo, patent medicines, instruments, etc.

Collector

Arizona Gastroenterology Consulants, Ltd.
Dr. Robert E. Kravetz, M.D.
6707 North 19th Ave.
Phoenix, AZ 85015
Phone: 602-242-2555
Collects medical artifacts.

Dealer

Arthur Davidson Ltd.
78-79 Jermyn St.
London SWIY 6NB England
Specializes in good medical and pharmaceutical items. *

Dealer

Hardings
Lynn Harding
103 West Aliso Street
Ojai, CA 93023
Phone: 805-646-0204
Specializes is buying and selling mechanical, industrial and scientific artifacts; also sells finely engineered replicas.

Expert

Medical Museum
Dr. Robert E. Kravetz, M.D.
Phoenix Baptist Hospital
Phoenix, AZ 85015
Phone: 602-242-2555
Medical museum curator, collector and historian; deals mainly with 18th and 19th century medical & pharmaceutical antiques.

Expert

Eli Buk
2nd Floor
151 Spring St.
New York, NY 10012
Specialist in historical science and technology. *

Expert

Don Fredgant
1625-52 Centerville Rd.
Tallahassee, FL 32308 *

Museum/Library

Armed Forces Medical Museum
Adrianne Noe, Curator
Bldg. 54
Walter Read Medical Center
Washington, DC 20306
Phone: 202-576-2438 or 202-576-0401
FAX: 202-576-2164
Historical collections containing over 1100 artifacts documenting the history of medicine; actively seeking medical instruments.

Museum/Library

Medical Museum
Dr. Robert E. Kravetz, M.D.
Phoenix Baptist Hospital
Phoenix, AZ 85015
Phone: 602-242-2555

Museum/Library

Hugh Mercer Apothecary Shop
c/o A.P.V.A.
1200 Charles St.
Fredericksburg, VA 22401
Phone: 703-373-3362

Museum/Library

Country Doctor Museum, The
P.O. Box 34
Bailey, NC 27807
Phone: 919-235-4165

Museum/Library

McDowell House & Apothecary Shop
125 S. Second St.
Danville, KY 40422
Phone: 606-236-2804

Museum/Library

Transylvania Museum
300 N. Broadway
Lexington, KY 40508
Phone: 606-233-8228

Museum/Library

Dittrick Museum of Medical History
James M. Edmonson, PhD
11000 Euclid Ave.
Cleveland, OH 44106
Phone: 216-368-3648
Collection of 75,000 artifacts: medical history, diagnostic instruments, microscopes, surgical and obstetric instruments, etc.

Museum/Library

International Museum of Surgical
Science & Hall of Fame
1524 North Lake Shore Drive
Chicago, IL 60610
Phone: 312-642-3555

Periodical

Greybird Publishing
Newsletter: Scientific, Medical & Mechanical Antiques
Richard Van Vleck
11824 Taneytown Pike
Taneytown, MD 21787
Phone: 301-447-2680
A quarterly newsletter for those interested in scientific, medical and mechanical devices; ads, auction reports, articles.

Civil War

Dealer

Antique Scientifica
Alex Peck
P.O. Box 710
Charleston, IL 61920
Phone: 217-348-1009
Wants surgical and bloodletting instruments, any Civil War (and pre-1890) medical gear, USA Hosp. Dept., etc.; anything Civil War. *

Dental

Collector

William Winburn
1502 Showalter Rd.
Grafton, VA 23692
Phone: 804-898-8246
Dental instruments especially extracting; modern or obsolete; also contents of old dental offices. *

Collector

Collector
5470 Folkestone Dr.
Dayton, OH 45459
Phone: 513-435-6849
Dental cabinets, instruments and catalogs.

Collector

Ken DuVal
P.O. Box 1668
Oceanside, CA 92054 *

Museum/Library

National Museum of Dentistry
666 W. Baltimore St.
Baltimore, MD 21201
Phone: 301-328-8314   FAX: 301-328-3028
Poster art advertising dentists or dental products, pre-1950 dentist's directories (e.g. Polk's, Beecher's), trade catalogs, etc.

Museum/Library

Medical University of South Carolina,
Macaulay Museum of Dental History
171 Ashley Avenue
Charleston, SC 29425
Phone: 803-792-2288

Museum/Library

Dr. John Harris Dental Museum
1370 Dublin Dr.
Columbus, OH 43215
Phone: 614-486-2700
Mailing address is as above, but located in Bainbridge, OH.

Museum/Library

Museum of Dentistry
295 S. Flower St.
Orange, CA 92668
Phone: 714-542-8808

Quackery

(see also HEALTH & BEAUTY ITEMS, Devices to Restore)

Collector

O. Lindan
1404 Dorsh Rd.
Cleveland, OH 44121
Phone: 216-382-7113
Wants old electrotherapeutic and controversial healing devices and related literature; also wants medical, scientific instruments.

Collector

Ed Keller
1205 Imperial Dr.
Pittsburg, KS 66762
Wants quack medical devices and old electrotherapeutic gadgets which shock, buzz, light up or remain silent.

Museum/Library

Lindan Hist. Coll. of
Electrotherapeutic & Controversial
O. Lindan
1404 Dorsh Rd.
Cleveland, OH 44121
Phone: 216-382-7113
Focuses on old electrotherapeutic and controversial healing devices and related literature.

Museum/Library

Museum of Questionable Medical Devices
549 Turnpike Rd.
Golden Valley, MN 55417
Phone: 612-545-1113

Museum/Library

National Museum of Medical Quackery,
The
3839 Lindell Boulevard
St. Louis, MO 63108

Museum/Library

Diablo Valley College Museum
Golf Club Road
Pleasant Hill, CA 94523
Phone: 415-685-1230

MENUS

(see also COOKBOOKS; RESTAURANT COLLECTIBLES)

Museum/Library

National Restaurant Association
1200 17th St. NW
Washington, DC 20036
Phone: 202-331-5960
Computer catalogued collection of thousands of menus from the 1930's to present.

Museum/Library

Cornell School of Hotel Administration
Library
Cornell University
Ithaca, NY 14854
Phone: 607-255-3673
Over 10,000 menus from the 1850's through the 1940's.

Museum/Library

Strong Museum, The
1 Manhattan Square
Rochester, NY 14607
Phone: 716-263-2700
Has a small collection of 100 menus dating back to the 1840's; fully catalogued on a computer database.

METAL ITEMS

(see also ALUMINUM, Hammered; BRASS ITEMS; BRONZE; CAST IRON ITEMS; COPPER ITEMS; PEWTER; SILVER; SILVERPLATE; TIN COLLECTIBLES)

Museum/Library

National Ornamental Metal Museum
374 West California Ave.
Memphis, TN 38106
Phone: 901-774-6380

Repro. Source

Kayne & Son Custom Forged Hardware
76 Daniel Ridge Rd.
Candler, NC 28715
Phone: 704-667-8868
Steel, brass, bronze reproductions of fireplace tools and accessories, hardware, military accouterments, etc. *

METEORITE COLLECTIBLES

(see also NATURAL HISTORY)

METTLACH

(see also STEINS)

MICROSCOPES

(see also INSTRUMENTS & DEVICES, Scientific)

Club/Association

Maryland Microscopical Society
Dr. Sam Koslov
8621 Polk St.
McLean, VA 22102
Phone: 301-953-5591
Focuses on instruments and devices; medical, surveying, photographic, microscopical, navigational, horological, astronomical, etc.

Collector

G.P.O., Inc.
P.O. Box 472
Mantua, NJ 08051
FAX: 609-468-9288
Wants pre 1900 microscopes, microscope slides and slide-making equipment.

Collector

Paul Ferraglio
3332 W. Lake Rd.
Canandaigua, NY 14424
Phone: 716-394-7663
Wants to buy antique brass microscopes, scientific and surveying instruments; also wants related books and catalogs.

Collector

Greybird Publishing
Richard Van Vleck
11824 Taneytown Pike
Taneytown, MD 21787
Phone: 301-447-2680
Wants medical and scientific antiques of all sorts; especially microscopes, eye-related instruments, laboratory and demo devices.

Museum/Library

Armed Forces Medical Museum, Billings
Microscope Collection
Adrianne Noe, Curator
Bldg. 54
Walter Read Medical Center
Washington, DC 20306
Phone: 202-576-2438 or 202-576-0401
FAX: 202-576-2164
Approx. 1000 microscopes and 700 accessories; documents histological techniques by the inclusion of microtomes, accessories &

MILITARIA

(see also AVIATION; BOOKS; CANNONS; CIVIL WAR; EDGED WEAPONS; FIREARMS; INDIAN WARS; MILITARY HISTORY; NAZI ITEMS; ORDNANCE; SWORDS; VIET NAM ITEMS)

Auction Service

Graf Klenau OHG
8000 Munchen 1
Postfach 122, Germany
A well established auction house handling all kinds of worldwide military-related antiques of high quality. *

Auction Service

Jan K. Kube
Herzostrasse 34
8 Muchen 40, Germany
A well established auction house handling all kinds of worldwide military-related antiques of high quality. *

Auction Service

Wallis & Wallis
West Street Auction Galleries
Lewes
East Sussex BN7 2NJ England
Britain's specialist auctioneers of arms, armor, militaria and military orders.

Auction Service

Kelley's
553 Main Street
Woburn, MA 01801
Phone: 617-935-3389 or 617-272-9167
Conducts several auctions per year of militaria from the Revolution to present day.

Auction Service

Mohawk Arms Inc.
P.O. Box 399
Utica, NY 13503
Phone: 315-724-1234
Specializes in uniforms, headgear, badges, award documents, ephemera, daggers, swords, photo albums, prints, books, art items, etc.

Auction Service

AAG, Militaria Mail Auction
Stephen Flood
20 Grandview Ave.
Wilkes-Barre, PA 18702
Phone: 717-829-1500 or 717-822-5300
FAX: 717-822-9992
Specializing in mail-bid auctions of militaria from Revolutionary War to Viet Nam with emphasis on WWII; all countries.

Auction Service

Roger S. Steffen Historical Militaria
Roger S. Steffen
14 Murnan Road
Cold Spring, KY 41076
Phone: 606-431-4499
Conducts mail-bid auctions of military items and antique firearms. *

Auction Service

Manion's Auction House
P.O. Box 12214
Kansas City, KS 66112
Phone: 913-299-6692   FAX: 913-299-6792
The largest auction service in the U.S. handling only military-related antiques: items from U.S., Germany, Japan and other countries.

Auction Service

Centurion, The
219 North Jackson
El Dorado, AR 71730
Conducts militaria mail-bid auctions. *

Auction Service

Der Gauleiter
P.O. Box 721288
Houston, TX 77272
Conducts bi-monthly auctions of military items specializing in Third Reich. *

Auction Service

RECAPT Historical Militaria Auction Service
Robert C. Thomas, Jr.
P.O. Box 1792
Santa Ana, CA 92702
Phone: 714-748-7459   FAX: 714-748-7492
Specializes in the sale of historical militaria.

Collector

Fred Robbins
210 Brunswick Ave.
Gardiner, ME 04345
Phone: 207-582-5005
Wants revolution, Civil War, flintlocks, head gear, Samurai swords, military daguerreotypes, G.A.R., presentation swords, etc. *

Collector

Gene Christian
3849 Bailey Ave.
Bronx, NY 10463
Phone: 212-548-0243
Wants Foreign Legion, Devils Island, China (USMC, 15th, Gunboats, W. Russians, Warlords), Military kukris w/marked blades.

Collector

Glen Hyatt
907 Easternview Dr.
Fredericksburg, VA 22405
Phone: 703-371-5680
WWI and WWII uniforms, equipment, memorabilia; particularly aviation. *

Collector

Ertel
Box 1150
Des Plaines, IL 60017
Phone: 708-699-1159
Wants Japanese samurai swords, all war souvenirs; any U.S. or foreign item; particularly swords, daggers, firearms. *

Collector

Ron L. Willis
2110 Fox Ave.
Moore, OK 73160
Phone: 405-793-9604 or 405-521-3484
Wants U.S. Navy - any period - patches, wings, uniforms, books, documents, edged weapons, photos, plaques, flags, etc.

Dealer

Fred Robbins
210 Brunswick Ave.
Gardiner, ME 04345
Phone: 207-582-5005
Wants militaria, flintlocks, percussion guns, uniforms, bugles, Samurai swords, spike helmets, Civil War veterans, etc. *

Dealer
Mohawk Arms Inc.
P.O. Box 399
Utica, NY 13503
Phone: 315-724-1234

Dealer
Allenwood Americana Antiques
Ken & Gloria Kipp
Box 116
Allenwood, PA 17810
Phone: 717-538-1440
Longtime, established militaria dealer with over 20 years experience; especially interested in WWI and WWII memorabilia; buys and sells.

Dealer
Phoenix Militaria, Inc.
Terry Hannon, Pres.
P.O. Box 245
Lyon Station, PA 19536-0245
Phone: 215-682-1010 or 800-446-0909
                    FAX: 215-682-1066
Buys/sells general militaria; also sells militaria collecting books & periodicals.

Dealer
San Juan Precious Metals Corp.
Ron Gordon
4818 San Juan Ave.
Jacksonville, FL 32210-3232
Phone: 904-387-3486
Wants German, US, Japanese, Vietnam military items: helmets, flags, uniforms, badges, swords, coins, daggers, etc.

Dealer
Roger S. Steffen Historical Militaria
Roger S. Steffen
14 Murnan Road
Cold Spring, KY 41076
Phone: 606-431-4499 *

Dealer
Seven Acres Antique Village & Museum
Randy Donley
8512 S. Union Rd.
Union, IL 60180
Phone: 815-923-2214
Buys and sells souvenirs and relics from all wars: uniforms, helmets, medals, weapons, guns, swords, etc.

Expert
AAG, Militaria Mail Auction
Stephen Flood
20 Grandview Ave.
Wilkes-Barre, PA 18702
Phone: 717-829-1500 or 717-822-5300
                    FAX: 717-822-9992
Buys and sells militaria from Revolutionary War to Viet Nam with emphasis on WWII; all countries.

Expert
Courtney Wilson
8398 Court Ave.
Ellicott City, MD 21043
Phone: 301-465-6827
Military antiques 1700-1900: appraiser, consultant, broker, dealer; arms, uniforms, equipment, memorabilia - especially Civil War.

Expert
Robert Fisch
c/o Greenberg Publishing Co.
7566 Main St.
Sykesville, MD 21784
Phone: 301-795-7447
Author of "Field Equipment of the Infantry: 1914 - 1945."

Expert
Sheperd Paine
Suite 160
6427 W. Irving Park Rd.
Chicago, IL 60634
Phone: 312-777-0499
Wants British, French and German pre-1914 uniforms, helmets, swords; familiar with military items from most countries & periods.

Museum/Library
U.S. Marine Corps Museum/Library
Marine Corps Historical Center
Washington Navy Yard
Washington, DC 20374
Phone: 202-433-3534

Museum/Library
U.S. Navy Museum
Bldg. 76
Washington Navy Yard
Washington, DC 20374
Phone: 212-433-4882

Museum/Library
U.S. Army Transportation Museum
Director
Bldg. #300, Besson Hall
ATTN: ATZF-PTM
Fort Eustis, VA 23604-5260
Phone: 804-878-1115
Collects, exhibits and interprets the history of U.S. Army transportation activities from the Revolutionary War to present.

Museum/Library
Parris Island Museum, The
Marine Corps Recruit Depot
Parris Island, SC 29905
Phone: 803-525-2951

Museum/Library
National Infantry Museum
U.S. Army Infantry Center
Fort Benning, GA 31905
Phone: 405-544-4762

Museum/Library
U.S. Air Force Museum
Richard L. Uppstrom, Dir.
Wright-Patterson A.F.B, OH 45433-6518
Phone: 513-255-3286   FAX: 513-255-3910
World's largest aviation museum with 10 1/2 acres of aircraft and other exhibits under roof.

Museum/Library
Seven Acres Antique Village & Museum
Randy Donley
8512 S. Union Rd.
Union, IL 60180
Phone: 815-923-2214
Large display of souvenirs and relics from all wars: uniforms, helmets, medals, weapons, guns, swords, etc.

Museum/Library
Liberty Memorial Museum, The
100 West 26th St.
Kansas City, MO 64108
Phone: 816-221-1918

Periodical
Magazine: Men at Arms
222 West Exchange Street
Providence, RI 02903

Periodical
New Breed Magazine Inc.
Magazine: New Breed
P.O. Box 428
Nanuet, NY 10954
*A monthly magazine with articles focusing on military adventure, history and law, weapons and ballistics reports, etc. *

Periodical
Phoenix Militaria, Inc.
Magazine: Military Collector Magazine
Terry Hannon, Ed.
P.O. Box 245
Lyon Station, PA 19536-0245
Phone: 215-682-1010 or 800-446-0909
                    FAX: 215-682-1066
A quarterly magazine for the military collector and related businesses.

Periodical
Phoenix Militaria, Inc.
Directory: Phoenix Militaria's Sourcebook & Directory
Terry Hannon, Ed.
P.O. Box 245
Lyon Station, PA 19536-0245
Phone: 215-682-1010 or 800-446-0909
                    FAX: 215-682-1066
A complete listing of militaria dealers, service companies and organizations.

Periodical

Wildcat Enterprises, Inc.
Journal: <u>Wildcat Collectors Journal</u>
Richard Cecilio
15158 N.E. 6 Ave.
Miami, FL 33162
Phone: 305-945-3228
Featuring classified ads to buy/sell/trade guns, knives, medals and related militaria; subscribers get FREE 40 word ad.

Periodical

Newsletter: <u>Doughboy, The</u>
P.O. Box 3912
Missoula, MT 59806 *

Periodical

Magazine: <u>Military History</u>
P.O. Box 373
Mt. Morris, IL 61054-7967
A guide through history focusing on armed conflicts.

Periodical

Magazine: <u>Military Collectors News</u>
P.O. Box 702073
Tulsa, OK 74170 *

Armored Vehicles

Club/Association

Dallas/Ft. Worth Arrowhead Chapter of the Military Vehicle Preservation
Newsletter: <u>Pintlehook</u>
Mark Chapin, Ed.
P.O. Box 921
Keller, TX 76248
Phone: 817-379-6875

Club/Association

Military Vehicle Collectors Club
Newsletter: <u>Army Motors</u>
P.O. Box 260607
Lakewood, CO 80226
Phone: 303-450-9184 *

Museum/Library

American Armoured Foundation
Bill Gasser
2383 5th Ave.
Ronkonkoma, NY 11779
Phone: 516-588-0033
Museum of armored vehicles, weapons and militaria dedicated in the honor of all veterans.

Museum/Library

Patton Museum of Cavalry & Armor
David Holt, Librarian
P.O. Box 208
Fort Knox, KY 40121-0208
Phone: 502-624-3812
Established to preserve historical materials relating to Cavalry and Armor and to make these properties available for public use.

Periodical

Magazine: <u>Military Vehicles</u>
P.O. Box 1748
Union, NJ 07083
A bi-monthly magazine for military vehicle enthusiasts.

British

Dealer

British Regalia Imports
P.O. Box 50473
Nashville, TN 37205
*Insignia, crests, tankards, canes, berets, weaponry, etc. *

German

Club/Association

Imperial German Military Collectors Association
Newsletter: <u>Kaiserzeit</u>
82 Atlantic St.
Keyport, NJ 07735
Phone: 201-739-1799
*Interested in items relating to pre-1918 Imperial Germany. *

Repro. Source

Richard & John Holt
4 Marion St.
Nesconset, NY 11767
Offers fully illustrated catalog of over 100 WWII German reproduction badges.

Insignia

Club/Association

American Society of Military Insignia Collectors
Magazine: <u>Trading Post</u>
George H. Duell, Jr.
526 Lafayette Ave.
Palmerton, PA 18701
Newsletter available only to members and contains member ads of items wanted and for sale.

Collector

Al Berhalter
50 Lamp Post Dr.
Barnegat, NJ 08005
Phone: 609-698-6398
*Wants WWI, WWII, Korea, Viet Nam military patches; single or collection. *

Marine Corps Related

Collector

Dick Weisler
53-07 213th St.
Bayside, NY 11364
Phone: 718-428-9829 or 718-626-7110
Wants recruiting posters, sheet music, belt buckles, cigarette lighters, steins, trucks, toy soldiers, documents, trench art, etc.

Medals

Club/Association

Orders & Medals Society of America
Newsletter: <u>Medal Collector, The</u>
John E. Lelle, Sec.
P.O. Box 484
Glassboro, NJ 08028
Interested in collecting and studying military and civil orders, decorations and medals of all countries.

Collector

Joe Copley
Box 43
New Castle, NH 03854-0043
Phone: 603-436-0297
Wants war medals: Mexican War, Civil War, any named items.

Collector

Cecil Lawhorn
Rt. 1, Box 176
Edwards, MO 65326
*Wants U.S. military campaign medals: Civil War, China Relief (1900-1901), WWI, China Service, Spanish War, etc. *

Collector

Grissom's
Box 12001
Chula Vista, CA 92012
Medals, U.S. of foreign; old and new.

Submarine Related

Collector

Ken Blazier
2937 Elda St.
Duarte, CA 91010
Wants WWII submarine memorabilia.

U-Boats

Club/Association

Sharkhunters
Magazine: <u>Sharkhunters KTB (Kriegs Tag Buch)</u>
Harry Cooper
P.O. Box 1539
Hernando, FL 32642
Phone: 904-637-2917   FAX: 904-637-6289
Locates and preserves the history of the German and Italian U-Boat forces; recognized leading authority on the subject.

Museum/Library

Museum of Science & Industry
Keith R. Gill
57th St. & Lake Shore Drive
Chicago, IL 60637
Phone: 312-684-1414   FAX: 312-684-5580

Uniforms

Club/Association

Association of American Military
Uniform Collectors
Newsletter: Footlocker
Gil Sanow, Ed.
P.O. Box 1876
Elyria, OH 44036
Phone: 316-365-5321
*Members are interested in improving their per-
sonal collections and in sharing information,
ideas and knowledge about military uniforms.*

Collector

Robert Gormley
334 Brownsburg Rd.
Newtown, PA 18940
Wants army uniforms from Civil War to WWII. *

WWI Items

Collector

R. Trawnik
1228 Lausanne
Dallas, TX 75298
Phone: 214-941-2445
*Wants WWI German spiked helmets, uniforms,
etc. Any condition.* *

WWI Items (Posters)

Collector

Ken Khuans
155 Harbor Drive #4812
Chicago, IL 60601
*Collector wants WWI posters; also books relating
to WWI posters.*

WWII Items

Collector

Richard Harrow
85-23 210 St.
Hollis Hills, NY 11427-1311
Phone: 718-740-1088
*Wants any item relating to WWII: allied forces,
anti-fascist propaganda, Jewish Holocaust, soldier benevolent aid, etc.* *

Expert

Dick Bitterman
1701 West Chase Ave.
Chicago, IL 60626
Phone: 312-743-3330 *

WWII Items (Aviation)

Collector

Tim Gordon
1750 W. Kent
Missoula, MT 59801
Phone: 406-728-1812
*Wants "nose art", jackets, patches, fliers' wings,
goggles, parachutes, leather boots, etc.*

MILITARY HISTORY

(see also AVIATION, Military; AVIATION
MEMORABILIA; BOOKS, Collector
(Militaria); CIVIL WAR; INDIAN WARS;
MARINE CORPS ITEMS; MILITARIA)

Club/Association

Company of Military Historians
Newsletter: Military Collector & Historian
N. Main St.
Westbrook, CT 06498
Phone: 203-399-9460 *

Club/Association

Western Front Association
Journal: Stand Ho!
Richard A. Baumgartner
743 11th Ave.
Huntingdon, WV 25701
*Organization founded for the purpose of fostering
interest in the study of WWI, and the memory of
those who fought therein.*

Collector

Mr. Earle
520 Grant
Hinsdale, IL 60521
*Wants Division histories of the WWI American
Expeditionary Forces, 1917-1919; also handwrit-
ten diaries or journals.*

Museum/Library

War Memorial Museum of Virginia, The
9285 Warwick Blvd.
Newport News, VA 23607
Phone: 804-247-8523 or 804-247-8522
*Museum interprets U.S. military history from
1775 to present; featuring over 60,000 artifacts.*

Periodical

MHQ Inc.
Magazine: MHQ: The Quarterly Journal of
Military History
Robert Cowley, Ed.
29 W. 38 St.
New York, NY 10018
Phone: 212-398-1550   FAX: 212-840-6790
*A quarterly magazine containing a wide variety of
articles on military history.*

Unit Histories

Collector

Bill Baumann
P.O. Box 319
Esperance, NY 12066
Phone: 518-875-6753
*Unit histories from WWII, Korea & Vietnam:
Army, Marine and Air Force fighter/bomber
squadrons.*

Collector

Michael Waskul
Box 1355
Ypsilanti, MI 48197

*Wants military unit histories Civil War through
Vietnam; especially desire WWII.* *

Museum/Library

U.S. Military History Institute
Carlisle Barracks
Room 1A518
Carlisle, PA 17013
Phone: 717-245-3152
*Specialized library to research military unit his-
tories.*

Museum/Library

U.S. Army Library
The Pentagon
Room 1A518
Washington, DC 20310
*Specialized library to research military unit his-
tories.*

Museum/Library

U.S. Army Center of Military History,
Museum Branch
20 Massachusetts Ave. NW
Washington, DC 20314
Phone: 202-272-0310
*Specialized library to research military unit his-
tories.*

Museum/Library

U.S. Marine Corps Museum/Library
Marine Corps Historical Center
Washington Navy Yard
Washington, DC 20374
Phone: 202-433-3534
*Specialized library to research military unit
histories.*

Museum/Library

Library of Congress
10 First St. SE
Washington, DC 20540
Phone: 202-287-5000
*Specialized library to research military unit his-
tories.*

Museum/Library

U.S. Air Force Historical Research
Center
Maxwell AFB
Montgomery, AL 36112
*Specialized library to research military unit his-
tories.*

Museum/Library

U.S. Army Military Police Corps
Regimental Museum
bldg. 3182
Fort McClellan, AL 36205
Phone: 205-848-3522 or 205-848-3050
*Gift shop provides military police memorabilia on
site and by mail order.*

Museum/Library

Women's Army Corps Museum
USAMP CS/TC & FM
Fort McClellan, AL 36205-5000
Phone: 205-848-3512 or 205-848-5559

MILLING

(see also SACKS, Flour & Sugar)

Club/Association

Society for the Preservation of Old
Mills (SPOOM)
Newsletter: SPOOM
William R. Rigler, Pres.
RR 21, Box 152
Wartrace, TN 37183
Phone: 615-455-1935
*Organization focuses on the milling industry:
mills, millwrights, equipment, techniques; ads,
mills for sale, millwrights, stones, etc.*

MINERALS

(see also GEMS & JEWELRY; LAPIDARY;
NATURAL HISTORY; SAND)

Museum/Library

Mineralogical Museum of Harvard
University
24 Oxford Street
Cambridge, MA 02138
Phone: 617-495-4758

Museum/Library

Pennsylvania State University Earth &
Mineral Sciences Museum & Art Gallery
Streidle Bldg. On Pollack Road
Philadelphia, PA 16802
Phone: 814-865-6427

Museum/Library

Colburn Memorial Mineral Museum
P.O. Box 1617
Asheville, NC 28802
Phone: 704-254-7162

Museum/Library

Arizona Mining Museum
Mineral Bldg.
State Fairgrounds
Phoenix, AZ 85007
Phone: 602-255-3791

MINIATURES

(see also ART, Portraits (Miniature); BOOKS,
Miniature; BOTTLES, Miniature; DOLL
HOUSES & FURNISHINGS; PIANOS,
Miniature; TRUCKS, Miniature)

Club/Association

National Association of Miniature
Enthusiasts
Magazine: Miniature Gazette
P.O. Box 69
Carmel, IN 46032
Phone: 317-571-8094
*N.A.M.E. serves the miniature collector and
builder; the monthly magazine contains articles,
ads, dealer listings, etc.*

Expert

Lillian Baker
15237 Chanera Ave.
Gardena, CA 90249
Phone: 213-329-2619
Author of "Creative and Collectible Miniatures."

Museum/Library

Museums at Stony Brook, The
Newsletter: Dialogue
1208 Rte. 25A
Stony Brook, NY 11790
Phone: 516-751-0066   FAX: 516-751-0353
*Large collection of American Art, decoys, horse-
drawn vehicles, costumes, and miniature period
rooms; museum shop.*

Museum/Library

Toy & Miniature Museum of Kansas City
Sandi Russell
5235 Oak St.
Kansas City, MO 64112
Phone: 816-333-2055
*Museum housed in an elegant mansion features
collections of miniatures, antique dolls' houses
and antique toys.*

Periodical

Magazine: International Dolls' House News
June Stowe, Ed.
P.O. Box 79
Southampton S09 7EZ England
*In publication for over 24 years; specialist maga-
zine devoted to doll houses and miniatures both
old and new.*

Periodical

Magazine: Dollmaker, The
P.O. Box 247
Washington, NJ 07882
*Contains how-to articles focusing on the making
of dolls and doll heads. **

Periodical

Magazine: Doll Castle News
P.O. Box 247
Washington, NJ 07882
Phone: 201-689-6513 or 201-689-7042
*A magazine focusing on dolls, miniatures, doll
houses and related items; ads, paper doll section,
needlework, patterns, etc.*

Periodical

Newsletter: Mott's Miniature Workshop News
P.O. Box 5514
Fullerton, CA 92635 *

Repro. Source

Little House of Miniatures
606 G Ave.
Grundy Center, IA 50638
Phone: 319-824-6259
*Complete mail-order source for miniatures:
wallpaper, carpet, electric wiring, building supplies, etc. **

Supplier

Lynne's Miniature Treasurers
Dept. 24
North Wales, PA 19454
*Offers a diversified catalog of miniature items and
supplies. **

Supplier

Masterpiece Museum Miniatures
P.O. Box 5280
Austin, TX 78763
*Offers a diversified line of miniature items and
supplies. **

Supplier

Many Goode's Catalogue
P.O. Box 5161
Torrance, CA 90510
*Offers a diversified line of miniature items and
supplies. **

Airplanes

(see also AVIATION MEMORABILIA;
TOYS, Airplane Related)

Club/Association

International Miniature Aircraft
Association, Inc.
Robert A. Blaney, Sec.
3380 14 Parkview Road
Long Valley, NJ 07853

Furniture

Museum/Library

Washington Dolls' House & Toy Museum
5236 44th Street NW
Washington, DC 20015
Phone: 202-244-0024

Museum/Library

Art Institute of Chicago, Thorne
Miniature Rooms
Michigan Ave. at Adams Street
Chicago, IL 60603
Phone: 312-443-3600

Periodical

Magazine: <u>Miniature Collector</u>
James Keough, MangPub
P.O. Box 631
Boiling Springs, PA 17007
Phone: 717-258-5684   FAX: 717-258-4465
Focuses on doll houses and 1/12, 1/2, and 1/4 inch scale miniatures.

Repro. Source

Duane Sylor
49 Horner Rd.
Angelica, NY 14709
Phone: 716-466-7700
Sells authentically crafted 1/2 scale traditionally painted furniture accenting Early American decor; great for dolls, teddies, tots.

Ladders

Collector

D.M. Werner
Box 580
Greenville, PA 16125
Wants miniature wood or metal stepladders or extension ladders. *

Vehicles

Club/Association

Motoring in Miniature Association
147 Pin Oak Drive
Williamsville, NY 14221
Phone: 716-689-9830 *

MINING RELATED ITEMS

(see also SCRIP)

Club/Association

Historical Construction Equipment
Association
Newsletter: <u>Equipment Echoes</u>
P.O. Box 328
Grand rapids, OH 43522
Phone: 419-832-0808
Dedicated to preserving the history of construction, surface mining and dredging equipment and related memorabilia, trade

Collector

Brad Ross
107 Westminster Drive
St. Clairsville, OH 43950
Phone: 614-695-1468
Wants mine antiques: lamps (carbide, safety, oilwick), signs, hats, containers, surveying instruments, blasting items, etc. *

Museum/Library

Matchless Mine Museum
414 W. 7th St.
Leadville, CO 80461
Phone: 719-486-0371

Museum/Library

Bisbee Mining & Historical Museum
P.O. Box 14
Bisbee, AZ 85603
Phone: 602-432-7071

Coal Mining

Collector

Frank Frazzini
227 Castner Ave.
Donora, PA 15033 *

Collector

George Nestor
701 Rose St.
Nanty Glo, PA 15943
Phone: 814-749-0244
Coal mine items wanted. All categories. *

Collector

William Blake
506 Driftwood Dr. Lot A
Charleston, WV 25306
Phone: 304-925-3780
Coal mine items wanted; all categories: carbide lights, safety lamps, oil wicks, etc.

Museum/Library

Museum of Anthracite Mining
Pine & 17th St.
Ashland, PA 17921
Phone: 717-875-4708

Lamps

(see also LAMPS & LIGHTING)

Club/Association

Old Mine Lamp Collectors Society of
America
Newsletter: <u>Underground Lamp Post, The</u>
Henry A. Pohs
4537 Quitman St.
Denver, CO 80212
Phone: 303-455-3922
Focuses on old non-electric mining lamps and related items.

Collector

Len Gaska
1688 E. Corson St.
Pasadena, CA 91106
Phone: 818-405-0647 or 818-585-3339
Carbide & other miners' lamps wanted.

Expert

Henry A. Pohs
4537 Quitman St.
Denver, CO 80212
Phone: 303-455-3922
Mine lighting historian; buys, sells, trades old non-electric mining lamps and related items; author of book on subject.

MODEL KITS

Expert

David Welch
RR 2, Box 233
Murphysboro, IL 62966
Phone: 618-687-2282
Specializing in Aurora figure kits; buying any pre-1977 TV, science-fiction, comic, movie of monster related kits.

Cars

Periodical

Magazine: <u>Plastic Fanatic</u>
19088 Santa Maria Avenue
Castro Valley, CA 94546 *

Plastic

Club/Association

Society for the Preservation and
Encouragement of Scale Model Kit
Magazine: <u>Kit Collectors Clearinghouse</u>
John W. Burns
3213 Hardy Drive
Edmond, OK 73013
Phone: 405-341-4640
A bi-monthly magazine for kit collectors; buy and sell ads, re-issue notices, information on vacuum-formed and "garage" kits, etc.

Club/Association

Kit Collectors International
Newsletter: <u>Vintage Plastic</u>
P.O. Box 38
Stanton, CA 90680
Phone: 714-826-5216 *

Club/Association

International Plastic Modelers Society
Journal: <u>IPMS/USA Modelers Journal</u>
P.O. Box 2890
Sacramento, CA 95812-2890
Journal includes review of new kits and accessories, scratch-building, convention articles, IPMS news, etc.

Collector

Jim Crane
15 Clemson Ct.
Newark, DE 19711
Phone: 302-738-6031
Wants Aurora, Revell; built or unbuilt; any condition; also catalogs.

Expert

John W. Burns
3213 Hardy Drive
Edmond, OK 73013
Phone: 405-341-4640
Author of "The 1987-1988 Collectors Value Guide for Scale Model Plastic Kits"; wants to buy unbuilt plastic model kits.

MODELS

(see also AIRPLANES, Model; MODEL
KITS; NAUTICAL COLLECTIBLES;
ROCKETS, Model Rocket Kits; SOLDIERS,
Model; TRAINS, Toy (O-Scale Kits))

Supplier

Superior Aircraft Materials
Mike Taibi
12020 Centralia Ave. #G
Hawaiian Gardens, CA 90716
Phone: 213-865-3220
*Specializes in supplying wood materials (balsa,
spruce, plywood) for the model builder.*

Auto/Truck/Motorcycle

Collector

Robert Olds
364 Vinewood
Tallmadge, OH 44278
Phone: 216-633-5938
Wants scale models of cars, trucks and motorcycles. *

Cars

Club/Association

Automotive Modelers Society
Newspaper: Scale Wheels
934 Montford Dr.
Charlotte, NC 28209
*Club for builders & collectors of scale vehicles;
annual convention, membership roster, local club
affiliates, bi-monthly newsletter.*

Club/Association

Model Car Collectors Association
Journal: Model Car Collectors Association
 Journal
5113 Sugar Loaf Dr. SW
Roanoke, VA 24018
Phone: 703-744-8109
*Dedicated to the promotion & enjoyment of the
model car hobby; a bi-monthly journal features kit
reviews, how-tos, free member ads.*

Collector

Ken Katz
354 Townline Rd.
Commack, NY 11725
Phone: 516-462-5808
*Wants models of automotive vehicles: plastic,
friction, built or unbuilt kits, promotional
models. **

Collector

Bob Shives
P.O. Box 976
Chambersburg, PA 17201-0976
Phone: 717-263-9316
*Wants promotional car models; also metal banks
by Banthrico, Master-Caster and National Products; also early Revell kits.*

Misc. Service

Edward Soltis
57 Morningside Ave.
Yonkers, NY 10703
*Will quote price for building any kit; 1/25th
plastic kits, 1/43 and 1/25 diecasts, etc.; ask for
pictures; many satisfied customers.*

Periodical

Magazine: Model Auto Review
P.O. Box MT1
Leeds LS17 6TA England
*MAR is a glossy magazine with over 100 color and
many more b/w photos; covering model cars,
trucks, buses, military vehicles.*

Periodical

MODELAUTO
P.O. Box MT1
Leeds LS17 6TA England
*Worldwide mail order specializing in 1:43 and
1:50 scales, but other models stocked as well; see
advertisement in "Model Auto Review."*

Periodical

Magazine: Model Collectors Digest
P.O. Box 8943
Waukegan, IL 60079
Focuses primarily on model cars.

Periodical

Newsletter: Traders Horn
J.F. Atkinson
1903 Schoettler Valley Rd.
Chesterfield, MO 63017
Phone: 314-532-3871
*The oldest and largest periodical dedicated to the
sales and trading of diecast toy vehicles, promotional models and model kits.*

Periodical

MCJ Associates
Magazine: Model Car Journal
Dennis Doty
P.O. Box 154135
Irving, TX 75015-4135
Phone: 214-790-5346
*Complete coverage of the model car hobby; kits,
diecast, promos, resin models, histories, events
list, ads, how-tos; since 1974.*

Engineering

Supplier

Coles' Power Models, Inc.
P.O. Box 788
Ventura, CA 93001
*Catalog of model engineering supplies; drawings,
castings, nuts, bolts, taps & dies, small tools,
books, fittings, sundries, etc. **

Gas-Powered

Collector

Bruce Pike
RD #1 Box 291
Aliquippa, PA 15001
Phone: 412-378-0449
*Wants old spark ignition model airplane engines;
also gas-powered race cars.*

MONEY

(see also COINS & CURRENCY)

MONTANA COLLECTIBLES

Collector

Tim Gordon
1750 W. Kent
Missoula, MT 59801
Phone: 406-728-1812
*Wants any pre-1930 item marked "Montana":
calendars, advertising, photos, post cards, history
books, tokens, trade cards, etc.*

MORMON ITEMS

Dealer

Neil Burnett
P.O. Box 1
Provo, UT 84603
Phone: 801-373-1111
Wants old Mormon books, old pamphlets, histories, etc.

MOTORCYCLES

Club/Association

Antique Motorcycle Club of America
Magazine: Antique Motorcycle, The
Dottie Wood, Sec.
14943 York Rd.
Sparks, MD 21152
Phone: 301-771-4456
*A club of 4000 members worldwide dedicated to
the preservation, restoration and enjoyment of
antique motorcycles.*

Club/Association

Vintage Motor Bike Club
Newsletter: Vintage Motor Bike Club
 Newsletter
330 East North Street
Coldwater, OH 45828
Phone: 419-678-3347
Features articles, ads, diagrams, and how-to articles for members. *

Collector

Richard L. Weiss
R.D. #2, Box 641
Breinigsville, PA 18031
Phone: 215-285-4122
*Specialized wants: Smith, Briggs & Stratton,
Merkel, Steffy motor wheels; Whizzer & pre-1940
American motorcycles; whole or parts.*

Periodical

TAM Communications, Inc.
Journal: Bike Journal
Buzz Kanter, Pub.
6 Prowitt Street
Norwalk, CT 06855
Phone: 203-855-0008 or 203-854-5962
For collectors and others interested in older motorcycles.

Periodical

TAM Communications, Inc.
Magazine: American Iron Magazine
Buzz Kanter, Pub.
6 Prowitt Street
Norwalk, CT 06855
Phone: 203-855-0008 or 203-854-5962
For collectors and others interested in American motorcycles.

Periodical

TAM Communications, Inc.
Magazine: British Cycle
Buzz Kanter, Pub.
6 Prowitt Street
Norwalk, CT 06855
Phone: 203-855-0008 or 203-854-5962
For collectors and others interested in British motorcycles.

Periodical

TAM Communications, Inc.
Magazine: Italian Motorcycle Times
Buzz Kanter, Pub.
6 Prowitt Street
Norwalk, CT 06855
Phone: 203-855-0008 or 203-854-5962
For collectors and others interested in Italian motorcycles.

Periodical

Newsletter: Motorcycle Trader
P.O. Box 73
Folly Beach, SC 29439
*Carries buy, sell, and trade ads for motorcycle enthusiasts. **

Periodical

Magazine: Classic Motorcycle, The
Jim Lance
c/o Publishers Mini Systems
P.O. Box 301369
Escondido, CA 92030-9957
Phone: 619-747-8327   FAX: 619-432-6560
British magazine about motor cycling's golden era; auctions, parts, restorations and much more for the do-it-yourself'r.

Cushman

Club/Association

Cushman Club of America
Magazine: Cushman Club of America Member Magazine
5817 E. Village Lane - Rt. 18
Springfield, MO 65804 *

Indian

Museum/Library

Indian Motorcycle Museum
33 Hendee Street
Springfield, MA 01139
Phone: 413-737-2624

Moto Guzzi

Club/Association

Moto Guzzi Owners Club
Frank Wedge, Dir.
RR #1, Box 136
Ellsworth, KS 67443-9
Focuses on the collection and restoration of Moto Guzzi motorcycles and related items.

Collector

Bob Mounce
704 E. Twelfth St.
Streator, IL 61364
Phone: 815-672-2827
Collects, rides and exchanges information with other collectors of Moto Guzzi motorcycles.

Collector

Keith Krenz
73 Circle Dr.
Streator, IL 61364
Collects, rides and exchanges information with other collectors of Moto Guzzi motorcycles.

Collector

Bernard L. Mei
614 Little St.
Streator, IL 61364
Collects, rides and exchanges information with other collectors of Moto Guzzi motorcycles.

MOUNTS

(see also ANIMAL TROPHIES)

MOVIE MEMORABILIA

(see also DISNEY COLLECTIBLES; MAGAZINES, Movie; MOVIE POSTERS; PERSONALITIES (MOVIE STARS); TELEVISION SHOWS & MEMORABILIA; WIZARD OF OZ)

Auction Service

Phillips Fine Art & Auctioneers
Henry Kurtz
406 East 79th St.
New York, NY 10022
Phone: 212-570-4830   FAX: 212-570-2207
Specializes in the sale of jewelry, paintings, prints, silver, coins, stamps, toys (especially lead soldiers), and movie memorabilia.

Club/Association

International Film Collector
15 Wallace Avenue
West Worthing
West Sussex BN11 5RA England *

Club/Association

Movie Star Fan Club
Magdalena DeMirgian
37 Landon Avenue
Watertown, MA 02172 *

Club/Association

Manuscript Society, The
Magazine: Manuscripts
350 N. Niagara St.
Burbank, CA 91505
An organization of collectors, dealers, librarians, archivists, scholars and others interested in autographs and manuscripts.

Club/Association

Hollywood Studio Collectors Club
Newsletter: Hollywood Studio Magazine
Suite 450
3960 Laurel Canyon Blvd.
Studio City, CA 91604
Phone: 818-990-5450
Focuses on movies, movie collectibles, and movie stars.

Club/Association

Newspaper: Hollywood Movie Archives
P.O. Box 1566
Apple Valley, CA 92307

Collector

Mitch Kaidy
921 Crittenden Rd.
Rochester, NY 14623
Phone: 716-424-4746
*Wants movie memorabilia paper collectibles. **

Dealer

Bill Day Movie Memorabilia
Bill Day
643 Pleasant St.
P.O. Box 344
Canton, MA 02021
Phone: 617-828-4386
Wants posters, magazines, autographs, silent & talkies.

Dealer

Casey's Collectible Corner
Dennis & Mary Luby
H.C.R. Box 31, Rte. 30
No. Blenheim, NY 12131
Phone: 607-588-6464
Buys and sells collectible toys: comic characters, TV shows and personalities; also space and monster toys, sports collectibles, etc.

Dealer

Quest-Eridon Books
Loraine Burdick
5 Court Place
Puyallup, WA 98372
Buys/sells movie magazines, theater advertising, memorabilia, stills, clippings on specific stars by request, Shirley Temple, pre-1960.

Man./Prod./Dist.

Film Favorites
Gene Arnold
P.O. Box 133
Canton, OK 73724
Phone: 405-886-3358
Makes b/w still photos from old movies (famous, obscure, silent, sound); will research titles upon request; also radio and TV shows.

Museum/Library

Library & Museum of the Performing Arts, Shelby Cullom Davis Museum
111 Amsterdam Ave.
New York, NY 10023
Phone: 212-870-1613

Museum/Library

American Film Institute, The
2021 N. Western Ave.
Los Angeles, CA 90027
Phone: 213-856-7600

Periodical

C.K. Hall & Company
Directory: Motion Pictures, Television & Radio
70 Lincoln Street
Boston, MA 02111
*A catalog of manuscript and special collections in the western U.S. ***

Periodical

Newspaper: Nostalgia World
P.O. Box 231
New Haven, CT 06473-0231
Phone: 203-239-4891
*Contains articles focusing on show business collectibles. ***

Periodical

Empire Publishing, Inc.
Newspaper: Big Reel
Route 3, P.O. Box 83
Madison, NC 27025
Phone: 919-427-5850   FAX: 919-427-7372
A monthly tabloid for movie and television memorabilia collectors and fans: ads, news, current & nostalgic feature articles, obits, etc.

Periodical

Magazine: American Movie Classics
P.O. Box 2065
Marion, OH 43305

Periodical

Newspaper: Movie Collector's World
P.O. Box 309
Fraser, MI 48026
Phone: 313-774-4311   FAX: 313-774-5450
Largest movie memorabilia collecting publication existing; posters, stills, videos, etc. offered in each issue.

Periodical

Classic Images
Newspaper: Classic Images
P.O. Box 809
Muscatine, IA 52761
Monthly tabloid featuring articles and advertisement directed at film buffs.

Periodical

Newspaper: Classic Images
P.O. Box 4079
Davenport, IA 52808 *

Periodical

Magazine: Filmfax
P.O. Box 1900
Evanston, IL 60204
A magazine of unusual film and television; a bimonthly with 100 pgs. of rare photos and articles about your favorite films & TV shows.

Back To The Future

Club/Association

Back To the Future Fan Club
Magazine: Back To the Future Magazine
P.O. Box 111000
Aurora, CO 80011 *

George Lucas Films

Club/Association

Lucasfilm Fan Club
Magazine: Lucasfilm Magazine
P.O. Box 111000
Aurora, CO 80011 *

Gone With The Wind

Club/Association

GWTW Collectors Club
Newsletter: GWTW Collectors Club Newsletter
8105 Woodview Rd.
Ellicott City, MD 21043
Phone: 301-465-4632 *

Club/Association

Tara Collectors Club
Newsletter: Jonesboro Wind
P.O. Box 1200
Jonesboro, GA 30237 *

Collector

Robert Buchanan
277 W. 22nd St.
New York, NY 10011
Phone: 212-989-3917
Wants any GWTW items; also any Vivien Leigh and Clark Gable.

Horror Films & Literature

(see also DRACULA)

Club/Association

Dracula & Company
Newsletter: Nocturnal News
P.O. Box 213
Metairie, LA 70004
Phone: 504-734-8414 *

Indiana Jones

Collector

Cindy Oakes
34025 W. 6 Mile
Livonia, MI 48152
Phone: 313-591-3252
Wants Indiana Jones dolls, figurines, playsets, etc.

Planet Of The Apes

Collector

David London
9605 Hall Road
Potomac, MD 20859
Phone: 301-299-2953
*Wants comics and "Planet of the Apes" movie memorabilia. ***

Silent Films

Collector

Yellowback Press
Magazine: Yellowback Library
Gil O'Gara
P.O. Box 36172
Des Moines, IA 50315
Phone: 515-287-0404
Wants silent movies on 35mm nitrate film.

Expert

Bijou Dream
Richard Alan Davis
9500 Old Georgetown Rd.
Bethesda, MD 20814-1724
Phone: 301-530-5904   FAX: 301-530-8532
Wants silent movie items: posters, lobby cards, programs, stills, Star Garment Co. hangers with head/shoulder of movie stars.

Star Wars

Collector

Cindy Oakes
34025 W. 6 Mile
Livonia, MI 48152
Phone: 313-591-3252
Wants Star Wars figures, jewelry, vehicles, autographs.

Trade Publications

Collector

George Reed
5239 Howland St.
Philadelphia, PA 19124
Phone: 215-743-5201

Wants movie trade publications made for the movie theater owners and operators: Exhibitors Herald World, Film Daily Yearbook, etc. *

Westerns

(see also COWBOY HEROES)

Club/Association

Old Time Western Film Club
Newsletter: Western Film Newsletter
Milo Holt
P.O. Box 142
Silver City, NC 27344
Interested in promoting the showing of old westerns and in the collecting of memorabilia relating thereto.

Club/Association

Westerns & Serials Fan Club
Magazine: Favorite Westerns & Serial World
Norman Kietzer
Route One, Box 103
Vernon Center, MN 56090
Phone: 507-549-3677
A club for collectors as well as non-collectors interested in westerns and serials, and in related memorabilia.

Periodical

World of Yesterday, The
Journal: Under Western Skies
Route 3, Box 263 - H
Waynesville, NC 28786
Phone: 704-648-5647
Periodic journal focusing on the old west of the Silver Screen & TV.

MOVIE POSTERS

(see also MOVIE MEMORABILIA; POSTERS)

Collector

Sam Sarowitz
23 E. 10th St.
New York, NY 10003
Phone: 212-477-2499
Wants movie posters, lobby cards; 1900-1960 only; small or large collections bought.

Collector

Bob Johnson
P.O. Box 71687
Marietta, GA 30007-1687
Serious collector wants movie posters from 1930's-1960's: science fiction, horror, Tarzan, detective/mystery, classic movies.

Collector

Jim Ashton
902 Progress
Middletown, IN 47356
Phone: 317-354-2308 *

Collector

Dwight Cleveland
1815 N. Orchard St. #8
Chicago, IL 60614-5136
Phone: 312-266-9152
Wants lobby cards, 1-sheets, window cards, glass slides, studio annuals, etc.

Collector

Gene Arnold
2234 South Blvd.
Houston, TX 77098
Phone: 713-528-1880
Wants any old movie posters or 11" x 14" lobby cards.

Collector

Bruce Hershenson
P.O. Box 3364
Long Beach, CA 90803
Phone: 213-493-7079
Wants high quality original posters from major Hollywood films. *

Dealer

Dave Bowers
Box 1224
Wolfeboro, NH 03894
Phone: 603-569-5095 or 800-458-4646
Wants American film posters from 1895-1915

Dealer

World Famous Collectors Originals
P.O. Box 17522
Memphis, TN 38117
Phone: 901-682-6761
Wants posters, lobbies, stills. Serving the movie investor/collector since 1980. *

Dealer

Luton's Posters
2780 Frayser Blvd.
Memphis, TN 38127
Phone: 901-357-1649
Cash paid for old movie posters. One item to thousands. *

Dealer

Celebrity Graphics
P.O. Box 385
Flushing, MI 48433
Phone: 313-659-8751
Wants movie posters, lobby cards, any vintage, any quantity.

Expert

Saturday Matinee
Ron Donnelly
Box 7047
Panama City, FL 32413 *

Expert

American Collectibles Exchange
Jon Warren
P.O. Box 2512
Chattanooga, TN 37409
Phone: 615-821-8121
Author of "Warren's Movie Poster Price Guide." *

Museum/Library

Motion Picture Arts Gallery
Ira Resnick, Dir.
133 E. 58th St.
New York, NY 10022
Phone: 212-223-1009
Cinematic history in collection of movie posters.

Teen Movies

Collector

Jim Weaver
405 Dunbar
Pittsburgh, PA 15235
Wants '50's teen movie posters: hot rod, bad girl, juvenile delinquent, rock 'n' roll, etc.; send lists and offers.

MOVIE PROJECTORS

Collector

Edward Stuart
3025 Ontario Road NW #203
Washington, DC 20009
Phone: 202-332-6511
Wants pre-1952 Bell & Howell movie projectors (those with brown wrinkle finish), 8mm or 16mm, silent only; also B&H mod. 130 sound.

MOVING & STORAGE ASSOCIATIONS

(see also REPAIRS & RESTORATIONS)

Club/Association

National Moving & Storage Association
Newspaper: M & S Times
Estelle Tredway
1500 North Beauregard Street
Alexandria, VA 22311
Phone: 703-671-8813   FAX: 703-671-6712
Members are providers of goods & services of use to moving & storage agents & warehousemen; also publishes "Direction" monthly journal.

Club/Association

Claims Prevention & Procedure Council
Newsletter: CPPC Newsletter
P.O. Box 301
Oak Forest, IL 60452
Phone: 708-535-CPPC   FAX: 708-535-2773
A moving industry related organization of repairmen, van lines, appraisers, insurance companies, lawyers and claims adjusters.

MOXIE

(see also SOFT DRINK COLLECTIBLES, Moxie)

MUGS

(see also GLASS, Mugs; GLASSES, Drinking; STEINS (MODERN))

MUSIC

(see also MUSICAL INSTRUMENTS; PERSONALITIES (MUSICIANS); PIANO ROLLS; RECORDS; SHEET MUSIC)

Book Seller

Jellyroll Productions
Box 29
Boyne Falls, MI 49713
Phone: 800-627-9218
Specializes in books relating to the hobby of music & music memorabilia collecting; artists, titles, posters, price guides, etc.

Dealer

Roundup Records
P.O. Box 154
North Cambridge, MA 02140
Phone: 617-661-6308   FAX: 617-868-8769
Mail order CD's, LP's, cassettes; specializing in hard to find blues, country, R&B, Rock 'n' Roll, jazz, bluegrass, etc.

Periodical

Krause Publications, Inc.
Newspaper: Music Mart
700 E. State St.
Iola, WI 54990
Phone: 715-445-2214 or 800-258-0929
FAX: 715-445-4087
All-advertising marketplace for fans of all music genres; buy, sell, and trade recorded music & music memorabilia.

Country

Dealer

Country Sales
P.O. Box 191
Floyd, VA 24091
Phone: 703-745-2001 *

Dealer

Elderly Instruments
P.O. Box 14210
Lansing, MI 48901
Phone: 517-372-7890 *

Dealer

Down Home Music, Inc.
Newsletter: Down Home Music Newsletter
6921 Stockton Ave.
El Cerrito, CA 94530
Phone: 415-525-1494   FAX: 415-525-2906
Specializes in hard-to-find recordings of blues, folk music, country, ethnic, early rock 'n' roll and jazz.

Museum/Library

Country Music Hall of Fame & Museum, Country Music Foundation
4 Music Square, East
Nashville, TN 37203
Phone: 615-255-2245

Periodical

Disc Collector Publications
Newsletter: Disc Collector
P.O. Box 315
Cheswold, DE 19936
Phone: 302-674-3632
Focuses on bluegrass and old time country music.

Cowboy

Periodical

Magazine: Song of the West
Mary Rogers, Pub.
P.O. Box 110
Hygiene, CO 80503
Phone: 303-223-8411
Historical and contemporary magazine on cowboy and Western music; articles, artist features, album reviews, events, ads.

Dixieland & Ragtime

Periodical

West Coast Rag
Newspaper: West Coast Rag
Pat & Woody Laughnan
1750 N. Farris
Fresno, CA 93704
Phone: 209-237-5947   FAX: 209-237-3027
Clearinghouse for advertisers, readers and collectors of vintage music, instruments, vintage music books; also concerts and festivals.

Periodical

f0311Maple Leaf Club
Newsletter: Rag Times, The
Richard Zimmerman, Ed.
105 Rickey Ct.
Grass Valley, CA 95949
A bi-monthly newsletter with everything about ragtime - past and present; since 1967.

Jazz

Collector

Chuck Moore
P.O. Box 280
Gladstone, OR 97027
*Wants Jazz LP's, singles, 78's; also older books, magazines, sheet music on jazz. **

Museum/Library

North Texas State University, Duke Ellington Collection
P.O. Box 13377 NTSU
Denton, TX 76203
Phone: 817-565-2386

Rock 'n' Roll

Club/Association

American Bandstand 1950's Fan Club
Magazine: Bandstand Boogie
P.O. Box 131
Adamstown, PA 19501
Phone: 717-738-2513
Focuses on "American Bandstand" from the 1950's and 1960's.

'60's

Dealer

Liverpool Productions
Charles F. Rosenay
397 Edgewood Ave.
New Haven, CT 06511
Phone: 203-865-8131   FAX: 203-562-5260
Buys and sells '60's music and memorabilia relating to the Beatles, British Invasion, Monkees and Beach Boys.

MUSIC BOXES

(see also MUSICAL INSTRUMENTS, Mechanical)

Club/Association

Musical Box Society International
Newsletter: News Bulletin
Mrs. Clarence Fabel, Sec.
Rt. 3, Box 205
Morgantown, IN 46160
Phone: 812-988-7545
The Society is dedicated to the study and preservation of all types of instruments that mechanically produce music.

Collector

Grand Illusions
Martin Roenigk
26 Barton Hill
East Hampton, CT 06424
Phone: 203-267-8682
Wants all types of mechanical music instruments: music boxes, player organs, coin pianos, singing birds, Wurlitzer 78 rpm jukeboxes, etc.

Collector

Bob Welch
P.O. Box 370
New Paltz, NY 12561 *

Collector

Dave Ogden
P.O. Box 223
Northbrook, IL 60062
Phone: 708-564-2893
Wants disc and cylinder music boxes; Regina; also monkey organs.

Collector

Arnold Levin
P.O. Box 223
Northbrook, IL 60062
Phone: 708-564-2893

Wants large cylinder and disc music boxes, e.g. Regina and Polyphon; buys, sells, and repairs. *

Collector
Ralph Schack
P.O. Box 58806
Los Angeles, CA 90058 *

Collector
Jim Brady
2725 E. 56th St.
Indianapolis, IN 46220
Phone: 317-259-4307
Music boxes wanted; any type or condition; also jukeboxes.

Dealer
Meekins Music Box Co.
P.O. Box 161
Collingswood, NJ 08108 *

Dealer
Bornand Music Box Company
R.C. Bornand
139 Fourth Ave.
Pelham, NY 10803
Phone: 914-738-1506

Dealer
Denny R. Smith
4408 Foxton Ct.
Dayton, OH 45414
Phone: 513-279-0417
Buying horn phonographs, music boxes, cylinders, parts.

Expert
William H. Edgerton
P.O. Box 88
Darien, CT 06820
Phone: 203-655-0566   FAX: 203-655-8066
Buys, sells, repairs pianos and rolls, musical boxes, player organs, nickelodeons, and automata.

Expert
Antique Music Box Restoration
Christian Eric
1825 Placentia Ave.
Costa Mesa, CA 92627
Phone: 714-548-1542   FAX: 714-631-6206
Specialists in antique musical boxes, emphasis on early cylinder, miniature and sur plateau mechanisms; author on subject.

Museum/Library
Lockwood-Matthews Mansion Museum
295 West Ave.
Norwalk, CT 06850
Phone: 203-838-1434

Museum/Library
Musical Museum, The
P.O. Box 901
Deansboro, NY 13328
Phone: 315-841-8774

Museum/Library
Miles Musical Museum
P.O. Box 488
Eureka Springs, AR 72632
Phone: 501-253-8961

Periodical
Newsletter: Jerry's Musical News
4624 West Woodland Road
Edina, MN 55424
Phone: 612-926-7775
Focusing on radios, music boxes, and phonographs. *

Repair Service
Chet Ramsay Antiques
Chet Ramsay
RD #1, Box 383
Coatesville, PA 19320
Phone: 215-384-0514
Wants all types of music boxes; buy, sell and repair; also wants parts.

Repair Service
Paul Smith
408 E. Leeland Heights Blvd.
Lehigh Acres, FL 33936
Phone: 813-728-9694
Repairs curious or unusual devices. *

Repair Service
Clarence W. Fabel
Box 205, Route 3
Morgantown, IN 46160
Repairs cylinder music boxes.

Repair Service
Regina Music Box Co., Inc.
7013 W. Crandall Ave.
Worth, IL 60482
Repairs disc music boxes; also has parts and new discs. *

Repair Service
K.R. Powers Antique Music Boxes
K.R. Powers
28 Alton Circle
Rogers, AR 72756
Phone: 501-263-2643
Disc and cylinder music box restoration, sales and repairs.

Repair Service
Antique Music Box Restoration
Christian Eric
1825 Placentia Ave.
Costa Mesa, CA 92627
Phone: 714-548-1542   FAX: 714-631-6206

Specialists in antique musical boxes, emphasis on early cylinder, miniature and sur plateau mechanisms; fine restoration.

MUSICAL INSTRUMENTS
Club/Association
American Musical Instrument Society
Newsletter: Newsletter (and Journal) of the AMIS
Dr. Margaret Banks
c/o The Shrine to Music Museum
414 East Clark St.
Vermillion, SD 57069
Phone: 605-677-5306 or 605-677-5073
Inter. organization founded to promote the study of the history, design and use of musical instruments; all periods and cultures.

Expert
Glenn Kramer
20E Taylor Lane
Fishkill, NY 12524
Phone: 914-896-6390 *

Expert
Vintage Instruments
Frederick W. Oster
1529 Pine Street
Philadelphia, PA 19102
Phone: 215-545-1100   FAX: 215-473-3634
Dealers/appraisers of rare and antique musical instruments: violins, cellos, bows, guitars, banjos, mandolins, strings, woodwinds, brass.

Museum/Library
Yale University Collection of Musical Instruments
P.O. Box 2117
New Haven, CT 06520
Phone: 203-436-4935

Museum/Library
Musical Museum, The
P.O. Box 901
Deansboro, NY 13328
Phone: 315-841-8774

Museum/Library
University of Michigan, Stearns Collection of Musical Instruments
Newsletter: Stearns Newsletter, The
School Of Music
Ann Arbor, MI 48109-2085
Phone: 313-763-4389
A collection of over 2000 musical instruments from around the world.

Museum/Library
Shrine To Music Museum, The
Dr. Margaret Banks, Curator
414 East Clark St.
Vermillion, SD 57069
Phone: 605-677-5306   FAX: 605-677-5073

Nationally accredited museum and center for the study of the history of musical instruments; collects American & European musical items.

Museum/Library

Miles Musical Museum
P.O. Box 488
Eureka Springs, AR 72632
Phone: 501-253-8961

Periodical

Magazine: Concertina & Squeezebox
Joel M. Cowan
P.O. Box 6706
Ithaca, NY 14851
The quarterly magazine for free reed aficionados; if you can squeeze it, this magazine covers it: concertinas, accordions, squeezeboxes.

Periodical

Newsletter: Zonophone Newsletter
Box 955
Ashtabula, OH 44004 *

Periodical

Newsletter: Jean's Musical News
Box 366
Madison, MI 48854
Mainly classified advertising relating to phonographs. *

Repair Service

Vintage Instruments
Frederick W. Oster
1529 Pine Street
Philadelphia, PA 19102
Phone: 215-545-1100   FAX: 215-473-3634
Dealers/appraisers of rare and antique musical instruments: violins, cellos, bows, guitars, banjos, mandolins, strings, woodwinds, brass.

Accordions

Collector

Jared Snyder
511 Carpenter Lane
Philadelphia, PA 19119
Wants anything accordion related: photographs, illustrations, postcards, etc. with emphasis on button accordions and exotic locales.

Bagpipes

Collector

R.L.S.
Box 40507
Albuquerque, NM 87196
Wants Bagpipes, Scottish kilts, pins, badges, buckles, caps, swords, jackets, jewelry, etc.

Drums

Collector

David Taylor
P.O. Box 87
Sylvania, OH 43560
Phone: 419-882-5547

Wants old drums and early brass horns. *

Folk

Periodical

Magazine: Mugwumps
15 Arnold Place
New Bedford, MA 02740
Phone: 617-993-0156
This publication focuses on folk musical instruments such as dulcimers and autoharps. *

Horns (Brass)

Collector

David Taylor
P.O. Box 87
Sylvania, OH 43560
Phone: 419-882-5547
Wants old drums and early brass horns. *

Collector

Shirley Orlando
8671 Carmel Circle
Huntington Beach, CA 92647
Wants string and wind instruments: guitars, banjos, violins, mandolins, saxophones, and other brass/woodwind instruments. *

Museum/Library

Streitwieser Foundation Trumpet Museum
Franz X. Streritwieser
880 Vaughan Road
Pottstown, PA 19464
Phone: 215-327-1351   FAX: 215-970-9752
A major collection over 750 brass instruments; also prints, recordings, books, figurines, sheet music, etc.; seeking additions.

Kazoos

Man./Prod./Dist.

American Kazoo Company
8703 S. Main St.
Eden, NY 14057
Phone: 716-992-3960
The only metal kazoo factory in the world. Since 1907. *

Mechanical

(see also MUSIC BOXES)

Club/Association

Australian Collectors of Mechanical
Musical Instruments
c/o 4 Lobellia St.
Chatswood, N.S.W. 2067
Australia

Club/Association

Society of Friends of Mechanical
Musical Instruments
Jurgen Hocker
Eichenweg 6
D-5060 Gerisch, Gladbach
Germany

Dealer

Musical Wonder House Museum, The
Danilo Konvalinka
P.O. Box 604
Wiscasset, ME 04578
Phone: 207-882-7163
Buys & sells music boxes, wind-up phonographs, player pianos & rolls, cylinder records, complete or parts; full repair services.

Expert

William H. Edgerton
P.O. Box 88
Darien, CT 06820
Phone: 203-655-0566   FAX: 203-655-8066
Buys, sells, repairs pianos and rolls, musical boxes, player organs, nickelodeons, and automata.

Expert

Mechanical Music Center
Fran Mayer
Box 1078
S. Norwalk, CT 06854
Phone: 203-852-1780 *

Museum/Library

Musical Wonder House Museum, The
Danilo Konvalinka
P.O. Box 604
Wiscasset, ME 04578
Phone: 207-882-7163
America's unique Music Museum in an 1852 sea captain's mansion; restored pieces in rooms furnished with antiques of the period.

Museum/Library

Smithsonian Institution
Division of Musical History
Washington, DC 20560

Museum/Library

Music Library
Neil Ratliff
Hornbrake 3210
College Park, MD 20742

Mechanical (Player Organs)

Club/Association

Netherlands Mechanical Organ Society
(KDV)
J.L.M. Van Dinteren
Postbus 147
6160 A C Geleen
Netherdands

Mechanical (Player Pianos)

(see also PIANO ROLLS)

Club/Association

Northwest Player Piano Association
Raymond Ince
4 Barrowby Lane
Leeds LS15 8PT England

Club/Association

Nederlandse Pianola Vereniging (Dutch
Pianola Association)
Kortedijk 10
2871 CB Schoonhouen
Netherdands

Club/Association

Player Piano Group
Frances Broadway
36 Snyder Road
Stoke Newington
London N16 7UF England

Club/Association

Automatic Musical Instrument Collectors
Association (AMICA)
Magazine: AMICA News Bulletin
Michael A. Barnhart, Mem.
919 Lantern Glow Trail
Dayton, OH 45431-2915
Phone: 513-254-5580
*Purpose is to foster preservation and appreciation
of instruments and recordings of roll-actuated
instruments, especially piano type.*

Supplier

Player Piano Co., Inc.
704 East Douglas
Wichita, KS 67202
Phone: 316-263-3241 or 316-263-1714
*Complete line of player piano restoration supplies,
service manuals, music rolls; catalog if mailed free
upon request.*

Organs

(see also CAROUSELS & CAROUSEL
FIGURES)

Club/Association

Reed Organ Society, Inc. - The Musical
Museum
Magazine: Reed Organ Society Bulletin
Arthur H. Sanders
P.O. Box 901
Deansboro, NY 13328
Phone: 315-841-8774
*Focuses to all aspects of reed organs: music, con-
struction, historical value, repair, etc.*

Repair Service

Pump & Pipe Shop, The
7698 Kraft Ave.
Caledonia, MI 49316
Phone: 616-891-8743
*Specializes in the restoration, buying and selling
of reed organs; also buys parts.*

Pianos

(see also PIANOS, Miniature)

Museum/Library

Museum of the American Piano, The
Roland Loest, Cur.
211 West 58th Street
New York, NY 10019
Phone: 212-246-4646
*Collection of about 25 primarily American pianos
spanning a period from the late 1700's to 1940's;
also related tools, machines.*

String

Club/Association

Fretted Instrument Guild of America
2344 South Oakley Ave.
Chicago, IL 60608 *

Club/Association

Ann Pertoney
2344-D Oakley Ave.
Chicago, IL 60608

Collector

Shirley Orlando
8671 Carmel Circle
Huntington Beach, CA 92647
*Wants string and wind instruments: guitars,
banjos, violins, mandolins, saxophones, and
other brass/woodwind instruments. *

Collector

David Gerton
3110 S.W. Arnold
Portland, OR 97219
Phone: 503-244-9695
*Old violins, violas, cellos, basses, bows, any con-
dition. *

Dealer

Music Emporium, Inc., The
2018 Massachusetts Ave.
Cambridge, MA 02140
Phone: 617-661-2099
*Wants old guitars, banjos, mandolins, concer-
tinas, wooden flutes or other stringed instruments
in any condition.*

Dealer

Mandolin Brothers, Ltd.
Newsletter: Vintage News, The
Stanley M. Jay
629 Forest
Staten Island, NY 10310
Phone: 718-981-3226 or 718-981-8585
                    FAX: 718-816-4416
*Buys and sells guitars, banjos, mandolins, 1833-
1969, especially Gibson, Martin, Fender,
Gretsch, Rickenbacker, Stromberg, etc.*

Dealer

Gruhn Guitars, Inc.
George Gruhn
410 Broadway
Nashville, TN 37203
Phone: 615-256-2033   FAX: 615-255-2021

*Specializes in vintage or custom-made fretted
instruments; issues tri-weekly catalog of over 100
vintage guitars, mandolins and banjos.*

Dealer

Elderly Instruments
Stan Werbin
P.O. Box 14210
Lansing, MI 48901
Phone: 517-372-7890 or 517-372-7880
                    FAX: 517-372-5155
*Specializes in American made fretted stringed
instruments: by Martin, Gibson, Vega, B&D,
D'Angelico, Stromberg, Mauer, Fender, etc.*

Museum/Library

C.F. Martin Guitar Museum
Mike Longworth
Box 329
Nazareth, PA 18064
Phone: 215-759-2837   FAX: 215-759-5757

Periodical

Magazine: Strings Magazine
David M. Brin, Ed.
P.O. Box 767
San Anselmo, CA 94960
Phone: 415-485-6946   FAX: 415-485-0831
*The magazine for players and makers of bowed
instruments; also publishes annual auction Price
Guide and annual Resource Guide.*

Periodical

Magazine: Acoustic Guitar
P.O. Box 767
San Anselmo, CA 94960
Phone: 415-485-6946   FAX: 415-485-0831
*The magazine for players and makers of bowed
instruments; also publishes the annual "Musical
String Instrument Auction Price Guide."*

Repair Service

Powell's String Instrument Repair
Box 115
Belmont, WV 26134
Phone: 304-665-2559
*Repairs; also buying guitars, banjos, mandolins;
all makers. *

Supplier

C.F. Martin Guitar Co.
Box 329
Nazareth, PA 18064
Phone: 215-759-2837   FAX: 215-759-5757
*Offers Woodworker's Dream Catalog for
Woodworkers & Luthiers; tools, materials, parts
for the fretted instrument maker.*

String (Violins)

Club/Association

American Federation of Violin and Bow
Makers, Inc.
William L. Monical, Pres.
288 Richmond Terrace
Staten Isl., NY 10301
Phone: 800-633-2777
*Founded to elevate national standards of
craftmanship & professional conduct; issues Jour-
neyman's and Master's degrees upon*

Collector

Musician
Planetarium Station
Box 11
New York, NY 10024
*Buying handmade violins and bows, professional
quality only.*

Dealer

Providence Violin Shop
Robert Portukalian
1279 North Main St.
Providence, RI 02904
Phone: 401-521-5145
*Wants quality handcrafted or factory-made vio-
lins.*

Expert

Wiliam L. Monical, Inc., Dealers &
Restorers of Fine Violins
William L. Monical
288 Richmond Terrace
Staten Isl., NY 10301
Phone: 718-816-7878 or 718-816-7176
*Specializes in bowed string instruments of modern
& Baroque violin and viola da gamba families:
sales, restoration, appraisals, cases.*

NAPKIN RINGS

Figural

Dealer

Sandra Whitson
P.O. Box 272
Lititz, PA 17543
Phone: 717-626-4978
*Buys and sells fine quality Victorian figural
napkin rings.*

Expert

Paul & Paula Brenner
1215 Grand Ave.
Spencer, IA 51301
Phone: 712-262-4113 *

NATURAL HISTORY

(see also FOSSILS; LAPIDARY;
METEORITE COLLECTIBLES;
MINERALS)

Book Seller

Natural History Books
Donald E. Hahn
Box 1004
Cottonwood, AZ 86326
Phone: 602-634-5016 or 602-634-1217
*Offers technical publications about earth and bio-
logical sciences, astronomy, anthropology, ar-
chaeology and meteorites.*

NAUTICAL COLLECTIBLES

(see also DIVING EQUIPMENT;
SCRIMSHAW; SHIPPING; SHIP
RELATED; STAMP COLLECTING, Covers
(Naval); TITANIC MEMORABILIA;
WHALING)

Auction Service

Richard A. Bourne Auction Co., Inc.
P.O. Box 141
Hyannis Port, MA 02647
Phone: 508-775-0797

Auction Service

Maritime Auctions
Chuck Deluca
P.O. Box 322
York, ME 03909
Phone: 207-363-4247

Club/Association

Nautical Research Guild
Journal: Nautical Research Journal
62 Marlboro Street
Newburyport, MA 01950-3130
Phone: 508-462-6970
*Focuses on the story of the ship, the technologies of
marine transportation, the shipwrights and
sailors.*

Club/Association

Sea Heritage Foundation
Newspaper: Sea Heritage News
254-26 75th Ave.
Alen Oaks, NY 11004
Phone: 718-343-9575 *

Dealer

Quester Maritime Collection
P.O. Box 446
Stonington, CT 06378
Phone: 203-535-3860   FAX: 203-535-3533
*Buys, sells, consults on 19th & 20th century
marine paintings, ships models, bronzes, cam-
paign furniture, etc.*

Dealer

Roger & Beverly Pfost
P.O. Box 2
Tailor's Isl., MD 21669
Phone: 301-397-3457

Dealer

Martifacts, Inc.
Raymond & Lyn Newman
P.O. Box 8604
Jacksonville, FL 32239-0604
Phone: 904-645-0150   FAX: 904-645-0150
*Buys/sells authentic brass and/or wood nautical
items salvaged from ships: lights, compasses,
clocks, bells, hatch covers, sextants, etc.*

Dealer

Oarhouse
Bill Wheeler
733 Edgewater Dr.
Dunedin, FL 34698
Phone: 813-733-SHIP
Buys and sells books on nautical subjects.

Museum/Library

Peabody Museum of Salem
East India Square
Salem, MA 01970
Phone: 617-745-1876

Museum/Library

Mariners' Museum, The
100 Museum Drive
Newport News, VA 23606
Phone: 804-595-0368

Museum/Library

Museum of Science & Industry
Keith R. Gill
57th St. & Lake Shore Drive
Chicago, IL 60637
Phone: 312-684-1414   FAX: 312-684-5580

Museum/Library

Allen Knight Maritime Museum
P.O. Box 805
Monterey, CA 93942
Phone: 408-375-2553

Museum/Library

National Maritime Museum, Fort Mason
Bldg. 201
San Francisco, CA 94123
Phone: 415-556-3002

Periodical

Shipcraft Guild
Newsletter: Binnacle
15 State St.
New York, NY 10004
Phone: 201-435-5205
*Focusing on model ship building, maritime affairs
and museums. *

Periodical

Magazine: Nautical Brass
Bill Momsen, Pub.
Dept. CI
P.O. Box 3966
N. Ft. Myers, FL 33918-3966
Phone: 813-997-1458

Covers collecting, restoring, and identifying nautical antiques; also pirates, shipwrecks, naval history.

Repair Service

Brass 'n Bounty
68 Front Street
Marblehead, MA 01945
Phone: 617-631-3864
Repairs nautical antiques such as telescopes, sextants, etc.

Repair Service

New York Nautical Instrument & Service Corp.
140 West Broadway
New York, NY 10012
Phone: 212-962-4522
Repairs nautical instruments such as sextants, barometers, marine clocks, compasses, etc. *

Merchant Marine
Collector

Ian A. Millar
1806 Bantry Trail
Kernersville, NC 27284
Wants memorabilia of the WWI Merchant Marine (U.S. or England): pins, badges, caps, uniforms, medals, awards, photos, etc.; send price.

Ship Models
Dealer

American Marine Model Gallery
R. Michael Wall
12I Derby Square
Salem, MA 01970
Phone: 508-745-5777   FAX: 508-745-5778
Representing the finest work of internationally acclaimed model makers; all models fully documented; 92 pg. illustrated catalog $10.

Repair Service

American Marine Model Gallery
R. Michael Wall
12I Derby Square
Salem, MA 01970
Phone: 508-745-5777   FAX: 508-745-5778
Offers complete restoration services, custom models, cases, appraisals.

NAZI ITEMS

(see also MILITARIA; SWORDS, 3rd Reich)

Collector

Brent Smith
5106 Southwind Rd.
Greensboro, NC 27405
Phone: 919-288-5061
Buying WWII Nazi war souvenirs - daggers, helmets, hats, medals, books, paper items, etc. *

Collector

K. Wiley
719 Baldwin SE
Grand Rapids, MI 49503
Phone: 616-451-8410
Wants Japanese swords, daggers, sword parts. Also German 3rd Reich daggers, swords, bayonets. References available.

Collector

Carl Schmidt
P.O. Box 331
Cedarburg, WI 53012
Wants Nazi WWII war relics with swastikas; send photo and state price.

Dealer

John Gunderson
64 Philip
Lake George, NY 12845
Phone: 518-668-2221
Wants pre-1945 NAZI memorabilia: flags, buckles, poletops, Hitler, etc.

Dealer

Distributing Co. (DISCO)
J. Streicher
P.O. Box 331 - I
Cedarburg, WI 53012
Buys and sells Nazi war souvenirs and daggers; illustrated catalog $25 (refundable).

Periodical

Magazine: Military Collectors News
P.O. Box 702073
Tulsa, OK 74170 *

Periodical

Magazine: Der Gauleiter
P.O. Box 721288
Houston, TX 77272
Phone: 713-495-4904
A monthly magazine with articles, features, and collector & dealer ads offering relics for sale. Specializes in Third Reich items.

Repro. Source

Hutchinson House
P.O. Box 41021
Chicago, IL 60641
Sells large selection of reproduction Nazi medals and badges; also war mementos from other countries; illustrated catalog $1.

NEEDLEWORK

(see also TEXTILES)

NETSUKES

(see also ORIENTALIA)

Club/Association

Netsuke Kenkyukai Society
Journal: Netsuke Kenkyukai Study Journal
P.O. Box 11248
Torrance, CA 90510-1248
Phone: 415-885-4157   FAX: 415-893-9702

Dealer

Bill Egleston
509H Brentwood Rd.
Marshalltown, IA 50158
Phone: 515-752-4579
Specializing in mail order sale of Oriental art, netsukes, etc.

Periodical

Newsletter: Netsuke & Ivory Carving Newsletter-Video
Joan L. Cervi
3203 Adams Way
Ambler, PA 19002
Phone: 215-628-2026
A wholesaler who offers VHS videos and a monthly newsletter about imported netsuke, ivory carvings and other Orientalia.

NEWSPAPERS

(see also COMIC STRIPS, Sunday Newspaper; PAPER COLLECTIBLES)

Auction Service

Vintage Cover Story
Bob Raynor
P.O. Box 975
Burlington, NC 27215
Phone: 919-584-6990
Buys, sells historic newspapers from 1760 through 1945; also conducts periodic mail/phone bid auctions of old collectible newspapers.

Club/Association

Newspaper Collectors Society of America
Magazine: Collectible Newspapers
Rick Brown
Box 19134
Lansing, MI 48901
Phone: 517-372-8381   FAX: 517-485-9115
Send #10 SASE and $1.50 for a 32 page primer (with extensive value guide) about old and historic newspapers.

Club/Association

International Newspaper Collectors Club
Newsletter: Newes, The
P.O. Box 5090
Phoenix, AZ 85010
Phone: 602-273-7288 *

Collector

Joe Weber
604 Centre St.
Ashland, PA 17921
Phone: 717-875-4787 or 717-875-4401

Wants to buy pre-1890 newspapers, especially those discussing important events; also papers from Pennsylvania; will advise others.

Dealer

Original Historic Newspapers
Mark E. Mitchell
3002 Winter Pine Ct.
Fairfax, VA 22031
Phone: 703-591-3150   FAX: 703-395-3152
Buys and sells 1620-1885 original high quality newspapers and periodicals; including Amer. Rev., Civil War, Harper's Weekly.

Dealer

Vintage Cover Story
Bob Raynor
P.O. Box 975
Burlington, NC 27215
Phone: 919-584-6990
Buys, sells historic newspapers from 1760 through 1945; also conducts periodic mail/phone bid auctions of old collectible newspapers.

Expert

Jim Lyons
P.O. Box 580
Los Altos, CA 94023
Phone: 415-948-5666
Specializes in rare newspapers. Author of "Collecting American Newspapers."

NIGHT LIGHTS

(see also LAMPS & LIGHTING, Miniature)

Collector

Wesley & Betty Strain
832 Carson Rd.
Ferguson, MO 63135
Phone: 314-524-5608
Wants old glass night lights in the shape of parrots, monkeys, owls, rabbits, Santas, etc.; no new or ceramic lights.

NORMAN ROCKWELL

(see also ILLUSTRATORS, Norman Rockwell; COLLECTIBLES (MODERN), Norman Rockwell)

NORTH VIET NAM & VIET CONG ITEMS

(see also VIET NAM ITEMS)

Club/Association

North Vietnamese & Viet Cong Collecting Group
10109 Earthstone Ct.
Raleigh, NC 27609 *

NUMISMATICS

(see also COINS & CURRENCY; MEDALS, ORDERS & DECORATIONS; SOUVENIR CARDS; TOKENS)

NUTS RELATED COLLECTIBLES

Museum/Library

Nut Museum, The
303 Ferry Road
Old Lyme, CT 06371
Phone: 203-434-7636

OCCUPIED JAPAN

Club/Association

O. J. Club, The
Newsletter: Upside Down World of an O.J. Collector, The
Florence Archambault
29 Freeborn St.
Newport, RI 02840
Phone: 401-846-9024
Focuses on Japanese-made items marked "Occupied Japan."

Club/Association

Occupied Japan Collectors Club, The
Newsletter: Occupied Japan Collectors Club Newsletter
18309 Faysmith Ave.
Torrence, CA 90504 *

Collector

Linda Trew
9015 Lake Braddock Dr.
Burke, VA 22015-2132
Phone: 703-978-9793
*Wants figurines only: Scottie dogs, shelf sitters, ethnic figurines and mermaids; no cups, plates, fans or metal items. ***

Expert

Florence Archambault
29 Freeborn St.
Newport, RI 02840
Phone: 401-846-9024

Expert

Gene Florence
Box 22186
Lexington, KY 40522 *

OCEAN LINER COLLECTIBLES

(see also NAUTICAL COLLECTIBLES; TITANIC MEMORABILIA; TRANSPORTATION COLLECTIBLES)

Club/Association

Steamship Historical Society of America, Inc.
Magazine: Steamboat Bill
Suite #4
300 Ray Drive
Providence, RI 02906
Phone: 401-274-0805

Club/Association

Oceanic Navigation Research Society, Inc.
Journal: Ship To Shore
Charles Ira Sachs
P.O. Box 8005
Studio City, CA 91608-0005
Phone: 818-985-1345
ONRS focuses on the history of liner travel from 1840-1930; ships tours & cruises offered; journal features rare memorabilia, articles.

Collector

Edward Roehrs
RFD #852
Arceibo, PR 00612
*Wants items relating to North German Lloyd, Hamburg Amerika Line, shipping, etc. ***

Collector

Ted Hindmarsh
Box 481
Halifax, MA 02338
Phone: 617-293-6617
*Wants all items: brochures, deck plans, souvenirs, postcards, models, menus, etc. ***

Collector

Ken Schultz
Box M753
Hoboken, NJ 07030
Phone: 201-656-0966
Wants all items relating to ocean liners: brochures, deck plans, souvenirs, postcards, models, menus, etc.

Collector

David Zwicke
12 East 3rd St.
Moonachie, NJ 07074
*Wants ocean liner and truck lines models, buttons, paper, china, calendars, souvenirs, etc. ***

Collector

Randy Ridgely
447 Oglethorpe Ave.
Athens, GA 30606
Wants railroad, steamship and airline items.

Collector

World Wide Ocean Liner Memorabilia
P.O. Box 518022
Perrysburg, OH 43551
Phone: 419-874-8525
*Anything with name or picture of Normandie, SS United States, Queen Elizabeth, France, etc. ***

Collector

Mr. Gardner
Box 1031
Desert Hot Springs, CA 92240
Wants old liner cabin plans, view booklets, etc. that promote ship travel.

Collector

E.S. Radcliffe
3732 Colonial Lane SE
Port Orchard, WA 98366
Phone: 206-876-8615
Wants pre-1940 ocean liner related items: brochures, labels, cards, tableware, books, souvenirs and all paper items.

Dealer

R. Faber
230 E. 15th St.
New York, NY 10003
Phone: 212-228-7353
Wants booklets, china, deck plans, models, souvenirs, posters, etc. from Lusitania, Titanic, Normandie, Queen Mary, Andrea Doria, etc.

Dealer

Robert L. Loewenthal
10161 SW 1st Court
Plantation, FL 33324
Phone: 305-474-4246
Wants ocean line memorabilia: postcards, china, books, pictures, silverplate, posters, deck plans, models, etc.

Expert

Charles Ira Sachs
P.O. Box 8798
Universal City, CA 91608-0794
Phone: 818-985-1345
Buys/sells/specializes/lectures on ocean liner history & memorabilia; posters, postcards and related material for collectors/museums.

Museum/Library

South Street Seaport Museum, The
207 Front St.
New York, NY 10038
Phone: 212-732-5168

Museum/Library

University of Baltimore, Steamship
Historical Society Collection
414 Pelton Ave.
Staten Island, NY 10310
Phone: 301-625-3134
Mailing address is as above, but located at 1420 Maryland Ave., Baltimore, MD.

OFFICE EQUIPMENT

(see also ADDING MACHINES;
CALCULATORS; TYPEWRITERS)

OIL DRILLING COLLECTIBLES

Museum/Library

Hill City Oil Museum
821 West Main Street
Hill City, KS 67642
Phone: 913-674-5621

Museum/Library

California Oil Museum
1003 Main Street
Santa Paula, CA 93060
Phone: 805-525-6672

OLD SLEEPY EYE

Club/Association

Old Sleepy Eye Collectors Club of
America
Newsletter: Sleepy Eye Newsletter
Jim Martin
P.O. Box 12
Monmouth, IL 61462
Phone: 309-734-2703 or 309-734-4933

Expert

David & Betty Hallam
P.O. Box 175
Monmouth, IL 61462
Phone: 309-734-4933 *

OLYMPIC GAMES COLLECTIBLES

(see also PINS; SPORTS COLLECTIBLES;
STAMP COLLECTING, Topical (Sports
Related))

Collector

Jim Clark
6100 Walnut Street
Kansas City, MO 64113
Phone: 816-243-5430 or 816-361-4311
                              FAX: 816-243-5450
Wants anything related to the Olympics: pins, dolls, coins, toys, mascots, displays, and anything marked with the Olympic rings.

Collector

Alan Polsky
4305 Redwood Ave. #10
Venice, CA 90292
Phone: 213-827-2436
Wants any original Olympic memorabilia: medallions, badges worn by athletes, press and officials, programs, pint, torches, etc.

Collector

Sherwin Podolsky
16035 Tupper
Sepulveda, CA 91343
                              FAX: 818-892-0510
Wants official reports, programs, posters, tickets, posted envelopes (covers), Organizing Committee stationery, postcards, etc.

Pins & Buttons

Club/Association

International Pin Collectors Club
Newsletter: IPCC Newsletter
P.O. Box 430
Marcy, NY 13403
Phone: 315-736-5651 or 315-736-4019

Interested in all sorts of pins: Olympic, Coca Cola, sports, Desert Storm, media, etc.

Dealer

Newsletter: Olympic Collectors Newsletter,
The
Bill Nelson
P.O. Box 41630
Tucson, AZ 85717-1630
Phone: 602-629-0868 or 602-629-0387
Monthly newsletter with news, tips, and sources of where to write for free pins and buttons; world's largest retailer of Olympic items.

OPERA MEMENTOS

(see also THEATRICAL MEMORABILIA)

Museum/Library

Nordica Homestead Museum
Holly Road
Farmington, ME 04938
Phone: 207-778-2042

Museum/Library

Marcella Sembrich Memorial Studio
3236 Congress St.
Fairfield, CT 06430
Phone: 518-644-9839
The mailing address is as noted above. The museum is located in Bolton Landing, NY.

OPTICAL ITEMS

(see also BINOCULARS; EYEGLASSES;
INSTRUMENTS & DEVICES;
KALEIDOSCOPES; MEDICAL, DENTAL
& PHARMACEUTICAL; MICROSCOPES;
STANHOPES; TOYS)

ORDNANCE

(see also MILITARIA)

Auction Service

Crittenden Schmitt Archives
Dr. J.R. Schmitt
Court House P.O. Box 4253
Rockville, MD 20849
Only video auctions in the world of ordnance material: collector ammunition, bombs, grenades, mines; inert only, from all countries.

Expert

Crittenden Schmitt Archives
Dr. J.R. Schmitt
Court House P.O. Box 4253
Rockville, MD 20849
Family in business since 1849; full line of consulting expertise in all areas of munitions: grenades, land mines, bombs, etc.

Badges

Collector
Crittenden Schmitt Archives
Dr. J.R. Schmitt
Court House P.O. Box 4253
Rockville, MD 20849
Wants only metal badges & pins relating to bomb squads, explosive ordnance disposal units, ammunition & weapons companies of the world.

ORIENTALIA

(see also ARMS & ARMOR; ART, Oriental; BRONZES; CERAMICS (ORIENTAL); CLOISONNE; IVORY; JADE; NETSUKES; PRINTS, Woodblock (Japanese); SNUFF BOTTLES)

Collector
Don Hartman
P.O. Box 3703
West Palm Beach, FL 33402
Phone: 407-640-4135
*Wants antique ivory, cloisonne, porcelains, bronzes, jades, hardstone carvings, books, pottery, netsukes, enamels, snuff bottles. ***

Collector
Marty Webster
2756 Kimberly
Ann Arbor, MI 48104
Phone: 313-665-2030
Wants oriental antiques: Chinese, Japanese, and Korean.

Dealer
Oriental Antiques by Susan Akins
Susan Akins
3740 Howard Ave.
Kensington, MD 20895
Phone: 301-946-4609
All Oriental items including Indonesia, Southeast Asia and India; also African items.

Dealer
Gaijin
Sharon & Arno Ziesnitz
7835 Painted Daisy Drive
Springfield, VA 22152
Phone: 703-451-1033
Want fine works of art: netsuke, inro, ojime, sword accessories, cloisonne, satsuma, ivory and wood carvings.

Expert
Briskin Antiques
Edith & Barry Briskin
304 Hamilton
Birmingham, MI 48011
Phone: 313-540-4332 *

Expert
Richard Silverman
838 N. Doheny Dr. #1102
Los Angeles, CA 90069
Phone: 213-273-3838
Specializes in Japanese prints and ceramics; netsuke and inro; also Indian and Nepalese items.

Museum/Library
Art Institute of Chicago
Michigan Ave. at Adams Street
Chicago, IL 60603
Phone: 312-443-3600

Museum/Library
Pacific Asia Museum
Newsletter: Pacific Asia Museum Member
　　Newsletter
46 N. Los Robles Ave.
Pasadena, CA 91101
Phone: 818-449-2742　　　FAX: 818-449-2754

Museum/Library
Asian Art Museum of San Francisco, The
Avery Brundage Collection
Golden Gate Park
San Francisco, CA 94118
Phone: 415-558-2993

Periodical
Journal: Orientalia Journal
P.O. Box 94
Little Neck, NY 11363
*A monthly newsletter about all types of Chinese and Japanese art. ***

Repro. Source
Arts of Asia
3203 Adams
Ambler, PA 19002
Importer of statues, netsuke, roof tiles, snuff bottles, etc., etc., wholesale prices; 60-pg. catalog $5.

Repro. Source
Oriental Discount
Paul & Michelle Noble
12219 Nebel St.
Rockville, MD 20852
Phone: 301-881-3637
Sells (new) ceramics, carved stone, lacquered screens, furniture, embroidery, etc.

Repro. Source
Peking Arts
12141 Nebel St.
Rockville, MD 20852
Phone: 301-258-8117
Sells (new) ceramics, carved stone, lacquered screens, furniture, embroidery, etc.

Repro. Source
Ben Shaool Wholesale
Ben Shaool
28 S. Potomac St.
Hagerstown, MD 21740
Phone: 301-797-5800
Importer of Oriental ivory, porcelain, reverse paintings, rugs; also bronzes, clocks, lacquered furniture.

Repro. Source
Manny's Oriental Rugs
Manny Shaool
72 W. Washington St.
Hagerstown, MD 21740
Phone: 301-797-7434
Importer of Oriental ivory, porcelain, reverse paintings, rugs; also bronzes, clocks, lacquered furniture.

Repro. Source
Chinese Antiques & Art
9615 Las Tunas Dr.
Temple City, CA 91780
Phone: 818-286-8696 or 818-286-8698
Carries porcelain, bronze, lacquer ware, jade, cloisonne, antique furniture, ivory, antique clocks, carvings and much more.

Japanese Items

(see also ARMS & ARMOR; FIREARMS, Japanese Matchlock; OCCUPIED JAPAN; PRINTS, Woodblock (Japanese))

Auction Service
Robert C. Eldred & Co.
P.O. Box 796
East Dennis, MA 02641
Phone: 508-385-3116

Collector
Mark Walberg
P.O. Box 130
Sunbury, PA 17801
Phone: 717-286-1617 or 717-286-1416
Wants Japanese swords and sword fittings, guns, rifles, cannons, daggers, head gear, stirrups and saddles, and Samurai items, etc.

Lacquer

Repair Service
Fine Art of Asia
Janet Francine Cobert
P.O. Box 2976
Beverly Hills, CA 90213
Phone: 213-475-8160
Restores Oriental lacquer and ceramic wares.

OSBORNES IVOREX

Collector
Andy Jackson
823 Carlson Ave.
West Chester, PA 19382
Phone: 215-692-0269 or 215-272-7900

Wants wall plaques, figurines, calendars and advertising brochures; will buy, sell or trade.

OUTBOARD MOTORS

(see also BOATS)

Club/Association

Antique Outboard Motor Club
Magazine: Antique Outboarder
E830 35th Ave.
Spokane, WA 99203 *

OUTHOUSES

Collector

David Norwood
P.O. Box 653
New Hope, PA 18939
Wants outhouse related items: postcards, banks, books, articles, miniatures, almost anything.

Collector

J. W. Courter
R.R. #1
Simpson, IL 62985
Phone: 618-949-3884
Wants items relating to outhouses: post cards, books, old photographs, plans, catalogs, models, etc.

OUTLAW & LAWMAN

(see also WESTERN AMERICANA)

Club/Association

National Association for Outlaw &
Lawman History
Newsletter: NAOLH Newsletter
Hank Clark
P.O. Box 812
Waterford, CA 95386
Phone: 209-874-2640
Members interested in Western outlaw and lawmen history and artifacts; sponsors annual Rendezvous.

Collector

Gordon Becker
1210 N. Jefferson
Dixon, IL 61021
Phone: 815-288-1629
*Wants Buffalo Bill and Annie Oakley items, pre-1920; also other Old West lawmen, outlaw, gun-fighter items. *

OWL COLLECTIBLES

Club/Association

Russell's Owl Collectors Club
Newsletter: ROCO Newsletter
P.O. Box 1292
Bandon, OR 97411
Phone: 503-396-2688 *

Expert

Donna Howard
P.O. Box 5491
Fresno, CA 93755
Phone: 209-439-4845

Periodical

Newsletter: Owl's Nest
Donna Howard
P.O. Box 5491
Fresno, CA 93755
Phone: 209-439-4845

OYSTER RELATED COLLECTIBLES

Collector

Robert & Helene Blom
P.O. Box 19
Cedarbrook, NJ 08018
Wants oyster tins, bottles, crocks, wood boxes, and any other items relating to oysters or to the oyster industry.

Collector

Vivian & James Karsnitz
1428 Jerry Lane
Manheim, PA 17545
Phone: 717-665-4202
Wants to buy oyster cans.

Collector

Goerge P. Juergens
35 Farrah Dr.
Elkton, MD 21921
Phone: 301-398-5041
Buying oyster advertising items: signs, posters, gal.-qt.-pt. cans, wooden boxes, bail handle tins, trade cards, etc.

OZ

(see also WIZARD OF OZ)

PADLOCKS

(see also LOCKS)

PAPER COLLECTIBLES

(see also ADVERTISING COLLECTIBLES; AUTOGRAPHS; HISTORICAL AMERICANA; MAPS; NEWSPAPERS; POSTCARDS; POSTERS; REPAIRS & RESTORATIONS; SHEET MUSIC)

Auction Service

Waverly Auctions
Dale Sorenson
4931 Cordell Ave.
Bethesda, MD 20814
Phone: 301-951-8883   FAX: 301-718-8375
Specializes in the auction of graphic art, books, paper, atlases, prints, postcards and other paper ephemera.

Club/Association

Ephemera Society, The
12 Fitzroy Square
London W1P 5HQ England *

Club/Association

Ephemera Society of Canada, The
36 Macauley Drive
Thornhill
Ontario L3T 5S5 Canada
Phone: 416-492-5958
Dedicated to the preservation, study and display of Canada's printed heritage.

Club/Association

Ephemera Society of America Inc., The
Newsletter: Ephemera News
P.O. Box 37
Schoharie, NY 12157
Phone: 518-295-7978
Focuses on the preservation and study of ephemera (short-lived printed matter); also publishes "The Ephemera Journal" annually.

Club/Association

National Association of Paper &
Advertising Collectors
Newspaper: Paper & Advertising Collector
(P.A.C.)
P.O. Box 500
Mount Joy, PA 17552
Phone: 717-653-9797

Collector

R. Wenzel
839 W. Fullerton
Chicago, IL 60614
Phone: 312-248-4642
*Wants trade cards, rewards of merit, 19th century scrap albums, bound vols. of sheet music; also other ephemera. *

Dealer

Past & Present
Susan Nicholson
P.O. Box 595
Lisle, IL 60532
Phone: 708-964-5240
Buys and sells rare and unusual postcards, Victorian valentines, periodicals, advertising trade cards, etc.

Dealer

Rebel Peddler, The
P.O. Box 3092
Springfield, MA 01101
Phone: 413-781-1995
*Wants comics, bubble gum cards, radio premiums, sports items, advertising items, political items, posters, old magazines, etc. *

Dealer

Yesterday's Paper, Inc.
Suite 11
31815 Camino Capistrano
San Juan Capistrano, CA 92675
Phone: 714-248-0945
Buys and sells anything made of old paper: books, maps, prints, comics, catalogs, posters, newspapers, documents, Disneyana, etc.

Expert

Ken Prag Paper Americana
Ken Prag
Box 531
Burlingame, CA 94011
Phone: 415-566-6400
Eager to buy old stocks and bonds, quality picture postcards, western stereoviews, old timetables and brochures, etc.

Museum/Library

Crane Museum
30 South St.
Dalton, MA 01226
Phone: 413-648-2600
Operated by the Crane Paper Company.

Periodical

Magazine: Paper Collectors' Marketplace
Doug Watson
P.O. Box 12899
Scandinavia, WI 54977
Phone: 715-467-2379
Monthly magazine for collectors of autographs, paperbacks, postcards, advertising, photographica, magazines; all types of paper

Periodical

Newsletter: Paper Pile Quarterly
P.O. box 2815
Palm Springs, CA 92263
For collectors of small paper collectibles and advertising, paper items, post cards, etc.

Arcade Cards

Club/Association

Arcade Collectors International
Newsletter: Penny Arcade
R.J. Schulhof
3621 Silver Spur Lane
Acton, CA 93510
Phone: 800-798-9823   FAX: 805-269-2854
Ads, news, research, price lists, check list of arcade cards, especially Exhibit Supply Co. & Nutoscope Co.

Historical

Auction Service

Rita-Mobley Auctions Inc.
P.O. Box 53
South Glastonbury, CT 06073
Phone: 203-633-3076
Specializing in historical items, ephemera, autographs, photographs, etc.

Dealer

Remember When Antiquities
P.O. Box 629
Acton, ME 04001
Phone: 207-477-8111
*Wants autographs, books, historical ephemera, sports memorabilia. ***

Repro. Source

Faksimile
152 Mercer St.
New York, NY 10012
Phone: 212-226-7658
*Creates one-of-a-kind facsimiles of old rare historical documents; recreating the idiosyncrasies and texture of the originals. ***

Repro. Source

Historical Documents Co.
8 N. Preston St.
Philadelphia, PA 19104
Phone: 215-387-8076
*Antiqued reproductions of historical documents, banknotes, posters, and maps. ***

Illustrated

Periodical

Newsletter: Paper Collecting Illustrator Collectors News, The
Denis C. Jackson, Ed.
P.O. Box 1958
Sequim, WA 98382
Phone: 206-683-2559
A monthly publication for collectors of magazines and other paper illustrations; free classifieds for subscribers.

Victorian Certificates

Repro. Source

Victorian Certificates
Mark Sutton
2035 St. Andrews Circle
Carmel, IN 46032
Phone: 317-844-5648
Reproduces Victorian-era certificates; add your own photos & calligraphy; commemorate weddings, anniversaries, births or baptisms.

Western

(see also WESTERN AMERICANA)

Auction Service

American West Archives
Warren Anderson
P.O. Box 100
Cedar City, UT 84721
Phone: 801-586-9497 or 801-586-7323
Buys and sells paper Americana associated with the Western US: old documents, letters, photos, stocks, maps, autographs, prints, etc.

PAPERDOLLS

(see also DOLLS, Paper)

PAPER MONEY

(see also COINS & CURRENCY, Paper Money)

PAPERWEIGHTS

(see also GLASS)

Club/Association

Cambridge Paperweight Circle
Newsletter: CPC Newsletter
Dennis H. Gould, Hon.Sec.
The Friars House
1 Free School Lane
Cambridge CB2 3QA England
The only paperweight club in the U.K. with members worldwide; newsletter covers paperweight activity, auctions, and new books.

Club/Association

Caithness Collectors Society
Newsletter: Art in Crystal News
Bldg #12
141 Lanza Ave.
Garfield, NJ 07026
Focuses on new paperweights.

Club/Association

Paperweight Collectors Association, Inc.
Newsletter: Paperweight Collector's Bulletin
Emanuel Lacher, Pres.
150 Fulton Ave.
Garden City Park, NY 11040
Phone: 516-741-3090   FAX: 506-741-3985
1200 member association of paperweight collectors; antique and modern; dealers, artists, makers of contemporary weights.

Club/Association

Paperweight Collectors Association of Texas
Joyce Glore
1631 Aguarena Springs Dr. #408
San Marcos, TX 78666
Also publishes an annual magazine about new and old paperweights.

Collector

Stanley Block
P.O. Box 51
Trumbull, CT 06611
Phone: 203-261-3223

Collector

Shirley M. Hobart
Box 128
McIntyre, PA 15756
Phone: 412-726-9098
Buys, sells and trades pre-1940 glass paperweights; also wants old jewelry, clothing and buttons.

Collector

Michael Bozek
350 So. Ave. 57
Los Angeles, CA 90042 *

Dealer

Gem Antiques
1088 Madison Ave.
New York, NY 10028
Phone: 212-535-7399
Wants antique and fine contemporary paperweights. *

Expert

L.H. Selman, Ltd.
Lawrence H. Selman
761 Chestnut St.
Santa Cruz, CA 95060
Phone: 800-538-0766   FAX: 408-427-0111
Buys and sells antique paperweights; also repairs and polishes paperweights. Author of "Art of the Paperweight."

Man./Prod./Dist.

House of Glass, Inc., The
Joe Rice
R.R. 3, Box 153
Elwood, IN 46036
Phone: 317-552-6841
Makes paperweights all signed by owner, Joe Rice; also makes all sorts of other solid glass: ashtrays, pears, ringholders, etc.

Museum/Library

Wheaton Historical Village Association
Museum of Glass
Glasstown Rd.
Millville, NJ 08332
Phone: 609-825-6800

Museum/Library

Corning Museum of Glass, The
One Museum Way
Corning, NY 14830-2253
Phone: 607-937-5371   FAX: 607-937-3352
Over 24,000 glass objects, innovative exhibits, videos, models; glass history, archaeology, and early manufacturing.

Museum/Library

Degenhart Paperweight & Glass Museum, Inc.
65323 Highland Hills Rd.
P.O. Box 186
Cambridge, OH 43725
Phone: 614-432-2626
Over 1000 paperweights on exhibit; video, research library, gift shop.

Museum/Library

Bergstrom-Mahler Museum
Alex Vance, ExDir
165 N. Park Ave.
Neenah, WI 54956
Phone: 414-751-4658 or 414-751-4672

The museum houses one of the world's finest collections of glass paperweights.

Periodical

Wheaton Historical Village Association
Museum of Glass
Newsletter: Gatherer, The
Glasstown Rd.
Millville, NJ 08332
Phone: 609-825-6800
This is a free newsletter about the glassworks at Wheaton Village and the paperweights currently being made there.

Periodical

L.H. Selman, Ltd.
Newsletter: Paperweight News
Lawrence H. Selman
761 Chestnut St.
Santa Cruz, CA 95060
Phone: 800-538-0766   FAX: 408-427-0111
Entertaining newsletter with notes, articles and even puzzles on the subject of paperweights.

Repair Service

Studio Hannah
Charles Hannah
P.O. Box 769
Flemington, NJ 08822
Phone: 201-782-7468 *

Repair Service

George N. Kulles
115 Little Creek Drive
Lockport, IL 60441
Phone: 708-301-0996
Restores and polishes damaged paperweight surfaces; author of "Identifying Antique Paperweights - Millifiore and Lampwork."

Repair Service

Castle's Fair
Larry Castle
885 Taylor Ave.
Ogden, UT 84404
Phone: 801-393-8131
Over ten years experience; all work is hand held using water-cooled diamond equipment to heal fractures.

PAPERWEIGHTS (MODERN)

Dealer

Dennis H. Gould
The Friars House
1 Free School Lane
Cambridge CB2 3QA England
Specialist dealer in modern European paperweights; interested in exchanging modern American artists for U.K. makers.

PASSPORTS

Collector

Dan M. Jacobson
P.O. Box 277101
Sacramento, CA 95827-7101
Issues periodic lists of tokens for sale.

PATCHES

(see also BADGES; FIRE FIGHTING MEMORABILIA; MILITARIA, Insignia; POLICE & SHERIFF MEMORABILIA)

Club/Association

National Cap & Patch Association
Newsletter: NCPA Newsletter
Rt. 1 P.O. Box 164
Deer Park, WI 54007
Phone: 715-269-5411 *

Man./Prod./Dist.

Gerry White Pin, Patch & Cap Co.
2422 McIntosh Rd.
Sarasota, FL 34232
Phone: 813-371-2518
Custom made patches, hat pins, caps, mugs, etc.

PATENT MODELS

Expert

Glenn McAndrews
402 E. Warren St.
Lebanon, OH 45036
Phone: 513-932-5448

Expert

Doug Weisehan
R.R. 3 Box 202
St. Charles, MO 63301
Specializes in salesman's samples and patent models; also antique toys, farm toys, metal farm signs. *

Museum/Library

Patent Model Museum
400 North 8th Street
Fort Smith, AR 72901
Phone: 501-782-9014

PATENTS

Misc. Service

U.S. Department of Commerce
Office of Patents & Trademarks
Washington, DC 20231
Send $2 for "General Information Concerning Patents" which lists regional patent libraries; or $1.50 for copy of a patent.

Misc. Service

U.S. Patent & Trademark Office,
Scientific Library, Foreign Patents
2021 Jefferson Davis Highway
Arlington, VA 22202
Can obtain copies of foreign patents for $10.

PEACE MOVEMENT ITEMS

(see also '60's MEMORABILIA)

Museum/Library

World Peace Museum, The
Meredith & Tom Hughes
P.O. Box 791
Great Falls, VA 22066
Phone: 703-759-6714
Seek all collectibles and ephemera relating to peace, peace movements and peace makers.

PEARL HARBOR

Expert

Harvey Dolin & Co.
Harvey & Sandy Dolin
5 Beekman St.
New York, NY 10038
Phone: 212-267-0216
Wants any item pertaining to Pearl Harbor.

PEEP SHOWS

(see also STANHOPES)

PENCILS

(see also PENS & PENCILS)

PENCIL SHARPENERS

Collector

Robert Kwalwasser
168 Camp Fatima Rd.
Renfrew, PA 16053
Wants old pencil sharpeners.

Collector

Kraker
9800 McMillan Ave.
Silver Spring, MD 20910
Pencil sharpeners, figural, hand-held; also unusual book banks.

Expert

Donna Leese
c/o AntiqueWeek
P.O. Box 90
Knightstown, IN 46148
Phone: 800-876-5133 *

PENNSYLVANIA GERMAN HERITAGE

Museum/Library

Hershey Museum
James McMahon
170 W. Hersheypark Dr.
Hershey, PA 17033
Phone: 717-534-3439
Focused collection of objects detailing the town of Hershey history, regional PA German heritage, native American material culture.

PENS & PENCILS

Club/Association

Pen Fancier's Club
Magazine: Pen Fancier's Magazine
Judith & Cliff Lawrence
1169 Overcash Dr.
Dunedin, FL 34698
Phone: 813-734-4742
Old fountain pens, pen parts and mechanical pencils.

Club/Association

Society for the Collection of
Brand-Name Pencils
Newsletter: Branded Pencil, The
603 East 105th Street
Kansas City, MO 64131
Phone: 816-942-1466 *

Club/Association

American Pencil Collectors Society
Newsletter: Pencil Collector, The
Robert J. Romey, Pres.
2222 S. Millwood
Wichita, KS 67213
Phone: 316-263-8419
Members focus on the collecting of pens & pencils: unsharpened lead pencils with advertisements or addresses, old mechanical

Collector

Richard Carvell
249 Sportsmans Ave.
Freeport, NY 11520
Phone: 516-623-1325 or 800-767-7367
Wants old fountain pens; any large size pen; any ornate pens; also gold filled & silver filigree; pre-1910 pearl overlay and solid gold.

Collector

Mrs. Ky
P.O. Box J
Port Jefferson Sta., NY 11776
Phone: 516-584-4246
Will buy old fountain pens, writing implements, related ephemera, pen advertising items (no magazine ads); also unusual gold & silver pens.

Collector

Bill Retskin
3417 Clayborne Ave.
Alexandria, VA 22306-1410
Phone: 703-768-1051   FAX: 703-768-4719
Wants pre-1965 mechanical advertising pencils.

Collector

Judson H. Bell
10124 Inverness Way
Port St. Luce, FL 34986
Phone: 407-489-0480
Buys high quality fountain pens and parts, 1880-1940; prefer sterling and 14k overlays; one or entire collection.

Collector

Stephen Berger
7759 Seminary Ridge
Worthington, OH 43085
Phone: 614-885-6083
Wants Parker, Shaeffer, Waterman, Conklin, Wahl-Eversharp.

Collector

Bob Johnson
Box 684
West Chester, OH 45069
Wants all model fountain pens or parts.

Collector

Jim Beattie
23050 Rebecca Dr.
Elkhart, IN 46517
Phone: 219-875-6617
Wants quality old fountain pens or parts, 1870-1970.

Collector

Andy Brenner
814 9th St.
Sheldon, IA 51201
*Wants pens by Parker, LeBoeuf, John Holland, Wahl-Eversharp, Waterman, Dunn, Swan, Moore, Conklin, Mont Blanc, and Houston. *

Collector

Richard Hartzog
P.O. Box 4143
Rockford, IL 61110-0643
*Wants gold and silver fountain pens. *

Collector

Bob Arnell
P.O. Box 313
Grandview, MO 64030
Phone: 816-966-0544
*Wants fountain pens and watches. *

Expert

Stuart Schneider
P.O. Box 64
Teaneck, NJ 07666
Phone: 201-261-1983
Wants old Waterman, Parker, Shaeffer, and Wahl-Eversharp pens; author of books of the subject; offers repairs of quality pens.

Expert

Judith & Cliff Lawrence
1169 Overcash Dr.
Dunedin, FL 34698
Phone: 813-734-4742
Old fountain pens, pen parts and mechanical pencils.

Expert
Vintage Fountain Pens
Jack Price
3520 N. High St.
P.O. Box 8212
Columbus, OH 43214
Phone: 614-267-8468
Old pens purchased, sold and repaired.

Expert
Dick Bitterman
1701 West Chase Ave.
Chicago, IL 60626
Phone: 312-743-3330 *

Expert
Fountain Pen Hospital - Texas
Glen Benton Bowen
P.O. Box 6007
Kingwood, TX 77325
Phone: 713-359-4363 or 713-359-4385
            FAX: 713-359-4468
Repairs, buys and sells; offers a consignment catalog, PENFINDER, of the world's most valuable and rare pens; author of pen book.

Periodical
Hudson Valley Graphics
Newsletter: Pens
Stuart Schneider
P.O. Box 64
Teaneck, NJ 07666
Phone: 201-261-1983
A quarterly newsletter focusing on fountain pens.

Periodical
World Publications
Magazine: Pen World Magazine
Glen Benton Bowen
P.O. Box 6007
Kingwood, TX 77325
Phone: 713-359-4363 or 713-359-4385
            FAX: 713-359-4468
Bi-monthly magazine to provide histories of pen companies and their products; full color reproductions of worlds most valuable pens.

PERAMBULATORS
Museum/Library
Victorian Perambulator Museum
Janet L. Pallo
26 East Cedar St.
Jefferson, OH 44047
Phone: 216-576-9588
Only Victorian perambulator museum in the U.S.; over 100 examples along with related items such as sleighs, dolls, etc.

PERSONALITIES
(see also POLITICAL COLLECTIBLES)

PERSONALITIES (ARTISTS)
(see also ILLUSTRATORS)

Daniel Chester French
Museum/Library
Chesterwood
P.O. Box 827
Stockbridge, MA 01262
Phone: 413-298-3579

Edna Hibel
(see also COLLECTIBLES (MODERN),
Edna Hibel)

Club/Association
Edna Hibel Collectors Society
Marilyn & Sol Winn
RD #1 381A Sackett Lake
Monticello, NY 12701
Phone: 914-794-1887 *

Grant Wood
Collector
Jerry A. McCoy
1960 Biltmore St. NW #5
Washington, DC 20009-1538
Phone: 202-462-4790
Wants anything relating to Grant Wood: autographs, lithographs, etc.

Saint-Gaudens
Museum/Library
Saint-Gaudens National Historic Site
Rt. 2, Box 73
Cornish, NH 03745
Phone: 603-675-2175

Salvador Dali
Museum/Library
Salvador Dali Museum
Newsletter: Dali Newsletter
Wayne Atherholt
1000 Third Street, S.
St. Petersburg, FL 33701
Phone: 813-823-3767   FAX: 813-894-6068
Permanent home of the world's most comprehensive collection of Dali's works; oil and watercolor paintings, drawings, graphics, etc.

Walt Kelly
(see also CARTOON ART, Walt Kelly)

PERSONALITIES (CRIMINALS)

Al Capone
Collector
Davis Wilcox
P.O. Box 11203
Indianapolis, IN 46201
Phone: 317-636-6204
Wants any Al Capone items; especially belt buckle. *

Expert
Chicago's Roaring 20's
Michael Y. Graham
345 Cleveland Ave.
Libertyville, IL 60048
Phone: 708-362-4808
Specializes in prohibition-era (1919-1933) gangster, speak-easy, political, breweriana, and saloon-items; emphasis on Chicago area.

PERSONALITIES (ENTERTAINERS)

Al Jolson
Club/Association
International Al Jolson Society, Inc.
Magazine: Jolie/The World of Al Jolson
2981 Westmoor Drive
Columbus, OH 43204
Phone: 614-274-1507
Dedicated to perpetuating the memory of the STAR that was and still is in memory "THE WORLD'S GREATEST ENTERTAINER!" - AL JOLSON.

Female Singers
Club/Association
Girl Groups Fan Club, The
Magazine: Girl Groups Gazette, The
Louis Wendruck
P.O. Box 69A04
West Hollywood, CA 90069
Phone: 213-650-5112
Fan Club for female singers and female singing groups of the '60's; quarterly magazine; sells T-shirts, records, memorabilia.

Frank Sinatra
Collector
Scott Sayers
1800 Nueces
Austin, TX 78701
Phone: 512-478-3483   FAX: 512-473-2447
Wants any Frank Sinatra related collectibles including records, toys, books, etc.; issues an auction list quarterly.

Jack Benny
Club/Association
International Jack Benny Fan Club
Newsletter: Jack Benny Times
Lura Lee, Pres.
15430 Lost Valley Dr.
Fort Wayne, IN 46845
Phone: 219-637-2287
Forum for acquisition and trading of memorabilia relating to Jack Benny & his associates; also JB audio tape lending library.

PERSONALITIES (FAMOUS)

Charles A. Lindbergh
(see also AVIATION)

Club/Association

C.A.L./NX211 Collectors Society
Newsletter: Spirit of St. Louis
Janet & Dick Hoerle, ExSec
727 Youn Kin Parkway, South
Columbus, OH 43207
Phone: 614-497-9517
Organized to perpetuate the memory of the man and the machine; interested in items concerning Charles A. Lindbergh (1902-1974).

Club/Association

Charles A. Lindbergh Collectors Club
Newsletter: Lindbergh Notes
c/o Aerophilatelic Federation
P.O. Box 1239
Elgin, IL 60121
Phone: 708-888-1907
Interested in philatelic items concerning Charles A. Lindbergh (1902-1974); covers, records, related airmail services, etc.

Collector

Kathy Myrick
Box 54 Crowley Isl. Rd.
Corea, ME 04624

Collector

Stanley King
260 Fifth Ave.
New York, NY 10001
A life long interest in collecting Lindbergh related material.

Collector

Lou Lufker
184 Dorothy Road
West Islip, NY 11795
*Major Lindbergh collector. ***

Collector

Robinson
8020 Westvale Dr.
Ft. Worth, TX 76116
Wants Lindbergh memorabilia; anything about Lindy or the Spirit of St. Louis.

Collector

Lyndon Sheldon
2019 Essex
Colorado Springs, CO 80909

Museum/Library

Missouri Historical Society
Jefferson Memorial Bldg.
Forest Park
St. Louis, MO 63112
Phone: 314-361-1424

Dionne Quintuplets

Club/Association

Dionne Quint Collectors
Newsletter: Quint News
P.O. Box 2527
Woburn, MA 01888
Phone: 617-933-2219

Collector

J. Rodolfos
60 B Eastern Ave.
Woburn, MA 01801
Wants Dionne quintuplet items.

Collector

Mrs. Donald Hulit
236 Cape Rd.
Standish, ME 04084
Phone: 207-642-3091
Dionne quintuplet item including games, china, paper, advertising, etc.

Collector

Marceil Drake
R.R. #3
Roanoke, IN 46783-8902
Phone: 219-672-2475
Wants Dionne quintuplet items: games, china, toys, paper advertising, etc.; anything related to Dionne quintuplets or Quintland.

PERSONALITIES (HISTORICAL)

Abraham Lincoln

Collector

Donald Ackerman
149 E. Joseph St.
Moonachie, NJ 07074
Phone: 201-807-0881 or 201-413-1644
Devoted collector eager to buy Abe Lincoln memorabilia: campaign flags, ribbons, banners, posters, photographic badges, glass, china.

Collector

Cary Demont
P.O. Box 19312
Minneapolis, MN 55419
Phone: 612-922-1617
Wants Lincoln related items: campaign badges, tintypes, ribbons, banners, portraits, flags and the unusual; also Jeff Davis & slavery.

George Washington

Museum/Library

Mount Vernon-Ladies' Association of the Union
M. Christine Meadows, Cur.
Mount Vernon, VA 22121
Phone: 703-780-2000

Jenny Lind

Collector

Barbara & Walt Gydesen
19 Logan St.
New Britain, CT 06051
Phone: 203-224-1583
Wants any material from sheet music to advertising items relating to Jenny Lind, "The Swedish Nightingale."

Lafayette

Collector

Andrew B. Golbert
R.R. 1, Box 1820
North Ferrisburg, VT 05473
Phone: 802-453-2525
Wants any Lafayette ephemera, particularly relating to his visit to the U.S. in 1824-25: ribbons, medals, tokens, prints, books, etc.

Napoleon

Club/Association

Napoleonic Society of America
Newsletter: Member's Bulletin
Robert M. Snibbe
1115 Ponce De Leon Blvd.
Clearwater, FL 34616
Phone: 813-586-1779
Founded in 1983 to provide a means of communicating and sharing views on Napoleon as a man and as a military genius; also memorabilia.

Collector

James Hilty
216 S. Broad St.
Holly, MI 48442
Phone: 313-634-1400
*Wants letters, diaries, maps, documents, books, etc. ***

Collector

W.R. Morat
3942 Park Ave.
Memphis, TN 38111
Phone: 901-458-2633
Wants Napoleon or his family & marshalls; books, pictures, statues, paintings, plates, tables, etc.; especially in America after exile.

Sir Winston S. Churchill

Club/Association

Churchill Society, International
Newsletter: Finest Hour
1847 Stonewood Dr.
Baton Rouge, LA 70816
Phone: 504-752-3313
Educational/charitable assoc. devoted to preserving the memory, thought, writings, of Sir Winston S. Churchill (1874-1965).

PERSONALITIES (INVENTORS)

Thomas Alva Edison

Museum/Library

Thomas Edison Birthplace Museum
P.O. Box 451
Milan, OH 44846
Phone: 419-499-2135
An Edison exhibit featuring phones, lamps, fans, photos, and other items related to Thomas Edison.

PERSONALITIES (LITERARY)

Charles Dickens

Collector

Gerald DiMinico
105 Park St.
Montclair, NJ 07042
Wants Charles Dickens material.

Edgar Allan Poe

Museum/Library

Edgar Allan Poe House & Museum
c/o CHAP
417 E. Fayette St., Room 1037
Baltimore, MD 21202
Phone: 301-396-4866

Horatio Alger, Jr.

(see also BOOKS, Horatio Alger, Jr.)

Club/Association

Horatio Alger Society
Newsletter: Newsboy, The
Cart T. Hartmann, Sec.
4907 Allison Drive
Lansing, MI 48910
Phone: 517-882-3203
To further the philosophy of Horatio Alger, Jr. and to encourage the spirit of Strive & Succeed.

Jack London

Museum/Library

Jack London State Historic Park Museum
Newsletter: Jack London Museum Newsletter
20 E. Spain St.
Sonoma, CA 95476
Phone: 707-938-5216
Wants Jack London books, magazines, letters and other memorabilia; mailing address as noted above, but located in Glen Ellen, CA.

Mark Twain

Club/Association

Mark Twain Society - Jersey City State
College
George Daneluck
2039 Kennedy Memorial Bldg.
Jersey City, NJ 07035

Collector

Cindy Lovell
2230 Silver Palm
Edgewater, FL 32032
Wants Mark Twain memorabilia: first editions, autographs, photos, anything. *

Museum/Library

Mark Twain Memorial
351 Farmington Ave.
Hartford, CT 06105
Phone: 203-247-0998

Museum/Library

Mark Twain Home & Museum
208 Hill St.
Hannibal, MO 63401
Phone: 314-221-9010

Sir Arthur Conan Doyle

Collector

Robert C. Hess
Robert Hess
559 Potter Blvd.
Brightwaters, NY 11718
Phone: 516-665-8365
Wants Sherlock Holmes/Sir Arthur Conan Doyle items: figurines, sculpture, statuary, dolls, original artwork, illustrations, etc.

Zane Grey

Club/Association

Zane Grey's West Society
Newsletter: Zane Grey Review
Carolyn Timmerman, Sec.
708 Warwick Ave.
Fort Wayne, IN 46825
Members are collectors of Zane Grey books and memorabilia.

PERSONALITIES (MILITARY)

Audie Murphy

Museum/Library

Confederate Research Center - Audie
Murphy Exhibit
Dr. B.D. Patterson
P.O. Box 619
Hillsboro, TX 76645
Phone: 817-582-2555
Special Audie Murphy memorabilia collection on display.

Gen. George S. Patton

Museum/Library

Patton Museum of Cavalry & Armor
David Holt, Librarian
P.O. Box 208
Fort Knox, KY 40121-0208
Phone: 502-624-3812
The "Patton Gallery" and the Emert L. "Red" Davis Library contains Gen. George S. Patton, Jr. artifacts and reference materials.

PERSONALITIES (MOVIE STARS)

Al Jolson

Collector

Markowitz
964 Hillside Blvd.
New hyde Park, NY 11040
Wants anything unique, unusual or uncommon related to Al Jolson or brother Harry: posters, lobby cards, heralds, etc.

Marilyn Monroe

Club/Association

Marilyn Monroe International Fan Club
P.O. Box 7544
Northridge, CA 91327
Phone: 818-831-1611

Collector

Cindy Oakes
34025 W. 6 Mile
Livonia, MI 48152
Phone: 313-591-3252
Wants dolls, jewelry, autographs, etc.

Collector

Lynn MacCarroll
4970 Palmyra
Las Vegas, NV 89102
Phone: 702-871-9383
Wants anything relating to Marilyn Monroe. *

Expert

Denis C. Jackson
P.O. Box 1958
Sequim, WA 98382
Phone: 206-683-2559
Author of "The Price & ID Guide to Marilyn Monroe."

Natalie Wood

Collector

Lynn MacCarroll
4970 Palmyra
Las Vegas, NV 89102
Phone: 702-871-9383
Wants anything relating to Natalie Wood. *

Shirley Temple

Collector

Rita Dubas
8811 Colonial Rd.
Brooklyn, NY 11209
Phone: 718-745-7532
Wants Shirley Temple items: unusual, advertising, foreign, photos, dolls; anything pertaining to Shirley. *

Collector

Cindy Lovell
2230 Silver Palm
Edgewater, FL 32032

Wants Shirley Temple memorabilia: first editions, autographs, photos, anything. *

Dealer
Frank Garcia
13701 SW 66th St. B-301
Miami, FL 33183
Phone: 305-383-9006
Wants early Shirley Temple items: jewelry, uncut paper dolls, sheet music, lobby cards, press books, clothing, etc.

Periodical
Newsletter: Shirley Temple Collector News
8811 Colonial Rd.
Brooklyn, NY 11209
Phone: 718-745-7532 *

Periodical
Shirley Temple Collectors By the Sea
Newsletter: Lollipop News
P.O. Box 6203
Oxnard, CA 93031
Phone: 708-904-0787 *

PERSONALITIES (MUSICIANS)

Band Leaders

Collector
John L. Micholas
172 Liberty St.
Trenton, NJ 08611
Phone: 609-530-5568 or 609-599-9672
Wants Glen Miller, Bunny Berigan, autographs, recordings, photos, sheet music, magazines, films, anything related.

Beatles

Club/Association
Beatles Fan Club of Great Britain
123 Marina
St Leonards On Sea
East Sussex TN3 80BN England *

Club/Association
Beatles Now
P.O. Box 307
Walthamstow
London E17 4LL England *

Club/Association
Harrison Alliance, The
Patti Murawski
67 Cypress St.
Bristol, CT 06010 *

Club/Association
Beatles Fan Club
Magazine: Good Day Sunshine
Charles F. Rosenay
397 Edgewood Ave.
New Haven, CT 06511
Phone: 203-865-8131   FAX: 203-562-5260

For Beatles fans and collectors of all ages; tours, conventions and special Beatles events, news, reviews, collectors column, etc.

Club/Association
Working Class Hero Club
Newsletter: Working Class Hero, The
B. Whatmough
3311 Niagara St.
Pittsburgh, PA 15213-4223
Non-profit organization for and by true Beatles fans; quarterly newsletter covers news, pictures and articles about the Beatles.

Club/Association
Beatles Connection
Newsletter: Beatles Connection
P.O. Box 1066
Pinellas Park, FL 34665 *

Collector
Cindy Oakes
34025 W. 6 Mile
Livonia, MI 48152
Phone: 313-591-3252
Wants original 1960's items only: porcelain Beatles, Remco Beatles, cloth Beatles dolls, Beatles nodders, Beatles blow-up dolls, etc.

Collector
Gretchen Dziadosz
333 Grentree Lane NE
Ada, MI 49301
Phone: 616-676-2961
Wants original 1960's items only.

Dealer
Beatles Compuloque
P.O. Box 1020
Stanton, CA 90680 *

Dealer
Ed Schreiber
Dept. 186 CIC
P.O. Box 2704
Huntington Beach, CA 92647
Phone: 714-846-4310
Wants Beatles related memorabilia: lunch boxes, record player, guitars, drums, gum cards, magazines, Yellow Sub. and movie items.

Dealer
Ticket To Ryde
P.O. Box 3393
Lacey, WA 98503 *

Expert
Joseph Hilton
6 Wheelwright Dr.
Durham, NH 03824
Phone: 603-659-8533
Collecting original 1960's items only: Beatles lunch boxes, games, toys, Yellow Submarine items, promo displays, anything Beatles.

Expert
Charles F. Rosenay
397 Edgewood Ave.
New Haven, CT 06511
Phone: 203-865-8131   FAX: 203-562-5260
Editor of Beatles Fan Club magazine; produces Beatles conventions; trades and sells memorabilia by mail; recognized expert.

Expert
Rick Rann
P.O. Box 877
Oak Park, IL 60303
Phone: 708-442-7907
Toys, dolls, guitars, record player, hair spray, records, concert tickets, movie items, magazines; co-author of book on same.

Expert
Jeff Augsburger
P.O. Box 311
River Forest, IL 60305
Toys, dolls, guitars, record player, hair spray, records, concert tickets, movie items, magazines; co-author of book on same.

Expert
Marty Eck
P.O. Box 311
River Forest, IL 60305
Toys, dolls, guitars, record player, hair spray, records, concert tickets, movie items, magazines; co-author of book on same.

Periodical
Beat Publications
Magazine: Beatles Monthly Book
45 St. Mary's Road
Ealing
London W5 5RQ England
A monthly magazine. *

Periodical
Newsletter: Rockwire Service Report
Box 56
Rego Park, NY 11374 *

Periodical
Goody Press, The
Magazine: Beatlefan
Bill King
P.O. Box 33515
Decatur, GA 30033
Phone: 404-633-5587
A bi-monthly magazine for Beatles fans; a news-oriented, professional publication; articles, books for sale, ads, etc.

Periodical
Magazine: Instant Karma
Marsha Ewing
P.O. Box 256
Sault Ste. Marie, MI 49783
Phone: 906-632-2231 or 906-635-0140
FAX: 906-632-4411

News, ads, opinions.

Periodical
Newsletter: Wright Thing, The
Barbara Fenwick
P.O. Box 18807
Minneapolis, MN 55418 *

Periodical
Newsletter: McCartney Observer, The
Doylene Kindsvater
220 E. 12th St.
La Crosse, KS 67548 *

Elton John
Collector
D. Edmond Miller
P.O. Box 4516
Durham, NC 27706-4516
Wants recordings and autograph material by Elton John.

Elvis
Club/Association
Graceland News Fan Club
Magazine: Graceland News
Josh Cooke
P.O. Box 452
Rutherford, NJ 07070
Phone: 201-933-4622
Formed in 1976; publishes Elvis Presley related newspapers and collector magazines.

Club/Association
Elvis Forever TCB Fan Club
Newsletter: Elvis Forever TCB Fan Club
    Newsletter
P.O. Box 1066
Pinellas Park, FL 34665 *

Club/Association
International Federation of Elvis
Presley Fan Clubs
2412 Repton Dr.
Fort Wayne, IN 46815 *

Collector
Cindy Oakes
34025 W. 6 Mile
Livonia, MI 48152
Phone: 313-591-3252
Wants dolls, jewelry, autographs, etc.

Museum/Library
Graceland
P.O. Box 16508
Memphis, TN 38186
Phone: 800-238-2000

James Dean
Club/Association
We Remember Dean International
Sylvia Bongiovanni, Ed
P.O. Box 5025
Fullerton, CA 92635
Formed in respectful memory of actor James Dean;bi-monthly newsletter includes Dean articles, current news, where to buy memorabilia,

Museum/Library
James Dean Gallery, The
David Loehr
425 North Main St.
P.O. Box 55
Fairmount, IN 46928
Phone: 317-948-3326
Houses the world's largest collection of memorabilia dealing with James Dean; wants James Dean plates, posters, records, novelties etc.

Liberace
Collector
N. Graf
902 Apricot
Winters, CA 95694
Wants anything Liberace: pictures, magazines, records, scrapbooks, posters, books, autographs, sheet music, etc.; send price & describe.

Museum/Library
Liberace Foundation for the Performing
& Creative Arts/Liberace Museum
Newsletter: Liberace Museum Newsletter
1775 E. Tropicana
Las Vegas, NV 89119
Phone: 702-798-5598   FAX: 702-798-7386
A non-profit foundation museum and gift shop with proceeds funding scholarships.

Monkees
Club/Association
Liverpool Productions' Monkees
Buttonmania Club
Charles F. Rosenay
397 Edgewood Ave.
New Haven, CT 06511
Phone: 203-865-8131   FAX: 203-562-5260

Rascals/Starliters
Club/Association
Rascals/Starlifters Fan Club
James A. Farley Building
P.O. Box 481
New York, NY 10116-0481
Phone: 201-763-6451
The Young Rascals, Joey Dee & the Starliters; free information and pen pal service for fans of the Rascals & all Rascal-related artists.

PETROLIANA
(see also GAS STATION COLLECTIBLES)

PEWTER
Club/Association
Pewter Collectors Club of America
Newsletter: Pewter Collectors Club of
    American Newsletter
William Paddock
29 Chesterfield Rd.
Scarsdale, NY 10583
Association of private collectors and interested parties; annual national as well as regional meetings.

Collector
William Paddock
29 Chesterfield Rd.
Scarsdale, NY 10583

Collector
Collector
P.O. Box 1301
Havertown, PA 19083
Phone: 215-446-4839
*Wants pewter porringers, tankards, teapots, plates, mugs, etc. *

Dealer
Twin Tankard
P.O. Box 2634
Columbia, MD 21045
Phone: 301-236-9391
*Wants antique steins, plates, chargers, etc. *

Museum/Library
Hershey Museum
James McMahon
170 W. Hersheypark Dr.
Hershey, PA 17033
Phone: 717-534-3439
Focused collection of objects detailing the town of Hershey history, regional PA German heritage, native American material culture.

Periodical
Newsletter: Pewter Bulletin
B.B. Hillmann
740 Highview Dr.
Wyckoff, NJ 07481 *

PEZ CONTAINERS
(see also CANDY CONTAINERS)

Collector
Charles Beesley
P.O. Box 400
St. Michaels, MD 21663
Phone: 301-745-9206
Wants Pez candy dispensers; one item or entire collection - anything PEZ.

Collector
David Welch
RR 2, Box 233
Murphysboro, IL 62966
Phone: 618-687-2282

Wants anything relating to Pez; paying up to $100 for certain containers.

Periodical
Newsletter: Optimist Pezzimist
P.O. Box 606
Dripping Springs, TX 78620

PHILATELICS
(see also STAMP COLLECTING)

PHONOGRAPHS
Book Seller
Antique Phonograph Collectors Club
Allen Koenigsberg
502 E. 17th St.
Brooklyn, NY 11226
Phone: 718-941-6835
Carries the most complete list of phonograph related books, catalogs, manuals, discographies, posters and magazines.

Club/Association
Antique Phonograph Collectors Club
Magazine: Antique Phonograph Monthly, The
Allen Koenigsberg
502 E. 17th St.
Brooklyn, NY 11226
Phone: 718-941-6835
Published 10 times each year; historical and current articles on phonograhs and musical instruments; also display and classified ads.

Club/Association
Michigan Antique Phonograph Society, Inc.
Newsletter: In The Groove
2609 Devonshire
Lansing, MI 48910
Phone: 517-482-7996
A highly recommended newsletter contains articles, member ads about antique phonographs, records and music boxes.

Club/Association
Vintage Radio & Phonograph Society, Inc.
Newsletter: Reproducer, The
C.F. Crandell, Pres.
P.O. Box 165345
Irving, TX 75016
Phone: 214-337-2823 or 214-315-2553
Purpose is to preserve early radios, phonographs, and related material and to conduct historical research of same.

Club/Association
American Phonograph Society, The
Journal: Journal of the American Phonograph Society
P.O. Box 5046
Berkeley, CA 94705 *

Collector
Paul Newth
26 Gail Dr.
Ellington, CT 06029
Wants cylinder phonographs and cylinder records.
*

Collector
Alvin Heckard
R.D. 1, Box 88
Lewistown, PA 17044
Phone: 717-248-7071 or 717-248-2816
Wants wind up type phonographs, parts, literature and advertising.

Collector
Ken Danckaert
231 Kennedy Ct.
Severna Park, MD 21146
Phone: 301-544-0260
*Want windup phonographs and parts; bought and sold; also repairs. *

Collector
Stuart Stein
P.O. Box 303
Frederick, MD 21701
Phone: 301-663-8369
Wants all wind-up phonographs, horn type.

Collector
Lon & Carol Sears
158 Ridgeway Rd.
Cincinnati, OH 45216
Phone: 513-821-8678
*Want windup phonographs and vintage radios; buy, sell, and repair; also parts and records. *

Dealer
Denny R. Smith
4408 Foxton Ct.
Dayton, OH 45414
Phone: 513-279-0417
Buying horn phonographs, music boxes, cylinders, parts.

Expert
Seven Acres Antique Village & Museum
Randy & Larry Donley
8512 S. Union Rd.
Union, IL 60180
Phone: 815-923-2214
Experts in antique phonographs; buys, sells, collects and repairs.

Expert
Steve Oliphant
5255 Allott Ave.
Van Nuys, CA 91401
Phone: 818-789-2339   FAX: 213-276-5632
Adviser and dealer of old phonographs; buys entire collections or individual pieces.

Museum/Library
Edison National Historic Site
Main St. at Lakeside Ave.
West Orange, NJ 07052
Phone: 201-736-5050
A museum with exhibits in all fields of Edison's contributions.

Museum/Library
Seven Acres Antique Village & Museum
Randy & Larry Donley
8512 S. Union Rd.
Union, IL 60180
Phone: 815-923-2214
Large exhibit of Edison phonographs, cylinder and disc music machines, and other music memorabilia.

Periodical
New Amberola Phonograph Co. The
Magazine: New Amberola Graphic, The
37 Caledonia St.
St. Johnsbury, VT 05819
A quarterly publication for collectors of early phonographs & records from the years 1895-1935; articles, book reviews, ads, auctions, etc.

Periodical
Magazine: Antique Phonograph Monthly
Allen Koenigsberg
502 E. 17th St.
Brooklyn, NY 11226
Phone: 718-941-6835
Published 10 times each year; historical and current articles on phonographs and musical instruments; also display and classified ads.

Periodical
Newspaper: Horn Speaker, The
Jim Cranshaw
P.O. Box 1193
Mabank, TX 75147
Phone: 903-848-0304
A newspaper for collectors and historians interested in antique radios and phonographs.

Repair Service
Antique Phonograph Center
Floyd Silver
Hwy. 206
P.O. Box 274
Vincentown, NJ 08088
Phone: 609-859-8617
Antique phonographs sales, service; complete restorations of Edison, Victor and Columbia phonographs.

Supplier
Ron Sitko
26 Tekakwitha Court
Clifton Park, NY 12065
*Sells parts for old phonographs. *

Supplier
Victorian Talking Machine Co.
261 Robinson Ave.
Newburgh, NY 12550
Phone: 914-561-0132
Sells and repairs antique phonographs; phonograph books and supplies; steel needles.

PHOTOGRAPHS

(see also 3-D PHOTOGRAPHICA;
CAMERAS & CAMERA EQUIPMENT;
PHOTOGRAPHY; REPAIR &
RESTORATIONS, Paper Items; STEREO
VIEWERS & STEREOGRAPHS)

Auction Service
Swann Galleries, Inc.
104 E. 25th St.
New York, NY 10010
Phone: 212-254-4710   FAX: 212-979-1017
Oldest/largest U.S. auctioneer specializing in rare books, autographs & manuscripts, Judaica, photographs, and works of art on paper.

Auction Service
Larry Gottheim Fine Early Photographs
33 Orton Ave.
Binghamton, NY 13905
Phone: 607-797-1685
*Conducts mail-bid auctions of fine early photographs, tintypes, daguerreotypes, etc. **

Club/Association
Photographic Collectors Club of Great
Britain
Magazine: Photographica World
Michael Pritchard, Ed.
5 Station Industrial Estate
Prudhoe
Northumberland NE42 6NP Eng.
Club aims to promote the study and collection of photographic equipment and images by publications, meetings, auctions and shows.

Club/Association
Association of International
Photography Art Dealers
93 Standish Rd.
Hillsdale, NJ 07642
Phone: 201-664-4600
Publishes the "AIPAD Membership Directory and Illustrated Catalogue" ($20) and a 35-page brochure "On Collecting Photographs" ($5).

Collector
Williams
29 Pinebrook
Morrisonville, NY 12962
*Wants quality daguerreotypes and ambrotypes. **

Collector
Doug Jordan
Box 20194
St. Petersburg, FL 33742
Phone: 813-577-9627

*Wants pre-1900 photos of all types. **

Collector
Levin
7440 East Prairie Rd.
Skokie, IL 60076
Phone: 312-675-7440
*Daguerreotypes, ambrotypes, tin types and paper. Especially outdoor scenes, occupationals and children. **

Collector
Collector
3100 Southfork Rd.
Cody, WY 82414
Phone: 307-587-2094
*Glass plates and negatives; any subjects. **

Collector
Norman Kulkin
727 N. Fuller Ave.
Los Angeles, CA 90046
Phone: 213-653-6929
Buy, sell, trade stereoviews, daguerreotypes, Civil War photos, anything in photographica 1839-1939.

Dealer
J. & L. Photography
Box 813
Levittown, NY 11756
Phone: 516-731-7772
*Wants daguerreotypes, stereoviews, tintypes, albums, CDV's, cameras, equipment, etc. **

Dealer
Gallery for Fine Photography, A
5423 Magazine Street
New Orleans, LA 70115 **

Dealer
Fraenkel Gallery
Jeffrey Fraenkel
49 Geary St.
San Francisco, CA 94108
Phone: 415-981-2661
With co-owner Frish Brandt specializes in 19th and 20th century photographers.

Expert
Larry Gottheim
33 Orton Ave.
Binghamton, NY 13905
Phone: 607-797-1685
*Specializes in fine early photographs, tintypes, daguerreotypes, etc. **

Museum/Library
Center for Creative Photography
843 E. University
Tucson, AZ 85719
Phone: 602-621-7968

Periodical
Camerashopper
Magazine: Camera Shopper Magazine
1 Magnolia Hill
West Hartford, CT 06117-2022
Phone: 203-233-9922   FAX: 203-233-5122
Buy, sell, trade magazine for used, classic and antique photographica including vintage photographs.

Periodical
Photographic Arts Center, The
Newsletter: Photograph Collector, The
Robert S. Persky
163 Amsterdam Ave. #201
New York, NY 10023-0099
Phone: 212-838-8640   FAX: 212-873-7065
For photograph collectors, dealers and curators; also publishes "The Photographic Art Market," as annual compilation of auction prices.

Brady's

Collector
David Holcomb
2897 Blendon Woods Blvd.
Columbus, OH 43231
Phone: 614-891-2717
*Wants Lincoln photographs and other photos from Brady's National Portrait Gallery. **

Cases

Dealer
Eugene R. Groves
P.O. Box 2471
Baton Rouge, LA 70821-2471
Phone: 504-387-3221   FAX: 504-346-8049
Wants early photo cases 1840-1865; big size, mother-of-pearl, tortoise, patriotic, signed, wall frames, etc.

Daguerreotypes

Dealer
George Rinhart
Upper Grey
Colebrook, CT 06021
Phone: 230-379-9773 **

Dealer
Eugene R. Groves
P.O. Box 2471
Baton Rouge, LA 70821-2471
Phone: 504-387-3221   FAX: 504-346-8049
Wants quality daguerreotypes: outdoors, occupationals, military, blacks, Louisiana, animals, signed, toys, large groups, etc.

Medical

Museum/Library

Armed Forces Medical Museum
Michael Rhode
Bldg. 54
Walter Read Medical Center
Washington, DC 20306
Phone: 202-576-2438 or 202-576-0401
FAX: 202-576-2164
Federal government museum archives that collects catalog material related to the history of medicine, especially military medicine.

Military

Periodical

Magazine: Military Images
R.D. 1, Box 99A
Henryville, PA 18332
Phone: 717-629-9152
Focuses on military images from 1839 to 1900.

Negatives

Collector

Don Culver
3083 Balsam
Edgewood, KY 41017
Wants glass or film negatives of obsolete forms of transportation, railroad, architecture, peoples, rivers, dams, floods, wars, etc. *

Yard-Long Pictures

Dealer

Meisel Primavera Gallery
Louis & Susan Meisel
133 Prince St.
New York, NY 10012
Wants photos usually 3 to 6 times as long as they are high; encompass a 180 to 360-degree shot. *

PHOTOGRAPHY

(see also 3-D PHOTOGRAPHICA;
CAMERAS & CAMERA EQUIPMENT;
PHOTOGRAPHS; STEREO VIEWERS &
STEREOGRAPHS)

Club/Association

Photographic Historical Society of New England, Inc.
Journal: Photographica Journal
West Newton Station
P.O. Box M
Boston, MA 02165 *

Club/Association

American Photographic Historical Society, Inc.
Magazine: Photographica
520 W. 44th St.
New York, NY 10036
Phone: 212-594-5056
Publishes "Photographica" quarterly and "In Focus" monthly.

Club/Association

Photographic Historical Society, Inc., The
Newsletter: PHS Newlsletter
R. Fricke
P.O. Box 39563
Rochester, NY 14604
Conducts a monthly meetings and a tri-annual symposium.

Club/Association

Photographic Society of America
Richard Frieners
1305 Foxglove Dr.
Batavia, IL 60510

Club/Association

Western Photographic Collectors Association, Inc.
Magazine: Photographist, The
P.O. Box 4294
Whittier, CA 90607
Phone: 213-693-8421
Non-profit organization dedicated to the dissemination of information on, and to stimulate interest in, all aspects of photographica.

Museum/Library

International Center of Photography
1130 5th Avenue
New York, NY 10128
Phone: 212-860-1777

Museum/Library

International Museum of Photography at George Eastman House
Magazine: Image
900 East Ave.
Rochester, NY 14607
Phone: 716-273-3361
Devoted to the history, technology and aesthetics of photography.

Museum/Library

International Photographic Historical Association
Newsletter: INPHO News
David Silver
P.O. Box 16074
San Francisco, CA 94116
Phone: 415-681-4356 or 415-292-2006
Corresponding research & resource center for those interested in studying/collecting objects pertaining to the history of photography.

Periodical

Rochester Institute of Technology, Graphics Arts Research Center
Newsletter: Graphic Arts Research Center Newsletter
1 Lomb Memorial Drive
Rochester, NY 14623 *

PIANO ROLLS

(see also MUSICAL INSTRUMENTS, Mechanical (Player Pianos))

Auction Service

QRS Music Rolls, Inc.
Dan Wilke
1026 Niagara St.
Buffalo, NY 14213
Phone: 716-885-4600   FAX: 716-885-7510
Offers bi-monthly auctions by mail of original antique piano rolls; sorry, no consignments accepted.

Collector

Deno Buralli
P.O. Box 6
Spring Grove, IL 60081
Reproducing rolls and standard 88-note rolls.

Dealer

Sheet Music Center
Box 367
Port Washington, NY 11050
Wants sheet music and piano rolls. *

Dealer

A.M.R. Publishing Co.
Frank Adams
P.O. Box 3007
Arlington, WA 98223
Phone: 206-659-6434   FAX: 206-659-5994
Buys and sells original player piano rolls.

Repro. Source

QRS Music Rolls, Inc.
1026 Niagara St.
Buffalo, NY 14213
Phone: 716-885-4600 or 800-247-6557
FAX: 716-885-7510
World's oldest manufacturer of player piano rolls; thousands of songs, old and new, by famous pianists of past and present.

Repro. Source

Play-Rite Music Rolls
401 S. Broadway
Turlock, CA 95380
Phone: 209-667-1996 or 800-826-5539
FAX: 209-667-8241
Sells new 10 to 16 tune "O" rolls for player pianos.

PIANOS

Miniature

(see also MUSICAL INSTRUMENTS, Pianos)

Club/Association

Miniature Piano Enthusiast Club
Newsletter: Musically Yours!
Janice E. Kelsh
Suite 202
5815 N. Sheridan Rd.
Chicago, IL 60660
Phone: 312-271-2970
Established in 1990 to promote the hobby of miniature piano collecting; annual convention.

Collector

Janice E. Kelsh
Suite 202
5815 N. Sheridan Rd.
Chicago, IL 60660
Phone: 312-271-2970
Interested in obtaining miniature pianos of all kinds; also wants old postcards depicting pianos.

PIE BIRDS

(see also KITCHEN COLLECTIBLES)

Collector

Hicker' Nut Hill Antiques
Genie Prather
Rt. 2, Box 532
Tyler, TX 75704 *

Expert

Alan Pedel
Marwood Lee
Barnstable
Devonshire EX331HQ England
Searches the heart of the English countryside for rare and lovely pie birds.

PIG COLLECTIBLES

Collector

Tony & Marie Shank
P.O. Box 778
Marion, SC 29571
Wants pottery pigs, but no banks. *

Expert

Mary Hamburg
20 Cedar St.
Danville, IL 61832
Phone: 217-446-2323 *

PIN-UP ART

(see also PLAYBOY ITEMS)

Collector

John Crawford
3442 Manor Hill
Cincinnati, OH 45220
Phone: 513-221-6050
Wants Vargas, Petty, Mozert, Elvgren, others; especially Esquire items.

Expert

Dick Bitterman
1701 West Chase Ave.
Chicago, IL 60626
Phone: 312-743-3330 *

PINS

(see also BUTTONS, Pinback; OLYMPIC GAMES COLLECTIBLES, Pins & Buttons)

Dealer

Newsletter: Olympic Collectors Newsletter, The
Bill Nelson
P.O. Box 41630
Tucson, AZ 85717-1630
Phone: 602-629-0868 or 602-629-0387
Monthly newsletter with news, tips, and sources; for collectors of Olympic, Sports, Disney, Coca Cola pins; large selection in stock.

Foreign

Club/Association

International Federation of Falerists
Box 8, University Center Bldg.
Univ. Of Manitoba, Manitoba
Winnipeg R3T 2N2 Canada
Focuses on the collecting of small medallic pinback buttons and badges (znachki) from the Soviet countries. *

PIONEERS

American

Collector

Lewis Leigh
Box 397
Fairfax, VA 22030
Wants papers, letters, journals, uniforms, weapons & flags of American soldiers, seamen, pioneers, adventurers: 1607-1919. *

PIPES

(see also SMOKING COLLECTIBLES)

Club/Association

Universal Coterie of Pipe Smokers, The
Magazine: Pipe Smoker's Ephemeris, The
Tom Dunn, Ed.
20-37 120th St.
College Point, NY 11356
An irregular quarterly magazine for pipe smokers and anyone interested in pipes, smoking, or related matters.

Club/Association

Pipe Collectors Club of America
Magazine: Pipe Smokers Pipeline
Robert C. Hamlin
P.O. Box 5179
Woodbridge, VA 22194-5179
Phone: 703-878-7655 or 703-878-3657
FAX: 703-878-7657

Club/Association

Pipe Collectors of the World
Box 11652
Houston, TX 77193 *

Collector

Bob Spore
400 Riverside Dr.
Pasadena, MD 21122
Phone: 301-437-2715
Collector seeking pre-smoked briar pipes; sells and appraises pipe collections; member T.U.C.O.P.S., P.C.C.A. *

Collector

Benjamin Rapaport
5101 Willowmeade Dr.
Fairfax, VA 22030
Wants meerschaum, opium, porcelain, Meissen, chinoiserie, Wedgwood, metal, cloisonne, champleve, etc. pipes. *

Expert

James Kesterson
3881 Fulton Grove Rd.
Cincinnati, OH 45245
Phone: 513-752-0949
Wants smoked or new briar pipes: brands like Barling, Caminetto, Charatan, Comoy, Dunhill, GBD, Larsen, Sasieni, Savinelli, etc.

Museum/Library

U.S. Tobacco Museum
100 W. Putnam Ave.
Greenwich, CT 06830
Phone: 203-869-5531

Museum/Library

National Tobacco-Textile Museum
P.O. Box 541
Danville, VA 24543
Phone: 804-797-9437

Museum/Library

Museum of Tobacco Art & History
800 Harrison St.
Nashville, TN 37203
Phone: 615-271-2349 or 615-271-2163
FAX: 615-271-2285
Museum traces history of tobacco from American Indians to present; collection of pipes, Cigar Store figures, snuff boxes, art, etc.

Meerschaum

Collector

Bernard Berlly
24 School House Ln.
Lake Success, NY 10020-1323
Phone: 516-829-2777   FAX: 516-829-2779
Wants antique carved meerschaum pipes.

PLANTERS PEANUTS ITEMS

Club/Association

Peanut Pals
Newsletter: Peanut Papers
Bob Walthall
P.O. Box 4465
Huntsville, AL 35815
Phone: 205-881-9198
Focuses on Planters Peanut's history and collectibles.

Collector

Neil Williams
323 Trafton Rd.
Springfield, MA 01108
Mr. Peanut wanted. Seeking older, unusual Planter's Peanut items. *

Expert

Judy Posner
R.D. 1 Box 273
Effort, PA 18330
Phone: 717-629-6583   FAX: 717-629-0521

PLASTIC COLLECTIBLES

(see also BOXES; CHARMS; TOYS, Plastic;
TRAINS, Toy (Plasticville); TUPPERWARE)

Club/Association

Society for Decorative Plastics
Newsletter: Collectible Plastics
P.O. Box 1099
Forestville, CA 95436 *

Expert

Catherine Yronwode
6632 Covey Rd.
Forestville, CA 95436
Phone: 707-887-2424
Specializes in pre-1950 collectible plastic items: powder boxes, mirror frames, napkin rings, etc. *

PLATES

(see also COLLECTIBLES (MODERN),
Collector Plates)

PLAYBOY ITEMS

(see also PIN-UP ART)

Collector

David Kveragas
1943 Timberlane
Clarks Summit, PA 18411-9539
Phone: 717-581-3429
Wants of Pin-Up illustrations by Vargas, Elugren, Armstrong, etc.; also authentic Playboy Playmate autographs, photos, photos, etc.

PLAYING CARDS

(see also GAMBLING COLLECTIBLES;
GAMES)

Club/Association

International Playing Card Society
188 Sheen Lane
East Sheen
London SW14 8LF England *

Club/Association

English Playing Card Society, The
Newsletter: English Playing Card Society
  Newsletter
Major R.T. Welsh
11 Pierrepont Street
Bath
Avon BA1 1LA England
For collectors, researchers, museums, archivists, manufacturers, etc. who are interested in English playing cards and card games.

Club/Association

Playing Card Collectors Association
Newsletter: PCCA Bulletin
P.O. Box 783
Bristol, WI 53104
Phone: 414-857-9334 *

Club/Association

Chicago Playing Card Collectors, Inc.
Newsletter: Chicago Playing Card Collector
Bernice De Somer, Dir.
1559 West Platt Blvd.
Chicago, IL 60626
Phone: 312-274-0250
Focuses on the history of playing cards; newsletter offers buy/sell/trade ads, articles, etc.

Club/Association

52 Plus Joker
Magazine: Clear the Decks
Bill Coomer, Sec.
1024 South Benton
Cape Girardeau, MO 63701
For those interested in collecting playing cards, antique and unusual decks.

Club/Association

American Game Collectors Association
Newsletter: Game Times
Joe Angiolillo, Pr.
4628 Barlow Dr.
Bartlesville, OK 74006
Focuses on board games as well as puzzles, playing cards, tops, toys, dolls, yo-yos, and outdoor and tabletop action games.

Collector

Ray Hartz
P.O. Box 1002
Westerville, OH 43081
Phone: 614-891-6296   FAX: 614-891-2392
Will pay top dollar for old, unusual playing card and game decks, complete and in excellent condition; U.S. or foreign.

Expert

Full House
Gene Hochman
P.O. Box 4057
Boynton Beach, FL 33424-4057
Conducts mail auctions specializing in playing cards and other gambling memorabilia. *

Expert

Parnell Publishing
Shami & Kathryn Maxwell
P.O. Box 16432
Phoenix, AZ 85011
Phone: 602-279-2358   FAX: 602-279-2358
Author of "Price Guide of Old & Unusual Playing Cards."

Museum/Library

Cincinnati Art Museum
Eden Park
Cincinnati, OH 45202
Phone: 513-721-5204

Museum/Library

Playing Card Museum
Margery B. Griffith, Dir.
Park & Beech Sts.
Cincinnati, OH 45212
Phone: 513-396-5700   FAX: 513-396-6321
Resource for research materials dealing with playing cards; largest playing card collection in the world.

Periodical

Magazine: Playing Card
188 Sheen Lane
East Sheen
London SW1 48LF England *

Repro. Source

U.S. Games Systems Inc.
179 Ludlow St.
Stamford, CT 06902
Phone: 203-353-8400
Authentic reproductions of antique decks from the 15th to 20th centuries. *

POCKET KNIVES

(see also KNIVES, Pocket)

POCKET MIRRORS

(see also ADVERTISING COLLECTIBLES)

Collector

Jerome Schaeper
705 Philadelphia St.
Covington, KY 41011
Phone: 606-581-3729
Tokens, medals, badges, pocket mirrors.

Dealer
Dave Beck
P.O. Box 435
Mediappolis, IA 52637
Phone: 319-394-3943
Buys and sells advertising watch fobs, mirrors and pinbacks; send stamp for illustrated mail auction catalog.

Expert
Chuck Thompson
P.O. Box 11652
Houston, TX 77293
Phone: 713-442-7200

POCKET-SIZE COLLECTIBLES
Collector
B.H. Axler
P.O. Box 1288
Ansonia, NY 10023
Wants any "Pocket Item", i.e. items or gadgets designed to fit in the pocket: tools, lighters, compacts, folding cups, etc.

POLICE & SHERIFF MEMORABILIA
(see also OUTLAW & LAWMAN; WESTERN AMERICANA)

Club/Association
Police Insignia Collectors Association
Newsletter: Police Insignia Collectors Association Newsletter
15 Pond Pl.
Cos Cob, CT 06807
Phone: 203-661-3927 *

Club/Association
Law Enforcement Badge & Patch Collectors Society
P.O. Box 444
Los Alamitos, CA 90720 *

Collector
Robert Kwalwasser
168 Camp Fatima Rd.
Renfrew, PA 16053
Wants police items, political parade torches, canes, guns, tinder pistols.

Collector
Robert Fischer
P.O. Box 9763
Baldwin, MD 21013
Wants old police badges.

Dealer
Baird Co.
P.O. Box 7638
Moreno Valley, CA 92303
Phone: 714-597-4409   FAX: 714-597-0625
Publishes lists of law enforcement memorabilia available; also conducts specialty mail auctions of same.

Expert
Gene's Badges & Emblems
Gene Matzke
2345 S. 28th
Milwaukee, WI 53215-2925
Phone: 414-383-8995
Wants police/fire/sheriffs & related law enforcement badges; also old cabinet police photos, handcuffs, leg irons and related items.

Expert
George E. Virgines
Box 193 - Suburban Route
Rapid City, SD 57701
*Author of "Badges of Law and Order." ***

Museum/Library
New York City Police Academy Museum
235 E. 20th St.
New York, NY 10003
Phone: 212-477-9753

Museum/Library
Suffolk County Police Department Museum
30 Yaphank Ave.
Yaphank, NY 11980
Phone: 516-345-6011

Museum/Library
American Police Hall of Fame & Museum
Magazine: Chief of Police and Police Times
3801 Biscayne Blvd.
Miami, FL 33137
Phone: 305-573-0202   FAX: 305-573-9819
Over 10,000 items on display; equipment, uniforms, firearms, etc. from the 1700's; wants anything related to law enforcement.

Museum/Library
American Police Center & Museum
1705-25 S. State St.
Chicago, IL 60616
Phone: 312-431-0005

Repro. Source
Franklin Mint
U.S. Route 1
Franklin Center, PA 19091
Phone: 215-959-6553 or 800-523-7622
    FAX: 215-459-6880
Reproduction police and sheriffs' badges.

POLITICAL COLLECTIBLES
(see also AUTOGRAPHS; BUTTONS, Pinback; CERAMICS, Political Related; HISTORICAL AMERICANA; PERSONALITIES; PROHIBITION ITEMS)

Auction Service
Ben Corning
10 Lilian Road Ext.
Framingham, MA 01701
Phone: 617-872-2229
*Specializes in mail-bid auctions of political items and historical Americana. ***

Auction Service
Rex Stark Auctions
Rex Stark
49 Wethersfield Road
Bellingham, MA 02019
Phone: 508-966-0994
Conducts mail auctions of quality historical Americana: political, early military, advertising, sports, etc.

Auction Service
David Frent
P.O. Box 455
Oakhurst, NJ 07755
Phone: 201-922-0768
Specializes in mail-bid auctions of political items and historical Americana.

Auction Service
Historicana
Robert Coup
P.O. Box 348
Leola, PA 17540-0348
Phone: 717-656-7780
Specializes in mail-bid auctions of character collectibles, Disneyana, political items & historical Americana; sample catalog $2.

Auction Service
Ohio Boys Video Auction - the Dixeys
626 Arlington Avenue
Mansfield, OH 44903
*Specializes in mail-bid auctions of political items and historical Americana. ***

Auction Service
Anderson Auction
Al Anderson
P.O. Box 644
Troy, OH 45373
Phone: 513-339-0850
Specializes in mail-bid auctions of political items and historical Americana.

Auction Service
Political Gallery, The
Tom Slater
1325 W. 86th St.
Indianapolis, IN 46260
Phone: 317-257-0863
Specializing in mail-bid auctions of Disneyana, historical Americana, toys, political items, and other collectibles.

Auction Service
Local, The
Robert M. Platt
P.O. Box 159
Kennedale, TX 76060
Specializing in the mail-bid auctions of pin-back political buttons of governors, congressional members, mayors, state officials, etc.

Club/Association

Society of Political Item Enthusiasts
Newsletter: Campaign Treasures
Box 159
Kennedale, TX 76060
Phone: 817-535-6283 *

Club/Association

American Political Items Collectors
(APIC)
Newspaper: Political Bandwagon
P.O. Box 340339
San Antonio, TX 78234
Phone: 512-655-8277
Dedicated to the collection, study and preservation of materials relating to the political campaigns of the U.S.

Collector

A. Lear
Box 53
Pipersville, PA 18947
Wants political bandannas, flags, pennants.

Collector

Peggy Dillard
P.O. Box 210904
Nashville, TN 37221
Send SASE and photocopy of political campaign items and receive free appraisal and offer in the mail.

Collector

Americana Resources
Suite 299
18222 Flower Hill Way
Gaithersburg, MD 20879
Wants presidential, paper items: buttons, ribbons, banners, 3-D. *

Collector

Don Beck
Box 15305
Ft. Wayne, IN 46885
Phone: 219-486-3010
Lincoln to Kennedy political pins, medals, flags, banners, autographs.

Collector

Paul Bengston
9283 Franlo Road
Eden Prairie, MN 55347-3000
Phone: 612-829-1326 or 612-522-3868
FAX: 612-522-0025
Wants pre-1964 political buttons, badges, ribbons, banners, tokens, flags, autographs, and related collectibles; send photocopy.

Collector

Cary Demont
P.O. Box 19312
Minneapolis, MN 55419
Phone: 612-922-1617

Wants political pre-1964 buttons, pins, flags, ribbons, banners, and the unusual; also suffrage, prohibition, slavery, and Lindbergh.

Collector

Larry Leedom
7217 Via Rio Nido
Downey, CA 90241
Wants 1840-1896 Presidential campaign ribbons, badges, pins and sulphides.

Collector

John Gearhart
3532 NE 124th
Portland, OR 97230
Phone: 503-255-8108
Buttons, posters, ribbons, banners, etc.

Dealer

Rex Stark
49 Wethersfield Road
Bellingham, MA 02019
Phone: 508-966-0994
Buys & sells political Americana; offers catalog of historical/political Americana for sale.

Dealer

Paul Longo Americana
Paul Longo
P.O. Box 490
South Orleans, MA 02662
Phone: 508-255-5482
Wants political pins, buttons, ribbons, banners, autographs, badges, etc.

Dealer

Robert M. Levine
14342 S. Outer 40 Drive
Chesterfield, MO 63017
Phone: 314-469-6322   FAX: 314-469-6383
Wants any political item; new or old; single or in quantity.

Dealer

Ronald E. Wade
229 Cambridge
Longview, TX 75601
Phone: 903-236-9615
Political buttons/pins JFK and older, posters, 3-dimensional political items, e.g. clocks, glassware, bandanas, etc.

Expert

Richard Friz
RFD 2, Box 155
Peterborough, NH 03458
Phone: 603-563-8155 *

Expert

Hake's Americana & Collectibles Auction
Ted Hake
P.O. Box 1444
York, PA 17405
Phone: 717-848-1333   FAX: 717-848-4977

Specializing in mail-bid auctions of Disneyana, historical Americana, toys, premiums, political items, character and other collectibles.

Expert

U.I. "Chick" Harris
Box 20614
St. Louis, MO 63139
Phone: 314-352-8623
Collector/specialist in all types of political Americana; conducts specialized mail-auctions of political and historical Americana.

Museum/Library

National Museum of American History
14th & Constitution Ave. NW
Washington, DC 20560
Phone: 202-357-2700

Museum/Library

Western Reserve Historical Society
10825 East Blvd.
Cleveland, OH 44106
Phone: 216-721-5722

Museum/Library

Presidential Museum, The
622 North Lee Street
Odessa, TX 79761
Phone: 915-332-7123

Periodical

Newsletter: Frontrunner Newsletter, The
RFD2, Box 155
Peterborough, NH 03458
A bi-monthly publication. *

Periodical

Newspaper: Political Collector, The
P.O. Box 5171
York, PA 17405
Phone: 717-846-0418
A monthly newspaper.

Periodical

Magazine: Political Bandwagon, The
Jeannine Coup
P.O. Box 348
Leola, PA 17540-0348
Phone: 717-656-7780
A monthly publication focusing on political collectibles; sample copy $1.

Franklin D. Roosevelt

Club/Association

Franklin D. Roosevelt Political Items
Collectors
Newsletter: New Deal, The
Robert M. Platt
6604 Anglin Drive
Fort Worth, TX 76119
Phone: 817-535-6283
A quarterly publication of the FDR chapter of the American Political Items Collectors (APIC).

George Bush

Club/Association

Bush Political Items Collectors
Newsletter: Bush Bandwagon
Ronald E. Wade
229 Cambridge
Longview, TX 75601
Phone: 903-236-9615

John F. Kennedy

Club/Association

Kennedy Political Items Collectors
(KPIC)
Newsletter: Hyannisporter
Harvey Goldberg, Ed.
P.O. Box 922
Clark, NJ 07066
Phone: 908-382-4652
*kpic is a world-wide organization for collectors of
Kennedy (and other) political campaign items.*

Richard Nixon

Club/Association

Nixon Political Items Collectors
Newsletter: Checkers
55 Warren Ave.
Plymouth, MA 02360
Phone: 617-746-0344 *

Ronald Reagan

Club/Association

Reagan Political Items Collectors
Newsletter: Reagan Review
Rt. 1, Box 258B
Denison, TX 75020
Phone: 214-465-2514 *

Wendell Willkie

Club/Association

Willkie Political Items Collectors
Newsletter: Willkie-Ites
144 E. Main St.
Bogota, NJ 07603
Phone: 201-342-1070 *

POLYNESIAN COLLECTIBLES

Dealer

Wholesale Rug
2448 Lincoln Hwy.
East Lancaster, PA 17602
Phone: 717-872-2598
*Wants cultural art and artifacts from all the
Polynesian islands; war clubs, items of personal
adornment; also pre-1925 Hawaiian items.*

POOL TABLES

(see also BILLIARD RELATED ITEMS)

PORCELAIN

(see also CERAMICS; DINNERWARE;
FIGURINES; OCCUPIED JAPAN;
ORIENTALIA; REPAIRS &
RESTORATIONS; TABLEWARE)

POSTAGE STAMPS

(see also STAMP COLLECTING)

POSTCARDS

Auction Service

Sally S. Carver Postcard Mail Auctions
179 South St.
Chestnut Hill, MA 02167
Phone: 617-469-9175
*Specializes in better quality postcards. *

Auction Service

McClintock PC Sales
John H. McClintock
P.O. Box 1765
Manassas, VA 22110
Phone: 703-368-2757
*Conducts 4 to 5 illustrated postcard mail auctions
per year; also promotes 9 postcard shows per year.*

Club/Association

Deltiologists of America
Magazine: Postcard Classics
Dr. James Lewis Lowe, Dir.
P.O. Box 8
Norwood, PA 19074
Phone: 215-485-8572
*International postcard society for collectors,
dealers, librarians, and archivist.*

Club/Association

Monumental Postcard Club
Newsletter: MPC Newsletter
Sandy Waters
3013 St. Paul St.
Baltimore, MD 21218-3943
*Non-profit organization open to the public; an-
nual club-sponsored show in October with dealers
from all over the world.*

Club/Association

International Postcard Association,
Inc.
V. Lee Cox, Pres.
Box 66, 1217 F.S.K. Hwy.
Keymar, MD 21757
Phone: 301-775-0188 or 301-775-0190
A club primarily for collectors of postcards.

Club/Association

Postcard History Society
Newsletter: Postcard History Society Bulletin
John H. McClintock, Dir
P.O. Box 1765
Manassas, VA 22110
Phone: 703-368-2757

Club/Association

International Federation of Postcard
Dealers, Inc.
Newsletter: IFPD Newsletter
John H. McClintock, Sec
P.O. Box 1765
Manassas, VA 22110
Phone: 703-368-2757

Club/Association

Denver Postcard Club
Newsletter: DPC Newsletter
George Van Trump, Jr.
P.O. Box 260170
Lakewood, CO 80226
Phone: 303-985-3508

Club/Association

International Postcard Collectors Club,
Von Der Ahe Library
Loyola-Marymount University
7101 W. 80th Street
Los Angeles, CA 90045 *

Collector

Bob & Kay Schies
452 East Bissell Ave.
Oil City, PA 16301
Phone: 814-677-3182
Buying pre-1930 postcards, any amount.

Collector

John H. McClintock
P.O. Box 1765
Manassas, VA 22110
Phone: 703-368-2757
Also promotes postcard shows.

Collector

Gary Olsen
505 S. Royal Ave.
Front Royal, VA 22630
Phone: 703-635-7157 or 703-635-7158
FAX: 703-635-1818
*Wants postcards with maps, music themes, real
estate subjects and/or famous "persons" autog-
raphs.*

Dealer

Cartomania Plus
Siegfried Feller
8 Amherst Rd.
Pelham, MA 01002
Phone: 413-253-3115

Dealer

Joseph Jordan Antiques
Joseph Jordan
Rte. 1
Cape Neddick, ME 03902
Phone: 207-363-2544 *

Dealer

S. Dobres Postcards
Sheldon Dobres
P.O. Box 1855
Baltimore, MD 12203-1855
Phone: 301-486-6569 or 301-539-3070
Postcards bought and sold; top prices paid for pre-1950 U.S. and foreign postcards.

Dealer

Mashburn Books & Cards
P.O. Box 609
Enka, NC 28728
Phone: 704-667-1427 *

Dealer

Shiloh Postcards
Box 20004
Sclayton, GA 30525
*Sells supplies, wholesale card lots and better cards, including original famous art cards. **

Expert

Sally Carver
179 South St.
Chestnut Hill, MA 02167
Phone: 617-469-9175
*Specializes in all better-quality pre-1930 postcards. **

Expert

Deltiologists of America
Dr. James Lewis Lowe, Dir.
P.O. Box 8
Norwood, PA 19074
Phone: 215-485-8572

Expert

Memory Lane Postcards, Inc.
V. Lee Cox
Box 66, 1217 F.S.K. Hwy.
Keymar, MD 21757
Phone: 301-775-0188 or 301-775-0190

Expert

Past & Present
Susan Nicholson
P.O. Box 595
Lisle, IL 60532
Phone: 208-964-5240
Buys and sells rare and unusual postcards, Victorian valentines, periodicals, advertising trade cards, etc.

Museum/Library

Lake County Museum, Curt Teich Postcard Archives
Journal: Image File
Katherine Hamilton-Smith
Lakewood Forest Preserve
Wauconda, IL 60084
Phone: 708-526-8638   FAX: 708-526-0024
Archive of N.A. postcards from 1898-1974; formerly industrial archives of Curt Teich Printing Co., Chicago; also postcard albums.

Periodical

Reflections of a Bygone Age
Magazine: Picture Postcard Monthly
Brian & Mary Lund
15 Debdale Lane
Keyworth
Nottinghamshire NG12 SHT Eng.
Magazine designed for collectors of old picture postcards whatever your interest, theme or area; events, clubs, checklists, values, etc.

Periodical

Magazine: Postcard Dealer, The
John H. McClintock
P.O. Box 1765
Manassas, VA 22110
Phone: 703-368-2757

Periodical

Barr Enterprises
Newspaper: Barr's Post Card News
70 S. 6th St.
Lansing, IA 52151-0310
Phone: 319-538-4500 or 800-397-0145
                          FAX: 319-538-4038
A weekly deltiology newspaper containing postcard events, shows, news, articles, club directory, current prices, ads, etc.

Periodical

Magazine: Postcard Collector
121 N. Main St.
P.O. Box 337
Iola, WI 54945
Phone: 715-445-5000 or 800-331-0038
                          FAX: 715-445-4053
The Hobby's leading publication; best source to buy, sell, learn about postcards.

Periodical

Gloria's Corner
Newsletter: Gloria's Corner
Gloria Jackson, Ed.
P.O. Box 507
Denison, TX 75021-0507
Phone: 903-463-3662 or 903-463-4878
                          FAX: 903-463-3426
A bi-monthly newsletter about postcards; trades, buying, selling, auctions, etc.

Aviation Related

(see also AVIATION MEMORABILIA)

Club/Association

Post Card Collectors Club
c/o Aerophilatelic Federation
P.O. Box 1239
Elgin, IL 60121
Phone: 708-888-1907
Members collect aviation related postcards, may be blank or depict planes, blimps, balloons, rockets or missiles.

Bank Related

Collector

Wilson's Syngraphics
John & Nancy Wilson
P.O. Box 27185
Milwaukee, WI 53227
Phone: 414-545-8636
Wants any pre-1934 paper money issued in the U.S.; also wants any postcards depicting banks.

Chuck Wagon Related

Misc. Service

Food Celebrity Service
Newsletter: Packaged Chili & Jerky Report
Chuck Thompson
P.O. Box 11652
Houston, TX 77293
Phone: 713-442-7200
Cowboy Chuck Wagon food researcher, historian, storyteller; wants postcards of old chuck wagons; columnist and lecturer.

Dance Related

Collector

Dr. William G. Sommer, MD
9 W. 10th St.
New York, NY 10011
Phone: 212-260-0999
Wants post cards depicting Africa-American dancing, e.g. Cake Walk, Jitterbug; also Waltz, Tango, etc. & dance items in other media.

Florida Related

Collector

Steve Hess
P.O. Box 3476
De Land, FL 32720-3476
Phone: 904-736-1067
Buying Florida postcards: small town, depots, blacks; anything pre-1915 Florida.

Foreign

Dealer

Jerry's Cards & Collectibles
Jerry Rubackin
Box 1271
Framingham, MA 01701
Phone: 508-788-0946
Always wants Honeymooners items and foreign postcards from Philippines and Switzerland.

Pennsylvania Related

Collector

Richard A. Wood
P.O. Box 22165
Juneau, AK 99802
Phone: 907-586-6748 or 907-789-8450
Wants postcards of Penna. Pike County towns: Milford, Twin Lakes, Shohola, Parker's Glen, Walker Lake, Woodtown; also ALASKA postcards.

Piano Related

Collector

Janice E. Kelsh
Suite 202
5815 N. Sheridan Rd.
Chicago, IL 60660
Phone: 312-271-2970
Interested in obtaining miniature pianos of all kinds; also want postcards depicting pianos.

Pontiac & Olds Related

Collector

Alfred Sherman
247 Parkview Ave. Apt. 5P
Bronxville, NY 10708
Phone: 914-965-4200
Wants 1942, 1946, 1947, 1948 Pontiac and Oldsmobile postcards.

Sports Related

Collector

Sportcards & Collectibles
166 Grove St.
Shelton, CT 06484
Wants sports postcards picturing boxing, baseball, football, stadiums, players, etc.; also buys sports cards - boxful or singles.

Washington DC Related

Collector

Newsletter: Wright Flyer
Jerry A. McCoy
1960 Biltmore St. NW #5
Washington, DC 20009-1538
Phone: 202-462-4790
Wants only real photo postcards of Washington, DC.

POSTCARDS (MODERN)

Periodical

Reflections of a Bygone Age
Magazine: Collect Modern postcards
Brian Lund
15 Debdale Lane
Keyworth
Nottinghamshire NG12 SHT Eng.
A bi-monthly magazine for collectors of modern picture postcards from 1950; featuring new issues, events, shops, values, etc.

POSTERS

(see also ADVERTISING COLLECTIBLES,
Posters; MARINE CORPS ITEMS;
MILITARIA; MOVIE POSTERS)

Auction Service

Miscellaneous Man
George Theofiles
Box 1776
New Freedom, PA 17349
Phone: 717-235-4766   FAX: 717-235-2853
Conducts mail-bid poster auctions.

Auction Service

Poster Mail Auction Co.
R. Neil/ Elaine Reynolds
#2 Patrick St.
Box 133
Waterford, VA 22190
Phone: 703-822-3574
Conducts 4 to 6 mail/telephone auctions per year of original vintage posters; 4 catalogs for $12.

Club/Association

Poster Society
Newsletter: P.S. Newsletter
138 W. 18th St.
New York, NY 10011
Phone: 201-247-4510 *

Collector

Nancy Steinbock Posters & Prints
Nancy Steinbock
197 Holmes Dale
Albany, NY 12208
Phone: 518-438-1577
Buys and sells posters 1880-present; subjects: war, travel, circus, literary, political, advertising, etc.; American or foreign.

Dealer

Fine Old Posters
R. Neil/ Elaine Reynolds
1015 King Street
Alexandria, VA 22314
Phone: 703-684-3656
Buys and sells hundreds of original vintage posters.

Expert

Fusco & Four, Associates
Tony Fusco
One Murdock Terrace
Brighton, MA 02135
Phone: 617-787-2637   FAX: 617-782-4430
Author of "Official Identification & Price Guide to Posters"; offers curatorial services for vintage 1870-1940 poster collectors.

Expert

Miscellaneous Man
George Theofiles
Box 1776
New Freedom, PA 17349
Phone: 717-235-4766   FAX: 717-235-2853
Since 1970 offering catalogs of rare posters and early advertising and ephemera on hundreds of subjects. Descriptive flyer available.

POSTMARKS

(see also STAMP COLLECTING, Postmarks)

POTATO RELATED COLLECTIBLES

Museum/Library

Potato Museum, The
Newsletter: Peelings
Meredith & Tom Hughes
P.O. Box 791
Great Falls, VA 22066
Phone: 703-759-6714
Exhibits the social history and influence of the potato worldwide; extensive potato library, archives and memorabilia collection.

POT LIDS

Collector

James Hagenbuch
102 Jefferson St.
East Greenville, PA 18041
Phone: 215-679-5849
Wants American pot lids for personal collection.

Expert

Daniel M. Sourbeer Antiques
Daniel Sourbeer
Box 10614
St. Petersburg, FL 33733
Phone: 813-866-3873
*Wants lids from small 19th-century ceramic containers that at one time held ointments, creams, or soaps. ***

POTTERY

(see also CERAMICS; COOKIE JARS;
DINNERWARE; FIGURINES; FLOWER
"FROGS"; REPAIRS & RESTORATIONS;
SALT & PEPPER SHAKERS; STEINS;
TILES)

POWDER HORNS

(see also ARMS & ARMOR; FIREARMS)

Collector

David A. Galliher
2500 W. Berwyn Rd.
Muncie, IN 47304
Phone: 317-289-2233
Wants early powder horns, engraved or with historical significance.

POWDER JARS

Collector

Darryl Rehr
11433 Rochester Ave. #303
Los Angeles, CA 90025
Phone: 213-447-5229
Wants all kinds of frosted figural glass powder jars with animals or other figures on the lid; please send photo.

PREHISTORIC ARTIFACTS

(see also ARCHAEOLOGICAL ARTIFACTS;
FOSSILS; INDIAN ITEMS; MINERALS)

Collector

Scott Young
P.O. box 8452
Port St. Lucie, FL 34985
Phone: 407-878-5634
Buys, sells, trades American Indian relics, prehistoric pottery points, tools, bone, etc.; one item or whole collection.

Collector

Hothem House
Lar Hothem
P.O. Box 458
Lancaster, OH 43130
Phone: 614-653-9030
Wants prehistoric American Indian artifacts.

Dealer

Rich Relics
Richard B. Troyanowski
P.O. Box 432
Sandia Park, NM 87047
Phone: 505-281-2611 or 505-281-2329
Buys/sells prehistoric/historic Indian artifacts, cowboy, militaria, old world antiquities & coins, fossils & ethnographic collectibles.

PREMIUMS

(see also CEREAL BOX PREMIUMS; COLLECTIBLES; RADIO SHOW PREMIUMS; TELEVISION SHOWS & MEMORABILIA)

PRINTING EQUIPMENT

(see also BOOK ARTS)

Club/Association

American Printing History Association
Newsletter: APHA Newsletter
Grand Central Station
P.O. Box 4922
New York, NY 10163 *

Collector

David W. Peat
1225 Carroll White
Indianapolis, IN 46219
Phone: 317-357-6895 or 317-351-4606
Wants antique printers type, catalogs of printers type (typefounders specimen books), small presses, other 19th cent. printing items.

Collector

James L. Weygand
P.O. Box 215
Nappanee, IN 46550
Phone: 219-773-4832
Wants table-top printing presses, catalogs, instruction booklets, literature, equipment, accessories, etc.

Museum/Library

Printers Row Printing Museum
731 S. Plymouth Ct.
Chicago, IL 60605
Phone: 312-987-1059

Type Founding Items

Collector

David W. Peat
1225 Carroll White
Indianapolis, IN 46219
Phone: 317-357-6895 or 317-351-4606
Wants old type casting (founding) equipment: hand molds, mats (matrices) for casting antique type, Bruce type caster, catalogs.

PRINTS

(see also ART; ILLUSTRATORS; COLLECTIBLES (MODERN), Prints; REPAIR & RESTORATIONS, Paper Items; WALLACE NUTTING)

Club/Association

American Historical Print Collectors Society
Magazine: Imprint
P.O. Box 1532
Fairfield, CT 06430
Phone: 914-795-5266
Objects are to the foster preservation, study and exhibition of historical American prints from the 17th through the 19th century.

Club/Association

American Antique Graphics Society
Joe Davidson
5185 Windfall Rd.
Medina, OH 44256
Phone: 216-723-7172
Members interested in graphic arts prints: from medieval, natural history to cigar labels.

Dealer

Fusco & Four, Associates
Tony Fusco
One Murdock Terrace
Brighton, MA 02135
Phone: 617-787-2637   FAX: 617-782-4430
Specializing in 20th century European and American works on paper, 1900-1950, especially WPA, regionalists, and urban social realists.

Dealer

Old Print Shop
Kenneth Newman
150 Lexington Ave. at 30th St.
New York, NY 10016
Phone: 212-683-3950
Wants 18th-20th century American prints; Currier & Ives, Endicott Hill, large folio American town views, marines, maps, historicals.

Dealer

W. Graham Arader III
1000 Boxwood Court
King Of Prussia, PA 19406
Phone: 215-825-6570
Buys & sells Audubon and other fine prints: Indians, natural history, sporting,, Currier & Ives, etc.; also maps, paintings and books.

Dealer

Old Print Gallery, The
James & Judith Blakely
1220 31st St. NW
Washington, DC 20007
Phone: 202-965-1818   FAX: 202-965-1869
Wants antique prints: city views, historical scenes, Currier & Ives, Western, natural history, sporting, military and nautical scenes.

Dealer

Print Portfolio
Monica Burdeshaw
4701 Sangamore Rd.
Bethesda, MD 20816
Phone: 301-229-5800
Buys and sells fine prints.

Dealer

Museum Shop, Ltd.
Richard Kornemann
30 East Patrick St.
Frederick, MD 21701
Phone: 301-695-0424
Specializes on Japanese ukiyoe woodblock prints, and 1930's era by Grant Wood, Whistler, T.H. Benton, WPA artists, etc.

Dealer

Aunti-Q
A. Thomas Fleming
2200 Columbia Pike, Apt. #105
Arlington, VA 22204-4422
Phone: 703-920-9093
Wants to buy paintings and prints.

Dealer

Newsletter: Art Collectors Quarterly, The
Elaine Kwan, ISA
860 Cedar Lane
Northbrook, IL 60062
Phone: 708-564-1660 or 708-205-1459
FAX: 708-664-1660
A quarterly newsletter serving as a vehicle for the interchange of artwork in the marketplace.

Dealer

Gallery Graphics, Inc.
P.O. Box 502
Noel, MO 64854
Phone: 417-475-6367
*Wants color prints, pictures, calendars, trade cards and pre-1930 books; wants prints by Pears Soap, Louis Icart, and others. *

Dealer
Antiques & Art Galleries
Steve Whysel
101 N. Main
Bentonville, AR 72712
Phone: 501-273-7701 or 501-444-9911
Wants pre-1920 etchings of botanicals (flowers), birds, fishing and horse racing scenes, Civil War soldiers, horses, battles, etc.

Periodical
Journal: Journal of the Print World
1000 Winona Road
Meredith, NH 03253-9599
Phone: 603-279-6479
A quarterly newspaper with articles, advertising and classifieds focusing on antique and contemporary prints and artists.

Periodical
Newsletter: Print Trader
67-62 79th Street
Middle Village, NY 11379
A newsletter about American print artists and their work. *

Periodical
Magazine: American Print Review
P.O. Box 6909
Chicago, IL 60680
Has ads and articles about print auctions, prices, etc. *

Periodical
Art On Paper Incorporated
Magazine: Prints Magazine
P.O. Box 1468
Alton, IL 62002
Phone: 618-402-1468
Magazine for collectors of prints and other art collectibles. *

Audubon

Dealer
Audubon Prints & Books
Ed Kenney
Suite 520
499 South Capitol Street SW
Washington, DC 20003
Phone: 703-759-5567 or 202-484-3334
Buys & sells natural history prints and books by John James Audubon; also prints by Wilson, Gould, Catesby, Bodmer, Catlin and others.

Dealer
Newsletter: Audubon Newsletter
Joel & Jean Mattison
4700 North Habana Ave.
Tampa, FL 33614
Phone: 813-879-2908
The Mattisons publish a newsletter focusing on articles about and values of Audubon prints.

Museum/Library
John James Audubon State Park and Museum
P.O. Box 576
Henderson, KY 42420
Phone: 502-826-2247 or 502-827-1893
FAX: 502-826-2286

Botanical

Museum/Library
Hunt Institute for Botanical Documentation
Newsletter: Huntia
James J. White
c/o Carnegie Mellon Univ.
Pittsburgh, PA 15213
Phone: 412-268-2434
Collection documents botanical imagery from the Renaissance onward.

Currier & Ives

Collector
Bob Bascom Prints
Bob Bascom
Box 4334
Burlington, VT 05406
Phone: 802-893-4082
Wants Currier and Ives original prints; also other medium or large 19th century American prints.

Dealer
Dealer
P.O. Box 157
Orleans, MA 02653
Wants Currier and Ives, and Kellogg original prints; also pre-1970 dolls. *

Dealer
Robert Searjeant
Box 23942
Rochester, NY 14692 *

Expert
Rudisill's Alt Print Haus
John & Barbara Rudisill
3 Lakewood
Medfield, MA 02052
Phone: 508-359-2261
Buys and sells original Currier & Ives prints.

Museum/Library
Museum of the City of New York
5th Avenue at 103rd St.
New York, NY 10029
Phone: 212-534-1672

Frederic Remington

Expert
Harold Samuels
Star Route Box 1281
Corrales, NM 87048 *

French Boudoir

Dealer
David Chase Gallery
Cliff Catania
P.O. Box 330
Ephrata, PA 17522
Phone: 717-733-4243   FAX: 717-733-4243
Wants Icart-like etchings by Ablett, Grellet, Felix, Helleu, Milliere, Robbe, Hardy, Meunier, etc.

Icart

Collector
Ed Meschi
Box 550
Monroeville, NJ 08343
Phone: 609-358-7293
Wants Louis Icart etchings.

Collector
Carol Haley
760 Madison Ave.
New York, NY 10021
Phone: 212-988-5181 *

Collector
Bill Holland
107 S. 18th St.
Philadelphia, PA 19103
Phone: 215-647-7099
Wants Louis Icart etchings. *

Collector
Diana Peters
2685 S.W. 17th Ave.
Coconut Grove, FL 33133
Phone: 305-854-4651 *

Dealer
H & D Press, Inc.
Carole Hibel
P.O. Box 1284
Staten Isl., NY 10314
Phone: 800-426-3357

Dealer
David Chase Gallery
Cliff Catania
P.O. Box 330
Ephrata, PA 17522
Phone: 717-733-4243   FAX: 717-733-4243
Buys and sells original Icart etchings; assisting major collectors. Author of "Complete Etchings of Louis Icart" (1990-Schiffer Pub.)

Dealer
Adrienne Leff
9479 South Dixie Hwy.
Miami, FL 33156
Phone: 305-667-4214   FAX: 305-661-3449
Wants original Louis Icart etchings, oils and complete books.

Expert

Cherub Antiques Gallery
Ron Faucette
2918 "M" St. NW
Washington, DC 20007
Phone: 202-337-2224 *

Illustrators

Dealer

Fromer's Antiques
Barb & Dan Fromer
Box 224
New Market, MD 21774
Phone: 301-831-6712
Antique tools; also wants Maxfield Parrish prints.

Leroy Neiman

Dealer

Hammer Graphics Gallery
Ralph Olsen
33 W. 57th St.
New York, NY 10019
Phone: 212-644-4405

Prang-Mark

Club/Association

Prang-Mark Society
Newsletter: Prang-Mark Society Newsletter
P.O. Box 306
Watkins Glen, NY 14891
Phone: 607-535-4004 *

Vanity Fair

Collector

Paul Davis
306 Landsende Rd.
Devon, PA 19333
Phone: 215-644-1216
Wants Vanity Fair caricature prints.

Wildlife

Museum/Library

American Museum of Natural History
Central Park West & 79th St.
New York, NY 10024
Phone: 212-769-5000

Woodblock (American)

Dealer

P. Hastings Falk, Inc.
Pete Falk
170 Boston Post Rd., Box 150
Madison, CT 06443
Phone: 203-245-2246
Buys and sells color woodblock prints by American artists; 1890's to 1920's.

Woodblock (Jacoulet)

Auction Service

Robert C. Eldred & Co.
P.O. Box 796
East Dennis, MA 02641
Phone: 508-385-3116
Specializes in the sale of 20th century Japanese-style woodblock prints by artist Paul Jacoulet.

Woodblock (Japanese)

(see also ART, Oriental; ORIENTALIA)

Club/Association

Ukiyo-E Society of America, Inc.
Newsletter: President's Newsletter
Anita V. Beenk, Pres.
FDR Station
P.O. Box 665
New York, NY 10150
Promotes the study/appreciation of Japanese woodblock prints through monthly meetings, seminars & exhibitions; also publishes Journal.

Collector

Georgia Cash
10799 SW 44th St.
Miami, FL 33165
Phone: 305-223-6050

Dealer

Ronin Gallery
Roni Neuer
605 Madison Ave.
New York, NY 10022
Specializes in Japanese woodblock prints and publishes catalogs on specialty artists.

Dealer

John Bradley Gallery
John Bradley
RR 3 Box 502 Burlingham Rd.
Pine Bush, NY 12566
Phone: 914-744-3642

Dealer

Gilbert Luber Gallery
1220 Walnut Street
Philadelphia, PA 19107
Specializes in Japanese woodblock prints; also carries general books on Japanese prints and art.

Expert

Schweitzer Japanese Prints, Inc.
Paul R. Schweitzer
6313 Lenox Rd.
Bethesda, MD 20817
Phone: 301-229-6574

Museum/Library

Honolulu Academy of Fine Arts
900 S. Beretania St.
Honolulu, HI 96814
Phone: 808-538-3693

Yard-Long

Expert

Those Wonderful Yard-Long Prints & More
Bill & June Keagy
P.O. Box 106
Bloomfield, IN 47424
Phone: 812-384-3471
Co-authors with Charles and Joan Rhoden of "Those Wonderful Yard-Long Prints"; also wants to buy yard-long prints.

Expert

Charles G. Rhoden
605 N. Main
Georgetown, IL 61846
*Co-author of "Those Wonderful Yard-Long Prints." ***

Repro. Source

Nostalgia Print Company
1118 Junlatta St.
Burlington, KS 66839

PROHIBITION ITEMS

(see also BREWERIANA; PERSONALITIES (CRIMINAL); POLITICAL COLLECTIBLES; SALOON COLLECTIBLES; WHISKEY INDUSTRY ITEMS)

Club/Association

Partisan Prohibition Historical Society
P.O. Box 2635
Denver, CO 80201
Phone: 303-572-0646 *

Collector

Cary Demont
P.O. Box 19312
Minneapolis, MN 55419
Phone: 612-922-1617
Wants political pre-1964 buttons, pins, flags, ribbons, banners, and the unusual; also suffrage, prohibition, slavery, and Lindbergh.

Expert

Chicago's Roaring 20's
Michael Y. Graham
345 Cleveland Ave.
Libertyville, IL 60048
Phone: 708-362-4808
Specializes in prohibition-era (1919-1933) gangster, speak-easy, political, breweriana, and saloon-items; emphasis on Chicago area.

Expert

Richard M. Bueschel
414 N. Prospect Manor Ave.
Mt. Prospect, IL 60056
Phone: 708-253-0791
Wants speakeasy photos, business cards, paper ephemera, bootleg liquor, flappers, rum running liquor trade personalities, etc.

PUPPETS

(see also VENTRILOQUIST ITEMS)

Club/Association

Puppeteers of America, Inc.
Magazine: Puppetry Journal
Gayle Schluter, Membr
5 Cricklewood Path
Pasadena, CA 91107

Museum/Library

Ontario Puppetry Association Museum
171 Avondale Avenue
Willowdale
Ontario M2N 2V4 Canada
Phone: 416-222-9029

Museum/Library

Bread & Puppet Museum
Rte. 122
Glover, VT 05839
Phone: 802-525-3031
A giant collection of puppets, masks and related graphics and paintings.

Museum/Library

Library & Museum of the Performing Arts, Shelby Cullom Davis Museum
111 Amsterdam Ave.
New York, NY 10023
Phone: 212-870-1613

PURSES

(see also CLOTHING & ACCESSORIES, Vintage)

Collector

Barbara Rossi
712 27th Ave.
San Mateo, CA 94403 *

Expert

Irene Spaulding
P.O. Box 38
Amherst, NH 03031
Specialist in antique purses and vintage clothing.

Expert

Evelyn Haertig
P.O. Box 5457
Carmel-By-The-Sea, CA 93921 *

Museum/Library

Boston Museum of Fine Arts
465 Huntington Avenue
Boston, MA 02115
Phone: 617-267-9300
An outstanding collection of purses.

Repair Service

Abraham & Strauss
420 Fulton St.
Brooklyn, NY 11233 *

PUZZLES

(see also GAMES)

Expert

Anne D. Williams
Economics Dept.
Bates College
Lewiston, ME 04240
Phone: 207-783-8732
Wants jigsaw puzzles and related ephemera & company records; wood, die-cut, etc.; author of many publications/books about puzzles.

Jigsaw

Club/Association

American Game Collectors Association
Newsletter: Game Times
Joe Angiolillo, Pr.
4628 Barlow Dr.
Bartlesville, OK 74006
Focuses on board games as well as puzzles, playing cards, tops, toys, dolls, yo-yos, and outdoor and tabletop action games.

Collector

Donald Sheldon
P.O. Box 3313
Trenton, NJ 08619
Phone: 609-588-5403
Wants jigsaw and frame tray puzzles with outerspace scenes, pre-1965; also outerspace game boards, greeting cards, coloring books, toys.

Collector

Puzzle Pit, The
Harry L. Rinker
5093 Vera Cruz Road
Zionsville, PA 18092
Phone: 215-965-1122   FAX: 215-965-1124
Wants wooden, cardboard jigsaw puzzles: those with advertising, mystery, personality, cartoon character, depression era, WWII theme.

Collector

Jim Rohacs
9721 Lomond Dr.
Manassas, VA 22110
Phone: 703-369-5578
Wants pre-1950's puzzles.

Expert

Chris McCann
658 MacElroy Road
Ballston Lake, NY 12019
Phone: 518-877-7303
Researcher of cardboard jigsaw puzzles of the Depression era; has computer database of more than 3000 titles; wants more.

Repro. Source

Harold Fessler
3103 34th Ave. Dr., W.
Bradenton, FL 34205
Phone: 813-756-9891

Custom wooden jigsaw puzzles made from your poster or print; other puzzles in stock.

Mechanical

Collector

Tom Rodgers
1466 West Wesley Rd.
Atlanta, GA 30327
Phone: 404-351-7744
Wants mechanical puzzles: puzzle jugs, trick locks, puzzle trade cards, folding puzzles, paper & string puzzles, etc.; NO jigsaws.

Expert

Jerry Slocum
P.O. Box 1635
Beverly Hills, CA 90213
Phone: 213-273-2270   FAX: 213-273-2270
Wants mechanical & dexterity puzzles, trick locks, trick matchsafes, folding puzzles, advertising string puzzles, puzzle trade cards.

Mechanical (Rubik's Cubes)

Collector

Just Puzzles
Peter M. Beck
54 Richwood Place
Denville, NJ 07834
Phone: 201-627-1458
Wants to buy any type of Rubik's cube memorabilia; buys and sells all forms of mechanical puzzles; send SASE for brochure.

PYROGRAPHY ITEMS

Collector

John Lewis
912 W. 8th St.
Loveland, CO 80537
Want quality "burnt wood" items such as plaques, boxes and furniture; also wants catalogs, wood burning kits, and books on pyrography. *

QUILTS

(see also FOLK ART; REPAIRS & RESTORATIONS, Textiles; TEXTILES)

Club/Association

National Quilting Association, Inc., The
Magazine: Patchwork Patter
P.O. Box 393
Ellicott City, MD 21043
Phone: 301-461-5733
Purpose is to stimulate, maintain and record interest in all matters pertaining to the making, collecting and preserving of quilts.

Club/Association

American Quilter's Society
Newsletter: American Quilter
P.O. Box 3290
Paducah, KY 42001 *

Collector

Michael Council
689 S. 3rd St.
Columbus, OH 43206
Phone: 614-444-0700 or 800-544-4117
Wants pre-1950 quilts and paisley shawls.

Collector

Evelyn Gibson
137 E. Main St.
Galesburg, IL 61401
Phone: 309-343-2001 *

Dealer

Kittelberger Galleries
Bryan Kittelberger
82 1/2 E. Main St.
Webster, NY 14580
Phone: 716-265-1230

Dealer

John Saul
P.O. Box 448
Tyler, TX 75701
Phone: 214-593-4668 *

Dealer

Missouri Antiques
David & Marci Van Ausdall
666-840 Spring Creek Dr.
Westwood, CA 96137
Phone: 916-256-3041
Buys and sells antique quilts, linens, textiles and antique sewing items.

Expert

Ardis & Robert James Quilt Collection, The
Ardis & Robert James
80 Ludlow Dr.
Chappaqua, NY 10514
Phone: 914-666-3774
Buys, sells, exhibits, lends, lectures and writes about quilts; collection featured in several publications.

Expert

Heritage Antiques, Inc.
Suzy McLennan Anderson
65 East Main St.
Holmdel, NJ 07733
Phone: 908-946-8801
Authenticates, buys, sells, appraises, lectures; author of "The Collectors Guide to Quilts."

Expert

Yvonne Khin
9459 Longs Mill Rd.
Rocky Ridge, MD 21778-8507
Phone: 301-898-0091
Author of "Collector's Dictionary of Quilt Names and Patterns" (1980).

Museum/Library

New England Quilt Museum
256 Market St.
Lowell, MA 01852
Phone: 617-452-4207

Museum/Library

Doll & Quilts Barn
Yvonne Khin
9459 Longs Mill Rd.
Rocky Ridge, MD 21778-8507
Phone: 301-898-0091
Quilt museum offering quilt repairs, enlarging, duplicating, quilting classes, storage, and research.

Periodical

Newsletter: Vintage Quilt Newsletter
311 West 6th
Alice, TX 78332

Periodical

Magazine: Quilters Newsletter
P.O. Box 394
Wheat Ridge, CO 80033
Phone: 303-420-4272 *

Repair Service

Doll & Quilts Barn
Yvonne Khin
9459 Longs Mill Rd.
Rocky Ridge, MD 21778-8507
Phone: 301-898-0091
Quilt museum offering quilt repairs, enlarging, duplicating, quilting classes, storage, and research.

RADIO SHOW PREMIUMS

(see also CHARACTER COLLECTIBLES; COLLECTIBLES; COWBOY HEROES)

Auction Service

Memory Tree
1546-10 Simpson St.
Madison, WI 53713
Phone: 608-222-2418   FAX: 608-222-6935
Conducts specialty mail auctions of cereal boxes and backs, character items, premiums, rings and classes.

Collector

Bruce Thalberg
23 Mountain View Dr.
Weston, CT 06883
Phone: 203-227-8175
Wants Lone Ranger, Sky King, Space Patrol, Tom Mix, Roy Rogers, The Shadow, Capt. Midnight, Terry & the Pirates, etc. items.

Collector

David Welch
RR 2, Box 233
Murphysboro, IL 62966
Phone: 618-687-2282
Wants all give-away or send-away items offered through radio programs and relating to TV, sports, comic, cartoon or movie characters.

Collector

Rex Miller
Rt. 1, Box 457
East Prairie, MO 63845
Phone: 314-649-5048
*Wants Capt. Midnight, Ellery Queen, rings, Superman items, etc. *

Collector

Jim Harmon
634 South Orchard Dr.
Burbank, CA 91506
*Wants radio premiums and tapes, comic books, and comic strips. *

Expert

Norm & Cathy Vigue
62 Bailey St.
Stoughton, MA 02072
Phone: 617-344-5441

Expert

Tomart Publications
Tom Tumbusch
P.O. Box 292102
Dayton, OH 45429
Phone: 513-294-2250
Buys radio, cereal, comic book, etc. premiums, i.e. rings, badges, etc.; author of "Illustrated Radio Premium Catalog & Price Guide."

Periodical

Magazine: Box Top Bonanza
Joel Smilgis
3403 46th Ave.
Moline, IL 61265
Phone: 309-797-3677
A bi-monthly magazine focusing on radio & TV premiums, character, comic, western, and adventure collectibles.

Captain Midnight

Collector

DeWayne Nall
P.O. Box 555
Cleburne, TX 76033
Phone: 817-641-5148
Wants rings, scopes, decoders, manuals, anything relating to Capt. Midnight.

Jimmie Allen

Collector

Jack Deveny
6805 Cheyenne Trail
Edina, MN 55439-1158
Phone: 612-941-2457
Wants Jimmie Allen Flying Club wings, I.D. bracelets, knife, whistles, maps, blotters, membership cards, aircraft models, etc.

Western Stars

(see also COWBOY HEROES)

Collector

Mark Dubiel
2336 Yemans
Hamtramck, MI 48212
*Wants Lone Ranger, Hopalong, Daniel Boone,
Gabby Hayes, Dale Evans, Annie Oakley, Sky
King, Buffalo Bill, Tom Mix, Gene Autry, etc.* *

RADIOS

(see also RADIO Shows, Old Time;
TELEGRAPH ITEMS; TELEVISIONS)

Club/Association

New England Antique Radio Club
Sue Bunis
RR1, Box 36
Bradford, NH 03221
Phone: 603-938-5051
For antique radio collectors, restorers and enthusiasts; also holds quaterly swap meets.

Club/Association

Antique Wireless Association
Newsletter: Old Timer's Bulletin
Bruce Kelley
#4 Main St.
Holcomb, NY 14469
Phone: 716-657-7489
*Purpose is to document and preserve the history of
radio and television artifacts.*

Club/Association

Antique Radio Club of America
Newsletter: Antique Radio Gazette, The
James Rankin
3445 Adaline Dr.
Stow, OH 44224

Club/Association

North American Radio Archives
Newsletter: NARA News
P.O. Box 118781
Cincinnati, OH 45211 *

Club/Association

Indiana Historical Radio Society
Dr. Edmund E. Taylor
245 N. Oakland Ave.
Indianapolis, IN 46201-3360
Phone: 317-638-1641
*Society of antique radio collectors who meet quarterly in Indiana; sponsors swap-meets, auctions,
museum projects, contests.*

Club/Association

Vintage Radio & Phonograph Society,
Inc.
Newsletter: Reproducer, The
C.F. Crandell, Pres.
P.O. Box 165345
Irving, TX 75016
Phone: 214-337-2823 or 214-315-2553

*Purpose is to preserve early radios, phonographs,
and related material and to conduct historical
research of same.*

Club/Association

Southern California Antique Radio
Society
Magazine: California Antique Radio Gazette_w08
Edward Sheldon
656 Gravilla Place
La Jolla, CA 92037

Collector

Radio Man, The
Marty & Sue Bunis
RR 1, Box 36
Bradford, NH 03221
Phone: 603-938-5051
*Collector of old and unusual radios, especially
novelty sets and 1950's/1960's transistors. Authors of book of antique radios.*

Collector

Alvin Heckard
R.D. 1, Box 88
Lewistown, PA 17044
Phone: 717-248-7071 or 717-248-2816
*Wants wood table model radios, colored bakelite
and plastic radios; also any parts, tubes, literature, service manuals, advertising, etc.*

Collector

Dave Walters
13805 Florida Ave.
Cresaptown, MD 21502
Phone: 310-729-3133
Wants old radios and radio tubes; pre-1940.

Collector

Donald O. Patterson
636 Cambridge Road
Augusta, GA 30909
Phone: 404-738-7227
*Wants 1920's battery radios; Zenith Stratosphere;
novelty radios, e.g. 1939 RCA World's Fair, etc.*

Collector

Gary B. Schneider
9511 Sunrise Blvd. #J-23
North Royalton, OH 44133
Phone: 216-582-3094
*Wants pre-1940 radio items: radios, tubes, parts,
speakers; also technical radio magazines, catalogs, books, advertising, etc.*

Collector

Larry Spilkin
P.O. Box 5039
Southfield, MI 48086-5039
Phone: 313-642-3722
Wants Catalin & Bakelite radios especially colored, marbelized or Art Deco styles.

Collector

Jerry Probst
P.O. Box 45
Janesville, WI 53547-0045
Phone: 608-752-2816   FAX: 608-752-7691
Wants AM and battery radios.

Collector

Paul Thompson
315 Larkspur Dr.
Santa Maria, CA 93455
Phone: 805-934-2778
*Wants Atwater Kent "breadboard" radios and
parts for same; also early battery radios, crystal
sets, parts, speakers, tubes and magazines.*

Dealer

Radio Relics
Brian Berry
P.O. Box 75
Germantown, MD 20875
Phone: 301-540-6349
*Wants old tube-type radios; also early electric
clocks and small appliance.*

Dealer

Lee's Antiques
Carole & Bob Lee
8612 Wiles Court
Middletown, MD 21769
Phone: 301-371-9578
Buys, sells and repairs old electric radios.

Dealer

Jerry's Vintage Radio
17665 1/1 Sierra Hwy.
Canyon Country, CA 91351
*Buy, sell, trade and restore old radios; electronic
repair, wood repair and restoration, plastic repair
& paint, tubes & parts, etc.*

Dealer

Steve Oliphant
5255 Allott Ave.
Van Nuys, CA 91401
Phone: 818-789-2339   FAX: 213-276-5632
*Dealer in old phonographs and radios; buys entire
collections or individual pieces.*

Expert

Vintage TV's
Harry Poster
Box 1883
S. Hackensack, NJ 07606
Phone: 201-794-9606
*Unusual radios bought; paying $100 to $12,000
for mirror, celluloid & novelty radios; buying early
transistor radios; please send photo.*

Expert

Ralph Williams
R.D. #1, Box 44
Orient, NY 11957
Phone: 516-323-3646 *

Expert

Gary B. Schneider
9511 Sunrise Blvd. #J-23
North Royalton, OH 44133
Phone: 216-582-3094
Founding publisher of "Antique Radio Classified"; author of "1988 Official Price Guide to Antiques - Radio Classification."

Expert

Antique Radio Labs
James Fred
R.R. 1, Box 41
Cutler, IL 46920
Specializing in 1920-1950 radios. *

Expert

Doug Heimstead
1349 Hillcrest Dr.
Fridley, MN 55432
Phone: 612-571-1387
Specializes in Art Deco, mirrored, Bakelite and novelty radios. *

Museum/Library

New England Wireless & Steam Museum, Inc.
697 Tillinghart Rd.
East Greenwich, RI 02818
Phone: 401-884-1710

Museum/Library

Museum of Broadcast Communication
800 South Wells St.
Chicago, IL 60607
Phone: 312-987-1500

Museum/Library

Antique Wireless Association's
Electronic Museum
Bruce Kelley
#4 Main St.
Holcomb, NY 14469
Phone: 716-657-6260
Open limited hours May through October; call or write before visiting; please enclose SASE if requesting a reply.

Museum/Library

A.W.A. Electronic Communication Museum
Main Street
Holcomb, NY 14469
Phone: 716-657-7489

Museum/Library

Auman Antique Television Museum
Larry Auman
Route #1, Box 368
Dover, OH 44622
Phone: 216-343-2297 or 216-364-1058
Museum shows early days of electronic entertainment: 1940's movie theater, 1920's-1930's radios, 1939-1950 TV's, and related

Museum/Library

Ed Taylor Radio Museum
Dr. Edmund E. Taylor
245 N. Oakland Ave.
Indianapolis, IN 46201-3360
Phone: 317-638-1641
Collection includes radio equipment, memorabilia, electric meters, electro-medical devices, Tesla coil, 2000 book technical library.

Museum/Library

Valparaiso Techincal Institute, Wilbur H. Cummings Museum of Electronics
Hershman Hall
Valparaiso, IN 46384
Phone: 219-462-2191
Includes phonographs, early TV's, radios, first-generation computers, speakers, antennae, vacuum tubes, and other electronic instruments.

Museum/Library

Museum of Science & Industry
Keith R. Gill
57th St. & Lake Shore Drive
Chicago, IL 60637
Phone: 312-684-1414   FAX: 312-684-5580

Periodical

Newsletter: Antique Radio Classified
P.O. Box 802
Carlisle, MA 01741
Antique radio's largest monthly about old radios, Art Deco, TV's, ham equip. - '40's, '50's, books, telegraph, etc.

Periodical

Newsletter: Electronics Trader
P.O. Box 73
Folly Beach, SC 29439
Phone: 803-588-2344
A bi-weekly newsletter with buy, sell, and trade ads for phonographs, old radios, jukeboxes, records, vacuum tubes, speakers, etc. *

Periodical

Magazine: Radio Age
636 Cambridge Road
Augusta, GA 30909
Phone: 404-738-7227
Published monthly since 1975 for collectors interested in the history of radio and television; restoration, articles by early

Periodical

Newsletter: Nostalgia Digest & Radio Guide
Box 421
Morton Grove, IL 60053
Phone: 708-965-7763
A bi-monthly publication with old radio-related articles, photos, columns, etc. *

Periodical

Newspaper: Horn Speaker, The
James Cranshaw
P.O. Box 1193
Mabank, TX 75147
Phone: 903-848-0304
A newspaper for collectors and historians interested in antique radios and phonographs.

Repair Service

John Okolowicz
624 Cedar Hill Rd.
Ambler, PA 19002
Phone: 215-542-1597
Wants pre-1950 radios and TV's in unusual or ornate plastic or wooden cabinets; especially those made by Emerson or Stromberg Carlson.

Repair Service

David T. Boyd
13917 Wisteria Drive
Germantwon, MD 20877
Phone: 301-948-8070 or 301-972-2777
Restores old tube-type radios and televisions from the 20's and 30's through the 1960's; also buys and sells.

Repair Service

DH Distributors
David Headley
P.O. box 48623
Wichita, KS 67201
Phone: 316-684-0050
Repairs and restores tube-type radios and audio equipment; chassis and cabinet restorations for tube-type radios; schematics.

Supplier

Old Tyme Radio Co.
Suite 317
2445 Lyttonsville Road
Silver Spring, MD 20910
Phone: 301-585-8776
Carries hard-to-find radio parts: vintage tubes, AK style battery cable, hook up wire, audio transformers, vintage headphones, etc.

Supplier

Puett Electronics
Newsletter: Antique Radio Topics
J.W.F. Puett
P.O. Box 28572
Dallas, TX 75228
Phone: 214-321-0927 or 214-327-8721
Mail order business in its 19th year servicing the antique radio collector; sells anything for old radios. Send for catalog.

Supplier

Antique Electronic Supply
6221 S. Maple Ave.
Tempe, AZ 85283
Phone: 602-820-5411   FAX: 602-820-4643

Large catalog carrying tubes, supplies, capacitors, transformers, chemicals, test equipment, wire, parts, tools, literature, etc.

Transistor

Collector

Bob Roberts
P.O. Box 152
Guilderland, NY 12084
Novelty transistor radios or telephones in unusual shapes (gas pumps, food items, cartoon characters, cars, etc.) *

Collector

J.L. Wilson
2007 Water Edge Dr.
Birmingham, AL 35244
Wants early, small transistor radios from the 1950's and early 1960's such as by Regency, Raytheon, Toshiba, Sony, Zenith, etc.

RADIO SHOWS

Old Time

Club/Association

Oldtime Radio-show Collectors
Association
Reg Hubert, Pres.
45 Barry Street
Sudbury
Ontario P3B 3H6 Canada
Phone: 705-560-3095 or 705-560-2957
O.R.C.A. is a non-profit association of people interested in the listening to and the preservation of oldtime radio shows.

Club/Association

Radio Collectors of America
Newsletter: RCA Newsletter
Ardsley Circle
Brokton, MA 02402
Purpose is to collect, preserve and enjoy old radio shows. Does not collect old radios, the emphasis is strictly on radio shows. *

Club/Association

Old Time Radio Club
Newsletter: OTRC Newsletter
Jerri Collins
56 Christen Ct.
Lancaster, NY 14086
Phone: 716-683-6199
A nationally oriented local chapter.

Club/Association

Old Time Radio Collectors Traders
Society
Fred B. Korb, Jr.
725 Cardigan Ct.
Naperville, IL 69565
Phone: 708-416-8968
Society members are amateur radio operators or sponsored by same; meetings held on 7.238MHZ, 7AM CST, Sundays; W9ZMR is net control.

Club/Association

Radio History Association of Colorado
Newsletter: RHAC Newsletter
Vicki Blake, Mem.
P.O. Box 1908
Englewood, CA 80150
Active local chapter, nice newsletter; organizes western area convention. *

Club/Association

Old Time Hollywood Radio
1680 North Vine Street #918
Hollywood, CA 90028 *

Club/Association

Society To Preserve & Encourage Radio
Drama, Variety & Comedy
P.O. Box 1587
Hollywood, CA 90028
Phone: 213-947-9800
Local club with many national members; good library.

Club/Association

Manuscript Society, The
Magazine: Manuscripts
350 N. Niagara St.
Burbank, CA 91505
An organization of collectors, dealers, librarians, archivists, scholars and others interested in autographs and manuscripts.

Collector

David L. Easter
1900 Angleside Road
Fallston, MD 21047
Phone: 301-877-2949
Interested in all old time radio shows, especially in science fiction program; American, BBC or South African.

Collector

Fred B. Korb, Jr.
725 Cardigan Ct.
Naperville, IL 69565
Phone: 708-416-8968
Looking for any new programs in circulation; member of O.R.C.A.T.S.

Dealer

Can Corner, The
Box 1173
Linwood, PA 19061
Jack Benny, Amos & Andy, Big Band specials, WWII broadcasts, old commericals for Chevrolet, Nash & Studebaker, etc.; send for list.

Museum/Library

Museum of Broadcasting, The
25 West 52nd St.
New York, NY 10022
Phone: 212-752-4690

Periodical

Friends of Old-Time Radio
Newsletter: Hello Again
Jay A. Hickerson
Box 4321
Hamden, CT 06514
Phone: 203-248-2887
For collectors of old-time radio shows; sponsors an annual convention; send SASE for sample copy of newsletter.

Periodical

Newsletter: NARA News
Janis DeMoss
5291 Jacks Creek Pike
Lexington, KY 40515

Periodical

Royal Promotions
Magazine: Old Time Radio Digest
Herb Brandenburg
4114 Montgomery Rd.
Cincinnati, OH 45212
Phone: 513-841-1267

Periodical

Newsletter: Old Time Radio News
959 Drayton
Ferndale, MI 48220 *

Repro. Source

Old Time Radio Co.
P.O. Box 9032
Grand Rapids, MI 49509
Phone: 800-334-3225

Old Time (Lum & Abner)

Club/Association

National Lum & Abner Society
Tim Hollis, ExSec
Rt. 3, Box 110
Dora, IL 35062
For fans of LUM & ABNER.

Old Time (Straight Arrow)

Club/Association

POW-WOW
Newsletter: POW-WOW
Bill Harper
301 East Buena Vista Ave.
North Augusta, SC 29841
Phone: 803-278-0437
POW-WOW is the definitive source for information on the Nabisco Straight Arrow Promotion 1948-1954.

Old Time (Vic & Sade)

Club/Association

Friends of Vic & Sade
Newsletter: FVS Newsletter
Mrs. Barbara Schwarz
7232 N. Keystone Ave.
Lincolnwood, IL 60646-2025
Phone: 708-679-2706
Devoted fans of VIC & SADE focusing on searching for and sharing recorded episodes as well as information on the program and cast.

RADIO TUBES

Supplier

DH Distributors
David Headley
P.O. Box 48623
Wichita, KS 67201
Phone: 316-684-0050
Buys and sells receiving, transmitting and industrial vacuum tubes.

RAILROAD COLLECTIBLES

(see also RAILROADS; TRANSPORTATION COLLECTIBLES)

Auction Service

Depot Attic, The
Fred N. Arone
377 Ashford Ave.
Dobbs Ferry, NY 10522
Phone: 914-693-5858
Conducts auctions specializing in railroad paper ephemera, books hardware, silverware and chinaware; all misc. railroad items.

Club/Association

Railroad Enthusiasts
456 Main St.
West Townsend, MA 01474 *

Club/Association

Railroadiana Collectors Association, Inc.
Magazine: Railroadiana Express
Joe Mazanek
795 Aspen
Buffalo Grove, IL 60089
Phone: 312-537-0891

Collector

Schreibman
Box 121
Mountaindale, NY 12763
Phone: 718-225-4006
Railroad timetables, annual passes, badges, depot items. *

Collector

Nestle's Railroadiana
RD 2, Ray Rd./Box 105
Greenwich, NY 12834
Phone: 518-692-2867

Buys and sells all sorts of railroadiana: timetables, guides, maps, advertising info., menus, old books and magazines, etc.

Collector

John Fowler
3021 Newark St. NW
Washington, DC 20008
Phone: 202-686-1411
Wants railroad timetables, china, silverware, menus, baggage, checks, pre-1900 passes; also Chesapeake Bay steamship memorabilia. *

Collector

Bruce Heiner
Box 630
Ellicott City, MD 21043
Phone: 301-750-7232
Timetables, bonds, stocks; also complete railroadiana collections. *

Collector

John Kelly
Route 2, Box 489
Smithsburg, MD 21783
Phone: 301-824-7458
Wants B&O Railroad, Western MD railroad items. *

Collector

David Freeman
P.O. Box 191
Floyd, VA 24091
Phone: 703-343-5358   FAX: 703-343-3240
Buys collections and accumulations of railroad passes, match books, pre-1950 timetables and playing cards, railroad sheet music.

Collector

Randy Ridgely
447 Oglethorpe Ave.
Athens, GA 30606
Wants railroad china, silver, pocket watches, etc.; also steamship and airline items.

Collector

R. Hebel
226 Tebbs
Lawrenceburg, IN 47025
Phone: 812-537-0150
All railroad items.

Collector

Richard Wright
P.O. Box 8051
Rowland Hts., CA 91748-0051
Phone: 714-681-4647
Wants railroad items such as china, silverware, lanterns, etc.; all inquires answered.

Dealer

Depot Attic, The
Fred N. Arone
377 Ashford Ave.
Dobbs Ferry, NY 10522
Phone: 914-693-5858
Retail store & auction specializing in railroad paper ephemera, books hardware, silverware and chinaware; all misc. railroad items.

Dealer

Private Car Limited
3rd & A Streets
Belleville, IL 62220 *

Dealer

Antiques & Artifacts
Scott Arden
20457 Highway 126
Noti, OR 97461
Phone: 503-935-1619
Leading RR mail order dealer for 20 years; catalog $1; buys and sells fine old transportation items, mostly non-paper;

Expert

Golden Spike Enterprises Inc.
Alan Altman
P.O. Box 422
Williamsville, NY 14221
Phone: 716-689-9074

Expert

Railroad Antiques
Gene Price
Box 278
Erwin, TN 37650 *

Museum/Library

Charleston Railroad Artifacts Museum
P.O. Box 10081
Charleston, SC 29411
Phone: 803-744-1092

Museum/Library

National Railroad Museum
Ray Sauvey
2285 S. Broadway
Green Bay, WI 54304-7245
Phone: 414-435-7623 or 414-435-7245

Museum/Library

Frisco Railroad Museum
c/o Chamber Of Commerce
Van Buren, AR 72956
Phone: 501-474-2761

Periodical

Magazine: Key, Lock & Lantern
P.O. Box 15
Spencerport, NY 14559 *

B & O Items

Collector

Charles Boice
7003 Charles Ridge Rd.
Towson, MD 21204
Phone: 301-321-7149
Baltimore & Ohio R.R. memorabilia and china.

Dealer

John R. Hickman
772 Tiffany Dr.
Gaithersburg, MD 20878
Phone: 301-926-5818
*Baltimore & Ohio R.R. memorabilia and china; also other transportation memorabilia from steamships and airlines. **

Repro. Source

B & O Railroad Museum
901 Pratt Street
Baltimore, MD 21223
Phone: 301-237-3746
Sells B & O railroad china and other B & O related items.

China

Collector

Robert D'Achille
Box 57 H.C. 79
Whitney Point, NY 13862
Phone: 607-862-3914
Wants any railroad china especially Railroad-marked; must be in good condition (no hairlines, cracks or chips, etc.)

Dealer

Golden Spike Enterprises Inc.
Alan Altman
P.O. Box 422
Williamsville, NY 14221
Phone: 716-689-9074

Expert

Great Delaware & New England Antiques
Trading Company
Gerry &Christie Geisler
P.O. Box 1065
Chatham, NJ 07928 *

Expert

Douglas W. McIntyre
20 Cleveland Place
Lockport, NY 14094
Author of "The Official Guide to Railroad Dining Car China."

Museum/Library

B & O Railroad Museum, Chessie Shop
901 Pratt Street
Baltimore, MD 21223
Phone: 301-237-3746
Shop sells B&O railroad china.

China (Penna. RR)

Repro. Source

Right Track Trading Co.
P.O. Box 186
Strasburg, PA 17579
*Offering reproductions of Pennsylvania Railroad Tuscan Keystone pattern dining car china, glass-ware and other items! **

Dining Items

Collector

Peter Tilp
P.O. Box 580
Summit, NJ 07901
Phone: 201-376-2995
Wants railroad dining car china, silverware, flatware, glassware, napkins, menus, and related items.

Dealer

Charles Goodman
636 W. Grant Ave.
Charleston, IL 61920
Phone: 217-345-6771
Wants railroad dining car china, silverware, flatware, glassware, napkins, menus, and related items; offers catalog of items for sale.

Equipment

Club/Association

Mid-Continent Railway Historical
Society
Newsletter: Railway Gazette
Box 55
North Freedom, WI 53951
Phone: 608-522-4261
*Interested in 1885-1915 rolling stock and other equipment; also railroad lore. **

Hat Badges

Expert

Jim Younger
4628 Old Dragon
Ellicott City, MD 21043
Phone: 301-964-1949
Wants railroad hat badges (all 'roads and occupa-tions), hats, uniforms, and brotherhood (Unions) lapel pins, RR fiction books.

Lanterns

Collector

Jake
P.O. Box 503
Falls Church, VA 22046
Marked railroad lanterns and marked globes: $200 for green, amber, blue marked RR globes.

Expert

David Dreimiller
Suite #4
33200 Brainbridge Rd.
Solon, OH 44139
Phone: 216-662-7820
Author of "Signal Lights" which covers railroad signal lamps and lanterns; also buys lanterns and manufacturer's sales literature.

Paper Items

Collector

Carl Loucks
199 Wayland
North Haven, CT 06473
Wants railroad timetables, brochures, guides, maps, menus; also trolley, air and bus.

Passes

Collector

C. Hazlett
R.D. 3 Box 605
Hollidaysburg, PA 16648
Phone: 814-695-0128
*Wants railroad passes and other transportation annual employees passes before 1920. **

Photographic Negatives

Collector

Don Culver
3083 Balsam
Edgewood, KY 41017
*Wants photographic negatives especially of steam diesel locomotives and anything else pertaining to railroads. **

Uniforms

(see also BUTTONS, Railroad/Transit
Uniforms)

RAILROADS

(see also STEAM-OPERATED, Models &
Equipment)

Club/Association

Chesapeake & Ohio Historical Society,
Inc.
Magazine: Chesapeake & Ohio Historical
   Magazine
P.O. Box 79
Clifton Forge, VA 24422
Phone: 703-862-2210
Monthly articles on history of the C&O RR and predecessors (PM RR in Mich., HV RR in Ohio, etc.), as well as successor CSX Transp.

Club/Association

Motor Car Collectors of America
Newsletter: Speeder
5 Bay View Hills
Wever, IA 52658

Members interested in the preservation and operation of railroad track cars, handcars, motor cars and velocipedes.

Club/Association
Railroad Club of America, Inc., The
Journal: Railroad Capital, The
William Shapotkin, Pres
P.O. Box 8292
Chicago, IL 60680
Phone: 708-251-2262
Founded in 1934 for the purpose of coordinating interests and activities of those interested in any matter pertaining to railroads.

Club/Association
Railway & Locomotive Historical Society
3363 Riviera West Drive
Kelseyville, CA 95451 *

Museum/Library
Museum of Transportation
15 Newton St.
Brookline, MA 02146
Phone: 617-522-6140

Museum/Library
New York Museum of Transportation
P.O. Box 136
West Henrietta, NY 14586
Phone: 716-533-1113

Museum/Library
California State Railroad Museum
125 I St.
Sacramento, CA 95814

Periodical
Newsletter: U.S. Rail News
P.O. Box 7007
Huntington Woods, MI 48070-7007 *

Periodical
Magazine: Rail
Jim Lance
c/o Publishers Mini Systems
P.O. Box 301369
Escondido, CA 92030-9957
Phone: 619-747-8327   FAX: 619-432-6560
British magazine for the railroad buff: new lines, history, expansion, railtours and new developements in wagons in the U.K.

Steam
Periodical
Magazine: Steam Railway
Jim Lance
c/o Publishers Mini Systems
P.O. Box 301369
Escondido, CA 92030-9957
Phone: 619-747-8327   FAX: 619-432-6560
British magazine with news, video & book reviews and plenty of steam railway history; color photos; a must for the railroad enthusiast.

Switchback
Collector
Robert Gormley
334 Brownsburg Rd.
Newtown, PA 18940
*Wants switchback railroad souvenirs. *

RATIONING RELATED ITEMS
(see also MILITARIA, WWII Items;
TOKENS, Ration)

Collector
Lee Poleske
Box 871
Seward, AK 99664
Wants OPA tokens and other WWII ration items.

RAZORS
(see also BARBER SHOP COLLECTIBLES;
SHAVING COLLECTIBLES)

RECORDED SOUND
(see also RADIO SHOWS, Old Time;
RECORDS)

Club/Association
Association for Recorded Sound
Collections, Inc.
Journal: ARSC Journal
P.O. Box 10162
Silver Spring, MD 20914
Phone: 301-593-6552
Dedicated to the preservation and study of recordings in the fields of music and speech: Edison cylinders, rare discs, oral history, etc.

RECORDS
(see also MUSIC; PHONOGRAPHS)

Auction Service
Antique Phonograph Center
Floyd Silver
Hwy. 206
P.O. Box 274
Vincentown, NJ 08088
Phone: 609-859-8617
Conducts special mail auctions of rare and unusual 78 rpm Edison diamond discs and cylinder records; $2 for catalog.

Collector
R. Hess
P.O. Box 963
New York, NY 10023-0963
Wants 1948-1965 LP records (33 1/3 rpm): Jazz, R&B, R'n R, Blues, pop, soundtracks, Latin; also related books, photos, mags., etc.

Collector
Dave A. Reiss
3920 Eve Drive
Seaford, NY 11783
Phone: 516-785-8336
Collects 78 rpm's, 1900 to 1930's: popular, classical, jazz, personalities, dance records, gospel, country & western, ethnic.

Dealer
Backnumber Records
Steven Smolian
8807 Postoak Road
Potomac, MD 20854
Phone: 301-983-3244 or 800-228-7833
Wants used records - LP's & 78's, audio collectibles; classical and jazz music a specialty; also appraises records.

Dealer
Gurley's
Box 995
Princeton, NC 27569 *

Dealer
Worldwide Collectors
28 Baker Dr.
Savannah, GA 31410 *

Dealer
Coin Machine Trader
Ted & Betty Salveson
569 Kansas SE
P.O. Box 602
Huron, SD 57350
Phone: 605-352-3870
Specializes in old phonograph records.

Dealer
Shellac Shack
L.R. (Les) Docks
P.O. Box 691035
San Antonio, TX 78269-1035
Phone: 512-492-6021
Buying vintage popular records, especially 78's: jazz, blues, hillbilly, pop, rockabilly, etc.; wants list for $2 (refundable).

Dealer
Disc Collector
7829 E. Parker Rd.
Parker, CO 80134
Phone: 303-841-3000
*Specializing in oldies from the 50's to 70's. *

Dealer
CVC Collectables
P.O. Box 219
Los Angeles, CA 90066
Phone: 213-313-0102
*Interested in LP's and 45's; also in promotional items and radio shows. *

Dealer

Hot Platters
Edward Odel
Dept. CC
P.O. Box 4213
Thousand Oaks, CA 91359-1213
Phone: 213-467-4692
Interested in LP's and 45's; also sheet music, posters, books and magazines; catalogs $3; also offers a record auction service.

Dealer

Collectors Sound, The
L. Stanley Baumruk
Suite 384
15840 Ventura Blvd.
Encino, CA 91436
Interested in LP's and 45's from 50's to the 70's. *

Expert

Shellac Shack
L.R. (Les) Docks
P.O. Box 691035
San Antonio, TX 78269-1035
Phone: 512-492-6021
Author of "American Premium Record Guide" (Books Americana),

Expert

Guideline
Jerry Osborne
P.O. Box 255
Port Townsend, WA 98363
Phone: 206-385-3029
Author of "The Official Price Guide to Records." *

Periodical

Beat Publications
Magazine: Record Collector
45 St. Mary's Road
Ealing
London W5 5RQ England
A monthly magazine. *

Periodical

New Amberola Phonograph Co. The
Magazine: New Amberola Graphic, The
37 Caledonia St.
St. Johnsbury, VT 05819
A quarterly publication for collectors of early phonographs & records from the years 1895-1935; articles, book reviews, ads, auctions, etc.

Periodical

Newspaper: Record Collectors Monthly
P.O. Box 75
Mendham, NJ 07945
Phone: 201-543-9520
Covers collectible records primarily from 1950 to 1968; 45's, LP's, some 78's; Rock 'n' Roll, R & B, vocal groups, POP' music of the era.

Periodical

Krause Publications, Inc.
Magazine: Goldmine
Jeff Tamarkin, Ed.
700 E. State St.
Iola, WI 54990
Phone: 800-258-0929 or 715-445-2214
FAX: 715-445-4087
Bi-weekly magazine containing articles, ads about records & recording artists from 1940's to present; the record & CD marketplace.

Periodical

Newsletter: Roaring 20's
1545 Raymond
Glendale, CA 91201
Phone: 213-242-8961
A quarterly focusing the collecting of vintage radios and radio parts. *

Periodical

Journal: Record Collectors Journal
P.O. Box 1200
Covina, CA 91722 *

Periodical

Discoveries, Inc.
Magazine: DISCoveries Magazine
Jerry Osborne, Pub.
P.O. Box 255
Port Townsend, WA 98368-2923
Phone: 206-385-1200 or 800-666-DISC
FAX: 206-385-6572
The record collector's magazine; articles on artists, ads for 10's of thousands of CD's & related music memorabilia from 1930's to present.

Supplier

Bags Unlimited
7 Canal Street
Rochester, NY 14608
Phone: 800-767-BAGS
Sells record collector supplies: poly and paper sleeves, mailers, filer pads, album jackets, storage boxes, divider cards, etc.

Supplier

MARSCO
1713 Central St.
Evanston, IL 60201
Phone: 708-328-7100
Carries paper and plastic sleeves for LP's and sheet music covers.

Country & Bluegrass

Collector

David Freeman
P.O. Box 191
Floyd, VA 24091
Phone: 703-343-5358   FAX: 703-343-3240
Buys and sells 1922-1980 country & bluegrass 78's, 45's & LP's; also songbooks; over 25 years experience; also specialty record auctions.

Jazz

Club/Association

International Association of Jazz
Record Collectors
Journal: IAJRC Journal
Phil Oldham, Ed.
8412 Royal Meadow Drive
Indianapolis, IN 46217-4865
Phone: 317-888-0861
Promotes exchange of information and research on jazz, its musicians and recordings.

Periodical

Magazine: Joslin's Jazz Journal
Box 213
Parsons, KS 67357
JJJ is the ultimate marketplace for original 78's, LP's, radio transcriptions, video tapes, and associated literature and memorabilia.

Jazz & Big Band

Club/Association

Collectors Record Club
Newsletter: CRC Newsletter
1206 Decatur St.
New Orleans, LA 70116
Phone: 504-525-1776 *

Rock 'n' Roll

Collector

Dealer
Flyer: Rockin' Richard 50's - 60's
        Entertainment Guide
Rockin' Richard
Box 222
Northford, CT 06472
Phone: 203-484-2023
Hosts New Haven, CT's longest running collector show on 88.7 FM (WNHV), Tuesday 8-11 PM; reviews recordings and products; hosts conv.

RELIGIOUS COLLECTIBLES

(see also JUDAICA; MORMON ITEMS; STAMP COLLECTING, Topical (Religion Related))

Club/Association

Medals of Antiquity Restored for
Christianity - M.A.R.C.
Newsletter: M.A.R.C., The
Emilio C. Botticelli
10 Dean St.
Worcester, MA 01609
Phone: 508-831-1309
All types of old religious medals; club focuses on medal history, values, varieties, makers, rarity, countries of origin, etc.

Relics

Collector

Tim Gordon
1750 W. Kent
Missoula, MT 59801
Phone: 406-728-1812
Wants small locket-size Catholic saint relics with pieces of cloth, chips of bone, etc.; about the size of a quarter with a glass cover.

REPAIRS & RESTORATIONS

(see also BAROMETERS; CLOCKS; DOLLS; FRAMES; MOVING & STORAGE; MUSIC BOXES; NAUTICAL COLLECTIBLES; PHONOGRAPHS; RADIOS; TELEPHONES; TOYS; etc.)

Misc. Service

Burlesque Repair Service
Andrew Gelinas
18 W. 3rd. St.
Bethlehem, PA 18015
Phone: 215-867-3313 or 215-867-1665
FAX: 215-867-4999
Sells customized computer program for household goods repair firms.

Supplier

A. Ludwig Klein & Son, Inc.
Route 63
P.O. Box 205
Harleysville, PA 19438
Phone: 215-256-9004 or 800-869-5633
Sells china and glass restoration supplies.

Art

Periodical

American Institute for Conservation of Historic & Artistic Works
Directory: AIC Directory
Suite #340
1400 16th St. NW
Washington, DC 20036
Phone: 202-232-6636
The AIC Directory lists competent conservators of paper, textiles, photographs, furniture, and more - over 2000 members.

Repair Service

Peter Kostoulakos
15 Sayles St.
Lowell, MA 01851
Phone: 508-453-8888
Conservation of oil paintings on canvas or solid supports; oil paintings cleaned and restored.

Repair Service

Art Conservation Laboratory
Barbara H. Beardsley
Raymond, NH 03077
Phone: 603-895-2639
Offers art conservation and art forgery detection services. *

Repair Service

Fine Art Restoration
John Squadra
RFD #2 Box 1440
Brooks, ME 04921
Phone: 207-722-3464
Specializing in the conservation and restoration of oil paintings; send photo of painting, incl. size; estimate returned; has crates.

Repair Service

Washington Conservation Studio
Justine S. Wimsatt
4230 Howard St.
Kensington, MD 20895
Phone: 301-564-1036
For 20 years has provided professional restoration of paintings, murals, icons, frames and related objects.

Repair Service

H.I. Gates
118 E. Church St.
Frederick, MD 21701
Phone: 301-663-3717
Conservator of paintings.

Repair Service

Robert & Marie Kuehne
9910 Green Valley Rd.
Union Bridge, MD 21791
Phone: 301-898-7921
Oil painting conservation/restoration; 20 yrs. experience; please call for expert info. & advice; FREE brochure available on request.

Repair Service

Bardwell Conservation, Ltd.
Margaret Bardwell
11373 Park Dr.
Fairfax, VA 22030
Phone: 703-385-8451
Conservation and restoration of paintings executed on canvas, metal or wood (including icons); also frames and small painted furniture.

Repair Service

Antique & Art Restoration By Wiebold
413 Terrace Place
Terrace Park, OH 45174
Phone: 513-831-2541
Silver repair and replating; restoration of bronzes, combs, brushes, knife blades, mirrors, frames, paintings, ceramics, glass, etc.

Repair Service

Balboa Art Conservation Center
Frances Prichatt
P.O. Box 3755
San Diego, CA 92103
Phone: 619-236-9702
Provides conservation services for art and paper items. *

Repair Service

Fine Art Conservation Laboratories
Scott M. Haskins
P.O. Box 23557
Santa Barbara, CA 93131
Phone: 805-564-3438   FAX: 805-963-0705
Specializes in the preservation of paintings, murals, works of art on paper and period frames.

Supplier

Gainsborough Products Company, Ltd.
3545 Mt. Diablo Blvd.
Lafayette, CA 94549
Phone: 415-283-4187 or 800-227-2186
Lining canvas and compound, repair putty, varnish remover, manuals, etc.

Cane & Basketry

Supplier

Able To Cane
P.O. Box 429
Warren, ME 04864
Phone: 207-273-3747
Source for cane, wicker and basket supplies; also repairs of antique seats, natural & fiber rush, Shaker tape seating, cane, splint, etc. *

Supplier

Connecticut Cane & Reed Co.
134 Pine St.
P.O. Box 762
Manchester, CT 06040
Phone: 203-646-6586   FAX: 203-649-2221
Largest selection of materials and books; source for cane, wicker and basket supplies; all types of materials to reseat a chair.

Supplier

Peerless Rattan & Reed
P.O. Box 636
Yonkers, NY 10701
Phone: 914-968-4046
Source for cane, wicker and basket supplies.

Supplier

Canecraft
Lilian Cummings
RD1 Box 126-A
Andreas, PA 18211
Phone: 717-386-2441
Sells cane, reed and rushing material for seating chairs, making baskets, and repairing wicker furniture; also instruction books.

Supplier

Barap Specialties
835 Bellows
Frankfort, MI 49635
Source for flat reed, fiber rush, decorative head nails, cane webbing and reed for reweaving chair seats, hardware, etc.

Supplier

Cane & Basket Supply Co.
1283 S. Cochran Ave.
Los Angeles, CA 90019
Phone: 213-939-9644   FAX: 213-939-7237
Source for cane, wicker and basket supplies.

Supplier

Franks Cane & Rush Supply
Mike Frank
P.O. Box 3025
Huntington Beach, CA 92605
Phone: 714-847-0707   FAX: 714-843-5645
Quality supplier of unusual supplies for the craftsman; mainly wicker repair and basketry; sorry, no restoration of repairs.

Ceramics

Repair Service

Fine Wares Restoration
Sharon Smith Abbott
Highland Ridge Road
P.O. Box 753
Bridgton, ME 04009
Phone: 207-647-2093
Restores ceramics & glass for private collectors and museums; member of the Amer. Inst. for Conservation of Historic & Artistic Works.

Repair Service

Jonathan Mark Gershen Porcelain,
Pottery & Glass Restoration
Jonathan Mark Gershen
1463 Pennington Road
Ewing Township, NJ 08618
Phone: 609-882-9417
Second generation restorer and long time member of the AICHAW; clients include museums, collectors and dealers from all over.

Repair Service

Harry A. Eberhardt & Son
2010 Walnut St.
Philadelphia, PA 19103
America's oldest repair firm. *

Repair Service

Grady Stewart Expert Porcelain
Restorations
2019 Sansom St.
Philadelphia, PA 19103
Phone: 215-567-2888
Offering repairs for museums, dealers, collectors; quality repairs of fine porcelain, pottery, stoneware, dolls.

Repair Service

Shepherd Studio
Mildred R. Shepherd
5527 Third St., South
Arlington, VA 22204
Phone: 703-671-1789
Offers conservation and restoration of objects of art; specializing in the repair of porcelain, glass, ivory, china and pottery.

Repair Service

Gregory A. Ehler
4786 Lee Highway
Arlington, VA 22207
Phone: 703-525-2470
Provides museum quality restoration of fine porcelain, pottery and enamels; member of Wash. D.C. Professional Restoration Associates.

Repair Service

Paul Barron Company
P.O. Box 2023
Decatur, GA 30030
Small firm. Excepts all kinds of china repairs. *

Repair Service

Lauraine Dunn Studios
Lauraine Dunn
181 N.E. 82nd St. #201
Miami, FL 33138
Phone: 305-758-7174
Well-established firm. Handles both decorative porcelain as well as dinnerware, fine art, metal, etc.

Repair Service

Antique & Art Restoration By Wiebold
413 Terrace Place
Terrace Park, OH 45174
Phone: 513-831-2541
Silver repair and replating; restoration of bronzes, combs, brushes, knife blades, mirrors, frames, paintings, ceramics, glass, etc.

Repair Service

Glass Doctor & Porcelain Clinic
Ross Jasper
3126 Fairview St.
Davenport, IA 52802
Phone: 319-322-5512
Restores figurines, toys, glass.

Repair Service

Morla W. Tjossem
911 E. Hancock St.
Appleton, WI 54911
Phone: 414-734-5463
China Mending and Restoration Course instructor on the Lawrence University campus; practicing restorer.

Repair Service

Wesley Art Service
P.O. Box 848
Los Gatos, CA 95031
China restorations of figurines. *

Supplier

Atlas Minerals & Chemicals, Inc.
Farmington Road
Mertztown, PA 19539
Phone: 215-682-7171
Offers a master mending kit for china and glass including materials and instructions to repair glass, china, porcelain, pottery, etc. *

Figurines

(see also REPAIRS & RESORATIONS, Ceramics; REPAIRS & RESTORATIONS, General)

Furniture

(see also REPAIRS & RESTORATIONS, Woodworking)

Repair Service

Manning Furniture Repair Co.
Dan Manning
P.O. Box 212
Allendale, NJ 07401
Phone: 201-825-8450   FAX: 201-825-8301
Specializing in cargo claims handling, and furniture and antiques repair services.

Repair Service

Burlesque Repair Service
Andrew Gelinas
18 W. 3rd. St.
Bethlehem, PA 18015
Phone: 215-867-3313 or 215-867-1665
                    FAX: 215-867-4999
Specializing in cargo claims handling and repair services for moving, insurance, retail companies; full shop facilities.

Repair Service

John Eaton
9064 Canterbury Riding
Laurel, MD 20707
Phone: 301-498-2351
Offers moving claims inspections and repairs; antiques restoration.

Repair Service

Shontere Restoration, Inc.
Belinda Shontere
P.O. Box 1805
Mitchellville, MD 20717
Phone: 301-870-3669 or 800-937-3786
                    FAX: 301-934-0511
Specializing in furniture repair and restoration.

Repair Service

Glade Valley Furniture Repair
John Pyle
10464 Glade Road
Walkersville, MD 21793
Phone: 301-898-3795

Repair Service

Heny Miller
9200 Maple St.
Manassas, VA 22110
Phone: 703-368-4502

Repair Service

Finishing Touch
Dennis Bell
118 Kent Berry Court
Gastonia, NC 28054
Phone: 704-868-8538

*Offers cargo claims handling furniture repairs. ***

Repair Service

Image Maintenance Assurance, Inc.
Dave Kummerow
P.O. Box 8407
Bartlett, IL 60103
Phone: 708-830-7965   FAX: 708-830-1458
Specializing in cargo claims handling and repair services; wood finishes, upholstery, fiberglass, vinyl, porcelain, etc.

Repair Service

Pacific Northwest Claim Service
Ray Spencer
1045 12th Ave. NW, Unit F3
Issaquah, WA 98027
Phone: 206-392-2500   FAX: 206-392-7525
Specializing in cargo claims handling and in complete repair services.

Furniture & Upholstery

(see also REPAIRS & RESTORATIONS, Upholstery)

Repair Service

West Interior Services, Inc.
Tom Kuhns
P.O. Box 200
Brackenridge, PA 15014
Phone: 412-224-2215   FAX: 412-226-3233
Specializes in moving or ins. claims; furniture repair, refinishing & restoration, architectural refinishing; fire, smoke, water damage.

Repair Service

Charles Jourdant Furniture Repair
Charles Jourdant
611 Alabama Ave.
North Beach, MD 20714
Phone: 301-855-6563   FAX: 301-257-0752
Furniture repair, refinishing and upholstering.

Furniture (Antique)

Repair Service

John Sutton Antique Restorations
John Sutton
14 North Henry St.
Brooklyn, NY 11222
Phone: 718-389-6101
Specializes in the restoration of 17th and 18th century English, French and American furniture.

Repair Service

Heritage Restorations
Stephen Rice
7200-10 Westmore Ave.
Rockville, MD 20850-1261
Phone: 301-762-3126
European trained craftsmen specializing in wooden objects d'Art & antique furniture restoration; duplicating finishes, inlays, etc.

Repair Service

Walter Raynes
4900 Wetheredsville
Baltimore, MD 21207
Phone: 301-448-3515
Specializes in the restoration and conservation of antique furniture only.

Repair Service

Begleiter Antique Restorations
Phil Goodman
6801 Reisterstown Rd.
Baltimore, MD 21215
Phone: 301-764-7467

Repair Service

Robert Esterly Antiques Repairing, Refinishing, Reproductions
Robert Esterly
6675 Mt. Phillip Rd.
Frederick, MD 21702
Phone: 301-694-0287 or 301-371-7430
Specializing in the repair, restoration and refinishing of antique furniture.

Repair Service

Antique Restorations, Inc.
Bruce M. Schuettinger
17 N. Alley
P.O. Box 244
New Market, MD 21774
Phone: 301-865-3009
Specializing in the restoration and conservation of antique wooden furniture and artifacts: veneer, caning, inlay, gilding, etc.

General

(see also REPAIRS & RESTORATIONS, Ceramics)

Periodical

Directory: Antique Repair Directory
Joseph V. Cifala
P.O. Box 537
Edgewater, MD 21037
Phone: 301-261-7640
Free listings for repairers of coin operated machines, porcelains, glass, furniture, etc.

Repair Service

Helige Ande Arts
Ingrid Sanborn
85 Church St.
West Newbury, MA 01985
Phone: 508-363-2253
Specializes in graining, stenciling, marbleizing, reverse painting on glass, and early paint matching; custom of restoration work.

Repair Service

Trefler & Sons Antique Restoring Studio, Inc.
Leon Trefler
99 Cabot St.
Needham, MA 02194
Phone: 617-444-2685   FAX: 617-444-0659
Restores ceramics, prints, paintings, furniture, paper, frames, crystal, porcelain, marble, ivory, cloisonne, metals, jade, etc.

Repair Service

Stoneledge, Inc.
17 Robert St.
Wharton, NJ 07885
Phone: 201-989-8800
Fine and decorative art restorers and conservators: paintings, ceramics, scultpures, ivory, etc. for collectors, dealers & museums.

Repair Service

Hess Restorations
Marina Pastor
200 Park Ave. South
New York, NY 10003
Phone: 212-260-2255 or 212-979-1143
Since 1945 specializing in repairs and restorations of most objects of art; highly recommended by museums and leading galleries.

Repair Service

A. Ludwig Klein & Son, Inc.
Route 63
P.O. Box 145
Harleysville, PA 19438
Phone: 215-256-9004 or 215-256-6426
Specializing in the repair and restoration of all types of glass, china and porcelain as well as ivory, jade, brass, pewter.

Repair Service

Nonomura Studios
David Sim
3432 Connecticut Ave. NW
Washington, DC 20008
Phone: 202-363-4025
Restores china, glassware, screens, scrolls, ivory, paintings, jade, lamps, furniture, etc.

Repair Service

Mario's Conservation Services
Sidney Williston
1738 14th St. NW
Washington, DC 20009
Phone: 202-234-5795
Restorers of decorative arts objects: metal, ivory, icons, frames, gold leaf, glass grinding and drilling.

Repair Service

Museum Shop, Ltd.
Richard Kornemann
30 East Patrick St.
Frederick, MD 21701
Phone: 301-695-0424

Highly-recommended conservator of oils, paper (etchings, lithographs, engravings, maps), icons, Oriental art, photos, 23k gold leaf, etc.

Repair Service
Wood & Stone Inc.
Harold Vogel
10115 Residency Rd.
Manassas, VA 22111
Phone: 703-369-1236 or 202-631-1236

Repair Service
Shepherd Studio
Mildred R. Shepherd
5527 Third St., South
Arlington, VA 22204
Phone: 703-671-1789
Offers conservation and restoration of objects of art; specializing in the repair of porcelain, glass, ivory, china and pottery.

Repair Service
International Conservation
Laboratories, Ltd.
5311 Patterson Ave.
Richmond, VA 23226
Phone: 804-282-7308
Restores ceramics, prints, paintings, clocks, music boxes, jewelry, electroplate, textiles, etc. *

Repair Service
Rikki's Studio Inc.
Gilbert Kerry Hall
2809 Bird Ave.
Coconut Grove, FL 33133
Phone: 305-446-2230 or 305-446-2022
Restorers and conservators of crystal, paintings, porcelains (European and Oriental), coromandel and objects d'Art.

Repair Service
Lauraine Dunn Studios
Lauraine Dunn
181 N.E. 82nd St. #201
Miami, FL 33138
Phone: 305-758-7174
Well-established firm. Handles both decorative porcelain as well as dinnerware, fine art, metal, etc.

Repair Service
Old World Restorations, Inc.
Douglas A. Eisele
The Columbia/Stanley Bldg.
347 Stanley Avenue
Cincinnati, OH 45226
Phone: 513-321-1911 or 800-878-1911
           FAX: 513-321-1914
Fine restoration and conservation of paintings, porcelain, glass, china, art pottery, metals, crystal, frames, ivory, gold leaf, etc.

Repair Service
David Jasper's Glass Clinic
David Jasper
RR3, Box 330
Sioux Falls, SD 57106
Phone: 605-361-7524
Four generations of restorers. Glass, porcelain, painting, dolls, figurines, ivory, lamps.

Gilding
Repair Service
Society of Gilders
Newsletter: Society of Gilders Newsletter
42 Maple Place
Nutley, NJ 07110
Phone: 201-667-5251
Publishes a list of its members; also gives workshops and lectures on the art of gilding.

Repair Service
Mario's Conservation Services
Sidney Williston
1738 14th St. NW
Washington, DC 20009
Phone: 202-234-5795
Restorers of decorative arts objects: metal, ivory, icons, frames, gold leaf, glass grinding and drilling.

Repair Service
Gold Leaf Studios, Inc.
William Adair
P.O. Box 50156
Washington, DC 20091
Phone: 202-638-4660
Gilding of anything gold leafed: frames, sculpture, sconces, etc.

Repair Service
Chelsea Lane Studion
Stanley Robertson
4717 S. Chelsea Ln.
Bethesda, MD 20814
Phone: 301-656-9344
Gilding of anything gold leafed: frames, sculpture, sconces, etc.

Repair Service
Museum Shop, Ltd.
Richard Kornemann
30 East Patrick St.
Frederick, MD 21701
Phone: 301-695-0424
23k gold leafing of antiques, picture frames, signs, etc.; also complete art and frame restoration.

Glass
(see also GLASS, Curved)

Repair Service
Rosine Green Associates, Inc.
45 Bartlett Crescent
Brookline, MA 02146
Phone: 212-674-8960

Well-known firm restores and rebuilds all kinds of glass articles. *

Repair Service
Bevel Glass Works, Inc.
Jerry Lewis
900 Hacienda
Belville, TX 77418
Phone: 407-865-5711
Makes replacement beveled glass and mirrors, engraved glass and mirrors, shelves with plate grooves, etc.

Repair Service
Crystal Workshop
Edward Poore
P.O. Box 475
Sagamore, MA 02561
Phone: 508-888-1621
Glass items made to order; also repairs stemware, cut glass, and art glass.

Repair Service
Fine Wares Restoration
Sharon Smith Abbott
Highland Ridge Road
P.O. Box 753
Bridgton, ME 04009
Phone: 207-647-2093
Restores ceramics & glass for private collectors and museums; member of the Amer. Inst. for Conservation of Historic & Artistic Works.

Repair Service
Art Cut Glass Studio
R.D. 1, Box 10 Fawn Frive
Matawan, NJ 07747
Phone: 201-583-7648

Repair Service
Jonathan Mark Gershen Porcelain,
Pottery & Glass Restoration
Jonathan Mark Gershen
1463 Pennington Road
Ewing Township, NJ 08618
Phone: 609-882-9417
Second generation restorer and long time member of the AICHAW; clients include museums, collectors and dealers from all over.

Repair Service
Flemington Cut Glass
156 Main St.
Flemington, NJ 08822
Phone: 201-782-3017

Repair Service
Gem Monogram & Cut Glass Corp.
628 Broadway
New York, NY 10012
Phone: 212-674-8960

Repair Service

Glass Restorations
308 East 78th St.
New York, NY 10021
Phone: 212-517-3287

Repair Service

Ray Errett - Glass Repair Specialist
Ray Errett
281 Chestnut St.
Corning, NY 14830
Phone: 607-962-6026 or 607-937-5371
Restores glass figurines, sculpture crystal, cut glass; works at Corning.

Repair Service

Corning Museum of Glass, The
Mr. Manwarren
1 Museum Way
Corning, NY 14830-2253
Phone: 607-937-5371
*Repairs broken teeth on cut glass. ***

Repair Service

Shay O'Brien Crystal
Shay O'Brien
Rout 2, Box 223K
Acme, PA 15610
Phone: 412-547-4618
Restores antique crystal cut glass; recuts teeth; reproductions from blanks.

Repair Service

Michael Andras
P.O. Box 250
Bear Rocks, PA 15610
Phone: 412-547-6419
Glass engraver and cutter.

Repair Service

Van Parys Studio
6338 Germantown Ave.
Philadelphia, PA 19144 *

Repair Service

Crystal Restoration Co.
Scenic Plaza, Highway 28
West Union, SC 29696
Phone: 803-638-9323
*Crystal repair only. ***

Repair Service

McCurley Glass Repair
Don & Joyce McCurley
Rt. #1, Box 738
Big Pine Key, FL 33043
Phone: 305-872-2359
Repairs glass and crystal; also carries large stock of replacement stoppers for bottles.

Repair Service

Calvin's Glass Repair
John Calvin
303 East First Ave.
Lenoire City, TN 37771
Phone: 615-968-3872
*Crystal repair only. ***

Repair Service

Chaudron Glass & Mirror Co., Inc.
Henry Chaudron
1801 Lovegrove St.
Baltimore, MD 21202
Phone: 301-685-1568
Resilvers mirrors; also specializes in cutting and hand-beveling plate glass.

Repair Service

David Jasper's Glass Clinic
David Jasper
RR3, Box 330
Sioux Falls, SD 57106
Phone: 605-361-7524
Four generations of restorers. Glass, porcelain, painting, dolls, figurines, ivory, lamps.

Repair Service

Josef Puehringer
1141 Central Ave.
Wilmette, IL 60091
Phone: 312-256-6055
*Cuts and engraves glass. ***

Repair Service

K. Matsumoto
226 South Wabash Ave.
Chicago, IL 60604 *

Repair Service

Zoe Restorations
5657 W. 50th St.
Shawnee Mission, KS 66201 *

Repair Service

18054 Ventura Blvd.
Eucino, CA 91316 *

Supplier

Atlas Minerals & Chemicals, Inc.
Farmington Road
Mertztown, PA 19539
Phone: 215-682-7171
*Offers a master mending kit for china and glass including materials and instructions to repair glass, china, porcelain, pottery, etc. ***

Lamps & Lighting

Repair Service

Lamp House
223 W. Market St.
Hallam, PA 17406
Phone: 717-757-6989
*Replacement shades, antique lamp restoration, custom lamps. ***

Repair Service

Light Ideas
1037 Taft Street
Rockville, MD 20850
Phone: 301-424-5483   FAX: 301-424-5791
Repairs lighting fixtures - chandeliers, crystal, early electric fans; also carries parts, repairs shades, beaded fringe.

Repair Service

A-Bit-of-Antiquity
Richard Dudley
1412 Forest Lane
Woodbridge, VA 22191
Phone: 703-491-2878
Expert restoration, repair, deplating & polishing of gas and electric lamps; specializing in oil lighting; carries old parts & shades.

Supplier

Crystal Mountain Prisms
P.O. Box 31
Westfield, NY 14787
Phone: 716-326-3676
*Sells prisms, chains, bobeches, pendants, drops, etc. ***

Supplier

Burdoch Victorian Lamp Co.
1145 Industrial Ave.
Escondido, CA 92025
Phone: 619-745-3275
Carries a line of replacement handsewn embroidered Victorian lamp shades; 30 styles and 9 colors.

Supplier

Kirk Lane Co.
2541 Pearle Buck Rd.
Bristol, PA 19007
Phone: 215-785-1251   FAX: 215-785-1651
Source for lamp parts including sockets, bases, harps, finials, chimneys, shades, etc.

Supplier

Campbell Lamps
Bill Campbell
1108 Pottstown Pike
West Chester, PA 19380
Phone: 215-696-8070
*Sells replacement glass shades, chimneys, metal parts, etc. ***

Supplier

Roy Electric Co., Inc.
1054 Coney Island Ave.
Brooklyn, NY 11230
Phone: 718-434-7002 or 800-366-3347
*Sells Victorian lamp shades, antique lighting fixtures, and parts. ***

Supplier

B & P Lamp Supply, Inc.
843 Old Morrison Highway
McMinnville, TN 37110
Phone: 615-473-3016
Offers a wide variety of lamp reproduction parts. Wholesale only. Handpainted shades, adaptors, burners, art glass shades, etc.

Supplier

American Lamp Supply Co.
Tom Teeter
51 Vaughans Gap Road
Nashville, TN 37205
Phone: 615-352-2357   FAX: 615-352-9423
*Sells Aladdin lamps and parts. **

Supplier

Brass Light Gallery
Steve Kaye
131 South First St.
Milwaukee, WI 53204
Phone: 414-271-8300 or 800-243-9595
                    FAX: 414-271-7755
Specializes in parts for gas wall sconces and chandeliers, and for early electric lamps; also does lamp repairs including metal work.

Supplier

Crystal Import Co.
521 W. Rosecrans Ave.
Gardenia, CA 90248
Phone: 213-323-8452   FAX: 213-323-8468
*Source for lamp crystals, chains, spindles, bobesches and bent arms. **

Leather

Repair Service

Wood & Leather Craft
H.C.R. 3, Box 9
Callicoon, NY 12723
Repairs and replaces leather table tops; also does custom tooling.

Repair Service

Bruce Hamilton
551 Main St.
P.O. Box 587
West Newbury, MA 01985
Repairs and replaces leather and cloth table tops.

Repair Service

Tom's Desk Leathers
403 Simcoe St.
Newmarket
Ontario L3Y 2M4 Canada
Phone: 416-836-6004
Repairs and replaces leather table tops; catalog carries samples of leathers (including hand antiqued and distressed) & tooling designs.

Supplier

Pecard
P.O. Box 263
Eugene, OR 97440

Sells the very best antique leather preservative - moisturizes, preserves, colorless, softens, odorless, long-lasting, safe.

Marble

Repair Service

U.S. Tile & Marble Co.
45 Q St. SW
Washington, DC 20024
Phone: 202-554-4370
Repairs broken marble slabs.

Repair Service

Jack T. Irwin, Inc.
601 East Gude Drive
Rockville, MD 20852
Phone: 301-762-5800
*Cuts and repairs marble tops. **

Supplier

Gawet Marble & Granite, Inc.
Route 4
Center Rutland, VT 05736
*Carries products for the cleaning and care of marble. **

Metal Items

Repair Service

Orum Silver Co., Inc.
Joseph J. Pistilli
51 S. Vine St.
P.O. Box 805
Meriden, CT 06450
Phone: 203-237-3037
Repairing, restoring, replating of antique and old silver, gold, nickel; brass & copper plating; cleaning, buffing, polishing.

Repair Service

Estes-Simmons Silverplating, Inc.
1050 Northside Dr., NW
Atlanta, GA 30318
Phone: 404-875-9581
Repairs silver, silverplate, gold, pewter, brass and copper; also replates silver.

Repair Service

Smith-Hoover Metalsmiths
James Smith-Hoover
228 7th St. SE
Washington, DC 20001
Phone: 202-544-3818
*Fine metal and glass refinishing process. **

Repair Service

Bethesda Art Metal Work
4955 Bethesda Ave.
Bethesda, MD 20814
Phone: 301-656-1445 *

Repair Service

Awesome Metal Restorations, Inc.
Boris Paskvan
10524 Detrick Ave.
Kensington, MD 20895
Phone: 301-929-7955
European expert restores gold, gilt, bronze, silver, silver plating, icons, metal accessories, sculptures, etc. for museums, homes, ins.

Repair Service

Abercombie & Co.
9159A Brookeville Rd.
Silver Spring, MD 20910
Phone: 301-585-2385
Replates silverplate; repairs all sorts of metal; silver, brass, copper; also welding.

Repair Service

Creative Metal Design
Pete Markey
7935 Edgewood Church Rd.
Frederick, MD 21702
Phone: 301-473-5995
Specializes in ornamental ironwork, hand forged originals; metal repairs; made the Statue of Liberty gates.

Repair Service

Jarnel Iron & Forge
David Nelson
221 Rowland
Hagerstown, MD 21740
Phone: 301-733-0441
Recasts replacement parts in various metals; also iron work.

Repair Service

Equestrian Forge
Alexander Bigler
P.O. Box 1950
Leesburg, VA 22075
Phone: 703-777-2110
Recasts replacement parts in various metals; also casts portrait sculptures.

Repair Service

Senti-Metal Co.
Silverplating Division
1919 Memory Lane
Columbus, OH 43209
*Replates silverplated items. **

Repair Service

Antique & Art Restoration By Wiebold
413 Terrace Place
Terrace Park, OH 45174
Phone: 513-831-2541
Silver repair and replating; restoration of bronzes, combs, brushes, knife blades, mirrors, frames, paintings, ceramics, glass, etc.

Repair Service

Jerry Probst
P.O. Box 45
Janesville, WI 53547-0045
Phone: 608-752-2816   FAX: 608-752-7691
Repairs silver back hair brushes.

Repair Service

Watkins & Sons
Jay A. Watkins
469 Vernon Way
El Cajon, CA 92020
Phone: 619-441-9441
Silversmithing and repair; silver, brass, copper, aluminum, refinishing; 25 years experience.

Mirrors

Repair Service

Chaudron Glass & Mirror Co., Inc.
Henry Chaudron
1801 Lovegrove St.
Baltimore, MD 21202
Phone: 301-685-1568
Resilvers mirrors; also hand-bevels plate glass.

Painted Finishes

Repair Service

Medusa
149 Sycamore St.
Somerville, MA 02145-2738
Reproduces faux marble, stencils, trompe l'oeil, etc. finishes.

Paper Items

Misc. Service

American Institute for Conservation of
  Historic & Artistic Works
Directory: AIC Directory
Suite #340
1400 16th St. NW
Washington, DC 20036
Phone: 202-232-6636
Cleaning, restoring, deacidification; in general to advance the knowledge and practice of the conservation of cultural property.

Misc. Service

Art Lab - The Restoration Workshop
  Class
David E. Hargis
P.O. Box 6986
Houston, TX 77265
Phone: 713-668-7711
Offers individual classes in the art of paper restoration; admission by application only.

Repair Service

Center for Conservation & Technical
Studies, The
Arthur Beale
Fogg Art Museum
Harvard University
Cambridge, MA 02138 *

Repair Service

Bridgitte Boyadjian
43 Fern Street
Lexington, MA 02173
Phone: 617-862-9395
Paper restoration and conservation; fine prints, drawings, watercolors and manuscripts.

Repair Service

Christa M. Gaehde
55 Falmouth Road
Arlington, MA 02174 *

Repair Service

Mary Todd Glaser
73 E. Linden Avenue
Englewood, NJ 07631 *

Repair Service

Carolyn Horton
430 W. 22nd Street
New York, NY 10011 *

Repair Service

Old Print Shop, The
Kenneth Newman
150 Lexington Ave. at 30th St.
New York, NY 10016
Phone: 212-683-3950
Paper conservator: preservation, restoration, cleaning, deacidification, encapsulation.

Repair Service

Museum of Modern Art
11 W. 53rd. Street
New York, NY 10019 *

Repair Service

Florence Hodes
145 Central Park West
New York, NY 10023 *

Repair Service

Conservation Center of the Institute of
Fine Arts
New York University
1 East 78th Street
New York, NY 10028 *

Repair Service

Brooklyn Museum, The
200 Eastern Parkway
Brooklyn, NY 11238
Phone: 718-638-5000 *

Repair Service

Edith MacKennan
11 Rosalind Road
Poughkeepsie, NY 12601 *

Repair Service

Pennsylvania Academy of Fine Arts
Broad & Cherry Streets
Philadelphia, PA 19102 *

Repair Service

Marilyn Kemp Weidner, FAIC
612 Spruce Street
Philadelphia, PA 19106
Phone: 215-627-2303 or 215-627-0188
Offers conservation treatment for art, artifacts, library & archival materials on paper; collection surveys and care consultations.

Repair Service

Archival Restoration Associates, Inc.
P.O. Box 1395
North Wales, PA 19454
Phone: 215-699-0165
Quality restorations of books, paper, photographs, parchment, and watercolors; estimates determined by condition of individual

Repair Service

Old Print Gallery, The
James Von Ruster
1220 31st St. NW
Washington, DC 20007
Phone: 202-965-1818   FAX: 202-965-1869
Paper conservator: preservation, restoration, cleaning, deacidification, encapsulation.

Repair Service

Kendra Lovette
6611 Park Heights Ave.
Baltimore, MD 21215
Phone: 301-764-6770
Paper conservator and repairer; anything on paper.

Repair Service

Dobson Studios
Janice & Dennis Dobson
810 N. Daniel St.
Arlington, VA 22201
Phone: 703-243-7363
Conservator of Oriental screens, scrolls and wood block prints; repairs and restoration to other paper items as well.

Repair Service

Conservation of Art On Paper, Inc.
Christine Smith, Dir.
Suite 110
3110 Mt. Vernon Ave.
Alexandria, VA 22305
Phone: 703-836-7757
Collections surveys, lectures/workshops, paper conservator: preservation, restoration, cleaning, deacidification, encapsulation.

Repair Service

Murray Lebwohl Studio, Inc.
1212 I Street
Alexandria, VA 22307 *

Repair Service
David Swift
6436 Brownlee Dr.
Nashville, TN 37205
Phone: 615-352-0308
Paper conservator: preservation, restoration, cleaning, deacidification, encapsulation. *

Repair Service
John Pofelski
190 South Wood Dale Road
Wood Dale, IL 60191 *

Repair Service
Art Institute of Chicago
Michigan Ave. at Adams Street
Chicago, IL 60603
Phone: 312-443-3600 *

Repair Service
Wynne H. Phelan
3721 Ella Lee Lane
Houston, TX 77027 *

Repair Service
Art Lab
David E. Hargis
P.O. Box 6986
Houston, TX 77265
Phone: 713-668-7711
Offers professional restoration of all paper collectibles, movie material, golden age comics, toy boxes & original art.

Supplier
University Products, Inc.
517 Main St.
P.O. Box 101
Holyoke, MA 01041-0101
Phone: 800-336-4847 or 800-628-1912
                              FAX: 413-532-9281
Carries safe products for the long term storage of postcards, posters, stamps, textiles, costumes; acid free archival supplies.

Supplier
TALAS
213 West 35th Street
New York, NY 10001-1996
Phone: 212-736-7744   FAX: 212-465-8722
Archival supplies for artists, restorers, collectors, bookbinders, conservators, calligraphers, museums, archives, libraries, etc.

Supplier
S & W Framing Supplies, Inc.
P.O. Box 340
New Hyde Park, NY 11040
General line of archival supplies including mat boards, document storage boxes, framing and photographic supplies. *

Supplier
Light Impressions Corp.
P.O. Box 940
Rochester, NY 14603
Phone: 800-828-9629 or 800-828-6216
                              FAX: 716-442-7318
General line of archival supplies including mat boards, document storage boxes, framing and photographic supplies.

Supplier
Conservation Resources International,
Inc.
8000 H Forbes Place
Springfield, VA 22151
Archival supplies for works of art on paper; document and photographic storage materials. *

Supplier
Hollinger Corporation
P.O. Box 6185
Arlington, VA 22206
Archival supplies for works of art on paper; document and photographic storage materials.

Supplier
Conservation Materials, Ltd.
P.O. Box 2884
Sparks, NV 89431
General line of archival supplies including mat boards, document storage boxes, framing and photographic supplies. *

Supplier
Restorations
P.O. Box 2000
Nevada City, CA 95959
Phone: 916-477-5527
Restoration services & supplies for baseball cards, comics, magazines; crease removal, corner repairs, spines rebuilt; free catalog.

Porcelain

(see also REPAIRS & RESTORATIONS, Ceramics)

Reverse Painting On Glass

Repair Service
Helige Ande Arts
Ingrid Sanborn
85 Church St.
West Newbury, MA 01985
Phone: 508-363-2253
Highly skilled at reproducing reverse paintings on glass.

Textiles

Repair Service
Textile Conservation Center, Museum of American Textile History
800 Mass. Ave.
North Andover, MA 01845
Phone: 508-686-0191

TCC provides evaluation, treatment and educational services that pertain to the conservation and preservation of historic

Repair Service
Shallcross & Lorraine
State House Post Office
Box 133
Boston, MA 02133
Phone: 617-720-2133
Reweaves and repairs Indian rugs, tapestries, needlework, etc.

Repair Service
Stephen & Carol Huber
82 Plants Dam Rd.
East Lyme, CT 06333
Phone: 203-739-0772   FAX: 203-739-0261
Specializes in the repair and conservation of antique needlework.

Repair Service
Testfabrics, Inc.
P.O. Box 420
Middlesex, NJ 08846
Phone: 201-469-6446   FAX: 201-469-1147
Provides textile conservation services.

Repair Service
Applebaum & Himmelstein
444 Central Park West
New York, NY 10025
Phone: 212-666-4630
Repairs silk textiles.

Repair Service
Textile Conservation Workshop
Patsy Orlofsky
Main Street
South Salem, NY 10590
Phone: 914-736-5805
Textile conservation lecturer and consultant; also does conservation and repairs of all types of textiles.

Repair Service
Thanewold Associates
P.O. Box 104
Zieglerville, PA 19492
Phone: 215-287-9158
Needlework repairs and conservation including samplers.

Repair Service
C. P. & Asst.
Clarissa Palmai
5416 Harwood Rd.
Bethesda, MD 20814
Phone: 301-656-6381
Offers textile conservation, consultation and lecturing.

Repair Service

Linens Limited
240 North Milwaukee St.
Milwaukee, WI 53202
Phone: 414-223-1123   FAX: 414-223-1126
Specializes in the repair of linens.

Repair Service

Emily Sanford
451 Gould Ave.
Hermosa Beach, CA 90254
Phone: 213-374-7412
*Restoration of textiles and oriental rugs. ***

Upholstery

Man./Prod./Dist.

Sleep Tite Mattress Company
8 Moore Street
Middletown, OH 45042
Phone: 513-422-9206
*Specializes in custom made mattresses and box springs for hard-to-fit antique beds. ***

Supplier

John K. Burch Co.
1818 Underwood Blvd.
Delran, NJ 08075
Phone: 800-257-9112
Mail order source for upholstering supplies; also fabric books.

Supplier

Douglas Industries, Inc.
412 Boston Ave.
Egg Harbor City, NJ 08215
Phone: 800-257-8551
Source for foam and fabrics.

Supplier

Carrousel Foam
1940 S. West Blvd.
Vineland, NJ 08360
Phone: 609-692-1777
Source for foam.

Supplier

Jack Raskin's Upholstery Supplies
1810-20 E. Boston St.
Philadelphia, PA 19125
Phone: 800-523-3213
Mail order source for upholstering supplies.

Supplier

Minute-Man Upholstery Supply Company of
North Carolina
P.O. Box 6534
High Point, NC 27262
Phone: 800-457-0029
Mail order source for upholstering supplies.

Supplier

Lexol Division, The, Corona Products
Company
P.O. Box 1214
Atlanta, GA 30301
Phone: 404-524-5434
*Sells a very good product for softening old and stiff leather. ***

Wicker

Repair Service

Garnett's Wicker Shop
Garnett Drake
Route 6, Box 39
Decatur, AL 35603 *

Repair Service

Wickery, The
Bea Niles
644 College St.
Milton, WI 53563 *

Woodworking

(see also REPAIRS & RESTORATIONS,
Furniture)

Repair Service

Original Woodworks
360 North Main St.
Stillwater, MN 55082
Phone: 612-430-3622
A full service shop specializing in antique restorations including furniture and architectural elements.

Supplier

Woodcraft
P.O. Box 4000
Woburn, MA 01888
Phone: 800-225-1153
Mail order source for complete line of woodworking tools, supplies and books.

Supplier

Period Furniture Hardware Co., Inc.
Charles Street Station
P.O. Box 314
Boston, MA 02114
Phone: 617-227-0758   FAX: 617-227-2987
Supplies fine quality reproduction hardware for furniture and the home; specializes in solid brass fittings and accessories.

Supplier

Trendlines
375 Beacham Street
Chelsea, MA 02150
Phone: 800-767-9999
Mail order source for a good mix of woodworking tools.

Supplier

Tremont Nail Company
Elm Street at Route 28
Wareham, MA 02571
Carries twenty different styles of historic cut nails.

Supplier

Brookstone
127 Vose Farm Road
Peterborough, NH 03458
Phone: 603-924-9541
Mail order source for hard to find tools and devices.

Supplier

Horton Brasses
P.O. Box 95
Cromwell, CT 06416
Phone: 203-635-4400   FAX: 203-635-6473
Sells reproduction hardware of finest quality, manufactured in CT of solid brass; exactly replicates originals; styles from 1600-1920.

Supplier

Micro Mark
340 Snyder Ave.
Berkeley Heights, NJ 07922
Mail order source for small tools only, e.g. X-Acto.

Supplier

Garrett Wade Company, Inc.
161 Avenue Of The Americas
New York, NY 10013-1299
Phone: 800-221-2942   FAX: 212-255-8552
Reproduction English solid brass hardware; also 220 page catalog of the world's finest specialty woodworking tools: planes, chisels, etc.

Supplier

Constantine
2050 Eastchester Road
Bronx, NY 10461
Phone: 800-223-8087   FAX: 212-792-2110
A complete line of tools, hardware, finishing supplies, marquetry kits, books, moldings, parts, veneers, hardwoods, etc.

Supplier

Mohawk Finishing Products
Rt. 30 Perth Rd.
Amsterdam, NY 12010
Phone: 800-545-0047
Major supplier of finishing tools, supplies and materials.

Supplier

Wood Finishing Supply Co., Inc.
1267 Mary Drive
Macedon, NY 14502
Phone: 315-986-4517
Mail order source for wood finishing supplies and brass hardware.

Supplier
Cyder Creek Wood Shoppe, Inc.
Box 19
Whitesville, NY 14897
Phone: 800-642-9663
Mail order source for wood turners' hand tools, books and supplies.

Supplier
18th Century Hardware Co., Inc.
John M. Fisher
131 East 3rd St.
Derry, PA 15627
Phone: 412-694-2708
Clean, polish & repair brass items; makes, sells reproduction hardware; clean and electrify brass lamps; offers catalog.

Supplier
Hoosier Emporium, The
Rick Zirpoli
Route 529, Box 264
Milanville, PA 18443
Phone: 717-729-7080
Manufactures & distributes authentically reproduced "want lists" and cardboard inserts for Hoosier, Sellers, etc. style kitchen cabinets.

Supplier
Ye Old Cowpath Antiques
59 Cowpath Road
Souderton, PA 18964
*Source for slip-on bedrail extenders. ***

Supplier
Ball & Ball
463 W. Lincoln Highway
Exton, PA 19341
Publishes a hardware catalog; also has a recasting service.

Supplier
American Machine & Tool Company
P.O. Box 70
Oyersford, PA 19468
Phone: 215-948-0400
Mail order source for hand tools and machinery.

Supplier
Industrial Abrasives Co.
Box 14955
Reading, PA 19612
Carries a large line of sand paper and other abrasives.

Supplier
Paxton Hardware Ltd.
P.O. Box 256
Upper Falls, MD 21156
Phone: 301-592-8505   FAX: 301-592-2224
Supplies brass reproduction hardware in period styles; 74 pg. catalog also contains pulls, knobs, locks, hinges, lamp parts, shades, etc.

Supplier
Bedell Manufacturing Company
P.O. Box 626
Merrifield, VA 22116
Phone: 703-573-7090
*Source for Victorian platform rocker replacement springs. ***

Supplier
Woodworking Tools & Books
1045 N. Highland Ave., NE
Atlanta, GA 30306
Phone: 800-241-6748
Mail order source for hand tools, machinery, workbenches, books, videos, and supplies.

Supplier
A & H Brass & Supply
1402 W. Market St.
Johnson City, TN 37601
Phone: 615-928-8220
Carries a wide selection of hardware, caning supplies, trunk parts, fiberboard seats, etc.

Supplier
Bob Morgan Woodworking Supplies
1123 Bardstown Road
Louisville, KY 40204
Phone: 502-456-2545
Mail order source for hardwoods, veneers, hand tools, and supplies.

Supplier
Cherry Tree Toys, Inc.
P.O. Box 369
Belmont, OH 43718
Phone: 614-484-4363
Mail order source for children's toys, doll houses, whirligig kits, parts, books and supplies.

Supplier
Farmerstown Furniture
Junior & Robert Hershberger
3155 S.R. 557
Baltic, OH 43804
Phone: 216-893-2464
Catalog of specialty products such as spool cabinet decals, highchair trays, iron bed parts, parts for iceboxes and Hoosier cabinets, etc.

Supplier
Leichtung Workshops
4944 Commerce Parkway
Cleveland, OH 44128
Phone: 800-321-6840
Mail order source for hand tools, supplies and small kits.

Supplier
Shopsmith Tool Guide
3931 Image Dr.
Dayton, OH 45414
Phone: 800-543-7586 or 800-762-7555
Mail order source for hand tools and supplies. Visit local Shopsmith Store or order by phone.

Supplier
Phyllis Kennedy Hardware
Phyllis & Phil Kennedy
9256 Holyoke Court
Indianapolis, IN 46268
Phone: 317-872-6366
Hardware for antique furniture, Hoosier cabinets and trunks; manufacturer of flour bins and sifters for Hoosier cabinets.

Supplier
Gaston's
2626 N. Walnut
Bloomington, IN 47408
Phone: 812-339-9111
*Wood finishing stains, lacquers, antique hardware, hard to find items. Call or write for free catalog. ***

Supplier
Doug's Furniture Refinishing & Supply
144 Sheldon
Climax, MI 49034
Phone: 616-746-4104
*Carries strippers, finishers, sanders, sandpaper and belts, carvings, reproduction hardware, glue, screws, chair seats, etc. ***

Supplier
Woodsmith Store
P.O. Box 1035
Des Moines, IA 50306
Phone: 800-444-7002
Mail order source for woodworking tools, hardware, and project plans and supplies.

Supplier
Silvo Hardware Co.
P.O. Box 92069
Milwaukee, WI 53202
Phone: 800-331-1261
Mail order source for hand tools and hardware.

Supplier
Heirloom Antique Brass Co.
P.O. Box 146
Dundas, MN 55019
Phone: 507-645-9341
Wholesale to dealers only; Victorian, Eastlake, and turn-of-the-century hardware.

Supplier
Restore-It Supply Co.
P.O. Box 10600
White Bear Lake, MN 55110
Phone: 612-429-2222
Sells restoration products such as tools, veneers, seat weaving supplies, decals, etc.

Supplier
Woodworkers' Store, The
21801 Industrial Blvd.
Rogers, MN 55374-9514
Phone: 612-428-4101 or 612-428-2199
                    FAX: 612-428-8668

Mail order source for hand tools, inlays, veneers, hardware, and hardwoods.

Supplier
Van Dykes Supply Company
P.O. Box 278
Woonsocket, SD 57385
Phone: 800-843-3320 or 605-796-4425
Mail order source for refinishing supplies; also issues a catalog of taxidermy supplies.

Supplier
Craftsman Wood Service Co.
1734 W. Cortland Ct.
Addison, IL 60101
Phone: 312-629-3100
Mail order source for hand tools, hardware, and finishing supplies.

Supplier
Star Chemical Co.
360 Shore Drive
Hinsdale, IL 60521
Phone: 708-654-8650
Major supplier of finishing tools, supplies and materials.

Supplier
Sears Power & Hand Tool Specialog
925 S. Homan Avenue
Chicago, IL 60607
Call your local Sears store catalog department for a copy of this Specialog.

Supplier
Clark Manufacturing Co.
Route 2
Raymore, MO 64083
Phone: 816-331-6851
*Manufacturers replacement pierced tins for pie safes. ***

Supplier
Wise Company, The
Noel & Bernice Wise
Dept. CIC
P.O. Box 118
Arabi, LA 70032-0118
Phone: 504-277-7551 or 504-277-7551
Hard to find antique reproduction hardware; also repairs old locks and makes new keys for old locks.

Supplier
Good Pickins'
Box 665
Jefferson, TX 75657
*Mail order source for old ice box hardware. ***

Supplier
Woodworker's Supply of New Mexico
5604 Alameda Place, NE
Albuquerque, NM 87113
Phone: 800-645-9292
Mail order source for hand tools, machinery, and hardware.

Supplier
Muff's Antiques
135 S. Glassell St.
Orange, CA 92666
*Mail order source for kitchen cabinet hardware (Hoosiers) including hinges, labels, canisters, castors, and rolls; also ice box parts. ***

Supplier
Harbor Freight Tools
3491 Mission Oaks Blvd.
Camarillo, CA 93011-6010
Phone: 800-423-2567   FAX: 805-388-0760
Absolutely the lowest prices on quality name brand tools, equipment, machinery for both the home and professional workshop; free catalog.

Supplier
Woodline the Japan Woodworker
1731 Clement Ave.
Alameda, CA 94501
Phone: 415-521-1810
Mail order source for highest quality woodworking tools from Japan.

Supplier
Finishing Touch, The
5636 College Ave.
Oakland, CA 94618
Phone: 415-652-4908
*Source for replacement pressed leather seats made of oak-tanned hides; also carries caning products and instructions. ***

Supplier
American Home Supply
P.O. Box 697
Campbell, CA 95009
Phone: 408-246-1962   FAX: 408-248-1308
Carries the largest selection of antique reproduction hardware on the West Coast; has a 99.9% stock rate.

Supplier
Anglo American Brass Company
Box 9792
San Jose, CA 95157-0792
Phone: 800-AAB-RASS
Publishes a hardware catalog; brass hardware, household hinges, glass knobs, brass casters, nickel plate ice box hardware, wooden casters.

Supplier
Ritter & Son Hardware
38001 Old Stage Road
P.O. Box 578
Gualala, CA 95445-9984
Phone: 707-884-3363 or 800-358-9120
              FAX: 707-884-1515
Supplier of furniture restoration hardware: carved oak gingerbread, Hoosier hardware, cast & stamped brass pulls, handles, etc.

Supplier
Old Hotel Antiques
P.O. Box 94
Sutter Creek, CA 95685
Phone: 209-267-5901
*Source for replacement solid oak replacement high chair trays. ***

Supplier
Bridge City Tool Works
1104 N.E. 28th Ave.
Portland, OR 97232
Phone: 503-282-6997
Mail order source for fine woodworking hand tools.

REPRODUCTION SOURCES

(see also BRASS ITEMS; BRONZES; FURNITURE; ORIENTALIA; SCRIMSHAW; and other individual categories)

General Line (Antiques)
Repro. Source
Verouden's Furniture, Ltd.
P.O. Box 312
Innerkip
Ontario NOJ 1MO Canada
Phone: 519-469-3256
*Various categories of reproduction furniture, carriages, carousel horses, etc. ***

Repro. Source
Sturbridge Yankee Workshop
Blueberry Rd.
Westbrook, ME 04092

Repro. Source
Artique Inc.
259 Godwin Ave.
Midland Park, NJ 07432
Phone: 201-444-8989
Repro. glassware, clay pipes, fraktur, advertising memorabilia, Christmas tree ornaments, wrought iron items, pottery, flags.

Repro. Source
B. Shackman & Co., Inc.
85 Fifth Ave.
New York, NY 10003
Phone: 212-989-5162
*Antique replica books, dolls, doll house furniture, miniatures, toys, Christmas ornaments. ***

Repro. Source
Metropolitan Museum of Art
Special Service Dept.
Middle Village, NY 11381
Phone: 312-673-6006

Repro. Source

Montgomery Wholesale Liquidators
151 Ward St., Route 17K
Montgomery, NY 12549
Phone: 914-457-9405
*Has large catalog of reproduction furniture and accessories. *

Repro. Source

Fred & Dottie's
Box 221, RD 3
Birdsboro, PA 19508
Phone: 215-582-1506
Repro furniture, wicker, glass, cast iron toys and banks, carousel animals, carriages, etc.

Repro. Source

Merritt's Antiques, Inc.
R.D. 2
Douglassville, PA 19518
Phone: 215-689-9541 or 800-345-4101
                    FAX: 215-689-4538
Carries a large line or reproduction clocks, ceramics, brass, dolls, furniture, glass, etc.

Repro. Source

Henry Francis DuPont Winterthur Museum
Direct Mail Marketing Office
Winterthur, DE 19735
Phone: 800-441-8229

Repro. Source

Avalon Forge
409 Gun Rd.
Baltimore, MD 21227
Phone: 301-242-8431
Offers documented 18th century replicas for living history such as military goods, farm and home items.

Repro. Source

Colonial Williamsburg
P.O. Box CH
Williamsburg, VA 23187
Phone: 800-446-9240

Repro. Source

Battlefield Antiques, Inc.
829 Chickamauga Ave.
Rossville, GA 30741
Phone: 404-861-3690
*Has large catalog of reproduction furniture and accessories. *

Repro. Source

Ideal Imports, Inc.
1340 Stirling Road
Dania, FL 33004
Phone: 305-922-1942   FAX: 305-922-6108
Sells new creations: bronzes, paintings, lamps, wood and more; special attention given to authentic patina.

Repro. Source

Verouden's Furniture, Ltd.
129 W. Lake St.
South Lyon, MI 48178
Phone: 313-437-9650
*Various categories of reproduction furniture, carriages, carousel horses, etc. *

Repro. Source

AA Importing Company, Inc.
7700 Hall St.
St. Louis, MO 63147
Phone: 314-383-8800 or 800-325-0602
                    FAX: 314-383-2608
Repro. Orientalia, porcelains, stoneware, cast iron banks and toys, simulated ivory, weathervanes, oak furniture; to the trade only.

Repro. Source

Burton's Antiques & Antique
Reproductions
Jim "Bud" Burton
9333 Harwin Drive
Houston, TX 77036
Phone: 713-789-9333 or 713-977-5885
                    FAX: 713-789-8181
Carries furniture and aluminum reproductions such as light poles, carousel horses, patio tables & chairs, etc.

Repro. Source

Barn Haus
28121 Timberline
San Antonio, TX 78260
*Sells reproduction Victorian street lights, carousel horses, etc. *

Repro. Source

J.K. Reed
Ron McKeown
1805 SE Union Avenue
Portland, OR 97214
Phone: 503-235-3156 or 800-537-7305
                    FAX: 503-231-2530
Carries reproductions of Victorian-style accent pieces: bird cages, rocking horses, doll carriages, iron tricycles, carousel horses, etc.

RESTAURANT COLLECTIBLES

(see also BOB'S BIG BOY ITEMS; FAST FOOD COLLECTIBLES; FOOD COLLECTIBLES; MENUS)

Collector

Glenn Grush
8400 Sunset Blvd.
Los Angeles, CA 90069
Phone: 213-656-4758
Wants restaurant memorabilia: Bob's Big Boy, Coon Chicken Inn, Sambo's; nodders, ceramic display pieces, tableware with logos, etc.

RESTRAINT DEVICES

(see also KEYS; LOCKS)

Handcuffs

Expert

International Handcuff Exchange
Michael Griffin
356 W. Powell Rd.
Powell, OH 43065
Phone: 614-846-0585
Buys/sells all types of handcuffs, leg irons, locks, magicians escape items, old or new; offers large quarterly list of items for sale.

Handcuffs & Leg Shackles

Dealer

Wheeler-Tanner ESCAPES
Joseph & Pamela Tanner
P.O. Box 349
Great Falls, MT 59403
Phone: 406-453-4961
Specialize in handcuffs, leg shackles, balls & chains, restraints, padlocks, locks & locking devices of all kinds (including railroad).

REVOLUTIONARY WAR ITEMS

Collector

Larry Jarvinen
313 Condon Rd.
Manistee, MI 49660
Phone: 616-723-5063
Wants muskets, lamps, pipes, chests, swords, polearms, tools, silverware, compasses, bayonets, canteens, etc.

Expert

Antiques Americana
K.C. Owings
Box 19
N. Abington, MA 02351
Phone: 617-857-1655 *

REWARDS OF MERIT

Collector

R. Wenzel
839 W. Fullerton
Chicago, IL 60614
Phone: 312-248-4642
*Wants trade cards, rewards of merit, 19th century scrap albums, bound vols. of sheet music; also other ephemera. *

RIDING TOYS

(see also BICYCLES; TOYS, Pedal Vehicles; TRICYCLES; WAGONS)

RIPLEY'S BELIEVE IT OR NOT

Collector

Dan Paulun
215 South Maple
West Lafayette, OH 43845
Phone: 614-545-9743

Wants anything Ripley: blotters, calendars, posters, museum & odditorium postcards and booklets, newspaper & magazine ads, etc.

ROBJ

Collector
Charles Sorkin
19 Chatsworth Ave.
Larchmont, NY 10538
Phone: 914-235-4718
Wants Robj porcelains: figural bottles, inkwells, powder jars, statuettes; any piece marked "Robj"; call collect.

Expert
Cocktails & Laughter Antiques
Randall Monsen
P.O. Box 1503
Arlington, VA 22210
Phone: 703-938-2129 *

ROCKETS
(see also MODEL KITS)

Club/Association
National Association of Rocketry
182 Madison Dr.
Elizabeth, PA 15037 *

Model Rocket Kits

Collector
Mark Mayfield
1207 Briarhill Lane
Atlanta, GA 30324
Phone: 404-321-5640
*Wants model rocket kits especially Saturn 1B, Little Joe II, Honest John, Pershing, X-Wing Fighter, Cineroc, Camroc. *

ROCK 'N' ROLL
(see also AUTOGRAPHS; MAGAZINES, Scandal/Cult/R 'n' R; MUSIC, Rock 'n' Roll; PERSONALITIES (MUSICIANS); RECORDS; SHEET MUSIC)

ROGERS GROUPS

Club/Association
Rogers Group, The
Newsletter: Newsletter of the Rogers Group
George Humphrey
4932 Prince George Ave.
Beltsville, MD 20705
Phone: 301-937-7899
Focuses on the life and works of John Rogers (1829-1904), American sculptor.

Dealer
Carmen's Garden of Treasures
Carme Pederson
114 E. 32nd St.
New York, NY 10016
Phone: 212-683-9197

Expert
George Humphrey
4932 Prince George Ave.
Beltsville, MD 20705
Phone: 301-937-7899
Interested in the life and works of John Rogers (1829-1904), American sculptor.

Museum/Library
John Rogers Studio & Museum of the New Cannan Historical Society
13 Oenoke Ridge
New Canaan, CT 06840
Phone: 203-966-1776

Museum/Library
Lightner Museum
P.O. Box 334
St. Augustine, FL 32085
Phone: 904-824-2874

ROLLER COASTERS
(see also AMUSEMENT PARK ITEMS)

Club/Association
American Coaster Enthusiasts, Inc.
Magazine: Rollercoaster!
Ray J. Ueberroth, Pres
P.O. Box 8226
Chicago, IL 60680
Phone: 301-385-1222   FAX: 301-385-1222
Promotes the preservation, appreciation and enjoyment of the roller coaster; 4000 members in 40 states and 17 countries.

ROSE O'NEILL COLLECTIBLES
(see also DOLLS, Kewpie)

Club/Association
International Rose O'Neill Club
Newsletter: Kewpiesta Kourier, The
Box E
Nixa, MO 65714
Phone: 417-725-3291
*Interested in Kewpie dolls and other items designed by Rose O'Neill (1874-1944). *

Expert
Lois Holman
309 Walnut Lane
Branson, MO 65616
Phone: 417-334-3273 *

Expert
Denis C. Jackson
P.O. Box 1958
Sequim, WA 98382
Phone: 206-683-2559
Author of "The Price & Identification Guide to Rose O'Neill"; covering magazine covers, advertising, paper items from Puck, etc.

ROYALTY COLLECTIBLES

British

Collector
Britannia Past
Edward J. Sperling
P.O. Box 977
Kennebunkport, ME 04046
Phone: 207-967-5989
Buys and sells by mail order British Royalty commemoratives: china, glass, silver, paper, textile, etc.

Dealer
British Royalty Commemoratives
Audrey B. Zeder
6755 Coralite CC
Long Beach, CA 90808
Phone: 213-421-0881
Buys, sells, British Royal commemorative items: ceramics, tins, magazines & souvenirs for all British royalty events; list $3.

Expert
Holloway House
Al Bolton
P.O. Box 210
Lititz, PA 17543
Phone: 717-627-4567 *

Expert
British Royalty Commemoratives
Audrey B. Zeder
6755 Coralite CC
Long Beach, CA 90808
Phone: 213-421-0881
Author of "British Royal Commemoratives."

ROYCROFT
(see also ARTS & CRAFTS, Roycroft)

RUBBER ITEMS

Museum/Library
Goodyear World of Rubber
1201 East Market Street
Akron, OH 44316
Phone: 216-796-2044

Clothing

Collector
Collector
Box 292
Villanova, PA 19085
Wants rubber raincoats, hats, rain suits, capes; any color; or photographs of firemen, policemen, fishermen, etc. wearing same.

Syringe Outfits

Collector
Brunswick
Box 9729
Baltimore, MD 21204

Wants hot bottles, bulbs, enamel cans, etc.: pre-1965 or foreign; also books, accessories, boxes, ads, catalogs, photos on use, etc.

RUGS

Repro. Source

Family Heir-Loom Weavers
David C. Kline
R.D. #3, Box 59E
Red Lion, PA 17356
Phone: 717-246-2431
Makers of fancy jacquard coverlets, ingrain carpets & other historic textiles; carpets in the Abe Lincoln home & various other sites.

Hooked

(see also FOLK ART)

Repair Service

Angela Lyons
127 Boston Post Rd.
Wayland, MA 01778
Phone: 617-358-4354
Repairs hooked rugs. *

Repair Service

Linda Eliasom
Box 542
Manchester, VT 05254
Phone: 802-867-2252
Repairs hooked rugs. *

Oriental

Club/Association

California Rug Society
6091 Claremont Ave.
Oakland, CA 94618
Phone: 415-655-0167
Provides information on the age, care, and authenticity of oriental rugs. *

Dealer

David Zahirpour Oriental Rugs
David Zahirpour
4918 Wisconsin Ave. NW
Washington, DC 20016
Phone: 202-338-4141 or 202-244-1800
Specialist in Oriental rugs; cleans and repairs; hand washing, stain removal, carpet reweaving and restoration, appraisals, etc.

Dealer

J & J Oriental Rug Gallery
B. Joseph Nabatkhorian
1200 King St.
Alexandria, VA 22314
Phone: 703-548-0000 or 800-343-3843
Wants used oriental rugs, any size or condition.

Dealer

Gerald W. Thompson Oriental Rugs
Gerald W. Thompson
P.O. Box 193
Shepherdstown, WV 25443
Phone: 304-876-2218
Specialist in antique and semi-antique oriental rugs with 20 years experience; also does repairs, appraisals, and lecturing.

Dealer

Aaron's Oriental Rug Gallery
Bob Anderson
1217 Broadway
Ft. Wayne, IN 46802
Phone: 219-422-5184
Pays cash for oriental rugs. Will travel. Free appraisals.

Dealer

Ciamak Khodad
817 West Lill St.
Chicago, IL 60614-2309
Phone: 800-848-RUGS
Wants old oriental rugs.

Expert

Persian Carpet, The
Dr. Douglas Lay
5634 Chapel Hill Boulevard
Durham, NC 27707
Phone: 919-968-0366 *

Expert

Sharon Kerwick
1633 NE 24th St.
Ft. Lauderdale, FL 33305
Phone: 305-565-9031

Expert

Val Arbab
P.O. Box 684
La Jolla, CA 92038
Phone: 619-453-4686
Appraises all oriental rugs and textiles; also buys, sells and brokers collectible and old decorative rugs.

Man./Prod./Dist.

Peerless Imported Rugs
3028 North Lincoln Ave.
Chicago, IL 60657
Phone: 800-621-6573

Periodical

Magazine: Oriental Rug Review
P.O. Box 709
Meredith, NH 03253
Phone: 603-744-9191   FAX: 603-744-6933
Published bi-monthly and focuses primarily on old rugs; book reviews, auctions, articles, etc.

Periodical

Magazine: Decorative Rug
R.F.D. 2 Beech Hill Rd.
Meredith, NH 03253 *

Periodical

Magazine: HALI
P.O. Box 4312
Philadelphia, PA 19118
Phone: 215-843-3090
An internationally recognized scholarly magazine about Oriental rugs.

Oritenal

Periodical

Museum Books, Inc.
Magazine: Rug News
34 West 37th Street
New York, NY 10018
Phone: 212-563-2771   FAX: 212-563-2798
Contains articles about the construction and quality of new Oriental rugs, primarily; also auction reports, shows, buy & sell ads.

RUSSEL WRIGHT

(see also CERAMICS (AMERICAN), Russel Wright Designs)

Collector

Dennis Boyd
211 S. Mulberry St.
Richmond, VA 23220
Wants Russel Wright dinnerware, sterling, stainless flatware, aluminum items, etc. *

Dealer

Racoons Tale
Edward E. Stump
6 High Street
Mullica Hill, NJ 08062
Phone: 609-478-4488 or 609-467-1265
Wants Russel Wright items: china dinnerware, modern, Iroquois, sterling & highlights; also anything unusual.

RUSSIAN ITEMS

Collector

Norman Roule
Amemb
APO, NY 09038-0001
Wants Russian books, postcards, autographs, coins, stamps, medals, regarding revolution and before WWI and Russian Civil War. *

Dealer

American-Russian Trade Company
P.O. Box 278183
Sacramento, CA 95826-8183
Phone: 916-366-8850
Buys and sells Imperial Russian items: enamels, metal, art; civil, military, religious, etc.; send photo or photocopy and price, please.

Museum/Library
Hillwood, The Marjorie Merriweather
Post Collection
4155 Linnean Ave. NW
Washington, DC 20008
Phone: 202-686-0410

Enamels

Expert
Melvin & Barb Alpern
14 Carter Rd.
West Orange, NJ 07052
Phone: 201-731-9427 *

Repair Service
Manhattan Art & Antiques Center, Shop
26
Clifford Baron
1050 Second Avenue
New York, NY 10022
Phone: 212-688-8510
Repairs Russian enamels. *

Faberge

Museum/Library
Forbes Magazine Collection
60 Fifth Avenue
New York, NY 10011
Phone: 212-206-5548
Collection of Russian Faberge eggs.

Museum/Library
Walters Art Gallery
600 N. Charles Street
Baltimore, MD 21201
Phone: 301-547-9000

Museum/Library
Virginia Museum of Fine Arts, Lillian
Thomas Pratt Collection
2800 Grove Ave.
Richmond, VA 23221-2466
Phone: 804-367-0888   FAX: 804-367-9393
*Fine arts museum covering the entire range of
history of art.*

Museum/Library
Cleveland Museum of Art, India Early
Minshall Collection
11150 East Boulevard
Cleveland, OH 44106
Phone: 216-421-7340

Samovars

Collector
Jerome M. Marks Agency
Jerome M. Marks
962 Sibley Tower Bldg.
Rochester, NY 14604
Phone: 716-546-2017   FAX: 716-546-3184
Wants to buy older Russian samovars.

SACKS

Flour & Sugar
(see also MILLING)

Collector
Sacks Appeal
Ross Hartsough
98 Bryn Mar Rd.
Winnipeg
Manitoba R3T 3P5 Canada
Phone: 204-269-1022
*Wants colorful flour, sugar, etc. sacks; especially
with cut-out patterns imprinted on the sack.*

SADDLES
(see also HORSE COLLECTIBLES;
WESTERN AMERICANA)

Collector
Gregg
Joy Road
Woodstock, CT 06281
Phone: 203-928-9204
*Wants side saddles or anything relating to side
saddles; saddlery catalogs, antique riding clothes
and accessories, etc.* *

SAFES
(see also LOCKS)

Club/Association
National Antique Safe Association
Magazine: Safe World
P.O. Box 110099
Aurora, CO 80011 *

Collector
Edward Stuart
3025 Ontario Road NW #203
Washington, DC 20009
Phone: 202-332-6511
*Wants pre-1900 safe locks, combination or key
operated types; also old brass or iron safe name
plates, or safe or safe lock catalogs.*

SALOON COLLECTIBLES
(see also ALCOHOLICS ANONYMOUOS
ITEMS; BREWERIANA; COCKTAIL
SHAKERS; PROHIBITION ITEMS;
WHISKEY INDUSTRY ITEMS)

Expert
Robert Doyle
R.D. 3 Box 137
Fishkill, NY 12524
Phone: 914-896-9492 *

Expert
Richard M. Bueschel
414 N. Prospect Manor Ave.
Mt. Prospect, IL 60056
Phone: 708-253-0791

*Wants pre-prohibition saloon photos, equipment,
catalogs, drink-mixers, books and other ephemera;
author of book on same.*

Expert
Baker's Lady Luck Emporium
Roger V. Baker
P.O. Box 620417
Woodside, CA 94062
Phone: 415-851-7188
*Specializing in saloon collectibles: gambling, bar
bottles, shaving mugs, razors, Bowie knives, dagg-
ers, barber items, match safes.*

SALT & PEPPER SHAKERS

Collector
Judy Posner
R.D. 1 Box 273
Effort, PA 18330
Phone: 717-629-6583   FAX: 717-629-0521
*Wants figural salt & pepper shakers: Black Ameri-
cana, Disneyana, Ceramic Art Studio, Regal
China, advertising figurals, etc.*

Dealer
Helene Guarnaccia
52 Coach Lane
Fairfield, CT 06430
Phone: 203-374-6034
List available upon request.

Dealer
Salt & Pepper Man, The
Larry Carey
P.O. Box 329
Mechanicsburg, PA 17055
Phone: 717-766-0868
Buys novelty salt and pepper shake collections.

Dealer
Lois' Collectibles of Antique Market
III
Lois & Ralph Behm
413 W. Main St.
St. Charles, IL 60174
Phone: 708-377-5599 *

Dealer
Peggy Cole
134 E. Laveta
Orange, CA 92666
Phone: 715-997-7379
*Wants nodder and black Americana figural salt &
pepper shakers.*

Expert
Bea Morgan
Lakeview Terrace
Sandy Hook, CT 06482
Phone: 203-426-5425 *

Expert
Melva Davern
Box 81914
Pittsburgh, PA 15217

Author of "The Collector's Encyclopedia of Salt &
Pepper Shakers." *

Museum/Library
Judith Basin Museum
P.O. Box 299
Stanford, MT 59479
Phone: 406-566-2572
2500 piece salt & pepper shaker collection.

Art Glass
Club/Association
Antique & Art Glass Salt Shaker
Collector's Society
Newsletter: Pioneer, The
M/M William Avery
2832 Rapidan Trail
Maitland, FL 32751
Phone: 407-629-1168
Promotes and encourages the collection and study
of salt shakers of the Antique Victorian and Art
Glass type; quarterly newsletter.

Collector
M/M Charles Lockwood
Box 228
Almond, NY 14804
Phone: 607-276-5565
Wants Victorian art and pattern glass shakers
and shakers containing agitators to break up the
salt; either singles or pairs.

Expert
World of Salt Shakers
Mildred & Ralph Lechner
P.O. Box 554
Mechanicsville, VA 23111
Phone: 804-737-3347
Directors of the Antique & Art Glass Salt Shaker
Collectors Society.

Novelty
Club/Association
Novelty Salt & Pepper Shakers Club
Newsletter: Novelty Salt & Pepper Shakers
  Club Newsletter
Irene Thornburg
581 Joy Road
Battle Creek, MI 49017
Phone: 616-963-7954
Focuses on novelty salt and pepper shakers; also
anything picturing shakers; offers "singles match-
ing service" for members.

Collector
Irene Thornburg
581 Joy Road
Battle Creek, MI 49017
Phone: 616-963-7954

Van Tellingen (Bendel)
Dealer
Sally Oge
2344 104th Ave.
Otsego, MI 49078
Phone: 616-694-6209

SALTS
Open
Club/Association
New England Society of Open Salts
Collectors
Newsletter: Salt Talk
Ed Berg, Pres.
587 Dutton Rd.
Sudbury, MA 01776
Phone: 617-443-3613 or 603-568-5553
Meets semi-annually usually in N. Reading,
MA.

Club/Association
Open Salt Collectors of the Atlantic
Region
Newsletter: OSCAR Newsletter
P.O. Box 5112
Lancaster, PA 17604-0112
Phone: 717-569-1980 or 301-447-6216
Meets quarterly at or near members' homes.

Dealer
Delaware Salt Box
Ed & Kay Berg
401 Nottingham Road
Newark, DE 19711
Phone: 302-731-5749
Issues lists of open salts for sale about 4 times per
year.

Dealer
Memory Lane Antiques
Betty Bird
107 Ida St.
Mount Shasta, CA 96067
Phone: 916-926-4331
Buying fancy open salts and/or salt spoons; prefer
art glass, colored glass and silver; any number.

Expert
Daniel Snyder
43 Main St.
Leroy, NY 14482
Phone: 716-768-6470
Specializes in master open salts. *

Expert
Patricia Johnson
P.O. Box 1221
Torrance, CA 90505
Phone: 213-373-5262
Author of "5000 Open Salts."

Periodical
Newsletter: Salty Comments
Ed Berg
401 Nottingham Road
Newark, DE 19711
Phone: 302-731-5749
The newsletter covers research on open salt dishes.

Supplier
Gem Monogram & Cut Glass Corp.
623 Broadway
New York, NY 10012
Phone: 212-674-8960
Carries a line of replacement glass liners for open
salts. *

SALVATION ARMY ITEMS
Collector
Rex Mcculley
P.O. Box 9415
Colorado Springs, CO 80932
Wants Salvation Army song sheets, posters (WWI
vintage), magazine covers, pins and buttons, etc.
*

SAMPLERS
(see also FOLK ART; REPAIRS &
RESTORATIONS, Textiles; TEXTILES)

Expert
Hanes & Ruskin Antiques
Joyce Hanes
Box 802
Westbrook, CT 06498
Phone: 203-399-5229 *

Expert
Heritage Antiques, Inc.
Suzy McLennan Anderson
65 East Main St.
Holmdel, NJ 07733
Phone: 908-946-8801
Authenticates, buys, sells, appraises, lectures; au-
thor of "The Collectors Guide to Quilts."

Museum/Library
Cooper-Hewitt Museum, The Smithsonian
Institution's Nat. Museum of Design
2 East 91st St.
New York, NY 10128
Phone: 212-860-6868

SAND
Club/Association
International Sand Collectors Society
Newsletter: Sand Paper, The
Karolyn B. Diefenbach, Dir
43 Highview Ave.
Old Greenwich, CT 06870-1703
Phone: 203-637-2801 or 203-637-0093
Serious and whimsical collections for purposes of
keepsake, analysis, bon hommarie; collector of
sand, soil, ore, or minerals.

SANTA CLAUS

(see also CHRISTMAS COLLECTIBLES)

SCALES

(see also INSTRUMENTS & DEVICES, Scientific)

Club/Association

International Society of Antique Scale
Collectors
Magazine: Equilibrium
Bob Stein, Pres.
Suite 1706
176 W. Abrams St.
Chicago, IL 60603
Phone: 312-263-7500   FAX: 312-263-7748
Focusing on antique scales.

Collector

Lenoard Pohutsky
Suite 104
20853 Farmington Rd.
Farmingtonhills, MI 48335
Phone: 313-477-5399
Wants old postal & gold scales, small scales, counterfeit detectors for coins, misc. weights, trade cards picturing scales, etc.

Collector

Chuck Thompson
P.O. Box 11652
Houston, TX 77293
Phone: 713-442-7200

Expert

Tod Carley
811 E. Central Rd., Apt. 304
Arlington Heights, IL 60005 *

Egg

Collector

Paul Neuhauser
819 Strong St.
Napoleon, OH 43545 *

Toy

Collector

Donald Gorlick
P.O. Box 24541
Seattle, WA 98124
Wants old toy scales; small tin scales like the old penny toys; any small toy scale but not the pencil sharpener type scales.

SCHMOO MEMORABILIA

Collector

Lee Garmon
1529 Whittier St.
Springfield, IL 62704
Phone: 217-789-9574

*Al Capp designed the Schmoo (a gourd-shaped character) in 1948; wants Schmoo books, banks, glass tumblers, figurines, etc. *

SCHOOLHOUSE RELATED MEMORABILIA

Expert

Schoolmaster Auctions
Ken Norris
P.O. Box 476
Grandfalls, TX 79742
Phone: 915-547-2421
*Wants hand bells, slates, dip pens, marbles, class rings, rulers, pencil boxes, potbelly stoves, student and teacher desks, etc. *

SCIENCE FICTION COLLECTIBLES

(see also COMIC BOOKS; SPACE ADVENTURE COLLECTIBLES; TOYS, Super Hero)

Club/Association

Galaxy Patrol
Newsletter: Galaxy Patrol Newsletter
Dale L. Ames
22 Colton Street
Worcester, MA 01610
Focuses on memorabilia relating to radio and TV show space heroes.

Collector

Dale L. Ames
22 Colton Street
Worcester, MA 01610
Interested in collectibles associated with science fiction TV & radio shows & recordings of the programs themselves; also sic-fi comics.

Collector

Russell K. Watkins
1220 Brighton Way
Lakeland, FL 33803
Phone: 813-646-9318
*Wants books, pulps, Burroughs, Weird Tales, The Shadow, Astounding Burroughs and Fantasy Press Books. *

Collector

Scott K. Watson
1301 Avenue F
Ft. Madison, IA 52627
Phone: 319-372-4830
*Wants comics, books, fanzines, magazines, science fiction, horror and fantasy, hardcover and paperbacks; also monster magazines. *

Collector

Edy J. Chandler
Box 20664
Houston, TX 77225
Phone: 713-781-6146
*Wants books, fanzines, robots, character merchandise, Star Wars items, etc. *

Dealer

American Collectibles Exchange
Jon Warren
P.O. Box 2512
Chattanooga, TN 37409
Phone: 615-821-8121
Specializes in Science Fiction and Fantasy items.

Dealer

Star Trader
Steve Benz
9809 Hayes
Overland Park, KS 66212
Phone: 913-648-5461
Buys, sells and trades science fiction collectibles from Star Trek to present.

Dealer

Stephen Buhner Bookseller
Stephen Buhner
8563 Flagstaff Road
Boulder, CO 80302
Phone: 303-443-1096 *

Dealer

One Book Shop, The
710 S. Forest Avenue
Tempe, AZ 85281
Phone: 602-967-3551
*Interested in science fiction collector comics. *

Dealer

Pantechnicon
Myron Cohen-Ross
P.O. Box 1038
Agoura Hills, CA 91301
Phone: 805-495-0299   FAX: 818-889-8972
Wants comics, character memorabilia, books, comic books, Fanzines, movie memorabilia, etc.; anything science fiction or fantasy.

Expert

Don & Maggie Thompson
c/o House Of Collectibles
201 East 50th St.
New York, NY 10022
Phone: 800-638-6460 *

Museum/Library

University of California, Dr. J. Eaton
Fantasy & Science Fiction Collection
Special Collections Department
P.O. Box 5900
Riverside, CA 92517
Phone: 714-787-3233 or 714-784-7324
                                FAX: 714-787-3285

SCOTTISH COLLECTIBLES

Collector

R.L.S.
Box 40507
Albuquerque, NM 87196
Wants Bagpipes, Scottish kilts, pins, badges, buckles, caps, swords, jackets, jewelry, etc.

SCRIMSHAW

(see also FOLK ART; IVORY; NAUTICAL COLLECTIBLES; WHALING)

Museum/Library

Old Dartmouth Historical Society &
Whaling Museum
18 Johnny Cake Hill
New Bedford, MA 02704
Phone: 508-997-0046

Museum/Library

Cold Spring Harbor Whaling Museum
P.O. Box 25
Cold Spring Harbor, NY 11724
Phone: 516-367-3418

Museum/Library

National Maritime Museum, Fort Mason
Bldg. 201
San Francisco, CA 94123
Phone: 415-556-3002

Periodical

Newsletter: Whalebone
P.O. Box 2834
Fairfax, VA 22031 *

SCRIP

(see also LOGGING RELATED ITEMS;
MINING RELATED ITEMS; TOKENS)

Club/Association

National Scrip Collectors Association
Newsletter: Scrip Talk
Walter Caldwell, Sec.
P.O. Box 29
Fayetteville, WV 25840
Phone: 304-574-0105
*Promotes collecting of coal, lumber and all mining
scrip (metal & paper), merchant tokens, and
mining artifacts including mining lamps.*

Depression

Expert

Neil Shafer
P.O. Box 17138
Milwaukee, WI 53217
Phone: 414-352-5962
*Co-author of "Standard Catalog of Depression
Scrip of the United States"; the 1930's including
Canada and Mexico.*

SCULPTURE

(see also ART; BRONZES; FOLK ART;
ROGERS GROUPS)

SEALS

Christmas & Charity

Club/Association

Christmas Seal & Charity Stamp Society
Newsletter: Seal News
5825 Dorchester Ave.
Chicago, IL 60637
Phone: 612-721-1981 *

Club/Association

International Seal, Label & Cigar Band
Society
Newsletter: Inter. Seal, Label & Cigar Band
 Soc. Bulletin
8915 E. Bellevue St.
Tucson, AZ 85715
Phone: 602-296-1048
*Interested in hotel, cigar box, beer, fruit crate, etc.
labels; also matchcovers, charity stamps, Christ-
mas seals, sugar packets, etc. *

Sealing Wax

Collector

Irwin Prince
142 Fairway Dr.
Indianapolis, IN 46260
Phone: 317-255-1913
*Wants wood, sterling, bronze, agate, glass, crys-
tal, ivory, bone, mother-of-pearl, etc. desk-type
sealing wax seals. *

SEASHELLS

Club/Association

Conchologists of America
Journal: American Conchologist
1222 Holsworth Ln.
Louisville, KY 40222
Phone: 502-423-0469
Members interested in the collection of seashells.

Expert

Minque's Molluscs
Mique & C.E. Pinkerton
1324 Westmoreland Dr.
Warrenton, VA 22186
Phone: 703-347-3839
*Wants seashells and seashell related items; also
books about seashells.*

Museum/Library

Delaware Museum of Natural History
Route 52, Box 3937
Greenville, DE 19807
Phone: 302-658-9111

Museum/Library

Rollins College, Beal-Maltbie Shell
Museum
Campus Box 2753
Winter Park, FL 32789
Phone: 305-646-2364

Museum/Library

Lionel Train & Seashell Museum
R.A. Paul
8184 North Tamiami Trail
Sarasota, FL 34243
Phone: 813-355-8184
*Collection of Lionel trains and seashells; great gift
shop offering sales and service of Lionel and other
makes of toy trains.*

Museum/Library

Banka's Shell Museum
P.O. Box 1537
Conrad, MT 59425
Phone: 406-278-3749

SERVICE STATION COLLECTIBLES

(see also GAS STATION COLLECTIBLES)

SEWING ITEMS & GO-WITHS

Collector

Collector
Rt. 1, Box 262
Middlebourne, WV 26149-9748
Phone: 304-386-4434   FAX: 304-386-4868
*Unusual sewing tools, small early sewing ma-
chines; fancy hair ornaments.*

Collector

Gold Hatpin, The
Diane Richardson
P.O. Box 993
Oak Park, IL 60303-0993
Phone: 708-848-3247
*Wants needle cases, thimbles, scissors, darning
eggs, sewing birds, thread winders, figural tape
measures, tatting shuttles, tool sets.*

Collector

Wynneth Mullins
P.O. Box 381807
Duncansville, TX 75138-1807
Phone: 214-780-8278
*Wants sewing thimbles and other sewing related
tools.*

Machines

Club/Association

International Sewing Machine Collectors
Society
Magazine: ISMACS News
Maggie Shell
48 Nightingale House
Thomas Moore St.
London E1 9UB England
*The world's only society for collectors of antique
sewing machines.*

Collector

Jerry Probst
P.O. Box 45
Janesville, WI 53547-0045
Phone: 608-752-2816   FAX: 608-752-7691

Dealer

Maggie Shell
48 Nightingale House
Thomas Moore Street
London E1 9UB England
Collects, buys and sells antique sewing machines as part of a mechanical-antique business.

Expert

Carter Bays
143 Spring Lake Rd.
Columbia, SC 29206
One of the nation's leading sewing machine collectors.

Repair Service

Simple Machine, The
Cathy & Stephen Racine
18 Masonic Home Rd. - Rt. 31
P.O. Box 234
Charlton, MA 01507
Phone: 508-248-6632
Buys, sells, repairs and restores old treadle sewing machines; also carries parts, belts, needles, bobbins and manuals.

Pincushions

Collector

R.L. Rice
612 E. Front St.
Bloomington, IL 61701
Wants cloth, cardboard, etc. pincushions. *

Thimbles

Club/Association

Thimble Society of London
Magazine: Thimble Society of London Magazine
C/5, Chenil Gallery
181 King's Road, Chelsea
London SW3 England *

Club/Association

Dorset Thimble Society
Newsletter: At Your Fingertips
Pinecroft, 28 Avon Road
Westmoors, Wimborne
Dorset BH22 0EG England *

Club/Association

Empire State Thimble Collectors
Barbara Acchino
8289 Northgate Dr.
Rome, NY 13440-1941
Phone: 716-652-4284
A non-profit organization of collectors who share an interest in the study, research and sharing of information about thimbles.

Club/Association

Thimble Collectors International
Newsletter: TCI Bulletin
Dickey Everson, Mem.
6411 Montego Bay Rd.
Louisville, KY 40228
Phone: 502-239-6274
A worldwide association of thimble collectors.

Club/Association

Thimble Guild, The
Newsletter: Thimble Guild
Wynneth Mullins
P.O. Box 381807
Duncansville, TX 75138-1807
Phone: 214-780-8278

Expert

Estelle Zalkin
7524 West Treasure Dr.
Miami Beach, FL 33141 *

Periodical

Newsletter: Thimbletter
Lorraine M. Crosby
93 Walnut Hill Road
Newton Highlands, MA 02161-1836
Phone: 617-969-9358
An informal bi-monthly newsletter, letters from subscribers, Q & A, for sale or trade, ads, new sources, misc. information.

SHAKER ITEMS

(see also FURNITURE (ANTIQUE))

Auction Service

Willis Henry Auctions
22 Main St.
Marshfield, MA 02050
Phone: 617-834-7774

Club/Association

Shaker Museum Foundation
Newsletter: Shaker Museum Newsletter
149 Shaker Museum Rd.
Old Chatham, NY 12136
Phone: 518-794-9100 *

Dealer

Douglas H. Hamel Antiques
RFD #10, Box 100
Concord, NH 03301
Phone: 603-798-5912
Buys and sells good quality Shaker items; helping to build major private and public collections for 20 years.

Dealer

Dr. M. Stephen Miller
Six Park Place
New Britain, CT 06052
Phone: 203-561-3342
Buys and appraises Shaker items.

Museum/Library

Hancock Shaker Village
P.O. Box 898
Pittsfield, MA 01202
Phone: 413-443-0188
200-year-old site; 20 restoned buildings house largest and finest collection of shaker furnishings and artifacts.

Museum/Library

Shaker Museum, The
Shaker Museum Road
Old Chatham, NY 12136
Phone: 518-794-9100
A 200-year-old Shaker site encompassing 20 restored buildings housing the largest and finest collection of Shaker furnishings & artifacts.

Museum/Library

Shaker Historical Museum
16740 S. Park Blvd.
Shaker Heights, OH 44120
Phone: 216-921-1201

Periodical

Magazine: Shaker Spirit
P.O. Box 1309
Point Pleasant, NJ 08742 *

Periodical

Newsletter: Shaker Messenger, The
Diana Van Kolken
P.O. Box 1645
Holland, MI 49422-1645
Phone: 616-396-4588
Focuses on the Shakers and their work products.

SHAVING COLLECTIBLES

(see also BARBER SHOP COLLECTIBLES)

Collector

Darryl Rehr
11433 Rochester Ave. #303
Los Angeles, CA 90025
Phone: 213-447-5229
Wants unusual safety razors, shavers, sharpeners and other paraphernalia associated with shaving.

Razors

Collector

D. Perkins
2317 N. Kessler Blvd.
Indianapolis, IN 46222
Phone: 317-638-4519
Wants early fancy or odd safety razors in tins or sets; also fancy handled straight razors.

Expert

Robert Doyle
R.D. 3 Box 137
Fishkill, NY 12524
Phone: 914-896-9492 *

Expert

Charles D. Stapp
7037 Haynes Rd.
Georgetown, IN 47122
Phone: 812-923-3483
Advisor to "Schroeder's Antique Price Guide."

Razors (Safety)

Club/Association

Safety Razor Collectors Guild
W. Will, Dir.
P.O. Box 885
Crescent City, CA 95531
Promotes interest in collecting and preserving safety-razors, blades and related items; no dues, but please include SASE with inquiries.

Collector

E. Wittkopf
4614 Manistee
Ft. Wayne, IN 46815
*Wants old safety razors, odd names and styles. ***

Periodical

Newsletter: Will's Safety-Razor & Safety-Razor-Blade Newsltr.
W. Will, Ed.
P.O. Box 522
Crescent City, CA 95531
Provides information & communication for collectors, groups, dealers interested in safety-razors, blades and related items; buy/sell

Razor Sharpeners

Collector

Darryl Rehr
11433 Rochester Ave. #303
Los Angeles, CA 90025
Phone: 213-447-5229
Collects gadgets used to sharpen safety razor blades (no Twinplex or Kriss Kross, please); send description or photocopy.

SHAWLS

Kashmir (Paisley)

(see also TEXTILES)

Collector

Frank Ames
254 West 73rd St.
New York, NY 10023
Phone: 212-787-0090 *

Collector

Michael Council
689 S. 3rd St.
Columbus, OH 43206
Phone: 614-444-0700 or 800-544-4117
Wants pre-1950 quilts and paisley shawls.

SHEET MUSIC

(see also HYMNS; MUSIC; PAPER COLLECTIBLES)

Auction Service

Beverly A. Hamer Sheet Music Sales
Beverly A. Hamer
P.O. Box 75
East Derry, NH 03041
Phone: 603-432-3528
Wants old collectible sheet music; publishes a set price list and conducts auctions of collectible sheet music; free search service.

Club/Association

Ragtime Society
P.O. Box 520, Station A
Weston
Ontario M9N 3N3 Canada *

Club/Association

New York Sheet Music Society
Newsletter: New York Sheet Music Society Newsletter
Bob Lippet, Pres.
P.O. Box 1214
Great Neck, NY 11023

Club/Association

Remember That Song
Newsletter: Remember That Song
Lois Cordey, Ed.
Suite 103-306
5821 N. 67th Ave.
Glendale, AZ 85301
Phone: 602-435-2136   FAX: 602-842-0064
RTS News is a 20-35 pg. illustrated newsletter consisting of articles and printed vintage music; also sheet music ads and auctions.

Club/Association

National Sheet Music Society, Inc.
Newsletter: National Sheet Music Society Newsletter
1597 Fair Park Ave.
Los Angeles, CA 90041

Club/Association

City of Roses Sheet Music Collectors Club
Margaret Horning, Sec.
13447 Bush St. S.E.
Portland, OR 97236
Phone: 503-761-3817
Sponsors an annual sheet music sale and show.

Collector

Chuck Seton
Ervilla Dr.
Larchmont, NY 10538 *

Collector

Kurt Stein
833 Crestview Dr.
Springfield, PA 19064

*Wants pre-1866 sheet music: bound or single copies. ***

Collector

Gary Olsen
505 S. Royal Ave.
Front Royal, VA 22630
Phone: 703-635-7157 or 703-635-7158
          FAX: 703-635-1818
Wants sheet music with covers depicting sports, WWI, or first names in the titles.

Dealer

Beverly A. Hamer Sheet Music Sales
Beverly A. Hamer
P.O. Box 75
East Derry, NH 03041
Phone: 603-432-3528
Wants old collectible sheet music; publishes a set price list and conducts auctions of collectible sheet music; free search service.

Dealer

Sheet Music Center
Box 367
Port Washington, NY 11050
*Wants sheet music and piano rolls. ***

Expert

Sandy Marrone
113 Oakwood Dr.
Cinnaminson, NJ 08077
Phone: 609-829-6104
Willing to answer questions about sheet music; would prefer discussing by phone but will answer mail if SASE enclosed.

Expert

Mt. Washington Antiques
Jeannie Peters
3742 Kellogg
Cincinnati, OH 45226
Phone: 513-231-6584 *

Museum/Library

American Antiquarian Society
185 Salisbury Street
Worcester, MA 01609
Phone: 508-755-5221

Museum/Library

Broadcast, Music, Inc. (BMI)
320 West 57th Street
New York, NY 10019

Museum/Library

American Society of Composers, Authors & Publishers (ASCAP)
1 Lincoln Plaza
New York, NY 10023

Museum/Library

Sonneck Society for American Music &
Music in America
Newsletter: SSAMMA Newsletter
14-34 155th Street
Whitestone, NY 11357

Periodical

Magazine: Sheet Music Magazine
352 Evelyn Street
Paramus, NJ 07653-0933 *

Periodical

Newsletter: Sheet Music Exchange
P.O. Box 69
Quicksburg, VA 22847 *

Supplier

MARSCO
1713 Central St.
Evanston, IL 60201
Phone: 708-328-7100
Carries paper and plastic sleeves for LP's and sheet
music covers.

Dance Related

Collector

Dr. William G. Sommer, MD
9 W. 10th St.
New York, NY 10011
Phone: 212-260-0999
Wants sheet music depicting Africa-American
dancing, e.g. Cake Walk, Jitterbug; also Waltz,
Tango, etc. & dance items in other media.

Rock 'N' Roll

Collector

Jim Weaver
405 Dunbar
Pittsburgh, PA 15235
Wants 1950's-1960's rock 'n' roll photo cover sheet
music; send lists and offers.

SHIPPING

(see also NAUTICAL COLLECTIBLES)

Chesapeake Bay Steamship

Collector

John Fowler
3021 Newark St. NW
Washington, DC 20008
Phone: 202-686-1411
Wants railroad timetables, china, silverware,
menus, baggage, checks, pre-1900 passes; also
Chesapeake Bay steamship memorabilia. *

Great Lakes Related

Collector

J.A. Baumhofer
P.O. Box 65493
St. Paul, MN 55165
Phone: 612-698-7151 or 612-224-3210
                                    FAX: 612-291-9179
Great Lakes ships, books, pictures, photos;
Green's or other directories.

SHIP RELATED

(see also NAUTICAL COLLECTIBLES;
TITANIC MEMORABILIA)

S.S. Normandie

Collector

W. LaPoe
11986 Lakeside Place NE
Seattle, WA 98125 *

U.S.S. Constitution

Collector

Tim O'Callaghan
46878 Bettyhill
Plymouth, MI 48170
Phone: 313-459-4636
Wants USS Constitution "Old Ironsides" items,
especially items made from the ship in the 1920's
and sold to raise money for restoration.

Warships

Club/Association

International Naval Research
Organization
Magazine: Warship International
George F. Dale, Sec.
P.O. Box 3249
1st St Station
Radford, VA 24143
Dedicated to the study of post-1860 naval vessels:
histories, elements of ballistics, design, careers,
etc.

SHOULDER PATCHES

(see also PATCHES)

SHRUNKEN HEADS

(see also SKELETONS)

SIGNS

(see also ADVERTISING COLLECTIBLES;
GAS STATION COLLECTIBLES;
HIGHWAY COLLECTIBLES; LAMPS &
LIGHTING, Neon; MARINE CORPS
ITEMS)

SILHOUETTES

(see also FOLK ART)

Collector

Janette Pike
9 Brookwood Ct.
Ashville, NC 28804
Wants framed silhouettes or silhouettes on boxes,
china, glass, jewelry, lamps, etc.; also wants books
about silhouettes. *

Collector

Lester Sender
3482 Lee Road
Shaker Heights, OH 44120
Phone: 216-752-2435   FAX: 216-991-7461
Buys and sells pre-1920 American and Continen-
tal silhouettes.

Expert

Hanes & Ruskin Antiques
Joyce Hanes
Box 802
Westbrook, CT 06498
Phone: 203-399-5229 *

Expert

W. Lehman Guyton
13801 York Rd. H-11
Cockeysville, MD 21030 *

Expert

Whitehall Shop
Alda Horner
1215 E. Franklin Street
Chapel Hill, NC 27514
Phone: 919-942-6720

Museum/Library

Essex Institute
132 Essex St.
Salem, MA 01970
Phone: 617-744-3390

Museum/Library

National Portrait Gallery
8th & F Streets NW
Washington, DC 20560
Phone: 202-357-1407

SILVER

(see also FLATWARE; REPAIRS &
RESTORATIONS, Metal Items;
SILVERPLATE; SPOONS; TABLEWARE)

Collector

Diane Cramer
P.O. Box 1243
Whittier, CA 90609
Phone: 213-696-6738
Wants American sterling silver & coin silver
serving pieces & holloware; also unusual sil-
verplate & applied silver or other metals.

Dealer

Beverly Bremer Silver Shop
3164 Peachtree Rd. NE
Atlanta, GA 30305
Phone: 404-261-4009
Appraises, buys, sells and matches sterling silver flatware; also buys and sells new and antique sterling silver holloware & giftware.

Dealer

Steve Duffy
20 Bridle Dr.
Winsted, CT 06098
Phone: 203-379-5749
Specializes in sterling silver flatware.

Dealer

Gary Niederkorn Silver
Newspaper: Silver Edition
Gary Niederkorn
2005 Locust St.
Philadelphia, PA 19103
Phone: 215-567-2606
Specializes in 19th and 20th cent. silver novelties, jewelry napkin rings, Judaica, picture frames, etc.; also Tiffany, Jensen, Mexican.

Dealer

Pillsbury-Michel Inc.
Robin Michel
P.O. Box 358
Ephraim, WI 54211
Phone: 414-854-4790 or 713-522-4790
*Buys and sells antique to contemporary silver: flat & hollow wares; English, American and Continental. ***

Dealer

Silver Vault, The
Rod Tinkler
P.O. Box 421
Barrington, IL 60011
Phone: 708-381-3101
Buy, sell, trade, appraise American, English and Continental silver.

Dealer

Pillsbury-Michel Inc.
William M. Pillsbury
Suite 508
2615 Waugh Dr.
Houston, TX 77006
Phone: 713-522-4790 or 414-854-4790
Buys and sells antique to contemporary silver: flat & hollow wares; English, American and Continental.

Expert

Fendelman & Schwartz
Jeri Schwartz
555 Old Long Ridge Rd.
Stamford, CT 06903
Phone: 203-322-7854

Appraises and liquidates estates; author of the "Official Identification and Price Guide to Silver & Silverplate."

Expert

Sterling Shop, The
P.O. Box 595
Silverton, OR 97381
Phone: 503-873-6315
Sterling and silverplate flatware matching service.

Museum/Library

Boston Museum of Fine Arts
465 Huntington Avenue
Boston, MA 02115
Phone: 617-267-9300

Museum/Library

Wadsworth Atheneum
600 Main Street
Hartford, CT 06103
Phone: 203-278-2670

Museum/Library

Yale University Art Gallery
Box 2006 Yale Station
New Haven, CT 06520
Phone: 203-432-0600

Museum/Library

Bayou Bend Collection, The
P.O. Box 130157
Houston, TX 77219
Phone: 713-529-8773

Periodical

Jewelers' Circular-Keystone Book Club
Index: Jewelers Sterling Flatware Pattern Index
One Chilton Way
Radnor, PA 19089-0140
Phone: 215-964-4480
A compilation of sterling silver flatware patterns.

Periodical

Price Guide: Silver Update
Nanette Monmonier
3366 Oak West Dr.
Ellicott City, MD 21043
Phone: 301-750-3282
Provides current prices for American and popular foreign silver manufacturers of flatware, holloware and silverplate.

Periodical

Magazine: Silver
Diane Cramer, Ed.
P.O. Box 1243
Whittier, CA 90609
Phone: 213-696-6738
Top quality magazine for silver collectors; well illustrated articles; 19th century silver & plate from archives; new information.

Baltimore

Dealer

Imperial Half Bushel
Pat Dugan
831 N. Howard St.
Baltimore, MD 21201
Phone: 301-462-1192
Specializes in Baltimore silver.

European

Expert

Fox in Flanders, A
Suzy Van Massenhove
3703 Whispering Lane
Falls Church, VA 22041
Phone: 703-256-3094

Georg Jensen

Collector

P. Norman
1124 Roan Lane
Alexandria, VA 22302
*Georg Jensen sterling flatware, holloware or odd pieces. ***

Expert

Sharon Kerwick
1633 NE 24th St.
Ft. Lauderdale, FL 33305
Phone: 305-565-9031
Specializes in Georg Jensen and other silver.

Man./Prod./Dist.

Jensen of Denmark, Inc. SVEND
1010 Boston Post Rd.
Rye, NY 10580
Phone: 914-967-6026

Gorham

Man./Prod./Dist.

Gorham, Inc.
P.O. Box 906
Mount Kisco, NY 10549
Phone: 914-242-9300 or 800-225-1460
FAX: 914-242-9379

International

Man./Prod./Dist.

International Silver Co.
P.O. Box 9114
East Boston, MA 02128-9114
Phone: 617-561-2200   FAX: 617-569-8484

Kirk Stieff

Man./Prod./Dist.

Kirk Stieff Co., The
800 Wyman Park Dr.
Baltimore, MD 21211
Phone: 301-338-6000

SILVER

264

Lunt

Man./Prod./Dist.

Lunt Silversmiths
298 Federal St.
Greenfield, MA 01301
Phone: 413-774-2774   FAX: 413-774-4393

Old Newbury

Man./Prod./Dist.

Old Newbury Crafters
36 Main St.
Amesbury, MA 01913
Phone: 617-388-0983

Oneida

Man./Prod./Dist.

Oneida Silversmiths
Kenwood Station
Oneida, NY 13421
Phone: 315-361-3000

Reed & Barton

Man./Prod./Dist.

Reed & Barton
144 W. Britannia Street
Taunton, MA 02780
Phone: 508-824-6611   FAX: 508-822-7269
Produces china, crystal, silver, silverplate, and stainless flatware, collectible plates, bells, dolls, ornaments and accessories.

Towle

Man./Prod./Dist.

Towle Silversmiths
P.O. Box 9115
E. Boston, MA 02128
Phone: 617-561-2200   FAX: 617-569-8484

Wallace

Man./Prod./Dist.

Wallace Silversmiths
175 McClellan Hwy.
E. Boston, MA 02128
Phone: 617-561-2200   FAX: 617-569-5814

SILVERPLATE

(see also FLATWARE; SILVER; TABLEWARE)

Collector

Sarah Eigen
230 E. 15 St.
New York, NY 10003
Phone: 212-982-0719
Wants pre-1900 silverplate holloware & flatware; Japanese or Aesthetic style; geometric decorations with bugs, blossoms, etc.

Expert

Artiques
Dick & Ellie Archer
419 Sevilla Dr.
St. Augustine, FL 32086
Phone: 904-797-4678
*Specializing in Victorian silverplate: figurals, fancy holloware, and collectibles. ***

Periodical

Magazine: Silver
Diane Cramer, Ed.
P.O. Box 1243
Whittier, CA 90609
Phone: 213-696-6738
Top quality magazine for silver collectors; well illustrated articles; 19th century silver & plate from archives; new information.

SILVERPLATED FLATWARE

(see also FLATWARE)

SILVERWARE

(see also FLATWARE)

'60'S MEMORABILIA

(see also PEACE MOVEMENT ITEMS)

Collector

Rick Synchef
16 Midway Ave.
Mill Valley, CA 94941
Phone: 415-381-4448
Wants 1960's "counterculture" memorabilia: hippie, political, music, drug, etc.: handbills, leaflets, books, etc.; also beatnik material.

SKELETONS

(see also ANIMAL TROPHIES)

Collector

H. Pofenius
8 Hillgrass
Irvine, CA 92715
Phone: 714-854-7575
Wants shruken heads from South American Indian tribes for personal collection.

Dealer

Long Island Trading Post
2088 Front St.
East Meadow, NY 11554
Phone: 516-794-1212
Wants stuffed real animals, heads, birds; also skulls and skeletons.

Dealer

Bone Room, The
5495 Claremont
Oakland, CA 94618
Phone: 415-652-4286
Wants old skeletons, skulls, horns, teeth, tusks and shruken heads.

SLAVERY ITEMS

(see also BLACK MEMORABILIA)

Collector

Cary Demont
P.O. Box 19312
Minneapolis, MN 55419
Phone: 612-922-1617
Wants political pre-1964 buttons, pins, flags, ribbons, banners, and the unusual; also suffrage, prohibition, slavery, and Lindbergh.

SLIDE RULES

(see also INSTRUMENTS & DEVICES, Scientific)

Collector

G.L. Netherland
4201 Vauxhall Road
Richmond, VA 23234
*Wants slide rules, protractors, old engineering instruments from the 1920's or earlier. ***

SMOKEY THE BEAR ITEMS

Collector

Wehr
P.O. Box 341
East Hampton, CT 06424
Wants Smokey the Bear items: dolls, all toys, large salt and pepper shakers, paper items, posters, cookie jars, clothing, etc.

Collector

Pete Nowicki
1531 39th Ave.
San Francisco, CA 94122
Phone: 415-566-7506
Collector seeks all licensed Smokey Bear items for collection: toys, dolls, posters, etc.

SMOKING COLLECTIBLES

(see also ADVERTISING COLLECTIBLES, Trade Cards (Tobacco); CIGAR BANDS, BOXES & LABELS; CIGAR STORE COLLECTIBLES; LIGHTERS; PIPES; MATCHCOVERS)

Collector

D. Nordlinger Stern
1336 54th Ave., N.E.
St. Petersburg, FL 33703
Phone: 813-527-1212   FAX: 813-525-4090
Wants tobacco memorabilia, particularly W. Duke and Duke's Mixture.

Collector

Terry Allen
1705 2nd Ave.
Manchester, TN 37355
*Wants tobacco products such as sacks, packs, tins, cigar bands, boxes and old cigarette packs; also cabinets, cases, boxes, display items. ***

Museum/Library

U.S. Tobacco Museum
100 W. Putnam Ave.
Greenwich, CT 06830
Phone: 203-869-5531

Museum/Library

Valentine Museum
1015 East Clay
Richmond, VA 23219
Phone: 804-649-0711

Museum/Library

Museum of Tobacco Art & History
800 Harrison St.
Nashville, TN 37203
Phone: 615-271-2349 or 615-271-2163
FAX: 615-271-2285
Museum traces history of tobacco from American Indians to present; collection of pipes, Cigar Store figures, snuff boxes, art, etc.

Advertising

Collector

Cindy Porman
22044 Roosevelt Rd.
South Bend, IN 46614
Phone: 219-291-6414
Copenhagen snuff related items or Weyman Bros. related items, crocks, pocket tin store displays & related advertising items.

SNOW BABIES

Collector

Sue Coffee
10 Saunders Hollow
Old Lyme, CT 06371
Phone: 203-434-5641
Wants old snow babies, German or Japan.

Expert

Mary Jo Walczak
5312 Brophy Dr.
Toledo, OH 43611
*Specializes in snow babies (1-5 inch long porcelain baby figurines.) ***

SNOWDOMES

Club/Association

Snow Biz
Newsletter: Snow Biz Newsletter
Nancy McMichael
P.O. Box 53262
Washington, DC 20009
Phone: 202-234-7484   FAX: 202-234-7484
Snow Biz aims to enhance the knowledge, enjoyment and collections of snowdome/waterglobe enthusiasts.

Collector

Helene Guarnaccia
52 Coach Lane
Fairfield, CT 06430
Phone: 203-374-6034

Collector

Miriam Bein
79 Riggs Place
South Orange, NJ 07079
Phone: 201-378-9434

Collector

Bruce Baron
4705 Henry Hudson Pkwy., 2E
Bronx, NY 10471

Collector

Donna Divon
P.O. Box 756
Yonkers, NY 10704

Collector

Hanson
P.O. Box 1222
Edgewood, MD 21040-1222 *

Expert

Nancy McMichael
2205 California St., NW
Washington, DC 20008
Phone: 202-234-7484

SNOWMOBILES

Club/Association

Antique Snowmobile Club of America
Newsletter: Iron Dog Tracks
W. 6110 Lost Arrow Rd.
Fond-Du-Lac, WI 54935
Phone: 414-921-6944 *

SNUFF BOTTLES

(see also ORIENTALIA)

Club/Association

International Chinese Snuff Bottle
Society
Journal: Chinese Snuff Bottle Journal
John Ford
2601 North Charles St.
Baltimore, MD 21218
Phone: 301-467-9400

Collector

Robert S. Block
42 Bassett St.
Trumbull, CT 06460
Phone: 203-783-1690
Wants to buy Chinese snuff bottles.

SODA FOUNTAIN COLLECTIBLES

Club/Association

Ice Screamers, The
Newsletter: Ice Screamer, The
Ed Marks
P.O. Box 5387
Lancaster, PA 17601-0387
Phone: 717-569-8284

Collector

David Cosmo
P.O. Box 522
Somers, NY 10589
*Wants signs, syrup dispensers, straw holders, crushed fruit jars, ice cream cone holders, milkshake mixers, etc. ***

Collector

Ed Marks
P.O. Box 5387
Lancaster, PA 17601
*Wants ice cream ephemera, books, pamphlets, dippers, scoops, salesman's samples, toys; anything relating to ice cream. ***

Collector

William A. Shaner, Jr.
403 N. Charlotte St.
Pottstown, PA 19464
Phone: 215-326-0165
Wants soda fountain and ice cream items; especially Burdan's ice cream trays, signs, ads, paper items, etc.

Collector

Tom Collins
3616 Camelot Dr.
Annandale, VA 22003
Phone: 703-560-4714
*Wants ice cream related items, scoops, etc. ***

Collector

Richard O. Gates
P.O. Box 187
Chesterfield, VA 23832
Phone: 804-748-0382 or 804-794-5146
Wants 50's soda fountain items; also jukeboxes, pinballs, Coca Cola machines & signs or literature related to any of the above.

Collector

Bob Shipley
1818 Grace Street
Riverside, CA 92504
*Wants ice cream scoops. ***

Expert

Harold & Joyce Screen
2804 Munster Rd.
Baltimore, MD 21234
Phone: 301-661-6765
Historian wants "Soda Fountain" mag., fountain equip. & supply catalogs, pre-1910 druggist journals, any early fountain photos, etc.

Expert
Wayne Smith
P.O. Box 418
Walkersville, MD 21793 *

Expert
"Mr. Ice Cream"
Allan Mellis
1115 W. Montana
Chicago, IL 60614
Phone: 312-327-9123
Wants rare scoops, postcards, pewter molds, ice cream trays, and ice cream-related watch fobs, magazines, valentines, buttons, etc.

SOFT DRINK COLLECTIBLES
(see also BOTTLES; SODA FOUNTAIN COLLECTIBLES)

Dealer
Buck Fever Studio
Box 230 961 Country Club Rd.
Marion, VA 24354
*Wants Coca-Cola (especially Lady calendars and signs), Pepsi Cola, Hires, Moxie, Nu Grape, Orange Crush, Dr. Pepper, Cherry Smash, etc. **

Expert
Allan Smith
1806 Shields Dr.
Sherman, TX 75090
Phone: 214-893-3626
*Wants Coca-Cola, Pepsi Cola, Dr. Pepper, RC Cola advertising items; also Red Goose, Buster Brown Shoes and western stars items. **

Coca-Cola
(see also ADVERTISING COLLECTIBLES, Tin Vienna Art Plates)

Auction Service
Nostalgia Publications
Allan Petretti
21 S. Lake Dr.
Hackensack, NJ 07601
Phone: 201-488-4536
Conducts semi-annual mail-bid auctions of coca-cola related advertising items; catalogs are $8 for three auctions.

Club/Association
Coca-Cola Collectors Club International
Newsletter: Coca-Cola Collectors News
P.O. Box 546
Holmdel, NJ 07733

Collector
Marty
Box 50
Willow Grove, PA 19090
Coca-cola items pre-1950 wanted.

Collector
Bill Combs
1002 Grove Hill Rd.
Baltimore, MD 21227
Phone: 301-242-8793
President of local coca-cola collector club; wants Coca-Cola & Pepsi trays, signs, light-ups, etc.

Collector
Richard O. Gates
P.O. Box 187
Chesterfield, VA 23832
Phone: 804-748-0382 or 804-794-5146
Wants coin-operated machines including jukeboxes, pinballs, Coca Cola machines & signs or literature related to any of the above.

Collector
Thom Thompson
123 Shaw Ave.
Versailles, KY 40383
Phone: 606-873-8787 or 606-255-2727
Advanced collector seeks older memorabilia.

Collector
Robb Johnson
1155 Crescent Lake Rd.
Pontiac, MI 48054
Phone: 313-673-2804
*Coca-cola items: signs, cardboard, dispensers & machines; all items; the older the better. **

Dealer
Bill Ricketts
P.O. Box 9605-B
Ashville, NC 28805
Phone: 704-669-2205 or 704-669-8881
Buys, sells and trades Coca-Cola memorabilia: trays, signs, posters, calendars, bottles, etc.; send SASE for list of items for sale.

Dealer
C.C. Cowboys
Marion Lathan
Rt. 1, Box 430
Chester, SC 29706
Phone: 803-377-8225 or 803-581-3000
Wants Coca Cola items: signs, clocks, calendars, thermometers, trays, toys, bottles, sheet music, etc.

Dealer
Al Wilson
P.O. Box 3904
Evergreen, CO 80439
Phone: 303-670-0362 *

Expert
Nostalgia Publications
Allan Petretti
21 S. Lake Dr.
Hackensack, NJ 07601
Phone: 201-488-4536
Author of "Petretti's Coca-Cola Collectibles Price Guide."

Expert
Pause That Refreshes Museum & Retail
Shoppe, The
Duane Bouliew
328 S. Main St.
Frankenmuth, MI 48734

Expert
Randy S. Schaeffer
611 N. 5th St.
Reading, PA 19601
Phone: 215-373-3333 or 215-683-4401
Advanced collector seeking the old, rare and unusual in Coca-Cola collectibles; also provides expert appraisals and evaluations.

Expert
William E. Bateman
611 N. 5th St.
Reading, PA 19601
Phone: 215-373-3333 or 215-683-4401
Advanced collector seeking the old, rare and unusual in Coca-Cola collectibles; also provides expert appraisals and evaluations.

Expert
Richard Mix
P.O. Box 558
Marietta, GA 30061-0558
Phone: 404-422-9083   FAX: 404-422-5649
Author of "The Mix Guide to Commemorative Coca-Cola Bottles."

Expert
Cocaholics
Gale DeCourtivron
4811 Remington Dr.
Sarasota, FL 34234
Phone: 813-351-1560
*Specializes in Coca-Cola memorabilia; Cocaholics hot line: 813-355-COLA. **

Expert
Shelly Goldstein
P.O. Box 301
Woodland Hills, CA 91364
Author of "The Index to Coca-Cola Collectibles."
*

Man./Prod./Dist.
KEM Manufacturing Company
Bill Ricketts
120 Cherry St.
Black Mountain, NC 28711
Phone: 704-669-2205 or 704-669-8881
Manufacturer of miniature Coca-Cola six packs, key chains and cigarette lighters; sold only to authorized outlets.

Museum/Library
Coca-Cola Company Archives
P.O. Drawer 1734
Atlanta, GA 30301
Phone: 414-676-3491

Request information about your Coca-Cola collectibles directly from the Company.

Museum/Library

World of Coca-Cola Pavilion, The
55 Martin Luther King Drive
Atlanta, GA 30303-3505
Phone: 404-676-5151
A 45,000 square foot attraction containing high-tech, interactive exhibits and archival materials from the company's 104-yr. history.

Museum/Library

Coca-Cola Memorabilia Museum of
Elizabethtown, Inc.
Box 647
Elizabethtown, KY 42701
Phone: 502-737-4000

Repro. Source

M & B Enterprises
Box 373
Burlington, IN 46913
Phone: 317-566-3715
*16 1/2" x 1 1/4" raised metal, painted colors Coca-Cola bottle advertising thermometer; $9.95 plus $1.50 S/H. ***

Coca-Cola Machines

Dealer

Fun-Tronics
Steve & Nancy Ebner
P.O. Box 3145
Gaithersburg, MD 20878
Phone: 301-371-5246
*Specializing in restoration supplies for vintage coke machines and dealers in related collectibles. ***

Supplier

Fun-Tronics
Steve & Nancy Ebner
P.O. Box 3145
Gaithersburg, MD 20878
Phone: 301-371-5246
*Specializing in restoration supplies for vintage coke machines and dealers in related collectibles. ***

Dr. Pepper

Club/Association

Dr. Pepper 10-2-4 Collector's Club
Newsletter: Lions Roar
Patsy M. Roberts
1529 John Smith
Irving, TX 75061
The 10-2-4 club is a national organization of people dedicated to the study of the history and collecting of Dr. Pepper Co. memorabilia.

Collector

Bob Thiele
620 Tinker
Pawhuska, OK 74056-4039

Wants early and unusual Dr. Pepper items: celluloid, early paper items, tokens, jewelry, pens, pencils, clothing, fountain pens, etc.

Collector

Wilton A. Lanning, Jr.
6433 Summit Ridge
Waco, TX 76710
Phone: 817-776-3130 or 817-772-2434
        FAX: 817-776-3153
Collector of Dr. Pepper, Circle A and Artesian Mfg. & Bottling memorabilia: bottles, signs, thermometers, advertising, etc.

Expert

Pepper's Deli
Bill Ricketts
120 Cherry St.
Black Mountain, NC 28711
Phone: 704-669-2205 or 704-669-8881
Buy/sell/trade pre-1960 Dr. Pepper advertising items; especially interested in old trays, signs, calendars; anything Dr. Pepper.

Museum/Library

Dr. Pepper Company Historian/Librarian
P.O. Box 225086
Dallas, TX 75265
Request information about your collectibles directly from the Company if they are still in business.

Museum/Library

Dr. Pepper Museum and Free Enterprise
Institute
Newsletter: Bottlecaps
300 S. 5th Street
Waco, TX 76701
Phone: 317-757-1024 FAX: 817-757-3562
The museum focuses on the soft drink industry.

Hires Root Beer

Collector

Steve Sourapas
1413 Northwest 198th
Seattle, WA 98177
Phone: 206-542-1791
Advanced collector seeks pre-1930 good to mint condition items.

Moxie

Club/Association

Moxie Enthusiasts Collectors Club of
American (MECCA)
Magazine: Moxie Magazine, The
Frank N. Potter
Route 375, Box 164
Woodstock, NY 12498
Phone: 914-679-5390

Expert

Frank N. Potter
Route 375, Box 164
Woodstock, NY 12498
Phone: 914-679-5390
Author of "The Book of Moxie."

Misc. Service

Kennebec Fruit Company
Frank Anicett
2 Main St.
Lisbon Falls, ME 04252
Phone: 207-353-8173
Each year sponsors a Moxie Festival in Lisbon Falls, ME; offers contemporary Moxie collectibles.

Painted-Label Soda Bottles

Club/Association

Procurers of Painted-Label Sodas
Newsletter: PPLS Newsletter
P.O. Box 8154
Houston, TX 77004
Phone: 713-523-4346 *

Expert

Gary Brent Kincade
P.O. Box 712
Weston, WV 26452
Phone: 304-842-3773

Pepsi-Cola

Club/Association

Pepsi-Cola Collectors Club
Newsletter: PCCC Newsletter
Bob Stoddard
P.O. Box 1275
Covina, CA 91722
Phone: 714-593-8750

Collector

Bill Ricketts
P.O. Box 9605-B
Ashville, NC 28805
Phone: 704-669-2205 or 704-669-8881
Wants to buy Pepsi-Cola items: advertising, trays, signs, posters, calendars, novelty items, bottles, etc.; please price and describe.

Expert

Michael Hunt
P.O. Box 546
Brownsburg, IN 46112
Phone: 317-852-7874
*Co-author of "Pepsi-Cola Collectibles." ***

Expert

Bill Vehling
P.O. Box 41233
Indianapolis, IN 46241
Co-author along with Michael Hunt of "Pepsi-Cola Collectibles."

Expert

Bob Stoddard
P.O. Box 1275
Covina, CA 91722
Phone: 714-593-8750
Author of "Introduction to Pepsi Collecting."

Museum/Library

Pepsi-Cola Company Archives
Anderson Hill Road
Purchase, NY 10577
Request information about your collectibles directly from the Company if they are still in business.

7-Up

Collector

Brian Adamson
6732 Arlington Street
Vancouver
British Col., V5S 3N9 Canada
Wants 7-Up related colletibles: thermometers, calendars, signs, etc.; also wants Pepsi and Orange Crush items.

Soft Drink Cans

Club/Association

National Pop Can Collectors
Newsletter: Can-O-Gram
Dave Brackett, Memb.
1124 Tyler St.
Fairfield, CA 94533
Phone: 707-426-5553
Worldwide network of collectors focusing on soda cans & bottles as well as other soda memorabilia; articles, free ads and roster.

Museum/Library

Museum of Beverage Containers &
Advertising, The
1055 Ridgecrest Drive
Goodlettsville, TN 37072
Phone: 615-859-5236   FAX: 615-859-5238
The largest collection of soda and beer cans in the world; buy, sell, trade beer & soda advertising items.

SOLDIERS

Model

Club/Association

Miniature Figure Collectors of America
Newsletter: Guidon, The
1988 Foster Dr.
Hatfield, PA 19440
Phone: 215-855-2232
Interested in military history, miniature figures of military personnel in uniform, dioramic scenes. *

Toy

(see also TOYS, Playsets)

Auction Service

Wallis & Wallis
Glenn Butler
West Street Auction Galleries
Lewes
East Sussex BN7 2NJ England
Britain's specialist auctioneers of die-cast & tin plate toys & models including model soldiers.

Auction Service

Toy Soldier Information Service
Hank Anton
92 Swain Ave.
Meriden, CT 06450
Phone: 203-237-5356
Conducts monthly dimestore toy soldier auction *

Auction Service

Phillips Fine Art & Auctioneers
Henry Kurtz
406 East 79th St.
New York, NY 10022
Phone: 212-570-4830   FAX: 212-570-2207
Specializes in the sale of jewelry, paintings, prints, silver, coins, stamps, toys (especially lead soldiers), and movie memorabilia.

Auction Service

Gene Parker
Rt. 1 Box 108
Sugar Grove, IL 60554
Conducts auctions and publishes lists of dimestore soldiers. *

Club/Association

Toy Soldier Collectors of America
Newsletter: Communique
John Giddings, Trea.
6924 Stone's Throw Cir. #8202
St. Petersburg, FL 33710
Phone: 813-381-1412
An information center for all toy soldier collectors worldwide.

Club/Association

Military Miniature Society of Illinois
Newsletter: Scabbard, The
P.O. Box 394
Skokie, IL 60077
Sponsors an annual exhibition on the 3rd Saturday in October; features the best work from the U.S., Canada and Europe.

Collector

Bill Lango
127 74th St.
North Bergen, NJ 07047
Phone: 201-861-2979   FAX: 201-854-1738
Interested in Barclay vehicles, animals and soldiers from original and new molds.

Collector

Tony & Jacki Grecco
P.O. Box 3490
Poughkeepsie, NY 12603
Phone: 914-462-8829 *

Collector

Lee Schaffer
504 Hillside Ave.
Rochester, NY 14610
Phone: 716-244-6747
Wants toy soldiers, farm, zoo, civilian figures; especially Barclay, Manoil and Britains.

Collector

Joe Wallis
P.O. Box 2294
Washington, DC 20013
Wants Britains toy soldiers. *

Collector

Don Pielin
1009 Kenilworth
Wheeling, IL 60090 *

Collector

Edward K. Poole
926 Terrace Mt. Drive
Austin, TX 78746
Wants toy soldiers, 1/36th scale ID vehicles and old wooden military vehicle kits. *

Collector

Bill Hanlon
5063 Camino Alta Mira
Castro Valley, CA 94546
Phone: 415-886-0976
Interested in plastic toy soldiers. *

Dealer

Hank Anton
92 Swain Avenue
Meriden, CT 06450
Phone: 203-237-5356 *

Dealer

London Bridge Collector's Toys
Ron & Joanne Ruddell
1344 Rt. 100 S.
Trexlertown, PA 18087
Phone: 215-395-2500 *

Dealer

Jack Matthews
1255 23rd Street NW
Washington, DC 20037
Wants German composition and tinplate toys, WWII paper items and dimestore toy soldiers. *

Dealer

Memorable Things
P.O. Box 10505
Towson, MD 21204 *

Dealer

Allen W. Smith
102 N. Cherry St.
Falls Church, VA 22046
Phone: 703-237-2164
Wants dimestore toy soldiers: lead, rubber, composition, paper; Auburn, Marx, Manoil, Barclay, Built-Rite,etc.; any number.

Dealer

K. Warren Mitchell
1008 Forward Pass
Pataskala, OH 43062
Phone: 614-927-1661
Wants all kinds of old toy soldiers especially Britains, "dimestore", Mignot, Heyde (no plastic toys, please.)

Expert

Barry Carter
c/o AntiqueWeek
P.O. Box 90
Knightstown, IN 46148
Phone: 800-876-5133 *

Expert

Fred Wilhemn
828 Hermes Ave.
Leucadia, CA 92024
Phone: 619-753-8264 *

Museum/Library

Jim Morris' Toy & Soldier Museum
Jim Morris
1100 Cherry St.
Vicksburg, MS 39180

Periodical

Magazine: Plastic Warrior
Paul Stadlinger
905 Harrison St.
Allentown, PA 18103
A British bi-monthly focusing on leading European figures: firms (Britains, Timpo, etc.), reviews, Q&A, letters, news, ads, etc.

Periodical

Vintage Castings Inc.
Magazine: Toy Soldier Review
127 74th St.
North Bergen, NJ 07047
Phone: 201-861-2979   FAX: 201-854-1738
A worldwide quarterly magazine for the toy soldier enthusiast.

Periodical

Newsletter: Old Toy Soldier Newsletter
209 North Lombard
Oak Park, IL 60302
Phone: 312-383-6525
A bi-monthly newsletter. *

Supplier

Costal Enterprises
Howard Wehner
P.O. Box 1053
Brick, NJ 08723
Sells molds, casting supplies, soldier sets and cast soldiers. *

SOUVENIR & COMMEMORATIVE ITEMS

(see also GLASS, Souvenir & Commemorative; CERAMICS, Souvenir & Commemorative; HISTORICAL AMERICANA; STATUE OF LIBERTY COLLECTIBLES)

Periodical

Newsletter: Antique Souvenir Collectors News
Box 562
Great Barrington, MA 01230
Phone: 413-528-5490
The nationwide marketplace for antique souvenirs of all kinds: souvenir china, spoons, photos, glass, postcards - anything souvenir.

Periodical

Newspaper: Travel Collector
P.O. Box 40
Manawa, WI 54949-0040
Phone: 414-596-1944
Monthly newspaper that focuses on souvenir and commemorative glass and ceramic items in addition to other souvenir collectibles.

Plates

Collector

David Ringering
1509 Wilson Terrace
Glendale, CA 91206
Phone: 818-241-8469
Wants to buy rolled edge, 10" souvenir/historical plates; also any other souvenirs with scenes of cities, towns, etc.

Summer Resort Items

Collector

D.W. Francis
Box 16
Wadsworth, OH 44281
Wants 1880-1930 summer resort souvenirs: Atlantic City, Coney Island, Cedar Point, etc. - post cards, booklets, pennants, tickets, etc. *

SPACE ADVENTURE COLLECTIBLES

(see also CHARACTER COLLECTIBLES; RADIO SHOW PREMIUMS; SCIENCE FICTION COLLECTIBLES; TELEVISION SHOWS & MEMORABILIA; TOYS, Space & Robot)

Expert

Tomart Publications
Tom Tumbusch
P.O. Box 292102
Dayton, OH 45429
Phone: 513-294-2250
Author of "Space Adventure Collectibles."

SPACE EXPLORATION

(see also APOLLO XI MEMORABILIA)

Museum/Library

Alabama Space & Rocket Center
Tranquility Base
Huntsville, AL 35807
Phone: 800-633-7280

Museum/Library

International Space Hall of Fame, The
Space Center
Magazine: SpaceLog
P.O. Box 533
Alamogordo, NM 88310
Phone: 505-437-2840 or 800-545-4021
                         FAX: 505-437-7722
The ISHF is a four-story museum which chronicles the history of man's exploration of space; from earliest rockets to space shuttle.

SPECTACLES

(see also EYEGLASSES)

SPINNING WHEELS

Repair Service

Mick Holloway
P.O. Box 453
Winchester, IN 47394
Collects and repairs spinning wheels.

SPOONS

(see also SILVER; SOUVENIR & COMMEMORATIVE ITEMS)

Club/Association

Silver Spoon Club, The
Newsletter: Finial, The
Glenleigh Park, Stickler St.
Austell
Cornwall PL26 7JB England
The Silver Spoon Club of Great Britain is a postal club exclusively for collectors of fine silver spoons.

Souvenir

Club/Association

Scoop Club, The
Journal: Spoony Scoop Newsletter
Margaret Alves
84 Oak Ave.
Shelton, CT 06484
Phone: 203-924-4768

A club for collectors of souvenir spoons; newsletter offers research material on silver spoons; identification; values, etc.

Club/Association
Northeastern Spoon Collectors Guild
Ann A. Marek
52 Hillcrest Ave.
Morristown, NJ 07960
Phone: 201-539-9846
NSCG is dedicated to the perpetuation of the spoon collecting hobby.

Club/Association
American Spoon Collectors
Newsletter: Spooners Forum
4922 State Line
Westwood Hills, KS 66205
Phone: 913-831-0912

Expert
Bill Boyd
4922 State Line
Westwood Hills, KS 66205
Phone: 913-831-0912
Wants souvenir spoons with embossed, enameled or engraved handles and bowls; also World's Fair subjects, full-figured people, etc.

SPORTING COLLECTIBLES
(see also ANIMAL TROPHIES; ART, Sporting; DECOYS; FISHING COLLECTIBLES; TARGET SHOOTING MEMORABILIA; TRAP SHOOTING; TRAPS)

Dealer
Vivian Karsnitz Antiques
Vivian & James Karsnitz
1428 Jerry Lane
Manheim, PA 17545
Phone: 717-665-4202
Buys decoys, shotshells, 2-pc. shotshell boxes, prints (especially Lynn Bogue Hunt), early sporting magazines, glass target balls.

Periodical
Krause Publications, Inc.
Magazine: Trapper & Predator Caller, The
700 East State St.
Iola, WI 54990
Phone: 800-258-0929 or 715-445-2214
　　　　　　　　　FAX: 715-445-4087
A monthly magazine about hunting, trapping and predator calling.

Duck Game Calls
Collector
Harry Warner
740 West Clover
Memphis, TN 38119
Wants to buy pieces or collections. *

Expert
Howard Harlan
4920 Franklin Rd.
Nashville, TN 37220
Co-author along with W. Crew Anderson of "Duck Calls, An Enduring American Folk Art."

SPORTS COLLECTIBLES
(see also ART, Sports; AUTOGRAPHS, Sports Related; COLLECTIBLES (MODERN), Sports Related; SPORTS HISTORY; TRADING CARDS, Non-Sport)

Collector
Ken Domonkos
P.O. Box 9
Hamburg, NJ 07419
Phone: 201-209-7784
Sports memorabilia and baseball cards.

Collector
Mark Dubiel
2336 Yemans
Hamtramck, MI 48212
Wants auto racing, tennis, Olympics, boxing, hockey, bowling, basketball, football, baseball, soccer, horse racing, golf, etc. items. *

Collector
Adelson Sports
Bob, Ken & Mike Adelson
13610 N. Scottsdale
Scottsdale, AZ 85254
Phone: 602-596-1913
Sports memorabilia: yearbooks, ticket stubs, pennants, World Series and All Star programs for all sports, etc.

Collector
Goodwin Goldfaden
44663 Calhoun Ave.
Sherman Oaks, CA 91423
Phone: 818-986-4914
All sports related items from 1860 to date.

Collector
John Buonaguidi
2830 Rockridge Dr.
Pleasant Hill, CA 94523
Wants any sports related item: baseball cards, World Series programs; autographed baseballs and photos, boxing posters, advertising, etc. *

Dealer
Paul Longo Americana
Paul Longo
P.O. Box 490
South Orleans, MA 02662
Phone: 508-255-5482
Wants baseball and other sports memorabilia: sports cards, balls, autographs, uniforms, pennants, yearbooks, statues, silks, etc.

Dealer
Stephan A. Tuchman
184 Hempstead Ave.
West Hempstead, NY 11552
Phone: 516-486-1400　　FAX: 516-486-1716
Wants all quality sports collectibles and memorabilia: baseball, golf, boxing, etc.

Misc. Service
Nationwide Publishing, Co.
P.O. Box 38
Bountiful, UT 84011
Offers listing of names, addresses and phone numbers of traders, buyers and sellers of baseball & other sports cards and memorabilia.

Museum/Library
New England Sports Museum
1175 Soldiers Field Rd.
Boston, MA 02134
Phone: 617-787-7678

Periodical
Magazine: Sports Card Review
RFD 1, Box 350
Winthrop, ME 04364
Monthly magazine with articles and ads fro sports cards and sports memorabilia collectors; buy, sell, trade nationwide.

Periodical
Just Sports Inc.
Price Guide: Just Sports Card Pricing Guide
P.O. Box 7446
Freeport, NY 11520
A monthly price guide to baseball, football, basketball and hockey sports cards. *

Periodical
Magazine: Tuff Stuff
P.O. Box 1637
Glen Allen, VA 23060
Phone: 804-266-0140 or 800-899-TUFF
　　　　　　　　　FAX: 804-266-6874
The complete monthly sports price guide publication including baseball, football, basketball and hockey; also non-sports cards.

Periodical
Krause Publications, Inc.
Newspaper: Sports Collectors Digest
Tom Mortenson, Ed.
700 E. State St.
Iola, WI 54990
Phone: 715-445-2214 or 800-258-0929
　　　　　　　　　FAX: 715-445-4087
A weekly newsmagazine for collectors of sports memorabilia; everything from baseball cards to game-worn uniforms.

Periodical

Krause Publications, Inc.
Magazine: Baseball Card News
Jon Brecka, Ed.
700 E. State St.
Iola, WI 54990
Phone: 800-258-0929 or 715-445-2214
FAX: 715-445-4087
The hobby's leading newspaper containing up-dates on new collectibles for baseball, football, hockey, basketball and other card sets.

Periodical

Global Sports Productions, Ltd.
Directory: Sports Address Bible, The
Ed Kobak
717 Eleventh St.
Sanat Monica, CA 90402
Phone: 213-395-6533
A reference guide with addresses, phone & fax numbers & contact persons for teams, organizations, sports collecting info., etc.

Auto Racing

Club/Association

Antique Auto Racing Association
Newsletter: AARA Newsletter
Box 486
Fairview, NC 28730
Phone: 704-628-3428 *

Collector

George Koyt
8 Lenora Ave.
Morrisville, PA 19067
Phone: 215-295-4908
Wants all types of auto racing items: programs, postcards, books, toys, games, anything auto racing, A to Z, old/new, large or small.

Museum/Library

National Museum of Racing & Hall of Fame
Union Ave.
Saratoga Springs, NY 12866
Phone: 518-584-0400

Museum/Library

Stock Car Hall of Fame Joe Weatherly Museum
P.O. Box 500
Darlington, SC 29532
Phone: 803-393-2103

Museum/Library

International Motor Sports Hall of Fame
Don Naman, ExDir
P.O. Box 1018
Talladega, AL 35160
Phone: 205-362-5002 or 205-362-5003
FAX: 205-362-3717
Preserves the worldwide history of motor sports; over $7M in racing vehicles and memorabilia on display; Hall of Fame.

Auto Racing (Indy 500)

Club/Association

National Indy 500 Collectors Club
Newsletter: Short Chute, The
John E. Blazier
10505 N. Delaware St.
Indianapolis, IN 46280
Phone: 317-848-4750
Goal is to preserve the history of the Indy 500 Mile Race; newsletter has club notes, member spotlight, articles, want, sell, trade, etc.

Collector

John E. Blazier
10505 N. Delaware St.
Indianapolis, IN 46280
Phone: 317-848-4750
Founder of the National Indy 500 Collectors Club.

Museum/Library

Indianapolis Motor Speedway Hall of Fame Museum
P.O. Box 24152
Speedway, IN 46224
Phone: 317-248-6747

Baseball

Auction Service

Lelands
151 W. 28th St. #7E
New York, NY 10001
Phone: 212-971-3111 *

Club/Association

Society for American Baseball Research
Journal: Baseball Research Journal
P.O. Box 93183
Cleveland, OH 44101-5183
Concentrates on the historical aspects of baseball rather than on baseball memorabilia.

Collector

Steve Freedman
Central Station
P.O. Box 2054
East Orange, NJ 07019
Phone: 201-743-2091
*Wants all baseball-related items; especially relating to New York area teams - Brooklyn Dodgers, NY Giants, Yankees, and Mets. *

Collector

Rob Lifson
P.O. Box 1923
Hoboken, NJ 07030
Phone: 201-792-9324 *

Collector

Ken Feldan
2 Hemlock Lane
Marlboro, NJ 07746
Phone: 201-536-5974

*Wants advertising signs, posters of ball players, photos, autographs, everything. *

Collector

Mark Rucker
137 Circular Street
Saratoga Springs, NY 12866
*A leading collector of baseball memorabilia. *

Collector

Dennis Goldstein
516 Manford Rd. SW
Atlanta, GA 30310
Phone: 404-758-4743 or 404-763-2014
FAX: 404-761-6353
Baseball historian looking for early photographs, books, programs, memorabilia.

Collector

William Mastro
25 Brook Lane
Palos Park, IL 60464
Phone: 708-361-2117
Advanced collector wants baseball cards and baseball memorabilia.

Dealer

Hall's Nostalgia
David Hall
21-25 Mystic St.
Box 408
Arlington, MA 02174 *

Expert

John Selsam
R.D. #1, Box 240A
Lewisburg, PA 17837
Phone: 717-326-1921 *

Museum/Library

National Baseball Hall of Fame & Museum, Inc.
P.O. Box 590
Cooperstown, NY 13326
Phone: 607-547-9988   FAX: 607-547-5980

Periodical

Krause Publications, Inc.
Magazine: Fantasy Baseball
Greg Ambrosious, Ed.
700 E. State St.
Iola, WI 54990
Phone: 715-445-2214 or 800-258-0929
FAX: 715-445-4087
Complete guide to fantasy baseball league; every major league player ranked from scrub to star; hottest hobby with more than 1M players.

Periodical

Baseball Cards Unlimited
Newsletter: Your Season Ticket
Rick Toms, Editor
106 Liberty Rd.
Woodsboro, MD 21798
Phone: 301-845-6076

Focuses on local MD, VA, DE, PA baseball card shows and auctions; also contains short articles, ads, tips, etc.

Periodical

Newspaper: Baseball Hobby News
Frank Barning
4540 Kearny Villa Rd.
San Diego, CA 92123
Phone: 619-565-2848   FAX: 619-565-6608
Monthly magazine published since 1979 for collectors of sports memorabilia with an emphasis on baseball; includes price guide.

Periodical

Magazine: Diamond Angle, The
J.G. Floto, Pub.
P.O. Box 409
Kaunakakai, HI 96748
Phone: 808-558-8366
A journal feature articles, book reviews, trivia, lore, monthly card columns; sells cards plus has nationwide dealer ads.

Baseball Cards

Collector

Clarence Law
Rt. 1 Box 42
Farmland, IN 47340
Phone: 317-468-8258
Wants baseball cards; any year, any publication.
*

Collector

Chuck Moore
P.O. Box 280
Gladstone, OR 97027
Phone: 503-654-9974
Wants baseball cards, publications, memorabilia; also older football and basketball memorabilia.

Dealer

Shortt Stop
Michael Shortt
557 Richmond Ave.
Syracuse, NY 13204 *

Dealer

Bubba's Baseball Cards
Steve White
3301 Bluebird Ct.
Ijamsville, MD 21754
Phone: 301-831-6992
Buy, sell, trade baseball, football, basketball and hockey cards (all brands) and memorabilia; 1952 to present.

Dealer

Texas Sportscard Company
2816 Center Street
Deer Park, TX 77536
Phone: 713-476-9964

Man./Prod./Dist.

Major League Marketing (Score & SportFlics)
25 Ford Road
Westport, CT 06880
Phone: 203-227-8882
A baseball card company.

Man./Prod./Dist.

Topps Company, Inc., The
254 36th St.
Brooklyn, NY 11232
A baseball card company.

Man./Prod./Dist.

Fleer Corp.
10th & Somerville
Philadelphia, PA 19141
A baseball card company.

Man./Prod./Dist.

Leaf, Inc. (Donruss)
P.O. Box 2038
Memphis, TN 38101
A baseball card company.

Man./Prod./Dist.

Upper Deck Company
23705 Via Del Rio
Yorba Linda, CA 92686
Phone: 714-692-1013
A baseball card company.

Museum/Library

Metropolitan Museum of Art, The
Jefferson Burdich Collection
5th Avenue & 82nd Street
New York, NY 10028
Phone: 212-879-5500

Museum/Library

National Baseball Hall of Fame & Museum, Inc.
P.O. Box 590
Cooperstown, NY 13326
Phone: 607-547-9988   FAX: 607-754-5980

Museum/Library

Larry Fritsch Collection, The
Larry Fritsch
P.O. Box 863
Stevens Point, WI 54481
Phone: 715-344-8687

Periodical

Newsletter: Old Judge, The
P.O. Box 137
Centerbeach, NY 11720 *

Periodical

Magazine: Trader Speaks, The
3 Pleasant Dr.
Lake Ronkonkoma, NY 11779
Phone: 516-981-6915

*A monthly magazine with articles and ads for cards. **

Periodical

Price Guide: Beckett Baseball Card Monthly
P.O. Box 1915
Marion, OH 43305-1915
The bible of card collecting - a monthly baseball card price guide and advertiser; also show calendar.

Periodical

Krause Publications, Inc.
Magazine: Sports Collectors Digest
700 E. State St.
Iola, WI 54990
Phone: 800-258-0929 or 715-445-2214
    FAX: 715-445-4087
A weekly newsmagazine for collectors of sports memorabilia; everything from baseball cards to game-worn uniforms.

Periodical

Krause Publications, Inc.
Magazine: Baseball Cards
KitSteve Kiefer, Ed.
700 E. State St.
Iola, WI 54990
Phone: 715-445-2214 or 800-258-0929
    FAX: 715-445-4087
Full color magazine featuring cards from all eras; news, columns, feature stories, price guides; ads for cards and related items.

Periodical

Krause Publications, Inc.
Magazine: Baseball Card Price Guide Monthly
Jeff Kurowski, Ed.
700 E. State St.
Iola, WI 54990
Phone: 800-258-0929 or 715-445-2214
    FAX: 715-445-4087
Hobby's most complete monthly price guide listing values for more than 45,000 cards; also ads for cards and related items.

Supplier

Columbia Sportcards & Supplies
Suite 300
10632 Little Patuxent
Columbia, MD 21044
Phone: 301-964-8022
*Carries Allstate display cases, issues catalog of supplies. **

Baseball Gloves

Club/Association

Glove Collector Club, The
Newsletter: Glove Collector, The
Joe Phillips
14057 Rolling Hills Lane
Dallas, TX 75240
Phone: 214-699-1808
Bi-monthly newsletter contains buy/sell/trade ads and articles about old baseball gloves.

Repro. Source

Joe Phillips
14057 Rolling Hills Lane
Dallas, TX 75240
Phone: 214-699-1808
Deals in re-issue USA made baseball gloves.

Baseball Photos

Dealer

Mike Andersen
9-G Bond St.
Boston, MA 02118-2116
Buys & sells vintage baseball photos; wants autographed show biz photos; sells booklet of show biz addresses.

Baseball Uniforms

Collector

Dick Dobbins
P.O. Box 193
Alamo, CA 94507
*Leading collector of baseball uniforms. **

Basketball

Museum/Library

Naismith Memorial Basketball Hall of Fame
P.O. Box 179
Springfield, MA 01101-0179
Phone: 413-781-6500

Periodical

Krause Publications, Inc.
Magazine: Football Basketball & Hockey
    Collector
Don Butler, Ed.
700 E. State St.
Iola, WI 54990
Phone: 800-258-0929 or 715-445-2214
                    FAX: 715-445-4087
News, columns and features on football, basketball and hockey cards and related memorabilia; articles, Q&A, pricing info., cards,

Bowling

Museum/Library

National Bowling Hall of Fame & Museum
111 Stadium Plz.
St. Louis, MO 63102
Phone: 314-231-6340

Boxing Newsletter: Boxing Collectors Newsletter 59 Bosson Street Revere, MA 02151 *

Collector

Ron McNair
186 Battery Ave.
Brooklyn, NY 11209
Phone: 718-833-9588
Wants books, ring magazines, memorabilia, libraries, etc.

Bullfighting

Museum/Library

Bullfight Museum
5001 Alameda
El Paso, TX 79905
Phone: 915-772-2711

Crew Rowing

Collector

Pete Falk
170 Boston Post Rd., Box 150
Madison, CT 06443
Phone: 203-245-2246
Wants 19th century cigarette & trade cards, posters, broadsides, stereoviews, prints, sheet music, & books on rowing.

Curling

Collector

D.M. Sgriccia
5216 Sherry Ln.
Howell, MI 48843
Wants to buy curling stones, memorabilia, trophies, books, prints, etc.

Museum/Library

Turner's Curling Museum
417 Woodlawn Crescent
Weyburn
Saskatchewan S4H 0X5 Canada
Phone: 306-842-3604

Football

Museum/Library

National Football Museum, Inc.
212 George Halas Dr. NW
Canton, OH 44708
Phone: 216-456-8207

Periodical

Krause Publications, Inc.
Magazine: Football Basketball & Hockey
    Collector
Don Butler, Ed.
700 E. State St.
Iola, WI 54990
Phone: 800-258-0929 or 715-445-2214
                    FAX: 715-445-4087
News, columns and features on football, basketball and hockey cards and related memorabilia; articles, Q&A, pricing info., cards,

Football Cards

Expert

Michael Moyer
324 North 16th St.
Allentown, PA 18102
Phone: 215-434-0892 *

Golf

Auction Service

Sporting Antiquities
Kevin C. McGrath
47 Leonard Road
Melrose, MA 02176
Phone: 617-662-6588
Sells antique golf collectibles through auction and private sales; buys high quality gold paintings, prints, clubs, books, balls, etc.

Auction Service

Old Golf Shop, Ltd.
John & Morton Olman
325 W. Fifth St.
Cincinnati, OH 45202
Specialize in golf auctions.

Club/Association

Golf Collectors Society
Journal: Bulletin, The
Charles H. Yaws, Dir.
P.O. Box 491
Shawnee Mission, KS 66201
Phone: 913-649-4618
An international society for the preservation of the treasures and traditions of the Royal and Ancient game; largest in the world.

Collector

Highlands Golf
Art DiProspero
152 Bamford Ave.
Oakville, CT 06779
Phone: 203-274-8471
Wants wooden shaft golf clubs, early trophies; pre-1920 golf books, golf bronzes, modern "classic" clubs, golf paintings & prints, etc.

Collector

Tom Lupinacci
1349 Newfield Ave.
Stamford, CT 06905
Phone: 203-322-8231 *

Collector

Collector
32 Sterling Dr.
Lake Grove, NY 11755
Phone: 516-585-9017
Wants golf memorabilia: programs, balls, score cards, wooden shafted clubs, post cards, photos, autographs, statues, china, trophies.

Collector

D. Perkins
2317 N. Kessler Blvd.
Indianapolis, IN 46222
Phone: 317-638-4519
Wants wooden shaft golf clubs, early trophies or any antique sports related item.

Collector

Frank R. Zadra
Rt. 3 Box 3318
Spooner, WI 54801
Phone: 715-635-2791
Wants old golf related items: unusual golf clubs, old balls, books, bronzes, quality china and ceramics, and miscellaneous related items.

Collector

Bob Lucas
108 Aberdeen Ct.
Geneva, IL 60134
Phone: 312-232-2665
Old golf items, wood-shafted clubs, books, prints, china, etc.

Collector

Richard Hartzog
P.O. Box 4143
Rockford, IL 61110-0643
*Pre-1930 ephemera only. ***

Collector

Mike Brooks
7335 Skyline
Oakland, CA 94611
Phone: 415-339-1751
Wants golf items and memorabilia.

Expert

Joseph Murdoch
638 Wagner Rd.
Lafayette, PA 19444
Phone: 215-828-4492 *

Museum/Library

PGA/World Golf Hall of Fame
P.O. Box 1908
Pinehurst, NC 28374
Phone: 800-334-GOLF

Golf Ball Markers

Collector

Norman Boughton
1356 Buffalo Rd.
Rochester, NY 14624
Phone: 716-235-3696
Wants golf markers (used to mark a spot on the green), any material; especially those identifiable to a particular course or golfer.

Golf Paintings

Collector

William Graham
845 Lincoln
Winnetka, IL 60093
Old golf paintings: glass, pottery, postcards, paper; pre-1920.

Harness Racing

Museum/Library

Trotting Horse Museum
Newsletter: Hall of Fame Trotters News
P.O. Box 590
Goshen, NY 10924
Phone: 914-294-6330

Hockey

Museum/Library

U.S. Hockey Hall of Fame
P.O. Box 657
Eveleth, MN 55734
Phone: 218-744-5167

Periodical

Krause Publications, Inc.
Magazine: Football Basketball & Hockey
  Collector
Don Butler, Ed.
700 E. State St.
Iola, WI 54990
Phone: 800-258-0929 or 715-445-2214
                    FAX: 715-445-4087
News, columns and features on football, basketball and hockey cards and related memorabilia; articles, Q&A, pricing info., cards,

Lacrosse

Museum/Library

National Lacrosse Foundation & Hall of Fame, The
Magazine: Lacrosse Magazine
113 West University Parkway
Baltimore, MD 21210
Phone: 301-235-6882   FAX: 301-366-6735
Promotes and preserves the sport of lacrosse; museum includes displays and archives, and is the sport's largest resource center.

Little League

Museum/Library

Peter J. McGovern Little League Museum
P.O. Box 3485
South Williamsport, PA 17701
Phone: 717-326-3607

Pocket Schedules

Collector

J. Golen
1501 N. Mildred
Dearborn, MI 48128
Phone: 313-278-0381
*Pocket schedules: baseball, football, basketball, hockey; pre-1970. ***

Programs

Expert

Bud Glick
2846 Lexington Lane
Highland Park, IL 60035
Phone: 708-576-3521 or 708-433-7484

Wants Official baseball World Series programs, All Star programs and NFL Championship football programs.

Rodeo

Club/Association

Rodeo Historical Society
Newsletter: Wild Bunch
1700 N.E. 63rd St.
Oklahoma City, OK 73111
Phone: 405-478-2250 *

Museum/Library

ProRodeo Hall of Champions & Museum of the American Cowboy
101 Pro Rodeo Drive
Colorado Springs, CO 80919
Phone: 719-593-8840

Roller Skating

Museum/Library

National Museum of Roller Skating
Newsletter: Historical Roller Skating Overview
P.O. Box 81846
Lincoln, NE 68510
Phone: 402-489-8811

Snow Skiing

Collector

Gary Schwartz
680 Hawthorne Sr.
Tiburn, CA 94920
*Wants pre-1940 books, company catalogs, magazines, post cards, sheet music, posters, photographs, etc. relating to skiing. ***

Museum/Library

New England Ski Museum
Newsletter: NESM Newsletter
E. John B. Allen
P.O. Box 267
Franconia, NH 03580
Phone: 603-823-7177   FAX: 603-823-8088
Museum contains library research materials, photo collections, etc.; available free to members or on a fee basis to the public.

Museum/Library

National Ski Hall of Fame & Museum
P.O. Box 191
Ishpeming, MI 49849
Phone: 906-486-9281

Museum/Library

Colorado Ski Museum - Ski Hall of Fame
15 Vail Rd.
Vail, CO 81658
Phone: 303-476-1876 or 303-476-1879
Traces 100 years of Colorado's ski heritage through displays containing equipment, artifacts and photographs.

Museum/Library

Western American Skisport Museum
P.O. Box 38
Soda Springs, CA 95728
Phone: 916-426-3313
The mailing address is as noted above, but the museum is located at the Boreal Ridge Ski Area, Donner Pass, CA.

Soaring

Museum/Library

National Soaring Museum
Harris Hill, RD 3
Elmira, NY 14903
Phone: 607-734-3128

Soccer

Museum/Library

National Soccer Hall of Fame, The
Albert L. Colone
5-11 Ford Ave.
Oneonta, NY 13820
Phone: 607-432-3351 or 607-432-3645
　　　　　　　　　FAX: 607-432-9357
Information on soccer history, especially American; wants all forms of memorabilia relating to soccer including photographs.

Softball

Museum/Library

National Softball Association of
America
Newsletter: National Softball Hall of Fame
　　Newsletter
2801 N.E. 50th St.
Oklahoma City, OK 73111
Phone: 405-424-5266

Surfing

Collector

Dan Pincetich
318 Cutty Ct.
Pacifica, CA 94044
Phone: 415-355-5264
Wants wood paddleboards (Blake, Mitchell, etc.); also wood surfboards, pre-1960 brochures, ads, books, photos, patches, etc.

Swimming

Museum/Library

International Swimming Hall of Fame
Bob Duenkel
1 Hall Of Fame Dr.
Fort Lauderdale, FL 33316
Phone: 305-462-6536　　FAX: 305-525-4031
Seeks photos, memorabilia, etc. regarding the great athletes and history of the aquatic sports; swimming, diving, water polo, etc.

Tennis

Collector

D. Brenner
550 Rowland Rd.
Stone Mountain, GA 30083
Wants tennis memorabilia: programs, books, guides, equipment, tickets, autographs, magazines, autographs; also football, basketball,

Museum/Library

International Tennis Hall of Fame &
Tennis Museum
194 Bellevue Ave.
Newport, RI 02840
Phone: 401-849-3990

Tennis Rackets

Collector

Ralph Nix
Box 655
Red Bay, AL 35582
*Wants early lawn tennis rackets and other tennis memorabilia. ***

Thoroughbred Racing

Collector

Gary Gatanis
3283 Cardiff
Toledo, OH 43606
Wants Kentucky Derby memorabilia.

Collector

Sport of Kings Society
Newsletter: Castaways
1406 Anden Lane
Madison, WI 53711
*Focuses on horse racing memorabilia. ***

Collector

Gary Medeiros
1319 Sayre St.
San Leandro, CA 94579
Thoroughbred racing and Kentucky Derby memorabilia.

Museum/Library

Aiken Thoroughbred Racing Hall of Fame
& Museum
P.O. Box 2213
Aiken, SC 29802
Phone: 803-649-7700

Museum/Library

Kentucky Derby Museum, The
P.O. Box 3513
Louisville, KY 40201
Phone: 502-637-1111

Thoroughbred Racing Cards

Dealer

Horse Star Cards, Inc.
P.O. Box 1415
Louisville, KY 40201
Phone: 502-222-5518
Specializes in Kentucky Derby Trading Cards.

Track & Field

Collector

Ed Kozloff
10144 Lincoln
Huntington Woods, MI 48070
Phone: 313-544-9099
Wants running memorabilia: track & field, road races, olympic material, medals, ribbons, trophies, annuals, books, magazines, etc.

Museum/Library

National Track & Field Hall of Fame
Suite 140
200 South Capitol Avenue
Indianapolis, IN 46206
Phone: 317-638-9155

Weightlifting

Museum/Library

Bob Hoffman Weightlifting Hall of Fame
Box 1707
York, PA 17405
Phone: 717-767-6481

Wrestling

Museum/Library

National Wrestling Hall of Fame
405 W. Hall Of Fame Ave.
Stillwater, OK 74075
Phone: 405-377-5242

SPORTS HISTORY

Club/Association

North American Society for Sport
History
Newsletter: North American Soc. for Sport
　　History Newsletter
Penn State University
101 S. White Bldg.
University Park, PA 16802
Phone: 814-865-7591 *

Club/Association

Sports Hall of Oblivion
Chuck Hershberger, GM
P.O. Box 69025
Pleasant Ridge, MI 48069
Phone: 313-543-9412
The Sports Hall of Oblivion is an organization dedicated to preserving the memory of defunct sports teams (HS, College, semi-pro, pro.)

SPRINKLERS

(see also WATER SPRINKLERS)

STAGECOACH ITEMS

(see also WESTERN AMERICANA)

Dealer

Macdonald's Historical Collections
J.F. Macdonald
1316 NE 113th
P.O. Box 56371
Portland, OR 97220
Phone: 503-255-7256
Wants items relating to stage travel: tickets, vouchers, broadside ads, Wells Fargo items, stereoscope views, strong boxes, etc.

STAINED GLASS

(see also ARCHITECTURAL ELEMENTS;
REPAIRS & RESTORATIONS, Lamps &
Lighting)

Collector

Bob Ward
365 Neiffer Rd.
Schwenksville, PA 19473
Phone: 215-287-9495
Wants stained glass windows.

Expert

Architectural Antiques
H. Weber Wilson
24 Frankliln St.
Newport, RI 02840
Phone: 401-846-7010
Repairs leaded stained glass and is an author of book on same; also sells architectural antiques.

Expert

Carl Heck Antiques
Carl Heck
Box 8416
Aspen, CO 81612
Phone: 303-925-8011
Specializes in antique stained and beveled glass and Tiffany windows; also leaded and reverse-painted lamps. *

Periodical

Magazine: Glass Patterns Quarterly
P.O. Box 131
Westport, KY 40077

Periodical

Magazine: Glass Art Magazine
P.O. Box 1507
Broomfield, CO 80038-1507
A bi-monthly magazine which includes glass industry news including upcoming museum and gallery exhibitions.

Supplier

Blenko Glass Company, Inc.
P.O. Box 67
Milton, WV 25541
Phone: 304-743-9081   FAX: 304-743-0547

Supplies hand-blown "antique" glass for stained glass windows.

STAINLESS STEEL FLATWARE

(see also FLATWARE)

STAMP BOXES

Club/Association

Stamp Box Collectors Society
Journal: Journal of the Stamp Box Collectors
Society
P.O. Box 54
Stanmore
Middlesex HA7 4ED England *

STAMP COLLECTING

(see also SEALS, Christmas & Charity;
STAMP BOXES)

Auction Service

Harmers of New York, Inc.
14 East 33rd. Street
New York, NY 10016
Phone: 212-532-3700
Harmers specializes in the sale of stamps, but also sells paper items such as autographs, manuscripts, maps, etc.

Club/Association

Collectors Club Philatelist
Newsletter: Collectors Club Philatelist
22 E. 35th St.
New York, NY 10016
Phone: 212-683-0559 *

Club/Association

Modern Postal History Society
Journal: Modern Postal History Journal
Terence Hines
Box 629
Chappaqua, NY 10514-0629
Focuses on the collection, documentation and study of postal history, practices and policies; emphasizing material from 1930 to date.

Club/Association

American Philatelic Society
Magazine: American Philatelist
P.O. Box 8000
State College, PA 16803
Phone: 814-237-3803
Provides services to 58,000 collectors in more than 100 countries.

Club/Association

Ben Franklin Stamp Club, U.S. Postal
Service
Philatelic Appairs, USPS
475 L'Enfant Plaza
Washington, DC 20260
*Ben Franklin Stamp Clubs are sponsored by the USPS and are in elementary schools throughout the U.S. *

Club/Association

Local Post Collectors Club
c/o Aerophilatelic Federation
P.O. Box 1239
Elgin, IL 60121-1239
Phone: 708-888-1907
Members gather and disperse data on modern local posts worldwide since most catalogs do not list any of these issues.

Club/Association

Council of Philatelic Organizations
Les Winick
P.O. Box 1625
Homewood, IL 60430
Phone: 708-799-8888   FAX: 708-799-8889
Column on stamp collecting provided at no charge to newspapers; also offers three booklets to learn more about the stamp collecting hobby.

Dealer

Bob Morris
706 Pawnee St.
Bethlehem, PA 18015
Phone: 215-865-9052 or 717-523-2072
Purchases U.S. and foreign stamps, envelopes and philatelic literature; will appraise in the PA, NJ, NY and DE area.

Dealer

M. Mitchell - Stamps 'N' Covers
Milton & Marion Mitchell
3401 Hallaton Ct.
Silver Spring, MD 20906
Phone: 301-598-7959
Purchases and appraises stamp collections and estates.

Dealer

Dalton & Dalton
Box 487
Muncie, IN 47305
Phone: 317-288-9488
*Stamp collections wanted, large or small; since 1949. *

Dealer

MCS
Box 18061
West St. Paul, MN 55118
Phone: 612-641-9909
*Stamps and coins bought. *

Expert

Alfred J. Moses
P.O. Box 3547
Riverside, CA 92519
*Writes stamp column for "Collectors News." *

Man./Prod./Dist.

Starmont Recycling Sales
Blaine Moore
2602 Hilltop Dr.
Marshalltown, IA 50158
Phone: 515-752-5077

Recycles discarded stamps, labels, coupons into bookmarks, lamp shades, paperweights, key rings, dinner mats, and other things.

Misc. Service

Citizens' Stamp Advisory Committee,
Stamp Information Branch, USPS
475 L'Enfant Plaza, Room 5800
Washington, DC 20260-6753
Ideas for stamps may be sent to the Citizens' Stamp Advisory Committee.

Museum/Library

Cardinal Spellman Philatelic Museum, Inc. at Regis College
235 Wellesley St.
Weston, MA 02193
Phone: 617-894-6735

Museum/Library

Wineburgh Philatelic Research Library
P.O. Box 830643
Richardson, TX 75083-0643
Phone: 214-690-2570 or 214-690-9243

Periodical

Newsletter: MiniPhil
Jacques Herrijgers
1 Nachtegaallaan, B-1701
Itterbeek, Belgium
A quarterly international advertising sheet for stamp collectors only; a bilingual publication (French and English.)

Periodical

Link House Publications
Magazine: Stamp Magazine
Link House, Dingwall Ave.
Croydon
Surrey CR9 2TA England
Britain's leading stamp publication; articles, G.B. covers, stamps, cancellations, postcards, auction news, stamp shows, etc.

Periodical

Hager Sales
Newsletter: Collectors Exchange
P.O. Box 404
N. Grafton, MA 01536
Classifieds for stamp collectors and hobbyists. •

Periodical

Philatelic Foundation
Newletter: Philatelic Foundation Bulletin
21 E. 40th St.
New York, NY 10016
Phone: 212-889-6483
Profiles stamp collectors and their collections.

Periodical

Newspaper: Mekeel's Weekly Stamp News
P.O. Box 5050
White Plains, NY 10602 •

Periodical

H.L. Lindquist Publications
Newspaper: Stamps
John MicGlire, Pub.
85 Canisteo St.
Hornell, NY 14843
Phone: 607-324-2212   FAX: 607-324-1753
The weekly publication of philately; features the latest in philatelic news, collections, ads, auctions, etc.

Periodical

H.L. Lindquist Publications
Journal: Stamp Auction News
John MicGlire, Pub.
85 Canisteo St.
Hornell, NY 14843
Phone: 607-324-2212   FAX: 607-324-1753
A monthly market journal with recent auction prices realized; prices, ads, auction house profiles, vendor ads, etc.

Periodical

Newspaper: Linn's Stamp News
Mike Laurence, Ed.
P.O. Box 29
Sidney, OH 45365
Phone: 513-498-0801   FAX: 513-498-0814
Offers "The Stamp Collectors Yellow Pages" listing services for stamp collectors.

Periodical

Scott Publishing Co.
Magazine: Scott's Stamp Monthly
P.O. Box 828
Sidney, OH 45365
Phone: 513-498-0802   FAX: 513-498-0808
Magazine features notices of new stamp issues (using copyrighted Scott Numbering system) and other articles for the collector.

Periodical

Newsletter: Circuit, The
825 East Torrey
New Braunfels, TX 78130 •

Periodical

Newspaper: Stamp Collector
David M. Schiller, ExDir
520 E. First St.
P.O. Box 10
Albany, OR 97321
Phone: 503-928-3569   FAX: 503-967-7262
Weekly newspaper for stamp collectors.

Supplier

Scott Publishing Co.
Magazine: Scott's Stamp Monthly
P.O. Box 828
Sidney, OH 45365
Phone: 513-498-0802   FAX: 513-498-0808
Publisher of catalogs, albums and various stamp supplies.

Air Mail Related

(see also AIRLINE MEMORABILIA)

Club/Association

Aerophilatelic Federation of the Americas
Magazine: AFA News
P.O. Box 1239
Elgin, IL 60121-1239
Phone: 708-888-1907
The AFA is an association of 16 full supporting clubs and 19 member clubs devoted to various aero specialties of stamp collecting.

Periodical

Aerophilatelic Federation of the Americas
Magazine: Jack Knight Air Log, The
P.O. Box 1239
Elgin, IL 60121-1239
Phone: 708-888-1907
A quarterly magazine with news, reports, articles, comments, etc. relating to aero, astro and specialized philately interests.

Air Mail Related (Canada)

Club/Association

Canadian Airmail Collectors Club
c/o Aerophilatelic Federation
P.O. Box 1239
Elgin, IL 60121-1239
Phone: 708-888-1907
Members collect covers relating to Canadian airmail: also airport dedications, airline history, labels, postcards, timetables, etc.

Air Mail Related (Latin Amer.)

Club/Association

Latin American Airmail Collectors Club
c/o Aerophilatelic Federation
P.O. Box 1239
Elgin, IL 60121-1239
Phone: 708-888-1907
Members focus on collecting the stamps and covers of Central and South American.

Air Mail Related (Mexican)

Club/Association

Mexican Airmail Collectors Club
c/o Aerophilatelic Federation
P.O. Box 1239
Elgin, IL 60121-1239
Phone: 708-888-1907
Members are interested in sharing knowledge about the aerophilately of Mexico, especially the early airmail history of the country.

Air Mail Related (Rocket)

Club/Association

Rocket Mail Society
c/o Aerophilatelic Federation
P.O. Box 1239
Elgin, IL 60121-1239
Phone: 708-888-1907
Members interested in the theory that mail can and should be delivered by rockets to speed service and delivery.

Air Mail Related (Uruguay)

Club/Association

Uruguay Collectors Club
c/o Aerophilatelic Federation
P.O. Box 1239
Elgin, IL 60121-1239
Phone: 708-888-1907
Members are interested in the aerophilatelic items of Uruguay: stamps, covers, cards, labels, etc.

Amelia Earhart Related

Club/Association

Amelia Earhart Collectors Club
c/o Aerophilatelic Federation
P.O. Box 1239
Elgin, IL 60121-1239
Phone: 708-888-1907
Members specialize in stamps and covers pertaining to Amelia Earhart.

Concord Related

Club/Association

Concorde Collectors Club
c/o Aerophilatelic Federation
P.O. Box 1239
Elgin, IL 60121-1239
Phone: 708-888-1907
Members of this new club are involved in collecting stamps, proofs, souvenir covers, etc. relating to the Concorde SST.

Confederate

Club/Association

Confederate Stamp Alliance
Magazine: Confederate Philatelist
P.O. Box 14
Manitowoc, WI 54221
Focuses on the mail and postal systems used during the Civil War period. The bi-monthly booklet contains extensively researched articles.

Dealer

Confederate Philately, Inc.
Jack E. Molesworth
88 Beacon Street
Boston, MA 02108
Phone: 617-523-2522
Buys and sells; has large and comprehensive stock of Confederate stamps, covers, and related items.

Dealer

Brian Michael Green
Brian & Maria Green
P.O. Box 1816
Kernersville, NC 27285-1816
Phone: 919-993-5100
Buy & sell Confederate States stamps, postally used envelopes & related material, military correspondences & Generals' letters, etc.

Covers

Collector

Robert & Marie Kuehne
9910 Green Valley Rd.
Union Bridge, MD 21791
Phone: 301-898-7921
Wants old U.S. & American Civil War Confederate stamps on envelopes.

Expert

James Kesterson
3881 Fulton Grove Rd.
Cincinnati, OH 45245
Phone: 513-752-0949
Wants 19th century U.S. stamps on envelopes (covers); also stampless and illustrated covers; any amount.

Covers (Air Mail Related)

Club/Association

Jack Knight Air Mail Society
c/o Aerophilatelic Federation
P.O. Box 1239
Elgin, IL 60121-1239
Phone: 708-888-1907
Members specialize in the collecting of airmail flight covers from the U.S. and throughout the world.

Covers (Balloon Related)

Club/Association

Balloon Post Collectors Club
c/o Aerophilatelic Federation
P.O. Box 1239
Elgin, IL 60121-1239
Phone: 708-888-1907
Members collect covers that have been flown by balloon, or that commemorate balloon flights, races or festivals.

Covers (First Day)

Auction Service

FDC Publishing Co.
Michael Mellone
P.O. Box 206
Stewartsville, NJ 08886
Conducts monthly mail auctions exclusively for First Day Covers.

Club/Association

First Day Cover Collectors Club
c/o Aerophilatelic Federation
P.O. Box 1239
Elgin, IL 60121-1239
Phone: 708-888-1907
Members are interested in collecting, producing, documenting stamps canceled on the first day of issue; cachets, programs, cancels, etc.

Club/Association

American First Day Cover Society
Newsletter: First Days
1611 Corral Dr.
Houston, TX 77090
Phone: 713-444-8327 *

Man./Prod./Dist.

Postal Commemorative Society
47 Richards Ave.
P.O. Box 57491
Norwalk, CT 06857-4910
Sells a series of new first day covers.

Museum/Library

National First Day Cover Museum, The
Judy Sargent
702 Randall Avenue
Cheyenne, WY 82001
Phone: 307-634-5911 or 307-771-3202
The world's only museum dedicated to the preservation and display of First Day Covers.

Covers (Naval)

Club/Association

Universal Ship Cancellation Society
Magazine: Log
Lorraine Kozicki
35 Montague Circle
East Hartford, CT 06118
Dedicated to the collection and study of Naval and maritime Postal History; interested in covers from ships and related installations.

Covers (War Related)

Club/Association

War Cover Club
Chris Kulpinski, Sec.
P.O. Box 464
Feasterville, PA 19047
Members interested in war related mails and postal history: soldier & POW mail, occupation, internments, camp cancels, propaganda, etc.

Duck/Fish & Game

(see also STAMP COLLECTING; Revenue & Tax Stamps)

Dealer

Dr. Duck
Lynn Troute
117 N. Durkin Dr.
Springfield, IL 62702

Federal and State duck stamps available; send for free list; also buying duck stamps used, mint or on licenses.

Expert

David R. Torre
P.O. Box 4298
Santa Rosa, CA 95402
Phone: 707-838-2565
Wants pictorial and non-pictorial waterfowl and fishing stamps; also pre-1930 pictorial hunting & fishing licenses from any state.

Errors

Club/Association

Errors, Freaks & Oddities Collectors Club
Newsletter: EFO Collector
J. E. McDevitt
1903 Village Rd., W.
Norwood, MA 02062
Phone: 617-769-6531 *

Japanese

Expert

Nippon Philatelics
Frnk L. Allard, Jr.
Drawer 7300
Carmel, CA 93921
Phone: 408-625-2643 or 408-624-4617
FAX: 408-624-4617
Wants anything Japanese: postcards, mail, stamps, posters, postal stationary, First Day Covers, photos, etc.; price lists available.

Postmarks

Club/Association

Post Mark Collectors Club
Newsletter: PMCC Bulletin
7629 Homestead Drive
Baldwinsville, NY 13027

Collector

David E. Lyman
4026 Sancrest Court
Mississauga
Ontario L5L 3Y5 Canada
Wants large pre-1950 collections of postmarks, cut, any size; all states and countries on piece; write before shipping.

Revenue & Tax Stamps

(see also BANK CHECKS; STAMP COLLECTING, Duck/Fish & Game)

Club/Association

State Revenue Society
Newsletter: State Revenue Newsletter
Terence Hines
Box 629
Chappaqua, NY 10514-0629

For collectors whose prime aim is the collection, identification and cataloging of state and local revenue philately.

Club/Association

American Revenue Association
Newsletter: American Revenuer
701 S. First Ave.
Arcadia, CA 91006
*Interested in U.S. and foreign revenue and tax stamps and stamped paper. ***

Souvenir Cards

Club/Association

Souvenir Card Collectors Society
Journal: Souvenir Card Journal
P.O. Box 4155
Tulsa, OK 74159
Phone: 918-747-6724
Souvenir cards are 8 1/2" x 11" cards with engraved reproductions of philatelic or numismatic designs from original plates.

Spanish

Club/Association

Spanish Philatelic Society
Newsletter: SPS Newsletter
Bob Penn
P.O. Box 3804
Gettysburg, PA 17325
Bi-monthly newsletter; Spain, colonies, Spanish Civil War, new issues; buy and sell ads.

Topical

Club/Association

American Topical Association
Magazine: Topical Time
Don Smith
P.O. Box 630
Johnstown, PA 15907-0630
Phone: 814-539-6301
Topicalists save stamps relating to a specific topic such as birds, space, buildings, transportation, etc.; collect by the subject

Topical (Christmas Related)

Club/Association

Christmas Philatelic Club
Newsletter: Yule Log
Vaughn H. Augustin, Sec.
6900 W. Quincy Ave. 9E
Littleton, CO 80123
Phone: 393-933-4287
For those interested in collecting Christmas stamps from around the world: seals, covers, postcards and any related Christmas material.

Topical (Dog Related)

Club/Association

Dogs On Stamps Study Unit
Journal: DOSSU Journal
Morris Raskin
3208 Hana Road
Edison, NJ 08817-2552
Phone: 908-248-1865
Purpose is to further the collection and study of philatelic postal material that pertains to dogs.

Topical (Golf Related)

Club/Association

International Philatelic Golf Society
Newsletter: Tee Time
P.O. Box 2183
Norfolk, VA 23501 *

Topical (Map Related)

Club/Association

Carto-Philatelists
Magazine: Carto-Philatelist
303 South Memorial Drive
Appleton, WI 54911 *

Topical (Religion Related)

Club/Association

Collectors of Religion On Stamps
Magazine: COROS Chronicle
208 East Circle Street
Appleton, WI 54915
Phone: 414-734-2417 or 414-832-5808

Topical (Scout Related)

Club/Association

Scouts On Stamps Society International
Journal: SOSSI Journal
253 Sheldon Ave.
Downers Grove, IL 60515 *

Topical (Sports Related)

Club/Association

Sports Philatelists International
Journal: Journal of Sports Philately
C.A. Reiss, Sec.
322 Riverside Dr.
Huron, OH 44839
Phone: 419-433-5315
Promotes information on sports stamps, cancels; check lists & articles related to sports and the Olympics.

STANHOPES

Collector

T.A. Coppens
1057 Forest Lakes Dr.
Naples, FL 33942
Little novelty viewers with peep holes showing scenes, Lord's Prayer, etc.; found in letter openers, pipes, souvenir trinkets, knives, etc.

Collector

Donald Gorlick
P.O. Box 24541
Seattle, WA 98124
Wants tiny viewers made of bone or metal sometimes found in crucifixes, pens, letter openers, needle holders, etc.

STANLEY TOOLS

(see also TOOLS, Stanley)

STAR TREK

(see also TELEVISION SHOW
MEMORABILIA, Star Trek)

STATUE OF LIBERTY COLLECTIBLES

Collector

Mike Brooks
7335 Skyline
Oakland, CA 94611
Phone: 415-339-1751
Buying early souvenir models, books, medals, advertising, donor certificates, unveiling invitations, Bartholdi related items, etc.

Expert

Harvey Dolin & Co.
Harvey & Sandy Dolin
5 Beekman St.
New York, NY 10038
Phone: 212-267-0216
Wants any item pertaining to the Statue of Liberty.

STEAM-OPERATED

Models & Equipment

(see also AUTOMOBILES, Steam; BOATS,
Steam; ENGINES; FARM MACHINERY;
HORNS & WHISTLES; INDUSTRY
RELATED ITEMS; RAILROADS; TOYS,
Steam/Hot Air)

Club/Association

International Brotherhood of Live
Steamers
369 Towhee Dr.
Bonny Doon, CA 95060
Phone: 408-426-3872
Interested in steam-operated models, equipment, and machinery; especially railroads. *

Club/Association

Northwest Steam Society
Newsletter: Steam Gage
P.O. Box 9727
Seattle, WA 98109
Phone: 206-321-1924
Interested in steam-operated models, equipment, and machinery; especially railroads. *

Museum/Library

Hamilton Museum of Steam & Technology,
The
900 Woodward Ave.
Hamilton
Ontario, Canada
Phone: 416-549-5525
Exhibits of industrial history; children's activities.

Museum/Library

Live Steam Museum
RTE 1 Box 11A
Alamo, TX 78516
Phone: 512-787-1941

Periodical

Magazine: Live Steam Magazine
P.O. Box 629
Traverse City, MI 49685
Phone: 616-941-7160
A magazine for the amateur machinist, or live steam hobbyist; steam locomotives, tractors, stationary engines, boats, etc.

Periodical

Magazine: Home Shop Machinist
P.O. Box 1810
Traverse City, MI 49685
Phone: 619-946-3712 or 800-447-7367
A magazine for the amateur machinist, or live steam hobbyist; articles, how-to's, plans, ads, etc.

STEIFF

(see also DOLLS; TEDDY BEARS)

Club/Association

Steiff Collectors Club
Newsletter: Steiff Life
Beth Savino
c/o The Toy Store
7856 Hill Ave.
Holland, OH 43528
Phone: 419-865-3899 or 800-862-8697
                               FAX: 419-865-2630
For collectors of contemporary and antique Steiff; a manufacturer sponsored club; offers product catalog of items for sale.

Expert

Bunny Walker
Box 502
Bucyrus, OH 44820
Phone: 419-562-8355 *

Museum/Library

Steiff Museum
Beth Savino
c/o The Toy Store
7856 Hill Ave.
Holland, OH 43528
Phone: 419-865-3899 or 800-862-8697
                               FAX: 419-865-2630

STEINS

Auction Service

F.T.S. Inc.
Ron Fox
416 Throop St.
N. Babylon, NY 11704
Phone: 516-669-7232   FAX: 516-669-7232
Send for free quarterly stein auction catalogs with photos, descriptions and estimates.

Auction Service

Kirsner's Auctions
Gary Kirsner
P.O. Box 8807
Coral Springs, FL 33075
Phone: 305-344-9856   FAX: 305-344-4421
Six to seven cataloged auctions per year; steins and related items; also specialty038auctions of Limited Edition and retired collectibles.

Auction Service

Les Paul, Steinologist
Les Paul
Suite A
2615 Magnolia St.
Oakland, CA 94607
Phone: 415-832-2615   FAX: 415-832-2616
Conducts mail-bid stein auctions.

Club/Association

Stein Collectors International
Magazine: Prosit
Walt Vodges, Treas.
8113 Bondage Dr.
Gaithersburg, MD 20879
Members have an interest in beer steins; the quarterly "Prosit" has a variety of articles about steins; SCI has its own stein museum.

Collector

Allan Harrell
P.O. Box 14002
Chicago, IL 60614
Phone: 312-508-9542
Wants steins: Mettlach, regimentals, character, etc.

Dealer

Heinz-N-Steins
Heinz Roes
231 Maple Ave.
Glen Burnie, MD 21061
Phone: 301-760-0707
Wants all steins including Mettlach, regimentals, etc.; also occupational shaving mugs and WWI German military pipes, cups, etc.

Expert

F.T.S. Inc.
Ron Fox
416 Throop St.
N. Babylon, NY 11704
Phone: 516-669-7232   FAX: 516-669-723:
Specializes in Mettlach steins.

Expert
Glentiques, Ltd.
Gary & Beth Kirsner
P.O. Box 8807
Coral Springs, FL 33075
Phone: 305-344-9856   FAX: 305-344-4421
Wants quality steins: Mettlach, regimentals, character, glass, etc.; author of "The Beer Stein Book", (1990).

Repro. Source
Werner Sahm-Rastal
P.O. Box 13 37
D-5410
Hohr-Grenzhausen, Germany *

Repro. Source
SCHWATLO GmbH
Zeiring 26
D-6239 EPPSTEIN
Germany *

STEINS (MODERN)

(see also GLASSES, Drinking)

Dealer
Krafts & Kollectors
2400 Lincoln Highway East
Lancaster, PA 17602
Phone: 717-394-6404
For the collector of mugs and steins: Anheuser Busch, Strohs, Coors, Miller, Hamm's, Pabst, Yuengling, etc.; send SASE for list.

Dealer
Heartland of Kentucky Specialties
P.O. Box 428
Lebanon Jct., KY 40105
Phone: 502-833-2827
Hundreds of whiskey decanters by Jim Beam, Wild Turkey, Ski Country, McCormick and others; also beer steins, neon lights, mirrors, clocks.

Dealer
Bill Cress
Box 989
Alton, IL 62002
Phone: 618-466-3513
Buys and sells all of the new and lots of the old steins; quarterly lists of modern steins and mugs for sale.

Dealer
D & A Investments
Darrell Bowman
2055 E. Burnside Circle
Salt Lake City, UT 84109
Phone: 801-277-4767 or 800-336-2055
Buys and sells American breweriana mugs & steins; major brands of any period; send SASE for updated price list of mugs & steins for sale.

Periodical
Newsletter: Stein Line
Thomas A. Hejza, Pub.
P.O. Box 48716
Chicago, IL 60648-0716
                    FAX: 708-673-2634
Published bi-monthly about newly-released and previously-released steins: stein sales, auctions, foreign steins, values, photos, etc.

Advertising
Collector
Donald Shaurette
#21 1240 Bryant Ave.
St. Paul, MN 55075
Wants miniature steins; also wants beer steins that advertise brands or breweries. *

Budweiser
Collector
P. Scarna
P.O. Box 1071
Dania, FL 33004
Wants to buy Budweiser, Anheuser-Bush and Bush Gardens beer steins and mugs; please send description and price.

Collector
Al Miller
515 Sun Manor
Flushing, MI 48433
Phone: 313-659-1189
Wants Budweiser ceramic mugs and steins prior to 1981. *

Miniature
Collector
Donald Shaurette
#21 1240 Bryant Ave.
St. Paul, MN 55075
Wants miniature steins; also wants beer steins that advertise brands or breweries. *

STEREO VIEWERS & STEREOGRAPHS

(see also 3-D PHOTOGRAPHICA; CAMERAS & CAMERA EQUIPMENT; PHOTOGRAPHS)

Club/Association
National Stereoscopic Association
Magazine: Stereo World
P.O. Box 14801
Columbus, OH 43214
Phone: 614-263-4296
Members collect stereo views, stereoscopes, stereo cameras; View Master reels, viewers, packets; all other 3-D collectibles.

Club/Association
Stereo Club of Southern California
Newsletter: SCSC Newsletter
Susan Pinsky
P.O. Box 2368
Culver City, CA 90231
Phone: 213-837-2368   FAX: 213-558-1653
A club for people interested in sharing 3-D (stereo) photography; some equipment listed in club newsletter classifieds.

Collector
Henry Medina
181 Thomas St.
Brentwood, NY 11717
Phone: 516-273-1832 *

Collector
Norman Kulkin
727 N. Fuller Ave.
Los Angeles, CA 90046
Phone: 213-653-6929
Buy, sell, trade stereoviews, daguerreotypes, Civil War photos, anything in photographica 1839-1939.

Dealer
Russell Norton
P.O. Box 1070
New Haven, CT 06504-1070
Phone: 203-562-7800
Stereo views always wanted.

Expert
Antique Graphics
John Waldsmith
107 N. Sycamore
P.O. Box 191
Sycamore, OH 44882
Phone: 419-927-2930
Wants stereoscopic views, View-Master reels, photographica; conducts mail/phone auctions on regular basis; also direct sales.

Expert
Stereographica
Chuck Reincke
2141 Sweet Briar Rd.
Tustin, CA 92680
Phone: 714-832-8563
Buy, sell stereo cards, View Master, Tru-Vue and viewers; prefer higher quality and more unusual items.

Supplier
Reel 3-D Enterprises, Inc.
David Starkman
P.O. Box 2368
Culver City, CA 90231
Phone: 213-837-2368   FAX: 213-558-1653
Offers a catalog with complete line of items for the modern 3-D enthusiast: books, stereo viewers, mounting supplies, etc.

Alaska Related

Collector

Richard A. Wood
P.O. Box 22165
Juneau, AK 99802
Phone: 907-586-6748 or 907-789-8450
Wants stereoviews of Alaska, Klondike; also photographer L. Hensel views of PA (especially Pike County, PA) and NY.

STERLING SILVER FLATWARE

(see also FLATWARE)

STEVENGRAPHS

Club/Association

Stevengraph Collectors Association
Newsletter: SCA Newsletter
David L. Brown
2829 Arbutus Road, #2103
Victoria
B. C. V8N 5X5 Canada
Phone: 604-477-9896
Approx. 120 members worldwide; focuses on the various jacquard woven silk works (Stevengraphs) by Thomas Stevens of Coventry, England.

Expert

John High
415 E. 52nd St.
New York, NY 10022
Phone: 212-758-1692 *

Museum/Library

Herbert Art Gallery & Museum
Nick Dodd
Jordan Well
Coventry CV1 5RW England
Has the largest collection of Stevengraphs in public hands; also has a very large silk ribbon collection.

Museum/Library

Paterson Museum
2 Market St.
Paterson, NJ 07501
Phone: 201-881-3874

STOCKS & BONDS

(see also CIVIL WAR ARTIFACTS,
Confederate Bonds)

Club/Association

Bond & Share Society
Newsletter: BSS Newsletter
24 Broadway
New York, NY 10004
Phone: 212-943-1880 *

Collector

Scott J. Winslow Associates, Inc.
P.O. Box 6033
Nashua, NH 03063
Phone: 603-881-4071

*Wants obsolete stock certificates and bonds. *

Collector

Fred Herrigel
Box 80
Oakhurst, NJ 07755
Obsolete stock certificates and pre-1920 postcard collections.

Collector

Centennial Documents
Richard Urmston
P.O. Box 5262
Clinton, NJ 08809
Phone: 908-703-6009   FAX: 908-730-9566
Wants stocks & bonds; send photocopy of items for sale.

Collector

Bob Pyne
P.O. Box 149064
Orlando, FL 32814
Wants older bank checks; also Confederate money, stocks and bonds.

Collector

Herb D. Rice
3883 Turtle Creek Blvd. #2317
Dallas, TX 75219
Wants old, obsolete stock certificates.

Dealer

Paul Longo Americana
Paul Longo
P.O. Box 490
South Orleans, MA 02662
Phone: 508-255-5482
Wants pre-1910 stocks and bonds; any amount.

Dealer

La Barre Galleries
George H. La Barre
P.O. Box 746
Hollis, NH 03049
Phone: 603-882-2411
Major dealer and expert in autographs, and stocks and bonds.

Dealer

Buttonwood Galleries
Phyllis Barrella
Throggs Neck Station
P.O. Box 1006
Bronx, NY 10465
Phone: 718-743-9535
Specializing in high quality pre-1910 stock certificates and bonds.

Dealer

Norrico Inc.
Frank Hammelbacher
6509 99 St.
Rego Park, NY 11375
Phone: 718-897-3699   FAX: 718-275-3666

Wants stocks/bonds, pre-1900; especially railroads, mining, telegraph, and the unusual

Dealer

Foxes' Den Antiques
Georgia Fox
P.O. Box 846
Sutter Creek, CA 95685
Phone: 209-267-0774
Wants old stocks & bonds, especially relating to gold mining in California or Nevada.

Expert

American West Archives
Warren Anderson
P.O. Box 100
Cedar City, UT 84721
Phone: 801-586-9497 or 801-586-7323
Buys and sells issued American stocks & bonds 1840-1930; especially mining, energy, transportation; offers mail order catalog.

Expert

Greentree Stocks
Bill Yatchman
P.O. Box 1688
Sedona, AZ 86336
Phone: 602-282-6547
*Author of "The Stock & Bond Collectors Price guide." *

Expert

Ken Prag Paper Americana
Ken Prag
Box 531
Burlingame, CA 94011
Phone: 415-566-6400
Eager to buy old stocks and bonds, quality picture postcards, western stereoviews, old timetables and brochures, etc.

Periodical

Magazine: Scrip
58 Inglehurst Gardens
Redbridge, Ilford
Essex 1G4 5HE England *

Periodical

R.M. Smythe & Company
Magazine: Friends of Financial History
24 Broadway
New York, NY 10004
Phone: 212-943-1880 *

Periodical

Krause Publications, Inc.
Newspaper: Bank Note Reporter
Dave Harper, Ed.
700 East State St.
Iola, WI 54990
Phone: 800-258-0929 or 715-445-2214
                    FAX: 715-445-4087
Monthly news source and marketplace for collectors of U.S. and world paper money, notes, checks and related fiscal paper.

STOCK TICKERS

(see also TELEGRAPH ITEMS)

Collector

Collector
P.O. Box 1447
New York, NY 10274
Phone: 718-317-1838
Wants early models with glass dome; also pre-1900 Poor's Manual. *

STOVES

Club/Association

Antique Stove Association
Newsletter: Stove Parts Needed Newsletter
Clifford Boram, Sec.
417 N. Main St.
Monticello, IN 47960
For those interested in antique stoves and related items; you must join to receive the benefits which are for members only.

Expert

Clifford Boram
417 N. Main St.
Monticello, IN 47960
Phone: 218-583-6465
Author of "How to Get Parts Cast for Your Antique Stove," will answer inquires ONLY if SASE is enclosed.

Repair Service

Bryant Stove Works
Beatrice Bryant
Rts. 139 & 220
P.O. Box 2048
Thorndike, ME 04986
Phone: 207-568-3498
Large collection on display ; also sells parts and restores antique (1780's-1940's) cook stoves, parlor stoves, and gas stoves.

Repair Service

Tomahawk Foundry, Inc.
2337 29th St.
Rice Lake, WI 54868
Phone: 715-234-4498
Makes replacement parts for cast iron stoves.

Supplier

Custom House
South Shore Drive
Owl's Head, ME 04854
Phone: 207-594-5985
Carries replacement parts for antique stoves. *

STREETCAR LINE COLLECTIBLES

Club/Association

Central Electric Railfans' Association
William M. Shapotkin, Mem.
P.O. Box 503
Chicago, IL 60690
Phone: 312-346-3723

Interested in history and equipment of electric railroading: urban, rapid transit, suburban, trunk line and industrial electric railways.

Collector

Jonathan Thomas
1208 Main St.
Southbury, CT 06488-2159
Collector and historian of pre-1930 U.S. trolleys/streetcars; wants fare counters, badges, car bells, registers, signs, documents, etc.

Museum/Library

Baltimore Streetcar Museum
P.O. Box 4881
Baltimore, MD 21211
Phone: 301-547-0264

STRING HOLDERS

Collector

John Reece
1426 Turnesa Dr.
Titusville, FL 32780
Wants string holders of all kinds: wall or hanging type; chalkware or china. *

Expert

Reynolds Toys
Charles Reynolds
2836 Monroe St.
Falls Church, VA 22042
Phone: 703-533-1322
Wants string holders made of metal, glass or wood; not interested in chalk or china types.

STUFFED TOYS

(see also STEIFF; TEDDY BEARS)

SUBWAY ITEMS

Museum/Library

New York Transit Museum
81 Willoughby St., Rm. 802
Brooklyn, NY 11201
Phone: 718-330-3060 or 718-330-3063
FAX: 718-522-2339
Features displays, exhibits, archive information regarding the New York Subway System.

SUFFRAGE ITEMS

Collector

Cary Demont
P.O. Box 19312
Minneapolis, MN 55419
Phone: 612-922-1617
Wants political pre-1964 buttons, pins, flags, ribbons, banners, and the unusual; also suffrage, prohibition, slavery, and Lindbergh.

SUGAR PACKETS

Club/Association

Sugar Packet Clubs International
Newsletter: Sugar Packet, The
Mitzt Geiser
15601 Burkhart Road
Orville, OH 44667
Phone: 216-682-7486
Specializing in the international trading and exchange of information on sugar sacs and sugar cubes.

Collector

Herb Schingoethe
156 S. Western Ave.
Aurora, IL 60506
Wants old sugar packets; wrappers, collections or accumulations.

SUGAR SHAKERS

Collector

Bob Hendel
1385 York Ave. #12G
New York, NY 10021
Phone: 212-772-9070
Wants large and small collections; very interested in "diner" shakers. *

SUNDIALS

Collector

Myron Palay
4242 Lorain Ave.
Cleveland, OH 44113-3771
Phone: 216-961-7903
Wants dials, astrolabes, books, prints, photos, catalogs; anything sundial related.

SUPER HEROES

(see also COLLECTIBLES; COMIC BOOKS; RADIO SHOW PREMIUMS; TOYS, Super Hero)

Batman

Collector

Batman Addict
Joe Desris
1202 60th Street, #107
Kenosha, WI 53140
Phone: 414-657-4737   FAX: 414-657-4733
Batman addict; only known cure: more collectibles! Wants anything Batman related from 1930's-1990's.

Captain Midnight

Collector

Bob Hritz
21 W. 262 Belden Ave.
lombard, IL 60148
Phone: 708-620-0156

Wants Captain Midnight items: Ovaltine glass jars, CM advertising, premiums, rings, pins, lobby cards, flight commander manual, etc.

Phantom

Collector

Robert J. Griffin
P.O. Box 76
Mattawan, MI 49071
Phone: 616-387-3024
Wants to buy memorabilia relating to The Phantom.

Superman

Dealer

Danny Fuchs
209-80 18th Ave.
Bayside, NY 11360
Phone: 718-225-9030
Buys and sells all types of pre-1960 Superman collectibles: toys, games, figurines, puzzles, novelties, premiums, etc. rare or unusual.

Expert

Danny Fuchs
209-80 18th Ave.
Bayside, NY 11360
Phone: 718-225-9030
"America's foremost Superman Collector"; co-author of "The Adventures of Superman Collecting."

SUPPLIERS

(see also REPAIRS & RESTORATIONS, Lighting; REPAIRS & RESTORATIONS, Upholstery; REPAIRS & RESTORATIONS, Woodworking; etc.)

SURVEYING INSTRUMENTS

(see also INSTRUMENTS & DEVICES, Scientific)

Collector

Barry Nichols
8139 East Britton Dr.
Niagara Falls, NY 14304
Wants surveying tools: instruments, compasses, chains, etc.

Collector

Dale Beeks
Box 2515H
Coeur D'Arlene, ID 83814
Phone: 208-667-0830
*Wants transits, compasses, link-chains; also fine microscopes, pre-1900 typewriters, calculating devices, medical items & quackery. ***

SWANKYSWIGS

(see also GLASSES, Drinking)

Expert

Ian Warner
P.O. Box 55
Brampton
Ontario L6V 2K7 Canada
Specializing in Wade porcelain and swankyswigs.
*

Expert

M. Fountain
201 Alvena
Wichita, KS 67203
Phone: 316-943-1925
*Swankyswigs were decorated glasses originally filled with Kraft Cheese Spreads. ***

SWIZZLE STICKS

Club/Association

International Swizzle Stick Collectors Association
Newsletter: Swizzle Stick News
Ray P. Hoare
P.O. Box 1117
Bellingham, WA 98227-1117
Collectors helping collectors; 6 years in operation; sponsors convention every other year.

SWORDS

(see also ARMS & ARMOR; CIVIL WAR ARTIFACTS; EDGED WEAPONS; MILITARIA; NAZI ITEMS)

Dealer

Frederick's Swords
Fred Coluzzi
6919 Westview
Oak Forest, IL 60452
Phone: 708-687-3647
Wants antique swords and daggers from all countries and all periods; issues 3 to 4 catalogs per year.

Museum/Library

Fort Ticonderoga
Box 390
Ticonderoga, NY 12883
Phone: 518-585-2821

3rd Reich

Collector

K. Wiley
719 Baldwin SE
Grand Rapids, MI 49503
Phone: 616-451-8410
Wants Japanese swords, daggers, sword parts. Also German 3rd Reich daggers, swords, bayonets. References available.

TABLEWARE

(see also CERAMICS; DINNERWARE; FLATWARE; GLASS, Elegant; GLASS, Crystal)

Dealer

Diane's Carriage House
Diane Thulin
8808 C&D Pear Tree Court
Alexandria, VA 22309
Phone: 703-780-4413

Man./Prod./Dist.

New York Merchandise Mart
41 Madison Ave.
New York, NY 10010
Phone: 212-686-1203
Showplace for purveyors of new tableware including gifts, glassware, ceramicware, silverware and decorative accessories.

Man./Prod./Dist.

225 The International Showcase
225 Fifth Ave.
New York, NY 10010
Phone: 212-685-6377 or 800-235-3512
Showplace for purveyors specializing in the sale of new giftware & decorative accessories; also tableware.

Man./Prod./Dist.

Atlanta Market Center
240 Peachtree St. NW
Atlanta, GA 30303
Phone: 404-220-3000
The major wholesale source for gifts, accessories, floor coverings, furniture, glass, china, tablewares, etc.

Periodical

Magazine: China Glass & Tableware
1115 Clifton Ave.
Clifton, NJ 07013
Phone: 201-779-1600   FAX: 201-779-3242
Trade magazine for new gifts, decorative accessories, and tabletop wares; buyer's resource directory guide available with subscription.

Periodical

Geyer-McAllister Publications, Inc.
Magazine: Gifts & Decorative Accessories
51 Madison Ave.
New York, NY 10010
Phone: 212-689-4411
Trade magazine for new gifts, decorative accessories, and tabletop wares; buyer's resource directory guide available with subscription.

TARGETS

Shooting Gallery

(see also TARGET SHOOTING MEMORABILIA)

Dealer

Argyle Antiques
Richard Tucker
P.O. Box 262
Argyle, TX 76226
Phone: 817-464-3752 or 817-335-6133

Buys and sells figural cast iron items: windmill weights, shooting targets, water sprinklers; no repros. or repaired items wanted.

TARGET SHOOTING MEMORABILIA

(see also SPORTS COLLECTIBLES; TARGETS, Shooting Gallery)

Collector
Allen Hallock
P.O. Box 2747
San Rafael, CA 94902
Phone: 415-924-1967 or 415-453-3300
　　　　　　　　FAX: 415-453-9256
Civilian target shooting memorabilia, 1875-1915: trophies, medals, souvenirs, photos, targets, documents, steins, etc.

Target Balls
Collector
Art Snyder
110 White Oak Drive
Butler, PA 16001-3446
Phone: 412-287-0278
Buys/sells/trades antique glass target balls, ball traps or throwers, glass house or sporting ads pertaining to same; anything related.

Collector
Williamson
Box 715
Cambridge, MD 21613
*Also wants "Field & Stream" magazines prior to 1915; Hazelton Books 1914 & 1917. ***

Collector
Alex Kerr
4709 Forman Ave.
N. Hollywood, CA 91602
Phone: 818-762-6320

Expert
Ralph Lindsay
P.O. Box 21
New Holland, PA 17557 *

TAXI RELATED COLLECTIBLES
Collector
Taxi Toys & Memorabilia
Nathan Willensky
5 East 22nd St. #24C
New York, NY 10010
Phone: 212-677-0900 or 212-982-2156
　　　　　　　　FAX: 212-995-1065
Buy and trades anything Taxi - toys and memorabilia; Taxis only.

TEAPOTS
Club/Association
Handle On the Teapot Enthusiast
Association
Newsletter: Hot Tea
Tina M. Carter, Ed.
882 South Mollison Ave.
El Cajon, CA 92020
Phone: 619-440-5043
An association for teapot collectors; newsletter features articles on teapots, coffeepots, childrens' sets, miniatures, etc.

Expert
Tina M. Carter
882 South Mollison Ave.
El Cajon, CA 92020
Phone: 619-440-5043

Periodical
Newsletter: Tea Talk
Diana Rosen
419 N. Larchmont Blvd. #225
Los Angeles, CA 90004
Phone: 213-871-6901 or 213-652-9306
　　　　　　　　FAX: 213-828-2444
A quarterly newsletter on the pleasures of tea; complete source for places to go, articles, features and anecdotes about TEA.

TEDDY BEARS
(see also DOLLS; STEIFF)

Club/Association
American Bear Club
Newsletter: American Bear Club Newsletter
Box 179
Huntington, NY 11743
Phone: 516-271-8990 *

Club/Association
Good Bears of the World
Magazine: Bear Tracks
P.O. Box 13097
Toledo, OH 43613
Phone: 419-531-5365 or 419-475-3946
"Good Bears" spread love & understanding by giving away Teddy Bears to comfort every hurt, abused child or lonely, forgotten adult.

Club/Association
Teddy Bear Boosters Club
P.O. Box 520
Stanton, CA 90680
Phone: 714-827-0345 *

Collector
Bill Boyd
4922 State Line
Westwood Hills, KS 66205
Phone: 913-831-0912

Collector
Magazine: Teddy Tribune, The
Barbara Wolters
254 W. Sidney
St. Paul, MN 55107
Phone: 612-291-7571
10 issues of Teddy Tribune per year; everything about teddy bears; send for free brochure.

Museum/Library
Frannie's Teddy Bear Museum
George B. Black, Jr.
2511 Pine Ridge Road
Naples, FL 33942
Phone: 813-598-2711　　FAX: 813-598-9239
Collects and displays teddy bears and related items from teddy bear artists; developing teddy bear archives from the antique to present.

Periodical
Magazine: Teddy Bear Review
170 Fifth Ave.
New York, NY 10010

Periodical
Hobby House Press, Inc.
Magazine: Teddy Bear & Friends
Rene M. Trezise
900 Frederick St.
Cumberland, MD 21502-9985
Phone: 301-759-3770　　FAX: 301-759-4940
First professional journal devoted to bears and other plush toys; new bears, research on old bears, bear prices, crafts, patterns, etc.

Periodical
Newsletter: Grizzly Gazette, The
8622 E. Oak Street
Scottsdale, AZ 85257
Phone: 602-941-8972 *

Periodical
Newspaper: National Doll & Teddy Bear
　Collector
Harmony Coburn, Pub.
215 Greenbridge Drive, #117
Lake Oswego, OR 97035
Phone: 503-636-5960
A monthly newspaper with a West Coast perspective; for doll and teddy bear collectors, dealers and artists.

TELEGRAPH ITEMS

(see also ELECTRICITY RELATED ITEMS; MAGAZINES, Radio & Wireless; RADIOS; STICKERS, Radio Stations; STOCK TICKERS)

Club/Association
Telsa Coil Builders' Association
Newsletter: TCBA News
Harry Goldman
3 Amy Lane
Queensbury, NY 12804
Phone: 518-792-1003

TCBA is a clearinghouse on the history of electricity, wireless, etc.; acts as consultants for high voltage historical equipment.

Club/Association

Antique Wireless Association
Newsletter: Old Timer's Bulletin
Bruce Kelley
#4 Main St.
Holcomb, NY 14469
Phone: 716-657-7489
Purpose is to document and preserve the history of radio and television artifacts.

Club/Association

Morse Telegraph Club
Newsletter: Dots & Dashes
712 South 49
Lincoln, NE 68510
Phone: 402-489-4062 *

Collector

Brasspounder
Roger W. Reinke
5301 Neville Court
Alexandria, VA 22310-1113
Phone: 703-971-4095 or 202-377-1139
Wants telegraph instruments, stock tickers, and related items such as call boxes, signs, early paper; condition not important.

Collector

Charles Goodman
636 W. Grant Ave.
Charleston, IL 61920
Phone: 217-345-6771
Wants telegraph books, instruments, keys, sounders, relays, resonators, Western Union items, old stock tickers, etc.

Museum/Library

New England Wireless & Steam Museum, Inc.
697 Tillinghart Rd.
East Greenwich, RI 02818
Phone: 401-884-1710

Museum/Library

American Radio Relay League Museum of Amateur Radio
225 Main St.
Newington, CT 06111
Phone: 203-666-1541

TELEPHONE COMPANY ITEMS

Bell-Shaped Paperweights

Expert

Jacqueline C. Linscott
3557 Nicklaus Dr.
Titusville, FL 32780
Phone: 407-267-9170
Wants in old, cobalt blue, bell-shaped paperweights used as give-aways by early telephone companies; author of book on same.

TELEPHONES

Club/Association

Telephone Artifacts Association
417 Arbor Ave.
Monroe, MI 48161 *

Club/Association

Telephone Collectors International, Inc.
Newsletter: Singing Wires
George W. Howard
19 North Cherry Dr.
Oswego, IL 60543
Phone: 708-554-8154
For antique telephone collectors; sponsors two shows annually where old phones and related items are displayed, bought and sold.

Club/Association

Antique Telephone Collectors Association
Newsletter: Antique Telephone Collectors Newsletter
P.O. Box 94
Abilene, KS 67410
Phone: 913-263-1757 or 407-267-9170
Members interested in anything relating to the history or artifacts of old telephones and the telephone companies.

Collector

Paul G. Engelke
23399 Rio Del Mar Dr.
Boca Raton, FL 33486-8504
Phone: 407-338-3332
Wants early wooden wall and candlestick phones, porcelain telephone signs, small coin phones, wooden coin phones, etc. but no paper.

Collector

John Huckeby
R.D. 6 Box 232
New Castle, IN 47362
Phone: 317-533-6369
Old telephones, complete or parts.

Dealer

Phone Wizard
Bruce Patterson
106 S. King St.
P.O. Box 70
Leesburg, VA 22075
Phone: 703-777-0000   FAX: 703-777-1233
Publishes a catalog ($3) providing genuine antique and Art Deco phones. Offers parts, conversions and repair service.

Dealer

Jim & Shirley's Antiques
146 N. Glassell St,
Orange, CA 92666
Phone: 714-639-9662 or 213-598-1914
Specializes in antique telephones and Victrolas: sales, repairs and conversions.

Expert

Phone-Tiques
Tom Guenin
Box 454
Chardon, OH 44024
*Specializes in antique telephones and their restorations. *

Expert

Dan Golden
5375-C Avenida Encinas
Carlsbad, CA 92008-4362
Phone: 619-438-8383 *

Museum/Library

Telephone Museum
Journal: Telephone Museum Journal
Bell Bldg.
Two E. First St.
Monroe, MI 48161
Phone: 313-243-6227

Museum/Library

Jefferson Telephone Museum
105 W. Harrison
Jefferson, IA 50129
Phone: 515-386-2626

Museum/Library

Illinois Bell's Oliver P. Parks Telephone Museum
529 South 7th Street
Springfield, IL 62721
A private museum based on a personal collection and including over 100 antique telephones.

Museum/Library

Museum of Independent Telephony
412 S. Campbell
Abilene, KS 67410
Phone: 913-263-2681
Established to honor approx. 6000 non-Bell companies formed when patent coverage expired to meet the demands for telephone service.

Museum/Library

Telephone Pioneer Museum
1209 Moutain Rd. Pl. NE
Albuquerque, NM 87110
Phone: 505-256-2105

Museum/Library

Telephone Museum
1145 Larkin St.
San Francisco, CA 94109
Phone: 415-441-3918

Periodical

Magazine: Crown Jewels of the Wire
John & Carol McDougald
Box 1003
St. Charles, IL 60174-1003
Phone: 708-513-1544

60-page monthly magazine of insulator and telephone history; glass, porcelain; foreign columns; classified ads, show dates, etc.

Repair Service

Chicago Old Telephone Company
P.O. Box 189
Lemon Springs, NC 28355
Phone: 919-774-6625
*Repair, service, parts. ***

Repair Service

House of Telephones
Odis W. LeVrier
15 East Ave. D
San Angelo, TX 76903
Phone: 915-655-4174 or 915-655-5122
                    FAX: 915-655-4177
Repairs antique telephones and carries parts.

Repair Service

Billard's Old Telephones
21710 Regnart Rd.
Cupertino, CA 95014
Phone: 408-252-2104
*Repairs telephones and publishes "Old Telephones and Parts Catalog." ***

Supplier

Chicago Old Telephone Company
P.O. Box 189
Lemon Springs, NC 28355
Phone: 919-774-6625
Carries parts for old telephones; also repairs.

Supplier

Phoneco, Inc.
Ron & Mary Knappen
207 E. Mill Rd.
P.O. Box 70
Galesville, WI 54630
Phone: 608-582-4124 or 608-582-2863
                    FAX: 608-582-4593
Buys, sells, refurbishes any old telephone; also sells old and new parts; catalogs, history, price guide, diagrams and restoration help.

Novelty

Collector

Bob Roberts
P.O. Box 152
Guilderland, NY 12084
*Novelty transistor radios or telephones in unusual shapes (gas pumps, food items, cartoon characters, cars, etc.) ***

TELESCOPES

(see also ASTRONOMICAL ITEMS; INSTRUMENTS & DEVICES, Scientific)

TELEVISIONS

(see also RADIOS)

Collector

Donald O. Patterson
636 Cambridge Road
Augusta, GA 30909
Phone: 404-738-7227
Wants pre-1940 televisions (RCA TRK-9,12 or GE HM 225, 171) direct view or mirror in the lid.

Dealer

Vintage TV's
Harry Poster
Box 1883
S. Hackensack, NJ 07606
Phone: 201-794-9606
Publishes an annual price guide, "Sight Sound Style", to vintage TV's and valuable radios.

Expert

Arnold Chase
9 Rushleigh Rd.
West Hartford, CT 06117
Phone: 203-521-5280 *

Expert

Mike Brooks
7335 Skyline
Oakland, CA 94611
Phone: 415-339-1751

Museum/Library

Auman Antique Television Museum
Larry Auman
Route #1, Box 368
Dover, OH 44622
Phone: 216-343-2297 or 216-364-1058
Museum shows early days of electronic entertainment: 1940's movie theater, 1920's-1930's radios, 1939-1950 TV's, and related

Periodical

Magazine: Radio Age
636 Cambridge Road
Augusta, GA 30909
Phone: 404-738-7227
Published monthly since 1975 for collectors interested in the history of radio and television; restoration, articles by early

Repair Service

John Okolowicz
624 Cedar Hill Rd.
Ambler, PA 19002
Phone: 215-542-1597
Wants pre-1950 radios and TV's in unusual or ornate plastic or wooden cabinets; especially those made by Emerson or Stromberg Carlson.

Repair Service

David T. Boyd
13917 Wisteria Drive
Germantwon, MD 20877
Phone: 301-948-8070 or 301-972-2777
Restores old tube-type radios and televisions from the 20's and 30's through the 1960's; also buys and sells.

Supplier

Antique Electronic Supply
6221 S. Maple Ave.
Tempe, AZ 85283
Phone: 602-820-5411   FAX: 602-820-4643
Large catalog carrying tubes, supplies, capacitors, transformers, chemicals, test equipment, wire, parts, tools, literature, etc.

TELEVISION SHOWS & MEMORABILIA

(see also CHARACTER COLLECTIBLES; COLLECTIBLES; GAMES, Board (TV Related); MOVIE MEMORABILIA; SUPER HEROES)

Club/Association

Manuscript Society, The
Magazine: Manuscripts
350 N. Niagara St.
Burbank, CA 91505
An organization of collectors, dealers, librarians, archivists, scholars and others interested in autographs and manuscripts.

Collector

Sacks Appeal
Ross Hartsough
98 Bryn Mar Rd.
Winnipeg
Manitoba R3T 3P5 Canada
Phone: 204-269-1022
Wants anything TV related: magazines, toys, gum cards, games, comics, TV program sound tracks, sheet music, etc.

Collector

Bruce Thalberg
23 Mountain View Dr.
Weston, CT 06883
Phone: 203-227-8175
Wants Lone Ranger, Sky King, Space Patrol, Tom Mix, Roy Rogers, The Shadow, Capt. Midnight, Terry & the Pirates, etc. items.

Dealer

TVC Enterprise
Diane L. Albert
P.O. Box 1088
Easton, MA 02334-1088
Phone: 508-238-1179
28 pg. catalogs of TV, movie, rock 'n roll & other music, theater & other media-related collectibles & memorabilia for sale; send SASE.

Dealer

Casey's Collectible Corner
Dennis & Mary Luby
H.C.R. Box 31, Rte. 30
No. Blenheim, NY 12131
Phone: 607-588-6464
Buys and sells collectible toys: comic characters, TV shows and personalities; also space and monster toys, sports collectibles, etc.

Dealer

Dennis Hasty
436 Hillside Ave., #11
Lockland, OH 45215
Wants TV character memorabilia. *

Dealer

Collectors Book Store
7014 Sunset Blvd.
Hollywood, CA 90028
Phone: 213-467-3296 *

Dealer

Jim's TV Collectibles
P.O. Box 4767
San Diego, CA 92164
Buys and sells TV cellectibles of all kinds, 1950-1990; 50 pg. catalog $2.

Dealer

Memory Shop West
1755 Market Street
San Francisco, CA 94103
Phone: 415-626-4873
Want photographs and memorabilia. *

Expert

TVC Enterprise
Diane L. Albert
P.O. Box 1088
Easton, MA 02334-1088
Phone: 508-238-1179
Consultant, freelance writer or researcher for production companies, books publishers etc. on the subject of TV nostalgia.

Expert

Hake's Americana & Collectibles Auction
Ted Hake
P.O. Box 1444
York, PA 17405
Phone: 717-848-1333   FAX: 717-848-4977
Author of "Hake's Guide to TV Collectibles."

Expert

David Welch
RR 2, Box 233
Murphysboro, IL 62966
Phone: 618-687-2282
Wants 1950's-1960's TV show related items: lunch boxes, games, toys, etc.

Museum/Library

Museum of Broadcasting, The
25 West 52nd St.
New York, NY 10022
Phone: 212-752-4690

Periodical

Empire Publishing, Inc.
Newspaper: Big Reel
Route 3, P.O. Box 83
Madison, NC 27025
Phone: 919-427-5850   FAX: 919-427-7372

A monthly tabloid for movie and television memorabilia collectors and fans: ads, news, current & nostalgic feature articles, orbits, etc.

Periodical

TVC Enterprise
Magazine: TV Collector, The
Diane L. Albert
P.O. Box 1088
Easton, MA 02334-1088
Phone: 508-238-1179
In-depth articles about old TV series, behind the scenes information, etc.; also collector ads for videotapes, memorabilia, etc.

Periodical

Magazine: Filmfax
P.O. Box 1900
Evanston, IL 60204
A magazine of unusual film and television; a bimonthly with 100 pgs. of rare photos and articles about your favorite films & TV shows.

Bewitched

Collector

Carol Ann Osman
363 Mansfield Ave.
Pittsburgh, PA 15220
Phone: 412-922-1865
Wants to buy anything from the TV series "Bewitched"; scripts, sheet music, games, books, toys, dolls, TV Guides, cels, drawings, etc.

Books & Magazines

Collector

Rick Nosker
8519 E. Sheridan
Scottsdale, AZ 85257
Wants books/magazines dealing with TV-related shows from the 1950's and 1970's; e.g. "The Untouchables", "Maverick", "Batman", etc. *

Dealer

TV Archives
P.O. Box 3
Blue Point, NY 11715
Wants pre-national New York City TV Guides, 1948-1953.

Dark Shadows

Club/Association

Dark Shadows Fan Club
Magazine: Dark Shadows Announcement, The
Louis Wendruck
P.O. Box 90A04
West Hollywood, CA 90069
Phone: 213-650-5112
Fan Club for TV's Gothic soap opera originally from the '60's; quarterly magazine; sells T-shirts, books, videos and memorabilia.

Collector

Steve Hall
P.O. Box 960398
Riverdale, GA 30296-0398
Wants Dark Shadows items: comics, books, models, games, cards, View-Masters, toys, misc.; anything from the TV show or movies.

Dennis The Menace

Collector

Pete Nowicki
1531 39th Ave.
San Francisco, CA 94122
Phone: 415-566-7506
Collector seeks all toys and collectibles relating to Dennis the Menace and his friends; no comics, please.

Doctor Who

Club/Association

Friends of Doctor Who
Newsletter: Friends of Doctor Who Newsletter
David Blaise
P.O. Box 14111
Reading, PA 19612-4111
Phone: 215-478-9200   FAX: 215-374-5570
The largest active Doctor Who fan organization in the United States.

Club/Association

St. Louis Celestial Intervention Agency
Newsletter: Time Lord Times
P.O. Box 733
St. Louis, MO 63188
One of the largest strictly Doctor Who clubs with local meetings in North America; excellent source for news and articles.

Club/Association

Doctor Who Fan Club of America
Newsletter: Whovian Times
P.O. Box 6024
Denver, CO 80206
Phone: 303-733-1717
"Whovians" are interested in the TV show, "Doctor Who", its cast and related memorabilia. *

Gilligan's Island

Club/Association

Original Gilligan's Island Fan Club, The
Newsletter: Gilligan's Island News
P.O. Box 25311
Salt Lake City, UT 84125-0311
Gilligan's is still afloat! Become a member of the OGIFC; a "castaway" membership includes t-shirts, newsletter plus more.

Gunsmoke

Collector

Hank Clark
P.O. Box 812
Waterford, CA 95386
Phone: 209-874-2640
*Wants television and radio "Gunsmoke" items;
autographs, photos, advertising, etc.*

Honeymooners/Jackie Gleason

Dealer

Jerry's Cards & Collectibles
Jerry Rubackin
Box 1271
Framingham, MA 01701
Phone: 508-788-0946
*Always wants Honeymooners and Jackie Gleason
items.*

I Dream Of Jeannie

Collector

Richard D. Barnes
389 West 100 South
Bountiful, UT 84010
Phone: 801-295-5762
*Collector/historian wants "Jeannie" scripts, press
photos, news articles, posters, books, toys, board
games, etc.*

Expert

Richard D. Barnes
389 West 100 South
Bountiful, UT 84010
Phone: 801-295-5762
*Author of IDofJ works including "Going Holly-
wood", a collectors guide to IDofJ, Barbara Eden
and other Hollywood collectibles.*

I Love Lucy

Club/Association

We Love Lucy/The International Lucille
Ball Fan Club
Newsletter: Lucy
P.O. Box 480216
Los Angeles, CA 90048
Phone: 213-475-0137
*Focuses on collectibles pertaining to the "I Love
Lucy" TV show and to Lucille Ball and other
characters.* *

Collector

Tiffany Stevens
478 Ward St.
Wallingford, CT 06492
*Focuses on collectibles pertaining to the "I Love
Lucy" TV show and to Lucille Ball and other
characters.*

Looney Tunes

Club/Association

Looney Tunes Fan Club of America
Suite 489
5 Manmar Dr.
Plainville, MA 02762

Lost In Space

Collector

Tod Evans
84 Elm St.
Westfield, NJ 07090
Phone: 201-789-9391
*Wants "Lost in Space" TV show items: anything
including models, figures, games, cards, models,
robots, etc.*

Man From U.N.C.L.E.

Club/Association

U.N.C.L.E. HQ
Newsletter: HQ Newsletter
Susan Cole
2710 Rohlwing Rd.
Rolling Meadows, IL 60008
Phone: 708-392-4869 or 708-438-0039
*Official fan club for the man/girl from
U.N.C.L.E.; focuses on the "Man from
U.N.C.L.E." reruns, the program and its
memorabilia.*

Mork & Mindy

Collector

Bob Holeman
305 Tanglewood Cr.
Lawton, OK 73505
*Wants "Mork and Mindy" TV show items: any-
thing including models, figures, games, cards,
models, robots, etc.* *

Star Trek

Club/Association

Star Trek Fan Club
Magazine: Official Star Trek Magazine
P.O. Box 111000
Aurora, CO 80011 *

Collector

Mitch & Chris Mitchell
6112 Clearbrook Dr.
Springfield, VA 22150
Phone: 703-451-4276

Collector

Cindy Oakes
34025 W. 6 Mile
Livonia, MI 48152
Phone: 313-591-3252
*Wants dolls, autographs and other Star Trek
memorabilia; also dolls from Star Trek The Movie
& New Generation series.*

Dealer

Star Tech
P.O. Box 456
Dunlap, TN 37327 *

Dealer

Star Trader
Steve Benz
9809 Hayes
Overland Park, KS 66212
Phone: 913-648-5461
*Buys, sells and trades all Star Trek memorabilia
from 1966 to present.*

Dealer

Lincoln Enterprises
P.O. Box 69470
Los Angeles, CA 90069 *

Periodical

Magazine: Starlog Magazine
475 Park Ave. South
New York, NY 10016 *

Periodical

Newsletter: Intergalactic News
P.O. Box 1516
Longwood, FL 32750 *

The Addams Family

Club/Association

Munsters & The Addams Family Fan Club
Magazine: Munsters & The Addams Family
Reunion
Louis Wendruck
P.O. Box 69A04
West Hollywood, CA 90069
Phone: 213-650-5112
*Fan Club for the '60's TV shows "The Munsters"
& "The Addams Family"; quarterly magazine;
sells T-shirts, photos, videos, memorabilia.*

The Munsters

Club/Association

Munsters & the Addams Family Fan Club
Magazine: Munsters & the Addams Family
Reunion
Louis Wendruck
P.O. Box 69A04
West Hollywood, CA 90069
Phone: 213-650-5112
*Fan Club for the '60's TV shows "The Munsters"
& "The Addams Family"; quarterly magazine;
sells T-shirts, photos, videos, memorabilia.*

Westerns

(see also COWBOY HEROES)

Club/Association

Westerns & Serials Club
Magazine: Western & Serials
Route 1, Box 103
Vernon Center, MN 56090

Club/Association
TV Western Collectors Fan Club
Newsletter: Television Western Collectors
  Newsletter
P.O. Box 1361
Boyes Hot Springs, CA 95416

TEXTILES

(see also CLOTHING & ACCESSORIES;
COVERLETS; LOOMS; QUILTS; REPAIRS
& RESTORATIONS, Textiles; RUGS;
SAMPLERS; SHAWLS, Kashmir (Paisley))

Club/Association
Costume Society of America, The
Newsletter: Costume Society of America
  Newsletter
55 Edgewater Dr.
P.O. Box 73
Earleville, MD 21919
Phone: 301-275-2329   FAX: 301-275-8936
*Dedicated to creating understanding of the field of
costume and to the study and preservation of
historic dress.*

Club/Association
Knitting Guild of America, The
Magazine: Cast On
Kathy Buder
P.O. Box 1606
Knoxville, TN 37901
Phone: 615-524-2401   FAX: 615-524-2401
*Provides education for hand & machine knitters;
"Cast On" contains articles, ads, seminars, corre-
spondence courses, competition, etc.*

Collector
Elizabeth Bright
26 Williams Cr.
Lexington, NC 27292
*Old quilts, samplers, large Marseilles spreads,
extra fancy white linens, unusual needlework.*

Dealer
Old Village Fabrics
157 Bedford Rd.
Pleasantville, NY 10570
Phone: 914-769-0233
Old fabric, buttons, quilts, quilt pieces, quilt tops.
*

Dealer
Diane McGee Estate Clothing Company
Diane McGee
5225 Jackson
Omaha, NE 68106
Phone: 402-551-0727
*Mail order only; specializing in vintage linens and
other textiles.*

Expert
Ita Aber
1 Fanshaw Rd.
Yonkers, NY 10705
Phone: 914-968-4863 or 212-877-6400
              FAX: 212-877-3107
*Specializes in lace, linens, and needlework; also
repairs; author of "The Art of Judaic Needlework."*

Expert
Cooperstown Textile School
S. Rabbit Goody
P.O. Box 455
Cooperstown, NY 13326
Phone: 607-264-8400 or 518-284-2896
*CTS offers 4-day workshops in textile identifica-
tion, dating & basic conservation; also teaches
weaving and makes historic reproductions.*

Museum/Library
Museum of American Textile History
800 Massachusetts Ave.
North Andover, MA 01845
Phone: 617-686-0191
*Outstanding collection of textiles and textile mak-
ing machinery and equipment.*

Museum/Library
Textile Museum, The
Newsletter: Textile Museum Newsletter, The
2320 'S' Street NW
Washington, DC 20008
Phone: 202-667-0441
*Oldest museum of textiles in the western hemi-
sphere; rotating exhibitions; library has 13,000
textile related volumes; museum shop.*

Museum/Library
Valentine Museum
1015 East Clay
Richmond, VA 23219
Phone: 804-649-0711

Embroidery

Museum/Library
Cooper-Hewitt Museum, The Smithsonian
Institution's Nat. Museum of Design
2 East 91st St.
New York, NY 10128
Phone: 212-860-6868

Embroidery (Stumpwork)

Club/Association
Stumpwork Society
Newsletter: Stumpwork Society Chronicle
Sylvia C. Fishman
P.O. Box 122
Bogota, NJ 07603
Phone: 201-224-3622   FAX: 201-224-3075
*Interested in antique stumpwork embroidery; res-
toration, preservation and collection.*

Folk Art

Dealer
Heritage Antiques
Box 844
Bellville, TX 77418
*Wants bedspreads, carpets, coverlets, clothing,
needlework, quilts, hooked rugs, samplers, shawls,
table linens, etc.*

Lace & Linens

Club/Association
International Old Lacers, Inc.
Magazine: International Old Lacers Bulletin
366 Bradley Ave.
Northvale, NJ 07647
Phone: 201-768-0795 *

Dealer
Pahaka
Pahaka September
19 Fox Hill
Upper Saddle River, NJ 07458
Phone: 201-327-1464
*Buys and sells quality lace, curtains, bed and
table linens, fabrics, embroidery, etc.*

Dealer
Jean Hoffman
236 East 80th Street
New York, NY 10021
Phone: 212-861-8256 or 212-535-6930
Buys and sells antique lace, linens, and textiles.

Dealer
Dealer
111 Parkway
Cleveland, MS 38732
*Wants 1850-1939 natural fiber linens: whites or
ecru with lots of handwork; also lace in good
condition, cutwork, and drawnwork. **

Dealer
Lace Merchant, The
Elizabeth M. Kurella
P.O. Box 222
Plainwell, MI 49080
Phone: 616-685-9792
*Offers many pieces of antique lace for sale; com-
plete catalog of slides and slide programs with
scripts available for $3.*

Dealer
Emma's Trunk
Jan Spencer
1701 Orange Tree Lane
Redlands, CA 92374
Phone: 714-798-7865 or 714-798-4141
*Wants FANCY aprons, bedspreads, Christening
gowns, collars, cuffs, doilies, handkerchiefs,
napkins, etc.; write before sending items.*

Expert
Whitehall Shop
Alda Horner
1215 E. Franklin Street
Chapel Hill, NC 27514
Phone: 919-942-3179

Expert
Linda & Kenneth Ketterling Antiques
Linda & Ken Ketterling
3202 E. Lincolnshire Blvd.
Toledo, OH 43606
Phone: 419-536-5531

Expert
Maryanne Dolan
138 Belle Avenue
Pleasant Hill, CA 94523
Phone: 415-935-2366
Author of "Old Lace & Linens."

Museum/Library
Ipswich Historical Society
53 S. Main St.
Ipswich, MA 01938
Phone: 508-356-2811

Museum/Library
Henry Morrison Flagler Museum,
Whitehall Mansion, The
P.O. Box 696
Palm Beach, FL 33480
Phone: 407-655-2833

Museum/Library
Lace Museum, The
1424 Brookdale
Mountain View, CA 94040
Phone: 415-967-2310

Periodical
Lace Merchant, The
Newsletter: Lace Collector, The
Elizabeth M. Kurella, Pub.
P.O. Box 222
Plainwell, MI 49080
Phone: 616-685-9792
Quarterly newsletter (12 pgs. illustrated); how to identify & appraise antique lace; what to use, save; market info, prices.

Repair Service
Unique Art Lace Cleaners
5926 Delmar Blvd.
St. Louis, MO 63112
Phone: 314-725-2900
Cleans and repairs old textiles, linens and lace.

Needlework

Dealer
Carol Huber
82 Plants Dam Rd.
East Lyme, CT 06333
Phone: 203-739-0772   FAX: 203-739-0261

Buys and sells early needlework including samplers, pictures and related items.

Needlework (Judaic)
(see also JUDAICA)

Expert
Ita Aber
1 Fanshaw Rd.
Yonkers, NY 10705
Phone: 914-968-4863 or 212-877-6400
                    FAX: 212-877-3107
Consultations, restorations and commissions; works with architects and decorators; lecturer, historian, author of book on same.

THANKSGIVING COLLECTIBLES
(see also HOLIDAY COLLECTIBLES)

THEATRICAL MEMORABILIA
(see also DANCE MEMORABILIA; MAGICIANS PARAPHERNALIA; OPERA MEMENTOS; VAUDEVILLE MEMORABILIA)

Club/Association
Theatre Historical Society of America
Journal: Marquee
2215 W. North Ave.
Chicago, IL 60647
Phone: 312-252-7200
THSA focuses on the history of theater structures; has extensive collection of photographs, clippings, programs, books,

Collector
D. Eliot
529 W. 42nd St. #5R
New York, NY 10036
Phone: 212-563-5444
*Wants theater souvenirs; pre-1920; especially commemorative items, e.g. 50th performance, 100th, etc. ***

Museum/Library
Boothbay Theater Museum, The
Corey Lane
Boothbay, ME 04537
Phone: 207-633-4536

Museum/Library
Theatre Museum of the Museum of the City of New York
5th Avenue at 103rd St.
New York, NY 10029
Phone: 212-955-7161

THERMOMETERS

Club/Association
Thermometer Collectors Club of America
Newsletter: Thermometer News
Warren D. Harris
6130 Rampart Dr.
Carmichael, CA 95608
Phone: 916-966-3490 or 916-487-6964

Expert
Warren Harris
6130 Rampart Dr.
Carmichael, CA 95608
Phone: 916-966-3490 or 916-487-6964
Wants decorative pre-1940 non advertising, non commercial, non clinical thermometers of every kind; mercury-in-the-tube type.

3-D PHOTOGRAPHICA
(see also CAMERAS & CAMERA EQUIPMENT; PHOTOGRAPHY, 3-D; STEREO VIEWERS & STEREOGRAPHS; VIEW-MASTERS)

Collector
Sheldon Aronowitz
487 Palmer Ave.
Teaneck, NJ 07666
Phone: 201-837-9508 or 201-854-7100
Wants View-Master, Tru-View, Stori-View, Anaglyph, Lenticular, holograms, stereo cards.

Expert
3-D Entertainment
Walter Sigg
P.O. Box 208
Swartswood, NJ 07877
Phone: 201-383-2437
Buys and sells View-Master, Tru-View, 3-D cameras, projectors, reels, and most 3-D items.

Expert
Roger T. Nazeley
4921 Castor Ave.
Philadelphia, PA 19124
Phone: 215-535-9021 or 215-743-8999
                    FAX: 215-289-5445
Buy, sell, trade View-Master reels and packets, Tru-Vue cards & film strips, look-a-like View-Masters, etc.; author of book on subject.

Expert
Antique Graphics
John Waldsmith
107 N. Sycamore
P.O. Box 191
Sycamore, OH 44882
Phone: 419-927-2930
Wants stereoscopic views, View-Master reels, photographica; conducts mail/phone auctions on regular basis; also direct sales.

Periodical

Magazine: Reel 3-D News
P.O. Box 35
Duarte, CA 91010
Phone: 213-357-8345
A magazine about 3-D photography and 3-D equipment collecting. *

View-Masters

Collector

Howard & Jean Hazelcorn
P.O. Box 1066
Teaneck, NJ 07666
Phone: 201-836-6293

TIFFANY ITEMS

(see also GEMS & JEWELRY; GLASS; LAMPS & LIGHTING; SILVER)

Collector

Harvey Weinstein
22 Halifax Dr.
Morganville, NJ 07751
Phone: 201-536-4467
Wants glass by Tiffany, Handel, Pairpoint. *

Collector

Bill Holland
107 S. 18th St.
Philadelphia, PA 19103
Phone: 215-647-7099
Wants anything by Tiffany Co. *

Dealer

Champaign Collector
Dan Hamelberg
Suite 200
303 S. Mattis
Champaign, IL 61821
Phone: 217-351-6012
Wants glass, lamps, silver, etc. *

Expert

Neustadt Museum of Tiffany Art, Inc., The
Dr. Egon Neustadt
124 West 79th St.
New York, NY 10024
Phone: 212-874-0872
Author of "The Lamps of Tiffany", an authoritative survey of Tiffany glass, jewels, and lamp bases and shades.

Expert

Team Antiques
P.O. Box 1052
Great Neck, NY 11023
Phone: 516-487-1826
Over 26 years experience in cataloging and selling Tiffanyana by mail-order.

Man./Prod./Dist.

Tiffany Co.
5th Ave. at 57th St.
New York, NY 10022
Phone: 212-755-8000
Main Tiffany store; Tiffany items also retailed through regional stores.

Museum/Library

University of Conecticut, The William Benton Museum of Art
Box U-140
Storrs, CT 06268
Phone: 203-486-4520
Houses the Dr. Egon Neustadt collection of Tiffany lamps and windows.

Museum/Library

Chrysler Museum, The
Olney Rd. & Mowbray Arch
Norfolk, VA 23510
Phone: 804-622-1211

TILES

(see also CERAMICS)

Book Seller

Tile Heritage Foundation
Joe Taylor
P.O. Box 1850
Healdsburg, CA 95448
Phone: 707-431-8453
Offers a large line of books about tile: terra cotta, foreign, decorated tiles, Delftware, English medieval, Victorian tiles, etc.

Club/Association

Tiles & Architectural Ceramics Society
Newsletter: Glazed Expressions
Ironbridge Gorge Museum
Ironbridge, Telford
Shropshire TF8 7AW England *

Periodical

Tile Heritage Foundation
Magazine: Flash Point
Joe Taylor
P.O. Box 1850
Healdsburg, CA 95448
Phone: 707-431-8453
Dedicated to promote appreciation for tiled surfaces; promotes preservation of rare & unusual ceramics; library on old tile.

Victorian

Expert

Blue Boar Antiques
Pamela & Allan Luttig
P.O. Box 423
Grand Ledge, MI 48837

TIN COLLECTIBLES

Containers

(see also ADVERTISING COLLECTIBLES; ADVERTISING COLLECTIBLES, Tin Vienna Art Plates; FOLK ART, Tinware)

Club/Association

Tin Container Collectors Association
Newsletter: Tin Type
P.O. Box 440101
Aurora, CO 80044

Periodical

Magazine: Can-O-Rama
27 Main Street
Walnut Hill, IL 62893 *

TITANIC MEMORABILIA

(see also NAUTICAL COLLECTIBLES)

Club/Association

Titanic Historical Society
Magazine: Titanic Commutator, The
Edward Kamunda
P.O. Box 51053
Indian Orchard, MA 01151-0053
Phone: 413-543-4770
Focuses on all aspects of the "Titanic", her sister ship the "Britannic", and the White Star Line.

Club/Association

Titanic International, Inc.
Magazine: Voyage
Suite D
31 Schanck Rd.
Freehold, NJ 07728 *

Collector

Dominic Rolla
1215 Spruce St.
Philadelphia, PA 19107
Wants newspapers, books, sheet music, artifacts. *

Expert

Edward Kamunda
P.O. Box 51053
Indian Orchard, MA 01151-0053
Phone: 413-543-4770
Wants newspapers, books, sheet music, artifacts.

TOASTERS

Collector

Richard Mathes
P.O. Box 1408
Springfield, OH 45501
Wants old fireplace, stove top and pre-1940 electric toasters.

Electric

(see also ELECTRICAL APPLIANCES)

Collector

William Blakeslee
116 Bethlehem Pike
P.O. Box 243
Ambler, PA 19002
Wants unusual electric toasters: Mecky, Trimble, Foldex, Coleman, Cozy, Monarch, Helion, Thoro, Birtman, Pelouze; send photo, markings.

Collector

Joe Lukach
7111 Deframe Ct.
Arvada, CO 80004
Phone: 303-422-8970
Wants unusual electric toasters 1908-1940, good non-corroded condition; especially ones with attached toast racks & of porcelain.

Expert

Howard & Jean Hazelcorn
P.O. Box 1066
Teaneck, NJ 07666
Phone: 201-836-6293
Authors of "Price Guide to Old Electric Toasters."

Expert

Toastmaster Antique Appliances
Jim A. Barker
P.O. Box 592
Hawley, PA 18428
Phone: 717-253-1951
Wants interesting electric toasters 1908-1940; also porcelain; by Estate, Pelouze, Mecky Toastrite, Mesco, etc.

TOBACCO RELATED COLLECTIBLES

(see also SMOKING COLLECTIBLES)

TOKENS

(see also CIVIL WAR ARTIFACTS, Tokens; COINS & CURRENCY; CREDIT CARDS & CHARGE COINS; EXONUMIA; SCRIP)

Auction Service

City Coin & Token Company
904 W. Broadway
Muskogee, OK 74401
Phone: 918-683-2646 *

Club/Association

Token & Medal Society
Journal: Token & Medal Society Journal
Cindy Grellman
P.O. Box 951988
Lake Mary, FL 32795
Phone: 407-321-8747
Promote and stimulates "exonumia", the study of non-government issue tokens and medals.

Club/Association

Active Token Collectors Organization
Newsletter: ATCO Newsletter
P.O. Box 1573
Stone Falls, SD 57101
Phone: 605-334-6910
*Interested in merchant trade tokens. *

Club/Association

American Numismatic Association
Magazine: Numismatist, The
Robert J. Leuver, ExDir
818 N. Cascade Ave.
Colorado Springs, CO 80903-3279
Phone: 719-632-2646 or 800-367-9723
FAX: 719-632-2646
Worldwide assoc. of collectors of coins, paper money, medals and tokens; over 33,000 members; offers collector services and benefits.

Collector

Jerome Schaeper
705 Philadelphia St.
Covington, KY 41011
Phone: 606-581-3729
Wants tokens, medals, badges, pocket mirrors.

Collector

Richard Hartzog
P.O. Box 4143
Rockford, IL 61110-0643
*Wants any tokens, medals, exonumia: badges, buttons, world's Fair items, political items, banners, etc. *

Dealer

Walter Korzik
P.O. Box 5294
Hamden, CT 06518
Phone: 203-281-0609 *

Dealer

Charles Kirtley
P.O. Box 2273
Elizabeth City, NC 27909 *

Dealer

S C Coin & Stamp Co. Inc.
Cy Phillips, Jr.
P.O. Drawer 3069
Arcadia, CA 91006
Phone: 818-445-8277 or 800-367-0779
Tokens, medals, coins, currency, badges, expo. and fair items, scrap gold and silver.

Dealer

Dan M. Jacobson
P.O. Box 277101
Sacramento, CA 95827-7101
Issues periodic lists of tokens for sale.

Museum/Library

Museum of the American Numismatic Association
Magazine: Numismatist, The
Robert W. Hoge, Cur.
818 N. Cascade Ave.
Colorado Springs, CO 80903
Phone: 719-632-2646   FAX: 719-634-4085
A museum collection including 400,000 items; largest numismatic circulating library with books and A/V material free to members.

Cardboard

Collector

Dan Benice
Box 10068
Rockville, MD 20850
Phone: 301-929-3060
*Wants cardboard tokens, passes, chits, coupons, premium tickets, discount cards, old tickets, etc. *

Food Stamp

Periodical

Newsletter: Food Stamp Change Newsletter
P.O. Box 40888
San Francisco, CA 94140
Phone: 415-648-8634
*Focusing on articles of interest to food stamp and token collectors. *

Free Drink

Collector

Gabby Talkington
4703 Upland Dr.
Richmond, CA 94803
Phone: 415-223-1142 or 415-273-3268
Wants "Free Drink" tokens from anywhere in the U.S. for personal collection.

Love

Club/Association

Love Token Society
Newsletter: Love Letter
P.O. Box 59699
Chicago, IL 60659
Phone: 312-338-5977 *

Merchants

Collector

Jim & Rita Hinton
P.O. Box 104284
Jefferson City, MO 65110-4284
Phone: 314-636-7567 or 314-636-2700
Wants merchant tokens that say "Good For"; prefers those listing town names.

Ration

Club/Association

Society of Ration Token Collectors
Newsletter: Ration Board, The
Samuel M. Hevener
3583 Everett Rd.
Richfield, OH 44286
Society collects, trades, sells paper & token home front ration items (for food, clothing, gasoline, tires, etc.); send SASE for info.

Sales Tax

Club/Association

American Tax Token Society
Newsletter: ATTS Newsletter
George Van Trump, Jr.
P.O. Box 260170
Lakewood, CO 80226
Phone: 303-985-3508
Interested in collecting tokens, scrip, punch cards, coupons, receipts, etc. relating to the history and collection of sales taxes.

Transportation (Fare)

Club/Association

American Vecturist Association
Newsletter: Fare Box, The
J.M. Coffee, Ed.
P.O. Box 1204
Boston, MA 02104-1204
Phone: 617-277-8111
Interested in collecting metal and plastic fare tokens.

Collector

Lee Schumacher
10609 Eastern
Kansas City, MO 64134
Wants bus, streetcar, ferry, bridge tokens; also passes, paper tickets, transfers, etc.; also Civil War, hard-times tokens. *

Expert

J.M. Coffee
P.O. Box 1204
Boston, MA 02104-1204
Phone: 617-277-8111
Co-author of the Atwood-Coffee "Catalogue of Transportation Tokens."

TOOLS

(see also BLACKSMITHING ITEMS; INDUSTRY RELATED ITEMS; MACHINERY & EQUIPMENT)

Auction Service

Richard Crane Auctions
Richard Crane
63 Poor Farm Rd.
Hillsboro, NH 03244
Phone: 603-478-5723
Specializes in the auction of antique tools.

Club/Association

Early American Industries Association, The
Newsletter: Shavings, The
John S. Watson, Treas.
Empire State Plaza Station
P.O. Box 2128
Albany, NY 12220-0128
Phone: 518-439-2215
Interested in old tools, implements, utensils, vehicles, "Whatsits"; and to discover, identify and preserve same.

Club/Association

Potomac Antique Tools & Industries Association (PATINA)
Newsletter: Patinagram
Richmond Brooks, Pres.
18816 Rolling Acres Way
Olney, MD 20832
Phone: 301-774-6747
Organization for men and women having an interest in the tools, crafts, techniques or manufacturing processes of the past.

Club/Association

Ohio Tool Collectors Association
Newsletter: Ohio Tool Box
George E. Woodard, Sec.
P.O. Box 261
London, OH 43140
Interested in tools used for any function including construction, writing, household, etc.

Club/Association

Mid-West Tool Collectors Association
Magazine: Gristmill
Ann Henley
808 Fairway Dr.
Columbia, MO 65201

Collector

Richard A. Wood
P.O. Box 22165
Juneau, AK 99802
Phone: 907-586-6748 or 907-789-8450
Wants old woodworking hand tools, pre-1860 machinery, and tool ephemera such as joiners' price lists, catalogs, pre-1900 paper, etc.

Dealer

Falcon-Wood
Peter & Annette Habicht
RFD 1, Box 176
Sheffield, MA 01257
Phone: 413-229-7745
Issues well illustrated catalogs of older and more interesting tools; send $6 to be placed on the mailing list.

Dealer

Fromer's Antiques
Barb & Dan Fromer
Box 224
New Market, MD 21774
Phone: 301-831-6712
Antique tools; also wants Maxfield Parrish prints.

Dealer

Murphy B. Clifton
5416 Ferndale St.
Springfield, VA 22151
Phone: 703-256-4907
Wants antique tools of all kinds.

Dealer

Bob Kaune
511 West 11th
Port Angeles, WA 98382
Phone: 206-452-2292
Issues catalog of primarily 19th and 20th century tools with a good selection of Stabley product.

Expert

Tools of Distinction
Jim Calison
60 Reservoir Rd.
Wallkill, NY 12589
Phone: 914-895-8035
Wants Stanley tools and other old hand woodworking tools.

Expert

Ed Hobbs
4417 Inwood Rd.
Raleigh, NC 27603
Writes column for Antique Week. *

Museum/Library

American Precision Museum Association, Inc.
P.O. Box 679
Windsor, VT 05089
Phone: 802-674-5781

Museum/Library

Mercer Museum of the Bucks County Historical Society
Pine & Ashland Streets
Doylestown, PA 18901
Phone: 215-345-0210

Museum/Library

World O'Tools Museum
Hunter M. Plinkton
Rte. 1, Box 180
Waverly, TN 37185
Phone: 615-296-3218
Always interested in old or odd mechanical tools; also related books and catalogs.

Periodical

Journal: Fine Tool Journal, The
Vern Ward
R.D. #2, Box 245B
Pittsford, VT 05763-9707
A monthly newsletter and advertiser for tool collectors.

English

Dealer

Bristol Design, Ltd.
14 Perry Road
Bristol BS1 5BG England
Issues a catalog with quality illustrations of fine English tools; subscription is $20 (partly refundable.)

Folding Rules

Collector

John Goetz
P.O. Box 1570
Cedar Ridge, CA 95924
Phone: 916-272-4644
Wants folding rules in good condition; made to measure rope, timber, contents of barrels; also for carpenters, engineers, machinists, etc.

Keen Kutter

Expert

Tools of Distinction
Jim Calison
60 Reservoir Rd.
Wallkill, NY 12589
Phone: 914-895-8035 *

Planes

Club/Association

British-American Rhykenological Society
60 Harvest Lane
Levittown, NY 11756 *

Stanley

Expert

Tool Merchant
John Walter
P.O. Box 6471
Akron, OH 44312
Phone: 800-542-1993
*Author of "Antique & Collectible Stanley Tools: A Guide to Identification and Value." *

Wrenches

Collector

Robert Rauhauser
Box 766
Thomasville, PA 17364-9622
Wants wrenches with names; especially cut-out (see throughs) wrenches; any farm machinery wrenches; specialty wrenches.

TOOTHPICK HOLDERS

Club/Association

National Toothpick Holders Collectors Society
Newsletter: Toothpick Bulletin
Joyce Ender
P.O. Box 246
Sawyer, MI 49125
Phone: 616-426-3800
Society members interested in collecting toothpick holders of all shapes and materials; monthly newsletter, annual conventions.

Expert

Newsletter: Toothpick Bulletin
Judy Knauer
1224 Spring Valley Lane
West Chester, PA 19380
Phone: 215-431-3477
Collector, lecturer, and author on old glass toothpick holders.

Expert

Joyce Ender
P.O. Box 246
Sawyer, MI 49125
Phone: 616-426-3800

TOYS

(see also CHILDREN'S THINGS; CRACKER JACK TOYS; DOLLS; GAMES; MINIATURES; MODEL KITS; RADIO PREMIUMS; SOLDIERS; SUPER HEROES; TRAINS; TRUCKS)

Auction Service

Sotheby's
34-35 New Bond Street
London W1A 2AA England
Conducts specialty auctions of tinplate toys, diecasts, trains, antique dolls, teddy bears, automata.

Auction Service

Wallis & Wallis
Glenn Butler
West Street Auction Galleries
Lewes
East Sussex BN7 2NJ England
Britain's specialist auctioneers of die-cast & tin plate toys & models including model soldiers.

Auction Service

Toy-A-Day
Box 98
South Hadley, MA 01075
Phone: 203-879-5799 or 203-879-5899
Specializes in the mail bid auction sale of contemporary collectible toys.

Auction Service

Skinner, Inc.
357 Main Street
Bolton, MA 01740
Phone: 508-779-6241 or 617-236-1700
FAX: 508-779-5144
Established in 1962, Skinner Inc. is the fifth largest auction house in the US.

Auction Service

New England Auction Gallery
Martin Krim
16 Herbert Ave.
West Peabody, MA 01960
Phone: 508-535-3140   FAX: 508-535-7522
Mail-bid auction service for toys and collectibles.

Auction Service

Richard W. Withington, Inc.
R.D. 2, Box 440
Hillsboro, NH 03244
Phone: 603-464-3232

Auction Service

Smith House Toy Sales
Herb & Barb Smith
P.O. Box 33605
Eliot, ME 03903
Phone: 207-439-4614
*Conducts four specialty mail-bid toy auctions each year. *

Auction Service

Lloyd Ralston Toy Auction
173 Post Rd.
Fairfield, CT 06430
Phone: 203-366-3399 or 203-255-1233

Auction Service

Sotheby's
1334 York Ave. at 72nd Street
New York, NY 10021
Phone: 212-606-7000

Auction Service

Christie's East
219 E. 67th St.
New York, NY 10021
Phone: 212-606-0400

Auction Service

Phillips Fine Art & Auctioneers
406 East 79th St.
New York, NY 10022
Phone: 212-570-4830   FAX: 212-570-2207
Specializes in the sale of jewelry, paintings, prints, silver, coins, stamps, toys (especially lead soldiers), and movie memorabilia.

Auction Service

Stephen Leonard Auctions
P.O. Box 127
Albertson, L.I., NY 11507
Phone: 516-742-0979

Auction Service

Hake's Americana & Collectibles Auction
Ted Hake
P.O. Box 1444
York, PA 17405
Phone: 717-848-1333   FAX: 717-848-4977
Specializing in mail-bid auctions of Disneyana, historical Americana, toys, premiums, political items, character and other collectibles.

Auction Service

Barrett/Bertoia Auctions
1217 Glenwood Dr.
Vineland, NJ 18630
Phone: 609-692-4092
Specializing in antique toys and collectibles sales.

Auction Service

Noel Barrett Auctions
P.O. Box 1001
Carversville, PA 18913
Phone: 215-297-5109

Auction Service

Ted Maurer Auctions
1003 Brookwood Dr.
Pottstown, PA 19464
Phone: 215-323-1573 or 215-367-5024

Auction Service

Richard Opfer Auctioneering, Inc.
1919 Greenspring Dr.
Timonium, MD 21093
Phone: 301-252-5035   FAX: 301-252-5863

Auction Service

Phil Savino
Rt. 2, Box 76
Micanopy, FL 32667
Conducts mail-bid auctions of various toy categories. *

Auction Service

Auction Under the Big Top
Tommy Sciortino
3723 N. Nebraska Aave.
Tampa, FL 33603
Phone: 818-248-5387 or 813-932-1782
             FAX: 813-248-5387
Specializes in the sale of circus equipment and memorabilia, carousels, amusement devices, coin-ops, toys, etc.

Auction Service

American Eagle Auction Company
6724 York Rd., SW
Pataskala, OH 43062

Auction Service

Global Toy Merchants
Rex & Kathy Barrett
P.O. Box 254
Medinah, IL 60157

Club/Association

Antique Toy Collectors of America, Inc., The
Newsletter: Toy Chest
Robert R. Grew
c/o Carter, Ledyard & Milburn
Two Wall St. - 13th Floor
New York, NY 10005
Phone: 212-238-8803   FAX: 212-732-3232
An organization focusing on antique toys and games.

Club/Association

Southern California Toy Collector's Club
Carl Natter
Suite 300
1760 Termino
Long Beach, CA 90804
Phone: 213-597-4351
Members interested in all types of toys from 19th century tin toys to GI Joe and Barbie.

Collector

Martin Krim
16 Herbert Ave.
West Peabody, MA 01960
Phone: 508-535-3140   FAX: 508-535-7522
Wants wind-up and battery toys, toy cars, robots and space toys.

Collector

Steve Leonard
Box 127
Albertson, NY 11507
Phone: 516-742-0979
Wants antique mechanical toys, etc.

Collector

Larry Bruch Toys
Larry Bruch
P.O. Box 121
Mountaintop, PA 18707
Phone: 717-474-9202
All kinds of pre-1960 toys wanted: German, American: metal cars, airplanes, boats; comic characters, cast iron toys and banks, etc.

Collector

Charles F. Wilding
10207 Greenacres Dr.
Silver Spring, MD 20903-1402
Phone: 301-434-6209
Wants antique toys, all kinds.

Collector

Harry Hill
18938 Planters Lane
Keedysville, MD 21756
Phone: 301-432-5006 *

Collector

Jim Conley
2758 Coventry Lane
Canton, OH 44708
Phone: 216-477-7725
Buys and sells cars, trucks, tin windups, Buddy L, Metal Craft, Smith Miller, Tonka, Lehmann, Bing, Ives, Marx, etc.; sellers call collect.

Collector

J. Michael
521 West McCarty St.
Indianapolis, IN 46255
Phone: 317-875-7192 *

Collector

Gary L. Linden
P.O. Box 243
River Forest, IL 60305
Wants Marx and other plastic toys. *

Dealer

Childhood Memories, Inc.
Vincent G. Krug
P.O. Box 96
Ashford, CT 06278
Phone: 203-429-8876
Wants older tin, wood, cast iron and composition toys; especially relating to Easter, Halloween, and Christmas.

Dealer

Pin-On
Helene G. Pollack
120 Bennets Farm Road
Ridgefield, CT 06877
Phone: 203-438-8286
Wants Disneyana and Betty Boop comic character items; also any comic character pin back buttons.

Dealer

Bill Bertoia
1217 Glenwood Drive
Vineland, NJ 08630
Phone: 609-692-4092 *

Dealer

J. Kellner
1222 7th St.
Huntington, WV 25701
Phone: 304-523-3287
Wants all old toys and banks; buys and sells. *

Dealer

Ed & Audrey Hyers
P.O. Box 18448
Asheville, NC 28814
Phone: 704-252-2155
Buys and sells quality 19th-century American toys, specializing in American tin toys.

Dealer
Brian L. Carter
29750 N. Hilltop
Orange Village, OH 44022
Phone: 216-831-4684
Wants old battery operated toys and tin wind up toys; airplanes, cars, comic character; all kinds; any condition.

Dealer
Toy Scouts, Inc.
Bill & Joanne Bruegman
330 Merriman Rd.
Akron, OH 44303-1552
Phone: 216-836-0668 or 216-864-6751
Specializes in 1950-60's toys: TV, cartoon, monsters, super heroes, games, cereal premiums, model kits, etc.; anything baby-boomer era.

Dealer
Doug Moore
57 Hickory Ridge Circle
Cicero, IN 46034
Phone: 317-877-1741
*Wants tin wind-ups, Buddy L toys, character toys, and cast iron toys. ***

Dealer
Continental Hobby House
P.O. Box 193
Sheboygan, WI 53082
Phone: 414-693-3371   FAX: 414-693-8211
Extensive list of toy trains (catalog $5); parts list ($5); HO train catalog ($5); wants all types of toys and trains especially European.

Dealer
Ken Schmitz
2405 West Carrington
Oak Creek, WI 53154
*Wants space character toys, western toys, and comic character figures, books, and games. ***

Dealer
Gullivers
Allan Kessler
2727 W. Howard St.
Chicago, IL 60645
Phone: 312-465-2060
*Wants early Disney items, comic characters, tin wind-ups, and celluloid toys. ***

Dealer
Collectorholics
Joe & Carolyn Thurmond
15006 Fuller
Grandviwe, MO 64030
Phone: 816-322-0906
Buys, sells, trades TV Guides, Western items, Star Trek, military toys, banks, novelty radios, radio premiums, Disney, etc.

Dealer
John D. McKenna
6570 Ashcroft Dr.
Colorado Springs, CO 80918
Phone: 719-592-0131
Buys, sells & collects pre-1960 toys in all categories especially early American tin, cast iron automotive and horsedrawn toys.

Expert
Richard Friz
RFD 2, Box 155
Peterborough, NH 03458
Phone: 603-563-8155
*Author of "The Official Price Guide to Collectible Toys." ***

Expert
Edmund Weinberg
77 Memorial Parkway
Atlantic Heights, NJ 07716 *

Expert
Darrow's Fun Antiques
Gary Darrow
309 E. 61st St.
New York, NY 10021
Phone: 212-838-0730
Buys & sells any type of antique toy: comic character, windup, friction, pedal cars, Tootsie Toys, GI Joe, lead soldiers, etc.

Expert
Rinker Enterprises, Inc.
Harry L. Rinker
P.O. Box 248
Zionsville, PA 18092
Phone: 215-965-1122   FAX: 215-965-1124
Researches, writes about and appraises all forms of 19th and 20th century toys, games and puzzles.

Expert
Bill Brophy
P.O. Box 1282
Fairfax, VA 22030 *

Expert
Hoosier Peddler, The
Dave Harris
5400 S. Webster St.
Kokomo, IN 46902
Phone: 317-453-6172
*Specializing in rare comic toys & tin wind-ups, antique advertising & Disneyana. ***

Expert
Nobel House
Carol & Jerry Dinelli
P.O. Box 964
Mundelein, IL 60060
Phone: 312-949-8588
*Writes column on antique and collectible toys. Has cataloged toy reproductions. ***

Expert
David Welch
RR 2, Box 233
Murphysboro, IL 62966
Phone: 618-687-2282
Wants 1950's-1960's tin robots; also 1930's-1960's Disney, Popeye, Betty Boop and monster toys.

Expert
J-L Collectibles
Jim & Leslie Smith
P.O. Box 472113
Garland, TX 75047-2113
Phone: 214-271-8917 or 214-840-2517
            FAX: 214-840-2517
Buys/sells battery-operated, friction, cast iron & wind-up toys; also diecast Tootsie Toys & Corgi, Japanese tin cars, planes & motorcycle.

Expert
Long's Americana
Earnest & Ida Long
P.O. Box 90
Mokelumne Hill, CA 95245
Phone: 209-286-1348
Specializes in toys, banks, games and other children's items; publishes "Dictionary of Toys, Vol I & II" and "Penny Lane."

Museum/Library
Forbes Magazine Collection
60 Fifth Avenue
New York, NY 10011
Phone: 212-206-5548

Museum/Library
Museum of the City of New York
5th Avenue at 103rd St.
New York, NY 10029
Phone: 212-534-1672

Museum/Library
Strong Museum, The
1 Manhattan Square
Rochester, NY 14607
Phone: 716-263-2700

Museum/Library
Washington Dolls' House & Toy Museum
5236 44th Street NW
Washington, DC 20015
Phone: 202-244-0024

Museum/Library
Western Reserve Historical Society
10825 East Blvd.
Cleveland, OH 44106
Phone: 216-721-5722

Museum/Library
Eugene Field House & Toy Museum
634 Broadway St.
St. Louis, MO 63102
Phone: 314-421-4689

Museum/Library

Toy & Miniature Museum of Kansas City
Sandi Russell
5235 Oak St.
Kansas City, MO 64112
Phone: 816-333-2055
Museum housed in an elegant mansion features collections of miniatures, antique dolls' houses and antique toys.

Museum/Library

Hobby City Doll & Toy Museum
1238 South Beach Blvd.
Anaheim, CA 92804
Phone: 714-527-2323

Periodical

Magazine: International Toy & Doll Collector
P.O. Box 9
Halstead
Essex, England *

Periodical

Newspaper: Toy Collecting
200 Nuncargate Road
Kirby in Ashfield
Nottingham, England
A monthly newspaper.

Periodical

Magazine: Name of the Game
P.O. Box 721
Plainview, CT 06062
Phone: 203-793-2383

Periodical

Magazine: Action Figure News & Review
556 Monroe Turnpike
Monroe, CT 06468
Phone: 203-452-7286
AFN is a full size magazine dedicated to the collecting of action figures and toys from 1964 to present; articles, ads, shows, etc.

Periodical

Toy Scouts, Inc.
Magazine: Model & Toy Collector Magazine
Bill & Joanne Bruegman
330 Merriman Rd.
Akron, OH 44303-1552
Phone: 216-836-0668   FAX: 216-864-6751
Focuses on collectible toys, models and various other memorabilia from the '50's to the present.

Periodical

Magazine: YesterDaze TOYS
Terri Steele, Pub.
275 State Rd.
Box 57
Otisville, MI 48463-0057
Phone: 313-631-4593
The monthly meeting place for toy collectors; if children played with it, this magazine covers it; old to not-so-old toys.

Periodical

Sharpe Publications
Magazine: Toy Collector Marketplace
1550 Territorial Road
Benton Harbor, MI 49022
Phone: 619-925-2178
A bi-monthly magazine for toy collectors. *

Periodical

Krause Publications, Inc.
Newspaper: Toy Shop
Bob Lemke, Pub.
700 East State St.
Iola, WI 54990
Phone: 715-445-2214 or 800-258-0929
                                    FAX: 715-445-4087
A monthly fully indexed newspaper containing classified ads for toys, tin soldiers, dolls, die-cast toys, models, trains, etc.

Periodical

Magazine: U.S. Toy Collector
P.O. Box 4244
Missoula, MT 59806
A monthly magazine about toy vehicles.

Periodical

Magazine: Antique Toy World
4419 Irving Park
Chicago, IL 60641
Phone: 312-725-0633
A monthly magazine serving toy collectors and dealers; 150-200 pages of all types of toys; ads, articles, etc.

Repair Service

Marc Olimpio's Antique Toy Restoration Center
Marc Olimpio
P.O. Box 1505
Wolfeboro, NH 03894
Phone: 603-569-6739
Specializes in early handpainted German and French-American tin toys, iron and pressed steel, and cast iron.

Repair Service

Gary J. Moran
3 Finch Court
Commack, NY 11725
Phone: 516-864-9444
Antique toy repairs, including battery operated, friction and wind-up toys; call or write for free estimate; broken toys purchased.

Repair Service

Toy Doctor
RR 1, Box 202
Eades Road
Red Creek, NY 13143
Phone: 315-754-8846
Repairs battery operated toys; robots and space toys a specialty. *

Repair Service

Pete Dibenedetto
568 Minnesota Avenue
Buffalo, NY 14215
Specializing in the repair of plastic toys. *

Repair Service

Newbraugh Brothers Toys
P.O. Box 32, R.D.1
Cogan Station, PA 17728
Phone: 717-435-0447
Custom painting of toys and trains. *

Repair Service

Joe Freeman
1313 N. 15th St.
Allentown, PA 18102
Phone: 215-434-0290   FAX: 215-821-8897
Specializes in the repair of tin toys; tin toy autos, boats, merry-go-rounds, etc.; repairs mechanisms, makes missing parts.

Repair Service

Russ Harrington's Repair & Restoration Service
Rus Harrington
1805 Wilson Point Road
Baltimore, MD 21220
Specializes in mechanical and still banks, and in iron toys. *

Repair Service

Jerry Shook
6528 Cedar Brook Dr.
New Albany, OH 43054
Phone: 614-855-7796
Makes rubber & plastic replacement parts for toys: wind ups, robots, battery operated, etc.; also for dolls; send SASE for parts list.

Repair Service

Ed's Toy Shop
953 East Richmond
Kokomo, IN 46901
Phone: 317-459-0325
Complete overhaul and repair of old toys.

Repair Service

Classic Tin Toy Co.
P.O. Box 193
Sheboygan, WI 53082
Phone: 414-693-3371   FAX: 414-693-8211
Repair and total restoration of all makes of old toys including tin, cast iron and tinplate trains.

Repair Service

Donald Walters
Route 1, Box 51
Curtiss, WI 54422
Phone: 715-654-5440
Repairs and repaints farm and other toys; glass beading, customizing, baked-on paint for smooth, shiny finish.

Repair Service

Phantom Antique Toy Restoration
Buddy George
1038 North Utica
Tulsa, OK 74110
Specializes in pressed-steel toys and pedal cars. *

Supplier

Thomas Toys
P.O. Box 405
Fenton, MI 48430
Phone: 313-629-8707
Carries antique toy car replacement parts.

Agriculture Related

(see also TOYS, Farm)

Airplane Related

(see also AIRLINE MEMORABILIA, Models
(Desk))

Collector

Perry R. Eichor
703 N. Almond Dr.
Simpsonville, SC 29681
Phone: 803-967-8770
*Wants aircraft toys and literature; member of
Antique Toy Collectors of America.*

Expert

G.R. Webster
P.O. Box 749
Teanec, NJ 07666
Phone: 203-629-4999
*Interested in airplane toys and models: diecast
toys, ID models, travel agency and desk models,
etc.*

Periodical

Magazine: Plane News, The
G.R. Webster
P.O. Box 749
Teanec, NJ 07666
Phone: 203-629-4999
*A quarterly magazine on aviation toys and models
(not plastic kits): diecast, ID models, travel
agency and desk models, etc.*

Battery Operated

Expert

Don Hultzman
5026 Sleepy Hollow Rd.
Medina, OH 44256
Phone: 216-225-2668
*Buys/sells battery and wind-ups; wants toys in
any condition; also expert repairs - undetectable &
guaranteed.*

Repair Service

J-L Collectibles
Jim & Leslie Smith
P.O. Box 472113
Garland, TX 75047-2113
Phone: 214-271-8917 or 214-840-2517
                              FAX: 214-840-2517
*Offers mechanical repair of most battery operated
and wind up toys.*

Battery Operated (Figural)

Collector

Adam Zidek
Route #5 Box 166
High Point, NC 27263
Wants figural battery toys; most any condition. *

BB Guns

Collector

Lee Woolf
321 Meeting House Lane
Narberth, PA 19072
Phone: 215-667-9378
*Wants Daisy BB guns, rifles, pistols; Red Rider
Targeteer.* *

Collector

Terry Burger
2323 Lincoln
Beatrice, NE 68310
Phone: 402-228-2797
*Wants pre-1915, preferably cast iron-framed
guns: Daisy, Atlas, Matchless, New rapid, etc.*

Museum/Library

Daisy International Air Gun Museum
P.O. Box 220
Rogers, AR 72757
Phone: 501-636-1200

Periodical

Newsletter: Toy Gun Collectors of America
    Newsletter
Jim Buskirk
312 Starling Way
Anaheim, CA 92807
Phone: 714-998-9615
*Subscription newsletter published quarterly: pho-
tos, information, articles; also free want ads for
subscribers.*

Bell

Collector

Dr. Greg Zeminick
Suite 160
1350 Kirts
Troy, MI 48084
Phone: 313-642-8129   FAX: 313-244-9495
Wants bell toys.

Boats & Outboards

Collector

Rich Pumphrey
1001 Fairwinds Dr.
Annapolis, MD 21401
Phone: 301-757-3795
*Wants toy outboard motors & boats: late 50's to
mid-60's, K+O Fleetline, Craftmaster, Mercury, Evinrude, Johnson, etc.*

Buses

Collector

Eugene R. Farha
P.O. Box 633
Cedar Grove, WV 25039
*Wants obsolete tinplate and plastic toy buses,
especially Greyhound and Trailways.*

Canadian

Club/Association

CTM Farm Toy & Collectors Club
Magazine: Canadian Toy Menia
Box 489
Rocanville
Saskatchewan S0A 3L0 Canada *

Cap Pistols

Club/Association

Toy Gun Purveyors
Newsletter: Toy Gun Newsletter
Box 243
Burke, VA 22015
Phone: 703-569-6665
*Over 500 members worldwide who share memories
and knowledge about toy guns; annual show each
year in the Wash., DC area.*

Collector

Dennis Carper
229 West Street
Winchester, VA 22601
Phone: 703-667-7939
Wants toy cap pistols: cast iron only. *

Collector

Terry Burger
2323 Lincoln
Beatrice, NE 68310
Phone: 402-228-2797

Collector

Charles W. Best
6288 South Pontiac
Englewood, CO 80111 *

Periodical

Newsletter: Toy Gun Collectors of America
    Newsletter
Jim Buskirk
312 Starling Way
Anaheim, CA 92807
Phone: 714-998-9615

Subscription newsletter published quarterly: photos, information, articles; also free want ads for subscribers.

Repro. Source

Reynolds Toys
Charles Reynolds
2836 Monroe St.
Falls Church, VA 22042
Phone: 703-533-1322
Offers limited editions of new original cap pistol reproductions of sand-cast aluminum.

Cars

Collector

Steve Butler
2912 Memory Lane
Silver Spring, MD 20904
Phone: 301-890-1739 or 301-492-6445
Wants automotive (cars and trucks) toys 1920-1960: iron, steel, cast metal, plastic.

Collector

Richard McCoy
1119 Michigan Ave.
St. Joseph, MI 49085
Wants toy cars from 1900 to 1960; especially larger pressed-steel types by Buddy L, Structo, etc.; also pedal cars and live steam toys.

Periodical

Newsletter: McElwee's Small Motor News
40 Fornof Lane
Pittsburgh, PA 15212 *

Cars (Kingsburg)

Collector

Martin Waarvick
Rt. 3, Box 3260
Wapato, WA 98951
Phone: 509-848-2632
*Wants Kingsburg toy cars 300 series; also battery operated 1950's Mickey the Magician, Haunted House and others. *

Cars (Miniature)

Club/Association

Capitol Miniature Auto Collectors Club
Newsletter: C.M.A.C.C. Bulletin
Charles F. Wilding
10207 Greenacres Dr.
Silver Spring, MD 20903-1402
Phone: 301-434-6209
Club sponsors two shows per year.

Dealer

Toys for Collectors
P.O. Box 1406
Attleboro Falls, MA 02763
*Offers catalog of hundreds of models for sale. *

Periodical

Magazine: Automobile Miniature
9, Rue De Saussure, 75017
Paris, France
*Eleven issues per year. *

Periodical

Model Collectors Warehouse
Newsletter: Model Collectors Digest
P.O. Box 8943
Waukegan, IL 60079-8943
Access to 1000's of out-of-production kits, promos & automotive toys, free ads, Model car club directory & news, swap meet calendar, etc.

Cars (Racing)

Club/Association

H.O. Slot Car Collecting & Racing Club
Newsletter: HOSCCRC Newsletter
Bob Beers
284 Willets Lane
West Islip, NY 14795
Phone: 516-661-8597
For the slot car collector, racer and enthusiast.

Collector

Gabriel Bogdonoff
614 Porter Rd.
Howell, NJ 07731
Phone: 201-363-4064
Wants toy race cars; can be gas powered, friction, wind up; also wants Japanese tin autos and Smith Miller trucks in any condition.

Character

(see also CHARACTER COLLECTIBLES)

Auction Service

New England Auction Gallery
Martin Krim
P.O. Box 2273
West Peabody, MA 01960
Phone: 508-535-3140   FAX: 508-535-7522
Full color illustrated catalogs; specializes in sales of Disney, TV and cartoon items from 1920-1970: toys, wind ups, robots, space toys.

Collector

Martin Krim
16 Herbert Ave.
West Peabody, MA 01960
Phone: 508-535-3140   FAX: 508-535-7522
Wants tin & celluloid toys from Japan, Germany, etc.; character items from TV shows, westerns, stars from the 50-60's; robot & space toys.

Collector

Richard Trautwein
437 Dawson St.
Sault Ste. Marie, MI 49783
Phone: 906-635-0356
Wants windup, battery, tin, pull, cast iron toys: Barney Google, Charlie Chaplin, Mickey Mouse, Donald Duck, Popeye, etc.

Dealer

Just Kids
326 Main Street
Huntington, NY 11743
Phone: 516-423-8849
Specializes in character toys: Roy Rogers, monsters, 50's-70's TV, Barbie, GI Joe, Batman, Superman, cartoon characters, Westerns, etc.

Dealer

Casey's Collectible Corner
Dennis & Mary Luby
H.C.R. Box 31, Rte. 30
No. Blenheim, NY 12131
Phone: 607-588-6464
Buys and sells collectible toys: comic characters, TV shows and personalities; also space and monster toys, sports collectibles, etc.

Dealer

O.E. & Julia Gernand
Rural Route 2
Yorktown, IN 47396
*Wants character toys and wind-ups. *

Dealer

Ken Schmitz
2405 West Carrington
Oak Creek, WI 53154
*Wants space character toys, westerns, comic characters, figures, books, games, etc. *

Dealer

Marc Belich
2014 South 81st. St.
West Allis, WI 53219
*Wants character toys of all kinds. *

Expert

Character Toys
David K. Longest
P.O. Box 2183
Clarksville, IN 47131-2183
*Author of "Toys Antique & Collectible." *

Construction Sets

Collector

George Wetzel
221 Hickory St.
Park Forest, IL 60466
Phone: 708-747-5841
Wants Erector sets, Meccano, Anchor stone blocks, Arkirecto, any old building toys.

Collector

Arlan Coffman
Suite 275
1223 Wilshire Blvd.
Santa Monica, CA 90403
Phone: 213-394-2397
Wants architectural construction toys: Erector sets, building blocks, villages, Lincoln Logs & figures, etc.

Construction Sets (Blocks)

Club/Association

Anchor Block Foundation
Magazine: Anchor House News
George Hardy
980 Plymouth Street
Pelham, NY 10803
Phone: 914-738-2935   FAX: 914-738-0008
Anchor House Found. is a club whose members have interests in and build with Anchor Blocks; semi-annual meetings in The Netherlands.

Museum/Library

Anker Museum
Newsletter: Ankerhuis Nieuws
Opaalstraat 204
Alphen a/d Rijn
Netherlands NL-2403 XK
Museum of Richter's Anchor Blocks (Richter's Anker Steenbouwdoozen.)

Construction Sets (Erector)

Club/Association

A.C. Gilbert Heritage Society
Newsletter: A.C. Gilbert Heritage Society
  Newsletter
Bill & Judy Harrison, Ed.
594 Front St.
Marion, MA 02738
Phone: 508-748-2540
For erector set enthusiasts; send SASE for news and information.

Club/Association

Southern California Meccano & Erector
Club
Newsletter: S.C.M.E.C. Newsletter
Clyde T. Suttle, Sec.
6062 Cerulean Ave.
Garden Grove, CA 92645-2722
Publishes a very good quarterly newsletter; holds regional meetings.

Collector

Wally Krocsko
Box 84
Burgettstown, PA 15021
Phone: 412-947-5671
Wants Gilbert, Meccano, etc. erector sets.

Collector

Elmer Wagner
256 S. Pitt St.
Carlisle, PA 17013
Phone: 717-243-3539
Wants A. C. Gilbert Erector sets, parts, manuals, catalogs, etc.

Collector

William M. Bean
6520 Imperial Woods Rd.
Dayton, OH 45459
Phone: 513-435-6196 or 513-436-9991

Wants Erector Sets by Gilbert, Meccano, Structiron, etc.; also sets that make the Erector airplane, Zeppelin; also advertising pieces.

Expert

Al Sternagle
R.D. #2, Box 400
Holidaysburg, PA 16648
Send $11 for "Erector Parts List"; author of several articles about Erectors.

Repair Service

Marion Designs
Bill & Judy Harrison
594 Front St.
Marion, MA 02738
Phone: 508-748-2540
Buy, sell, trade, restore and remanufacture Erector sets; also offers electroplating service.

Supplier

Elmer Wagner
256 South Pitt St.
Carlisle, PA 17013
Send for free 20-page parts catalog.

Diecast

Club/Association

Diecast Exchange Club
Newsletter: Diecast Exchange Club Newsletter
P.O. Box 1066
Pinellas Park, FL 34665 *

Collector

Cartel
Box 3428
York, PA 17402
*Wants tin toys and diecast, especially Dinky, Matchbox, Corgi. ***

Collector

Carl Natter
Suite 300
1760 Termino
Long Beach, CA 90804
Phone: 213-597-4351
Wants to buy cast iron toys from the 1930's, Tootsie Toy and other diecast cars and trucks.

Dealer

Specialty Diecast Co.
Tom Pilla
370 Miller Road
Medford, NJ 08055
Phone: 609-654-8484 or 609-654-2281
                    FAX: 609-654-2281
Sells old and new diecast toys: Dinky, Corgi, Matchbox, Revell, etc.

Ertl Replicas

Club/Association

Ertl Collectors Club
Newsletter: Ertl Replica, The
Mike Meyer, Ed.
Highways 136 & 20
Dyersville, IA 52040
Phone: 319-875-2000
Provides new product and historical information to collectors of Ertl replica toys.

Farm

(see also TOYS, Playsets)

Book Seller

Diamond Enterprises & Book Publishers
Div. of Yesteryear Toys & Books, Inc.
Box 537
Alexandria Bay, NY 13607
Phone: 613-475-1771 or 613-475-1782
                    FAX: 613-475-3748
Offers a complete line of hobby and toy publications; specialty in hobby steam and farm toys including antique tractor books.

Club/Association

Antique Engine, Tractor & Toy Club
Newsletter: AETTC Newsletter
David Semmel
Box 385, RT. #1 Pine Street
Slatington, PA 18080
Phone: 215-767-4768
Organized in 1986 with over 425 members; dedicated to preservation and enjoyment of old time farm engines, tractors and related toys.

Club/Association

Farm Toy Collectors Club
Box 38
Boxholm, IA 50040

Collector

Lee Schaffer
504 Hillside Ave.
Rochester, NY 14610
Phone: 716-244-6747
Civilian, farm and zoo figures; also vehicles and equipment.

Collector

Mark S. McCracken
R.D. 1, Box 184
Vanderbilt, PA 15486
Phone: 412-677-4650
Wants toy tractors, equipment, trucks, barns, animals, sales literature; all kinds in any condition.

Collector

Le Erin Plasterer
1800 McDowell Rd.
Greencastle, PA 17225
Phone: 717-597-3598
*Wants antique peddle farm tractor toys; also other farm related items. ***

Collector

Jim Proctor
1395 South Concord Rd.
West Chester, PA 19382
Phone: 215-399-0802

Collector

Terpbroson
Earl Terpstra
8104 Famos Ct.
Springfield, VA 22153
Phone: 703-455-2834 or 703-922-4522
Wants farm and construction toys.

Collector

Paul Ashby
602 Circle Dr.
Enid, OK 73703
Phone: 405-237-8442
*Wants toy tractors and other farm-related toys. ***

Dealer

Action Toys
Newsletter: Action Toys Newsletter
P.O. Box 31551
Billings, MT 59107
Phone: 406-248-4121
Issues bi-monthly newsletter containing list of toys for sale; also contains price guide, stories, background info.

Expert

Bernard L. Scott
117 Highview Drive
Cocoa, FL 32922
Phone: 407-632-0665
*Specializes in battery-operated, friction, and wind-up toys. ***

Periodical

Magazine: Tractor Classics
P.O. Box 191
Listowel
Ontario N4H 3HE Canada
Phone: 519-291-1656
Canada's farm toy magazine: new toy information, toy show reviews, free ads, etc.

Periodical

Newsletter: Miniature Tractor & Implement
1881 Eagley Rd.
East Springfield, PA 16411-9739
Phone: 814-922-3460 *

Periodical

Magazine: Toy Tractor Times, The
P.O. Box 156
Osage, IA 50461-0156
Phone: 515-732-3530   FAX: 515-732-5135
Features farm toys with an emphasis on toy tractors; articles, ads, shows, new releases, etc.

Periodical

Turtle River Toy Co.
Newsletter: Turtle River Toy News
R.R. 1, Box 44
Manvel, ND 58256-9763
Phone: 701-699-3577
A monthly newsletter focusing on tractors and farm related toys.

Periodical

Turtle River Toy Co.
Newsletter: Oliver Collectors News, The
R.R. 1, Box 44
Manvel, ND 58256-9763
Phone: 701-699-3577
A monthly newsletter focusing on Oliver tractors and implements, and Oliver toys.

Periodical

Toy Farmer Ltd.
Magazine: Toy Farmer
Claire D. Scheibe
HC 2 Box 5
LaMoure, ND 58458
Phone: 701-883-5206 or 701-883-5207
                    FAX: 701-883-5208
Toy Farmer sponsors the annual National Farm Toy Shoy in Dyersville, IA.

Periodical

Magazine: Farm Antiques News
Gary Van Hoozer, Ed.
414 Main St.
P.O. Box 96
Tarkio, MO 64491-0096
Phone: 816-736-5668 or 816-736-4528
                    FAX: 816-736-5700
For collectors, restorers, traders of all types/sizes of old (pre-1950) farm items: tractors, horse & other machinery, toys, etc.

Supplier

Dakota Toys
Rt. 3, Box 179
Arlington, SD 57212
Phone: 605-983-5987
Catalog contains toy parts, decals, paints, kits, 1/64 items, books, scratch building materials, tools and diorama materials.

Fisher-Price

Collector

Al Kamine
30 Larkspur Lane
Clifton, NJ 07013
Phone: 201-471-8922
*Wants Fisher-Price toys, parts, pieces, and catalogs. ***

Collector

John J. Murray
Box 29
Eden, NY 14057

The foremost collector of older Fisher-Price toys; co-author with Bruce R. Fox of "Fisher-Price 1931-63"; send SASE for info. on

Collector

Frank Frazzini
227 Castner Ave.
Donora, PA 15033
*Wants Fisher-Price pull toys only. ***

Collector

Kathy Bailey
1526 Canterbury
Murray, KY 42071
Phone: 502-759-4717
*Wants toys from the 30's, 40's, & 50's. ***

Dealer

Art Westson
40 Leaside Dr.
West Seneca, NY 14224
Phone: 716-674-7582 *

Gas Station Related

Collector

Mary Ruga
Miller Ave.
Dorothy, NJ 08317
*Wants toy gas station trucks, old or new; also wants toy service station and related service station toys. ***

Repro. Source

Art Bransky
R.D. 2, Box 558
Breinigsville, PA 18031
Phone: 215-285-6180
Makes repro. plastic/mylar window panes & graphics, wood panels, gas pump graphics, etc. for toy gas stations, bus garages, supermarkets.

German & Japanese

Collector

Martin Krim
P.O. Box 2273
West Peabody, MA 01960
Phone: 508-535-3140   FAX: 508-535-7522
Wants German and Japanese toys c. 1900; also comic character toys, windups, battery, etc.; celluloid, tin etc.

Hot Wheels

Collector

William Gehman
554 W. Broad St.
New Holland, PA 17557
Phone: 717-354-8374
*Wants anything to do with Hot Wheels including sizzlers. ***

Marklin

Collector
Ronald Wiener
Packard Bldg. - 12th Floor
111 S. 15th St.
Philadelphia, PA 19102
Phone: 215-977-2266   FAX: 215-977-2346
Wants Marklin (German) metal toys and toy trains, 1895-1960 in original and excellent condition, especially pre-1942 O gauge.

Matchbox

Club/Association
American International Matchbox
Newsletter: A.I.M. Newsletter
522 Chestnut St.
Lynn, MA 01904
Phone: 617-595-4135 *

Club/Association
Matchbox U.S.A.
Newsletter: Matchbox U.S.A.
Charles Mack
62 Saw Mill Rd.
Durham, CT 06422
Phone: 203-349-1655
Conducts annual conventions and shows.

Club/Association
Matchbox Collectors Club
Newsletter: MCC Newsletter
P.O. Box 119
Wood Ridge, NJ 07075

Club/Association
Pennsylvania "Matchbox" Collectors Club
Newsletter: Pennsylvania "Matchbox"
    Collectors Club Newsletter
1515 North 12th Street
Reading, PA 19604 *

Expert
Dana Johnson
104 NW Lava Road
Bend, OR 97701
Phone: 503-382-8410
Author of "Matchbox Bluebook - A Collector's Guide to Current Prices."

Mickey Mouse

Collector
Debra Krim
16 Herbert Ave.
West Peabody, MA 01960
Phone: 508-535-3140   FAX: 508-535-7522
Wants 1930's Mickey Mouse items: empty boxes, figurals, wind ups, bisque figurines, games, jewelry, etc.

Ohio Art

Dealer
Dealer
One Toy Street
Bryan, OH 43506
Wants factory made lithographed toys since 1908.
*

Optical
(see also STREO VIEWERS & STEREOGRAPHS)

Auction Service
Christie's South Kensington, Ltd.
Michael Pritchard
85 Old Brompton Road
London SW7 3LD England
Specializes in the sale of optical toys such as persistence of vision devices, stereoscopes, magic lanterns/slides, etc.

Collector
Christian Bailly
110 E. 57th St.
New York, NY 10022
Phone: 212-421-7546
Wants to buy antique magic lanterns, slides, and all pre-1914 optical toys of all kinds.

Collector
Davis Weiss
2072 77th St.
Brooklyn, NY 11214
*Wants animation effects (Zoetropes), anamorphoses (distorted pictures corrected in reflecting cylinder), Magic mirror, etc. *

Paper

Dealer
Paper Soldier, The
Barb & Jonathan Newman
8 McIntosh Lane
Clifton Park, NY 12065
Phone: 518-371-9202 or 518-371-5130
Paper toys bought and sold. Paper dolls, paper soldiers, toy theaters, planes, ships, paper and cardboard houses, etc.

Pedal Vehicles
(see also BICYCLES; TRICYCLES; WAGONS)

Club/Association
National Pedal Vehicle Association
Bruce Beimers
1720 Rupert, N.E.
Grand Rapids, MI 49505
Phone: 616-361-9887
Focuses on bicycles and pedal cars.

Collector
Art Bransky
R.D. 2, Box 558
Breinigsville, PA 18031
Phone: 215-285-6180
Wants streamline child's wagons and tricycles; also pre-1950 pedal cars and any unusual riding toy.

Collector
Frank Martin
RD #2 Reuther Dr.
Warren, OH 44481
Phone: 216-538-2213
Wants old pedal cars and other pedal toys.

Collector
Darwin Hunkler
2248 S. Cty, Rd. 350 W.
Russiaville, IN 46979
Phone: 317-453-1210
*Wants pedal cars, large steel toys, Buddy-L, Keystone, Sturdy Toy, Kingsbury, etc. *

Collector
Elmer Duellman
Rt. 2 Box 26
Fountain City, WI 54629 *

Collector
Jack Callaway
P.O. Box 6906
Lincoln, NE 68506
*Wants toys and pedal cars. *

Collector
Nate Stoller
960 Reynolds Dr.
Ripon, CA 95366
Phone: 209-956-5244 or 209-529-5300
Wants to buy or trade pre-1960 pedal cars.

Periodical
Newsletter: Wheel Goods Trader, The
P.O. Box 435
Fraser, MI 48026-0435
Magazine for collectors of wheeled vehicles: pedal cars, pedal airplanes; classifieds, calendar, etc.

Repair Service
Pedal Power
Ed Weirick
RFD #3, Box 190
Ellsworth, ME 04605
Phone: 207-667-2115
*Wants original pedal cars; also does custom design and restoration. *

Playsets

Auction Service
Toy-A-Day
Peter Fritz
Box 6026
Wolcott, CT 06716
Phone: 203-879-5799 or 203-879-5899

Conducts monthly auction of playsets, games, TV toys and post-WWII through Star Wars super heroes.

Collector

Thomas P. Terry
5894 Lakeview Ct. E.
Onalaska, WI 54650
Phone: 608-781-1894
Wants complete or partial Marx playsets: figures, accessories, individual pieces; western towns, ranches, wars, space, jungle, etc.

Dealer

Terry Geppert
4532 W. 102nd St.
Minneapolis, MN 55437
Phone: 612-831-7454

Dealer

P.O. Box 5161
Dearborn, MI 48128
Phone: 313-277-0751
Buys and sells post-WWII toys by Ideal, Marx, Superior; playsets and plastic figures; soldiers, farms, cowboys, etc.

Expert

Tim Geppert
2818 McKeag Dr.
Fort Collins, CO 80526
Phone: 303-225-9782
Author of "Guide for Non-Metallic Toy Soldiers of the U.S."
(see also SOLDIERS, Toy)

Periodical

Specialty Publishing Co.
Magazine: Plastic Figure & Playset Collector
Thomas P. Terry, Ed.
P.O. Box 1355
La Crosse, WI 54602-1355
Phone: 608-781-1894
A bi-monthly magazine devoted to Marx and related playsets and plastic figures from the 1950-1970's era.

Periodical

Magazine: Plastic Warrior
Paul Stadlinger
905 Harrison St.
Allentown, PA 18103
A British bi-monthly focusing on leading European figures: firms (Britains, Timpo, etc.), reviews, Q&A, letters, news, ads, etc.

Sand

Collector

Donald Gorlick
P.O. Box 24541
Seattle, WA 98124
Wants sand toys (not very old); small box-like toy containing a clown or trapeze artist which spins when the box is inverted.

Schoenhut

Club/Association

Schoenhut Collectors Club
Newsletter: Schoenhut Newsletter
M/M Robert Zimmerman
45 Louis Ave.
West Seneca, NY 14224
Phone: 716-674-6657
A quarterly newsletter; articles, prices and announcements of shows and events of interest to Schoenhut collectors.

Club/Association

Schoenhut Toy Collectors
Norman Bowers
1916 Cleveland Street
Evanston, IL 60202
Phone: 708-866-6175 *

Collector

Harry R. McKeon, Jr.
18 Rose Lane
Flourtown, PA 19031-1910
Phone: 215-233-4904
Wants Schoenhut items: dolls, games, circus animals, toys, accessories; anything Schoenhut except pianos.

Dealer

Norman Bowers
1916 Cleveland Street
Evanston, IL 60202
Phone: 708-866-6175
Buys, sells, trades Shoenhut items; also still and mechanical banks.

Repair Service

Christmas Past
Blossom Abell
420 La For River Drive
P.O. Box 247
Algonquin, IL 60102
Phone: 708-658-4990
Repairs Schoenhut circus animals and figures including restringing.

Scientific Laboratory

Collector

Barry Lutsky
31 Longfield Dr.
Neshanic, NJ 08853
Phone: 201-369-7367
*Wants toys by A.C. Gilbert, Chemcraft; 1915-1950; also Erector Sets. *

Space & Robot

Auction Service

Lloyd Ralston Toy Auction
173 Post Rd.
Fairfield, CT 06430
Phone: 203-366-3399 or 203-255-1233

Collector

John & Jenny Tarrant
10221 Squire Meadows
St. Louis, MO 63123
Wants Japanese tin robots made in the 50's and 60's.

Dealer

Robots & Space Toys
Ernie Mannix
888 Seventh Ave. 9th Fl.
New York, NY 10106
Phone: 212-744-6447
Wants robots and space toys.

Dealer

Space Toys
P.O. Box 5161
Dearborn, MI 48128
Phone: 313-277-0751
Wants to buy space toy buildings, figures, premiums, 1950's TV space series' toys, Archer slot handed figures & accessories.

Squeak

Expert

Tiffee Jasso
P.O. Box 85
Likely, CA 96116 *

Star Wars

Collector

Whit Alexander
P.O. Box 2326
Florence, AL 35630 *

Steam/Hot Air

Collector

Lowell Wagner
10585 Knight
Waconia, MN 55387
Phone: 612-442-4036 or 612-933-2011
　　　　　　　　　　　FAX: 612-933-2824
Wants steam toys and hot air engines; also wants steam toy catalogs, steam plants, accessories, autos, tractors, boats, etc.

Dealer

Diamond Enterprises & Book Publishers
Div. of Yesteryear Toys & Books, Inc.
Box 537
Alexandria Bay, NY 13607
Phone: 613-475-1771 or 613-475-1782
　　　　　　　　　　　FAX: 613-475-3748
American and Canadian distributors of Mamod and Wilesco steam models; sales, parts and service.

Super Hero

(see also CHARACTER COLLECTIBLES; COMIC BOOKS; RADIO SHOW PREMIUMS; SCIENCE FICTION COLLECTIBLES; TELEVISION SHOWS & MEMORABILIA)

Collector

Dale L. Ames
22 Colton Street
Worcester, MA 01610

Dealer

Other Worlds Collectibles
Frank R. Pacella
P.O. Box 4596
Bay Terrace, NY 11360-4596
Publishes a mail-order catalog of toys for sale. *

Tin

Collector

Harry R. McKeon, Jr.
18 Rose Lane
Flourtown, PA 19031-1910
Phone: 215-233-4904
Wants tin toys made by Martin, Bing, Lehman, Gutherman, Ives, Strauss, etc.

Collector

Scott Smiles
440 SW 5th Avenue
Boynton Beach, FL 33435
Wants tin wind-up toys. *

Dealer

John D. McKenna
6570 Ashcroft Dr.
Colorado Springs, CO 80918
Phone: 719-592-0131
Buys, sells & collects pre-1960 toys in all categories especially early American tin, cast iron automotive and horsedrawn toys.

Repro. Source

Shylling Associates, Inc.
P.O. Box 233
Peabody, MA 01960-6733
Phone: 508-532-7540   FAX: 508-977-0271

Tops & Gyroscopes

(see also TOYS, Yo-Yo's)

Collector

Top Secret
Bruce R. Middleton
5 Lloyd Rd.
Newburgh, NY 12550
Phone: 914-564-2556
Buys, sells, trades tops, yo-yo's, spinners, figurals, peg tops, supported tops, diablos, gyroscopes, etc.; seeks other collectors.

Collector

Dan Lassanske
P.O. Box 839
Santa Margarita, CA 93453
Phone: 805-438-5630
Wants to buy old tops.

Collector

Allan Rumpf
3432 72nd Ave. SE
Mercer Isl., WA 98040
Phone: 206-232-5676
Collects tops, yo-yo's and diabolos (mostly wooden) from different countries; also wants photos, articles and books about tops.

Dealer

Toycrafter, The
Don Olney
1237 E. Main St.
Rochester, NY 14609
Phone: 716-288-9000   FAX: 716-654-7820
Buys, sells, trades new and old tops; also wants top related ads, photos, books, photos and videos of people doing tricks with tops.

Museum/Library

Spinning Top Exploratory Museum
Newsletter: Spin-Offs
Judith Schultz
492 North Pine
Burlington, WI 53105
Phone: 414-763-3946
1,000 tops and yo-yo's on exhibit (antique and modern); top games and experiments to try; 35 types to spin; sales of unique tops; demos.

Transportation

Dealer

Aquarius Antiques
Jim & Nancy Schaut
P.O. Box 10781
Glendale, AZ 85318
Phone: 602-878-4293
Publishes a quarterly catalog of one-of-a-kind transportation toys and memorabilia; toys, board games, trains; buy and sell.

Trucks & Equipment

Collector

N.W. Neil
Box 9352
Greensboro, NC 27429

Dealer

Hiram Hobby Co.
18413 Rt 700
Hiram, OH 44234
Phone: 216-834-8817 *

Periodical

Toy Parts Peddler
Newsletter: American Toy Trucker, The
Dennis & Marge Lowry
1143 46th Street
Des Moines, IA 50311
Phone: 515-277-7589
A monthly newsletter dedicated to toy trucks and related equipment.

Periodical

Toy Farmer Ltd.
Magazine: Toy Trucker & Contractor
Claire D. Scheibe
HC 2 Box 5
LaMoure, ND 58458
Phone: 701-883-5206 or 701-883-5207
                    FAX: 701-883-5208
The Toy Farmer sponsors an annual National Toy Truck and Construction Show in August.

Supplier

Toy Parts Peddler
Dennis & Marge Lowry
1143 46th Street
Des Moines, IA 50311
Phone: 515-277-7589
Supplies parts for post WWII toy trucks, construction toys, toy race cars, and related equipment.

Volkswagen

Club/Association

Volkswagen Toy Collectors of America
Box 1091
Tustin, CA 92680 *

Water Pistols

Collector

Jean B. Hall
10 Alden Dr.
Norwood, MA 02062
Phone: 617-762-3779
Wants water pistols, especially Captain Video, Jaws, Davy Crockett, Pac-Man, St. Louis Exposition 1904, etc.; also TV Sci-Fi items.

Yo-Yo's

(see also TOYS, Tops & Gyroscopes)

Collector

Les Gordon
6475 E. 550 St.
Whitestown, IN 46075-9763
Phone: 317-769-3382
Wants old yo-yo's and related pins, patches, advertisements, trophies, strings, books, paper, memorabilia, etc.

Collector

Bob Zeuschel
805 Westbrook Meadows Ct.
Ballwin, MO 63021
Wants yo-yo's by Duncan, Goody, Royal, Ja-Do, Flores, etc.

TRACTORS

(see also FARM MACHINERY)

Collector

Zane Prifogle
Rt 7 Box 29
Connersville, IN 47331
Phone: 317-825-5300
Wants sales catalogs, brochures, memorabilia, signs, magazines, for farm tractors; especially anything marked John Deere. *

Periodical

Stemgas Publishing Co.
Magazine: Gas Engine Magazine
P.O. Box 328
Lancaster, PA 17603
Phone: 717-392-0733   FAX: 717-392-1341
G.E.M. is the leading magazine for antique tractor and gas engine collectors.

Periodical

Magazine: Antique Power
Patrick Ertel
P.O. Box 838
Yellow Springs, OH 45387
Phone: 513-767-1344
Has regular columns about farm toys, tractor restoration, farm literature collecting and tractor history; free ads for subscribers.

Periodical

Turtle River Toy Co.
Newsletter: Turtle River Toy News
R.R. 1, Box 44
Manvel, ND 58256-9763
Phone: 701-699-3577
A monthly newsletter focusing on tractors and farm related toys.

Case

Expert

Charles H. Wendel
R.R. 1, Box 28-A
Atkins, IA 52206
Author of "150 Years of J.I. Case."

Fordson

Club/Association

Fordson Tractor Club
Newsletter: FTC Newsletter
250 Robinson Rd.
Cave Junction, OR 97523
Phone: 503-592-3203
Dedicated to the restoration, preservation, exhibition of the Fordson tractor; bi-annual newsletter, manuals, service bulletins, etc.

Ford Worthington

Club/Association

Worthington Register
Newsletter: Worthington News
R.D. 2, Box 44
Mertztown, PA 19539
Phone: 215-682-6453 *

John Deere

Club/Association

Two-Cylinder Club Worldwide
Magazine: Two-Cylinder
Dave Trumbauer
P.O. Box 2275
Waterloo, IA 50704
Phone: 319-232-3402 or 319-292-6870
                        FAX: 319-232-6080
Over 20,000 members who collect John Deer literature and memorabilia, and who restore early John Deere tractors, engines, and implements.

Collector

Jim Proctor
1395 South Concord Rd.
West Chester, PA 19382
Phone: 215-399-0802
Wants pre-1960 John Deere 2-cylinder tractors; also wants tractor sales literature.

Museum/Library

John Deere Historic Site
R.R. 3
Dixon, IL 61021
Phone: 815-652-4551

Oliver

Collector

Rick & Andrew Garnhart
4858 Holland CHurch Rd.
German Valley, IL 61039
Phone: 815-362-6531
Buy, sell, appraise Oliver tractors.

Periodical

Turtle River Toy Co.
Newsletter: Oliver Collectors News, The
R.R. 1, Box 44
Manvel, ND 58256-9763
Phone: 701-699-3577
A monthly newsletter focusing on Oliver tractors and implements, and Oliver toys.

TRADING CARDS

Non-Sport

(see also BUBBLE GUM CARDS; BUBBLE GUM & CANDY WRAPPERS; SPORTS COLLECTIBLES)

Collector

Dan Calandriello
53-C Beacon Village
Burlington, MA 01803
Phone: 617-229-9009
Wants 1930's era non-sports cards: gum, candy, silks, Mickey Mouse, Indian gum, Superman, Lone Ranger, all war cards.

Dealer

Card Coach, The
Newsletter: Non-Sport Report, The
Jim & Sue
P.O. Box 128
Plover, WI 54467
Phone: 715-341-5452
Wants non-sport cards and collectibles; publishes periodic catalog of cards and collectibles for sale; friendly, fast service since 1956.

Periodical

Magazine: Tuff Stuff
P.O. Box 1637
Glen Allen, VA 23060
Phone: 804-266-0140 or 800-899-TUFF
                        FAX: 804-266-6874
The complete monthly sports price guide publication including baseball, football, basketball and hockey; also non-sports cards.

TRAINS

Toy

Auction Service

Greenberg Publishing Company, Inc.
Bruce C. Greenberg
7566 Main St.
Sykesville, MD 21784
Phone: 301-795-7447

Book Seller

Greenberg Publishing Company, Inc.
Bruce C. Greenberg
7566 Main St.
Sykesville, MD 21784
Phone: 301-795-7447
Greenberg Pub. offers largest selection of toy train collector guides: Lionel, Amer. Flyer, Marx, LGB, Marklin, Williams, AMT, etc.

Club/Association

Toy Train Collectors Society
Newsletter: Century Limited
160 Dexter Terrace
Tonawanda, NY 14150
Phone: 716-694-3771 *

Club/Association

Train Collectors Association
Magazine: Train Collectors Quarterly
P.O. Box 248
Strasburg, PA 17579
Phone: 717-687-8623 or 717-687-8623
                        FAX: 717-687-0742

Purpose is to bring together persons interested in collecting and operating toy trains and related items.

Club/Association

National Model Railroad Association, Inc.
Magazine: NMRA Bulletin, The
4121 Cromwell Road
Chattanooga, TN 37421
Phone: 615-892-2846

Club/Association

Toy Train Operating Society, Inc.
Magazine: Bulletin, The
Suite 308
25 West Walnut Street
Pasadena, CA 91103
Phone: 818-578-0673
Formed to further the toy train hobby and to promote fellowship; members receive "The Bulletin" magazine and "Order Board" admagazine.

Collector

Walter Makolandra
70 Cass Ave.
Woonsocket, RI 02895-4739
Phone: 401-765-4756
Collector seeks Lionel, American Flyer, Marklin, Bing and other trains and related items.

Collector

Golden Spike International
Jan Rechenberg
1700 Grand Concourse
Bronx, NY 10457
Phone: 212-294-1614 *

Collector

Wally Krocsko
Box 84
Burgettstown, PA 15021
Phone: 412-947-5671
Wants Gilbert, Meccano, etc. erector sets.

Collector

Neil K. Yerger
7 Farm Road
Wayne, PA 19087-3303
Wants to buy Lionel, American Flyer, Williams, K-Line, Weaver, etc. toy trains and accessories.

Collector

Richard MacNary
4727 Alpine Drive
Lilburn, GA 30247
*Wants Marx trains, Coca-Cola vehicles, wood, cardboard, paper toys, soldiers. **

Collector

Phil Stuhltrager
6761 Shieldwood
Toledo, OH 43615
Phone: 419-841-6116

Wants old Lionel, American Flyer, Marklin trains.

Collector

Tom Tomasik
2511 Pineview Dr. NE
Grand Rapids, MI 49505
Phone: 616-361-9678

Collector

Gerald C. Wagner
4455 Hermosa Way
San Diego, CA 92103 *

Collector

Edwin Wilder
Box 175
Nordland, WA 98358
Model railroad car, locomotive, structure kits - used, old. Also old locomotives and toy trains.

Dealer

Frank Camileri
10 Front Street
East Rockaway, NY 11518
*Buys, sells and repairs Lionel, and American Flyer, HO, O, N gauge. **

Dealer

Upstairs Hobby Shop
Stephen Hajash
P.O. Box 41
Harrisonburg, VA 22801
*Specializing in Plasticville, K-Lineville, Littletown and Marx buildings; Lionel and American Flyer trains; bought and sold. **

Dealer

Richard Giedroyc
P.O. Box 4145
Sidney, OH 45365
Phone: 513-498-1872
*Wants toy trains by Ives, Lionel, American Flyer, Fundamentions, Dorfan, Marx, etc.; also clockwork toys, character toys, boats, etc. **

Expert

Greenberg Publishing Company, Inc.
Bruce C. Greenberg
7566 Main St.
Sykesville, MD 21784
Phone: 301-795-7447
Specializes in Lionel, American Flyer, Marx, LGB, Marklin, Williams, AMT, etc.

Expert

William M. Bean
6520 Imperial Woods Rd.
Dayton, OH 45459
Phone: 513-435-6196 or 513-436-9991
Writes articles for the Train Collectors Association Quarterly.

Museum/Library

Toy Train Museum of the Train Collectors Association
P.O. Box 248
Strasburg, PA 17579
Phone: 717-687-8976 or 717-687-8623
FAX: 717-687-0742

Periodical

Magazine: O Scale Railroading
Box 239
Nazareth, PA 18064
A bi-monthly magazine exclusively for the O Gauge collector and market.

Periodical

Kalmbach Publishing Co.
Magazine: Classic Toy Trains
Richard E. Christianson
P.O. Box 1612
Milwaukee, WI 53187-1612
Phone: 414-796-8776 or 800-446-5489
FAX: 414-796-0126
Bi-monthly magazine with articles on collecting, repairing, & operating Lionel, American Flyer, Marx, Ives, LGB & other toy trains.

Repair Service

Newbraugh Brothers Toys
P.O. Box 32, R.D.1
Cogan Station, PA 17728
Phone: 717-435-0447
*Custom painting of toys and trains. **

Repair Service

William Gough
9133 Simms Ave.
Baltimore, MD 21234
Phone: 301-256-1448 *

Repro. Source

Pride Lines Ltd.
John & Joyce Davanzo
651 West Hoffman Ave.
Lindenhurst, NY 11757
Phone: 516-225-0033
*Manufacturers of fine "investibles"; all metal, quality electric toy trains, streetcars, lamps, railroad figures and accessories, etc. **

Toy (Hornby)

Club/Association

Hornby Railway Collectors' Association
Journal: Journal of the HRCA, The
Christopher Groom, Sec.
The Shrubbery
Willington
Derbyshire DE6 6DR England

Toy (Lionel)

Club/Association

Lionel Operating Train Society
Magazine: Switcher
John P. Dalton
6832 Meadowdale Cir.
Cincinnati, OH 45243
Phone: 513-793-9133

Club/Association

Lionel Railroad Club
Newsletter: Inside Track
P.O. Box 748
Mt. Clemens, MI 48043
Phone: 313-949-4100 *

Club/Association

Lionel Collectors Club of America
Newsletter: Lion Roars
P.O. Box 479
LaSalle, IL 61301
Phone: 815-654-1705
Purpose is to promote and foster interest in Lionel electric trains.

Collector

Ronald Wiener
Packard Bldg. - 12th Floor
111 S. 15th St.
Philadelphia, PA 19102
Phone: 215-977-2266   FAX: 215-977-2346
Wants Marklin (German) metal toys and toy trains, 1895-1960 in original and excellent condition, especially pre-1942 O gauge.

Museum/Library

Lionel Train & Seashell Museum
R.A. Paul
8184 North Tamiami Trail
Sarasota, FL 34243
Phone: 813-355-8184
Collection of Lionel trains and seashells; great gift shop offering sales and service of Lionel and other makes of toy trains.

Periodical

Lionel Collector Series Marketmaker
Price Guide: Trainmaster
Roger P. Bryan
P.O. Drawer D
Gainsville, FL 32602
Phone: 904-377-7439 or 904-373-4908
                                      FAX: 904-374-6616
A quarterly publication; the number one Lionel Collector Series marketmaker/market report; geared to the advanced collector/investor.

Toy (Marklin)

Club/Association

Marklin Digital Special Interest Group
Newsletter: Digital SIG, The
P.O. Box 51319
New Berlin, WI 53151-0319
Phone: 414-784-8854   FAX: 414-784-1095

Provides its members with in-depth knowledge and insight into the advanced Marklin Digital control technology.

Club/Association

Marklin Club
Newsletter: HotTraks
P.O. Box 51559
New Berlin, WI 53151-0559
Phone: 414-784-8854   FAX: 414-784-1095
Dedicated to serving the interests of the Marklin enthusiast.

Expert

Robert Monaghan
c/o Greenberg Publishing Co.
7566 Main St.
Sykesville, MD 21784
Phone: 301-795-7447
Author of "Greenberg's Guide to Marklin OO/ HO."

Toy (O-Scale Kits)

Collector

Joe Weber
604 Centre St.
Ashland, PA 17921
Phone: 717-875-4787 or 717-875-4401
Wants o-scale (Lionel size) toy trains, i.e. kits assembled by the enthusiast; made by Scalecraft, Lobaugh, Ferris, Hines, Max Gray.

Toy (Plasticville Items)

Expert

Frank Hare
P.O. Box 218
Bethel Park, PA 15102 *

Toy (S-Gauge)

Periodical

Heimburger Publishing
Magazine: S-Gaugian
Donald Heimburger
7236 West Madison Ave.
Forest Park, IL 60130
The magazine focuses on S-gauge toy train operation, modeling, and collecting.

TRAMP ART

(see also FOLK ART; HOBO COLLECTIBLES)

Expert

Michael Cornish
195 Boston St.
Dorchester, MA 02125
Phone: 617-282-3853 or 617-965-1240
Buys, sells and repairs tramp art (layered and notched objects made from recycled wood c. 1870-1940); seeks unusual or furniture pieces.

Museum/Library

U.S. Tobacco Museum
100 W. Putnam Ave.
Greenwich, CT 06830
Phone: 203-869-5531

TRANSPORTATION COLLECTIBLES

(see also AIRLINE MEMORABILIA; AIRSHIPS; BUS LINE COLLECTIBLES; OCEAN LINER COLLECTIBLES; RAILROAD COLLECTIBLES; TRUCK LINE COLLECTIBLES)

Club/Association

Transport Ticket Society
4 Gladridge Close Courts Road
Early, Reading
Berks R66 2DL England
Interested in the collection of tickets, transfers, passes, tokens, and other items issued by companies in the fare collection process.

Club/Association

American Transit Collectors Association
Newsletter: Collectors Item
8304 16th St. #108
Silver Spring, MD 20910
Phone: 301-588-6579
Interested in the collection of tickets, transfers, passes, tokens, and other items issued by companies in the fare collection process. *

Dealer

Antiques & Artifacts
Scott Arden
20457 Highway 126
Noti, OR 97461
Phone: 503-935-1619
Leading RR mail order dealer for 20 years; catalog $1; buys and sells fine old transportation items, mostly non-paper;

Museum/Library

Owls Head Transportation Museum
Charles Chiarchiaro
Rt. 73, Box 277
Owls Head, ME 04854
Phone: 207-594-4418

Timetables

Club/Association

National Association of Timetable Collectors
Newsletter: First Edition, The
315 W. Charles St.
Champaign, IL 61820
Interested in timetables from airlines, steamships, railroads, and bus lines. *

TRAPS

Club/Association

North American Trap Collectors
Association
Newsletter: NATCA Newsletter
Tom Parr
P.O. Box 94
Galloway, OH 43119
Members interested in the preservation of all trapping devices (animal, fish, bird, insect), trap operations, fur trade industry, etc.

Collector

Ron B. Frodelius
Box 125
Fayetteville, NY 13066
Wants anything related to trapping; ads, books, catalogs, magazines, hunt-trader-trapper, fur-fish-game mags.; also outdoor sport books.

Collector

Terry Burger
2323 Lincoln
Beatrice, NE 68310
Phone: 402-228-2797

Expert

Boyd Nedry
728 Buth Dr.
Comstock Park, MI 49321
Phone: 616-784-1513
Specializes in unusual animal traps or related items: fly, mouse, mole, minnow, bear; any material: wood, glass, metal, etc.; any age.

Museum/Library

Museum of the Fur Trade
Magazine: MFT Quarterly
HC 74, Box 18
Chadron, NE 69337
Phone: 308-432-3843
Dedicated to the study of the American fur trade from colonial times to the present; not involved with present day trapping.

Periodical

Krause Publications, Inc.
Magazine: Trapper & Predator Caller, The
700 East State St.
Iola, WI 54990
Phone: 800-258-0929 or 715-445-2214
                    FAX: 715-445-4087
A monthly magazine about hunting, trapping and predator calling.

Rat/Mouse/Fly

Collector

Robert Kwalwasser
168 Camp Fatima Rd.
Renfrew, PA 16053
Wants old mouse, fly and rat traps.

Collector

Tom Edmonds
6306 East Pea Ridge Rd.
Huntington, WV 25705
Phone: 304-697-5280
Wants antique mousetraps; prefers live catch or capture traps.

Collector

Mike Brooks
7335 Skyline
Oakland, CA 94611
Phone: 415-339-1751
Specializes in the collection of unusual mouse traps.

TRAP SHOOTING

Museum/Library

Trap Shooting Hall of Fame & Museum
601 N. National Road
Vandalia, OH 45377
Phone: 513-898-1945

TREASURE HUNTING

(see also ARCHAEOLOGICAL ARTIFACTS; ARTIFACTS; BOTTLES; CIVIL WAR ITEMS; COINS & CURRENCY)

Club/Association

Federation of Metal Detector &
Archeological Clubs, Inc.
Newsletter: Quest, The
Joe Cook
12 High Street
West Milford, NJ 07480
Phone: 201-697-9490
The FMDAC is composed of over 190 clubs. Goals include the promoting and protecting of the metal detecting hobby.

Club/Association

Preservation of the Independent
Detectorist Club, The
Wayne K. Hunt
460 W. Berwick St.
Easton, PA 18402
Phone: 215-252-2988
A club within the Federation of Metal Detector & Archeological Clubs primarily for individuals unable to join a local FMDAC chapter.

Periodical

Magazine: Western & Eastern Treasures
    Magazine
Rosemary Anderson, MngEd
P.O. Box 1095
Arcata, CA 95521
Phone: 707-822-8442   FAX: 707-822-0973
A how-to magazine for those interested in the hobby of metal detecting: collectors of artifacts, bottles, coins, etc.

TREES & SHRUBS

Club/Association

International Society of Arboriculture
P.O. Box 71
Urbanes, IL 61801
Send for "Guide for Establishing Values of Trees and Other Plants" *

Misc. Service

Guardian Tree Experts
Greydon Tolson
12200 Nebel St.
Rockville, MD 20852
Phone: 301-881-8550
Appraises trees and shrubs.

TRICYCLES

(see also BICYCLES; TOYS, Pedal Vehicles; WAGONS)

Collector

Art Bransky
R.D. 2, Box 558
Breinigsville, PA 18031
Phone: 215-285-6180
Wants streamline child's wagons and tricycles; also pre-1950 pedal cars and any unusual riding toy.

TROLLEY LINE COLLECTIBLES

(see also STREETCAR LINE COLLECTIBLES)

TROLLS

Collector

Debbie Brown
541 South St. Clair Street
Painseville, OH 44077
Phone: 216-354-6412
Wants trolls & related items in any condition, any number: trolls, troll houses, handlebar covers, charms, outfits, animals, etc.

Expert

Jeanne Niswonger
305 West Beacon Road
Lakeland, FL 33803
Author of "Troll Dolls."

Expert

Susan Miller
606 East Wabash Ave.
Crawfordsville, IN 47993
Phone: 317-362-0352 *

TROPHIES

(see also ANIMAL TROPHIES)

TRUCK LINE COLLECTIBLES

(see also TRANSPORTATION COLLECTIBLES)

Collector

David Zwicke
12 East 3rd St.
Moonachie, NJ 07074
Wants ocean liner and truck lines models, buttons, paper, china, calendars, souvenirs, etc. *

TRUCKS

Club/Association

American Truck Historical Society
Magazine: Wheels of Time
P.O. Box 531168
Birmingham, AL 35253
Phone: 205-870-0566
Recognized by the Amer. Trucking Assoc. as the official archives for the trucking industry; collects & preserves the history of trucking.

Museum/Library

Van Horn Truck Museum
Highway 65 North
Mason City, IA 50401
Phone: 515-423-0550
Over 60 models of pre-1930 trucks; 1930 store front streets, circus room with large scale model circus one man spent 34 years making!

Periodical

Antique Truck Collectors of America, Inc.
Newsletter: Double Clutch
P.O. Box 291
Hershey, PA 17033
Phone: 717-533-9032
Focuses on antique trucks and other commercial vehicles.

Periodical

Krause Publications, Inc.
Price guide: Truck Prices
700 E. State St.
Iola, WI 54990
Phone: 800-258-0929 or 715-445-2214
FAX: 715-445-4087
Monthly price guide for every type of truck fan, collector, restorer, appraiser, RV hobbyist, history buff, dealer, etc.

Miniature

Club/Association

Miniature Truck Association
Newsletter: Miniature Truck News
3449 N. Randolph St.
Arlington, VA 22207
Phone: 703-524-2061
Interested in miniature toy vehicles of all types with a basic specialty in commercial truck replicas. *

TRUNKS

Dealer

Antique Trunk Co.
3706 W. 169th St.
Cleveland, OH 44111
Phone: 916-372-8228
Buy, sell, trade, restore, and repairs old trunks; also carries repair supplies.

Periodical

Newsletter: Antique Trunk Quarterly
P.O. Box 44336
Washington, DC 20026-4336 *

Repair Service

Trunks By Paul
Paul Berkowitz
14 Park Ave.
Gaithersburg, MD 20877
Phone: 301-840-0920
Buys and sells trunks; also offers trunk refinishing for others; carries full line of trunk hardware and accessories.

Repair Service

Original Woodworks
360 North Main St.
Stillwater, MN 55082
Phone: 612-430-3622
Specializing in complete antique trunk restoration; will transform your trunk inside and out into a treasured family heirloom.

Repair Service

House of Antique Trunks
753 B Northport Dr.
P.O. Box 508
West Sacramento, CA 95691-0508
Phone: 916-372-8228
Antique trunk restoration parts & accessories; doll trunk supplies; chromolithographs for lids; linings, adhesives, leather; repairs.

Supplier

Charlotte Ford Trunks
P.O. Box 536
Spearman, TX 79081
Phone: 806-659-3027
Publishes a parts catalog for trunk restorations.

TUPPERWARE

Museum/Library

Tupperware Museum, The
P.O. Box 2353
Orlando, FL 32802
Phone: 305-847-3111

TYPEWRITERS

(see also ADDING MACHINES; ADVERTISING COLLECTIBLES, Typewriter Related; CALCULATORS)

Club/Association

Early Typewriter Collectors Association
Magazine: ETCetera
Darryl Rehr, Ed.
11433 Rochester Ave. #303
Los Angeles, CA 90025
Phone: 213-477-5229
An internt'l. club for collectors of old office equipment; provides contact with worldwide network of over 500 members; free ads.

Collector

Peter Frei
P.O. Box 500
Brimfield, MA 01010
Phone: 800-942-8968
Wants old typewriters, adding machines, sewing machines, and old vacuum cleaners, etc.

Collector

John Moore
206 Thomas St.
South Plainfield, NJ 07080
Phone: 201-755-8491
Wants pre-1915 typewriters; any odd or unusual typewriter. *

Collector

William Porter
908 Pierce
Birmingham, MI 48009
Phone: 313-647-3876
Olivetti typewriters; also calculators old and new. *

Collector

Jerry Probst
P.O. Box 45
Janesville, WI 53547-0045
Phone: 608-752-2816   FAX: 608-752-7691

Collector

Richard B. Dickerson
620 South Sierra Bonita
Pasadena, CA 91106
Premier collector of typewriters. *

Collector

Mike Brooks
7335 Skyline
Oakland, CA 94611
Phone: 415-339-1751
20 year collector buying early oddball typewriters, braille writers, shorthand machines and other 19th century office machines.

Collector

Jim Rauen
6937 Glenview Dr.
San Jose, CA 95120
Phone: 408-268-2943
Typewriters and other office equipment prior to 1900. *

Dealer
Graham Forsdyke
158 Hampton Rd.
Chingford
London E4 8NT England
Buys, sells and collects mechanical antiques, especially early typewriters.

Expert
Paul Lippman
1216 Garden St.
Hoboken, NJ 07030
Phone: 201-656-5278
Author of "Collector's Guide to American Typewriters."

Expert
Darryl Rehr
11433 Rochester Ave. #303
Los Angeles, CA 90025
Phone: 213-447-5229
Wants pre-1915 typewriters & related advertising, especially typewriters w/o keyboards; send SASE for free information pamphlet.

Museum/Library
Milwaukee Public Museum
800 W. Wells St.
Milwaukee, WI 53233
Phone: 414-278-2702

Periodical
Anglo-American Typewriter Collector's Society
Magazine: Typewriter Times
Paul Lippman
1216 Garden St.
Hoboken, NJ 07030
Phone: 201-656-5278
Quarterly magazine with articles and photos about typewriter history and technology; auction prices, ads, book reviews, etc.

Ribbon Tins
Collector
Hobart D. Van Deusen
28 The Green
Watertown, CT 06795
Phone: 203-945-3456
Wants ribbon tins - small tin boxes used from 1880's to 1950 with graphic designs on them; has duplicates to sell; will help identify.

Collector
Darryl Rehr
11433 Rochester Ave. #303
Los Angeles, CA 90025
Phone: 213-447-5229
Wants tins of all sizes and makes, especially those with unusual shapes & graphics; any amount; send description or photocopy.

UFO'S & UNEXPLAINED PHENOMENA
Collector
Lucius Farish
Route 1, Box 220
Plumerville, AR 72127
Phone: 501-354-2558
Wants books, booklets, periodicals on UFO's, extraterrestrial life, Atlantis, Bigfoot, occultism, unexplained phenomena.

Collector
Samadhi Metaphysical Literature
D.E. Whelan
P.O. Box 170
Lakeview, AR 72642
Phone: 501-431-8830
Wants books/magazines: mysticism, astrology, Atlantis, herbalism, UFO, tarot, crystal balls, the unexplained, etc.; SASE catalog $1.

Misc. Service
UFO Newsclipping Service
Lucius Farish
Route 1, Box 220
Plumerville, AR 72127
Phone: 501-354-2558
Current press reports of UFOs/unexplained phenomena from around the world; newsclippings compiled in 20-page monthly issues; since 1969.

UMBRELLAS
(see also CANES & WALKING STICKS)

Repair Service
Uncle Sam Umbrella Shop
161 West 57th St.
New York, NT 10019
Phone: 212-582-1977
Repairs canes and umbrellas.

UNICORNS
Club/Association
Unicorns Unanimous
248 N. Larchmont Blvd.
Los Angeles, CA 90004 *

U.S. POSTAL SERVICE ITEMS
Club/Association
Cheswick Historical Society
Newsletter: Stamps, Old Letters & History
Steve Pavlina
208 Allegheny Ave.
Cheswick, PA 15024
Phone: 412-274-9106
Focuses on U.S. postal History.

Collector
Tom Mills
Bellevue Rd.
Berlin, MA 01503
*Wants fire alarm and police boxes, cast iron signs and U.S.P.O. pickup boxes; also wants porcelain license plates and signs. **

Dealer
Railway Mail Service Library
Dr. Frank R. Scheer, Curator
12 E. Rosemont Ave.
Alexandria, VA 22301-2325
Phone: 703-549-4095
Send LSASE for free illustrated want list; seeks postmarks, badges, letter boxes, post office-view post cards, etc.; any age or country.

VACUUM CLEANERS
Museum/Library
Hoover Historical Center
Newspaper: Center News
C.A. (Stacy) Krammes, Dir.
2225 Easton Street, NW
North Canton, OH 44720
Phone: 216-499-0287 or 216-499-9200
Boyhood home of W. H. Hoover; has extensive collection of antique and early electric vacuum cleaners & vacuum industry memorabilia.

VALENTINES
(see also HOLIDAY COLLECTIBLES; PAPER COLLECTIBLES)

Auction Service
Evalene Pulati
P.O. Box 1404
Santa Ana, CA 92702
Phone: 714-547-1355

Club/Association
National Valentine Collectors Association
Newsletter: National Valentine Collectors Bulletin
Evalene Pulati
P.O. Box 1404
Santa Ana, CA 92702
Phone: 714-547-1355
The quarterly newsletter focuses on collecting valentines; identification, values, ads.

Expert
Evalene Pulati
P.O. Box 1404
Santa Ana, CA 92702
Phone: 714-547-1355
Author of "Illustrated Valentine Price Guides."

VAUDEVILLE MEMORABILIA
Collector
Mr. J.S.
6 Chancery Ln.
Chico, CA 95926
Wants original Vaudeville sheet music, posters, photos and movie memorabilia.

VENTRILOQUIST ITEMS

(see also PUPPETS; THEATRICAL
MEMORABILIA)

Collector

Alan Ende
40 Morrow Ave.
Scarsdale, NY 10583
Wants dummies and anything relating to ventriloquism. *

Museum/Library

Vent Haven Museum, The
33 West Maple
Fort Mitchell, KY 41011
Phone: 606-341-0461

VETERANS

Civil War

(see also MEDALS, ORDERS &
DECORATIONS)

Club/Association

Civil War Veterans Historical
Association
Newsletter: Veteran, The
Marshall Brighenti, Sec.
RD #2, Box 61
Belle Vernon, PA 15012
Phone: 412-929-7311
*For those interested in preserving the memory of
Union and Confederate veterans of the American
Civil War; also memorabilia.*

Collector

Marshall/Julie Brighenti
RD 2, Box 61
Belle Vernon, PA 15012
Phone: 412-929-7311
*Wants Grand Army of the Republic items:
badges, ribbons, canes, glass, gold testimonial
badges, etc.; also Civil War 22nd PA items.*

Collector

David Maloney
1612 Shookstown Rd.
Frederick, MD 21702
Phone: 301-663-0818 or 301-695-8544
                    FAX: 302-695-6491
*Wants Union and Confederate veteran-related
items: Grand Army of the Republic, United Confederate Veterans, WRC, SUV; any related item.*

Expert

Sons of Union Veterans of the Civil War
Bill Little
55 Windbriar Ln.
Gettysburg, PA 17325
Phone: 717-334-4852
Gettysburg Sons of Union Veterans camp commander; collector of G.A.R and other veteran-related memorabilia and history. *

Expert

Sons of Union Veterans of the Civil War
Richard Schlenker
4112 Heatherfield Rd.
Rockville, MD 20853
Phone: 301-871-6868
S.U.V. commander-in-chief 1982-1983. *

Museum/Library

War Library & Museum of the Military
Order of the Loyal Legion of the U.S.
17th St. & Montgomery Ave.
Philadelphia, PA 19121
Phone: 215-763-6529

Museum/Library

Grand Army of the Republic Civil War
Museum & Library
4278 Griscom St.
Philadelphia, PA 19124-3954
Phone: 215-673-1688 or 215-289-6484
*Civil War Museum & Library; artifacts, personal
memorabilia, paintings, G.A.R. & S.U.V.C.W.
records; open first Sunday or by appt.*

Museum/Library

Grand Army of the Republic Memorial
Hall Museum
State Capitol 419 N.
Madison, WI 53702
Phone: 608-266-1680

Museum/Library

G.A.R. Hall & Museum
308 North Marshall
Litchfield, MN 55355
Phone: 612-693-8911
*Mailing address is as noted above. the museum is
located at 318 N. Marshall, Litchfield, MN.*

Museum/Library

Grand Army of the Republic Memorial &
Veteran's Military Museum
23 E. Downer Pl.
Aurora, IL 60505
Phone: 312-897-7221

Museum/Library

Grand Army of the Republic Memorial
Museum
78 E. Washington St.
Chicago, IL 60602
Phone: 312-269-2926

Periodical

Newsletter: Great Republic, The
Roger L. Heiple
P.O. Box 16
South Lyon, MI 48178
A newsletter about Civil War veterans, their history, activities and memorabilia.

Mexican War

Club/Association

Descendants of Mexican War Veterans
1114 Pacific
Richardson, TX 75081
*A national lineage society open to men and
women.*

VETERINARY MEDICINE ITEMS

Collector

Paul Ferraglio
3332 W. Lake Rd.
Canandaigua, NY 14424
Phone: 716-394-7663
*Wants to buy veterinary medicine items: old surgical instruments, animal medicine bottles and
tins, pamphlets, display cabinets, signs.*

VIET NAM ITEMS

(see also MILITARIA, Insignia; NORTH
VIET NAM & VIET CONG ITEMS)

Expert

Albert Mendez
142-35 38th Ave.
Flushing, NY 11354
Phone: 718-961-2866
*Specializing in Viet Nam military and police
items.*

Insignia

Dealer

M.A. Mendez
142-35 38th Ave.
Flushing, NY 11354
Phone: 718-961-2866
*Buys and sells US military insignia manufactured
in Viet Nam during the Vietnam War.*

VIEW-MASTERS

(see also 3-D PHOTOGRAPHICA, View-
Masters)

VOLKSWAGEN-SHAPED ITEMS

Collector

Mike Wilson
23490 S.W. 82nd
Tualatin, OR 97062
Phone: 503-638-7074
*Wants Volkswagen toys, memorabilia, literature,
etc.*

Collector

Michael Davis
East 1128 Glass
Spokane, WA 99207
*Wants VW toys, games, old advertising, books,
etc.*

WAGONS

(see also BICYCLES; TOYS, Pedal Vehicles; TRICYCLES)

Collector

Art Bransky
R.D. 2, Box 558
Breinigsville, PA 18031
Phone: 215-285-6180
Wants streamline child's wagons and tricycles; also pre-1950 pedal cars and any unusual riding toy.

WALLACE NUTTING

(see also FURNITURE, Wallace Nutting; PRINTS)

Auction Service

Michael Ivankovich Antiques, Inc.
Michael Ivanovich
P.O. Box 2458
Doylestown, PA 18901
Phone: 215-345-6094
Largest auction service for Wallace Nutting prints, books and furniture; conducts 3-4 auctions/yr., each with 300-500 WN pictures.

Club/Association

Wallace Nutting Collectors Club
Newsletter: Wallace Nutting Collectors
  Newsletter
Justine/George Monro
186 Mountain Ave.
North Caldwell, NJ 07006
Phone: 201-226-1713
Helps members learn more about Wallace Nutting, the man and his works.

Expert

Michael Ivankovich Antiques, Inc.
Michael Ivanovich
P.O. Box 2458
Doylestown, PA 18901
Phone: 215-345-6094
Wants pictures, books, furniture; leading collector; also conducts auctions of Wallace Nutting items; author of books on Nutting.

WASHING MACHINES

Maytag

Club/Association

Maytag Collectors Club
Newsletter: Maytag Collectors Club Newsletter
Nate & Charlene Stoller
960 Reynolds Dr.
Ripon, CA 95366
Phone: 209-575-2444
Over 175 members nationwide collecting all types of Maytag items.

Collector

Jeff Barthled
14018 NE 85th St.
Elk River, MN 55330
Phone: 612-441-7059

Expert

Orville Butler
21-10 Stouffer Pl.
Lawrence, KS 66044
Phone: 913-865-2809   FAX: 913-865-2809
Acts as consultant for identification and valuation of old Maytag appliances; assists in locating appliances for collectors.

Expert

Lee Maxwell
35901 WCR 31
Eaton, CO 80615
Phone: 303-454-3856
Collector of old and unusual washing machines, has collection of over 250 pre-1930 Maytag appliances; please send pictures & description.

Man./Prod./Dist.

Maytag Company Archives
Orville Butler, Hist.
1 Dependability Sq.
Newton, IA 50208
Phone: 515-792-7000
Private company archives include paper artifacts, production records, old catalogs; will help identify or date your Maytag machine.

Museum/Library

Jasper County Historical Museum
Hans J. Brosig, Dir.
1700 South 15th Ave. West
P.O. Box 834
Newton, IA 50208
Phone: 515-792-9118
Hold artifact collection of the Maytag Company: washing machines, seed cleaners, ironers, dryers, advertising & promotional items.

Supplier

Maytag Unlimited
3306 Amherst Pike
Madison Heights, VA 24572
Phone: 804-929-4468
New and used engine parts, restoration supplies, engines, etc.

WATCHES

(see also CLOCKS; INSTRUMENTS & DEVICES, Scientific)

Club/Association

National Association of Watch & Clock Collectors, Inc.
Magazine: Bulletin of the NAWCC
Thomas J. Bartels, ExDir
514 Poplar St.
Columbia, PA 17512-2130
Phone: 717-684-8261   FAX: 717-684-0878

The NAWCC is a non-profit and scientific association founded in 1943 and now serving the horological interests of 35,000 hobbyists.

Collector

J. Saeman
P.O. Box 151004
Columbus, OH 43215
Phone: 800-779-1504
*Wants watches, wristwatches, pocket watches: Patek Phillip, Rolex, Movado, LeCoultre, Gruen, Curves, etc. ***

Collector

Myron Palay
4242 Lorain Ave.
Cleveland, OH 44113-3771
Phone: 216-961-7903
Wants contents of watch and clock repair shops, 1 item or entire shop; also wants pre-1700 watches and clocks in any condition.

Collector

Bob Arnell
P.O. Box 313
Grandview, MO 64030
Phone: 816-966-0544
*Wants pens and watches. ***

Dealer

David Searless
University Place Suite 200
124 Mt. Auburn St.
Cambridge, MA 02138
Phone: 617-576-5810   FAX: 617-876-8114
Wants rare watches.

Dealer

Daugherty & Associates
945 Fourth Ave.
Huntington, WV 25701
Phone: 304-522-6758 or 800-444-4367
                           FAX: 304-522-6795
Wants Rolex, Patek Philippe, Vacheron & Constantin: moonphases, repeaters, chronographs, etc. regardless of age.

Dealer

Maundy International Watches
Miles Sandler
P.O. Box 13028
Overland Park, KS 66212
Phone: 800-235-2866 or 913-383-2880
Watches - buying Patek Philippe pocket & wrist watches and fine watches from USA & Europe; largest watch mail-order since 1976.

Dealer

Phil Hodson & Associates
Phil Hodson
Box 820428
Ft. Worth, TX 76182
Phone: 817-589-2112 or 800-726-2112

Wants Rolex, Patek Phillippe and others especially Rolex Daytona Cosmographs and Rolex Oyster Chronographs.

Expert
Arthur Guy Kaplan
P.O. Box 1942
Baltimore, MD 21203
Phone: 301-752-2090 or 301-664-8350
FAX: 301-783-2723
Author of "The Official Price Guide to Antique Jewelry."

Expert
Cooksey Shugart
P.O. Box 3147
Cleveland, TN 37320-347
Phone: 615-479-4813   FAX: 615-479-4813
Author of "The Official Price Guide to Watches."

Expert
Olde Time Antiques
Joe & Wilma Clark
2088 Creekview Ct.
Reynoldsburg, OH 43068
Phone: 614-863-2637 *

Museum/Library
American Clock & Watch Museum
Journal: Timepiece Journal
100 Maple St.
Bristol, CT 06010-5092
Phone: 203-583-6070
Preserves the history of American horology, especially Connecticut and Bristol's role; large displays of clocks & watches.

Museum/Library
National Association of Watch & Clock Collectors Museum, Inc., The
Patricia Tomes
514 Poplar St.
Columbia, PA 17512-2130
Phone: 717-684-8261   FAX: 717-684-0878
The NAWCC museum strives to illustrate the history of timekeeping with a collection of more than 8000 horological items.

Museum/Library
Time Museum, The
Dorothy Mastricola
7801 E. State St.
P.O. Box 5285
Rockford, IL 61125-0285
Phone: 815-398-6000   FAX: 815-398-4700
Has an extensive collection of time-measuring devices from all parts of the world dating from ancient instruments to the atomic clock.

Periodical
Magazine: Watch & Clock Review
2403 Champa St.
Denver, CO 80205
Phone: 303-296-1600   FAX: 303-295-2159

Monthly magazine primarily for new and vintage watch and clock retailers; features articles on watches, clocks and shops.

Character/Comic
Collector
Maggie Kenyon
1 Christopher St.
New York, NY 10014
Phone: 212-675-3213
Wants any comic/character watch, either old or new; will buy single or in quantity.

Collector
Joe Ramos
2207 Manning St.
Bronx, NY 10462
Phone: 212-828-1021
Wants comic & character watches from 30's-50's; any condition; also wants original boxes, bands, parts, etc.; also expert repairs.

Collector
David Welch
RR 2, Box 233
Murphysboro, IL 62966
Phone: 618-687-2282
Wants watches/clocks relating to sports, TV, cartoon, comic, movie characters with original boxes ONLY; also wants empty boxes.

Expert
Norm & Cathy Vigue
62 Bailey St.
Stoughton, MA 02072
Phone: 617-344-5441
Want mint boxed character watches; also point-of-sale signs for same.

Expert
Howard S. Brenner
106 Woodgate Terrace
Rochester, NY 14625
Phone: 716-482-3641
Specializes in mint/boxed examples of comic watches; author of "Collecting Comic Character Clock & Watches."

Periodical
Newsletter: Comic Watch Times
Howard S. Brenner
106 Woodgate Terrace
Rochester, NY 14625
Phone: 716-482-3641

Wrist
Dealer
Horological Artifacts
Paul Duggan
P.O. Box 63
Chelmsford, MA 01824
Phone: 617-256-5966 *

WATCH FOBS
Club/Association
Canadian Association of Watch Fob Collectors
John Carrington
P.O. Box 787
Caledonia
Ontario N0A 1A0 Canada
Phone: 416-765-4836 or 416-664-4576
Dedicated to the collection and preservation of advertising-type watch fobs.

Club/Association
International Watch Fob Association, Inc.
Newsletter: IWFA Newsletter
Ray Rothlisberger
RR 5
Burlington, IA 52601
Phone: 319-752-6749

Collector
John Cline
609 N. East St.
Carlisle, PA 17013
Wants road or farm machinery-related fobs, or fobs advertising fur, traps, powder and gun companies.

Expert
John M. Kaduck
P.O. Box 02152
Cleveland, OH 44102
*Author of "Collecting Watch Fobs." *

Expert
Tony George
29941 Briarcroft
El Toro, CA 92630
Phone: 714-951-1310 *

Advertising
Dealer
Dave Beck
P.O. Box 435
Mediappolis, IA 52637
Phone: 319-394-3943
Buys and sells advertising watch fobs, mirrors and pinbacks; send stamp for illustrated mail auction catalog.

WATER SPRINKLERS
(see also GARDEN HOSE NOZZLES)

Collector
Dale McNaught
202 Josephine Ave.
Madison, WV 25130
Phone: 304-369-6648
Wants old lawn sprinklers, anything pertaining to garden sprinklers & lawn sprinkling devices; brass, cast iron; figural; also advertising.

Dealer

Argyle Antiques
Richard Tucker
P.O. Box 262
Argyle, TX 76226
Phone: 817-464-3752 or 817-335-6133
Buys and sells figural cast iron items: windmill weights, shooting targets, water sprinklers; no repros. or repaired items wanted.

WAX CARVINGS

Museum/Library

Blair Museum of Lithophanes & Carved Waxes
Laurel Blair, Curator
2030 Robinwood Ave.
P.O. Box 4557
Toledo, OH 43620
Phone: 419-243-4115

WEANERS

Calf & Cow

(see also FARM COLLECTIBLES)

Collector

Steve Deer
P.O. Box 477
Greencastle, IN 46135
Phone: 317-653-9437
Wants rare and especially homemade calf and cow weaners.

WEATHERVANES

(see also FOLK ART)

WEAVING EQUIPMENT

(see also LOOMS)

WEDDING COLLECTIBES

(see also BRIDAL COLLECTIBLES)

WESTERN AMERICANA

(see also ART, Western; COWBOY HEROES; HORSE COLLECTIBLES; INDIAN ITEMS; OUTLAW & LAWMAN; PAPER COLLECTIBLES, Western; SADDLES; STAGECOACH ITEMS)

Book Seller

Maverick Distributors
Kenneth Asher
Drawer 7289
Bend, OR 97708
Phone: 503-382-2728 or 800-333-8046
Sells Western Americana books: Indian art & artifacts, bottles, cowboy & horse collectibles, fruit jars, railroad, logging, history. etc.

Club/Association

Working Cowboy
Newspaper: Rope Burns
Bobby Newton
c/o Chamber of Commerce
P.O. Box 35
Gene Autry, OK 73436
Phone: 405-389-5350
Largest listing of western events: bit-spur-collectible shows & auctions, rodeos, roundups, western trade & trappings, etc.

Club/Association

American Cowboy Culture Association
Newsletter: ACCA Newsletter
Alvin G. Davis
P.O. Box 4040
Lubbock, TX 79409
Phone: 806-742-2498
Purpose is to promote all areas of cowboy culture; publishes newsletter, sponsors events relating to cowboys.

Club/Association

National Bit, Spur & Saddle Collectors Association
Newsletter: Spur, The
P.O. Box 3098
Colorado Springs, CO 80934
Members interested in western Americana memorabilia; sponsors shows and auctions.

Club/Association

Western Americana Collectors Society
Roger V. Baker
P.O. Box 620417
Woodside, CA 94062
Phone: 415-851-7188
Interested in American Indian items, cowboy paraphernalia, firearms, knives, saloon antiques, gold rush, mining and other related items.

Collector

Joe Sherwood
P.O. Box 47
Millwood, NY 10546
Send SASE for Cowboy Collectable Guide which contains information about upcoming cowboy auctions and shows.

Collector

Bill Mackin
P.O. Box 70
Meeker, CO 81641
Phone: 303-878-4525
Wants pre-1940's cowboy and tack items: guns, cartridge belts, chaps, law badges, neckerchiefs, brands and brand books, spurs, etc.

Collector

Charlie Smith
1006 NE 4th Ave.
Milton-Freewater, OR 97862
Phone: 503-938-6298

*Wants inlaid spurs, fancy chaps, holsters with money belts, miniature western items, ivory poker chips, back bar bottles, etc. ***

Dealer

Treasure Hunt
L.R. Kauffman
P.O. Box 3862
New Haven, CT 06525
Wants pre-1900 western ephemera, view books, promotional booklets of towns and states; documents on mining, towns, Indians, etc.

Dealer

Trade Routes Antiques
Kurt House
4614 Travis
Dallas, TX 75205
Phone: 214-559-4440
Wants pre-1920 cowboy items: bits, spurs, guns, gunbelts, swords, badges, cattleman antiques, books, manufacturer's catalogs, etc.

Dealer

Old West Antiques & Cowboy Collectibles
Brian Label
1215 Sheridan Ave.
Cody, WY 82414
Phone: 397-587-9014
Issues three catalogs per year of western Americana collectibles: saddles, chaps, spurs, bridles, etc.; also auction news, ads.

Dealer

Argent Express
Hank Clark
P.O. Box 812
Waterford, CA 95386
Phone: 209-874-2640
Buys/sells Western American paper, books, weapons, autographs, vintage coins, photographs, gold & silversmithing, conchos & buttons.

Expert

Bill Mackin
P.O. Box 70
Meeker, CO 81641
Phone: 303-878-4525
Author of "Cowboy and Gunfighter Collectibles."

Expert

American West Archives
Warren Anderson
P.O. Box 100
Cedar City, UT 84721
Phone: 801-586-9497 or 801-586-7323
Buys and sells paper Americana associated with the Western US: old documents, letters, photos, stocks, maps, autographs, prints, etc.

Misc. Service
Food Celebrity Service
Newsletter: Packaged Chili & Jerky Report
Chuck Thompson
P.O. Box 11652
Houston, TX 77293
Phone: 713-442-7200
Cowboy Chuck Wagon food researcher, historian, storyteller; wants postcards of old chuck wagons; columnist and lecturer.

Museum/Library
Rockwell Museum, The
Cedar St. at Denison Pkwy.
Corning, NY 14830
Phone: 607-937-5386
Large collection of glass made by Frederic Carder while he was with Steuben Glass Works; also large collection of western Americana.

Museum/Library
Seven Acres Antique Village & Museum
Randy Donley
8512 S. Union Rd.
Union, IL 60180
Phone: 815-923-2214
Large display of all kinds of Americana, especially from the Wild West.

Museum/Library
Pony Express Museum
914 Penn St.
St. Joseph, MO 64503
Phone: 816-279-0559

Museum/Library
Texas Ranger Hall of Fame & Museum
P.O. Box 2570
Waco, TX 76702
Phone: 817-754-1433

Museum/Library
National Cowgirl Hall of Fame & Western Heritage Center
P.O. Box 1742
Hereford, TX 79045
Phone: 806-364-5252

Museum/Library
Gene Autry Western Heritage Museum
4700 Western Heritage Way
Los Angeles, CA 90027-1462
Phone: 213-677-2000   FAX: 213-660-5721
Collects items relating to the American West, including Western film memorabilia.

Museum/Library
Wells Fargo History Museum
333 S. Grand Ave.
Los Angeles, CA 90071
Phone: 213-253-7166

Museum/Library
Round Up Hall of Fame & Museum
P.O. Box 609
Pendleton, OR 97801
Phone: 800-524-2984

Periodical
Magazine: Westerner, The
P.O. Box 5232
Vienna, WV 26105
Phone: 304-295-3143
Features stories of the Old West, Western firearms, working cattle ranches, Western towns and museums, Western artists, stuntmen, etc.

Periodical
Magazine: Wild West
P.O. Box 385
Mt. Morris, IL 61054-7942
Focuses on the history of the Wild West - lawmen, outlaws, warriors & chiefs, dance hall girls, boomtowns, cattle rustlers, etc.

Periodical
Magazine: Western Horseman
P.O. Box 7980
Colorado Springs, CO 80933
A monthly magazine focusing on western horsemanship and lifestyle.

Periodical
Magazine: Cowboy Magazine
P.O. Box 126
La Veta, CO 81055
For people who enjoy reading about or participating in the cowboy lifestyle; cattle drives, cowboy antiques, rodeos, book reviews,

Periodical
Magazine: Boots
Box 766
Challis, ID 83226
A magazine about cowboy art, music and poetry.

Periodical
Magazine: American Cowboy Poet
P.O. Box 326
Eagle, ID 83616

Repro. Source
Old West Shop/Replica Products
P.O. Box 5232
Vienna, WV 26105
Phone: 304-295-7239
*Sells Russell and Remington prints, Remington bronzes, marshal badges, western guns, western movie posters. **

Photographs
Collector
Tim Gordon
1750 W. Kent
Missoula, MT 59801
Phone: 406-728-1812

Wants early photos stereoviews of the West: western street scenes, saloon interiors, cowboys, Indians, lawmen, hangings, etc.

Dealer
Treasure Hunt
L.R. Kauffman
P.O. Box 3862
New Haven, CT 06525
Issues illus. lists of photographic images of the west; wants pre-1900 western photos or stereo views of historical interest.

Spurs
Periodical
Magazine: Spur Collectors Quarterly
Box 882
Canyon, TX 79015
Phone: 806-655-9938 *

Whiskey Bottles
Club/Association
49'er Historical Bottle Club
John Goetz
P.O. Box 1570
Cedar Ridge, CA 95924
Phone: 916-272-4644
Always glad to provide information on West coast bottles or on club membership.

WESTERN ART & CRAFTS
(see also ART, Western)

Dealer
Kline's Gallery
Alt. 40
Boonsboro, MD 21713-0041
Phone: 301-432-6650
Sells new Southwest American Indian art and crafts: blankets, paintings, sculpture, bronzes, jewelry, etc.

WHALING
(see also NAUTICAL COLLECTIBLES; SCRIMSHAW)

Expert
Stuart M. Frank, Ph.D
P.O. Box 491
Sharon, MA 02067
Phone: 617-784-3017 or 617-784-3280
Specializing in maritime artworks & artifacts: maritime paintings and scrimshaw.

Expert
Mary Malloy
P.O. Box 491
Sharon, MA 02067
Phone: 617-784-3280
Research, consultation; maritime history, material culture, maritime tools & artifacts; NW Coast Indian art.

Museum/Library

Kendall Whaling Museum, The
Newsletter: KWM Newsletter
P.O. Box 297
Sharon, MA 02067
Phone: 617-784-5642
*International collection of whaling artworks &
artifacts specializing in paintings 1600-present,
scrimshaw, tools, gear, prints, etc.*

Museum/Library

New Bedford Whaling Museum
18 Johnny Cake Hill
New Bedford, MA 02740
Phone: 617-997-0046

Museum/Library

Cold Spring Harbor Whaling Museum
P.O. Box 25
Cold Spring Harbor, NY 11724
Phone: 516-367-3418

Museum/Library

Sag Harbor Whaling & Historical Museum
P.O. Box 1327
Sag Harbor, NY 11963
Phone: 516-725-0770

Museum/Library

Pacific Whaling Museum
Sea Life Park
Waimanalo, HI 96795
Phone: 808-259-5177

Periodical

Newsletter: Whalebone
P.O. Box 2834
Fairfax, VA 22031 *

WHISKEY INDUSTRY ITEMS

(see also CERAMICS (ENGLISH), Whisky
Pitchers; PROHIBITION ITEMS)

Museum/Library

Seagram Museum, The
57 Erb Street
Waterloo
Ontario N2L 6C2 Canada
Phone: 519-885-1857

Museum/Library

Oscar Getz Museum of Whiskey History
P.O. Box 41
Bardstown, KY 40004
Phone: 502-348-2999

WHITE HOUSE COLLECTIBLES

Collector

John Reed
1979 Country Club Drive
Huntington Valley, PA 19006
*China, crystal, documents, letters, Christmas
cards, paintings, bronzes, invitations, etc.; anything pertaining to the US presidents. **

China

Repro. Source

United States Historical Society
First & Main Streets
Richmond, VA 23219
Phone: 804-648-4736   FAX: 804-648-0002

WICKER

(see also REPAIR & RESTORATIONS,
Wicker)

Museum/Library

High Museum of Art, The
1280 Peachtree St.
Atlanta, GA 30309
Phone: 404-892-3600   FAX: 404-898-9578

Museum/Library

East Martello Museum
3501 South Roosevelt Blvd.
Key West, FL 33040
Phone: 305-296-3913

WINCHESTER COLLECTIBLES

Collector

James Anderson
P.O. Box 12704
New Brighton, MN 55112
Phone: 612-484-3198
*Items made by Winchester Repeating Arms Co.
(and other gun, cartridge or powder Co's.): tools,
posters, knives, fishing items, etc.*

Expert

American West Archives
Warren Anderson
P.O. Box 100
Cedar City, UT 84721
Phone: 801-586-9497 or 801-586-7323

Museum/Library

Winchester Mystery House, Antique
Products Museum
525 South Winchester Blvd.
San Jose, CA 95128
Phone: 408-247-2000
*Displays cutlery, flashlights, lawn mowers, fish-
ing tackle, and farm tools manufactured by the
Winchester Products company after WWI.*

WINDMILL COLLECTIBLES

Club/Association

Windmill Study Group
301 Thornbridge Dr.
Midland, TX 79703
*Interested in stamps dealing with windmills and
related subject. **

Museum/Library

Volendam Windmill Museum, Inc.
R.D. #1, Box 242
Milford, NJ 08848
Phone: 201-995-4365

Periodical

Newsletter: Windmillers' Gazette
Lindsay T. Baker
P.O. Box 507
Rio Vista, TX 76093
*Only periodical in American devoted exclusively
to windmills and wind power history; author of "A
Field Guide to American Windmills."*

Weights

Collector

Craig Emmerson
Suite 1200
10505 N. 69th St.
Scottsdale, AZ 85253
Phone: 602-998-2213 or 602-991-9638
                    FAX: 602-998-8968
*Collector wants single weights or entire collec-
tions: horses, roosters, bulls, hearts, bells, letters,
etc.; send photo and price.*

Dealer

Argyle Antiques
Richard Tucker
P.O. Box 262
Argyle, TX 76226
Phone: 817-464-3752 or 817-335-6133
*Buys and sells figural cast iron items: windmill
weights, shooting targets, water sprinklers; no rep-
ros. or repaired items wanted.*

Expert

Donald E. Sites
P.O. Box 201
Grinnell, KS 67738
Author of "Windmills and Windmill Weights."

Repro. Source

Treasure Chest
Doug Clemence
436 North Chicago
Salina, KS 67401
Sells reproduction windmill weights.

WINES

Museum/Library

Greyton H. Taylor Wine Museum
R.D. 2
Hammondsport, NY 14840
Phone: 607-868-4814

Periodical

Wine Price File
Book: Wine Price File
William H. Edgerton
P.O. Box 88
Darien, CT 06820
Phone: 203-655-0566   FAX: 203-655-8066
*A semi-annual publication; advice to collectors,
appraisals, valuations, consulting, restaurant
wine lists prepared.*

WIRELESS COMMUNICATIONS

(see also TELEGRAPH ITEMS)

WITCHES

Salem

Collector

C.J. Russell
P.O. Box 499
Winchester, NH 03470
*Wants items with a witch on them such as sterling silver, china, soda bottles, scissors, tea strainers etc. ** *

Collector

L. Richard
200 Knicker Bocker Rd.
Demarest, NJ 07627
*Wants Salem Witch items: postcards, novelties, souvenirs, memorabilia, old or new. ** *

Museum/Library

Salem Witch Museum
19 1/2 Washington Square North
Salem, MA 01970
Phone: 617-744-1692

WIZARD OF OZ

(see also MOVIE MEMORABILIA)

Club/Association

International Wizard of Oz Club, The
Newsletter: Baum Bugle, The
Fred M. Meyer
220 N. 11th St.
Escanaba, MI 49829
Promotes the study and collecting of items relating to L. Frank Baum (1856-1919), The Oz Books, toys, movies, etc.

Collector

Michael Gessel
P.O. Box 748
Arlington, VA 22216
Phone: 703-532-4261
Wants books, posters, games, and advertising related to "The Wizard of Oz"; also wants items by W. W. Denslow.

Collector

Edwin Wilder
Box 175
Nordland, WA 98358
Wants OZ books, all authors, all related.

Expert

Jay Scarfone
6 Westmont
Hershey, PA 17033
Wants all kinds of memorabilia from the 1939 movie "The Wizard of Oz"; ads, souvenirs, posters, lobby cards, coat hangers, dolls, etc.

WOOD

Identification

Misc. Service

Gordon Salter
2208 Lorelei Lane
Wilmington, DE 19810
*Send a wood sample for identification. ** *

Misc. Service

Dr. Michael Taras
5 S. Craggmore Dr.
Salem, SC 29676
Phone: 803-944-0655
*Send a wood sample for identification. ** *

Misc. Service

Center for Wood Anatomy Research, U.S.
Forest Products Laboratory
P.O. Box 5130
Madison, WI 53705
*Send a wood sample for identification. This is a free service offered by the U.S. Department of Agriculture. ** *

WOODBURNING CRAFT ITEMS

(see also PYROGRAPHY)

WOODEN MONEY

Club/Association

International Organization of Wooden
Money Collectors
Newsletter: Bunyan's Chips
P.O. Box 395
Goose Creek, SC 29445
Phone: 803-797-1260 *

Club/Association

Dedicated Wooden Money Collectors
Newsletter: Timber Lines
1028 Azalea Ct.
La Marque, TX 77568
Phone: 409-935-2136 *

Club/Association

American Wooden Money Guild
Newsletter: Old Woody Views
P.O. Box 30444
Tucson, AZ 85751
*"Lignadenarists" are interested in collecting wooden money. ** *

Nickels

Club/Association

American Nickel Collectors Association
Newsletter: Nickel News
Suite 163
736-D St. Andrews
Columbia, SC 29210 *

Collector

Norman Boughton
1356 Buffalo Rd.
Rochester, NY 14624
Phone: 716-235-3969
Wants wooden money issued for celebrations, used as money or issued by restaurant chains such as McDonald's.

WORLD'S FAIRS & EXPOSITIONS

Club/Association

World's Fair Collectors Society, Inc.
Newsletter: Fair News
Michael R. Pender, ExDir
P.O. Box 20806
Sarasota, FL 34276-3806
Phone: 813-923-2590
Focuses on collecting and preserving materials pertinent to the history of World's Fairs and International expositions.

Club/Association

1904 World's Fair Society
Newsletter: World's Fair Bulletin
Max Storm
529 Barcia
St. Louis, MO 63119
Phone: 314-968-2810

Club/Association

World's Fair, Inc.
Journal: World's Fair
Judith Rubin
P.O. Box 339 ABJ
Corte Madera, CA 94976
Phone: 415-924-6035
A quarterly journal of international expositions and events; people, pageantry, planning and politics; articles, ads; free sample.

Collector

Ken Schultz
Box M753
Hoboken, NJ 07030
Phone: 201-656-0966
Wants all items relating to world's fairs and expositions.

Collector

Richard Hebel
Box 1116
Carmel, IN 46032
Phone: 317-848-2977
*Wants '33 World's Fair Memorabilia. ** *

Collector

Max Storm
529 Barcia
St. Louis, MO 63119
Phone: 314-968-2810
Wants any type of memorabilia from the 1904 St. Louis World's Fair: clocks, padlocks, postcards, watches, china, tickets, paper, etc.

Dealer

Bill's St. Louis World's Fair
Willliam "Bill" Pieber
944 Warwick Lane
Ballwin, MO 63011
Phone: 314-227-8930 or 314-827-2889
FAX: 314-827-4353
Buys and sells St. Louis World's Fair (1904) and Louisiana Purchase Exposition items; also all World's Fair items.

Expert

Richard Friz
RFD 2, Box 155
Peterborough, NH 03458
Phone: 603-563-8155 *

Expert

Harvey Dolin & Co.
Harvey & Sandy Dolin
5 Beekman St.
New York, NY 10038
Phone: 212-267-0216
Wants any item pertaining to the 1939 New York World's Fair and the Columbian Fair.

Expert

Raymond's Antiques
Al Raymond
P.O. Box 509
Richfield Springs, NY 13439 *

Expert

Richard Hartzog
P.O. Box 4143
Rockford, IL 61110-0643 *

Expert

D.D. Woollard, Jr.
11614 Old St. Charles Rd.
Bridgeton, MO 63044
Phone: 314-739-4662
Buy, sell, trade World Fair & Exposition memorabilia: major interest in older fairs - 1893 Chicago, 1904 St. Louis, etc.

Museum/Library

Queens Museum, The
Newsletter: Q.M.N.Y. World's Fair
  Newsletter, The
New York City Bldg.
Flushing Meadows Corona Park
Flushing, NY 11368-3398
Phone: 718-592-2405
Focuses on the 1939 and 1964 World's Fairs.

Museum/Library

Buffalo & Erie County Historical
Society
25 Nottingham Ct.
Buffalo, NY 14216
Phone: 716-873-9644

Museum/Library

Atwater Kent Museum - the History
Museum of Philadelphia
15 S. 7th St.
Philadelphia, PA 19143
Phone: 215-922-3031

Museum/Library

Museum of Science & Industry
Keith R. Gill
57th St. & Lake Shore Drive
Chicago, IL 60637
Phone: 312-684-1414   FAX: 312-684-5580

Archives contains documents & photos of the 1893 Columbian Exposition and the 1933-1934 Century of Progress Exposition.

Museum/Library

Presido Army Museum
Presidio Of San Francisco
Bldg. 2
San Francisco, CA 94129
Phone: 415-561-3319

Museum/Library

Petaluma History Museum
20 Fourth St.
Petaluma, CA 94952
Phone: 707-778-4398
Museum of the 1939 San Francisco World's Fair held on Treasure Island, San Francisco Bay.

WORLD WAR MEMORABILIA

(see also MARINE CORPS ITEMS;
MILITARIA; RATIONING RELATED
ITEMS)

YELLOWSTONE PARK COLLECTIBLES

Collector

Jane Graham
109 South 4th Ave.
Bozeman, MT 59715
Wants anything related to Yellowstone Park pre-1930; also anything relating to Montana pre-1950.

ZEPPLINS

(see also AIRSHIPS)

APPENDIX A

AUCTION SERVICES

ADVERTISING COLLECTIBLES

James D. Julia, Inc.
P.O. Box 830
Fairfield, ME 04937
Phone: 207-453-7904   FAX: 207-453-2502

Dave Beck
P.O. Box 435
Mediappolis, IA 52637
Phone: 319-394-3943
Conducts mail auctions of advertising watch fobs, mirrors, pinback buttons, etc.; send stamp for illustrated auction catalog.

Trade Cards

Murray Cards (International) Ltd.
51 Watford Way
Hendon Central
London NW4 3JH England
Stocks and auctions trade cards; also publishes "Cigarette Card Values" - a catalog of cigarette and other trade cards.

Trade Cards (Tobacco)

Murray Cards (International) Ltd.
Newsletter: Cigarette Cards
51 Watford Way
Hendon Central
London NW4 3JH England
Stocks in excess of 20M cigarette & trade cards; monthly specialist auctions; publisher of card values & books on card collecting.

AMUSEMENT PARK ITEMS

Norton Auctioneers of Michigan, Inc.
David A. Norton
Pearl at Monroe
Coldwater, MI 49036
Phone: 517-279-9063
Specializing in the auctioning of amusement rides, carousels, amusement parks, arcades, museums, etc.

ANTIQUITIES

Hesperia Arts
Jonathan Rosen
29 West 57th Street
New York, NY 10019
Specializing in the sale of antiquities.

ARMS & ARMOR

Wallis & Wallis
West Street Auction Galleries
Lewes
East Sussex BN7 2NJ England
Britain's specialist auctioneers of arms, armour, militaria and military orders.

ART

James R. Bakker
370 Broadway Street
Cambridge, MA 02139
Phone: 617-864-7067 *

Philip C. Shute Gallery
Philip Shute
50 Turnpike Street
West Bridgewater, MA 02379
Phone: 508-588-0022 or 508-588-7833
Antique and custom furniture, art, silver, glass and china, collectibles, etc.

Young Fine Art Gallery, Inc.
P.O. Box 313
North Berwick, ME 03906 *

Mystic Fine Arts
47 Holmes Street
Mystic, CT 06255
Phone: 203-572-8873

Swann Galleries, Inc.
104 E. 25th St.
New York, NY 10010
Phone: 212-254-4710   FAX: 212-979-1017
Oldest/largest U.S. auctioneer specializing in rare books, autographs & manuscripts, Judaica, photographs, and works of art on paper.

Christie's East
219 E. 67th St.
New York, NY 10021
Phone: 212-606-0400

Sotheby's
1334 York Ave. at 72nd Street
New York, NY 10021
Phone: 212-606-7000

Christie's
502 Park Ave.
New York, NY 10022
Phone: 212-546-1000

William Doyle Galleries
175 E. 87th St.
New York, NY 10128
Phone: 212-427-2730

Weschler's
William P. Weschler, Jr.
909 E Street NW
Washington, DC 20004
Phone: 202-628-1281 or 800-331-1430
                    FAX: 202-628-2366
Conducts specialized auction sales of art, paintings, prints and graphics.

Frank Boos Gallery, Inc.
420 Enterprise Court
Bloomfield Hills, MI 48013
Phone: 313-332-1500

Chicago Art Gallery, Inc.
Richard Friedman
6039 Oakton Street
Skokie, IL 60077
Phone: 708-677-6080 or 708-677-6081

Selkirk Galleries
4166 Olive Street
St. Louis, MO 63108
Phone: 314-533-1700

Western Heritage Sale
1416 Avenue K
Plano, TX 75074
Phone: 214-423-1500

Texas Art Gallery
1400 Main Street
Dallas, TX 75202
Phone: 214-747-8158

Oriental

Weschler's
William P. Weschler, Jr.
909 E Street NW
Washington, DC 20004
Phone: 202-628-1281 or 800-331-1430
                    FAX: 202-628-2366
Conducts specialized auction sales of antique Oriental Art.

ART DECO

Gallery 68 Auctions
3 Southvale Drive
Toronto
Ontario M46 1G1 Canada *

Christie's East 219 E. 67th St. New York, NY
10021 Phone: 212-606-0400
*Christie's East is well known in the collecting field
for its Art Deco auctions.*

Phillips Fine Art & Auctioneers
406 East 79th St.
New York, NY 10022
Phone: 212-570-4830   FAX: 212-570-2207
*Specializes in the sale of jewelry, paintings,
prints, silver, coins, stamps, toys (especially lead
soldiers), and movie memorabilia.*

William Doyle Galleries
175 E. 87th St.
New York, NY 10128
Phone: 212-427-2730
*Conducts four annual "Belle Epoque" auctions
featuring Art Deco.*

Saugerties Auction Service
16 Livingston Street
Saugerties, NY 12477
Phone: 914-246-9928
*Conducts specialized Art Deco auctions twice a
year.* *

Savoia & Fromm Auction Services
Route 23
South Cairo, NY 12482
Phone: 518-622-8000   FAX: 518-622-9453

Art Deco Auctions, Ltd.
19528 Ventura Blvd. #153
Tarzana, CA 91356
Phone: 818-996-3509
*Specializes in Art Deco posters, lithographs, etch-
ings, and original paintings including artists Icart
and Erte.* *

ARTS & CRAFTS

David Rago's American Arts & Crafts
Auction
Station E
P.O. Box 3592
Trenton, NJ 08629
Phone: 609-585-2546
*Specializing in the sale of American art pottery
and Arts and Crafts items.*

Don Treadway Auctions
Don Treadway
2128 Madison Rd.
Cincinnati, OH 45208
Phone: 513-321-6742   FAX: 513-871-7722
Specializes in the sale of Arts and Crafts pottery.

AUCTION SERVICES (ALL CATEGORIES)

Christie's South Kensington, Ltd.
85 Old Brompton Road
London SW7 3LD England
*Regular sales of furniture, paintings, silver, jew-
elry, ceramics, textiles, books and collectibles; free
verbal valuations weekdays.*

Phillips Auction Gallery
101 New Bond Street
London W1Y 0AS England

Pioneer Auction of Amherst
Jct. Rt. 111 & 63
N. Amherst, MA 01059
Phone: 413-253-9914 *

Caropreso Gallery
136 High Street
Lee, MA 01238
Phone: 413-243-3424 *

Douglas Auctioneers
Douglas B. Bilodeau
Route 5
South Deerfield, MA 01373
Phone: 413-665-3530   FAX: 413-665-2877
*Auction sales year-round, specializing in an-
tiques, fine art, estates, and appraising; also con-
ducts Auctioneering School.*

Skinner, Inc.
357 Main Street
Bolton, MA 01740
Phone: 508-779-6241 or 617-236-1700
                      FAX: 508-779-5144
*Established in 1962, Skinner Inc. is the fifth
largest auction house in the US.*

Willis Henry Auctions
22 Main St.
Marshfield, MA 02050
Phone: 617-834-7774

F.B. Hubley & Co., Inc.
364 Broadway
Cambridge, MA 02139
Phone: 617-876-2030 *

Marc J. Matz Gallery
366-B Broadway
Cambridge, MA 02139
Phone: 617-661-6200 *

Robert C. Eldred & Co.
P.O. Box 796
East Dennis, MA 02641
Phone: 508-385-3116

Richard A. Bourne Auction Co., Inc.
P.O. Box 141
Hyannis Port, MA 02647
Phone: 508-775-0797

Arman Absentee Auctions
P.O. Box 3239
Newport, RI 02840
Phone: 401-683-3100   FAX: 401-683-4044
*Specialize in mail-bid auctions for historical staf-
fordshire, quimper, American glass, paperweights,
bottles, etc.*

Gustave White Auctioneers
P.O. Box 59
Newport, RI 02840
Phone: 401-847-4250 *

Richard W. Withington, Inc.
R.D. 2, Box 440
Hillsboro, NH 03244
Phone: 603-464-3232

Northeast Auctions
Ronald Bourgeault
694 Lafayette Road
Hampton, NH 03842
Phone: 603-926-9800   FAX: 603-926-3545 *

Paul McInnis
356 Exeter Road
Hampton Falls, NH 03844
Phone: 603-778-8989 *

Sanders & Mock Associates, Inc.
Mark Hanson
P.O. Box 37
Tamworth, NH 03886
Phone: 603-323-8749 or 603-323-8784

Richard W. Oliver Auctions
Route One, Plaza One
Kennebunk, ME 04043
Phone: 207-985-3600   FAX: 207-985-7734

F.O. Bailey Auction Gallery
Joy Piscopo
141 Middle Street
Portland, ME 04101
Phone: 207-744-1479   FAX: 207-774-7914 *

James D. Julia, Inc.
P.O. Box 830
Fairfield, ME 04937
Phone: 207-453-7904   FAX: 207-453-2502

Duane Merrill
32 Beacon Street
S. Burlington, VT 05403
Phone: 802-878-2625 *

Winter Associates, Inc.
Regina Madigan
P.O. Box 823
Plainville, CT 06062
Phone: 203-793-0288 or 800-962-2530
*Conducts estate liquidations of antiques, fine fur-
niture, paintings, jewelry, porcelain, glass, etc.*

Litchfield Auction Gallery
Clarence W. Pico
425 Bantam Rd.
P.O. Box 1337
Litchfield, CT 06759
Phone: 203-567-3126   FAX: 203-567-3266
Auction announcements and catalogs available upon request (no subscription).

Berman's Auction Gallery
33 West Blackwell Street
Dover, NJ 07081
Phone: 201-361-3110

Bob Koty Professional Auctioneers
Bob & Clara Koty
P.O. Box 625
Freehold, NJ 07728
Phone: 908-780-1265
Specializes in the auction sale of antiques, collectibles, household contents, estates, etc.

Castner Auction & Appraisal Service
Leon Castner, Pres.
6 Wantage Ave.
Branchville, NJ 07826
Phone: 201-948-3868
Specializing in the sale of local estate contents including antiques and residential contents.

Swann Galleries, Inc.
104 E. 25th St.
New York, NY 10010
Phone: 212-254-4710   FAX: 212-979-1017
Oldest/largest U.S. auctioneer specializing in rare books, autographs & manuscripts, Judaica, photographs, and works of art on paper.

Lubin Galleries, Inc.
Irwin Lubin
30 West 26th Street
New York, NY 10010
Phone: 212-924-3777   FAX: 212-366-9190
Sells furniture, antiques, silver, bronzes, porcelains, oriental rugs, ethnographic art, jewelry, etc.

Christie's East
219 E. 67th St.
New York, NY 10021
Phone: 212-606-0400

Sotheby's
1334 York Ave. at 72nd Street
New York, NY 10021
Phone: 212-606-7000

Guernsey's Auction
108 1/2 East 73rd St.
New York, NY 10021
Phone: 212-794-2280   FAX: 212-744-3638
Auctions unique commodities and collections, e.g. vintage automobiles, marine art, animation cels, Soviet art, posters, etc.

Sotheby's Arcade Auction
1334 York Ave. at 72nd Street
New York, NY 10021
Phone: 212-606-7409
Focuses on the sale of collectibles: toys, dolls, games, banks, etc.

Christie's
502 Park Ave.
New York, NY 10022
Phone: 212-546-1000

Phillips Fine Art & Auctioneers
406 East 79th St.
New York, NY 10022
Phone: 212-570-4830   FAX: 212-570-2207
Specializes in the sale of jewelry, paintings, prints, silver, coins, stamps, toys (especially lead soldiers), and movie memorabilia.

Harmer Rooke Galleries
3 East 57th Street
New York, NY 10022
Phone: 212-751-1900   FAX: 212-758-1713

William Doyle Galleries
175 E. 87th St.
New York, NY 10128
Phone: 212-427-2730

South Bay Auctions, Inc.
485 Montauk Highway
East Moriches, NY 11940
Phone: 516-878-2909 or 516-878-2933
                           FAX: 516-878-1863

Marvin Cohen Auctions
Box 425, Routes 20 & 22
New Lebanon, NY 12125
Phone: 518-794-7477

Savoia & Fromm Auction Services
Route 23
South Cairo, NY 12482
Phone: 518-622-8000   FAX: 518-622-9453

Mid-Hudson Auction Galleries
1 Idlewild Ave.
Cornwall-On-Hudson, NY 12520
Phone: 914-534-7828 *

Doyle Auctioneers
R.D. 3 Box 137
Fishkill, NY 12524
Phone: 914-896-9492

Iroquois Auction Gallery
Box 66
Port Henry, NY 12974
Phone: 518-546-7003 *

Mapes Auctioneers & Appraisers
David W. Mapes
1600 Vestal Parkway West
Vestal, NY 13850
Phone: 607-754-9193   FAX: 607-786-3549

Collectors Auction Services
P.O. Box 13732
Seneca, PA 16346
Phone: 814-677-6070   FAX: 814-677-6070
An absentee mail bid auction handling quality antiques and collectibles.

Roan Bros. Auction Gallery
R.D. 3 Box 118
Cogan Station, PA 17728
Phone: 717-494-0170

Freeman/Fine Arts of Phila.
Leslie Lynch Lynch, ASA
1808-10 Chestnut St.
Philadelphia, PA 19103
Phone: 215-563-9275 or 215-563-9453
                           FAX: 215-563-8236
A full-service auction tradition since 1805 with new ideas to serve both buyer and seller with auction and appraisal services.

Alderfer Auction Company
501 Fairground Road
Hatfield, PA 19440
Phone: 215-368-5477   FAX: 215-368-9055

Pennypacker Auction Center
1540 New Holland Rd.
Reading, PA 19607 *

Weschler's
William P. Weschler, Jr.
909 E Street NW
Washington, DC 20004
Phone: 202-628-1281 or 800-331-1430
                           FAX: 202-628-2366
A full service auction service for art, antiques, decorative accessories, household furnishings, and commercial liquidations.

Sloan's
Ben Hastings
4920 Wyaconda Rd.
Rockville, MD 20852
Phone: 301-468-4911

Richard Opfer Auctioneering, Inc.
1919 Greenspring Drive
Timonium, MD 21093
Phone: 301-252-5035

Harris Auction Galleries
8783-875 N. Howard St.
Baltimore, MD 21201
Phone: 301-728-7040 *

Fredericktowne Auction Gallery
Thom Pattie
5305 Jefferson Pike
Frederick, MD 21701
Phone: 301-473-5566 or 800-962-1305

Jim Depew Galleries
1860 Piedmont Road, NE
Atlanta, GA 30324
Phone: 404-874-2286 *

Garth's Auction, Inc.
P.O. Box 369
Delaware, OH 43015
Phone: 614-362-4771

Wolf's Auctioneers
1239 West 6th St.
Cleveland, OH 44113
Phone: 216-575-9653 or 800-526-1991
                    FAX: 216-621-8011

Dumouchelle Art Galleries
Lawrence Dumouchelle
409 East Jefferson Ave.
Detroit, MI 48226
Phone: 313-963-6255 or 313-963-0248
                    FAX: 313-963-8199
A fine arts auction house; rugs, paintings, jewelry, porcelain, silver, art glass, toys, dolls, furniture, books, sculpture, etc.

Dunning's Auction Service, Inc.
755 Church Rd.
Elgin, IL 60123
Phone: 312-741-3483   FAX: 708-741-3589
Premier mid-American auction firm selling antiques, fine art, jewelry, American Indian art, and real estate.

Hanzel Galleries, Inc.
1120 South Michigan Avenue
Chicago, IL 60605
Phone: 312-922-6234

Chase Gilmore Art Galleries
724 West Washington
Chicago, IL 60606
Phone: 312-648-1690 *

Leslie Hindman Auctions
215 West Ohio St.
Chicago, IL 60610
Phone: 312-670-0010   FAX: 312-670-4248

Manion's Auction House
P.O. Box 12214
Kansas City, KS 66112
Phone: 913-299-6692   FAX: 913-299-6792
A mail-bid auction company specializing in militaria, baseball cards, toys, glass, railroad items, and other collectibles.

Woody Auction Company
P.O. Box 618
Douglass, KS 67039
Phone: 316-746-2694

Morton M. Goldberg Auction Galleries, Inc.
547 Baronne St.
New Orleans, LA 70113
Phone: 504-592-2300   FAX: 504-592-2311 *

Pettigrew Auction Company
1645 South Tejon Street
Colorado Springs, CO 80906
Phone: 719-633-7963

Butterfield & Butterfield
7601 Sunset Blvd.
Los Angeles, CA 90046
Phone: 213-850-7500

Butterfield & Butterfield
220 San Bruno Ave.
San Francisco, CA 94103
Phone: 415-861-7500

AUTOGRAPHS

T. Vennett-Smith Chartered Auctioneer
Richard Davie
11 Nottingham Road, Gotham
Nottingham NG11 OHE England
Great Britain's leading professional autograph auction house, specializing in bi-monthly auctions of fine and varied autographs.

Swann Galleries, Inc.
104 E. 25th St.
New York, NY 10010
Phone: 212-254-4710   FAX: 212-979-1017
Oldest/largest U.S. auctioneer specializing in rare books, autographs & manuscripts, Judaica, photographs, and works of art on paper.

AUTOMOBILES

Kruse International
P.O. Box 190
Auburn, IN 46706
Phone: 219-925-5600   FAX: 219-925-5467
Specializes in auctioning antique, classic and other special interest automobiles, planes, motorcycles, trucks, etc.

AVIATION MEMORABILIA

Dale C. Anderson Co.
Dale C. Anderson
4 W. Confederate Ave.
Gettysburg, PA 17325
Conducts mail bid auctions of military and civilian aviation memorabilia.

BICYCLES

Bill's Classic Cyclery
Bill Feasel
712 Morrison St.
Fremont, OH 43420
Phone: 419-334-7844   FAX: 419-334-2845
Conducts auctions specializing in the sale of classic bicycles, tricycles, wagons and toy pedal vehicles.

BOOKS

New Hampshire Book Auctions
Richard & Mary Sykes
92 Woodbury Rd.
P.O. Box 86
Weare, NH 03281
Phone: 603-529-1700 or 603-529-7432
Specializes in the auction of books, maps, prints and ephemera.

Swann Galleries, Inc.
104 E. 25th St.
New York, NY 10010
Phone: 212-254-4710   FAX: 212-979-1017
Oldest/largest U.S. auctioneer specializing in rare books, autographs & manuscripts, Judaica, photographs, and works of art on paper.

Waverly Auctions
Dale Sorenson
4931 Cordell Ave.
Bethesda, MD 20814
Phone: 301-951-8883   FAX: 301-718-8375
Specializes in the auction of graphic art, books, paper, atlases, prints, postcards and other paper ephemera.

Baltimore Book Co., Inc.
Chris Bready
2112 N. Charles St.
Baltimore, MD 21218
Phone: 301-659-0550
Buys and auctions books, prints, paintings, autographs, photographs, and ephemera.

Samuel Yudkin & Associates
2109 Popkins Lane
Alexandria, VA 22307
Phone: 703-768-1858
Booksellers who conduct book and print auctions. *

California Book Auction Galleries, Inc.
5225 Wilshire Blvd. #324
Los Angeles, CA 90036
Phone: 213-939-6202

California Book Auction Galleries, Inc.
Suite 730
965 Mission St.
San Francisco, CA 94103
Phone: 415-243-0650   FAX: 415-243-0789
Specialty auction house dealing in fine and rare books, manuscripts and maps.

BOTTLES

B.B.R. Auctions
2 Strafford Ave., Elsescar
Barnsley
S. Yorkshire S74 8AA England
England's leading specialists and auction house for antique bottles, pot lids and related advertising material.

Norman C. Heckler & Company
79 Bradford Corner Road
Woodstock Valley, CT 06282
Phone: 203-974-0682 or 203-974-1634
Specializes in the sale of early glass and bottles; Heckler & Co. sold a single bottle for $40,700 at auction in 1990.

Glass Works Auctions
James Hagenbuch
P.O. Box 187
East Greenville, PA 18041
Phone: 215-679-5849
Specializes in the auction of bottles, flasks, barber bottles, jars, bitters bottles, scent bottles, shaving mugs, and related go-withs.

Miniature Liquor

Frank Callan
P.O. Box 777
Brewster, MA 02631
Phone: 508-896-6491
Specializes in the auction of mini liquor bottles & figurals from all over the world; quarterly auction catalog has 800-1000 items.

BREWERIANA

Lynn Geyer Auctions
Lynn Geyer
329 West Butler Dr.
Phoenix, AZ 85021
Phone: 602-943-2283
Conducts annual specialized auction on all aspects of breweriana and soda-pop; also contemporary steins, mugs & drinking glasses.

CAMERAS & CAMERA EQUIPMENT

Christie's South Kensington, Ltd.
Michael Pritchard
85 Old Brompton Road
London SW7 3LD England
An international auction house specializing in the sale of rare and collectible cameras, photographic equipment and optical toys.

CAROUSELS & CAROUSEL FIGURES

Guernsey's Auction
108 1/2 East 73rd St.
New York, NY 10021
Phone: 212-794-2280   FAX: 212-744-3638
Specializes in the sale of carousel figures.

Auction Under the Big Top
Tommy Sciortino
3723 N. Nebraska Aave.
Tampa, FL 33603
Phone: 818-248-5387 or 813-932-1782
            FAX: 813-248-5387
Specializes in the sale of circus equipment and memorabilia, carousels, amusement devices, coin-ops, toys, etc.

CARTOON ART

Russ Cochran
P.O. Box 469
West Plains, MO 65775
Phone: 417-256-2224
Conducts phone bid auctions of original comic art and illustrations.

CERAMICS

Majolica

Michael G. Strawser
P.O. Box 332
Wolcottville, IN 46795
Phone: 219-854-2895 or 219-854-3979
Specializing in Majolica auctions in the U.S.

CERAMICS (AMERICAN)

Stoneware

Marlin G. Denlinger Auctions
R.R. 3, Box 3775
Morrisville, VT 05661
Phone: 802-888-2774
Conducts specialized auctions of decorated stoneware. *

Arthur Auctioneering
Wayne Arthur
R.D. 2 Box 155
Hughesville, PA 17737
Phone: 717-584-3697
Conducts specialized sales of decorated stoneware.

CEREAL BOXES

Memory Tree
1546-10 Simpson St.
Madison, WI 53713
Phone: 608-222-2418   FAX: 608-222-6935
Conducts specialty mail auctions of cereal boxes and backs, character items, premiums, rings and classes.

CHARACTER COLLECTIBLES

Memory Tree
1546-10 Simpson St.
Madison, WI 53713
Phone: 608-222-2418   FAX: 608-222-6935
Conducts specialty mail auctions of cereal boxes and backs, character items, premiums, rings and classes.

Cartoon & Comic

Comic Strip & Character Memorabilia
P.O.Box 385H
La Mirada, CA 90637
Phone: 213-943-9380
Conducts mail-bid auctions of cartoon and comic character memorabilia. *

CHRISTMAS COLLECTIBLES

Robert J. Connelly, ASA
666 Chenango St.
Binghamton, NY 13901
Phone: 607-722-9593   FAX: 607-722-1266
Conducts specialty Christmas sales.

Bruce & Shari Knight
2475 Signal Hill Road
Springfield, OH 45504
Conducts specialty Christmas sales. *

CIRCUS COLLECTIBLES

Auction Under the Big Top
Tommy Sciortino
3723 N. Nebraska Aave.
Tampa, FL 33603
Phone: 818-248-5387 or 813-932-1782
            FAX: 813-248-5387
Specializes in the sale of circus equipment and memorabilia, carousels, amusement devices, coin-ops, toys, etc.

COIN-OPERATED MACHINES

Home Amusement Co., Inc.
11910 Parklawn Drive
Rockville, MD 20852
Phone: 301-468-0070
Specialized auctions of carousel horses, slot machines, juke boxes, arcade games, collectibles, country store, trade stimulators, etc.

Auction Under the Big Top
Tommy Sciortino
3723 N. Nebraska Aave.
Tampa, FL 33603
Phone: 818-248-5387 or 813-932-1782
            FAX: 813-248-5387
Specializes in the sale of circus equipment and memorabilia, carousels, amusement devices, coin-ops, toys, etc.

COINS & CURRENCY

Spink & Son, Ltd.
King Street
St. James's
London SW1Y 6QS England
Auctioneers and dealers of coins (ancient to present), medals, orders, tokens, decorations and other numismatic items.

Bowers & Merena, Inc.
Box 1224
Wolfeboro, NH 03894
Phone: 603-569-5095 or 800-458-4646
FAX: 603-569-5319
Specializes in coin auctions.

Stack's Coin Galleries
123 West 57th St.
New York, NY 10019
Phone: 212-582-5955   FAX: 212-245-5018
Specializes in coin auctions.

Superior Galleries
9478 West Olympic Blvd.
Beverly Hills, CA 90212-4299
Phone: 800-421-0754   FAX: 213-203-0496
Specialists in the auctioning of coins. Offers grading services. *

Coins (Ancient)

Classic Numismatic Group, Inc.
Box 245
Quarryville, PA 17566-0245
Phone: 717-786-4013
Specializes in the auction sale of classical coins: Greek, Roman, Byzantine, Medieval, British, foreign, etc.

COLLECTIBLES

Nostalgia Publications, Inc.
Allan Petretti
21 South Lake Dr.
Hackensack, NJ 07601
Phone: 201-488-4536
Conducts mail-bid auctions of Coca-Cola and other advertising memorabilia and collectibles. *

Doyle Auctioneers
R.D. 3 Box 137
Fishkill, NY 12524
Phone: 914-896-9492

Hake's Americana & Collectibles Auction
Ted Hake
P.O. Box 1444
York, PA 17405
Phone: 717-848-1333   FAX: 717-848-4977
Specializing in mail-bid auctions of Disneyana, historical Americana, toys, premiums, political items, character and other collectibles.

Kurt R. Krueger Auctions
160 N. Washington St.
Iola, WI 54945
Phone: 715-445-3845
Specializing in the mail-bid auction of tokens, advertising, brewery items, Western Americana, autographs, sports, etc.

Mail Bid Auction
G.E. Moore
P.O. Box 414
Yucca Valley, CA 92286
FAX: 619-365-9668

Conducts mail-bid auctions of collectibles: books, coins, medals, Disney, theater, valentines, art, railroad, medical/dental, etc.

DECOYS

Bird

Richard W. Oliver Auctions
Route One, Plaza One
Kennebunk, ME 04043
Phone: 207-985-3600   FAX: 207-985-7734

James D. Julia, Inc.
Frank M. Schmidt
P.O. Box 830
Fairfield, ME 04937
Phone: 207-453-7904   FAX: 207-453-2502 *

DOLLS

Sotheby's
34-35 New Bond Street
London W1A 2AA England
Conducts specialty auctions of tinplate toys, diecasts, trains, antique dolls, teddy bears, automata.

Richard W. Withington, Inc.
R.D. 2, Box 440
Hillsboro, NH 03244
Phone: 603-464-3232

Theriault's Auction
P.O. Box 151
Annapolis, MD 21404
Phone: 301-224-3655   FAX: 301-224-2515

Cobb's Doll Auction
David M. Cobb
803 Franklin Ave.
Columbus, OH 43205
Phone: 614-252-8844
Conducts quarterly antique doll auctions; send $22 for catalog; send address for advance notice flyer.

McMasters' Auction
James E. McMasters
P.O. Box 1755
Cambridge, OH 43725
Phone: 800-842-3526 or 614-432-4320
FAX: 614-432-3191

International Doll Exhibitions & Auctions, Ltd.
P.O. Box 54
Morton Grove, IL 60053 *

Frasher's
Rt. 1, Box 142
Oak Grove, MO 64075
Phone: 816-625-3786 *

J & J Galleries
Paul Johnson
P.O. Box 20764
Kansas City, MO 64195-0764
Phone: 816-386-2972 or 312-878-0928
Specializing in antique dolls and related items. *

FARM MACHINERY

Blaine Renzel
P.O. Box 222
Emigsville, PA 17318
Phone: 717-764-6412
Specializes in the sale of old and new farm machinery and equipment.

Waverly Sale Co.
Bill Dean
Box 355
Waverly, IA 50677
Phone: 319-352-3177
Specializes in the sale of old and new farm machinery and equipment.

FIREARMS

J.C. Devine, Inc. Auctioneers
Savage Road
P.O. Box 413
Milford, NH 03055
Phone: 603-673-4967   FAX: 603-672-0328
Specializes in the sale of antique firearms and edged weapons. *

FIRE FIGHTING MEMORABILIA

Maritime Auctions
Chuck Deluca
P.O. Box 322
York, ME 03909
Phone: 207-363-4247
Author of "Firehouse Memorabilia - A Collector's Reference."

FISHING COLLECTIBLES

Richard A. Bourne Auction Co., Inc.
P.O. Box 141
Hyannis Port, MA 02647
Phone: 508-775-0797

Richard W. Withington, Inc.
R.D. 2, Box 440
Hillsboro, NH 03244
Phone: 603-464-3232

GAMBLING COLLECTIBLES

Full House
Gene Hochman
P.O. Box 4057
Boynton Beach, FL 33424-4057
Conducts mail auctions specializing in playing cards and other gambling memorabilia. *

GAMES

Richard W. Withington, Inc.
R.D. 2, Box 440
Hillsboro, NH 03244
Phone: 603-464-3232

GLASS

Skinner, Inc.
357 Main St.
Bolton, MA 01740
Phone: 508-779-6241 or 617-236-1700
                    FAX: 508-779-5144
Established in 1962, Skinner Inc. is the fifth largest auction house in the US.

Richard A. Bourne Auction Co., Inc.
P.O. Box 141
Hyannis Port, MA 02647
Phone: 508-775-0797

Arman Absentee Auctions
P.O. Box 3239
Newport, RI 02840
Phone: 401-683-3100   FAX: 401-683-4044
Specializing in mail-bid auctions of early American glass, historical Staffordshire, paperweights.

Glass Works Auctions
James Hagenbuch
P.O. Box 187
East Greenville, PA 18041
Phone: 215-679-5849
Specializes in the auction of bottles, flasks, barber bottles, jars, bitters bottles, scent bottles, shaving mugs, and related go-withs.

Art

Early Auction Co.
123 Main St.
Milford, OH 45150
Phone: 513-831-4833

Carnival

Woody Auction Company
P.O. Box 618
Douglass, KS 67039
Phone: 316-746-2694

Early American

Norman C. Heckler & Company
79 Bradford Corner Road
Woodstock Valley, CT 06282
Phone: 203-974-0682 or 203-974-1634
Specializes in the sale of early glass and bottles; Heckler & Co. sold a single bottle for $40,700 at auction in 1990.

GLASSES

Drinking

Glasses, Mugs & Steins Auction
Pete Kroll
P.O. Box 207
Sun Prairie, WI 53590
Phone: 608-837-4818
A semi-annual mail auction featuring collectible advertising glasses, mugs, & steins: beer, soda, cartoon, Disney, rootbeer, sports, etc.

HISTORICAL AMERICANA

Ben Corning
10 Lilian Road Ext.
Framingham, MA 01701
Phone: 617-872-2229
*Specializes in mail-bid auctions of political items and historical Americana. ***

Rex Stark Auctions
49 Wethersfield Road
Bellingham, MA 02019
Phone: 508-966-0994
Conducts mail auctions of quality historical Americana: political, early military, advertising, sports, etc.

Rita-Mobley Auctions Inc.
P.O. Box 53
South Glastonbury, CT 06073
Phone: 203-633-3076
Specializing in historical items, ephemera, autographs, photographs, etc.

William A. Fox Auctions, Inc.
676 Morris Avenue
Springfield, NJ 07081
Phone: 201-467-2366
Specializes in the sale of Americana, ephemera, and U.S. and foreign stamps and covers.

David Frent
P.O. Box 455
Oakhurst, NJ 07755
Phone: 201-922-0768
*Specializes in mail-bid auctions of political items and historical Americana. ***

Swann Galleries, Inc.
104 E. 25th St.
New York, NY 10010
Phone: 212-254-4710   FAX: 212-979-1017
Oldest/largest U.S. auctioneer specializing in rare books, autographs & manuscripts, Judaica, photographs, and works of art on paper.

Historicana
Robert Coup
P.O. Box 348
Leola, PA 17540
Phone: 717-656-7780
Specializes in mail-bid auctions of toys, collectibles, political items and historical Americana.

Ohio Boys Video Auction - the Dixeys
626 Arlington Avenue
Mansfield, OH 44903
*Specializes in mail-bid auctions of political items and historical Americana. ***

Anderson Auction
Al Anderson
P.O. Box 644
Troy, OH 45373
Phone: 513-339-0850
Specializes in mail-bid auctions of political items and historical Americana.

Political Gallery, The
Tom Slater
1325 W. 86th St.
Indianapolis, IN 46260
Phone: 317-257-0863
Specializing in mail-bid auctions of Disneyana, historical Americana, toys, political items, and other collectibles.

U.I. "Chick" Harris
Box 20614
St. Louis, MO 63139
Phone: 314-352-8623
Collector/specialist in all types of political Americana; conducts specialized mail-auctions of political and historical Americana.

HOLIDAY COLLECTIBLES

Holiday Auction, The
Cindy Chipps
4027 Brooks Hill Rd.
Brooks, KY 40109
Phone: 502-955-9238
Holds monthly mail auction of a wide variety of holiday items from the common to the very rare; send #10 SASE for free catalog.

HORSE-DRAWN VEHICLES

Martin Auctioneers Inc.
Larry L. Martin
P.O. Box 477
Intercourse, PA 17534
Phone: 717-768-8108   FAX: 717-768-7714
Specializes in the sale of horse drawn carriages, buggies, hitch wagons, tack and other horse-related items.

Carriages

Martin Auctioneers, Inc.
P.O. Box 71
Blue Ball, PA 17506
Phone: 717-768-8108
Specializes in the sale of carriages, sleds and other horse-drawn vehicles.

INDIAN ITEMS

Robert W. Skinner, Inc.
Route 117
Bolton, MA 01740
Phone: 508-779-6241 *

Jack Sellner P.O. Box 308 Fremont, CA
94537-0308
Conducts annual Indian auctions.

JUDAICA

Swann Galleries, Inc.
104 E. 25th St.
New York, NY 10010
Phone: 212-254-4710   FAX: 212-979-1017
Oldest/largest U.S. auctioneer specializing in rare books, autographs & manuscripts, Judaica, photographs, and works of art on paper.

MACHINERY & EQUIPMENT

Construction

Vilsmeier Auction Company, Inc.
Walter Vilsmeier
Rt. 309
Montgomeryville, PA 18936
Phone: 215-699-5833
Specializes in the sale of used machinery and equipment; tractor crawlers, loader backhoes, air compressors, graders, etc.

Forke Brothers
830 NBC Center
Lincoln, NE 68508
Phone: 402-475-3631
*Specializes in the sale of used machinery and equipment; tractor crawlers, loader backhoes, air compressors, graders, etc. *

Miller & Miller
2525 Ridgmar Blvd.
Fort Worth, TX 76116
Phone: 817-732-4888
*Specializes in the sale of used machinery and equipment; tractor crawlers, loader backhoes, air compressors, graders, etc. *

Ritchie Bros.
821 Weld County Rd. 27
Brighton, CO 80601
Phone: 800-547-3555
*Specializes in the sale of used machinery and equipment; tractor crawlers, loader backhoes, air compressors, graders, etc. *

MARBLES

Block's Box
Robert S. Block
P.O. Box 51
Trumbull, CT 06611
Phone: 203-261-3223 or 203-783-1690
Conducts mail-bid auctions of marbles received from collectors, dealers, estates, museums and others.

Dan & Gretchen Turner
P.O. Box 210992
Nashville, TN 37221
Phone: 615-952-3699
Conducts marble mail auctions using VHS video tape/catalog.

MEDALS

ORDERS & DECORATIONS

Wallis & Wallis
West Street Auction Galleries
Lewes
East Sussex BN7 2NJ England
Britain's specialist auctioneers of arms, armour, militaria and military orders.

Spink & Son, Ltd.
King Street
St. James's
London SW1Y 6QS England
Auctioneers and dealers of coins (ancient to present), medals, orders, tokens, decorations and other numismatic items.

MILITARIA

Graf Klenau OHG
8000 Munchen 1
Postfach 122, Germany
*A well established auction house handling all kinds of worldwide military-related antiques of high quality. *

Jan K. Kube
Herzostrasse 34
8 Muchen 40, Germany
*A well established auction house handling all kinds of worldwide military-related antiques of high quality. *

Wallis & Wallis
West Street Auction Galleries
Lewes
East Sussex BN7 2NJ England
Britain's specialist auctioneers of arms, armor, militaria and military orders.

Kelley's
553 Main Street
Woburn, MA 01801
Phone: 617-935-3389 or 617-272-9167
Conducts several auctions per year of militaria from the Revolution to present day.

Mohawk Arms Inc.
P.O. Box 399
Utica, NY 13503
Phone: 315-724-1234
Specializes in uniforms, headgear, badges, award documents, ephemera, daggers, swords, photo albums, prints, books, art items, etc.

AAG, Militaria Mail Auction
Stephen Flood
20 Grandview Ave.
Wilkes-Barre, PA 18702
Phone: 717-829-1500 or 717-822-5300
                    FAX: 717-822-9992
Specializing in mail-bid auctions of militaria from Revolutionary War to Viet Nam with emphasis on WWII; all countries.

Roger S. Steffen Historical Militaria
Roger S. Steffen
14 Murnan Road
Cold Spring, KY 41076
Phone: 606-431-4499
*Conducts mail-bid auctions of military items and antique firearms. *

Manion's Auction House
P.O. Box 12214
Kansas City, KS 66112
Phone: 913-299-6692   FAX: 913-299-6792
The largest auction service in the U.S. handling only military-related antiques.

Centurion, The
219 North Jackson
El Dorado, AR 71730
*Conducts militaria mail-bid auctions. *

Der Gauleiter
P.O. Box 721288
Houston, TX 77272
*Conducts bi-monthly auctions of military items specializing in Third Reich. *

RECAPT Historical Militaria Auction
Service
Robert C. Thomas, Jr.
P.O. Box 1792
Santa Ana, CA 92702
Phone: 714-748-7459   FAX: 714-748-7492
Specializes in the sale of historical militaria.

MOVIE MEMORABILIA

Phillips Fine Art & Auctioneers
Henry Kurtz
406 East 79th St.
New York, NY 10022
Phone: 212-570-4830   FAX: 212-570-2207
Specializes in the sale of jewelry, paintings, prints, silver, coins, stamps, toys (especially lead soldiers), and movie memorabilia.

NAUTICAL COLLECTIBLES

Richard A. Bourne Auction Co., Inc.
P.O. Box 141
Hyannis Port, MA 02647
Phone: 508-775-0797

Maritime Auctions
Chuck Deluca
P.O. Box 322
York, ME 03909
Phone: 207-363-4247

NEWSPAPERS

Vintage Cover Story
Bob Raynor
P.O. Box 975
Burlington, NC 27215
Phone: 919-584-6990
Buys, sells historic newspapers from 1760 through 1945; also conducts periodic mail/phone bid auctions of old collectible newspapers.

ORDNANCE

Crittenden Schmitt Archives
Dr. J.R. Schmitt
Court House P.O. Box 4253
Rockville, MD 20849
Only video auctions in the world of ordnance material: collector ammunition, bombs, grenades, mines; inert only, from all countries.

ORIENTALIA

Japanese Items

Robert C. Eldred & Co.
P.O. Box 796
East Dennis, MA 02641
Phone: 508-385-3116

PAPER COLLECTIBLES

Waverly Auctions
Dale Sorenson
4931 Cordell Ave.
Bethesda, MD 20814
Phone: 301-951-8883   FAX: 301-718-8375
Specializes in the auction of graphic art, books, paper, atlases, prints, postcards and other paper ephemera.

Historical

Rita-Mobley Auctions Inc.
P.O. Box 53
South Glastonbury, CT 06073
Phone: 203-633-3076
Specializing in historical items, ephemera, autographs, photographs, etc.

Western

American West Archives
Warren Anderson
P.O. Box 100
Cedar City, UT 84721
Phone: 801-586-9497 or 801-586-7323
Buys and sells paper Americana associated with the Western US: old documents, letters, photos, stocks, maps, autographs, prints, etc.

PHOTOGRAPHS

Swann Galleries, Inc.
104 E. 25th St.
New York, NY 10010
Phone: 212-254-4710   FAX: 212-979-1017
Oldest/largest U.S. auctioneer specializing in rare books, autographs & manuscripts, Judaica, photographs, and works of art on paper.

Larry Gottheim Fine Early Photographs
33 Orton Ave.
Binghamton, NY 13905
Phone: 607-797-1685
*Conducts mail-bid auctions of fine early photographs, tintypes, daguerreotypes, etc. ***

PIANO ROLLS

QRS Music Rolls, Inc.
Dan Wilke
1026 Niagara St.
Buffalo, NY 14213
Phone: 716-885-4600   FAX: 716-885-7510
Offers bi-monthly auctions by mail of original antique piano rolls; sorry, no consignments accepted.

POLITICAL COLLECTIBLES

Ben Corning
10 Lilian Road Ext.
Framingham, MA 01701
Phone: 617-872-2229
*Specializes in mail-bid auctions of political items and historical Americana. ***

Rex Stark Auctions
Rex Stark
49 Wethersfield Road
Bellingham, MA 02019
Phone: 508-966-0994
Conducts mail auctions of quality historical Americana: political, early military, advertising, sports, etc.

David Frent
P.O. Box 455
Oakhurst, NJ 07755
Phone: 201-922-0768
*Specializes in mail-bid auctions of political items and historical Americana. ***

Historicana
Robert Coup
P.O. Box 348
Leola, PA 17540
Phone: 717-656-7780
Specializes in mail-bid auctions of toys, collectibles, political items and historical Americana.

Ohio Boys Video Auction - the Dixeys
626 Arlington Avenue
Mansfield, OH 44903
*Specializes in mail-bid auctions of political items and historical Americana. ***

Anderson Auction
Al Anderson
P.O. Box 644
Troy, OH 45373
Phone: 513-339-0850
Specializes in mail-bid auctions of political items and historical Americana.

Political Gallery, The
Tom Slater
1325 W. 86th St.
Indianapolis, IN 46260
Phone: 317-257-0863
Specializing in mail-bid auctions of Disneyana, historical Americana, toys, political items, and other collectibles.

Local, The
Robert M. Platt
P.O. Box 159
Kennedale, TX 76060
Specializing in the mail-bid auctions of pin-bac political buttons of governors, congressional mem bers, mayors, state officials, etc.

POSTCARDS

Sally S. Carver Postcard Mail Auctions
179 South St.
Chestnut Hill, MA 02167
Phone: 617-469-9175
*Specializes in better quality postcards. ***

McClintock PC Sales
John H. McClintock
P.O. Box 1765
Manassas, VA 22110
Phone: 703-368-2757
Conducts 4 to 5 illustrated postcard mail auctions per year; also promotes 9 postcard shows per year.

POSTERS

Miscellaneous Man
George Theofiles
Box 1776
New Freedom, PA 17349
Phone: 717-235-4766   FAX: 717-235-2853
Conducts mail-bid poster auctions.

Poster Mail Auction Co.
R. Neil/Elaine Reynolds
#2 Patrick St.
Box 133
Waterford, VA 22190
Phone: 703-822-3574
Conducts 4 to 6 mail/telephone auctions per year of original vintage posters; 4 catalogs for $12.

RADIO SHOW PREMIUMS

Memory Tree
1546-10 Simpson St.
Madison, WI 53713
Phone: 608-222-2418   FAX: 608-222-6935

Conducts specialty mail auctions of cereal boxes and backs, character items, premiums, rings and classes.

RAILROAD COLLECTIBLES

Depot Attic, The
Fred N. Arone
377 Ashford Ave.
Dobbs Ferry, NY 10522
Phone: 914-693-5858
Conducts auctions specializing in railroad paper ephemera, books hardware, silverware and chinaware; all misc. railroad items.

RECORDS

Antique Phonograph Center
Floyd Silver
Hwy. 206
P.O. Box 274
Vincentown, NJ 08088
Phone: 609-859-8617
Conducts special mail auctions of rare and unusual 78 rpm Edison diamond discs and cylinder records; $2 for catalog.

SHAKER ITEMS

Willis Henry Auctions
22 Main St.
Marshfield, MA 02050
Phone: 617-834-7774

SHEET MUSIC

Beverly A. Hamer Sheet Music Sales
Beverly A. Hamer
P.O. Box 75
East Derry, NH 03041
Phone: 603-432-3528
Wants old collectible sheet music; publishes a set price list and conducts auctions of collectible sheet music; free search service.

SOFT DRINK COLLECTIBLES

Coca-Cola

Nostalgia Publications
Allan Petretti
21 S. Lake Dr.
Hackensack, NJ 07601
Phone: 201-488-4536
Conducts semi-annual mail-bid auctions of coca-cola related advertising items; catalogs are $8 for three auctions.

SOLDIERS

Toy

Wallis & Wallis
Glenn Butler
West Street Auction Galleries
Lewes
East Sussex BN7 2NJ England
Britain's specialist auctioneers of die-cast & tin plate toys & models including model soldiers.

Toy Soldier Information Service
Hank Anton
92 Swain Ave.
Meriden, CT 06450
Phone: 203-237-5356
Conducts monthly dimestore toy soldier auctions. *

Phillips Fine Art & Auctioneers
Henry Kurtz
406 East 79th St.
New York, NY 10022
Phone: 212-570-4830   FAX: 212-570-2207
Specializes in the sale of jewelry, paintings, prints, silver, coins, stamps, toys (especially lead soldiers), and movie memorabilia.

Gene Parker
Rt. 1 Box 108
Sugar Grove, IL 60554
Conducts auctions and publishes lists of dimestore soldiers. *

SPORTS COLLECTIBLES

Baseball

Lelands
151 W. 28th St. #7E
New York, NY 10001
Phone: 212-971-3111 *

Golf

Sporting Antiquities
Kevin C. McGrath
47 Leonard Road
Melrose, MA 02176
Phone: 617-662-6588
Sells antique golf collectibles through auction and private sales; buys high quality gold paintings, prints, clubs, books, balls, etc.

Old Golf Shop, Ltd.
John & Morton Olman
325 W. Fifth St.
Cincinnati, OH 45202
Specialize in golf auctions.

STAMP COLLECTING

Harmers of New York, Inc.
14 East 33rd. Street
New York, NY 10016
Phone: 212-532-3700
Harmers specializes in the sale of stamps, but also sells paper items such as autographs, manuscripts, maps, etc.

Covers (First Day)

FDC Publishing Co.
Michael Mellone
P.O. Box 206
Stewartsville, NJ 08886
Conducts monthly mail auctions exclusively for First Day Covers.

STEINS

F.T.S. Inc.
Ron Fox
416 Throop St.
N. Babylon, NY 11704
Phone: 516-669-7232   FAX: 516-669-7232
Send for free quarterly stein auction catalogs with photos, descriptions and estimates.

Kirsner's Auctions
Gary Kirsner
P.O. Box 8807
Coral Springs, FL 33075
Phone: 305-344-9856   FAX: 305-344-4421
Six to seven cataloged auctions per year; steins and related items; also specialty auctions of Limited Edition and retired collectibles.

Les Paul, Steinologist
Les Paul
Suite A
2615 Magnolia St.
Oakland, CA 94607
Phone: 415-832-2615   FAX: 415-832-2616
Conducts mail-bid stein auctions.

TOKENS

City Coin & Token Company
904 W. Broadway
Muskogee, OK 74401
Phone: 918-683-2646 *

TOOLS

Richard Crane Auctions
Richard Crane
63 Poor Farm Rd.
Hillsboro, NH 03244
Phone: 603-478-5723
Specializes in the auction of antique tools.

TOYS

Sotheby's
34-35 New Bond Street
London W1A 2AA England
Conducts specialty auctions of tinplate toys, diecasts, trains, antique dolls, teddy bears, automata.

Wallis & Wallis
Glenn Butler
West Street Auction Galleries
Lewes
East Sussex BN7 2NJ England
Britain's specialist auctioneers of die-cast & tin plate toys & models including model soldiers.

Toy-A-Day
Box 98
South Hadley, MA 01075
Phone: 20-879-5799 or 203-879-5899
Specializes in the mail bid auction sale of contemporary collectible toys.

Skinner, Inc.
357 Main Street
Bolton, MA 01740
Phone: 508-779-6241 or 617-236-1700
                    FAX: 508-779-5144
*Established in 1962, Skinner Inc. is the fifth
largest auction house in the US.*

New England Auction Gallery
Martin Krim
16 Herbert Ave.
West Peabody, MA 01960
Phone: 508-535-3140   FAX: 508-535-7522
Mail-bid auction service for toys and collectibles.

Richard W. Withington, Inc.
R.D. 2, Box 440
Hillsboro, NH 03244
Phone: 603-464-3232

Smith House Toy Sales
Herb & Barb Smith
P.O. Box 336
Eliot, ME 03903
Phone: 207-439-4614
*Conducts four specialty mail-bid toy auctions
each year.* *

Lloyd Ralston Toy Auction
447 Stratfield Road
Fairfield, CT 06432
Phone: 203-366-3399

Sotheby's
1334 York Ave. at 72nd Street
New York, NY 10021
Phone: 212-606-7000

Christie's East
219 E. 67th St.
New York, NY 10021
Phone: 212-606-0400

Phillips Fine Art & Auctioneers
406 East 79th St.
New York, NY 10022
Phone: 212-570-4830   FAX: 212-570-2207
*Specializes in the sale of jewelry, paintings,
prints, silver, coins, stamps, toys (especially lead
soldiers), and movie memorabilia.*

Stephen Leonard Auctions
P.O. Box 127
Albertson, L.I., NY 11507
Phone: 516-742-0979

Hake's Americana & Collectibles Auction
Ted Hake
P.O. Box 1444
York, PA 17405
Phone: 717-848-1333   FAX: 717-848-4977
*Specializing in mail-bid auctions of Disneyana,
historical Americana, toys, premiums, political
items, character and other collectibles.*

Historicana
Robert Coup
P.O. Box 348
Leola, PA 17540
Phone: 717-656-7780
*Specializes in mail-bid auctions of toys, collect-
ibles, political items and historical Americana.*

Barrett/Bertoia Auctions
1217 Glenwood Dr.
Vineland, NJ 18630
Phone: 609-692-4092
Specializing in antique toys and collectibles sales.

Noel Barrett Auctions
P.O. Box 1001
Carversville, PA 18913
Phone: 215-297-5109

Ted Maurer Auctions
1931 N. Charlotte Street
Pottstown, PA 19464
Phone: 215-323-1573

Richard Opfer Auctioneering, Inc.
1919 Greenspring Drive
Timonium, MD 21093
Phone: 301-252-5035

Phil Savino
Rt. 2, Box 76
Micanopy, FL 32667
*Conducts mail-bid auctions of various toy catego-
ries.* *

Auction Under the Big Top
Tommy Sciortino
3723 N. Nebraska Aave.
Tampa, FL 33603
Phone: 818-248-5387 or 813-932-1782
                    FAX: 813-248-5387
*Specializes in the sale of circus equipment and
memorabilia, carousels, amusement devices,
coin-ops, toys, etc.*

Character

New England Auction Gallery
Martin Krim
P.O. Box 2273
West Peabody, MA 01960
Phone: 508-535-3140   FAX: 508-535-7522
*Full color illustrated catalogs; specializes in sales
of Disney, TV and cartoon items from 1920-1970:
toys, wind ups, robots, space toys.*

Optical

Christie's South Kensington, Ltd.
Michael Pritchard
85 Old Brompton Road
London SW7 3LD England
*Specializes in the sale of optical toys such as
persistence of vision devices, stereoscopes, magic
lanterns/slides, etc.*

Space & Robot

Lloyd Ralston Toy Auction
447 Stratfield Road
Fairfield, CT 06432
Phone: 203-366-3399

TRAINS

Toy

Greenberg Publishing Company, Inc.
Bruce C. Greenberg
7566 Main St.
Sykesville, MD 21784
Phone: 301-795-7447

Continental Auctions
Heinz A. Mueller
P.O. Box 193
Sheboygan, WI 53801 *

VALENTINES

Evalene Pulati
P.O. Box 1404
Santa Ana, CA 92702
Phone: 714-547-1355

WALLACE NUTTING

Michael Ivankovich Antiques, Inc.
Michael Ivanovich
P.O. Box 2458
Doylestown, PA 18901
Phone: 215-345-6094
*Largest auction service for Wallace Nutting
prints, books and furniture; conducts 3-4 auc-
tions/yr., each with 300-500 WN pictures.*

APPENDIX B

MATCHING SERVICES

CERAMICS

Flow Blue

Country Oaks Antiques
7116 Shadow Oaks
Memphis, TN 38125
Buys and sells flow blue on national market; provides locator service; send $2 and LSASE for inventory list.

CERAMICS (AMERICAN DINNERWARE)

Gladding-McBean/Franciscan

Deleen Enge
912 N. Signal
Ojai, CA 93203
Phone: 805-646-2549
Specializing in mail order sales of Franciscan (trade name used by Gladding McBean and Co.) dinnerware; author of "Franciscan Ware."

Warwick China Co.

Ackerman Antiques
Box 2310
Athens, OH 45701

CERAMICS (CONTINENTAL)

Haviland

Harrison's Antiques
Peg Harrison
2417 Edgewater Dr.
Orlando, FL 32804
Phone: 305-425-6481
Matching service for Haviland, china, sterling and antique decorative accessories. *

Walker's Matching Service
Box 357
Athens, OH 45701
Phone: 614-593-5631
Buys and sells French or American patterns of Haviland.

E.C. Sales
Ed Cunningham
47 Coventry
Anderson, IN 46012
Phone: 317-643-4127
If possible, please send Schleiger number with your request. *

Seekers, The
9014 Roos Road
Houston, TX 77036
Phone: 713-777-4430
Send for list of all Haviland China matching services. *

Auld Lang Syne
7600 Highway 120
Jamestown, CA 94237
Phone: 209-984-DISH
Pattern locators.

CERAMICS (ORIENTAL)

Noritake

Noritake Co., Inc.
75 Seaview Drive
Secaucus, NJ 07094
Phone: 201-319-0600   FAX: 201-319-1962 *

COLLECTIBLES (MODERN)

Ornaments (Hallmark)

David & Pennie Scheirer
Suite 299
700-U E. Redlands Blvd.
Redlands, CA 92373
Phone: 714-794-9233
Will find lowest priced dealers for any particular Hallmark ornament or Merry Miniature; avoid the middleman markups; send SASE for info.

DINNERWARE

William Ashley Ltd.
Suite 209
50 Bloor St.
West Toronto M4W 3L8 Canada
Phone: 416-964-2500   FAX: 416-964-2500
Discontinued pattern service.

Old China Patterns Ltd.
1560 Brimley Rd.
Scarborough
Ontario M1P 3G9 Canada
Phone: 416-299-8880   FAX: 416-299-4721
International matching service for dinnerware by major English and American manufacturers. *

Ross Simmons
136 Route 5
Warwick, RI 02886
Phone: 401-463-3100 or 800-556-7376
                       FAX: 401-463-8599
Sells new, active patterns of Royal Doulton, Minton, Wedgwood, Noritake, Villeroy & Boch, Royal Worcester, Lenox, etc.

Thurber's
2158 Plainfield Pike, Unit 1
Cranston, RI 02921
Phone: 401-942-0488 or 800-848-7237
                       FAX: 401-942-5601

China By Pattern
P.O. Box 129
Farmington, CT 06034
Phone: 203-678-7079
International matching service. All china patterns/manufacturers. *

Lanac Sales
73 Canal St.
New York, NY 10002
Phone: 212-925-6422 *

Past & Presents
65-07 Fitchess St.
Rego Park, NY 11374
Phone: 718-896-5146
Matching and locating service for Coalport, Derby, Franciscan, Gorham, Lenox, Metlox, Mikasa, Minton, Noritake, and others.

Pattern Finders
P.O. Box 206
Port Jefferson Station, NY 11776
Phone: 516-928-5158
All major brands of dinnerware and crystal stocked in huge inventory; locating service for hard to find patterns; Rosenthal specialists.

Old China Patterns Ltd.
Dept. CIC
P.O. Box 290
Fineview, NY 13640
Phone: 315-482-3829   FAX: 315-482-5827
Buys and sells internationally; since 1966; specializing in English & American china; charter member Inter. Assoc. of Dinnerware Matchers.

China Match
Freda Bell
9 Elmford Rd.
Rochester, NY 14606
Phone: 716-426-2783 or 716-338-3781
Replacements of discontinued china, stoneware, glass and crystal stemware.

Replacements Ltd.
Lea Ann Mills
P.O. Box 26029
Greensboro, NC 27420
Phone: 919-697-3000   FAX: 919-697-3100
China, crystal and flatware (obsolete, active and inactive).

China Cabinet
P.O. Box 266
Clearwater, SC 29822
Phone: 803-593-9655
Features a number of Metlox Potteries patterns. *

China Chasers
2380 Peachtree Corners Circle
Norcross, GA 30092
Phone: 404-441-9146
China and crystal replacements. *

Johnson Brothers Replacements
3576 Clairmont Rd.
Atlanta, GA 30319
Phone: 404-634-1194 *

Joyful Ventures
P.O. Box 4995
Ocala, FL 32678 *

Abrahante's Tableware Matching Service
Suite 209
7175 SW 47th St.
Miami, FL 33155
Phone: 305-661-1456
American, English and Japanese manufacturers of discontinued patterns of china, crystal and flatware.

Jewel Box
P.O. Box 145
Albertville, AL 35950
Phone: 205-878-3301 *

China Mater
99 West Carlos Rd.
Memphis, TN 38117
Phone: 901-685-6983 *

Barron's
P.O. Box 994
Novi, MI 48376
Phone: 800-538-6340

Jacquelynn's China Matching Service
Jacquelynn Ives
219 N. Milwaukee St.
Milwaukee, WI 53202
Phone: 414-272-8880
Discontinued Coalport, Franciscan, Lenox, Minton, Spode, Royal Doulton, Wedgwood, Pickard, and other china patterns bought & sold.

China & Crystal Replacements
P.O. Box 187
Excelsior, MN 55331
Phone: 612-474-6418
Discontinued and active china, dinnerware and crystal bought and sold.

Patterns of the Past
513 S. Main St.
Princeton, IL 61356
Phone: 805-875-1944 *

Dining Elegance, Ltd.
Dept. CIC
P.O. Box 4203
St. Louis, MO 63163
Phone: 314-865-1408

Listing of patterns in stock sent upon request; $1.

International Dinnerware Matchers
  Association
E. Wallace
P.O. Box 4203
St. Louis, MO 63163
An association of dinnerware matchers. *

Locators, Inc.
908 Rock St.
Little Rock, AR 72202
Phone: 501-371-0858 or 800-367-9690
Carries out-of-production (discontinued) china and crystal, and discontinued as well as active sterling flatware patterns.

Seekers, The
9014 Roos Road
Houston, TX 77036
Phone: 713-523-9710 *

Ettelman's Discontinued China & Crystal
Mrs. David Solka, Pres.
P.O. Box 6491
Corpus Christi, TX 78466
Phone: 512-888-8391
Buy/sell inactive patterns of china by Caselton, Flintridge, Franciscan, Haviland, Lenox, Oxford and Syracuse.

International Association of Dinnerware
  Matchers
P.O. Box 50125
Austin, TX 78763-0125
Phone: 512-472-1548
IADM is a group of independent dinnerware matchers in the US & Canada organized to promote honesty and integrity within the profession.

A&A Dinnerware Locators
Larry & Anne McDonald
P.O. Box 50222
Austin, TX 78763-0222
Phone: 512-472-1548 or 512-264-1054
Locate/match discontinued china, earthenware, etc.; all major manufacturers: American, European, Japanese; primarily mail order.

Jo Hancock
2318 61st
Lubbock, TX 79412
Phone: 806-792-2557 *

Walter Drake Silver & China Exchange
94 Drake Building
Colorado Springs, CO 80940
Phone: 719-596-3140 or 800-525-9291
              FAX: 719-593-5321
Active and inactive silver and china tableware replacements. For their Insurance Replacement Department call 800-525-2274.

Wood Jewelers
848 East Main St.
Santa Paula, CA 93060
Phone: 805-525-5547 *

China Traders
Suite 220
690 Los Angeles Ave.
Simi Valley, CA 93065
Phone: 805-527-5440
A discontinued china replacement service; buys and sells most discontinued china patterns.

Silver Lane Antiques
P.O. Box 322
San Leandro, CA 94577
Phone: 415-483-0632
Buys and sells discontinued patterns by major American and English china companies; also American sterling flatware.

Table Treasures
P.O. Box 4265
Stockton, CA 95204
Phone: 209-463-3607
Buy, sell and locate discontinued patterns in china, earthenware and crystal. American, English and Japanese manufacturers.

Patterns Unlimited International
Warren & Betty Roundhill
Dept. CIC
P.O. Box 15238
Seattle, WA 98115
Phone: 206-523-9710
Buy, sell and appraise discontinued tableware patterns of china, silver and glass.

FLATWARE

Dirilyte

Mrs. Kay's Sterling, Stainless &
Silverplate
Dept. JA1-92
P.O. Box 74184
Los Angeles, CA 90004-0184
Phone: 213-661-6279
Matching service for DISCONTINUED FLATWARE only; takes trade-in's; does insurance appraisals; nation-wide network of pickers, suppliers.

Silverplate

Barron's
P.O. Box 994
Novi, MI 48376
Phone: 800-538-6340

Walter Drake Silver & China Exchange
94 Drake Building
Colorado Springs, CO 80940
Phone: 719-596-3140 or 800-525-9291
              FAX: 719-593-5321

Active and inactive silver and china tableware replacements. For their Insurance Replacement Department call 800-525-2274.

Mrs. Kay's Sterling, Stainless & Silverplate
Dept. JA1-92
P.O. Box 74184
Los Angeles, CA 90004-0184
Phone: 213-661-6279
Matching service for DISCONTINUED FLATWARE only; takes trade-in's; does insurance appraisals; nation-wide network of pickers, suppliers.

Abbey's Perfect Match
Attn: Coleen
P.O. Box 75603
Los Angeles, CA 90075
Phone: 213-913-3472
Purchases store closeouts of discontinued flatware; also offers great discounts on current patterns.

Stainless Steel

Barron's
P.O. Box 994
Novi, MI 48376
Phone: 800-538-6340

Mrs. Kay's Sterling, Stainless & Silverplate
Dept. JA1-92
P.O. Box 74184
Los Angeles, CA 90004-0184
Phone: 213-661-6279
Matching service for DISCONTINUED FLATWARE only; takes trade-in's; does insurance appraisals; nation-wide network of pickers, suppliers.

Abbey's Perfect Match
Attn: Coleen
P.O. Box 75603
Los Angeles, CA 90075
Phone: 213-913-3472
Purchases store closeouts of discontinued flatware; also offers great discounts on current patterns.

Sterling Silver

Ross Simmons
136 Route 5
Warwick, RI 02886
Phone: 401-463-3100 or 800-556-7376
FAX: 401-463-8599
Sells new, active patterns for Gorham, Reed & Barton, Wallace, Towle, Lunt, Kirk-Stieff, International.

Thurber's
2158 Plainfield Pike, Unit 1
Cranston, RI 02921
Phone: 401-942-0488 or 800-848-7237
FAX: 401-942-5601

Lanac Sales
73 Canal St.
New York, NY 10002
Phone: 212-925-6422 *

Past & Presents
65-07 Fitchess St.
Rego Park, NY 11374
Phone: 718-896-5146
Matching and locating service for Coalport, Derby, Franciscan, Gorham, Lenox, Metlox, Mikasa, Minton, Noritake, and others.

Edward G. Wilson Inc.
Edward Wilson
1802 Chestnut St.
Philadelphia, PA 19103
Phone: 215-563-7369
Replaces active, inactive, and obsolete sterling and coin silver.

Kent Lambert
113 N. Charles St.
Baltimore, MD 21202
Phone: 301-355-3390 *

Replacements Ltd.
Lea Ann Mills
P.O. Box 26029
Greensboro, NC 27420
Phone: 919-697-3000   FAX: 919-697-3100
China, crystal and flatware (obsolete, active and inactive).

Beverly Bremer Silver Shop
3164 Peachtree Road NE
Atlanta, GA 30305
Phone: 404-261-4009 *

Abrahante's Tableware Matching Service
Suite 209
7175 SW 47th St.
Miami, FL 33155
Phone: 305-661-1456
American, English and Japanese manufacturers of discontinued patterns of china, crystal and flatware.

Barron's
P.O. Box 994
Novi, MI 48376
Phone: 800-538-6340

Jane Rosenow
Rt. #1, Box 177
Galva, IL 61434
Phone: 309-932-3953
*100's of patterns. *

Locators, Inc.
908 Rock St.
Little Rock, AR 72202
Phone: 501-371-0858 or 800-367-9690

Carries out-of-production (discontinued) china and crystal, and discontinued as well as active sterling flatware patterns.

Walter Drake Silver & China Exchange
94 Drake Building
Colorado Springs, CO 80940
Phone: 719-596-3140 or 800-525-9291
FAX: 719-593-5321
Active and inactive silver and china tableware replacements. For their Insurance Replacement Department call 800-525-2274.

Mrs. Kay's Sterling, Stainless & Silverplate
Dept. JA1-92
P.O. Box 74184
Los Angeles, CA 90004-0184
Phone: 213-661-6279
Matching service for DISCONTINUED FLATWARE only; takes trade-in's; does insurance appraisals; nation-wide network of pickers, suppliers.

Silver Lane Antiques
P.O. Box 322
San Leandro, CA 94577
Phone: 415-483-0632
Buys and sells discontinued patterns by major American and English china companies; also American sterling flatware.

Sterling Shop, The
P.O. Box 595
Silverton, OR 97381
Phone: 503-873-6315
Sterling and silverplate flatware matching service.

Patterns Unlimited International
Warren & Betty Roundhill
Dept. CIC
P.O. Box 15238
Seattle, WA 98115
Phone: 206-523-9710
Buy, sell and appraise discontinued tableware patterns of china, silver and glass.

GLASS

Candlewick

Ackerman Antiques
Box 2310
Athens, OH 45701

Crystal

Thurber's
2158 Plainfield Pike, Unit 1
Cranston, RI 02921
Phone: 401-942-0488 or 800-848-7237
FAX: 401-942-5601

Past & Presents
65-07 Fitchess St.
Rego Park, NY 11374
Phone: 718-896-5146

Matching and locating service for Coalport, Derby, Franciscan, Gorham, Lenox, Metlox, Mikasa, Minton, Noritake, and others.

Pattern Finders
P.O. Box 206
Port Jefferson Station, NY 11776
Phone: 516-928-5158
All major brands of dinnerware and crystal stocked in huge inventory; locating service for hard to find patterns; Rosenthal specialists.

China Match
Freda Bell
9 Elmford Rd.
Rochester, NY 14606
Phone: 716-338-3781
Replacements of discontinued china, stoneware, glass and crystal stemware.

Replacements Ltd.
Lea Ann Mills
P.O. Box 26029
Greensboro, NC 27420
Phone: 919-697-3000   FAX: 919-697-3100
China, crystal and flatware (obsolete, active and inactive).

China Chasers
2380 Peachtree Corners Circle
Norcross, GA 30092
Phone: 404-441-9146
China and crystal replacements. *

Abrahante's Tableware Matching Service
Suite 209
7175 SW 47th St.
Miami, FL 33155
Phone: 305-661-1456
American, English and Japanese manufacturers of discontinued patterns of china, crystal and flatware.

Barron's
P.O. Box 994
Novi, MI 48376
Phone: 800-538-6340

China & Crystal Replacements
P.O. Box 187
Excelsior, MN 55331
Phone: 612-474-6418
Discontinued and active china, dinnerware and crystal bought and sold.

Dining Elegance, Ltd.
Dept. CIC
P.O. Box 4203
St. Louis, MO 63163
Phone: 314-865-1408
List of patterns in stock available upon request; $1.

Locators, Inc.
908 Rock St.
Little Rock, AR 72202
Phone: 501-371-0858 or 800-367-9690
Carries out-of-production (discontinued) china and crystal, and discontinued as well as active sterling flatware patterns.

A&A Dinnerware Locators
Larry & Anne McDonald
P.O. Box 50222
Austin, TX 78763-0222
Phone: 512-472-1548 or 512-264-1054
Locate/match discontinued crystal patterns; all major manufacturers: American, European, Japanese; primarily mail order.

Table Treasures
P.O. Box 4265
Stockton, CA 95204
Phone: 209-463-3607
Buy, sell and locate discontinued patterns in china, earthenware and crystal. American, English and Japanese manufacturers.

Patterns Unlimited International
Warren & Betty Roundhill
Dept. CIC
P.O. Box 15238
Seattle, WA 98115
Phone: 206-523-9710

Buy, sell and appraise discontinued tableware patterns of china, silver and glass.

Elegant

Red Horse Inn Antiques
420 1st Ave. N.W.
Plainview, MN 55964
Phone: 507-534-3511
Specializes in matching glass by Cambridge, Fostoria, Morgantown, Heisey, Tiffin, Duncan and Fry; no European glass companies in stock.

Ettelman's Discontinued China & Crystal
P.O. Box 6491
Corpus Christi, TX 78466
Phone: 512-888-8391
Buys/sells inactive patterns of elegant glassware by Cambridge, Duncan, Fostoria, Heisey, Lenox and Tiffin.

Lalique

Tops & Bottoms Club
Madeleine France
P.O. Box 15555
Plantation, FL 33318
Phone: 305-584-0009   FAX: 305-584-0014
Matches Lalique perfume bottle tops and bottoms.

Pattern

Kieningers
5159 Ridge Rd. East, R.D. 3
Williamson, NY 14589
Has thousands of pieces in stock; hundreds of patterns; will try to match. *

Val St. Lambert

Establishment Dubois
Avenue Brugman 219, 1180
Brussels, Belgium
Val St. Lambert also sold in the US through Bailey, Banks & Biddle stores. *

APPENDIX C

REPAIR AND RESTORATION SERVICES

ART

Oriental

Dobson Studios
Janice & Dennis Dobson
810 N. Daniel St.
Arlington, VA 22201
Phone: 703-243-7363
Conservator of Oriental screens, scrolls and wood block prints; repairs and restoration to other paper items as well.

AUTOMOBILES

Classic Coach Works
Bob Burroughs
4937-C Green Valley Rd.
Monrovia, MD 21770
Phone: 301-831-6666
Restores classic automobiles.

AUTOMOBILIA

Instruments

John Wolf & Co.
4550 Wood St.
Willoughby, OH 44094

BANKS

Sy Schreckinger
P.O. Box 104
East Rockaway, NY 11518
Offers professional, museum quality repair, restoration and cleaning of iron and tin mechanical and still banks.

BAROMETERS

Den of Antiquity
138 Charles Street
Boston, MA 02114
Phone: 617-367-6190
*Repairs and restores antique mercury barometers. **

Henry Witzenberger
15 Po Lane
Hicksville, NY 11801
Phone: 516-935-7432
*Repairs and restores antique mercury and aneroid barometers; also repairs clocks. **

Charles Edwin Antiques
Chuck Probst
P.O. Box 1340
Louisa, VA 23093
Phone: 703-967-0416
Buys, sells, repairs.

BILLIARD RELATED ITEMS

Time After Time
5 Padanaran Rd.
Danbury, CT 06811
*Wants pool tables, cues and accessories; buys, sells and restores. **

BOOKS

Book Doctor, The
P.O. Box 68
Harrisburg, OH 43126
Phone: 800-848-7918
*Does handcrafted bookbinding, family bible restorations, book restoration, leather binding, etc. **

Harden Ballantine Bookcrafts
202 North Walnut St.
Yellow Springs, OH 45387
Phone: 513-767-7417
*Bookbinder. Disbound books repaired. **

Don E. Sanders Bookbiner
Don E. Sanders
1116 Pinion Dr.
Austin, TX 78748
Phone: 512-282-4774
20 years experience; custom binding & cases, restoration and repair.

Adolphus Bindery
P.O. Box 2085
Austin, TX 78768
Phone: 512-444-6616
*Bookbinder specializing in restoration. **

BRASS ITEMS

Brass & Copper Polishing Shop
Don Reedy
13 South Carroll St.
Frederick, MD 21701
Phone: 301-663-4240 or 301-662-5503
Repairs and polishes brass and copper items.

CAMERAS & CAMERA EQUIPMENT

Cameratek
Cliff Ratcliff
1780 N. Market St.
Frederick, MD 21701
Phone: 301-695-9733
Professional repair service; also buy, sell, trade, used cameras.

CANES & WALKING STICKS

Uncle Sam Umbrella Shop
161 West 57th St.
New York, NT 10019
Phone: 212-582-1977
Repairs canes and umbrellas.

CAROUSELS & CAROUSEL FIGURES

R & F Designs, Inc.
William R. Finkenstein
95 Riverside Ave.
Bristol, CT 06010
Phone: 203-585-5411
Considered the best carousel restoration firm, examples: New Orleans, City Park, Derby Ride, Playland, Rye, NY.

Bill Hamlet
614 Polk Street
Raleigh, NC 27604
*Restores old carousel figures and carves new figures. **

Rosa P. Ragan
905 W. Johnson
Raleigh, NC 27605 *

Gray Sales, Inc. P.O. Box 14732 Surfside
Beach, SC 29587 Phone: 803-238-0251
*Does carousel figure restorations and appraisals. **

Joe Leonard Custom Woodworking
P.O. Box 510
Burton, OH 44021
*Restores old carousel figures and carves new figures. **

Floyd Girtz
1500 N. Pecan Avenue
Roswell, NM 88201
*Restores old carousel figures and carves new figures. **

Carol Perron
P.O. Box 14942
Portland, OR 97214
Phone: 503-235-2252

CLOCKS

Burt Dial Company
P.O. Box 774
Raymond, NH 03077
Phone: 603-895-2879
Specializes in reverse painting on glass for clock tablets and doors, and in the restoring of clock dials.

Charles Miller
1721 Stanton St.
York, PA 17404
Phone: 843-0363
Member NAWCC, AWI. *

Antique Clock Repair
Joel Vernick
10807 Kenilworth Ave.
P.O. Box 81
Garrett Park, MD 20896
Phone: 301-933-0654 or 301-933-4689
Over 30 years experience in clock repair.

Harvey Flemister
512 Highgate Terrace
Silver Spring, MD 20904
Phone: 301-622-3686
Many years experience in the repair and restoration of antique clocks and watches.

Dorothy Briggs
410 Ethan Allen Ave.
Takoma Park, MD 20912
Phone: 301-270-4166
Specializes in the restoration of painted clock dials as well as reverse painting on glass. *

Old Clockworks, The
Lee M. Flemister
10201 Kings Arms Tavern Court
Ellicott City, MD 21043
Phone: 301-854-5514

Dial House, The
Martha & Dick Smallwood
2287 Buchanan Highway
Dallas, GA 30132
Phone: 404-445-2877
Antique clock dials only; preserved, restored or replaced; call or write before shipping.

COIN-OPERATED MACHINES

Joseph S. Jancuska
619 Miller St.
Luzerne, PA 18709
Phone: 717-287-3478
Buys, sells, repairs and appraises slot machines, trade stimulators, gum & nut machines & other coin-operated machines.

DOLLS

Victorian Doll Museum & Chili Doll
   Hospital
Linda Greenfield
4332 Buffalo Road
North Chili, NY 14514
Phone: 716-247-1030
Recognized expert in doll restoration; repairs all types of dolls; restringing, leather body repair, replacement of cloth bodies.

Doll Heaven
502 Broadway
New Haven, IN 46774
Phone: 219-493-6428
Doll restoration & repair; specializing in broken bisque and composition dolls; modern, antique, collector dolls; all materials.

International Doll Restoration Artists
   Association
Magazine: IDRAA Workshop
Route 2, Box 7
Worthington, MN 56187 *

FANS

Mechanical

Light Ideas
1037 Taft Street
Rockville, MD 20850
Phone: 301-424-5483   FAX: 301-424-5791
Repairs early electric fans; also carries parts.

FIREARMS

Gunsmithing

Gun Center, The
William A. Kelley, Jr.
5831 Buckeystown Pike
Frederick, MD 21701
Phone: 301-694-6887
Offers a full line of gunsmithing services: repair, hot blueing, custom metal and stock work, etc.

Dilliott Gunsmithing, Inc.
Route 3, Box 3430
Dandridge, TN 37725
Phone: 615-397-9204
Repair and restoration of antique firearms; make obsolete parts; bluing and parkerizing.

Scott's Creek Armory, Inc.
Richard Binger
Rt. 1, Box 70
Morgantown, IN 46160
Phone: 317-878-5489
Buys and sells flintlocks and cartridge rifles and muskets; specializing in gunsmithing and restoration.

FIRE FIGHTING MEMORABILIA

Little Century
H. Thomas & Pat Laun
215 Paul Ave.
Syracuse, NY 13206
Phone: 315-437-4156 or 315-654-3244
Repairs fire fighting antiques and collectibles; wood and metal parts fabricated.

FRAMES

Restoration of Antique Frames
R. Wayne Reynolds
P.O. Box 28
Stevenson, MD 21153
Phone: 301-484-1028
Conserves and restores gessoed and gold-leafed items such as frames, plaster items, moldings, etc. *

FURNITURE (ANTIQUE)

Brass Beds

Bedpost, The
32 S. High St.
East Bajor, PA 18013
Phone: 215-588-4667
Manufactures brass and iron beds; also repairs antique brass beds and provides parts.

GEMS & JEWELRY

Thompsons Studio, Inc.
Back Meadow Road
Damariscotta, ME 04543
Phone: 207-563-5280
Repairs jewelry of any period. *

HORSE-DRAWN VEHICLES

Carriages

Chimney Farm Carriages
Charles C. Bent
R.F.D. 2
North Canaan, NH 03741
Phone: 603-523-4259
Restores horse-drawn vehicles. *

Woodlyn Coach Co.
Ivan Burkholder
4410 TR 628
Millersberg, OH 44654
Phone: 216-674-9124
Specializes in the repair and complete restoration of horse drawn carriages, buggies and wagons; also builds new hitch wagons.

A & D Buggy Shop
Alvin Raber
4682 RT. 5 TR 628
Millersburg, OH 44654
Phone: 614-599-6131
Specializes in the repair and restoration of horse drawn carriages and buggies.

INDIAN ITEMS

White Deed Indian Traders
Conrad "Duke" Glodowski
1834 Red Pine Lane
Stevens Point, WI 54481
Phone: 715-344-9217
Specializes in the repair and conservation of American Indian artifacts.

Salvatore Macri
5518 East Pinchot Ave.
Phoenix, AZ 85018
Phone: 602-959-1933
Restores fine porcelain and prehistoric and historic Indian artifacts. *

KNIVES

Garry L. Wackerhagen
2910 McNutt Ave.
Maryville, TN 37801
Phone: 615-977-WACK
Knife repair and restorations; reasonable rates.

Wendell Carson
Rt. 4, Box 314
New Albany, MS 38652 *

Charles Jones
P.O. Box 282
Belton, TX 76513
Specializes in the repair of Case knives. *

Skip Bryan
1852 Albany
Loveland, CO 80537
Specializes in the repair of old knives. *

Pocket

Ken Lukes
405 E. Wake Ham Ave.
Santa Ana, CA 92701
Phone: 714-542-8553

LAMPS & LIGHTING

Aladdin

A-Bit-of-Antiquity
Richard Dudley
1412 Forest Lane
Woodbridge, VA 22191
Phone: 703-491-2878
Expert restoration, repair, deplating & polishing of gas and electric lamps; specializing in oil lighting; carries old parts & shades.

Tiffany/Handel/Pairpoint

Joan Meyer
104 Colwyn Lane
Bala Cynwyd, PA 19004
Phone: 215-664-3174
Expert craftsmanship, only Tiffany glass used, all work guaranteed; also wants Tiffany glass, sheets, scraps. *

LAPIDARY

Hegeman & Co.
Richard P. Hegeman
Suite 307
334 Westminster St.
Providence, RI 02903
Phone: 401-831-6812

Cutters of all precious/semi-precious stones; specializing in the repair & restoration of all types of jewelry & gemstone replacements.

MARBLES

Jack Leslie
Rt. 4, Box 60
Liberty, MO 64068
Phone: 816-455-2110
Restores and regrinds glass marbles. *

Castle's Fair
Larry Castle
885 Taylor Ave.
Ogden, UT 84404
Phone: 801-393-8131
Restores and regrinds glass marbles; over ten years experience and more that 6000 marbles restored.

MUSIC BOXES

Chet Ramsay Antiques
Chet Ramsay
RD #1, Box 383
Coatesville, PA 19320
Phone: 215-384-0514
Wants all types of music boxes; buy, sell and repair; also wants parts.

Paul Smith
408 E. Leeland Heights Blvd.
Lehigh Acres, FL 33936
Phone: 813-728-9694
Repairs curious or unusual devices. *

Clarence W. Fabel
Box 205, Route 3
Morgantown, IN 46160
Phone: 812-988-7545
Repairs cylinder music boxes. *

Regina Music Box Co., Inc.
7013 W. Crandall Ave.
Worth, IL 60482
Repairs disc music boxes; also has parts and new discs. *

K.R. Powers Antique Music Boxes
K.R. Powers
28 Alton Circle
Rogers, AR 72756
Phone: 501-263-2643
Disc and cylinder music box restoration, sales and repairs.

Antique Music Box Restoration
Christian Eric
1825 Placentia Ave.
Costa Mesa, CA 92627
Phone: 714-548-1542   FAX: 714-631-6206
Specialists in antique musical boxes, emphasis on early cylinder, miniature and sur plateau mechanisms; fine restoration.

MUSICAL INSTRUMENTS

Vintage Instruments
Frederick W. Oster
1529 Pine Street
Philadelphia, PA 19102
Phone: 215-545-1100   FAX: 215-473-3634
Dealers/appraisers of rare and antique musical instruments: violins, cellos, bows, guitars, banjos, mandolins, strings, woodwinds, brass.

Organs

Pump & Pipe Shop, The
7698 Kraft Ave.
Caledonia, MI 49316
Phone: 616-891-8743
Specializes in the restoration, buying and selling of reed organs; also buys parts.

String

Powell's String Instrument Repair
Box 115
Belmont, WV 26134
Phone: 304-665-2559
Repairs; also buying guitars, banjos, mandolins; all makers. *

NAUTICAL COLLECTIBLES

Brass 'n Bounty
68 Front Street
Marblehead, MA 01945
Phone: 617-631-3864
Repairs nautical antiques such as telescopes, sextants, etc.

New York Nautical Instrument & Service
  Corp.
140 West Broadway
New York, NY 10012
Phone: 212-962-4522
Repairs nautical instruments such as sextants, barometers, marine clocks, compasses, etc. *

Ship Models

American Marine Model Gallery
R. Michael Wall
12I Derby Square
Salem, MA 01970
Phone: 508-745-5777   FAX: 508-745-5778
Offers complete restoration services, custom models, cases, appraisals.

ORIENTALIA

Lacquer

Fine Art of Asia
Janet Francine Cobert
P.O. Box 2976
Beverly Hills, CA 90213
Phone: 213-475-8160
Restores Oriental lacquer and ceramic wares.

PAPERWEIGHTS

Studio Hannah
Charles Hannah
P.O. Box 769
Flemington, NJ 08822
Phone: 201-782-7468 *

George N. Kulles
115 Little Creek Drive
Lockport, IL 60441
Phone: 708-301-0996
Restores and polishes damaged paperweight surfaces; author of "Identifying Antique Paperweights - Millifiore and Lampwork."

Castle's Fair
Larry Castle
885 Taylor Ave.
Ogden, UT 84404
Phone: 801-393-8131
Over ten years experience; all work is hand held using water-cooled diamond equipment to heal fractures.

PHONOGRAPHS

Antique Phonograph Center
Floyd Silver
Hwy. 206
P.O. Box 274
Vincentown, NJ 08088
Phone: 609-859-8617
Antique phonographs sales, service; complete restorations of Edison, Victor and Columbia phonographs.

PURSES

Abraham & Strauss
420 Fulton St.
Brooklyn, NY 11233 *

QUILTS

Doll & Quilts Barn
Yvonne Khin
9459 Longs Mill Rd.
Rocky Ridge, MD 21778-8507
Phone: 301-898-0091
Quilt museum offering quilt repairs, enlarging, duplicating, quilting classes, storage, and research.

RADIOS

John Okolowicz
624 Cedar Hill Rd.
Ambler, PA 19002
Phone: 215-542-1597
Wants pre-1950 radios and TV's in unusual or ornate plastic or wooden cabinets; especially those made by Emerson or Stromberg Carlson.

David T. Boyd
13917 Wisteria Drive
Germantwon, MD 20877
Phone: 301-948-8070 or 301-972-2777

Restores old tube-type radios and televisions from the 20's and 30's through the 1960's; also buys and sells.

DH Distributors
David Headley
P.O. box 48623
Wichita, KS 67201
Phone: 316-684-0050
Repairs and restores tube-type radios and audio equipment; chassis and cabinet restorations for tube-type radios; schematics.

REPAIRS & RESTORATIONS

Art

Peter Kostoulakos
15 Sayles St.
Lowell, MA 01851
Phone: 508-453-8888
Conservation of oil paintings on canvas or solid supports; oil paintings cleaned and restored.

Art Conservation Laboratory
Barbara H. Beardsley
Raymond, NH 03077
Phone: 603-895-2639
Offers art conservation and art forgery detection services. *

Fine Art Restoration
John Squadra
RFD #2 Box 1440
Brooks, ME 04921
Phone: 207-722-3464
Specializing in the conservation and restoration of oil paintings; send photo of painting, incl. size; estimate returned; has crates.

Van Cline & Davenport, Ltd.
Stephen Van Cline
792 Franklin Ave.
Franklin Lakes, NJ 07417
Phone: 201-891-4588
Specializes in fine art, paintings, watercolors, and drawings; also repairs and restores paintings.

Washington Conservation Studio
Justine S. Wimsatt
4230 Howard St.
Kensington, MD 20895
Phone: 301-564-1036
For 20 years has provided professional restoration of paintings, murals, icons, frames and related objects.

H.I. Gates
118 E. Church St.
Frederick, MD 21701
Phone: 301-663-3717
Conservator of paintings.

Robert & Marie Kuehne
9910 Green Valley Rd.
Union Bridge, MD 21791
Phone: 301-898-7921
Oil painting conservation/restoration; 20 yrs. experience; please call for expert info. & advice; FREE brochure available on request.

Bardwell Conservation, Ltd.
Margaret Bardwell
11373 Park Dr.
Fairfax, VA 22030
Phone: 703-385-8451
Conservation and restoration of paintings executed on canvas, metal or wood (including icons); also frames and small painted furniture.

Antique & Art Restoration By Wiebold
413 Terrace Place
Terrace Park, OH 45174
Phone: 513-831-2541
Silver repair and replating; restoration of bronzes, combs, brushes, knife blades, mirrors, frames, paintings, ceramics, glass, etc.

Balboa Art Conservation Center
Frances Prichatt
P.O. Box 3755
San Diego, CA 92103
Phone: 619-236-9702
Provides conservation services for art and paper items. *

Fine Art Conservation Laboratories
Scott M. Haskins
P.O. Box 23557
Santa Barbara, CA 93131
Phone: 805-564-3438   FAX: 805-963-0705
Specializes in the preservation of paintings, murals, works of art on paper and period frames.

Beveled Glass

Chaudron Glass & Mirror Co., Inc.
Henry Chaudron
1801 Lovegrove St.
Baltimore, MD 21202
Phone: 301-685-1568
Resilvers mirrors; also hand-bevels plate glass.

Ceramics

Fine Wares Restoration
Sharon Smith Abbott
Highland Ridge Road
P.O. Box 753
Bridgton, ME 04009
Phone: 207-647-2093
Restores ceramics & glass for private collectors and museums; member of the Amer. Inst. for Conservation of Historic & Artistic Works.

Jonathan Mark Gershen Porcelain, Pottery &
  Glass Restoration
Jonathan Mark Gershen
1463 Pennington Road
Ewing Township, NJ 08618
Phone: 609-882-9417
*Second generation restorer and long time member
of the AICHAW; clients include museums, collectors and dealers from all over.*

Harry A. Eberhardt & Son
2010 Walnut St.
Philadelphia, PA 19103
*America's oldest repair firm. *

Grady Stewart Expert Porcelain Restorations
2019 Sansom St.
Philadelphia, PA 19103
Phone: 215-567-2888
*Offering repairs for museums, dealers, collectors;
quality repairs of fine porcelain, pottery, stoneware, dolls.*

Shepherd Studio
Mildred R. Shepherd
5527 Third St., South
Arlington, VA 22204
Phone: 703-671-1789
*Offers conservation and restoration of objects of
art; specializing in the repair of porcelain, glass,
ivory, china and pottery.*

Gregory A. Ehler
4786 Lee Highway
Arlington, VA 22207
Phone: 703-525-2470
*Provides museum quality restoration of fine porcelain, pottery and enamels; member of Wash. D.C.
Professional Restoration Associates.*

Paul Barron Company
P.O. Box 2023
Decatur, GA 30030
*Small firm. Excepts all kinds of china repairs. *

Lauraine Dunn Studios
Lauraine Dunn
181 N.E. 82nd St. #201
Miami, FL 33138
Phone: 305-758-7174
*Well-established firm. Handles both decorative
porcelain as well as dinnerware, fine art, metal,
etc.*

Antique & Art Restoration By Wiebold
413 Terrace Place
Terrace Park, OH 45174
Phone: 513-831-2541
*Silver repair and replating; restoration of bronzes,
combs, brushes, knife blades, mirrors, frames,
paintings, ceramics, glass, etc.*

Glass Doctor & Porcelain Clinic
Ross Jasper
3126 Fairview St.
Davenport, IA 52802
Phone: 319-322-5512
Restores figurines, toys, glass.

Morla W. Tjossem
911 E. Hancock St.
Appleton, WI 54911
Phone: 414-734-5463
China Mending and Restoration Course instructor on the Lawrence University campus; practicing restorer.

Wesley Art Service
P.O. Box 848
Los Gatos, CA 95031
*China restorations of figurines. *

Furniture

Manning Furniture Repair Co.
Dan Manning
P.O. Box 212
Allendale, NJ 07401
Phone: 201-825-8450   FAX: 201-825-8301
Specializing in cargo claims handling, and furniture and antiques repair services.

Burlesque Repair Service
Andrew Gelinas
18 W. 3rd. St.
Bethlehem, PA 18015
Phone: 215-867-3313 or 215-867-1665
                    FAX: 215-867-4999
*Specializing in cargo claims handling and repair
services for moving, insurance, retail companies;
full shop facilities.*

John Eaton
9064 Canterbury Riding
Laurel, MD 20707
Phone: 301-498-2351
Offers moving claims inspections and repairs; antiques restoration.

Shontere Restoration, Inc.
Belinda Shontere
P.O. Box 1805
Mitchellville, MD 20717
Phone: 301-870-3669 or 800-937-3786
                    FAX: 301-934-0511
Specializing in furniture repair and restoration.

Glade Valley Furniture Repair
John Pyle
10464 Glade Road
Walkersville, MD 21793
Phone: 301-898-3795

Heny Miller
9200 Maple St.
Manassas, VA 22110
Phone: 703-368-4502

Finishing Touch
Dennis Bell
118 Kent Berry Court
Gastonia, NC 28054
Phone: 704-868-8538
*Offers cargo claims handling furniture repairs. *

Image Maintenance Assurance, Inc.
Dave Kummerow
P.O. Box 8407
Bartlett, IL 60103
Phone: 708-830-7965   FAX: 708-830-1458
*Specializing in cargo claims handling and repair
services; wood finishes, upholstery, fiberglass, vinyl, porcelain, etc.*

Pacific Northwest Claim Service
Ray Spencer
1045 12th Ave. NW, Unit F3
Issaquah, WA 98027
Phone: 206-392-2500   FAX: 206-392-7525
*Specializing in cargo claims handling and in
complete repair services.*

Furniture & Upholstery

West Interior Services, Inc.
Tom Kuhns
P.O. Box 200
Brackenridge, PA 15014
Phone: 412-224-2215   FAX: 412-226-3233
*Specializes in moving or ins. claims; furniture
repair, refinishing & restoration, architectural refinishing; fire, smoke, water damage.*

Charles Jourdant Furniture Repair
Charles Jourdant
611 Alabama Ave.
North Beach, MD 20714
Phone: 301-855-6563   FAX: 301-257-0752
Furniture repair, refinishing and upholstering.

Furniture (Antique)

Heritage Restorations
Stephen Rice
7200-10 Westmore Ave.
Rockville, MD 20850-1261
Phone: 301-762-3126
*European trained craftsmen specializing in
wooden objects d'Art & antique furniture restoration; duplicating finishes, inlays, etc.*

Walter Raynes
4900 Wetheredsville
Baltimore, MD 21207
Phone: 301-448-3515
*Specializes in the restoration and conservation of
antique furniture only.*

Begleiter Antique Restorations
Phil Goodman
6801 Reisterstown Rd.
Baltimore, MD 21215
Phone: 301-764-7467

Robert Esterly Antiques Repairing,
    Refinishing, Reproductions
Robert Esterly
6675 Mt. Phillip Rd.
Frederick, MD 21702
Phone: 301-694-0287 or 301-371-7430
Specializing in the repair, restoration and refinishing of antique furniture.

Antique Restorations, Inc.
Bruce M. Schuettinger
17 N. Alley
P.O. Box 244
New Market, MD 21774
Phone: 301-865-3009
Specializing in the restoration and conservation of antique wooden furniture and artifacts: veneer, caning, inlay, gilding, etc.

General

Helige Ande Arts
Ingrid Sanborn
85 Church St.
West Newbury, MA 01985
Phone: 508-363-2253
Specializes in graining, stenciling, marbleizing, reverse painting on glass, and early paint matching; custom of restoration work.

Trefler & Sons Antique Restoring
    Studio, Inc.
Leon Trefler
99 Cabot St.
Needham, MA 02194
Phone: 617-444-2685   FAX: 617-444-0659
Restores ceramics, prints, paintings, furniture, paper, frames, crystal, porcelain, marble, ivory, cloisonne, metals, jade, etc.

Stoneledge, Inc.
17 Robert St.
Wharton, NJ 07885
Phone: 201-989-8800
Fine and decorative art restorers and conservators: paintings, ceramics, sculptures, ivory, etc. for collectors, dealers & museums.

Hess Restorations
Marina Pastor
200 Park Ave. South
New York, NY 10003
Phone: 212-260-2255 or 212-979-1143
Since 1945 specializing in repairs and restorations of most objects of art; highly recommended by museums and leading galleries.

A. Ludwig Klein & Son, Inc.
Route 63
P.O. Box 145
Harleysville, PA 19438
Phone: 215-256-9004 or 215-256-6426
Specializing in the repair and restoration of all types of glass, china and porcelain as well as ivory, jade, brass, pewter.

Nonomura Studios
David Sim
3432 Connecticut Ave. NW
Washington, DC 20008
Phone: 202-363-4025
Restores china, glassware, screens, scrolls, ivory, paintings, jade, lamps, furniture, etc.

Mario's Conservation Services
Sidney Williston
1738 14th St. NW
Washington, DC 20009
Phone: 202-234-5795
Restorers of decorative arts objects: metal, ivory, icons, frames, gold leaf, glass grinding and drilling.

Museum Shop, Ltd.
Richard Kornemann
30 East Patrick St.
Frederick, MD 21701
Phone: 301-695-0424
Highly-recommended conservator of oils, paper (etchings, lithographs, engravings, maps), icons, Oriental art, photos, 23k gold leaf, etc.

Wood & Stone Inc.
Harold Vogel
10115 Residency Rd.
Manassas, VA 22111
Phone: 703-369-1236 or 202-631-1236

Shepherd Studio
Mildred R. Shepherd
5527 Third St., South
Arlington, VA 22204
Phone: 703-671-1789
Offers conservation and restoration of objects of art; specializing in the repair of porcelain, glass, ivory, china and pottery.

International Conservation
Laboratories, Ltd.
5311 Patterson Ave.
Richmond, VA 23226
Phone: 804-282-7308
Restores ceramics, prints, paintings, clocks, music boxes, jewelry, electroplate, textiles, etc. *

Rikki's Studio Inc.
Gilbert Kerry Hall
2809 Bird Ave.
Coconut Grove, FL 33133
Phone: 305-446-2230 or 305-446-2022
Restorers and conservators of crystal, paintings, porcelains (European and Oriental), coromandel and objects d'Art.

Lauraine Dunn Studios
Lauraine Dunn
181 N.E. 82nd St. #201
Miami, FL 33138
Phone: 305-758-7174

Well-established firm. Handles both decorative porcelain as well as dinnerware, fine art, metal, etc.

Old World Restorations, Inc.
Douglas A. Eisele
The Columbia/Stanley Bldg.
347 Stanley Avenue
Cincinnati, OH 45226
Phone: 513-321-1911 or 800-878-1911
                    FAX: 513-321-1914
Fine restoration and conservation of paintings, porcelain, glass, china, art pottery, metals, crystal, frames, ivory, gold leaf, etc.

David Jasper's Glass Clinic
David Jasper
RR3, Box 330
Sioux Falls, SD 57106
Phone: 605-361-7524
Four generations of restorers. Glass, porcelain, painting, dolls, figurines, ivory, lamps.

Gilding

Society of Gilders
Newsletter: Society of Gilders Newsletter
42 Maple Place
Nutley, NJ 07110
Phone: 201-667-5251
Publishes a list of its members; also gives workshops and lectures on the art of gilding.

Mario's Conservation Services
Sidney Williston
1738 14th St. NW
Washington, DC 20009
Phone: 202-234-5795
Restorers of decorative arts objects: metal, ivory, icons, frames, gold leaf, glass grinding and drilling.

Gold Leaf Studios, Inc.
William Adair
P.O. Box 50156
Washington, DC 20091
Phone: 202-638-4660
Gilding of anything gold leafed: frames, sculpture, sconces, etc.

Chelsea Lane Studio
Stanley Robertson
4717 S. Chelsea Ln.
Bethesda, MD 20814
Phone: 301-656-9344
Gilding of anything gold leafed: frames, sculpture, sconces, etc.

Museum Shop, Ltd.
Richard Kornemann
30 East Patrick St.
Frederick, MD 21701
Phone: 301-695-0424
23k gold leafing of antiques, picture frames, signs, etc.; also complete art and frame restoration.

Glass

Rosine Green Associates, Inc.
45 Bartlett Crescent
Brookline, MA 02146
Phone: 212-674-8960
*Well-known firm restores and rebuilds all kinds of glass articles. *

Crystal Workshop
Edward Poore
P.O. Box 475
Sagamore, MA 02561
Phone: 508-888-1621
Glass items made to order; also repairs stemware, cut glass, and art glass.

Fine Wares Restoration
Sharon Smith Abbott
Highland Ridge Road
P.O. Box 753
Bridgton, ME 04009
Phone: 207-647-2093
Restores ceramics & glass for private collectors and museums; member of the Amer. Inst. for Conservation of Historic & Artistic Works.

Art Cut Glass Studio
R.D. 1, Box 10 Fawn Frive
Matawan, NJ 07747
Phone: 201-583-7648

Jonathan Mark Gershen Porcelain, Pottery & Glass Restoration
Jonathan Mark Gershen
1463 Pennington Road
Ewing Township, NJ 08618
Phone: 609-882-9417
Second generation restorer and long time member of the AICHAW; clients include museums, collectors and dealers from all over.

Flemington Cut Glass
156 Main St.
Flemington, NJ 08822
Phone: 201-782-3017

Gem Monogram & Cut Glass Corp.
628 Broadway
New York, NY 10012
Phone: 212-674-8960

Glass Restorations
308 East 78th St.
New York, NY 10021
Phone: 212-517-3287

Ray Errett - Glass Repair Specialist
Ray Errett
281 Chestnut St.
Corning, NY 14830
Phone: 607-962-6026 or 607-937-5371
Restores glass figurines, sculpture crystal, cut glass; works at Corning.

Corning Museum of Glass, The
Mr. Manwarren
1 Museum Way
Corning, NY 14830-2253
Phone: 607-937-5371
*Repairs broken teeth on cut glass. *

Shay O'Brien Crystal
Shay O'Brien
Rout 2, Box 223K
Acme, PA 15610
Phone: 412-547-4618
Restores antique crystal cut glass; recuts teeth; reproductions from blanks.

Michael Andras
P.O. Box 250
Bear Rocks, PA 15610
Phone: 412-547-6419
Glass engraver and cutter.

Van Parys Studio
6338 Germantown Ave.
Philadelphia, PA 19144 *

Crystal Restoration Co.
Scenic Plaza, Highway 28
West Union, SC 29696
Phone: 803-638-9323
*Crystal repair only. *

McCurley Glass Repair
Don & Joyce McCurley
Rt. #1, Box 738
Big Pine Key, FL 33043
Phone: 305-872-2359
Repairs glass and crystal; also carries large stock of replacement stoppers for bottles.

Calvin's Glass Repair
John Calvin
303 East First Ave.
Lenoir City, TN 37771
Phone: 615-968-3872
*Crystal repair only. *

David Jasper's Glass Clinic
David Jasper
RR3, Box 330
Sioux Falls, SD 57106
Phone: 605-361-7524
Four generations of restorers. Glass, porcelain, painting, dolls, figurines, ivory, lamps.

Josef Puehringer
1141 Central Ave.
Wilmette, IL 60091
Phone: 312-256-6055
*Cuts and engraves glass. *

K. Matsumoto
226 South Wabash Ave.
Chicago, IL 60604 *

Zoe Restorations
5657 W. 50th St.
Shawnee Mission, KS 66201 *

Lamps & Lighting

Lamp House
223 W. Market St.
Hallam, PA 17406
Phone: 717-757-6989
*Replacement shades, antique lamp restoration, custom lamps. *

Light Ideas
1037 Taft Street
Rockville, MD 20850
Phone: 301-424-5483   FAX: 301-424-5791
Repairs lighting fixtures - chandeliers, crystal, early electric fans; also carries parts, repairs shades, beaded fringe.

A-Bit-of-Antiquity
Richard Dudley
1412 Forest Lane
Woodbridge, VA 22191
Phone: 703-491-2878
Expert restoration, repair, deplating & polishing of gas and electric lamps; specializing in oil lighting; carries old parts & shades.

Marble

U.S. Tile & Marble Co.
45 Q St. SW
Washington, DC 20024
Phone: 202-554-4370
Repairs broken marble slabs.

Jack T. Irwin, Inc.
601 East Gude Drive
Rockville, MD 20852
Phone: 301-762-5800
*Cuts and repairs marble tops. *

Metal Items

Orum Silver Co., Inc.
Joseph J. Pistilli
51 S. Vine St.
P.O. Box 805
Meriden, CT 06450
Phone: 203-237-3037
Repairing, restoring, replating of antique and old silver, gold, nickel; brass & copper plating; cleaning, buffing, polishing.

Smith-Hoover Metalsmiths
James Smith-Hoover
228 7th St. SE
Washington, DC 20001
Phone: 202-544-3818
*Fine metal and glass refinishing process. *

Bethesda Art Metal Work
4955 Bethesda Ave.
Bethesda, MD 20814
Phone: 301-656-1445 *

Awesome Metal Restorations, Inc.
Boris Paskvan
10524 Detrick Ave.
Kensington, MD 20895
Phone: 301-929-7955
European expert restores gold, gilt, bronze, silver, silver plating, icons, metal accessories, sculptures, etc. for museums, homes, ins.

Abercombe & Co.
9159A Brookeville Rd.
Silver Spring, MD 20910
Phone: 301-585-2385
Replates silverplate; repairs all sorts of metal; silver, brass, copper; also welding.

Creative Metal Design
Pete Markey
7935 Edgewood Church Rd.
Frederick, MD 21702
Phone: 301-473-5995
Specializes in ornamental ironwork, hand forged originals; metal repairs; made the Statue of Liberty gates.

Jarnel Iron & Forge
David Nelson
221 Rowland
Hagerstown, MD 21740
Phone: 301-733-0441
Recasts replacement parts in various metals; also iron work.

Equestrian Forge
Alexander Bigler
P.O. Box 1950
Leesburg, VA 22075
Phone: 703-777-2110
Recasts replacement parts in various metals; also casts portrait sculptures.

Senti-Metal Co.
Silverplating Division
1919 Memory Lane
Columbus, OH 43209
Replates silverplated items. *

Antique & Art Restoration By Wiebold
413 Terrace Place
Terrace Park, OH 45174
Phone: 513-831-2541
Silver repair and replating; restoration of bronzes, combs, brushes, knife blades, mirrors, frames, paintings, ceramics, glass, etc.

Jerry Probst
P.O. Box 45
Janesville, WI 53547-0045
Phone: 608-752-2816   FAX: 608-752-7691
Repairs silver back hair brushes.

Watkins & Sons
Jay A. Watkins
469 Vernon Way
El Cajon, CA 92020
Phone: 619-441-9441
Silversmithing and repair; silver, brass, copper, aluminum, refinishing; 25 years experience.

Mirrors

Chaudron Glass & Mirror Co., Inc.
Henry Chaudron
1801 Lovegrove St.
Baltimore, MD 21202
Phone: 301-685-1568
Resilvers mirrors; also hand-bevels plate glass.

Painted Finishes

Medusa
149 Sycamore St.
Somerville, MA 02145-2738
Reproduces faux marble, stencils, trompe l'oeil, etc. finishes.

Paper Items

Center for Conservation & Technical Studies, The
Arthur Beale
Fogg Art Museum
Harvard University
Cambridge, MA 02138 *

Bridgitte Boyadjian
43 Fern Street
Lexington, MA 02173
Phone: 617-862-9395
Paper restoration and conservation; fine prints, drawings, watercolors and manuscripts.

Christa M. Gaehde
55 Falmouth Road
Arlington, MA 02174 *

Mary Todd Glaser
73 E. Linden Avenue
Englewood, NJ 07631 *

Carolyn Horton
430 W. 22nd Street
New York, NY 10011 *

Old Print Shop, The
Kenneth Newman
150 Lexington Ave. at 30th St.
New York, NY 10016
Phone: 212-683-3950
Paper conservator: preservation, restoration, cleaning, deacidification, encapsulation.

Museum of Modern Art
11 W. 53rd. Street
New York, NY 10019 *

Florence Hodes
145 Central Park West
New York, NY 10023 *

Conservation Center of the Institute of Fine Arts
New York University
1 East 78th Street
New York, NY 10028 *

Brooklyn Museum, The
200 Eastern Parkway
Brooklyn, NY 11238
Phone: 718-638-5000 *

Edith MacKennan
11 Rosalind Road
Poughkeepsie, NY 12601 *

Pennsylvania Academy of Fine Arts
Broad & Cherry Streets
Philadelphia, PA 19102 *

Marilyn Kemp Weidner, FAIC
612 Spruce Street
Philadelphia, PA 19106
Phone: 215-627-2303 or 215-627-0188
Offers conservation treatment for art, artifacts, library & archival materials on paper; collection surveys and care consultations.

Archival Restoration Associates, Inc.
P.O. Box 1395
North Wales, PA 19454
Phone: 215-699-0165
Quality restorations of books, paper, photographs, parchment, and watercolors; estimates determined by condition of individual

Old Print Gallery, The
James Von Ruster
1220 31st St. NW
Washington, DC 20007
Phone: 202-965-1818   FAX: 202-965-1869
Paper conservator: preservation, restoration, cleaning, deacidification, encapsulation.

Kendra Lovette
6611 Park Heights Ave.
Baltimore, MD 21215
Phone: 301-764-6770
Paper conservator and repairer; anything on paper.

Dobson Studios
Janice & Dennis Dobson
810 N. Daniel St.
Arlington, VA 22201
Phone: 703-243-7363
Conservator of Oriental screens, scrolls and wood block prints; repairs and restoration to other paper items as well.

Conservation of Art On Paper, Inc.
Christine Smith, Dir.
Suite 110
3110 Mt. Vernon Ave.
Alexandria, VA 22305
Phone: 703-836-7757

Collections surveys, lectures/workshops, paper conservator: preservation, restoration, cleaning, deacidification, encapsulation.

Murray Lebwohl Studio, Inc.
1212 I Street
Alexandria, VA 22307 *

David Swift
6436 Brownlee Dr.
Nashville, TN 37205
Phone: 615-352-0308
*Paper conservator: preservation, restoration, cleaning, deacidification, encapsulation. ***

John Pofelski
190 South Wood Dale Road
Wood Dale, IL 60191 *

Art Institute of Chicago
Michigan Ave. at Adams Street
Chicago, IL 60603
Phone: 312-443-3600 *

Wynne H. Phelan
3721 Ella Lee Lane
Houston, TX 77027 *

Art Lab
David E. Hargis
P.O. Box 6986
Houston, TX 77265
Phone: 713-668-7711
Offers professional restoration of all paper collectibles, movie material, golden age comics, toy boxes & original art.

Reverse Painting On Glass

Helige Ande Arts
Ingrid Sanborn
85 Church St.
West Newbury, MA 01985
Phone: 508-363-2253
Highly skilled at reproducing reverse paintings on glass.

Textiles

Textile Conservation Center, Museum of American Textile History
800 Mass. Ave.
North Andover, MA 01845
Phone: 508-686-0191
TCC provides evaluation, treatment and educational services that pertain to the conservation and preservation of historic textiles.

Shallcross & Lorraine
State House Post Office
Box 133
Boston, MA 02133
Phone: 617-720-2133
Reweaves and repairs Indian rugs, tapestries, needlework, etc.

Stephen & Carol Huber
82 Plants Dam Rd.
East Lyme, CT 06333
Phone: 203-739-0772   FAX: 203-739-0261
Specializes in the repair and conservation of antique needlework.

Testfabrics, Inc.
P.O. Box 420
Middlesex, NJ 08846
Phone: 201-469-6446   FAX: 201-469-1147
Provides textile conservation services.

Applebaum & Himmelstein
444 Central Park West
New York, NY 10025
Phone: 212-666-4630
Repairs silk textiles.

Textile Conservation Workshop
Patsy Orlofsky
Main Street
South Salem, NY 10590
Phone: 914-736-5805
Textile conservation lecturer and consultant; also does conservation and repairs of all types of textiles.

Thanewold Associates
P.O. Box 104
Zieglerville, PA 19492
Phone: 215-287-9158
Needlework repairs and conservation including samplers.

C. P. and Asst.
Clarissa Palmai
5416 Harwood Rd.
Bethesda, MD 20814
Phone: 301-656-6381
Offers textile conservation, consultation and lecturing.

Linens Limited
240 North Milwaukee St.
Milwaukee, WI 53202
Phone: 414-223-1123   FAX: 414-223-1126
Specializes in the repair of linens.

Emily Sanford
451 Gould Ave.
Hermosa Beach, CA 90254
Phone: 213-374-7412
*Restoration of textiles and oriental rugs. ***

Wicker

Garnett's Wicker Shop
Garnett Drake
Route 6, Box 39
Decatur, AL 35603 *

Wickery, The
Bea Niles
644 College St.
Milton, WI 53563 *

Woodworking

Original Woodworks
360 North Main St.
Stillwater, MN 55082
Phone: 612-430-3622
A full service shop specializing in antique restorations including furniture and architectural elements.

RUGS

Hooked

Angela Lyons
127 Boston Post Rd.
Wayland, MA 01778
Phone: 617-358-4354
*Repairs hooked rugs. ***

Linda Eliasom
Box 542
Manchester, VT 05254
Phone: 802-867-2252
*Repairs hooked rugs. ***

RUSSIAN ITEMS

Enamels

Manhattan Art & Antiques Center, Shop 26
Clifford Baron
1050 Second Avenue
New York, NY 10022
Phone: 212-688-8510
*Repairs Russian enamels. ***

SEWING ITEMS & GO-WITHS

Machines

Simple Machine, The
Cathy & Stephen Racine
18 Masonic Home Rd. - Rt. 31
P.O. Box 234
Charlton, MA 01507
Phone: 508-248-6632
Buys, sells, repairs and restores old treadle sewing machines; also carries parts, belts, needles, bobbins and manuals.

SPINNING WHEELS

Mick Holloway
P.O. Box 453
Winchester, IN 47394
Collects and repairs spinning wheels.

STOVES

Bryant Stove Works
Beatrice Bryant
Rts. 139 & 220
P.O. Box 2048
Thorndike, ME 04986
Phone: 207-568-3498
Large collection on display ; also sells parts and restores antique (1780's-1940's) cook stoves, parlor stoves, and gas stoves.

Tomahawk Foundry, Inc.
2337 29th St.
Rice Lake, WI 54868
Phone: 715-234-4498
Makes replacement parts for cast iron stoves.

TELEPHONES

Chicago Old Telephone Company
P.O. Box 189
Lemon Springs, NC 28355
Phone: 919-774-6625
Repair, service, parts. *

House of Telephones
Odis W. LeVrier
15 East Ave. D
San Angelo, TX 76903
Phone: 915-655-4174 or 915-655-5122
FAX: 915-655-4177
Repairs antique telephones and carries parts.

Billard's Old Telephones
21710 Regnart Rd.
Cupertino, CA 95014
Phone: 408-252-2104
Repairs telephones and publishes "Old Telephones and Parts Catalog." *

TELEVISIONS

John Okolowicz
624 Cedar Hill Rd.
Ambler, PA 19002
Phone: 215-542-1597
Wants pre-1950 radios and TV's in unusual or ornate plastic or wooden cabinets; especially those made by Emerson or Stromberg Carlson.

David T. Boyd
13917 Wisteria Drive
Germantwon, MD 20877
Phone: 301-948-8070 or 301-972-2777
Restores old tube-type radios and televisions from the 20's and 30's through the 1960's; also buys and sells.

TEXTILES

Lace & Linens

Unique Art Lace Cleaners
5926 Delmar Blvd.
St. Louis, MO 63112
Phone: 314-725-2900
Cleans and repairs old textiles, linens and lace.

TOYS

Marc Olimpio's Antique Toy Restoration
Center
Marc Olimpio
P.O. Box 1505
Wolfeboro, NH 03894
Phone: 603-569-6739

Specializes in early handpainted German and French-American tin toys, iron and pressed steel, and cast iron.

Gary J. Moran
3 Finch Court
Commack, NY 11725
Phone: 516-864-9444
Antique toy repairs, including battery operated, friction and wind-up toys; call or write for free estimate; broken toys purchased.

Toy Doctor
RR 1, Box 202
Eades Road
Red Creek, NY 13143
Phone: 315-754-8846
Repairs battery operated toys; robots and space toys a specialty. *

Pete Dibenedetto
568 Minnesota Avenue
Buffalo, NY 14215
Specializing in the repair of plastic toys. *

Newbraugh Brothers Toys
P.O. Box 32, R.D.1
Cogan Station, PA 17728
Phone: 717-435-0447
Custom painting of toys and trains. *

Mint & Boxed, Inc.
Joe Freeman
1313 N. 15th Street
Allentown, PA 18102
Phone: 215-434-0290   FAX: 215-821-8897
Specializes in the repair of tin toys; tin toy autos, boats, merry-go-rounds, etc.; repairs mechanisms, makes missing parts.

Russ Harrington's Repair & Restoration
Service
Rus Harrington
1805 Wilson Point Road
Baltimore, MD 21220
Specializes in mechanical and still banks, and in iron toys. *

Jerry Shook
6528 Cedar Brook Dr.
New Albany, OH 43054
Phone: 614-855-7796
Makes rubber & plastic replacement parts for toys: wind ups, robots, battery operated, etc.; also for dolls; send SASE for parts list.

Ed's Toy Shop
953 East Richmond
Kokomo, IN 46901
Phone: 317-459-0325
Complete overhaul and repair of old toys.

Classic Tin Toy Co.
P.O. Box 193
Sheboygan, WI 53082
Phone: 414-693-3371   FAX: 414-693-8211
Repair and total restoration of all makes of old toys including tin, cast iron and tinplate trains.

Donald Walters
Route 1, Box 51
Curtiss, WI 54422
Phone: 715-654-5440
Repairs and repaints farm and other toys; glass beading, customizing, baked-on paint for smooth, shiny finish.

Phantom Antique Toy Restoration
Buddy George
1038 North Utica
Tulsa, OK 74110
Specializes in pressed-steel toys and pedal cars. *

Battery Operated

J-L Collectibles
Jim & Leslie Smith
P.O. Box 472113
Garland, TX 75047-2113
Phone: 214-271-8917 or 214-840-2517
FAX: 214-840-2517
Offers mechanical repair of most battery operated and wind up toys.

Construction Sets (Erector)

Marion Designs
Bill & Judy Harrison
594 Front St.
Marion, MA 02738
Phone: 508-748-2540
Buy, sell, trade, restore and remanufacture Erector sets; also offers electroplating service.

Pedal Vehicles

Pedal Power
Ed Weirick
RFD #3, Box 190
Ellsworth, ME 04605
Phone: 207-667-2115
Wants original pedal cars; also does custom design and restoration. *

Schoenhut

Christmas Past
Blossom Abell
420 La For River Drive
P.O. Box 247
Algonquin, IL 60102
Phone: 708-658-4990
Repairs Schoenhut circus animals and figures including restringing.

TRAINS

Toy

Newbraugh Brothers Toys
P.O. Box 32, R.D.1
Cogan Station, PA 17728
Phone: 717-435-0447
Custom painting of toys and trains. *

William Gough
9133 Simms Ave.
Baltimore, MD 21234
Phone: 301-256-1448 *

TRUNKS

Trunks By Paul
Paul Berkowitz
14 Park Ave.
Gaithersburg, MD 20877
Phone: 301-840-0920
Buys and sells trunks; also offers trunk refinishing for others; carries full line of trunk hardware and accessories.

Original Woodworks
360 North Main St.
Stillwater, MN 55082
Phone: 612-430-3622
Specializing in complete antique trunk restoration; will transform your trunk inside and out into a treasured family heirloom.

House of Antique Trunks
753 B Northport Dr.
P.O. Box 508
West Sacramento, CA 95691-0508
Phone: 916-372-8228
Antique trunk restoration parts & accessories; doll trunk supplies; chromolithographs for lids; linings, adhesives, leather; repairs.

UMBRELLAS

Uncle Sam Umbrella Shop
161 West 57th St.
New York, NT 10019
Phone: 212-582-1977
Repairs canes and umbrellas.

APPENDIX D

SUPPLIERS

ANTIQUES DEALERS & COLLECTORS, SUPPLIES FOR

Ship's Treasurers
P.O. Box 590
Milton, MA 02186
Phone: 617-964-8010
Carries baseball card polypropylene sleeves.

Russell Norton
P.O. Box 1070
New Haven, CT 06504-1070
Phone: 203-562-7800
Carries clear 2.5 mil polypropylene archival sleeves.

Flip Cards & Supplies
181 Route 46 West
Lodi, NJ 07644
Phone: 201-472-8077   FAX: 201-472-6559
Carries supplies for the sports card and memorabilia collector: snap-tight card holders, top load and screw down card holders, etc.

Antique Dealers Supply
Warren Abrams
P.O. Box 717
Matawan, NJ 07747
Phone: 908-583-3345   FAX: 908-290-9345
Carries table covers, aluminum show cases, canopies, lights, alarms, etc.

Mylan Enterprises
P.O. Box 194
Morris Plains, NJ 07950
Phone: 201-538-6186
Carries a wide assortment of wrapping pads, and bubble pacs and bags.

Source, The
P.O. Box 350349
Brooklyn, NY 11235

Intense Tents
Box 538
Round Lake, NY 12151
Phone: 518-899-6190
Supplier of canopy tent units.

Seidman Supply Co.
3366 Kensington Ave.
Philadelphia, PA 19134
Phone: 215-423-8896   FAX: 215-423-9242
Carries supplies for the sports card and memorabilia collector: ball cubes and holders; sorting trays, shoeboxes, acrylic card holders.

John P. Scott Woodworking
1300 Evergreen Ave.
Richmond, VA 23224
Phone: 804-231-1942
Manufacturers lighted bases to display paperweights, glass and crystal.

Corbox Co.
6701 Hubbard Avenue
Cleveland, OH 44127
Phone: 800-321-7286
Supplier of Corbox carry-all boxes with attached covers. *

Roberts Colonial House, Inc.
Paul B. Roberts
570 W. 167th Street
South Holland, IL 60473
Phone: 312-331-6233   FAX: 708-331-0538

Sells plate hangers, plate stands, plexiglass display cubes, quilted vinyl china cases, and over 1600 other items; send for catalog.

J-Mounts/Militaire Promotions
Suite 160
6427 W. Irving Park Rd.
Chicago, IL 60634
Phone: 312-777-0499
Sell J-mount display boxes; glass-top display boxes for small collectibles: jewelry, watches, buttons, badges, etc.; all sizes.

Garrett's
Rt. 1, Box 97
Eudora, KS 66025
Phone: 913-542-2339 or 800-447-7508
Sells black collector frames and aluminum or cherry sales/display/show cases.

Collectors Supply Company
8415 "G" Street
Omaha, NE 68127
Phone: 401-592-1786   FAX: 402-592-9015
Album pages, plastic bags, displays, etc.

Charlie's
4908 E. 15th St.
Tulsa, OK 74112
Phone: 918-749-1010 or 800-433-7083
Sells hand-crafted aluminum display cases.

Jones West Packaging Co.
Dept. DL-1
P.O. Box 1084
Rohnert Park, CA 94927
Phone: 707-795-8552

Supplier of all sizes of ZIP CLOSE plastic bags in small or large quantities; since 1981; credit cards accepted.

BARBER SHOP COLLECTIBLES

Barber Poles

William Marvy Company
Robert Marvy
1540 St. Clair Ave.
St. Paul, MN 55105
Phone: 612-698-0726   FAX: 612-698-4048
Manufacturers barber poles and replacement parts: domes, motors, glass and paper cylinders, etc.

BASKETS

Connecticut Cane & Reed Co.
134 Pine St.
P.O. Box 762
Manchester, CT 06040
Phone: 203-646-6586   FAX: 203-649-2221
Largest selection of materials and books; source for cane, wicker and basket supplies; all types of materials to reseat a chair.

BEADS

Gampel Supply Corp.
39 West 37th St.
New York, NY 10018 *

Har Man Importing Company
48 West 37th St.
New York, NY 10018 *

Berger Specialty Company
413 East 8th St.
Los Angeles, CA 90010 *

Bead Store, The
417 Castro St.
San Francisco, CA 94114 *

Venerable Bead, The
2990 Adeline
Berkeley, CA 94703 *

BEER CANS

Soda Mart - Can World
1055 Ridgecrest Dr.
Goodlettsville, TN 37072
Phone: 615-859-5236   FAX: 615-859-5238
Sells breweriana books; also cleans and de-rusts on cans, and sells supplies for the beer can collector.

BOTTLES

Perfume & Scent

Paradise & Co.
2902 Neal Road
Paradise, CA 95969
Phone: 916-872-5020   FAX: 916-872-5020

Repairs; also replacement hardware and atomizer bulbs and tassels for perfume bottles.

CAROUSELS & CAROUSEL FIGURES

Sally Craig
336 W. High Street
Elizabeth, PA 17022
*Carries hair tails and stirrups. *

Brass Ring, The
5746 La Cumbre Road
Somis, CA 93066
*Carries custom stands. *

CLOCKS

Mason & Sullivan Co. Classics in the Making
586 Higgins Crowell Road
West Yarmouth, Cape Cod, MA 02673
Phone: 800-227-7418
Mail order source for quality kits; boats, guitars, steam engines, kaleidoscopes, instruments, etc.; also supplies.

Modern Technical Tools & Supply Company
211 Nevada Street
Hicksville, NY 11801
Phone: 516-931-7875
*Carries clock movements and related tools and materials for the clockmaker, hobbyist or technician. *

S. LaRose, Inc.
234 Commerce Place
Greensboro, NC 27420
Phone: 919-275-0462
*Carries a complete line of clock parts. *

M. Beresh, Inc.
Suite 353
21770 Greenfield
Oak Park, MI 48237
Phone: 313-968-2930
*Carries complete line of clock parts. *

KLOCKIT
P.O. Box 636
Lake Geneva, WI 53147
Phone: 800-556-2548
Mail order source for clock movements, hands, faces, hardware, music boxes, barometers, parts, tools, etc.

American Clockmaker, The
P.O. Box 326
Clintonville, WI 54929
Phone: 715-823-5101
Mail order source for clock movements, kits, parts and supplies; including shelf, grandfather and German cuckoo clocks.

Turncraft Clock Imports Co.
P.O. Box 27288
Golden Valley, MN 55427-0288
Phone: 800-544-1711

Mail order source of fine clock movements, kits, parts and supplies.

Bernard Edwards Dial Co.
1331 Southwind Drive
Northbrook, IL 60062
Phone: 708-272-2563
*Specializing in clock dials only. *

Timesavers
P.O. Box 171
Wheeling, IL 60090
Phone: 312-394-4818
*Carries a complete line of clock parts. *

Aguilar Jewelers' Supply
520 "E" Street, Room 408
San Diego, CA 92101
Phone: 714-232-2993
*Carries complete line of clock parts. *

Otto Frei - Jules Borel
Box 796
Oakland, CA 94604
Phone: 415-832-0355
Carries complete line of clock parts.

CLOTHING & ACCESSORIES

Vintage

Mini-Magic
3675 Reed Road
Columbus, OH 43220
*Focus on fabrics and supplies for doll people but also sells acid-free tissue and other conservation supplies. *

COIN-OPERATED MACHINES

Evans & Frink
Rick Frink
2977 Eager
Howell, MI 48843
Supplies reelstrips, pay cards, decals, instruction sheets, and mint wrappers for slot machines and trade stimulators.

Jukeboxes

Jukebox Junction
P.O. Box 1081
Des Moines, IA 50311
*Publishes a catalog of reproduction jukebox parts and literature. *

Slot Machines

Antique Slot Machine Part Co.
Tom Krahl
140 N. Western Ave.
Carpentersville, IL 60110
Phone: 708-428-8476
Publishes a catalog of reproduction slot machine parts; also repairs.

DOLLS

Dollspart Supply Co.
46-50 54th Ave.
Maspeth, NY 11378
Phone: 718-361-1833 or 800-336-3655
　　　　　　　　　　　FAX: 718-361-5833
Sells full range of doll books and parts: eyes, wigs, bodies, clothing, tools, etc.

Joyce's Doll House Parts
20188 Williamson
Mt. Clemens, MI 48043-7498
Phone: 313-791-0469　　FAX: 313-791-6193
Replacement limbs for the collector; nearly 300 styles in porcelain, bisque or china, wigs, eyes, sewing needs, etc.; catalog.

ENGINES

Gasoline

Starbolt Engine Supplies
Bill Starky
3403 Buckeystown Pike
Adamstown, MD 21710
Phone: 301-874-2821
Sells parts for old gas engines. Mail order only.

FIREARMS

Knife & Gun Finishing Supplies
P.O. Box 13522
Arlington, TX 76013
Carries equipment and supplies for buffing, polishing, and making guns.

GEMS & JEWELRY

Kassoy
32 W. 47th Street
New York, NY 10036
Phone: 800-452-7769
Mail order source for tools, supplies and instruments for the jewelry trade.

Nasco
901 Janesville Ave.
Fort Atkinson, WI 53538
Phone: 414-563-2446 or 800-558-9595
*Carries supplies for jewelry arts and crafts: wire, chains, tools, findings, beads, etc. ***

American Gem & Mineral Suppliers
　Association
1299 Armando St.
Upland, CA 91789
Phone: 714-981-8588
Members are retailers, manufacturers, wholesalers, importers, distributors, or publishers in the gem, mineral, lapidary fields.

GLASS

Curved

B & L Antiqurie, Inc.
P.O. Box 453-6217
Lexington, MI 48450-0453
Phone: 800-523-6523　　FAX: 313-359-7498
Curved glass for china cabinets & convex picture frame glass; special bends and cuts such as serpentine and J bends quoted on request.

M.D. King
403 E. Montgomery
Knoxville, IA 50138
Phone: 515-842-6394
Curved glass for china cabinets; all sizes; will ship.

Hoffer Glass
George J. Hoffer
613 W. College Ave.
Appleton, WI 54911
Phone: 414-731-8101
Curved glass for china cabinets; send width, length and a radius template; will quote picked up or shipped UPS.

Universal Glass Co.
P.O. Box 2097
Alma, AR 72921
Phone: 800-446-5504
Curved glass for china cabinets; call for quote or brochure.

KNIVES

Masecraft Supply
902 Colony Road
Meriden, CT 06450
*Carries equipment and supplies for buffing, polishing, and making knives. ***

Anderson Cutlery & Supply Co.
Box 383
Newton, CT 06470
*Carries equipment and supplies for buffing, polishing, and making knives. ***

Sheffield Knifemakers Supplies
P.O. Box 141
De Land, FL 32720
*Carries equipment and supplies for buffing, polishing, and making knives. ***

Knife & Gun Finishing Supplies
P.O. Box 13522
Arlington, TX 76013
Carries equipment and supplies for buffing, polishing, and making knives.

LAMPS & LIGHTING

Chandeliers

Lighting Designs
1500 Rockville Pike
Rockville, MD 20852
Phone: 301-468-7300

Carries large selection of crystal chandeliers and parts for same.

LIDS

Abercombie & Co.
9159A Brookeville Rd.
Silver Spring, MD 20910
Phone: 301-585-2385
Carries replacement metal tops for bottles and shakers.

Lid Lady, The
Virginia Bodiker
7790 East Ross Road
New Carlisle, OH 45344
Carries replacement lids for ceramic, glass, metal, and plastic vessels and containers.

MINIATURES

Lynne's Miniature Treasurers
Dept. 24
North Wales, PA 19454
*Offers a diversified catalog of miniature items and supplies. ***

Masterpiece Museum Miniatures
P.O. Box 5280
Austin, TX 78763
*Offers a diversified line of miniature items and supplies. ***

Many Goode's Catalogue
P.O. Box 5161
Torrance, CA 90510
*Offers a diversified line of miniature items and supplies. ***

MODELS

Superior Aircraft Materials
Mike Taibi
12020 Centralia Ave. #G
Hawaiian Gardens, CA 90716
Phone: 213-865-3220
Specializes in supplying wood materials (balsa, spruce, plywood) for the model builder.

Engineering

Coles' Power Models, Inc.
P.O. Box 788
Ventura, CA 93001
*Catalog of model engineering supplies; drawings, castings, nuts, bolts, taps & dies, small tools, books, fittings, sundries, etc. ***

MUSICAL INSTRUMENTS

Mechanical (Player Pianos)

Player Piano Co., Inc.
704 East Douglas
Wichita, KS 67202
Phone: 316-263-3241 or 316-263-1714

Complete line of player piano restoration supplies, service manuals, music rolls; catalog if mailed free upon request.

String

C.F. Martin Guitar Co.
Box 329
Nazareth, PA 18064
Phone: 215-759-2837   FAX: 215-759-5757
Offers Woodworker's Dream Catalog for Woodworkers & Luthiers; tools, materials, parts for the fretted instrument maker.

PHONOGRAPHS

Ron Sitko
26 Tekakwitha Court
Clifton Park, NY 12065
Sells parts for old phonographs. *

Victorian Talking Machine Co.
261 Robinson Ave.
Newburgh, NY 12550
Phone: 914-561-0132
Sells and repairs antique phonographs; phonograph books and supplies; steel needles.

RADIOS

Old Tyme Radio Co.
Suite 317
2445 Lyttonsville Road
Silver Spring, MD 20910
Phone: 301-585-8776
Carries hard-to-find radio parts: vintage tubes, AK style battery cable, hook up wire, audio transformers, vintage headphones, etc.

Puett Electronics
Newsletter: Antique Radio Topics
J.W.F. Puett
P.O. Box 28572
Dallas, TX 75228
Phone: 214-321-0927 or 214-327-8721
Mail order business in its 19th year servicing the antique radio collector; sells anything for old radios. Send for catalog.

Antique Electronic Supply
6221 S. Maple Ave.
Tempe, AZ 85283
Phone: 602-820-5411   FAX: 602-820-4643
Large catalog carrying tubes, supplies, capacitors, transformers, chemicals, test equipment, wire, parts, tools, literature, etc.

RADIO TUBES

DH Distributors
David Headley
P.O. box 48623
Wichita, KS 67201
Phone: 316-684-0050
Buys and sells receiving, transmitting and industrial vacuum tubes.

RECORDS

Bags Unlimited
7 Canal Street
Rochester, NY 14608
Phone: 800-767-BAGS
Sells record collector supplies: poly and paper sleeves, mailers, filer pads, album jackets, storage boxes, divider cards, etc.

MARSCO
1713 Central St.
Evanston, IL 60201
Phone: 708-328-7100
Carries paper and plastic sleeves for LP's and sheet music covers.

REPAIRS & RESTORATIONS

A. Ludwig Klein & Son, Inc.
Route 63
P.O. Box 205
Harleysville, PA 19438
Phone: 215-256-9004 or 800-869-5633
Sells china and glass restoration supplies.

Art

Gainsborough Products Company, Ltd.
3545 Mt. Diablo Blvd.
Lafayette, CA 94549
Phone: 415-283-4187 or 800-227-2186
Lining canvas and compound, repair putty, varnish remover, manuals, etc.

Cane & Basketry

Able To Cane
P.O. Box 429
Warren, ME 04864
Phone: 207-273-3747
Source for cane, wicker and basket supplies; also repairs of antique seats, natural & fiber rush, Shaker tape seating, cane, splint, etc. *

Connecticut Cane & Reed Co.
134 Pine St.
P.O. Box 762
Manchester, CT 06040
Phone: 203-646-6586   FAX: 203-649-2221
Largest selection of materials and books; source for cane, wicker and basket supplies; all types of materials to reseat a chair.

Peerless Rattan & Reed
P.O. Box 636
Yonkers, NY 10701
Phone: 914-968-4046
Source for cane, wicker and basket supplies.

Canecraft
Lilian Cummings
RD1 Box 126-A
Andreas, PA 18211
Phone: 717-386-2441
Sells cane, reed and rushing material for seating chairs, making baskets, and repairing wicker furniture; also instruction books.

Barap Specialties
835 Bellows
Frankfort, MI 49635
Source for flat reed, fiber rush, decorative head nails, cane webbing and reed for reweaving chair seats, hardware, etc.

Cane & Basket Supply Co.
1283 S. Cochran Ave.
Los Angeles, CA 90019
Phone: 213-939-9644   FAX: 213-939-7237
Source for cane, wicker and basket supplies.

Franks Cane & Rush Supply
Mike Frank
P.O. Box 3025
Huntington Beach, CA 92605
Phone: 714-847-0707   FAX: 714-843-5645
Quality supplier of unusual supplies for the craftsman; mainly wicker repair and basketry; sorry, no restoration of repairs.

Ceramics

Atlas Minerals & Chemicals, Inc.
Farmington Road
Mertztown, PA 19539
Phone: 215-682-7171
Offers a master mending kit for china and glass including materials and instructions to repair glass, china, porcelain, pottery, etc. *

Glass

Atlas Minerals & Chemicals, Inc.
Farmington Road
Mertztown, PA 19539
Phone: 215-682-7171
Offers a master mending kit for china and glass including materials and instructions to repair glass, china, porcelain, pottery, etc. *

Lamps & Lighting

Crystal Mountain Prisms
P.O. Box 31
Westfield, NY 14787
Phone: 716-326-3676
Sells prisms, chains, bobeches, pendants, drops, etc. *

Kirk Lane Co.
2541 Pearle Buck Rd.
Bristol, PA 19007
Phone: 215-785-1251   FAX: 215-785-1651
Source for lamp parts including sockets, bases, harps, finials, chimneys, shades, etc.

Campbell Lamps
Bill Campbell
1108 Pottstown Pike
West Chester, PA 19380
Phone: 215-696-8070
Sells replacement glass shades, chimneys, metal parts, etc. *

B & P Lamp Supply, Inc.
843 Old Morrison Highway
McMinnville, TN 37110
Phone: 615-473-3016
Offers a wide variety of lamp reproduction parts. Wholesale only. Handpainted shades, adaptors, burners, art glass shades, etc.

American Lamp Supply Co.
Tom Teeter
51 Vaughans Gap Road
Nashville, TN 37205
Phone: 615-352-2357   FAX: 615-352-9423
Sells Aladdin lamps and parts. *

Brass Light Gallery
Steve Kaye
131 South First St.
Milwaukee, WI 53204
Phone: 414-271-8300 or 800-243-9595
                                  FAX: 414-271-7755
Specializes in parts for gas wall sconces and chandeliers, and for early electric lamps; also does lamp repairs including metal work.

Crystal Import Co.
521 W. Rosecrans Ave.
Gardenia, CA 90248
Phone: 213-323-8452   FAX: 213-323-8468
Source for lamp crystals, chains, spindles, bobesches and bent arms. *

Leather

Pecard
P.O. Box 263
Eugene, OR 97440
Sells the very best antique leather preservative - moisturizes, preserves, colorless, softens, odorless, long-lasting, safe.

Marble

Gawet Marble & Granite, Inc.
Route 4
Center Rutland, VT 05736
Carries products for the cleaning and care of marble. *

Paper Items

University Products, Inc.
517 Main St.
P.O. Box 101
Holyoke, MA 01041-0101
Phone: 800-336-4847 or 800-628-1912
                                  FAX: 413-532-9281
Carries safe products for the long term storage of postcards, posters, stamps, textiles, costumes; acid free archival supplies.

TALAS
213 West 35th Street
New York, NY 10001-1996
Phone: 212-736-7744   FAX: 212-465-8722
Archival supplies for artists, restorers, collectors, bookbinders, conservators, calligraphers, museums, archives, libraries, etc.

S & W Framing Supplies, Inc.
P.O. Box 340
New Hyde Park, NY 11040
General line of archival supplies including mat boards, document storage boxes, framing and photographic supplies. *

Light Impressions Corp.
P.O. Box 940
Rochester, NY 14603
Phone: 800-828-9629 or 800-828-6216
                                  FAX: 716-442-7318
General line of archival supplies including mat boards, document storage boxes, framing and photographic supplies.

Conservation Resources International, Inc.
8000 H Forbes Place
Springfield, VA 22151
Archival supplies for works of art on paper; document and photographic storage materials. *

Hollinger Corporation
P.O. Box 6185
Arlington, VA 22206
Archival supplies for works of art on paper; document and photographic storage materials.

Conservation Materials, Ltd.
P.O. Box 2884
Sparks, NV 89431
General line of archival supplies including mat boards, document storage boxes, framing and photographic supplies. *

Restorations
P.O. Box 2000
Nevada City, CA 95959
Phone: 916-477-5527
Restoration services & supplies for baseball cards, comics, magazines; crease removal, corner repairs, spines rebuilt; free catalog.

Upholstery

John K. Burch Co.
1818 Underwood Blvd.
Delran, NJ 08075
Phone: 800-257-9112
Mail order source for upholstering supplies; also fabric books.

Douglas Industries, Inc.
412 Boston Ave.
Egg Harbor City, NJ 08215
Phone: 800-257-8551
Source for foam and fabrics.

Carrousel Foam
1940 S. West Blvd.
Vineland, NJ 08360
Phone: 609-692-1777
Source for foam.

Jack Raskin's Upholstery Supplies
1810-20 E. Boston St.
Philadelphia, PA 19125
Phone: 800-523-3213
Mail order source for upholstering supplies.

Minute-Man Upholstery Supply Company of North Carolina
P.O. Box 6534
High Point, NC 27262
Phone: 800-457-0029
Mail order source for upholstering supplies.

Lexol Division, The, Corona Products Company
P.O. Box 1214
Atlanta, GA 30301
Phone: 404-524-5434
Sells a very good product for softening old and stiff leather. *

Woodworking

Woodcraft
P.O. Box 4000
Woburn, MA 01888
Phone: 800-225-1153
Mail order source for complete line of woodworking tools, supplies and books.

Period Furniture Hardware Co., Inc.
Charles Street Station
P.O. Box 314
Boston, MA 02114
Phone: 617-227-0758   FAX: 617-227-2987
Supplies fine quality reproduction hardware for furniture and the home; specializes in solid brass fittings and accessories.

Trendlines
375 Beacham Street
Chelsea, MA 02150
Phone: 800-767-9999
Mail order source for a good mix of woodworking tools.

Tremont Nail Company
Elm Street at Route 28
Wareham, MA 02571
Carries twenty different styles of historic cut nails.

Brookstone
127 Vose Farm Road
Peterborough, NH 03458
Phone: 603-924-9541
Mail order source for hard to find tools and devices.

Horton Brasses
P.O. Box 95
Cromwell, CT 06416
Phone: 203-635-4400   FAX: 203-635-6473
Sells reproduction hardware of finest quality, manufactured in CT of solid brass; exactly replicates originals; styles from 1600-1920.

Micro Mark
340 Snyder Ave.
Berkeley Heights, NJ 07922
Mail order source for small tools only, e.g. X-Acto.

Garrett Wade Company, Inc.
161 Avenue Of The Americas
New York, NY 10013-1299
Phone: 800-221-2942   FAX: 212-255-8552
Reproduction English solid brass hardware; also 220 page catalog of the world's finest specialty woodworking tools: planes, chisels, etc.

Constantine
2050 Eastchester Road
Bronx, NY 10461
Phone: 800-223-8087   FAX: 212-792-2110
A complete line of tools, hardware, finishing supplies, marquetry kits, books, moldings, parts, veneers, hardwoods, etc.

Mohawk Finishing Products
Rt. 30 Perth Rd.
Amsterdam, NY 12010
Phone: 800-545-0047
Major supplier of finishing tools, supplies and materials.

Wood Finishing Supply Co., Inc.
1267 Mary Drive
Macedon, NY 14502
Phone: 315-986-4517
Mail order source for wood finishing supplies and brass hardware.

Cyder Creek Wood Shoppe, Inc.
Box 19
Whitesville, NY 14897
Phone: 800-642-9663
Mail order source for wood turners' hand tools, books and supplies.

18th Century Hardware Co., Inc.
John M. Fisher
131 East 3rd St.
Derry, PA 15627
Phone: 412-694-2708
Clean, polish & repair brass items; makes, sells reproduction hardware; clean and electrify brass lamps; offers catalog.

Hoosier Emporium, The
Rick Zirpoli
Route 529, Box 264
Milanville, PA 18443
Phone: 717-729-7080
Manufactures & distributes authentically reproduced "want lists" and cardboard inserts for Hoosier, Sellers, etc. style kitchen cabinets.

Ye Old Cowpath Antiques
59 Cowpath Road
Souderton, PA 18964
*Source for slip-on bedrail extenders. **

Ball & Ball
463 W. Lincoln Highway
Exton, PA 19341
Publishes a hardware catalog; also has a recasting service.

American Machine & Tool Company
P.O. Box 70
Royersford, PA 19468
Phone: 215-948-0400
Mail order source for hand tools and machinery.

Industrial Abrasives Co.
Box 14955
Reading, PA 19612
Carries a large line of sand paper and other abrasives.

Paxton Hardware Ltd.
P.O. Box 256
Upper Falls, MD 21156
Phone: 301-592-8505   FAX: 301-592-2224
Supplies brass reproduction hardware in period styles; 74 pg. catalog also contains pulls, knobs, locks, hinges, lamp parts, shades, etc.

Bedell Manufacturing Company
P.O. Box 626
Merrifield, VA 22116
Phone: 703-573-7090
*Source for Victorian platform rocker replacement springs. **

Woodworking Tools & Books
1045 N. Highland Ave., NE
Atlanta, GA 30306
Phone: 800-241-6748
Mail order source for hand tools, machinery, workbenches, books, videos, and supplies.

A & H Brass & Supply
1402 W. Market St.
Johnson City, TN 37601
Phone: 615-928-8220
Carries a wide selection of hardware, caning supplies, trunk parts, fiberboard seats, etc.

Bob Morgan Woodworking Supplies
1123 Bardstown Road
Louisville, KY 40204
Phone: 502-456-2545
Mail order source for hardwoods, veneers, hand tools, and supplies.

Cherry Tree Toys, Inc.
P.O. Box 369
Belmont, OH 43718
Phone: 614-484-4363
Mail order source for children's toys, doll houses, whirligig kits, parts, books and supplies.

Farmerstown Furniture
Junior & Robert Hershberger
3155 S.R. 557
Baltic, OH 43804
Phone: 216-893-2464
Catalog of specialty products such as spool cabinet decals, highchair trays, iron bed parts, parts for iceboxes and Hoosier cabinets, etc.

Leichtung Workshops
4944 Commerce Parkway
Cleveland, OH 44128
Phone: 800-321-6840
Mail order source for hand tools, supplies and small kits.

Shopsmith Tool Guide
3931 Image Dr.
Dayton, OH 45414
Phone: 800-543-7586 or 800-762-7555
Mail order source for hand tools and supplies. Visit local Shopsmith Store or order by phone.

Phyllis Kennedy Hardware
Phyllis & Phil Kennedy
9256 Holyoke Court
Indianapolis, IN 46268
Phone: 317-872-6366
Hardware for antique furniture, Hoosier cabinets and trunks; manufacturer of flour bins and sifters for Hoosier cabinets.

Gaston's
2626 N. Walnut
Bloomington, IN 47408
Phone: 812-339-9111
*Wood finishing stains, lacquers, antique hardware, hard to find items. Call or write for free catalog. **

Doug's Furniture Refinishing & Supply
144 Sheldon
Climax, MI 49034
Phone: 616-746-4104
*Carries strippers, finishers, sanders, sandpaper and belts, carvings, reproduction hardware, glue, screws, chair seats, etc. **

Woodsmith Store
P.O. Box 1035
Des Moines, IA 50306
Phone: 800-444-7002
Mail order source for woodworking tools, hardware, and project plans and supplies.

Silvo Hardware Co.
P.O. Box 92069
Milwaukee, WI 53202
Phone: 800-331-1261
Mail order source for hand tools and hardware.

Heirloom Antique Brass Co.
P.O. Box 146
Dundas, MN 55019
Phone: 507-645-9341

Wholesale to dealers only; Victorian, Eastlake, and turn-of-the-century hardware.

Restore-It Supply Co.
P.O. Box 10600
White Bear Lake, MN 55110
Phone: 612-429-2222
Sells restoration products such as tools, veneers, seat weaving supplies, decals, etc.

Woodworkers' Store, The
21801 Industrial Blvd.
Rogers, MN 55374-9514
Phone: 612-428-4101 or 612-428-2199
FAX: 612-428-8668
Mail order source for hand tools, inlays, veneers, hardware, and hardwoods.

Van Dykes Supply Company
P.O. Box 278
Woonsocket, SD 57385
Phone: 800-843-3320 or 605-796-4425
Mail order source for refinishing supplies; also issues a catalog of taxidermy supplies.

Craftsman Wood Service Co.
1734 W. Cortland Ct.
Addison, IL 60101
Phone: 312-629-3100
Mail order source for hand tools, hardware, and finishing supplies.

Star Chemical Co.
360 Shore Drive
Hinsdale, IL 60521
Phone: 708-654-8650
Major supplier of finishing tools, supplies and materials.

Sears Power & Hand Tool Specialog
925 S. Homan Avenue
Chicago, IL 60607
Call your local Sears store catalog department for a copy of this Specialog.

Clark Manufacturing Co.
Route 2
Raymore, MO 64083
Phone: 816-331-6851
*Manufacturers replacement pierced tins for pie safes. *

Wise Company, The
Noel & Bernice Wise
Dept. CIC
P.O. Box 118
Arabi, LA 70032-0118
Phone: 504-277-7551 or 504-277-7551
Hard to find antique reproduction hardware; also repairs old locks and makes new keys for old locks.

Good Pickins'
Box 665
Jefferson, TX 75657
*Mail order source for old ice box hardware. *

Woodworker's Supply of New Mexico
5604 Alameda Place, NE
Albuquerque, NM 87113
Phone: 800-645-9292
Mail order source for hand tools, machinery, and hardware.

Muff's Antiques
135 S. Glassell St.
Orange, CA 92666
*Mail order source for kitchen cabinet hardware (Hoosiers) including hinges, labels, canisters, castors, and rolls; also ice box parts. *

Harbor Freight Tools
3491 Mission Oaks Blvd.
Camarillo, CA 93011-6010
Phone: 800-423-2567   FAX: 805-388-0760
Absolutely the lowest prices on quality name brand tools, equipment, machinery for both the home and professional workshop; free catalog.

Woodline the Japan Woodworker
1731 Clement Ave.
Alameda, CA 94501
Phone: 415-521-1810
Mail order source for highest quality woodworking tools from Japan.

Finishing Touch, The
5636 College Ave.
Oakland, CA 94618
Phone: 415-652-4908
*Source for replacement pressed leather seats made of oak-tanned hides; also carries caning products and instructions. *

American Home Supply
P.O. Box 697
Campbell, CA 95009
Phone: 408-246-1962   FAX: 408-248-1308
Carries the largest selection of antique reproduction hardware on the West Coast; has a 99.9% stock rate.

Anglo American Brass Company
Box 9792
San Jose, CA 95157-0792
Phone: 800-AAB-RASS
Publishes a hardware catalog; brass hardware, household hinges, glass knobs, brass casters, nickel plate ice box hardware, wooden casters.

Ritter & Son Hardware
38001 Old Stage Road
P.O. Box 578
Gualala, CA 95445-9984
Phone: 707-884-3363 or 800-358-9120
FAX: 707-884-1515
Supplier of furniture restoration hardware: carved oak gingerbread, Hoosier hardware, cast & stamped brass pulls, handles, etc.

Old Hotel Antiques
P.O. Box 94
Sutter Creek, CA 95685
Phone: 209-267-5901
*Source for replacement solid oak replacement high chair trays. *

Bridge City Tool Works
1104 N.E. 28th Ave.
Portland, OR 97232
Phone: 503-282-6997
Mail order source for fine woodworking hand tools.

SALTS

Open

Gem Monogram & Cut Glass Corp.
623 Broadway
New York, NY 10012
Phone: 212-674-8960
*Carries a line of replacement glass liners for open salts. *

SHEET MUSIC

MARSCO
1713 Central St.
Evanston, IL 60201
Phone: 708-328-7100
Carries paper and plastic sleeves for LP's and sheet music covers.

SOFT DRINK COLLECTIBLES

Coca-Cola Machines

Fun-Tronics
Steve & Nancy Ebner
P.O. Box 3145
Gaithersburg, MD 20878
Phone: 301-371-5246
*Specializing in restoration supplies for vintage coke machines and dealers in related collectibles. *

SOLDIERS

Toy

Costal Enterprises
Howard Wehner
P.O. Box 1053
Brick, NJ 08723
*Sells molds, casting supplies, soldier sets and cast soldiers. *

SPORTS COLLECTIBLES

Baseball Cards

Columbia Sportcards & Supplies
Suite 300
10632 Little Patuxent
Columbia, MD 21044
Phone: 301-964-8022
*Carries Allstate display cases, issues catalog of supplies. *

STAINED GLASS

Blenko Glass Company, Inc.
P.O. Box 67
Milton, WV 25541
Phone: 304-743-9081   FAX: 304-743-0547
Supplies hand-blown "antique" glass for stained glass windows.

STAMP COLLECTING

Scott Publishing Co.
Magazine: Scott's Stamp Monthly
P.O. Box 828
Sidney, OH 45365
Phone: 513-498-0802   FAX: 513-498-0808
Publisher of catalogs, albums and various stamp supplies.

STEREO VIEWERS & STEREOGRAPHS

Reel 3-D Enterprises, Inc.
David Starkman
P.O. Box 2368
Culver City, CA 90231
Phone: 213-837-2368   FAX: 213-558-1653
Offers a catalog with complete line of items for the modern 3-D enthusiast: books, stereo viewers, mounting supplies, etc.

STOVES

Custom House
South Shore Drive
Owl's Head, ME 04854
Phone: 207-594-5985
*Carries replacement parts for antique stoves. ***

TELEPHONES

Chicago Old Telephone Company
P.O. Box 189
Lemon Springs, NC 28355
Phone: 919-774-6625
Carries parts for old telephones; also repairs.

Phoneco, Inc.
Ron & Mary Knappen
207 E. Mill Rd.
P.O. Box 70
Galesville, WI 54630
Phone: 608-582-4124 or 608-582-2863
                        FAX: 608-582-4593
Buys, sells, refurbishes any old telephone; also sells old and new parts; catalogs, history, price guide, diagrams and restoration help.

TELEVISIONS

Antique Electronic Supply
6221 S. Maple Ave.
Tempe, AZ 85283
Phone: 602-820-5411   FAX: 602-820-4643
Large catalog carrying tubes, supplies, capacitors, transformers, chemicals, test equipment, wire, parts, tools, literature, etc.

TOYS

Thomas Toys
P.O. Box 405
Fenton, MI 48430
Phone: 313-629-8707
Carries antique toy car replacement parts.

Farm

Dakota Toys
Rt. 3, Box 179
Arlington, SD 57212
Phone: 605-983-5987
Catalog contains toy parts, decals, paints, kits, $\frac{1}{4}$ items, books, scratch building materials, tools and diorama materials.

Trucks & Equipment

Toy Parts Peddler
Dennis & Marge Lowry
1143 46th Street
Des Moines, IA 50311
Phone: 515-277-7589
Supplies parts for post WWII toy trucks, construction toys, toy race cars, and related equipment.

TRUNKS

Charlotte Ford Trunks
P.O. Box 536
Spearman, TX 79081
Phone: 806-659-3027
Publishes a parts catalog for trunk restorations.

INDEX TO MAJOR CATEGORIES

INDEX TO SUBCATEGORIES

SEE INDEX TO MAJOR CATEGORIES *FOR EXTENSIVE CROSS-REFERENCES*

Collector's Information Clearinghouse
Antiques & Collectibles Resource Directory
LISTING APPLICATION AND CHANGE FORM

1. List your SPECIALTY AREA: _____

2. Check the ENTRY CLASSIFICATION that applies to this Specialty Area (make copies of this form as necessary):

- Auction Service
- Book Seller
- Club/Association
- Collector
- Dealer

- Matching Service
- Museum/Library
- Periodical
- Vendor/Supplier
- Expert

- Repair/Restoration Service
- Reproduction Source
- Manufacturer, Producer or Distributor

- Other (please specify): _____

3. NAME (exactly as you wish it listed): _____

4. NAME of your business, club, association, museum, etc.: _____

_____

Annual Dues (for Clubs, Associations and Societies): $ _____

5. PERIODICALS (magazines, newsletters, newspapers, etc.) that you publish (please ensure that complimentary subscriptions of each are sent to CIC, Attn: File Editor, P.O. Box 2049, Frederick, MD 21702-1049 for review).

Periodical #1: _____
    Format: _____ Frequency: _____
    Annual Subscription Fee: _____ or _____ FREE to members

Periodical #2: _____
    Format: _____ Frequency: _____
    Annual Subscription Fee: _____ or _____ FREE to members

6. MAILING ADDRESS:

Street (for UPS): _____
P.O. Box: _____
City: _____ State: _____ Zip: _____
Country: _____
_____ This is a permanent address   _____ This address changes as club officers change

7. TELEPHONE #1: _____ **TELEPHONE #2:** _____
    FAX: _____

8. COMMENT LINE: (Describe your club, association, periodical or service. For the collector or dealer, describe your wants. If you are an author, please list your most recent book dealing with this specialty area. Please limit your comment to 200 characters. Attach brochures, flyers, business cards, etc.)

_____
_____
_____

Date: _____ Signature: _____ Title: _____

Collector's Information Clearinghouse ● P.O. Box 2049, Frederick, MD 21702-1049 ● (301) 695-8544 ● Fax (301) 695-6491